# THESE TRUTHS

# THESE TRUTHS

★ ★ ★ ★

*A History of
the United States*

# JILL LEPORE

**W. W. NORTON & COMPANY**

*Independent Publishers Since 1923*

New York   London

Some material in this book originally appeared in a different form in *The New Yorker*.

"Mr. Roosevelt Regrets." Copyright © 1943 by the Pauli Murray Foundation, from *Dark Testament and Other Poems* by Pauli Murray. All rights reserved. Reprinted with permission of Charlotte Sheedy Literary Agency and Liveright Publishing Corporation. "Superman" from *Collected Poems, 1953–1993* by John Updike, copyright © 1993 by John Updike. Used by permission of Alfred A. Knopf, an imprint of the Knopf Doubleday Publishing Group, a division of Penguin Random House LLC. All rights reserved.

For information about permission to reproduce selections from this book, write to Permissions, W. W. Norton & Company, Inc., 500 Fifth Avenue, New York, NY 10110

For information about special discounts for bulk purchases, please contact W. W. Norton Special Sales at specialsales@wwnorton.com or 800-233-4830

Manufacturing by LSC Communications Harrisonburg
Book design by Lovedog Studio
Production manager: Anna Oler

Library of Congress Cataloging-in-Publication Data

Names: Lepore, Jill, 1966– author.
Title: These truths : a history of the United States / Jill Lepore.
Description: First edition. | New York : W. W. Norton & Company, [2018] |
Includes bibliographical references and index.
Identifiers: LCCN 2018019180 | ISBN 9780393635249 (hardcover)
Subjects: LCSH: United States—History. | Civil rights—United States—History. |
United States—Politics and government.
Classification: LCC E178 .L57 2018 | DDC 973—dc23
LC record available at https://lccn.loc.gov/2018019180

W. W. Norton & Company, Inc.
500 Fifth Avenue, New York, N.Y. 10110
www.wwnorton.com

W. W. Norton & Company Ltd.
15 Carlisle Street, London W1D 3BS

2 3 4 5 6 7 8 9 0

---

PREVIOUS SPREAD

*Americans assembled on the National Mall for the 1963 March on Washington.*

*We must disenthrall ourselves,*
*and then we shall save our country.*

—Abraham Lincoln, 1862

# CONTENTS ★ ★ ★ ★

*Introduction:* The Question Stated                                      xi

*Part One*
## THE IDEA   (1492–1799)

| | | |
|---|---|---|
| *One* | The Nature of the Past | 3 |
| *Two* | The Rulers and the Ruled | 31 |
| *Three* | Of Wars and Revolutions | 72 |
| *Four* | The Constitution of a Nation | 109 |

*Part Two*
## THE PEOPLE   (1800–1865)

| | | |
|---|---|---|
| *Five* | A Democracy of Numbers | 153 |
| *Six* | The Soul and the Machine | 189 |
| *Seven* | Of Ships and Shipwrecks | 232 |
| *Eight* | The Face of Battle | 272 |

*Part Three*
## THE STATE   (1866–1945)

| | | |
|---|---|---|
| *Nine* | Of Citizens, Persons, and People | 311 |
| *Ten* | Efficiency and the Masses | 361 |

*Eleven*    A Constitution of the Air                              421

*Twelve*    The Brutality of Modernity                             472


*Part Four*

# THE MACHINE (1946–2016)

*Thirteen*   A World of Knowledge                                   521

*Fourteen*   Rights and Wrongs                                      589

*Fifteen*    Battle Lines                                           646

*Sixteen*    America, Disrupted                                     719


*Epilogue:* The Question Addressed                                  785


*Acknowledgments*                                                   791


*Notes*                                                             793


*llustration Credits*                                               881


*Index*                                                             889

*Introduction*

# THE QUESTION
# STATED

THE COURSE OF HISTORY IS UNPREDICTABLE, AS IRREG-
ular as the weather, as errant as affection, nations rising and falling by whim and chance, battered by violence, corrupted by greed, seized
by tyrants, raided by rogues, addled by demagogues. This was all true
until one day, Tuesday, October 30, 1787, when readers of a newspaper
called the *New-York Packet* found on the front page an advertisement for
an almanac that came bound with tables predicting the "Rising and Setting of the Sun," the "Judgment of the Weather," the "Length of Days
and Nights," and, as a bonus, something entirely new: the Constitution of
the United States, forty-four hundred words that attempted to chart the
motions of the branches of government and the separation of their powers
as if these were matters of physics, like the transit of the sun and moon
and the comings and goings of the tides.[1] It was meant to mark the start
of a new era, in which the course of history might be made predictable
and a government established that would be ruled not by accident and
force but by reason and choice. The origins of that idea, and its fate, are
the story of American history.

The Constitution entailed both toil and argument. Knee-breeched,
sweat-drenched delegates to the constitutional convention had met all
summer in Philadelphia in a swelter of secrecy, the windows of their
debating hall nailed shut against eavesdroppers. By the middle of September, they'd drafted a proposal written on four pages of parchment. They
sent that draft to printers who set the type of its soaring preamble with a
giant W, as sharp as a bird's claw:

We the People of the United States, in Order to form a more perfect Union, establish Justice, insure domestic Tranquility, provide for the common defence, promote the general Welfare, and secure the Blessings of Liberty to ourselves and our Posterity, do ordain and establish this Constitution for the United States of America.

As summer faded to fall, the free people of the United States, finding the Constitution folded into their newspapers and almanacs, were asked to decide whether or not to ratify it, even as they went about baling hay, milling corn, tanning leather, singing hymns, and letting out the seams on last year's winter coats, for mothers and fathers grown fatter, and letting down the hems, for children grown taller.

They read this strange, intricate document, and they debated its plan. Some feared that the new system granted too much power to the federal government—to the president, or to Congress, or to the Supreme Court, or to all three. Many, like sixty-one-year-old George Mason of Virginia, a delegate who'd refused to sign it, wanted the Constitution to include a bill of rights. ("A bill might be prepared in a few hours," Mason had begged at the convention, to no avail.)[2] Others complained about this clause or that, down to commas. It was not an easy thing to read. A few suggested scrapping it and starting all over again. "Cannot the same power which called the late convention, call another?" one citizen wondered. "Are not the people still their own masters?"[3]

Much of what they said is a matter of record. "The infant periods of most nations are buried in silence, or veiled in fable," James Madison once remarked.[4] Not the United States. Its infancy is preserved, like baby teeth kept in a glass jar, in the four parchment sheets of the Constitution, in the pages of almanacs that chart the weather of a long-ago climate, and in hundreds of newspapers, where essays for and against the new system of government appeared alongside the shipping news, auction notices, and advertisements for the return of people who never were their own masters—women and children, slaves and servants—and who had run away, hoping to ordain and establish, for themselves and their posterity, the blessings of liberty.

The season of ratification was an autumn of ordinary bustle and business. In that October 30, 1787, issue of the *New-York Packet*, a schoolmaster announced that he was offering lessons in "reading, writing, arithmetic, and merchants' accounts" in rooms near city hall. The estate of Gearey, Champion, and Co., consisting chiefly of "a large and general Assortment of Drugs and Medicines," was to be auctioned. Many-masted sailing ships from London and Liverpool and trim schooners from St. Croix, Baltimore, and Norfolk had dropped anchor in the depths of the harbor; sloops from Charleston and Savannah had tied their painters to the docks. A Scotsman offered a reward for the return of his stolen chestnut-colored mare, fourteen hands high, "lofty carriage, trots and canters very handsome." A merchant with a warehouse on Peck Slip wanted readers to know that he had for sale dry codfish, a quantity of molasses, ground ginger in barrels, York rum, pickled codfish, writing paper, and men's shoes. And the *Columbian Almanack* was for sale, with or without the Constitution as an appendix, at the printers' shop, where New Yorkers might also inquire after two people, for a price:

> TO BE SOLD. A LIKELY young NEGRO WENCH, 20 years of age, she is healthy and had the small pox, she has a young male child.

The mother was said to be "remarkably handy at housework"; her baby was "about 6 months old," still nursing. Their names were not mentioned.[5] They were not ruled by reason and choice. They were ruled by violence and force.

Between the everyday atrocity of slavery and the latest news from the apothecary there appeared on page 2 of that day's *New-York Packet* an essay titled THE FEDERALIST No. 1. It had been written, anonymously, by a brash thirty-year-old lawyer named Alexander Hamilton. "You are called upon to deliberate on a new Constitution for the United States of America," he told his readers. But more was at stake, too, he insisted; the wrong decision would result in "the general misfortune of mankind." The United States, he argued, was an experiment in the science of politics, marking a new era in the history of government:

> It seems to have been reserved to the people of this country, by their conduct and example, to decide the important question, whether societies of men are really capable or not of establishing good government from reflection and choice, or whether they are

forever destined to depend for their political constitutions on accident and force.[6]

This was the question of that autumn. And, in a way, it has been the question of every season since, the question of every rising and setting of the sun, on rainy days and snowy days, on clear days and cloudy days, at the clap of every thunderstorm. Can a political society really be governed by reflection and election, by reason and truth, rather than by accident and violence, by prejudice and deceit? Is there any arrangement of government—any constitution—by which it's possible for a people to rule themselves, justly and fairly, and as equals, through the exercise of judgment and care? Or are their efforts, no matter their constitutions, fated to be corrupted, their judgment muddled by demagoguery, their reason abandoned for fury?

This question in every kind of weather is the question of American history. It is also the question of this book, an account of the origins, course, and consequences of the American experiment over more than four centuries. It is not a simple question. I once came across a book called *The Constitution Made Easy*.[7] The Constitution cannot be made easy. It was never meant to be easy.

THE AMERICAN EXPERIMENT rests on three political ideas— "these truths," Thomas Jefferson called them—political equality, natural rights, and the sovereignty of the people. "We hold these truths to be sacred & undeniable," Jefferson wrote in 1776, in a draft of the Declaration of Independence:

> that all men are created equal & independent, that from that equal creation they derive rights inherent & inalienable, among which are the preservation of life, & liberty, & the pursuit of happiness; that to secure these ends, governments are instituted among men, deriving their just powers from the consent of the governed.

The roots of these ideas are as ancient as Aristotle and as old as Genesis and their branches spread as wide as the limbs of an oak. But they are this nation's founding principles: it was by declaring them that the nation came to be. In the centuries since, these principles have been cherished, decried, and contested, fought for, fought over, and fought against. After Benjamin Franklin read Jefferson's draft, he picked up his quill, scratched out the words "sacred & undeniable," and suggested that "these truths" were, instead, "self-evident." This was more than a quibble. Truths that are sacred and undeniable are God-given and divine, the stuff of religion. Truths that are self-evident are laws of nature, empirical and observable, the stuff of science. This divide has nearly rent the Republic apart.

Still, this divide is nearly always overstated and it's easy to exaggerate the difference between Jefferson and Franklin, which, in those lines, came down, too, to style: Franklin's revision is more forceful. The real dispute isn't between Jefferson and Franklin, each attempting, in his way, to reconcile faith and reason, as many have tried both before and since. The real dispute is between "these truths" and the course of events: Does American history prove these truths, or does it belie them?

Before the experiment began, the men who wrote the Declaration of Independence and the Constitution made an extraordinarily careful study of history. They'd been studying history all their lives. Benjamin Franklin was eighty-one years old, hunched and crooked, when he signed the Constitution in 1787, with his gnarled and speckled hand. In 1731, when he was twenty-five, straight as a sapling, he'd written an essay called "Observations on Reading History," on a "little Paper, accidentally preserv'd."[8] And he'd kept on reading history, and taking notes, asking himself, year after year: What does the past teach?

The United States rests on a dedication to equality, which is chiefly a moral idea, rooted in Christianity, but it rests, too, on a dedication to inquiry, fearless and unflinching. Its founders agreed with the Scottish philosopher and historian David Hume, who wrote, in 1748, that "Records of Wars, Intrigues, Factions, and Revolutions are so many Collections of Experiments."[9] They believed that truth is to be found in ideas about morality but also in the study of history.

It has often been said, in the twenty-first century and in earlier centuries, too, that Americans lack a shared past and that, built on a cracked foundation, the Republic is crumbling.[10] Part of this argument has to do with ancestry: Americans are descended from conquerors and from the conquered, from people held as slaves and from the people who held them, from the Union and from the Confederacy, from Protestants and from Jews, from Muslims and from Catholics, and from immigrants and from people who have fought to end immigration. Sometimes, in American history—in nearly all national histories—one person's villain is another's hero. But part of this argument has to do with ideology: the United States is founded on a set of ideas, but Americans have become so divided that they no longer agree, if they ever did, about what those ideas are, or were.

I wrote this book because writing an American history from beginning to end and across that divide hasn't been attempted in a long time, and it's important, and it seemed worth a try. One reason it's important is that understanding history as a form of inquiry—not as something easy or comforting but as something demanding and exhausting—was central to the nation's founding. This, too, was new. In the West, the oldest stories, the *Iliad* and the *Odyssey*, are odes and tales of wars and kings, of men and gods, sung and told. These stories were memorials, and so were the histories of antiquity: they were meant as monuments. "I have written my work, not as an essay which is to win the applause of the moment," Thucydides wrote, "but as a possession for all time." Herodotus believed that the purpose of writing history was "so that time not erase what man has brought into being." A new kind of historical writing, less memorial and more unsettling, only first emerged in the fourteenth century. "History is a philosophical science," the North African Muslim scholar Ibn Khaldun wrote in 1377, in the prologue to his history of the world, in which he defined history as the study "of the causes and origins of existing things."[11]

Only by fits and starts did history become not merely a form of memory but also a form of investigation, to be disputed, like philosophy, its premises questioned, its evidence examined, its arguments countered. Early in the seventeenth century, Sir Walter Ralegh began writing his own *History of the World*, from a prison in the Tower of London where he was allowed to keep a library of five hundred books. The past, Ralegh explained, "hath made us acquainted with our dead ancestors," but it also casts light on the present, "by the comparison and application of other men's fore-passed miseries with our own like errors and ill deservings."[12] To study the past is to unlock the prison of the present.

This new understanding of the past attempted to divide history from faith. The books of world religions—the Hebrew Bible, the New Testament, and the Quran—are pregnant with mysteries, truths known only by God, taken on faith. In the new history books, historians aimed to solve mysteries and to discover their own truths. The turn from reverence to inquiry, from mystery to history, was crucial to the founding of the United States. It didn't require abdicating faith in the truths of revealed religion and it relieved no one of the obligation to judge right from wrong. But it did require subjecting the past to skepticism, to look to beginnings not to justify ends, but to question them—with evidence.

"I offer nothing more than simple facts, plain arguments, and common sense," Thomas Paine, the spitfire son of an English grocer, wrote in *Common Sense*, in 1776. Kings have no right to reign, Paine argued, because, if we could trace hereditary monarchy back to its beginnings—"could we take off the dark covering of antiquity, and trace them to their first rise"—we'd find "the first of them nothing better than the principal ruffian of some restless gang." James Madison explained Americans' historical skepticism, this deep empiricism, this way: "Is it not the glory of the people of America, that, whilst they have paid a decent regard to the opinions of former times and other nations, they have not suffered a blind veneration for antiquity, for custom, or for names, to overrule the suggestions of their own good sense, the knowledge of their own situation, and the lessons of their own experience?"[13] Evidence, for Madison, was everything.

"A new era for politics is struck," Paine wrote, his pen aflame, and "a new method of thinking hath arisen."[14] Declaring independence was itself an argument about the relationship between the present and the past, an argument that required evidence of a very particular kind: historical evidence. That's why most of the Declaration of Independence is a list of historical claims. "To prove this," Jefferson wrote, "let facts be submitted to a candid world."

*Facts, knowledge, experience, proof.* These words come from the law. Around the seventeenth century, they moved into what was then called "natural history": astronomy, physics, chemistry, geology. By the eighteenth century they were applied to history and to politics, too. *These truths:* this was the language of reason, of enlightenment, of inquiry, and of history. In 1787, then, when Alexander Hamilton asked "whether societies of men are really capable or not of establishing good government from reflection and choice, or whether they are forever destined to depend for their political constitutions on accident and force," that was the kind of question a scientist asks before beginning an experiment. Time alone would tell. But time has passed. The beginning has come to an end. What, then, is the verdict of history?

This book attempts to answer that question by telling the story of American history, beginning in 1492, with Columbus's voyage, which tied together continents, and ending in a world not merely tied together but tangled, knotted, and bound. It chronicles the settlement of American colonies; the nation's founding and its expansion through migration, immigration, war, and invention; its descent into civil war; its entrance into wars in Europe; its rise as a world power and its role, after the Second World War, in the establishment of the modern liberal world order: the rule of law, individual rights, democratic government, open borders, and free markets. It recounts the nation's confrontations with communism abroad and discrimination at home; its fractures and divisions, and the wars it has waged since 2001, when two airplanes crashed into the two towers of the World Trade Center eight blocks from the site of a long-gone shop where the printers of the *New-York Packet* had once offered for sale a young mother and her six-month old baby and the *Columbian Almanack,* bound with the Constitution, or without.

With this history, I've told a story; I've tried to tell it fairly. I have written a beginning and I have written an ending and I have tried to cross a divide, but I haven't attempted to tell the whole story. No one could. Much is missing in these pages. In the 1950s, the historian Carl Degler explained the rule he'd used in deciding what to leave in and what to leave out of his own history of the United States, a lovely book called *Out of Our Past.* "Readers should be warned that they will find nothing here on the Presidential administrations between 1868 and 1901, no mention of the American Indians or the settlement of the seventeenth-century colonies," Degler advised. "The War of 1812 is touched on only in a footnote."[15] I, too, have had to skip over an awful lot. Some very important events haven't even made it into the footnotes, which I've kept clipped and short, like a baby's fingernails.

In deciding what to leave in and what to leave out, I've confined myself to what, in my view, a people constituted as a nation in the early twenty-first century need to know about their own past, mainly because this book is meant to double as an old-fashioned civics book, an explanation of the origins and ends of democratic institutions, from the town meeting to the party system, from the nominating convention to the secret ballot, from talk radio to Internet polls. This book is chiefly a political history. It pays very little attention to military and diplomatic history or to social and cultural history. But it does include episodes in the history of American law and religion, journalism and technology, chiefly because these are places where what is true, and what's not, have sometimes gotten sorted out.

Aside from being a brief history of the United States and a civics primer, this book aims to be something else, too: it's an explanation of the nature of the past. History isn't only a subject; it's also a method. My method is, generally, to let the dead speak for themselves. I've pressed their words between these pages, like flowers, for their beauty, or like insects, for their hideousness. The work of the historian is not the work of the critic or of the moralist; it is the work of the sleuth and the storyteller, the philosopher and the scientist, the keeper of tales, the sayer of sooth, the teller of truth.

What, then, of the American past? There is, to be sure, a great deal of anguish in American history and more hypocrisy. No nation and no people are relieved of these. But there is also, in the American past, an extraordinary amount of decency and hope, of prosperity and ambition, and much, especially, of invention and beauty. Some American history books fail to criticize the United States; others do nothing but. This book is neither kind. The truths on which the nation was founded are not mysteries, articles of faith, never to be questioned, as if the founding were an act of God, but neither are they lies, all facts fictions, as if nothing can be known, in a world without truth. Between reverence and worship, on the one side, and irreverence and contempt, on the other, lies an uneasy path, away from false pieties and petty triumphs over people who lived and died and committed both their acts of courage and their sins and errors long before we committed ours. "We cannot hallow this ground," Lincoln said at Gettysburg. We are obliged, instead, to walk this ground, dedicating ourselves to both the living and the dead.

A last word, then, about storytelling, and truth. "I have begun this letter five times and torn it up," James Baldwin wrote, in a letter to his nephew begun in 1962. "I keep seeing your face, which is also the face of your father and my brother." His brother was dead; he meant to tell his nephew about being a black man, about the struggle for equality, and about the towering importance and gripping urgency of studying the past and reckoning with origins. He went on,

I have known both of you all your lives, have carried your Daddy in my arms and on my shoulders, kissed and spanked him and watched him learn to walk. I don't know if you've known anybody from that far back; if you've loved anybody that long, first as an infant, then as a child, then as a man, you gain a strange perspective on time and human pain and effort. Other people cannot see what I see whenever I look into your father's face, for behind your father's face as it is today are all those faces which were his.[16]

No one can know a nation that far back, from its infancy, with or without baby teeth kept in a jar. But studying history is like that, looking into one face and seeing, behind it, another, face after face after face. "Know whence you came," Baldwin told his nephew.[17] The past is an inheritance, a gift and a burden. It can't be shirked. You carry it everywhere. There's nothing for it but to get to know it.

# THESE TRUTHS

## Part One

THE

IDEA

★ ★ ★ ★

*1492–1799*

*In the beginning, all the World was America.*

—John Locke,
Second Treatise on Government,
1689

# *One*

# THE NATURE
# OF THE PAST

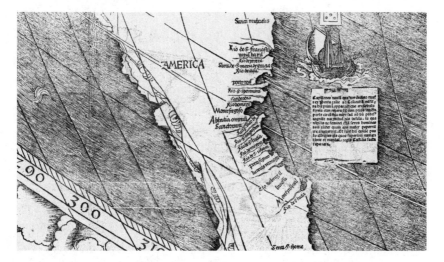

*"America" first appeared as the name of an undefined
land mass on a map of the world made in 1507.*

"WE SAW NAKED PEOPLE," A BROAD-SHOULDERED SEA
captain from Genoa wrote in his diary, nearing land after weeks
of staring at nothing but blue-black sea. Or, at least, that's what Christopher Columbus is thought to have written in his diary that day in October 1492, ink trailing across the page like the line left behind by a snail
wandering across a stretch of sand. No one knows for sure what the sea
captain wrote that day, because his diary is lost. In the 1530s, before it
disappeared, parts of it were copied by a frocked and tonsured Dominican
friar named Bartolomé de Las Casas. The friar's copy was lost, too, until
about 1790, when an old sailor found it in the library of a Spanish duke.
In 1894, the widow of another librarian sold to a duchess parchment
scraps of what appeared to be Columbus's original—it had his signature,

*On an ink-splotched sketch of northwest Haiti, Columbus
labeled "la española," Hispaniola, "the little Spanish island."*

and the year 1492 on the cover. After that, the widow disappeared, and,
with her, whatever else may have been left of the original diary vanished.[1]

All of this is unfortunate; none of it is unusual. Most of what once
existed is gone. Flesh decays, wood rots, walls fall, books burn. Nature
takes one toll, malice another. History is the study of what remains, what's
left behind, which can be almost anything, so long as it survives the rav-
ages of time and war: letters, diaries, DNA, gravestones, coins, television
broadcasts, paintings, DVDs, viruses, abandoned Facebook pages, the
transcripts of congressional hearings, the ruins of buildings. Some of
these things are saved by chance or accident, like the one house that, as
if by miracle, still stands after a hurricane razes a town. But most of what
historians study survives because it was purposely kept—placed in a box
and carried up to an attic, shelved in a library, stored in a museum, photographed or recorded, downloaded to a server—carefully preserved and
even catalogued. All of it, together, the accidental and the intentional,
this archive of the past—remains, relics, a repository of knowledge, the
evidence of what came before, this inheritance—is called the historical
record, and it is maddeningly uneven, asymmetrical, and unfair.

Relying on so spotty a record requires caution. Still, even its absences
speak. "We saw naked people," Columbus wrote in his diary (at least,
according to the notes taken by Las Casas). "They were a people very
poor in everything," the sea captain went on, describing the people he
met on an island they called Haiti—"land of mountains"—but that
Columbus called Hispaniola—"the little Spanish island"—because he

thought it had no name. They lacked weapons, he reported; they lacked tools. He believed they lacked even a faith: "They appear to have no religion." They lacked guile; they lacked suspicion. "I will take six of them from here to Your Highnesses," he wrote, addressing the king and queen of Spain, "in order that they may learn to speak," as if, impossibly, they had no language.[2] Later, he admitted the truth: "None of us understands the words they say."[3]

Two months after he reached Haiti, Columbus prepared to head back to Spain but, off the coast, his three-masted flagship ran aground. Before the ship sank, Columbus's men salvaged the timbers to build a fort; the sunken wreckage has never been found, as lost to history as everything that the people of Haiti said the day a strange sea captain washed up on shore. On the voyage home, on a smaller ship, square-rigged and swift, Columbus wondered about all that he did not understand about the people he'd met, a people he called "Indians" because he believed he had sailed to the Indies. It occurred to him that it wasn't that they didn't have a religion or a language but that these things were, to him, mysteries that he could not penetrate, things beyond his comprehension. He needed help. In Barcelona, he hired Ramón Pané, a priest and scholar, to come along on his next voyage, to "discover and understand . . . the beliefs and idolatries of the Indians, and . . . how they worship their gods."[4]

Pané sailed with Columbus in 1493. Arriving in Haiti, Pané met a man named Guatícabanú, who knew all of the languages spoken on the island, and who learned Pané's language, Castilian, and taught him his own. Pané lived with the natives, the Taíno, for four years, and delivered to Columbus his report, a manuscript he titled *An Account of the Antiquities of the Indians*. Not long afterward, it vanished.

The fates of old books are as different as the depths of the ocean. Before *An Account of the Antiquities of the Indians* disappeared, Columbus's son Ferdinand, writing a biography of his father, copied it out, and even though Ferdinand Columbus's book remained unpublished at his death in 1539, his copy of Pané's extraordinary account had by then been copied by other scholars, including the learned and dogged Las Casas, a man who never left a page unturned. In 1570, a scholar in Venice was translating Pané's *Antiquities* into Italian when he died in prison, suspected of being a spy for the French; nevertheless, his translation was published in 1571, with the result that the closest thing to the original of

Pané's account that survives is a poor Italian translation of words that had already been many times translated, from other tongues to Guatícabanú's tongue, and from Guatícabanú's tongue to Castilian and then, by Pané, from Castilian.[5] And yet it remains a treasure.

"I wrote it down in haste and did not have sufficient paper," Pané apologized. He'd collected the Taíno's stories, though he'd found it difficult to make sense of them, since so many of the stories seemed, to him, to contradict one another. "Because they have neither writing nor letters," Pané reported, "they cannot give a good account of how they have heard this from their ancestors, and therefore they do not all say the same thing." The Taíno had no writing. But, contrary to Columbus's initial impressions, they most certainly did have a religion. They called their god Yúcahu. "They believe that he is in heaven and is immortal, and that no one can see him, and that he has a mother," Pané explained. "But he has no beginning." Also, "They know likewise from whence they came, and where the sun and the moon had their beginning, and how the sea was made, and where the dead go."[6]

People order their worlds with tales of their dead and of their gods and of the origins of their laws. The Taíno told Pané that their ancestors once lived in caves and would go out at night but, once, when some of them were late coming back, the Sun turned them into trees. Another time, a man named Yaya killed his son Yayael and put his bones in a gourd and hung it from his roof and when his wife took down the gourd and opened it the bones had been changed into fish and the people ate the fish but when they tried to hang the gourd up again, it fell to the earth, and out spilled all the water that made the oceans.

The Taíno did not have writing but they did have government. "They have their laws gathered in ancient songs, by which they govern themselves," Pané reported.[7] They sang their laws, and they sang their history. "These songs remain in their memory rather than in books," another Spanish historian observed, "and this way they recite the genealogies of the caciques, kings, and lords they have had, their deeds, and the bad or good times they had."[8]

In those songs, they told their truths. They told of how the days and weeks and years after the broad-shouldered sea captain first spied their island were the worst of times. Their god, Yúcahu, had once foretold that they "would enjoy their dominion for but a brief time because a clothed people would come to their land who could overcome them and kill them."[9] This had come to pass. There were about three million people on that island, land of mountains, when Columbus landed; fifty years later, there were only five hundred; everyone else had died, their songs unsung.

# I.

STORIES OF ORIGINS nearly always begin in darkness, earth and water and night, black as doom. The sun and the moon came from a cave, the Taíno told Pané, and the oceans spilled out of a gourd. The Iroquois, a people of the Great Lakes, say the world began with a woman who lived on the back of a turtle. The Akan of Ghana tell a story about a god who lived closer to the earth, low in the sky, until an old woman struck him with her pestle, and he flew away. "In the beginning, God created the heaven and the earth," according to Genesis. "And the earth was without form, and void; and darkness was upon the face of the deep."

Darkness was on the face of the deep in geological histories, too, whose evidence comes from rocks and bones. The universe was created about fourteen billion years ago, according to the traces left behind by meteors and the afterlives of stars, glowing and distant, blinking and dim. The earth was formed about four billion years ago, according to the sand and rocks, sea floors and mountaintops. For a very long time, all the lands of the earth were glommed together until, about three hundred million years ago, those glommed-together lands began breaking up; parts broke off and began drifting away from one another, like the debris of a sinking ship.

Evidence of the long-ago past is elusive, but it survives in the unlikeliest of places, even in the nests of pack rats, mammals that crept up in North America sixty million years ago. Pack rats build nests out of sticks and stones and bones and urinate on them; the liquid hardens like amber, preserving pack rat nests as if pressed behind glass. A great many of the animals and plants that lived at the time of ancient pack rats later became extinct, lost forever, saved only in pack rat nests, where their preserved remains provide evidence not only of evolution but of the warming of the earth. A pack rat nest isn't like the geological record; it's more like an archive, a collection, gathered and kept, like a library of old books and long-forgotten manuscripts, a treasure, an account of the antiquities of the animals and plants.[10]

The fossil record is richer still. Charles Darwin called the record left by fossils "a history of the world imperfectly kept." According to that record, *Homo sapiens*, modern humans, evolved about three hundred thousand years ago, in East Africa, near and around what is now Ethiopia. Over the next hundred and fifty thousand years, early humans spread into the Middle East, Asia, Australia, and Europe.[11] Like pack rats, humans store and keep and save. The record of early humans, however imperfectly kept, includes not only fossils but also artifacts, things created by people (the word contains its own meaning—*art* + *fact*—an *artifact* is a fact made by art). Artifacts and the fossil record together tell the story of how, about twenty thousand years ago, humans migrated into the Americas from Asia when, for a while, the northwestern tip of North America and the northeastern tip of Asia were attached when a landmass between them rose above sea level, making it possible for humans and animals to walk between what is now Russia and Alaska, a distance of some six hundred miles, until the water rose again, and one half of the world was, once again, cut off from the other half.

In 1492, seventy-five million people lived in the Americas, north and south.[12] The people of Cahokia, the biggest city in North America, on the Mississippi floodplains, had built giant plazas and earthen mounds, some bigger than the Egyptian pyramids. In about 1000 AD, before Cahokia was abandoned, more than ten thousand people lived there. The Aztecs, Incas, and Maya, vast and ancient civilizations, built monumental cities and kept careful records and calendars of exquisite accuracy. The Aztec city of Tenochtitlán, founded in 1325, had a population of at least a quarter-million people, making it one of the largest cities in the world. Outside of those places, most people in the Americas lived in smaller settlements and gathered and hunted for their food. A good number were farmers who grew squash and corn and beans, hunted and fished. They kept pigs and chickens but not bigger animals. They spoke hundreds of languages and practiced many different faiths. Most had no written form of language. They believed in many gods and in the divinity of animals and of the earth itself.[13] The Taíno lived in villages of one or two thousand people, headed by a cacique. They fished and farmed. They warred with their neighbors. They decorated their bodies; they painted themselves red. They sang their laws.[14] They knew where the dead went.

In 1492, about sixty million people lived in Europe, fifteen million fewer than lived in the Americas. They lived and were ruled in villages and towns, in cities and states, in kingdoms and empires. They built magnificent cities and castles, cathedrals and temples and mosques, libraries and universities. Most people farmed and worked on land surrounded by fences, raising crops and cattle and sheep and goats. "Be fruitful, and multiply, and replenish the earth, and subdue it," God tells Adam and Eve in Genesis, "and have dominion over the fish of the sea, and over the fowl of the air, and over every living thing that moveth upon the earth." They spoke and wrote dozens of languages. They recorded their religious tenets and stories on scrolls and in books of beauty and wonder. They were Catholic and Protestant, Jewish and Muslim; for long stretches of time, peoples of different faiths managed to get along and then, for other long stretches, they did not, as if they would cut out one another's hearts. Their faith was their truth, the word of their God, revealed to their prophets, and, for Christians, to the people, through the words spoken by Jesus—the *good-spell*, or "good news"—their Gospel, written down.

Before 1492, Europe suffered from scarcity and famine. After 1492, the vast wealth carried to Europe from the Americas and extracted by the forced labor of Africans granted governments new powers that contributed to the rise of nation-states.

A nation is a people who share a common ancestry. A state is a political community, governed by laws. A nation-state is a political community, governed by laws, that, at least theoretically, unites a people who share a common ancestry (one way nation-states form is by violently purging their populations of people with different ancestries). As nation-states emerged, they needed to explain themselves, which they did by telling stories about their origins, tying together ribbons of myths, as if everyone in the "English nation," for instance, had the same ancestors, when, of course, they did not. Very often, histories of nation-states are little more than myths that hide the seams that stitch the nation to the state.[15]

The origins of the United States can be found in those seams. When the United States declared its independence in 1776, plainly, it was a state, but what made it a nation? The fiction that its people shared a common ancestry was absurd on its face; they came from all over, and, having waged a war against England, the very last thing they wanted to celebrate was their Englishness. In an attempt to solve this problem, the earliest historians of the United States decided to begin their accounts with Columbus's voyage, stitching 1776 to 1492. George Bancroft published his *History of the United States from the Discovery of the American Continent to the Present* in 1834, when the nation was barely more than a half-century old, a fledgling, just hatched. By beginning with Columbus, Bancroft made the United States nearly three centuries older than it was, a many-feathered old bird. Bancroft wasn't only a historian; he was also a politician: he served in the administrations of three U.S. presidents, including as secretary of war during the age of American expansion. He believed in manifest destiny, the idea that the United States was fated to cross the continent, from east to west. For Bancroft, the nation's fate was all but sealed the day Columbus set sail. By giving Americans a more ancient past, he hoped to make America's founding appear inevitable and its growth inexorable, God-ordained. He also wanted to celebrate the United States, not as an offshoot of England, but instead as a pluralist and cosmopolitan nation, with ancestors all over the world. "France contributed to its independence," he observed, "the origin of the language we speak carries us to India; our religion is from Palestine; of the hymns sung in our churches, some were first heard in Italy, some in the deserts of Arabia, some on the banks of the Euphrates; our arts come from Greece; our jurisprudence from Rome."[16]

Yet the origins of the United States date to 1492 for another, more troubling reason: the nation's founding truths were forged in a crucible of violence, the products of staggering cruelty, conquest and slaughter, the assassination of worlds. The history of the United States can be said to begin in 1492 because the idea of equality came out of a resolute rejection of the idea of inequality; a dedication to liberty emerged out of bitter protest against slavery; and the right to self-government was fought for, by sword and, still more fiercely, by pen. Against conquest, slaughter, and slavery came the urgent and abiding question, "By what right?"

To begin a history of the United States in 1492 is to take seriously and solemnly the idea of America itself as a beginning. Yet, so far from the nation's founding having been inevitable, its expansion inexorable, the history of the United States, like all history, is a near chaos of contingencies and accidents, of wonders and horrors, unlikely, improbable, and astonishing.

To start with, weighing the evidence, it's a little surprising that it was western Europeans in 1492, and not some other group of people, some other year, who crossed an ocean to discover a lost world. Making the journey required knowledge, capacity, and interest. The Maya, whose territory stretched from what is now Mexico to Costa Rica, knew enough astronomy to navigate across the ocean as early as AD 300. They did not, however, have seaworthy boats. The ancient Greeks had known a great deal about cartography: Claudius Ptolemy, an astronomer who lived in the second century, had devised a way to project the surface of the globe onto a flat surface with near-perfect proportions. But medieval Christians, having dismissed the writings of the ancient Greeks as pagan, had lost much of that knowledge. The Chinese had invented the compass in the eleventh century, and had excellent boats. Before his death in 1433, Zheng He, a Chinese Muslim, had explored the coast of much of Asia and eastern Africa, leading two hundred ships and twenty-seven thousand sailors. But China was the richest country in the world, and by the late fifteenth century no longer allowed travel beyond the Indian Ocean, on the theory that the rest of the world was unworthy and uninteresting. West Africans navigated the coastline and rivers that led into a vast inland trade network, but prevailing winds and currents thwarted them from navigating north and they seldom ventured into the ocean. Muslims from North Africa and the Middle East, who had never cast aside the knowledge of antiquity and the calculations of Ptolemy, made accurate maps and built sturdy boats, but because they dominated trade in the Mediterranean Sea, as well as overland trade with Africa, for gold, and with Asia, for spices, they didn't have much reason to venture farther.[17]

It was somewhat out of desperation, then, that the poorest and weakest Christian monarchs on the very western edge of Europe, fighting with Muslims, jealous of the Islamic world's monopoly on trade, and keen to spread their religion, began looking for routes to Africa and Asia that wouldn't require sailing across the Mediterranean. In the middle of the fifteenth century, Prince Henry of Portugal began sending ships to sail along the western coast of Africa. Building forts on the coast and founding colonies on islands, they began to trade with African merchants, buying and selling people, coin for flesh, a traffic in slaves.

Columbus, a citizen of the bustling Mediterranean port of Genoa, served as a sailor on Portuguese slave-trading ships beginning in 1482. In 1484, when he was about thirty-three years old, he presented to the king of Portugal a plan to travel to Asia by sailing west, across the ocean. The king assembled a panel of scholars to consider the proposal but, in the end, rejected it: Portugal was committed to its ventures in West Africa, and the king's scholars saw that Columbus had greatly underestimated the distance he would have to travel. Better calculated was the voyage of Bartolomeu Dias, a Portuguese nobleman, who in 1487 rounded the southernmost tip of Africa, proving that it was possible to sail from the Atlantic to the Indian Ocean. Why sail west, across the Atlantic, when a different way to sail to the East had already been found?

Columbus next brought his proposal to the king and queen of Spain, who at first rejected it; they were busy waging wars of religion, purging their population of people who had different ancestors and different beliefs. Early in 1492, after the last Muslim city in Spain fell to the Spanish crown, Ferdinand and Isabella ordered that all Jews be expelled from their realm and, confident that their pitiless Inquisition had rid their kingdom of Muslims and Jews, heretics and pagans, they ordered Columbus to sail, to trade, and to spread the Christian faith: to conquer, and to chronicle, to say what was true, and to write it down: to keep a diary.

To WRITE SOMETHING down doesn't make it true. But the history of truth is lashed to the history of writing like a mast to a sail. Writing was invented in three different parts of the world at three different moments in time: about 3200 BCE in Mesopotamia, about 1100 BCE in China, and about AD 600 in Mesoamerica. In the history of the world, most of the people who have ever lived either did not know how to write or, if they did, left no writing behind, which is among the reasons why the historical record is so maddeningly unfair. To write something down is to make a fossil record of a mind. Stories are full of power and force; they seethe with meaning, with truths and lies, evasions and honesty. Speech often has far more weight and urgency than writing. But most words, once spoken, are forgotten, while writing lasts, a point observed early in the seventeenth century by an English vicar named Samuel Purchas. Purchas, who had never been more than two hundred miles from his vicarage, carefully studied the accounts of travelers, because he proposed to write a new history of the world.[18] Taking stock of all the differences between the peoples of all ages and places, across continents and centuries, Purchas was most struck by what he called the "literall advantage": the significance of writing. "By writing," he wrote, "Man seems immortall."[19]

A new chapter in the history of truth—foundational to the idea of truth on which the United States would one day stake and declare its independence—began on Columbus's first voyage. If any man in history had a "literall advantage," that man was Christopher Columbus. In Haiti in October 1492, under a scorching sun, with two of his captains as witnesses, Columbus (according to the notes taken by Las Casas) declared that "he would take, as in fact he did take, possession of the said island for the king and for the queen his lords." And then he wrote that down.[20]

This act was both new and strange. Marco Polo, traveling through the East in the thirteenth century, had not claimed China for Venice; nor did Sir John Mandeville, traveling through the Middle East in the fourteenth century, attempt to take possession of Persia, Syria, or Ethiopia. Columbus had read Marco Polo's *Travels* and Mandeville's *Travels*; he seems to have brought those books with him when he sailed.[21] Unlike Polo and Mandeville, Columbus did not make a catalogue of the ways and beliefs of the people he met (only later did he hire Pané to do that). Instead, he decided that the people he met had no ways and beliefs. Every difference he saw as an absence.[22] Insisting that they had no faith and no civil government and were therefore infidels and savages who could not rightfully own anything, he claimed possession of their land, by the act of writing. They were a people without truth; he would make his truth theirs. He would tell them where the dead go.

Columbus had this difference from Marco Polo and Mandeville, too: he made his voyages not long after Johannes Gutenberg, a German blacksmith, invented the printing press. Printing accelerated the diffusion of knowledge and broadened the historical record: things that are printed are much more likely to last than things that are merely written down, since printing produces many copies. The two men were often paired. "Two things which I always thought could be compared, not only to Antiquity, but to immortality," wrote one sixteenth-century French philosopher, are "the invention of the printing press and the discovery of the new world."[23] Columbus widened the world, Gutenberg made it spin faster.

But Columbus himself did not consider the lands he'd visited to be a new world. He thought only that he'd found a new route to the old world. Instead, it was Amerigo Vespucci, the venturesome son of a notary from Florence, Italy, who crossed the ocean in 1503 and wrote, about the lands he found, "These we may rightly call a new world." The report Vespucci brought home was soon published as a book called *Mundus Novus*, translated into eight languages and published in sixty different editions. What Vespucci reported discovering was rather difficult to believe. "I have found a continent more densely peopled and abounding in animals than our Europe or Asia or Africa," he wrote.[24] It seemed a Garden of Eden, a place only ever before imagined. In 1516, Thomas More, a counselor to England's king, Henry VIII, published a fictional account of a Portuguese sailor on one of Vespucci's ships who had traveled just a bit farther, to an island where he found a perfect republic, named Utopia (literally, no place)—the island of nowhere.[25]

What did it mean to find someplace where nowhere was supposed to be? The world had long seemed to consist of three parts. In the seventh century, the Archbishop Isidore of Seville, writing an encyclopedia called the *Etymologiae* that circulated widely in manuscript—as many as a thousand handwritten copies survive—had drawn the world as a circle surrounded by oceans and divided by seas into three bodies of land, Asia, Europe, and Africa, inhabited by the descendants of the three sons of Noah: Shem, Japheth, and Ham. In 1472, *Etymologiae* became one of the very first books ever to be set in type and the archbishop's map became the first world map ever printed.[26] Twenty years later, it was obsolete.

Discovering that nowhere was somewhere meant work for mapmakers, another kind of writing that made claims of truth and possession. In 1507, Martin Waldseemüller, a German cartographer living in northern France who had in his hands a French translation of *Mundus Novus,* carved onto twelve woodblocks a new map of the world, a Universalis Cosmographia, and printed more than a thousand copies. People pasted the twelve prints together and mounted them like wallpaper to make a giant map, four feet high by eight feet wide. Wallpaper fades and falls apart: only a single copy of Waldseemüller's map survives. But one word on that long-lost map has lasted longer than anything else Waldseemüller ever wrote. With a nod to Vespucci, Waldseemüller, inventing a word, gave the fourth part of the world, that unknown utopia, a name: he labeled it "America."[27]

*A drawing originally made in the seventh century by Isidore of Seville became, in 1472, the first printed map of the world; twenty years later, it was obsolete.*

This name stuck by the merest accident. Much else did not last. The Taíno story about the cave, the Iroquois story about the turtle, the Akan story about the old woman with the pestle, the Old Testament story of Adam and Eve—these stories would be unknown, or hardly known, if they hadn't been written down or recorded. That they lasted mattered. Modernity began when people fighting over which of these stories was true began to think differently about the nature of truth, about the nature of the past, and about the nature of rule.

## II.

IN 1493, WHEN COLUMBUS returned from his unimaginable voyage, a Spanish-born pope granted all of the lands on the other side of the ocean, everything west of a line of longitude some three hundred miles west of Cape Verde, to Spain, and granted what lay east of that line, western Africa, to Portugal, the pope claiming the authority to divvy up lands inhabited by tens of millions of people as if he were the god of Genesis. Unsurprisingly, the heads of England, France, and the Netherlands found this papal pronouncement absurd. "The sun shines for me as for the others," said the king of France. "I should like to see the clause

*Artists working for the sixteenth- century mestizo Diego Muñoz Camargo illustrated the Spanish punishment for native converts who abandoned Christianity.*

of Adam's will which excludes me from a share of the world."[28] Nor did Spain's claim go uncontested on the other side of the world. A Taíno man told Guatícabanú that the Spanish "were wicked and had taken their land by force."[29] Guatícabanú told that to Ramón Pané, who wrote it down. Ferdinand Columbus copied that out. And so did a scholar in a prison in Venice. It was as if that Taíno man had taken down from his roof a gourd full of the bones of his son and opened it, spilling out an ocean of ideas. The work of conquest involved pretending that ocean could be poured back into that gourd.

An ocean of ideas not fitting into a gourd, people in both Europe and the Americas groped for meaning and wondered how to account for differ- ence and sameness. They asked new questions, and they asked old ques- tions more sharply: Are all peoples one? And if they are, by what right can one people take the land of another or their labor or, even, their lives?

Any historical reckoning with these questions begins with counting and measuring. Between 1500 and 1800, roughly two and a half million Europeans moved to the Americas; they carried twelve million Africans there by force; and as many as fifty million Native Americans died, chiefly of disease.[30] Europe is spread over about four million square miles, the Americas over about twenty million square miles. For centuries, geography had constrained Europe's demographic and economic growth; that era came to a close when Europeans claimed lands five times the size of Europe. Taking possession of the Americas gave Europeans a surplus of land; it ended famine and led to four centuries of economic growth, growth without precedent, growth many Europeans understood as evidence of the grace of God. One Spaniard, writing from New Spain to his brother in Valladolid in 1592, told him, "This land is as good as ours, for God has given us more here than there, and we shall be better off."[31] Even the poor prospered.

The European extraction of the wealth of the Americas made possible the rise of capitalism: new forms of trade, investment, and profit. Between 1500 and 1600 alone, Europeans recorded carrying back to Europe from the Americas nearly two hundred tons of gold and sixteen thousand tons of silver; much more traveled as contraband. "The discovery of America, and that of a passage to the East Indies by the Cape of Good Hope, are the two greatest and most important events recorded in the history of mankind," Adam Smith wrote, in *The Wealth of Nations*, in 1776. But the voyages of Columbus and Dias also marked a turning point in the development of another economic system, slavery: the wealth of the Americas flowed to Europe by the forced labor of Africans.[32]

Slavery had been practiced in many parts of the world for centuries. People tended to enslave their enemies, people they considered different enough from themselves to condemn to lifelong servitude. Sometimes, though not often, the status of slaves was heritable: the children of slaves were condemned to a life of slavery, too. Many wars had to do with religion, and because many slaves were prisoners of war, slaves and their owners tended to be people of different faiths: Christians enslaved Jews; Muslims enslaved Christians; Christians enslaved Muslims. Since the Middle Ages, Muslim traders from North Africa had traded in Africans from below the Sahara, where slavery was widespread. In much of Africa, labor, not land, constituted the sole form of property recognized by law, a form of consolidating wealth and generating revenue, which meant that African states tended to be small and that, while European wars were fought for land, African wars were fought for labor. People captured in African wars were bought and sold in large markets by merchants and local officials and kings and, beginning in the 1450s, by Portuguese sea captains.[33]

Columbus, a veteran of that trade, reported to Ferdinand and Isabella in 1492 that it would be the work of a moment to enslave the people of Haiti, since "with 50 men all of them could be held in subjection and can be made to do whatever one might wish."[34] In sugar mines and gold mines, the Spanish worked their native slaves to death while many more died of disease. Soon, they turned to another source of forced labor, Africans traded by the Portuguese.

Counting and keeping accounts on the cargo of every ship, Europeans found themselves puzzled by an extraordinary asymmetry. People moved from Europe and Africa to the Americas; wealth moved from the Americas to Europe; and animals and plants moved from Europe to the Americas. But very few people or animals or plants moved from the Americas to Europe or Africa, at least not successfully. "It appears as if some invisible barrier existed preventing passage Eastward, though allowing it Westward," a later botanist wrote.[35] The one-way migration of people made self-evident sense: people controlled the ships and they carried far more people west than east, bringing soldiers and missionaries, settlers and slaves. But the one-way migration of animals and plants was, for centuries, until the late nineteenth-century age of Darwin and the germ theory of disease, altogether baffling, explained only by faith in divine providence: Christians took it as a sign that their conquest was ordained by God.

The signs came in abundance. When Columbus made a second voyage across the ocean in 1493, he commanded a fleet of seventeen ships carrying twelve hundred men, and another kind of army, too: seeds and cuttings of wheat, chickpeas, melons, onions, radishes, greens, grapevines, and sugar cane, and horses, pigs, cattle, chickens, sheep, and goats, male and female, two by two. Hidden among the men and the plants and the animals were stowaways, seeds stuck to animal skins or clinging to the folds of cloaks and blankets, in clods of mud. Most of these were the seeds of plants Europeans considered to be weeds, like bluegrass, daisies, thistle, nettles, ferns, and dandelions. Weeds grow best in disturbed soil, and nothing disturbs soil better than an army of men, razing forests for timber and fuel and turning up the ground cover with their boots, and the hooves of their horses and oxen and cattle. Livestock eat grass; people eat livestock: livestock turn grass into food that humans can eat. The animals that Europeans brought to the New World—cattle, pigs, goats, sheep, chickens, and horses—had no natural predators in the Americas but they did have an abundant food supply. They reproduced in numbers unfathomable in Europe. Cattle populations doubled every fifteen months. Nothing, though, beat the pigs. Pigs convert one-fifth of everything they eat into food for human consumption (cattle, by contrast, convert one-twentieth); they feed themselves, by foraging, and they have litters of ten or more. Within a few years of Columbus's second voyage, the eight pigs he brought with him had descendants numbering in the thousands. Wrote one observer, "All the mountains swarmed with them."[36]

Meanwhile, the people of the New World: They died by the hundreds. They died by the thousands, by the tens of thousands, by the hundreds of thousands, by the tens of millions. The isolation of the Americas from the rest of the world, for hundreds of millions of years, meant that diseases to which Europeans and Africans had built up immunities over millennia were entirely new to the native peoples of the Americas. European ships, with their fleets of people and animals and plants, brought along, unseen, battalions of diseases: smallpox, measles, diphtheria, trachoma, whooping cough, chicken pox, bubonic plague, malaria, typhoid fever, yellow fever, dengue fever, scarlet fever, amoebic dysentery, and influenza, diseases that had evolved alongside humans and their domesticated animals living in dense, settled populations—cities—where human and animal waste breeds vermin, like mice and rats and roaches. Most of the indigenous peoples of the Americas, though, didn't live in dense settlements, and even those who lived in villages tended to move with the seasons, taking apart their towns and rebuilding them somewhere else. They didn't accumulate filth, and they didn't live in crowds. They suffered from very few infectious diseases. Europeans, exposed to these diseases for thousands of years, had developed vigorous immune systems, and antibodies particular to bacteria to which no one in the New World had ever been exposed.

The consequence was catastrophe. Of one hundred people exposed to the smallpox virus for the first time, nearly one hundred became infected, and twenty-five to thirty-three died. Before they died, they exposed many more people: smallpox incubates for ten to fourteen days, which meant that people who didn't yet feel sick tended to flee, carrying the disease as far as they could go before collapsing. Some people who were infected with smallpox could have recovered, if they'd been taken care of, but when one out of every three people was sick, and a lot of people ran, there was no one left to nurse the sick, who died of thirst and grief and of being alone.[37] And they died, too, of torture: already weakened by disease, they were worked to death, and starved to death. On the islands in the Caribbean, so many natives died so quickly that Spaniards decided very early on to conquer more territory, partly to take more prisoners to work in their gold and silver mines, as slaves.

Spanish conquistadors first set foot on the North American mainland in 1513; in a matter of decades, New Spain spanned not only all of what became Mexico but also more than half of what became the continental United States, territory that stretched, east to west, from Florida to California, and as far north as Virginia on the Atlantic Ocean and Canada on the Pacific.[38] Diseases spread ahead of the Spanish invaders, laying waste to wide swaths of the continent. It became commonplace, inevitable, even, first among the Spanish, and then, in turn, among the French, the Dutch, and the English, to see their own prosperity and good health and the terrible sicknesses suffered by the natives as signs from God. "Touching these savages, there is a thing that I cannot omit to remark to you," one French settler wrote: "it appears visibly that God wishes that they yield their place to new peoples." Death convinced them at once of their right and of the truth of their faith. "The natives, they are all dead of small Poxe," John Winthrop wrote when he arrived in New England in 1630: "the Lord hathe cleared our title to what we possess."[39]

Europeans craved these omens from their God, because otherwise their title to the land and their right to enslave had little foundation in the laws of men. Often, this gave them pause. In 1504, the king of Spain assembled a group of scholars and lawyers to provide him with guidance about whether the conquest "was in agreement with human and divine law." The debate turned on two questions: Did the natives own their own land (that is, did they possess "dominion"), and could they rule themselves (that is, did they possess "sovereignty")? To answer these questions, the king's advisers turned to the philosophy of antiquity.

Under Roman law, government exists to manage relations of property, the king's ministers argued, and since, according to Columbus, the natives had no government, they had no property, and therefore no dominion.

*An Aztec artist rendered the Spanish conquistadors, led by Cortés, invading Mexico.*

Regarding sovereignty, the king's ministers turned to Aristotle's *Politics*. "That some should rule and others be ruled is a thing not only necessary, but expedient," Aristotle had written. "From the hour of their birth, some are marked out for subjection, others for rule." All relations are relations of hierarchy, according to Aristotle; the soul rules over the body, men over animals, males over females, and masters over slaves. Slavery, for Aristotle, was not a matter of law but a matter of nature: "he who is by nature not his own but another's man, is by nature a slave; and he may be said to be another's man who, being a human being, is also a possession." Those who are by nature possessions are those who have a lesser capacity for reason; these people "are by nature slaves," Aristotle wrote, "and it is better for them as for all inferiors that they should be under the rule of a master."[40]

The king was satisfied: the natives did not own their land and were, by nature, slaves. The conquest continued. But across the ocean, a trumpet of protest was sounded from a pulpit. In December 1511, on the fourth Sunday of Advent, Antonio de Montesinos, a Dominican priest, delivered a sermon in a church on Hispaniola. Disagreeing with the king's ministers, he said the conquistadors were committing unspeakable crimes. "Tell me, by what right or justice do you hold these Indians in such cruel and horrible slavery? By what right do you wage such detestable wars on these people who lived mildly and peacefully in their own lands, where you have consumed infinite numbers of them with unheard of murders and desolations?" And then he asked, "Are they not men?"[41]

Out of this protest came a disquieting decision, in 1513: the conquistadors would be required to read aloud to anyone they proposed to conquer and enslave a document called the Requerimiento. It is, in brief, a history of the world, from creation to conquest, a story of origins as justification for violence.

"The Lord our God, Living and Eternal, created the Heaven and the Earth, and one man and one woman, of whom you and we, all the men of the world, were and are descendants, and all those who come after us," it begins. It asks that any people to whom it was read "acknowledge the Church as the Ruler and Superior of the whole world, and the high priest called Pope, and in his name the King and Queen." If the natives accepted the story of Genesis and the claim that these distant rulers had a right to rule them, the Spanish promised, "We in their name shall receive you in all love and charity, and shall leave you your wives, and your children, and your lands, free without servitude." But if the natives rejected these truths, the Spanish warned, "we shall forcibly enter into your country, and shall make war against you in all ways and manners that we can, and shall subject you to the yoke and obedience of the Church and of their Highnesses; we shall take you and your wives and your children, and shall make slaves of them."[42]

With the Requerimiento in hand, with its promises of love and charity and its threats of annihilation and devastation, the Spanish marched across the North American continent. In 1519, determined to ride to glory, Hernán Cortés, mayor of Santiago, Cuba, led six hundred Spaniards and more than a thousand native allies thundering across the land with fifteen cannons. In Mexico, he captured Tenochtitlán, a city said to have been grander than Paris or Rome, and destroyed it without pity or mercy. His men burned the Aztec libraries, their books of songs, their histories written down, a desolation described in a handful of surviving *icnocuicatl*, songs of their sorrow. One begins,

*Broken spears lie in the roads;*
*we have torn our hair in our grief.*

*The houses are roofless now, and their walls*
*are red with blood.*[43]

In 1540, a young nobleman named Francisco Vásquez de Coronado
led an army of Spaniards who were crossing the continent in search of
a fabled city of gold. In what is now New Mexico, they found a hive of
baked-clay apartment houses, the kind of town the Spanish took to calling a pueblo. Dutifully, Coronado had the Requerimiento read aloud.
The Zuni listened to a man speaking a language they could not possibly
understand. "They wore coats of iron, and warbonnets of metal, and carried for weapons short canes that spit fire and made thunder," the Zuni
later said about Coronado's men. Zuni warriors poured cornmeal on the
ground, and motioned to the Spanish they dare not cross that line. A battle began. The Zuni, fighting with arrows, were routed by the Spaniards,
who fought with guns.[44]

The conquest raged on, and so did the debate, even as the lines
between the peoples of the Americas, Africa, and Europe blurred. The
Spanish, unlike later English colonizers, did not travel to the New World
in families, or even with women: they came as armies of men. They seized
and raped women and they loved and married them and raised families
together. La Malinche, a Nahua woman who was given to Cortés as a
slave and who became his interpreter, had a son with him, born about
1523, the freighted symbol of a fateful union. In much of New Spain, the
mixed-race children of Spanish men and Indian women, known as mestizos, outnumbered Indians; an intricate caste system marked gradations
of skin color, mixtures of Europeans, Native Americans, and Africans,
as if skin color were like dyes made of plants, the yellow of sassafras, the
red of beets, the black of carob. Later, the English would recognize only
black and white, a fantasy of stark and impossible difference, of nights
without twilight and days without dawns. And yet both regimes of race,
a culture of mixing or a culture of pretending not to mix, pressed upon
the brows of every person of the least curiosity the question of common
humanity: Are all peoples one?

Bartolomé de Las Casas had been in Hispaniola as a settler in 1511,
when Montesinos had preached and asked, "Are they not men?" Stirred,
he'd given up his slaves and become a priest and a scholar, a historian of
the conquest, which is what led him, later, to copy parts of Columbus's

*Mexican* casta, *or* caste, *paintings purported to chart sixteen different possible intermarriages of Spanish, Indian, and African men and women and their offspring.*

diary and Pané's *Antiquities*. In 1542, Las Casas wrote a book called *Brevísima Relación de la Destrucción de las Indias*, history not as justification but as a cry of conscience. With the zeal of a man burdened by his own guilt, he asked, "What man of sound mind will approve a war against men who are harmless, ignorant, gentle temperate, unarmed, and destitute of every human defense?"[45] Eight years later, a new Spanish king summoned Las Casas and other scholars to his court in the clay-roofed city of Valladolid for another debate. Were the native peoples of the New World barbarians who had violated the laws of nature by, for instance, engaging in cannibalism, in which case it was lawful to wage war against them? Or were they innocent of these violations, in which case the war was unlawful?

Las Casas argued that the conquest was unlawful, insisting that charges of cannibalism were "sheer fables and shameless nonsense." The opposing argument was made by Juan Ginés de Sepúlveda, Spain's royal historian, who had never been to the New World. A translator of Aristotle, Sepúlveda cited Aristotle's theory of natural slavery. He said that the difference between the natives and the Spaniards was as great as that "between apes and men." He asked, "How are we to doubt that these people, so uncultivated, so barbarous, and so contaminated with such impiety and lewdness, have not been justly conquered?"[46]

The judges, divided, failed to issue a decision. The conquest continued. Broken spears clattered to the ground and the walls ran red with blood.

## III.

To ALL OF THIS, the English came remarkably late. The Spanish had settled at Saint Augustine, Florida, in 1565 and by 1607 were settling the adobe town of Santa Fe, nearly two thousand miles away. The French, who made their first voyages in 1534, were by 1608 building what would become the stone city of Quebec, a castle on a hill. The English sent John Cabot across the Atlantic in 1497, but he disappeared on his return voyage, never to be seen again, and the English gave barely any thought to sending anyone after him. The word "colony" didn't even enter the English language until the 1550s. And although England chartered trading companies—the Muscovy Company in 1555, the Turkey Company, in 1581, and the East India Company, in 1600—all looked eastward, not westward. About America, England hesitated.

In 1584, Elizabeth, the fierce and determined queen of England, asked one of her shrewdest ministers, Richard Hakluyt, whether she ought to found her own colonies in the Americas. She had in mind the Spanish and their idolatries, and their cruelties, and their vast riches, and their tyranny. By the time Elizabeth began staring west across the ocean, Las Casas's pained history of the conquest had long since been translated into English, lavishly illustrated with engravings of atrocities, often under the title *Spanish Cruelties* and, later, as *The Tears of the Indians*. The English had come to believe—as an article of faith, as a matter of belonging to the "English nation"—that they were nobler than the Spanish: more just, wiser, gentler, and dedicated to liberty. "The Spaniards governe in the Indies with all pride and tyranie," Hakluyt reminded his queen, and, as

*Elizabeth rests her hand on a globe,*
*laying claim to North America.*

with any people who are made slaves, the natives "all yell and crye with one voice *Liberta, liberta*."[47] England could deliver them.

England's notion of itself as a land of liberty was the story of the English nation stitched to the story of the English state. The Spanish were Catholic, but, while conquistadors had been building a New Spain, the English had become Protestant. In the 1530s, Henry VIII had established the Church of England, defiantly separate from the Church of Rome. Occupied with religious and domestic affairs, England had been altogether tentative in venturing forth to the New World. When Henry VIII died, in 1547, his son Edward became king, but by 1552, Edward was mortally ill. Hoping to avoid the ascension of his half-sister Mary, who was a Catholic, Edward named as his successor his cousin Lady Jane Grey. But when Edward died, Mary seized power, had Jane beheaded, and became the first ruling queen of England. She attempted to restore Catholicism and persecuted religious dissenters, nearly three hundred of whom were burned at the stake. Protestants who opposed her rule on religious grounds decided to argue that she had no right to reign because she was a woman, claiming that for the weak to govern the strong was "the subversion of good order." Another of Mary's Protestant critics complained that her reign was a punishment from God, who "haste set to rule over us an woman whom nature hath formed to be in subjeccion unto man." Mary's Catholic defenders, meanwhile, argued that, politically speaking, Mary was a man, "the Prince female."

When Mary died, in 1558, Elizabeth, a Protestant, succeeded her, and Mary's supporters, who tried to argue against Elizabeth's right to rule, were left to battle against their own earlier arguments: they couldn't very well argue that Elizabeth couldn't rule because she was a woman, when they had earlier insisted that her sex did not bar Mary from the throne. The debate moved to new terrain, and clarified a number of English ideas about the nature of rule. Elizabeth's best defender argued that if God decided "the female should rule and govern," it didn't matter that women were "weake in nature, feable in bodie, softe in courage," because God would make every right ruler strong. In any case, England's constitution abided by a "rule mixte," in which the authority of the monarch was checked by the power of Parliament; also, "it is not she that ruleth but the lawes." Elizabeth herself called on yet another authority: the favor of the people.[48] A mixed constitution, the rule of law, the will of the people: these were English ideas that Americans would one day make their own, crying, "Liberty!"

Elizabeth eyed Spain, which had been warring with England, France, and a rebelling Netherlands (the Dutch did not achieve independence from Spain until 1609). She set out to fight Spain on every field. On the question of founding colonies in the Americas, Hakluyt submitted to Elizabeth a report that he titled "A particular discourse concerning the greate necessitie and manifold comodyties that are like to growe to this Realme of Englande by the Western discoveries lately attempted." How much the queen was animated by animosity to Spain is nicely illustrated in the title of a report submitted to her at the very same time by another adviser: a "Discourse how Her Majesty may annoy the King of Spain."[49]

Hakluyt believed the time had come for England to do more than attack Spanish ships. Establishing colonies "will be greately for the inlargement of the gospell of Christe," he promised, and "will yelde unto us all the commodities of Europe, Affrica, and Asia." And if the queen of England were to plant colonies in the New World, word would soon spread that the English "use the natural people there with all humanitie, curtesie, and freedome," and the natives would "yielde themselves to her government and revolte cleane from the Spaniarde."[50] England would prosper; Protestantism would conquer Catholicism; liberty would conquer tyranny.

Elizabeth was unpersuaded. She was also distracted. In 1584, she'd expelled the Spanish ambassador after discovering a Spanish plot to invade England by way of Scotland. She liked the idea of an English foothold in the New World, but she didn't want the Crown to cover the cost. She decided to issue a royal patent—a license—to one of her favorite courtiers, the dashing Walter Ralegh, writer, poet, and spy, granting him the right to land in North America south of a place called Newfoundland: A new-found-land, a new world, a utopia, a once-nowhere.

Ralegh was an adventurer, a man of action, but he was also a man of letters. Newly knighted, he launched an expedition in 1584. He did not sail himself but sent out a fleet of seven ships and six hundred men, providing them with a copy of Las Casas's "book of Spanish crueltyes with fayr pictures," to be used to convince the natives that the English, unlike the Spanish, were men of mercy and love, liberty and charity. Ralegh may well also have sent along with his expedition a copy of a new book of essays by the French philosopher Michel de Montaigne. Like William Shakespeare, Ralegh was deeply influenced by Montaigne, whose 1580 essay "Of Cannibals" testifies to how, in one of the more startling ironies in the history of humanity, the very violence that characterized the meeting between one half of the world and the other, which sowed so much destruction, also carried within it the seeds of something else.[51]

"Barbarians are no more marvelous to us than we are to them, nor for better cause," Montaigne wrote. "Each man calls barbarism whatever is not his own practice."[52] They are to us as we are to them, each true: out of two truths, one.

Ralegh's men made landfall on an island on the Outer Banks of what is now North Carolina, sweeping beaches edged with seagrass and stands of pine trees and palms. The ships sailed away, leaving behind 104 men with very little by way of supplies; the supply ship had been damaged, nearly running aground on the shoals. The site had been chosen because it was well hidden and difficult to reach. It may have been a good hideout for pirates, but it was a terrible place to build a colony. The settlers planned to wait out the winter, awaiting supplies they hoped would arrive in the spring. Meanwhile, they intended to look for gold and for a safer, deeper harbor. They built a fort, surrounded by palisades. They aimed its guns out over the wide water, believing their enemy to be Spain. They built houses outside the protection of the fort. They had very little idea that the people who already lived in the Outer Banks might pose a danger to them.

They sent home glowing reports of a land of ravishing beauty and staggering plenty. Ralph Lane, the head of the expedition, wrote that "all the kingdoms and states of Christendom, their commodities joined in one together, do not yield either more good or more plentiful whatsoever for public use is needful, or pleasing for delight." Yet when the supply ship was delayed, the colonists, in the midst of plenty, began to starve. The natives, to whom the colonists had been preaching the Gospel, began telling them, "Our Lord God was not God, since he suffered us to sustain much hunger." In June, a fleet arrived, commanded by Sir Francis Drake, a swashbuckler who'd sailed across the whole of the globe. He carried a cargo of three hundred Africans, bound in chains. Drake told the colonists that either he could leave them with food, and with a ship to look for a safer harbor, or else he could bring them home. Every colonist opted to leave. On Drake's ships, they took the places of the Africans, people that Drake may have simply dumped into the cobalt sea, unwanted cargo.

Another expedition sent in 1587 to what had come to be called Roanoke fared no better. John White, an artist and mapmaker who had carefully studied the reports of the first expedition, aimed to establish a permanent colony not on the island but in nearby Chesapeake Bay, in a city to be called Ralegh. Instead, one blunder followed another. White sailed back to England that fall, in hopes of securing supplies and support. His timing could hardly have been less propitious. In 1588, a fleet of 150 Spanish ships attempted to invade England. Eventually, the armada was defeated. But with a naval war with Spain raging, White had no success in scaring up more ships to sail to Roanoke, leaving the settlement marooned.

Any record of the fate of the English colony at Roanoke, like most of what has ever happened in the history of the world, was lost. When White finally returned, in 1590, he found not a single Englishman, nor his daughter, nor his grandchild, a baby named Virginia, after Elizabeth, the virgin queen. Nearly all that remained of the settlement were the letters "CRO" carved into the trunk of a tree, a sign that White and the colonists had agreed upon before he left, a sign that they'd packed their things and headed inland to find a better site to settle. Three letters, and not one letter more. They were never heard from again.

"We found the people most gentle, loving and faithful, void of all guile and treason and such as lived after the manner of the Golden Age," Arthur Barlowe, one of Ralegh's captains, had earlier written home, describing Roanoke as a kind of Eden.[53] The natives weren't barbarians; they were ancestors, and the New World was the oldest world of all.

In the brutal, bloody century between Columbus's voyage and John White's, an idea was born, out of fantasy, out of violence, the idea that there exists in the world a people who live in an actual Garden of Eden, a state of nature, before the giving of laws, before the forming of government. This imagined history of America became an English book of genesis, their new truth.

"In the beginning," the Englishman John Locke would write, "all the world was America." In America, everything became a beginning.

# Two

# THE RULERS
# AND THE RULED

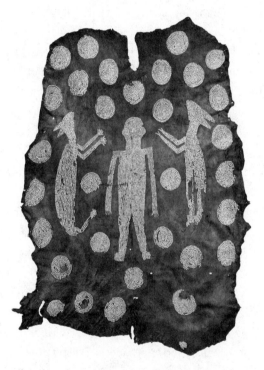

*This deerskin cloak, likely worn by Powhatan,*
*was by the middle of the seventeenth century*
*housed in a museum in Oxford, England.*

**T**HEY SKINNED THE DEER WITH KNIVES MADE OF STONE
and scraped the hides of flesh and fat with a rib bone. They soaked
the hides in wood ash and corn mash and stretched them on a frame of
sticks before sewing them together with thread made of tendons, twisted.
Onto these stitched and tanned hides, they embroidered hundreds of tiny
shells of seashore snails, emptied and dried, into the pattern of a man,

flanked by a white-tailed deer and a mountain lion in a field of thirty-four circles.

This man was their ruler, the animals his spirits, and the circles the villages over which he ruled. One of his names was Wahunsunacock, but the English called him Powhatan. He may have worn the deerskin as a cloak; he may have used it to honor his ancestors. He may have given it to the English as a gift, in 1608, when their king, James, sent to him the gift of a scarlet robe, one robe for another. Or, the English might have stolen it. Somehow, someone carried it to England on a ship. In 1638, an Englishman who saw it in a museum in England, called the sinew-stitched deerskin decorated with shells "the robe of the King of Virginia." But if it was Powhatan's cloak, it also served as a map of his realm.[1]

The English called Powhatan "king," for the sake of diplomacy, but it was the king of England who claimed to be the king of Virginia: James considered Powhatan among his subjects. The nature and history of the two kings' reigns casts light on matters with which England's colonists would wrestle for more than a century and a half: Who rules, and by what right?

Powhatan was born about 1545. At the death of his father, he inherited rule over six neighboring peoples; in the 1590s, he'd begun expanding his reign. On the other side of the ocean, James was born in 1566; the next year, when his mother died, he became king of Scotland. In 1603, after the death of his cousin Elizabeth, James was crowned king of England. The separation of the Church of England from the Church of Rome had elevated the monarchy, since the king no longer answered to the pope, and James believed that he, like the pope, was divinely appointed by God. "As to dispute what God may doe is Blasphemie," he wrote, in a treatise called *The True Law of Free Monarchies*, "so is it Sedition in subjects to dispute what a King may do"—as if he were both infallible and above the rule of law.[2]

James, a pope-like king, proved more determined to found a colony in the New World than Elizabeth had been. In 1606, he issued a charter, granting to a body of men permission to settle on "that parte of America commonly called Virginia," land that he claimed as his property, since, as the charter explained, these lands were "not now actually possessed by any Christian Prince or People" and the natives "live in Darkness," meaning that they did not know Christ.[3]

Unlike the Spanish, who set out to conquer, the English were determined to settle, which is why they at first traded with Powhatan, instead of warring with him. James granted to the colony's settlers the right to "dig, mine, and search for all Manner of Mines of Gold, Silver, and Copper," the very kind of initiatives taken by Spain, but he also urged them to convert the natives to Christianity, on the ground that, "in propagating of Christian Religion to such People," the English and Scottish might "in time bring the Infidels and Savages, living in those parts, to human Civility, and to a settled and quiet Government."[4] They proposed, he insisted, to bring not tyranny but liberty.

James's charter, like Powhatan's deerskin, is also a kind of map. ("Charter" has the same Latin root as "chart," meaning a map.) By his charter, James granted land to two corporations, the Virginia Company and the Plymouth Company: "Wee woulde vouchsafe unto them our licence to make habitacion, plantacion and to deduce a colonie . . . at any Place upon the said-Coast of Virginia or America, where they shall think fit and convenient."[5] Virginia, at the time, stretched from what is now South Carolina to Canada: all of this, England claimed.

England's empire would have a different character than that of either Spain or France. Catholics could make converts by the act of baptism, but Protestants were supposed to teach converts to read the Bible; that meant permanent settlements, families, communities, schools, and churches. Also, England's empire would be maritime—its navy was its greatest strength. It would be commercial. And, of greatest significance for the course of the nation that would grow out of those settlements, its colonists would be free men, not vassals, guaranteed their "English liberties."[6]

At such a great distance from their king, James's colonists would remain his subjects but they would rule themselves. His 1606 charter decreed that the king would appoint a thirteen-man council in England to oversee the colonies, but, as for local affairs, the settlers would establish their own thirteen-man council to "govern and order all Matters and Causes." And, most importantly, the colonists would retain all of their rights as English subjects, as if they had never left England. If the king meant his guarantee of the colonists' English liberties, privileges, and immunities as liberties, privileges, and immunities due to them if they were to return to England, the colonists would come to understand them as guaranteed in the colonies, a freedom attached to their very selves.[7]

Over the course of the seventeenth and early eighteenth centuries, the English established more than two dozen colonies, founding a sea-born empire of coastal settlements that stretched from the fishing ports of Newfoundland to the rice fields of Georgia and, in the Caribbean, from Jamaica and Antigua to Bermuda and Barbados. Beginning with the Virginia charter, the idea of English liberties for English subjects was planted on American soil and, with it, the king's claim to dominion, a claim that rested on the idea that people like Powhatan and his people lived in darkness and without government, no matter that the English called their leaders kings.

And yet England's own political order was about to be toppled. At the beginning of English colonization, the king's subjects on both sides of the ocean believed that men were created unequal and that God had granted to their king the right to rule over them. These were their old truths. At the end of the seventeenth century, John Locke, imagining an American genesis and borrowing from Christian theology, would argue that all men were born into a state "of equality, wherein all the power and jurisdiction is reciprocal, no one having more than another," each "equal to the great-est, and subject to no body."[8] By 1776, many of the king's subjects in many of his colonies so wholly agreed with this point of view that they accepted Thomas Paine's "plain truth," that, "all men being originally equals," noth-ing was more absurd than the idea that God had granted to one person and his heirs the right to rule over all others. "Nature disapproves it," Paine insisted, "otherwise she would not so frequently turn it into ridicule by giving mankind an ass for a lion."[9] These became their new truths.

What had happened between the Virginia charter and the Declaration of Independence to convince so many people that all men are created equal and that governments derive their just powers from the consent of the governed? The answer lies in artifacts as different as a deerskin cloak and a scarlet robe and in places as far from one another as the ruins of ancient castles and the hulls of slave ships, each haunted by the rattling of iron-forged chains.

# I.

VIRGINIA'S FIRST CHARTER was prepared in the office of Attorney General Edward Coke, a sour-tempered man with a pointed chin, a sys-

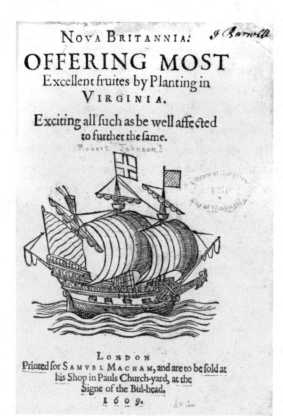

*The Virginia Company recruited colonists with advertisements that lavishly promised an Eden-like bounty.*

tematic mind, and an ungovernable tongue. Coke, who invested in the Virginia Company, was the leading theorist of English common law, the body of unwritten law established by centuries of custom and cases, to which Coke sought to apply the precepts of rationalism. "Reason is the life of the law," Coke wrote, and "the common law itself is nothing else but reason." In 1589, when he was thirty-seven, Coke became a member of Parliament. Five years later, Elizabeth appointed him attorney general. In 1603, after James threw Sir Walter Ralegh in the Tower of London, Coke prosecuted Ralegh for treason, for plotting against the king. "Thou viper," Coke said to Ralegh in court, "thou hast an English face, but a Spanish heart." Ralegh languished in prison for thirteen years, writing his history of the world, before he was beheaded. Meanwhile, his conviction freed the right to settle Virginia—a right Elizabeth had granted to Ralegh—to be newly issued by James, under Coke's watchful eye. Two months after issuing the colony's charter, James appointed Coke chief justice of the court of common pleas.[10]

To settle the new colony, the Virginia Company rounded up men who were eager to make their own fortunes, along with soldiers who'd fought in England's religious wars against Catholics and Muslims. Burly and fearless John Smith, all of twenty-six, had already fought the Spanish in France and in the Netherlands and, with the Austrian army, had battled the Turks in Hungary. Captured by Muslims, he'd been sold into slavery, from which he'd eventually escaped. Engraved on his coat of arms, with three heads of Turks, was his motto, *vincere est vivere*: to conquer is to live.[11] George Sandys, Virginia's treasurer, had traveled by camel to Jerusalem and had written at length about Islam; William Strachey, the colony's secretary, had traveled in Istanbul. Much like the Spanish, these men and their investors wanted to found a colony in the New World to search for gold to fund wars to defeat Muslims in the Old World, even as they pledged not to inflict "Spanish cruelties" on the American natives.[12]

In December 1606, 105 Englishmen—and no women—boarded three ships, carrying a box containing a list of the men appointed by the Virginia Company to govern the colony, "not to be opened, nor the governours knowne until they arrived in Virginia." During the voyage, Smith was confined belowdecks, shackled and in chains, accused of plotting a mutiny to "make himselfe king."[13] In May 1607, when the expedition finally landed on the banks of a brackish river named after their king, the box was opened, and it was discovered that Smith, though still a prisoner, was on that list.[14] Unclapped came his chains.

Whatever "quiet government" the company's merchants had intended, the colonists proved ungovernable. They built a fort and began looking for gold. But a band of soldiers and gentlemen-adventurers proved unwilling to clear fields or plant and harvest crops; instead, they stole food from Powhatan's people, stores of corn and beans. Smith, disgusted, complained that the company had sent hardly any but the most useless of settlers. He counted one carpenter, two blacksmiths, and a flock of footmen, and wrote the rest off as "Gentlemen, Tradesmen, Servingmen, libertines, and such like, ten times more fit to spoyle a Commonwealth, than either begin one, or but helpe to maintaine one."[15]

In 1608, Smith, elected the colony's governor, made a rule: "he who does not worke, shall not eat."[16] By way of diplomacy, he staged an elaborate coronation ceremony, crowning Powhatan "king," and draping upon his shoulders the scarlet robe sent by James. Whatever this gesture meant to Powhatan, the English intended it as an act of their sovereignty, insisting that, in accepting these gifts, Powhatan had submitted to English rule: "Powhatan, their chiefe King, received voluntarilie a crown and a scepter, with a full acknowledgment of dutie and submission."[17] And still the English starved, and still they raided native villages. In the fall of 1609, the colonists revolted—auguring so many revolts to come—and sent Smith back to England, declaring that he had made Virginia, under his leadership, "a misery, a ruine, a death, a hell."[18]

The real hell was yet to come. In the winter of 1609–10, five hundred colonists, having failed to farm or fish or hunt and having succeeded at little except making their neighbors into enemies, were reduced to sixty. "Many, through extreme hunger, have run out of their naked beds being so lean that they looked like anatomies, crying out, we are starved, we are starved," wrote the colony's lieutenant governor, George Percy, the eighth son of the earl of Northumberland, reporting that "one of our Colline murdered his wife Ripped the Childe outt of her woambe and threwe it into the River and after Chopped the Mother in pieces and salted her for his food."[19] They ate one another.

Word of this dire state of affairs soon reached England. Like nearly everything else reported from across the ocean, it set minds alight. The philosopher Thomas Hobbes, who served on the board of the Virginia Company, eyed the descent of the colony into anarchy with more than passing interest. In 1622, four years after Powhatan's death, the natives rose up in rebellion and tried to oust the English from their land, killing hundreds of new immigrants in what the English called the "Virginia massacre." Hobbes, working out a theory of the origins of civil society by deducing an original state of nature, pondered the violence in Virginia. "The savage people in many places of America . . . have no government at all, and live at this day in that brutish manner," he would later write, in *The Leviathan*, a treatise in which he concluded that the state of nature is a state of war, "of every man against every man."[20]

Miraculously, the colony recovered; its population grew and its economy thrived with a new crop, tobacco, a plant found only in the New World and long cultivated by the natives.[21] With tobacco came the prospect of profit, and a new political and economic order: the colonists would rule themselves and they would rule over others. In July 1619, twenty-two English colonists, two men from each of eleven parts of the colony, met in a legislative body, the House of Burgesses, the first self-governing body in the colonies. One month later, twenty Africans arrived in Virginia, the first slaves in British America, Kimbundu speakers from the kingdom of Ndongo. Captured in raids ordered by the governor of Angola, they had been marched to the coast and boarded the *São João Bautista,* a Portuguese slave ship headed for New Spain. At sea, an English privateer, the *White Lion,* sailing from New Netherlands, attacked the *São João Bautista,* seized all twenty, and brought them to Virginia to be sold.[22]

Twenty Englishmen were elected to the House of Burgesses. Twenty Africans were condemned to the house of bondage. Another chapter opened in the American book of genesis: liberty and slavery became the American Abel and Cain.

## II.

WAVES SLAPPED AGAINST the hulls of ships like the pounding of a drum. Mothers lulled children to sleep while men wailed, singing songs of sorrow. "It frequently happens that the negroes, on being purchased by the Europeans, become raving mad," wrote one slave trader. "Many of them die in that state." Others took their own lives, throwing themselves into the sea, hoping that the ocean would carry them to their ancestors.[23]

The English who crossed the ocean endured the hazards of the voyage under altogether different circumstances, but the perils of the passage left their traces on them, too, in memoirs and stories, and in their bonds to one another. In the summer of 1620, a year after the *White Lion* landed off the coast of Virginia, the *Mayflower,* a 180-ton, three-masted, square-rigged merchant vessel, lay anchored in the harbor of the English town of Plymouth, at the mouth of the river Plym. It soon took on its passengers, some sixty adventurers, and forty-one men—dissenters from the Church of England—who brought with them their wives, children, and servants. William Bradford, the dissenters' chronicler, called them "pilgrims."[24]

Bradford, who would become governor of the colony the dissenters would found, became, too, its chief historian, writing, he said, "in a plain style, with singular regard unto the simple truth in all things." Ten years before, Bradford explained, the pilgrims had left England for Holland, where they'd settled in Leiden, a university town known for learning and for religious toleration. After a decade in exile, they'd decided to make a new start someplace else. "The place they had thoughts on was some of those vast and unpeopled countries of America," Bradford wrote, "which are fruitful and fit for habitation, being devoid of all civil inhabitants, where there are only savage and brutish men which range up and down, little otherwise than the wild beasts." Though fearful of the journey, they placed their faith in a providential God, and set sail for Virginia. "All being compact together in one ship," Bradford wrote, "they put to sea again with a prosperous wind."

During the treacherous, sixty-six-day journey over what Bradford called the "vast and furious ocean," one man was swept overboard, saved only by grasping a halyard; the ship leaked; a beam split; and one of the masts bowed and nearly cracked. For two days, the wind grew so fierce that everyone on board had to crowd into the hull, huddled under rafters. When the storm quieted, the crew caulked the decks, fortified the masts, and raised the sails once more. Elizabeth Hopkins gave birth on the swaying ship; she named her son Oceanus. The ship, blown severely off course, dropped anchor not in Virginia but off the windswept coast of Cape Cod. Unwilling to risk the ocean again, the pilgrims rowed ashore to found what they hoped would be a new and better England, another beginning. And yet, wrote Bradford, "what could they see but a hideous and desolate wilderness, full of wild beasts and wild men"? They fell to their knees and praised God they were alive. The day they arrived, having sailed what Bradford described as a "sea of troubles," in a ship they imagined as a ship of state—the whole body of a people, in the same boat—they signed a document in which they pledged to "covenant and combine ourselves together into a civil body politic."[25] They named their agreement after their ship. They called it the Mayflower Compact.

The men who settled Virginia had been granted a charter by the king. But the men, women, and children who settled in what they called a New England had no charter; they'd fled the king, bridling against his rule. Religious dissent in seventeenth-century England was also a form of political dissent. It was punishable by both imprisonment and execution. But if James's divine right to rule was questioned by dissenters who fled his authority, it was being questioned, too, on the floor of Parliament. The battle between the king and Parliament would send tens of thousands more exiles across the vast and furious ocean, seeking political freedom in the colonies. It would also foster in them a deep and abiding spirit of rebellion against arbitrary rule.

Even as dissenters in New England struggled to survive their first winter in a settlement they named Plymouth, members of Parliament were beginning to challenge the tradition by which Parliament met only when summoned by the king. In 1621, Edward Coke, who, after Ralegh's beheading in 1618 had emerged as James's most cunning adversary, claimed that Parliament had the right to debate on all matters concerning the Commonwealth. The king had Coke arrested, confined him to the Tower of London, and dissolved Parliament. Ralegh had written a history of the world while in prison; Coke would write a history of the law.

To build his case against the king, Coke dusted off a copy of an ancient and almost entirely forgotten legal document, known as Magna Carta (literally, the "great charter"), in which, in the year 1215, King John had pledged to his barons that he would obey the "law of the land." Magna Carta wasn't nearly as important as Coke made it out to be, but by arguing for its importance, he made it important, not only for English history, but for American history, too, tying the political fate of everyone in England's colonies to the strange doings of a very bad king from the Middle Ages.

King John, born in 1166, was the youngest son of Henry II. As a young man, he'd studied with his father's chief minister, Ranulf de Glanville, who had dedicated himself to preparing one of the earliest commentaries on the English law, in which he had attempted to address the rather delicate question of whether a law can be a law if no one had ever written it down.[26] It would be "utterly impossible for the laws and rules of the realm to be reduced to writing," Glanville admitted. That said, unwritten laws are still laws, he insisted; they are a body of custom and precedent that together constitute "common law."[27]

Glanville's ruminations had led him to another and even more delicate question: If the law isn't written down, and even if it is, by what argument or force can a king be constrained to obey it? Kings had insisted on their right to rule, in writing, since the sixth century BC.[28] And, at least since the ninth century AD, they'd been binding themselves to the administration of justice by taking oaths.[29] In 1100, in the Charter of Liberties, Henry I, the son of William the Conqueror, promised to "abolish all the evil customs by which the kingdom of England has been unjustly oppressed," which, while not a promise that he kept, set a precedent that Glanville might have expected would act to restrain Henry I's grandson King John.[30]

Unfortunately, King John proved a tyrant, heedless of the Charter of Liberties. He levied taxes higher than any king ever had before and either carried so much coin outside his realm or kept so much of it in his castle that it was difficult for anyone to pay him with money. When his noblemen fell into his debt, he took their sons hostage. He had one noble-woman and her son starved to death in a dungeon. Rumor had it that he ordered one of his clerks crushed to death.[31]

In 1215, barons rebelling against the king captured the Tower of London.[32] When John agreed to meet with them to negotiate a peace and they gathered at Runnymede, a meadow by the Thames, the barons presented him with a very long list of demands, which were rewritten as a charter, in which the king granted "to all free men" in his realm—that is, not to the people, but to noblemen—"all the liberties written out below, to have and to keep for them and their heirs, of us and our heirs."[33] This was the great charter, the Magna Carta.

Magna Carta had been revoked almost immediately after it was written, and it had become altogether obscure by the time of King James and his battles with the ungovernable Edward Coke. But Coke, as brilliant a political strategist as he was a legal scholar, resurrected it in the 1620s and began calling it England's "ancient constitution." When James insisted on his sovereignty—an ancient authority, by which the monarch is above the law—Coke, countering with his ancient constitution, insisted that the law was above the king. "Magna Carta is such a fellow," Coke said, "that he will have no sovereign."[34]

Coke's resurrection of Magna Carta explains a great deal about how it is that some English colonists would one day come to believe that their king had no right to rule them and why their descendants would come to believe that the United States needed a written constitution. But Magna Carta played one further pivotal role, the role it played in the history of truth—a history that had taken a different course in England than in any other part of Europe.

The most crucial right established under Magna Carta was the right to a trial by jury. For centuries, guilt or innocence had been determined, across Europe, either by a trial by ordeal—a trial by water, for instance, or a trial by fire—or by trial by combat. Trials by ordeal and combat required neither testimony nor questioning. The outcome was, itself, the evidence, the only admissible form of judicial proof, accepted because it placed judgment in the hands of God. Nevertheless, the practice was easily abused—priests, after all, could be bribed—and, in 1215, the pope banned trial by ordeal. In Europe, it was replaced by a new system of divine judgment: judicial torture. But in England, where there existed a tradition of convening juries to judge civil disputes—like disagreements over boundaries between neighboring freeholds—trial by ordeal was replaced not by judicial torture but by trial by jury. One reason this happened is because, the very year that the pope abolished trial by ordeal, King John pledged, in Magna Carta, that "no free man is to be arrested, or imprisoned . . . save by the lawful judgment of his peers or by the law of the land."[35] In England, truth in either a civil dispute or criminal investigation would be determined not by God but by men, and not by a battle of swords but by a battle of facts.

This turn marked the beginning of a new era in the history of knowledge: it required a new doctrine of evidence and new method of inquiry and eventually led to the idea that an observed or witnessed act or thing—the substance, the *matter*, of fact—is the basis of truth. A judge decided the law; a jury decided the facts. Mysteries were matters of faith, a different kind of truth, known only to God. But when, during the Reformation, the Church of England separated from the Roman Catholic Church, protesting the authority of the pope and finding truth in the Bible, the mysteries of the church were thrown open, the secrets of priests revealed. The age of mystery began to wane, and, soon, the culture of fact spread from law to government.[36]

In seventeenth-century England, the meat of the matter between the king and Parliament was a dispute over the nature of knowledge. King James, citing divine right, insisted that his power could not be questioned and that it lay outside the realm of facts. "That which concerns the mystery of the king's power is not lawful to be disputed," he said.[37] To dispute the divine right of kings was to remove the king's power from the realm of mystery, the realm of religion and faith, and place it in the realm of fact, the realm of evidence and trial. To grant to the colonies a charter was to establish law on a foundation of fact, a repudiation of government by mystery.

By what right did the king rule? And how might Parliament constrain him? After James died, in 1625, his son, Charles, was crowned king, but Charles, too, believed in the divine right of kings. Three years later, Coke, now seventy-six, and having returned to Parliament, objected to Charles's exerting his royal prerogative to billet soldiers in his subjects' homes and to confine men to jail, without trial, for refusing to pay taxes. Coke claimed that the king's authority was constrained by Magna Carta.[38] At Coke's suggestion, Parliament then prepared and delivered to King Charles a Petition of Right, which cited Magna Carta to insist that the king had no right to imprison a subject without a trial by jury. If Coke had been successful, England's American colonies would have been less so. Instead, in 1629, the king, having forbidden Coke from publishing his study of Magna Carta, dissolved Parliament. It was this act that led tens of thousands of the king's subjects to flee the country and cross the ocean, vast and furious.

Between 1630 and 1640, the years during which King Charles ruled without Parliament, a generation of ocean voyagers, some twenty thousand dissenters, fled England and settled in New England. One of these people was John Winthrop, a stern and uncompromising man with a Vandyke beard and a collar of starched ruffles, who decided to join a new expedition to found a colony in Massachusetts Bay. Unlike Bradford's pilgrims, who wanted to separate from the Church of England, Winthrop was one of a band of dissenters known as Puritans—because they wanted to purify the Church of England—who lost their positions in court after the dissolution of Parliament. In 1630, Winthrop, who would become the first governor of Massachusetts, wrote an address called "A Model of Christian Charity" to his fellow settlers. The *Mayflower* compact had described the union of Plymouth's settlers into a body politic, but Winthrop described the union of his people in the body of Christ, held together by the ligaments of love. "All the parts of this body being thus united are made so contiguous in a special relation as they must needs partake of each other's strength and infirmity, joy and sorrow, weal and woe," he said, citing 1 Corinthians 12. "If one member suffers, all suffer with it; if one be in honor, all rejoice with it." In this, their New England, he said, they would build a city on a hill, as Christ had urged in his Sermon on the Mount (Matthew 5:14): "A city that is set on a hill cannot be hid."[39]

Colonies sprouted along the Atlantic coast like cattails along the banks

*In 1629, Massachusetts Bay*
*adopted a colony seal that,*
*by way of justifying settlement,*
*pictured a nearly naked*
*Indian, begging the English to*
*"Come Over and Help Us."*

of a pond. Roger Williams, once Coke's stenographer, joined the mission to Massachusetts Bay, although for his commitment to religious toleration he was banished in 1635. The next year, he founded Rhode Island. In 1624, the Dutch had settled New Netherland (which later became New York); in 1638, Swedish colonists settled New Sweden, a colony that straddled parts of latter-day New Jersey, Pennsylvania, and Delaware. Even colonies that weren't Puritan were founded by dissenters of one kind or another. Maryland, named after Charles I's Catholic wife, Henrietta Maria, started in 1634 as a sanctuary for Catholics. Connecticut, like Rhode Island, was founded in 1636, New Haven in 1638, New Hampshire in 1639.

English migrants often came as families and they sometimes came as whole towns, hoping to found a Christian commonwealth, a religious community bound to the common wealth of all, public good over private gain. "The care of the public must oversway all private respects," Winthrop said. "For it is a true rule that particular estates cannot subsist in the ruin of the public." They expected the world to be watching. "The eyes of all people are upon us," Winthrop said. Theirs was an ordered world, a world of hierarchy and deference. They considered the family a "little commonwealth," the father its head, just as a minister is the head of a congregation and the king is the head of his people. They built towns around commons—lands owned in common, for pasturing animals. They did not consider a commitment to the public good, the common weal, to be at odds with the desire for prosperity. They believed in providence: everything happened for a reason, ordained by God.

Wealth was a sign of God's favor, its accretion for its own sake a great sin. New Englanders expected to thrive by farming and by trade. "In America, religion and profit jump together," wrote Edward Winslow, of Plymouth.[40] They governed themselves through town meetings. Their lives centered on their churches, or meetinghouses: they built more than forty of them in their first two decades. In England, they'd raised money by promising to "propagate the Gospel," that is, to convert the Indians to Christianity. Massachusetts adopted as a colony seal a drawing of a nearly naked Indian mouthing the words "Come Over and Help Us," a reference to the biblical Macedonians, awaiting Christ. In 1636, New England Puritans founded a school in Cambridge for educating "English and Indian youth": Harvard College. The next year, in Connecticut, war broke out between the colonists and the Pequot Indians. At the end of the war, the colonists decided to turn captured Indians into slaves and to sell them to the English in the Caribbean. In 1638, the first African slaves in New England arrived in Salem, on board a ship called the *Desire* that had carried captured Pequots to the West Indies, where they'd been traded, as Winthrop noted in his diary, for "some cotton and tobacco, and negroes." There would never be very many Africans in New England, but New Englanders would have slave plantations, on the distant shores. Nearly half of colonial New Englanders' wealth would come from sugar grown by West Indian slaves.[41]

The English in the colonies understood their rights as "free men" as deriving from an "ancient constitution" that guaranteed that even kings were subject to the "laws of the land." These same people sold Indians and bought Africans. By what right did they rule them, in their city on a hill?


# III.

ENGLAND'S AMERICA WAS disproportionately African. England came late to founding colonies and it came late to trafficking in slaves, but nearly as soon as it entered that trade, it dominated it. One million Europeans migrated to British America between 1600 and 1800 and two

*European slave traders inspecting people for purchase
sometimes licked their skin, believing it possible to determine
whether they were healthy or sick by the taste of their sweat.*

and a half million Africans were carried there by force over that same stretch of centuries, on ships that sailed past one another by day and by night.[42] Africans died faster, but as a population of migrants, they outnumbered Europeans two and a half to one.

Much as the English had told lurid tales of "Spanish cruelties" in the Americas, they had long condemned the Portuguese for trading in Africans. An English trader named Richard Jobson told a Gambian man who tried to sell him slaves in 1621 that the Portuguese "were another kinde of people different from us." The Portuguese bought and sold people, like animals, but the English, Jobson said, "were a people, who did not deale in any such commodities, neither did wee buy or sell one another, or any that had our owne shapes."[43]

But in the 1640s, when English settlers in Barbados began planting sugar, they set these long-held reservations aside. Growing sugar takes more work than growing tobacco. To grow this difficult but wildly profitable new crop, Barbadian planters bought Africans from the Spanish and the Dutch and, soon enough, from the English. In 1663, not long after the English entered the slave trade, they founded the Company of Royal Adventurers of England Trading with Africa. In the last twenty-five years of the seventeenth century, English ships, piloted by English sea captains, crewed by English sailors, carried more than a quarter of a million men, women, and children across the ocean, shackled in ships' holds.[44] Theirs was not a ship of state crossing a sea of troubles, another *Mayflower*, their bond a covenant. Theirs was a ship of slavery, their bonds forged in fire. They whispered and wept; they screamed and sat in silence. They grew ill; they grieved; they died; they endured.

Many of the Africans bought by English traders were Bantu speakers and came from the area around what is now Senegambia; some were Akan speakers, from what is now Ghana; others spoke Igbo, and came from what is now Nigeria. During the march to the coast, on the journey across the Atlantic, on islands in the Caribbean, on the continent, and above all on board those ships, they died in staggering numbers. They believed that they lived after death. *Nyame nwu na mawu*, they said, in Akan: "God does not die, so I cannot die."[45]

By what right did the English hold these people as their slaves? They looked to the same ancient authorities as had Juan Sepúlveda, in his debate with Bartolomé de Las Casas at Valladolid in 1550—and found them insufficient. Under Roman law, all men are born free and can only be made slaves by the law of nations, under certain narrow conditions— for instance, when they're taken as prisoners of war, or when they sell themselves as payment of debt. Aristotle had disagreed with Roman law, insisting that some men are born slaves. Neither of these traditions from antiquity proved to be of much use to English colonists attempting to codify their right to own slaves, because laws governing slavery, like slavery itself, had disappeared from English common law by the fourteenth century. Said one Englishman in Barbados in 1661, there was "no track to guide us where to walk nor any rule sett us how to govern such Slaves."[46] With no track or rule to guide them, colonial assemblies adopted new practices and devised new laws with which they attempted to establish a divide between "blacks" and "whites." As early as 1630, an Englishman in Virginia was publicly whipped for "defiling his body in lying with a negro."[47] Adopting these practices and passing these laws required turning English law upside down, because much in existing English law undermined the claims of owners of people. In 1655, a Virginia woman with an African mother and an English father sued for her freedom by citing English common law, under which children's status follows that of their father, not their mother. In 1662, Virginia's House of Burgesses answered doubts about "whether children got by any English-man upon a Negro woman should be slave or ffree" by reaching back to an archaic Roman rule, *partus sequitur ventrem* (you are what your mother was). Thereafter, any child born of a woman who was a slave inherited her condition.[48]

In one of the more unsettling ironies of American history, laws drafted to justify slavery and to govern slaves also codified new ideas about liberty and the government of the free. In 1641, needing to provide some legal support for trading Indians for Africans, the Massachusetts legislature established The Body of Liberties, a bill, or list, of one hundred rights, many of them taken from Magna Carta. (A century and a half later, seven of them would appear in the U.S. Bill of Rights.) The Body of Liberties includes this prohibition: "There shall never be any bond slaverie, villi-nage or Captivitie amongst us unles it be lawfull Captives taken in just warres, and such strangers as willingly selle themselves or are sold to us." Drawing on Roman law, the provision about slavery offered specific legal cover for selling into slavery Pequot and other Algonquians captured by the colonists during the Pequot War in 1637 and for the sale and pur-chase of Africans—described under the language of "strangers," that is, foreigners who "are sold to us"—so that there would be no legal question to debate.[49] Not for another century and a half would New Englanders be willing to open the legality of slavery to debate.

Tied to England, to the Caribbean, and to West Africa by the path steered by ships that sailed between them, colonists plotted the course of their laws. Even as England's colonists justified the taking of slaves and insisted on their right to rule over them absolutely and without restraint, the king's subjects were fighting to restrain his authority. Under what con-ditions do some people have a right to rule, or to rebel, and others not? In 1640, King Charles at last summoned a meeting of Parliament in hopes of raising money to suppress a rebellion in Scotland. The newly summoned Parliament, striking back, passed a law abridging the king's authority, including requiring that Parliament meet at least once every three years, with or without a royal summons. War between supporters of the king and backers of Parliament broke out in 1642. During this battle, the legal fiction of the divine right of kings was replaced by another legal fiction: the sovereignty of the people.[50]

This idea, which would ride across the ocean on the crest of every wave, rested on the notion of representation. Parliaments had first met in the thirteenth century, when the king began summoning noblemen to court to *parler*, demanding that they pledge to obey his laws and pay his taxes. After a while, those noblemen began pretending that they weren't making these pledges for themselves alone but that, instead, in some meaningful way, they "represented" the interests of other people, their vassals. In the 1640s, those parleying noblemen, now called Parliament, challenged the king, countering his claim to sovereignty with a claim of their own: they argued that they represented the people and that the people were sovereign. They said this was because, in some time immemorial, the people had granted them authority to represent them. Royalists pointed out that this was absurd. How can "the people" rule when "they which are the people this minute, are not the people the next minute"? Who even *are* the people? Also, when, exactly, did they empower Parliament to represent them? In 1647, the Levellers, hoping to remedy this small problem, drafted An Agreement of the People, with the idea that every Englishman would sign it, granting to his representatives the power to represent him.[51] This didn't quite come to pass. Instead, in 1649, the king was tried for treason and beheaded.

Out of this same quarrel came foundational ideas about freedom of speech, freedom of religion, and freedom of the press, ideas premised on the belief, heretical to the medieval church, that there is no conflict between freedom and truth. In 1644, the Puritan poet John Milton— later the author of *Paradise Lost*—published a pamphlet in which he argued against a law passed by Parliament requiring printers to secure licenses from the government for everything they printed. No book should be censored before publication, Milton argued (though it might be condemned after printing), because truth could only be established if allowed to do battle with lies. "Let her and falsehood grapple," he urged, since, "whoever knew Truth to be put to the worst in a free and open encounter?" This view depended on an understanding of the capacity of the people to reason. The people, Milton insisted, are not "slow and dull, but of a quick, ingenious and piercing spirit, acute to invent, subtle and sinewy to discourse, not beneath the reach of any point the highest that human capacity can soar to."[52]

In Rhode Island, Roger Williams dedicated himself to the cause of the "liberty of conscience," the idea that the freer people are to think, the more likely they are to arrive at the truth. In a letter written in 1655, Williams borrowed from Plato's *Republic* the idea of a political society as like passengers on board a ship—a metaphor adored by people who had crossed a desperately dangerous ocean. "There goes many a ship to sea, with many hundred souls in one ship, whose weal and woe is common, and is a true picture of a commonwealth, or a human combination or society," Williams wrote, and sometimes "both papists and protestants, Jews and Turks, may be embarked in one ship." The shipmaster ought to protect their freedom to worship as they wished, Williams insisted, by insuring "that none of the papists, protestants, Jews, or Turks, be forced to come to the ship's prayers of worship, nor compelled from their own particular prayers or worship, if they practice any."[53]

Williams, who notably included in his commonwealth Catholics and all manner of Protestants but also Jews and Muslims, imagined a particularly capacious ship, at a time when religious and political dissent was flourishing. Between 1649 and 1660, England had no king, and became a commonwealth, and people took seriously the idea of a common wealth, everyone in the same boat as everyone else, and it also got a little easier to pretend that there existed such a thing as the people, and that they were the sovereign rulers of . . . themselves. In England, new sects thrived, from Baptists to Quakers. The Diggers advocated communal ownership of land. The Levellers argued for political equality. Meanwhile, on the other side of the ocean, the colonies grew, and the colonists came to see themselves as the people, too. Not to mention, much of British America was itself the product of religious and political rebellion, each colony its own experiment in the rule of the people and freedom of speech. Most colonies established assemblies, popularly elected legislatures, and made their own laws. By 1640, eight colonies had their own assemblies. Barbados, settled by the English in 1627, was by 1651 insisting that Parliament had no authority over its internal affairs (which, in any event, chiefly concerned the law of slavery).

The restoration of the monarchy, in 1660, with the coronation of Charles II, represented not a lessening but a deepening commitment to religious toleration, the new king pledging "that no man shall be disquieted or called in question for differences of opinion in matter of religion."

*A Brief Account of the Province of* Pennſilvania *in* America, *lately granted under the Great Seal of* England *to* William Penn, *&c.*

THe King having been favourably pleaſed after a loᵍg Solicitation, in Right of my Fathers Services, and a conſiderable part of his Eſtate, to confer and ſettle upon me, and my Heirs, a Tract of Land in *America,* by the name of *Pennſylvania* ; with the powers requiſite to the well government thereof; I thought good to publiſh this abreviated account of the former Relation, as leſs troubleſom to Send or Read, for their Satisfa-ction, that are ſoberly deſirous and reſolved for thoſe parts of the World.

I.  *Something of the Place.*

The Place lies 600 Miles nearer the *Sun* than *England,* for *England* begins at the 5oth. Degree and ten Mi-nutes of *North* Latitude, and this place begins at 40. which is about the Latitude of *Naples* in *Italy,* or *Mom-pellier* in *France* : I ſhall ſay little in its praiſe to excite deſires in any ; whatever I could truly write as to the Soil, Air and Water, this ſhall ſatisfie me, that by the Bleſſing of God, and the Honeſty and Induſtry of man, it may be a good and Fruitful Land.

For Navigation, it is ſaid to have two Conveniencies, the one by lying Nineſcore Miles upon *Delaware* River, that is to ſay, about 70 Miles, before we come to the Falls, where a Veſſel of 200 Tuns may Sail, (and ſome Creeks and ſmall Harbours in that diſtance, where Ships may come nearer than the Rivers in the Country) and above the Falls for Boats, the other Convenience is through *Cheſpapeak-Bay,* the head falling within this La-titude.

For Timber & other Wood, there is Variety for the uſe of man, as Oak, Cheſnut, Wallnut, Popler, Cedar, Beech, &c.

For *Fowl, Fiſh* and *Wild Deer,* they are reported to be plentiful in thoſe parts, and *Engliſh* Proviſion grows there, and is to be had at reaſonable Rates : The Commodities that the Countrey is thought to be capable of, are *Silk, Flax, Hemp, Wine, Cider, Wood, Madder, Liquoriſt, Tobacco, Potaſtes and Iron* ; and it doth actually produce *Hides, Tallow, Pipeſtaves, Beef, Pork, Sheep, Wool, Corn* as *Wheat, Early, Rye,* and alſo *Furrs,* as your *Beaver, Peltree, Mincks, Racoons, Martins,* and ſuch like; ſtore of which is to be found among the *Indians,* that are profitable Commodities in *Europe.*

The way of Trading in thoſe Countries, is thus, they ſend to the *Southern* Plantations, *Corn, Beef, Pork, Fiſh,* and *Pipſtaves,* and take their Growth and bring for *England,* and return with *Engliſh* Goods to their own Countrey; their *Furrs* they bring for *England,* and either ſell them here, or carry them out again to other parts of *Europe* , where they will yield a better price : And for thoſe that will follow Merchandize and Navi-gation, there is conveniency, and *Timber* ſufficient for Shipping.

II.  *The Conſtitutions.*

For the Conſtitution of the Countrey, the Patent ſhows.  *Firſt, That the People and Governour have a* Le-giſlative *Power* ; *ſo that no Law can be made, nor Money raiſed, but by the peoples conſent.*

2dly.  *That the Rights and Freedoms of* England (the beſt and largeſt in *Europe* ) *ſhall be in force there.*

3dly.  *That making no Law againſt Allegiance* (which ſhould we, 'twere by the Law of *England* void of it ſelf that Moment) *we may Enact what Laws we pleaſe for the Good, Proſperity and Security of the ſaid Province.*

4thly.  That ſo ſoon as any are Ingaged with me, we ſhall begin a Scheam or Draught together, ſuch as ſhall give Ample Teſtimony of my ſincere Inclinations to Encourage Planters, and ſettle a Free, Juſt and In-duſtrious *Colony* there.

*In 1681, Charles II granted lands to the English Quaker*
*William Penn, who founded a "holy experiment"*
*in the eponymous colony of Pennsylvania.*

This spirit extended across the ocean, especially in the six Restoration colonies, those that were founded or came under English rule during Charles II's reign. New York and New Jersey became religious asylums for Quakers, Presbyterians, and Jews, as did Pennsylvania, granted by Charles II to the Quaker William Penn in 1681. Penn called Pennsylvania his "holy experiment" and hoped it would form "the seed of a nation." In his 1682 Frame of Government, a constitution for the new colony, he provided for a popularly elected general assembly and for freedom of worship, decreeing "That all persons living in this province, who confess and acknowledge the one Almighty and eternal God, to be the Creator,

Upholder and Ruler of the world; and that hold themselves obliged in conscience to live peaceably and justly in civil society, shall, in no ways, be molested or prejudiced for their religious persuasion or practice, in matters of faith and worship, nor shall they be compelled, at any time, to frequent or maintain any religious worship, place or ministry whatever."[54] Peace rested on tolerance.

With each new charter, with each new constitution, with each new slave code, England's American colonists upended assumptions and rewrote laws governing the relationship between the rulers and the ruled. In the tumult of a century of civil strife, the water between England and America became a kind of looking glass: people drafting new laws saw in their reflections political philosophers; political philosophers saw in their reflections colonial lawmakers. Few people contemplated this relationship more closely than John Locke, a political philosopher who also served as colonial lawmaker.

Locke, a tutor at Christ Church, Oxford, had a hollow face and a long nose; he looked like a bird of prey. He never married. One of his students was the son of the Earl of Shaftesbury, who was the chancellor of the exchequer, and a rather ill man. In 1667, Locke left Oxford and became Shaftesbury's personal secretary, in charge as well of his medical care; he moved into Exeter House, Shaftesbury's London residence, in the Strand. It happened that Shaftesbury was deeply involved in colonial affairs, serving and establishing various councils on trade and plantations, including the board of proprietors for the colony of Carolina. (Charles had granted the colony to eight members of Parliament who had supported his restoration to the throne.) Locke became the colony's secretary.

As secretary, Locke wrote and later revised the colony's constitution, not long after writing his *Letters concerning Toleration*, and at the very time when he was drafting *Two Treatises on Civil Government*, works that would later greatly influence the framers of the U.S. Constitution.[55] Without ever crossing the ocean, Locke dug deep into the soil of the colonies and planted seeds as small as the nibs of his pen.

Consistent with his argument in his *Letters concerning Toleration*, Locke's *Fundamental Constitutions of Carolina* established freedom of religious expression. People who did "not acknowledge a God and that God is publicly and solemnly to be worshiped" were to be barred from settling and owning land, but, aside from that, *any* belief was acceptable, the constitution decreeing that "heathens, Jews and other dissenters from the purity of Christian Religion may not be scared and kept at a distance." Moreover, and in this same spirit—and here weighing in on a debate that had begun in 1492 and had occupied the Spanish throne for the better part of a century—Carolina's constitution established that the heathenism of the natives was not sufficient grounds to take their lands: "The Natives of that place," the constitution stipulated, "are utterly strangers to Christianity whose Idollatry Ignorance or mistake gives us noe right to expell or use them ill."[56] By what right, then, did the English claim their land?

The answer to this question rested in Locke's philosophy. The *Fundamental Constitutions* established a government as a matter of practice, while in the *Two Treatises on Civil Government* Locke attempted to explain, as a matter of philosophy, how governments come to exist. He began by imagining a state of nature, a condition *before* government:

> To understand political power right, and derive it from its original, we must consider, what state all men are naturally in, and that is, a state of perfect freedom to order their actions, and dispose of their possessions and persons, as they think fit, within the bounds of the law of nature, without asking leave, or depending upon the will of any other man.

This was more than a thought experiment; this was a known place: "In the beginning," he wrote, "all the world was America."

This state of nature, for Locke, was a state of "perfect freedom" and "a state also of equality." Locke's egalitarianism derived, in part, from his ideas about Christianity, and the equality of all people before God, "there being nothing more evident, than that creatures of the same species and rank, promiscuously born to all the same advantages of nature, and the use of the same faculties, should also be equal one amongst another without subordination or subjection." From this state of natural, perfect equality, men created civil society—government—for the sake of order, and the protection of their property.

To understand how governments came to exist, then, required understanding how people come to hold property. This, for Locke, required looking to the example of America. Half of the references to America in Locke's *Second Treatise* come in the chapter called "Of Property." [57] He considered, for instance, kings like Powhatan, whose deerskin cloak Locke might well have held in his hands, fingering its snail shells, since the cloak was housed in a museum at Oxford. "The Kings of the Indians in America," Locke wrote, "are little more than Generals of their Armies," and the Indians, having no property, have "no Government at all." Kings like Powhatan had no sovereignty, according to Locke, because they did not cultivate the land; they only lived there. "God gave the World to Men in Common," Locke wrote, but "it can not be supposed he meant it should always remain common and uncultivated. He gave it to the use of the Industrious and Rational, (and Labour was to be his Title to it)." People who leave "great Tracts of Ground" to waste—that is, uncultivated—and who owned land in common, have therefore not "joyned with the rest of Mankind." A people who do not believe land can be owned by individuals not only cannot contract to sell it, they cannot be said to have a government, because government only exists to protect property.

It's not that this idea was especially new. In *Utopia* in 1516, Thomas More had written that taking land from a people that "does not use its soil but keeps it idle and waste" was a "most just cause for war."[58] But Locke, spurred both by a growing commitment to religious toleration and by a desire to distinguish English settlement from Spanish conquest, stressed the lack of cultivation as a better justification for taking the natives' land than religious difference, an emphasis with lasting consequences.

In both the Carolina constitution and in his *Two Treatises on Government*, Locke treated both property and slavery. "Slavery" is, in fact, the very first word in the *Two Treatises*, which begins: "Slavery is so vile and miserable an estate of man, and so directly opposite to the generous temper and courage of our nation, that it is hardly to be conceived that an Englishman, much less a gentleman, should plead for it." This was an attack on Sir Robert Filmer, who had argued, in a book called *Patriarcha*, that the king's authority derives, divinely, from Adam's rule and cannot be protested. For Locke, to believe that was to believe that the subjects of the king were nothing but his slaves. Locke argued that the king's subjects were, instead, free men, because "the natural liberty of man is to be free from any superior power on earth, and not to be under the will or legislative authority of man, but to have only the law of nature for his rule." All men, Locke argued, are born equal, with a natural right to life, liberty, and property; to protect those rights, they erect governments by consent. Slavery, for Locke, was no part either of a state of nature or of civil society. Slavery was a matter of the law of nations, "nothing else, but the state of war continued, between a lawful conqueror and a captive." To introduce slavery in the Carolinas, then, was to establish, as funda-mental to the political order, an institution at variance with everything about how Locke understood civil society. "Every Freeman of Carolina, shall have absolute power and Authority over his Negro slaves," Locke's constitution read. That is to say, notwithstanding the vehement assertion of a natural right to liberty and the claim that absolute power is a form of tyranny, the right of one man to own another—impossible to conceive in a state of nature or under a civil government, impossible to imagine under any arrangement except a state of war—was not only possible, but lawful, in America.[59]

The only way to justify this contradiction, the only way to explain how one kind of people are born free while another kind of people are not, would be to sow a new seed, an ideology of race. It would take a long time to grow, and longer to wither.

## IV.

THE REVOLUTION IN AMERICA, when it came, began not with the English colonists but with the people over whom they ruled. Long before shots were fired at Lexington and Concord, long before George Wash-ington crossed the Delaware, long before American independence was thought of, or even thinkable, a revolutionary tradition was forged, not by the English in America, but by Indians waging wars and slaves wag-ing rebellions. They revolted again and again and again. Their revolutions came in waves that lashed the land. They asked the same question, unre-lentingly: *By what right are we ruled?*

It often seemed to England's colonists as if these rebellions were part of a conspiracy, especially when they came one after another, as they did in 1675 and 1676, a century before the English began their own struggle for independence. In June of 1675, a federation of New England Algonquians, led by a sachem named Metacom (the English called him "King Philip"), attempted to oust the foreigners from their lands, attacking town after town. The Indians, one Englishman wrote, had "risen round the country." Before it was over, more than half of all the English towns in New England had been either destroyed or abandoned. Metacom was shot, drawn, quartered, and beheaded, his severed head placed on a pike in Plymouth, a king's punishment. His nine-year-old son was sold as a slave and shipped to the Caribbean, where a slave rebellion had just broken out in Barbados. The English in Barbados believed that the Africans there "intended to Murther all the White People"; their "grand design was to choose them a King." (Panicked, the legislature on the island swiftly passed a law banning the buying of any Indian slaves carried from New England, for fear that they would only add to the rebellion.) New England and Barbados, one New Englander remarked, had "tasted of the same cup."

That cup spilled over. Even as war was raging in New England and rebellion was seizing Barbados, natives began attacking English towns in Maryland and Virginia, leading Virginia governor William Berkeley to declare that "the Infection of the Indianes in New-England" had spread southward. Berkeley's refusal to retaliate against the Indians led to a rebellion incited by a colonist named Nathaniel Bacon, who led a band of five hundred men to Jamestown, which they burned to the ground. More mayhem would have surely followed had not Berkeley lost his governorship and Bacon died of dysentery.[60]

Wars and rebellions and rumors of more filled the pages of colonial letters and newspapers. Word spread wide and far, and invariably had this effect: racial lines hardened. Before King Philip's War, ministers in New England had attempted to convert the natives to Christianity, to teach them English, with the idea that they would eventually live among the English. After the war, these efforts were largely abandoned. Bacon's Rebellion hardened lines between whites and blacks. Before Bacon and his men burned Jamestown, poor Englishmen had very little political power. As many as three out of every four Englishmen and women who sailed to the colonies were either debtors or convicts or indentured servants; they weren't slaves, but neither were they free.[61] Property requirements for voting meant that not all free white men could vote. Meanwhile, the fact that slaves could be manumitted by their masters meant that it was possible to be both black and free and white and unfree. But after Bacon's Rebellion, free white men were granted the right to vote, and it became nearly impossible for black men and women to secure their freedom. By 1680, one observer could remark that "these two words, Negro and Slave" had "grown Homogeneous and convertible": to be black was to be a slave.[62]

Fear of war and rebellion haunted every English colony, lands of terror, and of terrifying political instability and physical vulnerability. In 1692, nineteen women and men were convicted of witchcraft in the Massachusetts town of Salem. What looked like witchcraft, though, appears to have been the aftermath of Indian attacks, the haunting memories of terrible suffering. During the witch trials, when Mercy Short said the Devil had tormented her by burning her, she described the Devil as "a Short and a Black Man . . . not of Negro, but of a Tawney, or an Indian colour." Two years before Satan and his witches afflicted Mercy Short, she had been captured by Abenakis, who raided her family's home in a town in New Hampshire, killing her parents and three of her brothers and sisters. Mercy Short had been forced to walk into Canada. Along the way, she witnessed atrocity upon atrocity: a five-year-old boy chopped to pieces, a young girl scalped, and a fellow captive "Barbarously Sacrificed," bound to a stake, and tortured with fire, the Abenakis cutting off his flesh, bit by bit. Witches call the Devil "a Black Man," the Boston minister Cotton Mather observed, "and they generally say he resembles an Indian." Mather took that to mean that blacks and Indians were devils, of a sort, instruments of evil. But what haunted Mercy Short wasn't the working of witchcraft; it was the working of terror.[63]

Even in years and places where there were no attacks, there was news of them, from other places, and, always, there was a terror of them. There were uprisings everywhere, and where there were not uprisings, there was fear of uprisings. Some of the plots that the settlers were forever suspecting, detecting, and suppressing were real, and some were imagined, but they all have this in common: parties of men, slaves or Indian, were planning to topple the government and erect their own.

Wars, rebellions, and rumors: what the colonists feared was revolution. On the Danish island of St. John's in 1733, ninety African slaves seized control of the island and held it for half a year. On Antigua in 1736, a group of black men "formed and resolved to execute a Plot, whereby all the white Inhabitants of the Island were to be murdered, and a new Form of Government to be established by the Slaves among themselves, and they entirely to possess the Island," its leader, a man named Court, having "assumed among his Country Men . . . the Stile of KING."[64] Sometimes, rebels faced trial; more usually they did not. In waging war against Indians, the English tended to abandon any ideas they had earlier held, about under what circumstances war was just; they tended to wage those wars first, and justify them afterward. And in suppressing and punishing slave rebellions, they abandoned their ideas about trial by jury and the abolition of torture. In Antigua, men charged with conspiracy were tortured under the terms of a new law making grotesque punishments legal; black men were broken on the wheel, starved to death, roasted over a slow fire, and gibbeted alive. On Nantucket in 1738, English colonists believed they had detected a conspiracy of the island's Indians "to destroy all the English, by first setting Fire to their Houses, in the Night, and then falling upon them with their Fire Arms." One Indian's explanation for this plot was "that the English at first took the Land from their Ancestors by Force, and have kept it ever since."[65]

Conquest was always fragile, slavery forever unstable. In Jamaica, where blacks outnumbered whites by as many as twenty to one, Africans led by a man named Cudjoe fled plantations and built towns—the English called them "maroon" towns—in the mountains in the island's interior. The First Maroon War ended in 1739 with a treaty under which the British agreed to acknowledge five Maroon towns, and granted Cudjoe and his followers their freedom and more than fifteen hundred acres of land. It had been a war for independence.

Word of rebellions in Jamaica and Antigua reached the Carolinas and Georgia in a matter of weeks, New England only days later. English colonists on the mainland had family on the islands—and so did their slaves, who, like their owners, traded gossip and news with the arrival of every ship. In 1739, more than a hundred black men rose up in arms and killed more than twenty whites in the Stono Rebellion in South Carolina, a colony where blacks outnumbered whites by two to one. "Carolina looks more like a negro country than like a country settled by white people," one visitor wrote.[66] The rebels hoped to make their way to Spanish Florida, where the Spanish had promised fugitive slaves their freedom. As they marched, they shouted, "Liberty!" They were led by a man named Jemmy. Born in Angola, he spoke Kikongo, English, and Portuguese, and, as was very often true of the leaders of slave rebellions, could read and write.[67]

What laws might quiet these rebellions, what punishments avert these revolutions? This was the question debated by colonial legislatures, in meetinghouses built of brick and wood and stone, even as Indians and Africans threatened to tear those meetinghouses down. In 1740, in the aftermath of the Stono Rebellion, the South Carolina legislature passed An Act for the Better Ordering and Governing Negroes, a new set of rules for relations between the rulers and the ruled. It restricted the movement of slaves, set standards for their treatment, established punishments for their crimes, explained the procedures for their prosecution and codified the rules of evidence for their trials; in capital cases, the charges were to be heard by two justices and a jury comprising at least three men. The law also made it a crime for anyone to teach a slave to write, in hopes of averting the next Jemmy, reading and preaching liberty.[68] The English, as Samuel Purchas had remarked, enjoyed a "literall advantage" over the people they ruled, and they meant to keep it.

Word of rebellions spread so fast in the colonies because, while suppressed among slaves, literacy was growing among the colonists, who had begun to print their own pamphlets and books and, especially, their own newspapers. The first printing press brought to Britain's colonies arrived in Boston in 1639, and the first newspaper in British America, *Publick Occurrences,* appeared there in 1690. Censored, it lasted for only a single issue, but a second newspaper, the *Boston News-Letter,* started in 1704, and carried on, printed from a shop on a narrow, cramped street in the narrow and cramped town of Boston, not far from the Common, where sheep grazed and where, at every hour, the lowing of cows could be heard as an unending thrum beneath the tolling of church bells.[69]

At first, colonial printers reported mostly news from Europe but, more and more, they began reporting the goings-on in neighboring colonies. They also began questioning authority, and insisting on their liberty and, in particular, on the liberty of the press. Its fiercest advocate would be Benjamin Franklin, born in Boston in 1706, the son of a Puritan candle maker and soap-boiler.

Benjamin Franklin was the youngest of his father's ten sons; his sister Jane, born in 1712, was the youngest of their father's seven daughters. Benjamin Franklin taught himself to read and write, and then he taught his sister, at a time when girls, like slaves, were hardly ever taught to write (they were, however, taught to read, so that they could read the Bible). He wanted to become a writer. His father could only afford to send him to school for two years (and sent Jane not at all). Another of their brothers,

James, became a printer, and at sixteen, Benjamin became his apprentice, just when James Franklin began printing an irreverent newspaper called the *New-England Courant.*[70]

The *New-England Courant* brooked no censor: it was the first "unlicensed" newspaper in the colonies; that is, the colonial government did not grant it a license, and did not review its content before publication. James Franklin decided to use his newspaper to criticize both the government and the clergy, at a time when the two were essentially one, and Massachusetts a theocracy. "The Plain Design of your Paper is to Banter and Abuse the Ministers of God," Cotton Mather seethed at him. In 1722, James Franklin was arrested for sedition. While he was in prison, his little brother and hardworking apprentice took over printing the *Courant,* and there appeared on the masthead, for the first time, the name BENJAMIN FRANKLIN.[71]

While his little sister remained at home dipping candles and boiling soap, young Benjamin Franklin decided to thumb his nose at the government by printing excerpts from a work known as *Cato's Letters,* written by two radicals, an Englishman, John Trenchard and a Scot, Thomas Gordon. *Cato's Letters* comprises 144 essays about the nature of liberty, including freedom of speech and of the press. "Without freedom of thought," Trenchard and Gordon wrote, "there can be no such thing as wisdom; and no such thing as publick liberty, without freedom of speech: Which is the right of every man."[72] Jane Franklin read those essays as well, and maybe, raised and schooled in a family of rebels, she began to wonder about the rights of every woman, too.

James Franklin fought his prosecution, got out of prison, and kept on printing, but in 1723, young Benjamin Franklin thumbed his nose at his brother, too, and ran away from his apprenticeship, which also meant that he abandoned his sister Jane. Not long after, at the age of fifteen, she was married. Benjamin Franklin began his rags-to-riches rise, a phrase that, at the time, was meant both figuratively and literally: paper is made of rags and Franklin, the first American printer to print paper currency, turned rags to riches. Jane, who would have twelve children and bury eleven of them, lived the far more common life of an eighteenth-century American and especially of a woman, born poor: rags to rags.

Leaving his sister in Boston, Benjamin Franklin eventually settled in the tidy Quaker town of Philadelphia and began printing his own newspaper, the *Pennsylvania Gazette*, in 1729. In its pages, he fought for freedom of the press. In a Miltonian 1731 "Apology for Printers," he observed "that the Opinions of Men are almost as various as their Faces" but that "Printers are educated in the Belief, that when Men differ in Opinion, both Sides ought equally to have the Advantage of being heard by the Publick; and that when Truth and Error have fair Play, the former is always an overmatch for the latter."[73]

The culture of the fact—the idea of empiricism that had spread from law to government—hadn't yet quite spread to newspapers, which were full of shipping news and runaway slave ads, and word of slave rebellions and Indian wars, and of the latest meeting of Parliament. Newspapers were interested in truth, but they established truth, as Franklin explained, by printing all sides, and letting them do battle. Printers did not consider it their duty to print only facts; they considered it their duty to print the "Opinions of Men," as Franklin put it, and let the best man win: truth will out.

But if the culture of the fact hadn't yet spread to newspapers, it had spread to history. In *Leviathan*, Thomas Hobbes had written that "The register of Knowledge of Fact is called History."[74] One lesson Americans would learn from the facts of their own history had to do with the limits of the freedom of the press, and this was a fact on which they dwelled, and a liberty they grew determined to protect.

After James Franklin's tangles with the law in Boston, the next battle over the freedom of the press was staged in New York, the busiest port on the mainland, where African slaves owned by the Dutch had once built a wall at the edge of town, and African slaves owned by the English had taken it down, leaving Wall Street behind. In 1732, a new governor arrived in New York to take up his office in city hall, built by Africans out of the stones that had once formed the wall.

William Cosby was a dandy and a lout. Like the governors of all but four of the mainland colonies, he'd been appointed by the king. He had neither any particular qualifications for the office nor any ties to the people over whom he would rule. He was greedy and corrupt. To topple him, a New York lawyer named James Alexander, a friend of Benjamin Franklin's, hired a German immigrant named John Peter Zenger to print a new newspaper, the *New-York Weekly Journal*. The first issue appeared in 1733. Much of the paper consisted of excerpts from *Cato's Letters* and like-minded essays written, anonymously, by Alexander. "No Nation Antient or Modern ever lost the Liberty of freely Speaking, Writing, or Publishing their Sentiments but forthwith lost their Liberty in general and became Slaves," Alexander wrote. By "slaves" he meant what Locke meant: a people subject to the tyranny of absolute and arbitrary rule. He most emphatically didn't mean the Africans who worked and lived in his own house. One in five New Yorkers was a slave. Slaves built the city, its hulking stone houses, its nail-knocked wooden wharves. They dug the roads, and their own graves, at the Negroes Burying Ground. They carried water for steeping tea and wood for burning. They loaded and unloaded the ships, steps from the slave market. But the liberty to freely speak, write, and publish was not theirs.[75]

Cosby, brittle and high-handed, like many an imperious and thin-skinned ruler after him, could not abide criticism. He ordered all copies of Zenger's paper burned, and had Zenger, a poor tradesman who was doing another man's bidding, arrested for seditious libel.

At a time when political parties were frowned upon by nearly every-one as destructive of the political order—"Party is the madness of many, for the gain of a few," remarked the poet Alexander Pope in 1727—two political factions nevertheless emerged in the hurly-burly city of New York: the Court Party, which supported Cosby, and the Country Party, which opposed him. "We are in the midst of Party flames," lamented Daniel Horsmanden, a petty, small-minded placeman appointed by Cosby to the Supreme Court. But three thousand miles from London, weeks of sailing time away from any relief from the abuses of a tyrannical governor, New Yorkers began to believe that parties might be "not only necessary in free Government, but of great service to the Public." As one New Yorker wrote in 1734, "Parties are a check upon one another, and by keeping the Ambition of one another within Bounds, serve to maintain the public Liberty."[76]

The next year, Zenger was tried before the colony's Supreme Court, in that city hall of stone. Alexander, whose authorship of the essays remained unknown, served as Zenger's lawyer until the court's chief jus-tice, a Cosby appointee, had him disbarred. Zenger was then represented by Andrew Hamilton, an especially shrewd lawyer from Philadelphia. Hamilton did not dispute that Zenger had printed articles critical of the governor. Instead, he argued that everything that Zenger had printed was true—Cosby really was a dreadfully bad governor—and dared a jury to disagree. In his closing argument, he both drew on *Cato's Letters* and elevated the controversy in New York to epic proportions, in a rhetorical move that would become commonplace by the 1760s, as more colonies bridled at English rule. The question, Hamilton told the jury, "is not the Cause of a poor Printer, nor of *New-York* alone." No, "It is the best Cause. It is the Cause of Liberty."[77]

The jury found Zenger not guilty. Cosby died ignominiously the next year. But New Yorkers' zeal for parties did not abate. There was even talk, for a time, of a civil war. The Country Party went on to dispute the authority of Cosby's beleaguered successor, George Clarke, who reported to London, astounded, that New Yorkers believed that "if a Governor misbehave himself they may depose him and set up another."[78]

And yet the idea that a people might depose a tyrant and replace him with one of themselves as a ruler was not, of course, such an astonishing notion: it lay behind every slave rebellion. In the years after the Zenger trial, fear that just such a conspiracy was in the minds of the city slaves became an obsession of their owners. In 1741, when fires broke out across the city, and Clarke's own mansion—the governor's mansion— burned to the ground, many New Yorkers became convinced that the fires had been set by the city's slaves, plotting a rebellion, not unlike the rebellions that had taken place in the 1730s in Antigua, Barbados, Jamaica, and South Carolina—and, if more violent, not altogether unlike the rebellion waged by the Country Party against Cosby. Were these not yet more terrifying party flames?

"The Negroes are rising!" New Yorkers shouted from street corners. Many of the city's slaves had come to New York from the Caribbean; not a few had come from islands known for rebellion. Caesar, owned by a Dutch baker, was able to read and write, like Jemmy, the leader of South Carolina's Stono Rebellion. Caesar had also fathered a child with a white woman—another crossing of racial lines. He was one of the first men arrested in New York. There followed whispered rumors and tortured confessions. Daniel Horsmanden decided that "most of the Negroes in town were corrupted" and that they planned to murder all the whites and elect Caesar as their governor.

What happened in New York in the 1730s and 1740s set a pattern in American politics. At Horsmanden's urging, more than 150 black men in the city were arrested, thrown in prison, and interrogated. Many were tried. The outcomes of the trials of Zenger and men like Caesar could hardly have been more different. White New Yorkers had decided that they could bear the singe of party flames: political dissent, in the form of a newspaper and a political party opposed to the royally appointed governor, they could tolerate. But dissent in the form of a slave rebellion they could not. The very court that had acquitted Zenger tried and convicted thirty black men, sentencing thirteen to be burned at the stake and seventeen more to be hanged, along with four whites. "Bonfires of the Negros," one colonist called the executions in 1741. But these, too, were party flames. Most of the rest of the black men who had been arrested were taken from their families and sold to the Caribbean, a fate many considered to be worse than death. Caesar, who at the gallows refused to confess, was hung in chains, his rotting body displayed for months, in hopes that his "Example and Punishment might break the Rest, and induce some of them to unfold this Mystery of Iniquity."[79] But the mystery of iniquity wasn't conspiracy; it was slavery itself.

Waves of rebellion lashed the shores of the English Atlantic for more than a century, from Boston to Barbados, from New York to Jamaica, from the Carolinas and back again to London. "Rule, Britannia, rule the waves; / Britons never will be slaves," read a poem written in England in 1740 that became the empire's anthem, and America's anthem, too. It was lost on no one that the loudest calls for liberty in the early modern world came from a part of that world that was wholly dependent on slavery.

Slavery does not exist outside of politics. Slavery is a form of politics, and slave rebellion a form of violent political dissent. The Zenger trial and the New York slave conspiracy were much more than a dispute over freedom of the press and a foiled slave rebellion: they were part of a debate about the nature of political opposition, and together they established its limits. Both Cosby's opponents and Caesar's followers allegedly plotted to depose the governor. One kind of rebellion was celebrated, the other suppressed—a division that would endure. In American history, the relationship between liberty and slavery is at once deep and dark: the threat of black rebellion gave a license to white political opposition. The American political tradition was forged by philosophers and by statesmen, by printers and by writers, and it was forged, too, by slaves.

*Benjamin Franklin's 1754 woodcut served as both
a political cartoon and a map of the colonies.*

ON MAY 9, 1754, Benjamin Franklin, a man of parts, printed a wood-cut in the *Pennsylvania Gazette*. It was titled "JOIN, or DIE," and it pic-tured a snake, chopped into eight pieces, labeled, by their initials, from head to tail: New England, New York, New Jersey, Pennsylvania, Mary-land, Virginia, North Carolina, and South Carolina.

For centuries, the kings and queens of Europe had fought over how to divvy up North America, as if the land were a cake to be carved. They staked their claims on the ground, naming towns and waging wars, and they staked their claims with maps, drawing lines and coloring shapes. In 1681, a map called "North America Divided into its Principall Parts where are distinguished the several States which belong to the English, Spanish, and French" was bound in an atlas printed in London, with colors inked by hand. It took only passing notice of natives of these lands, vaguely noting the "Apache" near New Mexico. Like many maps, it became very quickly outdated. England and Scotland formed a union in 1707 and went on waging an on-again, off-again war with France and Spain that spilled over onto the North American continent, where both

Britain and France allied with Indians. The colonists named these wars after the kings or queens under whose reign they fell: King William's War (1689–1697), Queen Anne's War (1702–1713), and King George's War (1744–48). North America was divided into its principal parts, and then it was divided again, and again.

Franklin's "JOIN, or DIE" woodcut illustrated an article, written by Franklin, about the need for the colonies to form a common defense— against France and Spain, and against warring Indians and rebelling slaves. Franklin, forty-eight, by then a man of means and accomplishment, dressed a cut fancier than his Quaker townsmen and spoke with warmth and force. In April 1754, the governor of Pennsylvania had appointed him to serve as a commissioner to a meeting, scheduled for June, in Albany, New York, where delegates from the colonies were to negotiate a treaty with a confederation of Iroquois, the so-called Six Nations: the Mohawks, the Oneidas, the Onondagas, the Cayugas, the Senecas, and the Tusca-roras. "Our Enemies have the very great Advantage of being under one Direction, with one Council, and one Purse," Franklin wrote, suggesting it was this unity that Britain's mainland American colonies lacked.[80]

Since running away from his apprenticeship in Boston in 1723, Frank-lin had headed very many civic-minded schemes for the North Ameri-can colonies as they spread westward, farther from shore, farther from the islands, farther from London, and farther from one another. Many of those schemes involved closing the distance between the colonies, chiefly by improving communication between them.

Franklin, champion of the freedom of the press, promoted, in every way, the diffusion of knowledge. In 1731, he founded the first lending library in America, the Library Company of Philadelphia. In 1732, he began printing *Poor Richard's Almanack*, which reached across the colo-nies and gave Americans a common store of proverbs and even a shared political history, as when, on the page for the month of June, Franklin added this notation: "On the 15th of this month, anno 1215, was *Magna Charta* sign'd by King John, for declaring and establishing *English Lib-erty*." In 1736 Franklin was elected clerk of the Pennsylvania Provincial Assembly. The next year, he was appointed postmaster of Philadelphia, and began improvements to the postal service. "The first Drudgery of Set-tling new Colonies, which confines the Attention of People to mere Nec-essaries, is now pretty well over," he wrote in 1743, in a pamphlet titled *A*

*Proposal for Promoting Useful Knowledge among the British Plantations in America*. Everywhere in America there were "Men of Speculation," conducting experiments, recording observations, making discoveries. "But as from the Extent of the Country such Persons are widely separated, and seldom can see and converse or be acquainted with each other, so that many useful Particulars remain uncommunicated, die with the Discoverers, and are lost to Mankind." He therefore established the American Philosophical Society, the colonies' first learned society.[81]

In much the same spirit that Franklin founded a library and a philosophical society, he dedicated himself to his work as postmaster: he wanted ideas to circulate, blood in the colonies' veins. He went on a tour of the colonies inspecting the post roads. He calculated their distance, and the time it took to travel from farm to farm, from town to town. He was also taking a kind of a census, counting people, and measuring the distance between them.

By 1750, even though the overwhelming majority of migrants to England's colonies had gone to the Caribbean, four out of every five people living in British America lived in one of the thirteen mainland colonies. This ratio was a consequence of different rates of mortality in different parts of Britain's American empire. Migrants to the Caribbean died in heaps. In New England, English settlers enjoyed very long lives. The southern colonies had more in common with the Caribbean: a black majority and a high mortality rate. The middle colonies were mixed, a stew of Scots, Irish, English, Dutch, Germans, and Africans, a population healthier than that of the Caribbean but not as healthy as that of New England. Yet for all their differences, by some measures the mainland colonies were becoming more alike in the middle of the eighteenth century: "I found but little difference in the manners and character of the people in the different provinces I passed thro," wrote the Scottish doctor Alexander Hamilton in 1744, after making a tour on horseback with his African slave, Dromo, from Maryland to Maine.[82]

One way in which the mainland colonies were becoming more alike was that so many of them were bound up in a religious revival, a more expressive religion, less in awe of ministers, more gripped by the power of the spirit and the equality of all souls under heaven. George Whitefield, a passionate evangelical from England, drew crowds of thousands. Fastidious and zealous, Whitefield was also sickly and cross-eyed—the

*George Whitefield's preaching stirred ordinary Americans
and set them swooning, but it also inspired study, and
intellectual independence, represented here in the form
of a woman, in the lower left, wearing spectacles
to study Scripture.*

uncharitable called him "Dr. Squintum." Raised by a widowed innkeeper, he came from the humblest of people, and in the colonies he attracted, from town to town, what he called a "cloud of witnesses" from all ranks of society. He told his followers they could be born again, into the body of Christ, and urged them to cast off the teachings of more restrained ministers. "I am willing to go to prison and to death for you," he said. "But I am not willing to go to heaven without you."[83]

This, too, represented a kind of revolution: Whitefield emphasized the divinity of ordinary people, at the expense of the authority of their ministers. In 1739, a gathering of orthodox clergy in Philadelphia had ruled that all ministers must have a degree from Harvard, Yale, or a British or European university. But Whitefield was a people's preacher, preaching to farmers and artisans, seamen and servants.[84]

Franklin had his doubts about Whitefield, but about religion, as about much else, he practiced discretion. "Talking against religion is unchaining a Tiger," as he put it. On other matters, he had far more to say. Having traveled the colonies and measured their extent, and having tried to tally the people, he wrote in 1751 an essay about the size of the population, called "Observations concerning the Increase of Mankind, Peopling of Countries, &c."

Franklin wanted to know: What would be the fate of colonists if the colonies were to grow bigger than the place they'd come from? Land was cheap in the colonies, "so cheap as that a labouring Man, that understands Husbandry, can in a short Time save Money enough to purchase a Piece of new Land sufficient for a Plantation." And if that man marries and has children, he and his wife could be confident that there would be plenty of land for their children, too. Franklin guessed the population of the mainland colonies to be about "One Million English Souls," and his calculations suggested that this number would double every twenty-five years. At that rate, in only a century, "the greatest Number of Englishmen will be on this Side the Water."

Franklin's numbers were off; his estimates weren't too high; they were too low. At the time, more than 1.5 million people lived in Britain's thirteen mainland colonies. Those colonies were far more densely settled than New France or New Spain. Only 60,000 French settlers lived in Canada and 10,000 more in Louisiana. New Spain was even more thinly settled. It was also more difficult—impossible—in New Spain and New France to separate out the settlers from the natives, since so many formed families together. In Britain's North American colonies, such unions were less frequently acknowledged, most kept actively hidden.

Franklin, like many an American after him, lost his trademark equanimity when it came to the question of color. In Spanish America, a land of mestizos, slave owners commonly freed their slaves in their wills; by 1775, free blacks outnumbered black slaves. Something similar happened in New France, where the families of French traders and Indians were known as Métis. Both there and in New Spain, people from different parts of the world married and reared children together over generations. Color in many ways marked status, but it did not mark a line between slavery and freedom, and color meant color: reds and browns, pinks and yellows. Britain's mainland colonies established a far different and more brutal racial regime, one that imagined only two colors, black and white, and two statuses, slave and free. Laws forbade mixed-race marriage, decreed the children of a slave mother to be slaves, and discouraged or prohibited manumissions. The owners of slaves very often had children with their female slaves, but they did not raise them as their own children, or free them, or even acknowledge them; instead, they deemed them slaves, and called them "black." Franklin, reckoning with that racial line, added one more observation to his essay on population; he wrote about a new race, a people who were "white."

"The Number of purely white People in the World is proportionably very small," Franklin began. As he saw it, Africans were "black"; Asians and Native Americans were "tawny"; Spaniards, Italians, French, Russians, Swedes, and Germans were "swarthy." That left very few people, and chiefly the English, as the only "white people" in the world. "I could wish their Numbers were increased," Franklin said, adding, wonderingly, "But perhaps I am partial to the Complexion of my Country, for such Kind of Partiality is natural to Mankind."[85]

Franklin stumbled over his partiality for people of his own "complexion." Was it really "natural"? Perhaps. Plainly, he was troubled by it. But, with his trademark alacrity, he wrote all this down, and then he moved on to another subject, the bonds that hold people together: Join, or die.

At the Albany Congress in 1754, Franklin proposed a Plan of Union, to be administered by a "President General, To be appointed and Supported by the Crown, and a Grand Council to be Chosen by the Representatives of the People of the Several Colonies, met in their respective Assemblies." The Union was to include the seven colonies labeled in his snake—New York, New Jersey, Pennsylvania, Maryland, Virginia, North Carolina, and South Carolina—and the four colonies represented, in the snake, as "New England"—Massachusetts, Rhode Island, Connecticut, and New Hampshire.

Franklin's plan apportioned representatives for each of the eleven colonies in the Union according to the size of their populations (two each for sparsely settled New Hampshire and tiny Rhode Island, seven each for populous Virginia and Massachusetts). The government, meeting in Philadelphia, would have the power to pass laws, to make treaties, to raise money and soldiers "for the Defence of any of the Colonies," and to protect the coasts. Delegates to the Albany Congress approved the Plan of Union, and brought it back to their colony assemblies, which, fearing the loss of their own authority, rejected it. The British government, too, disapproved; as Franklin said, "it was judg'd to have too much of the *Democratic*." [86]

Franklin's Plan of Union failed. What lasted was the woodcut, which had a great deal in common with Powhatan's deerskin, stitched together a half century before. "JOIN, or DIE" is, among other things, a map, but it's a particular kind of map, known as a "dissected map." Dissected maps were the very first jigsaw puzzles, made by mapmakers, out of paper glued to wood. One of the first dissected maps was called "Europe Divided into its Kingdoms," made in London in the 1760s by a mapmaker who had apprenticed with the king's geographer; it was a toy, meant to teach children geography. It also taught children how to understand the nature of kingdoms, and of rule.

Franklin's "JOIN, or DIE" did some of that, too: it offered a lesson about the rulers and the ruled, and the nature of political communities. It made a claim about the colonies: they were parts of a whole.

# Three

# OF WARS AND REVOLUTIONS

*Boston-born artist John Singleton Copley left the colonies in 1774, never to return; in 1783, while living in London, he depicted the 1781 Battle of Jersey in a 12 × 8 foot painting—only a detail is shown here—and offered his own argument about American liberty by picturing, near its center, a black man firing a gun.*

BENJAMIN LAY STOOD BARELY OVER FOUR FEET TALL, hunchbacked and bowed, with a too-big head and a barrel chest and legs so spindly it did not appear possible they could bear his weight. As a boy in England, he'd worked on his brother's farm before being appren-

*In protest of slavery, Benjamin Lay rejected anything produced by slave labor, became a hermit, and lived in a cave.*

ticed to a glove maker, shearing and stitching skins. At twenty-one, he went to sea; in his hammock, by the light of tallow, he read books. Lay liked to call himself "a poor common sailor and an illiterate man," but in truth, he was widely read and well traveled. He sailed to Syria and to Turkey, where he met "four men that had been 17 Years Slaves"—Englishmen who'd been enslaved by Muslims. He swabbed decks with men who'd sailed on English slave-trading ships, carrying Africans. He heard tales of dark and terrible cruelties. In 1718, Lay sailed to Barbados, where he saw people branded and tortured and beaten, starved and broken; he decided that everything about this arrangement was an offense against God, who "did not make others to be Slaves to us."[1]

Lay and his also hobbled wife—a Quaker preacher with a crooked back—left Barbados after only eighteen months and returned to England. Maybe it was something about being so bowed, so easily dismissed, so set aside, that left them reeling at the horrors of slavery, the breaking of backs, the butchering of bodies. In 1732, they embarked for Pennsylvania to join William Penn's Holy Experiment. In Philadelphia, Lay turned bookseller, selling Bibles and primers along with the works of his favorite poets, like John Milton's *Paradise Lost*, and of his favorite philosophers, like *Seneca's Morals*, essays on ethics by an ancient Roman stoic.[2] He traveled from town to town and from colony to colony, only ever on foot—he would not spur a horse—to denounce slavery before governors and ministers and merchants. "What a Parcel of Hypocrites and Deceivers we are," he said.[3] His arguments fell on deaf ears. After his wife died, he lost his last restraint. In 1738, he went to a Quaker meeting in New Jersey carrying a Bible whose pages he'd removed; he'd placed inside the book a pig's bladder filled with pokeberry juice, crimson red. "Oh all you negro masters who are contentedly holding your fellow creatures in a state of slavery," he cried, entering the meetinghouse, "you who profess 'to do unto all men as ye would they should do unto you,'" you shall see justice "in the sight of the Almighty, who beholds and respects all nations and colours of men with an equal regard." Then, taking his Bible from his coat and a sword from his belt, he pierced the Bible with the sword. To the stunned parishioners, it appeared to burst with blood, as if by a miracle, spattering their heads and staining their clothes, as Lay thundered, from his tiny frame: "Thus shall God shed the blood of those persons who enslave their fellow creatures."[4]

The next month, Benjamin Franklin printed Lay's book, *All Slave-Keepers That keep the Innocent in Bondage, Apostates*, a rambling and furious three-hundred-page polemic. Franklin sold the book at his shop, two shillings a copy, twenty shillings a dozen. Lay handed out copies for free.[5] Then he became a hermit. Outside of Philadelphia, he carved a cave out of a hill. Inside, he stowed his library: two hundred books of theology, biography, poetry, and history. He'd decided to protest slavery by refusing to eat or drink or wear or use anything that had been made with forced labor. He also refused to eat animals. He lived on water and milk, roasted turnips and honey; he kept bees and spun flax and stitched clothes. Franklin used to visit him in his cave. Franklin at the time owned a "Negro boy" named Joseph. By 1750 he owned two more slaves, Peter and Jemima, husband and wife. Lay pressed him and pressed him: *By what right?*

Franklin, himself a runaway, knew, as every printer knew, and every newspaper reader knew, that every newspaper contained, within its pages, tales of revolution, in the stories of everyday escapes. Among them, in those years, were the following. Bett, who had "a large scar on her breast," ran away in 1750 from a man on Long Island. She was wearing nothing but a petticoat and a jacket in the bitter cold of January. Primus, who was thirty-seven, and missing the first joint of one of his big toes, probably a punishment for an earlier attempted escape, ran away from Hartford in 1753, carrying his fiddle. Jack, "a tall slim fellow, very black, and speaks good English," left Philadelphia in July of 1754. Sam, a carpenter, thirty, "a dark Mulatto," ran away from a shop in Prince George's County, Maryland, in the winter of 1755. "He is supposed to be lurking in Charles County," his owner wrote, "where a Mulatoo Woman lives, whom he has for some Time called his Wife; but as he is an artful Fellow, and can read and write, it is probable he may endeavor to make his Escape out of the Province." Will, forty, ran away from a plantation in Virginia in the summer of 1756; he was, his owner said, "much scar'd on his back with a whip."[6]

When Benjamin Franklin began writing his autobiography, in 1771, he turned the story of his own escape—running away from his apprenticeship to his brother James—into a metaphor for the colonies' growing resentment of parliamentary rule. James's "harsh and tyrannical Treatment," Franklin wrote, had served as "a means of impressing me with that Aversion to arbitrary Power that has stuck to me thro' my whole Life."[7] But that was also the story of every runaway slave ad, testament after testament to an aversion to arbitrary power.

In April 1757, before sailing to London, Franklin drafted a new will, in which he promised Peter and Jemima that they would be freed at his death. Two months later, when Franklin reached London, he wrote to his wife, Deborah, "I wonder how you came by Ben. Lay's picture." She had hung on the wall an oil portrait of the dwarf hermit, standing outside his cave, holding in one hand an open book.[8]

The American Revolution did not begin in 1775 and it didn't end when the war was over. "The success of Mr. Lay, in sowing the seeds of . . . a revolution in morals, commerce, and government, in the new and in the old world, should teach the benefactors of mankind not to despair, if they do not see the fruits of their benevolent propositions, or undertakings, during their lives," Philadelphia doctor Benjamin Rush later wrote. Rush signed the Declaration of Independence and served as surgeon general of the Continental army. To him, the Revolution began with the seeds sown by people like Benjamin Lay. "Some of these seeds produce their fruits in a short time," Rush wrote, "but the most valuable of them, like the venerable oak, are centuries in growing."[9]

In 1758, when Benjamin Lay's portrait hung in Benjamin Franklin's house, the Philadelphia Quaker meeting formally denounced slave trading;

Quakers who bought and sold men were to be disavowed. When Lay heard the news he said, "I can now die in peace," closed his eyes, and expired.[10] Within the year, another Pennsylvania Quaker, Anthony Benezet, published a little book called *Observations on the Inslaving, Importing and Purchasing of Negroes*, in which he argued that slavery was "inconsistent with the Gospel of Christ, contrary to natural Justice and the common feelings of Humanity, and productive of infinite Calamities."[11] Bett and Primus and Jack and Sam and Will had not run away for nothing.

There were not one but two American revolutions at the end of the eighteenth century: the struggle for independence from Britain, and the struggle to end slavery. Only one was won.

# I.

**BENJAMIN FRANKLIN WROTE** a new will before he sailed to London in 1757 because Britain and France were attacking each other's ships, and he feared his might get sunk. The fighting had broken out three years before, only weeks after Franklin printed his "JOIN, or DIE" snake, slithering across a page. The battling had begun not at sea but on land, in Franklin's own colony of Pennsylvania. Britain sorely wanted land that the French had claimed in the Ohio Valley, complaining, "the French have stripped us of more than nine parts in ten of North America and left us only a skirt of coast along the Atlantic shore."[12] Leaving that skirt behind, English settlers had begun advancing farther and farther inland, into territories occupied by native peoples but claimed by France. To stop them, the French had starting building forts along their borders. The inevitable skirmish came in May 1754, when a small force of Virginia militiamen and their Indian allies, led by twenty-one-year-old Lieutenant Colonel George Washington, ambushed a French camp at the bottom of a glen.

Born in 1732 in Westmoreland County, Virginia, Washington had inherited his first human property at the age of ten, traveled to the West Indies as a young man, and accepted his first military commission at the age of twenty. Tall, imposing, and grave, he cut a striking figure. He was, as yet, inexperienced, and his first battle proved disastrous for the Virginians, who retreated to a nearby meadow and hastily erected a small wooden garrison that they named, suitably, Fort Necessity. After losing a third of his men in a single day, like so many stalks of wheat hacked down by a scythe, the young lieutenant surrendered. Only weeks later, delegates from the colonies met in Albany to consider Franklin's proposal to form a defensive union, and, though they approved the plan, their colonial assemblies rejected it.

The war came all the same, a war over the trade in the East Indies, over fishing rights off the coast of Newfoundland, over shipping along the Mississippi River, and over sugar plantations on West Indian islands. Like all wars, its costs were borne most heavily by the poor, who did the fighting, while traders, who sold weapons and supplied soldiers, saw profits. "War is declared in England—universal joy among the merchants," wrote one New Yorker in 1756.[13] The colonists called it the French and Indian War, after the people they were fighting in North America, but the war stretched from Bengal to Barbados, drew in Austria, Portugal, Prussia, Spain, and Russia, and engaged armies and navies in the Atlantic and the Pacific, in the Mediterranean and the Caribbean. The French and Indian War did what Franklin's woodcut could not: as far north as New England, it brought Britain's North American colonies together. Not least, it also led to the publication of an *American Magazine*, printed in Philadelphia and sent to subscribers from Jamaica to Boston. As its editors boasted: "Our readers are a numerous body, consisting of all parties and persuasions, thro' *British America*."[14]

During earlier wars between the British and the French, the colonists had mostly done their own fighting, raising town militias and provincial armies. But in 1755, Britain sent regiments of its regular army to North America, under the command of the stubborn and tempestuous General Edward Braddock. Franklin viewed the appointment of Braddock as the Crown's attempt to keep the colonies weak. "The British Government not chusing to permit the Union of the Colonies, as propos'd at Albany, and to trust that Union with their Defence, lest they should thereby grow too military," he wrote, they "sent over General Braddock with two Regiments of Regular English Troops."[15] Charged with moving the French line, Braddock began to prepare to engage the French at Fort Duquesne, at the mouth of the Ohio River, on the western edge of the frontier. Franklin warned the general that his planned route, as serpentine as a snake's path, would expose his troops to Indian attack. "The slender Line near four Miles long, which your Army must make," he explained, "may expose it to be attack'd by Surprize in its Flanks, and to be cut like a Thread into several Pieces." Braddock, it would seem, gave Franklin a condescending smile, the same smile the king gave his subjects. "These Savages may indeed be a formidable Enemy to your raw American Militia," he said. "But upon the King's regular and disciplin'd Troops, Sir, it is impossible they should make any Impression."

Braddock and his troops proceeded with their march. Along the way, they plundered the people. Before long, many colonists found themselves fearing the British army as much as the French. "This was enough to put us out of Conceit of such Defenders if we had really wanted any," wrote Franklin bitterly. Braddock's troops were ignominiously defeated and Braddock was shot. During a beleaguered retreat, the dying general was carried off the field by Washington.[16]

Nothing daunted, William Pitt, the new secretary of state, determined to win the war and settle Britain's claims in North America once and for all. In his honor, when the British and American troops finally seized Fort Duquesne, they renamed it Fort Pitt. But Pitt's lasting legacy would lie in the staggering cost of the war. Before long, forty-five thousand troops were fighting in North America; half were British soldiers, half were American troops. Pitt promised the colonies the war would be fought "at His Majesty's expense." It was the breaking of that promise, and the laying of new taxes on the colonies, that would, in the end, lead the colonists to break with England.

Even before then, the most expensive war in history cost Britain the loyalty of its North American colonists. British troops plundered colonial homes and raided colonial farms. Like Braddock, they also sneered at the ineptness of colonial militias and provincial armies. In close quarters, in camps and on marches, few on either side failed to notice the difference between British and American troops. The British found the colonists inexpert, undisciplined, and unruly. But to the Americans, few of whom had ever been to Britain, it was the British who were wanting: lewd, profane, and tyrannical.[17]

A clash proved difficult to avoid. In the British army, rank meant everything. British officers were wealthy gentlemen; enlisted men were drawn from the masses of the poor. In the colonial forces, there were hardly any distinctions of rank. In Massachusetts, one in every three men served in the French and Indian War, whether they were penniless clerks or rich merchants. In any case, differences of title and rank that existed in Britain did not exist in the colonies, at least among free men. In England, fewer than one in five adult men could vote; in the colonies, that proportion was two-thirds. The property requirements for voting were met by so many men that Thomas Hutchinson, who lost a bid to become governor in 1749, complained that the town of Boston was an "absolute democracy."[18]

"There is more equality of rank and fortune in America than in any other country under the sun," South Carolina governor Charles Pinckney declared. This was true so long as no one figured in that calculation— as Pinckney never would—people who were property, a number that included Pinckney's forty-five slaves at Snee Farm, fifty-five people who constituted the source of his family's wealth. Among them were Cyrus, a carpenter (valued by Pinckney at £120); Cyrus's children, Charlotte (£80), Sam (£40), and Bella (£20); his granddaughter Cate (£70); and a very old woman named Joan, who might have been Cyrus's mother. Pinckney placed the value of this great-grandmother at zero; she was, to him, worthless.[19]

In 1759, British and American forces defeated the French in Quebec, a stunning victory that led the Iroquois to abandon their longstanding position of neutrality and join with the English, which turned the tide of the war. In August 1760, the English captured Montreal, and the North American part of the war ended only six hundred miles from where it began, at the ragged western edge of the British Empire.

Weeks later, young George III was crowned king of Great Britain. Twenty-two and strangely shy, he was a boy of a man, dressed in gold, his white-buckled shoes tripping on a train of ermine. He presented himself to an uneasy world as a defender of the Protestant faith and of English liberties. He had declared, as Prince of Wales, "The pride, the glory of Britain, and the direct end of its constitution is political liberty."[20] But by now, while his subjects in North America welcomed the coronation of their new king, they might as easily have recalled the wisdom of a proverb that Franklin had printed twenty years earlier in *Poor Richard's Almanac*: "The greatest monarch on the proudest throne, is oblig'd to sit upon his own arse."[21]

Mapmakers sharpened their quills to redraw the map of North America when peace was reached in 1763. Under its terms, France ceded Canada and all of New France east of the Mississippi to Britain; France

*London-printed maps commemorating the treaty that
ended the Seven Years' War in 1763 marked out the
importance of both the Caribbean and the continent.*

granted all its land to the west of the Mississippi, territory known as Louisiana, to Spain; and Spain yielded Cuba and half of Florida to Britain.
Britain's skirt of settlement along the Atlantic looked now like bolts of
fabric unfurled on the dressmaker's floor.

"We in America have certainly abundant reason to rejoice," the leading
Massachusetts lawyer James Otis Jr. wrote from Boston in 1763. "The
British dominion and power may now be said, literally, to extend from sea
to sea, and from the great river to the ends of the earth." If the war had
strained the colonists' relationship to the empire, the peace had strengthened both the empire and the colonists' attachment to it. Added Otis,
"The true interests of Great Britain and her plantations are mutual, and
what God in his providence has united, let no man dare attempt to pull
asunder."[22]

But the war had left Britain nearly bankrupt. The fighting had nearly
doubled Britain's debt, and Pitt's promise began to waver. Then, too, the
king's ministers determined that defending the empire's new North American borders would require ten thousand troops or more, especially after a

confederation of Indians led by an Ottawa chief named Pontiac captured British forts in the Great Lakes and Ohio Valley. Pontiac, it was said, had been stirred to action by a prophecy of the creation on earth of a "Heaven where there was no White people."[23] Fearing the cost of suppressing more Indian uprisings, George III issued a proclamation decreeing that no colonists could settle west of the Appalachian Mountains, a line that many colonists had already crossed.

In 1764, to pay the war debt and fund the defense of the colonies, Parliament passed the American Revenue Act, also known as the Sugar Act. Up until 1764, the colonial assemblies had raised their own taxes; Parliament had regulated trade. When Parliament passed the Sugar Act, which chiefly required stricter enforcement of earlier measures, some colonists challenged it by arguing that, because the colonies had no representatives in Parliament, Parliament had no right to levy taxes on them. The Sugar Act wasn't radical; the response to it was radical, a consequence of the growing power of colonial assemblies at a time when the idea of representation was gaining new force.

Taxes are what people pay to a ruler to keep order and defend the realm. In the ancient world, landowners paid in crops or livestock, the landless with their labor. Levying taxes made medieval European monarchs rich; only in the seventeenth century did monarchs begin to cede the power to tax to legislatures.[24] Taxation became tied to representation at the very time that England was founding colonies in North America and the Caribbean, which was also the moment at which the English had begun to dominate the slave trade. In the 1760s, the two became muddled rhetorically. Massachusetts assemblyman Samuel Adams asked, "If Taxes are laid upon us in any shape without our having a legal Representation where they are laid, are we not reduced from the Character of free Subjects to the miserable State of tributary Slaves?"[25]

Taxation without representation, men like Adams argued, is rule by force, and rule by force is slavery. This argument had to do, in part, with debt. "The Borrower is a slave to the Lender," as Franklin once put it in *Poor Richard's Almanack*.[26] Debtors could be arrested and sent to debtors' prison.[27] Debtors' prison was far more common in England than in the colonies, which were in many ways debtors' asylums.[28] But if there was an unusual tolerance for debt in the colonies, there was also an unusual amount of it, and in the 1760s there was, suddenly, rather a lot more of it. The governor of Massachusetts reported that "a Stop to all Credit was expected" and even "a general bankruptcy."[29] The end of the French and Indian War led to a contraction of credit, followed by a crippling depression and, especially in the South, several years of poor crops. Tobacco plantation owners in the Chesapeake found themselves heavily indebted to merchants in England, who, themselves strapped, were quite keen to collect those debts. These planters, in particular, found it politically useful to describe themselves as slaves to their creditors.[30] During these same years, though, the sugar colonies in the Caribbean prospered, not least because the Sugar Act enforced a monopoly: under its terms, colonists on the mainland had to buy their sugar from the British West Indies.[31] This difference did not pass unobserved. "Our Tobacco Colonies send us home no such wealthy planters as we see frequently arrive from our sugar islands," Adam Smith would remark in *The Wealth of Nations*.[32]

Parliament's next revenue act induced a still more strenuous response. A 1765 Stamp Act required placing government-issued paper stamps on all manner of printed paper, from bills of credit to playing cards. Stamps were required across the British Empire, and, by those standards, the tax levied in the colonies was cheap: colonists paid only two-thirds of what Britons paid. But in the credit-strained mainland colonies, this proved difficult to bear. Opponents of the act began styling themselves the Sons of Liberty (after the Sons of Liberty in 1750s Ireland) and describing themselves as rebelling against slavery. A creditor was "lord of another man's purse"; hadn't British creditors and Parliament itself swindled North American debtors of their purses, and their liberty, too? Was not Parliament making them slaves? John Adams, a twenty-nine-year-old Boston lawyer and leader of the Stamp Act opposition, wrote: "We won't be their negroes."[33]

The colonies were bound up in a growing credit crisis that would engulf the whole of the British Empire, from Virginia planters to Scottish bankers to East India Company tea exporters. But there were American particulars, too: with the Stamp Act, a tax on all printed paper, including newspapers, Parliament levied a tax that cost the most to the people best able to complain about it: the printers of newspapers. "It will affect Printers more than anybody," Franklin warned, begging Parliament to reconsider.[34] Printers from Boston to Charleston argued that Parliament was trying to reduce the colonists to a state of slavery by destroying the freedom of the press. The printers of the *Boston Gazette* refused to buy stamps and changed the paper's motto to "A free press maintains the majesty of the people." In New Jersey, a printer named William Goddard issued a newspaper called the *Constitutional Courant*, with Franklin's segmented snake on the masthead. This time, asked whether to join or die, the colonies decided to join.

In October, the month before the Stamp Act was to take effect, twenty-seven delegates from nine colonies met in a Stamp Act Congress in New York's city hall, where John Peter Zenger had been tried in 1735 and Caesar in 1741. The Stamp Act Congress collectively declared "that it is inseparably essential to the Freedom of a People, and the undoubted Right of Englishmen, that no Taxes be imposed on them, but with their own consent, given personally, or by their Representatives."[35] When they dined, they sent their leftovers to the debtors confined in a prison in the building's garret, making common cause with men deprived of their liberty by creditors.[36]

The sovereignty of the people, the freedom of the press, the relationship between representation and taxation, debt as slavery: each of these ideas, with origins in England, found a place in the colonists' opposition to the Stamp Act. Still, Parliament professed itself baffled. In 1766, Benjamin Franklin appeared before the House of Commons to explain the colonists' refusal to pay the tax. At sixty, Franklin presented himself as at once a man of the world and an American provincial, wily and plainspoken, sophisticated and homespun.

"In what light did the people of America use to consider the Parliament of Great Britain?" the ministers asked.

"They considered the Parliament as the great bulwark and security of their liberties and privileges, and always spoke of it with the utmost respect and veneration," was Franklin's reply.

"And have they not still the same respect for Parliament?"

"No; it is greatly lessened."

If the colonists had lost respect for Parliament, why had this come to pass? On what grounds did they object to the Stamp Tax? There was nothing in Pennsylvania's charter that forbade Parliament from exercising this authority.

It's true, Franklin admitted, there was nothing specifically to that effect in the colony's charter. He cited, instead, their understanding of "The common rights of Englishmen, as declared by Magna Charta," as if the colonists were the barons of Runnymede, King George their King John, and Magna Carta their constitution.

"What used to be the pride of the Americans?" Parliament wanted to know.

"To indulge in the fashions and manufactures of Great Britain."

"What is now their pride?"

"To wear their old clothes over again till they can make new ones."[37]

Here was Poor Richard, again with his proverbs.

And yet this defiance did not extend to Quebec, or to the sugar islands, where the burden of the Stamp Tax was actually heavier. Thirteen colonies eventually cast off British rule; some thirteen more did not. Colonists from the mainland staged protests, formed a congress, and refused to pay the stamp tax. But, except for some vague and halfhearted objections expressed on Nevis and St. Kitts, British planters in the West Indies barely uttered a complaint. (South Carolina, whose economy had more in common with the British West Indies than with the mainland colonies, wavered.) They were too worried about the possibility of inciting yet another slave rebellion.[38]

On the mainland, whites outnumbered blacks, four to one. On the islands, blacks outnumbered whites, eight to one. One-quarter of all British troops in British America were stationed in the West Indies, where they protected English colonists from the ever-present threat of slave rebellion. For this protection, West Indian planters were more than willing to pay a tax on stamps. Planters in Jamaica were still reeling from the latest insurrection, in 1760, when an Akan man named Tacky had led hundreds of armed men who burned plantations and killed some sixty slave owners before they were captured. The reprisals had been ferocious: Tacky's head was impaled on a stake, and, as in New York in 1741, some of his followers were hung in chains while others were burned at the stake. And still the rebellions continued, for which island planters began to blame colonists on the mainland: Did the Sons of Liberty realize what they were saying? "Can you be surprised that the Negroes in Jamaica should endeavor to Recover their Freedom," one merchant fumed, "when they dayly hear at the Tables of their Masters, how much the Americans are applauded for the stand they are making for theirs"?[39]

Unsurprisingly, the island planters' unwillingness to join the protest against the Stamp Act greatly frustrated the Sons of Liberty. "Their

SOULEVEMENT DES NEGRES
à la Jamaïque.

*en 1759.*

*People held in slavery in Jamaica rebelled throughout the middle decades of the eighteenth century, leaving Jamaican slave owners reliant on British military protection and unwilling to join colonists on the continent in rebelling against British rule.*

Negroes seem to have more of the spirit of liberty than they," John Adams complained, asking, "Can no punishment be devised for Barbados and Port Royal in Jamaica?" Adams was the rare man whose soaring ambition matched his talents. He would learn to restrain his passions better. But in the 1760s, his anger at those who refused to support the resistance was unchecked. The punishment the Sons of Liberty decided upon came in the form of a boycott of Caribbean goods. In language even more heated than Adams's, patriot printers damned "the SLAVISH Islands of Barbados and Antigua—Poor, mean spirited, Cowardly, Dastardly Creoles," for "their base desertion of the cause of liberty, their tame surrender of the rights of Britons, their mean, timid resignation to slavery."[40]

Planters bridled at the attack and floundered under the effects of the boycott. "We are likely to be miserably off for want of lumber and northern provisions," one Antigua planter wrote, "as the North Americans are determined not to submit to the Stamp Act."[41] But they did not yield. And some began to consider their northern neighbors to be mere blusterers. "I look on them as dogs that will bark but dare not stand," complained one planter from Jamaica.[42]

Nor were the West Indian planters wrong to worry that one kind of rebellion would incite another. In Charleston, the Sons of Liberty marched through the streets, chanting, "Liberty and No Stamps!" only to be followed by slaves crying, "Liberty! Liberty!" And not a few Sons of Liberty made this same leap, from fighting for their own liberty to fighting to end slavery. "The Colonists are by the law of nature free born, as indeed all men are, white or black," James Otis Jr. insisted, in a searing tract called *Rights of the British Colonists, Asserted*, published in 1764, only months after he had rejoiced about the growth of Britain's empire. Brilliant and unstable, Otis would later lose his mind (before his death in 1783, when he was struck by lightning, he had taken to running naked through the streets). But in the 1760s, he, better than any of his contemporaries, saw the logical extension of arguments about natural rights. He found it absurd to suggest that it could be "right to enslave a man because he is black" or because he has "short curl'd hair like wool." Slavery, Otis insisted, "is the most shocking violation of the law of nature," and a source of political contamination, too. "Those who every day barter away other men's liberty, will soon care little for their own," he warned.[43]

Otis's readers picked and chose which parts of his treatise to hold close and which parts to shed. But something had been set loose in the world, a set of unruly ideas about liberty, equality, and sovereignty. In 1763, when Benjamin Franklin visited a school for black children, he admitted that his mind had changed. "I . . . have conceiv'd a higher Opinion of the natural Capacities of the black Race, than I had ever before entertained," he wrote a friend. In Virginia, George Mason began to have doubts about slavery, sending to George Washington, in December of 1765, an essay in which he argued that slavery was "the primary Cause of the Destruction of the most flourishing Government that ever existed"—the Roman republic—and warning that it might be the destruction of the British Empire, too.[44]

Debt, taxes, and slavery weren't the only issues raised in the political debates of the 1760s. The intensity of the debate strengthened new ideas about equality, too. "Male and female are all one in Christ the Truth," Benjamin Lay had argued, expressing an idea that drew on a wealth of seventeenth-century Quaker writings about spiritual equality. "Are not women born as free as men?" Otis asked.[45] Even Benjamin Franklin's long-suffering sister Jane began to entertain this notion. In 1765, Jane Franklin lost her husband, a saddler and ne'er-do-well named Edward Mecom, who had sickened while in debtors' prison, and she'd begun taking in, as boarders, members of the Massachusetts Assembly. "I do not Pretend to writ about Politics," she once wrote to her brother, "tho I Love to hear them."[46] This was false modesty, a "fishing for commendation" about which her brother so often chided her. At her table, there was a lot for her to listen to, when, in 1766, Otis was elected as Speaker of the Massachusetts Assembly but the royally appointed governor refused to accept the results of the election. If Jane Franklin wasn't, as yet, willing to write about politics, she had heard much worth pondering. Not long after the governor overturned the results of the election, she wrote to her brother to ask that he send her "all the Pamphlets & Papers that have been Printed of yr writing."[47] She decided to make a study of politics.

In 1766, Parliament repealed the Stamp Act. The repeal "has hushed into silence almost every popular Clamour, and composed every Wave of Popular Disorder into a smooth and peaceful Calm," John Adams wrote in his diary.[48] "I congratulate you & my Countrymen on the Repeal," Franklin wrote to his sister.[49] The week after the news reached Boston, its town meeting voted in favor of "the total abolishing of slavery from among us."[50] Pamphleteers began arguing for a colony-wide antislavery law; others counseled waiting until the end of the battle with Parliament, because, even as it repealed the Stamp Act, Parliament had passed the Declaratory Act, asserting its authority to make laws "in all cases whatsoever." The next year, Parliament passed the Townshend Acts, taxes on lead, paper, paint, glass, and tea. When this, too, led to riots and boycotts, the prime minister sent to Boston two regiments of the British army to enforce the law.

"The whol conversation of this Place turns upon Politics," Jane reported to her brother. The Boston Town meeting resolved that "a series of occurrences . . . afford great reason to believe that a deep-laid and desperate plan of imperial despotism has been laid, and partly executed, for the extinction of all civil liberty." When troops fired into a crowd in March 1770, killing five men, the Sons of Liberty called it a "massacre" and cried for relief from the tyranny of a standing army. But on the islands, planters called not for less military presence but more, the colonial assembly on St. Kitts begging the king to send troops to protect the colonists from "the turbulent and savage dispositions of the Negroes ever prone to Riots and Rebellions."[51]

And still, the zeal for liberty raised the question of ending slavery. The Worcester Town Meeting called for a law prohibiting the importing and buying of slaves; by 1766, an antislavery bill had been introduced into the Massachusetts Assembly. But, mindful of how the question of slavery had severed the island colonies from the mainland, many in Massachusetts feared that further antislavery sentiment would sever the northern colonies from the southern. "If passed into an act, it should have a bad effect on the union of the colonies," one assemblyman wrote to John Adams in 1771, when the bill came up for a vote.[52] The next year, the Court of King's Bench in London took up the case of *Somerset v. Stewart*. Charles Stewart, a British customs officer in Boston, had purchased an African man named James Somerset. When Stewart was recalled to England in 1769, he brought Somerset with him. Somerset escaped but was recaptured. Stewart, deciding to sell him to Jamaica, had him imprisoned on a ship. Somerset's friends brought the case to court, where the justice, Lord Mansfield, found that nothing in English common law supported Stewart's position. Somerset was set free.

The Somerset case taught people held in slavery two lessons: first, they might look to the courts to secure their freedom, and, second, they had a better shot at winning it in Britain than in any of its colonies. They began to act. Relying on the same logic that James Otis Jr. had expounded, they petitioned the courts for their freedom: "We expect great things from men who have made such a noble stand against the designs of their fellow-men to enslave them," read a petition filed by four black men in Boston in April 1773. And they tried to escape to England: in Virginia that September, a slave couple ran away hoping to secure their freedom by reaching London, holding, as one observer put it, "a notion now too prevalent among the Negroes."[53]

This struggle for liberty was lost as the colonists returned, instead, to their battles with Parliament. The London-based East India Company was at risk of bankruptcy, partly due to the colonial boycott, but more due to a famine in Bengal, the military costs it incurred there, and collapsing stock value consequent to the empire-wide credit crash of 1772. In May of 1773, Parliament passed the Tea Act, which reduced the tax

No. X.    Engraved for Royal American Magazine.    Vol. I.

*Boston cannonaded*

*The able Doctor, or America Swallowing the Bitter Draught.*

*A British minister with the 1774 bill closing the port
of Boston in his pocket pours tea down the throat of
"America"—here, and often, depicted as a naked Indian
woman—while another looks under her skirt.*

on tea—as a way of saving the East India Company—but again asserted
Parliament's right to tax the colonies. Townspeople in Philadelphia called
anyone who imported the tea "an enemy of the country." Tea agents
resigned their posts in fear. That fall, three ships loaded with tea arrived
in Boston. On the night of December 16, dozens of colonists disguised as
Mohawks—warring Indians—boarded the boats and dumped chests of
the tea into the harbor. To punish the city, Parliament passed the Coercive Acts, which closed Boston Harbor and annulled the Massachusetts
charter, effective in June of 1774.

In Virginia, James Madison Jr., twenty-three, eyed the events in Massachusetts from Montpelier, his family's plantation in the Piedmont, east
of the Blue Ridge Mountains. He'd graduated from Princeton two years
before and was home tutoring his younger siblings. Far from the scene of
action, he followed the news avidly and took pains to understand why the
response to the tea tax was different in the northern and middle colonies
than in the southern colonies. At Princeton, a Presbyterian college—
a college of a dissenting faith—he'd made a study of religious liberty,

and, after the dumping of the tea, he concluded that Massachusetts and Pennsylvania had resisted parliamentary authority in a way that Virginia did not because the more northern colonies had no established religion. Religious liberty, Madison came to believe, is a good in itself, because it promotes an independence of the mind, but also because it makes possible political liberty. Hearing word of the Coercive Acts, he began to think, for the first time, of war. He wrote to his closest friend, William Bradford, in Philadelphia, and asked him whether it might not be best "as soon as possible to begin our defense."[54]

Meanwhile, at Mount Vernon, George Washington, who'd been elected to the Virginia legislature in 1758, had chiefly occupied himself managing his considerable tobacco estate.[55] He hadn't been much animated by the colonies' growing resistance to parliamentary authority until the passage of the Coercive Acts. In September, fifty-six delegates from twelve of the thirteen mainland colonies met in Philadelphia, in a carpenters' guild-hall, as the First Continental Congress. Washington served as a delegate from Virginia. But if protest over the Stamp Act had temporarily united the colonies, the Coercive Acts appeared to many delegates to be merely Massachusetts's problem. To Virginians, the delegates from Massachusetts seemed intemperate and rash, fanatical, even, especially when they suggested the possibility of an eventual independence from Britain. In October, Washington expressed relief when, after speaking to the "Boston people," he felt confident that he could "announce it as a fact, that it is not the wish or interest of that Government, or any other upon this Continent, separately or collectively, to set up for Independency." He was as sure "as I can be of my existence, that no such thing is desired by any thinking man in all North America."[56]

From Philadelphia, James Madison's friend William Bradford passed along fascinating tidbits of gossip about the goings-on at Congress. Bradford proved a resourceful reporter, and a better sleuth. From the librarian at the Library Company of Philadelphia—which supplied Congress with books—he'd heard that the delegates were busy reading "Vattel, Burlamaqui, Locke, and Montesquieu," leading Bradford to reassure Madison: "We may conjecture that their measures will be wisely planned since they debate on them like philosophers."[57]

Wise they may have been, but these philosophers immediately confronted a very difficult question that has dogged the Union ever since.

Congress was meant to be a representative body. How would representation be calculated? Virginia delegate Patrick Henry, an irresistible orator with a blistering stare, suggested that the delegates cast a number of votes proportionate to their colonies' number of white inhabitants. Given the absence of any accurate population figures, the delegates had little choice but to do something far simpler—to grant each colony one vote. In any case, the point of meeting was to become something more than a collection of colonies and the sum of their grievances: a new body politic. "The distinction between Virginians, Pennsylvanians, New Yorkers, and New Englanders is no more," Henry said. "I am not a Virginian, but an American."[58] A word on a long-ago map had swelled into an idea.

# II.

THE CONTINENTAL CONGRESS neither suffered the disunion and chaos of the Albany Congress nor undertook the deferential pleading of the Stamp Act Congress. Preparing for the worst, this new, more ambitious, and more expansive—*continental*—Congress urged colonists to muster their militias and stockpile weapons. It also agreed to boycott all British imports and to ban all trade with the West Indies, a severing of ties with the islands. The month the boycott was to begin, the Jamaica Assembly sent a petition to the king, with a bow and a curtsey. The Jamaicans began with an assurance that the island had no intention of joining the rebellion: "weak and feeble as this Colony is, from its very small number of white inhabitants, and its peculiar situation from the incumbrance of more than two hundred thousand slaves, it cannot be supposed that we now intend, or ever could have intended, resistance to Great Britain," the Jamaicans explained. And yet, they went on, they did agree with the continentals' fundamental grievance, declaring it "the first established principle of the Constitution, that the people of England have a right to partake, and do partake, of the legislation of their country."[59]

Unmoved, Congress offered Jamaica halfhearted thanks: "We feel the warmest gratitude for your pathetic mediation in our behalf with the crown." Neither the king nor Parliament proved inclined to reconsider the Coercive Acts. The tax burden against which the colonists were protesting was laughably small, and their righteousness was grating. Lord North, the prime minister, commissioned the famed essayist Samuel Johnson to write a response to the Continental Congress's complaints. Plainly, the easiest case to make against the colonists was to charge them with hypocrisy. In *Taxation No Tyranny*, Johnson asked, dryly, "How is it that we hear the loudest yelps for liberty among the drivers of negroes?" Johnson's opposition to slavery was far more than rhetorical; a free Jamaican, a black man named Francis Barber, was his companion, collaborator, and heir. ("To the next insurrection of negroes in the West Indies," Johnson declared, in a toast he offered during the war.) But Johnson's charge of hypocrisy amounted to no more than the charges made by Philadelphia doctor Benjamin Rush the year before: "Where is the difference," Rush wondered, "between the British Senator who attempts to enslave his fellow subjects in America, by imposing Taxes upon them contrary to Law and Justice, and the American Patriot who reduces his African Brethren to Slavery, contrary to Justice and Humanity?"[60]

By now, the seed planted by Benjamin Lay had borne fruit, and Quakers had formally banned slavery—excluding from membership anyone who claimed to own another human being. On April 14, 1775, one month before the Second Continental Congress was to meet in Philadelphia, two dozen men, seventeen of them Quakers, founded in that city the Society for the Relief of Free Negroes Unlawfully Held in Bondage. But once again, as in 1773, whatever the urgency of ending slavery, the attention of all the colonies was called away. Five days later, on April 19, 1775, blood spilled on the damp, dark grass of spring, on Lexington Green.

It began when General Thomas Gage, in charge of the British troops, seized ammunition stored outside of Boston, in nearby Charlestown and Cambridge, and sent seven hundred soldiers to do the same in Lexington and Concord. Seventy armed militiamen, or minutemen—farmers who pledged to be ready at a moment's notice—met them in Lexington, and more in Concord. The British soldiers killed ten of them, and lost two men of their own. The rebel forces then laid siege to Boston, occupied by the British army. Loyalists stayed in the city, but Loyalists in Boston were few: twelve thousand of the city's fifteen thousand inhabitants attempted to escape, the ragged and the dainty, the old and the young, the war's first refugees.

John Hancock, John Adams, and Samuel Adams rode in haste to Philadelphia. The evacuation cleaved families. *Boston Gazette* printer

Benjamin Edes carted his printing press and types to the Charles River and rowed across while, in Boston, his eighteen-year-old son was taken prisoner of war.[61] Jane Franklin, sixty-three, rode out of the city in a wagon with a granddaughter, leaving a grandson behind. "I had got Pact up what I Expected to have liberty to carey out intending to seek my fourtune with hundred others not knowing whither," she wrote to her brother, who was on his way back to America, after years in England, to join Congress.[62]

Shots having been fired, the debate at the Second Continental Congress, which convened that May, was far more urgent than at the First. Those who continued to hope for reconciliation with Great Britain—which described most delegates—had now to answer the aggrieved, more radical delegates from Massachusetts, who brought stories of trials and tribulations. "I sympathise most sincerely with you and the People of my native Town and Country," Benjamin Franklin wrote to his sister. "Your Account of the Distresses attending their Removal affects me greatly."[63] In June, two months after bullets were first fired in Massachusetts, Congress voted to establish a Continental army; John Adams nominated George Washington as commander. The resolute and nearly universally admired Washington, a man of unmatched bearing, and very much a Virginian, was sent to Massachusetts to take command—his very ride meant as a symbol of the union between North and South.

All fall, Congress was occupied with taking up the work of war, raising recruits and provisioning the troops. The question of declaring independence was put off. Most colonists remained loyal to the king. If they supported resistance, it was to fight for their rights as Englishmen, not for their independence as Americans.

Their slaves, though, fought a different fight. "It is imagined our Governor has been tampering with the Slaves & that he has it in contemplation to make great Use of them in case of a civil war," young James Madison reported from Virginia to his friend William Bradford in Philadelphia. Lord Dunmore, the royal governor of Virginia, intended to offer freedom to slaves who would join the British army. "To say the truth, that is the only part in which this colony is vulnerable," Madison admitted, "and if we should be subdued, we shall fall like Achilles by the hand of one that knows that secret."[64]

But the colonists' vulnerability to slave rebellion, that Achilles' heel, was hardly a secret: it defined them. Madison's own grandfather, Ambrose Madison, who'd first settled Montpelier, had been murdered by slaves in 1732, apparently poisoned to death, when he was thirty-six. In Madison's county, slaves had been convicted of poisoning their masters again in 1737 and 1746: in the first case, the convicted man was decapitated, his head placed atop a pole outside the courthouse "to deter others from doing the Like"; in the second, a woman named Eve was burned alive.[65] Their bodies were made into monuments.

No estate was without this Achilles' heel. George Washington's slaves had been running away at least since 1760. At least forty-seven of them fled at one time or another.[66] In 1763, a twenty-three-year-old man born in Gambia became Washington's property; Washington named him Harry and sent him to work draining a marsh known as the Great Dismal Swamp. In 1771, Harry Washington managed to escape, only to be recaptured. In November 1775, he was grooming his master's horses in the stables at Mount Vernon when Lord Dunmore made the announcement that Madison had feared: he offered freedom to any slaves who would join His Majesty's troops in suppressing the American rebellion.[67]

In Cambridge, where George Washington was assembling the Continental army, he received a report about the slaves at Mount Vernon. "There is not a man of them but would leave us if they believed they could make their escape," Washington's cousin reported that winter, adding, "Liberty is sweet."[68] Harry Washington bided his time, but he would soon join the five hundred men who ran from their owners and joined Dunmore's forces, a number that included a man named Ralph, who ran away from Patrick Henry, and eight of the twenty-seven people owned by Peyton Randolph, who had served as president of the First Continental Congress.[69]

Edward Rutledge, a member of South Carolina's delegation to the Continental Congress, said that Dunmore's declaration did "more effectually work an eternal separation between Great Britain and the Colonies— than any other expedient which could possibly have been thought of."[70] Not the taxes and the tea, not the shots at Lexington and Concord, not the siege of Boston; rather, it was this act, Dunmore's offer of freedom to slaves, that tipped the scales in favor of American independence.

Not that it ever tipped them definitively. John Adams estimated that about a third of colonists were patriots, a third were Loyalists, and a third never really made a decision about independence.[71] Aside from Dunmore's proclamation of freedom to slaves, the strongest impetus for independence came from brooding and tireless Thomas Paine, who'd immigrated to Philadelphia from England in 1774. In January 1776, Paine published an anonymous pamphlet called *Common Sense*, forty-seven pages of brisk political argument. "As it is my design to make those that can scarcely read understand," Paine explained, "I shall therefore avoid every literary ornament and put it in language as plain as the alphabet." Members of Congress might have been philosophers, reading Locke and Montesquieu. But ordinary Americans read the Bible, *Poor Richard's Almanack*, and Thomas Paine.

Paine wrote with fury, and he wrote with flash. "The cause of America is in a great measure the cause of all mankind," he announced. "'Tis not the affair of a city, a country, a province, or a kingdom, but of a continent—of at least one eighth part of the habitable globe. 'Tis not the concern of a day, a year, or an age; posterity are virtually involved in the contest, and will be more or less affected, even to the end of time."

His empiricism was homegrown, his metaphors those of the kitchen and the barnyard. "There is something absurd in supposing a continent to be perpetually governed by an island," he wrote, turning the logic of English imperialism on its head. "We may as well assert that because a child has thrived upon milk, that it is never to have meat."

But he was not without philosophy. Digesting Locke for everyday readers, Paine explained the idea of a state of nature. "Mankind being originally equals in the order of creation, the equality could only be destroyed by some subsequent circumstance," he wrote, a schoolteacher to his pupils. The rule of some over others, the distinctions between rich and poor: these forms of inequality were not natural, nor were they prescribed by religion; they were the consequences of actions and customs. And the most unnatural distinction of all, he explained, is "the distinction of men into kings and subjects."[72]

Paine made use, too, of Magna Carta, arguing, "The charter which secures this freedom in England, was formed, not in the senate, but in the field; and insisted upon by the people, not granted by the crown." He urged Americans to write their own Magna Carta.[73] But Magna Carta supplies no justification for outright rebellion. The best and most expedient strategy, Paine understood, was to argue not from precedent or doctrine but from nature, to insist that there exists a natural right to revolution, as natural as a child leaving its parent. "Let us suppose a small number of persons settled in some sequestered part of the earth, unconnected with the rest, they will then represent the first peopling of any country, or of the world," he began, as if he were telling a child a once-upon-a time story.[74] They will erect a government, to secure their safety, and their liberty. And when that government ceases to secure their safety and their liberty, it stands to reason that they may depose it. They retain this right forever.

Much the same language found its way into resolutions passed by specially established colonial conventions, held so that the colonies, untethered from Britain, could establish new forms of government. "All men are by nature equally free and independent, and have certain inherent rights, of which, when they enter into a state of society, they cannot, by any compact, deprive or divest their posterity," read the Virginia Declaration of Rights and Form of Government, drafted in May 1776 by brazen George Mason. "All power is vested in, and consequently derived from, the people." James Madison, half Mason's age, had been elected to the convention from Orange County. He proposed a revision to Mason's Declaration. Where Mason had written that "all men should enjoy the fullest toleration in the exercise of religion," Madison rewrote that clause to instead guarantee that "all men are equally entitled to the full and free exercise of it." The proposed change was adopted, and Madison became the author of the first-ever constitutional guarantee of religious liberty, not as something to be tolerated, but as a fundamental right.[75]

Inevitably, slavery cast its long and terrible shadow over these statements of principle: slavery, in fact, had made those statements of principle possible. Mason's original draft hadn't included the clause about rights being acquired by men "when they enter into a state of society"; these words were added after members of the convention worried that the original would "have the effect of abolishing" slavery.[76] If all men belonging to civil society are free and equal, how can slavery be possible? It must be, Virginia's convention answered, that Africans do not belong to civil society, having never left a state of nature.

Within eighteenth-century political thought, women, too, existed outside the contract by which civil society was formed. From Massachusetts, Abigail Adams wrote to her husband, John, in March of 1776, wondering whether that might be remedied. "I desire you would Remember the

Ladies, and be more generous and favourable to them than your ancestors," she began, alluding to the long train of abuses of men over women.
"Do not put such unlimited power into the hands of the Husbands," she
told him. She spoke of tyranny: "Remember all Men would be tyrants if
they could." And she challenged him to follow the logic of the principle of
representation: "If perticuliar care and attention is not paid to the Laid-
ies we are determined to foment a Rebelion, and will not hold ourselves
bound by any Laws in which we have no voice, or Representation."

Her husband would have none of it. "As to your extraordinary Code
of Laws, I cannot but laugh," he replied. "We have been told that our
Struggle has loosened the bands of Government every where. That Children and Apprentices were disobedient—that schools and Colledges were
grown turbulent—that Indians slighted their Guardians and Negroes
grew insolent to their Masters. . . . Depend upon it, We know better than
to repeal our Masculine systems."[77] That women were left out of the
nation's founding documents, and out of its founders' idea of civil society,
considered, like slaves, to be confined to a state of nature, would trouble
the political order for centuries.

AT THE CONTINENTAL CONGRESS, in June, Pennsylvania delegate John Dickinson drafted the Articles of Confederation. "The Name
of this Confederacy shall be 'The United States of America,'" he wrote,
possibly using that phrase for the first time. It may be that Dickinson
found the phrase "the united states" in a book of treaties used by Congress; it included a treaty from 1667 that referred to a confederation of
independent Dutch states as the "the united states of the Low Countries."
In Dickinson's draft, the colonies—now states—were to form a league of
friendship "for their Common Defence, the Security of their Liberties,
and their mutual & general Wellfare." The first draft brought before Congress called for each state's contribution to the costs of war, and of the
government, to be proportionate to population, and therefore called for a
census to be taken every three years. It would take many revisions and a
year and a half of debate before Congress could agree on a final version.
That final document stripped from Dickinson's original most of the powers his version had granted to Congress; the final Articles of Confederation are more like a peace treaty, establishing a defensive alliance among

sovereign states, than a constitution, establishing a system of government. Much was makeshift. The provision for a census of all the states together, for instance, was struck in favor of an arrangement by which a common treasury was to be supplied "in proportion to the value of all land within each state," and since, in truth, no one knew that value, what the states contributed would be left for the states to decide.[78]

Nevertheless, these newly united states edged toward independence. On June 7, 1776, fiery Virginia delegate Richard Henry Lee introduced a resolution "that these United Colonies are, and of right ought to be, free and independent States." A vote on the resolution was postponed, but Congress appointed a Committee of Five to draft a declaration: Benjamin Franklin, John Adams, Thomas Jefferson, New York delegate Robert R. Livingston, and Connecticut delegate Roger Sherman. Jefferson agreed to prepare a first draft.

The Declaration of Independence was not a declaration of war; the war had begun more than a year before. It was an act of state, meant to have force within the law of nations. The Declaration explained what the colonists were fighting for; it was an attempt to establish that the cause of the revolution was that the king had placed his people under arbitrary power, reducing them to a state of slavery: "The history of the present King of Great Britain is a history of repeated injuries and usurpations, all having in direct object the establishment of an absolute Tyranny over these States." Many readers found these words unpersuasive. In 1776, the English philosopher and jurist Jeremy Bentham called the theory of government that informed the Declaration of Independence "absurd and visionary." Its self-evident truths he deemed neither self-evident nor true. He considered them, instead, "subversive of every actual or imaginable kind of Government."[79]

But what Bentham found absurd and visionary represented the summation of centuries of political thought and political experimentation. "There is not an idea in it but what had been hackneyed in Congress for two years before," Adams later wrote, jealous of the acclaim that went to Jefferson. Jefferson admitted as much, pointing out that novelty had formed no part of his assignment. Of the Declaration, he declared, "Neither aiming at originality of principles or sentiment, nor yet copied from any particular and previous writing, it was intended to be an expression of the American mind."[80] But its ideas, those expressions of the American mind, were older still.

"We hold these truths to be sacred & undeniable," Jefferson began, "that all men are created equal & independant, that from that equal creation they derive rights inherent & inalienable, among which are the preservation of life, & liberty, & the pursuit of happiness; that to secure these ends, governments are instituted among men, deriving their just powers from the consent of the governed; that whenever any form of government shall become destructive of these ends, it is the right of the people to alter or to abolish it, & to institute new government." He'd borrowed from, and vastly improved upon, the Virginia Declaration of Rights, written by George Mason. Having established that a right of revolution exists if certain conditions are met, it remained to establish that those conditions obtained. The bulk of Jefferson's draft was a list of grievances, of charges against the king, calling him to account "for imposing taxes on us without our consent," for dissolving the colonists' assemblies, for keeping a standing army, "for depriving us of trial by jury," rights established as far back as Magna Carta. Then, in the longest statement in the draft, Jefferson blamed George III for African slavery, charging the king with waging "cruel war against human nature itself, violating its most sacred rights of life & liberty in the persons of a distant people who never offended him, captivating & carrying them into slavery," preventing the colonies from outlawing the slave trade and, "that this assemblage of horrors might want no fact of distinguished die, he is now exciting those very people to rise in arms among us." This passage Congress struck, unwilling to conjure this assemblage of horrors in the nation's founding document.

The Declaration that Congress did adopt was a stunning rhetorical feat, an act of extraordinary political courage. It also marked a colossal failure of political will, in holding back the tide of opposition to slavery by ignoring it, for the sake of a union that, in the end, could not and would not last.

In July, the Declaration of Independence was read aloud from town houses and street corners. Crowds cheered. Cannons were fired. Church bells rang. Statues of the king were pulled down and melted for bullets. Weeks later, when a massive slave rebellion broke out in Jamaica, slave owners blamed the Americans for inciting it. In Pennsylvania, a wealthy merchant, passionately stirred by the spirit of the times, not only freed his slaves but vowed to spend the rest of his life tracking down those he had previously owned and sold, and their children, and buying their freedom. And in August 1776, one month after delegates to the Continental Congress determined that in the course of human events it sometimes becomes necessary for one people to dissolve the bands which have connected them with another, Harry Washington declared his own independence by running away from Mount Vernon to fight with Dunmore's regiment, wearing a white sash stitched with the motto "Liberty to Slaves."[81]

## III.

DURING THE WAR, nearly one in five slaves in the United States left their homes, fleeing American slavery in search of British liberty. One American refugee renamed himself "British Freedom." New lyrics to "Yankee Doodle," rewritten as "The Negroes Farewell to America," were composed in London. In the new version, fugitive slaves leave the United States "for old Englan' where Liberty reigns / Where Negroe no beaten or loaded with chains."[82]

Not many succeeded in reaching the land where liberty reigned, or even in getting behind British battle lines. Instead, they were caught and punished. One slave owner who captured a fifteen-year-old girl who was heading for Dunmore's regiment punished her with eighty lashes and then poured hot embers into the gashes.[83] However desperate and improbable a flight, it must have seemed a good bet; the shrewdest observers expected Britain to win the war, not least because the British began with 32,000 troops, disciplined and experienced, compared to Washington's 19,000, motley and unruly. An American victory appeared an absurdity. But the British regulars, far from home, suffered from a lack of supplies, and while William Howe, commander in chief of British forces, set his sights first on New York and next on Philadelphia, he found that his victories yielded him little. Unlike European nations, the United States had no established capital city whose capture would have led to an American surrender. More importantly, time and again, Howe failed to press for a final, decisive defeat of the Americans, fearing the losses his own troops would sustain and the danger of heavy casualties when reinforcements were at such a distance.

Then, too, Britain's forces were spread thin, across the globe, waging the war on many fronts. For the British, the American Revolution formed

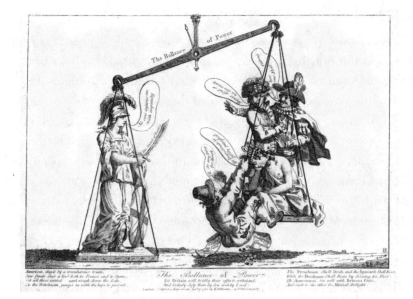

*This political cartoon, published in London, shows "Britain,"
on one side of the scale, warning, "No one injures me with
impunity," while, on the other side, "America," trampled
by her allies (Spain, France, and the Netherlands), cries,
"My Ingratitude is Justly punished."*

merely one front in a much larger war, a war for empire, a world war. Like
the French and Indian War, that war was chiefly fought in North America,
but it spilled out elsewhere, too, to West Africa, South Asia, the Mediterranean, and the Caribbean. In 1777, Howe captured Philadelphia while,
to the north, the British commander John Burgoyne suffered a humiliating
defeat at the Battle of Saratoga. This American victory helped John Jay,
John Adams, and Benjamin Franklin, serving as diplomats in France, to
secure a vital treaty: in 1778, France entered the conflict as an ally of the
United States, at which point Lord North, keen to protect Britain's much
richer colonies in the Caribbean from French attack, considered simply
abandoning the American theater. Spain joined the French-American
alliance in 1779. Germany entered the conflict by supplying paid soldiers
called, by Americans, Hessians. And, partly because the Dutch had been
supplying arms and ammunition to the Americans, Britain declared war
on Holland in 1780. The involvement of France brought the fighting to the
wealthy West Indies, where, beginning in 1778, the French captured the

British colonies of Dominica, Grenada, St. Vincent, Montserrat, Tobago, St. Kitts, and Turks and Caicos. The cessation of trade between the mainland and the British Caribbean exacted another kind of toll on Britain's profitable sugar colonies: Africans starved to death. On Antigua alone, a fifth of the slave population died during the war.[84]

To Americans, the Revolutionary War was not a world war but a civil war, between those who favored independence and the many who did not. John Adams, offhand, guessed that one in three colonists remained loyal to the Crown and another third hadn't quite decided, but Adams's guess did not begin to include the still greater numbers of Loyalists whom the British counted among their allies: the entire population of American slaves and nearly all Native American peoples. One reason the British continually failed to press their advantage was that they kept trying to change the field of fighting to a part of the colonies where they expected to find more Loyalist support, not only among the merchants and lawyers and farmers who remained loyal to the Crown but among their African and Indian allies. The battle, Howe's successor, Henry Clinton, believed, was "to gain the hearts & subdue the minds of America."[85] That strategy failed. And when that strategy failed, Britain didn't so much lose America as abandon it.

At first, the Crown courted compliance. In 1778, the king sent commissioners authorized to offer to repeal all acts of Parliament that had been opposed by the colonies since 1763, but when Congress demanded that the king recognize American independence, the commissioners refused. At this point, although Clinton held New York City and fighting continued to the west, the theater of war moved to the South: British ministers decided to make a priority of saving the wealthy sugar islands, to give up on the northern and middle mainland colonies, and to try to keep the southern colonies in order to restore the supply of food to the West Indies. Clinton captured Savannah, Georgia, in December 1778 and set his sights on Charleston, South Carolina, the largest city in the South. In Congress, this led to a debate about arming slaves. In May 1779, Congress proposed to enlist three thousand slaves in South Carolina and Georgia and to pay them with their freedom. "Your Negro Battallion will never do," warned John Adams. "S. Carolina would run out of their Wits at the least Hint of such a Measure."[86] He was entirely correct. The South Carolina legislature rejected the proposal, declaring, "We are much disgusted."[87] Clinton captured Charleston in May of 1780.

*Benjamin West, American-born History Painter to the
King, began a painting of the British and American
peace commissioners—including Benjamin Franklin, John
Adams, and John Jay—but never finished the canvas.*

In 1781, in hopes of taking the Chesapeake, the British general Lord
Cornwallis fortified Yorktown, Virginia, as a naval base. His troops were
soon besieged and bombarded by a combination of French and American
forces. The French were led by the dazzling Marquis de Lafayette, whose
service to the Continental army and impassioned advocacy of the American cause had included lobbying for French support. Cornwallis was vulnerable because British naval forces were occupied in the Caribbean. He
surrendered on October 19, not realizing that British forces were that very
day sailing from New York to aid him. Cornwallis's defeat at Yorktown
ended the fighting in North America, but it didn't end the war. The real
end, for Great Britain, came in 1782, in the West Indies, at the Battle of
the Saintes, when the British defeated a French and Spanish invasion of
Jamaica, an outcome that testified not to the empire's weaknesses but to
its priorities. Britain kept the Caribbean but gave up America.

Not surprisingly, the terms of the peace proved as messy and sprawling
as the war. Loyalists confronted the same decision as the empire itself:
whether to give up on America. "To go or not to—is that the question?"

one bit of Shakespearean doggerel went. "Whether 'tis best to trust the inclement sky . . . or stay among the Rebels! / And, by our stay rouse up their keenest rage." Most, not near so indecisive as Hamlet, left if they could: 75,000, about one in every forty people in the United States, evacuated with the British. They went to Britain and Canada, to the West Indies and India: they helped build the British Empire. "No News here but that of Evacuation," one patriot wrote from New York. "Some look smiling, others melancholy, a third Class mad." None were more desperate to escape the United States than the 15,000–20,000 ex-slaves who were part of that exodus, the largest emancipation in American history before Abraham Lincoln signed the Emancipation Proclamation in 1863.[88] In July of 1783, Harry Washington, who'd left Mount Vernon years before to join Dunmore's regiment, managed to reach New York City, where he boarded the British ship *L'Abondance*, bound for Nova Scotia. A clerk noted his departure in a ledger called the "Book of Negroes," listing the 2,775 runaway black men, women, and children who evacuated from the city with the British that summer: "Harry Washington, 43, fine fellow. Formerly the property of General Washington; left him 7 years ago."[89]

When Cornwallis surrendered at Yorktown, 60,000 Loyalists raced to get behind British lines. Knowing their property would be seized, if it hadn't been already—or that they themselves would be seized, as someone else's property—they chose to leave the United States for Britain or for other parts of its empire. They headed to New York, Savannah, or Charleston, cities still held by the British, and from which they would soon be disembarking. Out of 9,127 Loyalists who sailed from Charleston, 5,327 were fugitive slaves. In Virginia, the 2,000 black soldiers under Cornwallis's command who had survived the siege, described as "herds of Negroes," trudged through swamps and forests in hopes of reaching a British warship that Washington, under the terms of the surrender, had agreed to allow to sail to New York. They suffered from exhaustion; they suffered from hunger; they suffered from disease. Of thirty people who escaped Thomas Jefferson's Monticello, fifteen died of smallpox before reaching Cornwallis. Other fugitive slaves fled to the French. "We gained a veritable harvest of domestics," wrote one surprised French officer. Armed slave patrols pursued the fugitives, capturing hundreds of Cornwallis's soldiers and their families, including two people owned by Washington and five owned by Jefferson. In the race to reach British lines, pregnant women ran, too, in hopes that their newborns would earn their freedom papers in the form of a "BB" certificate: "Born Free Behind British Lines."[90]

Reaching New York or Charleston or Savannah was only the beginning of the journey. In New York, Boston King, a runaway from South Carolina, heard a rumor that all the slaves in the city, some two thousand, "were to be delivered up to their masters," and he was haunted by fear of American slave owners marching through the city, "seizing upon their slaves in the streets, or even dragging them out of their beds." King, a carpenter, wrote in his memoirs that blacks in the city were too frightened even to sleep. A Hessian officer reported that as many as five thousand slave owners entered the city to recapture their slaves. George Washington had in fact ordered the keeping of the "Book of Negroes" so that owners might later seek compensation for slaves carried off in British ships. In Charleston, soldiers patrolled the wharves to hold back the hundreds of people desperately seeking to realize what would be, for most of them, their last chance at securing the blessings of liberty for themselves and their posterity. Despite the patrols, dozens of people leapt off the docks and swam out to the last longboats heading to the British warships, including the aptly named *Free Briton*. The swimmers grabbed the rails of the crowded boats and tried to climb aboard. When they would not let go, the British soldiers on the boats tried to hack off their fingers.[91]

The Revolution was at its most radical in the challenge it presented to the institution of slavery and at its most conservative in its failure to meet that challenge. Still, the institution had begun to break, like a pane of glass streaked with cracks but not yet shattered. In January 1783, when Lafayette heard that the commissioners in Paris were near to arriving at a peace treaty, he wrote to Washington to congratulate him and to propose that together they finish work the Revolution had begun. "Let us unite in purchasing a small estate, where we may try the experiment to free the negroes," he suggested. "Such an example as yours might render it a general practice; and if we succeed in America," they could bring the experiment to the West Indies. "I should be happy to join you in so laudable a work," Washington wrote back, saying that he wished to meet to discuss the details.[92]

No thinking person was unaffected by the challenge the struggle for liberty posed to the institution of slavery, America's Achilles' heel. In Philadelphia in 1783, James Madison, leaving Congress, was packing up, preparing to return to Montpelier. He wasn't sure what to do about Billey, a twenty-three-year-old man that he'd brought with him from Virginia when he'd first come to serve in Congress. Billey had been Madison's property since his birth in 1759, when Madison was eight years old. In 1777, the Pennsylvania legislature passed the first abolition law in the Western world, decreeing that any child born to an enslaved woman after March 1, 1780, would be free after twenty-eight years of slavery, and banning the sale of slaves. New York's John Jay declared that to oppose emancipation would be to find of America that "her prayers to Heaven for liberty will be impious."[93] In 1782, the Virginia legislature passed a law that allowed slave owners to free their slaves: one Virginia Quaker said, upon manumitting his slaves, that he had been "fully persuaded that freedom is the natural Right of all mankind & that it is my duty to do unto others as I would desire to be done by in the Like Situation."[94] Not many followed his lead. In 1782, Madison had bought a cache of books in Philadelphia, including a copy of Hobbes's *Leviathan*, even though short of cash and complaining that he would soon be "under the necessity of selling a negro," meaning Billey.[95]

The terrible irony of the man who would draft the Constitution selling a man to buy philosophy was prevented by the terms of Pennsylvania's 1780 abolition law. Madison could not, in fact, sell Billey in Philadelphia. And in 1783, as he prepared to leave Philadelphia for Virginia, it was by no means certain, under Pennsylvania law, that he had any legal right to force Billey to go with him, either. "I have judged it most prudent not to force Billey back to Virginia even if it could be done," Madison reported to his father. "I am persuaded his mind is too thoroughly tainted to be a fit companion for fellow slaves in Virginia." That is, Billey, having spent three and a half years serving Madison in Philadelphia, a city where many black people were free, would be a problem on a plantation: he would incite rebellion. Trade in slaves was illegal in Pennsylvania. Madison might have tried to smuggle Billey out of the state, to sell him farther south, or into the Caribbean, but, he told his father, he was unwilling to "think of punishing him by transportation merely for coveting that liberty for which we have paid the price of so much blood, and have proclaimed so often to be the right, and worthy pursuit, of every human being." In the end, Madison decided to sell him, not as a slave but as an indentured servant, with a seven-year term. Billey renamed himself William Gardener, served out his seven-year term, became a free man, worked as merchant's agent, and raised a family with a wife who, when Jefferson was in Philadelphia, washed Jefferson's clothes.[96]

Gardener found his freedom in Philadelphia. Other men and women met more clouded fates. Nearly thirty thousand Loyalists had sailed from New York to Nova Scotia, among them Harry Washington. Washington settled in Nova Scotia with some fifteen hundred families, the largest free black community in North America, where they flocked around a Methodist preacher named Moses Wilkinson and a Baptist named David George. But, living alongside twelve hundred black slaves brought to Nova Scotia by white Loyalists, the free black community faced continuing challenges. "The White people were against me," George reported. After he attempted to baptize a white man and woman, a white mob tackled him on his pulpit. "It is known by experience that these Persons brought up in Servitude and Slavery want the assistance and Protection of a Master to make them happy," wrote one white Nova Scotian, of free blacks. Swindlers took over their land allotments, selling off "ye Black men's ground," as one surveyor observed with dismay, without "even a shadow of a license." The free black community began to wither. "Many of the poor people were compelled to sell their best gowns for five pounds of flour, in order to support life. When they had parted with all their clothes, even to their blankets, several of them fell down dead in the streets, thro' hunger," Boston King reported. "Some killed and ate their dogs and cats."[97] It was as terrible a disaster as Jamestown.

While American exiles struggled to survive in Canada, Benjamin Franklin was in Paris, negotiating the terms of the peace. "A Grate work Indeed you have Done God be Praised," his sister Jane wrote to him.[98] In September 1783, the American delegation signed the Treaty of Paris. Britain agreed to recognize the independence and sovereignty of the United States. The Americans agreed to make good on debts to British creditors. There were arrangements made for Loyalists and their property, and for the release of prisoners of war. Spain and France were largely cut out of the negotiations, and got very little from them, while Britain ended up with a very different and more far-flung empire than it had in 1775.

The terms of the peace cut the number of African slaves in Britain's empire in half, which meant that the antislavery movement in England gained a more attentive audience, and the proslavery lobby was vastly weakened. Quite the reverse applied in the United States. In the aftermath of the American Revolution, slave owners in states like South Carolina gained political power, while slave owners in the West Indies lost it. West Indian planters were outraged by Britain's decision to forbid trade between the islands and the United States, a decision that led to riots. A sizable number of the freed slaves who left the United States for other parts of the British Empire ended up in the Caribbean. In Jamaica, they began demanding the right to vote: they argued that taxation without representation was tyranny. In the end, the American challenge to empire contributed to a political and moral critique of slavery that was felt far more deeply in the British Empire than in the United States.[99]

The peace made, George Washington rode on a gray horse into the city of New York, where a flag of thirteen stripes and stars had been raised on a pole in Battery Park. Only hours before, the British flag had waved. The last British troops had left the city, occupied since 1776, the last British ship not yet quite out of sight. The city erupted in jubilation as Washington and his soldiers rode down Broadway. That night, Washington went to a tavern for a public dinner, where he raised his wine glass and offered thirteen toasts, to the new nation, to liberty, to America's allies, and more. "To the memory of those heroes who have fallen for our freedom!" And: "May America be an Asylum to the persecuted of the earth!" And finally: "May the remembrances of the day be a lesson to princes."[100]

England would have no slaves. And America would have no king.

*Four*

# THE CONSTITUTION
# OF A NATION

WE, the People of the United States, in order to form a more perfect Union, eſtabliſh Juſtice, inſure domeſtic Tranquility, provide for the common Defence, promote the General Welfare, and ſecure the Bleſſings of Liberty to Ourſelves and our Poſterity, do ordain and eſtabliſh this Conſtitution for the United States of

*Printers published the proposed Constitution as a broadside but*
*also included it in newspapers, almanacs, and pamphlets.*

JAMES MADISON, THIRTY-SIX, BOOKISH, AND WISE, reached Philadelphia on May 3, 1787, eleven days before the constitutional convention was meant to begin. He settled into his old rooms at Mrs. House's hotel, a boardinghouse at Fifth and Market Streets, where he'd stayed during meetings of the Continental Congress. To prepare for the convention, he reviewed his notes on the construction of republics. George Washington arrived on May 13, on the eve of the convention, not nearly as quietly, greeted by crowds, the pealing of church bells, a regiment of cavalry, and a thirteen-gun salute. When Washington reached Mrs. House's, where he'd planned to stay, the wealthy Philadelphia merchant Robert Morris met him there and insisted that Washington stay at his lavish mansion, a few blocks away. The next morning, Washington and Madison walked together to the Pennsylvania State House through a tender mist.[1]

Very few of the delegates had arrived. "There is less punctuality in the outset than was to be wished," Madison wrote to Jefferson, in Paris, on May 15, brooding.[2] Delay or no delay, from the start of the proceedings, Madison took careful notes, certain "of the value of such a contribution to the fund of materials for the History of a Constitution on which would be staked the happiness of a young people." Past an arched doorway, in the Assembly Room of the State House, its tall windows flooding the room with light, the convention met from May 14 to September 17, from a season of planting to a season of harvest. Madison didn't miss a single day, "nor more than a casual fraction of an hour in any day," he explained, "so that I could not have lost a single speech, unless a very short one."[3]

Madison spoke softly and haltingly, the very opposite of the way he wrote. He was making a record for himself, and he was also writing down what happened in Philadelphia that summer for Jefferson. Ever since Jefferson left the country, in 1784, Madison had been taking notes of congressional deliberations for him, too. But Madison understood that, above all, he was making a record for posterity, a record of how a constitution had come to be written.

To constitute something is to make it. A body is constituted of its parts, a nation of its laws. "The constitution of man is the work of nature," Rousseau wrote in 1762, "that of the state the work of art."[4] By the eighteenth century, a constitution had come to mean "that Assemblage of Laws, Institutions and Customs, derived from certain fix'd Principles of Reason . . . according to which the Community hath agreed to be govern'd."[5] Englishmen boasted that "England is now the only monarchy in the world that can properly be said to have a constitution."[6] But England's constitution is unwritten; instead of a single, written document, England's constitution is the sum of its laws, customs, and precedents. In a debate with the conservative Edmund Burke, Thomas Paine suggested that England's constitution did not, in fact, exist. "Can, then, Mr. Burke produce the English Constitution?" Paine asked. "If he cannot, we may fairly conclude that though it has been so much talked about, no such thing as a constitution exists, or ever did exist."[7] In America's book of genesis, the constitution would be written, printed, and preserved.

Centuries of speculation about a state of nature—a time before government—came to an end. It was no longer necessary to imagine how a people might erect a government: this could be witnessed. "We have no occasion to roam for information into the obscure field of antiquity, nor hazard ourselves upon conjecture," Paine wrote. "We are brought at once to the point of seeing government begin, as if we had lived in the beginning of time."[8] It was with this in mind that Madison proved so careful a historian. It was as if he were living at the beginning of time.

# I.

THE CONSTITUTION OF the United States was not the first written constitution in the history of the world. The world's first written, popularly ratified constitutions were drafted by the American states, beginning in 1776. Having dismantled their own governments, they took seriously— literally—the idea that they needed to create them anew, as if they had been returned to a state of nature.

Three states had adopted written constitutions even before Congress declared independence from England, because they found themselves otherwise without a government. "We conceive ourselves reduced to the necessity of establishing A FORM OF GOVERNMENT," a Constitutional Congress convened in New Hampshire declared in January 1776, after the Loyalist governor of New Hampshire fled the state, along with most members of his council.[9] Eleven of the thirteen states devised constitutions in 1776 or 1777. The work of writing these constitutions, Jefferson noted in 1776, was "the whole object of the present controversy."[10]

Most state constitutions were drafted by state legislatures; others were written by men elected as delegates to special conventions. In the spring of 1775, the irascible John Adams had urged Congress "to recommend to the People of every Colony to call such Conventions immediately and set up Governments of their own, under their own Authority; for the People were the Source of all Authority and the Original of all Power." New Hampshire had been the first to act. It was the first state to submit its constitution to the people for ratification, a process whose outcome was far from inevitable. In 1778, when the Massachusetts legislature drafted a constitution and presented it to the people for ratification, the people rejected it, and called for a special convention, which was held in Cambridge in 1779; Adams, one of its delegates, was the chief author of a new constitution that the people of Massachusetts ratified in 1780. That this act—the people voting on the very form of government—represented an extraordinary break with the past was not lost on Adams, who wrote, "How few of the human race have ever enjoyed an opportunity of making an election of government, more than of air, soil, or climate, for themselves or their children!"[11]

Each of the states was a laboratory, each new constitution another political experiment. Many state constitutions, like those of Virginia and Pennsylvania, included a Declaration of Rights. Pennsylvania's, written in September 1776, began by echoing the preamble to the Declaration of Independence, establishing "That all men are born equally free and independent, and have certain natural, inherent and inalienable rights, amongst which are, the enjoying and defending life and liberty, acquiring, possessing and protecting property, and pursuing and obtaining happiness and safety." Massachusetts's constitution insisted on a right to revolution, decreeing that when the government fails the people, "the people have a right to alter the government, and to take measures necessary for their safety, prosperity and happiness."[12]

For all the veneration of the "people," the word "democracy" retained an unequivocally negative connotation. Eighteenth-century Americans borrowed from Aristotle the idea that there are three forms of government: a monarchy, an aristocracy, and a polity; governments by the one, the few, and the many. Each becomes corrupt when the government seeks to advance its own interests rather than the common good. A corrupt monarchy is a tyranny, a corrupt aristocracy an oligarchy, and a corrupt polity a democracy. The way to avoid corruption is to properly mix the three forms so that corruption in any one would be restrained, or checked, by the others.

Between a government too monarchical and a government too democratic, Massachusetts lawyer and later member of Congress Fisher Ames would have rather had the former. "Monarchy is like a merchantman, which sails well, but will sometimes strike on a rock, and go to the bottom," Ames wrote in 1783, "whilst a republic is a raft, which would never sink, but then your feet are always in the water."[13]

Unlike the harrumphing Ames, many of the people who were drafting state constitutions apparently preferred to err on the side of democracy. In framing new governments, several states lowered property qualifications for voting. Under the terms of Pennsylvania's new constitution, any man who had lived in the state for a year and paid taxes—*any* taxes—could vote: where earlier two-thirds of white men could vote, 90 percent now could. Yet many men of means found this development alarming, believing that poor men, like women, lacked the capacity to make good political decisions because, dependent on others, their will was not their own. Massachusetts's constitution included property qualifications both for office seekers and for voters. As Adams explained, "Such is the Frailty of the human Heart, that very few Men, who have no Property, have any Judgment of their own."[14]

Most states arranged a government of three branches, with a governor as executive, a superior court as judicial, and a Senate and House of Representatives as legislative. But some states, attempting to correct for colonial arrangements, in which a royally appointed governor and his appointed council wielded the preponderance of power over a weak elected assembly, granted the greatest weight to lower houses of the legislature rather than to upper houses or to an executive. Pennsylvania's constitution, like its Quakers, was the most radical, and, in the eyes of many observers, alarmingly democratic. It called for annual elections, no governor, and a unicameral legislature whose members served limited terms. Any proposed law had to be printed and distributed to the people, who would have a year to consider it before the legislature voted.[15]

The states' constitutions were political experiments in more ways, too. The Declaration of Rights in Vermont's 1777 constitution specifically banned slavery: men might be indented as servants till the age of twenty-one, or women till the age of eighteen, but no one past that age could be held in bondage. (This provision would have made Vermont the first state to abolish slavery, except that in 1777 Vermont was not a state but an independent republic; it would not join the United States until 1791.)

In 1781, Bett, a slave in Massachusetts whose husband had fought and died in the war, filed a suit in which she argued that the state's new constitution had abolished slavery. Bett's owner, John Ashley, was a local judge. She'd heard him talking about natural rights with twenty-six-year-old Theodore Sedgwick, one of his law clerks. When Ashley's wife tried to strike Bett's sister with a kitchen shovel, Bett blocked the blow and was badly burned. Fleeing, she went to Sedgwick and decided, with his help, to sue for her freedom. "All men are born free and equal, and have certain natural, essential, and unalienable rights; among which may be reckoned the right of enjoying and defending their lives and liberties; that of acquiring, possessing, and protecting property; in fine, that of seeking and obtaining their safety and happiness," Adams had written, in Article I of the Massachusetts Constitution's Declaration of Rights. Citing Adams, Bett won her case and her liberty and gave herself a new name: Elizabeth Freeman.[16]

Two years later, the Massachusetts Supreme Judicial Court formally ruled that slavery was inconsistent with the state's constitution, adding, "Is not a law of nature that all men are equal and free? Is not the laws of nature the laws of God? Is not the law of God then against slavery?" The next year, Pennsylvania's 1775 Society for the Relief of Free Negroes Unlawfully Held in Bondage renamed itself the Pennsylvania Society for Promoting the Abolition of Slavery, and a judge in Vermont ruled in favor of a runaway slave whose master had produced a bill of sale proving his ownership: the judge said in order to retain his property in the form of another man he'd have to provide a bill of sale from "God Almighty."[17]

Inevitably, some state constitutions worked better than others. What clearly didn't work well were the Articles of Confederation, which had been hastily drawn up by the Continental Congress for the purpose of waging war against Britain, and even this they did not do well (regiments went unfed, soldiers unpaid, veterans unpensioned). Drafted in 1777, the Articles weren't ratified by the states until 1781—the delay was the result of the states' competing claims to western land—and even after the Articles were adopted, those claims remained largely unresolved. Efforts to revise the Articles proved fruitless, even though the Continental Congress had no standing to resolve disputes between states nor any authority to set standards or to regulate trade. The new nation was riddled, as a result, with thirteen different currencies and thirteen separate navies.

Most urgently, Congress lacked the authority to raise money, which it needed both to make good on its debts and to pay for troops in the Northwest Territory, a swath west of the Alleghenies, north of the Ohio River, and east of the Mississippi that the federal government had acquired from the states. The 1783 Treaty of Paris had required that the states repay their debts, and when the states defaulted on those debts, Great Britain threatened to default on a commitment, also made under the terms of the peace, to surrender its northwestern forts—Oswego, Niagara, and Detroit—to the United States.

*The value of paper currency fluctuated wildly, and by the
end of the Revolutionary War, money printed on behalf of
the Continental Congress had become nearly worthless.*

Even if Congress had fully possessed the power to tax, how to calculate
the tax burden of each state remained unsettled. Should each state pay
in proportion to the size of its population or in proportion to its property?
In much of the country, one kind of property took the form of people. For
purposes of taxation, then, would slaves count as people or as property?
In 1777, Pennsylvania's Samuel Chase had argued that only white inhabitants should count as people because, legally, blacks were no more people
"than cattle." This point seemed so essential to South Carolina's Thomas
Lynch that he had threatened that "if it is debated, whether their slaves
are their property, there is an end of the confederation," whereupon Benjamin Franklin made the wry observation that there was one plain way to
tell the difference between people and property: "sheep will never make
any insurrections."[18]

In 1781 and again in 1783, Congress tried to revise the Articles so as
to grant itself authority to collect taxes on imports. This led to a return
to the original debate about how to calculate each state's tax burden: by
the number of inhabitants or by the value of land. The value of land was
difficult to calculate—acreage alone is a poor guide, since a field is worth
more than a swamp—and, as Adam Smith had argued in *The Wealth*

*of Nations,* "the most decisive mark of the prosperity of any country is the increase of the number of its inhabitants." Population seemed both easier to calculate and a more sensible measure, for purposes not only of taxation but also of representation. This led to a compromise, involving a fraction. A committee on revenue proposed that "two blacks be rated as equal to one freeman." Other proposals followed, until "Mr. Madison said that in order to give a proof of the sincerity of his professions of liberality, he would propose that Slaves should be rated as 5 to 3."

It was very nearly arbitrary, this mathematical formula that would determine the course of American elections for seven decades. At the time, it was also moot: it was never implemented because the state legislatures refused to ratify any revenue-raising amendments.[19] But the proposed ratio—three to five—was not forgotten.

The confederation limped along, weak and hobbled. France and Holland pressed for payment of debts—in real money, not the paper promises on which the Republic floated. "Not worth a continental," a phrase used to describe the paper currency printed by Congress, entered the lexicon. Congress was unable to pay its creditors and, by 1786, the continental government was nearly bankrupt. The states, too, were in distress; they could levy taxes, but they couldn't reliably collect them. Massachusetts had levied taxes to retire the state's war debt; farmers who failed to pay could have their property seized and auctioned. Many of those farmers had fought in the war, and, beginning in August 1786, they decided to fight again: well over a thousand armed farmers in western Massachusetts, angry and alienated and led by a veteran named Daniel Shays, protested the government, blockading courthouses and seizing a federal armory.[20]

It seemed as if the infant nation might descend into civil war, beginning an unending cycle of revolution. "I wish our Poor Distracted State would atend to the many good Lessons" of history, Jane Franklin wrote to her brother, and not "keep always in a Flame."[21] Madison feared the rebellion would spread all the way to Virginia. Washington began to wonder whether the nation needed a king after all, writing to Madison, "We are fast verging to anarchy and confusion!" As Madison reported to Jefferson, Shays's Rebellion had "tainted the faith" of even the most committed republicans.[22]

A last-ditch effort to restore order by revising the Articles of Confederation was scheduled to begin on September 11, 1786, in Annapolis, at a special convention of delegates that included Madison, who had probably been behind the resolution to convene the meeting. To prepare, he threw himself into his reading of political history. He'd been assembling a library. In 1785, Jefferson shipped him crates of books from Paris. "Since I have been at home I have had leisure to review the literary cargo for which I am so much indebted to your friendship," he wrote to Jefferson in March 1786, reporting that Virginia had so much snow that winter that the tops of the Blue Ridge Mountains were still white. While the snow melted that spring, Madison composed a long essay called "Ancient & Modern Confederacies," an assessment of all the confederated governments he could discover in his reading: their structure, their strengths, and, above all, their weaknesses.[23]

It had been an unusually wet spring. Madison left Virginia in summer and wended through fields of sodden crops of wheat and rye. He rode all the way to New York on business before turning around to head back down to Maryland, still mulling over his reading, and giving Jefferson still more instructions for books he'd like to add to his library. "If you meet with 'Graecorum Respublicae ab Ubbone Emmio descriptae,' Lugd. Batavorum, 1632, pray get it for me," he pressed him.[24]

A road-weary Madison arrived in Annapolis in September vastly discouraged. So frayed was the spirit of union and so weak was the federal government that delegates from only five of the thirteen states turned up for the convention. They met at George Mann's tavern, a six-gabled brick hotel. Madison stabled his horse in Mann's barn. Without anything close to a quorum, twelve men from five states agreed to a resolution drafted by Alexander Hamilton of New York that delegates—ideally from all thirteen states—would gather in Philadelphia the next year "to devise such further provisions as shall appear to them necessary to render the constitution of the Federal Government adequate to the exigencies of the Union."[25]

If more delegates *had* turned up for the Annapolis Convention, they'd most likely have proposed a single amendment to the Articles, granting Congress the authority to raise revenue. The bad turnout, ironically, opened the possibility for more sweeping action. Still, when the resolution reached Congress, which met, then, in New York, Congress failed for

*James Madison took copious notes on the proceedings of the constitutional convention.*

weeks to consider it. Arguably, it was only the course of events in Massachusetts that spurred Congress to act. In January 1787, the governor of Massachusetts sent a three-thousand-man militia across the state in an attempt to suppress Shays's Rebellion and regain the federal armory (all of this without any authority from the federal government). The state instituted martial law. In New York, Congress finally acted, approving of the proposed Philadelphia convention "for the sole and express purpose of revising the Articles of Confederation."[26] No one said anything about drafting a constitution.

After Annapolis, Madison went home to Virginia and resumed his course of study. In April of 1787, he drafted an essay called "Vices of the Political System of the United States." It took the form of a list of eleven deficiencies, beginning with " 1. Failure of the States to comply with the Constitutional requisitions. . . . 2. Encroachments by the States on the federal authority. . . . 3. Violations of the law of nations and of treaties." And it closed with a list of causes for these vices, which he located primarily "in the people themselves." By this last he meant the danger that a majority posed to a minority: "In republican Government the majority however composed, ultimately give the law. Whenever therefore an apparent interest or common passion unites a majority what is to restrain them from unjust violations of the rights and interests of the minority, or of individuals?"[27] What force restrains good men from doing bad things? Honesty, character, religion—these, history demonstrated, were not to be relied upon. No, the only force that could restrain the tyranny of the people was the force of a well-constructed constitution. It would have to be as finely wrought as an iron gate.

# II.

BENJAMIN FRANKLIN, who was not done with his usefulness, spent the early days of May 1787 waiting for the laggard delegates to arrive and attending to his correspondence. His sister Jane wrote from Boston that she'd been reading about him. "I wanted to tell you how much Pleasure I Injoy in the constant and lively mention made of you in the News papers," she wrote, full of pride. Franklin was eighty-one years old; Jane was seventy-four. The news of his flurry of activity, she told him, winking, "makes you Apear to me Like a young man of Twenty-five."[28]

Franklin was the oldest of the seventy-five men who had been elected to represent twelve states at the convention. (Rhode Island, unwilling to grant the necessity of the meeting, refused to send a delegation.) Half of the delegates were lawyers. Nineteen delegates owned slaves. Only fifty-five showed up, and, since they came and went, there were usually only about thirty men on hand on any given day. When, on May 14, the day the convention was to begin, hardly any of the delegates had arrived, Madison blamed the weather.

Aside from Franklin and Madison, two more members of the Pennsylvania delegation, Gouverneur Morris and James Wilson, were already in town, and so were two more members of the Virginia delegation: George Washington and Edmund Randolph. These six men met on the night of May 16 at Franklin's newly enlarged house, its growth a measure of his own rise. As he explained to his sister, he'd built an addition and installed a door in his bedroom by which he could enter directly into his library, even in slippers and robe. "When I look at these Buildings, my dear Sister, and compare them with that in which our good Parents educated us, the Difference strikes me with Wonder," he wrote to her, remembering the tiny wooden house on the crooked street of Boston where they'd been born, in a smaller America.[29]

That night, by the light of candles in Franklin's dining room, the six early-comers to the convention agreed that, instead of merely revising the Articles, which were little more than a treaty of alliance among sovereign states, the convention ought to devise a national government. The next day, Madison set to work drafting what became known as the Virginia Plan. Franklin returned to his correspondence. "We are all well, and join in Love to you and yours," he wrote to his sister.[30] He pondered the state of the Union. His sister had one piece of advice. "I hope with the Asistance of such a Nmber of wise men as you are connected with in the Convention you will Gloriously Accomplish, and put a Stop to the nesesity of Dragooning, & Haltering, they are odious means," she wrote, urging her brother to support an end to the draft and capital punishment. "I had Rather hear of the Swords being beat into Plow-shares, & the Halters used for Cart Roops, if by that means we may be brought to live Peaceably with won a nother." Franklin's sister, like so many Americans, had suffered gravely during the war. She'd lost her home. One of her sons had died of wounds suffered during the Battle of Bunker Hill; another had gone mad. She'd had enough of guns and violence. Franklin tucked her letter away and governed his tongue. [31]

The convention began its work eleven days late, on May 25, when at last a quorum of twenty-nine delegates had arrived. Washington, almost as striking at fifty-five as he'd been as a young man, was unanimously elected president. (His beauty was marred only by his terrible teeth, which had rotted and been replaced by dentures made from ivory and from nine teeth pulled from the mouths of his slaves.)[32] Deeply and nearly universally admired, Washington represented to many Americans all that was noblest in a republic. Nothing better testified to his civic virtue than his resignation of his command at the end of the war: instead of seizing power, he had given it away.[33] His role as president of the constitutional convention was mostly ceremonial, but, as with so many ceremonial roles, it was an essential and even a stirring performance.

The deliberations began in earnest on May 29, when Edmund Randolph offered a polite expression of gratitude to the framers of the Articles of Confederation, who could hardly be faulted for that document's deficiencies, given that they had "done all that patriots could do, in the then infancy of the science, of constitutions, & of confederacies." Randolph was a formidable lawyer whose Loyalist father had fled Virginia in 1775 and whose uncle Peyton's slaves had joined Lord Dunmore's regiment. He knew mayhem. He said he considered "the prospect of anarchy from the laxity of government everywhere," and offered a series of resolutions about the means available to the convention for avoiding chaos.[34]

The immediate problem the delegates were charged with addressing—that chaos—was Congress's debt, its lack of cash, and its inability to raise taxes or to suppress popular revolt or to resolve conflicts between the states. But, like many other delegates, Randolph believed that the work of the convention was to counter the tendencies of the state constitutions. "Our chief danger arises from the democratic parts of our constitutions," he said. Massachusetts firebrand Elbridge Gerry agreed that the states suffered from an "excess of democracy." Randolph believed that the point of the convention was "to provide a cure for the evils under which the United States labored; that in tracing these evils to their origin every man had found it in the turbulence and follies of democracy: that some check therefore was to be sought for against this tendency of our Governments."[35]

Those delegates who opposed establishing a national government, and who thought they'd come to Philadelphia to revise the Articles of Confederation, could not appeal to the public, which might well have been severely alarmed by word of the goings-on in Independence Hall had they heard so much as a whisper. But the delegates had pledged to keep their deliberations secret—for a term of fifty years—a pledge that worked in favor of men like Madison. And, within the hall, it allowed for a full and frank airing of views.

The Constitution drafted in Philadelphia acted as a check on the Revolution, a halt to its radicalism; if the Revolution had tilted the balance between government and liberty toward liberty, the Constitution shifted it toward government. But in very many ways the Constitution also realized the promise of the Revolution, and particularly the promise of representation. In devising the new national government, the delegates adamantly rejected a proposal that the state legislators, rather than the people, elect members of Congress. "Under the existing Confederacy, Congress represent the *States* not the *people* of the States," George Mason said, "their acts operate on the *States* not on the individuals. The case will be changed in the new plan of Government. The people will be represented; they ought therefore to choose the Representatives."[36]

However much delegates at the convention might have railed at the excess of democracy in the state constitutions and regretted the lowering of property qualifications for voting in the states, they did not institute those requirements in the federal constitution. Franklin argued that, since poor men of no estate whatsoever had fought in the war, there could be no sound reason why they should not vote in the new government. "Who are to be the electors of the federal representatives?" Madison asked. "Not the rich, more than the poor; not the learned, more than the ignorant; not the haughty heirs of distinguished names, more than the humble sons of obscure and unpropitious fortune. The electors are to be the great body of the People of the United States." This was a matter as much of politics as of principle. Connecticut delegate Oliver Ellsworth put it plainly: "The people will not readily subscribe to the Natl. Constitution, if it should subject them to be disfranchised." Voting requirements were left to the states.

Nor did the Constitution institute property requirements for running for federal office. "Who are to be the objects of popular choice?" Madison asked. "Every citizen whose merit may recommend him to the esteem and confidence of his country." What could be more revolutionary than these words? "No qualification of wealth, of birth, of religious faith, or of civil profession is permitted to fetter the judgment or disappoint the inclination of the people," Madison insisted.[37]

In this same revolutionary spirit, the Constitution required congressmen to be paid, so that the office would not be limited to wealthy men. It required only a short residency for immigrants before they, too, became eligible to run for office. Delegates who argued for greater restriction faced immigrants like Hamilton, born in the West Indies, and James Wilson, born in Scotland, who wondered at the prospect of "his being incapacitated from holding a place under the very Constitution which he had shared in the trust of making."

But if these matters were resolved with relative ease, others proved far more difficult. The convention found itself facing a nearly unbreachable divide. How was fairly apportioned representation in Congress to be achieved in a national government composed of states of such different sizes? One proposal involved redrawing the map of the United States. "Lay the map of the confederation on the table," a New Jersey delegate suggested, and redraw it so that "all the existing boundaries be erased, and that a new partition of the whole be made into 13 equal parts."[38] But, as Madison pointed out, the problem wasn't only the size of the states. It was the nature of their population. "The States were divided into different interests not by their difference of size," he explained, ". . . but principally from the effects of their having or not having slaves."[39]

The problem of property in the form of people had become an even bigger problem than it had been before the Revolution. The years following the end of the war had witnessed the largest importation of African slaves to the Americas in history—a million people over a single decade. The slave population of the United States, 500,000 in 1776, had soared to 700,000 by 1787. After the Treaty of Paris, when Britain recognized the independence of the United States, it also regarded its former colonies as a foreign nation, which meant that American merchants were banned from British ports, including ports in the West Indies. As a result, a trade in slaves grew *within* the United States, as slave owners in the South sold their property to back country settlers in Kentucky, Louisiana, and Tennessee. Yet even as the number of slaves in the southern states was rising, it was falling in the North; by 1787, slavery had been effectively abolished in New England and much challenged in Pennsylvania and New York. Economically, it was significant in only five of the thirteen states, and in only two, South Carolina and Georgia, was it the crux of the economy.

At the convention, it proved impossible to set the matter of slavery aside, both because the question of representation turned on it and because any understanding of the nature of tyranny rested on it. When Madison argued about the inevitability of a majority oppressing a minority, he cited ancient history, and told of how the rich oppressed the poor in Greece and Rome. But he cited, too, modern American history. "We have seen the mere distinction of color made in the most enlightened period of time, the ground of the most oppressive dominion ever exercised by man over man."[40] In offering this illustration of oppression, Madison hadn't intended to make a point about slavery (although he did, inadvertently, make such a point, since what he said that day revealed that he thought "the mere distinction of color" was no basis for bondage); he was trying to convince his fellow delegates that a republic needed to be large, and with an abundance of factions, so that a majority could not oppress a minority. But slavery was how he understood oppression.

Slavery became the crucial divide in Philadelphia because slaves factored in two calculations: in the wealth they represented as property and in the population they represented as people. The two could not be separated.

The most difficult question at the convention concerned representation. States with large populations of course wanted representation in the federal legislature to be proportionate to population. States with small populations wanted equal representation for each state. States with large numbers of slaves wanted slaves to count as people for purposes of representation but not for purposes of taxation; states without slaves wanted the opposite. "If . . . we depart from the principle of representation in proportion to numbers, we will lose the object of our meeting," Pennsylvania's James Wilson warned on June 9.[41] That same day, or probably later that evening, Benjamin Franklin, catching up on his correspondence, distributed to notable antislavery leaders around the world copies of the new constitution of the Pennsylvania Society for Promoting the Abolition of Slavery, "for in this business the friends of humanity in every Country are of one Nation and Religion."[42] Franklin spoke at the convention on the question of representation, but it was Wilson, his fellow Pennsylvanian, who treated the matter squarely. Better than any other delegate, Wilson understood the nature of the political divide—a divide that would, in a matter of decades, sunder the Union.

On July 11, Wilson asked why, if slaves were admitted as people, they weren't "admitted as Citizens." And "then why are they not admitted on an equality with White Citizens?" And, if they weren't admitted as people, "Are they admitted as property? Then why is not other property admitted into the computation?"

The convention was very nearly at an impasse, broken only by a deal involving the Northwest Territory—a Northwest Ordinance decreeing that any new states entering the Union formed north of the Ohio River would be without slavery, while those south of the Ohio would continue slavery. This measure passed on July 13. Four days later, the convention adopted what's known as the Connecticut compromise, establishing equal representation in the Senate, with two senators for each state, and proportionate representation in the House of Representatives, with one representative for every 40,000 people (at the very last minute this number was changed to 30,000). And, for purposes of representation, each slave would count as three-fifths of a person—the ratio that Madison had devised in 1783. A federal census, conducted every ten years, was instituted to make the count.[43]

The most remarkable consequence of this remarkable arrangement was to grant slave states far greater representation in Congress than free states. In 1790, the first Census of the United States counted 140,000 free citizens in New Hampshire, which meant that the Granite State got four seats in the House of Representatives. But South Carolina, with 140,000 free citizens and 100,000 slaves, got six seats. The population of Massachusetts was greater than the population of Virginia, but Virginia had 300,000 slaves and so got five more seats. If not for the three-fifths rule, the representatives of free states would have outnumbered representatives of slave states by 57 to 33.[44]

During a break in the proceedings in August, Madison attended to his own affairs. A slave named Anthony, seventeen, had run away from Montpelier; Madison asked his erstwhile human property, Billey, now William Gardener, if he knew where Anthony might have gone.[45] Anthony had gone looking to be five-fifths of a person.

Franklin spent the break resting, and pondering the problem of slavery. He'd planned to introduce a proposal calling for a statement of principle condemning both the trade and slavery itself, but northern delegates had convinced him to withdraw it because the compromise was so fragile. Massachusetts delegate Rufus King spent the adjournment rethinking his concession to the three-fifths clause. And when deliberations resumed, King proposed that Congress at least be granted the authority to abolish the slave trade, whereupon the South Carolina delegation made clear that any attempt to restrict the trade would force them to leave the convention.

This Luther Martin could not abide. Martin, the son of New Jersey farmers, had been a schoolmaster before he became a lawyer; in 1778, he'd been appointed Maryland's attorney general. Martin declared that the trade in slaves "was inconsistent with the principles of the Revolution and dishonorable to the American character." He was short and red-faced, as slovenly as he was brilliant. "His genius and vices were equally remarkable," it was said.[46] But he proved a man of principle. He withdrew from the convention, refused to sign the Constitution, and opposed its ratification, warning that "national crimes can only be, and frequently are, punished in this world by national punishments."[47] John Rutledge dismissed Martin's argument. Rutledge, forty-eight, had served in the South Carolina assembly, the Stamp Act Congress, and the Continental Congress, and as governor of his state; he proved to be the South's most determined defender. "The true question at present," he insisted, "is whether the Southern states shall or shall not be parties to the Union."

New Englanders ceded the point. "Let every state import what it pleases," said Connecticut's Oliver Ellsworth. Ellsworth, a devout Christian, had prepared for a career in the ministry before becoming a lawyer. "The morality or wisdom of slavery are considerations belonging to the states themselves," he said. He also believed that the institution was on the wane: "Slavery, in time, will not be a speck in our country."

A compromise between those opposed to the slave trade and those in favor of it was reached with a motion that Congress should be prohibited from interfering with the slave trade for a period of twenty years. Madison was aggrieved. He'd have preferred no mention of slavery in the Constitution at all. "So long a term will be more dishonorable to the national character than to say nothing about it in the Constitution," he warned. Gouverneur Morris, who'd lost a leg to a carriage wheel and the use of an arm to a boiling pot of water, was appalled at the entire bargain, and decided to deliver a lecture. "The inhabitant of Georgia and S.C. who goes to the Coast of Africa, and in defiance of the most sacred laws of humanity tears away his fellow creatures from their dearest connections & damns them to the most cruel bondages, shall have more votes in a Govt. instituted for protection of the rights of mankind, than the Citizen of Pa. or N. Jersey who views with a laudable horror, so nefarious a practice." He said he "would sooner submit to a tax for paying for all the Negroes in the United States than saddle posterity with such a Constitution." As Morris pointed out, the delegates were there to build a republic, but there was nothing more aristocratic than slavery. He called it "the curse of heaven."[48]

The Constitution would not lift that curse. Instead, it tried to hide it. Nowhere do the words "slave" or "slavery" appear in the final document. "What will be said of this new principle of founding a right to govern Freemen on a power derived from slaves," Pennsylvania's John Dickinson wondered—correctly, as it would turn out. He predicted: "The omitting the *Word* will be regarded as an Endeavour to conceal a principle of which we are ashamed."[49]

Five days before the close of the convention, George Mason proposed adding a bill of rights. "A bill might be prepared in a few hours," he urged. But Mason's proposal was struck down; not a single state voted in favor of it, mainly because most states already had a bill of rights, but also because the delegates were exhausted and eager to go home.

By Monday, September 17, 1787, after four months of arduous debate, a polished draft was at last ready for signatures. After the document was read out loud for the very first time, Franklin, crippled by gout, struggled to rise from his chair but, as had happened many times during the convention, he found he was too weary to make a speech. Wilson, half Franklin's age, read his remarks instead.

"Mr. President," he began, addressing Washington, "I confess that there are several parts of this constitution which I do not at present approve, but I am not sure I shall never approve them." He suggested that he might, one day, change his mind. "For having lived long, I have experienced many instances of being obliged by better information, or fuller consideration, to change opinions even on important subjects, which I once thought right, but found to be otherwise. It is therefore that the older I grow, the more apt I am to doubt my own judgment, and to pay more respect to the judgment of others." Hoping to pry open the minds of delegates who were closed to the compromise before them, he reminded them of the cost of zealotry. "Most men indeed as well as most sects in Religion, think themselves in possession of all truth, and that wherever others differ from them it is so far error." But wasn't humility the best course, in such circumstances? "Thus I consent, Sir, to this Constitution," he closed, "because I expect no better, and because I am not sure, that it is not the best."[50]

It was four o'clock in the afternoon when the delegates began signing the bottom of the last of the document's four sheets of parchment. Mason was among the delegates who refused to sign. Washington sat in a chair in front of a window. Franklin understood the importance of political theater. He ventured that he had often wondered, during the many long days at the convention when he'd lost track of the time, whether the sun he could see outside the window, like the sun carved on the back of Washington's chair, was rising or setting. "But now at length," he said, "I have the happiness to know that it is a rising and not a setting sun."[51]

The day after the convention adjourned, what had been kept for so long strictly secret and had only so lately been written on parchment was copied and made public, printed in newspapers and on broadsheets, often with "We the People" set off in extra-large type. Washington sent a copy to Lafayette in Paris: "It is now a Child of fortune." As Madison explained, the Constitution is "of no more consequence than the paper on which it is written—a blank page—unless it be stamped with the approbation of those to whom it is addressed. . . . THE PEOPLE THEMSELVES."[52]

THE DECLARATION OF INDEPENDENCE had been signed by members of the Continental Congress; it had never been put to a popular vote. The Articles of Confederation had been ratified in the states, not by the people, but by the state legislatures. Except for the Massachusetts Constitution, in 1780, and the second New Hampshire Constitution, in 1784, no constitution, no written system of government, had ever before been submitted to the people for their approval. "This is a new event in the history of mankind," said the governor of Connecticut at his state's ratification convention.[53]

The debate over ratifying the Constitution produced some of the most heated political writing in American history, not only in American newspapers but in hundreds of broadsides and pamphlets. The argument in favor of ratification was made, eloquently and persuasively, in eighty-five essays, known as *The Federalist Papers*, published between October 1787 and May 1788 under the pen name Publius. Ambitious, young, red-haired Alexander Hamilton, who hadn't played much of a role at the constitutional convention, and who thought the Constitution created a

*A 1787 engraving pictures Federalists and Anti-Federalists*
*pulling in two different directions a wagon labeled*
*"Connecticut," stuck in a ditch and loaded with*
*debts and (worthless) paper money.*

government too democratic, wrote fifty-one of the essays. Madison wrote another twenty or so, and John Jay wrote the rest.

The debate, waged in ratifying conventions but, even more thrillingly, in the nation's weekly newspapers, established the structure of the new nation's two-party system. Against the Federalists stood the unfortunately named Anti-Federalists, who opposed ratification. If it hadn't been for the all-or-nothing dualism of this choice, and a partisan press, the United States might well have a multiparty political culture.

The Anti-Federalists generally charged that the Constitution amounted to a conspiracy against their liberties, not least because it lacked a bill of rights. Jefferson, from Paris, made this complaint: "A bill of rights is what the people are entitled to against every government on earth."[54] Anti-Federalists also argued that Congress was too small; here they cited John Adams, who'd written that a legislature "should be in miniature, an exact portrait of the people at large." Influenced by Montesquieu's *The Spirit of the Laws* (1748), Anti-Federalists believed that a republic had to be small and homogeneous; the United States was too big for this form of government. They also charged that the Constitution was difficult to read, and that its difficulty was further evidence that it was part of a conspiracy against the understanding of a plain man, as if it were willfully incomprehensible. "The constitution of a wise and free people," Anti-Federalists insisted, "ought to be as evident to simple reason, as the letters of our alphabet," as easy to read as *Common Sense*. "A constitution ought to be, like a beacon, held up to the public eye, so as to be understood by every man," Patrick Henry declared."[55]

Anti-Federalists, including former delegates to the convention, also contested the three-fifths clause. Luther Martin called it a "solemn mockery of and insult to God" and said that the clause "involved the absurdity of increasing the power of a state . . . in proportion as that state violated the rights of freedom."[56] Madison defended this decision, insisting that there was no other way to count slaves except as both persons and property, since this "is the character bestowed on them by the laws under which they live."[57]

Ratification proved to be a nail-biter. By January 9, 1788, five states— Connecticut, Delaware, Georgia, New Jersey, and Pennsylvania—had ratified. The debate that began in mid-January at the convention in Massachusetts grew heated. "You Perceive we have some quarilsome spirits against the constitution," Jane Franklin reported to her brother from Massachusetts. "But," she reassured him, "it does not appear to be those of Superior Judgment."[58] After Federalists promised they'd propose a bill of rights at the first session of the new Congress, Massachusetts, in a squeaker, voted in favor of ratification by a vote 187 to 168 in February. In March, Rhode Island, which had refused to send any delegates to the constitutional convention, refused to hold a ratifying convention. Maryland ratified in April, South Carolina in May, New Hampshire in June. That made nine states in favor, meeting the minimum required.

Practically, though, the approval of Virginia and New York was essential. At Virginia's convention, Patrick Henry argued that the Constitution was an assault on the sovereignty of the states: "Have they made a proposal of a compact between states? If they had, this would be a confederation: It is otherwise most clearly a consolidated government. The question turns, sir, on that poor little thing—the expression, We, the *people*, instead of the *states*, of America."[59] But Federalists eventually prevailed, by a vote of 89 to 79, on June 25, 1788.

On the Fourth of July, James Wilson, with full-throated passion, spoke at a parade in Philadelphia, while a ratifying convention met in New York. "You have heard of Sparta, of Athens, and of Rome; you have heard of their admired constitutions, and of their high-prized freedom," he told his audience. Then he asked a series of rhetorical questions. But were their constitutions written? The crowd called back, "No!" Were they written by the people? No! Were they submitted to the people for ratification? No! "Were they to stand or fall by the people's approving or rejecting vote?" No, again.

Three weeks later, New York ratified by the smallest of margins: 30 to 27.[60] By three votes, the Constitution became law. And yet the political battle raged on. The day after the vote, Thomas Greenleaf, the only Anti-Federalist printer in Federalist-dominated New York City, arrived home in the evening to find that a band of Federalists had fired musket balls into his house. He loaded two pistols, put them in a chest near his bed, and went to sleep, only to be awakened in the middle of the night by men shouting outside his house. When a mob began breaking down his door, smashing windows, and throwing stones, Greenleaf shot into the crowd from a second-story window, tried to reload, then decided to run. After he and his wife and children made a narrow escape out the back door, the mob swarmed his house and office and destroyed his type and printing press, a bad omen for a nation founded on the freedom of speech.[61]

Ratification had been an agony. It might very easily have gone another way. An unruly new republic had begun.

## III.

THE FIRST CONGRESS convened on March 4, 1789, in New York's city hall, where the German printer John Peter Zenger had been tried in 1735, where a black man named Caesar had met his fate in 1741, and where the Stamp Act Congress had deliberated in 1765, each another trial for freedom. Renamed Federal Hall, the building was refitted to its new purpose, enlarged, improved, and made majestic, with Tuscan columns and Doric pillars, according to a plan designed by the French

*George Washington was inaugurated on the balcony of Federal Hall, formerly New York's city hall.*

FEDERAL HALL
The Seat of CONGRESS

architect Pierre Charles l'Enfant, who, when the federal government moved to the banks of the Potomac, would one day design the nation's capital. In L'Enfant's hands, city hall grew to three times its original size, its aesthetic founding a new architectural style: Federal. Above a grand new balcony, facing Wall Street, a giant eagle, carrying thirteen arrows, appeared to burst out of the clouds. A new cupola boasted half-circle windows, eyes to the sky.[62]

For all its pomp, Federal Hall was a monument to republicanism: the building opened its doors to the people. The Constitution requires that "Each House shall keep a Journal of its Proceedings, and from time to time publish the same." The *Congressional Record* was published, because it had to be, but Congress decided to make its proceedings public in an altogether different way. Pennsylvania's 1776 Constitution had decreed that "the doors of the house . . . shall be and remain open for the admission of all persons who behave decently," and the House of Representatives followed this precedent, opening its doors from its first session. The representatives' hall, arched and octagonal, was two stories tall, with large galleries for spectators.[63]

The new president wasn't inaugurated until April 30; the delay was due to the time it took to conduct the first presidential election. Washington had run unopposed, but there remained the matter of counting the votes. Exactly how the new president was to assume his office was not immediately clear. The Constitution calls only for a president to take an oath, swearing to "preserve, protect and defend the Constitution of the United States."

Hours before Washington's inauguration was scheduled to take place, a special congressional committee decided that it might be fitting for the president to rest his hand on a Bible while taking the oath of office. Unfortunately, no one in Federal Hall had a copy of the Bible on hand. There followed a mad dash to find one. At midday, above a crowd assembled on Wall Street, Washington took his oath standing on a balcony, below that eagle bursting from the clouds.

He pledged, and then he kissed his borrowed Bible. After Washington was sworn in, he entered Federal Hall and delivered a speech that had been written by Alexander Hamilton. The Constitution does not call for an inaugural address. But Washington had a sense of occasion. He began by addressing his remarks to "Fellow-Citizens of the Senate and the House of Representatives." He was speaking to Congress, in that arched, octagonal room, but he invoked the people. "The preservation of the sacred fire of liberty, and the destiny of the Republican model of Government," Washington said, are "staked on the experiment entrusted to the hands of the American people."[64]

Nearly everything Washington did set a precedent. What would have happened if he had decided, before taking that oath of office, to emancipate his slaves? He'd grown disillusioned with slavery; his own slaves, and the greater number of slaves owned by his wife, were, to him, a moral burden, and he understood very well that for all the wealth generated by forced, unpaid labor, the institution of slavery was a moral burden to the nation. There is some evidence—slight though it is—that Washington drafted a statement announcing that he intended to emancipate his slaves before assuming the presidency. (Or maybe that statement, like Washington's inaugural address, had been written by Hamilton, a member of New York's Manumission Society.) This, too, Washington understood, would have established a precedent: every president after him would have had to emancipate his slaves. And yet he would not, could not, do it.[65] Few of Washington's decisions would have such lasting and terrible consequences as this one failure to act.

THE CONSTITUTION DOESN'T say much about the duties of the president. "The President shall be Commander in Chief of the Army and Navy of the United States," according to Article II, Section 2, and "he may require the Opinion, in writing, of the principal Officer in each of the executive Departments, upon any Subject relating to the Duties of their respective Offices." But the Constitution doesn't call for a cabinet. Nevertheless, the first Congress established several departments, to which Washington appointed secretaries: the Department of State, headed by Jefferson; the Department of the Treasury, headed by Hamilton, and the Department of War, headed by Henry Knox.

Congress's most pressing order of business was drafting a bill of rights. Madison, having prepared a bill "to make the Constitution better in the opinion of those who are opposed to it," presented a list of twelve amendments to the House on June 8. He had wanted the amendments written into the constitution, each in its proper place, but instead they were added at the end.[66]

While Madison's proposed amendments were debated and revised, Congress tackled the question of the national judiciary. Article III, Section 1, decrees that "The judicial Power of the United States, shall be vested in one supreme Court," but the details were left to Congress. On September 24, 1789, Washington signed the Judiciary Act, which established the number of justices, six; defined the authority of the court, which was narrow; and created the office of attorney general, to which Washington appointed Edmund Randolph.

Under the Constitution, the power of the Supreme Court is quite limited. The executive branch holds the sword, Hamilton had written in Federalist 78, and the legislative branch the purse. "The judiciary, on the contrary, has no influence over either the sword or the purse; no direction either of the strength or of the wealth of the society; and can take no active resolution whatever." All judges can do is judge. "The judiciary is beyond comparison the weakest of the three departments of powers,"

Hamilton concluded, citing, in a footnote, Montesquieu: "Of the three powers above mentioned, the judiciary is next to nothing."[67]

The Supreme Court had no rooms in Federal Hall. Instead, it met—when it met—in a drafty room on the second floor of an old stone building called the Merchants' Exchange, at the corner of Broad and Water Streets. The ground floor, an arcade, served as a stock exchange. Lectures and concerts were held upstairs. On the first day the court was called to session, only three justices showed up, and so, lacking a quorum, court was adjourned.[68]

The day after Washington signed the Judiciary Act, Congress sent Madison's twelve constitutional amendments to the states for ratification. Meanwhile, Congress took up other business, and was immediately confronted with the question of slavery. On February 11, 1790, a group of Quakers presented two petitions, one from Philadelphia and one from New York, urging Congress to end the importation of slaves and to gradually emancipate those already held. In the octagonal room in Federal Hall, after representatives from Georgia and South Carolina rose to condemn the petitions, Madison moved to put the petitions to a committee. The next day, Congress received a petition from the Pennsylvania Abolition Society urging Congress to "take such measures in their wisdom, as the powers with which they are invested will authorize, for promoting the abolition of slavery, and discouraging every species of traffic in slaves"; its signatories included Benjamin Franklin.

After several hours of debate—before spectators in the galleries—Congress voted 43 to 11 to refer all three petitions to a committee (seven of the eleven "no" votes came from Georgia and South Carolina). On March 8, the day scheduled for the committee report, southern delegates succeeded in delaying it. James Jackson of Georgia gave a two-hour speech, in which he said that the Constitution was a "sacred compact," and William Loughton Smith of South Carolina spoke for another two hours, opposing emancipation by insisting that if blacks were free they would marry whites, "the white race would be extinct, and the American people would be all of the mulatto breed."[69]

Not so many miles away from New York, men, women, and children who had once been owned by some of the people who were engaged in this debate were engaged in a debate of their own. Harry Washington, who had left New York for Halifax in 1783, wondered whether he ought to move his family to a new colony, in West Africa. The first expedition to Sierra Leone had sailed from London in May of 1787, just as the delegates to the constitutional convention were straggling into Philadelphia. As some four hundred emigrants prepared to sail, the African-born writer and former slave Quobna Ottobah Cugoano had warned them that "they had better swim to shore, if they can, to preserve their lives and liberties in Britain, than to hazard themselves at sea . . . and the peril of settling at Sierra Leone." They sailed all the same. Across the Atlantic, they'd founded a capital and elected as their governor a runaway slave and Revolutionary War veteran from Philadelphia named Richard Weaver. Five months later, plagued by disease and famine, 122 of the settlers had died. Even worse, and exactly as Cugoano had predicted, some were kidnapped and sold into slavery all over again. But for some, Sierra Leone was home. Frank Peters, kidnapped as a child, had spent most of his life as a field slave in South Carolina until he joined the British army in 1779. Two weeks after he arrived in Sierra Leone, at the age of twenty-nine, an old woman found him, held him, and pressed him close: she was his mother.[70]

Harry Washington decided, in the end, to join nearly twelve hundred black refugees from the United States who boarded fifteen ships in Halifax Harbor, bound for the west coast of Africa, along with black preachers Moses Wilkinson and David George. Before the convoy left the harbor, each family was handed a certificate "indicating the plot of land 'free of expence' they were to be given 'upon arrival in Africa.'" But when Washington reached Sierra Leone, he found that the colony's new capital, Freetown, was plagued by disease and weighed down by a poverty enforced by exorbitant rents. "We wance did call it Free Town," Wilkinson complained bitterly, but "we have a reason to call it a town of slavery."[71]

In New York, a slave town, the congressional committee charged with responding to the antislavery petitions finally presented its report. The Constitution forbade Congress from outlawing the slave trade until the year 1808 but provided for taxing imported goods, the committee reported, and that authority included the power to tax the slave trade heavily enough to discourage and even to end it. Madison, quiet of voice, stood to speak. He urged the committee to eliminate this allowance on revising the report. It had been a tiny window, the smallest of openings. Madison slammed it shut. The final report concluded, "Congress have no authority to interfere in the emancipation of slaves, or in the treatment of them within any of the States; it remaining with the several States alone to provide any regulations therein, which humanity and true policy may require." A resolution to accept the report passed 29 to 25, along sectional lines. It effectively tabled the question of slavery until 1808.[72]

Franklin, from his deathbed, attempted to protest. Earlier, he'd tried to reassure his sister, "As to the Pain I suffer, about which you make yourself so unhappy, it is, when compar'd with the long life I have enjoy'd of Health and Ease, but a Trifle."[73] But this was the merest dissembling. He was in agony. Writing in the *Pennsylvania Gazette*, he offered an attack on slavery, signing his essay "Historicus"—the voice of history.[74]

He died two weeks later. He was the only man to have signed the Declaration of Independence, the Treaty of Paris, and the Constitution. His last public act was to urge abolition. Congress would not hear of it.


THE DIVIDE OVER slavery, which had nearly prevented the forming of the Union, would eventually split the nation in two. There were other fractures, too, deep and lasting. The divide between Federalists and Anti-Federalists didn't end with the ratification of the Constitution. Nor did it end with the ratification of the Bill of Rights. On December 15, 1791, ten of the twelve amendments drafted by Madison were approved by the necessary three-quarters of the states; these became the Bill of Rights. They would become the subject of ceaseless contention.

The Bill of Rights is a list of the powers Congress does not have. The First Amendment reads, "Congress shall make no law respecting an establishment of religion, or prohibiting the free exercise thereof; or abridging the freedom of speech, or of the press; or the right of the people peaceably to assemble, and to petition the Government for a redress of grievances." Its tenets derive from earlier texts, including Madison's 1785 "Memorial Remonstrance against Religious Assessments" ("The Religion then of every man must be left to the conviction and conscience of every man"), Jefferson's 1786 Statute for Religious Freedom ("our civil rights have no dependence on our religious opinions any more than our opinions in physics or geometry"), and Article VI of the Constitution ("no religious test shall ever be required as a qualification to any office or public trust under the United States").[75]

Yet the rights established in the Bill of Rights were also extraordinary. Nearly every English colony in North America had been settled with an established religion; Connecticut's 1639 charter explained that the whole purpose of government was "to mayntayne and presearve the liberty and purity of the gospel of our Lord Jesus." In the century and a half between the Connecticut charter and the 1787 meeting of the constitutional convention lies an entire revolution—not just a political revolution but also a religious revolution. So far from establishing a religion, the Constitution doesn't even mention "God," except in naming the date ("the year of our Lord . . ."). At a time when all but two states required religious tests for office, the Constitution prohibited them. At a time when all but three states still had an official religion, the Bill of Rights forbade the federal government from establishing one. Most Americans believed, with Madison, that religion can only thrive if it is no part of government, and that a free government can only thrive if it is no part of religion.[76]

With the ratification of the Bill of Rights, new disputes emerged. Much of American political history is a disagreement between those who favor a strong federal government and those who favor the states. During Washington's first term, this dispute took the form of a debate over the economic plan put forward by Hamilton. Much of this debate concerned debt. First stood private debt. The depression that followed the war had left many Americans insolvent. There were so many men confined to debtors' prison in Philadelphia that they printed their own newspaper: *Forlorn Hope*.[77] Second stood the debts incurred by the states during the war. And third stood the debts incurred by the Continental Congress. Until these government debts were paid, the United States would have no lenders and no foreign investors and would be effectively unable to participate in world trade.

Hamilton proposed that the federal government not only pay off the debts incurred by the Continental Congress but also assume responsibility for the debts incurred by the states. To this end, he urged the establishment of a national bank, like the Bank of England, whose benefits would include stabilizing a national paper currency. Congress passed a bill establishing the Bank of the United States, for a term of twenty years, in February 1790. Before signing the bill into law, Washington consulted with Jefferson, who advised the president that Hamilton's plan was unconstitutional because it violated the all-purpose Tenth Amendment, which reads: "The powers not delegated to the United States by the Constitution, nor prohibited by it to the States, are reserved to the States respectively, or to the people." The Constitution does not specifically grant to Congress the power to establish a national bank, and, since the Tenth Amendment says that all powers not granted to Congress are held by either the states or by the people, Congress cannot establish a national bank. Washington signed anyway, establishing a precedent for interpreting the Constitution broadly, rather than narrowly, by agreeing with Hamilton's argument that establishing a national bank fell under the Constitution's Article I, Section 8, granting to Congress the power "To make all Laws which shall be necessary and proper," the very opposite of how Congress had interpreted its power to tax the slave trade.

Other elements of Hamilton's plan raised other objections. States that had already paid off their war debts, like Virginia and Maryland, objected to the federal government's assumption of state debt, since federal taxes levied in Virginia and Maryland would now be used to pay a burden incurred by states that had not yet paid their debts, like South Carolina and Massachusetts. The idea that this plan was unconstitutional, Hamilton believed, was "the first symptom of a spirit which must either be killed or will kill the constitution of the United States." Hamilton brokered a deal. Southerners were also averse to Hamilton's economic plan because it emphasized manufacturing over agriculture and therefore seemed disadvantageous to the southern states. Also on the congressional agenda was where to locate the nation's capital. The First Congress met for its first two sessions in New York and for its second two sessions in Philadelphia. The Continental Congress had also met in Baltimore and Princeton, and in half a dozen other places. Where it and the other branches of the federal government should permanently meet was a vexing question, given the sectional tensions that had plagued the Union from the start. In a deal worked out with Madison over dinner at Jefferson's rooms on Maiden Lane, in New York—and known as the "dinner table bargain"—Hamilton threw his support behind a plan to locate the nation's capital in the

South, in exchange for Madison's support and the support of his fellow southerners for Hamilton's plan for the federal government to assume the states' debts. In July 1790, Congress passed Hamilton's assumption plan, and voted to establish the nation's capital on a ten-mile square stretch of riverland along the Potomac River, in what was then Virginia and Maryland, and to found, as mandated in the Constitution, a federal district. It would be called Washington.[78]

Hamilton believed that the future of the United States lay in manufacturing, freeing Americans of their dependence on imported goods, and spurring economic growth. To that end, his plan included raising the tariff—taxes on imported goods—and providing federal government support to domestic manufacturers and merchants. Congress experimented, briefly, with domestic duties (including taxes on carriages, whiskey, and stamps). Before the Civil War, however, the federal government raised revenue and regulated commerce almost exclusively through tariffs, which, unlike direct taxes, skirted the question of slavery and were therefore significantly less controversial. Also, tariffs appeared to place the burden of taxation on merchants, which appealed to Jefferson. "We are all the more reconciled to the tax on importations," Jefferson explained, "because it falls exclusively on the rich." The promise of America, Jefferson thought, was that "the farmer will see his government supported, his children educated, and the face of his country made a paradise by the contributions of the rich alone."[79]

But Hamilton's critics, Jefferson chief among them, charged that Hamilton's economic plan would promote speculation, which, indeed, it did. To Hamilton, speculation was necessary for economic growth; to Jefferson, it was corrupting of republican virtue. This matter came to a head in 1792, when speculation led to the first financial panic in the new nation's history.

As with so many financial crises, the story began with ambition and ended with corruption. Hamilton had been befriended by John Pintard, an importer with offices at 12 Wall Street. Pintard had been elected to the state legislature in 1790; the next year, he'd become a partner of Leonard Bleecker, who happened to be the secretary of New York's Society for the Relief of Distressed Debtors: together, they auctioned stock. After Bleecker dissolved their partnership, Pintard began dealing with Hamilton's assistant secretary of the Treasury, William Duer, a rogue who had the idea of cornering stock in the Bank of the United States. With Pintard acting as his agent, Duer borrowed the life savings of "shopkeepers, widows, orphans, Butchers, Carmen, Gardners, market women." In 1792, when it became clear that over a million dollars' worth of bank notes, signed by Pintard, weren't worth the paper on which they were printed, Duer and Pintard's insolvency triggered the nation's first stock market crash. A mob attempted to stone Duer to death and then chased him to debtors' prison. Pintard hid in his Manhattan town house. "Would it not be prudent for him to remove to a State where there is a Bankrupt Act?" one friend wondered.[80] Pintard fled across the river to New Jersey, where he was eventually found, and sent to debtors' prison.

Even the most eminent of men could not escape confinement for debt. James Wilson, the most democratic delegate to the constitutional convention, and now a Supreme Court justice, fell so badly into debt that he was afraid to ride circuit, for fear of being captured by his creditors and clapped in chains. (He owed nearly $200,000 to Pierce Butler, who'd been a South Carolina delegate to the constitutional convention.) In 1797, Wilson joined Pintard in debtors' prison in New Jersey, and, although he managed to get out by borrowing $300 from one of his sons, he was thrown into another debtors' prison, in North Carolina, the next year, where his wife found him in ragged, stained clothes. He soon contracted malaria. Only fifty-six years old, he died of a stroke, raving, deliriously, about his debts.[81]

Hamilton determined that the United States should have unshakable credit. The nation's debts would be honored: private debt could be forgiven. In the new republic, individual debts—the debts of people who took risks—could be discharged. Pintard got out of debtors' prison by availing himself of a 1798 New Jersey insolvency law; later, he filed for bankruptcy under the terms of the first U.S. bankruptcy law, passed in 1800.[82] He was legally relieved of the obligation ever to repay his debts, his ledger erased. The replacement of debtors' prison with bankruptcy protection would change the nature of the American economy, spurring investment, speculation, and the taking of risks.

The Panic of 1792 had this effect, too: it led New York brokers to sign an agreement banning private bidding on stocks, so that no one, ever again, could do what Duer had done; that agreement marks the founding of what would become the New York Stock Exchange.

# IV.

"IT IS AN AGE of revolutions, in which everything may be looked for," Thomas Paine wrote from England in 1791, in the first part of *Rights of Man*. He soon fled England for France, where he wrote the second part. "Where liberty is, there is my country," Franklin once said, to which Paine is supposed to have replied, "Wherever liberty is not, there is *my* country."[83] The one country where Paine didn't try to rile up revolution was Haiti. It was an age of revolutions, but Paine wasn't looking for a slave rebellion.

Haiti, then known as Saint-Domingue, was the largest colony in the Caribbean, and the richest. France's most vital colony, its population consisted of 40,000 whites, 28,000 free people of color, and 452,000 slaves—half the slave population of the entire Caribbean. The world's leading producer of sugar and coffee, the island exported nearly as much sugar as Jamaica, Cuba, and Brazil combined.[84] Its revolution began in 1791.

The events that unfolded in Haiti followed France's own, tortured revolution, begun in the spring of 1789. Members of a special legislature called in response to France's own difficulties with war debt defied the king, formed themselves into a National Assembly, abolished the privileges of the aristocracy, and set about drafting a constitution. In August, Lafayette introduced into the assembly a Declaration of the Rights of Man and of the Citizen. Article I read, "Men are born and remain free and equal in rights."[85]

Paine was in Paris during the Reign of Terror, when Louis XVI was beheaded. Paine himself was arrested. He wrote most of the second part of *The Age of Reason* from a cell while the prison's inmates went daily to their deaths. In six weeks in the summer of 1794, more than thirteen hundred people were executed.[86]

The French Revolution had gone too far, a revolution that never stopped. But, though it terrified Americans, it held for most Americans not half the fear that was inspired by the revolution in Haiti in 1791, where hundreds of thousands of slaves cast off their chains. They were

*Federalists and Anti-Federalists had different
reactions to the Haitian revolution.*

led at first by a man named Boukman and, after Boukman's death, by an
ex-slave named Toussaint Louverture. Their slave rebellion was a war for
independence, the second in the Western world.

American owners of slaves were terrified by the events unfolding in
Haiti—their darkest fears realized. But to some radicals in New England,
the Haitian revolution was the inevitable next step in the progress of the
freedom of man. Abraham Bishop, a Connecticut Jeffersonian, was one of
a handful of Americans to welcome the revolution. "If Freedom depends
upon colour, and if the Blacks were born for slaves, those in the West-
India islands may be called Insurgents and Murderers," Bishop observed,
in a series of essays called "The Rights of Black Men," published in Boston. "But the enlightened mind of Americans will not receive such ideas,"
Bishop went on. "We believe that Freedom is the natural right of all rational beings, and we know that the Blacks have never voluntarily resigned
that freedom. Then is not their cause as just as ours?"

The answer his fellow Americans gave was a resounding no. Instead,
American newspapers reported on the Haitian revolution as a kind of
madness, a killing frenzy. "Nothing can be more distressing than the
situation of the inhabitants, as their slaves have been called into action,
and are a terrible engine, absolutely ungovernable," Jefferson wrote. So
far from extending statements about the equality of "all men" to all men,
white or black, the revolution on Saint-Domingue convinced many white

Americans of the reverse. Between 1791 and 1793, the United States sold arms and ammunition and gave hundreds of thousands of dollars in aid to the French planters on the island.[87] Federalists tended to be more worried about France than about Haiti. Republicans, especially southerners, were worried about a spreading revolution. Jefferson, calling the Haitians "cannibals," warned Madison, "If this combustion can be introduced among us under any veil whatever, we have to fear it."[88]

With the frightening specters of France and Haiti in mind, Americans worried about their own republic, a land of liberty and slavery. Madison had promised that the Constitution would insure its stability. A democracy, in which the people "assemble and administer the government in person," will always be subject to endless "turbulence and contention," he argued, but a republic, in which the people elect representatives to do the work of governing, can steer clear of that fate by electing men who will always put the public good before narrow or partisan interests, the good of all above the good of any part or party. Earlier political thinkers had suggested that this system could only work if a republic were small. Madison argued that it could only work if a republic were large, for two reasons. First, in a large republic, there would be more men to choose from, and so a better chance, purely as a matter of numbers, for the people to elect men who will guard the public interest. Second, in a large republic, candidates for office, in order to be known and to appeal to so large a number of voters, would need to be both notable and worthy.[89]

Yet the Constitution did not hold factions in check, and as early as 1791, Madison had begun to revise his thinking. In an essay called "Public Opinion," he considered a source of instability particular to a large republic: the people might be deceived. "The larger a country, the less easy for its real opinion to be ascertained," he explained. That is, factions might not, in the end, consist of wise, knowledgeable, and reasonable men. They might consist of passionate, ignorant, and irrational men, who had been led to hold "counterfeit" opinions by persuasive men. (Madison was thinking of Hamilton and his ability to gain public support for his financial plan.) The way out of this political maze was the newspaper. "A circulation of newspapers through the entire body of the people," he explained, "is equivalent to a contraction of territorial limits." Newspapers would make the country, effectively, smaller.[90]

It was an ingenious idea. It would be revisited by each passing generation of exasperated advocates of republicanism. The newspaper would hold the Republic together; the telegraph would hold the Republic together; the radio would hold the Republic together; the Internet would hold the Republic together. Each time, this assertion would be both right and terribly wrong.

But Madison was shrewd to sense the importance of the relationship between technologies of communication and the forming of public opinion. The American two-party system, the nation's enduring source of political stability, was forged in—and, fair to say, created by—the nation's newspapers. Newspapers had shaped the ratification debate between Federalists and Anti-Federalists, and by 1791 newspapers were already beginning to shape the first party system, a contest between Federalists and those who aligned themselves with a newly emerging opposition: the Democratic-Republican Party, more usually known as Jeffersonians or Republicans. Jefferson and Madison, who founded the Democratic-Republican Party, believed that the fate of the Republic rested in the hands of farmers; Hamilton and the Federalist Party believed that the fate of the Republic rested in the development of industry. Each party boasted its own newspapers. In the 1790s, while Federalists battled Jeffersonian Republicans, newspapers grew four times as fast as the population.[91]

Newspapers in the early republic weren't incidentally or inadvertently partisan; they were entirely and enthusiastically partisan. They weren't especially interested in establishing facts; they were interested in staging a battle of opinions. "Professions of impartiality I shall make none," wrote a Federalist printer. "They are always useless, and are besides perfect nonsense."[92] The printer of the *Connecticut Bee* promised to publish news

*Of turns of fortune, changes in the state,*
*The fall of fav'rites, projects of the great,*
*Of old mismanagements, taxations new,*
*All neither wholly false, nor wholly true.*[93]

Once much maligned as destructive of public life, parties, driven by newspapers, became its machinery. "The engine," said Jefferson, "is the press."[94]

In September of 1796, readers of newspapers found out that George Washington, sixty-four, would not run for a third term. It was an astonishing act, an abdication of power not unlike his retirement from the military after the war, and possibly the most important act of his presidency. He knew it would set a precedent, that no president should rule forever, or even for very long. By way of farewell, he addressed a letter to the American people, a speech never delivered, but instead published in newspapers across the country.

Madison had first drafted the letter of abdication in 1792, the first time that Washington had wanted to step down. But he'd been convinced to serve a second term in hopes of uniting the Federalist and Republican factions. Revised by Hamilton, the letter became known as Washington's Farewell Address. It appeared, first, on page two of a Philadelphia newspaper. Addressed "To the PEOPLE of the United States"; signed "G. Washington."

Washington's Farewell Address consists of a series of warnings about the danger of disunion. The North and the South, the East and the West, ought not to consider their interests separate or competing, Washington urged: "your union ought to be considered as a main prop of your liberty." Parties, he warned, were the "worst enemy" of every government, agitating "the community with ill-founded jealousies and false alarms," kindling "the animosity of one part against another," and even fomenting "riot and insurrection." As to the size of the Republic, "Is there a doubt whether a common government can embrace so large a sphere? Let experience solve it." The American experiment must go on. But it could only thrive if the citizens were supported by religion and morality, and if they were well educated. "Promote, then, as an object of primary importance, institutions for the general diffusion of knowledge," he urged. "In proportion as the structure of a government gives force to public opinion, it is essential that public opinion should be enlightened." [95]

There is something heartbreaking in Washington's Farewell Address, with its faith in reason, experience, and truth. Washington delivered his letter to the People of the United States in much the same spirit as Madison had urged and helped draft the Constitution itself. Washington hoped, he said, that Americans might "control the usual current of the passions." "Passion" or variants of the word appear seven times in the Farewell; it is the source of every problem; reason is its only remedy. Passion is a river. There would be no changing its course. Nor was George Washington free from its force.

As George and Martha Washington prepared to leave the capital for

Virginia, their slaves made different arrangements. Their enslaved cook, Hercules, escaped to New York, and Martha Washington's twenty-two-year-old slave seamstress, Ona Judge, escaped by ship to New Hampshire. Judge had learned that Martha Washington intended to give her as a wedding gift to her granddaughter. George Washington sent a slave catcher after her, but when the agent found the seamstress he reported that "popular opinion here is in favor of universal freedom," and it would create a spectacle if he were to seize her. Judge sent word to Washington that she would return to Mount Vernon only if granted her freedom, since she would "rather suffer death than return to slavery." Washington refused, on the ground that it would set a "dangerous precedent."[96] What to do about slavery, and precedent, weighed heavily on his mind, and on his conscience.

On December 12, 1799, after riding his horse through snow that turned to rain, Washington fell ill. Two days later, at four o'clock in the afternoon, in his bedchamber on the second floor of his mansion at Mount Vernon, as he lay dying, he asked his wife, Martha, to bring him two different wills that he had left on his desk. He read them over slowly and carefully and then asked her to burn one of them. Later that day, he breathed his last, surrounded by his wife, his doctor, his secretary, and four of his slaves: Caroline and Molly, housemaids; Christopher, a manservant; and Charlotte; a seamstress. When Washington died, the black people in that room outnumbered the white people.

During his second term, Washington had written to his secretary that he wished "to liberate a species of property which I possess, very repugnantly to my own feelings." He had arranged for this to be done, but only after his death. In the will that he did not have his wife burn—a second will that he had prepared only that summer—he had written: "Upon the decease of my wife . . . all the Slaves which I hold in my own right shall receive their freedom."

There were more than three hundred people enslaved at Mount Vernon; Washington owned 123; the rest were his wife's. Washington's will was published in newspapers from Maine to Georgia, as he knew it would be. Everyone at Mount Vernon knew the terms of his will. His 123 slaves would be freed only upon Martha Washington's death. His wife, understandably, feared she might be murdered.[97]

Harry Washington, who had once been Washington's property, might

*An 1800 print commemorating the life of Washington pictures him holding "The American Constitution," a tablet etched in stone.*

Washington giving the Laws to America.

have heard the news of his death, an ocean away, in another unruly republic. About half of Sierra Leone's black settlers rebelled against the colony's tyrannical government, said to be "as thorough Jacobins as if they had been trained and educated in Paris." In 1799, a group of revolutionaries led by Harry Washington tried to declare independence. The rebellion was swiftly put down, its instigators banished. Months after George Washington died at Mount Vernon, the exiled rebels of Sierra Leone elected, as their leader, Harry Washington.[98]

At George Washington's death, the nation fell into mourning, in a torrent of passion. People preached and prayed; they dressed in black and wept. Shops were closed. Funeral orations were delivered. "Mourn, O, Columbia!" declared a newspaper in Baltimore. The Farewell Address was printed and reprinted, read and reread, stitched, even, into pillows.

"Let it be written in characters of gold and hung up in every house," one edition of the Address urged. "Let it be engraven on tables of brass and marble and, like the sacred Law of Moses, be placed in every Church and Hall and Senate Chamber."

Let it be written. Americans read their Washington. And they looked at him, in prints and portraits. One popular print, *Washington Giving the Laws to America*, showed the archangel Gabriel in the heavens carrying an American emblem while Washington, dressed in a Roman toga and seated among the gods, holds a stylus in one hand and, in his other hand, a stone tablet engraved with the words "The American Constitution."[99] It was as if the Constitution had been handed down from the heavens, tablets etched out of stone, sacred and infallible, from God to the first American president. Where were the centuries of ideas and decades of struggle? What of the hardscrabble American people and their fiercely fought debates? What of the near fisticuffs over ratification? What of the feuds and the failures and the compromises, the trials of facts, the battles between reason and passion?

In the quiet of a room in a house not too far away, James Madison pulled out of a cabinet the notes he had taken down, day after day, at the constitutional convention, that sweltering summer in Philadelphia. He read over them and wondered at them, and then he settled to the work of revision, word by word. He puttered away, in secret, page after page. In his desk, he kept safe, for another day, the story of how the Constitution had been written, and of its fateful compromises.

# Part Two

# THE
# PEOPLE

★ ★ ★ ★

## 1800–1865

*They said, some men are too ignorant, and vicious,
to share in government. Possibly so, said we; and,
by your system, you would always keep them ignorant,
and vicious. We proposed to give all a chance; and we
expected the weak to grow stronger, the ignorant, wiser;
and all better, and happier together. We made the
experiment; and the fruit is before us.*

—Abraham Lincoln,
"Fragments on Government,"
1854

*Five*

# A DEMOCRACY OF NUMBERS

*Philadelphians of all ranks celebrate the Fourth of July
in 1812 in this watercolor by John Lewis
Krimmel, a German immigrant.*

I N 1787, WHILE FEDERALISTS AND ANTI-FEDERALISTS were fighting over the proposed Constitution in the mottled pages of American newspapers and on the creaky floors of convention halls, John Adams, minister to Britain, grumbled at his desk in Grosvenor Square, London, while Thomas Jefferson, minister to France, leaned over a desk of his own, undoubtedly fancier, at the Hôtel de Langeac on Paris's Champs-Elysées. Far from home, the two men who had together crafted the Declaration of Independence staged an epistolary debate about the Constitution, exchanging letters across the English Channel, as if they were holding a two-man ratifying convention, Adams worrying that the Constitution gave the legislature too much power, Jefferson fearing the same about the presidency. "You are afraid of the one—I, of the few," Adams wrote Jefferson. "You are Apprehensive of Monarchy; I, of Aristocracy." Both men agonized about elections, Jefferson fearing there would be too few, Adams that there would be too many. "Elections, my dear sir," Adams wrote, "I look at with terror."[1]

The debate between Adams and Jefferson hadn't ended after the Constitution was ratified. It hadn't ended after Washington was elected in 1788, or during his administration, when Adams served as his vice president, and Jefferson as his secretary of state, and it hadn't ended after Washington was elected again in 1792. Instead, in 1796, their debate helped establish the nation's first stable political parties.

Jefferson had been worried that the Constitution allowed for a president to serve again and again, till his death, like a king. Adams liked that idea. "So much the better," he'd written in 1787.[2] In 1796, when Washington announced that he wouldn't run for a third term, Adams and Jefferson each sought to replace him. Adams narrowly won. The two men next faced off in an election Jefferson called "the revolution of 1800." Whether or not it was a revolution, the election of 1800, the climax of a decades-long debate between Adams and Jefferson, led to a constitutional crisis. The Constitution hadn't provided for parties, and the method of electing the president could not accommodate them. Nevertheless, Adams ran as a Federalist and Jefferson as a Republican, which meant that, whatever the results of the voting, no one was quite sure of the outcome, especially after the two men received an equal number of votes in the Electoral College, a tie that, under the terms of the Constitution, was to be broken by a vote in the House of Representatives.

Jefferson heard rumors that if he won, Federalists would "break the Union"; he believed they hoped to change the law to allow for Adams to serve for life. "The enemies of our Constitution are preparing a fearful operation," he warned. Meanwhile, Alexander Hamilton sounded an alarm that if Adams were to be reelected, Virginians would "resort to the employment of physical force" to keep Federalists out of office. It was even said that some Federalists in Congress had decided they'd "go with-out a Constitution and take the risk of a civil war" rather than elect Jefferson. "Who is to be president?" asked one troubled congressman, and "what is to become of our government?"[3]

The ongoing argument between Adams and Jefferson was at once a rivalry between two ambitious men, bitter and petty, and a dispute about the nature of the American experiment, philosophical and weighty. In 1800, Adams was sixty-four and even more disputatious, vain, and learned than he'd been as a younger man. A founder of the American Academy of Arts and Sciences, he'd written a ponderous, three-volume *Defense of the Constitutions of Government of the United States*, explaining the fragile balance between an aristocracy of the rich and a democracy of the poor, a balance that could only be struck by a well-engineered constitution. "In every society where property exists, there will ever be a struggle between rich and poor," he wrote. "Mixed in one assembly, equal laws can never be expected. They will either be made by numbers, to plunder the few who are rich, or by influence, to fleece the many who are poor."[4]

Jefferson, fifty-seven, president of the American Philosophical Society, by turns moody and frantic, a searing writer, was no less learned, if far more inconsistent, than Adams. He placed his faith in the rule of the majority. The point of the American experiment, he believed, was "to shew by example the sufficiency of human reason for the care of human affairs and that the will of the majority, the Natural law of every society, is the only sure guardian of the rights of man."[5] Adams believed in restraining the will of the majority, Jefferson in submitting to it.

Both men subscribed to the Aristotelian notion that there exist three forms of government, that each could become corrupt, and that the perfect government was the one that best balanced them. Adams believed that the form of government most "susceptible of improvement" was a polity, and that such an improvement could be achieved—and the terrors of democracy avoided—if legislatures were to do a better job of representing the interests of the people by more exactly mirroring them. "The end to be aimed at, in the formation of a representative assembly, seems to be the sense of the people, the public voice," he wrote. "The perfection of the portrait consists in its likeness."[6]

Yet, for all Adams's talk of portraits and likenesses, the dispute between the two men turned not on art but on mathematics. Government by the people is, in the end, a math problem: Who votes? How much does each vote count?

Adams and Jefferson lived in an age of quantification. It began with the measurement of time. Time used to be a wheel that turned, and turned again; during the scientific revolution, time became a line. Time, the easiest quantity to measure, became the engine of every empirical inquiry: an axis, an arrow. This new use and understanding of time contributed to the idea of progress—if time is a line instead of a circle, things can get better and even better, instead of forever rising and falling in endless cycles, like the seasons. The idea of progress animated American independence and animated, too, the advance of capitalism. The quantification of time led to the quantification of everything else: the counting of people, the measurement of their labor, and the calculation of profit as a function of time. Keeping time and accumulating wealth earned a certain equivalency. "Time is money," Benjamin Franklin used to say.[7]

Quantification also altered the workings of politics. No matter their differences, Adams and Jefferson agreed that governments rest on mathematical relationships: equations and ratios. "Numbers, or property, or both, should be the rule," Adams insisted, "and the proportions of electors and members an affair of calculation."[8] Determining what that rule would be had been the work of the constitutional convention; fixing that rule would be the work of the election of 1800, and of the political reforms to follow, each another affair of calculation.

# I.

KINGS ARE BORN; presidents are elected. But how? In Philadelphia in 1787, James Wilson explained, the delegates had been "perplexed with no part of this plan so much as with the mode of choosing the President." At the convention, Wilson had proposed that the people elect the president directly. But James Madison had pointed out that since "the right of suffrage was much more diffusive in the Northern than the Southern States . . . the latter could have no influence in the election on the score of the Negroes." That is, in a direct election, the North, which had more voters, would have more votes. Wilson's proposal was defeated, 12 states to 1.[9] Some delegates to the convention had believed Congress should elect the president. This method, known as indirect election, allowed for popular participation in elections while steering clear of the "excesses of democracy"; it filtered the will of the many through the judgment of the few. The Senate, for instance, was elected indirectly: U.S. senators were chosen not by the people but by state legislatures (direct election of senators was not instituted until the ratification of the Seventeenth Amendment, in 1913). But, for the office of the presidency, indirect election presented a problem: having Congress choose the president violated the principle of the separation of powers.

Wilson had come up with another idea. If the people couldn't elect the president, and Congress couldn't elect the president, maybe some other body could elect the president. Wilson suggested that the people elect delegates to an Electoral College, a body of worthy men of means and reputation who would do the actual electing. This measure passed. But Wilson's compromise stood on the back of yet another compromise: the slave ratio. The number of delegates to the Electoral College would be determined not by a state's population but by the number of its representatives in the House. That is, the size of a state's representation in the Electoral College was determined by the rule of representation—one member of Congress for every forty thousand people, with people who were enslaved counting as three-fifths of other people.[10] The Electoral College was a concession to slave owners, an affair of both mathematical and political calculation.

These calculations required a census, which depended on the very new science of demography (a founding work, the first edition of Thomas Malthus's *Essay on the Principle of Population*, appeared in 1798). Article I, Section 2, of the Constitution calls for the population of the United States to be counted every ten years. Census takers were to count "the whole number of free Persons" and "all other Persons" but to exclude "Indians not taxed," meaning Indians who lived as independent peoples, even if they lived within territory claimed by the United States. This first federal census, conducted in 1790, counted 3.9 million people, including 700,000 slaves. The three-fifths clause not only granted slave-owning states a disproportionate representation in Congress but amplified their votes in the Electoral College. Virginia and Pennsylvania, for instance, had roughly equivalent free populations but, because of its slave population, Virginia had three more seats in the house and therefore six more electors in the Electoral College, with the result that, for thirty-two of the first thirty-six years of the Republic, the office of the president of the United States was occupied by a slave-owning Virginian, with John Adams the only exception.[11]

There remained still more contentious calculations. How delegates to the Electoral College would be chosen had been left to the states. In 1796, in seven out of sixteen states the people elected delegates; in the rest, state legislatures elected delegates. The original idea had been for delegates to use their own judgment in deciding how to cast their votes in the Electoral College, although they hadn't had to make much of a decision in 1788 and 1792, since Washington ran unopposed. But by 1796, two political parties having emerged and a decision needing to be made, party leaders had come to believe that delegates ought to do the bidding of the men who elected them. One Federalist complained that he hadn't chosen his elector "to determine for me whether John Adams or Thomas Jefferson is the fittest man for President of these United States . . . No, I chose him to act, not to think."[12]

This ambiguity had resulted in a botched election. Under the Constitution, the candidate with the most Electoral College votes becomes president; the candidate who comes in second becomes vice president. In 1796, Federalists wanted Adams as president and Thomas Pinckney as vice president. But in the Electoral College, Adams got seventy-one votes, Jefferson sixty-eight, and Pinckney only fifty-nine. Federalist electors had been instructed to cast the second of their two votes for Pinckney; instead, many had cast it for Jefferson. Jefferson therefore became Adams's vice president, to the disappointment of everyone.

During Adams's stormy administration, the distance between the two parties widened. Weakened by the weight of his own pride and not content with issuing warnings about the danger of parties, Adams attempted to outlaw the opposition. In 1798, while the United States was engaged in an undeclared war with France, Congress passed the Alien and Sedition Acts, granting to the president the power to imprison noncitizens he deemed dangerous and to punish printers who opposed his administration: twenty-five people were arrested for sedition, fifteen indicted, and ten convicted; that ten included seven Republican printers who supported Jefferson.[13] Jefferson and Madison believed that the Alien and Sedition laws violated the Constitution. If a president overreaches his authority, if Congress passes unconstitutional laws, what can states do? The Constitution does not grant the Supreme Court the authority to decide on the constitutionality of laws passed by Congress; that's a power that the court decided to exercise on its own, but, in 1798, it hadn't tried yet. Meanwhile, Jefferson and Madison and other Republicans came up with another form of judicial review: they argued that the states could decide on the constitutionality of federal laws. They wrote resolutions objecting to the Alien and Sedition Acts. Madison wrote a resolution for Virginia; Jefferson wrote one for Kentucky. "Unless arrested on the threshold," Jefferson warned, the Alien and Sedition laws would drive the states "into revolution and blood, and will furnish new calumnies against republican government, and new pretexts for those who wish it to be believed that man cannot be governed but by a rod of iron."[14]

The widening divide between the parties also marked a hardening of views on slavery. During the Haitian revolution, Jefferson, favoring France, wanted, at most, a remote relationship with an island of freed slaves. But the Adams administration, favoring England, wanted to renew trade with the Caribbean island and even to recognize its independence. "Nothing is more clear than, if left to themselves, that the Blacks of St Domingo will be incomparably less dangerous than if they remain the subjects of France," Timothy Pickering, Adams's secretary of state, wrote in 1799. Meanwhile, Africans in America found inspiration in news of events in Haiti. In the summer of 1800, a blacksmith named Gabriel, who became known as "the American Toussaint," led a slave rebellion in Virginia, marching under the slogan "Death or Liberty." The rebellion failed. Gabriel and twenty-six of his followers were tried and executed. Opponents of slavery predicted that Gabriel's rebellion would not be the last. "Tho Gabriel dies, a host remains," warned Timothy Dwight, the president of Yale. "Oppresse'd with slavery's galling chain."[15]

Jefferson believed that the election of 1800 would "fix our national character" and "determine whether republicanism or aristocracy would prevail." It did, in any event, establish a number of conventions of American politics, including the party caucus and a no-holds-barred style of political campaigning. Early in the year, Federalists and Republicans in Congress, keen to avoid a repetition of the confusion of 1796, held a meeting to decide on their party's presidential nominee. They called this meeting a "caucus." (The word is an Americanism; it comes from an Algonquian

*An election of 1800 campaign banner for Thomas Jefferson promised "John Adams No More."*

word for "adviser.") The Republicans settled on Jefferson, the Federalists on Adams, although Alexander Hamilton tried to convince Federalists to abandon Adams and instead throw their support behind his running mate, Charles Cotesworth Pinckney of South Carolina. "Great and intrinsic defects in his character unfit him for the office of chief magistrate," Hamilton wrote of Adams, citing "the unfortunate foibles of a vanity without bounds, and a jealousy capable of discoloring every object."[16] Adams held on to the nomination only by the grip of his talons.

The candidates themselves did not campaign; Americans deemed a candidate's addressing the people directly a form of demagoguery. When Adams made a detour while traveling from Massachusetts to Washington, a Republican newspaper editor demanded, "Why must the President go fifty miles out of his way to make a trip to Washington?" But the lack of participation of the candidates themselves by no means quieted the campaigning, which chiefly took place in the nation's newspapers. Voters argued in taverns and fields, and even by the side of the road, having the kind of conversations that the *Carolina Gazette* attempted to capture by printing "A DIALOGUE Between a *FEDERALIST* and a *REPUBLICAN*":

REPUBLICAN. Good morrow, Mr. Federalist; 'tis pleasant weather;
what is the news of the day? How are elections going, and who is
likely to be our president?

FEDERALIST. For my part I would rather vote for any other man in
the country, than Mr. Jefferson.

REPUBLICAN. And why this prejudice against Mr. Jefferson, I pray
you?

FEDERALIST. I do not like the man, nor his principles, from what
I have heard of him. First, because he holds not implicit faith
in the Christian Religion; 2dly, because I fear he is too great an
advocate for French principles and politics; and lastly, because I
understand he is violently prejudiced against every thing that is
of British connection.

They argue on. "What have you or anyone to do with Mr. J.'s religious
principles?" the Republican asks, after which their debate nearly ends in
fisticuffs.[17]

Republicans attacked Adams for abuses of office. Federalists attacked
Jefferson for his slaveholding— Americans will not "learn the principles
of liberty from the slave-holders of Virginia," cried one—and especially
for his views on religion. In *Notes on the State of Virginia*, Jefferson had
stated his commitment to religious toleration. "It does me no injury for my
neighbor to say there are twenty gods or no god," he'd written. "It neither
picks my pocket nor breaks my leg." From their pulpits, Federalist clergymen preached that such an opinion could lead to nothing but unchecked
vice, crime, and depravity. One New York minister answered Jefferson:
"Let my neighbor once perceive himself that there is no God, and he
will soon pick my pocket and break not only my *leg* but my *neck.*" And a
Federalist newspaper, *Gazette of the United States*, insisted that the election offered Americans a choice between "GOD—AND A RELIGIOUS
PRESIDENT" and "JEFFERSON—AND NO GOD!!!!"[18]

Republicans answered Federalist hyperbole with still more hyperbole.
In 1799, Federalists had unsuccessfully pursued the Philadelphia printer
William Duane for sedition. In 1800, Duane printed in his newspaper, the
*Aurora*, a pair of lists, contrasting the two candidates. With a second term
under Adams, the nation would endure more of "Things As They Are":

*The principles and patriots of the* Revolution *condemned.*
*The* Nation *in arms without a foe, and divided without a cause.*
*The reign of terror created by false alarms, to promote domestic feud*
    *and foreign war.*
*A Sedition Law.*
*An established church, a religious test, and an order of Priesthood.*

But if Jefferson were elected, the nation could look forward to "Things As
They Will Be":

*The Principles of the* Revolution *restored.*
*The* Nation *at peace with the world and united in itself.*
Republicanism *allaying the fever of domestic feuds, and subduing the*
    *opposition by the force of reason and rectitude.*
*The Liberty of the Press.*
*Religious liberty, the rights of conscience, no priesthood, truth, and*
    *Jefferson.*[19]

"Take your choice," James Callender, a Scottish satirist, wrote in a
pamphlet called *The Prospect before Us*, "between Adams, war and beg-
gary, and Jefferson, peace and competency." Aristocracy or republicanism, order or disorder, virtue or vice, terror or reason, Adams or Jefferson.
"Such papers cannot fail to have the best effect," Jefferson wrote privately
of Callender's pamphlet. For *The Prospect before Us*, Callender was convicted of sedition. Sentenced to six months' confinement, he wrote a second volume from jail. Thumbing his nose at his prosecutors, he titled one
chapter "More Sedition."[20]

The campaigning went on for rather a long time, partly because there
was no single national election day in 1800. Instead, voting stretched
from March to November. Voting was done in public, not in secret. It
also hardly ever involved paper and pen, and counting the votes—another
affair of calculation—usually meant counting heads or, rather, counting polls. A "poll" meant the top of a person's head. (In *Hamlet*, Ophelia
says, of Polonius, "His beard as white as snow: All flaxen was his poll."
Not until well into the nineteenth century did a "poll" come to mean the
counting of votes.) Counting polls required assembling—all in favor of
the Federalist stand here, all in favor of the Republican over there—and

in places where voting was done by ballot, casting a ballot generally meant tossing a ball into a box. The word "ballot" comes from the Italian *ballota*, meaning a little ball—and early Americans who used ballots cast pea or pebbles, or, not uncommonly, bullets. In 1799, Maryland passed a law requiring voting on paper, but most states were quite slow to adopt this reform, which, in any event, was not meant to make voting secret, voting publicly being understood as an act of republican citizenship.[21]

The revolution of 1800, as Jefferson saw it, was accomplished "by the rational and peaceable instrument of reform, the suffrage of the people"—a revolution in voting.[22] Nevertheless, out of a total U.S. population of 5.23 million, only about 600,000 people were eligible to vote. Only in Maryland could black men born free vote (until 1802, when the state's constitution was amended to exclude them); only in New Jersey could white women vote (until 1807, when the state legislature closed this loophole). Of the sixteen states in the Union, all but three—Kentucky, Vermont, and Delaware—limited suffrage to property holders or taxpayers, who made up 60–70 percent of the adult white male population. Only in Kentucky, Maryland, North Carolina, Rhode Island, and Virginia did voters choose their state's delegates to the Electoral College. In no state did voters cast ballots for presidential candidates: instead, they voted for legislators, or they voted for delegates. Which of these methods each state followed was part of what the election was about in the first place, since one method was more aristocratic, and the other more republican—that's what Jefferson meant by calling the election a revolution.[23]

Before the election was over, seven out of the sixteen states in the Union changed or modified their procedures for electing delegates to the Electoral College. This began in the spring of 1800, after Republicans made a strong showing in local elections in New England, and the Federalist-dominated legislatures of Massachusetts and New Hampshire repealed the popular vote and put the selection of Electoral College delegates into their own hands. Some efforts to manipulate the voting were thwarted. When, in an election engineered by Jefferson's running mate, Aaron Burr, New Yorkers elected a Republican legislature, Hamilton tried to convince the state's governor, John Jay, to convene the lame-duck Federalist legislature to change the rules, throwing the election of delegates to the people so that the new legislature would not be able to choose Jeffersonian electoral delegates. Hamilton couldn't stand Adams, but he considered Jefferson a "contemptible hypocrite."[24] What he proposed was patently unethical. But if the result would be "to prevent an *atheist* in Religion, and a *fanatic* in politics from getting possession of the helm of State," Hamilton told Jay, "it will not do to be overscrupulous." Jay refused.[25]

When the Electoral College met in December 1800, one error of its design became immediately clear: Adams lost, but the winner remained uncertain. Republican electors were supposed to vote for Jefferson and Burr. For Jefferson to become president, at least one Republican elector had to remember to *not* vote for Burr, so that Jefferson would win and Burr place second. That someone forgot. Instead, Jefferson and Burr both received seventy-three votes in the Electoral College to Adams's sixty-five and Pinckney's sixty-four, the Federalists having remembered to give their presidential candidate one more vote than his running mate. (This problem was fixed in 1804, with the Twelfth Amendment, which separated the election of the president and the vice president.) The Jefferson-Burr tie was thrown to the House, dominated by lame-duck Federalists. Jefferson's party had just won sixty-seven House seats, compared to the Federalists' thirty-nine, but these new congressmen had not yet taken office.[26] Between Jefferson and Burr, Congress eventually decided in favor of the Virginian. Meanwhile, from New England, Federalist Timothy Pickering dubbed Jefferson a "Negro President" because twelve of his electoral votes were a product of the three-fifths clause. Without these "Negro electors," as northerners called them, he would have lost to Adams, sixty-five to sixty-one. "The election of Mr. Jefferson to the presidency," John Quincy Adams remarked, represented "the triumph of the South over the North—of the slave representation over the purely free."[27]

ON FEBRUARY 17, 1801, Jefferson was at last elected president. "I shall leave in the stables of the United States seven Horses and two Carriages with Harness," Adams wrote him. "These may not be suitable for you: but they will certainly save you a considerable Expense."[28] Jefferson was inaugurated on March 4, 1801, one day after the Sedition Act expired. He was the first president to be inaugurated in the new capital city of Washington. Spurning pomp, and refusing to ride on any of John Adams's seven horses or in either of his two carriages, he walked through the city's muddy streets, a man of the people. Bostonians insisted that he did not, in fact, walk but instead rode "into the temple of Liberty on the shoulders of slaves."[29]

Jefferson's inauguration marked the first peaceful transfer of power between political opponents in the new nation, a remarkable turning point. The two-party system turned out to be essential to the strength of the Republic. A stable party system organizes dissent. It turns discontent into a public good. And it insures the peaceful transfer of power, in which the losing party willingly, and without hesitation, surrenders its power to the winning party.

Jefferson delivered his inaugural address to Congress, assembled in the unfinished Capitol, but he addressed it to the American people: "Friends and Fellow Citizens." It is one of the best inaugurals ever written. He spoke about "the contest of opinion," a contest waged in the pages of the nation's unruly newspapers. He tried to wave aside the bitter partisanship of the election and to defeat the spirit of intolerance manifest in the Sedition Act. "Every difference of opinion is not a difference of principle," he said. "We have called by different names brethren of the same principle. We are all Republicans, we are all Federalists. If there be any among us who would wish to dissolve this Union or to change its republican form, let them stand undisturbed as monuments of the safety with which error of opinion may be tolerated where reason is left free to combat it." Three weeks later, Jefferson wrote to Sam Adams: "The storm is over, and we are in port."[30]

The storm was not over. One of the last and most important decisions John Adams made before leaving the presidency was to appoint to the office of chief justice the Virginian John Marshall, who was Jefferson's cousin and also one of his fiercest political rivals. Federalists had lost power in the other two branches of government, but they seized it in the judicial branch and held it, a check against the suffrage of the people, a form of power more easily subject to abuse than any other.

A corrupt or too powerful judiciary had been one of the abuses that led to the Revolution. In 1768, Benjamin Franklin had listed judicial appointment as one of the "causes of American discontents," and, in the Declaration of Independence, Jefferson included the king's having "made Judges dependent on his Will alone" on his list of grievances.[31] "The judicial power ought to be distinct from both the legislative and executive, and independent," John Adams had argued in 1776, "so that it may be a check upon both."[32] But a tension exists between judicial independence and the separation of powers. Appointing judges to serve for life would seem to establish judicial independence, but what power would then check the judiciary? Another solution was to have judges elected by the people—the people would then check the judiciary—but the popular election of judges would seem to make the courts subject to all manner of political caprice. At the constitutional convention, no one had argued that the Supreme Court justices ought to be popularly elected, not because the delegates were unconcerned about judicial independence but because there wasn't a great deal of support for the popular election of anyone, including the president. And, although there was, for a time, some disagreement over whether the president or the Senate ought actually to do the appointing, the proposal that the president ought to appoint justices, and the Senate confirm them, and that these justices ought to hold their appointments "during good behavior," was established swiftly, and without much dissent.[33]

Nevertheless, this arrangement had proved controversial during the debate over ratification. In an essay called "The Supreme Court: They Will Mould the Government into Almost Any Shape They Please," one Anti-Federalist had pointed out that the power granted to the court was "unprecedented in a free country," because its justices are, finally, answerable to no one: "No errors they may commit can be corrected by any power above them, if any such power there be, nor can they be removed from office for making ever so many erroneous adjudications."[34]

This is among the reasons Hamilton had found it expedient, in Federalist 78, to emphasize the weakness of the judicial branch.[35] When it began, the Supreme Court, without even a building to call its own, really was nearly as weak as Hamilton pretended it would be. It served, at first, as an appellate court and a trial court and, under the terms of the 1789 Judiciary Act, a circuit court. People thought it was a good idea for the justices to ride circuit, so that they'd know the citizenry better. The justices quite disliked riding circuit and, in 1792, petitioned the president to relieve them of the duty, writing, "we cannot reconcile ourselves to the idea of existing in exile from our families." Washington, who had no children of his own, was unmoved.[36] At one point, the chief justice, John Jay, wrote to Washington to let him know that he was going to skip the next session because his wife was having a baby ("I cannot prevail upon myself to be then at a Distance from her," Jay wrote), and because there wasn't much on the docket, anyway. In 1795, Jay resigned his appointment as chief justice to become governor of New York, closer to home. Washington then asked Hamilton to take his place; Hamilton said no, as did Patrick Henry. When the Senate rejected Washington's next nominee for Jay's replacement, the South Carolinian John Rutledge, Rutledge tried to drown himself near Charleston, crying out to his rescuers, "He had long been a Judge & he knew no Law that forbid a man to take away his own life."[37] The court, in short, was troubled.

Before leaving office, Adams had tried to reappoint Jay as chief justice, but Jay had refused, writing to the president, "I left the Bench perfectly convinced that under a system so defective, it would not obtain the energy, weight, and dignity which are essential to its affording due support to the national government, nor acquire the public confidence and respect which, as the last resort of the justice of the nation, it should possess."[38] All of this changed with John Marshall.

In 1801, when Marshall was appointed chief justice, the president lived in the President's House, Congress met at the Capitol, and the court still lacked a home, having no building of its own. Marshall took his oath of office in a dank, dark, cold, "meanly furnished, very inconvenient" room in the basement of the Capitol, where the justices, who had no clerks, had no room to put on their robes or to deliberate. "The deaths of some of our most talented jurists," one architect remarked, "have been attributed to the location of this Courtroom." Cleverly, Marshall made sure all the justices rented rooms at the same boardinghouse, so that they could have someplace to talk together, unobserved.[39]

Nearly the very last thing Adams had done before leaving office was to persuade the lame-duck Federalist Congress to pass the 1801 Judiciary Act, reducing the number of Supreme Court Justices to five, a change slated to go into effect once the next vacancy came up. The only point of this chicanery was to make it so Jefferson wouldn't have the chance to name a justice to the bench until two justices left. The next year, the newly elected Republican Congress repealed the 1801 act and, furthermore, suspended the next two sessions of the Supreme Court.

Sessions of Congress were open to the public and their deliberations were published, in accordance with what James Wilson had called, at the constitutional convention, the people's "right to know." But Marshall decided that the deliberations of the Supreme Court ought to be cloaked in secrecy. He also urged the justices to issue unanimous decisions—a single opinion, ideally written by the chief justice—and to destroy all evidence of disagreement.

Marshall's critics considered these practices to be incompatible with a government accountable to the people. "The very idea of cooking up opinions in conclave begets suspicions," Jefferson complained.[40] But Marshall went ahead anyway. And, in 1803, in *Marbury v. Madison*, a suit against Jefferson's secretary of state, James Madison, Marshall granted to the Supreme Court a power it had not been granted in the Constitution: the right to decide whether laws passed by Congress are constitutional.

Marshall declared: "It is emphatically the province and duty of the judicial department to say what the law is."[41] One day, those words would be carved in marble; in 1803, they were very difficult to believe.

## II.

THE REPUBLIC WAS SPREADING like ferns on the floor of a forest. Between the first federal census and the second, the population of the United States increased from 3.9 to 5.3 million; by 1810, it was 7.2 million, having grown at the extraordinary rate of 35 percent every decade. By 1800, 500,000 people had moved from the eastern states to land along the Tennessee, Cumberland, and Ohio Rivers, portending a political shift to the West. Jefferson believed that the fate of the Republic lay in expansion: more land and more farmers. He believed that yeoman farmers, secure in their possessions and independent of the influence of other men, constituted the best citizens. "Dependence begets subservience and venality," he wrote. There was something romantic, too, in Jefferson's attachment to farming: "Those who labor in the earth are the chosen people of God." Influenced by Malthus, Jefferson believed that the new nation had to acquire more territory both to supply its growing population with food and to retain its republican character. Malthus postulated as a law of nature "the perpetual tendency in the race of man to increase beyond the means of subsistence." In a growing population, poverty in man was as inevitable as old age.[42] To this law, Thomas Jefferson expected the United States to prove an exception.

*Jefferson imagined an "empire of liberty," a republic of
yeoman farmers, equal and independent.*

Convinced that the fate of the Republic turned on farming, Jefferson feared manufacturing and the rise of the factory. Workers in steampowered factories in England, he thought, were the very opposite of the virtuous, independent citizens needed in a republic; they were dependent laborers, subservient and venal. Jefferson had a nail factory on his slave plantation, at Monticello, though it was small-scale, and what he hoped to avoid was the next stage of manufacturing, industrial production. But what he did not see, could not see, was that his fields were a factory, too, run not by machines but by the forced labor of more than a hundred enslaved human beings.

The first factories in the Western world weren't in buildings housing machines powered by steam: they were out of doors, in the sugarcane fields of the West Indies, in the rice fields of the Carolinas, and in the tobacco fields of Virginia. Slavery was one kind of experiment, designed to save the cost of labor by turning human beings into machines. Another kind of experiment was the invention of machines powered by steam. These two experiments had a great deal in common. Both required a capital investment, and both depended on the regimentation of time.[43] What separated them divided the American economy into two: an industrial North, and an agricultural South.

Jefferson's presidency was a long battle over which of these systems ought to prevail, which meant looking to the West. The Louisiana Territory, nearly a million square miles west of the Mississippi, had been under Spanish rule since 1763, inhabited by Spaniards, Creoles, Africans, and Indians generally loyal to Great Britain. Spain allowed Americans to freely navigate the Mississippi and to ship goods from the vital port city of New Orleans, an arrangement that was essential for western settlement. But in 1800 Napoleon Bonaparte, who had seized control of France in 1799, secretly purchased the territory. He then attempted to reinstitute slavery on Saint-Domingue, which he hoped would serve as the economic heart of his New World empire. Napoleon's troops captured and imprisoned Toussaint Louverture in 1802, but after war broke out between France and Britain the next year, Napoleon withdrew his forces from Saint-Domingue. The island's former slaves declared their independence in 1803, establishing the Republic of Haiti. The United States refused to recognize Haiti but profited from its independence; without it, Napoleon no longer had much use for the Louisiana Territory and, at war with Britain, was keenly in need of funds. Jefferson and Madison arranged for their fellow Virginian, James Monroe, to travel to Paris to offer Napoleon $2 million for New Orleans and Florida (he was authorized to pay as much as $10 million). Unexpectedly, Napoleon offered to sell the entire Louisiana Territory for $15 million. Monroe, seizing the opportunity, made the purchase. Its geographical and economic consequences were enormous: the size of the United States doubled.

But there were other consequences, too, both constitutional and political. The restoration of navigation rights along the Mississippi, and the use of the Port of New Orleans, were together a triumph. But under the Constitution, expenses have to be approved by the House and treaties by the Senate. Congress has the power to admit to the Union new states "established within the limits of the United States," but it does not specifically have the power to acquire new territory that would be incorporated into the Union. Views on the matter fell along party lines. New England–dominated Federalists argued that Jefferson's envoys had overstepped their authority and, further, that the purchase would make the Republic "too widely dispersed," resulting, ultimately, in the "dissolution of the government." Republicans argued that the purchase fell within the power to make treaties. Jefferson had no regrets about the purchase, but he did have qualms about its constitutionality. Since 1787, he'd argued for limiting the powers of the federal government; he believed that the Constitution would have to be amended before the treaty could be ratified. "I had rather ask an enlargement of power from the nation, where it is found necessary, than to assume it by a construction which would make our powers boundless." If the Constitution were so broadly constructed that the power to make treaties could be read as a power to purchase land from another country, the Constitution, Jefferson thought, would have been made "a blank paper." Yet, in the end, Jefferson deferred to his advisers, who argued against pursuing an amendment. Then, too, he thought this vast swath of territory might be "the means of tempting all our Indians on the East side of the Mississippi to remove to the West."[44]

In 1804, after reading a revised edition of Malthus's *Essay on the Principle of Population*, Jefferson concluded that "the greater part of his book is inapplicable to us" because of "the singular circumstance of the immense extent of rich and uncultivated lands in this country, furnishing an increase of food in the same ratio with that of population." Malthus might have derived a law of nature, Jefferson conceded, but America provided an exception. "By enlarging the empire of liberty," he wrote in 1805, "we . . . provide new sources of renovation, should its principles, in any time, degenerate, in those portions of our country, which gave them birth."[45]

This scarcely settled the question. In 1806, Jefferson secured the passage of a Non-Importation Act, banning certain British imports and, in 1807, an Embargo Act, banning all American exports. During the ongoing war between Britain and France, the British had been seizing American ships and impressing American seamen. Jefferson believed that banning all trade was the only way to remain neutral. No Americans ships were to sail to foreign ports. He insisted that all the goods Americans needed they could produce in their own homes. "Every family in the country is a manufactory within itself, and is very generally able to make within itself all the stouter and middling stuffs for its own clothing and household use," he wrote to Adams. "We consider a sheep for every person in the family as sufficient to clothe it, in addition to the cotton, hemp and flax which we raise ourselves." Jefferson—blind to slavery—believed in an agrarian independence that required precise limits on economic activity: "Manufactures, sufficient for our own consumption, of what we raise the raw material (and no more). Commerce sufficient to carry the surplus produce of agriculture, beyond our own consumption, to a market for exchanging it for articles we cannot raise (and no more). These are the true limits of manufactures and commerce. To go beyond them is to increase our dependence on foreign nations, and our liability to war."[46]

The embargo devastated the American economy. Jeffersonian agrarianism was not only backward-looking but also largely a fantasy. In 1793, when Jefferson first heard about the cotton gin, a machine that separates cotton fibers from the cotton bolls ("gin" is short for "engine"), he thought it would be excellent "for family use." As late as 1815 he was boasting that, as a result of the embargo, "carding machines in every neighborhood, spinning machines in large families and wheels in the small, are too radically established ever to be relinquished." That year, cotton and slave plantations in the American South were shipping seventeen million bales of cotton to England, to be carded and woven and spun in the coal-and-steam-powered mills in Lancaster and Manchester.[47]

Parliament abolished the slave trade in 1807; Congress followed in 1808, the first year that the trade could be ended, under the terms of the Constitution. But the cotton gin had by then made American slavery more profitable than ever. Congress repealed Jefferson's embargo when he left office in 1809 (following the precedent established by Washington in not running for a third term), but New Englanders continued to press for the development of manufacturing. Congress therefore authorized a new kind of counting to be part of the next federal census, in 1810: an inventory of American manufacturing, overseen by Tench Coxe, former assistant secretary of the Treasury. In 1812, no longer able to stay neutral in the Napoleonic Wars, Congress narrowly approved the request by Jefferson's successor, Madison, to declare war on Britain, the South supporting the declaration, and New England and the mid-Atlantic states mostly opposing it. It adversely affected northern manufacturing. It threatened an invasion from Canada. And it symbolized, to many Federalists, the daunting political dominance of the Republican Party. Not without cause, Federalists saw little distinction between the administrations of Jefferson and Madison, and would feel the same way about Madison's successor, James Monroe, Virginians elected under the three-fifths clause.

Much of the fighting in what came to be called the War of 1812 took place at sea and in Canada. Britain successfully defended its possessions to the north. In 1813, the British captured the nation's capital, Madison and his cabinet fled to Virginia, and, between the battle and a storm, the

President's House was all but destroyed. Three clerks at the War Office stuffed the original parchment Constitution of the United States into a linen sack and carried it to a gristmill in Virginia, which was a good idea, because the British burned the city down. Later, when someone asked James Madison where the Constitution had gone, he had not the least idea.[48] After the war, the rebuilt President's House was freshly painted— and became known as the White House.

The War of 1812 reminded northerners of the price the Republic had paid for the political calculation made in 1787. New Englanders hadn't wanted to wage the war in the first place, and yet they found themselves powerless against the slave-owning states, grown mightier through the extension of slavery into newly acquired territories. By 1804, after the acquisition of the Louisiana Territory, Massachusetts and Connecticut had called for the abolition of the three-fifths clause. Their calls grew more shrill in 1812, after the New England author of a polemic titled *Slave Representation* damned the three-fifths clause as "the rotten part of the Constitution" and urged that it be "amputated."[49] Eyeing the inevitable ushering into the Union of new states, one writer from Massachusetts calculated that "one slave in Mississippi has nearly as much power in Congress, as five free men in the State of New-York." Federalist fury reached a climax in 1814 at the Hartford Convention, where delegates from five New England states assembled in Connecticut to debate possible actions, including secession. Towns that had petitioned for the convention called for the end of slave representation. But three days after the convention sent its recommendation to the states, the last battle of the war began in New Orleans, where Andrew Jackson, a young general from Tennessee, led American troops to a stunning victory. The protest of New England was forgotten, the call to eradicate the three-fifths ratio ignored. On March 3, 1815, the last day Congress was in session, the resolutions of the Hartford Convention were read into the record and promptly tabled.[50]

The next day, at Monticello, Jefferson, seventy-two, pondered the future of the children he'd had with one of his slaves, a woman named Sally Hemings. Jefferson's wife, Martha Wayles, had died in 1782, when Jefferson was thirty-eight. While she lay on her deathbed, he had promised her he would never remarry. Sally Hemings was the much younger half-sister of Jefferson's wife; they had different mothers but the same father, John Wayles, who had six children with one of his slaves, a woman

*This political cari-cature, engraved and inked in Massachusetts about 1804 and sold in New Hampshire by 1807, depicts Jefferson as a rooster and Sally Hemings as his hen, testament to how widespread were rumors about the president's relationship with one of his slaves.*

named Elizabeth Hemings, herself the child of an African woman and an English man. "The whole commerce between master and slave is a perpetual exercise of the most boisterous passions, the most unremitting despotism on the one part, and degrading submission on the other," Jefferson wrote in 1782, the year of his wife's death. "The man must be a prodigy who can retain his manners and morals undepraved by such circumstances." In 1789, when sixteen-year-old Sally Hemings was working for and living in the residence of forty-six-year-old Jefferson in Paris, she became pregnant. She might have left him and gained her freedom; slavery was illegal in France. Instead, she extracted from him a promise, that if she stayed with him, he would set all of their children free.[51]

But he'd not quite managed to keep his children with Sally Hemings a secret. In 1800, printers had helped get Jefferson elected, but his view of them had grown dim over their scrutiny of his family life. (During his second term, an embittered Jefferson would suggest that newspapers ought to be divided into four sections: Truths, Probabilities, Possibilities, and Lies.)[52] Only days after his inauguration, he'd complained that printers "live by the zeal they can kindle, and the schisms they can create."[53] James Callender, who'd gone to prison for sedition for campaigning for Jefferson, had wanted a political appointment. Jefferson having failed to reward him with a position, Callender in 1802 published an essay in the *Richmond Recorder* in which he reported on longstanding rumors that Jefferson had fathered children with one of his slaves. "Her name," he wrote, "is SALLY." And, had Callender been willing to publish the story of this scandal earlier, he said, "the establishment of this single fact would have rendered his election impossible."[54] Sally Hemings had had seven children by Jefferson, bearing her last in 1808. Jefferson, whose election had been made possible by the three-fifths clause, lived in a world that made the political calculation that his seven children with Sally were worth no more than four and two-tenths.

On March 4, 1815, the day after Congress tabled a resolution to abolish the three-fifths clause, haunted by the tragedy of his own and the nation's malign political math, Jefferson attempted to calculate just how many generations would have to pass before a child with a full-blooded African ancestor could be called "white." Under Virginia law—absurdity heaped upon absurdity—to be seven-eighths white was to be, legally, magically, white.

"Let us express the pure blood of the white in the capital letters of the printed alphabet," Jefferson began, writing out his mathematical proof. "Let the first crossing be of $a$, a pure negro, with A, a pure white," he went on. "The unit of blood of the issue being composed of the half of that of each parent, will be $a/2 + A/2$. Call it, for abbreviation, $h$ (half blood)." This $h$ was Elizabeth Hemings, Sally's mother, the daughter of an Englishman, A, and an African woman, $a$. He labeled the second "pure white" B, a so-called quadroon, $q$, and the third "pure white" C. B was John Wayles, Sally's father, and $q$, Sally herself. C was the third president of the United States. He concluded his proof:

> Let the third crossing be of $q$ and C, their offspring will be $q/2 + C/2$ = $A/8 + B/4 + C/2$, call this $e$ (eighth), who having less than 1/4 of $a$, or of pure negro blood, to wit 1/8 only, is no longer a mulatto, so that a third cross clears the blood.[55]

To Jefferson, his children by Hemings were $e$, the third crossing, not black, because seven-eighths white: not three-fifths a person, but a whole.

Only four of Sally Hemings's children lived to adulthood. She knew and they knew what Jefferson knew: if they left Monticello, they could pass for white, if they chose, reinventing themselves as citizens, making their own calculations, in a republic of blood.

OTHER MEN'S CONSCIENCES troubled them differently. In December 1816, a group of northern reformers and southern slave owners met in Washington at Davis's Hotel for a meeting chaired by Henry Clay, the fast-talking Kentucky congressman and Speaker of the House. They'd gathered to discuss what to do about the nation's growing number of free blacks. In 1790, there had been 59,467; by 1800, there were 108,398; in 1810, 186,446, to some a threatening multitude. The census made clear that the American population was growing at a rate never seen anywhere before, in the history of the world. Yet it made this much clear, too: the original thirteen eastern states were losing power, relative to the newer, western states. The institution of slavery, so far from dying the natural death predicted by the framers of the Constitution, was growing in the West, even as it was declining in the East. Two new states had lately entered the Union as free states: Ohio in 1803 and Indiana in 1816. Two more had entered as slave states: Louisiana in 1812 and Mississippi in 1816. But population growth in free states was outpacing that in slave states. And the population of free blacks was growing at a rate more than double that of the population of whites.

In Washington, the men who met in Davis's Hotel decided upon a plan: they would found a colony in Africa, as Clay said, "to rid our country of a useless and pernicious, if not dangerous portion of its population." They elected a president, Bushrod Washington, George Washington's nephew and a Supreme Court justice. Andrew Jackson served as a vice president. They chose a name for their organization; they called it the American Colonization Society.[56]

By 1816, the divide between Republicans and Federalists had begun to align rather closely with the divide over the question of slavery. In his diary, John Quincy Adams, the son of the former president, who served as secretary of state for the new president, James Monroe, began calling the two parties the "slavery party" and the "free party."[57] Any extension of the Union threatened the balance between these two political forces. In 1819, Missouri, which had been settled by southerners, became the first part of the Louisiana Territory west of the Mississippi and north of the

Ohio River to seek to enter the Union as a state. To the bill granting Missouri admission, James Tallmadge, a congressman from New York, introduced an amendment that would have banned slavery in the state. When one critic of the amendment said it would destroy the Union, Tallmadge replied, "Sir, if a dissolution of the Union must take place, let it be so!"[58]

The Tallmadge Amendment passed narrowly in the House but failed in the Senate. The debate that followed lasted more than two years. In wrestling with this question, members of Congress had the advantage of an extraordinary wealth of information about the population but suffered from a lack of historical perspective on the Constitution itself. The fifty-year vow of silence pledged by delegates to the constitutional convention—which prevented James Madison from publishing his *Notes*—meant that whatever logic there was to the three-fifths compromise was essentially unknowable. In November 1819, Madison, living in retirement in Virginia, answered a query about Missouri, explaining his view that the Constitution probably did not grant Congress the power to make the prohibition of slavery a condition of entering the Union and that, in any case, once Missouri became a state, it would have the right to institute slavery. For Madison, a member of the Colonization Society, the matter could be divided into a moral question, a matter of political arithmetic, and a constitutional one, a matter of law.

"Will it or will it not better the condition of the slaves, by lessening the number belonging to individual masters, and intermixing both with greater masses of free people?" Madison asked. "Will the aggregate strength, security, tranquility and harmony of the whole nation be advanced or impaired by lessening the proportion of slaves to the free people in particular sections of it?"[59]

Tallmadge and his supporters condemned the politics of slavery, assailing the injustice of slave representation, and insisted that whatever bargain had been made at the constitutional convention need not extend into states that had not existed in 1787. Their opponents, instead of defending slavery, insisted on the impracticability of emancipation by arguing that black people would never be able to live among white people as equals. "There is no place for the free blacks in the United States—no place where they are not degraded," one argued. "If there was such a place, the society for colonizing them would not have been formed."[60] Behind Madison's remarks about "lessening the proportion of slaves to the free people," behind Jefferson's tortured calculations about how many generations would have to pass before his own children could pass for "white," lay this hard truth: none of these men could imagine living with descendants of Africans as political equals.

And yet Jefferson made good on his promise to Sally Hemings. His two oldest children with Sally, Beverly and Harriet, left Monticello, apparently with his approval. "Harriet. Sally's run," Jefferson wrote in 1822 in his "Farm Book," where he kept track of his human property. Harriet Hemings hadn't run. She was twenty-one, and Jefferson had set her free. "She was nearly as white as anybody, and very beautiful," recalled one of Jefferson's overseers, who also said that Jefferson ordered him to give fifty dollars to Harriet, and had paid for her ride, by stage, to Philadelphia. From there she traveled on to Washington, where her brother Beverly had already settled. "She thought it to her interest, on going to Washington, to assume the role of a white woman," said Harriet's brother Madison, the only one of Sally Hemings's children to live his life as a black man. He seems never to have forgiven his sister. But he kept her secret. "I am not aware that her identity as Harriet Hemings of Monticello has ever been discovered," he said. "Harriet married a white man in good standing in Washington City, whose name I could give," he said, "but will not."[61]

On the floor of Congress, men pounded on their desks, and they rose to make speeches, and they listened, intently or indifferently. Into the stale air of the room wafted another proposal. Southerners like Henry Clay and John Tyler began to make a mathematical argument about "diffusion": if slavery were allowed in states like Missouri, people who wanted to own slaves would have to buy them from states like Virginia, and then slavery as an institution would grow in the West, but the number of slaves would be small. Meanwhile, the number of slaves in the East would continue to decline, and in both places the ratio of slaves to white people would be low, which, it was expected, would make the condition of slaves better, and would lessen the likelihood that they would have children with whites. Might the blood of the nation be cleared?

"Diffusion is about as effectual a remedy for slavery as it would be for smallpox," scoffed a Baltimore attorney named Daniel Raymond, in a thirty-nine-page pamphlet called *The Missouri Question*. Raymond was a member of the American Colonization Society, but, he argued, the idea "that the Colonization Society can under any circumstances, have any perceptible effect in eradicating slaves from our soil, is utterly chimerical." It was a matter of Malthusianism: "as population increases in a geometrical ratio, it is utterly impossible by that means, to make any perceptible diminution of the number of blacks in our country. On the contrary, the curse of slavery will continue to increase and that in a geometrical ratio too, in spite of the utmost efforts of the Society." Slavery would not simply disappear, Raymond insisted: "It is an axiom as true as the first problem in Euclid, that if left to itself it will every year become more inveterate and more formidable."[62]

Southerners attacked Raymond on the floor of the Senate. Among other things, they pointed out that a moral objection that was geographically bounded—those who opposed slavery in the West promised they would leave it alone in the South—was hardly a deeply held conviction. Virginia senator James Barbour asked, "What kind of ethics is that which is bounded by latitude and longitude, which is inoperative on the left, but is omnipotent on the right bank of a river?" But Raymond's math, at any rate, turned out to be right. Calculating the growth of the slave population based on its known rate of increase, Raymond predicted that the number of slaves in the United States, less than 900,000 in 1800, would be 1.9 million by 1830. He was very close; it would be 2 million.[63]

Month after month of pencil to paper, adding and subtracting, multiplying and dividing, did not settle the matter of the ratio of white people to black people in the United States. Nor did the colonization scheme. (Only about three thousand African Americans ever left for Liberia.) The Missouri question was settled, more or less, by accident. In 1820, Maine, which had been part of Massachusetts, petitioned to be admitted to the Union as a free state. Alabama had been admitted to the Union the summer before, as a slave state, making the number of free and slave states equal, at twelve each. Congress, eager to end the impasse over Missouri, devised a compromise that would retain the balance between slave and free states. Under the Missouri Compromise, a deal deftly brokered by Clay, ever after known as "the Great Compromiser," Missouri was admitted as a slave state and Maine as a free state, and a line was set at 36°30' latitude, the southern border of Missouri: any states formed out of territories above that line would enter the Union as free states, and any states below that line would enter as slave states. The three-fifths clause survived. But John Quincy Adams did not believe it would survive for long. "Take it for granted that the present is a mere preamble—a title page to a great, tragic volume," he wrote in his diary. "The President thinks this question will be winked away by a compromise. But so do not I. Much am I mistaken if it is not destined to survive his political and individual life and mine."[64] He was not mistaken.

# III.

THE FIRST FIVE PRESIDENTS of the United States, Washington, Adams, Jefferson, Madison, and Monroe, were diplomats, soldiers, philosophers, and statesmen, founders of the nation. Even Monroe, the youngest of the five men, and the least distinguished of them, had fought in the Revolutionary War and served in the Continental Congress. But by 1824, that generation had passed. John Quincy Adams had been intended—at least by his father—as their successor, groomed, from childhood, for the presidency. "You come into life with advantages which will disgrace you if your successes are mediocre," John Adams told him. "And if you do not rise . . . to the head of your country, it will be owing to your own Laziness, Slovenliness, and Obstinacy."[65]

John Quincy Adams was hardly a shirker. He'd begun keeping a diary in 1779, when he was twelve and on a diplomatic mission to Europe with his father. After finishing his studies and passing the bar, he'd served as Washington's minister to the Netherlands and Portugal, as his father's minister to Prussia, and as Madison's minister to Russia. He spoke fourteen languages. As secretary of state, he'd drafted the Monroe Doctrine, establishing the principle that the United States would keep out of wars in Europe but would consider any European colonial ventures in the Americas as acts of aggression. By the time he decided to seek the presidency, he'd also served as a U.S. senator and as a professor of logic at Brown and professor of rhetoric and oratory at Harvard.

In 1824, it was said that American voters faced a choice between "John Quincy Adams, / Who can write / And Andrew Jackson, / Who can fight."[66] If the battle between John Adams and Thomas Jefferson had determined whether aristocracy or republicanism would prevail (and, with Jefferson, republicanism won), the battle between Andrew Jackson and John Quincy Adams would determine whether republicanism or democracy would prevail (and, with Jackson, democracy would, eventually, win). Jackson's rise to power marked the birth of American populism. The argument of populism is that the best government is that most closely directed by a popular majority. Populism is an argument about the people, but, at heart, it is an argument about numbers.[67]

A national hero after the Battle of New Orleans, Jackson had gone on to lead campaigns against the Seminoles, the Chickasaws, and the Choctaws, pursuing a mixed strategy of treaty-making and war-making, with far more of the latter than the former, as part of a plan to remove all Indians living in the southeastern United States to lands to the west. He was provincial, and poorly educated. (Later, when Harvard gave Jackson an honorary doctorate, John Quincy Adams refused to attend the ceremony, calling him "a barbarian who could not write a sentence of grammar and hardly could spell his own name.")[68] He had a well-earned reputation for being ferocious, ill-humored, and murderous, on the battlefield and off. When he ran for president, he had served less than a year in the Senate. Of his bid for the White House Jefferson declared, "He is one of the most unfit men I know of for such a place."[69]

Jackson made a devilishly shrewd decision. He would make his lack of certain qualities—judiciousness, education, political experience—into strengths. He would run as a hot-tempered military man who'd pulled himself up by his own bootstraps. To do this, he needed to tell the story of his life. Within weeks of his victory at the Battle of New Orleans, in preparation for a political career, he hired a biographer, sixty-five-year-old David Ramsay, a South Carolina legislator and physician and gifted historian whose books included a two-volume *History of the American Revolution* (1789) and a heroic *Life of George Washington* (1807). But before Ramsay could begin work on the biography, he was shot in the back on the streets of Charleston. Jackson hired his aide-de-camp John Reid, who drafted four chapters before he, too, died an unfortunate and unexpected death. "The book must be finished," Jackson insisted. He turned, next, to a twenty-six-year-old lawyer named John Eaton who had served under Jackson during the Creek War and the War of 1812; Eaton was Jackson's "bosom friend and adopted son," according to Margaret Bayard Smith, a novelist and remarkably astute observer of Washington society and politics. (Her husband, Samuel Harrison Smith, was a president of the Bank of the United States.) Eaton's *Life of Andrew Jackson* appeared in 1817. The next year, Eaton was elected to the Senate, and in 1823, when Jackson joined him in Washington, the two senators from Tennessee shared lodgings.[70]

Andrew Jackson, man of the people, was the first presidential candidate to campaign for the office, the first to appear on campaign buttons, and nearly the first to publish a campaign biography. In 1824, when Jackson announced his bid for the presidency, Eaton, who ran Jackson's campaign, shrewdly revised his *Life of Andrew Jackson*, deleting or dismissing everything in Jackson's past that looked bad and lavishing attention on anything that looked good and turning into strengths what earlier had been considered weaknesses: Eaton's Jackson wasn't uneducated; he was self-taught. He wasn't ill-bred; he was "self-made."[71]

The election of 1824 also altered the very method of electing a president. Why should a party's nominee be selected by a caucus in Congress? The legislative caucus worked only so long as voters didn't mind that they had virtually no role in electing the president.[72] Calls for the beheading of "King Caucus" had begun in 1822, when the *New York American* asked: "Why should not a general convention of Republican delegates from the different states assemble at Washington a few months prior to the period for electing a President and decide, by a majority, the choice of an individual for that elevated office"? Two years later, popular opposition to the caucus had grown. After word got out to the press about a caucus meeting to be held in the House, only 6 out of 240 legislators were willing to appear before a disgruntled public, which flooded the galleries shouting, "Adjourn! Adjourn!" And so it did.[73]

With the caucus dead, John Quincy Adams, John C. Calhoun, and Henry Clay simply declared their candidacies. Jackson looked for a popular mandate: he was nominated by the Tennessee legislature. The momentum behind Jackson's candidacy drew, as well, on the power of newly enfranchised voters. When new states entered the Union, they held conventions to draft and ratify their own state constitutions: they almost always adopted more democratic arrangements than those that prevailed in the thirteen original states. They abolished property requirements for

*Andrew Jackson's 1824 bid for the presidency
introduced all manner of paraphernalia,
including this campaign sewing box.*

voting, replaced judicial appointment with judicial elections, and provided for the popular election of delegates to the Electoral College. The new and more democratic state constitutions put pressure on older states to revise their own constitutions. By 1821, property qualifications for voting no longer existed in twenty-one out of twenty-four states. Three years later, eighteen out of twenty-four states held popular elections for delegates to the Electoral College. More and poorer white men came to the polls and were elected to office, much to the dismay of conservatives like Chancellor James Kent of New York who, at New York's 1821 constitutional convention, complained, "The notion that every man that works a day on the road, or serves an idle hour in the militia, is entitled as of right to an equal participation in the whole power of government, is most unreasonable and has no foundation in justice." He believed in proportionate representation—representation proportionate to wealth: "Society is an association for the protection of property as well as of life, and the individual who contributes only one cent to the common stock, ought not to have the same power and influence in directing the property concerns of the partnership, as he who contributes his thousands."[74]

*Paper ballots were in general use by the 1820s, usually in the form of "party tickets" for an entire slate of candidates, like this Democratic Party ticket from Ohio in 1828.*

JACKSON
AND THE
PEOPLE'S TICKET.
———
Governor,
John W. Campbell.
Congress,
James Findlay.
Senator,
Jonathan Cilley.
Representatives,
Alexander Duncan,
Elijah Hayward,
Robert T. Lytle
Sheriff,
John C. Avery.
Commissioner,
Leonard Armstrong.
Auditor,
John T. Jones.
Coroner,
David Jackson, jr.

As the kind of people who could vote changed, so did the method of voting. Early paper voting had been unwieldy and inconvenient; voters were expected to bring to the polls a scrap of paper on which they could write the names of their chosen candidates. With the electorate expanding, this system became even more impractical. Party leaders began to print ballots, usually in partisan newspapers, usually in long strips, listing an entire slate as a "party ticket." The ticket system consolidated the power of the parties and contributed to the expansion of the electorate: party tickets meant that voters didn't need to know how to write or even how to read; each party ticket was printed on a different color paper, and each was stamped with a party symbol.

In 1824, Jackson won both the popular vote and a plurality, though not a majority, of the electoral vote. The election was thrown to the House, which chose John Quincy Adams after Henry Clay threw his support behind him. Adams then appointed Clay his secretary of state. Jefferson wrote to John Adams to congratulate him on his son's election. Having retired from politics, the two men had renewed the friendship of their youth. "Every line from you exhilarates my spirits," Adams replied.[75]

Jackson, furious at what he deemed a "corrupt bargain," resigned from the Senate in 1825, returned to the Hermitage, and bided his time while the electorate swelled. Between 1824 and 1828, it more than doubled, growing from 400,000 to 1.1 million. Men who had attended the constitutional convention in 1787 shook their gray-haired heads and warned that Americans had crowned a new monarch, King Numbers.[76]

ON JULY 4, 1826, the United States celebrated its jubilee, the fiftieth anniversary of the Declaration of Independence. In cities and towns, Americans paraded and sang and raised glasses and listened to speeches. Many of those speeches celebrated the new spirit of democracy, the defeat of the contempt for the people that had been part of the nation's founding. "There may be those who scoff at the suggestion that the decision of the whole is to be preferred to the judgment of the enlightened few," said the historian George Bancroft, speaking in Boston. "They say in their hearts that the masses are ignorant; that farmers know nothing of legislation; that mechanics should not quit their workshops to join in forming public opinion. But true political science does indeed venerate the masses." The voice of the people, Bancroft insisted, "is the voice of God."[77]

Nothing more clearly marked the end of the founding era than the coincidence of the deaths of two men, on that very day: Thomas Jefferson, the pen of the Declaration, and John Adams, the voice of independence. Adams, ninety, died at his home in Massachusetts. "He breathed his last about 6 o'clock in the afternoon," reported one newspaper, "while millions of his fellow-countrymen were engaged in festive rejoicings at the nation's jubilee, and in chanting praises to the immortal patriots whose valour and virtue accomplished their country's freedom and independence."[78] He had been declining for years. He'd lost his teeth and his eyesight. He slept in an overstuffed armchair in his library, in a dressing coat and a cotton cap, surrounded by his books; he left them, in his will, to his son John Quincy. Cannons fired on the Fourth were nearly drowned out by the sound of thunder, an afternoon storm. Having been carried to his bed, Adams stirred and whispered, "Thomas Jefferson survives." At twenty past six, he died. But in Virginia, Jefferson, eighty-three, had died at ten minutes before one.

In a will that Jefferson had made months before, he'd freed the last two of his children with Sally Hemings, Madison and Eston; he did not mention Sally. Invited to celebrate the Fourth of July in Washington, Jefferson had instead sent a letter of regret, and words upon the day, celebrating this self-evident truth: "the mass of mankind has not been born with saddles on their backs, nor a favored few, booted and spurred, ready to ride them." He was dying. Suffering and in pain, he'd been dosed with laudanum. He'd slept through most of July 2 and July 3 and then refused the medicine. He died on the Fourth, while the bells in nearby Charlottesville tolled the anniversary of American independence.

Sally Hemings's brother John built Jefferson's coffin. Six months later, to pay his debts, Jefferson's entire estate, including 130 slaves, was sold at an auction. The Fossett children, cousins of Sally Hemings's, were among the "130 VALUABLE NEGROES" sold to the highest bidder.[79] Hemings, fifty-three years old, was appraised at fifty dollars, but she was not sold at auction; she had, by then, quietly left Monticello for Charlottesville, where she lived until her death. From Monticello, she brought with her a pair of Jefferson's eyeglasses to remember him by—a man of sight, and of blindness.[80]

Their daughter Harriet Hemings was twenty-seven and still living in Washington in 1828 when Andrew Jackson finally defeated John Quincy Adams, in an election that marked the founding of the Democratic Party, Jackson's party, the party of the common man, the farmer, the artisan: the people's party.

Jackson won a whopping 56 percent of the popular vote. Four times as many white men cast a ballot in 1828 as in 1824. They voted in throngs. They voted by casting ballots, not balls but slips of paper: Jackson tickets, with which they cast their votes for Jackson delegates to the Electoral College, and for an entire slate of Democratic Party candidates. The majority ruled. Watching the rise of American democracy, an aging political elite despaired, and feared that the Republic could not survive the rule of the people. Wrote John Randolph of Virginia, "The country is ruined past redemption."[81]

On a mild winter's day, March 4, 1829, twenty thousand Americans turned up in Washington for Andrew Jackson's unruly inauguration.

*Jackson's inauguration in 1829 brought an unprecedented crowd
to the Capitol—a crowd that followed him to the White House.*

Steamboats from Alexandria offered discounted passage across the Potomac.[82] "Thousands and thousands of people, without distinction of rank,
collected in an immense mass round the Capitol," wrote Margaret Bayard
Smith. Jackson was the first president to deliver his inaugural address to
the American people. Following the practice established by Jefferson,
he walked to the Capitol instead of riding. Harriet Hemings might have
watched, from a sidewalk.

John Marshall administered the oath of office. Margaret Bayard Smith
said that when Jackson began to speak, "an almost breathless silence,
succeeded and the multitude was still, listening to catch the sound of
his voice."

His voice rising, he celebrated the triumph of numbers. "The first principle of our system," Jackson said, "is that the majority is to govern." He
bowed to the people. Then, all at once, the people nearly crushed him
with their affection. "It was with difficulty he made his way through the
Capitol and down the hill to the gateway that opens on the avenue," Smith
reported. Supreme Court Justice Joseph Story attended the swearing-in
and then left, bemoaning "the reign of KING MOB."[83]

Even after the president mounted a horse, the people followed him.
"Country men, farmers, gentlemen, mounted and dismounted, boys,

women and children, black and white," Smith wrote. "Carriages, wagons and carts all pursuing him to the President's house." They followed Jackson from the steps of the Capitol all the way to the White House, where, for the first time, the doors were opened to the public. A "rabble, a mob, of boys, negros, women, children, scrambling fighting, romping," wrote Smith. "Ladies fainted, men were seen with bloody noses and such a scene of confusion took place as is impossible to describe,—those who got in could not get out by the door again, but had to scramble out of windows." There was a real worry that the people might press the president to death before the day came to an end. "But it was the People's day," she wrote, "and the People's President and the People would rule."[84] The rule of numbers had begun.

## Six

# THE SOUL AND THE MACHINE

*In the 1830s, railroads emerged as a symbol of progress, pictured, as in this engraving, as if cutting through the wilderness and carrying civilization across the continent.*

MARIA W. STEWART, DARK AND BEAUTIFUL, CARRIED A manuscript tucked under her arm as she picked her way through the cobbled streets of Boston to the offices of the *Liberator*, at 11 Merchants' Hall, down by the docks. "Our souls are fired with the same love of liberty and independence with which your souls are fired," she'd written in an essay she hoped to publish. The descendant of slaves, she'd been born free, in Connecticut, in 1803. Orphaned at five, she'd been bound as a servant to a clergyman till she turned fifteen. In August of 1826, weeks after the fiftieth anniversary of the signing of the Declaration of Independence and the deaths of John Adams and Thomas Jefferson, she'd married a much older man: she was twenty-three; her husband, James W. Stewart, described as "a tolerably stout well-built man; a light, bright mulatto," had served as a sailor during the War of 1812; captured, he'd been a prisoner of war. "It is the blood of our fathers, and the tears of our brethren that have enriched your soils," Maria Stewart wrote in her first, revolutionary essay about American history. "AND WE CLAIM OUR RIGHTS."[1]

William Lloyd Garrison, the editor of the *Liberator*, was two years younger than Stewart. He'd apprenticed as a typesetter and worked as a printer and an editor and failed, again and again, before founding his most radical newspaper. A thin, balding white man, he slept on a bed on the floor of his cramped office, a printing press in the corner; he kept a cat to catch rats. Stewart told Garrison she wished to write for his newspaper, to say what she thought needed saying to the American people. Impressed with her "intelligence and excellence of character," he later recalled, he published the first of her essays in 1831 in a column called the Ladies' Department. "This is the land of freedom," Stewart wrote. "Every man has a right to express his opinion." And every woman, too. She asked, "How long shall the fair daughters of Africa be compelled to bury their minds and talents beneath a load of iron pots and kettles?"[2]

Stewart was a born-again Christian, caught up in a religious revival that swept the country and reached its height in the 1820s and 1830s in the factory towns that grew like kudzu along the path cut by the Erie Canal, from the Hudson River to the Great Lakes, where the power of steam and the anxiety of industrialization were answered by the power of Christ and the assurance of the Gospel. Before the revival began, a scant one in ten Americans were church members; by the time it ended, that ratio had risen to eight in ten.[3] The Presbyterian minister Lyman Beecher called it "the greatest work of God, and the greatest revival of religion, that the world has ever seen."[4]

The revival, known as the Second Great Awakening, infused American politics with the zealotry of millennialism: its most ardent converts believed that they were on the verge of eliminating sin from the world, which would make possible the Second Coming of Christ, who was expected to arrive in as short a time as three months and to come, not to the holy lands, to Bethlehem or Jerusalem, but to the industrializing United States, to Cincinnati and Chicago, to Detroit and Utica. Its ministers preached the power of the people, offering a kind of spiritual Jacksonianism. "God has made man a moral free agent," said the thundering, six-foot-three firebrand Charles Grandison Finney.[5] And the revival was revolutionary: by emphasizing spiritual equality, it strengthened protests against slavery and against the political inequality of women.

"It is not the color of the skin that makes the man or the woman," wrote Stewart, "but the principle formed in the soul."[6] The democratization of American politics was hastened by revivalists like Stewart who believed in the salvation of the individual through good works and in the equality of all people in the eyes of God. Against that belief stood the stark and brutal realities of an industrializing age, the grinding of souls.

# I.

**THE UNITED STATES** was born as a republic and grew into a democracy, and, as it did, it split in two, unable to reconcile its system of government with the institution of slavery. In the first decades of the nineteenth century, democracy came to be celebrated; the right of a majority to govern became dogmatic; and the right to vote was extended to all white men, developments much derided by conservatives who warned that the rule of numbers would destroy the Republic. By the 1830s, the American experiment had produced the first large-scale popular democracy in the history of the world, a politics expressed in campaigns and parades, rallies and conventions, with a two-party system run by partisan newspapers and an electorate educated in a new system of publicly funded schools.

The great debates of the middle decades of the nineteenth century had to do with the soul and the machine. One debate merged religion and politics. What were the political consequences of the idea of the equality of souls? Could the soul of America be redeemed from the nation's original sin, the Constitution's sanctioning of slavery? Another debate merged politics and technology. Could the nation's new democratic traditions survive in the age of the factory, the railroad, and the telegraph? If all events in time can be explained by earlier events in time, if history is a line, and not a circle, then the course of events—change over time—is governed by a set of laws, like the laws of physics, and driven by a force, like gravity. What is that force? Is change driven by God, by people, or by machines? Is progress the progress of *Pilgrim's Progress*, John Bunyan's 1678 allegory—the journey of a Christian from sin to salvation? Is progress the extension of suffrage, the spread of democracy? Or is progress invention, the invention of new machines?

A distinctively American idea of progress involved geography as destiny, picturing improvement as change not only over time but also over space. In 1824, Jefferson wrote that a traveler crossing the continent from west to east would be conducting a "survey, in time, of the progress of man from the infancy of creation to the present day," since "in his progress he would meet the gradual shades of improving man." His traveler—a surveyor, at once, of time and space—would begin with "the savages of the Rocky Mountains": "These he would observe in the earliest stage of association living under no law but that of nature, subscribing and covering themselves with the flesh and skins of wild beasts." Moving eastward, Jefferson's imaginary traveler would then stop "on our frontiers," where he'd find savages "in the pastoral state, raising domestic animals to supply the defects of hunting." Next, farther east, he'd meet "our own semi-barbarous citizens, the pioneers of the advance of civilization." Finally, he'd reach the seaport towns of the Atlantic, finding man in his "as yet, most improved state."[7]

Maria Stewart's Christianity stipulated the spiritual equality of all souls, but Jefferson's notion of progress was hierarchical. That hierarchy, in Jackson's era, was the logic behind African colonization, and it was also the logic behind a federal government policy known as Indian removal: native peoples living east of the Mississippi were required to settle in lands to the west. A picture of progress as the stages from "barbarism" to "civilization"—stages that could be traced on a map of the American continent—competed with a picture of progress as an unending chain of machines.

The age of the machine had begun in 1769, in Glasgow, when James Watt patented an improvement on the steam engine. People had tapped into natural sources of power for manufacturing before—with water-wheels and windmills—but Watt's models produced five times the power of a waterwheel, and didn't need to be sited on a river: a steam engine could work anywhere. Watt reckoned the power of a horse at ten times the power of a man; he defined one "horse power" as the energy required to lift 550 pounds by one foot in one second. Powered by steam, manufacturing became, in the nineteenth century, two hundred times more efficient than it had been in the eighteenth century. That this invention would eventually upend political arrangements is prefigured in a likely apocryphal story told at the time about Watt and the king of England. When King George III went to a factory to see Watt's engine at work, he was told that the factory was "manufacturing an article of which kings were fond."[8]

What article is that, he asked? The reply: Power.

There followed machine upon machine, steam-driven looms, steam-driven boats, making for faster production, faster travel, and cheaper goods. Steam-powered industrial production altered the economy, and it also altered social relations, especially between men and women and between the rich and the poor. The anxiety and social dislocation produced by those changes fueled the revival of religion. Everywhere, the flame of revival burned brightest in factory towns.

Before the rise of the factory, home and work weren't separate places. Most people lived on farms, where both men and women worked in the fields. In the winter, women spent most of their time carding, spinning and weaving wool, sheared from sheep. In towns and cities, shopkeepers and the masters of artisanal trades—bakers, tailors, printers, shoemakers—lived in their shops, where they also usually made their goods. They shared this living space with journeymen and apprentices. Artisans made things whole, undertaking each step in the process of manufacturing: a baker baked a loaf, a tailor stitched a suit. With the rise of the factory came the division of labor into steps done by different workers.[9] With steam power, not only were the steps in the manufacturing process divided, but much of the labor was done by machines, which came to be known as "mechanical slaves."[10]

New, steam-powered machines could also spin and weave—and even weave in ornate, multicolored patterns. In 1802, Joseph-Marie Jacquard, a French weaver, invented an automated loom. By feeding into his loom stiff paper cards with holes punched in them, he could instruct it to weave in any pattern he liked. Two decades later, the English mathematician Charles Babbage used Jacquard's method to devise a machine that could "compute"; that is, it could make mathematical calculations. He called it the Difference Engine, a giant mechanical hand-cranked calculating machine that could tabulate any polynomial function. Then he invented another machine—he called it the Analytical Engine—that could apply the act of mechanical tabulation to solve any problem that involved logic.

*The textile mills of Lowell, Massachusetts, on the
banks of the Merrimack River, were the first in
the United States to use power looms.*

Babbage never built a working machine, but Ada Lovelace, a mathematician and the daughter of Lord Byron, later prepared a detailed description and analysis of the principles and promises of Babbage's work, the first account of what would become, in the twentieth century, a general-purpose computer.[11]

In the United States, with its democracy of numbers, a calculating computer, a machine that could count, would one day throw a wrench in the machinery of government. But long before that day came, Americans devised simpler machines. Watt jealously guarded his patents. In 1810, an American merchant named Francis Cabot Lowell toured England's textile mills and made sketches from memory. In New England, working from those sketches, he designed his own machines and began raising money to build his own factory. Lowell died in 1817. His successors opened the Lowell mills on the Merrimack River in 1823. Every step, from carding to cloth, was done in the same set of factories: six brick buildings erected around a central clock tower. Inspired by the social reformer Robert Owen, Lowell had meant his system as a model, an alternative to the harsh conditions found in factories in England. He called it "a philanthropic manufacturing college." The Lowell mill owners hired young women, transplants from New England farms. They worked twelve hours a day and attended lectures in the evening; they published a monthly magazine. But the utopia that Francis Cabot Lowell imagined did not last. By the 1830s, mill owners had cut wages and sped up the pace of work, and when women protested, they were replaced by men.[12]

Factories accelerated production, canals acceleration transportation. The Erie Canal, completed in 1825, took eight years to dig and covered 360 miles. Before the canal, the wagon trip from Buffalo to New York City took twenty days; on the canal, it took six. The price of goods plummeted; the standard of living soared. A mattress that cost fifty dollars in 1815, which meant that almost no one owned one, cost only five dollars in 1848.[13] One stop on the Erie Canal was Rochester, a mill town on the shore of Lake Ontario that processed the grain from surrounding farms. In 1818, Rochester exported 26,000 barrels of flour a year. Its mills were small, made up of twelve to fifteen men working alongside a master, in a single room, in the master's house. There was, as there had been in such shops for centuries, a great deal of drinking: workers were often paid not in wages but in liquor. Work wasn't done by the clock but by the task. By the end of the 1820s, after the completion of the canal, these small shops had become bigger shops, typically divided into two rooms and employing many more men, each doing a smaller portion of the work, and generally working by the clock, for wages. "Work" came to mean not simply labor but a place, the factory or the banker's or clerk's office: a place men went every day for ten or twelve hours. "Home" was where women remained, and where what they did all day was no longer considered work—that is, they were not paid. The lives of women and men diverged. Wage workers became less and less skilled. Owners made more and more money. Rochester was exporting 200,000 barrels of flour a year by 1828 and, by end of the 1830s, half a million. In 1829, a newspaper editor who used the word "boss" had to define it ("a foreman or master workman, of modern coinage"). By the early 1830s, only the boss still worked in the shop; his employees worked in factories. Masters, or bosses, no longer lived in shops, or even in the neighborhoods of factories: they moved to new neighborhoods, enclaves of a new middle class.[14]

That new middle class soon grew concerned about the unruliness of workers, and especially about their drinking. Inspired by a temperance crusade led by the revivalist Lyman Beecher, a group of mill owners formed the Rochester Society for the Promotion of Temperance. Its members pledged to give up all liquor and to stop paying their workers in

*The tent meetings of the Second Great Awakening had much in
common with Jacksonian-era political rallies, but, where men
dominated party politics, women dominated the revival movement.*

alcohol. Swept up in the spirit of evangelical revival, they began to insist
that their workers join their churches; and they ultimately fired those who
did not. In this effort, they were led, principally, by their wives.

Women led the temperance movement, spurred to this particular crusade not least because drunken husbands tended to beat their wives.
Few laws protected women from such assaults. Husbands addicted to
drinking also spent their wages on liquor, leaving their children hungry.
Since married women had no right to own property, they had no recourse
under the law. Convincing men to give up alcohol seemed the best solution. But the movement was also a consequence of deeper and broader
changes. With the separation of home from work there emerged an ideology of separate spheres: the public world of work and politics was the
world of men; the private world of home and family was the world of
women. Women, within this understanding, were the gentler sex, more
nurturing, more loving, more moral. One advice manual, *A Voice to the
Married*, told wives that they should make the home a haven for their
husbands, "an Elysium to which he can flee and find rest from the story
strife of a selfish world." These changes in the family had begun before
industrialization, but industrialization sped them up. Middle-class and
wealthier women began having fewer children—an average of 3.6 chil-

dren per woman in the 1830s, compared to 5.8 a generation earlier. No new method of contraception made this possible: declining fertility was the consequence of abstinence.[15]

Lyman Beecher wielded enormous influence in this era of reform, and so did his indomitable daughter Catherine, who advocated for the education of girls and published a treatise on "domestic economy"—advice for housewives.[16] But the most powerful preacher to this new middle class, and especially to its women, was Charles Grandison Finney.

Finney had been born again in 1821, when he was twenty-nine, and the Holy Spirit descended upon him, as he put it, "like a wave of electricity." He was ordained three years later by a female missionary society. He held big meetings and small, tent meetings and prayer groups. He looked his listeners in the eye. "A revival is not a miracle," he said. "We are either marching towards heaven or towards hell. How is it with you?" Women didn't always constitute the majority of converts, but their influence was felt on many who did convert. Another female missionary society invited Finney to Rochester in 1830, where he preached every night, and three times on Sunday, for six months. He preached to all classes, all sexes, and all ages but above all to women. Church membership doubled during Finney's six-month stay in Rochester—driven by women. The vast majority of new joiners—more than 70 percent—followed the faith of their mothers but not of their fathers. One man complained after Finney visited: "He stuffed my wife with tracts, and alarmed her fears, and nothing short of meetings, day and night, could atone for the many fold sins my poor, simple spouse had committed, and at the same time, she made the miraculous discovery, that she had been 'unevenly yoked.'" By exercising their power as moral reformers, the wives and daughters of factory owners brought their men into churches. Factory owners began posting job signs that read "None but temperate men need apply." They even paid their workers to go to church. The revival was, for many Americans, heartfelt and abiding. But for many others, it was not. As one Rochester millworker said, "I don't give a damn, I get five dollars more in a month than before I got religion."[17]

If the sincerity of converts was often dubious, another kind of faith was taking deeper root in the 1820s, an evangelical faith in technological progress, an unquestioning conviction that each new machine was making the world better. That faith had a special place in the United States, as if machines had a distinctive destiny on the American continent. In prints and paintings, "Progress" appeared as a steam-powered locomotive, chugging across the continent, unstoppable. Writers celebrated inventors as "Men of Progress" and "Conquerors of Nature" and lauded their machines as far worthier than poetry. The triumph of the sciences over the arts meant the defeat of the ancients by the moderns. The genius of Eli Whitney, hero of modernity, was said to rival that of Shakespeare; the head of the U.S. Patent Office declared the steamboat "a mightier epic" than the *Iliad*.[18]

In 1829, Jacob Bigelow, the Rumford Professor of Physical and Mathematical Sciences at Harvard, delivered a series of lectures called "The Elements of Technology." Before Bigelow, "technology" had meant the arts, mostly the mechanical arts. Bigelow used the word to mean the application of science for the benefit of society. For him, the "march of improvement" amounted to a kind of mechanical millennialism. "Next to the influence of Christianity on our moral nature," he later proclaimed, technology "has had a leading sway in promoting the progress and happiness of our race." His critics charged him with preaching "the gospel of machinery."[19]

The Welshman Thomas Carlyle, calling the era "the Age of Machinery," complained that faith in machines had grown into a religious delusion, as wrong and as dangerous as a belief in witchcraft. Carlyle argued that people like Bigelow, who believed that machines liberate mankind, made a grave error; machines are prisons. "Free in hand and foot, we are shackled in heart and soul with far straighter than feudal chains," Carlyle insisted, "fettered by chains of our own forging."[20] America writers, refuting Carlyle, argued that the age of machinery was itself making possible the rise of democracy. In 1831, an Ohio lawyer named Timothy Walker, replying to Carlyle, claimed that by liberating the ordinary man from the drudgery that would otherwise prohibit his full political participation, machines drive democracy.[21]

Opponents of Andrew Jackson had considered his presidency not progress but decay. "The Republic has degenerated into a Democracy," one Richmond newspaper declared in 1834.[22] To Jackson's supporters, his election marked not degeneration but a new stage in the history of progress. Nowhere was this argument made more forcefully, or more influentially, than in George Bancroft's *History of the United States from the Discovery of the American Continent to the Present*. The book itself, reviewers noted, voted for Jackson. The spread of evangelical Christianity, the invention of new machines, and the rise of American democracy convinced Bancroft that "humanism is steady advancing," and that "the advance of liberty and justice is certain." That advance, men like Bancroft and Jackson believed, required Americans to march across the continent, to carry these improvements from east to west, the way Jefferson had pictured it. Democracy, John O'Sullivan, a New York lawyer and Democratic editor, argued in 1839, is nothing more or less than "Christianity in its earthly aspect." O'Sullivan would later coin the term "manifest destiny" to describe this set of beliefs, the idea that the people of the United States were fated "to over spread and to possess the whole of the continent which Providence has given for the development of the great experiment of liberty."[23]

To evangelical Democrats, Democracy, Christianity, and technology were levers of the same machine. And yet, all along, there were critics and dissenters and objectors who saw, in the soul of the people, in the march of progress, in the unending chain of machines, in the seeming forward movement of history, little but violence and backwardness and a great crushing of men, women, and children. "Oh, America, America," Maria Stewart cried, "foul and indelible is thy stain!"[24]

**STEWART HAD STUDIED** the Bible from childhood, a study she kept up her whole life, even as she scrubbed other people's houses and washed other people's clothes. "While my hands are toiling for their daily sustenance," she wrote, "my heart is most generally meditating upon its divine truths."[25] She considered slavery a sin. She took her inspiration from Scripture. "I have borrowed much of my language from the holy Bible," she said.[26] But she also borrowed much of her language—especially the language of rights—from the Declaration of Independence. That the revival of Christianity coincided with the fiftieth anniversary of the Declaration, an anniversary made all the more mystical when the news spread that both Jefferson and Adams had died that very day, July 4, 1826, as if by the hand of God, meant that the Declaration itself took on a religious cast. The self-evident, secular truths of the Declaration of Independence became, to evangelical Americans, the truths of revealed religion.

To say that this marked a turn away from the spirit of the nation's founding is to wildly understate the case. The United States was founded

*An unidentified woman, about the age of Maria W. Stewart when she first wrote for the* Liberator, *posed for a daguerreotype, holding a book, an emblem of her learnedness.*

during the most secular era in American history, either before or since. In the late eighteenth century, church membership was low, and anticlerical feeling was high. It is no accident that the Constitution does not mention God. Philadelphia physician Benjamin Rush wondered, politely, whether this error might be corrected, assuming it to have been an oversight. "Perhaps an acknowledgement might be made of his goodness or of his providence in the proposed amendments," he urged.[27] No correction was made.

The United States was not founded as a Christian nation. The Constitution prohibits religious tests for officeholders. The Bill of Rights forbids the federal government from establishing a religion, James Madison having argued that to establish a religion would be "to foster in those who still reject it, a suspicion that its friends are too conscious of its fallacies to trust it to its own merits."[28] These were neither casual omissions nor accidents; they represented an intentional disavowal of a constitutional relationship between church and state, a disavowal that was not infrequently specifically stated. In 1797, John Adams signed the Treaty of Tripoli, securing the release of American captives in North Africa, and promising that the United States would not engage in a holy war with Islam because "the Government of the United States of America is not, in any sense, founded on the Christian religion."[29]

But during the Second Great Awakening, evangelicals recast the nation's origins as avowedly Christian. "Upon what was America founded?" Maria Stewart asked, and answered, "Upon religion and pure principles."[30] Lyman Beecher argued that the Republic, "in its constitution and laws, is of heavenly origin."[31] Nearly everything took on a religious cast during the revival, not least because of the proliferation of preachers. In 1775, there had been 1,800 ministers in the United States; by 1845, there were more than 40,000.[32] They were Baptist, Methodist, Presbyterian, Congregationalist, Episcopalian, Universalist, and more, very much the flowering of religious expression that Madison had predicted would result from the prohibition of an established religion. The separation of church and state allowed religion to thrive; that was one of its intentions. Lacking an established state religion, Americans founded new sects, from Shakers to Mormons, and rival Protestant denominations sprung up in town after town. Increasingly, the only unifying, national religion was a civil religion, a belief in the American creed. This faith bound the nation together, and provided extraordinary political stability in an era of astonishing change, but it also tied it to the past, in ways that often proved crippling. In 1816, when Jefferson was seventy-three and the awakening was just beginning, he warned against worshipping the men of his generation. "This they would say themselves, were they to rise from the dead," he wrote: ". . . laws and institutions must go hand in hand with the progress of the human mind." To treat the founding documents as Scripture would be to become a slave to the past. "Some men look at constitutions with sanctimonious reverence, and deem them like the ark of the covenant, too sacred to be touched," Jefferson conceded. But when they do, "They ascribe to the men of the preceding age a wisdom more than human."[33]

Abolitionists adopted a different posture. They didn't worship the founders; they judged them. In the spring of 1829, William Lloyd Garrison, who'd entered the evangelical movement as an advocate of temperance and had only lately begun to concern himself with the problem of slavery, was asked to deliver a Fourth of July address before a Massachusetts branch of the Colonization Society, at the Park Street Church in Boston. He declared that the holiday was filled with "hypocritical cant about the inalienable rights of man."[34]

This complicated position, a sense of the divinity of the Declaration of Independence, mixed with fury at the founders themselves, came, above all, from black churches, like the church where Maria Stewart and her husband were married, the African Meeting House on Belknap Street, in Boston's free black neighborhood, on a slope of Beacon Hill known as "Nigger Hill."[35] Their friend David Walker, a tall, freeborn man from North Carolina, lived not far from the meetinghouse, and kept a slop shop on Brattle Street, selling gear to seamen; he likely traded with James W. Stewart, who earned his living outfitting ships. Walker was born in Wilmington, North Carolina. His father was a slave, his mother a free black woman. Sometime between 1810 and 1820, he'd moved from Wilmington to Charleston, South Carolina, probably drawn to its free black community and to its church. At the very beginning of the revival, in 1816, the African Methodist Episcopal Church was founded in Philadelphia. Charleston opened an AME church in 1817; Walker joined.

While men like Finney preached to the workers and bosses of Rochester, New York, black evangelicals preached to free blacks who were keenly aware of the very different effects of the age of the machine on the lives of slaves and slave families. Cotton production in the South doubled between 1815 and 1820, and again between 1820 and 1825. Cotton had become the most valuable commodity in the Atlantic world. The Atlantic slave trade had been closed in 1808, but the new and vast global market for cotton created a booming domestic market for slaves. By 1820, more than a million slaves had been sold "down the river," from states like Virginia and South Carolina to the territories of Alabama, Louisiana, and Mississippi. Another million people were sold, and shipped west, between 1820 and 1860. Mothers were separated from their children, husbands from wives. When the price of cotton in Liverpool went up, so did the price of slaves in the American South. People, like cotton, were sold by grades, advertised as "Extra Men, No.1 Men, Second Rate or Ordinary Men, Extra Girls, No.1 Girls, Second Rate or Ordinary Girls." Slavery wasn't an aberration in an industrializing economy; slavery was its engine. Factories had mechanical slaves; plantations had human slaves. The power of machines was measured by horsepower, the power of slaves by hand power. A healthy man counted as "two hands," a nursing woman as a "half-hand," a child as a "quarter-hand." Charles Ball, born in Maryland during the American Revolution, spent years toiling on a slave plantation in South Carolina, and time on an auction block, where buyers inspected his hands, moving each finger in the minute action required to pick cotton. The standard calculation, for a cotton crop, "ten acres to the hand."[36]

David Walker, living in Charleston, bore witness to those sufferings, and he prayed. So did Denmark Vesey, a carpenter who worshipped with Walker at the same AME church. In 1822, Vesey staged a rebellion, leading a group of slaves and free blacks in a plan to seize the city. Instead, Vesey was caught and hanged. Slave owners blamed black sailors, who, they feared, spread word in the South of freedom in the North and of independence in Haiti. After Vesey's execution, South Carolina's legislature passed the Negro Seaman Acts, requiring black sailors to be held in prison while their ships were in port.[37] Walker decided to leave South Carolina for Massachusetts, where he opened his shop for black sailors and helped found the Massachusetts General Colored Association, the first black political organization in the United States. Meanwhile, he helped runaways. "His hands were always open to contribute to the wants of the fugitive," the preacher Henry Highland Garnet later wrote. And he studied; he "spent all his leisure moments in the cultivation of his mind."[38] He also began helping to circulate in Boston the first black newspaper, *Freedom's Journal*, published in New York beginning in 1827. "We wish to plead our own cause," its editors proclaimed. "Too long have others spoken for us."[39]

In the fall of 1829, the year Jacob Bigelow and Thomas Carlyle were arguing about the consequences of technological change, David Walker published a short pamphlet that struck the country like a bolt of lightning: *An Appeal to the Colored Citizens of the World, but in Particular, and Very Expressly, to those of the United States of America.* Combining the exhortations of a revivalist preacher with the rabble-rousing of a Jacksonian political candidate, Walker preached that, without the saving redemption of abolition, there would come a political apocalypse, the wages of the sin of slavery: "I call men to witness, that the destruction of the Americans is at hand, and will be speedily consummated unless they repent."

Walker claimed the Declaration of Independence for black Americans: "'We hold these truths to be self-evident—that ALL men are created EQUAL!! that they *are endowed by their Creator with certain inalienable rights*; that among these are life, *liberty*, and the pursuit of happiness!!'" He insisted on the right to revolution. Addressing his white readers, he wrote, "Now, Americans! I ask you candidly, was your sufferings under Great Britain, one hundredth part as cruel and tyrannical as you have rendered ours under you?" He described American expansion, the growth of the Union from thirteen states to twenty-four, as a form of violence: "the whites are dragging us around in chains and in handcuffs, to their new States and Territories, to work their mines and farms, to enrich them and their children." And he damned manifest destiny as a fraud, resting on the belief of millions of Americans "that we being a little darker than they, were made by our Creator to be an inheritance to them and their children forever." He called the scheme of Henry Clay's American Colonization Society the "colonizing trick": "This country is as much ours as it is the whites, whether they will admit it now or not, they will see and believe it by and by." And he warned: "Are Mr. Clay and the rest of the Americans, innocent of the blood and groans of our fathers and us, their children?—Every individual may plead innocence, if he pleases, but God will, before long, separate the innocent from the guilty." He asked black men to take up arms. "Look upon your mother, wife and children," he urged, "and answer God Almighty; and believe this, that it is no more harm for you to kill a man, who is trying to kill you, than it is for you to take a drink of water when thirsty." And, remarking on the history of the West Indies, he warned the owners of men: "Read the history particularly of Hayti, and see how they were butchered by the whites, and do you take warning." In an age of quantification, Walker made his own set of calculations: "God has been pleased to give us two eyes, two hands, two feet, and some sense in our heads as well as they. They have no more right to hold us in slavery than we have to hold them." And then: "I do declare it, that one good black man can put to death six white men."[40]

The preaching of David Walker, even more than the preaching of Lyman Beecher or Charles Grandison Finney, set the nation on fire. It was prosecutorial; it was incendiary. It was also widely read. Walker had made elaborate plans to get his *Appeal* into the hands of southern slaves. With the help of his friends Maria and James Stewart, he stitched copies into the linings of clothes he and Stewart sold to sailors bound for Charleston, New Orleans, Savannah, and Wilmington. The *Appeal* went through three editions in nine months. The last edition appeared in June of 1830; that August, Walker was found dead in the doorway of his Boston shop. There were rumors he'd been murdered (rewards of upward of $10,000 had been offered for him in the South). More likely, he died of tuberculosis. James and Maria Stewart moved into his old rooms on Belknap Street.[41]

Walker had died, but he had spread his word. In 1830, a group of slaves plotting a rebellion were found with a copy of the *Appeal*. With Walker, the antislavery argument for gradual emancipation, with compensation for slave owners, became untenable. Abolitionists began arguing for immediate emancipation. And southern antislavery societies shut their doors. As late as 1827, the number of antislavery groups in the South had outnumbered those in the North by more than four to one. Southern antislavery activists were usually supporters of colonization, not of emancipation. Walker's *Appeal* ended the antislavery movement in the South and radicalized it in the North. Garrison published the first issue of the *Liberator* on January 1, 1831. It begins with words as uncompromising as Walker's: "I am in earnest—I will not equivocate—I will not excuse—I will not retreat a single inch—AND I WILL BE HEARD."[42]

That summer, in Virginia, a thirty-year-old revivalist preacher named Nat Turner planned a slave rebellion for the Fourth of July. Turner's rebellion was at once an act of emancipation and of evangelism. Both of his parents were slaves. His mother had been born in Africa; his father escaped to the North. The wife of Turner's owner had taught him to read when he was a child; he studied the Bible. He worked in the fields, and he also preached. In 1828, he had a religious vision: he believed God had called him to lead an uprising. "White spirits and black spirits engaged in battle," he later said, ". . . and blood flowed in streams." He delayed until August, when, after killing dozens of whites, he and his followers were caught. Turner was hanged.

The rebellion rippled across the Union. The Virginia legislature debated the possibility of emancipating its slaves, fearing "a Nat Turner might be in every family." Quakers submitted a petition to the state legislature calling for abolition. The petition was referred to a committee, headed by Thomas Jefferson's thirty-nine-year-old grandson, Thomas Jefferson Randolph, who proposed a scheme of gradual emancipation. Instead, the legislature passed new laws banning the teaching of slaves to read and write, and prohibiting, too, teaching slaves about the Bible.[43] In a nation founded on a written Declaration, made sacred by evangelicals during a religious revival, reading about equality became a crime.

Alexis de Tocqueville, the sharp-eyed French political theorist and historian, landed in New York in May 1831, for a nine-month tour of the United States. Nat Turner waged his rebellion in Virginia that August. Maria Stewart's first essay appeared in the *Liberator* that October. "If ever America undergoes great revolutions, they will be brought about by the presence of the black race on the soil of the United States," Tocqueville predicted. "They will owe their origin, not to the equality, but to the inequality of condition."[44] Even as Tocqueville was writing, those revolutions were already being waged.

## II.

**MARIA STEWART WAS** the first woman in the United States to deliver an address before a "mixed" audience—an audience of both women and men, which happened to have been, as well, an audience of both blacks and whites. She spoke, suitably, in a hall named after Benjamin Franklin. She said she'd heard a voice asking the question: "'Who shall go forward, and take of the reproach that is cast upon the people of color? Shall it be a woman?' And my heart made this reply—'If it is thy will, be it even so, Lord Jesus!'"[45]

Stewart delivered five public addresses about slavery between 1831 and 1833, the year Garrison founded the American Anti-Slavery Society, in language that echoed hers. At the society's first convention, Garrison declared, "We plant ourselves upon the Declaration of our Independence and the truths of Divine Revelation, as upon the Everlasting Rock."[46]

*Shall it be a woman?* One consequence of the rise of Jacksonian democracy and the Second Great Awakening was the participation of women in the reformation of American politics by way of American morals. When suffrage was stripped of all property qualifications, women's lack of political power became starkly obvious. For women who wished to exercise power, the only source of power seemingly left to them was their role as mothers, which, they suggested, rendered them morally superior to men—more loving, more caring, and more responsive to the cries of the weak.

Purporting to act less as citizens than as mothers, cultivating the notion of "republican motherhood," women formed temperance societies, charitable aid societies, peace societies, vegetarian societies, and abolition societies. The first Female Anti-Slavery Society was founded in Boston in 1833; by 1837, 139 Female Anti-Slavery Societies had been founded across the country, including more than 40 in Massachusetts and 30 in Ohio. By then, Maria Stewart had stopped delivering speeches, an act that many women, both black and white, considered too radical for the narrow ambit of republican motherhood. After 1835, she never again spoke in public. As Catherine Beecher argued in 1837, in *An Essay on Slavery and Abolitionism, with Reference to the Duty of American Females*, "If the female advocate chooses to come upon a stage, and expose her person, dress, and elocution to public criticism, it is right to express disgust."[47]

While women labored to reform society behind the scenes, men protested on the streets. The eighteen-teens marked the beginning of a decades-long struggle between labor and business. During the Panic of 1819, the first bust in the industrializing nineteenth century, factories had closed when the banks failed. In New York, a workingman's wages fell from 75 cents to 12 cents a day. Those who suffered the most were men too poor to vote; it was, in many ways, the suffering of workingmen during that Panic of 1819 that had led so many men to fight for the right to vote, so that they could have a hand in the direction of affairs. Having secured the franchise, they attacked the banks and all manner of monopolies. In 1828, laborers in Philadelphia formed the Working Men's Party. One writer in 1830 argued that commercial banking was "the foundation of artificial inequality of wealth, and, thereby, of artificial inequality of power."[48]

Workingmen demanded shorter hours (ten, instead of eleven or twelve) and better conditions. They argued, too, against "an unequal and very excessive accumulation of wealth and power into the hands of a few." Jacksonian democracy distributed political power to the many, but industrialization consolidated economic power in the hands of a few. In Boston, the top 1 percent of the population controlled 10 percent of wealth in 1689, 16 percent in 1771, 33 percent in 1833, and 37 percent in 1848, while the lowest 80 percent of the population controlled 39 percent of the wealth in 1689, 29 percent in 1771, 14 percent in 1833, and a mere 4 percent in 1848. Much the same pattern obtained elsewhere. In New York, the top 1 percent of the population controlled 40 percent of the wealth in 1828 and 50 percent in 1845; the top 4 percent of the population controlled 63 percent of the wealth in 1828 and 80 percent in 1845.[49]

Native-born workingmen had to contend with the ease with which factory owners could replace them with immigrants who were arriving in unprecedented numbers, fleeing hunger and revolution in Europe and seeking democracy and opportunity in the United States. Many parts of the country, including Iowa, Minnesota, and Wisconsin, recruited immigrants by advertising in European newspapers. Immigrants encouraged more immigrants, in the letters they wrote home to family and friends, urging them to pack their bags. "This is a free country," a Swedish immigrant wrote home from Illinois in 1850. "And nobody needs to hold his hat in his hand for anyone else." A Norwegian wrote from Minnesota, "The principle of equality has been universally accepted and adopted."[50]

In 1831, twenty thousand Europeans migrated to the United States; in 1854, that number had risen to more than four hundred thousand. While two and a half million Europeans had migrated to all of the Americas between 1500 and 1800, the same number—two and a half million— arrived specifically in the United States between 1845 and 1854 alone. As a proportion of the U.S. population, European immigrants grew from 1.6 percent in the 1820s to 11.2 percent in 1860. Writing in 1837, one Michigan reformer called the nation's rate of immigration "the boldest experiment upon the stability of government ever made in the annals of time."[51]

The largest number of these immigrants were Irish and German. Critics of Jackson—himself the son of Irish immigrants—had blamed his election on the rising population of poor, newly enfranchised Irishmen. "Everything in the shape of an Irishman was drummed to the polls," one newspaper editor wrote in 1828.[52] By 1860, more than one in eight Americans were born in Europe, including 1.6 million Irish and 1.2 million Germans, the majority of whom were Catholic. As the flood of immigrants swelled, the force of nativism gained strength, as did hostility toward Catholics, fueled by the animus of evangelical Protestants.

In 1834, Lyman Beecher delivered a series of anti-Catholic lectures. The next year, Samuel F. B. Morse, a young man of many talents, best known as a painter, published a virulent treatise called *Imminent Dangers to the Free Institutions of the United States through Foreign Immigration*, urging the passage of a new immigration law banning all foreign-born Americans from voting.[53] Morse then ran for mayor of New York (and lost). Meanwhile, he began devising a secret code of dots and dashes, to be used on the telegraph machine he was designing. He believed there existed a Catholic plot to take over the United States. He believed that, to defeat such a plot, the U.S. government needed a secret cipher. Eventually, he decided that a better use of his code, not secret but public, would be to use it to communicate by a network of wires that he imagined would one day stretch across the entire continent. It wouldn't be long, he predicted in 1838, before "the whole surface of this country would be channeled for those nerves which are to diffuse, with the speed of thought, a knowledge of all that is occurring throughout the land; making, in fact, one neighborhood of the whole country."[54]

Could a mere machine quiet the political tumult? In Philadelphia in 1844, riots between Catholics and Protestants left twenty Americans dead. The single biggest wave of immigration in the period came between 1845 and 1849, when Ireland endured a potato famine. One million people died, and one and a half million left, most for the United States, where they landed in Eastern Seaboard cities, and settled there, having no money to pay their way to travel inland. (Patrick Kennedy, the great-grandfather of the first Catholic to be elected president of the United States, left Ireland in 1849.) They lived in all-Irish neighborhoods, generally in tenements, and worked for abysmal wages. New York lawyer George Templeton Strong, writing in his diary, lamented their foreignness: "Our Celtic fellow citizens are almost as remote from us in temperament and constitution as the Chinese." The Irish, keen to preserve their religion and their communities, built Catholic churches and parochial schools and mutual aid societies. They also turned to the Democratic Party to defend those institutions. By 1850, one in every four people in Boston was Irish. Signs at shops began to read, "No Irish Need Apply."[55]

Germans, who came to the United States in greater numbers than the Irish, suffered considerably less prejudice. They usually arrived less destitute, and could afford to move inland and become farmers. They tended to settle in the Mississippi or Ohio Valleys, where they bought land from earlier German settlers and sent their children to German schools and German churches. The insularity of both Irish and German communities contributed to a growing movement to establish tax-supported public elementary schools, known as "common schools," meant to provide a common academic and civic education to all classes of Americans. Like the extension of suffrage to all white men, this element of the American experiment propelled the United States ahead of European nations. Much of the movement's strength came from the fervor of revivalists. They hoped that these new schools would assimilate a diverse population of native-born and foreign-born citizens by introducing them to the traditions of American culture and government, so that boys, once men, would vote wisely, and girls, once women, would raise virtuous children. "It is our duty to make men moral," read one popular teachers' manual, published in 1830. Other advocates hoped that a shared education would diminish partisanship. Whatever the motives of its advocates, the common school movement emerged out of, and nurtured, a strong civic culture.[56]

Yet for all the abiding democratic idealism of the common school movement, it was animated, as well, by nativism. One New York state assemblyman warned: "We must decompose and cleanse the impurities which rush into our midst. There is but one rectifying agent—one infallible filter—the SCHOOL." And critics suggested that common schools, vaunted as moral education, provided, instead, instruction in regimentation. Common schools emphasized industry—working by the clock. This curriculum led workingmen to voice doubts about the purpose of such an education, with *Mechanics Magazine* asking in 1834: "What is the education of a common school? Is there a syllable of science taught in one, beyond the rudiments of mathematics? No."[57]

Black children were excluded from common schools, leading one Philadelphia woman to point out the hypocrisy of defenders of slavery who based their argument on the ignorance of Americans of African descent: "Conscious of the unequal advantages enjoyed by our children, we feel indignant against those who are continually vituperating us for the ignorance and degradation of our people." Free black families supported their own schools, like the African Free School in New York, which, by the 1820s, had more than six hundred students. In other cities, black families fought for integration of the common schools and won. In 1855, the Massachusetts legislature, urged on by Charles Sumner, made integration mandatory. This occasioned an outcry. The *New York Herald* warned: "The North is to be Africanized. Amalgamation has commenced. New England heads the column. God save the Commonwealth of Massachusetts!" No other state followed. Instead, many specifically passed laws making integration illegal.[58]

With free schools, literacy spread, and the number of newspapers rose, a change that was tied to the rise of a new party system. Parties come and go, but a party system—a stable pair of parties—has characterized American politics since the ratification debates. In American history the change from one party system to another has nearly always been associated with a revolution in communications that allows the people to shake loose of the control of parties. In the 1790s, during the rise of the first party system, which pitted Federalists against Republicans, the number of newspapers had swelled. During the shift to the second party system, which, beginning in 1833, pitted Democrats against the newly founded Whig Party, not only did the number of newspapers rise, but their prices plummeted. The newspapers of the first party system, which were also known as "commercial advertisers," had consisted chiefly of partisan commentary and ads, and generally sold for six cents an issue. The new papers cost only one cent, and were far more widely read. The rise of the so-called penny press also marked the beginning of the triumph of "facts" over "opinion" in American journalism, mainly because the penny press aimed at a different, broader, and less exclusively partisan, audience. The *New York Sun* appeared in 1833. "It shines for all" was its common-man motto. "The object of this paper is to lay before the public, at a price within the means of everyone, ALL THE NEWS OF THE DAY," it boasted. It dispensed with subscriptions and instead was circulated at newsstands, where it was sold for cash, to anyone who had a ready penny. Its front page was filled not with advertising but with news. The penny press was a "free press," as James Gordon Bennett of the *New York Herald* put it, because it wasn't beholden to parties. (Bennett, born in Scotland, had immigrated to the United States after reading Benjamin Franklin's *Autobiography*.) Since the paper was sold at newsstands, rather than mailed to subscribers, he explained, its editors and writers were "entirely ignorant who are its readers and who are not." They couldn't favor their readers' politics because they didn't know them. "We shall support no party," Bennett insisted. "We shall endeavor to record facts."[59]

During the days of the penny press, Tocqueville observed that Americans had a decided preference for weighing the facts of a matter themselves:

They mistrust systems; they adhere closely to facts and study facts with their own senses. As they do not easily defer to the mere name of any fellow man, they are never inclined to rest upon any man's authority; but, on the contrary, they are unremitting in their efforts to find out the weaker points of their neighbor's doctrine.[60]

The people wished to decide, not only on how to vote, but about what's true, and what's not.

# III.

IF THOMAS JEFFERSON rode to the White House on the shoulders of slaves, Andrew Jackson rode to the White House in the arms of the people. By the people, Jackson meant the newly enfranchised workingman, the farmer and the factory worker, the reader of newspapers. In office, he pursued a policy of continental expansion, dismantled the national bank, and narrowly averted a constitutional crisis over the question of slavery. He also extended the powers of the presidency. "Though we live under the form of a republic," Justice Joseph Story said, "we are in fact under the absolute rule of a single man." Jackson vetoed laws passed by Congress (becoming the first president to assume this power). At one point, he dismissed his entire cabinet. "The man we have made our President has made himself our despot, and the Constitution now lies a heap of ruins at his feet," declared a senator from Rhode Island, "When the way to his object lies through the Constitution, the Constitution has not the strength of a cobweb to restrain him from breaking through it."[61] His critics dubbed him "King Andrew."

Jackson's first campaign involved implementing the policy of Indian removal, forcibly moving native peoples east of the Mississippi River to lands to the west. This policy applied only to the South. There were Indian communities in the North—the Mashpees of Massachusetts, for instance—but their numbers were small. James Fennimore Cooper's *The Last of the Mohicans* (1826) was just one in a glut of romantic paeans to the "vanishing Indian," the ghost of Indians past. "We hear the rustling of their footsteps, like that of the withered leaves of autumn, and they are gone forever," wrote Justice Story in 1828. Jackson directed his policy of Indian removal at the much bigger communities of native peoples of the Southeast, the Cherokees, Chickasaws, Chocktaws, Creeks, and Semi-

*The Cherokees devised their own writing system, adopted their own constitution, and began printing their own newspaper, the* Phoenix, *in 1828.*

noles who lived on homelands in Alabama, Florida, Georgia, Louisiana, Mississippi, and Tennessee, Jackson's home state.[62]

To this campaign, Jackson brought considerable military experience. In 1814, he'd led a coalition of U.S. and Cherokee forces against the Creeks. After that war, the Creeks ceded more than twenty million acres of their land to the United States. In 1816 and 1817, Jackson then compelled his Cherokee allies to sign treaties selling to the United States more than three million acres for about twenty cents an acre. When the Cherokees protested, Jackson reputedly said, "Look around, and recollect what happened to our brothers the Creeks."[63] But the religious revival interfered with removal. In 1816, evangelicals from the American Board of Commissioners of Foreign Missions began attempting to convert the Cherokee, declaring a mission "to make the whole tribe English in their language, civilized in their habits, and Christian in their religion," a mission that, if accomplished, would seem to defeat the logic of removal in the name of "progress." Meanwhile, the Cherokee decided to proclaim their political equality and declare their independence as a nation.[64]

For centuries, Europeans had based their claims to lands in the New World on arguments that native peoples had no right to the land they inhabited, no sovereignty over it, because they had no religion, or because they had no government, or because they had no system of writing. The Cherokees, with deliberation and purpose, challenged each of these arguments. In 1823, when the federal government tried to get the Cherokees to agree to move, the Cherokee National Council replied, "It is the fixed and unalterable determination of this nation never again to cede one foot of land." A Cherokee man named Sequoyah, who'd fought under Jackson during the Creek War, invented a written form of the Cherokee language, not an alphabet but a syllabary, with one character for every syllable. In 1825, the Cherokee Nation began printing the *Phoenix*, in both English and, using the syllabary, in Cherokee. In 1826, it established a national capital, at New Echota (just outside of what's now Calhoun, Georgia), and in 1827 the National Council ratified a written constitution.[65]

South Carolina–born John C. Calhoun, Monroe's secretary of war, pressed them: "You must be sensible that it will be impossible for you to remain, for any length of time, in your present situation, within the limits of Georgia, or any other State." To whch the Cherokees replied: "We beg leave to observe, and to remind you, that the Cherokees are not foreigners, but original inhabitants of America; and that they now inhabit and stand on the soil of their own territory; . . . and that they cannot recognize the sovereignty of any State within the limits of their territory."[66]

Jacksonians argued that, in the march of progress, the Cherokees had been left behind, "unimproved," but the Cherokees were determined to call that bluff by demonstrating each of their "improvements." In 1825, Cherokee property consisted of 22,000 cattle, 7,600 horses, 4,600 pigs, 2,500 sheep, 725 looms, 2,488 spinning wheels, 172 wagons, 10,000 plows, 31 grist mills, 10 sawmills, 62 blacksmith shops, 8 cotton gins, 18 schools, 18 ferries, and 1,500 slaves. The writer John Howard Payne, who lived with Cherokees in the 1820s, explained, "When the Georgian asks—shall savages infest our borders thus? The Cherokee answers him—'Do we not read? Have we not schools? churches? Manufactures? Have we not laws? Letters? A constitution? And do you call us savages?'"[67]

They might have prevailed. They had the law of nations on their side. But then, in 1828, gold was discovered on Cherokee land, just fifty miles from New Echota, a discovery that doomed the Cherokee cause. When

Jackson took office, in March 1829, he declared Indian removal one of his chief priorities and argued that the establishment of the Cherokee Nation violated Article IV, Section 3 of the U.S. Constitution: "no new States shall be formed or erected within the Jurisdiction of any other State" without that state's approval.

Jackson's Indian Removal Act aroused the ire of reformers and revivalists. David Walker had argued that Indian removal was just another version of the "colonizing trick." Catharine Beecher, disavowing public speaking but advocating letter-writing, led an effort to submit a female petition opposing Indian removal to Congress. After considerable debate, the bill narrowly passed, the vote falling along sectional lines, New Englanders voting 28–9 against and southerners 60–15 in favor in the House while, in the Senate, New Englanders voted nearly uniformly against, and southerners unanimously in favor. The middle states were more divided. And yet the debate itself had raised, for everyone, broader questions about the nature of race, one senator from New Jersey inquiring, "Do the obligations of justice change with the color of the skin?"[68]

There remained the matter of the lawfulness of the act, and the question of its enforcement. The Cherokees argued that the state of Georgia had no jurisdiction over them, and the case went to the Supreme Court. In *Cherokee Nation v. Georgia* (1831), Chief Justice John Marshall said, "If courts were permitted to indulge their sympathies, a case better calculated to excite them can scarcely be imagined." In his opinion, Marshall fatefully defined the Cherokee as "domestic dependent nations," a new legal entity—not states and not quite nations, either. In another case the next year, *Worcester v. Georgia* (1832), Marshall elaborated: "The Cherokee Nation, then, is a distinct community, occupying its own territory, . . . in which the laws of Georgia can have no force, and which the citizens of Georgia have no right to enter. . . . The Acts of Georgia are repugnant to the Constitution, laws, and treaties of the United States."[69]

In New England, Marshall's decision led tribes like the Penobscots and the Mashpees to press for their own independence. In 1833, the Mashpee people published *An Indian's Appeal to the White Men of Massachusetts*, arguing, "As our brethren, the white men of Massachusetts, have recently manifested much sympathy for the red men of the Cherokee nation . . . we, the red men of the Mashpee tribe, consider it a favorable time to speak. We are not free. We wish to be so."[70] Marshall's rulings in the Cherokee cases—which touched on the nature of title—inevitably occasioned a pained discussion about the European settlement of North America and the founding of the United States. In 1835, Edward Everett, a Massachusetts legislator who'd led the fight against Indian removal in Congress, balked at the hypocrisy of northern writers and reformers: "Unless we deny altogether the rightfulness of settling the continent,— unless we maintain that it was from the origin unjust and wrong to introduce the civilized race into America, and that the whole of what is now our happy and prosperous country ought to have been left, as it was found, the abode of barbarity and heathenism,—I am not sure, that any different result could have taken place."[71] Jackson agreed, asking, "Would the people of Maine permit the Penobscot tribe to erect an independent government within their State?"[72]

In the end, Jackson decided to ignore the Supreme Court. "John Marshall has made his decision," he is rumored to have said (the rumor appears to have been a wild one). "Now let him enforce it."[73] The leaders of a tiny minority of Cherokees signed a treaty, ceding the land to Georgia and setting a deadline for removal at May 23, 1838. By the time the deadline came, only 2,000 Cherokees had left for the West; 16,000 more refused to leave their homes. U.S. Army General Winfield Scott, a fastidious career military man from Virginia known as "Old Fuss and Feathers," arrived to force the matter. He begged the Cherokees to move voluntarily. "I am an old warrior, and have been present at many a scene of slaughter," he said, "but spare me, I beseech you, the horror of witnessing the destruction of the Cherokees." On the forced march 800 miles westward and, by Jefferson's imagining, backward in time, one in four Cherokees died, of starvation, exposure, or exhaustion, on what came to be called the Trail of Tears. By the time it was over, the U.S. government had resettled 47,000 southeastern Indians to lands west of the Mississippi and acquired more than a hundred million acres of land to the east. In 1839, in Indian Territory, or what is now Oklahoma, the Cherokee men who'd signed the treaty were murdered by unknown assassins.[74]

By then, Jackson's two terms in office had come to an end. But during the years he occupied the White House, between 1829 and 1837, ignoring a decision made by the Supreme Court had been neither the last nor the least of Andrew Jackson's assertions of presidential power. Especially fraught was Jackson's relationship with his first vice president, John C. Calhoun, Monroe's former secretary of war, a fellow so stern and unyielding that one particularly shrewd observer dubbed him "cast-iron man."[75] Calhoun had served as John Quincy Adams's vice president, too, and his relationship with Jackson had been strained from the start. Matters worsened when Calhoun led South Carolina's attempt to "nullify" a tariff established by Congress. Like the struggle over Indian removal, the debate over the tariff stretched the limits of the powers of the Constitution to hold the states together.

One night in 1832, at a formal dinner, Jackson and Calhoun battled the matter out over drinks. The president offered a toast to "Our federal Union—it must be preserved." After Jackson sat down, Calhoun rose from his seat to offer his own toast: "The Union—next to our liberty, the most dear; may we all remember that it can only be preserved by respecting the rights of the states." The much lesser political skills of former New York governor Martin Van Buren, also at the dinner that night, were in evidence when he rose to give a third toast, to "mutual forbearance and reciprocal concession."[76] Between Jackson and Calhoun, there would be no forbearance, and very little concession.

Although the tariff cut the duty on imports in half, it still worried southerners, who argued that it put the interest of northern manufacturers above southern agriculturalists. The South provided two-thirds of American exports (almost entirely in the form of cotton) and consumed only one-tenth of its imports, leading its politicians to oppose the tariff by endorsing a position that came to be called "free trade."[77]

To protest the tariff, Calhoun wrote a treatise on behalf of the South Carolina legislature in which he developed a theory of constitutional interpretation under which he argued that states had the right to declare federal laws null and void. Influenced by the Kentucky and Virginia Resolves, drafted by Jefferson and Madison in 1798, and also by the Hartford Convention, in 1812, in which northern states had threatened to secede from the Union over their opposition to the war with Britain, Calhoun argued that if a state were to decide that a law passed by Congress was unconstitutional, the Constitution would have to be amended, and if such an amendment were not ratified—if it didn't earn the necessary approval of three-quarters of the states—the objecting state would have the right to secede from the Union. The states had been sovereign before the Constitution was ever written, or even thought of, Calhoun argued, and they remained sovereign. Calhoun also therefore argued against majority rule; nullification is fundamentally anti-majoritarian. If states can secede, the majority does not rule.[78]

The nullification crisis was less a debate about the tariff than it was a debate about the limits of states' rights and about the question of slavery, an early augury of the civil war to come. South Carolina had the largest percentage of slaves of any region in the country. Coming in the wake of David Walker's *Appeal* and the challenge posed by the Cherokee Nation to the State of Georgia, nullification represented South Carolina's attempt to reject the power of the federal government to set laws it found unfavorable to its interests.

Jackson responded with a proclamation in which he called Calhoun's theory of nullification a "metaphysical subtlety, in pursuit of an impracticable theory." Jackson's case amounted to this: the United States is a nation; it existed before the states; its sovereignty is complete. "The Constitution of the United States," Jackson argued, "forms a government, not a league."[79] In the end, Congress adopted a compromise tariff and South Carolina accepted it. "Nullification is dead," Jackson declared. But the war was far from over. The nullification crisis hardened the battle lines between the sectionalists and the nationalists, while Calhoun became the leader of the proslavery movement, declaring that slavery is "indispensable to republican government."[80]

Jackson's feud with Calhoun meant that he had not the least wish for him to continue as his vice president during a second term. Reluctant simply to drop Calhoun from the ticket for fear of political reprisal, Jackson cast about for a subtler means by which he could get rid of his cast-iron man. His eyes fell upon a new and short-lived political party, the Anti-Masons. In September of 1831, the Anti-Masons held the first presidential nominating convention in American history. Founded on the opposition to secret cabals, like Masons or political caucuses, the Anti-Masons had decided to borrow the idea of holding a gathering of delegates, like the constitutional conventions that had been held, year after year, in the states. Unfortunately, the man the Anti-Masons chose as their nominee turned out to be . . . a Mason. But the Anti-Masons' nominating convention left two legacies: the practice of granting to each state delegation a number of votes equal to the size of its delegation in the Electoral College, and the rule by which a nomination requires a three-quarters vote. Two months after the Anti-Masons met, yet another short-lived party, the National Republican Party, held a convention of its own, in which roll was called of states, not in alphabetical order but in "geographical order," beginning with Maine, and working down the coast, causing no small consternation among the gentlemen from Alabama.[81] Henry Clay, asked by letter if he would be willing to be nominated by the short-lived National Republicans, wrote back to say yes but added that it was impossible for him to attend the convention in Baltimore "without incurring the imputation of presumptuousness or indelicacy." Clay accepted the nomination, and set a precedent that lasted until Franklin Delano Roosevelt: for more than a century, no nominee accepted the nomination in person, and Roosevelt only did it because he was trying to put the point across that he was promising to offer Americans a "new deal."[82]

Still, the practice of nominating a presidential candidate at a national party convention might not have become an American political tradition if Jackson hadn't decided that the Democratic Party ought to hold one, too, so that he could get rid of his disputatious vice president. Jackson and his advisers realized that if they left the nomination to the state legislatures, where Calhoun had a great deal of support, they'd be stuck with him again. Jackson therefore contrived to have the New Hampshire legislature call for a national convention and to nominate Jackson as president and his pliable former secretary of state, New York governor Martin Van Buren, as his running mate.

The election of 1832 turned on the question of the national bank. Like the battles over Indian removal and the tariff, Jackson's battle with the bank tested the power of the presidency. The issue was longstanding. Because the Constitution barred states from printing money, banks chartered by state legislatures printed their own money, not legal tender but banknotes, signed by bank presidents. Three hundred forty-seven banks opened up in the United States between 1830 and 1837. They printed their own money, producing more than twelve hundred different kinds of bills. Under this notoriously unstable arrangement, counterfeiting was rife, and so was swindling, especially by land banks, set up to speculate on western land.

In 1816, Congress had chartered a Second Bank of the United States, to help the nation recover from the devastation of the war with England.

In 1819, the Supreme Court had upheld the constitutionality of the bank.[83] The Bank of the United States served as the depository of all federal money; it handled its payments and revenues, including taxes. Nevertheless, it was a private bank reporting to stockholders. Its economic influence was extraordinary. By 1830, its holdings of $35 million amounted to twice the annual expenses of the federal government. To its severest critics, the national bank looked like an unelected fourth branch of the government.[84] Jackson hated all banks. "I do not dislike your bank any more than all banks," he told the bank's president, Nicholas Biddle. Jackson believed that the Bank of the United States undermined the sovereignty of the people, defied their will, and, like all banks, had "a corrupting influence" on the nation by allowing "a few Monied Capitalists" to use public revenue, to "enjoy the benefit of it, to the exclusion of the many."[85]

In January 1832, with Jackson nearing the end of his term, Biddle submitted to Congress a request to renew the bank's charter, even though that charter wasn't due to expire until 1836. Congress obliged. Clay promised, "Should Jackson veto it, I will veto him!"[86] But in July 1832, Jackson did veto the bank bill, delivering an 8,000-word message in which he made clear that he believed the president has the authority to decide on the constitutionality of laws passed by Congress.

"It is maintained by the advocates of the bank that its constitutionality in all its features ought to be considered as settled by precedent and by the decision of the Supreme Court," Jackson said. "To this conclusion, I cannot assent."[87] Biddle called Jackson's veto message "a manifesto of anarchy." But the Senate proved unable to override the veto. The Bank War, said Edward Everett, "is nothing less than a war of Numbers against Property."[88] Jackson, man of the people, King of Numbers, won in a rout.

# IV.

JACKSON'S BANK VETO unmoored the American economy. With the dissolution of the Bank of the United States, the stability it had provided, ballast in a ship's hull, floated away. Proponents of the national bank had insisted on the need for federal regulation of paper currency. Jackson and his supporters, known as "gold-bugs," would have rather had no paper money at all. In 1832, $59 million in paper bills was in circulation, in

1836, $140 million. Without the national bank's regulatory force, very little metal backed up this blizzard of paper, American banks holding only $10.5 million in gold.[89]

Both speculators and the president looked to the West. "The wealth and strength of a country are its population, and the best part of the population are cultivators of the soil," Jackson said, echoing Jefferson.[90] Fleeing worsening economic conditions in the East and seeking new opportunities, Americans moved west, alone and with families, on wagons and trails, on canals and steamboats, to Ohio, Indiana, Illinois, Alabama, Mississippi, Missouri, Louisiana, Arkansas, and Michigan. They homesteaded on farms; they built cabins out of rough-hewn logs. They started newspapers and argued about politics. They built towns and churches and schools. "I invite you to go to the West, and visit one of our log cabins, and number its inmates," said one Indiana congressman. "There you will find a strong, stout youth of eighteen, with his better half, just commencing the first struggles of independent life. Thirty years from that time, visit them again; and instead of two, you will find in that same family twenty-two. This is what I call the American multiplication table."[91]

Still, slavery haunted every step of westward settlement. Elijah Lovejoy, born in Maine, settled in St. Louis, where he printed abolitionist tracts, the distribution of which was illegal in slave states, leading abolitionists to call for "free speech" against southerners' demands for "free trade." In 1836, proslavery rioters destroyed Lovejoy's press. Lovejoy moved across the river, to the free state of Illinois, where he and his black typesetter, John Anderson, reopened their business with a new press. That press, too, was destroyed by a mob, and when a third press arrived, Lovejoy, who was armed, was shot in the chest and killed, a martyr to the cause of free speech.

To survey land and supervise settlement, Congress chartered the General Land Office. Surveyors laid the land out in grids of 640 acres. These they divided into 160-acre lots, as the smallest unit to be offered for sale. By 1832, during a boom in land sales—the office was receiving 40,000 patents a year—that minimum purchase was reduced to 40 acres. In 1835, Congress increased the number of clerks working at the Land Office from 17 to 88. Yet still they could not keep up with the volume of paperwork.

From the South, American settlers crossed the border into Mexico, which had won independence from Spain in 1821. Mexico had trouble

*Pioneers heading west gathered at settlements like Major
John Dougherty's trading post on the Missouri River.*

managing its sprawling north; much of the land between its populous
south, including its capital, Mexico City, and its most distant territory,
Alta California, was desert, and chiefly occupied by Apaches, Utes, and
Yaqui Indians. As one Mexican governor said, "Our territory is enormous,
and our Government weak." As early as 1825, John Quincy Adams had
instructed the American minister to Mexico to try to negotiate a new
boundary; the Mexican government needed the money but it wouldn't sell
its own land. As its minister, Manuel de Mier y Terán, argued: "Mexico,
imitating the conduct of France and Spain, might alienate or cede unpro-
ductive lands in Africa or Asia. But how can it be expected to cut itself off
from its own soil?"

Mexico wouldn't sell its own land, but the Mexican territories of Coahuila and Texas, along the Gulf of Mexico, and west of the state of Louisiana, proved particularly attractive to American settlers in search of new
lands for planting cotton. "If we do not take the present opportunity to
people Texas," one Mexican official warned, "day by day the strength of
the United States will grow until it will annex Texas, Coahuila, Saltillo,
and Nuevo León." (At the time, Texas included much of what later
became Kansas, Colorado, Wyoming, New Mexico, and Oklahoma.) In
1835, Americans in Texas rebelled against Mexican rule, waging a war

under the command of a political daredevil named Sam Houston. In 1836, Texas declared its independence, founding the Republic of Texas, with Houston its president. Mexico's president, General Antonio López de Santa Anna, warned that, if he were to discover that the U.S. government had been behind the Texas rebellion, he would march "his army to Washington and place upon its Capitol the Mexican flag."[92]

When Houston sent a proposal to Congress requesting annexation, the measure failed, for three reasons. First, Jackson feared annexation would provoke a war with Mexico, which did not recognize Texas's independence. Second, from the point of view of the United States, which, along with Great Britain and France, did recognize Texas's independence, Texas was a foreign country, which meant that its annexation was an altogether different issue than it had been in 1825, when John Quincy Adams, as secretary of state, had sought to acquire the territory. Finally, if Texas were admitted to the Union, it would enter as a slave state. Quincy Adams, who, having lost the presidency, had become a member of the House, filibustered the annexation proposal for three weeks. The people of the United States, he said, "dearly as they loved the Union, would prefer its total dissolution to the act of annexation of Texas." The American Anti-Slavery Society flooded Congress with tens of thousands of abolitionist petitions. When Quincy Adams tried to get the petitions a hearing, southern legislators silenced him under the terms of a "gag rule" that banned from the floor of Congress any discussion of antislavery petitions, another triumph for opponents of free speech.[93]

Southern slave owners, a tiny minority of Americans, amounting to about 1 percent of the population, deployed the rhetoric of states' rights and free trade (by which they meant trade free from federal government regulation), but in fact they desperately needed and relied on the power of the federal government to defend and extend the institution of slavery. The weakness of their position lay behind their efforts to silence dissent. Beginning in 1836, Ohio Democrat Thomas Morris introduced petitions denouncing slavery, calling for its abolition in the District of Columbia and urging the overturning of a ban on sending abolitionist literature through the mail, only to have the petitions suppressed. Morris, uncouth and self-taught, had been raised by his Baptist preacher father to hate slavery. Early in 1838, he damned "the putrid mass of prejudice, which interest has created, to keep the colored race in bondage." Later that year, he told an Ohio newspaper that he had "always believed slavery to be wrong, in principle, in practice, in every country and under every condition of things." Unsurprisingly, he was not reelected. In February 1839, knowing that he would never again hold public office, he let loose, delivering the fiercest antislavery speech yet voiced on the Senate floor. Borrowing from the Jacksonian indictment of the "money power," he coined the phrase "slave power." Morris described the struggle as a battle between democracy and two united aristocracies: "the aristocracy of the North," operating "by the power of a corrupt banking system, and the aristocracy of the South," which operated "by the power of the slave system." Morris closed by stating his faith that democracy would prevail, and "THE NEGRO WILL YET BE SET FREE."[94]

The debate over Texas, along with the election of 1836, illustrated just how powerfully Andrew Jackson and John Quincy Adams shaped national politics, long after the end of each of their presidencies. Jackson held the strings of the Democratic Party, while Quincy Adams steered the erratic course of the Whig Party. Jackson decided not to run for a third term, but, just as he'd connived to rid himself of Calhoun in 1832, he was determined to choose his successor. Once again, King Andrew masqueraded as the champion of the common man.

In 1835, Jackson issued a call for a Democratic nominating convention, in an extraordinary letter published, first, in a Tennessee newspaper:

> I consider the true policy of the friends of republican principles to send delegates, fresh from the people, to a general convention, for the purpose of selecting candidates for the presidency and vice-presidency; and, that to impeach that selection before it is made, or to resist it when it is fairly made, as an emanation of executive power, is to assail the virtue of the people, and, in effect, to oppose their right to govern.[95]

For all his flummery about the virtue of the people and their right to govern, the point of this convention was to assure the nomination of Jackson's handpicked successor, Martin Van Buren, and to allow for Van Buren to contrive for his choice, Richard Johnson, to win the vice presidential nomination. The calumny did not go unnoticed. Tennessee, whose support for Jackson had long since begun to waver, refused to send a delegation to

SPECIE CLAWS.

*During the Panic of 1837, a destitute family cowers when debt collectors come to the door, demanding hard money; fading portraits of Jackson and Van Buren hang on the wall behind them.*

the convention, held in Baltimore. Unwilling to forfeit Tennessee's fifteen electoral votes at the convention, Van Buren's convention manager, New York senator Silas Wright, went to a tavern and found a Tennessean who just happened to be in the city—Edward Rucker, who became a one-man, fifteen-vote delegation. ("Ruckerize" became a verb: it means to commit political skullduggery by packing a convention.) [96]

But Quincy Adams's party found itself in still greater disarray. Disorganized and dispersed, the Whigs failed to hold a nominating convention and could not decide on a single candidate; four different Whigs ran for president, splitting the party and leaving a wide path for the Democratic candidate, Van Buren, to ride to electoral victory.

Van Buren took office in March 1837. Five weeks later, the nation's financial system fell apart in the worst financial disaster in American history, second only to the crash of 1929. "The stock market collapsed. The blackness of darkness still hangeth over it," one New Yorker wrote from Wall Street that April. By the fall of 1837, nine out of ten eastern factories had closed. The poor broke into shops, only to find their shelves empty. What began with the Panic of 1837 ended only after a seven-yearlong depression, well into a decade of despair known as "The Hungry Forties."[97]

Whigs dubbed the new president Martin Van Ruin, which was unfair, since the fall was the result of Jackson's decisions, not Van Buren's, the consequence, above all, of unregulated banking industry. But if the suffering was Jacksonian, so was its relief: the Panic of 1837 democratized bankruptcy protection and led to the abolition of debtors' prisons. In 1810, a New York lawyer named Joseph Dewey Fay, who claimed to have spent sixteen years in debtors' prison, had estimated that in the aftermath of the Panic of 1809, 10 percent of New York's freemen had been arrested for debt. "Americans boast that they have done away with torture," Fay had written, "but the debtors' prison is torture." Fay had gone to Albany and successfully lobbied the legislature to pass an expanded insolvency law for imprisoned debtors. Twenty-five hundred debtors availed themselves of discharge in the law's first nine months. Earlier bankruptcy laws had protected only stockbrokers, but the new law set a precedent: it was the first legislation anywhere to offer bankruptcy to everyone. In 1819, the Supreme Court had ruled it unconstitutional. Still, a turn had come: New York abolished debtors' prison in 1831, and in 1841, Congress passed a federal law offering bankruptcy protection to everyone. Within two years, 41,000 Americans had filed for bankruptcy. Two years later, the law was repealed, but state laws continued to offer bankruptcy protection and, still more significantly, debtors' prisons were gone for good. In Britain and all of Europe except Portugal, offenders were still being thrown in debtors' prison (a plot that animated many a nineteenth-century novel); in the United States, debtors could declare bankruptcy and begin again.

The forgiveness of debts fostered a spirit of risk taking that fueled American enterprise. Tocqueville marveled at "the strange indulgence which is shown to bankrupts in the United States." In this, he observed, "Americans differ, not only from the nations of Europe, but from all the commercial nations of our time." A nation of debtors, Americans came to see that most people who fall into debt are victims of the business cycle and not of fate or divine retribution or the wheel of fortune. The nation's bankruptcy laws, even as they came and went again, made taking risks less risky for everyone, which meant that everyone took more risks.[98]

Martin Van Ruin didn't stand much of a chance at reelection in 1840.

**The People's Line--Take care of the Locomotive**
*Sold at 104 Nassau, and 18 Division Streets, New-York.*

*An 1848 cartoon pictured William Henry Harrison as
the engine of a train fueled by hard cider and pulling a
log cabin while President Martin Van Buren, driving
"Uncle Sam's Cab," pulled by a blindered horse,
stumbles on a pile of (Henry) Clay.*

Voters blamed both him and his party for the misery caused by Jackson. The Whigs, unsurprisingly, but in a move that would become characteristic of American campaigning, argued that the Democrats, the so-called party of the people, had in fact failed the people. The Democratic Party, Whigs claimed, had become the party of tyranny and corruption, and the Whigs were the *real* people's party. "The Whigs are THE Democrats, if there must be a party by that name," one Whig insisted.[99]

For their presidential candidate, the Whigs nominated seventy-two-year-old William Henry Harrison, ran him as a war hero, and tried to pitch him as a Jacksonian man of the people, and even a frontiersman, which required considerable stretching of the truth. Harrison had served as governor of the Indiana Territory, and as a senator from Ohio, but he came from eminent forebears: his father, a Virginia plantation owner, had signed the Declaration of Independence. Writing in 1839, Harrison's campaign biographer tried, in *The People's Presidential Candidate*, to present the staggeringly wealthy Harrison as a humble farmer who had "never been rich." Harrison exerted himself, delivering, at a hotel in Ohio, the first-ever presidential campaign speech, but his campaign urged him not to say too much. "Let him then rely entirely on the past," they advised. "Let him say not one single word about his principles, or his creed—let him say nothing—promise nothing." Critics dubbed him "General Mum." Democrats mocked Harrison by suggesting that, so poor as he was, he lived in a log cabin and drank nothing but hard cider. Whigs took this as a political gift. Calling Harrison the "Log Cabin Candidate," they campaigned in log cabins mounted on wheels and hitched to horses, handing out mugs of hard cider along the road. Harrison, of course, lived in a mansion, but after the log cabin campaign of 1840, few presidential candidates, whether they started out poor or whether they started out rich, failed to run as log cabin candidates.[100]

Busy dueling for the mantle of "party of the people," neither the Whigs nor the Democrats offered a plausible solution to the problem of slavery; they barely addressed it. This led to the founding of new parties, including the evangelical Liberty Party, formed in 1839. "We must abolish slavery," the party pledged, "& as sure as the sun rises we shall in 5 or 6 years run over slavery at full gallop unless she pulls herself up & gets out of the way of Liberty's cavalry." Its bid to evangelical Whigs: "Vote as you pray."[101]

The religious revival that had brought women into moral reform also carried them into politics. In the 1820s and 1830s, Jacksonian democracy involved a lot of brawls. When the reformer Fanny Wright tried to attend a convention in 1836, she was called a "female man." But while Democrats banned women from their rallies, Whigs welcomed them. In the 1840s, as one contemporary observed, "the ladies were Whigs."[102] Beginning with the Whig Party, long before women could vote, they brought into the parties a political style they'd perfected first as abolitionists and then as prohibitionists: the moral crusade, pious and uncompromising. No election has been the same since.

During the years that Democrats ran against Whigs, both parties incorporated both Jacksonian populism—the endless appeals to "the people"—and the spirit of evangelical reform (campaign rallies borrowed their style and zeal from revival meetings). Walt Whitman complained about "the neverending audacity of elected persons," damning men in politics as members of the establishment, no matter their appeals to the people. But those appeals were hardly meaningless: undeniably, the nature of

American democracy had changed. Not only were more men able to vote, but more men *did* vote: voter turnout rose from 27 percent in 1824 to 58 percent in 1838 and to 80 percent in 1840.[103]

Harrison won by a landslide. He then promptly died of pneumonia. His vice president and successor, John Tyler, came to be called "His Accidency," but the log cabin, like the female reformer, proved long-lived. So did the battle for the soul of the nation in an age of machines.

The United States is "the country of the Future," Ralph Waldo Emerson proclaimed in February 1844, rhapsodizing about "a country of beginnings, of projects, of vast designs and expectations." That spring, Samuel F. B. Morse sat at a desk in the chambers of the U.S. Supreme Court and tapped out a message on his new telegraph machine, along wires stretched between Washington and Baltimore, paid for by Congress. His first message, in a code no longer secret: "What hath God wrought"? Meanwhile, a railroad line that began in Boston reached Emerson's hometown of Concord, Massachusetts. "I hear the whistle of the locomotive in the woods," Emerson wrote in his journal. "It is the voice of the civility of the Nineteenth Century saying, 'Here I am.'"[104]

The United States had been founded as a political experiment; it seemed natural that it should advance and grow through other kinds of experimentation. By December, telegraph wires would be installed along lines cut by train tracks through woods and meadows and even mountains, and Americans began imagining a future in which both the railroad and the telegraph would reach all the way across the continent. "The greatest revolution of modern times, and indeed of all time, for the amelioration of Society, has been effected by the Magnetic Telegraph," the *New York Sun* announced, proclaiming "the annihilation of space."[105] Time was being annihilated, too: news spread in a flash. As penny press printer James Gordon Bennett of the *New York Herald* pointed out, the telegraph appeared to make it possible for "the whole nation" to have "the same idea at the same time." "The progress of the age has almost outstripped human belief," Daniel Webster said. "The future is known only to Omniscience."[106]

The progress of the age—the rapid growth of the population, the unending chain of machines, and the astonishing array of goods—combined to produce an unceasing and often uneasy fascination with what lay ahead: What next? Political economists, in particular, busied themselves with working out a system for understanding the relationship between the present and the future. In Paris, a philosopher named Karl Marx began making predictions about the consequences of capitalism. He saw in the increase in the production of goods a decrease in the value of labor and a widening inequality between the rich and the poor. "The worker becomes all the poorer the more wealth he produces," Marx argued in 1844. "The devaluation of the world of men is in direct proportion to the increasing value of the world of things."[107] American thinkers pondered this problem, too. Emerson wrote,

> 'Tis the day of the chattel,
> Web to weave, and corn to grind;
> Things are in the saddle,
> and ride mankind.[108]

In the United States, the political debate about the world of people and the world of things contributed to the agonized debate about slavery: Can people be things? Meanwhile, the geographical vastness of the United States meant that the anxiety about the machinery of industrial capitalism took the form not of Marxism, with its argument that "the history of all hitherto existing society is the history of class struggles," but instead of a romance with nature, and with the land, and with all things rustic. Against the factory, Americans posed not a socialist utopia but the log cabin. "It did not happen to me to be born in a log cabin," Webster, a three-time presidential aspirant, sighed, despairing of his biographical deficiency in the age of the log cabin presidency.[109] But the most famous log cabin in nineteenth-century America was the one built in 1844 by Emerson's twenty-seven-year-old friend Henry David Thoreau.

The year the railroad reached Concord, Thoreau built a log cabin on a patch of land Emerson owned, on Walden Pond, a kettle pond a little more than a mile outside of town. He dug a cellar at the site of a woodchuck's burrow. He borrowed an axe and hewed framing timbers out of white pine. "We boast that we belong to the Nineteenth Century and are making the most rapid strides of any nation," Thoreau wrote, from the ten-by-fifteen-foot cabin he built over that cellar, at a cost of $28.12. He used the boards from an old shanty for siding. He mixed his own plaster, from lime ($2.40—"that was high") and horsehair ($0.31—"more than I needed"). He moved in, fittingly, on the Fourth of July. The chimney he built before winter, from secondhand bricks, marked real progress, but he didn't think the same could be said for the nation's "rapid strides" and "vast designs." He had the gravest of doubts about what the machine was doing to the American soul, the American people, and the land itself. The telegraph? "We are in great haste to construct a magnetic telegraph from Maine to Texas; but Maine and Texas, it may be, have nothing important to communicate." The postal system? "I never received in my life more than one or two letters that were worth the postage." The nation's much-vaunted network of newspapers? "We are a race of tit-men, and soar but little higher in our intellectual flights than the columns of the daily paper." Banks and railroads? "Men have an indistinct notion that if they keep up this activity of joint stocks and spades long enough all will at length ride somewhere, in next to no time, and for nothing; but though a crowd rushes to the depot, and the conductor shouts 'All aboard!' when the smoke is blown away and the vapor condensed, it will be perceived that a few are riding, but the rest are run over."[110]

Instead of Marx, America had Thoreau. Thoreau's experiment wasn't a business; it was an antibusiness; he paid attention to what things cost because he tried never to buy anything. Instead, he bartered, and lived on 27 cents a week. At his most entrepreneurial, he planted a field of beans and realized a profit of $8.71. "I was determined to know beans," he wrote in a particularly beautiful and elegiac chapter called "The Bean-Field." He worked, for cash, only six weeks out of the year, and spent the rest of his time reading and writing, planting beans and picking huckleberries. "Mr. Thoreau is thus at war with the political economy of the age," one critic complained. Thoreau had chosen not to be ridden by the machine, "not to live in this restless, nervous, bustling, trivial Nineteenth Century, but to stand or sit thoughtfully while it goes by."[111]

One pressing question woke him up every morning, as regularly as the screech of the whistle of the train that chugged by his cabin, on tracks built just up the hill from Walden Pond, where he'd hoped to still his soul. Were all these vast designs and rapid strides worth it? Thoreau thought not. He came to this truth: "They are but improved means to an unimproved end."[112] And still the trains chugged along, and the factories hummed, and the banks opened and closed, and the presses printed newspapers, and the telegraph wires reached across the nation, in one great and unending thrum.

# Seven

# OF SHIPS
# AND SHIPWRECKS

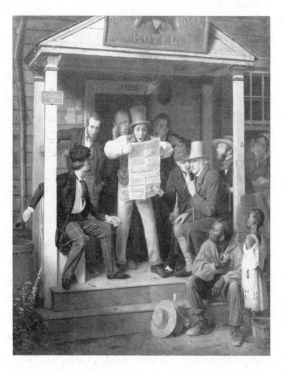

*In Richard Caton Woodville's 1848 painting, a crowd gathers
on and around the porch of the "American Hotel"—a symbol of
the Union—eagerly awaiting the "War News from Mexico."*

THE DAY ABEL UPSHUR DIED, THE FATE OF THE UNION
turned on the question of Texas. On the afternoon of February 28,
1844, Upshur, John Tyler's secretary of state, boarded the USS *Princeton*, an iron-hulled, steam-powered warship, for a short trip along the icy
waters of the Potomac. Tyler boarded, too, and so did all but one member
of his cabinet, along with hundreds more dignitaries, soldiers, and sailors,

and invited guests, in top hats and uniforms and snugly buttoned gowns, wrapped in woolen cloaks. James Madison's aging widow, Dolley, was there, shivering against the wind, along with John C. Calhoun's young son Patrick, a second lieutenant in the army, and General Juan Almonté, the straight-backed and stalwart Mexican ambassador, his cuffs embroidered with gold, his epaulets like wings.

The U.S. Senate was about to vote on a treaty to annex Texas, a long-sought land of ranges and plains, of cattle towns and rushing rivers. Upshur, fifty-three and balding, with a broad forehead and a long, slender nose, had stayed up late the night before, counting votes and pondering war. Mexico considered Texas one of its provinces, if a rebelling one. If the Senate approved annexation, Upshur knew, Mexico might well declare war on the United States. Upshur, who, before he became secretary of state, had been secretary of the navy, expected that war to be waged at sea, in the Gulf of Mexico, and he had been building up the fleet, preparing for battle. The USS *Princeton* was the navy's most formidable warship; the point of setting forth on the Potomac was to offer—to Almonté—a demonstration of the ship's fearsome cannon, the largest gun ever mounted on a battleship. It was called the Peacemaker.

As the ship steamed along the river, the gun was fired three times, each with a thundering, earth-shaking roar. Obeying the orders of the ship's doctor, the guests kept their hands over their ears and their mouths wide open, to blunt the force of the shock wave. Almonté seemed suitably daunted. There was to be one more display: a salute to George Washington as the great ship steamed past Mount Vernon.[1]

Tyler, a gaunt and ungainly man, had staked his presidency on annexation. But his presidency had been weak from the start, and by the time the treaty was drafted, he was a president without a party. A southern aristocrat who despised populism, Tyler had been nominated as Harrison's running mate because he'd been a vocal critic of both Jackson and Van Buren, and because Whigs hoped he would carry his crucial home state, Virginia. He'd hardly been queried on his politics, nor had voters been informed of them. As one campaign song had it, "We will vote for Tyler therefore / without a why or wherefore." But Tyler did have political positions, strenuously held: he had long advocated states' rights. An opponent of the national bank, Tyler didn't like anything national; he once complained about the signs he saw all over Washington, DC: "National Hotel,

National boot-black, National black-smith, National Oyster-house."[2] In April 1841, after Harrison died weeks after his inauguration, Congress had twice passed legislation renewing the charter of the national bank. And twice Tyler had vetoed it. By September, every member of Tyler's cabinet except his secretary of state, Daniel Webster, had resigned in protest. Two days later, fifty Whig members of Congress gathered on the steps of the Capitol and banished the president from the party. Protesters rallied outside the White House. Fearful for his safety, Tyler had established a presidential police force (it later became the Secret Service). His only respite from the incessant political assault had come during a time of tragedy: his wife, Letitia, suffered a stroke. Having borne eight children, she died in the White House in September 1842. When Charles Dickens met Tyler while on a headlong tour of the United States that year, the novelist wrote that the president "looked somewhat worn and anxious, and well he might; being at war with everybody."[3]

Abel Upshur came to be Tyler's secretary of war after Webster, the last remaining member of Tyler's original cabinet, resigned in May 1843 to protest the plan to annex Texas. Webster believed that the Republic was already large enough, and that any extension would diminish the spirit of the Union. How could people so different, spread across thousands of miles, even choose a ruler? He wondered "with how much of mutual intelligence, and how much of a spirit of conciliation and harmony, those who live on the St. Lawrence and the St. John might be expected ordinarily to unite in the choice of a President, with the inhabitants of the banks of the Rio Grande del Norte and the Colorado."[4]

When Webster's replacement died of a burst appendix, Tyler appointed Upshur. He might have seen something of himself in him. Upshur, like Tyler, was a southern aristocrat, disdainful of the people (they "read but little," he said, "and they do not think at all"). Upshur believed that slavery solved the problem of the tensions between capital and labor by giving even a white man of desperate circumstances a reason to accept the economic order: "However poor, or ignorant or miserable he may be, he has yet the consoling consciousness that there is a still lower condition to which he can never be reduced."[5]

Tyler and Upshur were convinced that the stability of the American republic rested on expansion. The Monroe Doctrine, crafted by John Quincy Adams in 1823, had warned Europeans not to found any new colonies in the Western Hemisphere, partly in order to keep the path clear for Americans. As one British newspaper observed at the time, "The plain *Yankee* of the matter is that the United States wish to monopolize to themselves the privilege of colonizing . . . every . . . part of the American continent."[6] Nevertheless, Great Britain's North American territory, acquired long before the Monroe Doctrine, stretched all the way across the continent, while, in the Pacific Northwest, both Britain and the United States claimed the vast swath of land known as the Oregon Territory. Upshur feared Britain was making a bid to extend its borders to the south. Britain had been selling steam-powered warships to Mexico and offering to buy California. Upshur also believed rumors (which turned out to be false) that Britain had offered loans to Texas if it would abolish slavery, with an eye, presumably, to making Texas part of the British Empire, in which slavery had been abolished in 1833. Tyler's plan was to annex Texas and have it enter the Union as a slave state, with the hope that he could arrange for the admission of Oregon as a free state, maintaining the balance of free states to slave.

Tyler and Upshur may have wanted to annex Texas in order to extend slavery into the West. But they steered clear of talking about it that way. They talked the language not of slavery but of liberty, making the argument—embraced by everyone from Jefferson to Tocqueville— that the acquisition of new territory provided economic opportunities to the poor, opportunities not available in Europe, because anyone could leave industry behind, move to the woods, build a cabin, fell trees, and plow fields.

In this new age of steam, when every metaphor, suddenly, had to do with engines, people talked about the West as a "safety valve," releasing pent-up pressure to avoid an explosion. "The public lands are the great regulator of the relations of Labor and Capital," said Horace Greeley, publisher of the *New York Tribune*, "the safety valve of our industrial and social engine." (Greeley, who, with his slumped shoulders and flat face, looked rather like a frog, was the most widely read editorial writer of his generation.) Supporters of the annexation of Texas went further, applying this metaphor to the problem of slave rebellion. "If we shall annex Texas," a Democratic senator from South Carolina promised in 1844, "it will operate as a safety-valve to let off this superabundant slave population from among us."[7]

And the debate might have gone that way, were it not for what happened on board the USS *Princeton* February 28. As the ship passed Mount Vernon, the crew lit the Peacemaker for its final salute. Suddenly, the gun exploded. Seven men were killed in the blast, including Upshur, along with Tyler's secretary of the navy and a New York merchant named David Gardiner, whose twenty-four-year-old daughter, Julia, was below-decks with the president. If Tyler had been topside, he, too, would likely have been killed. Instead, he carried a fainting Julia Gardiner in his arms off the ship and onto a rescue boat.

The death of Upshur had serious political consequences. To replace him, Tyler appointed Calhoun as his new secretary of state. And Cast-Iron Calhoun talked about Texas *only* with reference to slavery.

As the debate over annexation intensified, John Quincy Adams, seventy-six, his face grown haggard but his political will unbroken, warned that if Texas were annexed, the North would secede; Calhoun, as lionlike at sixty-two as he had been in his youth, warned that the South would secede if it were not. The rivalry between the two men, begun with the "corrupt bargain" of 1828, continued undiminished, even if the explosion on the Potomac set them both back on their heels.

After a brief period of mourning, Congress resumed its business. "The treaty for the annexation of Texas to this Union was this day sent into the Senate," Quincy Adams wrote in his diary in April, "and with it went the freedom of the human race."[8] Henry Clay called it "Mr. Tyler's abominable treaty."[9] Quincy Adams insisted that annexing Texas would turn the Constitution into a "menstruous rag."[10]

In June, the Senate failed to ratify the treaty by a vote of 35 to 16 that fell along sectional lines. Days later, when President Tyler married Julia Gardiner, white flowers wreathed in her hair, the *New York Herald* said of the wedding: "The President has concluded a treaty of immediate annexation, which will be ratified without the aid of the Senate of the United States."[11]

Tyler, a better bridegroom than a president, decided to run for reelection even though no party would have him. He therefore more or less invented a third party—a one-man party—and called for a convention to nominate him under the banner of "Tyler and Texas." He did not name a running mate; Texas was his running mate.

MARRIAGE OF TEXAS.

*President Tyler officiates at a wedding between the Texas star and America in a political cartoon from a New Orleans newspaper in 1844— the year Tyler himself married.*

Tyler's hope, in running, was to convince the Democrats to nominate him at their own convention. But Andrew Jackson, edging toward eighty in a not altogether quiet retirement at his slave plantation, had changed his mind about annexation. Earlier, he'd opposed it, fearing a war with Mexico. Now he favored it. But Van Buren did not. Jackson, still controlling the party, decided to thwart Van Buren's attempt to win the Democratic nomination. Jackson called a meeting at the Hermitage. "General Jackson says the candidate for the first office should be an annexation man, and from the Southwest," wrote James K. Polk, a Jackson loyalist. Polk became that man.[12]

Polk was forty-eight and wiry and had eyes like caverns and hair like smoke. A former Speaker of the House and governor of Tennessee, he was unknown outside his home state. "Who is James K. Polk?" became the motto of his opposition. Tyler, assured that the Democrats would fight for annexation, dropped out of the race.[13]

Henry Clay had been trying to become president of the United States since he was a boy in short pants in the hills of Virginia. He'd already run three times, but in 1844, when he was sixty-seven, the Whigs chose him once more. Clay opposed annexation, but not strenuously enough for abolitionists who left the Whigs to join the Liberty Party. The National Convention of Colored Men—men who hoped, one day, to be able to vote—endorsed the Liberty Party, too.

The race between Polk and Clay, a referendum on annexation, was extraordinarily close. In the end, Polk won the popular vote by a razor-thin margin of 38,000 votes out of 2.6 million cast. Tyler, limping to the end of his term, took Polk's victory as a mandate for annexation and pressed the House for a vote. On January 25, 1845, the House passed a resolution in favor of annexation, 120–98, having devised a compromise under which the eastern portion of Texas would enter the Union as a slave state, but not the western portion. On February 28, the one-year anniversary of the disaster on the USS *Princeton*, the Senate approved that resolution by just two votes. It would fall to Polk to sign the formal treaty, but it was Tyler who signed the resolution, on March 1, three days before Polk took office. In a slight to his cast-iron secretary of state, he handed the pen he used to sign it not to Calhoun but to his new bride, Julia Gardiner, as if Texas were her wedding gift.

Two days later, General Almonté, with epaulets like wings, was recalled to Mexico. Both nations braced for war. American soldiers pointed their guns to the southwest, ready to fire shots across a border. But soon enough the United States would be at war with itself, a nation looking down the barrel of its own gun.


## I.


IN THE 1840S AND 1850S, the United States faced a constitutional crisis that recast the parties and deepened the national divide. Expansion, even more than abolition, pressed upon the public the question of the constitutionality of slavery. How or even whether this crisis would be resolved was difficult to see not only because of the nature of the dispute but also because there existed very little agreement about who might resolve it: Who was to decide whether a federal law was unconstitutional?

One man of unbounded temerity had said that the Supreme Court could decide. In 1803, in *Marbury v. Madison*, Chief Justice John Marshall had asserted that "it is emphatically the province and duty of the judicial department to say what the law is." Marshall may have established a precedent for judicial review, but he had hardly made it a practice. Before his death, in 1835, at the age of seventy-nine, he served on the court for thirty-four years; *Marbury* is the only time the Marshall Court overturned a federal law.

Another man of similar disposition had said that the states had this authority. When, in 1832, Calhoun, on behalf of South Carolina, had argued that the states can simply nullify acts of Congress, his argument had failed, and making it had nearly destroyed his career.

A third man, not to be undone in the matter of audacity, insisted that this power lay with the president alone. When Jackson vetoed the Bank Act, he had demonstrated that the president has the power to block legislation, but while Jackson sorely wished he had the authority to pronounce laws unconstitutional, this was the merest fancy.

In the midst of all this clamoring among the thundering white-haired patriarchs of American politics, there emerged the idea that the authority to interpret the Constitution rests with the people themselves. Or, at least, this became a rather fashionable thing to say. "It is, Sir, the people's Constitution, the people's government, made for the people, made by the people, and answerable to the people," Daniel Webster roared from the floor of Congress.[14] Every man could read and understand the Constitution, Webster insisted. As to the actual state of affairs, there was considerable disagreement. In 1834, Justice Joseph Story published a schoolbook in which he attempted to illustrate the nation's laws to its children. "The Constitution is the will, the deliberate will, of the people," he explained.[15] Tocqueville rhapsodized that the American people knew their Constitution as if by heart. "I scarcely ever met with a plain American citizen who could not distinguish with surprising facility the obligations created by the laws of Congress from those created by the laws of his own state," the Frenchman reported.[16] He thought that the American people were fitted to their Constitution like a hand to a glove. But William Grimes, who escaped from slavery in Virginia 1814 and became a barber in Connecticut—and who was the sort of person Tocqueville never interviewed—had a different idea about just how fitted were the people and the parchment: "If it were not for the stripes on my back which were made while I was a slave," Grimes wrote, "I would in my will, leave my skin a legacy to the government, desiring that it might be taken off and made into parchment and then bind the Constitution of glorious happy and free America."[17] Americans' deepest and most abiding divide turned on this starkly different reading of their Constitution, in what meaning lay between the ink written onto parchment and the scars etched on a black man's back.

A great many people on both sides of this divide had hoped that the long-awaited publication of James Madison's *Notes* on the debates at the constitutional convention would cast so much light on the question of slavery as to resolve it. Madison had been asked, time and again, to resolve disputes by revealing their contents. But he refused, steadfast in keeping his vow of secrecy. For years, for decades, Madison had added to and revised his record of what was said and done in the Pennsylvania State House in the long, hot summer of 1787. He'd puttered away at it. The Constitution couldn't be rewritten or easily amended—but Madison's *Notes* could. As the years passed, and Madison grew old, he observed how many other nations had followed the United States' lead and written their own constitutions: France, Haiti, Poland, the Netherlands, Switzerland. By 1820, at least sixty constitutions had been written in Europe alone; eighty more would be written by 1850. Very few of those constitutions lasted.[18]

In 1836, Madison turned eighty-five and collapsed at the breakfast table. "The Sage of Montpelier Is No More!" announced the *Charleston Courier*, in a column blocked in black.[19] He was the last delegate to the constitutional convention to die. Madison's will, made public that summer, revealed two facts that agitated each side in the debate over slavery: he had not freed his slaves, and he had arranged for a sizable part of the proceeds of the publication of his *Notes* to go the American Colonization Society. The next year, the fifty-year reign of secrecy came to a close. But so nervous were members of Congress about what the *Notes* might contain, and how their publication would turn the political winds, that when Dolley Madison asked Congress to pay for the printing, the panicked House could hardly manage to hold a vote.[20]

In the end, Congress approved the expense, and the *Notes* were finally printed in 1840. Far from settling the issue of whether the Constitution did or did not sanction slavery, publication gave partisans on all sides more ammunition for their arguments. Radical abolitionists, finding in the *Notes* evidence of coldhearted deal making in Philadelphia, came to consider the Constitution unredeemable. William Lloyd Garrison, peering out from narrow spectacles, would infamously call the Constitution "a Covenant with Death and an Agreement with Hell." But other opponents of slavery quoted from Madison's *Notes* to argue that the Constitution most specifically did not sanction slavery. In *The Unconstitutionality of Slavery*, Massachusetts lawyer Lysander Spooner damned Garrison for damning the Constitution and wondered why abolitionists were so scared of using it as a weapon: "If they have the constitution in their hands, why, in heaven's name do they not out with it, and use it?"[21]

The *Notes*, it appeared, could be read as variously as the Constitution itself. As one shrewd observer remarked, "The Constitution threatens to be a subject of infinite sects, like the Bible." And, as with many sects, those politicians who most strenuously staked their arguments on the Constitution often appeared the least acquainted with it. Remarked New York governor Silas Wright, "No one familiar with the affairs of our government, can have failed to notice how large a proportion of our statesmen appear never to have read the Constitution of the United States with a careful reference to its precise language and exact provisions, but rather, as occasion presents, seem to exercise their ingenuity . . . to stretch both to the line of what they, at the moment, consider expedient."[22]

And so it came to pass that in 1846, when the United States faced war with Mexico, Americans had yet to settle some seemingly elemental matters relating to their system of government. Annexing Texas meant trying to stretch the already taut parchment of the Constitution across still vaster distances. And the possibility of annexing conquered parts of Mexico meant something else, too—not merely extending the Republic but founding an empire.

**A NATION HAS** borders but the edges of an empire are frayed.[23] While abolitionists damned the annexation of Texas as an extension of the slave power, more critics called it an act of imperialism, inconsistent with a republican form of government. "We have a republic, gentlemen, of vast extent and unequalled natural advantages," Daniel Webster pointed out. "Instead of aiming to enlarge its boundaries, let us seek, rather, to strengthen its union."[24] Webster lost that argument, and, in the end, it was the American reach for empire that, by sundering the Union, brought about the collapse of slavery.

No American president made that reach for empire with more bluster and determination than James K. Polk. Texas was only the beginning. Polk also wanted to admit Florida as a slave state, and, he hoped, Cuba. ("As the pear, when ripe, falls by the law of gravity into the lap of the husbandman," Calhoun had once said, "so will Cuba eventually drop into the lap of the Union.")[25] But when Polk sent an agent to Spain, he was told that, rather than sell Cuba to the United States, Spain "would prefer seeing it sunk in the Ocean."[26]

More immediately, Polk wanted to acquire Oregon, an expanse of achingly beautiful land that included all of what later became Oregon, Idaho, and Washington, and much of what later became Montana and Wyoming. "Our title to the country of Oregon is clear and unquestionable," Polk announced, as if willing this to be true. Britain, Russia, Spain, and Mexico had all made claims to the Oregon Territory. Americans, though, had been staking their claim by moving there. They'd been heading west from Missouri along the arduous Oregon Trail, a series of old Indian roads that cut across mountains and unfurled over valleys and snaked along streams. In 1843, some eight hundred Americans traveled the Oregon Trail, carrying their children in their arms and pulling everything they owned in wind-swept wagons. With Polk's pledge behind them, hundreds became thousands. They traveled in caravans, guided by little more than books like Lansford W. Hastings's *Emigrants' Guide to Oregon and California* and John C. Frémont's *Report of an Exploration . . . between the Missouri River and the Rocky Mountains* (1843) or his *Report of the Exploring Expedition to Oregon and California* (1845). Frémont, born in Georgia in 1813, had been commissioned as a second lieutenant in the U.S. Army Corps of Topographical Engineers. During a series of extraordinary expeditions, he mapped much of the West. How much of this territory did Americans want? The answer became a rallying cry: "The Whole of Oregon!"[27]

To the southwest, Polk had no intention of ending his reach with the annexation of Texas. Nor did John O'Sullivan, editor of the *Democratic Review*. "Texas is now ours," O'Sullivan wrote in 1845, and California would soon be, too: "it will be idle of Mexico to dream of dominion."[28] Immediately after Mexico severed diplomatic relations with the United States, Polk sent an envoy to Mexico with $25 million in hopes of buying three stretches of land: the Nueces Strip, a patch of disputed territory claimed by both Texas and Mexico; New Mexico; and Alta California, north of Baja California and including parts of what became Arizona, Nevada, Colorado, Utah, and Wyoming. When Mexico refused to treat with the Polk delegation, Polk ordered U.S. troops into the Nueces Strip; they set up camp along the Rio Grande. To lead them, Polk passed over more experienced generals in favor of Zachary Taylor, a fellow southerner unlikely to question his questionable orders.

Polk hoped to provoke a confrontation and soon got what he was after. During a skirmish on April 25, 1846, Mexican forces killed eleven U.S. soldiers. Polk asked Congress to declare war. "Mexico has passed the boundary of the United States, has invaded our territory and shed American blood upon the American soil," he insisted.[29] Not everyone was convinced that Mexico had fired first, or that the Americans who were killed had been standing on American soil when they were shot. In Congress, a gangly young House member from Illinois named Abraham Lincoln introduced resolutions, the so-called spot resolutions, demanding to know the exact spot where American blood was first shed on American soil. He earned the nickname Spotty Lincoln. He did not prevail.

Congress granted Polk his declaration, and war came, but opposition escalated, not least because troubling news from Mexico traveled to American cities in record-breaking time. At the outbreak of the war, the publisher of the *New York Sun* established an ad hoc news-gathering network involving boats and stagecoaches and early telegraph operators. The *Sun*'s scheme came to be called "the wire service" and, later, the Associated Press.[30]

Polk's very slender victory at the polls proved a thin reed on which to wage a war of aggression in the name of the American people. Nor did Congress escape heightened scrutiny. In the quarrelsome 1840s, visitors to Congress very often found its deliberations contemptible, but no one was more severe on this subject than the author of *Pickwick Papers*. During his stay in Washington, Charles Dickens, who had started out as a police reporter, visited the House and Senate every day, sitting in the galleries, taking notes. He found the rooms in the Capitol attractive and well appointed—"both houses are handsomely carpeted," he allowed—and the Senate was "dignified and decorous," its deliberations "conducted with much gravity and order." But meetings of the House of Representatives, he said, were "the meanest perversion of virtuous Political Machinery that the worst tools ever wrought." Its members were cowardly, petty, cussed, and degraded. Dickens, for all the flair of his pen, had by no means exaggerated. Although hardly ever reported in the press, the years between 1830 and 1860 saw more than one hundred incidents of violence between congressmen, from melees in the aisles to mass brawls on the floor, from fistfights and duels to street fights. "It is the game of these men, and of their profligate organs," Dickens wrote, "to make the strife of politics so fierce and brutal, and so destructive of all self-respect in worthy men, that sensitive and delicate-minded persons shall be kept aloof, and they, and such as they, be left to battle out their selfish views unchecked." Dickens knew a rogue when he heard one and a circus when he saw one.[31]

Nearly as soon as the war with Mexico began, members of Congress began debating what to do when it ended. They spat venom. They pulled guns. They unsheathed knives. Divisions of party were abandoned; the splinter in Congress was sectional. Before heading to the Capitol every morning, southern congressmen strapped bowie knives to their belts and tucked pistols into their pockets. Northerners, on principle, came unarmed. When northerners talked about the slave power, they meant that literally.[32]

If the United States were to acquire territory from Mexico, and if this territory were to enter the Union, would Mexicans become American citizens? Calhoun, now in the Senate, vehemently opposed this idea. "I protest against the incorporation of such a people," he declared. "Ours is the government of the white man."[33] And what about the territory itself: would these former parts of Mexico enter the Union as free states or slave? In 1846, David Wilmot, a thirty-two-year-old Democratic congressman from Pennsylvania who looked as meek as a schoolmaster, suggested that a proviso be added to any treaty negotiated to end the war, decreeing that "neither slavery nor involuntary servitude shall ever exist" in any territories acquired through the war with Mexico.

In 1846, the Wilmot Proviso passed, 83–64, in the House, a vote

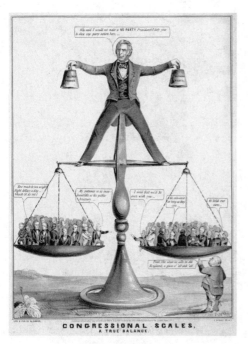

*Zachary Taylor tries to balance the congressional scales between the "Wilmot Proviso" and "Southern Rights."*

that fell entirely along sectional rather than party lines. Massachusetts abolitionist and staunch opponent of the war Charles Sumner predicted that the proviso would lead to "a new crystallization of parties, in which there shall be one grand Northern party of Freedom." Supporters of the Wilmot Proviso argued that slavery and democracy could not coexist. "It is not a question of mere dollars and cents," said one Wilmot supporter in the House.

> It is not a mere political question. It is one in which the North has a higher and deeper stake than the South possibly can have. It is a question whether, in the government of the country, she shall be borne down by the influence of your slaveholding aristocratic institutions, that have not in them the first element of Democracy.[34]

Members of Congress shook their fists. Southerners narrowed their eyes at northerners; northerners glared back at them. Men on both sides of the aisle stamped their feet. And the ground beneath the Capitol began to shake.

And yet, as different as were Wilmot's interests from Calhoun's, they

Americans who
objected to the
extension of slavery
often pictured Texans
(and Mexicans) as
mixed-race and
brutal. In this political
cartoon, "young
Texas," whose tattoos
read "Murder,"
"Slavery," and
"Rape," sits on
a whipped and
manacled slave.

YOUNG TEXAS IN REPOSE.

were both interested in the rights of white men, as Wilmot made plain. "I plead the cause of the rights of white freemen," he said. "I would preserve for free white labor a fair country, a rich inheritance, where the sons of toil, of my own race and own color, can live without the disgrace which association with negro slavery brings upon free labor."[35]

Protests against the war, as a war of aggression, and against the extension of slavery, as an injustice to black people, were sounded not from the elegantly carpeted floor of Congress but from pulpits and pews built of rough-hewn oak. Theodore Parker, a thirty-six-year-old Unitarian minister who had just returned from a tour of Europe, called on Americans to abolish slavery and disavow conquest. "Abroad we are looked on as a nation of swindlers and men-stealers!" he cried. "And what can we say in our defence? Alas, the nation is a traitor to its great idea—that all men are born equal, each with the same inalienable rights." Parker called for a revolution in the name of the nation and in the name of God, in the spirit of the nation's founding, and of its founding ideas.

"We are a rebellious nation; our whole history is treason; our blood was attainted before we were born; our Creeds are infidelity to the Mother church; our Constitution treason to our Father-land. What of that? Though all the Governors in the world bid us commit treason against Man, and set the example, let us never submit. Let God only be a Master to control our Conscience!"[36]

From the stillness of Walden Pond, Henry David Thoreau heeded that call to conscience. He refused to pay his taxes, in protest of the war. In 1846, he left the cabin where he'd listened to whip-poor-wills sing Vespers, and went to jail. In an essay on civil disobedience, he explained that, in a government of majority rule, men had been made into unthinking machines, spineless, and less than men, unwilling to cast votes of conscience. (Of the democracy of numbers, he asked, searchingly, "How many *men* are there to a square thousand miles in this country? Hardly one.") Prison, he said, was "the only house in a slave-state in which a free man can abide with honor."[37] When Emerson asked him why he had gone to jail, Thoreau is said to have answered, "Why did you not?" But Emerson had his own misgivings:

> Behold the famous States
> Harrying Mexico
> With rifle and with knife![38]

With that rifle and with that knife, Americans would soon begin to carve up their own country.

## II.

FREDERICK DOUGLASS SAT for his first photograph in 1841. He was twenty-three. He wore a dark suit with a stiff white collar and a polka-dotted tie. His skin was sepia, his hair black, his expression resolute. He stared straight into the camera. Born in Maryland in 1818, Douglass had taught himself to read and write from scraps of newspaper and old spelling books, and studied oratory on the sly. He escaped from slavery in 1838, disguised as a sailor. Living in New England, he began reading William Lloyd Garrison's *Liberator*. Three years later, he

*Frederick Douglass, the most photographed man in antebellum America, believed photography to be a democratic art.*

spoke for the first time at an antislavery meeting, on Nantucket. "Have we been listening to a thing, a piece of property, or to a man?" Garrison had asked, when he took the stage after Douglass finished speaking. "A man! A man!" came the cry from the crowd.[39] But Douglass provided his own testament, sitting for a daguerreotype, the ocular proof, eyeing the camera: I am a man.[40]

In the 1840s, Douglass became one of the nation's best-known speakers. In 1843 alone, he had more than one hundred speaking engagements. He spoke with force and eloquence. His bearing rivaled that of the greatest Shakespearean actors. Garrison wished Douglass would make himself humbler, and talk plainer, to appear more, that is, like Garrison's notion of an ex-slave. Bristling at Garrison's handling, Douglass told his own story and made his own way. In 1845, he published an autobiography that, by revealing details of his origins, exposed him to fugitive slave catchers and imperiled his life; he left the country. *Narrative of the Life of Frederick Douglass* was translated into French, German, and Dutch. Douglass, speaking in Europe, became the most famous black person in the world.[41] After buying his freedom, he returned to the United States in 1847 and started a newspaper, the *North Star*. Its motto and creed: "Right is of no Sex—Truth is of no Color—God is the Father of us all, and we are all Brethren."[42]

In the *North Star*, Douglass called for an immediate end to the war with Mexico. "We beseech our countrymen to leave off this horrid conflict, abandon their murderous plans, and forsake the way of blood," he urged. "Let the press, the pulpit, the church, the people at large, unite at once; and let petitions flood the halls of Congress by the million, asking for the instant recall of our forces from Mexico."[43] Douglass, who had faith in the power of photography, had faith in other technologies, too. Douglass believed that the great machines of the age were ushering in and accelerating an era of political revolution, of which protest of the war formed only one small part. "Thanks to steam navigation and electric wires," he wrote, "a revolution cannot be confined to the place or the people where it may commence but flashes with lightning speed from heart to heart."[44]

Other observers expected technological forces to work different miracles. As the nation split apart over the war with Mexico, many commentators came to believe that mighty machines could repair the breach. If the problem was the size of the Republic, the sprawl of its borders, the frayed edges of empire, couldn't railroads, and especially the telegraph, tie the Republic together? "Doubt has been entertained by many patriotic minds how far the rapid, full, and thorough intercommunication of thought and intelligence, so necessary to the people living under a common representative republic, could be expected to take place throughout such immense bounds," said one House member in 1845, but "that doubt can no longer exist."[45]

Samuel Morse's 1844 demonstration had proven that communication across even so great a distance as the width of the continent could be had in an instant. *What hath God wrought?* He had wrought, among other things, a wire service. Lawrence Gobright, the Associated Press's clear-eyed Washington correspondent, determined to use the new wire service to inform Americans of goings-on in Congress: "My business is to communicate facts," Gobright wrote about his barebones style. "My instructions do not allow me to make any comment upon the facts which I communicate."[46] But, for all the utopianism of Douglass and for all Gobright's worthiness, even Americans with an unflinching faith in machine-driven progress understood that a pulse along a wire could not stop the slow but steady dissolution of the Union.

In February 1847, Taylor's forces defeated a Mexican army commanded by Antonio López de Santa Anna near Monterrey. By summer, Mexico was prepared to negotiate a peace. Even as negotiators were tackling the matter of the border between the two nations, U.S. forces led by General Winfield Scott invaded Mexico City. By September, they had occupied the city. With the Americans wielding this tremendous bargaining power, an "All Mexico" movement arose, its adherents taking the position that the United States ought to acquire all of Mexico. Michigan senator Lewis Cass was among those who opposed this plan, on the grounds that it would be difficult to integrate the citizens of Mexico into the United States. "We do not want the people of Mexico either as citizens or subjects," Cass said. "All we want is a portion of territory, which they nominally hold, generally uninhabited, or, where inhabited at all, sparsely so."[47]

Polk's ambition seemed limitless. He considered trying to acquire all of Mexico, from 26° north all the way to the Pacific. In the end, the line was set at 36° north. Mexico held onto Baja California, Sonora, and Chihuahua but, in exchange for $15 million, ceded to the United States more than half of its land. Mexican nationals who remained in that territory were given the choice to cross the new border back into Mexico, retain their Mexican citizenship, or become American citizens "on an equality with that of the inhabitants of the other territories of the United States." Some 75,000–100,000 Mexicans chose to remain, largely in Texas and California, where, although promised political equality, they faced a growing racial animosity and economic losses, especially as their existing economy—trading and ranching—was replaced by prospecting, commercial agriculture, and industrial production.[48]

The war formally ended on February 2, 1848, with the signing of the Treaty of Guadalupe Hidalgo, under which the top half of Mexico became the bottom third of the United States. The gain to the United States was as great as the loss to Mexico. In 1820, the United States of America had spanned 1.8 million square miles, with a population of 9.6 million people; Mexico had spanned 1.7 million square miles, with a population of 6.5 million people. By 1850, the United States had acquired one million square miles of Mexico, and its population had grown to 23.2 million; Mexico's population was 7.5 million.[49]

As the United States swelled, Mexico shrank. Most of the land along the border between the two countries was barren and featureless. When the

Joint United States and Mexican Boundary Commission began the work of surveying, its members found it hard even to stay alive: most died by starvation. But the scale of the territory the United States acquired by the Treaty of Guadalupe Hidalgo was staggering. The Louisiana Purchase had doubled the size of the United States. In gaining territory from Mexico, the United States grew by 64 percent. The Superintendent of the Census, charged with measuring its extent, marveled that the territory comprising the United States had grown to "nearly ten times as large as the whole of France and Great Britain combined; three times as large as the whole of France, Britain, Austria, Prussia, Spain, Portugal, Belgium, Holland, and Denmark, together; one-and-a-half times as large as the Russian empire in Europe; one-sixth less only than the area covered by the fifty-nine or sixty empires, states, and Republics of Europe; of equal extent with the Roman Empire or that of Alexander, neither of which is said to have exceeded 3,000,000 square miles."[50]

Had the United States, an infant nation, become an empire? And in its imperial reach, would it fall, like Rome? "The United States will conquer Mexico," Emerson had predicted, "but it will be as the man who swallows the arsenic which brings him down. Mexico will poison us."[51]

These dismal fears were on the mind of eighty-year-old John Quincy Adams, hobbled and infirm, who objected to the war, and to the peace, with his dying breath. On February 21, 1848, the day Polk received the Treaty of Guadalupe Hidalgo, Quincy Adams collapsed in the House of Representatives, very nearly in the middle of giving a speech, a last gasp of opposition to the war and all that it stood for. He died two days later. Young Abraham Lincoln, who'd been there when Quincy Adams fell to the floor, was among the men appointed to make arrangements for the funeral, held in the House of Representatives. Calhoun served as a pallbearer. Until the death of Lincoln, the death of no other statesman was so closely reported, followed, and witnessed, a national pageant. Telegraph lines had only just been completed between Portland, Maine, and Richmond, Virginia, and as far west as Cincinnati; word of Quincy Adams's death spread faster than the wind. His glass-covered coffin traveled five hundred miles by train, stopping in one city after another, where thousands of Americans lined up to view it in an unprecedented, steam-powered parade of grief. The nation fell into mourning, pondering the awful matter of political poison, and the dread question of disunion.[52]

## III.

HORACE GREELEY HIRED Margaret Fuller as an editor at the *New York Tribune* in 1844. Fuller, thirty-four, nearsighted and frail, was the most learned woman in the United States, as comfortable writing literary criticism as she was discussing philosophy with Emerson. "Her powers of speech throw her writing into the shade," Emerson once wrote in his journal.[53]

Rebukes by the likes of Catherine Beecher, who condemned any woman who spoke in public, had silenced a great many women but not all, and certainly not Fuller or prominent abolitionists like the Grimké sisters. Angelina Grimké, raised in Charleston, South Carolina, and expelled from her church for speaking out against slavery, had written a reply to Beecher, an essay called "Human Rights Not Founded on Sex." She said, "The investigation of the rights of the slave has led me to a better understanding of my own."[54] Her sister Sarah made the argument historical: "The page of history teems with woman's wrongs, and it is wet with woman's tears."[55]

Sentiment was not Fuller's way; debate was her way. She was a scourge of lesser intellects. Edgar Allan Poe, whose work she did not admire, described her as wearing a perpetual sneer. In "The Great Lawsuit: Man *versus* Men, Woman *versus* Women," Fuller argued that the democratization of American politics had cast light on the tyranny of men over women: "As men become aware that all men have not had their fair chance," she observed, women had become willing to say "that no women have had a fair chance." Meanwhile, abolition—"partly because many women have been prominent in that cause"—had made urgent the fight for women's rights. In 1845, in *Woman in the Nineteenth Century,* Fuller argued for fundamental and complete equality: "We would have every path laid open to Woman as freely as to Man."[56] The book was wildly successful, and Greeley, who had taken to greeting Fuller with one of her catchphrases about women's capacity—"Let them be sea-captains, if you will"—sent her to Europe to become his newspaper's foreign correspondent. Fuller was in Rome, where she fell in love and gave birth to a son, when the women's rights movement was born in earnest in the United States, as

THE TELEGRAPHIC CANDIDATES.

*The leading 1848 presidential candidates race to the White
House by telegraph (Lewis Cass) and railroad (Zachary Taylor);
Henry Clay tries to gain on them in a rowboat; laggard Martin
Van Buren follows on a skinny horse; and a black man,
representing abolition, lies facedown in the dirt, defeated.*

part of the political mayhem of the revolutionary year of 1848, a presidential election year.[57]

Polk had pledged to serve only one term. Democrats struggled to name a replacement. By now, finding a candidate to run for president had become all but impossible; the parties were national, but, given that politics had become sectional, what man could attract voters in both the North and the South?

The contenders were decidedly lackluster, the cramped and short-sighted men of a cramped and shortsighted age. One Democratic Party prospect, Pennsylvania lawyer and lifelong bachelor James Buchanan, had served as Polk's secretary of state. Buchanan favored solving the territorial problem by extending the Missouri Compromise line all the way across the continent. Senator Lewis Cass, who'd served as Jackson's secretary of war, had a subtler mind. Cass favored a political scheme dubbed, by its supporters, "popular sovereignty," under which each state ought to decide, on entering the Union, whether it would allow or prohibit slavery. At the party's nominating convention, Cass prevailed, and delegates chose, as his running mate, William Butler, a general who had served in the War with Mexico with no particular distinction.

Military heroes were the fashion of the political year. The Whig Party courted two of the war's two better-known generals, Zachary Taylor and Winfield Scott, casting aside the two aging leaders of the party, Henry Clay and Daniel Webster. Taylor had never belonged to a political party; Scott was nearly as mysterious. Taylor only grudgingly agreed to declare himself a Whig. "I am a Whig," he said, adding, "but not an ultra Whig." As he himself admitted, he'd never even voted.[58] Nevertheless, he won the nomination. Clay, dismayed at the rise of the war heroes, declared, "I wish I could slay a Mexican."[59]

The rise of Cass and Taylor left Democrats and Whigs who opposed the extension of slavery into the territories without a candidate. They bolted and, at a convention held in Buffalo in June of 1848, formed the Free-Soil Party. Casting about in desperation for a man with a national reputation, they settled on ex-president Martin Van Buren and adopted as their motto "Free Soil, Free Speech, Free Labor, and Free Men!"[60]

The Free-Soil, Free-Speech movement came out of the dispute over the interpretation of the Constitution, but it was also tied to revolutions that convulsed Europe in 1848. Margaret Fuller filed reports from Italy, where she nursed fallen revolutionaries in a hospital in Rome. Reeling from those revolutions, the king of Bavaria asked the historian Leopold von Ranke to explain why his people had rebelled against monarchial rule, as had so many peoples in Europe that year. "Ideas spread most rapidly when they have found adequate concrete expression," Ranke told the king, and the United States had "introduced a new force in the world," the idea that "the nation should govern itself," an idea that would determine "the course of the modern world": free speech, spread by wire, would make the whole world free.[61]

Unlike the predominant U.S. response to the Haitian revolution, most Americans, following Margaret Fuller, greeted the revolutions in Europe as democratic revolutions, the people rising up against the tyranny of aristocracy and monarchy. Marx's *Communist Manifesto*, published that year, was hardly read, and soon forgotten (only to be rediscovered decades later). But it captured a sentiment that coursed across the American continent: the workers had lost control of the means of production.

People who rallied behind "free labor" insisted on the moral superiority of yeoman farming and wage work over slave labor. But the language of the struggle between labor and capital suffused free labor ideology. "Labor is prior to, and independent of capital," Lincoln said in 1859, and "in fact, capital is the fruit of labor."[62] But the battle, for Free-Soilers, wasn't really between labor and capital; it was between free labor (the producing classes) and the slave power (American aristocrats). The Free-Soil movement enjoyed its strongest support in two particular sorts of middling classes: laboring men in eastern cities and farming men in western territories. If it sounds, in retrospect, like Marx, its rhetoric in fact borrowed from the nature writings of Emerson and Thoreau. Unlike Thoreau, who cursed the railroads, Free-Soilers believed in improvement, improvement through the hard work of the laboring man, his power, his energy. "Our paupers to-day, thanks to free labor, are our yeoman and merchants of tomorrow," the *New York Times* boasted. "Why, who are the laboring people of the North?" Daniel Webster asked. "They are the whole North. They are the people who till their own farms with their own hands, freeholders, educated men, independent men." As laboring men moved westward, they carried this spirit with them, so long as they founded free states. The governor of Michigan argued, "Like most new States, ours has been settled by an active, energetic, and enterprising class of men, who are desirous of accumulating property rapidly."[63]

Free-Soilers and their bedfellows spoke of "Northern Progress and Southern Decadence," comparing the striving, energetic, and improving work of free labor to the corruption, decadence, and backwardness of slavery. Slavery reduced a man to "a blind horse upon a tread-mill," said Lincoln. Slavery had left the South in ruins, wrote New York senator William Seward: "An exhausted soil, old and decaying towns, wretchedly-neglected roads." As Horace Greeley put it, "Enslave a man and you destroy his ambition, his enterprise, his capacity."[64]

This attack by northerners led southerners to greater exertions in defending their way of life. They battled on several fronts. They described northern "wage slavery" as a far more exploitative system of labor than slavery. They celebrated slavery as fundamental to American prosperity. Slavery "has grown with our growth, and strengthened with our strength," Calhoun said. And they elaborated an increasingly virulent ideology of racial difference, arguing against the very idea of equality embodied in the American creed.

Some of these ideas came from the field of ethnology. The Swiss-born American naturalist Louis Agassiz advocated "special creation," the idea that God had created and distributed all the world's plants and animals separately, and strewn them across the lands and the seas, each to its proper place. With proslavery southerners, Agassiz also subscribed to polygenesis, the theory that God had created four different races, each in a separate Garden of Eden. But, as Frederick Douglass observed, slavery lay "at the bottom of the whole controversy," since the dispute between polygenists and monogenists was, at heart, a debate "between the slave-holders on the *one* hand, and the abolitionists on the other."[65]

Conservative Virginian George Fitzhugh, himself inspired by ethno-logical thinking, dismissed the "self-evident truths" of the Declaration of Independence as utter nonsense. "Men are not born physically, morally, or intellectually equal," he wrote. "It would be far nearer the truth to say, 'that some were born with saddles on their backs, and others booted and spurred to ride them,'—and the riding does them good." For Fitzhugh, the error had begun in the imaginations of the *philosophes* of the Enlighten-ment and in their denial of the reality of history. Life and liberty are not "inalienable rights," Fitzhugh argued: instead, people "have been sold in all countries, and in all ages, and must be sold so long as human nature lasts." Equality means calamity: "Subordination, difference of caste and classes, difference of sex, age, and slavery beget peace and good will." Progress is an illusion: "the world has not improved in the last two thou-sand, probably four thousand years." Perfection is to be found in the past, not in the future.[66] As for the economic systems of the North and the South, "Free laborers have not a thousandth part of the rights and liber-ties of negro slaves," Fitzhugh insisted. "The negro slaves of the South are the happiest, and, in some sense, the freest people in the world."[67]

The Free-Soil Party opposed every single one of Fitzhugh's claims. And, if it drew support from farmers and laborers, it also earned the loy-alty of free blacks. To support the party, Henry Highland Garnet, a black abolitionist in Troy, New York, reprinted David Walker's *Appeal*. The party held its first convention in Buffalo in the summer of 1848. Salmon Chase drafted the party's platform, which very closely followed Chase's interpretation of Madison's *Notes*. The Constitution couldn't be rejected,

Chase argued, it had to be reclaimed. His key ideas, he explained, were three: "1. That the original policy of the Government was that of slavery restriction. 2. That under the Constitution Congress cannot establish or maintain slavery in the territories. 3. That the original policy of the Government has been subverted and the Constitution violated for the extension of slavery, and the establishment of the political supremacy of the Slave Power."[68]

The Free-Soil Party had also drawn the support of women who'd been involved in the temperance and abolition movements, and who'd campaigned on behalf of the Whig Party in 1840 and 1844. On the heels of the Free-Soil convention in Buffalo, three hundred women and men held a women's rights convention in Seneca Falls, New York. Margaret Fuller was still in Italy, but it was her work that had served as a catalyst.

Elizabeth Cady Stanton, thirty-two, drafted a manifesto. The daughter of a New York Supreme Court Justice, Stanton had grown up reading her father's lawbooks. Earlier that spring, she'd been instrumental in securing the passage of a state Married Women's Property Act. Under most existing state laws, married women could not own property or make contracts; anything they owned became their husbands' upon marriage; the New York law allowed women "separate use" of their separate property. Stanton, whose husband, also a lawyer, would help found the Republican Party, was also a noted abolitionist. As Fuller had pointed out, the migration of abolitionism into party politics illustrated to women just how limited was their capacity to act politically when they could not vote. The women who gathered at Seneca decided to fight for all manner of legal reform and, controversially, for the right to vote. They felt, Stanton later wrote, "as helpless and hopeless as if they had been suddenly asked to construct a steam engine."

Stanton's Declaration of Sentiments did not merely call for piecemeal legislative reform but instead echoed the Declaration of Independence:

> When, in the course of human events, it becomes necessary for one portion of the family of man to assume among the people of the earth a position different from that which they have hitherto occupied, but one to which the laws of nature and of nature's God entitle them, a decent respect to the opinions of mankind requires that they should declare the causes which impel them to the separation.

And on it went. "The history of mankind is a history of repeated injuries and usurpations on the part of man toward woman, having in direct object the establishment of an absolute tyranny over her," Stanton wrote. "To prove this, let facts be submitted to a candid world." Man took woman's property, passed laws in which she had no voice, subjected her to taxation without representation, denied her an education, made her a slave to his will, forbade her from speaking in public, and denied her the right to vote.[69] One Whig newspaper called the convention "the most shocking and unnatural incident ever recorded in the history of womanity."[70] But nothing so weak as ridicule ever stopped Stanton, who refused to let the battle over the meaning of the Constitution be settled by men alone.

Margaret Fuller, the most accomplished American woman of the century, would miss that battle. With her babbling, toddling nearly two-year-old son and his father, and with the manuscript of her epic history of the revolution in Rome wrapped in a blue calico bag tucked into a portable wooden desk, she left Italy in 1849 and set sail for New York. Less than three hundred yards from the shore of Fire Island and mere miles from New York City, their ship ran aground on a sandbar in a raging storm. Other passengers pried planks from the deck of the ship and, using them as rafts, made their way to shore. Fuller, who was terrified of water and unwilling to let go of her baby, sat on the deck in a white nightdress and waited for a lifeboat from the island lighthouse while the ship beneath her broke to pieces, its masts splintering, its rigging whipping in the wind. A wave crashed over her and she was plunged into the fearsome sea.

Thoreau came from Massachusetts to comb the beach in search of her remains or any of her pages. Only the tiny bare body of her baby was ever found.[71]

# IV.

HISTORY TEEMS WITH mishaps and might-have-beens: explosions on the Potomac, storms not far from port, narrowly contested elections, court cases lost and won, political visionaries drowned. But over the United States in the 1850s, a sense of inevitability fell, as if there were a fate, a dismal dismantlement, that no series of events or accidents could thwart.

Near the end of 1849, Henry Wadsworth Longfellow, despairing for the Union, composed a poem about the American ship of state. Longfellow, born by the sea in Portland, Maine, in 1807, was America's best-known and best-loved poet. He was also the beloved and passionately loyal friend of six-foot-four Charles Sumner, who in the 1840s campaigned against the annexation of Texas and the War with Mexico while fighting against racial segregation in Boston schools. In 1842, Sumner had convinced Longfellow to put his pen to the antislavery cause, and Longfellow had dutifully written and published a little book of *Poems on Slavery.* Well known for his abolitionist views, Longfellow had in 1844 been urged by the Liberty Party to run for Congress. "Though a strong anti-Slavery man, I am not a member of any society, and fight under no single banner," he wrote, declining. "Partizan warfare becomes too violent—too vindictive for my taste; and I should be found but a weak and unworthy champion in public debate."[72]

By 1849, Longfellow, like most Americans who were paying attention, feared for the Republic. He began writing a poem, called "The Building of the Ship," about a beautiful, rough-hewn ship called the *Union.* But as he closed the poem, he could imagine nothing but disaster for this worthy vessel. In his initial draft, he closed the poem with these lines:

> . . . *where, oh where,*
> *Shall end this form so rare?*
> . . . *Wrecked upon some treacherous rock,*
> *Rotting in some loathsome dock,*
> *Such the end must be at length*
> *Of all this loveliness and strength!*

Then, on November 11, 1849, Sumner came to dinner at Longfellow's house in Cambridge, flushed with excitement about the Free-Soil Party. Sumner was running for Congress as a Free-Soiler; November 12 was Election Day. He convinced Longfellow that the Union might yet be saved, and that he ought to write a more hopeful ending to his poem. Longfellow drafted a revision that night and the next day went to the polls to vote for Sumner. Longfellow's new ending became one of his most admired verses:

*Sail on! Sail on! O Ship of State!*
*For thee the famished nations wait!*
*The world seems hanging on thy fate!*

He wrote to his publisher, "What think you of the enclosed, instead of the sad ending of 'The Ship'? Is it better?" It was better. Lincoln's secretary later said that after Lincoln read Longfellow's poem, "His eyes filled with tears and his checks were wet. He did not speak for some minutes, but finally said with simplicity, 'It is a wonderful gift to be able to stir men like that!'"[73]

By the middle of the nineteenth century, the struggle over slavery that had begun on the shores of the Atlantic had reached the shores of the Pacific—across three thousand miles hatched and crisscrossed with train tracks and telegraph wires. "The Union has been preserved thus far by miracles," John Marshall had written in 1832. "I fear they cannot continue." Another miracle, it seemed, was needed in 1850. The discovery of gold in California had led to a gold rush. Migrants came from the east, from neighboring Oregon, from Mexico, and from parts elsewhere, unimaginably far, even from Chile and China. In 1849, a California constitutional convention decreed that "neither slavery nor involuntary servitude, unless for the punishment of crimes, shall ever be tolerated in the State." (A resolution to prohibit "free negroes" from settling in the state was defeated.) With a constitution ratified by voters in the fall of 1849, the request to enter the Union went to Congress.[74]

It must have felt like living on a seesaw. Admitting California as a free state would have toppled the precarious balance between slave and free states. Congress seemed at an impasse. But over eight months of close negotiation, Henry Clay, much aided by Illinois senator Stephen Douglas, a short, brawny bulldog of a man, brokered a compromise or, rather, a series of compromises, involving a set of issues related to slavery. To appease Free-Soilers, California would be admitted as a free state; the slave trade would be abolished in Washington, DC; and Texas would yield to New Mexico a disputed patch of territory, in exchange for $10 million. (John C. Frémont, an opponent of slavery, was elected California's first senator.) To appease those who favored slavery, the territories of New Mexico, Nevada, Arizona, and Utah would be organized without mention of slavery, leaving the question to be settled by the inhabitants themselves, upon application for statehood. Douglas promoted the idea of popular sovereignty, proclaiming, "If there is any one principle dearer and more sacred than all others in free governments, it is that which asserts the exclusive right of a free people to form and adopt their own fundamental law."[75]

Unfree people, within Stephen Douglas's understanding, had no such rights. The final proslavery element of the Compromise of 1850, the Fugitive Slave Law, required citizens to turn in runaway slaves and denied fugitives the right to a jury trial. The law, said Harriet Jacobs, a fugitive slave living in New York, marked "the beginning of a reign of terror to the colored population."[76] Bounty hunters and slave catchers hunted down and captured former slaves and returned them to their owners for a fee. Little stopped them from seizing men, women, and children who had been born free, or who had been legally emancipated, and selling them to the South, too. Nothing so brutally exposed the fragility of freedom or the rapaciousness of slavery. "If anybody wants to break a law, let him break the Fugitive-Slave Law," Longfellow wrote bitterly. "That is all it is for."[77]

Harriet Tubman, who'd first run away when she was only seven years old, helped build a new American infrastructure: the Underground Railroad. Tubman, five feet tall, had been beaten and starved—a weight thrown at her head had left a permanent dent—but had escaped bondage in 1849, fleeing from Maryland to Philadelphia. Beginning in 1850, she made at least thirteen trips back into Maryland to rescue some seventy men, women, and children, while working, in New York, Philadelphia, and Canada, as a laundress, housekeeper, and cook. People took to calling her "Captain Tubman" or, more simply, "Moses." Once, asked what she would do if she were captured, she said, "I shall have the consolation to know that I had done some good to my people."[78]

The Compromise of 1850 lasted for barely four years, but in the interim it transformed the abolitionist movement and, once again, realigned the parties. In 1851, Charles Sumner, running as a Free-Soiler, won the Massachusetts senate seat long held by Daniel Webster, architect of the compromise that Sumner despised. That same year, Frederick Douglass broke with Garrison on the question of the Constitution. "I am sick and tired of arguing on the slaveholders' side," Douglass said. He had come to believe that the Constitution did not sanction slavery and could be used to end it.[79] "At a time like this, scorching irony, not convincing argument, is needed," Douglass said bitterly, in a blistering speech he delivered in Rochester on July 5, 1852. "What, to the American slave, is your 4th of July?" he asked.

> I answer; a day that reveals to him, more than all other days in the year, the gross injustice and cruelty to which he is the constant victim. To him, your celebration is a sham; your boasted liberty, an unholy license; your national greatness, swelling vanity; your sounds of rejoicing are empty and heartless; your denunciation of tyrants, brass fronted impudence; your shouts of liberty and equality, hollow mockery; your prayers and hymns, your sermons and thanksgivings, with all your religious parade and solemnity, are, to him, mere bombast, fraud, deception, impiety, and hypocrisy—a thin veil to cover up crimes which would disgrace a nation of savages.[80]

But even as Douglass called on Americans to realize the promise of the nation's founding documents, expansion to the West led to still more staggering constitutional distortions and moral contortions.

In 1854, the seesaw tipped once more, pressed down, on the proslavery end, by Stephen Douglas, who served as chair of the Senate's Committee on Territories. Congress had been talking about plans for a transcontinental railroad since the 1830s. Douglas wanted the railroad to go through Chicago. But between Chicago and the Pacific stood the so-called Permanent Indian Territory, the land to which Andrew Jackson had removed eastern Indians, including the Cherokees. Douglas argued that, in an age of improvement, in the country of the future, the very notion of a Permanent Indian Territory was absurd: "The idea of arresting our progress in that direction has become so ludicrous that we are amazed, that wise and patriotic statesmen ever cherished the thought. . . . How are we to develop, cherish, and protect our immense interests and possessions on the Pacific, with a vast wilderness fifteen hundred miles in breadth, filled with hostile savages, and cutting off all direct communication? The Indian barrier must be removed."[81]

When a bill organizing the Permanent Indian Territory into Kansas and Nebraska was introduced into Congress in January of 1854, Douglas proposed an amendment that amounted to a repeal of the Missouri

Compromise, which would have prohibited slavery from both territories. Instead, in accordance with the principle of popular sovereignty, the people of Kansas and Nebraska would decide. The Kansas-Nebraska Act effectively opened to slavery land that had previously been closed to it. Its consequences represented, to many northerners, an outrageous betrayal of the Constitution itself. New York senator Preston King predicted that "past lines of party will be obliterated with the Missouri line." Maine senator Hannibal Hamlin declared, "The old Democratic party is now the party of slavery."[82]

So far from serving as a safety value with which to release the pent-up pressure of the growing American population, expansion into the West had proved explosive. The Kansas-Nebraska controversy made the Democratic Party into the party of slavery, and it spelled the end of the American Party, also known as the Know-Nothing Party. The Know-Nothings had pledged never to vote for any foreign-born or Catholic candidate and campaigned for extending the period of naturalization to twenty-one years. They'd won control of the Massachusetts legislature and over 40 percent of the vote in Pennsylvania. One Pennsylvania Democrat said, "Nearly everybody seems to have gone altogether deranged on Nativism." In New York, Samuel F. B. Morse ran for Congress as a Know-Nothing and lost, but he spread his message by reprinting his nativist tract *Imminent Dangers* and began arguing that abolitionism was itself a foreign plot, a "long-concocted and skillfully planned intrigue of the British aristocracy."[83] ("Slavery per se is not a sin," Morse insisted. "It is a social condition ordained from the beginning of the world for the wisest purposes, benevolent and disciplinary, by Divine Wisdom.")[84] In February 1854, at their convention in Philadelphia, northern Know-Nothings proposed a platform plank calling for the reinstatement of the Missouri Compromise. When that motion was rejected, some fifty delegates from eight northern states bolted: they left the convention, and the party, to set up their own party, the short-lived North American Party. Nativism would endure as a force in American politics, but, meanwhile, nativists split over slavery.

The Kansas-Nebraska Act also drew forty-five-year-old Abraham Lincoln out of his law practice and back into politics. As a member of the House, Lincoln had opposed the war with Mexico and supported the Wilmot Proviso, but he'd hardly spoken about slavery. In the spring of

1854, he began meditating on the institution of slavery and, like a lawyer preparing for court, weighing possible arguments with which to defeat those who defended the institution. In a fragment written in April, he anticipated a line of debate:

If A. can prove, however conclusively, that he may, of right, enslave B.—why may not B. snatch the same argument, and prove equally, that he may enslave A?—

You say A. is white, and B. is black. It is *color*, then; the lighter, having the right to enslave the darker? Take care. By this rule, you are to be slave to the first man you meet, with a fairer skin than your own.

You do not mean *color* exactly? You mean the whites are *intellectually* the superiors of the blacks, and, therefore have the right to enslave them? Take care again. By this rule, you are to be slave to the first man you meet, with an intellect superior to your own.

But, say you, it is a question of *interest*; and, if you can make it your *interest*; you have the right to enslave another. Very well. And if he can make it his interest, he has the right to enslave you.[85]

Lincoln found a political home in a new political party, the Republican Party, founded in May 1854, in Ripon, Wisconsin, by fifty-four citizens determined to defeat the Kansas-Nebraska Act. Three of those fifty-four citizens were women. Their new party drew a coalition of former Free-Soilers, Whigs, and northern Democrats and Know-Nothings who opposed slavery. If the Democratic Party had become the party of slavery; the Republican Party would be the party of reform. In that spirit, it welcomed the aid of women: women wrote Republican campaign literature and made speeches on behalf of the party. One of the party's best, and best-paid, speakers was Anna Dickinson, who became the first woman to speak in the Hall of the House of Representatives.[86]

Joining the new party, Lincoln wrestled with the implications of the speeches and writing of far-seeing Frederick Douglass, who had staked the fundamental case against slavery in the common humanity of all people. In August 1854, still working out his best line of argument, Lincoln began speaking at political meetings. That fall, campaigning as a Republican, he decided to challenge Stephen Douglas for his seat in the Senate. He debated Douglas in Peoria before a fascinated crowd. Douglas spoke for three hours and then, after a dinner break, Lincoln spoke for just as long. Lincoln argued that what Douglas advocated was an abomination of the idea of democracy. The matter depended on whether "the negro is a man," Lincoln said.

> If he is *not* a man, why in that case, he who *is* a man may, as a matter of self-government, do just as he pleases with him. But if the negro *is* a man, is it not to that extent, a total destruction of self-government, to say that he too shall not govern *himself*? When the white man governs himself, that is self-government; but when he governs himself, and also governs *another* man, that is *more* than self-government—that is despotism. If the negro is a *man*, why then my ancient faith teaches me that "all men are created equal;" and that there can be no moral right in connection with one man's making a slave of another.

For this, for making democracy into the abomination of despotism, he said he hated the Kansas-Nebraska Act:

> I hate it because of the monstrous injustice of slavery itself. I hate it because it deprives our republican example of its just influence in the world—enables the enemies of free institutions, with plausibility, to taunt us as hypocrites—causes the real friends of freedom to doubt our sincerity, and especially because it forces so many really good men amongst ourselves into an open war with the very fundamental principles of civil liberty—criticizing the Declaration of Independence, and insisting that there is no right principle of action but *self-interest*.

Lincoln's was the language of free soil, free speech, and free labor. He grounded his argument against slavery in his understanding of American history, in the language of Frederick Douglass, and in his reading of the

Constitution. "Let no one be deceived," he said. "The spirit of seventy-six and the spirit of Nebraska, are utter antagonisms."[87]

Lincoln lost the race. And still he kept at work, refining his argument, as if he were hewing a log, cutting it into boards, and sanding them. "Most *governments* have been based, practically, on the denial of equal rights of men," he wrote, in a note to himself. "*Ours* began, by *affirming* those rights. . . . We made the experiment; and the fruit is before us. Look at it—think of it. Look at it, in its aggregate grandeur, of extent of country, and numbers of population—of ship, and steamboat, and rail.[88]

Kansas, left to decide whether it would enter the Union as a free or a slave state, broke out in outright war. Southerners moved into Kansas to vote for slavery; northerners moved into Kansas to vote against it. Eventually, they began shooting one another. Horace Greeley dubbed it "Bleeding Kansas." Soon there would be blood on the Senate floor. Lincoln privately confided his despair about what he described as the nation's "progress in degeneracy," a political regression:

> As a nation, we began by declaring that "*all men are created equal.*" We now practically read it "all men are created equal, *except negroes.*" When the Know-Nothings get control, it will read "all men are created equal, except negroes, and *foreigners, and Catholics.*" When it comes to this I should prefer emigrating to some country where they make no pretense of loving liberty—to Russia, for instance, where despotism can be taken pure, and without the base alloy of hypocrisy.[89]

In May of 1856, Charles Sumner delivered from his desk in the Senate a thundering speech called "The Crime Against Kansas," indicting the barbarism of slavery, comparing slavery to rape (and intimating that all slave owners raped their slaves), and warning of a civil war. "Even now, while I speak," Sumner shouted, "portents lower in the horizon, threatening to darken the land, which already palpitates with the mutterings of civil war." Two days later, Congressman Preston Brooks, a cousin of South Carolina senator Andrew Butler, who had cowritten the Kansas-Nebraska Act with Stephen Douglas, approached Sumner while Sumner was sitting at his desk on the Senate floor. "Mr. Sumner, I have read your speech twice over carefully," Brooks told Sumner. "It is a libel on South Carolina, and Mr. Butler, who is a relative of mine." Not waiting for a reply, Brooks then beat Sumner mercilessly with his cane, thwacking him on the head again and again. Longfellow, who had been quietly doing his own part in the fight against slavery—buying the freedom of fugitive slaves and funding free schools—wrote to Sumner to tell him that he was "the greatest voice on the greatest subject that had been uttered since we became a nation."[90] It would take Sumner more than three years to recover from his head injuries. In all that while, Massachusetts refused to elect a replacement, leaving his Senate seat empty.

"The South cannot tolerate free speech anywhere," the *Cincinnati Gazette* argued.[91] But what Brooks's caning of Sumner illustrated best was that the battle over slavery was a battle over the West. In the 1856 election, the Republican Party, incorporating Free-Soilers and acknowledging the growing political power of the West, nominated the Californian and famed explorer John C. Frémont for president, and only narrowly voted down Lincoln for vice president. The party adopted the slogan: "Free Speech, Free Soil, and Frémont!" It included on its platform opposition to the idea that slavery could be left to the states: "We deny the authority of Congress, of a Territorial Legislature, of any individual or association of individuals, to give legal existence to slavery in any Territory of the United States, while the present Constitution shall be maintained."[92]

Frémont, however, proved a lackluster campaigner. As more than one Republican pointed out, his wife, the formidably eloquent Jesse Benton Frémont, "would have been the better candidate."[93] The Whigs nominated the unmemorable Millard Fillmore, the president of their nominating convention declaring, "It has been preached that the Whig party is dead, but it is not so." He was wrong. The Whigs really were dead. In 1856, Democrats decided their best chance of winning an election was nominating a proslavery northerner, and chose James Buchanan. Polk once confided in his diary, "Mr. Buchanan is an able man, but in small matters without judgment and sometimes acts like an old maid."[94] A man of limited imagination, Buchanan's sole political virtue was the appearance of evenhandedness: during the maelstrom of the Kansas-Nebraska Act, he had been serving as ambassador to Great Britain, which made him appear, to American voters, unstained, as if a vote for Buchanan were a vote for union. In the general election, Buchanan campaigned by arguing that electing Frémont, a known opponent of the extension of slavery to the territories, would lead to a civil war; he won by a landslide.

The war Buchanan hoped to avert would come, with or without him. Frémont had been the first presidential candidate to promise to end the extension of slavery; Buchanan, who promised no such thing, was the first president whose inauguration was photographed. A blurry black-and-white print of the East Portico of the Capitol Building captured a crowd of men in top hats and ladies in hoop skirts, pressed against railings, on Wednesday, March 4, 1857. Buchanan was sworn in by Chief Justice Roger Taney, a wizened seventy-nine-year-old Maryland Democrat who'd been named to the court by Andrew Jackson. Buchanan proceeded to deliver an inaugural address in which he waved aside the small matter of slavery: "Most happy will it be for the country when the public mind shall be diverted from this question to others of more pressing and practical importance." He also expressed his contentment with a much-anticipated decision of Taney's Supreme Court in a case known as *Dred Scott v. Sandford*. Scott, born into slavery, had been carried into a free state and had sued for his freedom. Buchanan, from his perch at the Capitol, calling out across a sea of top hats, insisted that he was happy to leave to the court both this question and the broader question of the extension of slavery. "It is a judicial question, which legitimately belongs to the Supreme Court of the United States, before whom it is now pending, and will, it is understood, be speedily and finally settled," Buchanan said. "To their decision, in common with all good citizens, I shall cheerfully submit."[95]

This was, to say the least, decidedly disingenuous. In truth, Buchanan had lobbied for the postponement of the ruling, and had also pressured at least one justice, a northerner, to join the court's proslavery majority. The next day, the *Philadelphia Inquirer* reported that Judge Taney was at home, writing his opinion. "The decision in the Dred Scott case will be delivered tomorrow," reported a correspondent for the *New York Herald*.[96] The nation held its breath.

The debate had been raging since 1787. Does the Constitution sanction slavery, or does it not? Frederick Douglass had come to find the very question an absurdity. Taney did not.

He handed down his decision on March 6. Only once, in *Marbury v.*

*Madison*, had the Supreme Court overturned federal legislation. Taney chose, in *Dred Scott v. Sandford*, for the court to wield this power again. Writing for a 7–2 majority, he declared the Missouri Compromise unconstitutional. But it was his logic that staggered. Congress had no power to limit slavery in the states, Taney argued, because the men who wrote the Constitution considered people of African descent "beings of an inferior order, and altogether unfit to associate with the white race, either in social or political relations, and so far inferior that they had no rights which the white man was bound to respect." No "negro of the African race," he ruled, could ever claim the rights and privileges of citizenship in the United States.[97]

Word spread by telegraph to every corner of the sprawling Republic. Reaction came swiftly, a torrent of outcry, and, from proslavery agitators, hushed relief. A few daily newspapers, setting type overnight, managed to get news of the ruling into their pages on Saturday, March 7. The *Albany Journal* even editorialized, finding the ruling to be no surprise since "Five of the Judges are slaveholders, and two of the other four owe their appointments to their facile ingenuity in making State laws bend to Federal demands in behalf of 'the Southern institution.'" Most papers didn't report the decision until Monday, March 9, and lengthier accounts of the opinion didn't appear until March 13, when William Lloyd Garrison's *Liberator* ran a full column summarizing the court's opinion, beginning with this decree: "That negroes, whether slave or free, that is, men of the African race, are not citizens of the United States by the Constitution." The implications of the ruling stunned his readers. Even Americans who held no strong views on the question of slavery—and they were rare enough—were nonetheless shocked by the court's exercise of the authority to determine the unconstitutionality of the law. The *National Era* ran an essay called "The Supreme Court—The Oligarchy, The People" on March 19, predicting, accurately enough, that "so far from suppressing the agitation of Slavery, or reconciling the People to its pretensions, this action of the Supreme Court will furnish new materials for controversy, add fuel to the fire, arouse the popular mind still more against the domination of the Slave Power." That same day, the *Independent* ran a piece: "Can Judges Make Law?"[98] Its answer: No.

The full opinion of the court—a book running to more than six hundred pages—would not be printed until May of 1857. But by then, at meetings all over the country, black people and white people alike had condemned the ruling. "A large meeting of colored people" was held in Philadelphia in April, at which it was resolved that "the only duty the colored man owes to a Constitution under which he is declared to be an inferior and degraded being, having no rights which white men are bound to respect, is to denounce and repudiate it, and to do what he can by all proper means to bring it into contempt."[99] What were a people to do whose highest court denied the possibility of equality? "I groan with you over the iniquity of the times," Longfellow wrote Sumner. "It is deplorable; it is heart-breaking; and I long to say some vibrant word, that should have vitality in it, and force."[100]

Lincoln delivered his opinion on the ruling in a speech in Springfield. The court's opinion, he said, was "based on assumed historical facts which were not really true." Taney had argued that the equality asserted in the Declaration of Independence was never intended to apply to black people. If this were true, Lincoln asked, what was the value of Jefferson's words? Were "these truths" mere lies? Lincoln offered his own reading. "The assertion that 'all men are created equal' was of no practical use in effecting our separation from Great Britain," he argued, "and it was placed in the Declaration, not for that, but for future use. Its authors meant it to be, thank God, it is now proving itself, a stumbling block to those who in after times might seek to turn a free people back into the hateful paths of despotism."[101]

But the most powerful speech about the court's ruling in *Dred Scott* was the speech given by Frederick Douglass. Jubilant slave owners said *Dred Scott* had settled the question of slavery for good. Douglass, looking to history, disagreed. "The more the question has been settled," he wryly remarked, "the more it has needed settling." In spite of the bleakness of the ruling—he called it a "vile and shocking abomination"—he found much reason for hope. "You may close your Supreme Court against the black man's cry for justice, but you cannot, thank God, close against him the ear of a sympathising world, nor shut up the Court of Heaven." Taney's interpretation of the Constitution would be ignored, Douglass predicted. "Slavery lives in this country not because of any paper Constitution, but in the moral blindness of the American people."[102]

Dred Scott, fifty-eight, died only months later. He'd been working as a porter in a hotel in St. Louis while suffering from tuberculosis, a slow sickness, a constitutional weakening, as relentless as the disease that wracked the nation itself. Frederick Douglass watched, and looked for a cure, an end to suffering, a lifting of the American people's moral blindness. But it was as if the nation, like Oedipus of Thebes, had seen that in its own origins lay a curse, and had gouged out its own eyes.

White-bearded Henry Wadsworth Longfellow, head in his hands, elbows perched on his desk, might have cast his mind back on the original ending he'd written for "The Building of the Ship," in which the *Union*, its captain and sailors blinded in a storm, is "Lost, lost, wrecked and lost! / By the hurricane driven and tossed." Instead, with Lincoln, he steered the ship of his soul out of the storm of despair and readied his cannons.

*Eight*

# THE FACE
# OF BATTLE

*Photographs like Alexander Gardner's portraits of the dead at
Antietam chronicled the war and its many devastations.*

**A** PHOTOGRAPH STOPS TIME, TRAPPING IT LIKE A BUT-
terfly in a jar. No other kind of historical evidence has this quality
of instantaneity, of an impression taken in a moment, in a flicker, an eye
opened and then shut. Photographs also capture the ordinary, the humble, the speechless. The camera discriminates between light and dark
but not between the rich and the poor, the literate and the illiterate, the
noisy and the quiet. The emergence of photography altered the historical
record. It also shaped the course of American history.

In March of 1839, during a trip to Europe to promote his telegraph,
Samuel Morse visited the Parisian studio of the painter Louis Daguerre,
fellow artist, fellow inventor. Two months before, Daguerre had presented
to the French Academy of Sciences the results of experiments in which
he took pictures by exposing to light polished, silver-coated copper sheets
in the presence of the vapor of iodine crystals. The result was spectacular,

an uncanny, ghostly likeness. In April, Morse wrote a letter home to his brother Sidney, editor of the *New York Observer*, describing Daguerre's invention as "one of the most beautiful discoveries of the age."[1]

The first photograph seen in the United States would be displayed eight months later in a Broadway hotel in New York. Studios soon opened in cities and towns across the country, where photographers, adapting to a fast-changing technology, made portraits of copper (called daguerreotypes), of glass (ambrotypes), and of iron (tintypes). The art spread quickly; by the 1840s and 1850s, twenty-five million portraits were taken in the United States. Ordinary people couldn't afford a painted portrait, but nearly everyone could afford a photograph; it became a technology of democracy. "Talk no more of 'holding the mirror up to nature,'" wrote one newspaper editor. "She will hold it up to herself, and present you with a copy of her countenance for a penny."[2] They were "so life-like they almost speak," people said, but portraits were also closely associated with death, with being trapped in time, on glass, for eternity, and, even more poignantly, with equality.[3] With photography, Walt Whitman predicted, "Art will be democratized."[4]

Frederick Douglass, an early convert, became a theorist of photography. "Negroes can never have impartial portraits at the hands of white artists," he said. "It seems to us next to impossible for white men to take likenesses of black men, without most grossly exaggerating their distinctive features." But a photograph was no caricature. Douglass therefore sat, again and again, in a portraitist's studio: he became the most photographed man in nineteenth-century America, his likeness taken more often than Twain or even Lincoln. Douglass believed both that photography would set his people free by telling the truth about their humanity and that photography would help realize the promise of democracy by capturing rich and poor alike. "What was once the special and exclusive luxury of the rich and great is now the privilege of all," he said. "The humblest servant girl may now possess a picture of herself such as the wealth of kings could not purchase fifty years ago." Technological progress, he predicted, would usher in an age of equality, justice, and peace:

> The growing inter-communication of distant nations, the rapid transmission of intelligence over the globe—the worldwide ramifications of commerce—bringing together the knowledge, the skill,

and the mental power of the world, cannot but dispel prejudice, dissolve the granite barriers of arbitrary power, bring the world into peace and unity, and at last crown the world with justice, liberty, and brotherly kindness.[5]

But by then, the daguerreotype had been abandoned in favor of the paper print, set aside, one Philadelphian remarked, "like a dead language, never spoken, and seldom written."[6] And Americans would be fighting a war one against another, the first war whose devastation was captured by photography: fields of Union and Confederate soldiers, caught in the trap of time, in black and white.

## I.

EVEN AS THE Union was falling apart, Americans indulged in the fantasy that technology could hold it together, and, not only that, but that technology could bind all of the peoples of the world to one another. On September 1, 1858, New Yorkers held a parade celebrating the completion of a cable stretching across the bottom of the Atlantic Ocean. "SEVERED JULY 4, 1776," read one banner, "UNITED AUGUST 12, 1858." Fifteen thousand people marched from the Battery through the city, past Barnum's Museum, where the flags of Britain and the United States were tied together by telegraph wire. "Never before was anything purely human done in the history of the world and the race which stood for One-ness as the successful laying of the Atlantic Cable does!" cried one speaker. "We have hitherto lived in a hemisphere, and we now live on a globe—live not by halves, but as a whole—not as scattered members, but as the connected limbs of one organic body, the great common humanity."[7]

Morse had long predicted that the telegraph would usher in an age of world peace. "I trust that one of its effects will be to bind man to his fellow-man in such bonds of amity as to put an end to war," he insisted.[8] War was a failure of technology, Morse argued, a shortcoming of communication that could be remedied by way of a machine. Endowing his work with the grandest of purposes, he believed that the laying of telegraph wires across the American continent would bind the nation together into one people, and that the laying of cable across the ocean would bind Europe to the Americas, ushering in the dawn of an age of global harmony. And the telegraph did introduce radical changes into American life. By 1858, Chicago's Board of Trade was posting grain prices from all over the continent. The nation was tied together by 50,000 miles of wire, 1,400 stations, and 10,000 telegraph operators.[9] But war isn't a failure of technology; it's a failure of politics.

In the summer of 1858, while New Yorkers were celebrating the laying of the Atlantic cable (a cable that, not long afterward, failed), the people of Illinois witnessed a different and more ancient kind of communication: debate. The debates staged that year between Abraham Lincoln and Stephen Douglas proved to be the greatest argument over the American experiment since the constitutional convention. Those debates didn't avert the coming war between the states, but they illustrate, better than any other part of the historical record of a cloven time, the nature of the disagreement.

Debate is to war what trial by jury is to trial by combat: a way to settle a dispute without coming to blows. The form and its rules had been established over centuries. They derived from rules used in the courts and in Parliament, and even from the rules of rhetoric used in the writing of poetry. Since the Middle Ages and the founding of the first universities, debate had been the foundation of a liberal arts education. (Etymologically and historically, the *artes liberales* are the arts acquired by people who are free, or *liber*.)[10] In the eighteenth century, debate was understood as the foundation of civil society. In 1787, delegates to the constitutional convention had agreed to "to argue without asperity, and to endeavor to convince the judgment without hurting the feelings of each other." Candidates for office debated face-to-face. With the expansion of the franchise, debating spread: beginning in the 1830s, debating classes were offered to ordinary citizens as a form of civic education. Debating societies popped up in cities and even the smallest of towns, where anyone who could vote was expected to know how to debate, although this meant, in turn, that anyone who couldn't vote was expected *not* to debate. (Women, who couldn't vote, were not allowed to debate in public, and when they did, it was considered scandalous. In 1837, when Angelina Grimké agreed to debate two men, the local newspaper refused to publish the results.)[11]

Still, that didn't stop people who couldn't vote from studying argument. Frederick Douglass, as a boy of twelve, and while still a slave, read the debates in a schoolbook called *The Columbian Orator*, which included a "Dialogue between a Master and Slave":

> MASTER: You were a slave when I fairly purchased you.
> SLAVE: Did I give my consent to the purchase?
> MASTER: You had no consent to give. You had already lost the right of disposing of yourself.
> SLAVE: I had lost the power, but how the right? I was treacherously kidnapped in my own country. . . . What step in all this progress of violence and injustice can give a right?[12]

Studying this debate, Douglass had first begun to ask himself these questions: "Why are some people slaves, and others masters? Was there ever a time when this was not so?"[13] Douglass escaped slavery, but he also defeated his bondage by argument.

Banned in Congress under the gag rule, open debate about slavery nevertheless took place elsewhere—in 1855, in Connecticut, the southern aristocrat George Fitzhugh debated the abolitionist Wendell Phillips on the question of "The Failure of Free Society"—but it was uncommon.[14] That made the debates between Abraham Lincoln and Stephen Douglas all the more remarkable.

Lincoln and Douglas had given speeches back-to-back in 1854, during the Kansas-Nebraska crisis; but they'd never faced each other. In the spring and early summer of 1858, Lincoln, running for a U.S. Senate seat held by Douglas, had been following Douglas from campaign stop to campaign stop, listening to him speak and then speaking to the same crowd the next day, or even later on the same day, which gave Lincoln the last word but left him with a much smaller audience, since Democrats seldom stayed to listen to him. Lincoln's supporters urged him to challenge Douglas: "Let him act the honorable part by agreeing to meet you in regular Debate, giving a fair opportunity to all to hear both sides." On July 24, Lincoln wrote to his political rival, inviting him to debate: "Will it be agreeable to you and myself to divide time and address the same audiences?" Douglas, with some reluctance, agreed.[15]

Some twelve thousand people showed up for their first debate, at two o'clock in the afternoon on August 21, in Ottawa, Illinois. There were no seats; the audience stood, without relief, for three hours. The two men, standing together on a stage, looked as though they might have been displayed together in Barnum's Museum: Lincoln, six foot four and as straight as a tree, Douglas, a full foot shorter, his whole body clenched as tight as a fist. They'd agreed to strict rules: the first speaker would speak for an hour and the second for an hour and a half, whereupon the first speaker would offer a thirty-minute rebuttal.

"Ladies and gentlemen," Douglas began, "we are present here to-day for the purpose of having a joint discussion, as the representatives of the two great political parties of the State and Union, upon the principles in issue between those parties."

The audience was as rapt as it was rowdy. "Hit him again!" the crowd cried, when Douglas scored a point against Lincoln. Douglas reminded his audience of Lincoln's opposition to the *Dred Scott* decision.

"I ask you, are you in favor of conferring upon the negro the rights and privileges of citizenship?" he called to the crowd.

"No, no!" came the reply.

The debate turned on the interpretation offered by the two men, and by their parties, of the Declaration of Independence and the Constitution. Douglas argued that Lincoln misread the Declaration of Independence if he believed that it applied to blacks as well as whites. "This Government was made by our fathers on the white basis," Douglas said. "It was made by white men for the benefit of white men and their posterity forever." As to the institution of slavery, that was up to the electorate, Douglas insisted: "I care more for the great principle of self-government, the right of the people to rule, than I do for all the negroes of Christendom."

Douglas charged Lincoln with being a zealot. This Lincoln denied. "I will say here, that I have no purpose directly or indirectly to interfere with the institution of slavery in the States where it exists," he said when he took the stage. "I believe I have no lawful right to do so, and I have no inclination to do so." He contested Douglas's assertion that he, Lincoln, believed in the equality of the races. "I have no purpose to introduce political and social equality between the white and the black races," he said. "But I hold that, notwithstanding all this, there is no reason in the world why the negro is not entitled to all the natural rights enumerated in the Declaration of Independence, the right to life, liberty, and the pursuit of happiness." The crowd cheered. "I hold that he is as much entitled to these as the white man," he added, to another round of cheers.

Douglas argued that claiming that blacks were included in the Declaration of Independence amounted to slandering Jefferson. Lincoln replied (calling Douglas, a former Illinois Supreme Court justice, "Judge"):

> I believe the entire records of the world, from the date of the Declaration of Independence up to within three years ago, may be searched in vain for one single affirmation, from one single man, that the negro was not included in the Declaration of Independence; I think I may defy Judge Douglas to show that he ever said so, that Washington ever said so, that any President ever said so, that any member of Congress ever said so, or that any living man upon the whole earth ever said so, until the necessities of the present policy of the Democratic party, in regard to slavery, had to invent that affirmation.

As to which of the two men could speak best for Jefferson, Lincoln laid down a gauntlet:

> And I will remind Judge Douglas and this audience, that while Mr. Jefferson was the owner of slaves, as undoubtedly he was, in speaking upon this very subject, he used the strong language that "he trembled for his country when he remembered that God was just"; and I will offer the highest premium in my power to Judge Douglas if he will show that he, in all his life, ever uttered a sentiment at all akin to that of Jefferson.

"Hit him again!" the crowd continued to holler at each of the next debates, as if watching a political prize fight, boxers in the ring, taunting, jabbing, dodging. Newspapers printed full transcriptions, including all the interjections from the crowd, the bloodthirsty calls, the thunderous applause. Lincoln began keeping a scrapbook of pasted newspaper columns. An inveterate archivist, he also knew that one day he'd make use of that record.

Their final debate took place in Alton, Illinois, on October 15, just weeks before the election. Not for the first time and not for the last, Lincoln bemoaned the suppression of plain talk about slavery, the endless avoidance of the question at hand. "You must not say anything about it in the free states *because it is not here.* You must not say anything about it in the slave states *because it is there.* You must not say anything about it in the pulpit, because that is religion and has nothing to do with it. You must not say anything about it in politics *because that will disturb the security of 'my place.'* There is no place to talk about it as being a wrong, although you say yourself it *is* a wrong." And, as to the wrongness of slavery, he called it tyranny, and the idea of its naturalness as much an error as a belief in the divine right of kings. The question wasn't sectionalism or nationalism, the Democratic Party or the Republican Party. The question was right against wrong. "That is the issue that will continue in this country when these poor tongues of Judge Douglas and myself shall be silent," Lincoln said.[16]

In November, Lincoln narrowly lost to Douglas. But he had become a leader of the Republican Party—and indisputably its most powerful speaker. "Though I now sink out of view, and shall be forgotten," he wrote, "I believe I have made some marks which will tell for the cause of civil liberty long after I am gone."[17] But Lincoln had yet to leave his lasting mark.

The year Lincoln debated Douglas, John Brown, with eyes like water and hair like a forest, held a constitutional convention in a hushed river town in Canada, fifty miles east of Detroit, a last stop on the Underground Railroad. Brown, fifty-eight, had fathered twenty children. He spoke of prophecies and scourges. He'd once founded a secret society called the League of Gileadites. A tanner, sheep farmer, and failed businessman, he'd first had his portrait taken by a black daguerreotype artist named Augustus Washington. In Washington's portrait, Brown, lean and fearsome, with furrowed brow, stands beside the flag of the Underground Railroad and holds up a hand, as if he might break the very glass beneath which his image is trapped. In the 1850s, Brown became a militant abolitionist, fighting in Kansas with his sons. He sounded like a patriarch out of the Old Testament, Abraham sacrificing Isaac. In his 1858 constitution, Brown and his followers—forty-four black men and eleven white

*African American photographer Augustus Washington captured this likeness of John Brown in his daguerreotype studio in Connecticut in 1846 or 1847. Brown, his right hand raised as if taking an oath, stands in front of the flag of the Subterranean Pass-Way, his more militant version of the Underground Railroad.*

men—replaced "we the people" with "we, citizens of the United States and the oppressed people . . . who have no rights," proclaimed bondage to be "in utter disregard and violation of those eternal and self-evident truths set forth in our Declaration of Independence," and declared war on slavery.[18] They began stockpiling weapons.

In the 1850s, while antislavery conviction grew in the free states, pro-slavery fervor grew in the slave states, not least because the price of slaves was on the rise, from an average of $900 in 1850 to $1,600 ten years later. The high price meant that owners, who spared no pains in the hunting of men, women, and children, were less worried about slave rebellion than about a mass exodus from slave states to free, a much-feared and, in the South, widely reported "slave stampede" that was nothing so much as legions of people emancipating themselves.[19]

Some slave states, blaming the exodus on the influence of free blacks, tried to ban them. Arkansas required that all free blacks leave the state by the end of 1859 or be reenslaved. Meanwhile, some new states entering the Union adopted a "whites-only" policy: Oregon's proposed constitution, which also placed severe restrictions on the growing number of immigrants from China—"No Negro, Chinaman, or Mulatto shall have the right of suffrage"—both prohibited slavery and barred blacks from entering the state.[20]

The price of slaves grew so high that a sizable number of white southerners urged the reopening of the African slave trade. In the 1850s, legislatures in several states, including South Carolina, proposed reopening the trade. Adopting this measure would have violated federal law. Some "reopeners" believed that the federal ban on the trade was unconstitutional; others were keen to nullify it, in a dress rehearsal for secession.

While John Brown and his men were drafting a new constitution in Canada, the Louisiana House of Representatives passed an act to reopen the trade. In 1859, anticipating the success of this movement, men from Mississippi, Arkansas, and Louisiana formed the African Labor Supply Association. A Southern Commercial Convention meeting in Montgomery, Alabama, voted that "all laws, State and Federal, prohibiting the African slave trade, ought to be repealed." Not content to wait for any of these laws to pass, southern vigilantes known as "filibusters" outfitted ships with arms and ammunition and attempted to conquer Cuba, Nicaragua, Guatemala, El Salvador, Mexico, and Brazil in order to extend a market for slaves. A leading reopener, Leonidas Spratt of South Carolina, said, "If the trade is wrong so be the condition which results from it"; the two could not be separated. Alabama's William Yancey, born on the banks of the Ogeechee River in Georgia, said that the real issue was labor, and that the only difference between labor in the North and the South was that "one comes under the head of importation, the other under the head of immigration." He said, "If it is right to buy slaves in Virginia and carry them to New Orleans, why is it not right to buy them in Cuba, Brazil, or Africa and carry them there?"[21]

Proslavery southerners made these arguments under the banner of "free trade," their rhetorical answer to "free labor." To George Fitzhugh, all societies were "at all times and places, regulated by laws as universal and as similar as those which control the affairs of bees," and trade itself, including the slave trade, was "as old, as natural, and irresistible as the tides of the ocean."[22] In 1855, David Christy, the author of *Cotton Is King*, wrote about the vital importance of "the doctrine of Free Trade," which included abolishing the tariffs that made imported English goods more expensive than manufactured goods produced in the North. As one south-erner put it, "Free trade, unshackled industry, is the motto of the South."[23]

If proslavery southerners defended free trade and pro-labor northern-ers defended free soil and free labor, abolitionists defended free speech. If southern Democrats came to Congress armed and ready to fight, and northern Whigs, Democrats, and Free-Soilers had usually come unarmed, northern Republicans nevertheless went to Congress ready to do battle. One Massachusetts congressman, heading to Washington for the 1855 session of Congress, was met at the train station by his constituents, bear-ing a gift. It was a pistol, engraved "Free Speech."[24]

When the South began referring to its economy as "unshackled," mat-ters had plainly arrived at an ideological impasse. By the end of 1858, many observers had come around to Lincoln's point of view that the United States would either be one thing or another, but not both. Wil-liam H. Seward, a Florida-born senator from New York, called the dis-pute between the states an unavoidable conflict, moral, and absolute: "It is an irrepressible conflict between opposing and enduring forces, and it means that the United States must and will, sooner or later, become either entirely a slaveholding nation, or entirely a free-labor nation." Seward had no doubt which side would prevail, since his theory of his-tory was a theory of progress, in a march from slavery to freedom and from inequality to equality. "I know, and you know, that a revolution has begun," he told his audience. "I know, and the world knows, that revolu-tions never go backwards."[25]

John Brown believed that the conflict was irrepressible, too, but he didn't fear the nation slipping into it; he wanted to start it. In the spring of 1859, Brown and a party of his followers made their way to Maryland, where they planned a military operation that would begin with the seizing of a U.S. arsenal at Harpers Ferry, Virginia (now part of West Virginia). In August, Frederick Douglass went to Chambersburg, Pennsylvania, to meet with Brown, who had also tried, and failed, to enlist the support of Harriet Tubman. Brown and Douglass met at an abandoned stone quarry outside of town. Brown told Douglass about his plan. Douglass warned him against it, saying "it would . . . array the whole country against us." The more Doug-lass heard, the more he worried. He later wrote, "All his arguments, and all his descriptions of the place, convinced me that he was going into a perfect steel trap, and that once in he would never get out alive."[26]

On the night of Sunday, October 16, 1859, Brown and twenty-one men attacked the arsenal and captured it. They halted a train leaving Harpers Ferry but then let it go. As the train sped through the Maryland countryside to Baltimore, passengers threw hastily written notes out the windows, warning people about the insurrection. Barely twelve hours after the raid had begun, headlines were being telegraphed across the continent: "INSURRECTION . . . at Harper's Ferry . . . GENERAL STAMPEDE OF SLAVES."

Brown had fallen into the perfect steel trap that Douglass feared. He'd hoped that word of the attack would stir up a widespread revolt, that black men and women would take up arms. But while word spread across the country by telegraph, it did not reach the slave cabins on plantations in neighboring Maryland and Virginia; slaves, marooned and isolated from the technology of the telegraph, remained unaware of the insurrection. U.S. Marines and soldiers commanded by Robert E. Lee retook the arsenal, capturing Brown and killing or capturing all of his men. "The result proves the plan was the attempt of a fanatic or madman," Lee said. Among the men killed was Dangerfield Newby, a free black man who was hoping to rescue his wife, Harriet, and their children from slavery in Virginia. His pocket held a letter from Harriet: "if I thought I shoul never see you," she wrote him, "this earth would have no charms for me."[27]

Brown had planned to lead an armed revolution throughout the South. At the nearby farm and school where he and his men had assembled, soldiers found sixteen boxes of weapons and ammunition, along with boxes of papers, including thousands of copies of his 1858 constitution and maps of the South, printed on cambric cloth, and with places where blacks outnumbered whites marked with Xs. They also found, rolled up into a scroll, a "Declaration of Liberty by the Representatives of the Slave Population of the United States of America."

"We hold these truths to be Self Evident; That All Men are Created Equal," it began, proceeding to establish a right to revolution: "The history of Slavery in the Unites States, is a history of injustice & Cruelties inflicted upon the Slave in evry conceivable way, & in barbarity not surpassed by the most Savage Tribes. It is the embodiment of all that is Evil, and ruinous to a Nation; and subversive of all Good."[28]

News of Brown's attack convinced southern slave owners that their worst fears were right: abolitionists were murderers. The so-called Secret Six, northern men who'd funded Brown, either denied their involvement or fled. Douglass, who'd not supported Brown's plan but had known of it, escaped to Canada and then to England. "I am most miserably deficient in courage," he confessed. But what most outraged slave owners was the number and stature of northerners who, on learning of Brown's raid, celebrated him as a hero and a martyr. On October 30, in Concord, Henry David Thoreau, shoulders slumped, hat to his chest, delivered "A Plea for Captain John Brown." "Is it not possible that an individual may be right and a government wrong?" Thoreau asked. Brown, he said, was, for his commitment to equality, "the most American of us all."[29]

Thoreau's own commitment to abolition was strengthened by his reading a book just published in London. The same was true of many of his contemporaries. The book had made its way to Concord even as Brown was raiding Harpers Ferry: Charles Darwin's *On the Origin of Species*. Thoreau, a naturalist, a man of beans and bumblebees and frogs and herons, had been following Darwin's work, and when the book appeared, he read it with a passionate interest, filling the pages of six notebooks with his notes. Darwin's *Origin of Species* would have a vast and lingering influence on the world of ideas. Most immediately, it refuted the racial arguments of ethnologists like Louis Agassiz. And, in the months immediately following the book's publication—the last, unsettling months before the beginning of the Civil War—abolitionists took it as evidence of the common humanity of man.[30]

During his trial, fifty-nine-year-old Brown, who'd been wounded during the battle, lay on a cot, unable to stand. Found guilty of murder, conspiracy, and treason, he was allowed to speak at his sentencing, on November 2. This speech earned Brown still more support in the North. "If it is deemed necessary that I should forfeit my life for the furtherance of the ends of justice, and mingle my blood further with the blood of my children and with the blood of millions in this slave country, whose rights are disregarded by wicked, cruel and unjust enactments," he said, "I submit."[31]

Brown went to the gallows three weeks before Christmas, in the last month of the most tumultuous decade in American history. To northern abolitionists, his death marked the beginning of a second American Revolution. "The second of December, 1859," Henry Wadsworth Longfellow wrote in his diary. "This will be a great day in our history; the date of a new Revolution,—quite as much needed as the old one."[32] Longfellow, building upon the verses he'd written in *Poems on Slavery*, decided to write a poem to stir the North to the cause of emancipation, to tie one revolution to another. He called it "Paul Revere's Ride."[33]

In Virginia, fifteen hundred soldiers gathered to watch Brown's execution. Among them was John Wilkes Booth, serving with a troop from Richmond. Brown gave no speech on the gallows, but on the morning of his execution he handed a guard a note he'd scribbled on a scrap of paper: "I John Brown am now quite *certain* that the crimes of this *guilty land*: *will* never be purged *away*; but with Blood."[34]

Six days later, on December 8, 1859, the day of John Brown's funeral, Mississippi congressman Reuben Davis gave a speech in Congress: "John Brown, and a thousand John Browns, can invade us, and the Government will not protect us." The Union had betrayed the South, Davis argued. And so, he resolved, "To secure our rights and protect our honor we will dissever the ties that bind us together, even if it rushes us into a sea of blood."[35]

**WEEKS AFTER DAVIS'S** dire warning, lanky Abraham Lincoln visited Mathew Brady's studio in New York. He posed for a photograph standing by a small table over which he towered, his left hand resting on a stack of books that looked, compared to him, as if they belonged in a dollhouse. His face was gaunt, his eyes hollow. Later that day, Lincoln delivered a speech at Cooper Union that launched his campaign for the Republican nomination for the presidency. The portrait, made into a miniature tintype, became a presidential campaign button.

Like everyone else running for president that year, Lincoln believed that the election turned on the interpretation of the Constitution. He set about making the case, once again, against Stephen Douglas, who was seeking the Democratic nomination. And, in a reprise of what he'd said during the great debates of 1858, he insisted both that Douglas's interpretation of the Constitution was in error and that his argument amounted to anarchy: "Your purpose, then, plainly stated," Lincoln charged, "is that you will destroy the Government, unless you be allowed to construe and enforce the Constitution as you please."[36]

*Mathew Brady's
1860 daguerreotype
of Abraham Lincoln,
cropped, was reproduced
as a campaign button.*

Lincoln had labored over the scrapbook he'd assembled of newspaper transcriptions of his 1858 debates with Douglas. The time had come to put them to use. He faithfully edited them for publication, not changing the speeches, omitting only the "cheers" and "laughter" and other reactions from the crowds. *Political Debates Between Hon. Abraham Lincoln and Hon. Stephen A. Douglas* was first advertised on May 5, 1860, eleven days before the Republican National Convention, with promotional copy that boasted, fairly enough: "There is probably no better exposition of the doctrines of the Democratic and Republican Parties than is contained in this volume." When people invited Lincoln to speak, he very often told them to read the *Debates* instead. Douglas, incensed, complained that his speeches had been "mutilated," a charge without foundation, but one that suggests that Douglas knew, as Lincoln knew, that even if Douglas had won that election, Lincoln had won those debates.[37]

The Democratic Party held its national convention in Charleston, South Carolina, in April, just before the published *Debates* appeared. The platform committee had been unable to bind together the two arms of the party, producing both a Majority Report, endorsed by southern delegates, and a Minority Report, submitted by northerners, whereupon the Alabama, Mississippi, Louisiana, Texas, and Florida delegations walked out of the convention in protest of the platform's failure to include a guarantee of the rights of citizens to hold "all descriptions of property" (meaning slaves). Unable to nominate a candidate, the remaining delegates decided to hold a second convention—to gather in Baltimore in June.

The Republicans met in Chicago in May, in a massive building called the Wigwam, after its arched wooden ceiling. The party endorsed the Declaration of Independence and the Constitution—leading one delegate to observe that, while he also believed in the Bible and the Ten Commandments, he didn't see why these documents needed mentioning—but specifically disavowed any proslavery interpretation of the Constitution as "a dangerous political heresy."[38] For the nomination, Lincoln was something of a dark horse. But Lincoln's supporters successfully courted delegates and resorted, too, to political chicanery. The day the balloting began, Lincoln's campaign managers printed thousands of fake admission tickets and handed them out to Lincoln supporters, who then packed the hall and thundered their applause whenever Lincoln's name was mentioned. Lincoln won the nomination, to still more thunder.[39]

William Dean Howells, twenty-three and prodigiously talented, agreed to write a campaign biography for Lincoln.[40] Howells, at the time, was an unknown poet from Ohio; he would go on to become one of the century's most esteemed men of letters. He wrote his *Life of Abraham Lincoln* in a matter of weeks, as much as a satire of the form as an example of it. Howells had never met Lincoln and knew very little about him; what he did know was that campaign biographies were overwrought, ridiculous, and fabulous.[41] He had not the least idea who Lincoln's ancestors were; he somehow worked that out to be a credit to the candidate. "There is a dim possibility that he is of the stock of the New England Lincolns, of Plymouth colony," he wrote, "but the noble science of heraldry is almost obsolete in this country, and none of Mr. Lincoln's family seems to have been aware of the preciousness of long pedigrees." Later, in the White House, Lincoln checked Howells's book out of the Library of Congress, in order to check Howells's facts. He made corrections in the margins. Howells had claimed that in the 1820s Lincoln had been "a stanch Adams man"—a supporter of John Quincy Adams. Lincoln crossed out "Adams" and wrote "anti-Jackson." Among Howells's many tall tales, he'd told about how, as a young congressman, Lincoln had walked for miles to the Illinois legislature, Lincoln scribbled in the margin: "No harm, if true; but, in fact, not true. L."[42]

While Republicans campaigned for Honest Abe, Democrats gathered in Baltimore for their second convention in June. An American flag was hung in the front of the hall, embroidered with the hopeful motto: "We Will Support the Nominee." The convention opened with the proposal of a loyalty oath: "every person occupying a seat in this convention is bound in good honor and good faith to abide by the action of this convention, and support its nominee."[43] The deliberations fell apart. At one point, one delegate drew his pistol on another. For the nomination, the convention was deadlocked through fifty-seven roll calls. On June 22, 1860, the Democratic Party split: the South walked out. The next day, Caleb Cushing of Massachusetts, presiding, stepped down, declaring, "The delegations of a majority of the States of this Union have, either in whole or in part, in one form or another, ceased to participate in the deliberations of this body." But the convention ultimately nominated Douglas, as the candidate of the Northern Democratic Party, while the bolting southern delegates reconvened down the street, opened their own convention, and nominated John C. Breckinridge, U.S. senator from Kentucky, on their first ballot, the candidate for the Southern Democratic Party.[44]

In November, when Longfellow heard that Lincoln had won the election, he exulted. "It is the redemption of the country," he wrote in his diary. "Freedom is triumphant."[45] Lincoln won every northern state, all six states in which the Lincoln-Douglas debates had been published, and all four states in which black men could vote. But Lincoln had won hardly any votes in the South, and his election led to unrest in the North, too, including attacks on abolitionists. In December, when Frederick Douglass was slated to speak in Boston's Tremont Temple on the occasion of the anniversary of John Brown's execution, a mob broke into the hall to silence him. To answer them, Douglass days later delivered a blistering "Plea for Free Speech," in which, as had Longfellow, he placed abolition

**CHARLESTON MERCURY EXTRA:**

Passed unanimously at 1.15 o'clock, P. M., December 20th, 1860.

AN ORDINANCE

To dissolve the Union between the State of South Carolina and other States united with her under the compact entitled " The Constitution of the United States of America."

We, the People of the State of South Carolina, in Convention assembled, do declare and ordain, and it is hereby declared and ordained,

That the Ordinance adopted by us in Convention, on the twenty-third day of May, in the year of our Lord one thousand seven hundred and eighty-eight, whereby the Constitution of the United States of America was ratified, and also, all Acts and parts of Acts of the General Assembly of this State, ratifying amendments of the said Constitution, are hereby repealed; and that the union now subsisting between South Carolina and other States, under the name of "The United States of America," is hereby dissolved.

THE UNION IS DISSOLVED!

*Broadsides printed early in 1861 notified citizens of the seceding states that their legislatures had dissolved the Union by repealing their ratification of the 1787 Constitution.*

in the tradition of the nation's founding. "No right was deemed by the fathers of the Government more sacred than the right of speech," Douglass said, and "Liberty is meaningless where the right to utter one's thoughts and opinions has ceased to exist."[46]

Many in the South pressed for secession. Others urged patience. Two days after the election, the *New Orleans Bee* printed a one-word response to Lincoln's victory: "WAIT."[47] They did not wait for long. Six weeks after the election, South Carolinians held a convention in which they voted to repeal the state's ratification of the Constitution, declaring, "The union now subsisting between South Carolina and other States, under the name of 'The United States of America,' is hereby dissolved."[48] Six states followed—Mississippi, Florida, Alabama, Georgia, Louisiana, and Texas—and in February 1861 they formed the Confederate States of America, with, as president, former Mississippi senator Jefferson Davis, a man the Texan Sam Houston once called "as ambitious as Lucifer and as cold as a lizard."[49]

"The dissolution of the Union goes slowly on," Longfellow wrote in his diary, miserably. "Behind it all I hear the low murmur of the slaves, like the chorus in a Greek tragedy."[50]

## II.

AT HIS INAUGURATION, Jefferson Davis, tall and gaunt, insisted that only the Confederacy was true to the original Constitution. "We have changed the constituent parts, but not the system of government. The constitution formed by our fathers is that of these Confederate States."[51] But when delegates from the seven seceding states met in secret in Montgomery, Alabama, they adopted a constitution that had more in common with the Articles of Confederation ("We, the people of the Confederate States, each State acting in its sovereign and independent character . . .").

The truths of the Confederacy disavowed the truths of the Union. The Confederacy's newly elected vice president, a frail Georgian named Alexander Stephens, delivered a speech in Savannah in which he made those differences starkly clear. The ideas that lie behind the Constitution "rested upon the assumption of the equality of races," Stephens said, but "Our new government is founded upon exactly the opposite idea: its foundations are laid, its cornerstone rests, upon the great truth that the negro is not equal to the white man; that slavery . . . is his natural and moral condition. This, our new government, is the first, in the history of the world, based upon this great physical, philosophical, and moral truth."[52] It would become politically expedient, after the war, for ex-Confederates to insist that the Confederacy was founded on states' rights. But the Confederacy was founded on white supremacy.

The South having seceded, Lincoln was nevertheless inaugurated, as scheduled, on March 4, 1861. He'd grown a beard since Election Day, a development that, in a quieter year, might have caused more of a stir. He rode from his hotel to the ceremony with James Buchanan in an open carriage, driven by a black coachman, surrounded by battalions of cavalry and infantry: there was every reason to fear someone might try to kill

him. Riflemen positioned themselves in the windows of the Capitol, prepared to shoot anyone in the crowd who drew a gun.

Sworn into office by the Chief Justice Roger Taney, who'd presided over
*Dred Scott*, Lincoln went on to give the most eloquent inaugural address
in American history. "One section of our country believes slavery is right
and ought to be extended, while the other believes it is wrong and ought
not to be extended," he said. "This is the only substantial dispute." He
hoped that this dispute could yet be resolved by debate. He closed:

> We are not enemies, but friends. We must not be enemies. Though
> passion may have strained it must not break our bonds of affection.
> The mystic chords of memory, stretching from every battlefield and
> patriot grave to every living heart and hearthstone all over this broad
> land, will yet swell the chorus of the Union, when again touched, as
> surely they will be, by the better angels of our nature.[53]

The better angels did not prevail. Debate had failed.

"Slavery cannot tolerate free speech," Frederick Douglass had said, in
his "Plea for Free Speech."[54] The seventeenth-century battle for freedom
of expression had been fought by writers like John Milton, opposing the
suppression of religious dissent; the eighteenth-century struggle for the
freedom of the press had been fought by printers like Benjamin Franklin and John Peter Zenger, opposing the suppression of criticism of the
government; and the nineteenth century's fight for free speech had been
waged by abolitionists opposing southern slave owners, who had been
unwilling to subject slavery to debate.

Opposition to free speech had long been the position of slave owners, a
position taken at the constitutional convention and extended through the
gag rule, antiliteracy laws, bans on the mails, and the suppression of speakers. An aversion to political debate also structured the Confederacy, which
had both a distinctive character and a lasting influence on Americans'
ideas about federal authority as against popular sovereignty. Secessionists
were attempting to build a modern, proslavery, antidemocratic state. In
order to wage a war, the leaders of this fundamentally antidemocratic state
needed popular support. Such support was difficult to gain and impossible
to maintain. The Confederacy therefore suppressed dissent.[55]

"The people have with unexampled unanimity resolved to secede," one South Carolina convention delegate wrote in his diary, but this was wishful thinking.[56] Seven states of the lower South seceded before Lincoln's inauguration, but the eight states of the upper South refused to do the same. And even in the lower South, the choice to secede was not a simple one. Nor was it an easy victory.

The most ardent supporters of secession were the wealthiest plantation owners; the least ardent were the great majority of white male voters: poor men who did not own slaves. The most effective way to persuade these men to support secession was to argue that even though they didn't own slaves, their lives were made better by the existence of the institution, since it meant that they were spared the most demeaning work. Prosecessionists made this argument repeatedly, and with growing intensity. James D. B. DeBow's *The Interest in Slavery of the Southern Non-Slaveholder* (1860) was widely excerpted in newspapers, reminding poor white men that "No white man at the South serves another as a body servant, to clean his boots, wait on his table, and perform the menial services of his household."[57]

Nevertheless, rather than trusting a decision about secession to the voters, or even to a ratifying convention, Georgia legislator Thomas R. R. Cobb advised his legislature to make the decision itself: "Wait not till the grog shops and cross roads shall send up a discordant voice from a divided people." When Georgia did hold a convention, its delegates were deeply split. The secessionists cooked the numbers in order to insure their victory and proceeded to require all delegates to sign a pledge supporting secession even if they had voted against it. One of the first things the new state of Georgia did was to pass a law that made dissent punishable by death.[58]

As hard as secessionists fought for popular support, and as aggressively as they suppressed dissent, they were nevertheless only partially successful. Four states in the upper South only seceded after Confederate forces fired on U.S. troops at Fort Sumter, South Carolina, on April 12. Even then, Virginia kept on stalling until, on April 17, Governor Henry Wise walked into the Virginia convention and took out his pistol and said that, by his order, Virginia was now at war with the federal government, and that if anyone wanted to shoot him for treason, they'd have to wrestle his pistol away from him first. The convention voted 88–55 to recommend secession. That went to the state's electorate on May 23, which voted 125,950–20,373 in favor. Most who opposed it were in the western part of the state. In June, they held their own convention and effectively seceded from the state, to become West Virginia. Four more states in the upper South still refused to secede, even as the cords that tied the nation together were being cut. Telegraph wires were only just first stretching all the way across the American continent. The first message sent, from east to west, had read: "May the Union Be Perpetuated." After the firing on Fort Sumter, Lincoln ordered the telegraph wires connecting Washington to the South severed.[59]

By June of 1861, the Confederacy comprised fifteen states stretching over 900,000 square miles and containing 12 million people, including 4 million slaves, and 4 million white women who were disenfranchised. It rested on the foundational belief that a minority governs a majority. "The condition of slavery is with us nothing but a form of civil government for a class of people not fit to govern themselves," said Jefferson Davis.[60]

The Civil War inaugurated a new kind of war, with giant armies wielding unstoppable machines, as if monsters with scales of steel had been let loose on the land to maul and maraud, and to eat even the innocent. When the war began, both sides expected it to be limited and brief. Instead, it was vast and long, four brutal, wretched years of misery on a scale never before seen. In campaigns of singular ferocity, 2.1 million Northerners battled 880,000 Southerners in more than two hundred battles. More than 750,000 Americans died. Twice as many died from disease as from wounds. They died in heaps; they were buried in pits. Fewer than 2,000 Americans had died in battle during the entire War with Mexico. In a single battle of the Civil War, at Shiloh, Tennessee, in 1862, there were 24,000 casualties. Soldiers were terrified of being left behind or lost among the unnamed, unburied, unremembered dead. One soldier from South Carolina wrote home: "I have a horror of being thrown out in a neglected place or bee trampled on." On battlefields, the dead and dying were found clutching photographs of their wives and children. After yet another slaughter, Union general Ulysses S. Grant said a man could walk across the battlefield in any direction, as far as he could see, without touching the ground but only the dead.[61]

Fields where once waved stalks of corn and wheat yielded harvests

*Alexander Gardner, another kind of sharpshooter, took this photograph of a dead Confederate sharpshooter at Gettysburg.*

of nothing but suffering and death or, falling fallow, nothing but graves. All of this, each misery, its grand scale, for the first time in history, was captured on camera, archived, displayed, exhibited. A thousand photographers produced hundreds of thousands of photographs on battlefield after battlefield. After the first major battle fought in the North, in Maryland— the worst day in American military history, with 26,000 Confederate and Union soldiers killed, wounded, captured, or missing—Mathew Brady, in his National Photographic Portrait Gallery, on the corner of New York's Tenth Street and Broadway, opened *The Dead of Antietam*, an exhibit of photographs of the carnage taken by a Scottish immigrant named Alexander Gardner. "Mr. BRADY has done something to bring home to us the terrible reality and earnestness of war," the *New York Times* reported. "If he has not brought bodies and laid them in our dooryards and along the streets, he has done something very like it."[62]

On a scorched Wednesday, July 1, 1863, the turning point in the war came at the Battle of Gettysburg, Pennsylvania. By the third day of fighting, each side had lost more than 20,000 men, and the Confederate general, the fifty-six-year-old Virginian Robert E. Lee, began his retreat. Five thousand horses, fallen, were burned to stop their rotting, the smoke of those fires mingling with the steam that rose from the fetid remains of unburied men. Samuel Wilkeson, a reporter for the *New York Times*, went to report on the battle and found that his oldest son, a lieutenant, had been wounded in the leg and had died after his surgeons abandoned him when Confederates neared the barn where they were attempting an amputation. On July 4, America's eighty-seventh birthday, Wilkeson buried his son and filed his report. "O, you dead, who died at Gettysburg have baptized with your blood the second birth of freedom in America," he wrote in agony, before supplying his readers with a list of the dead and wounded.[63] The next day, Alexander Gardner and two of his team showed up with their cameras and took shots from which Gardner made some eighty-seven photographs, a field of ghosts. They lay in trenches, they lay on hilltops; they lay between trees, they lay atop rocks.

Gardner gathered them together in a book of the dead, *Gardner's Photographic Sketch Book of the War*, America's first book of photographs. Gardner had been an abolitionist, and the book included photographs of the dead and dying but it included, too, scenes of towns and streets and scenes that told the story of slavery. On a brick building of a trading house was printed: "Price, Birch & Co. Dealers in Slaves." Gardner titled it *Slave Pen, Alexandria, Virginia*.[64] Gardner was a Union soldier, his camera his weapon.

Four months after the carnage, Lincoln set out for Gettysburg. Thousands of bodies had lain, barely covered by dirt; hogs rutting in the fields had dug up arms and legs and heads. But with caskets provided by the War Department, the corpses had been uncovered, sorted, and catalogued; a third had been reburied, the rest waited. Lincoln had been invited to dedicate their burial. After an eighty-mile train ride, he arrived in Pennsylvania at dusk to find coffins still stacked at the station. The next morning, still in mourning for his own young son, he rode at the head of a march of one hundred men astride horses. The oration that day was given by Edward Everett. Lincoln, offering a dedication, spoke for a mere three minutes. With a scant 272 words, delivered slowly in his broad Kentucky accent, he renewed the American experiment.[65]

He spoke first of the dead: "We have come to dedicate a portion of that field, as a final resting place for those who here gave their lives that that nation might live. It is altogether fitting and proper that we should do this." But a cemetery is not only for the dead, he said:

It is for us the living, rather, to be dedicated here to the unfinished work which they who fought here have thus far so nobly advanced. It is rather for us to be here dedicated to the great task remaining before us—that from these honored dead we take increased devotion to that cause for which they gave the last full measure of devotion—that we here highly resolve that these dead shall not have died in vain—that this nation, under God, shall have a new birth of freedom—and that government of the people, by the people, for the people, shall not perish from the earth.[66]

He did not mention slavery. There would be those, after the war ended, who said that it had been fought over states' rights or to preserve the Union or for a thousand other reasons and causes. Soldiers, North and South, knew better. "The fact that slavery is the sole undeniable cause of this infamous rebellion, that it is a war of, by, and for Slavery, is as plain as the noon-day sun," a soldier writing for his Wisconsin regimental newspaper explained in 1862. "Any man who pretends to believe that this is not a war for the emancipation of the blacks," a soldier writing for his Confederate brigade's newspaper wrote that same year, "is either a fool or a liar."[67] By then, the emancipation had begun.

## III.

IT WAS AN American Odyssey. "They came at night, when the flickering camp-fires shone like vast unsteady stars along the black horizon," W. E. B. Du Bois later wrote, "old men, and thin, with gray and tufted hair; women with frightened eyes, dragging whimpering hungry children; men and girls, stalwart and gaunt."[68] They came, too, in daylight, and on horseback, by wagon and cart. They clambered aboard trains. They packed food and stole guns. They walked and they ran and they rode, carrying their children on their backs, dedicating themselves to the unfinished work of the nation: freeing themselves.

The Civil War was a revolutionary war of emancipation. The exodus began even before the first shots were fired, but the closer the Union army drew, the more the people fled. The families who lived on Jefferson Davis's thousand-acre cotton plantation, Brierfield, with its colonnaded mansion, in Mississippi, just south of Vicksburg, began leaving early in 1862. Another 137 people left Brierfield after the fall of Vicksburg and headed to Chickasaw Bayou, a Union camp. Confederate secretary of state Robert Toombs had boasted that the Confederacy would win the war and that he would one day call a roll of slaves at Bunker Hill. Wrote one newspaper reporter, after the arrival of Davis's former slaves at Chickasaw Bayou, "The President of the Confederate States may call the roll of his slaves at Richmond, at Natchez, or at Niagara, but the answer will not come."[69]

Lincoln announced on September 22, 1862, in a Preliminary Emancipation Proclamation, that he would free nearly every slave held in every Confederate state in exactly one hundred days—on New Year's Day 1863. He'd planned the announcement for a long time, wrestling with his conscience. "I said nothing to anyone," he later told his cabinet, "but I made the promise to myself and to my maker."[70] Across the land, people fell to their knees. Frederick Douglass said that the war had at last been "invested with sanctity." In New York, Horace Greeley declared that "in all ages there has been no act of one man and of one people so sublime as this emancipation." The *New York Times* deemed the Proclamation as important as the Constitution. "Breath alone kills no rebels," Lincoln cautioned. But a crowd of black men, women, and children nevertheless came to the White House and serenaded him, singing hosannas.[71]

The announcement set the South on fire. The *Richmond Examiner* called the promised Emancipation Proclamation the "most startling political crime, the most stupid political blunder, yet known in American history." Fifteen thousand copies of the Proclamation having been printed, the news made its way within days to slaves, whispered through windows, shouted across fields. Isaac Lane swiped a newspaper from his master's mail and read it aloud to every slave he could find. Not everyone was willing to wait as long as one hundred days. In October, men caught planning a rebellion in Culpeper, Virginia, were found to have in their possession newspapers in which the Proclamation had been printed; seventeen of those men were killed, their executions meant as a warning, the reign of a different hell.[72]

Frederick Douglass, who had led his people to the very gates of freedom, worried that Lincoln might abandon the pledge. "The first of January is to be the most memorable day in American Annals," he wrote. "But will that deed be done? Oh! That is the question." The promised emancipation

*On Emancipation Day, January 1, 1863, black men, women, and children celebrated outside Beaufort, South Carolina.*

turned the war into a crusade. But not all of Lincoln's supporters were interested in fighting a crusade against slavery. As autumn faded to winter, pressure mounted on the president to retract the promise. He held fast.

"Fellow citizens, we cannot escape history," Lincoln told Congress in December. "We shall nobly save, or meanly lose, the last best hope of earth." On Christmas Eve, day ninety-two, a worried Charles Sumner visited the White House. Would the president make good his pledge? Lincoln offered reassurance. On December 29, Lincoln read a draft of the Emancipation Proclamation to his cabinet. (It did not free slaves in states that had not seceded, nor those in territory in secessionist states held by the Union army.) Cabinet members suggested an amendment urging "those emancipated, to forbear from tumult." This Lincoln refused to add. But Salmon Chase, secretary of the Treasury, suggested a new ending, which Lincoln did adopt: "I invoke the considerate judgment of all mankind and the gracious favor of almighty God."[73]

On day ninety-six, Douglass declared, "The cause of human freedom and the cause of our common country are now one and inseparable." Ninety-seven, ninety-eight. Ninety-nine: New Year's Eve 1862, "watch night," the eve of what would come to be called the "Day of Days."

In the capital, crowds of African Americans filled the streets. In Norfolk, Virginia, four thousand slaves—who, living in a border state that was not part of the Confederacy, were not actually freed by the Emancipation Proclamation—paraded through the streets with fifes and drums, imitating the Sons of Liberty. In New York, Henry Highland Garnet, the black abolitionist, preached to an overflow crowd at the Shiloh Presbyterian Church. At exactly 11:55 p.m., the church fell silent. The parishioners sat in the cold, in the stillness, counting those final minutes, each tick of the clock. At midnight, the choir broke the silence: "Blow Ye Trumpets Blow, the Year of Jubilee has come." On the streets of the city, the people sang another song:

> *Cry out and shout all ye children of sorrow,*
> *The gloom of your midnight hath passed away.*

One hundred. On January 1, 1863, sometime after two o'clock in the afternoon, Lincoln held the Emancipation Proclamation in his hand and picked up his pen. He said solemnly, "I never, in my life, felt more certain that I was doing right than I do in signing this paper."[74]

In South Carolina, the Proclamation was read out to the First South Carolina Volunteer Infantry, a regiment of former slaves. At its final lines, the soldiers began to sing, quietly at first, and then louder:

> *My country, 'tis of thee,*
> *Sweet land of liberty,*
> *Of thee I sing!*[75]

American slavery had lasted for centuries. It had stolen the lives of millions and crushed the souls of millions more. It had cut down children, stricken mothers, and broken men. It had poisoned a people and a nation. It had turned hearts to stone. It had made eyes blind. It had left gaping wounds and terrible scars. It was not over yet. But at last, at last, an end lay within sight.

The American Odyssey had barely begun. From cabins and fields they left. Freed men and women didn't always head north. They often went south or west, traveling hundreds of miles by foot, on horseback, by stage, and by train, searching. They were husbands in search of wives,

wives in search of husbands, mothers and fathers looking for their children, children for their parents, chasing word and rumors about where their loved ones had been sold, sale after sale, across the country. Some of their wanderings lasted for years. They sought their own union, a union of their beloved.

**"MEN OF COLOR, TO ARMS!"** Frederick Douglass cried on March 2, 1863, calling on black men to join the Union army: "I urge you to fly to arms, and smite with death the power that would bury the Government and your liberty in the same hopeless grave." Congress had lifted a ban on blacks in the military in 1862, but with emancipation, Douglass began traveling through the North as a recruiting agent for the Fifty-Fourth Massachusetts Infantry, a newly formed all-black regiment. "The iron gate of our prison stands half open," Douglass wrote. "The chance is now given you to end in a day the bondage of centuries."[76]

The Confederacy, meanwhile, had called its own men to arms, instituting the first draft in American history. The Union had soon followed, instituting a draft of its own. In July 1863, white New Yorkers, furious at being called to fight what was plainly a war of emancipation, protested the draft during five days of violent riots that mainly involved attacking the city's blacks. Eleven men were lynched, and the more than two hundred children at the Colored Orphan Asylum only barely escaped when the building was set on fire.

The Confederate draft called on as many as 85 percent of white men between the ages of eighteen and thirty-five, a much broader swath of the population than served in the Union army. Seventy percent of Union soldiers were unmarried; the Confederate draft drew on married men, leaving their families at risk of destitution and starvation. "I have no head to my family," one Confederate woman wrote in 1863, the year the Confederate government also passed a "one-tenth tax," requiring citizens to give 10 percent of everything grown or raised on farms to the state.[77] Near the end of the war, the Confederate government, its army desperately short of both men and supplies, decided to do what had been for so long unthinkable: it began enlisting slaves as soldiers, to the great dismay of many Confederate soldiers, who'd been urged to fight to protect their rights as whites. One private from North Carolina wrote home to his mother, "I did not volunteer my services to fight for A free Negroes free country, but to fight for A free white mans free country."[78]

The Civil War expanded the powers of the federal government by precedents set in both the North and the South that included not only conscription but also a federal currency, income taxes, and welfare programs. The Union, faced with paying for the war against the Confederacy, borrowed from banks and, when money ran short, recklessly printed it, producing federal legal tender, the greenback. The House Ways and Means Committee considered levying a tax on land, willing to take the risk that such a measure would be eventually struck down as unconstitutional, because a land tax is a direct tax. But Schuyler Colfax, a Republican from Indiana, objected: "I cannot go home and tell my constituents that I voted for a bill that would allow a man, a millionaire, who has put his entire property into stock, to be exempt from taxation, while a farmer who lives by his side must pay a tax." A tax on income seemed a reasonable, and less regressive, alternative. A number of states—Pennsylvania, Virginia, Alabama, North Carolina, South Carolina, Maryland, and Florida—already taxed income. And Britain had partly funded the Crimean War by doing the same. Unlike a tax on real estate, an income tax was not, or at least not obviously, a direct tax, prohibited by the Constitution. Income also included earnings from stocks and so didn't exempt fat cats. In 1862, Lincoln signed a law establishing an Internal Revenue Bureau charged with administering an income tax, later turned into a graduated tax, taxing incomes over $600 at 3 percent and incomes more than $10,000 at 5 percent. The Confederacy, reluctant to levy taxes, was never able to raise enough money to pay for the war, which is one reason the rebellion failed.[79]

Yet ironically the Confederacy, a government opposed to federal power, exercised it to a far greater degree than the Union. The rhetoric of war had it that Southerners were fighting to protect their homes and especially their wives. But Confederate conscription led white women in the South to protest politically. They entered the political arena with much the same fervor that Northern women had for decades demonstrated in the fight for abolition. By 1862, large numbers of soldiers' wives had begun petitioning the government, seeking relief. Mary Jones, a soldier's widow from the river town of Natchez, Mississippi, wrote to her governor: "Every Body say I must be taken care of by the Confederate States

Frank Leslie's Illustrated Newspaper, *a Northern paper, in 1863
ran this before-and-after illustration of Southern women first
urging their men to rebellion and later staging bread riots.*

they did not tell my Deare Husband that I should Beg from Door to Door
when he went to fight for his country." These disenfranchised women
employed the rhetoric of wartime sacrifice as a claim to citizenship: "We
have given our men." They also began organizing collectively by staging
food riots. In November 1862, two petitioning women warned that "the
women talk of Making up Companys going to try to make peace for it is
more than human hearts can bear." Another woman warned the governor
of North Carolina, "The time has come that we the common people has
to hav bread or blood and we are bound boath men and women to hav it
or die in the attempt." The following spring, female mobs numbering in
the hundreds, and often armed with knives and guns, were involved in
at least twelve violent protests. "Bread or blood," rioting women shouted,
in Atlanta, in Richmond, in Mobile. In Salisbury, North Carolina, Mary
Moore had a message for her governor: "Our Husbands and Sons are now
separated from us by the cruel war not only to defend their humbly homes
but the homes and property of the rich man."[80]

In the end, the petitions written and protests staged by white Confederate women contributed to the creation of a new system of public welfare,

relief for soldiers' wives, a state welfare system bigger than any anywhere in the Union. The rise of the modern welfare system is often traced to the pension system instituted for Union veterans in the 1870s, but it was the Confederacy—and Southern white women—that laid its foundation.[81]

The war was not yet won and emancipation not yet achieved. As late as the summer of 1862, in the last weeks before the Emancipation Proclamation, Lincoln had insisted that the purpose of the war was to save the Union. "If I could save the Union without freeing any slave, I would do it," he wrote Horace Greeley, "and if I could save it by freeing all the slaves, I would do it, and if I could save it by freeing some and leaving others alone, I would also do that."[82] But by 1864, he had wholly changed his mind. Victory without abolition would be no victory at all.

The Emancipation Proclamation had freed all slaves within the Confederate states, but it had not freed slaves in the border states, and it had not made slavery itself impossible: that would require a constitutional amendment. While soldiers fought and fell on distant battlefields, Elizabeth Cady Stanton and Susan B. Anthony knocked on doors and gathered four hundred thousand signatures demanding passage of the Thirteenth Amendment, prohibiting slavery in the United States.[83] The measure was approved by the Senate, 33–6, on April 8, 1864. All Senate Republicans, three Northern Democrats, and five senators from border states voted in favor. But in the House, voting weeks before the Republican National Convention was scheduled to meet in Baltimore, the amendment fell thirteen votes short of the needed two-thirds majority.

A war-weary Abraham Lincoln had decided to run for reelection, even though no American president had served a second term since Andrew Jackson. His supporters handed out campaign buttons, tintype photographs of Lincoln, cased in metal. His face is sunken and craggy, as chiseled as a sea-swept rock. He lifts his chin and looks off into the distance as if offering a promise.[84] In the election, he confronted a meager opponent, George McClellan, an inept general whom Lincoln had relieved of his command. McClellan's support within the party was thin. At the Democratic Convention in August, a display outside the hall—coiled gas pipe with jets that were meant to ignite and spell out the words "McClellan, Our Only Hope"—failed and only sputtered, as helplessly as the candidate.[85] Three months later, Lincoln won 55 percent of the popular vote, the greatest margin since Jackson's reelection in 1828. His most sweeping victory came from the Union army: 70 percent of soldiers voted for him. Instead of voting for their former commander, McClellan, they cast their votes for Lincoln—and for emancipation.[86]

After the election, Lincoln pressed the House for passage of the Thirteenth Amendment by lobbying senators from border states. "We can never have an entire peace in this country so long as the institution of slavery remains," said James S. Rollins of Missouri, a former slave owner. When the amendment finally passed by the required two-thirds majority, on January 31, 1865, 119 to 56, the hall for a moment fell silent. And then members of Congress sank to their seats and "wept like children." Outside, a hundred-gun salute announced the result. From the battlefield, one black Union soldier wrote: "America has washed her hands at the clear spring of freedom."[87] Only time would tell whether the water from that spring could ever clean the stain of slavery.

Rain fell in Washington for weeks that winter as winds lashed the city, uprooting trees, as if the very weather were bringing the cruelty of war to the capital. On the morning of Lincoln's inauguration, March 4, the crowds came armed with umbrellas, bayoneted against the sky. They huddled in a swamp of puddles and mud. A fog fell over the city. But just as Lincoln rose to speak, the skies cleared and the sun broke through the clouds. With the heavy steps of his lumbering gait, Lincoln ascended the platform on the east front of the Capitol. Alexander Gardner captured him in a photograph of magnificent acuity. Lincoln wears no hat. He holds a sheaf of papers in his hand and looks down. He spoke but briefly. Slavery had been "the cause of the war," and yet "fondly do we hope, fervently do we pray, that this mighty scourge of war may speedily pass away": a prayer for the living and for the dead. And then he closed, with words that have since been etched into his memorial:

> With malice toward none, with charity for all, with firmness in the right as God gives us to see the right, let us strive on to finish the work we are in, to bind up the nation's wounds, to care for him who shall have borne the battle and for his widow and his orphan, to do all which may achieve and cherish a just and lasting peace among ourselves and with all nations.

John Wilkes Booth, twenty-six, watched from the balcony. "What an excellent chance I had to kill the President, if I had wished, on Inauguration Day!" he'd later say.[88]

On April 9, in the parlor of a farmhouse in Appomattox, Virginia, Confederate General Robert E. Lee surrendered his command to Union General Ulysses Grant. Two days later, Booth, a well-known Shakespearean actor, stood uneasily in a crowd, watching Lincoln deliver a speech in which the president explained the terms of the victory. "That means nigger citizenship," Booth muttered. Four days and some hours after that, at about 10:15 p.m. on April 14, Good Friday, Booth shot Lincoln with a derringer in Ford's Theatre, a playhouse six blocks from the White House.

Lincoln slumped in a chair, a walnut rocker, unconscious. An army surgeon leapt into the president's box, laid Lincoln out on the carpeted floor, removed his shirt, and looked for the wound. He and two other doctors then carried the president down a staircase, out of the playhouse, and into a first-floor room in a boardinghouse on Tenth Street. The president, fifty-six, was not expected to survive. Hoping he might speak before dying, more than a dozen people remained at his side through the night. They waited in vain. He never woke. He died in the morning, the first president of the United States to be killed while in office. Word of his death, spread by telegraph, was reported in newspapers on Saturday and mourned in churches on Sunday. "May we not have needed this loss," declared one minister, "in which we gain a national martyr."[89] It was Easter.

The death of Abraham Lincoln marked the birth of a new American creed: a religion of emancipation. It began with the mourning of a martyr. After four years of war, most Americans had black clothes ready to hand, the women their widow's weeds, the men their black cloaks and armbands. At the White House, the doctors who conducted the autopsy kept relics, one wrapping in paper "a splinter of bone from the skull." Lincoln had been a man of gigantic proportions, his body the subject of ceaseless fascination. The embalmers, arriving at the White House, promised, "The body of the President will never know decay."[90]

Four days later, when the casket was put on display, vendors sold mementos as mourners gathered to get a glimpse of the dead president.

*Mourners lined New York's Union Square in 1865 as Lincoln's funeral procession passed by while, perched on a rooftop, a photographer captured a bird's-eye shot of the scene.*

"We have lost our Moses," cried one elderly black woman waiting in line. "He was crucified for us," another black mourner said in Pennsylvania. Not all Americans mourned. "Hurrah!" one South Carolinian wrote in her diary. "Old Abe Lincoln has been assassinated!"[91]

Pallbearers carried Lincoln's casket onto a funeral train that snaked across the country, through fields and towns, for twelve days and nights. On May 4, 1865, his body was carried into a temporary vault in Springfield, Illinois, until a more permanent memorial could be built, a granite obelisk above a marble sarcophagus.[92] If he had uttered no dying words, he had left many last words, forever remembered, and etched in stone.

With the nation still draped in black, the Thirteenth Amendment, Lincoln's last legacy, went to the states. When it was finally ratified, on December 6, 1865, one California congressman declared, "The one question of the age is *settled*."[93] A great debate had ended. A terrible war had been won. Slavery was over. But the unfinished work of a great nation remained undone: the struggle for equality had only just begun.

Lincoln would remain a man trapped in time, in the click of a shutter and by the trigger of a gun. In mourning him, in sepia and yellow, in black and white, beneath plates of glinting glass, Americans deferred a different grief, a vaster and more dire reckoning with centuries of suffering and loss, not captured by any camera, not settled by any amendment, the injuries wrought on the bodies of millions of men, women, and children, stolen, shackled, hunted, whipped, branded, raped, starved, and buried in unmarked graves. No president consecrated their cemeteries or delivered their Gettysburg address; no committee of arrangements built monuments to their memory. With Lincoln's death, it was as if millions of people had been crammed into his tomb, trapped in a vault that could not hold them.

# Part Three

**THE STATE**

★ ★ ★ ★

*1866–1945*

*Decisions in a modern state tend to be made by
the interaction, not of Congress and the executive,
but of public opinion and the executive.*

—Walter Lippmann,
"The Basic Problem of Democracy,"
1919

*Nine*

# OF CITIZENS,
# PERSONS,
# AND PEOPLE

*Residents of Richmond, Virginia, celebrated the
anniversary of Emancipation Day in 1888, beneath
a banner of Abraham Lincoln.*

WHAT IS A CITIZEN? BEFORE THE CIVIL WAR, AND
for rather a long time afterward, the government of the United
States had no certain answer to that question. "I have often been pained
by the fruitless search in our law books and the records of our courts
for a clear and satisfactory definition of the phrase 'citizen of the United
States,'" Lincoln's exasperated attorney general wrote in 1862.[1] In 1866,
Congress charged two legal scholars with discovering the definition. "The
word citizen or citizens is found ten times at least in the Constitution of

the United States," one scholar wrote to the other, "and no definition of it is given anywhere."[2]

Congress raised the question while deliberating over the consequences of emancipation: millions of people once held as slaves had been freed. What it would mean for them to become citizens would depend, in part, on the meaning of "citizen." On this score, the Constitution proved maddeningly vague, referring to citizenship chiefly as a requirement for running for office, and in relation to the status of immigrants. Article II, Section 1, decreed, "No Person except a natural born Citizen, or a Citizen of the United States, at the time of the Adoption of this Constitution, shall be eligible to the Office of President." But even so seemingly straightforward a statement turned out to be murky. The words "natural born" were added only at the last minute, without recorded debate, after John Jay wrote a letter to George Washington suggesting that it might be "wise and seasonable to provide a strong check to the admission of foreigners into the administration of our national government and to declare expressly that the commander in chief of the American army shall not be given to, nor devolve on, any but a natural born citizen."[3] What and who is a "natural born citizen"? Jay didn't say.

Under English common law, a "natural born subject" is a person born within the king's realm or, depending on the circumstances, outside the king's realm, but to the king's subjects. A natural born citizen, though, isn't quite the same thing as a natural born subject, not least because most U.S. laws did not discriminate between "natural born" and "naturalized" citizens, since Americans—immigrants and the children of immigrants—rejected the fealty of blood. In Federalist No. 52, Madison explained that anyone interested in running for Congress need only have been a U.S. citizen for seven years, because "the door of this part of the federal government is open to merit of every description, whether native or adoptive, whether young or old, and without regard to poverty or wealth, or to any particular profession of religious faith."[4] People running for Congress didn't have to meet property requirements; they didn't have to have been born in the United States; and they couldn't be subjected to religious tests. This same logic applied to citizenship, and for the same reason: the framers of the Constitution understood these sorts of requirements as forms of political oppression. The door to the United States was meant to be open.

Before the 1880s, no federal law restricted immigration. And, despite periods of fervent nativism, especially in the 1840s, the United States welcomed immigrants into citizenship, and valued them. After the Civil War, the U.S. Treasury estimated the worth of each immigrant as equal to an $800 contribution to the nation's economy, eliciting a protest from Levi Morton, a congressman from New York, that this amount was far too low. On the floor of the House, Morton asked, "what estimate can we place upon the value to the country of the millions of Irishmen and Germans to whom we largely owe the existence of the great arteries of commerce extending from the Atlantic to the Pacific, and the results of that industry and skill which have so largely contributed to the wealth and property of the country?"[5]

Plainly, whatever else could be said of American citizenship, the idea was both liberal and capacious. Article IV, Section 2, of the Constitution established that "citizens of each state shall be entitled to all privileges and immunities of citizens in the several states," a stipulation that Alexander Hamilton believed to be "the basis of the Union."[6] A citizen of one state was the equal of a citizen from another state. But what made these people citizens? Under what conditions were residents *not* citizens? And what, exactly, were the privileges and immunities of citizenship?

Nineteenth-century politicians and political theorists interpreted American citizenship within the context of an emerging set of ideas about human rights and the authority of the state, holding dear the conviction that a good government guarantees everyone eligible for citizenship the same set of political rights, equal and irrevocable. Massachusetts senator Charles Sumner stated this view squarely in 1849, while discussing the constitution of his home state: "Here is the Great Charter of every human being drawing vital breath upon this soil, whatever may be his condition, and whoever may be his parents. He may be poor, weak, humble, or black,—he may be of Caucasian, Jewish, Indian, or Ethiopian race,—he may be of French, German, English, or Irish extraction; but before the Constitution of Massachusetts all these distinctions disappear. . . . He is a MAN, the equal of all his fellow-men. He is one of the children of the State, which, like an impartial parent, regards all its offspring with an equal care."[7]

The practice fell short of the ideal. On the one hand, all citizens, whether natural born or naturalized, were eligible to run for Congress, no federal laws restricted immigration, and all citizens were, at least theoretically, political equals, but on the other hand, no small number of laws and customs restricted citizenship. The Naturalization Act passed in 1798 extended the residency period required for an immigrant to become a citizen from five to fourteen years. That period was set back to five years in 1802, but under the terms of a law that declared that only a "free white person" could become a citizen. In 1857, in *Dred Scott*, the Supreme Court considered the question of black citizenship, asking, "Can a negro whose ancestors were imported into this country and sold as slaves become a member of the political community formed and brought into existence by the Constitution of the United States, and as such become entitled to all the rights, and privileges, and immunities, guaranteed by that instrument to the citizen?" Its resounding answer was no. And the citizenship of women was of such a limited scope that in 1859, Elizabeth Cady Stanton wrote bitterly to Susan B. Anthony: "When I pass the gate of the celestials and good Peter asks me where I wish to sit, I will say, 'Anywhere so that I am neither a negro nor a woman. Confer on me, great angel, the glory of White manhood, so that henceforth I may feel unlimited freedom.'"[8]

Adding to the confusion, restrictions on citizenship were unevenly enforced, as is made clear in the evidence of passport applications. The United States issued its first passport in 1782, but for a long time passports were issued not only by the federal government but also, and more usually, by states and cities, by governors, by mayors, and even by neighborhood notary publics. Moreover, not all citizenship documents took the form of passports. Black sailors were commonly issued something known as a "seaman's protection certificate," declaring that the bearer was a "Citizen of the United States of America"; Frederick Douglass used one of these certificates to make his escape from slavery.[9] (There existed, too, in the land of slavery, a proof of identity that served more like a certificate of *non*citizenship, an *anti*passport, a "slave pass": a paper signed by a slave owner, needed by any enslaved person moving through land controlled by slave patrols, armed bands of white men formed into militias.) A black man, identified as a "free person of color"—a term adapted from the French *gens de couleur libres,* and regularly used in the United States beginning in 1810—first obtained a passport in 1835, but that same year the Supreme Court considered the question of whether a passport is also a proof of citizenship and decided that it was not.[10]

This hodgepodge only gradually yielded to a more uniform system. In 1856, Congress passed a law declaring that only the secretary of state "may grant and issue passports," and that only citizens could obtain them. In August of 1861, Lincoln's secretary of state, William Seward, issued this order: "Until further notice, no person will be allowed to go abroad from a port of the United States without a passport either from this Department or countersigned by the Secretary of State." From then until the end of the war, this restriction was enforced; its aim was to prevent men from leaving the country in order to avoid military service. In 1866, a State Department clerk wrote that, in the issuing of passports, "there is no distinction made in regard to color," a policy well ahead of federal citizenship law, but it was just this sort of thing that led Congress to send those two legal scholars into the law books, looking, in vain, for a definition of the word "citizen."[11]

The Civil War raised fundamental questions not only about the relationship between the states and the federal government but also about citizenship itself and about the very notion of a nation-state. What is a citizen? What powers can a state exert over its citizens? Is suffrage a right of citizenship, or a special right, available only to certain citizens? Are women citizens? And if women are citizens, why aren't they voters? What about Chinese immigrants, pouring into the West? They were free. Were they, under American law, "free white persons" or "free persons of color" or some other sort of persons?

In the decades following the war, these questions would be addressed by a new party system and a new political order, while a newly empowered and authorized federal government supported the growth of industrial capitalism, which in turn produced inequalities of income and wealth that shook the foundation of the Republic. In that new political order, corporations would claim to be, in the eyes of the law, "persons," and the dispossessed, the farmers and factory workers who were left behind, would found a political party that insisted on their preeminent authority as "the people."

In 1866, Congress searched in vain for a well-documented definition of the word "citizen." Over the next thirty years, that definition would become clear, and it would narrow. In 1896, the U.S. passport office, in the Department of State, which had grown to thousands of clerks, began processing applications according to new "Rules Governing the Applica-

Lew Wa Ho worked at a dry goods shop in St. Louis;
the photograph was included in his Immigration Service
case file as evidence of employment.

tion of Passports," which required evidence of identity, including a close
physical description

> Age, _____ years; stature, _____ feet _____ inches (English measure);
> forehead, _____; eyes, _____; nose, _____; mouth, _____; chin,
> _____; hair, _____; complexion, _____; face, _____

as well as affidavits, signatures, witnesses, an oath of loyalty, and, by way
of an application fee, one dollar.[12]

In the unruly aftermath of the Civil War, the citizen was defined,
described, measured, and documented. And the modern administrative
state was born.

# I.

THE UNION'S DEFEAT of the Confederacy granted to the federal government unprecedented powers. The government exerted over the former
soldiers of the Confederacy the powers of a victor over the vanquished.
Over former slaves, it exerted powers designed to guarantee civil rights,

in an attempt to thwart the efforts of Southern states, which were determined to deny those rights to freedmen and women.

Long before the war ended, black men and women tried to anticipate and influence the government's postwar plans. Their priorities were clear: citizenship and property. In March 1863, Edwin Stanton, Lincoln's secretary of war, established the American Freedmen's Inquiry Commission. Its investigators reported that "the chief object of ambition among the refugees is to own property, especially to possess land, if it only be a few acres." In October 1864, in Syracuse, New York, the National Convention of Colored Men called for "full measure of citizenship" for black men—not women—and for legislative reforms that included allowing "colored men from all sections of the country" to settle on lands granted to citizens by the federal government through the Homestead Act. The Homestead Act, signed into law in 1862, had made available up to 160 acres of "unappropriated public lands" to individuals or heads of families who would farm them for five years and then pay a small fee. Thaddeus Stevens, a craggy-faced Pennsylvanian, led the self-styled Radical Republicans, that wing of the party staunchly committed to reconstructing the political order of Southern society. Stevens, who had been chairman of the House Ways and Means Committee under Lincoln, wanted to confiscate and distribute nearly four hundred million acres of Confederate land from some seventy thousand of the Confederacy's "chief rebels," and distribute forty acres to every adult freedman. The Bureau of Refugees, Freedmen, and Abandoned Lands (more generally known as the Freedmen's Bureau) supplied food and clothing to war refugees and to aid the settlement of freed people but, at freedmen's conventions, rumors spread that the bureau intended to give each freedman forty acres and a mule. "I picked out my mule," Sam McAllum, a Mississippi ex-slave later told an interviewer. "All of us did."[13]

As the war neared its close, Congress debated how to govern the peace. What should happen to the leaders of the Confederacy? Would they still have the rights of citizens? What should happen to their property? Thaddeus Stevens insisted that the federal government had to treat the former Confederacy as "a conquered people" and reform "the foundation of their institutions, both political, municipal and social," or else "all our blood and treasure have been spent in vain."[14]

But Lincoln was opposed to a vindictive peace, fearing that it would prevent the nation from binding its wounds. He proposed, instead, the so-called 10 percent plan, which included pardoning Confederate leaders and allowing a state to reenter the Union when 10 percent of its voters had taken an oath of allegiance. Radical Republicans in Congress rejected that plan and, at the end of 1864, passed the Wade-Davis Bill, which required a majority of voters to swear that they had never supported the Confederacy, and which would have meant the complete disenfranchisement of all former Confederate leaders and soldiers. Lincoln vetoed the bill. He did, however, eventually agree to place the South under military rule.

After Lincoln was assassinated and his vice president, Andrew Johnson, assumed the presidency, Johnson, a square-built former governor of Tennessee, attempted to turn the tide of the postwar plan, plotting a course markedly different from Lincoln's. Lincoln had chosen Johnson as his running mate in an effort to offer reassurance to border states. With Lincoln's death, Johnson set for himself the task of protecting the South. He talked not about "reconstruction" but about "restoration": he wanted to bring the Confederate states back into the Union as fast as possible, and to leave matters of citizenship and civil rights to the states to decide.

Freedmen continued to press their claims: Union Leagues, Republican clubs, and Equal Rights Leagues held "freedmen's conventions," demanding full citizenship, equal rights, suffrage, and land, and complaining about the amnesties and pardons issued by Johnson to former Confederate leaders. "Four-fifths of our enemies are paroled or amnestied, and the other fifth are being pardoned," declared one assembly of blacks in Virginia, charging Johnson with having "left us entirely at the mercy of these subjugated but unconverted rebels in everything save the privilege of bringing us, our wives and little ones, to the auction block."[15] By the winter of 1865–66, Southern legislatures consisting of former secessionists had begun passing "black codes," new, racially based laws that effectively continued slavery by way of indentures, sharecropping, and other forms of service. In South Carolina, children whose parents were charged with failing to teach them "habits of industry and honesty" were taken from their families and placed with white families as apprentices in positions of unpaid labor.[16] Slavery seemed like a monster that, each time it was decapitated, grew a new head.

And then rose the Ku Klux Klan, founded in Tennessee in 1866, a fraternal organization of Confederate veterans who dressed in white robes,

A pamphlet published in 1916 celebrated "the noble ride of the Ku Klux Klan of the Reconstruction Period" and insisted on its "rightful place in history as the saviour of the South, and, thereby, the saviour of the nation."

in order to appear, according to one original Klansman, as "the ghosts of the Confederate dead, who had arisen from their graves in order to wreak vengeance." The Klan really was a resurrection—not of the Confederate dead but of the armed militias that had long served as slave patrols that for decades had terrorized men, women, and children with fires, ropes, and guns, instruments of intimidation, torture, and murder.[17]

On February 2, 1866, the Senate passed the Civil Rights Act, the first federal law to define citizenship. "All persons born in the United States and not subject to any foreign power, excluding Indians not taxed, are hereby declared to be citizens of the United States," it began. It declared that all citizens have a right to equal protection under the law; its provisions included extending the Freedmen's Bureau. Five days after the Senate vote—a crucial, pivotal moment—Frederick Douglass visited the White House to seek the president's support during an extraordinarily tense meeting, a confrontation as remarkable and historic as any that has happened in those halls.

"You are placed in a position where you have the power to save or destroy us," Douglass told the president. "I mean our whole race."

Johnson, in a rambling, evasive, and self-justifying speech, assured Douglass that he was a friend to black people. "I have owned slaves and bought slaves," he said, "but I never sold one." In truth, Johnson had no intention of taking a stand against black codes or debating equal rights or signing a Civil Rights Act. After Douglass left, Johnson scoffed to an aide, "He's just like any nigger, and he would sooner cut a white man's throat than not."[18]

In March, after the House passed the Civil Rights Act, Johnson vetoed it. In April, Congress, wielding its power, overrode Johnson's veto. A landmark in the history of the struggle for power between the executive and legislative branches of the federal government, Congress's stand marked the first time that it had ever overridden a presidential veto.

As the federal government acted to define citizenship and protect civil rights, Johnson tried to halt these changes but proved unable to triumph over the Radical Republicans who dominated Congress and stood at the center of national power.[19] As Radical Republicans turned to the question of voting, they began work on constitutional amendments designed to prevent the disenfranchisement of freedmen: the Fourteenth and Fifteenth Amendments. There were ideals at stake, of course: making good on the promise of the nation's founding documents and the cause for which the war was fought. But there was also the matter of raw politics. The abolition of slavery rendered the three-fifths clause obsolete. With each black man, woman, and child counting not as three-fifths of a person but as five-fifths, Southern states gained seats in Congress. Black men, if they were able to vote, were almost guaranteed to vote Republican. For Republicans in Congress to maintain their hold on power, then, they needed to be sure the Southern states didn't stop black men from voting.

In pursuing this end, Radical Republicans were supported by the legions of women who had fought for abolition and emancipation and for women's rights. After Lincoln signed the Emancipation Proclamation, and after ratification of the Thirteenth Amendment, Elizabeth Cady

Stanton and Susan B. Anthony had begun to fight, equally hard, for the next amendment, which they expected to guarantee the rights and privileges of citizenship for all Americans—including women.

The Fourteenth Amendment, drafted by the Joint Committee on Reconstruction, marked the signal constitutional achievement of a century of debate and war, of suffering and struggle. It proposed a definition of citizenship guaranteeing its privileges and immunities, and insuring equal protection and due process to all citizens. "All persons born or naturalized in the United States, and subject to the jurisdiction thereof, are citizens of the United States and of the State wherein they reside," it began. "No state shall make or enforce any law which shall abridge the privileges or immunities of citizens of the United States; nor shall any state deprive any person of life, liberty, or property, without due process of law; nor deny to any person within its jurisdiction the equal protection of the laws."[20]

During the drafting of the amendment, the committee betrayed the national phalanx of women who for decades had fought for abolition and for black civil rights by proposing to insert, into the amendment's second section, a provision that any state that denied the right to vote "to any of the male inhabitants of such state" would lose representation in Congress. "Male" had never before appeared in any part of the Constitution. "If that word 'male' be inserted," Stanton warned, "it will take us a century at least to get it out."[21] She was not far wrong.

Women protested. "Can any one tell us why the great advocates of Human Equality . . . forget that when they were a weak party and needed all the womanly strength of the nation to help them on, they always united the words 'without regard to sex, race, or color'?" asked Ohio-born reformer Frances Gage. Charles Sumner offered this answer: "We know how the Negro will vote, but are not so sure of the women." How women would vote was impossible to know. Would black women vote the way black men voted? Would white women vote like black women? Republicans decided they'd rather not find out. "This is the negro's hour," they told women. "May I ask just one question based on the apparent opposition in which you place the negro and the woman?" Stanton asked Wendell Phillips. "My question is this: Do you believe the African race is composed entirely of males?"[22]

Over the protests of women, the word "male" stayed in the draft. But another term raised more eyebrows. "All *persons* born or naturalized in the United States . . . are citizens."[23] Why "persons"? To men who were keen to deny women equal rights, "persons" seemed oddly expansive. Was there a way in which this amendment could be read, even with the word "male," to support female claims for equal rights?

During the Senate debate, Jacob Howard, a Republican from Michigan, explained that the amendment "protects the black man in his fundamental rights as a citizen with the same shield which it throws over the white man." Howard assured his fellow senators that the amendment most emphatically did not guarantee black men the right to vote (even though he wished that it did); it only suggested, without providing any mechanism for enforcement, that states that barred men from voting would lose representation in Congress. On this point, Howard quoted James Madison, who'd written that "those who are to be bound by laws, ought to have a voice in making them." From the floor, Reverdy Johnson, a Democrat from Maryland, rose to ask how far such a proposition could logically be extended, especially given the amendment's use of the word "person":

MR. JOHNSON: Females as well as males?
MR. HOWARD: Mr. Madison does not say anything about females.
MR. JOHNSON: "Persons."
MR. HOWARD: I believe Mr. Madison was old enough and wise enough to take it for granted that there was such a thing as the law of nature which has a certain influence even in political affairs, and that by that law women and children are not regarded as the equals of men.[24]

It would take a century for this matter to reach Congress again, and then only accidentally, during the debate over the 1964 Civil Rights Act. Yet even with the Fourteenth Amendment's extension of certain protections only to "male inhabitants" and its narrowed understanding of the rights of persons, ratification was by no means assured. Andrew Johnson opposed the amendment and urged Southern states not to ratify it. Only Tennessee ratified (always ambivalent about the Confederacy, and the last state to secede, Tennessee became the first readmitted to the

Union). Meanwhile, in the fall of 1866, Radical Republicans were elected to Congress in huge numbers, cutting down Johnson at his knees. And yet, from his knees, still he swung at them. Republicans, deeming the expansion of federal power the only possible way to insure the civil rights of former slaves, passed four Reconstruction Acts. Johnson, swinging wildly, vetoed all four. Congress overrode each of his vetoes, crushing the president into the ground.

The Reconstruction Acts divided the former Confederacy into five military districts, each ruled by a military general. Each former rebel state was to draft a new constitution, which would then be sent to Congress for approval. In an act of constitutional coercion, Congress made readmission to the Union contingent on the ratification of the Fourteenth Amendment. Under the terms of Reconstruction, men who had been Confederate soldiers could not vote, but men who had been slaves could. In the former Confederacy, most white men who were able to vote were Democrats; 80 percent of eligible Republican voters were black men. Still, even with the protection of federal troops, black men were not always able to vote, especially as the Klan grew. Black men most often succeeded in casting ballots in the upper South. Ninety percent of black registered voters managed to vote in Virginia. In the deeper South, black men arrived early at the polls and in groups, often marching together, by prearrangement, to protect themselves against attack. One election supervisor from Alabama described the first day of voting in 1867: "there must have been present, near one thousand freedmen, many as far as thirty miles from their home, all eager to vote."[25]

While the battle to ratify the Fourteenth Amendment raged on, black men participated in more than Election Day. Eight hundred black men served in state legislatures. They filled more than a thousand public offices, mostly in town and county government. A black man was, briefly, governor of Louisiana. "Now is the black man's day—the whites have had their way long enough," said one politician. A northern journalist visiting the South Carolina legislature wrote: "The body is almost literally a Black Parliament. . . . The Speaker is black, the Clerk is black, the door-keepers are black, the little pages are black, the chairman of the Ways and Means is black, and the chaplain is coal black." Whites called it "Negro rule."[26]

In Washington, Johnson struggled to regain his feet. Early in 1868, he tried to fire Secretary of War Edwin Stanton, a Radical Republican and Lincoln appointee. But Stanton, hardheaded and uncompromising, barricaded himself in his office for two months. The nation reeled from one constitutional crisis to the next. The House began impeachment proceedings against the president, charging him with violating a recently passed Tenure of Office Act. Congress voted to impeach, 126 to 47, but the Senate vote, 35–19, fell one vote shy of the two-thirds required. Johnson had survived, but impeachment, a constitutional gun that had never before been fired, had for the first time been loaded.[27]

The Fourteenth Amendment was finally ratified in the summer of 1868. That summer, Johnson failed to win the Democratic nomination for president, while Ohio-born Ulysses S. Grant, veteran of the War with Mexico and hero of the Civil War, won the Republican nomination, campaigning on the pledge "Let us have peace." Black men who managed to vote despite the menace of the KKK nearly all voted for Grant.

Women tried to vote, too. Before the Fourteenth Amendment, women's rights reformers had fought for women's education and for laws granting to married women the right to control their own property; after the Fourteenth Amendment, the women's rights movement became the women's suffrage movement, which both narrowed and intensified it. In 1868, in a plan that was known as the New Departure, black and white women attempted to gain the right to vote by exercising it: they went to the polls and were arrested when they tried to cast ballots. During those same years, it became increasingly difficult for black men to vote, leading Congress to debate and propose yet another constitutional amendment, one that would raise still more questions about citizens, persons, and people, categories whose limits had long been tested by women and were being newly tested by immigrants from China.

CHINESE IMMIGRANTS BEGAN arriving in the United States in large numbers during the 1850s, following the gold rush. In 1849, California had 54 Chinese residents; by 1850, 791; by 1851, more than 7,000; by 1852, about 25,000. Most came from Kwangtung Province and sailed from Hong Kong, sent by Chinese trading firms known as "the Six Companies." Most were men. Landing in San Francisco, they worked as miners, first in California and then in Oregon, Nevada, Washington, Idaho,

In an 1886 cartoon, Uncle Sam kicks Chinese immigrants out of the United States, demonstrating the intensity of anti-Chinese feeling in the era of the Chinese Exclusion Act.

Montana, and Colorado. In the federal census of 1860, 24,282 out of 34,935 Chinese toiled in mines. Although some Chinese immigrants left mining—and some were forced out—many continued to mine well into the 1880s, often working in sites abandoned by other miners. An 1867 government report noted that in Montana, "the diggings now fall into the hands of the Chinese, who patiently glean the fields abandoned by the whites." Chinese workers began settling in Boise in 1865 and only five years later constituted a third of Idaho's settlers and nearly 60 percent of its miners. In 1870, Chinese immigrants and their children made up nearly 9 percent of the population of California, and one-quarter of the state's wage earners.[28]

Their rights, under state constitutions and statutes, were markedly limited. Oregon's 1857 constitution barred "Chinamen" from owning real estate, while California barred Chinese immigrants from testifying in court, a provision upheld in an 1854 state supreme court opinion, *People v. Hall*, which described the Chinese as "a race of people whom nature has marked as inferior, and who are incapable of progress or intellectual development beyond a certain point, as their history has shown."[29]

The Chinese American population was growing at its fastest clip in the 1860s, just as the federal government was debating the relationship between citizenship and race. The Fourteenth Amendment's provision for birthright citizenship—anyone born in the United States is a citizen—made no racial restriction. Under its terms, the children of Chinese immigrants born in the United States were American citizens. As Lyman Trumbull, a senator from Illinois, said during the debates over the amendment, "the child of an Asiatic is just as much a citizen as the child of a European."[30] (This interpretation of the amendment was upheld in an 1898 ruling by the Supreme Court, in *United States v. Wong Kim Ark*.) Trumbull, who'd helped write the Thirteenth Amendment, was one of a very small number of men in Congress who talked about Chinese immigrants in favorable terms, describing them as "citizens from that country which in many respects excels any other country on the face of the globe in the arts and sciences, among whose population are to be found the most learned and eminent scholars in the world." More typical was the view expressed by William Higby, a Republican congressman from California, and a onetime miner. "The Chinese are nothing but a pagan race," Higby said in 1866. "You cannot make good citizens of them."[31]

If the children of Chinese immigrants were U.S. citizens, what about the immigrants themselves? Chinese immigrants' most significant protection against discrimination in western states was an 1868 treaty between China and the United States. It provided that "Chinese subjects visiting or residing in the United States, shall enjoy the same privileges, immunities, and exemptions in respect to travel or residence, as may there be enjoyed by the citizens or subjects of the most favored nation."[32] That treaty, though, didn't make Chinese immigrants into citizens; it only suggested that they be treated like citizens.

And what about the voting rights of U.S.-born Chinese Americans? Much turned on the Fifteenth Amendment, proposed early in 1869. While the aim of the amendment was to guarantee African Americans the right to vote and hold office, its language inevitably raised the question of Chinese citizenship and suffrage. Opponents of the amendment found its entire premise scandalous. Garrett Davis, a Democratic senator from Kentucky, fumed, "I want no negro government; I want no Mongolian government; I want the government of the white man which our fathers incorporated."[33] Michigan's Jacob Howard urged that the Fifteenth Amendment specifically bar Chinese men by introducing language explaining that the amendment only applied to "citizens of the United States of African descent."[34] Presumably, Howard calculated that this revision, which amounted to Chinese exclusion, would improve the chances of the amendment's passage and ratification. But congressional enthusiasm for immigration thwarted his proposal. George F. Edmunds of Vermont called Howard's revision to the amendment an outrage, pointing out that his new language would enfranchise black men only by leaving out "the native of every other country under the sun."[35]

Rare was the American orator who could devise, out of a debate mired in invective, an argument about citizenship that rested on human rights. But Frederick Douglass, at the height of his rhetorical powers, made just this argument in a speech in Boston in 1869. Who deserves citizenship and political equality? Not people of one descent or another, or of one sex or another, but all people, Douglass insisted. "The Chinese will come," he said. "Do you ask, if I favor such immigration, I answer I would. Would you have them naturalized, and have them invested with all the rights of American citizenship? I would. Would you allow them to vote? I would." Douglass spoke about what he called a "composite nation," a strikingly original and generative idea, about a citizenry made better, and stronger, not in spite of its many elements, but because of them: "I want a home here not only for the negro, the mulatto and the Latin races; but I want the Asiatic to find a home here in the United States, and feel at home here, both for his sake and for ours."[36]

Douglass's expansiveness, his deep belief in equality, did not prevail. In its final language, the Fifteenth Amendment, ratified in 1870, declared that "the right of citizens of the United States to vote shall not be denied or abridged by the United States or by any state on account of race, color, or previous condition of servitude."[37] It neither settled nor addressed the question of whether Chinese immigrants could become citizens. And, in practice, it hardly settled what it proposed to settle— the voting rights of black men—for whom voting became only more difficult, and more dangerous, in the face of a rising tide of terrorism. Even though a Republican-controlled Congress passed the Force Act of 1870 and the Klan Act of 1871, making it illegal to restrict or interfere with suffrage, the Klan only increased its efforts to take back the South, rampaging across the land.

Nor did the Fifteenth Amendment settle the question of whether women could vote. On the one hand, it didn't guarantee women that right, since it didn't bar discrimination by sex (only discrimination by "race, color, or previous condition of servitude"); on the other hand, it didn't suggest that women couldn't vote. What it did do was to divide the equal rights movement, splitting the American Equal Rights Association, a civil rights organization, into two, Stanton and Anthony founding the National Woman Suffrage Association, which did not support the amendment, and the veteran reformer Lucy Stone and the poet Julia Ward Howe founding the rival American Woman Suffrage Association, which did. (The rift would be mended when the two organizations merged in 1890 as the National American Woman Suffrage Association.)

In 1870, five black women were arrested for voting in South Carolina. But by now, women had decided to test the limits of female citizenship not only by voting but also by running for office. Victoria Woodhull, a charismatic fortune-teller from Ohio who'd attended a suffrage convention in 1869, moved to New York, and reinvented herself as a stockbroker, became the first woman to run for president. She ran as a "self-nominated" candidate of the party she helped create, the Equal Rights Party. In 1871 she announced, "We are plotting revolution." Woodhull said she ran "mainly for the purpose of drawing attention to the claims of woman to political equality with man." Ingeniously, she argued that women had already had the right the vote, under the privileges and immunities clause of the Constitution, an argument she brought before a House Judiciary committee, making her the first woman to address a congressional committee. "As I have been the first to comprehend these Constitutional and legal facts, so am I the first to proclaim, as I now do proclaim to the women of the United States of America that they are enfranchised." Woodhull's candidacy ended in ignominy. She spent Election Day in prison on charges of obscenity, and in the end, the Supreme Court ruled against her interpretation of the Constitution, deciding, in *Minor v. Happersett*, that the Constitution "did not automatically confer the right to vote on those who were citizens."[38]

Woodhull's adventurous, glamorous, and shocking campaign helped ensure that the question commanded attention, even if that attention was, at best, polite. "The honest demand of any class of citizens for additional rights should be treated with respectful consideration," Republicans announced at their 1872 convention, a position that Stanton called not a plank but a splinter. At the party's 1876 convention, marking the centennial of the Declaration of Independence, Sarah Spencer, of the National Woman Suffrage Association, said, "In this bright new century, let me ask you to win to your side the women of the United States." She was hissed. At that same convention, Frederick Douglass, his raven hair now streaked with gray, became the first black person to speak before any nominating convention. Spencer had pleaded. Douglass pressed. "The question now is," he said, eyeing the crowd of rowdy delegates, silenced by his booming voice, "Do you mean to make good to us the promises in your constitution?"[39]

Their answer, apparently, was no. That fateful year, a century after the nation was founded, Reconstruction failed, felled by the seedy compromises, underhanded dealings, personal viciousness, and outright fraud of small-minded and self-gratifying men. Grant, dissuaded from running for a third term, stepped down in 1876. Roscoe Conkling, a big, bearded boxer and New York senator, was so sure he'd get the party's nomination that he picked his vice president and a motto—"Conkling and Hayes / Is the ticket that pays"—only to be defeated by his erstwhile running mate, the lackluster former governor of Ohio, Rutherford B. Hayes. When the Democrats met in St. Louis—the first time a convention was held west of the Mississippi—a delegation opposed to the nomination of the New York governor and dogged reformer Samuel Tilden hung a giant banner from the balcony of the Lindell Hotel. It read, "The City of New York, the Largest Democratic City in the Union, Uncompromisingly Opposed to the Nomination of Samuel J. Tilden for the Presidency Because He Cannot Carry the State of New York."[40] Tilden won the nomination anyway and, in the general election, he won the popular vote against Hayes. Unwilling to accept the result of the election, Republicans disputed the returns in Florida, Louisiana, and South Carolina. Eventually, the decision was thrown to an electoral commission that brokered a nefarious compromise: Democrats agreed to throw their support behind the man ever after known as Rutherfraud B. Hayes, so that he could become president, in exchange for a promise from Republicans to end the military occupation of the South. For a minor and petty political win over the Democratic Party, Republicans first committed electoral fraud and then, in brokering a compromise, abandoned a century-long fight for civil rights.

Political equality had been possible, in the South, only at the barrel of a gun. As soon as federal troops withdrew, white Democrats, calling themselves the "Redeemers," took control of state governments of the South, and the era of black men's enfranchisement came to a violent and terrible end. The Klan terrorized the countryside, burning homes and hunting, torturing, and killing people. (Between 1882 and 1930, murderers lynched more than three thousand black men and women.) Black politicians elected to office were thrown out. And all-white legislatures began passing a new set of black codes, known as Jim Crow laws, that segregated blacks from whites in every conceivable public place, down to the last street corner. Tennessee passed the first Jim Crow law, in 1881, mandating the separation of blacks and whites in railroad cars. Georgia became the first state to demand separate seating for whites and blacks in streetcars, in 1891. Courthouses provided separate Bibles. Bars provided separate stools. Post offices mandated separate windows. Playgrounds had separate swings. In Birmingham, for a black child to play checkers with a white child in a public park became a crime.[41] Slavery had ended; segregation had only begun.

# II.

MARY E. LEASE crossed the plains like a tornado. "Raise less corn and more hell," she said. She could talk for hours, her audience rapt. She stood almost six feet tall. "Tall and raw-boned and ugly as a mud hen," one reporter called her; "the people's party Amazon," said another. A writer who watched her said she had "a golden voice," an extraordinary contralto; to listen to her was to be hypnotized. A founder and principal orator of the populist movement, Lease believed that after the Civil War the federal government had conspired with corporations and bankers to wrest political power from ordinary people, like farmers and factory workers. "There is something radically wrong in the affairs of this Nation," Lease told a mesmerized crowd in 1891. "We have reached a crisis in the affairs of this Nation which is of more importance, more fraught with mighty consequence for the weal or woe of the American people, than was even that crisis that engaged the attention of the people of this Nation in the dark and bleeding years of civil strife." [42]

*A family unable to pay the mortgage on a farm
in western Kansas headed back east to Illinois,
having chronicled the journey on the canvas of their
wagon: "left Nov. 20, 1894; arrived Dec. 26, 1894."*

Lease had known that civil strife in her heart and by her hearth. Born in 1850, the daughter of Irish immigrants, she'd lost her father, two brothers, and an uncle in the Civil War; her uncle died at Gettysburg and her father starved to death as a prisoner of war. She never forgave the South, or the Democratic Party (which she called, all her life, "the intolerant, vindictive, slavemaking Democratic Party").[43] Married in 1873, she raised four children and lost two more to early death while farming in Kansas and Texas, and taking in washing, and also writing, and studying law. What was this new crisis endangering the nation that she talked about in hundreds of speeches, to applause as loud as a torrent of rain hitting the roof of a barn? "Capital buys and sells to-day the very heart-beats of humanity," she said. Democracy itself had been corrupted by it: "the speculators, the land-robbers, the pirates and gamblers of this Nation have knocked unceasingly at the doors of Congress, and Congress has in every case acceded to their demands."[44] The capitalists, she said, had subverted the will of the people.

The populist movement, marble in the flesh of American politics into the twenty-first century, started in the South and in the West. Lease and people like her drew on the agrarian republicanism of Thomas Jefferson and the common-man rhetoric of Andrew Jackson, but they also influenced the political commitments of Franklin Delano Roosevelt, serving as a bridge between populism and progressivism, the two great political reform movements that straddled the end of the nineteenth century and the beginning of the twentieth.

Lease fought for the farmers and wage laborers whose political voices, she believed, were being shouted down by capitalists. But she also fought for women's suffrage and for temperance and helped to diffuse a distinctive female political style—the moral crusade—throughout American politics. Prevented from entering the electorate, women who wanted to influence public affairs relied on forms of popular politics that, among men, were on the decline: the march, the rally, the parade. In the late nineteenth century, a curious reversal took place. Electoral politics, the politics men engaged in, became domesticated, the office work of education and advertising—even voting moved indoors. Meanwhile, women's political expression moved to the streets. And there, at marches, rallies, and parades, women deployed the tools of the nineteenth-century religious revival: the sermon, the appeal, the conversion.[45]

The female political style left its traces in every part of American politics, nowhere more deeply than in the populist tradition. Beginning in the twentieth century, it would drive the modern conservative movement.

What Lease described as a conspiracy between the federal government and capitalists, especially railroad company owners and bankers, had its roots in the Civil War itself, and in the federal government's shifting policy toward the West. Before the war, the controversy over slavery had limited federal involvement in the West, but when the South seceded, Democratic opposition in Congress disappeared, giving Republicans a free hand. Without Democrats fighting for slavery's expansion, Republicans had made haste to bring the West into the Union, and to exert authority over its economic development. A Republican Congress had approved the organization of new territories: the Dakotas (1861), Nevada (1861), Arizona (1863), Idaho (1863), and Montana (1864). In 1862 alone, in addition to the Homestead Act, the Republican Congress passed the Pacific Railway Act (chartering railroad companies to build the line from

Omaha, Nebraska, to Sacramento, California) and the National Bank Act (to issue paper money to pay for it all). After the war, political power moved from the states to the federal government and as the political influence of the South waned, the importance of the West rose. Congress not only sent to the states amendments to the Constitution that defined citizenship and guaranteed voting rights but also passed landmark legislation involving the management of western land, the control of native populations, the growth and development of large corporations, and the construction of a national transportation infrastructure.

The independent farmer—the lingering ideal of the Jeffersonian yeoman—remained the watchword of the West, but in truth, the family farming for subsistence, free of government interference, was far less common than a federally subsidized, capitalist model of farming and cattle raising for a national or even an international market. The small family farm—Jefferson's republican dream—was in many parts of the arid West an environmental impossibility. Much of the property distributed under the terms of the Homestead Act, primarily in the Great Basin, was semi-arid, the kind of land on which few farmers could manage a productive farm with only 160 acres. Instead, Congress typically granted the best land to railroads, and allowed other, bigger interests to step in, buying up large swaths for agricultural business or stock raising and fencing it in, especially after the patenting of barbed wire in 1874.[46]

With the overwhelming force of the U.S. Army, the federal government opened land for settlement by suppressing Indian insurrections, including a rebellion of more than six thousand Dakota Sioux. In measures that began as exigencies of war, the federal government forced native peoples off their land while providing corporations with incentives to build railroads. In a single ten-year span, Congress granted more than one hundred million acres of public lands to railroad companies. In 1870, only two million non-Indians lived west of the Missouri River; by 1890, that number had risen to more than ten million.[47]

As railroads owned by large corporations extended their tentacles like so many octopuses across vast lands owned by giant companies, the big business of beef-cattle raising grew. Railroads made it possible to carry massive herds to market in cities like Chicago, St. Louis, Omaha, and Kansas City. Buffalo that had long thrived on those lands were slaughtered nearly to extinction and replaced by Texas longhorns, five million of which were driven to railroad terminals in 1865 by cowboys of all backgrounds—white, black, Mexican, and Indian. By 1880, two million cattle were slaughtered in Chicago alone. In 1885, an American economist tried to reckon the extraordinary transformation wrought by what was now 200,000 miles of railroad, more than in all of Europe. It was possible to move one ton of freight one mile for less than seven-tenths of one cent, "a sum so small," he wrote, "that outside of China it would be difficult to find a coin of equivalent value to give a boy as a reward for carrying an ounce package across a street."[48]

The transformation of the West fueled the American economy, but it also produced instability, especially given rampant land speculation and the popularity of railroad stocks and bonds, novel financial instruments issued and managed by the federal government. That instability contributed to a broader set of political concerns that became Mary Lease's obsession, concerns known as "the money question," and traceable all the way back to Hamilton's economic plan: Should the federal government control banking and industry?

Federal land and railroad projects required vast amounts of spending at a time when Americans were uncertain how to pay their debts. Like the Continental currency printed during the Revolutionary War, greenbacks, issued during the Civil War and not backed up by gold, soon became all but valueless. After the war, gold-bugs argued for the collection and retirement of the greenbacks and the establishment of a gold standard; "silverites" supported a standard of specie-backed currency but not specifically gold. In 1869, Congress passed the Public Credit Act, promising to pay back its own debt in specie or specie-backed notes. But with all its borrowing and intricate financial instruments, the federal government, especially the administration of Ulysses S. Grant, became notorious for corruption and bribery.

Matters reached a crisis point in 1873, for Mary Lease and for the country, too. That spring, Lease and her husband and children moved to Kingman, Kansas, onto land they'd acquired through the Homestead Act. The Leases got their Kansas land for free, but Mary's husband, Charles, had to borrow hefty sums of money from a local bank to buy tools and pay land office fees. They lived in a sod house, where Mary pinned newspaper pages to the walls so that she could read while kneading dough. For a few months they scraped by, but within a year they were unable to repay their debts, and the bank repossessed their land.[49] Life on a Kansas farm was like trying to raise corn on a beach of sand. Better to raise hell.

In suffering financial ruin the dire year of 1873, the Leases were not alone. Eighteen-seventy-three saw the worst financial disaster since the Panic of 1837. Blame for the collapse rests on the desk of a white-whiskered Philadelphia banker named Jay Cooke, the latest in a long line of scoundrels that went all the way back to William Duer, whose swindling brought on the Panic of 1792. Cooke had made a great deal of money during the Civil War, investing in federal war bonds and in the Northern Pacific Railway, chartered by Congress in 1864. His brother Henry had been placed in charge of the Freedman's Savings Bank, chartered in 1865. Henry Cooke illegally invested the bank's money—the savings of freedmen—in his brother's railroad ventures. The proposed Northern Pacific was supposed to go through lands owned and occupied by the Sioux, who, in 1872, began fighting against the U.S. Army. Investors pulled out of Jay Cooke's scheme, and Henry Cooke's savings bank collapsed. Jay Cooke & Company closed and declared bankruptcy, a bankruptcy that led to a nationwide depression.[50] More than one hundred banks and nearly twenty thousand businesses failed. Even after the worst of the depression was over, the price of grain kept on falling. A farmer's profit on a bushel of corn had been forty-five cents in 1870; by 1889, the profit on that same bushel had fallen to ten cents.[51]

The populist revolt began when farmers started banding together and calling for cooperative farming and regulation of banks and railroads and an end to corporate monopolies. Nearly a million small farmers in the South and the Midwest flocked to an organization called the Grange. On July 4, 1873, they issued a Farmers' Declaration of Independence, calling for an end to "the tyranny of monopoly," which they described as "the absolute despotism of combinations that, under the fostering care of government and with wealth wrung from the people, have grown to such gigantic proportions as to overshadow all the land and wield an almost irresistible influence for their own selfish purposes in all its halls of legislation."[52]

Finance capitalism had brought tremendous gains to investors and created vast fortunes, inaugurating the era known as the Gilded Age, edged with gold. It spurred economic development and especially the growth of big businesses: big railroad companies, big agriculture companies, and, beginning in the 1870s, big steel companies. (Andrew Carnegie built his first steel mill in 1875.) But to poor farmers like Mary Lease and to the farmers who joined the Grange, finance capitalism looked like nothing so much, as Lease put it, as "a fraud against the people."[53]

It looked that way to wage laborers, too. The Knights of Labor, founded in 1869 and with seven hundred thousand members by the 1880s, crusaded against the kings of industry. "One hundred years ago we had one king of limited powers," the head of the Knights of Labor said. "Now we have a hundred kings, uncrowned ones, it is true, but monarchs of unlimited power, for they rule through the wealth they possess."[54] The laborers who raised their fists against the new uncrowned kings also hoped to crush beneath their feet the new peasants. No group of native-born Americans was more determined to end Chinese immigration than factory workers. The 1876 platform of the Workingmen's Party of California declared that "to an American death is preferable to life on par with a Chinaman."[55] In 1882, spurred by the nativism of populists, Congress passed its first-ever immigration law, the Chinese Exclusion Act, which barred immigrants from China from entering the United States and, determining that the Fourteenth Amendment did not apply to people of Chinese ancestry, decreed that Chinese people already in the United States were permanent aliens who could never become citizens.

The National Farmers' Alliance, formed in Texas in 1877 to fight for taxing of railroads and corporations and for the establishment of farm cooperatives and the removal of fences from public lands, soon spread into the Dakotas, Nebraska, Minnesota, Iowa, and Kansas.[56] Populists, whether farmers or factory workers, for all their invocation of "the people," tended to take a narrow view of citizenship. United in their opposition to the "money power," members of the alliance, like members of the Knights of Labor, were also nearly united in their opposition to the political claims of Chinese immigrants, and of black people. The Farmers' Alliance excluded African Americans, who formed their own association, the Colored Farmers' Alliance. Nor did populists count Native Americans within the body of "the people."

The long anguish of dispossession and slaughter that had begun in Haiti in 1492 opened a new chapter in the 1880s, on the eve of the four hundredth anniversary of Columbus's first voyage. Since the era of Andrew Jackson and the forced removal of the Cherokees from their homelands, the federal government's Indian policy rested on treaties that confined native peoples to reservations—"domestic dependent nations." This policy had led to decades of suffering, massacre, and war, as many people, especially on the Plains, where the Cheyenne and Sioux stood their ground, had resisted forced confinement. Plains warfare ended in 1886, when Geronimo, of the Bedonkohe band of the Chiricahua Apaches, became one of the last native leaders to surrender to the U.S. Army.[57] And still the conquest continued.

In 1887, Congress passed the Dawes Severalty Act, under whose terms the U.S. government offered native peoples a path to citizenship in a nation whose reach had extended across the lands of their ancestors. The Dawes Act granted to the federal government the authority to divide Indian lands into allotments and guaranteed U.S. citizenship to Indians who agreed to live on those allotments and renounce tribal membership. In proposing the allotment plan, Massachusetts senator Henry Laurens Dawes argued that the time had come for Indians to choose between "extermination or civilization" and insisted that the law offered Americans the opportunity to "wipe out the disgrace of our past treatment" and instead lift Indians up "into citizenship and manhood."[58]

But in truth the Dawes Act understood native peoples neither as citizens nor as "persons of color," and led to nothing so much as forced assimilation and the continued takeover of native lands. In 1887 Indians held 138 million acres; by 1900, they held only half of that territory. From the great debate at Valladolid in 1550 between Las Casas and Sepúlveda, debate about the morality of conquest had continued all but unabated across hundreds of years, during which each generation of Europeans and Americans who had confronted what by the middle of the nineteenth century they called the "Indian problem" had fallen short of their own understanding of justice.

———

POPULISTS' GRIEVANCES WERE many, and bitter. Their best-founded objection was their concern about the federal government's support of the interests of businesses over those of labor. This applied, in particular, to the railroads. In 1877, railroad workers protesting wage cuts went on strike in cities across the country. President Hayes sent in federal troops to end the strikes, marking the first use of the power of the federal government to support business against labor. The strikes continued, with little success in improving working conditions. Between 1881 and 1894, there was, on average, one major railroad strike a week. Labor was, generally and literally, crushed: in a single year, of some 700,000 men working on the railroads, more than 20,000 were injured on the job and nearly 2,000 killed.[59]

The lasting legacy of this battle came in the courts. When state legislatures tried to tax the railroads, as California did, federal judges eagerly entertained arguments that such taxes were unconstitutional—even going so far as accepting the argument that such laws violated the rights of corporations as "persons." In 1882, Roscoe Conkling represented the Southern Pacific Railroad Company's challenge to a California tax rule. He told the U.S. Supreme Court, "I come now to say that the Southern Pacific Railroad Company and its creditors and stockholders are among the 'persons' protected by the Fourteenth Amendment."[60]

Conkling, aside from having been a senator and a presidential candidate, had twice been nominated to serve on the U.S. Supreme Court (he'd declined, unwilling to bear the loss of his income as a corporate attorney). In offering an argument about the meaning and original intention of the word "person" in the Fourteenth Amendment, Conkling enjoyed a singular authority: he'd served on the Joint Committee on Reconstruction that had drafted the amendment and by 1882 was the lone member of that committee still living. With no one alive to contradict him, Conkling assured the court that the committee had specifically rejected the word "citizen" in favor of "person" in order to include corporations. (A legal fiction that corporations are "artificial persons" dates to the eighteenth century.) It's true that "the rights and wrongs of the freedmen were the chief spur and incentive" of the amendment, Conkling allowed, but corporations had been on the minds of its drafters, too. A New York newspaper, reporting that day's oral arguments, headlined its story "Civil Rights of Corporations."[61]

Much evidence suggests, however, that Conkling was lying. The record of the deliberations of the Joint Committee on Reconstruction does not support his argument regarding the committee's original intentions, nor is it plausible that between 1866 and 1882, the framers of the Fourteenth Amendment had kept mysteriously hidden their secret intention to guarantee equal protection and due process to corporations. But in 1886, when another railroad case, *Santa Clara County v. Southern Pacific Railroad*, reached the Supreme Court, the court's official recorder implied that the court had accepted the doctrine that "corporations are persons within the meaning of the Fourteenth Amendment."[62] After that, the Fourteenth Amendment, written and ratified to guarantee freed slaves equal protection and due process of law, became the chief means by which corporations freed themselves from government regulation. In 1937, Supreme Court Justice Hugo Black would observe, with grim dismay, that, over the course of fifty years, "only one half of one percent of the Fourteenth Amendment cases that came before the court had anything to do with African Americans or former slaves, while over half of the cases were about protecting the rights of corporations."[63] Rights guaranteed to the people were proffered, instead, to corporations.

## III.

**"MAN IS MAN,"** Mary E. Lease liked to say, but "woman is superman." Populism gave vent to the grievances of farmers and laborers against business and government. But the movement was built by women—women who believed they were morally superior to men.[64]

Lease entered politics by way of the Women's Christian Temperance Union (WCTU), a federation of women's clubs formed in Cleveland in 1874 and itself an outgrowth of a campaign against saloons known as the Woman's Crusade. She first spoke in public at a WCTU rally in Kansas, delivering a hair-raiser called "A Plea for the Temperance Ballot for Women."[65] Lease argued that, to end the scourge of alcohol—which, for women, served as shorthand for husbands who beat their wives and children and who spent their wages on drinking, leaving their families to starve—women needed the right to vote.

This argument reshaped the nation's political parties. In 1872, the Prohibition Party became the first party to declare itself in favor of women's suffrage. Seven years later, the WCTU, under the leadership of Frances

Willard, adopted "Home Protection" as its motto. The indefatigable Willard, who'd been president of a women's college and the first female dean of Northwestern University, lived by another motto: "Do Everything." When the Republican Party failed to support either Prohibition or suffrage, Willard defected from the GOP and founded the Home Protection Party, which in 1882 merged with the Prohibition Party. "Then and there," Willard wrote, American women entered politics, "and when they came they came to stay."[66]

Like Lease, Sarah E. V. Emery, a devout Universalist from Michigan, rose to prominence as a speaker and writer through the WCTU, the Knights of Labor, and the Farmers' Alliance. The Farmers' Alliance sold over 400,000 copies of Emery's anti-Semitic tract *Seven Financial Conspiracies Which Have Enslaved the American People.* "It is within the memory of many of my readers when millionaires were not indigenous to American soil," Emery wrote. "But that period has passed, and today we boast more millionaires than any other country on the globe; tramps have increased in a geometrical ratio; while strikes, riots and anarchists' trials constitute an exciting topic of conversation in all classes of society." Emery blamed this state of affairs on a conspiracy of Jewish bankers.[67]

To advance their causes, both populists and suffragists, rejected by the major parties, turned to third-party politics. If the Republican Party had turned its back on equal rights for women, the Democratic Party had still less interest in the cause. Susan B. Anthony hoped to deliver a speech at the 1880 Democratic National Convention, calling on the party "to secure to twenty millions of women the rights of citizenship." Instead, Anthony was left to look on, in silence, while her statement was read by a male clerk, after which, the *New York Times* reported, "No action whatever was taken in regard to it, and Miss Anthony vexed the convention no more."[68] Marietta Stow, a newspaper publisher, declared that it was "quite time that we had our own party" and ran for governor of California in 1882 as a candidate of the Woman's Independent Political Party. Two years later, Belva Lockwood, a DC attorney, campaigned as the presidential candidate of the Equal Rights Party. In 1886, Emery spoke on behalf of suffrage planks at both the Democratic Party and Prohibition Party conventions. But Judith Ellen Foster, who'd helped found the WCTU, condemned third parties at a Republican rally. Far from honoring woman, a third party only "appropriates her work and her influence to its own purposes," Foster warned. In 1892, Foster founded the Woman's National Republican Association. "We are here to help you," she told the party's male delegates at its convention that year, and, she added, echoing Willard, "we have come to stay."[69]

By then, Lease had helped found not a women's club or a women's party but a People's Party, which joined with a movement led by a California newspaperman named Henry George. A character straight out of a Melville novel, George, born in Philadelphia in 1839, had left school at fourteen and sailed to India and Australia as a foremast boy, on board a ship called the *Hindoo*. Romantics wrote about India as a place of jewels and jasmine; George was struck, instead, by its poverty. Returning to Philadelphia, he became a printer's apprentice, a position that many radicals before him had taken into politics. (Benjamin Franklin had been a printer's apprentice. So had William Lloyd Garrison.) Enticed by the West, he joined the crew of a navy lighthouse ship sailing around Cape Horn in 1858 because it was the only way he could afford to get to California. In San Francisco, he edited a newspaper; it soon failed. By 1865, married and with four children, he was begging in the streets to feed his family.[70]

He finally found work, first as a printer and then as a writer and editor, with the *San Francisco Times*. From the West, when the railroad had nearly crossed the continent, George wrote an essay called "What the Railroad Will Bring Us." His answer: the rich will get richer and the poor will get poorer. In a Fourth of July oration in 1877, he declared, "No nation can be freer than its most oppressed, richer than its poorest, wiser than its most ignorant."[71]

In *Progress and Poverty: An Inquiry into the Causes of Industrial Depressions and of Increase of Want with Increase of Wealth*, published in 1879, George argued that the very same technological progress that brought so many marvels brought wealth to the few and poverty to the many. "Discovery upon discovery, and invention after invention, have neither lessened the toil of those who most need respite, nor brought plenty to the poor," he wrote. He devised an economic plan that involved abolishing taxes on labor and instead imposing a single tax on land. Tocqueville had argued that democracy in America is made possible by economic equality;

people with equal estates will eventually fight for, and win, equal political rights. George agreed. But, like Mary Lease, he thought that financial capitalism was destroying democracy by making economic equality impossible. He saw himself as defending "the Republicanism of Jefferson and the Democracy of Jackson."[72]

George believed that the problem of inequality could not be solved without reforming elections. Suffragists suggested that the solution to corrupt elections was for women to vote, and some suggested it would be better to retract the franchise from poor white men (and give it to wealthier white women instead). But George, while granting that elections had become a national scandal, resisted the conclusion "that democracy is therefore condemned or that universal suffrage must be abandoned."[73] He didn't want poor white men to lose the right to vote, and he supported women's suffrage (though he vehemently opposed extending either suffrage or any other right of citizenship to Chinese immigrants or their children). He wanted white men to vote better.

In the age of popular politics, Election Day was a day of drinking and brawls. Party thugs stationed themselves at the polls and bought votes by doling out cash, called "soap," and handing voters pre-printed party tickets. Buying votes cost anything from $2.50, in San Francisco, to $20, in Connecticut. In Indiana, men sold their suffrages for no more than the cost of a sandwich.[74] Prohibitionists argued that the best way to battle corruption was to get alcohol out of elections. George argued for getting money out. In 1871, after the *New York Times* began publishing the results of an investigation into the gross corruption of elections in New York City under Democratic Party boss William Magear Tweed, George, who had spent considerable time in Australia and had married an Australian woman, proposed a reform that had been introduced in Australia in 1856. Under the terms of Australia's ballot law, no campaigning could take place within a certain distance of the polls, and election officials were required to print ballots and either to build booths or hire rooms, to be divided into compartments, where voters could mark their ballots in secret. Without such reforms, George wrote, "we might almost think soberly of the propriety of putting up our offices at auction."[75]

To promote the Australian ballot, George created a new party, the Union Labor Party. Mary Lease joined the party in Kansas. In 1886, George, having moved east, ran for mayor of New York on the Union

Labor ticket. The Democratic candidate, Abram Hewitt, won, but George beat the Republican, twenty-eight-year-old Theodore Roosevelt, a young man who only six years before had written a senior thesis at Harvard titled "The Practicability of Equalizing Men and Women Before the Law." Three years later, Henry George and Mary Lease helped to form the People's Party. "We are depending upon the votes of freemen for our success—votes of men who will not be bought or sold," Lease said at the party's Kansas convention in 1890. "Let our motto be more money and less misery."[76]

As the suffering of farmers and wage workers grew, so did the ranks of the People's Party, which became the most successful third party in American history. Between 1889 and 1893, the mortgages on so many farms were foreclosed that 90 percent of farmland fell into the hands of bankers. The richest 1 percent of Americans owned 51 percent of the nation's wealth, and the poorest 44 percent owned less than 2 percent. Populists didn't oppose capitalism; they opposed monopolism, which Lease called "the divine right of capital," predicting that it would go the way of "the divine right of kings." If they weren't quite socialists, they were certainly collectivists. "Henry George is not the representative of any political party, clan or 'ism,'" Lease said. "In the great struggle now going on between the millions who have not enough to eat and the plutocratic few who have a million times more than their craven bodies deserve; in the great struggle between human greed and human freedom, Henry George stands as a fearless exponent and defender of human rights."[77]

For all its passionate embrace of political equality and human rights and its energetic championing of suffrage, the People's Party rested on a deep and abiding commitment to exclude from full citizenship anyone from or descended from anyone from Africa or Asia. (Emery's anti-Semitism pervaded the movement as well, but it did not attach itself to arguments about citizenship.) Populism's racism and nativism rank among its longest-lasting legacies. Lease, in a wildly incoherent white suprema-cist screed called *The Problem of Civilization Solved*, wove together the population theories of Thomas Malthus and Thomas Jefferson with the colonization schemes endorsed by James Madison and the outright racism of the social Darwinist Herbert Spencer to propose that all manual labor be done by Africans and Asians. "Through all the vicissitudes of time, the Caucasian has arisen to the moral and intellectual supremacy of the world," she wrote, and the time had come for white people to realize their "destiny to become the guardians of the inferior races."[78]

Many of the reforms proposed by populists had the effect of diminishing the political power of blacks and immigrants. Chief among them was the Australian ballot, more usually known as the secret ballot, which, by serving as a de facto literacy test, disenfranchised both black men in the rural South and new immigrants in northern cities. In 1888, the Kentucky state legislature became the first in the nation to attempt the reform, in the city of Louisville. "The election last Tuesday was the first municipal election I have ever known which was not bought outright," one observer wrote to the *Nation* after Election Day.[79] Massachusetts passed a secret ballot law later that year. The measure seemed likely to suppress the Democratic vote, since literacy was lowest among the newest immigrants to northern cities, who tended to vote Democratic. In New York, the Democratic governor, David Hill, vetoed a secret ballot bill three times.[80] Hill's veto was only broken in 1890, after fourteen men carried a petition weighing half a ton to the floor of the New York legislature.[81]

Massachusetts and New York proved the only states to deliberate at length over the secret ballot. Quickest to adopt the reform were the states of the former Confederacy, where the reform appealed to legislatures eager to find legal ways to keep black men from voting. In 1890, Mississippi held a constitutional convention and adopted a new state constitution that included an "Understanding Clause": voters were required to pass oral examination on the Constitution, on the grounds that "very few Negroes understood the clauses of the Constitution." (Nor, of course, did most whites, though white men were not tested.) In the South, the secret ballot was adopted in this same spirit. Both by law and by brute force, southern legislators, state by state, and poll workers, precinct by precinct, denied black men the right to vote. In Louisiana, black voter registration dropped from 130,000 in 1898 to 5,300 in 1908, and to 730 in 1910. In 1893, Arkansas Democrats celebrated their electoral advantage by singing,

*The Australian ballot works like a charm*
*It makes them think and scratch*
*And when a Negro gets a ballot*
*He has certainly met his match.*[82]

Populists' other signal reform was the graduated income tax, a measure they believed essential to the survival of a democracy undermined by economic inequality. After the Civil War, a wartime federal income tax had been allowed to expire, over the protests of John Sherman, a Republican from Ohio who would go on to author the Sherman Antitrust Act (1890) and who, countering Jefferson, pointed out that tariffs unfairly burdened the poor. "We tax the tea, the coffee, the sugar, the spices the poor man uses," Sherman said. "Everything that he consumes we call a luxury and tax it; yet we are afraid to touch the income of Mr. Astor. Is there any justice in that? Is there any propriety in it? Why, sir, the income tax is the only one that tends to equalize these burdens between rich and poor."[83]

But the man who drove this point home was the inimitable William Jennings Bryan. Tall, broad-shouldered, and sturdy in a string tie and cowhide boots, Bryan carried populism from the Plains to the Potomac and turned the Democratic Party into the people's party. Born in Illinois in 1860, he'd snuck into the Democratic National Convention in St. Louis in 1876 when an obliging policeman had helped him in through a window. He'd gone to Illinois College and then to Union College of Law in Chicago. He made a particular study of oratory, at which he trained for years. Still, when he asked his mother's opinion of his first political speech in 1880, she said, "Well, there were a few good places in it—where you might have stopped!" Moving to Nebraska, he'd settled in Lincoln, a prairie town, in the Union's fastest-growing state. He was elected to Congress as a Democrat in 1890, when he was thirty. "Boy Bryan," he was called. He began his first run for the presidency when he was two months shy of the required age. He would live his life on the political stage and die, far diminished, in the glow cast by the footlights.[84]

Nearly everyone who ever heard Boy Bryan said he was the best speaker they'd ever known. In an age before amplification, Bryan may have been the only speaker most people had ever really *heard*: he could project his voice for three blocks, and at events where speaker after speaker took to the stage, very often only Bryan's rose above the distant mumble of lesser men. He was also mesmerizing. The first presidential candidate to campaign on behalf of the poor, Bryan delivered the leveling promise of the Second Great Awakening to American party politics and, in the end, to the Democratic Party. One Republican said, "I felt that Bryan was the first politician I had ever heard speak the truth and nothing but the truth," even though in every case, when he read a transcript of the speech in the newspaper the next day, he "disagreed with almost all of it."[85]

Lease didn't trust Bryan, mainly because she didn't trust anyone willing to join the Democratic Party but also she feared his lack of support for female suffrage. With Sarah Emery, Lease in 1891 signed the founding charter of the National Woman's Alliance, dedicated to uniting the causes of suffrage and populism; its Declaration of Purposes called for "full political equality of the sexes."[86] As the People's Party grew, and began winning municipal and state elections, Lease and Emery—and female suffrage—remained at its center. Emery became editor of the party's magazine, *New Forum*.[87] At the People's Party convention in Omaha in 1892, Lease seconded the nomination of the party's presidential candidate, James Weaver. Her twelve-year-old daughter, Evelyn Louise Lease, took the stage to call for a suffrage plank. "The motto of the Alliance is: 'Equal right to all and special privileges to none,'" little Evelyn said, "but you are not true to that motto if you do not give woman her rights."[88] But the People's Party betrayed Lease. The final platform, adopted on the Fourth of July, included a preamble written by a Minnesota farmer named Ignatius Donnelly. "We meet in the midst of a nation brought to the verge of moral, political, and material ruin," Donnelly began. "Corruption dominates the ballot-box, the Legislatures, the Congress, and touches even the ermine of the bench."[89] The platform called for the secret ballot, public ownership of the railroads, a graduated income tax, an eight-hour workday, and the direct election of U.S. senators (who were still being elected by state legislatures). Female suffrage was not among the party's demands. "We seek to restore the Government of the Republic to the hands of the 'plain people' with whom it originated," Donnelly said.[90] The plain people, the party's new leadership had determined, did not include women.

Advocates argued that the party's best chances of success lay in fusing with the Democratic Party. Lease, opposed to fusion because she hated Democrats, grew disillusioned with the populist revolt after the Kansas People's Party merged into the Democratic Party in 1892. The next year, she was urged to run for the U.S. Senate: "No one can come between me and the people of Kansas," she said, "and if I want to be United States senator they will give me the office." She also considered running for Congress in Kansas's Seventh District. But both times she decided against running, citing her worsening health.[91]

Calls for fusion only grew louder after 1893, when the nation fell once again into an economic depression, triggered by the bankruptcy of the Philadelphia & Reading Rail Road. Within months more than 8,000 businesses, 156 railroads, and 400 banks had collapsed. One in five Americans lost their jobs. "I take my Pen In hand to let you know that we are Starving to death," a young farm woman from Kansas wrote to her governor.[92] But the hard times also narrowed the agenda of the People's Party, which focused on the fight for "Free Silver": expanding the money supply by making silver, along with gold, the basis of currency. By now Lease was leaning toward socialism: "Nationalize the railroads, telegraph and all labor-saving machinery," she said in 1893, to "end the cause of industrial strikes and business disquietude."[93]

The suffering that followed the Panic of 1893 strengthened the income tax argument in Congress, where Bryan became its fiercest supporter. The time for an income tax seemed ripe. In the decades after the Civil War, the same labor-saving machinery that both created American prosperity and left many Americans behind in the new economy also advanced political debate about the distribution of wealth. The speed of transportation across the continent by railroad, and across the oceans by steam, meant that the United States was fully emerged in a global traffic of goods and labor, while new technologies of communication, especially the telephone and the transatlantic telegraph, raised new challenges to longstanding convictions about tariffs and taxes. By now, income taxes had become commonplace in Europe. Responding to the suggestion that if Congress passed an income tax, rich Americans would flee to Europe, Bryan wondered where they would possibly go. "In London, they will find a tax of more than 2 per cent assessed upon incomes," he said. "If they look for a place of refuge in Prussia, they will find an income tax of 4 per cent."[94]

In 1894, Bryan tacked an income tax amendment to a tariff bill, which managed to pass. But the populist victory—a 2 percent federal income tax that applied only to Americans who earned more than $4,000—didn't last long. The next year, in *Pollock v. Farmers' Loan and Trust Company*, the Supreme Court ruled 5–4 that the tax was a direct tax, and therefore unconstitutional, one justice calling the tax the first campaign in "a war of the poor against the rich."[95]

POPULISM ENTERED AMERICAN politics at the end of the nineteenth century, and it never left. It pitted "the people," meaning everyone but the rich, against corporations, which fought back in the courts by defining themselves as "persons"; and it pitted "the people," meaning white people, against nonwhite people who were fighting for citizenship and whose ability to fight back in the courts was far more limited, since those fights require well-paid lawyers.

Populism also pitted the people against the state. During populism's first rise, the state as a political entity became an object of formal academic study through political science, one of a new breed of academic fields known as the social sciences. Before the Civil War, most American colleges were evangelical; college presidents were ministers, and every branch of scholarship was guided by religion. After 1859, and the *Origin of Species,* the rise of Darwinism contributed to the secularization of the university, as did the influence of the German educational model, in which universities were divided into disciplines and departments, each with a claim to secular, and especially scientific, expertise. These social sciences—political science, economics, sociology, and anthropology—used the methods of science, and especially of quantification, to study history, government, the economy, society, and culture.[96]

Columbia University opened a School of Political Science in 1880, the University of Michigan in 1881, Johns Hopkins in 1882. Woodrow Wilson completed a PhD in political science at Johns Hopkins in 1886. He planned to write a "history of government in all the civilized States in the world," to be called *The Philosophy of Politics.* In 1889, he published a preliminary study called, simply, *The State.*[97]

For Wilson's generation of political scientists, the study of the state replaced the study of the people. The erection of the state became, in their view, the greatest achievement of civilization. The state also provided a bulwark against populism. In the first decades of the twentieth century, populism would yield to progressivism as urban reformers applied the new social sciences to the study of political problems, to be remedied by the intervention of the state.

The rise of populism and the social sciences reshaped the press, too. In the 1790s, the weekly partisan newspaper produced the two-party system. The penny press of the 1830s produced the popular politics of Jacksonian democracy. And in the 1880s and 1890s the spirit of populism and the empiricism of the social sciences drove American newspapers to a newfound obsession with facts.

The "journalist," like the political scientist, was an invention of the 1880s. *The Journalist*, a trade publication that identified journalism as a new profession that shared with the social scientist a devotion to facts, began appearing in 1883, the year Joseph Pulitzer took over the *New York World*.[98] Pulitzer, a Hungarian immigrant who hadn't known a word of English when he arrived in the United States, had served in an all-German regiment in the Civil War; after the war, he studied law in St. Louis and began working for a German-language newspaper. He made the *World* into one of the nation's most influential papers. "A newspaper relates the events of the day," Pulitzer said. "It does not manufacture its record of corruptions and crimes, but tells of them as they occur. If it failed to do so it would be an unfaithful chronicler."[99]

William Randolph Hearst began publishing the *New York Journal* in 1895. Hearst, born to great wealth in 1863 (his father had struck gold in California), had taken over his father's paper, the *San Francisco Examiner*, in 1887, after dropping out of college. In 1896, Adolph Ochs, the son of a Bavarian immigrant and lay rabbi, took over the *New York Times*. Ochs, raised in Tennessee, had started his career in newspapers by delivering the *Knoxville Chronicle* at the age of eleven; he left school three years later. He was thirty-eight when he bought the *Times* and pledged his intention to publish "without fear or favor."[100]

The newspapers of the 1880s and 1890s were full of stunts and scandals and crusades, even as they defended their accuracy. "Facts, facts piled up to the point of dry certitude was what the American people really wanted," wrote the reporter Ray Stannard Baker. Julius Chambers said that writing for the *New York Herald* involved "Facts; facts; nothing but facts. So many peas at so much a peck; so much molasses at so much a quart." A sign at the *Chicago Tribune* in the 1890s read: "WHO OR WHAT? HOW? WHEN? WHERE?" The walls at the *New York World* were covered with printed cards: "Accuracy, Accuracy, Accuracy! Who? What? Where? When? How? The Facts—The Color—The Facts!"[101]

In 1895, Pulitzer's *New York World* endorsed Mary Lease as candidate for mayor of Wichita. After she lost and her home in Wichita was foreclosed, she moved to New York and decided it was "the heart of America." She campaigned for Henry George, who was running for mayor. It looked as though he had a chance, but he died in his bed of a stroke five days before the election. His body lay in state at Grand Central Station. More than a hundred thousand mourners came to pay their respects. Lease delivered a eulogy. The *New York Times* reported, "Not even Lincoln had a more glorious death."[102]

In the summer of 1896, William Jennings Bryan, a man Ochs's *New York Times* called an "irresponsible, unregulated, ignorant, prejudiced, pathetically honest and enthusiastic crank," chugged across the plains in a custom railroad coach called the Great Nebraska Silver Train, which was decorated with giant signs that read "Keep Your Eye on Nebraska." He was heading for Illinois, to the Democratic National Convention at the Chicago Coliseum, a three-story building that took up an entire city block, where he would deliver one of the most effective and memorable speeches in American oratorical history.

Boy Bryan, in his baggy pants and black alpaca suit, had come to Chicago to fuse the People's Party into the Democratic Party, to turn the party of white southerners into the party, as well, of western farmers and northern factory workers, leaving the Republican Party to be the party of businessmen. The wind was at his back. The Democratic Party had for the first time endorsed an income tax, "so that the burdens of taxations may be equally and impartially laid, to the end that wealth may bear its due proportion of the expenses of the Government."[103] But naming Bryan as its presidential candidate would be a far greater step for the Democratic Party than adding a plank to its platform.

Bryan leapt to the stage. "I come to speak to you in defense of a cause as holy as the cause of liberty," he said, "the cause of humanity." The struggle between business and labor had been misunderstood, and rested on too narrow a definition of business. The people are "a broader class of businessmen": "The man who is employed for wages is as much a business man as his employer," Bryan said. "The farmer who goes forth in the morning and toils all days . . . and who by the application of brain

Judge *magazine in 1896 pictured William Jennings Bryan bearing his cross of gold, wielding a crown of thorns, and standing on an open Bible while a follower, behind him, waves a flag that reads "Anarchy."*

and muscle to the natural resources of the country creates wealth, is as much a business man as the man who goes upon the board of trade and bets upon the price of grain." Opposing the gold standard, the Republican Party's central economic policy, Bryan brought together his Jeffersonianism with his revivalist Christianity. "There are two ideas of government. There are those who believe that, if you will only legislate to make the well-to-do prosperous, their prosperity will leak through on those below. The Democratic idea, however, has been that if you legislate to make the masses prosperous, their prosperity will find its way up through every class which rests upon them."

As he closed, hollering to a crowd more than twenty thousand strong, he placed upon his head an imaginary crown of thorns: "We will answer their demand for a gold standard by saying to them: You shall not press down upon the brow of labor this crown of thorns." He stretched his arms wide and bowed his head. "You shall not crucify mankind upon a cross of gold." And then he shut his eyes and fell as still as death.

"My God! My God! My God!" the crowd began to chant.[104] They took off their hats and threw them up in the air. Those who didn't have hats took off their coats and threw them instead. Anyone who had an umbrella opened it. "Under the spell of the gifted blatherskite from Nebraska," a reporter for the *New York Times* wrote, "the convention went into spasms of enthusiasm."[105]

Bryan, the gifted blatherskite, was much mocked, especially in the big cities of the East, by newspapers favorable to business interests. The *Times* ran the headline, "The Silver Fanatics Are Invincible: Wild, Raging, Irresistible Mob Which Nothing Can Turn from Its Abominable Foolishness." Even Joseph Pulitzer's far more man-of-the-people *World* refused to endorse Bryan. Populists, meanwhile, feared that fusion would destroy their movement. "We will not crucify the People's Party on the cross of Democracy!" said one delegate from Texas.[106]

But, in the end, the People's Party threw its support behind Bryan, mounting no candidate of its own. Even Mary Lease gave him her grudging endorsement. At the People's Party convention in St. Louis, she seconded his nomination. And socialists supported him. Eugene Debs, the Indiana-born labor organizer and later the head of the Socialist Party, wrote to Bryan, "You are at this hour the hope of the Republic."[107]

Bryan ran against Republican former Ohio governor William McKinley, who represented the interests of businessmen and ran armed with a war chest of donations made by banks and corporations terrified of the possibility of a Bryan presidency. Ballot reform, far from keeping money out of elections, had ushered more money into elections, along with a new political style: using piles of money to sell a candidate's personality, borrowing from the methods of business by using mass advertising and education, slogans and billboards. McKinley ran a new-style campaign; Bryan ran an old-style campaign. Bryan barnstormed all over the country: he gave some six hundred speeches to five million people in twenty-seven states and traveled nearly twenty thousand miles. But McKinley's campaign coffers were fuller: Republicans spent $7 million; Democrats, $300,000. John D. Rockefeller alone provided the GOP with a quarter of a million dollars. McKinley's campaign manager, Cleveland businessman Mark Hanna, was nearly buried in donations from fellow businessmen. He used that money to print 120 million pieces of campaign literature. He hired fourteen hundred speakers to stump for McKinley; dubbing the populists Popocrats, they agitated voters to a state of panic.[108] As Mary Lease liked to say, money elected McKinley. Lease, disgusted by the election, left populism behind in favor of journalism: Pulitzer hired her as a reporter.[109]

On Election Day, nine out of ten American voters cast secret, government-printed ballots. McKinley won, with 271 electoral votes, to Bryan's 176. Black men hardly voted, women and Chinese Americans not at all. But for the first time in decades, no one was killed at the polls. Bryan and his wife collected clippings and published a scrapbook. They called it *The First Battle*.

# IV.

IN 1892, Americans marked the anniversary of Columbus's first voyage across the Atlantic by hosting the largest-ever world's fair, the Columbian Exposition, on six hundred acres of fairgrounds in Chicago, in more than two hundred buildings containing thousands of exhibits, pavilions representing forty-six nations, and, not least, the first Ferris wheel. Among the fair's hundreds of public lecturers stood two men who proposed to consider the course of American history from the vantage of the last years of the tumultuous nineteenth century. Frederick Jackson Turner, thirty-one, a dashing young historian with a mustache and a bow tie, wanted to explain the rise of American democracy, a triumph and a beacon. Frederick Douglass, seventy-five, an aging statesman, his hair a cloud of white, proposed to explain the rise of Jim Crow, a descent into a dark night.

Turner, born in Wisconsin in 1861, was one of the first Americans to receive a doctorate in history. At the exposition, he delivered his remarks before the American Historical Association, an organization that had been founded in 1884 and incorporated by an act of Congress in 1889 "for the promotion of historical studies, the collection and preservation of historical manuscripts and for kindred purposes in the interest of American history and of history in America."[110] History and journalism became professions at the same time and, like journalists, historians borrowed from the emerging social sciences, relying on quantitative analysis to understand how change happens. Where George Bancroft, in his *History of the United States*, had looked for explanations in the hand of providence, Frederick Jackson Turner looked to the census. The difference between Turner's methods and Bancroft's signaled a profound shift in the organization of knowledge, one that would have lasting consequences for the relationship between the people and the state and for civil society itself. Like Darwinism, the rise of the social sciences involved the abdication of other ways of knowing, and, indirectly, contributed to the rise of fundamentalism. Across newly defined academic disciplines, scholars abandoned the idea of mystery—the idea that there are things known only by God—in favor of the claim to objectivity, a development sometimes called "the disenchantment of the world."[111] When universities grew more secular, religious instruction became confined to divinity schools and theological seminaries. But in the 1880s and 1890s, those schools were dominated by liberal theologians like the Congregationalist Washington Gladden—men who were modernists. Gladden devised what came to be called the New Theology, accepting evolution as consistent with a living Christian faith and understanding its discovery as part of humanity's journey toward the Kingdom of God. A theologian at the University of Chicago's divinity school defined modernism as "the use of scientific, historical, and social methods in understanding and applying evangelical Christianity to the needs of living persons."[112] Increasingly, this is exactly what evangelicals who eventually identified themselves as fundamentalists found objectionable.[113] Their leader was William Jennings Bryan, who would earn the nickname "Mr. Fundamentalist."

Modernism shaped faith, and it shaped history. Turner titled his lecture "The Significance of the Frontier in American History," and in it he attempted to account for the sweep of history over four centuries. Influenced by both Jefferson and Darwin, Turner saw the American frontier as the site of political evolution, beginning with the "savages" of a "wilderness," proceeding to the arrival of European traders, and continuing through various forms of settlement, through the establishment of cities and factories, "the evolution of each into a higher stage," and culminating in the final stage of civilization: capitalism and democracy.[114]

Turner proposed this thesis at an exposition whose exhibits included some four hundred Native Americans on display in what amounted to human zoos. Turner derived his ideas about evolution from the same early anthropological work that shaped those exhibits. But he based his analysis of the frontier on a quantitative analysis of the findings of the 1890 census, the tool with which the state counted the people, a census that had been tallied in record-breaking time. The 1880 census had taken eight years to tabulate. But in 1890, the Census Bureau's Herman Hollerith, an engineer from Buffalo, New York, who'd taught mechanical engineering at MIT, introduced a reform that allowed for the census to be tallied in just a year. Inspired by the punching of railway tickets done by conductors to identify passengers by sex, height, and hair color, Hollerith made punch cards that could automatically tabulate all of the traits surveyed by census takers: the characteristics of citizens. Hollerith fed punch cards of twelve rows and twenty columns into a tabulating machine he'd designed. In 1896, he founded the Tabulating Machine Company, which would eventually merge with a number of others to become a firm called International Business Machines, better known as IBM.[115]

In "The Significance of the Frontier in American History," Turner used Hollerith's figures to calculate population densities across the country and, from them, to argue that there was no longer any discernible line between settled and unsettled parts of the continent. He argued that the frontier, which he described as "the meeting point between savagery and civilization," had been opened in 1492 and closed four centuries later but, while it lasted, in that meeting place, American democracy had been forged: "American democracy is fundamentally the outcome of the experiences of the American people in dealing with the West," by which he meant the experience of European immigrants to the United States in defeating its native peoples, taking possession of their homelands, and erecting there a civilization of their own. This, for Turner, was the story of America and the lesson of American history: evolution.[116]

Frederick Douglass, more than twice Frederick Jackson Turner's age, was scheduled to deliver his own lecture on August 25, 1893, the fair's designated "Colored People's Day." The Columbian Exposition was segregated, not by Jim Crow laws, which didn't extend to Illinois, but by racial convention, which did. Even the guards were all white; only the janitors were black. Douglass, who, as the former U.S. ambassador to Haiti, had represented the nation of Haiti at the Haitian pavilion, was the only eminent African American with a role at the fair, whose program had been planned by a board of 208 commissioners, all white.[117] There were, however, black people at the fair: on display. In the Hall of Agriculture, old men and women, former slaves, sold miniature bales of cotton, souvenirs, while, in a series of exhibits intended to display the Turnerian progress of humankind from savagery to civilization, black Americans were posed in a fake African village. "As if to shame the Negro," Douglass wrote, they "exhibit the Negro as a repulsive savage."[118]

Douglass had planned to deliver a lecture titled "The Race Problem in America." But Ida B. Wells, a thirty-one-year-old black woman with wide-set eyes and her hair piled on top of her head like a Gibson girl, went to see Douglass at the fair to try to convince him not to deliver the address and instead to boycott Colored People's Day, a travesty that Wells dubbed "Tambo and Bones 'Negro Day.'"[119]

The daughter of former slaves, Wells was born in Holly Springs, Mississippi, in 1862. In 1883, while working as a schoolteacher, she'd been asked to leave the "ladies' car" of a train and move to the car for blacks. She refused, took her case to court, and began writing for black newspapers. In 1892, after three black men who'd opened a People's Grocery were lynched, she began writing about "the threadbare lie that Negro men rape white women." Fierce and fearless, Wells urged black militancy and armed resistance against lynching and against Jim Crow. She recommended a Winchester rifle. "The more the Afro-American yields and cringes and begs," Wells wrote, "the more he is insulted, outraged and lynched." When Wells founded her own newspaper in Memphis, she called it *Free Speech*, carrying on the long tradition of making free speech the centerpiece of the struggle for racial justice. After a white mob burned the offices of *Free Speech* to the ground, she moved to New York, where she published under the pen name Exiled. In 1887, she was elected secretary of the black-run National Press Association. In 1892, when she published her first book, *Southern Horrors: Lynch Law in All Its Phases*, Douglass wrote a testimonial, saying that his own voice was feeble by comparison.[120]

In 1893, when Wells went to see Douglass at the Chicago World's Fair, they decided to go to lunch. Wells wanted to go to a restaurant across the street but wasn't sure if they'd be served: only whites were allowed. "Come, let's go there," said Douglass. The waiters looked at them, astonished, until they recognized Douglass. Pressed by Wells, Douglass, who was more than willing to condemn the fair, agreed to provide an introductory essay to a pamphlet called *The Reason Why the Colored American Is*

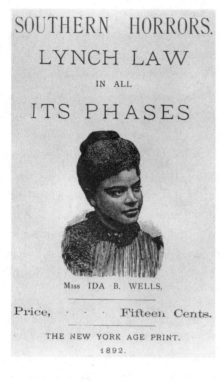

*Ida B. Wells's indictment of lynching was first published in 1892.*

*Not in the Columbian Exposition*, in which he insisted that any true representation of the American nation had to be honest, and that, as much as he wished he could tell the story of America as a story of progress, the truth was different. From slavery to Jim Crow, the history of the United States, he argued, "involves the necessity of plain speaking of wrongs and outrages endured, and of rights withheld, and withheld in flagrant contradiction to boasted American Republican liberty and civilization."[121]

Still, as hard as Wells tried to convince Douglass to boycott "Tambo and Bones 'Negro Day,'" he decided to go ahead with his address.[122] When the day came, he arrived to find the fair decked out with watermelons, and white hecklers waiting for him. With the careful, halting steps of an old man, he climbed to the stage. "Men talk of the Negro problem," he began. "There is no Negro problem," he said, his voice rising. "The problem is whether the American people have loyalty enough, honor enough, patriotism enough, to live up to their own Constitution."[123]

It was one of the last public speeches Frederick Douglass ever delivered—but not the very last. On September 3, 1894, an ailing Douglass made the journey from his home in Washington to speak in Manassas, Virginia, at the dedication of an industrial school for free black children—a school for learning how to build. "A ship at anchor, with halliards broken, sails mildewed, hull empty, her bottom covered with seaweed and barnacles, meets no resistance," Douglass said that day, turning the idea of a ship of state to the problem of Jim Crow. "But when she spread her canvas to the breeze and sets out on her voyage, turns prow to the open sea, the higher shall be her speed, the greater shall be her resistance. And so it is with the colored man." He paused to allow his listeners to conjure the scene, and its meaning, of a people struggling against the sea. "My dear young friends," Douglass closed. "Accept the inspiration of hope. Imitate the example of the brave mariner, who, amid clouds and darkness, amid hail, rain and storm bolts, battles his way against all that the sea opposes to his progress and you will reach the goal of your noble ambition in safety."[124]

Two years later, Douglass, seventy-seven, collapsed in the middle of an after-dinner conversation with his wife about the emancipation of women. He'd spent the day in suffrage meetings with Susan B. Anthony, one of his closest friends.[125] He'd had a heart attack. At his funeral, attended by thousands of mourners, the minister took as his text, "Know ye not that there is a Prince and a great man fallen this day in Israel?"[126] *Accept the inspiration of hope.*

MONTHS LATER, DOUGLASS'S challenge to the American people to live up to their own Constitution haunted the halls of the Supreme Court when the justices took up, once again, the matter of citizens, persons, and people. Homer Plessy, a shoemaker from New Orleans who looked white but who, under Louisiana's race laws was technically black, had been arrested for violating an 1890 Jim Crow law mandating separate railway cars for blacks and whites. Plessy had contrived to get arrested in order to challenge the Louisiana law. John Ferguson, a judge in a lower court, had ruled against Plessy, and in 1896, the Supreme Court heard the appeal, *Plessy v. Ferguson.*

By now, judicial review had come to be understood as the paramount power of the court, a power wielded by the state against the people as represented by their legislatures. In 1892, the president of the American Bar Association declared judicial review "the loftiest function and the most sacred duty of the judiciary—unique in the history of the world."[127]

In a 7–1 decision in *Plessy v. Ferguson*, the Supreme Court upheld the lower court's ruling—and thereby made the landmark ruling that Jim Crow laws did not violate the Constitution—by arguing that separate accommodations were not necessarily unequal accommodations. The Fourteenth Amendment promised all citizens the equal protection of the law. The majority in *Plessy v. Ferguson* asserted that separation and equality were wholly separate ideas. "We consider the underlying fallacy of the plaintiff's argument to consist in the assumption that the enforced separation of the two races stamps the colored race with a badge of inferiority. If this be so, it is not by reason of anything found in the act, but solely because the colored race chooses to put that construction upon it." The resulting legal principle—that public accommodations could be "separate but equal"—would last for more than half a century.

The sole dissenter, John Marshall Harlan, objecting to the establishment of separate classes of citizens, insisted that the achievement of the United States had been the establishment, by amendment, of a Constitution that was blind to race. "Our constitution is color-blind, and neither knows nor tolerates classes among citizens," Harlan wrote, and it is therefore a plain violation of the Constitution "for a state to regulate the enjoyment by citizens of their civil rights solely upon the basis of race." Consider the absurdities, contortions, and contradictions of Jim Crow laws and of the 1882 Chinese Exclusion Act, Harlan urged his colleagues. Under the terms of the Chinese Exclusion Act, immigrants from China could not become American citizens. But under the terms of Louisiana's railway car law, "a Chinaman can ride in the same passenger coach with white citizens of the United States, while citizens of the black race in Louisiana . . . are yet declared to be criminals, liable to imprisonment, if they ride in a public coach occupied by citizens of the white race."

Harlan was not attempting to protest discrimination against Chinese immigrants. Instead, he was pointing out the absurdity of a set of laws that grant more rights to noncitizens than to citizens. What all these laws had in common, Harlan argued, was that they were based on race. And yet a war had been fought and won to establish that laws in the United

States could not be based on race; nor could citizenship be restricted by race. The court's opinion in *Plessy*, Harlan warned, was so dreadfully in error as to constitutional principles that "the judgment this day rendered will, in time, prove to be quite as pernicious as the decision made by this tribunal in the *Dred Scott Case*."[128] This prediction proved true.

"How does it feel to be a problem?" W. E. B. Du Bois asked, the year after *Plessy v. Ferguson* established the doctrine of separate but equal. "One ever feels his two-ness,—an American, a Negro; two souls, two thoughts, two unreconciled strivings; two warring ideals in one dark body, whose dogged strength alone keeps it from being torn asunder."[129]

A citizen, a person, a people. Four centuries had passed since continents, separated by oceans, had met again. A century had passed since Jefferson had declared all men equal. Three decades had passed since the Fourteenth Amendment had declared all persons born or naturalized in the United States to be citizens. And now the Supreme Court ruled that those who would set aside equality in favor of separation had not violated the nation's founding truths. In one of the most wrenching tragedies in American history—a chronicle not lacking for tragedy—the Confederacy had lost the war, but it had won the peace.

## Ten

# EFFICIENCY AND
# THE MASSES

*The 120-acre Ford Motor plant in Highland Park,
Michigan, opened in 1910, the largest
manufacturing site in the world.*

WALTER LIPPMANN WORE A THREE-PIECE PINSTRIPE
suit the way a tiger wears his skin, but the clue to his acuity came
in the raised eyebrows, as pointed as the tip of an arrow. Educated at
Harvard, where he studied with William James and George Santayana,
he'd seemed destined for a distinguished if quiet career as a professor
of philosophy, or maybe history, when he decided, instead, to become a
reporter, the sort of man who tucked his pencil into his hat band, except
that he wasn't exactly that kind of reporter: he invented another kind, the

learned political commentator. "To read, if not to comprehend, Lippmann was suddenly the thing to do," wrote one much-wounded rival.

By 1914, when Lippmann was twenty-five, he'd already written two piercing books about American politics and helped launch the *New Republic*. He was heavyset and silent; his friends called him Buddha. He lived with a who's who of other young liberals in a narrow three-story red brick row house on Nineteenth Street in Washington that visitors, including Herbert Hoover, who once ate an unlit cigar there over dinner, named the House of Truth. Theodore Roosevelt called Lippmann the "most brilliant young man of his age in all the United States," which was but small comfort to older men, who found their ideas unraveled by Lippmann, like yarn in the clutches of a kitten. How did a man so young write with such authority, matched by so wide an appeal? Oliver Wendell Holmes said Lippmann's pieces were like flypaper: "If I touch it, I am stuck till I finish it."[1]

In the last decades of the nineteenth century and the first decades of the twentieth, when Lippmann came of age, industrialism brought great, glittering wealth to a few, prosperity to the nation, cheaper goods to the middle class, and misery and want to the many. The many now numbering more than ever before, talk of "the people" yielded to talk of "the masses," the swelling ranks of the poor, haggard and hungry. Like many Americans of his generation, Lippmann started out as a socialist, when even mentioning the masses hinted at socialism; *The Masses* was the name of a socialist monthly, published in New York, and, especially after the Russian Revolution of 1917, which brought the Bolshevists to power ("*bol'shinstvo*" means "the majority"), "the masses" sounded decidedly Red. But Lippmann soon began to write about the masses as "the bewildered herd," unthinking and instinctual, and as dangerous as an impending stampede. For Lippmann, and for an entire generation of intellectuals, politicians, journalists, and bureaucrats who styled themselves Progressives—the term dates to 1910—the masses posed a threat to American democracy. After the First World War, Progressives refashioned their aims and took to calling themselves "liberals."[2]

Only someone with so great a faith in the masses as Lippmann had when he started out could have ended up with so little. This change was wrought in the upheaval of the age. In the years following the realigning election of 1896, everything seemed, suddenly, bigger than before, more crowded, and more anonymous: looming and teeming. Even buildings were bigger: big office buildings, big factories, big mansions, big museums. Quantification became the only measure of value: how big, how much, how many. There were big businesses: big banks, big railroads, Big Oil. U.S. Steel, the first billion-dollar corporation, was formed in 1901 by consolidating more than two hundred companies in the iron and steel businesses. To fight monopolies, protect the people, and conserve the land, the federal government grew bigger, too; dozens of new federal agencies were founded in this era, from the National Bureau of Standards (1901) to the Forest Service (1905), the Coast Guard (1915), and the Bureau of Efficiency (1916), the last designed to handle the problem of bigness by the twin arts of organization and acceleration, a bureau of bureaus.

"Mass" came to mean anything that involved a giant and possibly terrifying quantity, on a scale so great that it overwhelmed existing arrangements—including democracy. "Mass production" was coined in the 1890s, when factories got bigger and faster, when the number of people who worked in them skyrocketed, and when the men who owned them got staggeringly rich. "Mass migration" dates to 1901, when nearly a million immigrants were entering the United States every year, "mass consumption" to 1905, "mass consciousness" to 1912. "Mass hysteria" had been defined by 1925 and "mass communication" by 1927, when the *New York Times* described the radio as "a system of mass communication with a mass audience."[3]

And the masses themselves? They formed a mass audience for mass communication and had a tendency, psychologists believed, to mass hysteria—the political stampede—posing a political problem unanticipated by James Madison and Thomas Jefferson, who believed that the size of the continent and the growth of its population would make the Republic stronger and its citizens more virtuous. They could not have imagined the vast economic inequality of the Gilded Age, its scale, its extravagance, and its agonies, and the challenge posed to the political order by millions of desperately poor men, women, and children, their opinions easily molded by the tools of mass persuasion.

To meet that challenge in what came to be called the Progressive Era, activists, intellectuals, and politicians campaigned for and secured far-reaching reforms that included municipal, state, and federal legislation. Their most powerful weapon was the journalistic exposé. Their biggest obstacle was the courts, which they attempted to hurdle by way of constitutional amendments. Out of these campaigns came the federal income tax, the Federal Reserve Bank, the direct election of U.S. senators, presidential primaries, minimum-wage and maximum-hour laws, women's suffrage, and Prohibition. Nearly all of these reforms had long been advocated for, in many cases first by William Jennings Bryan. Progressives' biggest failure was also Bryan's: their unwillingness to address, or even discuss, Jim Crow. Instead, they propped it up. And all of what Progressives accomplished in the management of mass democracy was vulnerable to the force that so worried the unrelenting Walter Lippmann: the malleability of public opinion, into mass delusion.

# I.

PROGRESSIVISM HAD ROOTS in late nineteenth-century populism; Progressivism was the middle-class version: indoors, quiet, passionless. Populists raised hell; Progressives read pamphlets. Populists had argued that the federal government's complicity in the consolidation of power in the hands of big banks, big railroads, and big businesses had betrayed both the nation's founding principles and the will of the people, and that the government itself was riddled with corruption. "The People's Party is the protest of the plundered against the plunderers—of the victim against the robbers," said one organizer at the founding of the People's Party in 1892.[4] "A vast conspiracy against mankind has been organized on two continents and is rapidly taking possession of the world," said another.[5] Progressives championed the same causes as Populists, and took their side in railing against big business, but while Populists generally wanted less government, Progressives wanted more, seeking solutions in reform legislation and in the establishment of bureaucracies, especially government agencies.[6]

Populists believed that the system was broken; Progressives believed that the government could fix it. Conservatives, who happened to dominate the Supreme Court, didn't believe that there was anything to fix but believed that, if there was, the market would fix it. Notwithstanding conservatives' influence in the judiciary, Progressivism spanned both parties. After 1896, when the Democratic Party convinced Bryan to run as a

Democrat instead of as a Populist, Democrats boasted that they had successfully folded Populists into their party. In 1905, Governor Jeff Davis of Arkansas said, "In 1896, when we nominated the grandest and truest man the world ever knew—William Jennings Bryan—for President, we stole all the Populists hate; we stole their platform, we stole their candidate, we stole them out lock, stock, and barrel." But Republicans were Progressives, too. "The citizens of the United States must effectively control the mighty commercial forces which they have themselves called into being," Theodore Roosevelt said. And, as Woodrow Wilson himself admitted, "When I sit down and compare my views with those of a Progressive Republican I can't see what the difference is."[7]

Much that was vital in Progressivism grew out of Protestantism, and especially out of a movement known as the Social Gospel, adopted by almost all theological liberals and by a large number of theological conservatives, too. The name dates to 1886, when a Congregationalist minister took to calling Henry George's *Progress and Poverty* a social gospel. George had written much of the book with evangelical zeal, arguing that only a remedy for economic inequality could bring about "the culmination of Christianity—the City of God on earth, with its walls of jasper and its gates of pearl!" (More skeptical and less religious liberals had long since lost faith with George's utopianism, Clarence Darrow shrewdly remarking, "The error I found in the philosophy of Henry George was its cocksureness, its simplicity, and the small value that it placed upon the selfish motives of men.")[8]

The Social Gospel movement was led by seminary professors—academic theologians who accepted the theory of evolution, seeing it as entirely consistent with the Bible and evidence of a divinely directed, purposeful universe; at the same time, they fiercely rejected the social Darwinism of writers like Herbert Spencer, the English natural scientist who coined the phrase "the survival of the fittest" and used the theory of evolution to defend all manner of force, violence, and oppression. After witnessing a coal miners' strike in Ohio in 1882, the Congregationalist Washington Gladden, a man never seen without his knee-length, double-breasted Prince Albert frock coat, argued that fighting inequality produced by industrialism was an obligation of Christians: "We must make men believe that Christianity has a right to rule this kingdom of industry, as well as all the other kingdoms of this world."[9]

Social Gospelers brought the zeal of abolitionism to the problem of industrialism. In 1895, Oberlin College held a conference called "The Causes and Proposed Remedies of Poverty." In 1897, Topeka minister Charles Sheldon, who got to know his parish by living among his poorest parishioners—spending three weeks in a black ghetto—sold millions of copies of a novel, *In His Steps: What Would Jesus Do?*, about a minister and his congregation who wonder how Christ would address industrialism (their answer: with Progressive reform). In 1908, Methodists wrote a Social Creed and pledged to fight to end child labor and to promote a living wage. It was soon adopted by the thirty-three-member Federal Council of Churches, which proceeded to investigate a steelworkers' strike in Bethlehem, ultimately taking the side of the strikers.[10]

William Jennings Bryan, hero of the plains, was a Social Gospeler in everything but name.[11] After losing the election in 1896, though, he threw off his cross of gold and dedicated himself to a new cause: the protest of American imperialism. Bryan saw imperialism as inconsistent with both Christianity and American democratic traditions. Other Progressives disagreed—Protestant missionaries in particular—seeing both Cuba and the Philippines as opportunities to gain new converts.

The Spanish-American War, what boosters called a "splendid little war," began in 1898. Cubans had been attempting to throw off Spanish rule since 1868, and Filipinos had been doing the same since 1896. Newspaper barons William Randolph Hearst and Joseph Pulitzer came to side with the Cuban rebels, and, eyeing a rich opportunity to boost their newspapers' circulation, they sent reporters and photographers not only to chronicle the conflict but, in Hearst's case, to stir it up. Newspaper lore has it that when one of Hearst's photographers cabled from Havana that war seemed unlikely, Hearst cabled back: "You furnish the pictures, and I'll furnish the war." President McKinley sent a warship to Cuba as a precaution, but in February 1898 that ship, the USS *Maine*, blew up in Havana, killing 250 U.S. sailors. The cause of the explosion was unknown—and it would later be revealed to have been an accident—but both Hearst and Pulitzer published a cable from the captain of the battleship to the assistant secretary of the navy, Theodore Roosevelt, informing him that the disaster was no accident. (The cable was later revealed to be a fake.) Newspaper circulation soared; readers clamored for war. When Congress obliged by declaring war on Spain,

*In 1898, newspaper publishers Joseph Pulitzer (left)
and William Randolph Hearst (right) used
the war to increase circulation.*

Hearst fired rockets from the roof of the *New York Journal*'s building.
Pulitzer came to regret his part in the rush to war, but not Hearst. On
his lead newspaper's front page, Hearst ran the headline HOW DO YOU
LIKE THE JOURNAL'S WAR?[12]

Thirty-nine-year-old Theodore Roosevelt, determined to see combat,
resigned his position as assistant secretary of the navy, formed the First
U.S. Volunteer Cavalry Regiment, charged up San Juan Hill, and came
back a hero. Even Bryan, thirty-eight, enlisted. He formed a volunteer
regiment from Nebraska, and went to Florida to prepare to fight, but was
never sent into combat, McKinley having apparently made sure Bryan, his
presidential rival, had no chance for glory.

Under the terms of the peace, Cuba became independent, but Spain
ceded Guam, Puerto Rico, and the Philippines to the United States, in
exchange for $20 million. A U.S. occupation and American colonial rule
were not what the people of the Philippines had in mind when they threw
off Spanish rule. The Philippines declared its independence, and Filipino
leader Emilio Aguinaldo formed a provisional constitutional government.
McKinley refused to recognize it, and by 1899 U.S. troops had fired on
Filipino nationalists. "I know that war has always produced great losses,"
Aguinaldo said in an address to the Filipino people. "But I also know by

experience how bitter is slavery." Bryan resigned his commission to protest the annexation, joining a quickly formed and badly organized Anti-
Imperialist League, whose supporters included Jane Addams, Andrew
Carnegie, William James, and Mark Twain. Bryan, their best speaker,
argued that the annexation of the Philippines betrayed the will of both
the Filipino people and the American people. "The people have not voted
for imperialism," he said, "no national convention has declared for it; no
Congress has passed upon it."[13]

From its start in 1899, the Philippine-American War was an unusually brutal war, with atrocities on both sides, including the slaughter
of Filipino civilians. U.S. forces deployed on Filipinos a method of torture known as "water cure," forcing a prisoner to drink a vast quantity
of water; most of the victims died. Meanwhile, in Washington, in the
debate over the annexation of the Philippines, Americans revisited unsettled questions about expansion that had rent the nation during the War
with Mexico and unsettled questions about citizenship that remained the
unfinished business of Reconstruction. The debate also marked the limits
of the Progressive vision: both sides in this debate availed themselves,
at one time or another, of the rhetoric of white supremacy. Eight million
people of color in the Pacific and the Caribbean, from the Philippines to
Puerto Rico, were now part of the United States, a nation that already, in
practice, denied the right to vote to millions of its own people because of
the color of their skin.

On the floor of the Senate, those who favored imperial rule over the
Pacific island argued that the Filipinos were, by dint of race, unable to govern themselves. "How could they be?" asked Indiana Republican Albert J.
Beveridge. "They are not of a self-governing race. They are Orientals." But
senators who argued against annexation pointed out that when the Confederacy had made this argument about blacks, the Union had fought a
war and staged an occupation over its disagreement with that claim. "You
are undertaking to annex and make a component part of this Government
islands inhabited by ten millions of the colored race, one-half or more of
whom are barbarians of the lowest type," said Ben Tillman, a one-eyed
South Carolina Democrat who'd boasted of having killed black men and
expressed his support for lynch mobs. "It is to the injection into the body
politic of the United States of that vitiated blood, that debased and ignorant people, that we object." Tillman reminded Republicans that they had

not so long ago freed slaves and then "forced on the white men of the South, at the point of the bayonet, the rule and domination of those ex-slaves. Why the difference? Why the change? Do you acknowledge that you were wrong in 1868?"[14]

The relationship between Jim Crow and the war in the Philippines was not lost on black soldiers who served in the Pacific. An infantryman from Wisconsin reported that the war could have been avoided had white American soldiers not applied to the Filipinos "home treatment for colored peoples" and "cursed them as damned niggers." Rienzi B. Lemus, of the Twenty-Fifth Infantry, reported on the contrast between what he read in American newspapers and what he saw in the Philippines. "Every time we get a paper from there," he wrote home to Richmond, Virginia, "we read where some poor Negro is lynched for supposed rape," while in the Philippines, only when "there was no Negro in the vicinity to charge with the crime," were two white soldiers sentenced to be shot for raping a Filipino woman.[15]

The war that began in Cuba in 1898 and was declared over in the Philippines in 1902 dramatically worsened conditions for people of color in the United States, who faced, at home, a campaign of terrorism. Pro-war rhetoric, filled with racist venom, only further incited American racial hatreds. "If it is necessary, every Negro in the state will be lynched," the governor of Mississippi pledged in 1903. Mark Twain called lynching an "epidemic of bloody insanities." By one estimate, someone in the South was hanged or burned alive every four days. The court's decision in *Plessy v. Ferguson* meant that there was no legal recourse to fight segregation, which grew more brutal with each passing year. Nor was discrimination confined to the South. Cities and counties in the North and West passed racial zoning laws, banning blacks from the middle-class communities. In 1890, in Montana, blacks lived in all fifty-six counties in the state; by 1930, they'd been confined to just eleven. In Baltimore, blacks couldn't buy houses on blocks where whites were a majority. In 1917, in *Buchanan v. Warley*, the Supreme Court availed itself of the Fourteenth Amendment not to guarantee equal protection for blacks but to guarantee what the court had come to understand as the "liberty of contract"—the liberty of businesses to discriminate.[16]

In the spring of 1899, while teaching at Atlanta University, W. E. B. Du Bois was walking from his rooms on campus to deliver to the offices

*Charles Mitchell was lynched in Urbana, Ohio, in 1897, one of thousands of black men lynched during the Jim Crow era.*

of a city newspaper a restrained essay about the lynching of Sam Hose, a black farmer, when he saw, displayed in a store window, Hose's knuckles. Hose had been dismembered, and barbecued, his body parts sold as souvenirs. Du Bois, who had earned a PhD in history at Harvard in 1895 before studying in Europe, had pioneered a new method of social science research that had become a hallmark of Progressive Era reform: the social survey. In 1896, he'd gone door-to-door in Philadelphia's Seventh Ward and personally interviewed more than five thousand people in order to prepare his study *The Philadelphia Negro*. In 1898, he'd delivered a meticulously argued academic lecture on "The Study of the Negro Problems," which, while brilliant, was cluttered with blather like "the phenomena of society are worth the most careful and systematic study." But on that spring day in 1899 when he saw what had once been Hose's hands, he turned around, walked back to his rooms, threw away his essay, and decided that "one could not be a calm, cool and detached scientist while Negroes were lynched, murdered and starved."[17]

A lot of other people decided that they, too, couldn't keep calm—and, like Du Bois, that they could no longer live in places like Georgia. "We are outnumbered and without arms," Ida B. Wells wrote. Instead, they packed up and left, in what came to be called the Great Migration, the movement of millions of blacks from the South to the North and West. Before the Great Migration began, 90 percent of all blacks in the United States lived in the South. Between 1915 and 1918, five hundred thousand African Americans left for cities like Milwaukee and Cleveland, Chicago and Los Angeles, Philadelphia and Detroit. Another 1.3 million left the South between 1920 and 1930. By the beginning of the Second World War, 47 percent of all blacks in the United States lived outside the South. In cities, they built new communities, and new community organizations. In 1909, in New York, Du Bois helped found the National Association for the Advancement of Colored People and the next year began editing its monthly magazine, *The Crisis*, explaining that its title came from the conviction that "this is a critical time in the history of the advancement of men"—a crisis for humanity.[18]

White Progressives, who borrowed from the social science methods pioneered by Du Bois, turned a blind eye to Jim Crow. Like Populists before them, when Progressives talked about inequality, they meant the condition of white farmers and white wage workers relative to business owners. Yet Progressives were undeniably influenced by the struggle for racial justice, not least by the investigative journalism methods pioneered by Wells, with her exposé of lynching: the exposé became Progressives' sharpest tool. After Theodore Roosevelt, alluding to *Pilgrim's Progress,* damned "the Man with the Muck-rake," who "consistently refuses to see aught that is lofty and fixes his eyes with solemn intentness only on that which is vile and debasing," investigative journalism came to be called muckraking.[19] It first became a national phenomenon at *McClure's*, a monthly magazine, when in 1902 its publisher, an Irish immigrant named Samuel Sidney McClure, gave an investigative assignment—designed to expose corruption and lawlessness—to each of his three best writers, charging Ray Stannard Baker with writing about unions, Ida Tarbell about Standard Oil, and Lincoln Steffens about big-city politics. (Steffens later hired as his assistant a very young Walter Lippmann.) None of these people liked being described as a writer who sees only filth. Tarbell, who'd earlier written biographies of Napoleon and Lincoln, considered herself

*In a 1910 magazine cover, top-hatted banker J. Pierpont Morgan grabs at all of New York City's banks—even a toddler's piggy bank.*

not a muckraker but a historian. And, as Baker later insisted, "We muck-raked not because we hated our world but because we loved it."[20]

Tarbell's indictment of Standard Oil, a catalogue of collusion and corruption, harassment, intimidation, and outright thuggery, first appeared as a nineteen-part series in *McClure's*. Standard Oil, Tarbell wrote, was the first of the trusts, the model for all that followed, and "the most perfectly developed trust in existence." Tarbell, who'd grown up next to an oil field—"great oil pits sunken in the earth"—had watched Standard Oil crush its competition. Often investigated by state and local governments, the company had left behind a paper trail, which Tarbell had followed, doggedly, in the archives. But it was her writing that brought her argument home. "There was nothing too good for them, nothing they did not hope and dare," she wrote of a group of young men starting out on their own in the industry, unaware of Standard Oil's methods. "At the very heyday of this confidence, a big hand reached out from nobody knew where, to steal their conquest and throttle their future."[21]

In the wake of Tarbell's indictment, Rockefeller, who'd founded Standard Oil in 1870, became one of the most despised men in America, a symbol of everything that had gone wrong with industrialism. That

Rockefeller was a Baptist and a philanthropist did not stop William Jennings Bryan from arguing that no institution should accept a penny from him (Bryan refused to serve on the board of his alma mater, Illinois College, until it broke ties with Rockefeller). "It is not necessary," Bryan said, "that all Christian people shall sanction the Rockefeller method of making money merely because Rockefeller prays."[22]

Muckraking fueled the engine of Progressivism. But the car was driven by two American presidents, Woodrow Wilson and Theodore Roosevelt, men who could hardly have been more different but who, between them, vastly extended the powers of the presidency while battling against combinations of capital that made corporations into monopolies.

WHEN WOODROW WILSON was a boy reading Sir Walter Scott, he made a paper navy, appointed himself its admiral, and wrote his fleet a constitution. His graduating class at Princeton named him the class's "model statesman." At the University of Virginia, he studied law and joined the debating society. A generation earlier, he'd have become a preacher, like his father, but instead he became a professor of political science.[23] In the academy and later in the White House, he dedicated himself to the problem of adapting a Constitution written in the age of the cotton gin to the age of the automobile.

A modernist, impatient with his ancestors, Wilson believed that the separation of powers had gotten thrown out of whack. In *Congressional Government*, he argued that Congress had too much power and used it unwisely, passing laws pell-mell and hardly ever repealing any. He applied the theory of evolution to the Constitution, which, he said, "is not a machine, but a living thing," and "falls, not under the theory of the universe, but under the theory of organic life." He came to believe that the presidency had been evolving, too: "We have grown more and more inclined from generation to generation to look to the President as the unifying force in our complex system, the leader both of his party and of the nation. To do so is not inconsistent with the actual provisions of the Constitution; it is only inconsistent with a very mechanical theory of its meaning and intention." A president's power, Wilson concluded, is virtually limitless: "His office is anything he has the sagacity and force to make it."[24]

A 1900 cartoon depicts
Theodore Roosevelt as
a centaur, branded
"GOP," bucking wildly
while firing two guns,
one labeled "Speeches,"
the other, "Wild Talk."

People with a writerly bent who were interested in understanding American democracy tended to produce, in those days, sweeping accounts of the nation's origins and rise. During the years when Frederick Douglass and Frederick Jackson Turner were wrestling with the story of America, Wilson wrote a five-volume *History of the American People* and young Theodore Roosevelt churned out a four-volume series called *The Winning of the West*. Wilson was more interested in ideas, Roosevelt in battles.

Roosevelt, who looked like a bear and roared like a lion, had finished a law degree at Columbia while serving in the New York State Assembly and spending a great deal of time at his ranch in western Dakota. But it was Roosevelt's fighting in the Spanish-American War that catapulted him to national fame. On his return from Cuba, he was elected the Republican governor of New York. Two years later, when McKinley faced the Democratic nominee, William Jennings Bryan, he named Roosevelt as his running mate.

"It was a mistake to nominate that wild man," McKinley's adviser Mark Hanna always said. But that wild man proved a tireless campaigner. "He ain't running, he's galloping," people said. In Roosevelt, Bryan met his match. Bryan traveled 16,000 miles on the campaign trail, so Roosevelt traveled 21,000. Bryan made 600 speeches, so Roosevelt made 673. Publicly, Roosevelt painted Bryan as a crackpot, with "communistic and socialistic doctrines"; privately, he remarked that Bryan was supported by "all the lunatics, all the idiots, all the knaves, all the cowards, and all the honest people who are slow-witted."[25] Bryan, to Roosevelt, was the candidate of the lame-brained.

When McKinley won, Democrats blamed Bryan, who, while he cornered the rural vote, had won not a single city except silver-mining Denver. Democracy appeared to be dooming the Democratic Party. In 1880, one half of the American workforce worked on farms; by 1920, only one-quarter did. A great many people worked in factories, and a rising number of them, especially women, worked in offices. In 1880, clerks made up less than 5 percent of the nation's workforce, nearly all of them men; by 1910, more than four million Americans worked in offices, and half were women. By 1920, most Americans lived and worked in cities. Bryan's followers were farmers, and so long as he led the party, it was hard to see how Democrats could win the White House. Said one character in a humor column, "I wondhur . . . if us dimmy-crats will iver ilict a prisidint again."[26]

In 1901, when McKinley was shot by an anarchist in Buffalo, Roosevelt, only forty-two, became the nation's youngest president. A great admirer of Lincoln, he wore on his hand a ring that contained a wisp of hair cut from the dead president's head. He bounded in and out of rooms and slapped senators on the back, but he read widely and deeply, and even though Pulitzer's *World* called him "the strangest creature the White House ever held," he knew how to work the press. He gave reporters a permanent room at the White House, and figured out that the best day to feed them stories was Sunday, so that their pieces would run at the beginning of the week; Roosevelt liked to say that he "discovered Monday." His lasting legacy was the regulatory state, the establishment of professional federal government and scientific agencies like the Forest and Reclamation Services. Not far behind was the series of wildlife refuges and national parks he created. Much of the rest was bluster. "I am not advocating anything revolutionary," Roosevelt himself said. "I am advocating action to prevent anything revolutionary."[27]

In the White House, Roosevelt pursued reforms long advocated by Populists. Announcing that "trusts are the creatures of the state," he set about using antitrust fervor to enact regulatory measures, principally through the Antitrust Division of the Justice Department.[28] Reelected in 1904, when he easily defeated Alton B. Parker, a conservative whom Democrats had nominated out of their vexation at Bryan, Roosevelt continued to move to the left, pursuing an agenda, not always successfully, of regulating the railroads, passing pure food and drug laws, and ending child labor.

Roosevelt also endorsed the income tax, a measure by now nearly universal in Europe. Between 1897 and 1906, supporters of the tax had introduced into Congress twenty-seven bills proposing to defeat, with a constitutional amendment, the Supreme Court's decision in *Pollock*, overturning the 1894 federal income tax. "I feel sure that the people will sooner or later demand an amendment to the constitution which will specifically authorize an income tax," Bryan said at a rally in Madison Square Garden before an adoring crowd of ten thousand, on his return from a yearlong trip around the world.[29]

The momentum for change came in the form of an earthquake that hit San Francisco in 1906, spreading fires across the city and, triggered by the collapse of insurance companies that were unable to cover hundreds of millions of dollars in earthquake-damage claims, a financial panic across the country. In the election of 1908, after Roosevelt pledged that he would not run for a third term, a pledge he much regretted, the Republicans nominated William Howard Taft, Roosevelt's secretary of war. The Democrats turned once again to Bryan, who demonstrated, for the third and final time, that, while he could raise a crowd to its feet and leave them weeping, he could not deliver the White House to his party.

President Taft, who had been a federal judge and who would go on to serve as chief justice of the United States, was perfectly willing to support a federal income tax, but he wanted to avoid signing a law that would end up going back to the Supreme Court: "Nothing has ever injured the prestige of the Supreme Court more than that last decision," he said about the court's decision in *Pollock*.[30] Taft decided to support a constitutional amendment, which went to the states for ratification in 1909.

Constitutional amendments are notoriously difficult to pass. The Sixteenth Amendment was not, and its success is a measure of the reach and intensity of the Progressive movement. It was ratified, handily and swiftly, in 42 of 48 states, six more than required, winning passage in state sen-

ates with an average support of 89 percent and, in state houses, 95 percent. In nineteen lower legislatures, the vote in favor was unanimous. The
Sixteenth Amendment became law in February 1913. The House voted on
an income tax bill in May. When the Bureau of Internal Revenue printed
its first 1040, the form was three pages, the instructions only one.[31] Americans later came to argue about the income tax more fiercely almost than
anything they'd argued about before, but when it started, they wanted it
desperately, and urgently.

INDUSTRIALISM HAD BUILT towers, tipped to the sky, and had
cluttered store shelves with trinkets, but it left workers with very little
economic security. Beginning in the 1880s, industrializing nations had
begun addressing this problem by providing "workingmen's insurance"—
health insurance, industrial accident compensation, and old-age pensions
for wage workers—along with various forms of family assistance, chiefly
to poor mothers or widows with dependent children. These programs created what came to be known as the modern welfare state. In the United
States, the earliest of these forms of assistance were tied to military service. Between 1880 and 1910, under the terms of benefits paid to Civil
War veterans and their widows and dependents, more than a quarter of
the federal budget went to welfare payments. When Pennsylvania congressman William B. Wilson introduced a pension plan for all citizens
over the age of sixty-five, he alluded to this tradition in the measure's
very title, calling it the Old-age Home Guard of the United States Army.
Beginning in the 1880s, reformers like Jane Addams and Florence Kelley, in Chicago, had been leading a fight for legislative labor reforms for
women, including minimum-wage and maximum-hour laws, and the abolition of child labor. Their first success came in 1883, when Illinois passed
a law for an eight-hour workday for women. And yet each of these Progressive reforms, from social insurance to protective legislation, faced a
legal obstacle: their critics called them unconstitutional.[32]

The Illinois Supreme Court struck down the eight-hour-workday law,
and, in a particularly remarkable set of decisions issued at a time when
courts were coming not only to support government intervention but also
to be tools of reform, the U.S. Supreme Court overruled much Progressive
labor legislation. The most important of these decisions came in 1905. In

a 5–4 decision in *Lochner v. New York,* the U.S. Supreme Court voided a state law establishing that bakers could work no longer than ten hours a day, six days a week, on the ground that the law violated a business owner's liberty of contract, the freedom to forge agreements with his workers, something the court's majority said was protected under the Fourteenth Amendment. The laissez-faire conservatism of the court was informed, in part, by social Darwinism, which suggested that the parties in disputes should be left to battle it out, and if one side had an advantage, even so great an advantage as a business owner has over its employees, then it should win. In a dissenting opinion in *Lochner,* Oliver Wendell Holmes accused the court of violating the will of the people. "This case is decided upon an economic theory which a large part of the country does not entertain," he began. The court, he said, had also wildly overreached its authority and had carried social Darwinism into the Constitution. "A Constitution is not intended to embody a particular economic theory," Holmes wrote. "The Fourteenth Amendment does not enact Mr. Herbert Spencer's *Social Statics.*"[33]

The *Lochner* decision intensified the debate about judicial review that had begun with *Marbury v. Madison* in 1803. Critics charged conservatives with "putting courts into politics and compelling judges to become politicians." Meanwhile, Progressives painted themselves as advocates of the people, and, continuing a long tradition in American politics, insisted that their political position represented the people's view of the Constitution—as against that of a corrupt judiciary. Roosevelt would eventually pledge to institute judicial recall—making it possible for justices to be essentially impeached—insisting, "the people themselves must be the ultimate makers of their own Constitution."[34]

From either political vantage, the heart of the struggle concerned the constitutionality of the provisions of a welfare state. Britain, which does not have a written constitution, established the foundations for what would become a comprehensive welfare state—complete with health insurance and old-age pensions—at the very time that the United States was failing to do the same. Wilson pointed out that the Constitution, written before mass industrialization, couldn't be expected to have anticipated it, and couldn't solve the problems industrialization had created, unless the Constitution were treated like a living thing that, like an organism, evolved. Critics further to the left argued that the courts had become an instrument of business interests. Unions, in fact, often failed to support labor reform legislation, partly because they expected it to be struck down by the courts as unconstitutional, and partly because they wanted unions to provide benefits to their members, which would be an argument for organizing. (If the government provided those social benefits, workers wouldn't need unions, or so some union leaders feared.)[35] Meanwhile, conservatives insisted that the courts were right to protect the interests of business and that either market forces would find a way to care for sick, injured, and old workers, or (for social Darwinists) the weakest, who were not meant to thrive, would wither and die.

For all of these reasons, American Progressives campaigning for universal health insurance enjoyed far less success than their counterparts in Britain. In 1912, one year after Parliament passed a National Insurance Act, the American Association for Labor Legislation formed a Committee on Social Insurance, the brainchild of Isaac M. Rubinow, a Russian-born doctor turned policymaker who would publish, in 1913, the landmark study *Social Insurance*. Rubinow had hoped that "sickness insurance" would eradicate poverty. By 1915, his committee had drafted a bill providing for universal medical coverage. "No other social movement in modern economic development is so pregnant with benefit to the public," wrote the editor of the *Journal of the American Medical Association*. "At present the United States has the unenviable distinction of being the only great industrial nation without compulsory health insurance," the Yale economist Irving Fisher pointed out in 1916.[36] It would maintain that unenviable distinction for a century.

Congress debated Rubinow's bill, which was also put forward in sixteen states. "Germany showed the way in 1883," Fisher liked to say, pointing to the policy's origins. "Her wonderful industrial progress since that time, her comparative freedom from poverty . . . and the physical preparedness of her soldiery, are presumably due, in considerable measure, to health insurance." But after the United States declared war with Germany in 1917, critics described national health insurance as "made in Germany" and likely to result in the "Prussianization of America." In California, the legislature passed a constitutional amendment providing for universal health insurance. But when it was put on the ballot for ratification, a federation of insurance companies took out an ad in the *San Francisco Chronicle* warning that it "would spell social ruin in the United States." Every voter in the state received in the mail a pamphlet with a picture of the kaiser and the words "Born in Germany. Do you want it in California?" The measure was defeated. Opponents called universal health insurance "UnAmerican, Unsafe, Uneconomic, Unscientific, Unfair and Unscrupulous."[37]

The fastest way through the constitutional thicket, it turned out, was to argue for welfare not for men but for women and children. By 1900, nearly one in five manufacturing jobs in the United States was held by a woman.[38] Women and children couldn't vote; in seeking labor reform and social insurance, they sought from the state not rights but protections. Mothers made claims on the state in the same terms as did veterans: a claim of services rendered. And even women who had not yet had children could be understood, for these purposes, as potential mothers. To that end, much of the early lobbying for protective legislation for women and children was done by the National Congress of Mothers, later known as the Parent Teacher Association, or the PTA. Founded in 1897 by Phoebe Apperson Hearst, the mother of the newspaper tycoon, and Alice McLellan Birney, the wife of a Washington, DC, lawyer, the National Congress of Mothers aimed to serve as a female auxiliary to the national legislature. "This is the one body that I put even ahead of the veterans of the Civil War," Theodore Roosevelt declared in 1908, "because when all is said and done it is the mother, and the mother only, who is a better citizen even than the soldier who fights for his country."[39]

Women were also consumers. In 1899, Florence Kelley, the daughter of an abolitionist who had helped found the Republican Party, became the first general secretary of the National Consumers League. Her motto: "Investigate, record, agitate." Kelley, born in Philadelphia in 1856, had studied at Cornell and in Zurich, where she became a socialist; in 1885, she translated the work of Friedrich Engels. In the 1890s, while working at Jane Addams's Hull House in Chicago, she'd earned a law degree at Northwestern. Eyeing the court's decision in *Lochner*, and understanding that the courts treated women differently than men, Kelley wondered whether maximum-hour legislation might have a better chance of success in the courts if the test case were a law aimed specifically at female workers. Already, state courts had made rulings in that direction. In 1902, the Nebraska Supreme Court decreed that "the state must be accorded the right to guard and protect women as a class, against such a condition; and the law in question, to that extent, conserves the public health and welfare."[40]

For women, who were not written into the Constitution, wining constitutional arguments has always required constitutional patching: cutting and pasting, scissors and a pot of glue. In an era in which the court plainly favored arguments that stopped short of actual equality—*Plessy v. Ferguson*, after all, had instituted the doctrine of "separate but equal" rather than provide equal protection to African Americans—Kelley tried arguing that women, physically weaker than men, deserved special protection.[41]

In 1906, the Oregon Supreme Court upheld a female ten-hour law that had been challenged by a laundryman named Curt Muller; Muller appealed to the U.S. Supreme Court. Kelley arranged for a lawyer named Louis Brandeis to argue the case for Oregon. Brandeis, known as "the people's attorney," was born in Kentucky in 1856, graduated from Harvard Law School in 1876, and married Alice Goldmark in 1891. Much of his legwork in the Muller case was done by the indefatigable reformer Josephine Goldmark, who worked for Kelley and was also Brandeis's sister-in-law.[42] Goldmark compiled the findings of hundreds of reports and studies by physicians, municipal health boards, public health departments, medical societies, factory inspectors, and bureaus of labor, demonstrating the harm done to women by working long hours. She presented Brandeis with a 113-page amicus brief that Brandeis submitted to the Supreme Court in 1908 in *Muller v. Oregon*. "The decision in this case will, in effect, determine the constitutionality of nearly all the statutes in force in the United States, limiting the hours of labor of adult women," Brandeis explained, arguing that overwork "is more disastrous to the health of women than of men, and entails upon them more lasting injury." The Oregon law was upheld.

*Muller v. Oregon* established the constitutionality of labor laws (for women), the legitimacy of sex discrimination in employment, and the place of social science research in the decisions of the courts. The "Brandeis brief," as it came to be called, essentially made muckraking admissible as evidence. Where the court in *Plessy v. Ferguson* had scorned any discussion of the facts of racial inequality, citing the prevailing force of tradition, *Muller v. Oregon* established the conditions that would allow for the presentation of social science evidence in the case that would overrule racial segregation, in *Brown v. Board of Education of Topeka*, in 1954.[43]

"History discloses the fact that woman has always been dependent upon man," Brandeis argued in *Muller v. Oregon*. "Differentiated by these matters from the other sex, she is properly placed in a class by herself, and legislation designed for her protection may be sustained, even when like legislation is not necessary for men and could not be sustained."[44] Kelley used this difference as a wedge. Between 1911 and 1920, laws providing relief for women in the form of mothers' and widows' pensions passed in forty states; between 1909 and 1917, maximum-hour laws for women passed in thirty-nine states; and between 1912 and 1923, minimum-wage laws for women passed in fifteen states.[45]

But Kelley and female protectionists had made a Faustian bargain. These laws rested on the idea that women were dependent, not only on men, but on the state. If women were ever to achieve equal rights, this sizable body of legislation designed to protect women would stand in their way.

MULLER V. OREGON set the brilliant Louis Brandeis in a new direction. He became interested in the new field of "efficiency" as a means of addressing the problems of relations between labor and business. Brandeis became convinced that "efficiency is the hope of democracy."[46]

The efficiency movement began when Bethlehem Steel Works, in Pennsylvania, hired a mechanical engineer from Philadelphia named Frederick Winslow Taylor to speed production, which Taylor proposed to do with a system he called "task management" or, later, "The Gospel of Efficiency." As Taylor explained in 1911 in his best-selling book, *The Principles of Scientific Management*, he timed the Bethlehem steelworkers with a stopwatch, identified the fastest worker, a "first-class man," from among "ten powerful Hungarians," and calculated the fastest rate at which a unit of work could be done. Thenceforth all workers were required to work at that rate or lose their jobs.[47] Taylor, though, had made up most of his figures. After charging Bethlehem Steel two and a half times what he could possibly have saved the company in labor costs, he, too, was fired.[48] Nevertheless, Taylorism endured.

Efficiency promised to speed production, lower the cost of goods, and improve the lives of workers, goals it often achieved. It was also a way to minimize strikes and to manage labor—particularly immigrant labor.

Before 1896, European immigrants to the United States had chiefly come from northern and western Europe, and especially from Germany and Ireland. After 1896, most came from the south and the east, and especially from Italy and Hungary. Slavs, Jews, and Italians, lumped together as the "new immigrants," also came in far greater numbers than Europeans had ever come before, sometimes more than a million a year. The number of Europeans who arrived in the twelve years between 1902 and 1914 alone totaled more than the number of Europeans who arrived in the four decades between 1820 and 1860.[49]

No one implemented the regime of efficiency better than Henry Ford. In 1903, Ford, the forty-year-old son of Michigan farmers, opened a motor car company in Detroit, where workers, timed by a clock, put together parts on an assembly line. By 1914, Ford's plant was manufacturing nearly a quarter of a million cars every year, cars that cost one-quarter of what he'd sold them for a decade earlier.[50] Before the automobile, only businesses owned large machines. As Walter Chrysler explained, "We were making the first machine of considerable size in the history of the world for which every human being was a potential customer."[51] If the railroad served as the symbol of progress in the nineteenth century, the automobile served as its symbol in the twentieth, a consumer commodity that celebrated individualism and choice. Announced Ford: "Machinery is the new Messiah."[52]

Efficiency reached into family life with the founding of "home economics."[53] Ford exerted particular control over the home lives of his largely immigrant workers, by way of a Sociological Department. "Employees should use plenty of soap and water in the home, and upon their children, bathing frequently," one pamphlet recommended. "Nothing makes for right living and health so much as cleanliness. Notice that the most advanced people are the cleanest." Ford also founded an English School, to Americanize his immigrant workers, using the same methods of assembly that he used in his plant. "There is a course in industry and efficiency, a course in thrift and economy, a course in domestic relations, one in community relations, and one in industrial relations," Ford's English

School announced. "This is the human product we seek to turn out, and as we adapt the machinery in the shop to turning out the kind of automobile we have in mind, so we have constructed our educational system with a view to producing the human product we have in mind."[54]

Brandeis came to believe that Taylorism could solve the problems of mass industrialism and mass democracy. While preparing to appear before the Interstate Commerce Committee on railroad freight rates, Brandeis called a meeting of efficiency experts.[55] In the Commerce Committee hearings, he argued that, instead of raising their freight rates, railroads ought to do their work more efficiently. With scientific management, Brandeis said, railroad companies could save one million dollars a day. He won the argument, but the people who worked on railroads and in factories soon began attempting to convince him that those savings came at their expense. The next year, when Brandeis gave a speech about efficiency to a labor union, one woman shouted at him, "You can call it scientific management if you want to, but I call it scientific driving."[56]

Some members of Congress suspected the same. In 1912, William B. Wilson, who'd gone down into the coal pits at the age of nine and joined the union at eleven, chaired a House Special Committee to Investigate the Taylor and Other Systems of Shop Management. When Taylor, called to testify, talked about "first-class men," Wilson inquired about workers who weren't first-class, men whom Taylor had described as dumb as dray horses. "Scientific management has no place for such men?" Wilson asked. "Scientific management has no place for a bird that can sing and won't sing," answered Taylor. "We are not . . . dealing with horses nor singing birds," Wilson told Taylor. "We are dealing with men who are a part of society and for whose benefit society is organized.[57]

Were men animals? Were men machines? Was machinery a messiah, and efficiency a gospel? With businesses driving workers to toil at breakneck speed, a growing number of Americans were drawn to socialism, especially since neither of the two major parties had any good answer to William B. Wilson's anguished exchange with Frederick Winslow Taylor. One union man in Schenectady said, "People got mighty sick of voting for Republicans and Democrats when it was a 'heads I win, tails you lose' proposition." In the presidential election of 1908, more than 400,000 people voted for the Socialist Party candidate, Eugene Debs. In 1911, Social-

*Photographer Jesse Tarbox Beals took this shot of
a suffrage parade in New York in 1910.*

ists were elected as the mayors of eighteen cities and towns and more than a thousand Socialists held offices in thirty states.[58]

Heads or tails was how the Democrats and Republicans looked to a lot of people in 1912, too, when Debs ran again, Woodrow Wilson won the Democratic nomination, and Theodore Roosevelt hoped to win the Republican one. Wilson believed that it was the obligation of the federal government to regulate the economy to protect ordinary Americans "from the consequences of great industrial and social processes which they cannot alter, control, or singly cope with." This scarcely distinguished him from Roosevelt. "The object of government is the welfare of the people," Roosevelt said. As Roosevelt put it, "Wilson is merely a less virile *me*."[59]

The election of 1912 amounted to a referendum on Progressivism, much influenced by the political agitation of women. "With a suddenness and force that have left observers gasping women have injected themselves into the national campaign this year in a manner never before dreamed of in American politics," the *New York Herald* reported, though only reporters who hadn't been paying attention saw anything sudden about it.[60]

Having fought for their rights formally since 1848, women had achieved the right to vote in eight states: Colorado (1893), Idaho (1896), Utah (1896), Washington (1910), California (1911), Arizona (1912), Kansas (1912) and Oregon (1912). They'd also begun fighting for a great deal more than suffrage. The word "feminism" entered English in the 1910s, as a generation of independent women, many of them college-educated—New Women, they were called—fought for equal education, equal opportunity, equal citizenship, and equal rights, and, not least, for birth control, a term coined by a nurse named Margaret Sanger when she launched the first feminist newspaper, *The Woman Rebel*, in 1914. In 1912 and again in 1916, suffragists marched on the streets of cities across the country, organized on the campuses of women's colleges, and staged hunger strikes. They waged old-style political campaigns, with buttons and banners. They flew in balloons. They decorated elephants and donkeys. Women who'd gone to prison for picketing took a train across the country in a Prison Special, wearing their prison uniforms. They dressed as statues; they wore red, white, and blue; they marched in chains. They waged a moral crusade, in the style of abolitionists, but on the streets, in the style of Jacksonian Democrats.[61]

Roosevelt, in an extraordinary campaign for direct democracy and social justice, hoped to wrest the Republican nomination from Taft partly by appealing to female voters, but mainly by availing himself of another Progressive reform: the direct primary. Progressive reformers, viewing nominating conventions as corrupt, had fought instead for state primaries, in which voters could choose their own presidential candidates. The first primary was held in 1899; the reform, led by Wisconsin's Robert La Follette, gained strength in 1905. "Let the People Rule" became Roosevelt's 1912 slogan. "The great fundamental issue now before the Republican Party and before our people can be stated briefly," he said. "It is: Are the American people fit to govern themselves, to rule themselves, to control themselves? I believe they are. My opponents do not." Thirteen states held primaries (all were nonbinding); Roosevelt won nine.[62]

As with the secret ballot, primaries were part Progressive reform, part Jim Crow. Roosevelt needed to win them because, at the Republican National Convention, he had no real chance of winning black delegates. Because the Republican Party had virtually no white support in the South, the only southern delegates were black delegates, men who had been appointed to party offices by the Taft administration. Roosevelt tried in vain to wrest them from their support for the president. "I like the Negro race," he said in a speech at an AME Church the day before the convention. But the next day the *New York Times* produced affidavits proving that Roosevelt's campaign wasn't so much trying to court black delegates as to bribe them. After Roosevelt lost the nomination to Taft, he formed the Progressive Party, whose convention refused to seat black delegates. "This is strictly a white man's party," said one of Roosevelt's supporters, a leader of the so-called Lily Whites.[63]

But the Progressive Party was not, in fact, strictly a white man's party; it was also a white woman's party. Roosevelt's new party adopted a suffrage plank and Roosevelt promised to appoint Jane Addams to his cabinet.[64] Addams gave the second nominating speech at the convention, after which she marched across the hall carrying a "Votes for Women" flag. Returning to her office, she found a telegram from a black newspaper editor that read: "Woman suffrage will be stained with Negro Blood unless women refuse all alliance with Roosevelt."[65]

Roosevelt's 1912 campaign marked a turn in American politics by venturing the novel idea that a national presidential administration answers national public opinion without the mediation either of parties, or of representatives in Congress. The candidate, Roosevelt suggested, is more important than the party. Roosevelt also used film clips and mass advertising in a way that no candidate had done before, gathering a national following through the tools of modern publicity and bypassing the party system by reaching voters directly. That he failed to win the presidency did not diminish the influence of this new conception of the nature of American political and constitutional arrangements.[66]

In the end, Roosevelt won 27 percent of the popular vote (more than any third-party candidate either before or since), but, having drawn most of those votes from Taft, Roosevelt's campaign allowed Wilson to gain the White House, the first southern president elected since the Civil War. Democrats controlled both houses of Congress, too, for the first time in decades. "Men's hearts wait upon us," Wilson said in his inaugural address, before the largest crowd ever gathered at an inauguration.[67] Wilson, having earned the endorsement of William Jennings Bryan, rewarded him by naming him his secretary of state. At the inauguration, Bryan sat right behind Wilson, a measure of the distance populism had traveled from the prairies of Kansas and Nebraska.

Few presidents have achieved so much so quickly as did Wilson, who delivered on an extraordinary number of his promised Progressive reforms. Learning from Roosevelt's good relationship with the press while in the White House, Wilson, in his first month, invited more than a hundred reporters to his office, fielded questions, and announced that he intended to do this regularly: in his first ten months alone, he held sixty press conferences. The author of *Congressional Government* also kept the Sixty-Third Congress in session for eighteen months straight, longer than Congress had ever met before. Congress obliged by lowering the tariff; reforming banking and currency laws; abolishing child labor; and passing a new antitrust act, the first eight-hour work-day legislation and the first federal aid to farmers.

Among Wilson's hardest fights was his nomination of Louis Brandeis to the Supreme Court, one of the most controversial in the court's history, not because Brandeis was the first Jew appointed to the court, though that was controversial in some quarters, but because Brandeis was a dogged opponent of plutocrats. Beyond the cases he'd argued, Brandeis had become something of a muckraker, publishing an indictment of the plutocracy, *Other People's Money and How the Bankers Use It*, parts of which sounded as though they could have been written by the likes of Mary E. Lease. "The power and the growth of power of our financial oligarchs comes from wielding the savings and quick capital of others," he wrote. "The fetters which bind the people are forged from the people's own gold." He pointed out that J. P. Morgan and the First National and National City Bank together held "341 directorships in 112 corporations having aggregate resources or capitalization of $22,245,000,000," a sum that is "more than three times the assessed value of all the real estate in the City of New York" and "more than the assessed value of all the property in the twenty-two states, north and south, lying west of the Mississippi River." During the Judiciary Committee debates over Brandeis's nomination, one senator remarked, "The real crime of which this man is guilty is that he has exposed the iniquities of men in high places in our financial system."[68]

Wilson fought hard for Brandeis, and won, and Brandeis's presence on the bench made all the difference to endurance of Progressive reform. But, like other Progressives, Wilson not only failed to offer any remedy for racial inequality; he endorsed it. On the fiftieth anniversary of the Battle of Gettysburg, he spoke on the battlefield at a reunion of more than fifty thousand Union and Confederate veterans. "A Reunion of whom?" asked the *Washington Bee*: black soldiers were not included. It was, instead, a reunion between whites in the North and the South, an agreement to remember the Civil War as a war over states' rights, and to forget the cause of slavery. "We have found one another again as brothers and comrades in arms, enemies no longer, generous friends rather, our battles long past, the quarrel forgotten," Wilson told the veterans at Gettysburg. A week later, his administration mandated separate bathrooms for blacks and whites working in the Treasury Department; soon he segregated the entire civil service, bringing Jim Crow to the nation's capital.[69]

"There may have been other Presidents who held the same sort of sentiments," wrote the NAACP's James Weldon Johnson, "but Mr. Wilson bears the discreditable distinction of being the first President of the United States, since Emancipation, who openly condoned and vindicated prejudice against the Negro."[70] Jim Crow thrived because, after the end of Reconstruction in 1877, reformers who had earlier fought for the cause of civil rights abandoned it for the sake of forging a reunion between the states and the federal government and between the North and the South. This wasn't Wilson's doing; this was the work of his generation, the work of the generation that came before him, and the work of the generation that would follow him, an abdication of struggle, an abandonment of justice.

# II.

WAR BROKE OUT in Europe in July of 1914, war on a scale that had never been seen before, a war run by efficiency experts and waged with factory-made munitions, a war without limit or mercy. Machines slaughtered the masses. Europe fell to its knees. The United States rose to its feet. The Great War brought the United States into the world. It marked the end of Europe's reign as the center of the Western world; that place, after the war, was held by the United States.[71]

At the start, Americans only watched, numb, shocked to discover that the nineteenth-century's great steam-powered ship of progress had carried its all-too-trusting passengers to the edge of an abyss. "The tide that bore us along was then all the while moving to *this* as its grand Niagara," wrote Henry James.[72] The scale of death in the American Civil War, so staggering at the time—750,000 dead, in four years of fighting—looked, by comparison, minuscule. Within the first eight weeks of the war alone, nearly 400,000 Germans were killed, wounded, sick, or missing. In 1916, over a matter of mere months, there were 800,000 military casualties in Verdun and 1.1 million at the Somme. But civilians were slaughtered, too. The Ottoman government massacred as many as 1.5 million Armenians. For the first time, war was waged by airplane, bombs dropped from a great height, as if by the gods themselves. Cathedrals were shelled, libraries bombed, hospitals blasted. Before the war was over, nearly 40 million people had been killed and another 20 million wounded.[73]

What sane person could believe in progress in an age of mass slaughter? The Great War steered the course of American politics like a gale-force wind. The specter of slaughter undercut Progressivism, suppressed socialism, and produced anticolonialism. And, by illustrating the enduring wickedness of humanity and appearing to fulfill prophecies of apocalypse as a punishment for the moral travesty of modernism, the war fueled fundamentalism.

Fundamentalists' dissent from Protestantism had to do with the idea of truth, a dissent that would greatly influence the history of a nation whose creed rests on a very particular set of truths. Fundamentalism began with a rejection of Darwinism. Some of fundamentalism's best-remembered preachers are southerners who moved west, like the Alabama-born Texas Baptist J. Frank Norris, six foot one and hard as oak. "I was born in the dark of the moon, in the dog-fennel season, just after a black cat had jumped upon a black coffin," Norris liked to say. Ordained in 1897, Norris went on to rail against "that hell-born, Bible-destroying, deity-of-Christ-denying, German rationalism known as evolution."[74] But fundamentalism began among educated northern ministers. Influenced by Scottish commonsense philosophers, early fundamentalists like the Princeton Theological Seminary's Charles Hodge maintained that the object of theology was to establish "the facts and principles of the Bible."

Darwinism, Hodge thought, would lead to atheism. He then declared the Bible "free from all error," a position his son, A. A. Hodge, also a professor at Princeton, carried further. (The younger Hodge insisted that it was the originals of the Scriptures that were free from error, not the copies; the originals do not survive. This distinction usually went unnoticed by his followers.)

By insisting on the literal truth of the Bible, fundamentalists dared liberal theologians and Social Gospelers into a fight, especially after the publication, beginning in 1910, of a twelve-volume series of pamphlets called *The Fundamentals: A Testimony to the Truth*. The purpose of a church is to convert people to Christ by teaching the actual, literal gospel, fundamentalists insisted, not by preaching good works and social justice. "Some people are trying to make a religion out of social service with Jesus Christ left out," the revivalist and ex–baseball player Billy Sunday complained in 1912. "We've had enough of this godless social service nonsense."[75]

William Jennings Bryan, Mr. Fundamentalist, was not actually a fundamentalist. For one, he believed in the Social Gospel; for another, he does not appear ever to have owned a copy of *The Fundamentals* and, as a man unconcerned with theological matters, he hardly ever bothered defending the literal truth of the Bible. "Christ went about doing good" was the sum of Bryan's theology. Bryan was confused for a fundamentalist because he led a drive to prohibit the teaching of evolution in the nation's schools. But Bryan saw the campaign against evolution as another arm of his decades-long campaign against the plutocracy, telling a cartoonist, "You should represent me as using a double-barreled shotgun fixing one barrel at the elephant as he tries to enter the treasury and another at Darwinism—the monkey—as he tries to enter the schoolroom."[76]

Bryan's difficulty was that he saw no difference between Darwinism and social Darwinism, but it was social Darwinism that he attacked, the brutality of a political philosophy that seemed to believe in nothing more than the survival of the fittest, or what Bryan called "the law of hate—the merciless law by which the strong crowd out and kill the weak."[77] How could a war without mercy not set this movement aflame? Germany was the enemy, the same Germany whose model of education had secularized American colleges and universities, which were now teaching eugenics, sometimes known as the science of human betterment, calling for the elimination from the human race of people deemed unfit to reproduce on the basis of their intelligence, criminality, or background.

Bryan wasn't battling a chimera. American universities were indeed breeding eugenicists. Zoologist Charles Davenport was a professor at Harvard when he wrote *Statistical Methods, with Special Reference to Biological Variation*. In 1910, in *Eugenics*, he defined the field as "the science of human improvement by better breeding." Biologist David Jordan was president of Stanford in 1906 when he headed a committee of the American Breeders' Association (an organization founded by Davenport) whose purpose was to "investigate and report on heredity in the human race" and to document "the value of superior blood and the menace to society of the inferior."[78]

Nor was this academic research without consequence. Beginning in 1907, with Indiana, two-thirds of American states passed forced sterilization laws. In 1916, Madison Grant, the president of the Museum of Natural History in New York, who had degrees from Yale and Columbia, published *The Passing of the Great Race; Or, the Racial Basis of European History*, a "hereditary history" of the human race, in which he identified northern Europeans (the "blue-eyed, fair-haired peoples of the north of Europe" that he called the "Nordic race") as genetically superior to southern Europeans (the "dark-haired, dark-eyed" people he called "the Alpine race") and lamented the presence of "swarms of Jews" and "half-breeds." In the United States, Grant argued, the Alpine race was overwhelming the Nordic race, threatening the American republic, since "democracy is fatal to progress when two races of unequal value live side by side."[79]

Progressives mocked fundamentalists as anti-intellectual. But fundamentalists were, of course, making an intellectual argument, if one that not many academics wanted to hear. In 1917, William B. Riley, who, like J. Frank Norris, had trained at the Southern Baptist Theological Seminary, published a book called *The Menace of Modernism*, whose attack on evolution included a broader attack on the predominance in public debate of liberal faculty housed at secular universities—and the silencing of conservative opinion. Conservatives, Riley pointed out, have "about as good a chance to be heard in a Turkish harem as to be invited to speak within the precincts of a modern State University." In 1919, Riley helped bring six thousand people to the first meeting of the World's Christian

Fundamentals Association. The horror of the war fueled the movement, convincing many evangelicals that the growing secularization of society was responsible for this grotesque parade of inhumanity: mass slaughter. "The new theology has led Germany into barbarism," one fundamentalist argued in 1918, "and it will lead any nation into the same demoralization."[80]

Even as Americans reeled at the slaughter in Europe, the United States edged toward war. "There will be no war while I am Secretary of State," Bryan had pledged when he joined Woodrow Wilson's administration.[81] But in 1915 Bryan resigned, unable to halt the drift toward American entry into the war.

Peace protests, mainly led by women, had begun just weeks after war broke out. At a Women's Peace Parade in New York in the summer of 1914, fifteen thousand women marched, dressed in mourning. Meanwhile, women were also marching for suffrage, the two causes twining together, on the theory that if women could vote, they'd vote against sending their sons and husbands to war.

In 1916, Wilson campaigned for reelection by pledging to keep the United States out of the war. The GOP nominated former Supreme Court justice Charles Evans Hughes, who took the opposing position. "A vote for Hughes is a vote for war," explained a senator from Oklahoma. "A vote for Wilson is a vote for peace."[82]

"If my re-election as President depends upon my getting into war, I don't want to be President," Wilson said privately. "He kept us out of war" became his campaign slogan, and when Theodore Roosevelt called that an "ignoble shirking of responsibility," Wilson countered, "I am an American, but I do not believe that any of us loves a blustering nationality."[83]

Wilson had withheld support from female suffrage, but women who could vote tended to favor peace. Suffragist Alice Paul decided that women, spurned by both parties, needed a party of their own. The National Woman's Party proceeded to parade through the streets of Denver with a donkey named Woodrow who carried a sign that read "It means freedom for women to vote against the party this donkey represents." Paul did not prevail. In the end it was women voters who, by rallying behind the peace movement, gained Wilson a narrow victory: he won ten out of the twelve states where women could vote.[84]

But as Wilson prepared for his second term, women fighting for equal rights dominated the news. In Brooklyn, Margaret Sanger and her sister Ethel Byrne, also a nurse, had opened the first birth control clinic in the United States. Sanger argued that the vote was nothing compared to the importance of birth control, especially for poor women, a position that might have seemed to align with conservative eugenicists, but which did not, since they were opposed to feminism. Arrested for violating a New York penal code that prevented any discussion of contraception, Ethel Byrne was tried in January 1917; the story appeared in newspapers across the country. Her lawyer argued that the penal code was unconstitutional, insisting that it infringed on a woman's right to the "pursuit of happiness." Byrne was found guilty on January 8; in prison, she went on a hunger strike. Two days later, Alice Paul and the National Woman's Party began a suffrage vigil outside the White House, carrying signs reading "Mr. President How Long Must Women Wait for Liberty?"[85]

Public support for suffrage plummeted as the United States grew closer to entering the war and questioning the president began to look like disloyalty. In January 1917, Wilson released an intercepted telegram from the German minister Arthur Zimmermann to the German ambassador in Mexico in which Zimmermann asked Mexico to enter the war as Germany's ally, promising to help "regain for Mexico the 'lost territories' of New Mexico, Arizona, and Texas should the U.S. declare War on Germany."[86] Days after Wilson was inaugurated, German U-boats sank three American ships. Wilson concluded that there was no longer any way to stay out of the war. At the beginning of April, he asked Congress to declare war.

"The world must be made safe for democracy," Wilson told Congress. Not everyone was persuaded. "I want especially to say, Mr. President, that I am not voting for war in the name of democracy," Ohio's Warren G. Harding said on the Senate floor. "It is my deliberate judgment that it is none of our business what type of government any nation on this earth may choose to have. . . . I voted for war tonight for the maintenance of American rights."[87]

Congress declared war. But Wilson's claim that the United States was fighting to make the world safe for democracy was hard for many to swallow. Wilson had in fact pledged not to make the world democratic, or even to support the establishment of democratic institutions everywhere, but instead to establish the conditions of stability in which democracy was possible. A war for peace it was not. The war required a massive mobilization: all American men between eighteen and forty-five had to register for the draft; nearly five million were called to serve. How were they to be persuaded of the war's cause? In a speech to new recruits, Wilson's new secretary of state, Robert Lansing, ventured an explanation. "Were every people on earth able to express their will, there would be no wars of aggression and, if there were no wars of aggression, then there would be no wars, and lasting peace would come to this earth," Lansing said, stringing one conditional clause after another. "The only way that a people can express their will is through democratic institutions," Lansing went on. "Therefore, when the world is made safe for democracy . . . universal peace will be an accomplished fact."[88]

Wilson, the political scientist, tried to earn the support of the American people with an intricate theory of the relationship between democracy and peace. It didn't work. To recast his war message and shore up popular support, he established a propaganda department, the Committee on Public Information, headed by a baby-faced, forty-one-year-old muckraker from Missouri named George Creel, best-known for an exposé on child labor called *Children in Bondage*. Creel applied the methods of Progressive Era muckraking to the work of whipping up a frenzy for fighting. His department employed hundreds of staff and thousands of volunteers, spreading pro-war messages by print, radio, and film. Social scientists called the effect produced by wartime propaganda "herd psychology"; the philosopher John Dewey called it the "conscription of thought."[89]

The conscription of thought also threatened the freedom of speech. To suppress dissent, Congress passed a Sedition Act in 1918. Not since the Alien and Sedition Acts of 1798 had Congress so brazenly defied the First Amendment. Fewer than two dozen people had been arrested under the 1798 Sedition Act. During the First World War, the Justice Department charged more than two thousand Americans with sedition and convicted half of them. Appeals that went to the Supreme Court failed. Pacifists, and feminists went to prison, and so, especially, did socialists. Ninety-six of the convicted were members of the Industrial Workers of the World (IWW), including its leader, Bill Haywood, sentenced to twenty years in prison. Eugene Debs was sentenced to a ten-year term for delivering a speech in which he'd told his listeners that they were "fit for something better than slavery and cannon fodder."[90]

Under this regime, W. E. B. Du Bois, the seemingly uncompromising leader and cofounder of the NAACP, was brought to heel. In 1915, in an *Atlantic* essay called "The African Roots of War," Du Bois had located the origins of the conflict in European powers' colonial rivalries in Africa, indicting the global order itself. "If we want real peace," Du Bois wrote, "we must extend the democratic ideal to the yellow, brown, and black peoples." But after the United States entered the war, Creel called thirty-one black editors and publishers to a conference in Washington and warned them about "Negro subversion." Du Bois wrote a resolution more or less pledging not to complain about race relations for the duration, promising that the African American was "not disposed to catalogue, in this tremendous crisis, all his complaints and disabilities." He then wrote the first of many editorials for *The Crisis*, making good on this promise. "Let us, while this war lasts, forget our special grievances and close our ranks shoulder to shoulder with our white fellow citizens and the allied nations that are fighting for democracy," he wrote, in words that might as well have been written by Creel himself. Du Bois asked black men who could not vote in the United States to give their lives to make the world "safe for democracy" and asked black people to hold off on fighting against lynchings, whose numbers kept rising.[91]

"Black bodies swinging in the southern breeze," Billie Holiday would later sing, in a wrenching eulogy. "Strange fruit hanging from the poplar trees."[92]

WALTER LIPPMANN, WRITING for the *New Republic*, had argued for the United States to enter the war. Once it did, he signed up and was recruited to a secret intelligence organization called the Inquiry, whose objective was to imagine the terms of the peace by redrawing the map of Europe. The Inquiry, needing a peerless stock of maps, took over the New York offices of the American Geographical Society. In that library, Lippmann, twenty-eight, drafted a report called "The War Aims and Peace Terms It Suggests." Revised by Wilson, Lippmann's report became Wilson's Fourteen Points, which the president submitted to a joint session of Congress on January 8, 1918, calling for a liberal peace that included free trade, freedom of the seas, arms reduction, the self-determination of colonized peoples, and a League of Nations.[93]

But the war had to be won before Wilson could begin to negotiate for that peace. And it had to be paid for. To that end, Wilson signed a tax bill, raising taxes on incomes, doubling a tax on corporate earnings, eliminating an exemption for dividend income, and introducing an estate tax and a tax on excess profits. Rates for the wealthiest Americans rose from 2 percent to 77, but most people paid no tax at all (80 percent of the revenue was drawn from the income of the wealthiest 1 percent of American families). Then, when taxes raised on income and business failed to cover the price of war, the federal government began selling war bonds. Twenty-two million Americans heeded the call to buy Liberty and Victory Bonds, leading to one unanticipated effect of the war: it introduced ordinary Americans to the experience of buying securities. The rhetoric of the war loan program advanced the idea of citizenship as a form of investment. One bulletin promised, "A financial interest in the Government, large or small though it may be, helps to make better citizens."[94]

Wars, as ever, expanded the powers of the state. It rearranged the relationship between the federal government and business, establishing new forms of cooperation, oversight, and regulation that amounted to erecting a welfare state for business owners. The National War Labor Board was charged with averting strikes so as not to impede munitions production, while the War Industries Board oversaw war-related manufacturing. The federal government managed the American economy with efficiency as its watchword. "Industrial history proves that reasonable hours, fair working conditions, and a proper wage scale are essential to high production," one army order advised. "During the war, every attempt should be made to conserve in every way all our achievements in the way of social betterment."[95]

The government asserted new forms of authority over the bodies of citizens, too. A "social purity" movement campaigned against the spread of venereal disease, which became the subject of military ordinances. "You wouldn't use another fellow's toothbrush," one army film pointed out. "Why use his whore?" Yet another moral campaign, Prohibition, long a female crusade, also became part of the wartime expansion of the powers of the state. It was approved by Congress in December 1917 as a war measure. "No drunken man was ever efficient in civil or military life," said Tennessee senator Kenneth McKellar. Outside of Congress, Americans were dubious. "A man would be better off without booze but the same is true of pie," was the position taken by Clarence Darrow.[96]

Lippmann, meanwhile, went to Europe to begin to work toward Wilson's planned peace. Appointed to the London office of an Inter-Allied Board for propaganda, Lippmann directed writings not at Americans but at Germans and Austrians. Airplanes and unmanned balloons sent behind enemy lines dropped millions of copies of his leaflets. Like everything he wrote, they were as sticky as flypaper. One he wrote as if he were a German prisoner of war: "Do not worry about me. I am out of the war. I am well fed. The American army gives its prisoners the same rations it gives its own soldiers: beef, white bread, potatoes, prunes, coffee, milk, butter." Copies were found in the rucksacks of a great many deserting German soldiers.[97] Lippmann got to wondering: were minds so easily led?

As the war drew to a close, the reckoning began. American losses were almost trivial compared to the staggering losses in European nations. Against America's 116,000 casualties, France lost 1.6 million lives, Britain 800,000, and Germany 1.8 million. Cities across Europe lay in ashes; America was untouched. Europe, composed of seventeen countries before the war, had splintered into twenty-six, all of them deeply in debt, and chiefly to Americans. Before the war, Americans owed $3.7 billion to foreigners; after the war, foreigners owed $12.6 billion to Americans. Even the terrifying influenza epidemic of 1918, which took 21 million lives worldwide, claimed the lives of only 675,000 Americans. The war left European economies in ruins, America's thriving. In the United States, steel production rose by a quarter between 1913 and 1920; everywhere else, it fell by a third.[98]

The Armistice came on November 11, 1918, when Germany agreed to terms of surrender tied to Wilson's Fourteen Points, which the Allies had not themselves wholeheartedly endorsed. In an extraordinary departure from convention, Wilson decided to head the United States' 1,300-person delegation to the Paris Peace Conference, in January 1919. This fell within his view of the scope of the presidency; not everyone agreed. Many Americans objected to an American president leaving American soil. And whose interests was he meant to represent? "Mr. Wilson has no authority whatever to speak for the American people at this time," said Theodore Roosevelt.[99] Article II, Section 2, of the Constitution stipulates that a president may negotiate a treaty, but ratification requires a two-thirds vote in the Senate. Notably—fatally—Wilson did not bring along with him to the conference even a single Republican senator.

Wilson was at first met with outpourings of affection and hope. Crowds lined the streets of Paris to greet him as "the God of Peace." This welcome did not do much to diminish his sense of mission. Lippmann reported, "The hotels were choked with delegations representing, and pretending to represent, and hoping to represent, every group of people in the world." Wilson was especially eagerly received by delegates from stateless and colonized societies—Egyptians, Indians, Chinese, Koreans, Arabs, Jews, Armenians, Kurds. A young Ho Chi Minh, the future leader of North Vietnam, then living in Paris, presented world leaders at Versailles with a petition titled "The Demands of the Vietnamese People": "All subject peoples are filled with hope by the prospect that an era of right and justice is opening to them." He tried to meet Wilson, with no success. But Wilson left a lasting legacy: his rhetoric of self-determination contributed to a wave of popular protests in the Middle East and Asia, including a revolution in Egypt in 1919; made the nation-state the goal of stateless societies; and lies behind the emergence and force of anticolonial nationalism.[100]

W. E. B. Du Bois made the journey to Paris four days after Wilson set sail, on a boat for members of the press. He was officially traveling on behalf of the NAACP, and as a scholar, aiming to gather material for a history of the war, but he was also there to attend a Pan-African Congress, which was held over three days at the Grand-Hotel, on the Boulevard des Capucines. And he may well have gone to Paris in an attempt to repair his reputation, gravely damaged by his having urged fellow black Americans to forget their grievances and make every sacrifice for the war. Thirty black men were lynched in 1917, twice as many the next year, and in 1919, seventy-six, including ten veterans, some still wearing their uniforms, having fought, some people thought, the wrong war.[101]

**IN FRANCE, WILSON** got much of what he wanted, but he did not get the peace he wanted, or the peace the world needed. Instead, the president fell ill in Paris, likely with the first in a series of strokes. Also, as the negotiations wore on, his presence was much resented.[102] "Nearly every experienced critic seems to be of opinion that he should have remained in America," H. G. Wells remarked. More bitterly resented was Wilson's wife, Edith, who appeared, to a devastated Europe, to be visiting in the role of tourist. "This may seem a trivial matter to note in a History of Mankind," Wells allowed, "but it was such small human things as this that threw a miasma of futility over the Peace Conference of 1919."[103]

The treaty makers, chiefly the United States, Britain, France, and Italy, redrew the map of Europe rather differently than it had been redrawn by Walter Lippmann, in the offices of the American Geographical Society. They balkanized Europe by establishing new states, including Czechoslovakia, Yugoslavia, Poland, and Finland. And they punished Germany. The treaty shackled German industry. It deprived Germany of control over its own affairs. It demanded from Germany $33 billion in reparations. "Looked at from above, below, and every side I can't see anything in this treaty but endless trouble for Europe," Lippmann wrote. The *New Republic*, concluding that "the League is not powerful enough to redeem the treaty," came out against it, a particularly difficult decision for Lippmann, who wrote the editorials condemning it. The magazine also serialized the publication of a shattering polemic called *The Economic Consequences of the Peace*, by a young British economist named John Maynard Keynes. Keynes called Wilson a fool, a "blind and deaf Don Quixote"[104] and pointed out that the peace treaty merely continued the deprivations of wartime, warning that it would bring misery to Europe—"the rapid depression of the standard of life of the European populations to a point which will mean actual starvation."

Wilson believed that any shortcomings of the terms of the peace could be addressed by the establishment of the League of Nations, since any problem created by the treaty, he reasoned, could be solved by the League. Only the League, he thought, could make peace last. Two days after returning to the United States, he delivered the Treaty of Versailles to the Senate and explained its provisions, including for the League of Nations, asking, "Dare we reject it and break the heart of the world?"[105]

In the Senate, what little support Wilson enjoyed came from fellow Democrats; Republicans proved implacable. The Republican chairman of the Senate Foreign Relations Committee, Henry Cabot Lodge, had the 264-page treaty printed, announced that he would convene hearings on the subject, and then all but tabled the matter, stonewalling for two weeks while he had every word read aloud.[106]

Wilson, still ailing, decided to canvass the nation and left Washington on September 3, 1919, for a seventeen-state train tour. "I promised our soldiers, when I asked them to take up arms, that it was a war to end wars," he told his wife. "If I do not do all in my power to put the Treaty into effect, I will be a slacker and never able to look those boys in the eye." In Nevada, his face began to twitch; in Utah, he sweated through his suit; by Wyoming he was incoherent. Finally, in Colorado, on October 2, 1919, he stumbled while mounting the stage. "I seem to have gone to pieces," he said. He lost the use of his left side. For five months, he was hidden in the West Wing of the White House, unseen, even by his cabinet.

Edith Wilson banned the public from the grounds. Even members of the Senate did not know the state of Wilson's condition. When the Senate sought compromise and the president proved unresponsive, the Senate could only conclude that he was uncompromising.[107] In March of 1920, the Senate rejected the Treaty of Versailles—and the League of Nations—by seven votes. The chance for a lasting peace came and, silently, went.

## III.

IN 1922, when Walter Lippmann turned thirty-two, he wrote a book called *Public Opinion*, in which he concluded that in a modern democracy the masses, asked to make decisions about matters far removed from their direct knowledge, had been asked to do too much. "Decisions in a modern state tend to be made by the interaction, not of Congress and the executive, but of public opinion and the executive," he'd once observed.[108] Mass democracy can't work, Lippmann argued, because the new tools of mass persuasion—especially mass advertising—meant that a tiny minority could very easily persuade the majority to believe whatever it wished them to believe.

The best hope for mass democracy might have seemed to be the scrupulously and unfailingly honest reporting of news, but this, Lippmann thought, was doomed to fall short, because of the gap between facts and truth. Reporters chronicle events, offering facts, but "they cannot govern society by episodes, incidents, and eruptions," he said.[109] To govern, the people need truth, sense out of the whole, but people can't read enough in the morning paper or hear enough on the evening news to turn facts into truth when they're driven like dray horses all day.

The solution Lippmann proposed to this problem was absurd, forged in the mind of a man who greeted the world with eyebrows arched. He suggested that the government open ten Bureaus of Intelligence, one for each department represented in the cabinet, where expert intellectuals, appointed for life ("with sabbatical years set aside for advanced study and training"), would put together all the facts and explain, to the masses, the truth.[110] He eventually came around to seeing how silly that was, but what actually happened was a lot worse: by the end of the decade, managing public opinion would become a business, in the form of "public relations."

Before then, women would gain the right to vote, the size of the electorate would double, and the problem would worsen. The Nineteenth Amendment, ratified in August 1920, was the last constitutional act of the Progressive Era. It proved a checkered victory. Women achieved the right to vote only after the style of party politics had changed, from the public, popular politics of parades and marches (and high voter turnout) to the private, domesticated politics of mass advertising (and lower voter turnout). As one feminist pointed out as early as 1926, "It is a misfortune for the woman's movement that it has succeeded in securing political rights for women at the very period when political rights are worth less than they have been at any time since the eighteenth century."[111]

Attaining the right to vote also divided the women's movement between those who wanted to pursue equal rights and those who, realizing that equal rights would render obsolete an entire body of protective labor legislation, did not. So-called equalizers formed the Women's League for Equal Opportunity and the Equal Rights Association; sought passage of the Equal Rights Amendment, first introduced into Congress in 1923; and viewed protectionism with cynicism and suspicion: "Labor men wanted protective laws for women only so that they could steal women's jobs under cover of chivalry," one equalizer would write in 1929. Protectionists, meanwhile, formed the League of Women Voters.[112] A half century later, as the Equal Rights Amendment at last neared ratification, this same divide, among women, would defeat it.

In the 1920 presidential election, the Republican Warren G. Harding easily triumphed over the Democrat, Ohio governor and Progressive reformer James Cox, and his relatively unknown running mate, the assistant secretary of the navy, Franklin Delano Roosevelt, chosen, in the main, for his famous last name. Wilsonian idealism and internationalism was over, and so was an era of reform. Harding rode to the White House on a rising tide of conservativism, a reaction against Progressive reforms that conservatives believed to be a betrayal of the nation's founding principles, and especially of the Constitution. "I must utter my belief in the divine inspiration of the founding fathers," Harding said in his inaugural address. He ordered the Librarian of Congress to take the original Constitution—the signed parchment—out of storage and erect for it a national shrine. He appointed as solicitor general James Montgomery Beck—Mr. Constitution—a former corporate lawyer who'd written a series of immensely popular books explaining the Constitution.[113]

"The Constitution is neither, on the one hand, a Gibraltar rock, which wholly resists the ceaseless washing of time or circumstance, nor is it, on the other hand, a sandy beach, which is slowly destroyed by the erosion of the waves," Beck wrote. "It is rather to be likened to a floating dock, which, while firmly attached to its moorings, and not therefore at the caprice of the waves, yet rises and falls with the tide of time and circumstance." Law professor Thomas Reed Powell, assessing Beck's work in a contemptuous review in the New Republic, remarked that Beck's Constitution moves neither forward nor backward: it "jiggles up and down," like Jell-O. Powell proposed to write a volume of "Becksniffian Songs of Innocence," to include this verse: "The Constitution is a dock, / That's moored, yet tosses to and fro. / It's not a beach; it's not a rock. / And that is why we love it so."[114] The feud between Beck and Powell was no petty squabble but instead suggested a deep and widening chasm. The argument over the nature of the Constitution had much in common with the argument between Protestants who believed the Bible to be literally true and those who did not. Beck was a constitutional fundamentalist, Powell a believer in evolution.

Harding's agenda of undoing Progressive reforms, outlined at his inauguration, brought together Solicitor General Beck's understanding of the Constitution with Frederick Winslow Taylor's gospel of efficiency. Taylorism had by now been applied to office work, to the very kind of work done by the government itself. Office workers sat at the new Modern Efficiency Desk, a metal slab topping file drawers, usually two on each side. They punched cards into time clocks and used typewriters and adding machines, manufactured by the Computing-Tabulating-Recording Company, founded in 1911 through a consolidation of companies that included Herman Hollerith's Tabulating Machine Company. A 1923 play called *The Adding Machine* lampooned the monotony of assembly-line office work and prefigured fears about machine automation. Its main character, "Mr. Zero," writes down numbers all day long, "upon a square sheet of ruled paper."[115] When his boss tells him that he will be replaced by an adding machine, he murders him. What any office worker might know how to do got smaller and smaller, like the skills of factory workers, while the businesses people worked for got bigger and bigger, including, by 1924, IBM. "We must study, through reading, listening, discussing, observing and thinking," said the company's founder, Thomas Watson. Its motto was THINK, which was what employees were asked to do, but observers worried, and more as the years passed, that thinking was becoming the work of machines.[116]

Harding wanted to Taylorize the federal government. "I speak for administrative efficiency," Harding said, in one of the worst inaugural addresses ever delivered, "for lightened tax burdens, for sound commercial practices, for adequate credit facilities, for sympathetic concern for all agricultural problems, for the omission of unnecessary interference of Government with business, for an end to Government's experiment in business, and for more efficient business in Government administration."[117]

With efficiency as his watchword, Harding assembled an extraordinary cohort of conservative businessmen in his cabinet who headed the federal government during some of the most prosperous years in American history. Between 1922 and 1928, industrial production rose by 70 percent, gross national product by almost 40 percent, per capita income by 30 percent, and real wages by 22 percent. The nation was electrified in the 1920s, too, as a new power grid reached business and residences alike: in

1916, only 16 percent of Americans lived in homes with electricity, but by 1927, that percentage had risen to 63.[118]

As secretary of Treasury, Harding appointed Andrew W. Mellon, an industrialist and philanthropist and the fourth wealthiest man in America after John D. Rockefeller Jr., Henry Ford, and Edsel Ford. Mellon, who would hold the office under three Republican presidents, Harding, Coolidge, and Hoover, aimed to bring efficiency to taxation. As Mellon argued in *Taxation: The People's Business* (1924), high taxes kill "the spirit of business adventure." Cutting taxes, Mellon insisted, would lower the cost of housing, reduce prices, raise the standard of living, create jobs, and "advance general prosperity." Mellon's bid for public support for his tax policy was greatly aided by the American Taxpayers' League, formerly known as the American Bankers' League—and bankrolled, in part, by members of the Mellon family—which sponsored, provided literature to, and paid the expenses of state tax clubs, whose members then testified before Congress, urging tax cuts. "Taxes are what we pay for civilized society," Oliver Wendell Holmes said in 1927— words later engraved on the front of the IRS Building in Washington—but Americans by no means uniformly agreed. During Mellon's tenure, Congress abolished the excess profits tax, cut the estate tax, exempted capital gains from income, and capped the top tax rate.[119]

As secretary of commerce, Harding appointed Herbert Hoover. Born into austere poverty in the Quaker town of West Branch, Iowa, and orphaned at the age of nine, Hoover had gone on to study geology at Stanford. As a mining engineer and organizational genius, he'd made a fortune in Australia and China and become a staggeringly successful international businessman, a millionaire ten times over by the time he retired from business at the age of thirty-seven to devote himself to public service and philanthropy. He'd lived most of his life outside the United States. Both during and after the war, he'd headed humanitarian relief efforts in Europe, helping to save tens of millions of lives. (When Wilson won the Nobel Peace Prize, not a few Europeans thought Hoover more deserving.) When he returned to the United States, he'd become a dazzlingly popular guest at Lippmann's House of Truth. "Many felt, as I did," Lippmann said, "that they had never met a more interesting man." In 1920, both parties had urged him to run for president, but, though he dipped a toe in the waters of the Republican primaries, he'd quietly lost the nomination to Harding.[120]

Hoover was an efficiency expert, best known for an influential 400-page report called *Waste in Industry*. So great was his fame that nearly anything involving the elimination of waste, including vacuum cleaning, took his name. Although opposed to big government, Hoover understood his role as secretary of commerce as giving him control over the entire American economy. From his office on the top floor of a building on the corner of Nineteenth Street and Pennsylvania Avenue, he brought the department's many bureaus into rooms below him. With daunting efficiency, he expanded Commerce—making himself "Under-Secretary of all other departments"—to realize his plan of a "new era." What Hoover designed was an associative state, bringing in business and labor leaders, farmers and fishermen, to cooperative meetings to order the government's priorities. During Hoover's tenure, the department's budget grew to almost six times its previous size, from $860,000 to $5 million. "Never before, here or anywhere else, has a government been so completely fused with business," the *Wall Street Journal* reported.[121]

During the 1920s, Americans' faith in progress turned into a faith in prosperity, fueled by consumption. "A change has come over our democracy," a journalist reported. "It is called consumptionism. The American citizen's first importance to his country is now no longer that of citizen but that of consumer."[122] By any measure, the American economy was getting bigger and bigger. The United States was the world's biggest lender, and its economy was the largest in the world; by 1929, it produced 42 percent of the world's output (Great Britain, France, and Germany together produced 28 percent).[123] Steel production and railroad income broke all records, graphs of growth reaching higher and higher, like the skyscrapers towering over New York's Fifth Avenue, Chicago's Michigan Avenue, and San Francisco's California Street.

And yet the nation turned inward. Before the war, most of the industrial world followed a policy of open borders for both goods and people. People left Europe for other parts of the world, especially the United States, while Europeans invested capital in building projects in their colonies. The devastation of the war and the brutal terms of the peace, especially for Germany, meant an end to these arrangements.[124] After the war, the United States became the center of global trade, and yet soon began closing its borders to both people and goods. In 1921 and 1922, Harding and a Republican Congress raised taxes on imports; and in 1921 and 1924, they placed restrictions on immigration. European countries, devastated by the war, were unable to send excess workers across the Atlantic and, unable to sell their manufactured goods in the United States, were left unable to repay to American lenders the money they owed them. In retaliation, European countries raised tariffs, too, depriving American farmers and manufacturers of a market.[125] And so began a vicious economic spiral. "It's a marvel, looking back on it now," Lippmann would later write ruefully, "that we could ever have so completely thought that a boom under such treacherous conditions was permanent."[126]

Harding's administration labeled its economic program a "return to normalcy." Its political program was a campaign against immigration, its cultural program an aesthetic movement known as the Colonial Revival. Both looked inward, and backward, inventing and celebrating an American heritage, a fantasy world of a past that never happened. Philanthropic industrialists fortified their vision of the nation's past, Henry Ford building an American history museum, John Rockefeller restoring Colonial Williamsburg, history as a life-sized dollhouse.[127] R. T. H. Halsey, who had a seat on the New York Stock Exchange, had led the effort to defend the banks against Theodore Roosevelt's attack on the "money trust." Relinquishing his seat on the exchange, he helped curate a new American Wing at the Metropolitan Museum of Art. Unveiled in 1924, it displayed American fine and decorative arts from before 1825. "Much of the America of today has lost sight of its traditions," Halsey warned. "Many of our people are not cognizant of our traditions and the principles for which our fathers struggled and died." For Halsey, the contemplation of the past was meant to provide a warning about the present: "The tremendous changes in the character of our nation and the influx of foreign ideas utterly at variance with those held by the men who gave us the Republic threaten, and unless checked, may shake, the foundations of our Republic."[128]

The year the American Wing opened, Congress passed the Immigration Act. It had two parts: an Asian Exclusion Act, extending the 1882 Chinese Exclusion Act, all but banned immigrants from anywhere in Asia, and a National Origins Act, which restricted the annual number of

*A 1921 cartoon depicts Uncle Sam deploying a funnel to stanch the flow of immigrants from Europe.*

THE ONLY WAY TO HANDLE IT.

European immigrants to 150,000 and established a quota by which the number of new arrivals was made proportional to their representation in the existing population. The act instantiated the eugenicist logic of Madison Grant's *Passing of the Great Race*. The purpose of the quota system was to end immigration from Asia and to curb the admission of southern and eastern Europeans, deemed less worthy than immigrants from other parts of Europe. Said Indiana Republican Fred S. Purnell, "There is little or no similarity between the clear-thinking, self-governing stocks that sired the American people and this stream of irresponsible and broken wreckage that is pouring into the lifeblood of America the social and political diseases of the Old World." New York Republican Nathan D. Perlman, a Jewish lawmaker and an opponent of immigration restriction, read into the *Congressional Record* the names of Americans, of all ethnicities, who'd been awarded the Distinguished Service Cross during the war. He argued in vain.[129]

The immigration restriction regime begun in 1924 hardened racial lines, institutionalized new forms of race-based discrimination, codified the fiction of a "white race," and introduced a new legal category into American life: the "illegal alien." Europeans, deemed "white," classified into their national origins, and ranked according to their desirability, could immigrate in limited numbers; entering the United States as legal aliens, they could become naturalized citizens. Chinese, Japanese, Indians, and other Asians, deemed nonwhite, could not immigrate into the United States legally, were deemed unassimilable, and were excluded from citizenship on racial grounds. More profoundly, the law categorized Europeans as belonging to nations—they were sorted by "national origin"—but categorized non-Europeans as belonging to "races"—they were sorted into five "colored races" (black, mulatto, Chinese, Japanese, and Indian).

Notably, the 1924 Immigration Act did not restrict immigration from Mexico, even though it, too, had been on the rise. Between 1890 and 1920, some 1.5 million Mexicans crossed into the United States, fleeing the dictator José de la Cruz Porfirio Díaz, especially after the revolt against him in 1910. Mexican Americans who had lived in the American Southwest for decades tended to retain their language and culture, and to live in urban barrios; they often resented these newer arrivals, *los recién llegados*. Newer Mexican immigrants were most often employed picking produce on newly irrigated agricultural tracts. In 1890, irrigated land in California, Nevada, Utah, and Arizona totaled about 1.5 million acres, but by 1902, there were 2 million irrigated acres in California alone. After the Chinese Exclusion Act of 1882, large growers had turned to Japanese laborers, but a so-called gentleman's agreement between Japan and the United States ended their migration in 1908, after which growers began sending employment agents over the border and into Mexico to recruit workers. In an era when the regime of scientific management maligned Hungarians, Italians, and Jews as near-animals who needed to be ruled not by the lash but by the stopwatch, business owners and policymakers tended to describe Mexican immigrants—desperately poor political refugees—as ideal workers. In 1908, U.S. government economist Victor S. Clark claimed that Mexican immigrants were "docile, patient, usually orderly in camp, fairly intelligent under competent supervision, obedient and cheap," and, in 1911, a U.S. congressional panel reported that while Mexicans "are not easily assimilated, this is not of very great importance as long as most of them return to their native land after a short time."[130]

But of course Mexicans who crossed the border in search of work did not always return to Mexico. During the debate over immigration restriction, Indiana congressman Albert H. Vestal asked, "What is the use of closing the front door to keep out undesirables from Europe when you permit Mexicans to come in here by the back door by the thousands and thousands?" Edward Taylor, a congressman from Colorado, answered that no one but Mexican immigrants would do the work they were hired to do: "The American laboring people will not get down on their hands and knees in the dirt and pull weeds and thin these beets, and break their backs doing that kind of work. In fact, there are very few people who can stand that kind of work. No matter how much they are paid, they cannot and will not do it." This did not quiet nativists, the American Eugenics Society warning: "Our great Southwest is rapidly creating for itself a new racial problem, as our old South did when it imported slave labor from Africa. The Mexican birth rate is high, and every Mexican child born on American soil is an American citizen, who, on attaining his or her majority, will have a vote. This is not a question of pocketbook or of the 'need of labor' or of economics. It is a question of the character of future races. It is eugenics, not economics." Congress, pressured by eugenicists and southern and western agriculturalists, in the end exempted Mexicans from the new immigration restriction regime, while also requiring not only passports but also visas for anyone entering the United States. Thus it erected hurdles that allowed Mexicans to cross the border to work temporarily but denied access to citizenship. Over time, Mexicans—assigned to a new category, "Mexican," in the federal census—would become most closely tied to the new legal, racialized category of "illegal alien." Before 1919, Mexicans who entered the United States at the border did not need to apply for entry. After the formation of the U.S. Border Patrol in 1924, soldiers armed points of entry, and deportation of "illegal aliens" became U.S. government policy.[131]

In effect, the new regime of immigration restriction extended the black-and-white racial ideology of Jim Crow to new European immigrants (by classing them as white, and eligible for citizenship) and to Asians and Mexicans (by classing them as nonwhite, and ineligible). It drew support from a second Ku Klux Klan that had emerged in 1915; by the 1920s, its five million members attacked Jews and Catholics as vehemently as they attacked blacks; the Klan had provided vocal support of immigration restriction. At the Democratic National Convention in New York in 1924, thousands of members of the KKK marched in the streets of the city, and the party was so disarrayed and disorganized—and so divided over matters relating to race—that the convention took a record-breaking 103 ballots to nominate the unmemorable John W. Davis.[132]

Driven by a combustible mix of nativism and eugenics, political scientist Lothrop Stoddard rewrote American history as a history of white people. "The problem of the Twentieth Century is the problem of the color-line," Du Bois had written in 1903.[133] Black intellectuals, especially the writers and artists of the Harlem Renaissance, countered the nostalgia of Colonial Revival with a new, critical attention to the nation's black past. It's time to "settle down to a realistic facing of facts," Alain Locke wrote in *The New Negro* (1925), a collection that included an essay called "The Negro Digs Up His Past."[134] Stoddard answered with a book called *The Rising Tide of Color Against the White World-Supremacy*, which blamed discontent and malaise in Europe on the darker races. Stumping for the Immigration Act, he argued that this same social problem had threatened to unravel the United States. By the end of the decade, he celebrated the triumph of immigration restriction. "We know that our America is a White America," Stoddard said, during a debate with W. E. B. Du Bois on a stage in Chicago. "And the overwhelming weight of both historical and scientific evidence shows that only so long as the American people remain white will its institutions, ideals and culture continue to fit the temperament of its inhabitants—and hence continue to endure."

"Your country?" Du Bois asked Stoddard. "How came it yours?" And then he pressed him: "Would America have been America without her Negro people?"[135]

Stoddard had no real answer. In the 1930s and into the 1940s, he applauded Hitler. He died disgraced and forgotten. But the debate he had with Du Bois over the nation's origins never ended.

## IV.

WE HOLD THESE TRUTHS *to be self-evident.* By 1926, a century and a half after the nation's birth, every word of its founding statement had been questioned. Who are we? What is true? What counts as evidence?

American politics had become riven by disputes over basic matters of fact. At the heart of those disputes lay rival interpretations of the Constitution, which rested on different understandings of its nature, an extension of the debate over the literal truth of the Bible. But Americans also expressed their political differences in debates over science and history, debates that were shaped by the new business of public relations.

Ivy Lee, one of the field's earliest practitioners, called it propaganda, which he defined as "the effort to propagate ideas." Lee, born in Georgia in 1877, the son of a Methodist minister, worked as a newspaper reporter before taking on assignments representing the interests of railroad corporations, attempting to get them better press. Among his earliest clients were John D. Rockefeller, who was attempting to recover from the damage to his reputation by Ida Tarbell's muckraking into Standard Oil, and Bethlehem Steel, suffering from the taint of Taylor-induced strikes. Carl Sandburg called Lee a "paid liar"; Upton Sinclair named him "Poison Ivy." In a speech to journalism teachers in the 1920s, Lee argued that facts don't exist or, at least, they can't be reported: "The effort to state an absolute fact is simply an attempt to achieve what is humanly impossible; all I can do is to give you *my interpretation of the facts.*"[136]

Journalists, especially reporters who'd served in the war, tended to disagree. In 1923, when two young army veterans, Henry Luce and Briton Hadden, decided to found a magazine, they wanted to call it *Facts.* In the end, they decided to call it *Time*, with the idea that, in the age of efficiency, it would save readers time. *Time* was meant to offer busy readers—and especially businessmen—a week's worth of news that could be read in an hour. Each issue was to contain 100 articles, none over 400 words long, full of nothing but the facts, put together, at first, by cutting sentences out of seven days' worth of newspapers and pasting them onto pages. Using a Taylor system of task management, Luce and Hadden sorted the news into categories, something that hadn't been done before. Despite its speed, brevity, and simplicity, *Time* claimed to be free from error, a record of events "accurately chronicled," which wasn't the same thing as making a claim for objectivity. "Show me a man who thinks he's objective, and I'll show you a man who's deceiving himself," Luce once said.[137] Objectivity was impossible; subjectivity led to the introduction of errors. The best that could be done would be to check every article for errors of fact. *Time* established the practice of fact-checking, and an elaborate method of checking, fact by fact, as if knowledge could be reduced to units, like parts on an assembly line.

To do this work, they hired young women just out of college. "Charged with verifying every word, they put a dot over each one to signify that they have," a visiting reporter observed. The author of an early manual for *Time*'s "checkers" advised them:

Checking is . . . sometimes regarded as a dull and tedious occupation, but such a conception of this position is extremely erroneous. Any bright girl who readily applies herself to the handling of the checking problem can have a very pleasant time with it and fill the week with happy moments and memorable occasions. The most important point to remember in checking is that the writer is your natural enemy. He is trying to see how much he can get away with. Remember that when people write letters about mistakes, it is you who will be screeched at. So protect yourself.

When readers wrote complaining of errors, *Time* published the letters, and printed corrections. Its editors kept a black book, in which every error was entered, with its correction.[138]

This practice reached a fervid intensity at the nearby offices of *Time*'s chief rival, *The New Yorker,* a magazine established in opposition to everything *Time* stood for—except for its obsession with facts. In the fall of 1924, Harold Ross, a former city newspaper reporter, and, like Luce and Hadden, a veteran of the First World War, wrote a prospectus for *The New Yorker*, a magazine that was not meant to save anyone even a moment of time. But, like Luce and Hadden, Ross disavowed error, fraud, and nonsense, especially of the PR kind. Ross promised, "It will hate bunk." "A SPECIAL EFFORT SHOULD BE MADE TO AVOID MISTAKES IN *THE NEW YORKER*," Ross announced, after they committed a doozy. One writer said Ross "clung to facts" the way "a drowning man clings to a spar." Later, he sent a memo to one of his editors: "Add Fact Checking to your list of chores."[139]

But if journalists were finding new devices to recommit themselves to accuracy in reporting, businesses were using the tools of public relations to make sure the press heard their particular side of every story. No man played a greater role in this transformation than Edward Bernays, a nephew of Sigmund Freud who used Freud's theory of the unconscious to help businesses sell their products to American consumers. Born in

Vienna, Bernays had grown up in New York. When the war started, he worked for George Creel's office of war propaganda and traveled with Wilson to the Paris peace talks, where, he liked to say, his services had been invaluable. Returning to civilian life, he began a career in public relations, which he described as "applied social science" but which *The Nation* called "The Higher Hokum." In 1924, Bernays met with Calvin Coolidge, who'd ascended to the presidency in 1923, after Harding's sudden death. Bernays decided Coolidge's image as a sturdy, crusty Vermonter would be improved by glamour, and so arranged to have Hollywood film stars visit the White House.[140]

"Good propaganda is an invisible government which sways the habits and actions of most of the people of the United States," Bernays explained. "Rightly employed, it is a quick and effective means of producing changes of social usefulness." Propaganda, used to run political campaigns, would make democracies run more efficiently: "Honest propaganda, efficiently applied, will save millions in the next political campaign," he predicted.[141]

In his 1928 book, *Propaganda,* Bernays explained that he'd also been influenced by Walter Lippmann's *Public Opinion*, having read Lippmann's concern for a gullible public as an opportunity for a canny publicist. "The conscious and intelligent manipulation of the organized habits and opinions of the masses is an important element in democratic society," Bernays insisted. For Bernays, propaganda was to the masses what the unconscious was to the mind, a people's "invisible governors."[142]

The tragedy that this spelled for the mass democracy of the United States played before the public on a stage in the small town of Dayton, Tennessee, over five long days in the summer of 1925, at the trial of a high school biology teacher named John Scopes, who was charged with the crime of teaching the theory of evolution. William Jennings Bryan, sixty-five, his broad head grown bald, led the prosecution, having captained the campaign to ban the teaching of evolution in the nation's public schools. Not all fundamentalists rejected evolution, believing, as R. A. Torrey, the editor of *The Fundamentals*, that a Christian could "believe thoroughly in the absolute infallibility of the Bible and still be an evolutionist of a certain type."[143] But Bryan's own views, like those of many fundamentalists, had hardened on the matter after the war, whose horrors so many tried but could not fathom, or reconcile with a loving God.

"Evolution is not truth," Bryan pointed out. "It is merely a hypothesis—

Shall Christianity Remain Christian?, *a pamphlet published in 1922, pictured a journey from doubt to atheism as an inevitable descent.*

it is millions of guesses strung together." But what he especially decried was its application to human societies. In 1921, in an essay called "The Menace of Darwinism," he had explained his support for a raft of Progressive reforms whose intention was to check the very idea that only the fittest should survive: "Pure-food laws have become necessary to keep manufacturers from poisoning their customers; child-labor laws have become necessary to keep employers from dwarfing the bodies, minds, and souls of children; anti-trust laws have become necessary to keep overgrown corporations from strangling smaller corporations and we are still in a death grapple with profiteers and gamblers in farm products." Bryan saw, in a secular modernity, the end of sympathy, compassion, and charity. He decried the heartlessness of science: "Men who would not cross the street to save a soul have traveled across the world in search of skeletons," he said in a 1923 speech to the West Virginia legislature. "The great need of the world today is to get back to God," he wrote. With Bryan, fundamentalism, which had begun as a theological dispute about facts and truth, became a populist movement about faith.[144]

In 1925, after Tennessee became the first state to ban the teaching of evolution, the American Civil Liberties Union convinced Scopes to test the law. The ACLU had been founded in 1917 to defend conscientious objectors, work that grew still more urgent during the Red Scare, the anti-

Bolshevik hysteria that had gripped the United States in the last years of the war. "The rights of both individuals and minorities are being grossly violated throughout the country," its founder wrote. It had since extended into peacetime its wartime mission of protecting Americans from assaults on civil liberties. Its interest in the Tennessee law, like Scopes's own, had nothing to do with religion and everything to do with free speech. (Scopes was himself a churchgoer and an admirer of Bryan, who had been the speaker at his high school graduation in Illinois in 1919.) The ACLU expected and planned for Scopes to be found guilty, after which the law could be appealed to a higher court.

That plan changed when Bryan was persuaded to join the prosecution and named as a counsel to the Tennessee attorney general. Bryan's involvement led Clarence Darrow to pledge to defend Scopes. Darrow was big and ornery, broad-shouldered and craggy, and liked to pretend he was a cracker-barrel philosopher, with his baggy pants and suspenders and string tie. "Everything about Darrow suggests a cynic," one reporter said. "Everything but one thing, and that is—an entire lack of real cynicism." In his long and justly famous career as the nation's best-known trial lawyer, he played a role in some two thousand trials; in more than a third of those cases, he was paid nothing. But the Scopes trial was the only trial in which he volunteered his services.[145]

Darrow and Bryan had both grown up on farms, become country lawyers, and fought for underdogs, and for the poor, their whole lives. They'd fought the same fight, Bryan as the "Great Commoner," Darrow as the "attorney for the damned." They spoke the same language. In 1903, when Darrow represented the United Mine Workers in Pennsylvania in arbitration, he told the court, "Five hundred dollars a year is a big price for taking your life and your limbs in your hand and going down into the earth to dig up coal to make somebody else rich."[146] Bryan could have said those words.

But Darrow knew that, for all that Bryan's campaign against the teaching of evolution was a campaign against social Darwinism, and a campaign for the underdog, it was also an assault on science. And Darrow couldn't take that, nor could most people who'd fought on the same side of the labor question as Bryan. By 1924, Eugene Debs, a longtime Bryan supporter, had taken to referring to Bryan as "this shallow-minded mouther of empty phrases, this pious canting mountebank, this prophet of the stone age."[147] Darrow agreed. He had been raised reading Charles Darwin and Frederick Douglass. His interest was in education. "I knew that education was in danger from the source that has always hampered it—religious fanaticism," he said. He considered Bryan "the idol of all Morondom."[148]

Dayton had two paved streets and a movie theater that fit seventy-five people. The trial became a circus as the town was flooded with more than one hundred journalists, dozens of preachers and psalm singers, and, not least, trained chimpanzees. "The thing is genuinely fabulous," H. L. Mencken reported to the *Baltimore Sun*. "I have stored up enough material to last me 20 years."[149]

No one disputed that Scopes had violated the law. The defense hoped to litigate the reasonableness of the law itself. It began by bringing in a parade of biologists to demonstrate that evolution is a science. "This is not the place to try to prove that the law ought never to have been passed," Bryan said. "The place to prove that, or to teach that, was to the legislature." But Bryan, as much as Darrow, if not more, wanted to put evolution on trial. The judge sided with Bryan and refused to allow the testimony of the biologists to be heard by the jury. The next day, it was so hot inside the courtroom that the judged moved the trial to the lawn in front of the courthouse. The defense then called none other than Bryan himself to the witness stand, as an expert on the Bible.

"You have given considerable study to the Bible, haven't you, Mr. Bryan?" Darrow asked.

"Yes, sir, I have tried to."

But Bryan was no theologian. For two long hours, Darrow sliced and diced him like a spring ham. Was the earth really made in six days? Had Jonah really been swallowed by a whale? If Eve was made of Adam's rib, how did Cain get his wife? Bryan, flustered, stammered. Darrow pressed. Bryan sweated and made very little sense.

"The only purpose Mr. Darrow has is to slur the Bible," Bryan complained.

"I object to your statement," said Darrow. "I am examining you on your fool ideas that no intelligent Christian on earth believes."[150]

The judge ordered Bryan's testimony expunged from the record, the jury found Scopes guilty, and, five days later, Bryan died in his sleep, taking a nap, while his wife was reading a newspaper on a porch outside his window. The Boy of the Plains, the Great Commoner, a three-time presidential candidate, had been felled, according to the wire service, "the victim of his last great battle."[151]

Fundamentalism did not die when Bryan's head fell on his pillow. Fundamentalism endured, and the challenge it posed to the nation's founding principles and especially to the nature of truth would be felt well into the twenty-first century. Darrow was not among those who believed that the Scopes trial, followed so swiftly by Bryan's death, had closed the book on fundamentalism. "I am pained to hear of Bryan's death," said a sober Darrow. "I have known Bryan since 1896 and supported him twice for the Presidency." But the idea that modernity had killed William Jennings Bryan took hold, and, mere weeks after his death, big-city reporters and above all H. L. Mencken were back to lampooning Bryan and his followers as dumb hicks, while privately, Mencken confessed that he was terrified of the people he'd met on that courthouse lawn in Dayton—their bigotry and fury set him shuddering. "I set out laughing," Mencken wrote to a friend, "and returned shivering."[152]

Walter Lippmann didn't shiver and he didn't lampoon. Instead, he sat down to think through the consequences of the argument Bryan had made in Dayton for freedom of religion, freedom of inquiry, and the separation of church and state. For Lippmann, the battle between Bryan and Darrow wasn't about evolution, it was about how people decide what's true—does truth derive from faith or from reason?—and, more deeply, what happens in a democracy when people can't agree about how they decide what's true. Does the majority rule?

Lippmann traced the question back to Thomas Jefferson. In Virginia's 1786 Bill for Establishing Religious Freedom, Jefferson had stated the principle that "to compel a man to furnish contributions of money for the propagation of opinions which he disbelieves and abhors, is sinful and tyrannical." In Tennessee's 1925 Act Prohibiting the Teaching of the Evolution Theory, the state legislature had banned "the teaching of the evolution theory in all the universities, normal and all other public schools of Tennessee, which are supported in whole or in part by the public school funds of the State."

Bryan, alluding to the principle stated by Jefferson, had asked, "What right has a little irresponsible oligarchy of self-styled intellectuals to demand control of the schools of the United States in which twenty-five millions of children are being educated at an annual expense of ten billions of dollars?" Didn't their demand for control violate not only the Tennessee statute but religious freedom itself?

Darrow had settled this question in his own mind. "I don't like onion soup, but you go ahead and have some," he liked to say. "I wouldn't force my prejudice on you."[153] Darrow liked to find refuge in an adage. But Lippmann found that formulation wanting, because it wasn't a matter of one man liking onion soup; it was a matter of the majority of voters liking onion soup, and voting to ban anything but onion soup from any restaurant that received government support. Not to mention, neither revealed religion nor a commitment to reason are onion soup: they are epistemologies.

Lippmann took Bryan's argument seriously.

"Jefferson had insisted that the people should not have to pay for the teaching of Anglicanism," he wrote. "Mr. Bryan asked why they should be made to pay for the teaching of agnosticism."[154]

What were the implications for democracy? If a majority of voters decided that Charles Darwin was wrong and that evolution shouldn't be taught in schools, what was everyone else supposed to do? If evolution was a strong and plausible and important theory of how change occurs in nature, how could the minority of people who found the theory persuasive even begin to argue with the majority, which, in a generation, would consist of people who had been taught something else?

Lippmann decided to work through this problem by imagining a dialogue in which Jefferson and Bryan take turns making their case to Socrates, Jefferson arguing for reason and Bryan arguing for religion, but both expressing their enthusiasm for popular rule. Each presents his case and agrees to abide by Socrates's decision.

JEFFERSON: And what do you conclude from all this?
SOCRATES: That the common people hate reason, and that reason is the religion of an élite, of great gentlemen like yourself.
BRYAN: Reason a religion? What do you mean?
SOCRATES: The common people have always known that reason is a religion. That is why they dislike it so violently.[155]

If the common people hate reason, Lippmann concluded, there's no way a government of the people can protect the freedom of thought. The person of faith cannot accept reason as the arbiter of truth without giving up on faith; the person of reason cannot accept that truth lies outside the realm of reason. The citizens being unable to agree on basic matters of fact, they cannot agree on how to educate their children together. "This is the propagandist's opportunity," Lippmann wrote.[156] With enough money, and with the tools of mass communication, deployed efficiently, the propagandist can turn a political majority into a truth.

Lippmann had talked himself into a corner. He'd thought his way into a problem the Constitution had not anticipated, a problem that suggested that, under these circumstances, people would not be able to rule themselves by reason and choice, as Alexander Hamilton had hoped, but would instead be ruled by accident and force. His mind grew clouded with dread. Efficiency could not solve this problem; efficiency was part of the problem. There had to be a solution.

"Gentlemen, the world is dark," Clarence Darrow once told a jury, leaning over the jury box with his broad-shouldered bulk. "But it is not hopeless."[157] There remained the question: Where did hope lie?

*Eleven*

# A CONSTITUTION
# OF THE AIR

*A family in Hood River, Oregon,
gathers around the radio in 1925.*

"**O**UR WHOLE BUSINESS SYSTEM WOULD BREAK DOWN IN** a day if there was not a high sense of moral responsibility in our business world," said bulldog-faced Herbert Hoover while campaigning for president in 1928, at the age of fifty-three. Hoover had earned the reputation of a savior, along with the nickname "Master of Emergencies," which was also the title of his campaign film, a chronicle of his relief work in Europe during the war and in Mississippi during the 1927 flood, featuring footage so moving—ashen, hollow children fed, at last—that it reduced theater audiences to tears. One of the most devoted and talented Americans ever to seek the White House, Hoover believed that the philosophy of moral progress that had animated both American politics and American protest since the nation's founding had come to be best represented by the leaders of American businesses, private citizens who, he thought, possessed a commitment to the public interest as unwavering as his own.[1] Nothing so well illustrated his idea of a government-business partnership as radio, an experimental technology in which Hoover, a consummate engineer, invested the hope of American democracy.

As secretary of commerce and undersecretary of everything, Hoover had convened a series of annual radio conferences at the White House between 1922 and 1925, bringing together government agencies, news organizations, and manufacturers, including the fledgling Radio Corporation of America. At the time, there were 220 radio stations in the United States, and 2.5 million radio sets. Telegraph and telephone lines had wired the Republic together by miles of cable, like so many strings of Christmas lights; radio, riding on waves of air, could go anywhere. Nevertheless, early radio sets worked like the telegraph and telephone and were used for point-to-point communication, often ship-to-shore. Hoover understood that the future of radio was in "broadcasting" (a usage coined in 1921), transmitting a message to receivers scattered across great distances, like sowing so many seeds across a field. He rightly anticipated that radio, the nation's next great mechanical experiment, would radically transform the nature of political communication: radio would make it possible for political candidates and officeholders to speak to voters without the bother and expense of traveling to meet them, and it would also make governing an intimate affair. NBC radio began broadcasting in 1926, CBS in 1928. By the end of the decade, nearly every household would have a wireless—often a homemade one. Hoover promised that broadcasting would make Americans "literally one people."[2]

Hoover refused to leave this to chance, or to the public-mindedness of businessmen. The chaos of the early airwaves convinced him that the government had a role to play in regulating the airwaves by issuing licenses to frequencies and by insisting that broadcasters answer to the public interest. "The ether is a public medium," he insisted, "and its use must be for the public benefit."[3] He pressed for passage of the Federal Radio Act, sometimes called the Constitution of the Air. Passed in 1927, it proved to be one of the most consequential acts of Progressive reform.

Under the terms of the Radio Act, the Federal Radio Commission (later the Federal Communications Commission) adopted an equal-time policy, and debates between political candidates became one of early radio's most popular features. Hoover would later grow troubled by the world radio had wrought. "Radio lends itself to propaganda far more easily than the press," he remarked in his memoirs. But his earlier technological utopianism was widely shared: wasn't radio, after all, the answer to the doubts about mass democracy expressed by the likes of Walter Lippmann? "If the future of our democracy depends upon the intelligence and cooperation of its citizens," RCA President James G. Harbord wrote in 1929, "radio may contribute to its success more than any other single influence."[4]

At the end of the 1920s, the nation's optimism appeared boundless, and not only about radio. "We in America today are nearer to the final triumph over poverty than ever before in the history of any land," Hoover said in the summer of 1928, accepting the Republican nomination. "We shall soon with the help of God be in sight of the day when poverty will be banished from this earth." American economic growth seemed unstoppable. "Everything indicates that business continues to make progress with production at a new high record," the *Wall Street Journal* reported in July 1928. "And there seems to be nothing in sight to check the upward trend." Stock market prices kept rising, at a time when stocks were no longer sold only to the wealthy. "Everybody Ought to be Rich," argued one investor, in a magazine article in which he proposed that Americans without savings buy stocks on an installment plan. By 1929, a quarter of U.S. households owned stocks, compared to less than 1 percent a generation before. When Hoover was elected president in November of 1928, the stock market teetered at a record high; its closing average was three times what it had been in 1918 and twice what it had been in 1924.[5]

Hoover rode to his inauguration on a rainy Monday in March in a Pierce-Arrow motor car as swank as his top hat. His reign appeared to mark the final triumph of the campaign for efficiency and prosperity, a mass democracy made orderly by public-spirited businessmen and efficiency engineers. "The modern technical mind was for the first time at the head of government," wrote pioneering *New York Times* reporter Anne O'Hare McCormick. "Almost with the air of giving genius its chance, we waited for the performance to begin." But, privately, Hoover worried that the American people believed him "a sort of superman."[6]

He set to work with his customary businessman's briskness. He had a telephone installed on his desk in the Oval Office. He scheduled his appointments at eight-minute intervals. He began reorganizing the federal government. "Back to the mines," he'd say, after a fifteen-minute lunch break. He worried about the runaway stock market but found himself unable to halt the bulls' stampede. The Dow Jones Industrial Average had soared to 240 in 1928; in the summer of 1929, it rose past 380.[7]

On October 21, 1929, Hoover, along with five hundred distinguished guests, including the owners of most of America's most powerful corporations, met at Henry Ford's Edison Institute, in Dearborn, Michigan, to celebrate the fiftieth anniversary of the invention of the incandescent lightbulb. Light's Golden Jubilee was the brainchild of Edward Bernays, whose publicity campaign in advance of the event including sending incandescent lightbulbs to the editors of all of the nation's newspapers. On the night of the gala, electric companies all over the country shut off their electricity for one minute to honor Thomas Edison. Eighty-two-year-old Edison then re-created the moment when he'd first lit a lightbulb, while on NBC an announcer reported breathlessly: "Mr. Edison has the two wires in his hand. Now he is reaching up to the old lamp; now he is making the connection. It lights!"[8]

That night, news came by radio that shares on the New York Stock Exchange had begun to fall. It was as if a light, too brightly lit, had shattered.

## I.

**DARKNESS HAD ALREADY** fallen on Europe, which was well into a depression by 1928, a consequence of the political settlement that had ended the First World War. Before the autumn of 1929, the United States had appeared beyond the reach of that shadow. But then, over three weeks, the Dow Jones fell from 326 to 198. Stocks lost nearly 40 percent of their value. At first, the market rallied; by March 1930, stocks traded on the Dow Jones had regained nearly 75 percent of the value they'd lost. Still, the economy teetered and then it tottered, a depression set in, and by late spring stock prices were once again plummeting.[9]

Hoover, master of emergencies, steered the country through the crash, but when the Depression began he did very little except to wait

*Dorothea Lange photographed farmers on relief
in California's Imperial Valley in 1936.*

for a recovery and attempt to reassure a panicked public. He believed in charity, but he did not believe in government relief, arguing that if the United States were to provide it the nation would be "plunged into socialism and collectivism." [10]

When Hoover did act, it was to sever the United States from Europe: he pulled up America's last financial drawbridge by convincing Congress to pass a new, punitive trade bill, the 1930 Tariff Act. Other nations, retaliating, soon passed their own trade restrictions. Up came their draw-bridges. World trade shrank by a quarter. U.S. imports fell. In 1929, the United States had imported $4.4 billion in foreign products; in 1930 imports declined to $3.1. Then U.S. exports fell. To protect American wheat farmers, the tariff on imported grain had been increased by almost 50 percent. But by 1931, American farmers found themselves able to sell only about 10 percent of their crops. Creditors seized farms and sold them off at auction. Foreign debtors, unable to sell their goods in the United States, proved unable to pay back their debts to American creditors.

Between 1929 and 1932, one in five American banks failed. The unemployment rate climbed from 9 percent in 1930, to 16 percent in 1931, to 23 percent in 1932, by which time nearly twelve million Americans—a number equal to the entire population of the state of New York—were out of work. By 1932, national income, $87.4 billion in 1929, had fallen to $41.7 billion. In many homes, family income fell to zero. One in four Americans suffered from want of food.[11]

Factories closed; farms were abandoned. Even the weather conspired to reduce Americans to want: a drought plagued the plains, sowing despair and reaping death. Soil turned to dust and blew away. Schools shut their doors, children grew thin, and even thinner, and babies died in their cradles. Farm families, displaced by debt and drought, wandered westward, carrying what they could in dust-covered jalopies. The experiment in democracy that had begun with American independence seemed on the very edge of defeat.

"At no time since the rise of political democracy have its tenets been so seriously challenged as they are today," was the proclamation of the *New Republic*, introducing a series on the future of self-government. All over the world, democracies were collapsing under the weight of the masses. The Russian, Ottoman, and Austrian Empires had fallen apart, producing, by 1918, more than a dozen new states, many of which, like Lithuania, Hungary, Bulgaria, and Poland, experimented with democracy but did not endure as democracies. The tally was bleak and, each year, bleaker, as one European nation after another turned to fascism or another form of authoritarianism.[12]

The long nineteenth-century's movement toward constitutional government, the rule of law, representative assemblies, and the abdication of dictatorship—the application to modern life of eighteenth-century ideas about reason and debate, inquiry and equality—had come to a halt, and begun a reversal. Hardly a week passed without another learned commentator declaring the experiment a failure. "Epitaphs for democracy are the fashion of the day," the legal scholar Felix Frankfurter remarked in 1930. "In 1931, men and women all over the world were seriously contemplating and frankly discussing the possibility that the Western system of Society might break down and cease to work," the British historian Arnold J. Toynbee observed that fateful year. "Representative democracy seems to have ended in a cul-de-sac," wrote the political theorist Harold Laski in 1932.[13]

The last peace had created the conditions for the next war. Out of want came fear, out of fear came fury. By 1930, more than three million Germans were unemployed and Nazi Party membership had doubled. Adolf Hitler, as addled as he was ruthless, came to power in 1933, invaded the Rhineland in 1936, Poland in 1939. The bells of history tolled a tragedy of ages. Japan, whose expansion had been prohibited by the League of Nations, invaded Manchuria in 1931 and Shanghai in 1937. Italy's dictator Benito Mussolini, Il Duce, thirsting for glory and for the triumphs and trophies of war, invaded Ethiopia in 1935. Tyrants ruled with the terror of lies, led by the Reich's Ministry of Propaganda. Mussolini predicted: "The liberal state is destined to perish."[14]

Much appeared to rest on the fate of the United States and its search for a new way, a third way, between laissez-faire capitalism and a state-run economy. "It has fallen to us to live in one of those conjunctures of human affairs which mark a crisis in the habits, the customs, the routine, the inherited method and the traditional ideas of mankind," Walter Lippmann announced in a speech in Berkeley in 1933. "The old relationships among the great masses of the people of the earth have disappeared," he said. "The fixed points by which our fathers steered the ship of state have vanished."[15]

Was the ship of state lost at sea? "We are still, all of us, more or less, primitive men—as lynchings illustrate dramatically and Fascism systematically," the historian Charles Beard wrote bitterly in 1934. The great masses of the people had insisted on their right to rule, but their rule, it turned out, was dangerous, so easily were they deceived by propaganda. "The liberal culture of modernity is quite unable to give guidance and direction to a confused generation which faces the disintegration of a social system and the task of building a new one," the theologian Reinhold Niebuhr wrote that year, in the aptly titled *Reflections on the End of an Era*.[16]

One set of political arrangements had come to an end; it remained to be seen what set of arrangements would replace them. After the stock market crash, voters rejected both Hoover's leadership and that of his party. In the 1930 midterm elections, Republicans lost fifty-two seats in the House. Advisers urged Hoover to address the nation in weekly ten-minute radio broadcasts, to offer comfort and solace and direction; he refused.

Few voices were less well suited to the new medium. Hoover spoke on the radio ninety-five times during his presidency but during the handful of broadcasts in which he did more than issue a strained greeting, he read from a script in a dreadful monotone. "No one with a spark of human sympathy can contemplate unmoved the possibilities of suffering that can crush many of our unfortunate fellow Americans if we shall fail them," he said once, reading a well-written and even stirring speech but sounding like an overworked principal at a middle-school graduation listlessly announcing the names of graduating students from a lectern in a gray-green auditorium.[17]

Franklin Delano Roosevelt was untroubled by any such awkwardness. He wore a wide-brimmed hat and wireless round eyeglasses. His daintiness, a certain fussiness of person, earned him the nickname "Feather Duster Roosevelt." But if he had a patrician style, he spoke on the radio with an easy intimacy and a ready charm, coming across as knowledgeable, patient, kind-hearted, and firm of purpose. He spoke, he liked to say, with the "quiet of common sense and friendliness."[18] Hoover, a man of humble origins, dedicated to public service, would come to be seen as having turned his back on the suffering of the poorest of Americans. Roosevelt, raised as an aristocrat, would be remembered as their champion.

Born in Hyde Park in 1882, Roosevelt as a young man had much admired his distant cousin, lion-hunting Theodore Roosevelt, and even emulated him. "Delighted!" he would say, and "Bully!" He was elected to the state senate in 1910, at the age of twenty-eight, as a Democrat. Three years later, Wilson appointed him assistant secretary of the navy. By 1920, he'd risen to the rank of presidential running mate. But the next year, his political career appeared to be over when, at the age of thirty-nine, he contracted polio and lost the use of both of his legs. Confined to a wheelchair in private, he disguised his condition from the public by using leg braces and a cane, walking only with great pain. It was his paralysis, his wife, Eleanor, said, that taught Roosevelt "what suffering meant."[19]

His acquaintance with anguish changed his voice: it made it warmer. Hoover understood the importance of radio; Roosevelt knew how to use it. In 1928, delivering a nominating address at the Democratic National Convention, the first convention broadcast on the air, Roosevelt felt—and sounded as though—he was addressing not the audience in Madison Square Garden but Americans across the country. He'd then honed his skills as a radio broadcaster as governor of New York, delivering regular "reports to the people" from WOKO in Albany. The state's newspapers

*Franklin Delano Roosevelt bypassed the press and*
*spoke to the people directly by radio.*

were predominantly Republican; to bypass them, Roosevelt delivered a
monthly radio address, reaching voters directly.

In 1932, he stumped for the Democratic nomination on behalf of a
new brand of liberalism that borrowed as much from Bryan's populism
as from Wilson's Progressivism. "The history of the last half century is
. . . in large measure a history of a group of financial Titans," Roosevelt
said in a rally in San Francisco. But "the day of the great promoter or the
financial Titan, to whom we granted anything if only he would build, or
develop, is over."[20]

When Roosevelt, at the governor's mansion in Albany, heard on the
radio that he'd been nominated at the Democratic National Convention
in Chicago, he called the hall and said that he was on his way. While
delegates—along with an expectant radio audience—waited, Roosevelt
flew to Chicago, his plane refueling in Cleveland. No presidential nominee had ever shown up to accept the nomination in person, but the times
were strange, Roosevelt said, and they called for change: "Let it from
now on be the task of our party to break foolish traditions." In his rousing
acceptance speech, broadcast live, he promised Americans a "new deal."

"I pledge you, I pledge myself, to a new deal for the American people," he told the roaring crowd in Chicago Stadium, straw hats waving. "Let us all here assembled constitute ourselves prophets of a new order of competence and of courage. This is more than a political campaign; it is a call to arms. Give me your help, not to win votes alone, but to win in this crusade to restore America to its own people."[21]

Republicans often said, as they'd said about William Jennings Bryan, that while listening to Roosevelt, they found themselves agreeing with him, even when they didn't. "All that man has to do is speak on the radio, and the sound of his voice, his sincerity, and the manner of his delivery, just melts me," one said. Hoover compared Roosevelt to Bryan not only in style but in substance, describing the New Deal as nothing more than "Bryanism under new words and methods." That wasn't really true, as a matter of politics and constituencies, but there were undeniable similarities. The New Deal "is as old as Christian ethics, for basically its ethics are the same," Roosevelt liked to say. "It recognizes that man is indeed his brother's keeper, insists that the laborer is worthy of his hire, demands that justice shall rule the mighty as well as the weak."[22]

Still, much was new in Roosevelt's presidency, beginning with his campaign. The stump speeches he delivered on stages all over the country were the first presidential campaign speeches recorded on film and screened in movie theaters as newsreels. After accepting the nomination, he began delivering nationwide radio addresses from the governor's mansion, each speech more disarming than the last.

"I hope during this campaign to use the radio frequently, to speak to you about important things that concern us all," he told his audience. "I want you to hear me tonight as I sit here in my own home, away from the excitement of the campaign, and with only a few of the family, and a few personal friends present." Most Americans had only ever heard national political candidates shouting, trying to project their voices across a banquet hall or a football field. Hearing Roosevelt speak quietly and calmly, as if he were sitting across the kitchen table, having a reasonable argument with you, earned him Americans' dedicated affection. "It was a God-given gift," his wife said. He "could talk to people so that they felt he was talking to them individually."[23]

In November, Roosevelt trounced Hoover, beating him 472 to 59 in the Electoral College and winning forty-two out of forty-eight states. The simplest explanation was that the public blamed Hoover for the Depression. But there was more to the rout. FDR's election also ushered in a new party system, as the Democratic and Republican Parties rearranged themselves around what came to be called the New Deal coalition, which brought together blue-collar workers, southern farmers, racial minorities, liberal intellectuals, and even industrialists and, still more strangely, women. With roots in nineteenth-century populism and early twentieth-century Progressivism, FDR's ascension marked the rise of modern liberalism.

But FDR's election and the New Deal coalition also marked a turning point in another way, in the character and ambition of his wife, the indomitable Eleanor Roosevelt. Born in New York in 1884, she'd been orphaned as a child. She married FDR, her fifth cousin, in 1905; they had six children. Nine years into their marriage, Franklin began an affair with Eleanor's social secretary, and when Eleanor found out, he refused to agree to a divorce, fearing it would end his career in politics. Eleanor turned her energies outward. During the war, she worked on international relief, and, after Franklin was struck with polio in 1921, she began speaking in public, heeding a call that brought so many women to the stage for the first time: she was sent to appear in her husband's stead.

Eleanor Roosevelt became a major figure in American politics in her own right just at a time when women were entering political parties. It was out of frustration with the major parties' evasions on equal rights that Alice Paul had founded the National Woman's Party in 1916.[24] Fearful that soon-to-be enfranchised female voters would form their own voting bloc, the Democratic and Republican Parties had then begun recruiting women. The Democratic National Committee (DNC) formed a Women's Division in 1917, and the next year, the Republicans did the same, the party chairman pledging "to check any tendency toward the formation of a separate women's party." After the ratification of the Nineteenth Amendment in 1920, Carrie Chapman Catt, head of the League of Women Voters, steered women away from the National Woman's Party and urged them to join one of the two major parties, advising, "The only way to get things in this country is to find them on the inside of the political party." Few women answered that call more vigorously than Eleanor Roosevelt, who became a leader of the Women's Division of the New York State Democratic Party while her husband campaigned and served as governor of the state. By 1928, she was one of the two

*Eleanor Roosevelt created an entirely new role for the First Lady, not least by spending time touring the country. In May 1935, she visited a coal mine in Bellaire, Ohio.*

most powerful women in American politics, head of the Women's Division of the DNC.[25]

Eleanor Roosevelt, lean and rangy, wore floral dresses and tucked flowers in the brim of floppy hats perched on top of her wavy hair, but she had a spine as stiff as the steel girder of a skyscraper. She hadn't wanted her husband to run for president, mainly because she had so little interest in becoming First Lady, a role that, with rare exception, had meant serving as a hostess at state dinners while demurring to the men when the talk turned to affairs of state. She made that role her own, deciding to use her position to advance causes she cared about: women's rights and civil rights. She went on a national tour, wrote a regular newspaper column, and in December 1932 began delivering a series of thirteen nationwide radio broadcasts. While not a naturally gifted speaker, she earned an extraordinarily loyal following and became a radio celebrity. From the White House, she eventually delivered some three hundred broadcasts, about as many as FDR. Perhaps most significantly, she reached rural women, who had few ties to the national culture except by radio. "As I have talked to you," she told her audience, "I have tried to realize that way up in the high mountain farms of Tennessee, on lonely ranches in the Texas plains, in thousands and thousands of homes, there are women listening to what I say."[26]

Eleanor Roosevelt not only brought women into politics and rein-vented the role of the First Lady, she also tilted the Democratic Party toward the interests of women, a dramatic reversal. The GOP had courted the support of women since its founding in 1854; the Demo-cratic Party had turned women away and dismissed their concerns. With Eleanor Roosevelt, that began to change. During years when women were choosing a party for the first time, more of them became Demo-crats than Republicans. Between 1934 and 1938, while the numbers of Republican women grew by 400 percent, the numbers of Democratic women grew by 700 percent.[27]

In January 1933, she announced that she intended to write a book. "Mrs. Franklin D. Roosevelt, who has been one of the most active women in the country since her husband was elected President, is going to write a 40,000-word book between now and the March inauguration," the *Boston Globe* reported, incredulous. "Every word will be written by Mrs. Roo-sevelt herself."[28]

*It's Up to the Women* came out that spring. Only women could lead the nation out of the Depression, she argued—by frugality, hard work, com-mon sense, and civic participation. The "really new deal for the people," Eleanor Roosevelt always said, had to do with the awakening of women.[29]

# II.

**FRANKLIN DELANO ROOSEVELT** rode to the Capitol in the back-seat of a convertible, seated next to Hoover, a blanket spread across their laps; after that cold day, March 4, 1933, the two men never met again. "This great nation will endure, as it has endured," FDR said in his inau-gural address, attempting to reassure a troubled nation as he braced him-self against the podium, bearing the weight of his body in great pain. "The only thing we have to fear is fear itself—nameless, unreasoning, unjustified terror."[30]

At the time, many Americans believed that the economic crisis was so dire as to require the new president to assume the powers of a dictator in order to avoid congressional obstructionism. "The situation is critical,

Franklin," Walter Lippmann wrote to Roosevelt. "You may have no alternative but to assume dictatorial powers."[31] *Gabriel Over the White House*, a Hollywood film coproduced by William Randolph Hearst and released to coincide with the March 1933 inauguration, depicted a fictional but decidedly Rooseveltian president who, threatened with impeachment, bursts into a joint session of Congress.

"You have wasted precious days, and weeks and years in futile discussion," he tells the assembled representatives. "We need action, immediate and effective action!" He declares a national emergency, adjourns Congress, and takes control of the government.

"Mr. President, this is dictatorship!" cries one senator.

"Words do not frighten me!" answers the president.[32]

"Do We Need a Dictator?" *The Nation* asked, the month the film was released, and answered, "Emphatically not!"[33]

Meanwhile, the world watched Germany. For a long time, American reporters had underestimated Hitler. Crackerjack world-famous journalist Dorothy Thompson interviewed Hitler in 1930 and dismissed him. "He is inconsequent and voluble, ill-poised, insecure," she wrote. "He is the very prototype of the Little Man." By 1933, what that little man intended was growing clearer, and Thompson would go on to do more to raise American awareness of the persecution of American Jews than almost any other writer. Nazism she would describe as "a repudiation of the whole past of Western man," a "complete break with Reason, with Humanism, and with the Christian ethics that are the basis of liberalism and democracy." Thrown out of Germany for her criticism of the Nazi government, she had her expulsion order framed and hung it on her wall.[34]

On January 30, 1933, Hitler was appointed chancellor of Germany. In parliamentary elections held on March 5—the last vote the German people would be allowed for a dozen years—the Nazi Party narrowly failed to win a majority. Six days later, Hitler told his cabinet of his intention to establish a Ministry of Propaganda. Joseph Goebbels, appointed as its head on March 13, reported in his diary four days later that "broadcasting is now totally in the hands of the state." Having seized control of the airwaves, Hitler seized control of what remained of the government. On March 23, he addressed the German legislature, the Reichstag, its doors barred. Speaking beneath a giant flag of a swastika, Hitler asked the Reichstag to pass the Law to Remedy the Distress of People and Reich, essentially abolishing its own authority and granting to Hitler the right to make law. The government then outlawed all parties but the Nazi Party. By October, Germany had withdrawn from the League of Nations. Jewish refugees trying to flee to the United States found themselves blocked by a grotesque paradox: Nazi law mandated that no Jew could take more than four dollars out of the country; American immigration laws banned anyone "likely to become a public charge."[35]

To many people around the world, Roosevelt was the hope of democratic government, and his New Deal the last best hope for a liberal order. "You have made yourself the Trustee for those in every country who seek to mend the evils of our condition by reasoned experiment within the framework of the existing social system," John Maynard Keynes wrote to the president. "If you fail, rational change will be gravely prejudiced throughout the world, leaving orthodoxy and revolution to fight it out. But if you succeed, new and bolder methods will be tried everywhere, and we may date the first chapter of a new economic era from your accession to office."[36]

Keynes's expectations were nothing compared to those of ordinary Americans. In FDR's first seven days in office, he received more than 450,000 letters and telegrams from the public. By no means was all the mail favorable, but FDR loved it all the same; it taught him what people were thinking. He made a point of reading a selection daily.[37]

People had been writing to presidents since George Washington was inaugurated, but, by volume, no other presidency had come anywhere close.[38] (Hoover received eight hundred letters a day; FDR eight thousand.) The rise of "fan mail"—the expression wasn't used before the 1920s—was a product of radio; radio stations and networks encouraged listeners to write to them and used their responses to refine their programming. In the 1930s, the National Broadcasting Corporation received ten million letters a year (not counting mail sent to its affiliates, sponsors, and stations). Like radio stations, the White House began reading, sorting, and counting its mail. Eleanor Roosevelt received three hundred thousand letters in 1933 alone. The mail came pouring down on Congress next. By 1935, the Senate received forty thousand letters a day. By the end of the 1930s, voters were writing letters to Supreme Court justices.[39]

If FDR listened carefully to ordinary Americans by reading voter mail, he also assembled an altogether unordinary team of advisers. Elected during a national emergency, Roosevelt assembled a "brain trust" that included Frances Perkins as his secretary of labor, the first female member of a presidential cabinet. How he both relied on his brain trust and put his own touch on their advice is suggested in how he handled radio scripts. "We are trying to construct a more inclusive society," Perkins wrote for him, in a draft of a speech he intended to give over the radio. When he delivered that speech, he said, instead: "We are going to make a country in which no one is left out."[40]

He began by shutting down the nation's banks. The rate of bank and business failures reached the highest point in history. Millions of Americans had lost every penny. The New York Stock Exchange and the Chicago Board of Trade had suspended trading, and the governors of thirty-two states had already shut their banks to prevent total collapse. In states where banks remained open, depositors could withdraw no more than 5 percent of their savings. Roosevelt shut the banks to prevent still further collapse. On March 5, the day after he was inaugurated, he asked Congress to declare a four-day bank holiday. Under the terms of the Emergency Banking Act, banks would be opened once they'd been found to be sound. On March 12, FDR spoke on the radio in what radio executives took to calling a "fireside chat"—the first of more than three hundred. Explaining his banking plan, he offered reassurance. "I want to tell you what has been done in the last few days, and why it was done, and what the next steps are going to be," he said. He offered a lesson: "When you deposit money in a bank, the bank does not put the money into a safe deposit vault." He asked for Americans' confidence. "I can assure you that it is safer to keep your money in a reopened bank than under the mattress."[41]

Roosevelt's ability to take such measures was greatly strengthened by the popular endorsement he was able to secure by way of the radio. People said that in the summer you could walk down a city street, past the open windows of houses and cars, and not miss a word of a fireside chat, since everyone was tuned in. "We have become neighbors in a new and true sense," FDR said, describing what coast-to-coast broadcasting had wrought. He'd listen to recordings of his addresses after he'd given them, to make improvements for the next time. He worked and reworked drafts so that, by the time he sat down at the microphone, he'd committed his speech to memory. Before every address, he took a nap to rest his voice. He spoke at an unusual speed—much slower than most radio announcers—and with an everyday vocabulary. Roosevelt's mastery of the airwaves resulted from his talent for and dedication to the form. But he also worked with his FCC chairman to block newspaper publishers from owning radio stations, thereby defeating William Randolph Hearst's attempt to expand his empire to radio and denying one of his key political opponents a place on the dial.[42]

Roosevelt was also dogged in his work with Congress. He met with legislators every day of the first hundred days of his administration and proposed—and Congress passed—a flurry of legislation intended to stabilize and reform the banking system, regulate the economy through government planning, provide economic relief through public assistance programs, reduce unemployment through a public works program, and allow farmers to keep their farms by securing better resources to rural Americans. "As a Nation," Perkins said, "we are recognizing that programs long thought of as merely labor welfare, such as shorter hours, higher wages, and a voice in the terms and conditions of work, are really essential economic factors for recovery."[43]

Roosevelt's agenda rested on the idea that government planning was necessary for the recovery and, to some degree, on the Keynesian belief that the remedy for depression was government spending, an agenda he adopted even before the publication, in 1936, of Keynes's *Theory of Employment, Interest, and Money*. FDR's banking reforms included the Emergency Banking Act; the Glass-Steagall Act, which established the Federal Deposit Insurance Corporation; and creation of the Securities Exchange Commission. The Public Works Administration oversaw tens of thousands of infrastructure projects, from repairing roads to building dams, as well as cultural and arts initiatives, including the Federal Writers' Project and the Federal Theatre Project. The Agricultural Adjustment Act addressed the problems faced by the more than one in three Americans who worked on farms.

FDR had dealt with many of these problems as a governor of New York. During the 1920s, more than three hundred thousand farms in New York were abandoned. Like many reformers associated with what came to be called the New Conservation, Roosevelt believed the greatest disparity of wealth in the United States was that between urban and rural Americans. Farming communities had worse schools, inadequate health care, and higher taxes. Poor land makes poor people, he believed. "I want to build up the land as, in part at least, an insurance against future depressions," Roosevelt said in 1931, the year he established the New York Power Authority. The Agricultural Adjustment Act, the Farm Security Administration, and other agricultural initiatives extended a better and fairer distribution of resources like land, power, and water to a national scale. Much of the greatest distress among rural Americans was felt in the Cotton Belt, a part of the country that FDR called "the Nation's No. 1 economic problem—the Nation's problem, not merely the South's."[44]

Reform, relief, and recovery were the three legs of FDR's agenda. Early results were promising, but the Depression continued. "When any prognosticator foretells the outcome of the acts of the New Deal, he is more or less of a guesser in this vale of tears," Charles Beard wrote in 1934. "What is an 'outcome' or a 'result'? Is it an outcome or result in 1936, 1950, or the year 2000?" The New Deal had barely begun but voters approved; Democrats fared well in the midterm elections, leading Roosevelt to push further. "Boys, this is our hour," his adviser Harry Hopkins said. "We've got to get everything we want—a works program, social security, wages and hours, everything—now or never." Or, not quite everything. In 1934 Isaac Rubinow, who'd fought for national health insurance during the 1910s, published *The Quest for Security* and urged FDR to include health care in the New Deal. But by now the American Medical Association, which had favored Rubinow's proposal before the war, had switched sides. Government meddling in medicine, the editor of the *Journal of the American Medical Association* said, came down to a question of "Americanism versus sovietism."[45]

Even without universal health care, the scope of the New Deal was remarkable. In 1935, Congress passed the National Labor Relations Act, granting to workers the right to organize, and established the Works Project Administration, to hire millions of people who built roads and schools and hospitals, as well as artists and writers. Meanwhile, Perkins drafted the Social Security Act, passed by Congress later that year. It established pensions, federal government assistance for fatherless families, and unemployment relief.

Still, the reforms had limits. The liberal policymakers who created the welfare state in the 1930s were averse to relief as such. "The Federal Government," FDR said, "has no intention or desire to force upon the country

*Sharecroppers were evicted from their homes in 1936
in Arkansas after joining a tenant farmers' union.*

or the unemployed themselves a system of relief which is repugnant to American ideals of individual self-reliance." And they were also squeamish about direct taxes, an aversion most manifest in the decision to fund the Social Security Act with an indirect tax on payroll. This allowed New Dealers to distinguish between old-age and unemployment programs (cast as insurance, paid for by annuities created from payroll taxes acting as insurance premiums) and poverty programs, like Aid to Dependent Children (cast as welfare). One legacy of this distinction was that Americans hostile to welfare seldom saw Social Security as part of it.[46]

**HUNGER, ACHING WANT,** was the great scourge of the 1930s. The land itself had grown barren. "When we picked the cotton, we could see the tracks where we plowed two or three months before," Willis Magby recalled of the drought in Beaton, Arkansas, west of Little Rock. "It hadn't rained enough to wash away the tracks." Magby was thirteen years old in 1933 when his parents piled him and his six younger siblings into an old Model T and drove from Arkansas to south Texas. The family slept on the ground at the side of the road, pawning the last of their scant belongings along the way to buy gasoline. Once in Texas, for weeks at a time they ate nothing but cornmeal soaked in rainwater. One winter, they lived off rabbits. Only in 1936, when Magby's father was able to get a government loan to buy a team of mules and plant a crop, did things start to look up.[47]

Nearly five in ten white families and nine in ten black families endured poverty at some point during the Depression. Black families fared worse, not only because more fell into poverty but also because the roads out of poverty were often closed to them: New Deal loan, relief, and insurance programs often specifically excluded black people.

Louise Norton, born in Grenada in 1900, met her husband, Earl Little, a Baptist minister, at a United Negro Improvement Association meeting in Philadelphia in 1917. In 1925, when the Littles were living in Omaha and Louise was pregnant with her son Malcolm and home alone with her three young children, mounted Klansmen came to their house, threatening to lynch the Reverend Little. Finding him not at home, they shattered all the windows. Driven out of Omaha, the Littles eventually settled in Lansing, Michigan, where still more vigilantes burned their home to the ground. In 1931, the Reverend Little was killed by a streetcar; much evidence suggests that his death was not an accident. After Little's death, the insurance company denied his widow his life insurance. For a while, Louise and the children lived on dandelions. In 1939, after giving birth to her eighth child, Louise Little was committed to an insane asylum at the Kalamazoo State Hospital, where she remained for the next quarter century. Her son Malcolm was moved into foster care and then a juvenile home, and eventually lived in Boston with his half-sister. He would one day change his name to Malcolm X.[48]

Yet if hard times widened some divisions, they narrowed others. People who were doing fairly well one day could be reduced to anguished indigence the next. Then, too, it was impossible not to bear witness. Massive unemployment had this side effect: people had more time on their hands to listen to the radio. One third of all movie theaters closed, but, between 1935 and 1941 alone, nearly three hundred new radio stations opened. By the end of the decade, the United States had more than half the world's radio sets, at a time when radio broadcasts chronicled and dramatized the suffering of the poor to a national audience, both in reporting and in the emerging genre of the radio drama, with a new vocabulary of sound effects, immediate and visceral.[49]

Much of the work of chronicling the suffering of those years was done by playwrights, photographers, historians, and writers, hired by the government under the auspices of the Works Progress Administration. Working for the Federal Writers Project and the Federal Theatre Project, including its Radio Division, they documented the lives of the ordinary, the rural, and especially the poor, in interviews, photographs, films, paintings, and radio broadcasts. Its critics called it the "Whistle, Piss, and Argue" department, but at a time when one in four people in publishing were out of work, the WPA's Federal Writers' Project provided employment to more than seven thousand writers, including Ralph Ellison, Zora Neale Hurston, John Cheever, and Richard Wright.[50] But it was radio that brought the sounds of suffering into the homes, even, of people who were still getting by, and even the rarer few who were prospering. James Truslow Adams's *The Epic of America* (1931), featuring the lives of the humblest Americans, was dramatized by the Federal Theatre of the Air. "There is no lack of excellent one-volume narrative histories of the United States, in which the political, military, diplomatic, social, and economic strands have been skillfully interwoven," Adams had written in his book's preface. *The Epic of America* was not that kind of book. Instead, Adams had tried "to discover for himself and others how the ordinary American, under which category most of us come, has become what he is to-day in outlook, character, and opinion." Adams, who'd wanted to call his book "The American Dream"—a term he coined—celebrated the struggles of the common man in language that would stir leaders of later generations, from Martin Luther King Jr. to Barack Obama.[51]

Much the same spirit pervaded the documentary projects of the WPA and of other New Deal programs, including the photography of Dorothea Lange and Walker Evans, undertaken on behalf of the Farm Security Administration. The head of the FSA's photography program required his staff to read Charles Beard's *History of the United States*—an eloquent and strident social history that championed the struggles of the poor. The WPA's folklore director, Benjamin Botkin, wanted to turn "the streets, the stockyards, and the hiring halls into literature." From more than ten thousand interviews, the Writers' Project produced some eight hundred books, including *A Treasury of American Folklore*, and a volume called *These Are Our Lives*, which included excerpts from more than two thousand interviews with Americans once held as slaves.[52]

If the Depression, and alike the New Deal, created a new compassion for the poor, it also produced a generation of politicians committed to the idea that government can relieve suffering and regulate the economy. In 1937, lanky former Texas schoolteacher Lyndon Baines Johnson was elected to Congress, where he worked to obtain federal funds for his district for projects like the construction of dams to improve farmland. When LBJ was a boy, his father had lost his farm. He'd grown up dirt-poor. Six foot three, with long ears and no discernible end to his energy, Johnson had hitchhiked to a state teachers college and, after graduating, taught at an elementary school in Cotulla, Texas, sixty miles north of the border. The students were Mexican American; there was no lunch break, because the children had no lunch to eat. Johnson organized a debating team and taught them how to fight for their ideas. When he ran for Congress, he printed signs that read "Franklin D. and Lyndon B." Like his hero, LBJ embraced the radio, campaigning on radio stations like KNOW in Austin and KTSA in San Antonio and once—in an act of inspired populist appeal—broadcasting from a barbershop.[53]

In Congress, Johnson regularly worked sixteen- and eighteen-hour days. He fought for the Bankhead-Jones Act in 1937, to help tenant farmers buy land. He campaigned for more improvements, too, and fought to have rural electrification placed in the hands not of power companies but farmers' cooperatives. He later said, "We built six dams on our river. We brought the floods under control. We provided our people with cheap power. . . . That all resulted from the power of the government to bring the greatest good to the greatest number."[54]

What was that number? New methods and new sources of information made it possible to measure the impact of the New Deal, as the age of quantification yielded to the age of statistics. In 1912, an Italian statistician named Corrado Gini, Chair of Statistics at the University of Cagliari, devised what came to be called the Gini index, which measures economic inequality on a scale from zero to one.[55] If all the income in the world were earned by one person and everyone else earned nothing, the world would have a Gini index of one. If everyone in the world earned exactly the same income, the world would have a Gini index of zero. In between zero and one, the higher the number, the greater the gap between the rich and the poor. Using federal income tax returns, filed beginning in 1913, it's possible to calculate the Gini index for the United States. In 1928, under the tax scheme endorsed by Secretary of the Treasury Andrew Mellon, the top 1 percent of American families earned 24 percent of all income. By 1938, after the reforms of the New Deal, the top 1 percent of American families earned only 16 percent of all income.[56] It was just this kind of redistribution, at a time when Americans were flirting with fascism, that alarmed conservatives. The sort of economic planning that Gini himself advocated was closely associated with nondemocratic states. In 1925, four years after he wrote an essay called "The Measurement of Inequality," Gini signed the "Manifesto of Fascist Intellectuals." His work as a scientist was so closely tied to the fascist state that after the regime fell he was tried for being "an apologist for Fascism."[57]

Americans, too, began hunting for apologists for fascism, and, especially, for communism, fishing for American subversives. During the Depression, some seventy-five thousand Americans had joined the Communist Party. In May 1938, Martin Dies Jr., a beefy thirty-seven-year-old conservative Democrat from Texas and a fly in Lyndon Johnson's eye, convened the House Un-American Activities Committee to investigate suspected communists and communist organizations. Dorothy Thompson railed against the committee: "little men—nasty little men—who run around pinning tags on people. This one is a 'Red'; this one is a 'Jew.' Since when has America become a race of snoopers?" But the snooping had been going on for a while. Much of Dies's work continued the campaign of harassment and intimidation waged by J. Edgar Hoover's FBI, which had for years been conducting surveillance on hundreds of black artists and writers, infiltrating their organizations and, in particular, harassing writers and artists of the Harlem Renaissance. As Richard Wright wrote, in "The FB Eye Blues," "Everywhere I look, Lord / I see FB eyes . . . I'm getting sick and tired of gover'ment spies."[58]

In congressional hearings, Dies directed his ire at writers and artists employed by the WPA, attempting to demonstrate that their work—their plays and poems and folklore collections and documentary photographs—contained hidden communist messages. In one notorious encounter, Dies called Hallie Flanagan, the director of the Federal Theatre Project. Flanagan, born in South Dakota, was an accomplished playwright and distinguished professor of drama at Vassar, where she'd founded its Experimental Theatre. When she appeared before Dies's committee, in December 1938, Alabama congressman Joseph Starnes asked her about a scholarly article she'd written in which she used the phrase "Marlow-esque madness." (The Theatre Project had funded productions of Mar-lowe's *Tragical History of Dr. Faustus* in New Orleans, Boston, Detroit, Atlanta and, directed by Orson Welles, in New York.)

"You are quoting from this Marlowe," Starnes said. "Is he a Communist?"

Spectators roared with laughter, but Flanagan answered solemnly.

"I was quoting from Christopher Marlowe."

"Tell us who Marlowe is," Starnes pressed.

"Put in the record," Flanagan said wearily, "that he was the greatest dramatist in the period of Shakespeare."[59]

Flanagan was right to be worried. The Federal Theatre Project had staged more than eight hundred plays. Dies's committee objected to only a handful—including *Woman of Destiny*, about a female president, and *Machine Age*, about mass production—but months after Flanagan's testimony, funding for both the Federal Theatre Project and the Federal Writers' Project stopped, Congress having struck a bargain with Dies little better than the deal Faustus struck with Lucifer.

## III.

FRANKLIN ROOSEVELT'S PRESIDENCY marked the beginning of a "new deal order," an American-led, rights-based liberalism that Lyndon Johnson would carry into the 1960s. In the nineteenth century, "liberalism" meant advocacy of laissez-faire capitalism. The meaning of the term changed during the Progressive Era, when self-styled Progressives, borrowing from Populism, began attempting to reform laissez-faire capitalism by using the tools of collective action and appeals to the people adopted by Populists; in the 1930s, these efforts came together as New Deal liberalism.[60]

All that while, a new kind of conservatism was growing, too. It consisted not only of businessmen who opposed government regulation of the economy but also of Americans, chiefly rural Americans, who objected to government interference in their lives. These two strands of conservatism were largely separate in the 1930s, but they'd already begun moving closer together, especially in their animosity toward the paternalism of liberalism.[61]

Not long into FDR's first term, businessmen who had supported him began to question his agenda. The du Pont brothers—Pierre, Irénée, and Lammot—belonged to a family that had made its fortune in paints, plastics, and munitions. In 1934, *Merchants of Death*, a bestseller that blamed arms manufacturers for the First World War, led to a congressional investigation, headed by North Dakota Republican senator Gerald P. Nye, who'd flouted his party to support Roosevelt. At the time, concern about munitions manufacturers crossed party lines, and so did a related concern about guns.

Americans had always owned guns, but states had also always regulated their manufacture, ownership, and storage. Carrying concealed weapons was prohibited by laws in Kentucky and Louisiana (1813), Indiana (1820), Tennessee and Virginia (1838), Alabama (1839), and Ohio (1859). Texas, Florida, and Oklahoma passed similar laws. The "mission of the concealed deadly weapon is murder," said one governor of Texas. "To check it is the duty of every self-respecting, law abiding man." Different rules obtained in the city and in the country. In western cities and towns, sheriffs routinely collected the guns of visitors, like checked baggage. In 1873, a sign in Wichita, Kansas read: "Leave Your Revolvers at Police Headquarters, and Get a Check." On the road into Dodge, a billboard read, "The Carrying of Firearms Strictly Prohibited." The shootout at the O.K. Corral, in Tombstone, Arizona, happened when Wyatt Earp confronted a man violating an 1879 city ordinance by failing to leave his gun at the sheriff's office.[62]

The National Rifle Association had been founded in 1871 by a former reporter from the *New York Times*, as a sporting and hunting association; most of its business consisted of sponsoring target-shooting competitions. Not only did the NRA not oppose firearms regulation, it supported and even sponsored it. In the 1920s and 1930s—the era of Nye's Munitions Committee—the NRA endorsed gun control legislation, lobbying for new state laws in the 1920s and 1930s. Concern about urban crime led to federal legislation in the 1930s. Public-safety-minded firearms regulation was uncontroversial. The NRA supported both the uniform 1934 National Firearms Act—the first federal gun control legislation—and the 1938 Federal Firearms Act, which together prohibitively taxed the private ownership of automatic weapons ("machine guns"), mandated licensing for handgun dealers, introduced waiting periods for handgun buyers, required permits for anyone wishing to carry a concealed weapon, and created a licensing system for dealers. In 1939, in a unanimous decision in *U.S. v. Miller*, the U.S. Supreme Court upheld these measures after FDR's solicitor general, Robert H. Jackson, argued that the Second Amendment is "restricted to the keeping and bearing of arms by the people collectively for their common defense and security." The text of the amendment, Jackson argued, makes clear that the right "is not one which may be utilized for private purposes but only one which exists where the arms are borne in the militia or some other military organization provided for by law and intended for the protection of the state."[63]

The 1934 and 1938 firearms legislation enjoyed bipartisan support, but the regulation of munitions manufacturing was more usually promoted by conservatives who were isolationists. For two years, Nye, railing against "merchants of death," led the most rigorous inquiry into the arms industry that any branch of the federal government has ever conducted. He convened ninety-three hearings. He thought that the ability to manufacture weapons should be restricted to the government. "The removal of the element of profit from war would materially remove the danger of more war," he said. From the vantage of the du Ponts, the prospect of handing the manufacture of weapons over to the government represented the worst possible instance of laissez-faire economics yielding to a planned economy. The du Ponts were concerned, too, about the growing strength of labor unions, the number of strikes, and the establishment of the Securities Exchange Commission. Irénée du Pont wrote: "It must have now become clear to every thinking man that the so-called 'New Deal,' advocated by the Administration, is nothing more or less than the Socialistic doctrine called by another name."[64]

To make this case to the American public, the du Ponts turned to the National Association of Manufacturers, whose president said, "The public does not understand industry, largely because industry itself has made no real effort to tell its story; to show the people of this country that our high living standards have risen almost altogether from the civilization which industrial activity has set up." To that end, the association hired a publicist named Walter W. Weisenberger, appointing him executive vice president. Weisenberger used the tools of radio and paid advertisement to oppose both labor agitation and government regulation by arguing that peace and prosperity were best assured by the leadership of businessmen and a free market. One campaign motto: "Prosperity dwells where harmony reigns."[65] The Association insisted that its efforts were educational, but a congressional investigation led by Wisconsin Progressive Robert M. La Follette concluded otherwise. Business leaders, the La Follette Committee reported, "asked not what the weaknesses and abuses of the economic structure had been, and how they could be corrected, but instead paid millions to tell the public that nothing was wrong and that grave dangers lurked in the proposed remedies."[66]

Other corporate leaders pursued similar aims. In July 1934, the du Ponts gathered fellow businessmen in the offices of General Motors in New York, where they founded a "propertyholders' association" to oppose the New Deal; by August, this association had been incorporated as the American Liberty League. In pamphlets and in speeches, the league argued that the voice of business was being drowned out by the "ravenous madness" of the New Deal. Leaguers particularly objected to Social Security, described as the "taking of property without due process of law." The majority of the league's funding came from only thirty very wealthy men; Democrats dubbed it the "Millionaires Union."[67] It went by other names, too. In the U.S. presidential election of 1936, the Liberty League supported the Republican nominee, Alf M. Landon, an oil executive and governor of Kansas, through the efforts of an organization called the Farmers' Independence Council. But the Farmer's Independence Council had the same mailing address as the Liberty League and a membership that consisted, not of any farmers, but instead of Chicago meatpackers. Most of its funding came from Lammot du Pont, who defended his lobbying as a "farmer" by insisting that his ownership of a 4,000-acre estate made him one.[68]

Many kinds of conservatism coexisted in the United States in the 1930s, not yet sharing an ideology. Businessmen who opposed the New Deal generally had little in common with conservative intellectuals. like Albert Jay Nock, editor of a magazine called *The Freeman* and author of *Our Enemy, the State* (1935). While he complained about a centralized state, Nock was chiefly concerned with the rise of mass democracy and mass culture as harbingers of the decline of Western civilization, believing that radical egalitarianism had produced a world of mediocrity and blandness. American conservative intellectuals were opposed to socialism; they were isolationists; many tended to be anti-Semitic. In 1941, Nock wrote an essay for *Atlantic Monthly* called "The Jewish Problem in America."[69]

Only after the war would the conservative movement find its base, and its direction. Meanwhile, the leftward drift of American politics in the 1930s was kept in check by the new businesses of political consulting and public opinion polling, the single most important forces in American democracy since the rise of the party system.

CAMPAIGNS, INC., the first political consulting firm in the history of the world, was founded by Clem Whitaker and Leone Baxter in California in 1933. Critics called it the Lie Factory.

Political consulting, when it started, had one foot in advertising and one foot in journalism. Political consulting is often thought of as a product of the advertising industry, but the reverse is closer to the truth. When modern advertising began, in the 1920s, the industry's big clients were interested in advancing a political agenda as much as, if not more than, a commercial one. Muckrakers and congressional investigations tended to make Standard Oil look greedy and Du Pont, for making munitions, sinister. Large corporations hired advertising firms to make themselves look better and to advance pro-business legislation.[70]

Political consulting's origins in journalism lie with William Randolph Hearst. Whitaker, thirty-four, started out as a newspaperman, or, really, a newspaper boy; he was already working as a reporter at the age of thirteen. By nineteen, he was city editor for the *Sacramento Union* and, two years later, a political writer for the *San Francisco Examiner*, a Hearst paper. In the 1930s, one in four Americans got their news from Hearst, who owned twenty-eight newspapers in nineteen cities. Hearst's papers were all alike: hot-blooded, with leggy headlines. Page one was supposed to make a reader blurt out, "Gee whiz!" Page two: "Holy Moses!" Page three: "God Almighty!" Hearst used his newspapers to advance his politics. In 1934, he ordered his editors to send reporters to college campuses, posing as students, to find out which members of the faculty were Reds. People Hearst thought were communists not infrequently thought

Hearst was a fascist; he'd professed his admiration for Hitler and Mussolini. Hearst didn't mind; he silenced his critics by attacking them in his papers relentlessly and ferociously. Some fought back. "Only cowards are intimated by Hearst," Charles Beard said. In February 1935, Beard addressed an audience of a thousand schoolteachers in Atlantic City and said, of Hearst, "No person with intellectual honesty or moral integrity will touch him with a ten-foot pole." The crowd gave Beard a standing ovation.[71]

Hearst endures, in American culture, in *Citizen Kane*, a film by Orson Welles released in 1941. The film bears so uncanny a resemblance to *Imperial Hearst*, a biography of Hearst published in 1936—with a preface by Beard—that the biographer sued the filmmakers. "I had never seen or heard of the book *Imperial Hearst*," Welles insisted in a deposition for a case that was eventually settled out of court. Welles argued that his Citizen Kane wasn't a character; he was a type: an American sultan. (The film was originally titled *American*.) If Kane, like Hearst, was a newspaper tycoon who turned to politics, that's because, according to Welles, "such men as Kane always tend toward the newspaper and entertainment world," despite hating the audience they crave, combining "a morbid preoccupation with the public with a devastatingly low opinion of the public mentality and moral character." A man like Kane, Welles said, believes that "politics as the means of communication, and indeed the nation itself, is all there for his personal pleasuring."[72] Hearst would not be the last American sultan.

Clem Whitaker, having been trained by Hearst, left the *San Francisco Examiner* to start a newspaper wire service, the Capitol News Bureau, distributing stories to over eighty papers. In 1933, Sheridan Downey, a progressive California lawyer originally from Wyoming, hired Whitaker to help him defeat a referendum sponsored by Pacific Gas and Electric. Downey also hired Leone Baxter, a twenty-six-year-old widow who had been a writer for the *Portland Oregonian*, and suggested that she and Whitaker join forces. When Whitaker and Baxter defeated the referendum, Pacific Gas and Electric was so impressed that it put the two on retainer, and Whitaker and Baxter, who later married, started doing business as Campaigns, Inc.[73]

Campaigns, Inc., specialized in running political campaigns for businesses, especially monopolies like Standard Oil and Pacific Telephone and Telegraph. Working for the left-wing Downey had been an aberration. As a friend said, they liked to "work the Right side of the street." In 1933, Upton Sinclair, an eccentric and dizzyingly prolific writer still best known for *The Jungle*, his 1906 muckraking indictment of the meat-packing industry, decided to run for governor of California. Sinclair, a longtime socialist, registered as a Democrat in order to seek the Democratic nomination, on a platform known as EPIC: End Poverty in California. After he unexpectedly won the nomination, he chose Downey as his running mate. (Their ticket was called "Uppie and Downey.") Sinclair saw American history as a battle between business and democracy, and, "so far," he wrote, "Big Business has won every skirmish."[74]

Emboldened by Roosevelt's winning of the White House, Sinclair decided to take a shot at the governor's office. Whitaker and Baxter, like most California Republicans, were horrified at the prospect of a Sinclair governorship.[75] Two months before the election, they began working for George Hatfield, a candidate for lieutenant governor on a Republican ticket headed by the incumbent governor, Frank Merriam. They locked themselves in a room for three days with everything Sinclair had ever written. "Upton was beaten," Whitaker later said, "because he had written books."[76] The *Los Angeles Times* began running on its front page a box with an Upton Sinclair quotation in it, a practice the paper continued every day for six weeks, right up until Election Day. For instance:

### SINCLAIR ON MARRIAGE:

THE SANCTITY OF MARRIAGE. . . . I HAVE HAD SUCH A BELIEF . . . I HAVE IT NO LONGER.[77]

The passage, as Sinclair explained in a book called *I, Candidate for Governor: And How I Got Licked*, was taken from his novel *Love's Pilgrimage* (1911), in which a fictional character writes a heartbroken letter to a man having an affair with his wife.[78] "Reading these boxes day after day," Sinclair wrote, "I made up my mind that the election was lost."[79]

The nation was founded on self-evident truths. But, as Sinclair argued, voters were now being led by a Lie Factory. "I was told they had a dozen men searching the libraries and reading every word I had ever published," he wrote. They'd find lines he'd written, speeches of fictional characters in novels, and stick them in the paper as if Sinclair had said them. "They had an especially happy time with *The Profits of Religion*," Sinclair said, referring to his 1917 polemic about institutionalized religion. "I received many letters from agitated old ladies and gentlemen on the subject of my blasphemy. 'Do you believe in God?' asked one." There was very little he could do about it. "They had a staff of political chemists at work, preparing poisons to be let loose in the California atmosphere on every one of a hundred mornings."[80]

"Sure, those quotations were irrelevant," Baxter later said. "But we had one objective: to keep him from becoming Governor." They succeeded. The final vote was Merriam, 1,138,000; Sinclair, 879,000.[81] No single development altered the workings of American democracy so wholly as the industry Whitaker and Baxter founded. "Every voter, a consumer; every consumer, a voter" became its mantra.[82] They succeeded best by being noticed least. Progressive reformers dismantled the party machine. But New Dealers barely noticed when political consultants replaced party bosses as the wielders of political power gained not by votes but by money.

Whitaker and Baxter won nearly every campaign they waged.[83] The campaigns they chose to run, and the way they decided to run them, shaped the history of California and of the country. They drafted the rules by which campaigns would be waged for decades afterward. The first thing they did, when they took on a campaign, was to "hibernate" for a week to write a Plan of Campaign. Then they wrote an Opposition Plan of Campaign, to anticipate the moves made against them. Every campaign needs a theme.[84] Keep it simple. Rhyming's good ("For Jimmy and me, vote 'yes' on 3"). Never explain anything. "The more you have to explain," Whitaker said, "the more difficult it is to win support." Say the same thing over and over again. "We assume we have to get a voter's attention seven times to make a sale," Whitaker said. Subtlety is your enemy. "Words that lean on the mind are no good," according to Baxter. "They must dent it." Simplify, simplify, simplify. "A wall goes up," Whitaker warned, "when you try to make Mr. and Mrs. Average American Citizen *work or think*."[85]

Make it personal, Whitaker and Baxter always advised: candidates are easier to sell than issues. If your position doesn't have an opposition, or if your candidate doesn't have an opponent, invent one. Once, when fighting an attempt to recall the mayor of San Francisco, Whitaker and Baxter waged a campaign against the Faceless Man—the idea was Baxter's—who might end up replacing him. Baxter drew a picture, on a tablecloth, of a fat man with a cigar poking out from beneath a face hidden by a hat, and then had him plastered on billboards all over the city, with the question "Who's Behind the Recall?" Pretend that you are the Voice of the People. Whitaker and Baxter bought radio ads, sponsored by "the Citizens Committee Against the Recall," in which an ominous voice said: "The real issue is whether the City Hall is to be turned over, lock, stock, and barrel, to an unholy alliance fronting for a faceless man." (The recall was defeated.) Attack, attack, attack. Said Whitaker: "You can't wage a defensive campaign and win!" Never underestimate the opposition.[86]

Never shy from controversy, they advised; instead, win the controversy. "The average American," Whitaker wrote, "doesn't want to be educated; he doesn't want to improve his mind; he doesn't even want to work, consciously, at being a good citizen. But there are two ways you can interest him in a campaign, and only two that we have ever found successful." You can put on a fight ("he likes a good hot battle, with no punches pulled"), or you can put on a show ("he likes the movies; he likes mysteries; he likes fireworks and parades"): "So if you can't fight, PUT ON A SHOW! And if you put on a good show, Mr. and Mrs. America will turn out to see it."[87]

Whitaker and Baxter, more effectively than any politician, addressed the problem of mass democracy with an elegant solution: they turned politics into a business. But their very success depended, in part, on the rise of another political industry: public opinion polling.

THE AMERICAN PUBLIC OPINION industry began as democracy's answer to fascist propaganda. By the end of 1933, Joseph Goebbels had established a Broadcasting Division within his Ministry of Propaganda and had undertaken production of cheap radio sets, the Volksempfanger, or "people's set," with the aim of ensuring that the government could reach every household, in a practice Goebbels liked to describe as "mind-bombing."[88] Fascists told the people what to believe; democrats asked them. But the scientific measurement of public opinion would come to rest on its ability to accurately predict the outcome of national elections.

*Joseph Goebbels, Germany's minister of propaganda,
made especially effective use of radio,
here used to address Hitler Youth.*

From the start, the industry embraced a paradox. Publicly and reliably predicting the outcome of an election would seem to undercut democracy, not promote it. Notwithstanding this paradox, polling proceeded.

Newspapers had been predicting local election results for decades, but predicting the outcome of a national election required a network of newspapers. In 1904, the *New York Herald*, the *Cincinnati Enquirer*, the *Chicago Record-Herald* and the *St. Louis Republic* joined forces to forecast elections, tallying their straws together. By 1916, the *Herald* had organized a group of newspapers in thirty-six states. That year, the *Literary Digest*, a national magazine, began mailing out ballots as a publicity stunt. The *Digest* used its polls to try to attract new subscribers; its plan was to collect more ballots than anyone else. In 1920, the *Digest* distributed eleven million ballots and, in 1924, more than sixteen million.[89] For reach, its only real rival was the chain of newspapers owned by William Randolph Hearst, which was able to report the results of polls in forty-three states. Although the *Literary Digest* sometimes miscalculated the popular vote, it always got the Electoral College winner right. In 1924, the *Digest's* forecast was right for all but two states and in 1928 for all but four.

A newspaperman named Emil Hurja figured out that this method was nevertheless bound to fail, since what matters is not the size of a stack of straws but its variety. Hurja tried to convince the Democratic National Committee to conduct its straw polls using ore sampling methods. "In mining you take several samples from the face of the ore, pulverize them, and find out what the average pay per ton will be," Hurja explained. "In politics you take sections of voters, check new trends against past performances, establish percentage shift among different voting strata, supplement this information from competent observers in the field, and you can accurately predict an election result." In 1928, the DNC dismissed Hurja as a crank, but by 1932 he was running FDR's campaign.[90] By 1932, the *Literary Digest*'s mailing list had grown to more than twenty million names. Most of those names were taken from telephone directories and automobile registration files. Hurja was one of the few people who understood that the *Digest* had consistently underestimated FDR's support because its sample, while very big, was not very representative: people who supported FDR were much less likely than the rest of the population to own a telephone or a car.[91]

Hurja was borrowing from the insights of social science. But the real innovation in public opinion measurement was a method that had been devised by social scientists in the 1920s, which was to use statistics to estimate the opinions of a vast population by surveying a statistically representative sample.

Political polling is the marriage of journalism and social science, a marriage made by George Gallup. "When I went to college, I wanted to study journalism, and later on go out and be an editor of a newspaper," Gallup said, remembering his days at the University of Iowa in the 1920s, but "in my day I couldn't get a degree in journalism, so I got my degree in psychology." He graduated in 1923, entered a graduate program in a new field, Applied Psychology, where everyone was talking about Walter Lippmann's 1922 book, *Public Opinion*, and Gallup got interested in the problem of measuring it. His first idea was to use the sample survey to understand how people read the news. In 1928, in a dissertation called "An Objective Method for Determining Reader Interest in the Content of a Newspaper," he argued that "at one time the press was depended upon as the chief agency for instructing and informing the mass of people," but that the growth of public schools meant that newspapers no longer filled that role and instead ought to meet "a greater need for entertainment." He had therefore devised a method to measure "reader interest," a way to know what parts of the paper readers found entertaining. He called it the "Iowa method": "It consists chiefly of going through a newspaper, column by column, with a reader of the paper." The interviewer would then mark up the newspaper to show what parts the reader had enjoyed. "The Iowa method offers the newspaper editor a scientific means for fitting his paper to his community," Gallup wrote: he could hire an expert in measurement to conduct a study to find out what features and writers his readers like best, and then stop printing the boring stuff.[92]

In 1932, when Gallup was a professor of journalism at Northwestern, his mother-in-law, Ola Babcock Miller, ran for lieutenant governor of Iowa. Her husband had died in office; her nomination was largely honorary and she was not expected to win. Gallup decided to apply his ideas about measuring reader interest to understanding her chances. After that, he moved to New York and began working for an advertising agency, where, while also teaching at Columbia, he perfected a method for measuring the size of a radio audience. He conducted some experiments in 1933 and 1934, trying to figure out how to better predict elections for newspapers and magazines, and started a company he named the Editors' Research Bureau. Gallup liked to call public opinion measurement "a new field of journalism." But he decided his work needed a scholarly pedigree. In 1935, he renamed the Editors' Research Bureau the American Institute of Public Opinion and established it in Princeton, New Jersey, which also made it sound more academic.[93]

Gallup's method was to survey public opinion by asking questions of a sample of the population carefully chosen to represent the whole of it. He said he was taking the "pulse of democracy." (Wrote a skeptical E. B. White: "Although you can take a nation's pulse, you can't be sure that the nation hasn't just run up a flight of stairs.") In 1935, to announce the publication of a new weekly column by Gallup, the Washington Post launched a blimp over the nation's capital trailing a streamer that read "America Speaks!"[94]

Gallup intended the measurement of public opinion to be a tool for democratic government, a tool intended to do the very opposite of the work of political consulting. Political consulting is the business of managing the opinions of the masses. Public opinion surveying is the business of finding out the opinions of the masses. Political consultants tell voters what to think; pollsters ask them what they think. But neither of these businesses gives a great deal of credit to the idea that voters ought to make independent judgments, or that they can.

New industries, new technologies, and the conduct of the war itself heightened longstanding concerns about the power of propaganda. Joseph Goebbels, who had completed his PhD in 1921, had been greatly influenced by Edward Bernays, and used the methods of American public relations in broadcasting messages by print, radio, film, and parades. Goebbels had a device installed in his office that allowed him to preempt national programming, and he deployed "radio wardens" to make sure Germans were listening to official broadcasts. The purpose of fascist propaganda is to control the opinions of the masses and deploy them in service of the power of the state. Germans had attempted to employ Bernays himself; he refused, but other American public relations firms had accepted commissions to produce pro-Nazi propaganda in the United States. Goebbels hoped to sow division in the United States, partly through a shortwave radio system, the Weltrundfunksender, or World Broadcasting Station, the Propaganda Ministry's "long-range propaganda artillery." By 1934 it was broadcasting pro-Germany English- and foreign-language propaganda to Africa, Latin America, the Far East, Southeast Asia, Indonesia, and Australia, though its broadcasts to North America far outstripped the scale of all of its other programs. To the United States, where it broadcast in "American English," the Weltrundfunksender sent false "news," chiefly having to do with claims about a "Communist Jewish conspiracy."[95]

Newspapers took to calling this sort of thing "fake news."[96] But some Americans worried that not much separated fake news from the work of Whitaker and Baxter's Lie Factory, or even from the forms of political persuasion deployed by the White House. Roosevelt's critics accused him of adapting the radio for purposes of propaganda. The Democratic National Committee's executive secretary talked about voters in much the same way as Whitaker and Baxter did: "The average American's mind works simply and it is not hard to keep him behind the President if we can properly inform him as to what is going on in Washington, what the President is trying to do, and the specific objectives he is seeking." This was best done, the DNC secretary pointed out, "from a source of confidence like the radio." But, in contrast to Europe, the government in the United States neither owned nor, in the end, controlled the radio.[97] And nothing in FDR's arsenal of persuasion came close to the deception practiced on voters by the nation's first political consultants.

Still, even Roosevelt's closest allies worried. Felix Frankfurter, an adviser to the president and a longtime friend of Walter Lippmann's—they'd lived together in the House of Truth—warned Roosevelt to keep clear of public relations professionals, calling men like Bernays "professional poisoners of the public mind, exploiters of foolishness, fanaticism, and self-interest."[98] FDR, though, was drawn not to Bernays but to Gallup. He trimmed his sails by the daily voter mail—and, more and more, by the weekly polls. Roosevelt was willing to use broad executive powers to accomplish his agenda, but not without popular support. With FDR, polling entered the White House and the American political process. And there it remained.

## IV.

ON JUNE 27, 1936, Roosevelt accepted his party's nomination at the University of Pennsylvania's Franklin Field before a crowd of 100,000. "This generation of Americans has a rendezvous with destiny," he said. The United States was now fighting to save democracy both "for ourselves and for the world."[99] Saving democracy at home required dismantling Jim Crow. This Roosevelt did not do.

Jim Crow defined New Deal politics. Between violence, poll taxes, literacy tests, and other forms of disenfranchisement, less than 4 percent of African Americans were registered to vote. Nevertheless, "the revenge of the slave is to place his masters in such subjection that they can make no decision, political, social, economic, or ethical, without reference to him," Anne O'Hare McCormick wrote in 1930. "Voteless, he dominates politics."[100]

FDR's reliance on public opinion surveys made this problem worse.

Gallup's early method is known as "quota sampling." He analyzed the electorate to determine what proportion of the people who vote are men, women, black, white, young, and old. The people who conducted his surveys had to fill a quota so that the survey respondents would constitute an exactly proportionate mini-electorate. But what Gallup presented to the American public as "public opinion" was the opinion of Americans who were disproportionately wealthy, white, and male. Nationwide, in the 1930s and 1940s, blacks constituted about 10 percent of the population but made up less than 2 percent of Gallup's survey group. Because blacks in the South generally could not vote, Gallup assigned no "Negro quota" in those states.[101] Instead of representing public opinion, polling essentially silenced the voices of African Americans.

Roosevelt's electoral coalition drew African Americans from the Republican Party; he consulted an informal group of advisers who came to be called his "black cabinet"; and he appointed the first African American federal judge. But New Deal programs were generally segregated, and Roosevelt failed to act to oppose lynching. After twenty-three lynchings in 1933, anti-lynching legislation was introduced into Congress. The next year, a man named Claude Neal, accused of rape and murder, was taken from a jail in Alabama and brought to Florida, where he was tortured, mutilated, and executed before four thousand spectators. In the Senate, southern Democrats waged a filibuster against the anti-lynching bill.[102] "If I come out for the anti-lynching bill now, they will block every bill I ask Congress to pass to keep America from collapsing," Roosevelt told the NAACP's Walter White. "Southerners, by reason of the seniority rule in Congress, are chairmen or occupy strategic places on most of the Senate and House committees." The anti-lynching bill died.[103]

Gallup's influence, meanwhile, grew. In 1936, in the pages of the *New York Herald-Tribune*, he predicted that *Literary Digest* would forecast that Alf Landon would defeat FDR in a landslide and that the *Digest* would be wrong. He was right on both counts.[104] This, though, was only the beginning of what Gallup intended to do. "I had the idea of polling on every major issue," he explained. As the world reeled and the end of liberal democracy appeared near to hand, Gallup argued that the measurement of public opinion was critical to the fight against fascism and the solution to the problem of mass democracy. In the fast-moving modern world,

"We need to know the will of the people at all times." Elections came only every two years but, by measuring the public's views on issues almost instantly, elected officials could better represent their constituents—more efficiently, and more democratically. Gallup believed that his method had rescued American politics from the political machine and restored it to the American pastoral: "Today, the New England town meeting idea has, in a sense, been restored." He was not alone. Elmer Roper, another early pollster, called the public opinion survey "the greatest contribution to democracy since the introduction of the secret ballot."[105]

*Time* coined the word "pollsters" in 1939, and, in the public mind, the word "polls" came to mean two different things: surveys of public opinion and forecasts of elections. When Gallup started, he conducted forecasts only in order to prove the accuracy of his surveys, there being no other way to demonstrate it.[106] That aside, the forecasts themselves were pointless.

Congress called for an investigation. "These polls are a racket, and their methods should be exposed to the public," Walter Pierce, a Democratic member of the House, wrote in 1939. (Pierce, like many critics of polling, which tended to show that Americans favored entering the war, was an isolationist.) Part of the concern was that polls were fraudulent. Another concern was that they were interfering with the proper function of elections and of government. Polls don't represent the people, one congressman wrote; Congress does: "Polls are in contradiction to representative government."[107]

A genuine antidote to fascism—a way to bolster representative government—was to promote open, fair-minded public debate. *America's Town Meeting of the Air* debuted on NBC Radio in 1935, ringing in each episode with the cry, "Oyez! Oyez! Come to the old town hall and talk it over!" *America's Town Meeting of the Air* aimed to break radio listeners out of their political bubbles. "If we persist in the practice of Republicans reading only Republican newspapers, listening only to Republican speeches on the radio, attending only Republican political rallies, and mixing socially only with those of congenial views," its moderator warned, "and if Democrats . . . follow suit, we are sowing the seeds of the destruction of our democracy." Each episode took the form of a formal debate about a policy question—for instance, "Does America need compulsory health insurance?" It went a long way toward achieving its object: the program spawned more than a thousand debating clubs, in which citizens listened together and, after the broadcast, staged their own face-to-face debates.[108]

Revealingly, FDR himself refused to debate on air. Candidates for local, statewide, and even national office had been debating on the radio since the early 1920s, but Roosevelt turned away all challengers, insisting, unconvincingly, that no president should debate on air because he might let slip a state secret. Republicans, frustrated, spliced bits of his speeches and other speeches into a rebuttal given by Republican senator Arthur Vandenberg and gave it to radio stations to broadcast as a "debate." Sixty-six stations were supposed to air the program; twenty-one, on learning that the debate was a fake, refused.[109]

Observers noted the dangers of radio—it appeared the perfect instrument for the propagandist—but just as many expressed much the same enthusiasm for radio as Frederick Douglass had expressed for photography, or as boosters of the Internet would express in years to come. Between 1930 and 1935, the number of radios in the United States doubled. "Distinctions between rural and urban communities, men and women, age and youth, social classes, creeds, states, and nations are abolished," wrote the psychologists Hadley Cantril and Gordon W. Allport in 1935. "As if by magic the barriers of social stratification disappear and in their place comes a consciousness of equality and of a community of interest."[110] Some of that, no doubt, did come to pass. But radio also created and strengthened both new and old forms of affiliation—and division.

Radio made fundamentalism into a national movement. In 1925, Paul Rader, the director of the Chicago Gospel Tabernacle, began broadcasting *The National Radio Chapel*. During the hardest years of the Depression, revivalist ministers railed against modernity and the suffering it had wrought, calling on listeners to return to God. *Radio Bible Class*, broadcast from Grand Rapids, Michigan, brought the tradition of Sunday and summer Bible study to communities that stretched as far as its radio signal could reach. New York's Calvary Baptist Church and the Bible Institute of Los Angeles were among those churches that owned their own radio stations. Fundamentalists founded new colleges in those years, too, and recruited students on air: Bob Jones College was founded in Florida in 1926 and moved to Cleveland, Tennessee, in 1933; William Jennings Bryan University was founded in Dayton, Tennessee, in 1930. Illinois's Wheaton College—the "Harvard of the Bible Belt"—had four hundred students in 1926 and eleven hundred in 1941; its students include Billy Graham. By 1939, the *Old Fashioned Revival Hour*, broadcast from Los Angeles over the Mutual network, reached an audience as large as twenty million.[111]

Radio also nourished populism. Charles Coughlin, a Catholic priest, began broadcasting Sunday Mass from a Michigan radio station in 1926 and in 1930 CBS decided to deliver his program, *The Golden Hour of the Little Flower*, over its national network. Turning from religion to politics and embracing a tacit anti-Semitism, Coughlin denounced "Wall Street financiers," and although at first an avid supporter of FDR, he by 1934 began considering his own bid for the White House. In May 1935 he addressed an audience of thirty thousand passionate supporters in Madison Square Garden, some carrying placards reading "Our Next President."[112]

Wild-eyed, fist-stamping Louisiana senator Huey Long rallied his followers by radio, too. Long, born in 1893, had passed the bar while working as a traveling salesman and been elected governor of Louisiana in 1928, the year FDR was elected governor of New York. A fiery populist, he'd ruthlessly accumulated political power in Louisiana before building a national political movement, the Share Our Wealth Society. Late in 1933, Long broke with FDR, calling him a dictator, and was soon attacking him on the radio. He bought coast-to-coast national airtime. "While I'm talking," he'd say at the beginning of a broadcast, "I want you to go to the telephone and call up five of your friends and tell them that Huey is on the air." Then he'd fill time for a few minutes, waiting for his audience to grow. Derided as a dangerous demagogue, he'd reached the peak of his power in September 1935, when he was gunned down in Baton Rouge by the son-in-law of one of his staunchest political enemies. "Every Man a King" had been Huey Long's motto. He died the death of Polonius, ridiculous. Coughlin, hoping to enlist Long's followers, merged his own organization with Long's Share Our Wealth Society and formed the Union Party, running as its presidential candidate against the man he'd taken to calling Franklin Double-Crossing Roosevelt.[113] He earned fewer than a million votes.

In November 1936, Roosevelt won reelection in another unprecedented electoral landslide, 523 to 8, and with more than 60 percent of the popular vote. Misjudging his power, he decided to forge ahead with continued reforms, a plan that required battling the Supreme Court.

EVEN BEFORE HE took office in 1933, FDR had begun lining up judicial support for his legislative agenda, meeting with Oliver Wendell Holmes, who told him, "You are in a war, Mr. President, and in a war there is only one rule, 'Form your battalion and fight!" At the end of his first hundred days in office, FDR had secured the passage of fifteen legislative elements of his New Deal. All had to do with the federal government's role in the regulation of the economy—and therefore, with the commerce clause in Article One, Section 8, of the Constitution, which granted to Congress the power "to regulate commerce with foreign nations, and among the several states, and with the Indian tribes." It would fall to the Supreme Court to decide whether or not the New Deal fell within this power.

The New Deal broadened and intensified the longstanding debate over the nature of the Constitution. "I don't believe in one generation deciding what the others shall do," wrote one philosophy professor in 1931. "Our forefathers didn't know anything about a country of 120,000,000 people, with automobiles, trains, and radios." How could a people committed to the idea of progress shackle themselves to the past? "Hopeful people today wave the flag," Thurman Arnold, FDR's assistant attorney general, said; "timid people wave the Constitution."[114]

Meanwhile, the court took on new trappings of power. In early 1933, just before leaving office, Hoover had laid the cornerstone for a new building for the court. Materials were shipped from all over the world: marble from Spain, Italy, and Africa; mahogany from Honduras. At a budget of $10 million, the plan was to build the largest marble building in the world. At the ceremony, after Hoover turned over a trowel's worth of dirt, Chief Justice Charles Evans Hughes delivered remarks recalling the court's long years of wandering, bumped from rooms in one federal building to another for a century and a half. "The court began its work a homeless department of the government," Hughes said, but "above the cornerstone we lay today will rise a memorial more sublime than monuments of war."[115]

Hughes, a reformer, had been appointed to the court twice; in between, he'd run for president. In 1906, running for governor of New York against William Randolph Hearst, Hughes had spent $619 against Hearst's $500,000—and won.[116] Once in office, Hughes pushed through the state legislature a clean elections law, limiting how much candidates were allowed to spend during a campaign. In 1910, Taft appointed Hughes to the Supreme Court, where, as a champion of civil liberties, he often joined with Holmes in dissent. Hughes resigned from the bench in 1916 to run for president; he lost, narrowly, to Wilson. He served as secretary of state under Harding and Coolidge before returning to the court under Hoover.

In Hughes's court, four conservative justices, known as the Four Horsemen, had consistently voted in favor of a liberty of contract, while the three liberals, Louis Brandeis, Benjamin Cardozo, and Harlan Stone, generally supported government regulation and found legislative efforts like minimum-wage laws to be consistent with the Constitution. That left Hughes and Owen Roberts as the deciding votes. In early rulings on New Deal legislation, the court, voting 5–4, Hughes and Roberts joining the liberals, let Roosevelt's agenda stand. "While an emergency does not create power," Hughes said, "an emergency may furnish the occasion for the exercise of the power."[117]

In the January 1935 session, the court heard arguments in another series of challenges to the New Deal. Anticipating that the court would rule against him, FDR drafted a speech. ("For use if needed," he wrote at the top.) But in February, the court again upheld his agenda, 5–4, leading one of the horsemen to cry, "The Constitution is gone!"[118] Roosevelt would need that speech by spring. On May 27, 1935, the court met in the Old Senate Chamber for the final time. On that day, in three unanimous decisions, the justices kicked the teeth out of the New Deal. Most importantly, it found that the National Recovery Administration, which Roosevelt had called the "most important and far-reaching legislation in the history of the American Congress," was unconstitutional, because Congress had exceeded the powers granted to it under the commerce clause. "The implications of this decision," FDR said, "are much more important than any decision probably since the *Dred Scott* case." Then he raged about the scant powers available to Congress to relieve a failing economy: "We have been relegated to the horse-and-buggy definition of interstate commerce."[119] But in the horse-and-buggy days, the court didn't have half as much power as it had claimed by 1935.

Six months later, when the court resumed, it met in its opulent new building, described by one reporter as an icebox decorated by a mad upholsterer. And then the Hughes Court went on a spree, striking down more than a dozen federal laws in less than eighteen months. Congress kept passing them; the court kept striking them down. At one point, FDR's solicitor general fainted in the courtroom. "Never before in the history of our country has the Supreme Court been called upon to adjudicate the constitutionality of so many acts of Congress which so vitally affected the life of every American as in the period 1933 to 1936," wrote a onetime constitutional law professor, in one of dozens of tracts published that attempted to explain this set of cases to voters. "Eight acts or portions of acts were declared unconstitutional, two were declared constitutional, and in four instances actions of executive officers or commissions were held to be outside the pale of the Constitution."[120]

The president began entertaining proposals about fighting back. One senator had an idea. "It takes twelve men to find a man guilty of murder," he said. "I don't see why it should not take a unanimous court to find a law unconstitutional." That would have required a constitutional amendment, a process that is notoriously corruptible. "Get me ten million dollars," Roosevelt said, "and I can prevent any amendment to the Constitution from being ratified by the necessary number of states."[121] He bided his time.

In November 1936, one week before Election Day, *The Nine Old Men*, an attack on the Hughes Court as feeble and daft, had begun appearing in the nation's newspapers and in bookstores; it became a best seller.[122] Inaugurated for a second term on January 20, 1937—Inauguration Day having been moved from March 4—Roosevelt immediately set about challenging the judicial branch. On February 5, he announced his plan to restructure the Supreme Court. Flushed with victory, and confident that Hughes's power was on the wane, Roosevelt floated his plan. Claiming that the justices were doddering and unable to keep up with the business at hand, he said that he would name an additional justice for every sitting justice over the age of seventy, which described six of them. The chief justice was seventy-four.

Roosevelt's overreach in 1937 resulted, in part, from his overestimation of the economic recovery. Believing the crisis to be nearly over, he cut federal expenditures, especially to the Works Progress Administration. A recession set in. "The Recession is more remarkable than the Depression," *Time* reported, citing a 35 percent decline in industrial production from the previous summer as "the swiftest decline in the history of U.S. business and finance." The brain trust was out of ideas. "We have pulled all the rabbits out of the hat and there are no more rabbits," one House Democrat said.[123] And still Roosevelt forged ahead.

In a fireside chat on March 9, 1937, Roosevelt compared the court crisis to the banking crisis, the subject of his first fireside chat. He argued that the time had come "to save the Constitution from the Court, and the Court from itself." This time, the radio magic didn't work. The president's approval rating had fallen from 65 percent to 51 percent. And, deftly, Hughes soon all but put the matter to rest. "The Supreme Court is fully abreast of its work," he reported on March 22, in a persuasive letter to the Senate Judiciary Committee. If efficiency were actually a concern, he wrote, there was a great deal of evidence to suggest that more justices would only slow things down.[124]

Then came the reversal. Beginning with *West Coast Hotel Co. v. Parrish*, a ruling issued on March 29, 1937, in a 5–4 opinion written by Hughes, sustaining a minimum-wage requirement for women, the Supreme Court began upholding the New Deal. Owen Roberts switched sides, a switch so sudden, and so crucial to the preservation of the court, that it was dubbed "the switch in time that saved nine." It looked purely political. "Even a blind man ought to see that the Court is in politics," Felix Frankfurter wrote to Roosevelt, "and understand how the Constitution is 'judicially construed.' It is a deep object lesson—a lurid demonstration—of the relation of men to the 'meaning' of the Constitution."[125]

On May 18, 1937, the Senate Judiciary Committee voted against moving the president's proposal out of committee. The court-packing plan was dead. Six days later, the Supreme Court upheld the old-age insurance provisions of the Social Security Act. The president, and his deal, had won. If the shift had more to do with law than with influence, it certainly didn't give that appearance, and it came at a cost of public confidence. In June 1937, H. L. Mencken published a satirical "Constitution for the New Deal" that began: "All governmental power of whatever sort shall be vested in a President of the United States."[126]

In 1938, FDR proposed a $5 billion spending plan, following the Keynesian argument that public spending was the best way to fight economic decline and stagnation. But Keynes himself was worried. In February, he wrote the president, "I am terrified lest progressive causes in all the democratic countries should suffer injury, because you have taken too lightly the risk to their prestige which would result from a failure measured in terms of immediate prosperity." In April, by a margin of 204 votes, a number that included 108 Democrats, Congress voted down FDR's plan to reorganize the executive branch, hire more White House staff, and move the Budget office from the Treasury Department to the White House. The bill would eventually pass, in a latter session, but leeway granted to Roosevelt in 1933 had been lost. As one critic of FDR wrote, "We have just witnessed, in Europe, what happens when one man is permitted too much power."[127] No one wanted to watch that closer to home.

ON MARCH 15, 1938, before a swastika-waving crowd of two hundred thousand German Austrians at Vienna's Heldenplatz, Plaza of Heroes, Adolf Hitler announced the Anschluss, the unification of Germany and Austria. Goebbels arranged for his Ministry of Propaganda to absorb the Austrian broadcasting system.[128] Having seized all branches of government and eliminated his political opposition in 1933, Hitler had stripped German Jews of citizenship beginning in 1935, with the Nuremberg Laws. He'd built an air force and raised an army. In 1936, he had sent a thirty-five-thousand-man army into the Rhineland and met no armed resistance. Later that year, he entered into an alliance called the Axis, with Japan and Italy. Pressing for a "Greater Germany," he'd at first forced Austria's chancellor to call for a referendum on unification, scheduled for March 13, 1938, but then, announcing that Germany would not accept the result of the referendum, he'd invaded what had been his homeland. Austrian forces had not resisted. Nor, despite Germany's having violated the Treaty of Versailles, did much of Europe.

Live, on-the-scene reporting began with that crisis, as did the breaking news bulletin, an interruption of regularly scheduled programming. During the whole of the crisis in Austria, American radio networks interrupted their regular programming to air news and opinion from Rome, Paris, London, and Berlin, often relayed by shortwave radio. Reporters interviewed witnesses on the spot, their microphones capturing the sounds of the streets, the clatter of horse hooves, the drone of sirens. In September, as Hitler tried to seize for Germany a portion of Czechoslovakia known as the Sudetenland and Europe teetered on the brink of war, radio announcers around the world provided, hour by hour, emergency updates. During the eighteen-day Munich crisis, NBC interrupted its programing 440 times. So pressing and urgent was the news that CBS stopped broadcasting ads. During those eighteen days, CBS reporter H. V. Kaltenborn, who never read from a script, made 102 broadcasts from New York, piecing together the on-the-scene reports, and slept, if he slept at all, on an army cot at CBS's Studio 9, with a microphone at his bedside.[129]

"The prime minister has sent the German Führer and Chancellor . . . the following message," the BBC reported on September 14, reading out loud a message sent to Hitler by Neville Chamberlain: "'In view of increasingly critical situation, I propose to come over at once to see you, with a view of trying to find a peaceful solution.'" Even as Chamberlain prepared to fly to Munich, Czech radio broadcasters struggled to counter Nazi propaganda. "Once again tonight we must perform the distasteful task of refuting further invented reports broadcast by the German wireless station," a Czech news anchor reported on September 18. "The Hungarian wireless station is apparently trying to compete with the Germans in the invention of false news."

"Hello America," said NBC correspondent Fred Bates on September 27. "This is London." Bates, his voice strained with anxiety, read aloud the leading editorials in the London newspapers, which made clear that, to Europe, the future of civilization itself had been cast into doubt. "I'm speaking to you this morning from the airport of the city of Munich," NBC's Max Jordan reported two days later, having been sent to the capital of Bavaria to report on the meeting of Hitler, Mussolini, Chamberlain, and the prime minister of France.[130] In what came to be called the Four-Power Pact, Italy, England, and France agreed to allow Germany to seize parts of Czechoslovakia. "What happened on Friday is called 'Peace,'"

*Newspapers around the country reported a panic during the 1938 broadcast of Orson Welles's The War of the Worlds.*

Dorothy Thompson said on her own radio broadcast the next day. "Actually, it is an international Fascist *coup d'etat*." The pact, she said, had been decided by four men in four hours, not one of whom had ever so much as set foot in Czechoslovakia, a country that Hitler would destroy and whose political minorities he would either murder or exile. The pact, Thompson said, means "the open establishment of terror."

Chamberlain, returning to London, announced that "all Europe may find peace" and, on a live radio broadcast, read aloud the agreement made with Hitler, even as his chief critic, Winston Churchill, damned him for appeasing Hitler in the altogether vain hope of avoiding war. "You were given the choice between war and dishonor," Churchill told Chamberlain. "You chose dishonor and you shall have war."[131]

The war Europe would have, the war the world would have, would be the first war waged in the age of radio, a war of the air. The fighting would unleash forces of savagery and barbarism. And the broadcasting of the war would suggest how, terrifyingly, "fake news" had become a weapon of tyrants. Nothing illustrated this better than a broadcast made, four weeks after the Munich crisis, by Orson Welles.

A little after eight in the evening of October 30, 1938, CBS Radio began its regular broadcast of Welles's *Mercury Theatre on the Air*, an hour-long radio drama that the network had signed on as part of its public-service programming mandate. That summer, Welles, twenty-three, had produced adaptations of *Dracula*, *The Count of Monte Cristo*, and the adventures of Sherlock Holmes. A theatrical prodigy, he had a genius for direction, a fascination with sound effects, and a particular talent for the art of spooking.

"The Columbia Broadcasting System and affiliated stations present Orson Welles and the *Mercury Theatre on the Air!*" the program always began, after which Welles would introduce that week's story. But on that evening, those in the audience who happened to miss the host's brief introduction found themselves listening to what seemed to be the nightly weather report, followed by a music program, into which a newsman broke in with an urgent announcement:

> Ladies and gentlemen, we interrupt our program of dance music to bring you a special bulletin from the Intercontinental Radio News. At twenty minutes before eight, central time, Professor Farrell of the Mount Jennings Observatory, Chicago, Illinois, reports observing several explosions of incandescent gas, occurring at regular intervals on the planet Mars.

After more music, another interruption brought the voice of a reporter named Carl Phillips, interviewing an astronomer at Princeton University. After another break, a much-shaken Phillips returned:

> Ladies and gentlemen, this is Carl Phillips again, out at the Wilmuth farm, Grovers Mill, New Jersey. . . . I hardly know where to begin, to paint for you a word picture of the strange scene before my eyes, like something out of a modern *Arabian Nights*. . . . I guess that's *it* . . . doesn't look very much like a meteor.

Suspense and tension heightening to panic, the radio network abandoned its dance music program for breathless reporting of an invasion from Mars, and of chaos in the streets as Americans tried to reach safety. The U.S. secretary of the interior addressed the "citizens of the nation" in hopes that their resistance might aid "the preservation of human supremacy on this earth." The ambition of the aliens was planetary. Said another voice: "Their apparent objective is to crush resistance, paralyze communi-cation, and disorganize human society."

The military took control of the airwaves. American cities, including New York, burned to the ground. "This may be the last broadcast," a despairing voice announced. "We'll stay here to the end. . . ." His voice breaks off as listeners hear the sound of his body falling. All that was heard next was what sounds like a shortwave radio operator:

> "2X2L calling CQ. . . . New York.
> Isn't there anyone on the air?"

Only then—but, according to the next day's newspaper reports, not before listeners all over the country panicked, called police, visited their parish priests to deliver their dying confessions, and ran screaming from their houses—did an announcer break in for a program identification, telling listeners that they'd been treated to "an original dramatization of *The War of the Worlds*."[132]

A decade of public relations and the authority of the radio had left Americans uncertain, anymore, about what was true. A contrite CBS announced that it would never again use "the technique of a simu-lated news broadcast." The FCC decided against reprisals. But all over the country commentators wondered what radio had wrought. Had the masses grown too passive, too eager to receive ready-made opinions?

Dorothy Thompson was grateful. "The greatest organizers of mass hys-terias and mass delusions today are states using the radio to excite terrors, incite hatreds, inflame masses, win mass support for policies, create idol-atries, abolish reason and maintain themselves in power." Having spent years trying to convince American readers of the rising tide of fascism, she concluded, "Welles has made a greater contribution to an understand-ing of Hitlerism, Mussolinism, Stalinism, anti-Semitism, and all the other terrorism of our times, more than will all the words about them that have been written."[133]

In 1938 and 1939, with CBS fighting $12 million in lawsuits over *The War of the Worlds*, Welles insisted that he never had any idea of the effect the broadcast was having, and certainly never meant to harm anyone.[134] But he later admitted that fifteen minutes into the broadcast, listeners had begun to panic, calling the station in terror. A New York policeman had even tried to break into the studio. "What's going on in there?" he'd called out. A station supervisor had asked Welles to stop the broadcast, or at least interrupt it, to reassure listeners.

"For God's sake, you're scaring people to death," the CBS supervisor said. "Please interrupt and tell them it's only a show."

"What do you mean interrupt?" Welles boomed. "They're scared? Good, they're supposed to be scared. Now let me finish."

Welles later insisted that his point, all along, had been to raise Americans' awareness about the perils of radio in an age of propaganda. "People suspect what they read in the newspaper," he said, but "when radio came . . . anything that came through that new machine was believed."[135] That didn't end with *The War of the Worlds*, which only made it harder for Americans to know what to believe. Except that this much they knew: something evil had been let loose upon the world.

On November 9, less than two weeks after the *War of the Worlds* broadcast, Nazis across Germany, Austria, and the Sudetenland burned more than seven thousand Jewish shops and more than a thousand synagogues. They murdered shopkeepers, and arrested more than thirty thousand Jews, a night known as Kristallnacht, after the smashed glass that littered the streets. "This is not a Jewish crisis," wrote Dorothy Thompson. "It is a human crisis."[136] It was as if the sky itself had shattered.

From the White House, Roosevelt said he "could scarcely believe that such things could occur in a twentieth-century civilization."[137] It was indeed difficult to believe. But a war of the worlds had begun.

## Twelve

# THE BRUTALITY
# OF MODERNITY

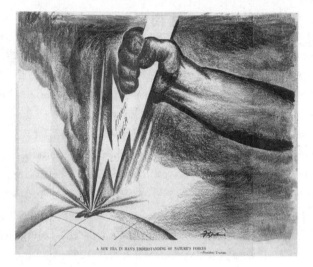

*The day after the United States bombed Hiroshima,*
*the* St. Louis Post-Dispatch *ran, as an editorial,*
*a crayon drawing titled* A New Era in Man's
Understanding of Nature's Forces.

THE 1939 WORLD'S FAIR WAS HELD ON TWELVE HUN-
dred acres in Queens, New York, a wasteland that had once been
an ash heap. Years of planning and building had gone into the work of
turning it into a fairground, a shimmering display of advances in politics,
business, science, and technology, right down to the scaled reproduction
of the Empire State Building. Its centerpiece was the Perisphere, a globe
two hundred feet in diameter and eighteen stories high that housed the
*Democracity* exhibit, a celebration of "the saga of democracy," which took
visitors to a world one hundred years in the future, to 2039, where highways carried people from suburbs like Pleasantville to the downtown of

Centerton.[1] The fair celebrated the defeat of the past; its theme was the World of Tomorrow. General Motors mounted an exhibit called *Futurama.* Westinghouse staged a "battle of the centuries" between Mrs. Drudge, who scrubbed, and Mrs. Modern, who used a dishwasher. Elektro the Moto-Man, a seven-foot-tall robot, suavely smoked a cigarette.[2]

On opening day, on April 30, 1939, in a ceremony held in the fair's Court of Peace, Franklin Delano Roosevelt, his hair gone gray at the temples, declared the World's Fair "open to all mankind." RCA, introducing the brand-new technology of television, sent out the address on NBC, which began broadcasting that day. A chorus line of women dressed in white performed a "Pageant of Peace." A lot of visitors to the World of Tomorrow were unimpressed. E. B. White had a cold the day he went. "When you can't breathe through your nose," he wrote, "Tomorrow seems strangely like the day before yesterday." *Harper's* offered a more mixed view: "It was the paradox of all paradoxes. It was good, it was bad; it was the acme of all crazy vulgarity; it was the pinnacle of all inspiration."[3]

It was also obsolete, even before it began. On opening day, the pavilions featuring Austria and Czechoslovakia were already anachronisms: those countries no longer existed. The allure of the future faded fast. After Hitler invaded Poland, in September, the Polish pavilion was draped in black. Belgium, Denmark, France, Luxembourg, and the Netherlands soon followed. By the time the fair closed, eighteen months after it opened, and bankrupt, half of the European countries represented at the World's Fair had fallen to Germany.[4]

The Second World War would bring the United States out of depression, end American isolationism, and forge a renewed spirit of civic nationalism. It would also call attention to the nation's unfinished reckoning with race, reshape liberalism, and form the foundation for a conservative movement animated by opposition to state power. By 1945, the future imagined six years before at the site of an old ash heap in Queens would look antique.

Still, the fair left its mark. Westinghouse had collected hundreds of items for a time capsule, to be opened five thousand years in the future, in the year 6939: everything from an alarm clock to an electric razor, along with seeds of grain provided by the U.S. Department of Agriculture, thousands of photographs, magazines, a dictionary, much of the *Encyclopedia Britannica* (14th edition, 1937), an RKO newsreel and a

motion-picture projector, and one hundred books, in the form of microfilm. ("A microscope is included to enable historians of the future to read
the microfilm; also included are instructions for making larger reading
machines such as those used with microfilm in modern libraries.") Not
everything was hokum. Among the "special messages from noted men of
our time," Albert Einstein had contributed a letter, written to tomorrow
from today.[5]

"People living in different countries kill each other at irregular time
intervals," Einstein reported of the world in 1939. And "anyone who thinks
about the future must live in fear and terror."[6] As Orson Welles had
warned, introducing *The War of the Worlds* the year before, "In the thirty-
ninth year of the twentieth century came the great disillusionment. . . ."

# I.

ON SEPTEMBER 1, 1939, the day Germany invaded Poland, a ceremony was taking place in Geneva. Officials from the League of Nations
dedicated a sculpture, a giant bronze globe, "To the Memory of Woodrow Wilson, President of the United States, Founder of the League of
Nations." Two days later, Britain and France, having fatefully appeased
Hitler at Munich the year before, declared war on Germany. Had the
United States not failed to join the League of Nations in 1919, some people thought, the world-shatteringly brutal war that followed might have
been avoided. "The United States now has her second opportunity to
make the world safe for democracy," said Henry Wallace, Roosevelt's secretary of agriculture. That fall, internationalists like Wallace who regretted the failure of the League of Nations began meeting, usually in secret,
to plan the peace—to imagine a new league. The Council on Foreign
Relations began preparing a report for the State Department.[7] Meanwhile, Roosevelt was trying to plan for war.

In the 1930s, both Congress and public opinion favored isolationism. In
1935, Congress passed the first of five Neutrality Acts, pledging that the
United States would keep clear of war in Europe. In 1936, when civil war
broke out in Spain, nearly three thousand private American citizens volunteered, and fought for democracy against a right-wing insurgency aided
by Hitler and Mussolini; more than a quarter of them lost their lives. But

the United States stayed out. A Gallup poll taken in 1937 reported that most Americans had no opinion about events going on in Spain.[8]

American indifference emboldened Germany. "America is not dangerous to us," Hitler said. "Everything about the behavior of American society reveals that it's half Judaized, and the other half Negrified," he said. "How can one expect a State like that to hold together—a country where everything is built on the dollar?" Americans' gullibility about Orson Welles's radio production of *The War of the Worlds* revealed Americans to be fools, Hitler thought, and Americans were too selfish to concern themselves with Europe: if he had a grudging respect for stolid Soviets, he saw Americans as fools distracted by baubles. "Transport a German to Kiev, and he remains a perfect German," Hitler said. "But transport him to Miami, and you make a degenerate out of him."[9]

Late in 1938, FDR had proposed a plan by which the United States would manufacture airplanes for Britain and France and build a 10,000-plane American air force. In 1939 he presented this plan, with a budget of $300 million, to Congress. "This program is but the minimum of requirements," the president said. While the Nazi war machine pummeled Europe, the president wanted Congress to repeal the Neutrality Acts, support American allies, and prepare American forces, a position that became known as his "short-of-war" strategy. Secretly, he had another worry, too. German chemists had discovered nuclear fission in 1938. Leo Szilard, a Hungarian scientist who had fled Germany, had come to New York with the news. Germany took over Czechoslovakia in March 1939. In August, Roosevelt received a letter written by Szilard and signed by Einstein, warning him about "extremely powerful bombs of a new type," fueled by uranium. "The United States has only very poor ores of uranium in moderate quantity," the physicist informed the president. But "I understand that Germany has actually stopped the sale of uranium from the Czechoslovakian mines which she has taken over." Roosevelt gathered together a secret advisory committee to investigate. It soon reported to him that uranium "would provide a possible source of bombs with a destructiveness vastly greater than anything now known."[10]

Before Germany invaded Poland, nearly half of Americans had been unwilling or unable even to commit themselves to favoring one side over the other in the conflict in Europe, not least because William Randolph

Hearst, who'd opposed U.S. involvement in the war in Europe in 1917 (calling for "America first!"), took the same position in 1938. Over NBC Radio he warned that the nations of Europe were "all ready to go to war, and all eager to get us to go to war," but that "Americans should maintain the traditional policy of our great and independent nation—great largely because it is independent."[11] A fringe fervently supported Hitler. Father Coughlin, who'd left broadcasting after failing to win the presidency, returned to radio in 1937, when he began to preach anti-Semitism and admiration for Hitler and the Nazi Party. To the extent that Hitler recip-rocated, it was to express his admiration not for the United States but for the Confederacy, whose defeat in the Civil War he much regretted: "the beginnings of a great new social order based on the principle of slavery and inequality were destroyed by the war," he wrote. Nazi propagandists, sowing discord, tried to make common cause with white southerners by urging the repeal of the Fourteenth and Fifteenth Amendments.[12] Coughlin played into their hands. In 1939, his audience, while dimin-ished, heeded his call to form a new political party, the Christian Front.[13] Dorothy Thompson ridiculed him. "I am 44 years old and if I have been menaced by Jews I haven't noticed it yet." (Her strategy was always to refuse to take Coughlin seriously. He once referred to her on the radio as "Dotty"; after that, she never failed, in her column, to call him "Chuck.") Twenty thousand Americans, some dressed in Nazi uniforms, gathered in a Madison Square Garden bedecked with swastikas and American flags, where they denounced the New Deal as the "Jew Deal," at a "Mass Demonstration for True Americanism." Thompson snuck into the rally, started laughing, and, even as she was dragged out by men dressed as storm troopers, kept calling out, "Bunk, bunk, bunk!"[14]

But if radio had first gained Coughlin his audience, it also helped bring him down, especially after an Episcopal priest from New Jersey named Father W. C. Kiernan launched a radio program whose purpose was to refute each of Coughlin's arguments. A callback to the protests of abo-litionists and anti-lynching crusaders from Frederick Douglass to Ida B. Wells, Kiernan called his program *Free Speech Forum*.[15]

After Britain and France declared war on Germany in September, *Fortune* magazine raced to add to its next issue a supplement called "The War of 1939," which included a map of Europe and a survey of public opinion.[16] "In the trouble now going on in Europe, which side would you like to see win?" *Fortune*'s survey asked. Eighty-three percent of Americans now chose "England, France, Poland and their friends." Only 1 percent chose "Germany and her friends."[17]

The forces of isolation, however, remained strong. *Fortune*'s map made Europe seem near. But in a speech on October 1, 1939, American aviator Charles Lindbergh, who in 1927 had been the first man to fly nonstop across the Atlantic alone, said, "One need only glance at a map to see where our true frontiers lie. What more could we ask than the Atlantic Ocean on the east and the Pacific on the west?" Europe might be engaged in an air war, and Americans might build an air force but, said Lindbergh, "An ocean is a formidable barrier, even for modern aircraft."[18]

Isolationists developed a vision of "Fortress America." Most isolationists were Republicans, while opposition to isolationism was strongest among southern Democrats, who were committed to global trade for their tobacco and cotton crops. But even committed isolationists understood that the world was shrinking. In February 1940, Michigan's Arthur Vandenberg wrote in his diary: "It is probably impossible that there should be such a thing as old fashioned isolation in this present foreshortened world when one can cross the Atlantic Ocean in 36 hours. . . . probably the best we can hope for from now on is 'insulation' rather than isolation."[19]

Opponents of Roosevelt's short-of-war strategy worried that it might backfire. If Americans were to sell tanks and ships to Britain and then, under attack from Germany, Britain were to surrender, American munitions would be seized by Germans. But Roosevelt's ability to rally Americans to England's aid was strengthened overnight when, on May 10, 1940, Winston Churchill became prime minister.

Churchill and Roosevelt had first met in London in 1918, when Roosevelt was a thirty-six-year-old assistant secretary of the navy and Churchill a forty-three-year-old former lord of the Admiralty. Twenty years later, after Churchill returned to the Admiralty, Roosevelt opened a channel of communication with him, eager to hear frank reports on events in Europe. Their relationship grew, Churchill the courter, Roosevelt the courted. "No lover ever studied the whims of his mistress as I did those of President Roosevelt," Churchill later said. The prime minister desperately needed to win over Roosevelt and secure U.S. supplies—and, ultimately, U.S. entry into the war—because Britain could not defeat Germany without the Americans. The course of the war and even the terms of the peace would depend, in no small part, on the course of their friendship. Between 1941 and 1945, they would spend 113 days together, including a holiday at Marrakech. Churchill, a poet and a painter, painted the sunset for the American president.[20]

If Churchill courted Roosevelt, he also courted American voters. On June 4, 1940, Churchill delivered a rousing speech to the House of Commons, broadcast on radio stations across the United States, pledging that Britain would fight as long as it took:

> We shall go on to the end, we shall fight in France, we shall fight on the seas and oceans, we shall fight with growing confidence and growing strength in the air, we shall defend our island, whatever the cost may be, we shall fight on the beaches, we shall fight on the landing grounds, we shall fight in the fields and in the streets, we shall fight in the hills; we shall never surrender . . . until in God's good time, the new world, with all its power and might, steps forth to the rescue and the liberation of the old.[21]

Roosevelt pounded this same message at home. Six days later, in a commencement address at the University of Virginia, at his son Franklin Jr.'s graduation, Roosevelt described the dream that the United States is "a lone island" as a nightmare, the "nightmare of a people without freedom," he said, "the nightmare of a people lodged in prison, handcuffed, hungry, and fed through the bars from day to day by the contemptuous, unpitying masters of other continents."[22]

Roosevelt had decided to run for an unprecedented third term, against the Republican challenger, Indiana businessman Wendell Willkie, who hoped to win over Democrats disenchanted with Roosevelt's reign. Whitaker and Baxter produced materials for Willkie's campaign, including a speaker's manual that offered advice about how to handle Democrats in the audience: "rather than refer to the opponent as the 'Democratic Party' or 'New Deal Administration' refer to the Candidate by name only." But Willkie was unwilling to run a divisive campaign. The president's short-of-war strategy had led him to propose the first ever peacetime draft; Willkie refused to oppose it. "If you want to win the election you will come out against the proposed draft," a reporter told Willkie. Willkie answered, "I would rather not win the election than do that."[23]

Americans had so far been spared the misery of war. But, notwith-standing Hearst and Lindbergh and Coughlin, Willkie's refusal to under-mine Roosevelt had spared Americans the burden of division. "Here we are, and our basic institutions are still intact, our people relatively pros-perous, and most important of all, our society relatively affectionate," Dor-othy Thompson wrote in the *New York Herald Tribune* the month before the election. "No country in the world is so well off."[24]

In September of 1940, Churchill refused to surrender to Germany, even after the German blitz took the lives of forty thousand Londoners. Germany, Italy, and Japan, the Axis Powers, signed a pact, acknowledg-ing one another's geographical spheres in the work of "their prime pur-pose to establish and maintain a new order of things," as if the world were theirs to divide. [25] In November, moved by Churchill's fortitude and fearful of the Axis menace, voters returned FDR to the White House. This unprecedented third term, along with the powers he'd assumed during the New Deal, the memory of the court-packing crisis, and the draft itself, added to the ongoing debate over whether the American sys-tem of government could endure the brutality of modernity. "Can our government meet the challenge of totalitarianism and remain demo-cratic?" political scientist Pendleton Herring asked. "Is the separation of powers between the legislative and executive branches compatible with the need for authority? In seeking firm leadership do we open ourselves to the danger of dictatorship?"[26] But for the most part, these questions were set aside until after the war.

On December 29, 1940, FDR again took to the radio, this time to talk about the distance of both time and space. "Never before since James-town and Plymouth Rock has our American civilization been in such danger as now," he said. The Monroe Doctrine of 1823 had been made obsolete, he said, by the speed of travel, even across the vast seas. "The width of those oceans is not what it was in the days of clipper ships. At one point between Africa and Brazil the distance is less than from Wash-ington to Denver, Colorado, five hours for the latest type of bomber. And at the North end of the Pacific Ocean America and Asia almost touch each other." And what of the Axis's "new order"? "They may talk of a 'new order' in the world, but what they have in mind is only a revival of the oldest and the worst tyranny." Americans would not do Europe's fighting for them but were duty-bound to provide arms to save the world from that tyranny. "No man can tame a tiger into a kitten by stroking it," he said. "There can be no appeasement with ruthlessness." Descending from the lofty to the practical, he said, "I appeal to the owners of plants—to the managers—to the workers—to our own Government employees—to put every ounce of effort into producing these munitions swiftly and without stint," he said. "We must be the great arsenal of democracy."[27]

Britain, overwhelmingly outgunned by Germany and with its own armaments fast dwindling, had run out of cash to buy tanks and ships and planes from the United States. FDR had a plan for that, the Lend-Lease Act: the United States would lend these things to Britain, to be returned after the war, in exchange of long-term leases of territory for American military bases. To reach Americans still wavering, Roosevelt aligned fighting the Axis with the United States' founding purpose, its self-evident truths. On January 6, 1941, in his annual address to Congress, he argued that the United States must exert its might in securing for the world "four essential human freedoms": freedom of speech, freedom of religion, freedom from want, and freedom from fear. (Answered one African American, "White folks talking about the Four Freedoms and we ain't got none.")[28]

As he readied for his third inauguration, Roosevelt took time to write a note to Churchill, which he trusted to his defeated opponent, Wendell Willkie, to deliver in person. "He is truly helping to keep politics out over here," Roosevelt said of Willkie. On a green sheet of White House stationary, Roosevelt wrote out, from memory, lines from the last stanza of Henry Wadsworth Longfellow's "Building of the Ship," the poem Longfellow had drafted in 1849 and revised after his friend Charles Sumner had convinced him to end with hope. "I think this verse applies to you people as it does to us," Roosevelt wrote Churchill:

> *Sail on, Oh Ship of State!*
> *Sail on, Oh Union strong and great.*
> *Humanity with all its fears*
> *With all the hope of future years*
> *Is hanging breathless on thy fate.*

Churchill read Roosevelt's letter on the radio. "What is the answer that I shall give in your name to this great man, the thrice-chosen head of a nation of a hundred and thirty million?" he asked his listeners. "Put your confidence in us, give us your faith and our blessing," he answered. "Give us the tools and we shall finish the job."[29]

Willkie, after meeting with Churchill, flew back to Washington in time to appear before the House Committee on Foreign Relations to offer his support for the Lend-Lease Act. When isolationists on the committee presented him with remarks he had made during the campaign, about Roosevelt rushing the United States into war, Willkie waved those remarks aside as campaign bluster. "He was elected President," Willkie said. "He is *my* President now."[30]

While Congress deliberated, Henry Luce took to the pages of *Life* to make the case for Lend-Lease. In 1919, Luce said, the United States had passed up "a golden opportunity . . . to assume leadership of the world." He urged Americans not to make that same mistake again. America must not only enter the war—he argued against "the moral and practical bankruptcy of any and all forms of isolationism"—but adopt a new role in the world. "The twentieth century is the American century," he insisted.[31]

Against the internationalism of Roosevelt, Willkie, and Luce stood the increasingly besieged and embittered ranks of "America Firsters." In testimony before the House Committee on Foreign Relations, Charles Lindbergh refused to make a distinction between the Axis and the Allies. "I want neither side to win," he answered.[32] Lindbergh, Henry Ford, and their followers adopted Hearst's America First motto in founding the America First Committee, which launched a publicity campaign against the Lend-Lease program by buying fifteen-minute ads on a forty-station radio network. So helpful were their efforts to the Germans that Nazi shortwave radio broadcast its approval from the Propaganda Ministry in Berlin: "The America First Committee is true Americanism and true patriotism."[33]

Congress nevertheless passed the Lend-Lease Act, which Roosevelt, relieved beyond measure, signed on March 11. A grateful Churchill called it "the most unsordid act in the history of any nation." The *New York Times* marked its passage as the long-delayed reversal of America's retreat from the world at the end of the last war.[34] Yet that spring and summer, Lindbergh drew crowds ten thousand strong, even as much of the world lay in the hands of the Axis. Hitler, having abandoned his pact with Stalin, had invaded the Soviet Union. Germany had seized virtually all of Europe; only Britain remained. Japan, feared for its pitilessness as a result of its invasion of Manchuria and Nanking, controlled nearly half of China. Lindberg fiercely opposed communism. "I would a hundred times rather see my country ally herself with England, or even with Germany with all her faults, than the cruelty, the godlessness, and the barbarism that exists in the Soviet Union," he insisted. His fevered anticommunism left him blind to other kinds of ruthlessness. He offered excuses for Nazi propaganda: "In time of war, truth is always replaced by propaganda. I do not believe we should be too quick to criticize the actions of a belligerent nation. There is always the question of whether we, ourselves, would do better under similar circumstances." (Much of the American Left suffered from a different blindness—to the ruthlessness of Stalinism.) But he was also animated by other passions, confiding to his diary his belief that the press, in the United States, was controlled by Jews—"Most of the Jewish interests in the country are behind war, and they control a huge part of our press and radio, and most of our motion pictures." Lindbergh, while defending Nazi propaganda, spoke out against what he considered to be American propaganda. At an America First rally in Des Moines, Iowa, in September, he named three forces as responsible for spreading it: "The British, the Jewish and the Roosevelt administration." Wendell Willkie, who had heroically cast down the campaign cudgel to lend his support to FDR and the war effort, called Lindbergh's speech "the most un-American talk made in my time by any person of national reputation."[35]

More moderate isolationists set their objections within the long tradition of opposition to American expansion and American imperialism, elaborating on arguments that had been made during the War with Mexico and the Spanish-American War. In May of 1941, Robert Taft, a Republican senator from Ohio, warned prophetically that American entry into the war would mean, ultimately, that the United States "will have to maintain a police force perpetually in Germany and throughout Europe." Taft said, "Frankly, the American people don't want to rule the world, and we are not equipped to do it. Such imperialism is wholly foreign to our ideals of democracy and freedom. It is not our manifest destiny or our national destiny."[36]

Roosevelt knew how to counter an argument about national destiny. That summer, in an elaborate ruse designed to fool the press, he appeared to leave Washington for a fishing trip in Maine. Even Eleanor didn't know the truth.[37] Instead, he headed out across the ocean to meet Winston Churchill. Each man came on a gray battleship of steel and glass; the American president arrived on board the *Augusta*, the British prime minister on the *Prince of Wales*. The portly Churchill, wearing the dark blue uniform of a navy man, crossed over to the *Augusta* to meet with Roosevelt, who was determined to stand to receive him, leaning heavily on his son Elliott. "The Boss insisted upon returning to the painful prison of his braces," an aide said, an arrangement all the more worrying on board a lurching ship. "Even the slight pitch of the *Augusta* meant pain and the possibility of a humiliating fall." But the president stayed on his feet.

"At last—we've gotten together," Roosevelt said, as the two men shook hands.

"We have," said Churchill.

They opened negotiations. Churchill hoped to convince Roosevelt to ask Congress to declare war. They resumed talks on board the *Prince of Wales*, Roosevelt again insisting on not using his wheelchair, holding onto Elliott with one hand and a rail with the other. Churchill didn't get what he wanted, but the two men forged a historic agreement. By telegram, they released a joint statement on August 14, containing, in eight points, their commitment, "after the final destruction of Nazi tyranny," to a postwar world of free trade, self-determination, international security, arms control, social welfare, economic justice, and human rights. Their agreement, dubbed the Atlantic Charter, established a set of principles that would later be restated at Bretton Woods and in the charter of the United Nations. They agreed to "respect the right of all peoples to choose the form of government under which they will live" and "to see sovereign rights and self-government restored to those who have been forcibly deprived of them." And they pledged themselves to what had been the tenets of Roosevelt's New Deal, "improved labour standards, economic advancement, and social security." And, bringing together Roosevelt's Four Freedoms with Churchill's knack for poetry, they pledged themselves to a peace in which "all the men in all the lands may live out their lives in freedom from fear and want."[38]

It was meant as a new deal for the world. But first, they would have to win the war.

## II.

EARLY IN THE SUN-STREAKED morning of December 7, 1941, the Imperial Japanese Navy launched more than 350 planes from aircraft carriers in the Pacific Ocean. They flew to Hawaii and began a surprise attack on an American naval base at Pearl Harbor, a torrent of bombs raining down from the sky like bolts of thunder thrown by an angry god. Japanese bombers sank four battleships, destroyed nearly 200 American planes, killed more than 2,400 Americans, and wounded another 1,100. Sixty-four Japanese military men were killed and one Japanese sailor was captured. Without issuing a declaration of war, and while the United States and Japan were still engaged in diplomacy, the Japanese had essentially wiped out the United States Pacific Fleet. Churchill called Roosevelt to ask if the news he'd heard could possibly be right.

"It's quite true," the president said. "We are all in the same boat now."

"This certainly simplifies things," Churchill said. "God be with you."[39]

Immediately, Roosevelt set about dictating the address he would deliver to Congress, marking the attack on a chronicle of time. "Yesterday comma December 7 comma 1941 dash a day which will live in world history dash the United States of America was suddenly and deliberately attacked by naval and air forces of the Empire of Japan period paragraph."[40] He thought better of it and rewrote his words with care, and with an ear for force. The next day, Americans turned to their radios to listen as the president, his voice unshaken, spoke to Congress, calling December 7, 1941, not "a date which will live in world history" but "a date which will live in infamy."

His hands bracing a podium crowded with microphones, he called upon the "righteous might" of the American people. Less than a half hour after the president finished his seven-minute speech, Congress declared war on Japan. As the nation set about the grim task of wartime mobilization, Roosevelt began the work of laying the groundwork for an argument that the United States ought to declare war on Germany, too. "We cannot measure our safety in terms of miles on any map," he told radio listeners on December 9, in a fireside chat in which he strategically tied Japan to Germany. "We expect to eliminate the danger from Japan, but it would serve us ill if we accomplished that and found that the rest of the world was dominated by Hitler and Mussolini."[41]

*A 1943 Office of War Information poster celebrated the combined strength of the Allied forces.*

Roosevelt would not need to press that argument. On December 11, Hitler declared war on the United States. This was Hitler's worst miscalculation, since it's by no means clear that Roosevelt would have been able to convince Congress to declare war on Germany if Hitler hadn't acted rashly. He'd underestimated Churchill, and he'd underestimated Roosevelt. Above all, he'd underestimated the United States.

However sudden, the decisive entry of the United States into the war in both Asia and Europe rested on years of preparation. American planning for the war had begun in the 1930s, with dedicated munitions manufacturing and the building of planes, tanks, and battleships, much of this taking place in the South. Under the terms of the draft for men between eighteen and forty-five, put in place in 1940, 31 million men registered, 17 million were examined, and 10 million served. Adding volunteers and women to that number, the total reached more than 15 million: 10.4 million in the army, 3.9 million in the navy, some 600,000 in the marines, and another 250,000 in the coast guard. Three million women entered the labor force. Three-quarters of those women were married. The female labor force doubled. Beginning in 1942, women joined the

*Wartime mobilization*
*called on women to join*
*the military, as in this*
*U.S. Navy recruiting*
*poster from 1942.*

Women's Army Corps and the navy's WAVES. By the time the war ended, in 1945, 12 million Americans were active-duty members of the military, compared with 300,000 in 1939.[42]

American manufacturing and farming were conscripted, too. Between 1940 and 1945, Americans produced 300,000 military planes, 86,000 tanks, 3 million machine guns, and 71,000 naval ships. Farm production increased by 25 percent. Farmers produced 477 million more bushels of corn in 1944 than they had in 1939. These supplies weren't just for American forces; the United States supplied Britain, France, the Soviet Union, China, and other allies. Fifteen percent of American output was shipped abroad.[43]

The federal budget grew at an astounding rate, from $9 billion in 1939 to $100 billion in 1945. Between 1941 and 1946, the federal government spent more than it had from 1789 to 1941. In 1939, less than 2 percent of American national output went to war; by 1944, 40 percent did. The GDP doubled. And the GNP rose from $91 billion to $166 billion, crushing doubts that the economy had reached its limit. Mobilization for war acted as a public works program, the largest ever. In Europe, even food was rationed during the war; in the United States, civilians enjoyed a wealth of consumer goods and increased buying power. The leanness of the Depression was over. "The pawnbroking business has fallen upon dark days," the *Wall Street Journal* observed in 1942.[44]

Even before the United States entered the war, FDR had claimed new powers for the office of the president. During the Civil War, Lincoln had invoked "presidential war power," but Roosevelt claimed a range of emergency powers never heard of before. In July 1939, he'd placed the secretaries of war and the navy under his own authority as commander in chief, removing them from the military chain of authority. After Germany invaded Poland, he'd issued an executive order declaring a "limited national emergency," a concept without precedent. Senator Robert Taft described the president as "a complete one-man dictatorship."

Within days of the attack on Pearl Harbor, Congress passed the War Powers Act, granting to the executive branch special powers to prosecute the war, including the power to surveil letters, telegraph messages, and radio broadcasts. Some of the new agencies created by the administration ultimately wielded little power. The War Production Board, created in January 1942, consisted chiefly of corporate executives doubtful about state planning. "The arsenal of democracy," I. F. Stone wrote, "is still being operated with one eye on the war and the other on the convenience of big business." Other wartime agencies had more authority. A Second War Powers Act, passed in March of 1942, granted the president authority over "special investigations and reports of census or statistical matters" and established the National War Labor Board and the Office of Price Administration, ceding considerable control over the economy to the federal government and, in particular, to the executive branch.[45]

Just as the administrative state had grown in both size and power during the First World War, it grew during the Second. The Pentagon opened in March 1943, having been built in sixteen months. The number of civil servants in the federal government grew from 950,000 in 1939 to 3.8 million in 1945. As federal spending skyrocketed, so did the national debt, which reached $258 billion in 1945 and called not only for war bonds but for an unprecedented rise in taxes. New Dealers sold tax hikes to the public as emergency measures, "taxes to beat the Axis," while the Revenue Act of

1942, which included a steeply progressive income tax, vastly broadened the tax base: 85 percent of American families filed a return.[46]

Business grew, and so did labor. Membership in trade unions rose from 6.6 million in 1939 to 12.6 million in 1945. Science grew, too. The Manhattan Project, a secret federal project to develop an atomic bomb, begun in 1939, had, by the end of the war, employed 130,000 staff, and cost $2 billion. The National Defense Research Committee (NDRC), established by FDR in 1940, was headed by Vannevar Bush, the so-called czar of research, who by 1941 was also head of the Office of Scientific Research and Development. Before the end of the war, the NDRC employed some two thousand scientists, including three out of four of the nation's physicists.[47]

Roosevelt liked to say that "Dr. New Deal" had been replaced with "Dr. Win-the-War" but the war itself, by extending the powers of the federal government, extended the New Deal.[48] The war also reshaped the role of the press. In the First World War, George Creel's government-run propaganda program had stirred up so much hysteria and hatred against Germany that Americans had taken to calling hamburgers "Salisbury steaks."[49] FDR, sharing Americans' bitter memories of earlier American wartime propaganda, had been reluctant to wield the power of government to tell the American people what to think about the war.[50] But the establishment of a government information agency had assumed a new urgency in 1940, after the publication of a book by Edmond Taylor, Paris bureau chief for the *Chicago Tribune*. In *The Strategy of Terror—Europe's Inner Front*, Taylor reported firsthand on the campaign of propaganda waged by the Nazis in France to break the will of the French people and divide the population. "Words exercise a strange tyranny over human affairs," Taylor wrote. He called propaganda "the invisible front."[51]

Two months before the attack on Pearl Harbor, Roosevelt issued an executive order establishing a new government information agency: the Office of Facts and Figures. To head it, he appointed Archibald MacLeish, a poet and writer whom he'd earlier named Librarian of Congress. The agency's mandate was not terribly clear. MacLeish said the executive order establishing it "read like a pass to a ball game." MacLeish's ideas about how to write about war could hardly have been more different than Creel's. MacLeish had fought in World War I, after which he lived in Paris, where he wrote poems about places where lay "upon the darkening plain / The dead against the dead and on the silent ground / The silent slain."[52]

After MacLeish returned to the United States from Paris, he'd been an editor for *Fortune* from 1929 to 1938 before serving as the Librarian of Congress. "Democracy is never a thing done," he said in 1939. "Democracy is always something that a nation must be doing." He believed that artists and writers have an obligation to fight "a revolution created out of disorder by a terror of disorder," and that the real battle was the battle for public opinion. "The principal battleground of this war is not the South Pacific," he said. "It is not the Middle East. It is not England, or Norway, or the Russian Steppes. It is American opinion."[53]

In directing the Office of Facts and Figures, MacLeish hoped not to produce propaganda but instead to educate the public about the danger of it. One of his office's earliest pamphlets, *Divide and Conquer*, relied heavily on Taylor's book to explain to Americans how the Nazi strategy of terror had worked in France. To illustrate, it quoted *Mein Kampf*. "At the bottom of their hearts the great masses of the people are more likely to be poisoned than to be consciously and deliberately bad," Hitler had written. "In the primitive simplicity of their minds they are more easily victimized by a large than by a small lie, since they sometimes tell petty lies themselves but would be ashamed to tell big ones." MacLeish's pamphlet aimed to defeat Nazi propaganda: "The United States is now subject to a total barrage of the Nazi strategy of terror. Hitler thinks Americans are suckers. By the very vastness of his program of lies, he hopes to frighten us into believing that the Nazis are invincible."[54]

Dorothy Thompson, who once described *Mein Kampf* as "eight hundred pages of Gothic script, pathetic gestures, inaccurate German, and unlimited self-satisfaction," had long been making the same argument. "The thing which we are all up against is propaganda," she said. "Sometimes I think that this age is going to be called the age of propaganda, an unprecedented rise of propaganda, propaganda as a weapon, propaganda as a technique, propaganda as a fine art, and propaganda as a form of government." The challenge to Western journalists, she said, was "to represent a theory of journalism, a theory of what journalism stands for, a thesis of journalism, a philosophy of journalism, in countries where this philosophy is fundamentally repudiated."[55]

In this same spirit, MacLeish insisted that his office wouldn't take positions but instead would give people the figures and facts: "The duty of government is to provide a basis for judgment; and when it goes beyond that, it goes beyond the prime scope of its duty." Journalists were doubtful. The *New York Herald Tribune* editorialized: "OFF is just going to superimpose its own 'well organized facts' upon the splendid confusion, interpret the interpreters, redigest those who now digest the digesters, explain what those who explain what the explainers of the explanations mean, and co-ordinate the coordinators of those appointed to co-ordinate the co-ordinations of the co-ordinated."[56]

MacLeish clung to his idealism, which he grounded in the nation's founding truths and in its founding commitment to truth. In an April 1942 speech at the annual meeting of the Associated Press, against the Nazi "strategy of terror," he proposed a new, American strategy:

> It is the strategy which is appropriate to our cause and to our purpose—the strategy of truth—the strategy which opposes to the frauds and the deceits by which our enemies have confused and conquered other peoples, the simple and clarifying truths by which a nation such as ours must guide itself.

To deploy the strategy of truth, he called upon American journalists: "No country has ever had at its disposal greater resources with which to fight the warfare of opinion than the practice of the profession of journalism in this country has produced."[57] Critics, not unreasonably, called MacLeish naïve: war requires deceit. And FDR himself had little interest in what MacLeish proposed. Early on, Roosevelt ordered MacLeish to announce that gasoline would be rationed, when it was perfectly clear to Americans that there was no shortage of gasoline. Instead, there was a very concerning shortage of rubber, but the president, knowing that revealing the rubber shortage would undermine the war cause, refused to allow MacLeish to reveal the truth.[58]

MacLeish soldiered on, especially keen to use the Office of Facts and Figures to mark the occasion, in 1941, of the 150th anniversary of the Bill of Rights. His surest vehicle was the radio. The Radio Division of the Office of Facts and Figures, headed by former CBS executive William

Lewis, commissioned writer Norman Corwin to compose a radio play about the Bill of Rights. *We Hold These Truths*, broadcast eight days after the attack on Pearl Harbor, was the first radio drama broadcast on all four networks. Its stars included Jimmy Stewart, Rudy Vallee, and Orson Welles, with music provided by the New York Philharmonic. *We Hold These Truths* was as much a call to arms as a celebration of the nation's founding creed, the original strategy of truth: "The Congress of the thirteen states, instructed by the people of the thirteen states, threw up a bulwark, wrote a hope, and made a sign for posterity against the bigots, the fanatics, bullies, lynchers, race-haters, the cruel men, the spiteful men, the sneaking men, the pessimists, the men who give up fights that have just begun."

MacLeish and Lewis then signed Corwin up to write a thirteen-week series called *This Is War!* Parts were hard-hitting, but, as FDR's critics pointed out, much of it aimed to shore up support for the president: it compared him to Washington and Lincoln.[59] Yet in courting public opinion, Roosevelt found MacLeish's Office of Facts and Figures too restrained, and in June of 1942 he replaced it with the Office of War Information, headed by former CBS reporter Elmer Davis, who was far more willing to use the methods of mass advertising than MacLeish had been. A frustrated MacLeish resigned and returned to the Library of Congress. Without MacLeish as a force of resistance, the agency drifted, much of the staff at one point resigning in protest over the hiring of a former advertising manager for Coca-Cola. Pulitzer Prize–winning reporter Henry Pringle made a mock Office of War Information poster. "Step right up and get your four delicious freedoms," it read. "It's a refreshing war."[60]

EVEN AS THE WAR raged on unremittingly, Roosevelt looked ahead to the peace, concerned not to repeat the travesty of Woodrow Wilson, the Treaty of Versailles, and the League of Nations. To that end, he invited Churchill to spend Christmas 1941 at the White House. During the visit, Roosevelt came up with the name for their planned new international organization, "United Nations." He hastened to the prime minister's room to get his agreement to it. Churchill had just emerged from a bath. Roosevelt entered his room and found him naked. "You see, Mr. President, I have nothing to hide from you," Churchill said calmly.[61]

Weeks later, on January 1, 1942, the United States, Britain, China, and the Soviet Union—the "Big Four"—adopted a "Declaration by United Nations." The document was signed on January 2 by twenty-six nations. All subscribed to the "common program of purposes and principles" of the Atlantic Charter and forswore the making of a separate peace. The Big Four also agreed to a military strategy: to concentrate on defeating Germany, first by bombing Germany and then by landing in France. The Allied victory against a far more loosely confederate Axis would depend on this unity of purpose.

The State Department, meanwhile, formed a secret fifteen-person Advisory Committee on Post-War Foreign Policy, headed by Undersecretary Sumner Welles. This study group devised much of the framework for the founding of the United Nations as an international organization. More publicly, Wendell Willkie dedicated himself to the work of convincing the Republican Party to abandon isolationism once and for all. "He who wins the war must maintain the peace," he said in February 1942, warning Republicans that to cede internationalism to the Democrats would destroy the GOP. That spring, he convinced the Republican National Committee to pass a resolution declaring that "our nation has an obligation to assist in bringing about comity, cooperation, and understanding among nations." Roosevelt asked Willkie to undertake a world tour to publicize the idea of a United Nations. He left in August, flying on a bomber named the *Gulliver.* Forty-nine days of travel included stops in Russia, the Middle East, and China. In a radio address that he gave when he got back, he called for an end to Western imperialism and the beginning of a new arrangement among nations. *One World,* the book he wrote about his trip and his vision, headed every best-seller list in the country, becoming only the third book published in the United States to sell more than a million copies. Roosevelt called for a United Nations, but it was Willkie who raised public support for it.[62]

Roosevelt's Office of War Information asked Americans to understand the war as a struggle between democracy and dictatorship, between freedom and fascism. For most soldiers, this meant something less lofty. When reporters asked GIs what they were fighting for, they generally said

*Soldiers communicated from the trenches by way of radio, here in the Philippine island of Leyte in 1944.*

that they were fighting for home. Ernie Pyle, a reporter from Indiana, hauled his Underwood typewriter along as he followed American infantrymen fighting in Europe and Africa. "I love the infantry," Pyle said, "because they are the mud-rain-frost-and-wind boys. . . . And in the end they are the guys that wars can't be won without." He wrote of the ordinary soldiers, the "dogfaces," and their bravery, and their misery, and the terribleness of their deaths. "Dead men had been coming down the mountain all evening, lashed onto the backs of mules," he wrote from Italy, describing a soldier who stopped to sit by the body of a captain, holding the dead man's hand. "Finally he put the hand down. He reached up and gently straightened the points of the captain's shirt collar, and then he sort of rearranged the tattered edges of his uniform around the wound, and then he got up and walked away down the road in the moonlight, all alone."[63]

They fought in the mountains and on the seas. In 1942, much of the American fighting took place in the Pacific, where the Allies hoped to halt the Japanese advance. In the spring, U.S. intelligence broke Japan's ciphers and, in the spring of 1942, defeated the Imperial Japanese Navy at the Hawaiian island of Midway. Allied troops then challenged and eventually defeated the Japanese in the Solomon Islands, at the Battle of Guadalcanal. In Guadalcanal, marines told reporter John Hersey that they were fighting for blueberry pie. "Home is where the good things are," Hersey wrote. "The generosity, the good pay, the comforts, the democracy, the pie."[64]

Meanwhile, on the home front, the federal government had instituted a policy of imprisoning people of Japanese ancestry, including American citizens. As early as 1934, the State Department had reported to FDR on the possibility of sabotage by Japanese Americans. In 1939, the president had asked the FBI to compile a list of possible subversives, a list known as the ABC list because of its ratings system: people on the list were labeled: A, immediately dangerous; B, potentially dangerous; or C, a possible Japanese sympathizer. In the hours after receiving word of the attack on Pearl Harbor, the FBI began rounding up suspects; by nightfall, the bureau had detained nearly eight hundred Japanese on the A list.[65]

On February 19, 1942, another day that would live in infamy, Roosevelt signed Executive Order 9066, authorizing the secretary of war to establish military zones. The U.S. Army issued Public Proclamation 1 in March, directing aliens to demarcated zones. Restrictions began with curfews and proceeded to relocation orders. Eventually, some 112,000 Japanese, a number that included 79,000 U.S. citizens, were ordered from their homes and imprisoned in camps in Arizona, California, Oregon, and Washington.[66] They packed what they could in duffel bags and stiff suitcases, their distress captured in pictures taken by photographers including Dorothea Lange.

Lange, who had been stricken by polio at the age of seven and walked with a painful limp, had become famous for the achingly sympathetic photographs she'd taken for the Farm Security Administration during the Depression. "Cripples know about each other," she said of her ability to capture suffering on film. Lange disagreed with Roosevelt's executive order. "She thought that we were entering a period of fascism," her assistant said, "and that she was viewing the end of democracy as we know it." Her photographs, commissioned by the War Relocation Authority for purposes of documentation, serve as testament to that objection. Lange's FSA photographs became iconic; her WRA photographs were, for

*Dorothea Lange photographed the forced relocation of Japanese Americans in California in 1942.*

decades, locked in archives, hidden from view, many of them stamped IMPOUNDED.[67]

Appeals to the courts proved unavailing. Gordon Hirabayashi, an American citizen and a Quaker who was a senior at the University of Washington, refused to abide by the curfew. "I consider it my duty to maintain the democratic standards for which this nation lives," Hirabayashi said. He turned himself in to the FBI but sought a legal remedy, arguing that the executive order was "unconstitutional because it discriminates against citizens of Japanese ancestry." In *Hirabayashi v. United States*, the Supreme Court in 1943 upheld the constitutionality of a curfew, if narrowly. "Distinctions between citizens solely because of their ancestry are by their very nature odious to a free people whose institutions are founded upon the doctrine of equality," Chief Justice Harlan Stone said, in the majority opinion, but in time of war, such discriminations "which are relevant to measures for our national defense and for the successful prosecution of the war" were perfectly constitutional. Justice Frank Murphy, while concurring, nevertheless regretted the ruling, which, he said, "goes to the very brink of constitutional power" and which he considered, whether constitutional or not, an American tragedy. "To say that any group cannot be assimilated is to admit that the great American experiment has failed." The curfew and internment orders had deprived American citizens of their liberty "because of their particular racial inheritance," and "in this sense it bears a melancholy resemblance to the treatment accorded to members of the Jewish race in Germany and in other parts of Europe."[68]

Fred Toyosaburo Korematsu, born in Oakland, California, in 1919, had tried to enlist in 1940. A welder at a defense plant, he refused to obey the relocation order, choosing to stay with his girlfriend, an Italian American. He had undergone plastic surgery to disguise his appearance; he pretended to be Mexican and eventually went into hiding. The ACLU took up his case, arguing that Executive Order 9066 was unconstitutional. In 1944, in *Korematsu v. United States*, the Supreme Court upheld the order in a 6–3 decision, relying on the opinion in *Hirabayashi* and emphasizing the danger posed to the United States by possible Japanese saboteurs who might aid a Japanese attack on the West Coast. Hoover appointee Justice Owen Roberts, in a strongly worded dissent, made a distinction between the two cases. "This is not a case of keeping people off the streets at night," he said. "It is the case of convicting a citizen as a punishment for not submitting to imprisonment in a concentration camp . . . solely because of his ancestry, without evidence or inquiry concerning his loyalty."[69]

And yet the war cultivated new forms of resistance to the racial order—unprecedented and sustained militant action. In the First World War, W. E. B. Du Bois, at the behest of George Creel, had urged African Americans to set aside the fight against Jim Crow for the duration. Eminent black leaders did not make this same case during the Second World War but instead put pressure on local and state institutions, and especially on the federal government, to dismantle segregation—as did men recruited to serve. "Every time I pick up the paper Some poor African American soldiers are getting shot lynch or hung, and framed up," a man from the Bronx wrote to Roosevelt. "I will be darned if you get me in your forces."[70]

The wartime economic boom that lifted so many Americans out of Depression-era poverty left African Americans out. In factories, their work was segregated and poorly paid. So too in the armed services. In the army, African Americans served in segregated, noncombat units, where they reported to white officers and did menial work; in the navy, they worked as cooks and stewards. They were forbidden from enlisting in the air force or marine corps. "The Negro soldier is separated from the white soldier as completely as possible," reported Henry Stimson, secretary of war. *The Crisis* editorialized: "A jim crow army cannot fight for a free world." James Baldwin worked in a defense plant in New Jersey in 1943, when he was nineteen. "The treatment accorded the Negro during the Second World War marks, for me, a turning point in the Negro's relation to America," he later wrote. "A certain hope died, a certain respect for white Americans faded."[71]

Scattered sit-ins had started in 1939. A leading legal architect of the movement was Pauli Murray. Murray, born in Baltimore in 1910, had graduated from Hunter College in 1928 and then worked for the National Urban League and for the WPA. One of her white forebears had been a trustee of the University of North Carolina, which rejected her application for admission in 1938 on the basis of her race. At the time, Murray was in search of a doctor to prescribe testosterone; she saw herself as male. Her struggle with her doctors met with no success. To challenge UNC, she approached Thurgood Marshall, a young lawyer leading the NAACP's campaign against segregation; Marshall discouraged her (Murray had moved to New York, and Marshall thought that a nonresident test case would be weaker than a claim made by a resident). In 1940, Murray was arrested in Virginia for refusing to give up a seat on a bus. Inspired by Henry David Thoreau's essay on civil disobedience, and having recently read a book called *War without Violence: A Study of Gandhi's Method and Its Accomplishments*, Murray had decided to try to apply Mahatma Gandhi's practice of Satyagraha, nonviolent direct action. The idea was to protest injustice without violence by waiting for one's political opponents to perform injustice, by their own violent suppression of a peaceful protest. Murray's own inclination was clench-fisted defiance of Jim Crow, but she forced herself to act, instead, with utmost courtesy. Murray next went to Howard University to study law, she said, "with the single-minded intention of destroying Jim Crow." Instead of fighting for equal facilities, Murray argued for dismantling the forty-five-year-old *Plessy* altogether by fighting against separate facilities. During her years at Howard, a time when most male students were away fighting the war, Murray planned sit-ins in Washington, DC, drugstores and cafeterias; participants carried signs that read "We Die Together, Why Can't We Eat Together?"[72]

In May 1941, A. Philip Randolph, the head of the Brotherhood of Sleeping Car Porters, called for a Negro March on Washington to be held that July. "I suggest that ten thousand Negroes march on Washington, D.C., the capital of the Nation, with the slogan, 'We loyal Negro American citizens demand our right to work and fight for our country,'" Randolph wrote. By June, more than a hundred thousand protesters were expected to march. Eleanor Roosevelt, hoping to convince Randolph to call off the march, met with him in New York, along with Bayard Rustin, a young civil rights activist who'd been helping to organize the event— and who would later go on to organize the 1963 March on Washington. "Mrs. Roosevelt led off by saying that Mr. Randolph knew of her affection, of her efforts on behalf of Negroes," Rustin recalled, "and that the President would be greatly embarrassed vis-a-vis our allies if, in the midst of our preparation for defense of freedom, this were to happen." Eleanor Roosevelt arranged for Randolph to meet with the president at the White House. The president, too, tried to dissuade him.

"You know, Mr. Randolph, that if you bring a hundred thousand blacks into Washington, there's absolutely no place for them to eat," he said. "Furthermore, there's no place for them to sleep, and even more serious there's no place in Washington where they can use toilet facilities."

"That is not my fault nor my problem," Randolph replied. "But you can issue an Executive Order before we get here opening up the toilets, opening up the restaurants, and making it possible for us to sleep in hotels."[73]

In the end, FDR signed Executive Order 8802, prohibiting racial discrimination in defense industries, and Randolph agreed to call off the march. Protests continued. Two black army sergeants in Norfolk, Virginia, refused to give up their seats on a bus; they were beaten and thrown in jail. A black U.S. Army nurse did the same in Montgomery, Alabama; the police who beat her broke her nose.[74] Martin Dies of the House Un-American Activities Committee blamed communists, charging that "throughout the South today subversive elements are attempting to convince the Negro that he should be placed on social equality with white people, that now is the time for him to assert his rights."[75] In 1942, FBI head J. Edgar Hoover, keen "to determine why particular Negroes or groups of Negroes or Negro organizations have evidenced sentiments for other 'dark races' (mainly Japanese) or by what forces they were influenced to adopt in certain instances un-American ideologies," conducted a nationwide investigation, including surveillance of hundreds of black lawyers, organizers, artists, and writers. It would result in a classified 730-page report called the *Survey of Racial Conditions in the United States,* code-named RACON. Far from proposing remedies in the form of civil rights, RACON warned of dangerous political subversives, by which Hoover and the Bureau meant African Americans working to dismantle Jim Crow. Hoover did not believe that the African American struggle for civil rights had come out of black communities; instead, he blamed the Communist Party, and he blamed the Axis. "It is believed the Axis Powers have endeavored to create racial agitation among American negroes which would cause disunity and would serve as a powerful weapon for adverse propaganda," the director wrote, in a memo to FBI field agents. "It is believed that the agitation has been incited among the American negroes by telling them that the present war is a 'race war' and that they should not fight against the Japanese, who are also of the colored race."[76]

By no means was the struggle against segregation confined to the South. In Detroit, white people barricaded the streets when the first black families moved in to a public housing project, the Sojourner Truth Homes, in February 1942. "WE WANT WHITE TENANTS IN OUR WHITE COMMUNITY," read one billboard. Tensions grew over the next year; in June of 1943 more than six thousand federal troops marched into Detroit to suppress the unrest. In New York that August, rumors that a white policeman had killed a black soldier led to riots that lasted two days, involved more than three thousand people, led to six hundred arrests, and left six people dead. "Don't you see, Mr. President," A. Philip Randolph wrote to Roosevelt, "this is not a repetition of anything that has happened before in the history of Negro-white relations?"[77] Roosevelt offered very little by way of reply.

Pauli Murray offered, that summer, a poem.

*A billboard in Detroit in 1942 called for
the continuation of segregated housing.*

*What'd you get, black boy
When they knocked you down in the gutter,
And they kicked your teeth out,
And they broke your skull with clubs*

*. . .*

*What'd the Top Man say, Black Boy?
"Mr. Roosevelt regrets. . . ."*[78]

After graduating first in her class at Howard, Murray was rejected from a graduate program at Harvard Law School, which did not admit women. She went instead to the University of California, where she wrote a dissertation on "The Right to Equal Opportunity in Employment." Beyond leading the effort to adapt the teachings of Gandhi to the civil rights movement, Murray would pioneer an interpretation of the Fourteenth Amendment that insisted that it could be used to fight not only Jim Crow, discrimination by race, but also "Jane Crow," discrimination by sex.[79]

FDR, confronted with a sustained and organized wartime campaign of sit-ins, protests, rallies, and boycotts, pledged to remedy one of the most galling forms of discrimination: black soldiers living in Jim Crow states generally could not vote. "Surely the signers of the Constitution did not intend a document which, even in wartime, would be construed to take away the franchise of any of those who are fighting to preserve the Constitution itself," the president said during a fireside chat in January 1944. But when proposed legislation guaranteeing soldiers the right to vote went to Congress, southern Democrats balked. Much amended, the measure that became law left enforcement to the states. As the *Pittsburgh Courier*, a black newspaper, explained, the new law "answers the demand for a soldier vote law while guaranteeing that the Negro vote be 'taken care of' by election in precincts, counties, and other state units, and therefore is satisfactory to all except Negroes."[80]

The American debate about the incompatibility of democracy and racism reached a new audience in 1944 with the publication of *An American Dilemma*, by a Swedish sociologist named Gunnar Myrdal, who'd been commissioned by the Carnegie Corporation to study race. The American dilemma, according to Myrdal, was the tension between, on the one hand, the American creed of human rights and personal liberty and, on the other, racial injustice. "The three great wars of this country have been fought for the ideals of liberty and equality, to which the nation was pledged," Myrdal wrote. "Now America is again in a life-and-death struggle for liberty and equality, and the American Negro is again watching for signs of what war and victory will mean in terms of opportunity and rights for him in his native land. To the white American, too, the Negro problem has taken on a significance greater than it has ever had since the Civil War."[81]

As a national consensus emerged about the need for Americans to find common cause and put their ethnic differences behind them, Hollywood filmmakers developed a convention later known as the "ethnic platoon," about a motley group of American soldiers who form a band of brothers. Eric Johnston, who had been an adviser to FDR, became head of the Motion Picture Association of America. "We'll have no more *Grapes of Wrath*," he announced. "We'll have no more films that deal with the seamy side of American life. We'll have no more films that treat the banker as a villain." A government pamphlet titled "A Manual for the Motion Picture Industry" explained that wartime films ought to be sure to include all manner of ethnic Americans as "the people," and that part of the fight in this war must be against "any form of racial discrimination or religious intolerance." *Lifeboat*, based on a story by John Steinbeck, directed by Alfred Hitchcock, and released in 1944, is the epitome of the genre. The military and civilian survivors of an attack by a German U-boat find themselves on a single lifeboat, with the U-boat captain. Only by conquering their own differences can they rescue themselves from his machinations. The rich socialite falls in love with the working-class Irishman; the black steward saves everyone.[82]

Whatever the influence of Gunnar Myrdal or Hollywood filmmakers on the wartime struggle for civil rights, that struggle was led by black Americans, intellectuals, reporters, artists, and activists. "To win a cheap military victory over the Axis and then continue the exploitation of subject peoples within the British Empire and the subordination of Negroes in the United States is to set the stage for the next world war—probably a war of color," the African American sociologist Horace Cayton wrote in *The Nation* in 1943. "Somehow, through some mechanism, there must be achieved in America and in the world a moral order which will include the American Negro and all other oppressed peoples. The present war must be considered as one phase of a larger struggle to achieve this new moral order."[83] Building that new order would be the work of the postwar world.

It was possible to begin to imagine that world in 1943, because the tide of the war had turned. U.S. and Canadian forces pushed back Japanese advances in the Pacific. Hitler's planned assault on Soviet forces at Kursk ended in a German retreat. Britain bombed Hamburg. Allies invaded Italy. In July 1943, Roosevelt, Churchill, and Stalin—the "Big Three"—met in Tehran, chiefly to plan the campaign against Germany. They also touched on the question of postwar international cooperation. Roosevelt and Stalin twice met together privately. ("Roosevelt believed that he would get along better with Stalin in Churchill's absence," the U.S. ambassador to the Soviet Union later said.) Roosevelt told Stalin about the plan, drafted by Sumner Welles, for a United Nations organization comprising three parts: an assembly, with delegates from all nations; an executive committee, of the Big Four, with six other regional delegates; and a security council of the "four policemen," who would have power to act with force to prevent aggression and secure the peace. (The idea of a "world's policeman" dates to the First World War, but in 1943, during a birthday dinner for Winston Churchill, FDR called upon the Allied powers—the United States, Great Britain, the Soviet Union, and China—to serve as the world's "four policemen.")

The meetings in Tehran, lavish dinners hosted by each leader in turn, were plagued by mistrust and, on Stalin's part, duplicity. Churchill felt that Roosevelt had betrayed him by meeting with and repeatedly siding with Stalin. "There I sat with the great Russian bear on one side of me, with paws outstretched," Churchill wrote, "and on the other side sat the great American buffalo." Stalin reveled in his ability to divide the two men. The Big Three agreed on a plan for attacking Germany. But the statement issued at the end of the Tehran conference made no reference to the United Nations.[84]

At home, Roosevelt's rhetoric took a turn toward what would become the UN's language of human rights. A fight for freedom became a fight for rights. In January 1944, in a message to Congress, Roosevelt announced his plan for a Second Bill of Rights. The first Bill of Rights had guaranteed certain political rights, but "as our nation has grown in size and stature," Roosevelt explained, "these political rights proved inadequate to assure us equality in the pursuit of happiness." Declaring certain "economic truths" to be "self-evident," his list of rights included "the right to a useful and remunerative job," "the right of every family to a decent home," "the right to adequate medical care," and "the right to a good education."[85]

*Time* declared, "Dr. Win-the-War has apparently called into consultation one Dr. Win-New-Rights." Wartime prosperity strengthened Roosevelt's hand in expanding the government's role in securing rights, and civil rights activists had demanded it. At the same time, liberals were losing political power, not gaining it, at least as measured by congressional elections. In 1942, Democrats lost 42 seats in the House and 8 in the Senate. They still held a majority of seats in both houses, but a far diminished one. In 1936, there were 242 more Democrats than Republicans in the House; in 1942, that majority had shrunk to 10. In 1938, Democrats held 60 more seats than Republicans in the Senate, a majority that, by 1942, had shrunk to 21. By 1943, Congress had eliminated a great many New Deal relief programs, including the Civilian Conservation Corps, the Works Progress Administration, the National Youth Administration, and the Home Owners' Loan Corporation. Other New Deal agencies were either dismantled or had their heads replaced with conservatives. I. F. Stone said that the New Deal was "beginning to commit hara kiri." In 1944, Archibald MacLeish gave voice to liberals' anticipation of a reactionary peace: "Liberals meet in Washington these days, if they can endure to meet at all, to discuss the tragic outlook for all liberal proposals, the collapse of all liberal leadership, and the inevitable defeat of all liberal aims. It is no longer feared, it is assumed, that the country is headed back to normalcy, that Harding is just around the corner."[86]

MacLeish was not far wrong. In 1945, Martin Dies reconvened his Un-American Activities Committee to investigate liberals suspected of being communists. Anticipating Joseph McCarthy, Dies warned of "hundreds of left-wingers and radicals who do not believe in our system of free enterprise" and claimed that "not less than two thousand outright Communists and Party-liners" were "still holding jobs in the government in Washington." The objects of Dies's ire included Frances Perkins and even Eleanor Roosevelt herself. "The First Lady of the Land," Dies said, "has been one of the most valuable assets which the Trojan Horse organization of the Communist Party have possessed."[87]

Liberalism survived—it remained the principal governing philosophy of the United States for decades—but it had been weakened. Socialism had been discredited. And conservatism, while still a hushed chorus of voices in a wilderness, gained strength in the form of a critique of statism. In 1941, James Burnham, a former liberal, published *The Managerial Revolution*, in which he argued that the nations that had descended into totalitarianism were those in which the greatest managerial power was held by the state. Practically, this kind of argument had the effect of galvanizing opposition to the income tax. The American Taxpayers' Association (formerly the American Bankers' League) argued for the repeal of the Sixteenth Amendment and, failing that, for a constitutional amendment calling for a 25 percent tax cap, a proposal initially made by Robert B. Dresser. Dresser served on the boards of both the American Taxpayers' Association and the Committee for Constitutional

Government, a businessmen's group organized in 1937 to oppose Roosevelt's court-packing plan.[88] The cap, introduced in Congress in 1938, died in committee, after which the two organizations began calling for a second constitutional convention. "Our present tax system is doing much to destroy the free enterprise system," a *New York Times* business reporter wrote in 1943, arguing that American taxpayers "should be given reasonable assurance now that their incomes and inheritances will not be confiscated in a process of converting our private enterprise system into some form of State socialism."[89] By 1944, after the Committee for Constitutional Government had distributed 82 million pieces of literature, half of the states required to call for a constitutional convention had voted in favor of Dresser's amendment, even though an investigation directed by the Treasury secretary reported that the measure would shift the burden of taxation from the wealthiest taxpayers to the poorest (only the top 1 percent of taxpayers would have seen their taxes cut, which is why its critics called it the Millionaires' Amendment).[90] By the end of the decade, only one lobbying group in the country was spending more than the Committee for Constitutional Government. Wright Patman, a congressional Democrat from Texas, called it "the most sinister lobby in America."[91]

THE ALLIES AT LAST invaded France on June 6, 1944, D-Day, determined to liberate a devastated and terrorized Europe. "You are about to embark upon the great crusade toward which we have striven these many months," General Dwight D. Eisenhower said in a message broadcast to the Allied Expeditionary Forces. "The eyes of the world are upon you." One million men eventually participated in the invasion along a fifty-mile stretch of the Normandy coast, the largest seaborne invasion in history. It began at fifteen minutes past midnight, when paratroopers from the 101st and 82nd Airborne Divisions fell from the sky, trying to drop behind enemy lines under cover of darkness. Infantrymen carrying heavy packs weighted with ammunition stormed five land-mined beaches, wading through neck-high water under fierce gunfire. A fleet of bombers and fighter jets attacked from the sky. "I've never seen so many ships in my life," said paratrooper Jim Martin, a twenty-two-year-old machinist from

Dayton, Ohio, about flying over and looking down at more than five thousand Allied naval vessels. "You could have walked across the English Channel, not that you'd have had to walk on water, you could just step from ship to ship."[92]

Aided by the French Resistance, the Allies defeated German forces and proceeded to push them from the west while Soviet troops continued to assault them from the east, the plan agreed upon at Tehran the year before. In the Pacific, U.S. forces defeated the Japanese in the Battle of the Philippine Sea and began bombing the Japanese islands. As victory in Europe neared, delegates from what were now forty-four Allied nations met in July 1944 in the White Mountains of New Hampshire, at Bretton Woods, to plan a postwar order that could avoid the fatal mistakes of the last peace. Columbia political science professor James T. Shotwell had been at Versailles in 1919 and, like many delegates, understood that the objective of the meeting at Bretton Woods was to learn the lesson of the decisions made there. "The magnitude of the Great Depression of 1930 was due to two things," Shotwell wrote, "the economic cost of the first World War and the acceptance of disastrous economic policies after it."[93] Disavowing the economic nationalism that had followed the end of the First World War, the Bretton Woods Conference committed itself to open markets and free trade, and to Keynesianism, founding the International Monetary Fund, which would establish a fixed rate of currency exchange. Keynes chaired the commission that established the international bank, which eventually became known as the World Bank.[94]

Even as this order was being built, a conservative assault on it began. Two months after Bretton Woods, Austrian-born political scientist Friedrich A. Hayek published an American edition of *The Road to Serfdom*, a work that established the fundamental framework of modern economic conservatism. Much of the argument Hayek made in *The Road to Serfdom* had been made, much earlier, by Herbert Hoover, in *The Challenge to Liberty* (1934). The New Deal, Hoover wrote, amounted to "the daily dictation by Government, in every town and village every day in the week, of how men are to conduct their daily lives." Under that and like schemes, "peoples and governments are blindly wounding, even destroying, those fundamental human liberties which have been the foundation and the inspiration of Progress since the Middle Ages."[95]

To Hoover, and to Hayek, it was as if time were running backwards, from freedom to serfdom.

Hayek, who taught at the London School of Economics, had been a critic of Keynesian economics since the 1930s. "I wish I could make my 'progressive' friends . . . understand that democracy is possible only under capitalism and that collectivist experiments lead inevitably to fascism of one sort or another," he'd written to Walter Lippmann in 1937. When governments assume control over economic affairs, Hayek warned, the people become slaves: "What is called economic power, while it can be an instrument of coercion, is, in the hands of private individuals, never exclusive or complete power, never power over the whole life of a person. But centralized as an instrument of political power it creates a degree of dependence scarcely distinguishable from slavery."[96]

Less important for what it said than for how many people read it, *The Road to Serfdom*, released in England in March of 1944, was published in the United States the following September, though it appeared first as an article in the *Saturday Evening Post*, was subsequently abridged in *Reader's Digest*, and was adopted as a Book-of-the-Month Club selection. Hayek's influence would begin to drive policy as early as 1947, when he and other economists met in Switzerland to talk about how to prevent Western democracies from falling into a "new kind of serfdom." They drafted a "Statement of Aims" declaring that "Over large stretches of the earth's surface the essential conditions of human dignity and free-dom have already disappeared. . . . Even that most precious possession of Western Man, freedom of thought and expression, is threatened by the spread of creeds which, claiming the privilege of tolerance when in the position of a minority, seek only to establish a position of power in which they can suppress and obliterate all views but their own."[97]

Liberals, of course, feared totalitarianism, too. As the Allies marched across Europe, reports of the devastation they found, the ruined cities, the slaughtered peoples, haunted Americans. What had man wrought? Over the course of the war, many liberals, especially those who'd flirted with communism, had changed their minds about the kinds of reforms they'd urged in the 1930s. As Reinhold Niebuhr put it, "The rise of totalitarianism has prompted the democratic world to view all collectiv-ist answers to our social problems with increased apprehension." Instead of arguing against monopolies and for the restraint of capitalism, many, especially after the war, abandoned their interest in economic reform and followed the lead of African Americans in a fight for rights, and especially for racial justice.[98]

Another fissure divided prewar from postwar liberals. Instead of arguing for and running public arts programs, public schools, public libraries, and public-minded radio and television programs, liberal intellectuals grew suspicious of mass culture, and, after the war, openly contemptuous of it. In the 1930s, it had been conservative intellectuals who were revolted by the masses; in the 1950s, it would be liberals—a trend that would only escalate over the following decades, and reach a crisis by the end of the century.[99] That crisis began with the death of Franklin Roosevelt.

## III.

ROOSEVELT HAD GROWN haggard. At his inauguration in January 1945, he was wan and weak and could hardly stand; during his brief speech, his whole body shook, as if he had been seized by a fever. There would be no rest. He had agreed to undertake a harrowing journey, halfway around the world, in wartime, to a summit with Churchill and Stalin. Two days after the inauguration, he boarded a train for an undisclosed location, his car outfitted with bulletproof windows and armor-plated siding. Disembarking from the train at Newport News, Virginia, he boarded the USS *Quincy*, a battleship specially equipped with ramps for his wheelchair, for an eleven-day, 5,000-mile voyage to Malta. As the ship entered the harbor of the Mediterranean island, Roosevelt sat on deck wearing a tweed cap and a brown coat, smiling when a band on the *Orion*, the British ship carrying Winston Churchill, played "The Star-Spangled Banner." Returning the favor, the band on board the *Quincy* played "God Save the King." From Malta, Roosevelt and Churchill were flown separately, each escorted by six fighter jets, on a seven-hour flight to Crimea, on the Black Sea, to meet with Joseph Stalin at a lavish villa, Livadia Palace, the summer retreat of the last czar, in the seaside resort town of Yalta.[100]

Roosevelt and Churchill had gone to Stalin, and not he to them. It had

*FDR and Winston Churchill conferred on a warship at
the outset of the Yalta Conference in 1945.*

been a terribly dangerous and long journey for the two friends, neither
of whom was well, but especially for Roosevelt, who was dying. At the
time the conference opened, Stalin enjoyed more support in the American press than he ever had before or ever would after. He appeared on the
cover of *Time* in a story celebrating the American ally's recent victories,
"as Joseph Stalin's armies thundered into the eastern Reich." A month
later, *Time*'s cover story, "Ghosts on the Roof," commentary in the form
of a strange fable written by senior writer Whittaker Chambers, fiercely
denounced Stalin for devising an entirely new politics—international
social revolution—by which he could "blow up countries from within."[101]
It would later be suggested that Roosevelt, his powers diminished, had
appeased Stalin at Yalta, with fateful consequences. As Stalin's ruthlessness later became altogether plain, it became clear, too, that the agreement reached at Yalta hadn't stopped Stalin from taking over Eastern
Europe and it may have made possible the communist takeover of China.
Later, too, there would follow intimations of intrigue and even of treason,
after it was revealed that Alger Hiss, an American delegate to the confer-

ence, was a Soviet spy. But Soviet archives, opened after the end of the Cold War, would reveal that he reported to the military, not to the political branch, and that his reports from Yalta had little or no effect on the proceedings. And by many measures, Roosevelt got from Stalin the most that it may have been possible for an American president to get.[102]

Churchill had brought with him his traveling map room, the British embassy having sent particular instructions: "Mr. Churchill hopes that his map room may be adjacent to his private quarters at Yalta, and it should be so placed as to be accessible to President Roosevelt when wheeled in his chair." Roosevelt, following the principles of the Atlantic Charter, arrived at Yalta determined not to slice and dice Europe and hand whole peoples over to imperial rule, as had been done at the end of the last war. He hoped to agree on a plan for how to win the war and to divide up Germany in a way that was agreeable to both Stalin and Churchill, in exchange for Stalin's agreement to enter the war with Japan.

The conference opened in the palace's ballroom on February 4. Churchill, who distrusted Stalin even more than Roosevelt did, repeatedly sought alliances with Roosevelt, to no avail, since Roosevelt was chiefly occupied trying to convince Stalin to join the fight against Japan. Neither Roosevelt nor Churchill enjoyed a particularly strong bargaining position. Both needed help from the Red Army, Churchill in Europe and Roosevelt in the Pacific. To secure Stalin's support, Roosevelt betrayed the principles of the Atlantic Charter in granting to Stalin, even before the war was over, territories in China, at the time an American ally. In the end, the three men agreed to a division of Germany into zones of occupation and to the prosecution of Nazi war criminals. In three months, Germany would surrender; in six months, Japan. But before either of those nations surrendered, Stalin had already begun to betray the pledges he'd made at Yalta.

On March 1, Roosevelt reported to Congress on the Yalta Conference, describing the United Nations as "a universal organization in which all peace-loving Nations will finally have a chance to join." He'd grown even thinner and paler. He spoke from a chair, unable to stand and bear the weight of his metal braces.[103] His hands trembled; he slurred his words. On April 12, while sitting for a portrait at his retreat, the Little White House, in Warm Springs, Georgia, he collapsed. He died at 3:35 p.m. of a cerebral hemorrhage.

His death was broadcast at 5:47 p.m.: "We interrupt this program to bring you a special news bulletin from CBS World News. . . ." Stations across the country canceled their regular programming for days and played only news reports, the president's favorite music, and tributes. A stricken Harry S. Truman, who'd taken the oath of office four hours after Roosevelt's death, said the next day, "There have been few men in all history the equal of the man into whose shoes I am stepping."[104]

Archibald MacLeish, three minutes into an address to the country on CBS, fell apart, weeping, as he said the words "our great president who is now so tragically dead at the moment of greatest need." Radio correspondents reported on the funeral train that carried the flag-draped coffin to Hyde Park as solemn crowds gathered at every train station along the way. CBS announcer Arthur Godfrey reported from Washington when Roosevelt's coffin was carried through the streets on a wagon led by six white horses, flanked by motorcycles, while a crowd, twenty people deep, watched from the sidewalk. "God give me the strength to do this," Godfrey said, as he lost control of himself when the coffin passed.[105]

ON APRIL 15, the day FDR was buried at his home in Hyde Park, CBS reporter Edward R. Murrow delivered, on American radio, the first eyewitness description of a Nazi concentration camp to reach the American public. At Buchenwald, he met the camp doctor. "We inspected his records," Murrow said, his deep voice deepening. "There were only names in the little black book, nothing more. Nothing about who these men were, what they had done, or hoped. Behind the names of those who had died, there was a cross. I counted them. They totaled 242—242 out of 1,200, in one month." Month after month they had died, unnamed, slaughtered, no prayers at their graves.[106]

Murrow, born in Polecat Creek, North Carolina, had been hired by CBS in 1935 to run its London office and coordinate its European coverage; he'd never trained as a reporter. But by 1938 and the Anschluss, he'd been conscripted into the work of reporting on fast-breaking news from the field. His first words on the radio, in what CBS decided to call a "special report," were: "This is Edward Murrow speaking from Vienna. It's now nearly 3:30 in the morning, and Herr Hitler has not yet arrived." In

1940, during the Blitz, he'd reported from the rooftops of London, transmitting a sense of such immediacy and intensity that he'd helped turn the tide of American opinion in favor of entering the war. "You laid the dead of London at our doors," Archibald MacLeish told him, "and we knew that the dead were our dead."[107]

By the spring of 1945, Murrow was both a veteran of the new art and science of foreign radio correspondence and a voice known, heard, and trusted across the United States. On April 11, soldiers from the U.S. Ninth Armored Infantry Battalion had reached Buchenwald, near Weimar; soldiers from the Eightieth Infantry Division had arrived the next day, along with a group of reporters, including Murrow. In 1943, in a meeting at the Polish embassy in Washington, U.S. Supreme Court Justice Felix Frankfurter had met Jan Karski, a Polish socialist who had escaped Belzec. Karski described the death camp. Frankfurter was unable to speak. A full ten minutes elapsed. "I am unable to believe you," he said finally. "Felix, you cannot tell this man to his face that he is lying," said the Polish ambassador. "I said that I am unable to believe him," Frankfurter replied. "There is a difference."[108]

At Buchenwald, on April 15, 1945, Murrow reported that he'd asked to see one of the barracks. "It happened to be occupied by Czechoslovaks," he said. "When I entered, men crowded around, tried to lift me to their shoulders. They were too weak. Many of them could not get out of bed." Murrow's voice tightened. "As we walked out into the courtyard, a man fell dead."[109]

Murrow did not use the word "Jew" at any point in his report. Nor did most reporters. *Life* described the people confined at Dachau as "the men of all nations that Hitler's agents had picked out as prime opponents of Nazism."[110] Eisenhower visited Ohrdruf, a smaller camp outside Buchenwald, reporting to George C. Marshall on the same day that Murrow reported on live radio from Buchenwald: "In one room, where they were piled up twenty or thirty naked men, killed by starvation, George Patton would not even enter. He said he would get sick if he did so. I made the visit deliberately in order to be in position to give *first-hand* evidence of these things if ever, in the future, there develops a tendency to charge these allegations merely to 'propaganda.'"[111]

Despite these reports, the scale of Nazi atrocities remained all but

*In 1945, General Dwight D. Eisenhower and other
U.S. generals stopped at a newly liberated concentration
camp at Ohrdruf, where the remains of burned
bodies were found on railroad tracks.*

unknown in the West. Only about a fifth of the prisoners at Buchenwald, Ohrdruf, and Dachau were, in fact, Jews; the rest were political prisoners and prisoners of war. The death camps, like Auschwitz, where nearly all the prisoners were Jews, had been closed before the Allies arrived, or else liberated by the Soviets. American reporters did not generally see them.[112] The extent of the genocide—the murder of six million Jews—would not reach the American public for years to come.

Three days after Eisenhower stopped at Ohrdruf, the 305th Infantry invaded the island of Iejima, near Okinawa. Reporter Ernie Pyle was in a jeep that was driven into a ditch by machine-gun fire. When Pyle raised his head to look around, he was shot in the temple, a hairsbreadth under his helmet. He was forty-four. He died on April 18, 1945, with the dogfaces he loved and whose war he'd chronicled better than any other writer. At the time he was shot, he'd been writing a column. A draft was found in his rucksack. It began, "And so it is over. . . ."[113]

It wasn't quite over, but very nearly. On April 24, Secretary of War

Henry Stimson sent a memo to the fledging President Truman, stamped SECRET. "I think it very important that I should have a talk with you as soon as possible." Truman had been told about the existence of the atomic bomb within hours of his swearing-in, but Stimson wanted to tell him, now, that the weapon was almost ready.[114]

In Europe, the Allied forces closed in on the Axis. On April 25, American forces fighting Germany from the west and Soviet forces driving from the east met on the Elbe River. Italian partisans caught up with Mussolini on April 28, shot him down, and dumped his body on the street, where a mob urinated on it, and hung him by his heels. Two days later, in a bunker in Berlin, Hitler committed suicide. Germany signed a total and unconditional surrender on May 7.

Stalin had already begun pressing his claims to influence over the territory Hitler had so brutally conquered. At Yalta, he'd promised to allow "free and unfettered elections" in Poland; by spring, he'd abandoned that pledge. On April 28, Churchill, astutely perceiving what this foretold, wrote to Stalin: "There is not much comfort in looking into a future where you and the countries you dominate, plus the Communist parties in many other States, are all drawn up on one side, and those who rally to the English-speaking nations and their Associates or Dominions are on the other."[115] There was little comfort in such a future, but it would come all the same.

The World of Tomorrow imagined by the smooth-talking planners of the 1939 World's Fair, a world of Elektro the Moto-Man and automatic dishwashing machines, would come, too. Its chorus line of women dressed in white, performing a "Pageant of Peace," had been followed by six years of horrifying warfare and genocide, the shocking brutality of modernity. "People living in different countries kill each other at irregular time intervals," Albert Einstein had written in 1939, and "anyone who thinks about the future must live in fear and terror."[116] And yet the fevered dream for world peace remained and seemed to many less a fantasy and closer to a reality when, on June 25, Truman attended the founding conference of the United Nations in San Francisco.

Delegates from fifty nations signed a charter that Truman called "a victory against war itself." The American experiment, begun at the height of the Enlightenment, was to see a new day. "Let us not fail to grasp this supreme chance to establish a world-wide rule of reason," Truman said, "to create an enduring peace under the guidance of God." As the conference closed, acting secretary general Alger Hiss boarded an army transport plane along with this cherished treasure, the United Nations Charter, locked in a seventy-five-pound safe, attached to a parachute that read "Finder! Do Not Open. Send to the Department of State, Washington."[117]

The United States, a nation founded in an act of severing, had tied its fate to the fate of the world. A nation that had refused to join the League of Nations had taken the lead in establishing its replacement.

It remained to be seen whether the moment would be fleeting or lasting, but it had been long in coming. The Depression, the New Deal, and Roosevelt's political rhetoric had taught Americans about the danger of an island. "We have learned that we cannot live alone, at peace; that our own well-being is dependent on the well-being of other nations, far away," Roosevelt had said in 1933, in his first inaugural address. "We have learned the simple truth, as Emerson said, that 'The only way to have a friend is to be one.'" And the millions of American sailors and soldiers and nurses and airmen who fought on all four corners of the globe gained a cosmopolitanism unknown to any previous generation of Americans. One GI, a "corporal with a rural background," told *Yank* magazine that, before the war, "I never got much more than fifteen miles from home," but "The Army's taken me through fifteen countries from Brazil to Iceland and from Trinidad to Czechoslovakia." In July 1945, the Office of War Information drafted "America in the World," a statement unimaginable in any other era in American history: "In this interdependent world, there is no region in which the United States can renounce its moral and ideological interest."[118]

Truman, meanwhile, faced a dire decision about how to end the war in Japan. In June 1945, Leo Szilard wrote to Truman, urging him against deploying the atomic bomb: "A nation which sets the precedent of using these newly liberated forces of nature for purposes of destruction may have to bear the responsibility of opening the door to an era of devastation on an unimaginable scale." Szilard was a great admirer of H. G. Wells, who'd predicted atomic warfare in a novel published in the dark days of 1914. Wells had imagined an atomic World of Tomorrow. "Power after power about the armed globe sought to anticipate attack by aggression.

They went to war in a delirium of panic, in order to use their bombs first," Wells wrote in his novel. "By the spring of 1959 from nearly two hundred centres, and every week added to their number, roared the unquenchable crimson conflagrations of the atomic bombs; the flimsy fabric of the world's credit had vanished, industry was completely disorganized, and every city, every thickly populated area, was starving or trembled on the verge of starvation."[119]

Szilard, fearing that Wells's long-ago predicted dystopia was at hand, began gathering signatures to send to Truman. When the military threatened to charge Szilard with espionage, J. Robert Oppenheimer decided to delay sending the petition. But Szilard pressed on, and by July 17, seventy scientists working on the Manhattan Project, having witnessed the first test of the atomic bomb, had signed his petition of protest.[120]

Outside of those scientists, the president, and a handful of military men with clearance, Americans did not know about the existence of the atomic bomb, but they who knew, knew fear. Weapons capable of destroying cities or even humanity itself had been the stuff of science fiction for decades. And the scale of destruction, between the First World War and the Second, augured nothing so much as yet more staggering destructive force.

Archibald MacLeish tapped into this fear in a campaign he waged to raise popular support for the United Nations. He arranged for so many pro–United Nations radio broadcasts that journalist and former America Firster John T. Flynn complained, "You cannot turn on the radio at any hour of the day—morning, noon, or night—whether you listen to the Metropolitan Opera or to a horse opera, a hill-billy ballad, a commentator or a newscaster, that you do not hear a plug for this great instrument of peace."[121] MacLeish's most powerful project was *Watchtower Over Tomorrow*, a fifteen-minute film screened at movie theaters across the country, queued up with the newsreels that appeared before feature films. Directed by Alfred Hitchcock, *Watchtower Over Tomorrow* opened with footage that Hitchcock took from a 1936 science fiction film, *Things to Come*, an adaptation of yet another dystopian novel written by Wells, which imagined a decades-long war and a new machine age in which a race of super-scientists have built a "space gun." In the footage used by Hitchcock, a giant crane lowers a bomb into the barrel of a giant missile that, launched in a giant cloud of dust, reaches the stars before falling to earth and exploding. "Death from the sky, from a bomb fired by an enemy, thousands of miles away, the bomb which could be the opening of World War Three," a narrator says. "It is to prevent the firing of such a bomb that we of the United Nations have struggled on the Italian Front, the Western Front, the Eastern Front, throughout the Balkans, halfway around the world, in China, in Burma, in the Atlantic, up and down the Pacific, wherever the enemy can be brought to bay, to make possible a peace more permanent than a breathing spell between devastating wars."[122]

*Watchtower Over Tomorrow* began appearing in theaters in the spring of 1945. The future that it imagined the United Nations would stop came all the same. That summer, on August 6, the United States dropped an atomic bomb on Hiroshima. Three days later, it dropped another on Nagasaki. Japan surrendered. "This is the greatest thing in history," Truman said.[123] The Second World War had ended. And, watchtower or no, an altogether new tomorrow had begun.

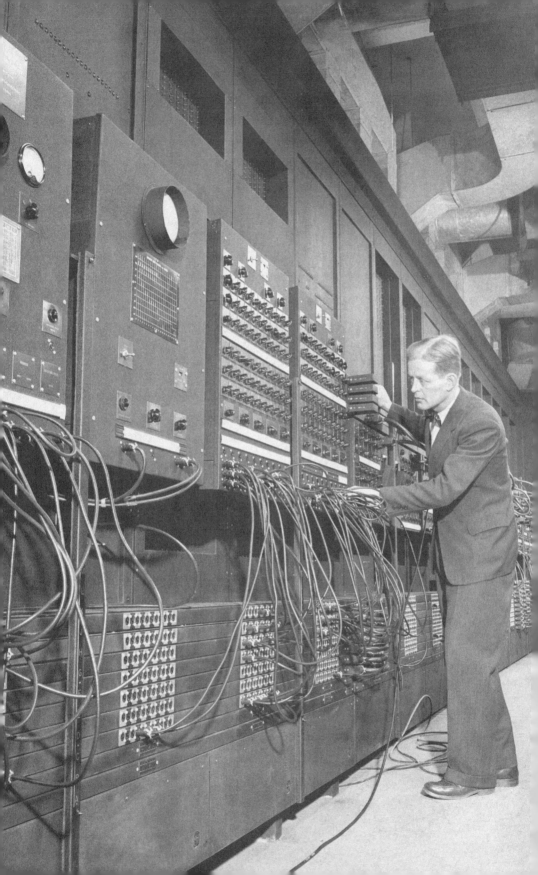

# Part Four

## THE MACHINE

★ ★ ★ ★

### 1946–2016

*Our challenges may be new. The instruments with which
we meet them may be new. But those values upon which our
success depends—honesty and hard work, courage and fair play,
tolerance and curiosity, loyalty and patriotism—these things
are old. These things are true. They have been the quiet force
of progress throughout our history. What is demanded,
then, is a return to these truths.*

—Barack Obama,
First Inaugural Address,
2009

*Thirteen*

# A WORLD OF KNOWLEDGE

*In an era of American abundance, TV sets in a
store window broadcast Eisenhower's announcement
of his decision to run for reelection in 1956.*

THE END OF TIME BEGAN AT EIGHT FIFTEEN ON THE
morning of August 6, 1945. "Miss Toshiko Sasaki, a clerk in the personnel department of the East Asia Tin Works, had just sat down at her
place in the plant office and was turning her head to speak to the girl at
the next desk," the writer John Hersey reported in *The New Yorker*. "Just
as she turned her head away from the windows, the room was filled with
a blinding light. She was paralyzed by fear, fixed still in her chair for a
long moment."

Everything fell, and Miss Sasaki lost consciousness. The ceiling
dropped suddenly and the wooden floor above collapsed in splinters

and the people up there came down and the roof above them gave way; but principally and first of all, the bookcases right behind her swooped forward and the contents threw her down, with her left leg horribly twisted and breaking underneath her. There, in the tin factory, in the first moment of the atomic age, a human being was crushed by books.[1]

*In the first moment of the atomic age, a human being was crushed by books:* the violence of knowledge.

Hiroshima marked the beginning of a new and differently unstable political era, in which technological change wildly outpaced the human capacity for moral reckoning. It wasn't only the bomb, and the devastation it wreaked. It was the computers whose development had made dropping the bomb possible. And it was the force of technological change itself, a political power unchecked by an eighteenth-century constitution and unfathomed by a nineteenth-century faith in progress.

Truman got word of the bombing on board a cruiser. The White House told the press the next day. The story went out over the radio at noon. Listeners reeled. John Haynes Holmes, a Unitarian minister and avowed pacifist, was on vacation at a cottage in Kennebunk, Maine. "Everything else seemed suddenly to become insignificant," he said, about how he felt when he heard the news. "I seemed to grow cold, as though I had been transported to the waste spaces of the moon." Days later, when the Japanese were forced to surrender, Americans celebrated. In St. Louis, people drove around the city with tin cans tied to the bumpers of their cars; in San Francisco, they tugged trolley cars off their tracks. More than four hundred thousand Americans had died in a war that, worldwide, had taken the lives of some sixty million people.[2]

And yet, however elated at the peace, Americans worried about how the war had ended. "There was a special horror in the split second that returned so many thousand humans to the primeval dust from which they sprang," one *Newsweek* editorial read. "For a race which still did not entirely understand steam and electricity it was natural to say: 'who next?'" Doubts gathered, and grew. "Seldom if ever has a war ended leaving the victors with such a sense of uncertainty and fear," CBS's Edward R. Murrow said. "We know what the bombs did to Hiroshima and Nagasaki," wrote the editors of *Fortune.* "But what did they do to the U.S. mind?"[3]

Part of the uncertainty was a consequence of the surprise. Americans hadn't known about the bomb before it fell. The Manhattan Project was classified. Even Truman hadn't known about it until after FDR's death. Nor had Americans known about the computers the military had been building, research that had also been classified, but which was dramatically revealed the winter after the war. "One of the war's top secrets, an amazing machine which applies electronic speeds for the first time to mathematical tasks hitherto too difficult and cumbersome for solution, was announced here tonight by the War Department," the *New York Times* reported from Philadelphia on February 15, 1946, in a front-page story introducing ENIAC, the Electronic Numerical Integrator and Computer, the first general-purpose electronic digital computer. Inside, the *Times* ran a full-page spread, including a photograph of the computer, the size of a room.[4] It was as if the curtain had been lifted, a magician's veil.

Like the atomic bomb, ENIAC was produced by the American military to advance the cause of war and relied on breakthroughs made by scientists in other parts of the world. In 1936, the English mathematician Alan Turing completed a PhD at Princeton and wrote a paper called "On Computable Numbers," in which he predicted the possibility of inventing "a single machine that can be used to compute any computable sequence."[5] The next year, Howard Aiken, a doctoral student at Harvard, poking around in the attic of a Harvard science building, found a model of Charles Babbage's early nineteenth-century Difference Engine; Aiken then proposed, to IBM, to build a new and better version, not mechanical but electronic. That project began at IBM in 1941 and three years later moved to Harvard, where Aiken, now a naval officer, was in charge of the machine, known as Mark I; Columbia astronomer L. J. Comrie called it "Babbage's dream come true." The Mark I was programmed by a longtime Vassar professor, the brilliant mathematician Grace Murray Hopper. "Amazing Grace," her colleagues nicknamed her, and she understood, maybe better than anyone, how far-reaching were the implications of a programmable computer. As she would explain, "It is the current aim to replace, as far as possible, the human brain."[6]

During the war, the Allied military had been interested in computers for two primary reasons: to break codes and to calculate weapons trajectories. At Bletchley Park, a six-hundred-acre manorial estate fifty miles northwest of London that became a secret military facility, Turing, who

*Vassar mathematician Grace Murray Hopper*
*programmed Mark I.*

would later be prosecuted for homosexuality and die of cyanide poisoning, had by 1940 built a single-purpose computer able to break the codes
devised by Germany's Enigma machine. At the University of Pennsylvania, physicist John Mauchly and electrical engineer Presper Eckert had
been charged with calculating firing-angle settings for artillery, work that
required iterative and time-consuming calculations. To do that work,
American scientists had been using an analog computer called a differential analyzer, invented at MIT in 1931 by FDR research czar Vannevar
Bush, an electrical engineer. Numbers were entered into the differential
analyzer by people who were known as "computers," and who were usually women with mathematics degrees, not unlike the "checkers," women
with literature degrees, who worked at magazines. But even when these
women entered numbers around the clock, it took a month to generate a
single artillery-trajectory table. In August 1942, Mauchly proposed using
vacuum tubes to build a digital electronic computer that would be much
faster. The U.S. War Department decided on April 9, 1943, to fund it.
Construction of ENIAC began in June 1943, but it wasn't fully opera-
tional until July 1945. ENIAC could make calculations a hundred times
faster than any earlier machine. Its first assignment, in the fall of 1945,
came from Los Alamos: using nearly a million punch cards, each pre-

pared and entered into the machine by a team of female programmers, ENIAC calculated the force of reactions in a fusion reaction, for the purpose of devising a hydrogen bomb.[7]

The machines built to plot the trajectories and force of missiles and bombs would come to transform economic systems, social structures, and the workings of politics. Computers are often left out of the study of history and government, but, starting at the end of the Second World War, history and government cannot be understood without them. Democracies rely on an informed electorate; computers, the product of long and deep study and experiment, would both explode and unsettle the very nature of knowledge.

The boundlessness of scientific inquiry also challenged the boundaries of the nation-state. After the war, scientists were among the loudest constituencies calling for international cooperation and, in particular, for a means by which atomic war could be averted. Instead, their work was conscripted into the Cold War.

The decision to lift the veil of secrecy and display ENIAC to the public came at a moment when the nation was engaged in a heated debate about the role of the federal government in supporting scientific research. During the war, at the urging of Vannevar Bush, FDR had created both the National Defense Research Committee and the Office of Scientific Research and Development. (Bush headed both.) Near the end of the war, Roosevelt had asked Bush to prepare a report that, in July 1945, Bush submitted to Truman. It was called "Science, the Endless Frontier."[8]

"A nation which depends upon others for its new basic scientific knowledge will be slow in its industrial progress and weak in its competitive position in world trade," Bush warned. "Advances in science when put to practical use mean more jobs, higher wages, shorter hours, more abundant crops, more leisure for recreation, for study, for learning how to live without the deadening drudgery which has been the burden of the common man for ages past."[9]

At Bush's urging, Congress debated a bill to establish a new federal agency, the National Science Foundation. Critics said the bill tied university research to the military and to business interests and asked whether scientists had not been chastened by the bomb. Scientific advances did indeed relieve people of drudgery and produce wealth and leisure, but the history of the last century had shown nothing if not that these benefits were spread so unevenly as to cause widespread political unrest and even revolution; the project of Progressive and New Deal reformers had been to protect the interests of those left behind by providing government supports and regulations. Could this practice be applied to the federal government's relationship to science? Democratic senator Harley M. Kilgore, a former schoolteacher from West Virginia, introduced a rival bill that extended the antimonopoly principles of the New Deal to science, tied university research to government planning, and included in the new foundation a division of social science, to provide funding for research designed to solve social and economic problems, on the grounds that one kind of knowledge had gotten ahead of another: human beings had learned how to destroy the entire planet but had not learned how to live together in peace. During Senate hearings, former vice president Henry Wallace said, "It is only by pursuing the field of the social sciences comprehensively" that the world could avoid "bigger and worse wars."[10]

Many scientists, including those who belonged to the newly formed Federation of Atomic Scientists, agreed, and two rivulets of protest became a stream: a revision of Kilgore's bill was attached to a bill calling for civilian control of atomic power. Atomic scientists launched a campaign to enlist the support of the public. "To the village square we must carry the facts of atomic energy," Albert Einstein said. "From there must come America's voice." Atomic scientists spoke at Kiwanis clubs, at churches and at synagogues, at schools and libraries. In Kansas alone, they held eight Atomic Age Conferences. And they published *One World or None: A Report to the Public on the Full Meaning of the Atomic Bomb*, essays by atomic scientists, including Leo Szilard and J. Robert Oppenheimer, and by political commentators, including Walter Lippmann. Albert Einstein, in his essay, argued for "denationalization."[11]

Against this campaign stood advocates for federal government funding of the new field of computer science, who launched their own publicity campaign, beginning with the well-staged unveiling of ENIAC. It had been difficult to stir up interest. No demonstration of a general-purpose computer could have the drama of an atomic explosion, or even of the 1939 World's Fair chain-smoking Elektro the Moto-Man. ENIAC was inert. Its vacuum tubes, lit by dim neon bulbs, were barely visible. When the machine was working, there was no real way to see much of anything happening. Mauchly and Eckert prepared press releases and, in advance of a scheduled press conference, tricked up the machine for dramatic effect. Eckert cut Ping-Pong balls in half, wrote numbers on them, and placed them over the tips of the bulbs, so that when the machine was working, the room flashed as the lights flickered and blinked. It blinked fast. The *Times* gushed, "The 'Eniac,' as the new electronic speed marvel is known, virtually eliminates time."[12]

The unintended consequences of the elimination of time would be felt for generations. But the great acceleration—the speeding up of every exchange—had begun. And so had the great atomization—the turning of citizens into pieces of data, fed into machines, tabulated, processed, and targeted, as the nation-state began to yield to the data-state.

## I.

THE END OF THE WAR marked the dawn of an age of affluence, a wide and deep American prosperity. It led both to a new direction for liberalism—away from an argument for government regulation of business and toward an insistence on individual rights—and to a new form of conservatism, dedicated to the fight against communism and deploying to new ends the rhetoric of freedom.

The origins of postwar prosperity lay in the last legislative act of the New Deal. In June 1944, FDR had signed the Serviceman's Readjustment Act, better known as the G.I. Bill of Rights. It created a veterans-only welfare state. The G.I. Bill extended to the sixteen million Americans who served in the war a series of benefits, including a free, four-year college education, zero-down-payment low-interest loans for homes and businesses, and a "readjustment benefit" of twenty dollars a week for up to fifty-two weeks, to allow returning veterans to find work. More than half of eligible veterans—some eight million Americans—took advantage of the G.I. Bill's educational benefits. Those who did enjoyed average earnings of $10,000–$15,000 more than those who didn't. They also paid more in taxes. By 1948, the cost of the G.I. Bill constituted 15 percent of the federal budget. But, with rising tax revenues, the G.I. Bill paid for itself almost ten times over. It created a new middle class, changed the face of American colleges and universities, and convinced many Americans

The G.I. Bill made it possible for a generation of Americans to attend college. In September 1947, three jubilant former servicemen leave a student union at Indiana University, waving their notices of admission.

that the prospects for economic growth, for each generation's achieving a standard of living higher than the generation before, might be limitless.[13]

That growth was achieved, in part, by consumer spending, as factories outfitted for wartime production were converted to manufacture consumer goods, from roller skates to color televisions. The idea of the citizen as a consumer, and of spending as an act of citizenship, dates to the 1920s. But in the 1950s, mass consumption became a matter of civic obligation. By buying "the dozens of things you never bought or even thought of before," *Brides* magazine told its readers, "you are helping to build greater security for the industries of this country."[14]

Critics suggested that the banality and conformity of consumer society had reduced Americans to robots. John Updike despaired: "I drive my car to supermarket, / The way I take is superhigh, / A superlot is where I park it, / And Super Suds are what I buy."[15] Nothing epitomized what critics called the "Packaged Society" so much as Disneyland, an amusement park that had opened in 1955 as a reimagined 1939 World's Fair, more provincial and more commercial, with a Main Street and a Tomorrowland. In Frontierland, Walt Disney explained, visitors "can return to frontier America, from the Revolutionary Era to the final taming of the great southwest," riding stagecoaches and Conestoga wagons over dusty trails and boarding the steamship *Mark Twain* within sight of the park's trademark turquoise-towered castle, a fairyland that sold itself as "The Happiest Place on Earth."[16]

Most of the buying was done by women: housewives and mothers. The home, which had become separated from work during the process of industrialization, became a new kind of political space, in which women met the obligations of citizenship by spending money. Domesticity itself took on a different cast, as changes to the structure of the family that had begun in the Depression and continued during the war were reversed. Before the war, age at first marriage had been rising; after the war, it began falling. The number of children per family had been falling; it began rising. More married women and mothers of young children had been entering the paid labor force; they began leaving it. Having bigger families felt, to many Americans, an urgent matter. "After the Holocaust, we felt obligated to have lots of babies," one Jewish mother later explained. "But it was easy because everyone was doing it—non-Jews, too." Expectations of equality between men and women within marriage diminished, as did expectations of political equality. Claims for equal rights for women had been strenuously pressed during the war, but afterwards, they were mostly abandoned. In 1940, the GOP had supported the Equal Rights Amendment (first introduced into Congress in 1923), and in 1944 the Democrats had supported it, too. The measure reached the Senate in 1946, where it won a plurality, but fell short of the two-thirds vote required to send an amendment to the states for ratification.[17] It would not pass Congress until 1972, after which an army of housewives, the foot soldiers of the conservative movement, would block its ratification.

The G.I. Bill, for all that it did to build a new middle class, also reproduced and even exacerbated earlier forms of social and economic inequality. Most women who had served in the war were not eligible for benefits; the women's auxiliary divisions of the branches of the military had been deliberately decreed to be civilian units with an eye toward avoiding providing veterans' benefits to women, on the assumption that they would be supported by men. After the war, when male veterans flocked to colleges and universities, many schools stopped admitting women, or reduced their number, in order to make more room for men. And, even among veterans, the bill's benefits were applied unevenly. Some five thousand soldiers and four thousand sailors had been given a "blue discharge" during the war as suspected homosexuals; the VA's interpretation of that discharge made them ineligible for any G.I. Bill benefits.[18]

African American veterans were excluded from veterans' organizations; they faced hostility and violence; and, most significantly, they were barred from taking advantage of the G.I. Bill's signal benefits, its education and housing provisions. In some states, the American Legion, the most powerful veterans' association, refused to admit African Americans, and proved unwilling to recognize desegregated associations. Money to go to college was hard to use when most colleges and universities refused to admit African Americans and historically black colleges and universities had a limited number of seats. The University of Pennsylvania had nine thousand students in 1946; only forty-six were black. By 1946, some one hundred thousand black veterans had applied for educational benefits; only one in five had been able to register for college. More than one in four veterans took advantage of the G.I. Bill's home loans, which meant that by 1956, 42 percent of World War II veterans owned their own homes (compared to only 34 percent of nonveterans). But the bill's easy access to credit and capital was far less available to black veterans. Banks refused to give black veterans loans, and restrictive covenants and redlining meant that much new housing was whites-only.[19]

Even after the Supreme Court struck down restrictive housing covenants in 1948, the Federal Housing Administration followed a policy of segregation, routinely denying loans to both blacks and Jews. In cities like Chicago and St. Louis and Los Angeles and Detroit, racially restrictive covenants in housing created segregated ghettos where few had existed before the war. Whites got loans, had their housing offers accepted, and moved to the suburbs; blacks were crowded into bounded neighborhoods within the city. Thirteen million new homes were built in the United States during the 1950s; eleven million of them were built in the suburbs. Eighty-three percent of all population growth in the 1950s took place in the suburbs. For every two blacks who moved to the cities, three whites moved out. The postwar racial order created a segregated landscape: black cities, white suburbs.[20]

The New Deal's unfinished business—its inattention to racial discrimination and racial violence—became the business of the postwar civil rights movement, as new forms of discrimination and the persistence of Jim Crow laws and even of lynching—in 1946 and 1947, black veterans were lynched in Georgia and Louisiana—contributed to a new depth of discontent. As a black corporal from Alabama put it, "I spent four years in the Army to free a bunch of Dutchmen and Frenchmen, and I'm hanged if I'm going to let the Alabama version of the Germans kick me around when I get home." Langston Hughes, who wrote a regular column for the *Chicago Defender*, urged black Americans to try to break Jim Crow laws at lunch counters. "Folks, when you go South by train, be sure to eat in the diner," Hughes wrote. "Even if you are not hungry, eat anyhow—to help establish that right."[21]

But where Roosevelt had turned a blind eye, Truman did not. He had grown up in Independence, Missouri, just outside of Kansas City, and worked on the family farm until the First World War, when he saw combat in France. Back in Missouri, he began a slow ascension through the Democratic Party ranks, starting with a county office and rising to the U.S. Senate in 1934. Roosevelt had chosen him as his running mate in 1944 chiefly because he was unobjectionable; neither wing of the Democratic Party was troubled by Truman. He had played virtually no role in White House affairs during his vice presidency, and was little prepared to move into the Oval Office upon Roosevelt's death. No president had faced a greater trial by fire than the decision that had fallen to Truman over whether or not to use the atomic bomb. Mild-mannered and myopic, Truman had a common touch. Unlike most American presidents, he had neither a college degree nor a law degree. For all his limitations as a president, he had an intuitive sense of the concerns of ordinary Americans. And, from the very beginning of his career, he'd courted black voters and worked closely with black politicians.

Unwilling to ignore Jim Crow, Truman established a commission on civil rights. *To Secure These Rights*, its 1947 report, demonstrated that a new national consensus had been reached, pointing to a conviction that the federal government does more than prevent the abuse of rights but also secures rights. "From the earliest moment of our history we have believed that every human being has an essential dignity and integrity which must be respected and safeguarded," read the report. "The United States can no longer countenance these burdens on its common conscience."[22]

Consistent with that commitment, Truman made national health insurance his first domestic policy priority. In September 1945, he asked Congress to act on FDR's Second Bill of Rights by passing what came to be called a Fair Deal. Its centerpiece was a call for universal medical insurance. The time seemed, finally, right, and Truman enjoyed some important sources of bipartisan support, including from Earl Warren, the Republican governor of California. What Truman proposed was a national version of a plan Warren had proposed in California: compulsory insurance funded with a payroll tax. "The health of American children, like their education, should be recognized as a definite public responsibility," the president said.[23]

Warren, the son of a Norwegian immigrant railroad worker, a striker who was later murdered, had grown up knowing hardship. After studying political science and the law at Berkeley and serving during the First World War, he'd become California's attorney general in 1939. In that position, he'd been a strong supporter of the Japanese American internment policy. "If the Japs are released," Warren had warned, "no one will be able to tell a saboteur from any other Jap." (Warren later publicly expressed pained remorse about this policy and, in a 1972 interview, wept over it.) On the strength of his record as attorney general, Warren had run for governor in 1942. Clem Whitaker and Leone Baxter had managed his campaign, which had been notoriously heated. "War-time voters live at an emotional pitch that is anything but normal," Whitaker had written in his Plan of Campaign. "This must be a campaign that makes people hear the beat of drums and the thunder of bombs—a campaign that stirs and captures the imagination; a campaign that no one who loves California can disregard. This must be A CALL TO ARMS IN DEFENSE OF CALIFORNIA!"[24]

Warren won, but he didn't like how he'd won. Just before the election, he fired Whitaker and Baxter. They never forgave him.

Late in 1944, Warren had fallen seriously ill with a kidney infection. His treatment required heroic and costly medical intervention. He began to consider the catastrophic effects a sudden illness could have on a family of limited means. "I came to the conclusion that the only way to

Keep politics out of this picture

*Leone Baxter and Clem Whitaker, who founded
Campaigns, Inc., in California in 1933, attained national
prominence at the end of the 1940s through their
successful defeat of Truman's health insurance plan.*

remedy this situation was to spread the cost through insurance," he later wrote. He asked his staff to develop a proposal. After conferring with the California Medical Association, he anticipated no objections from doctors. And so, in his January 1945 State of the State address, Warren announced his plan, a proposal modeled on the social security system: a 1½ percent withholding of wages would contribute to a statewide compulsory insurance program.[25] And then the California Medical Association hired Campaigns, Inc.

Earl Warren began his political career as a conservative and ended it as a liberal. Years later, Leone Baxter was asked by a historian what she made of Warren's seeming transformation. Warren's own explanation, the historian told Baxter, was this: "I grew up a poor boy myself and I saw the trials and tribulations of getting old without having any income and being sick and not being able to work." Baxter shot back, "He didn't see them until that Sunday in 1945." Then she ended the interview.[26]

What really changed Earl Warren was Campaigns, Inc. Whitaker and Baxter took a piece of legislation that enjoyed wide popular support and torpedoed it. Fifty newspapers initially supported Warren's plan; Whitaker and Baxter whittled that down to twenty. "You can't beat something with nothing," Whitaker liked to say, so they launched a drive for private health insurance. Their "Voluntary Health Insurance Week," driven by 40,000 inches of advertising in more than four hundred newspapers, was observed in fifty-three of the state's fifty-eight counties. Whitaker and Baxter sent more than nine thousand doctors out with prepared speeches. They coined a slogan: "Political medicine is bad medicine."[27] They printed postcards for voters to stick in the mail:

> *Dear Senator:*
>     *Please vote against all Compulsory Health Insurance Bills*
> *pending before the Legislature. We have enough regimentation in*
> *this country now. Certainly we don't want to be forced to go to "A*
> *State doctor," or to pay for such a doctor whether we use him or*
> *not. That system was born in Germany—and is part and parcel*
> *of what our boys are fighting overseas. Let's not adopt it here.*[28]

When Warren's bill failed to pass by just one vote, he blamed Whitaker and Baxter. "They stormed the Legislature with their invective," he complained, "and my bill was not even accorded a decent burial."[29] It was the greatest legislative victory at the hands of admen the country had ever seen. It would not be the last.


# II.

RICHARD MILHOUS NIXON counted his resentments the way other men count their conquests. Born in the sage-and-cactus town of Yorba Linda, California, in 1913, he'd been a nervous kid, a whip-smart striver. His family moved to Whittier, where his father ran a grocery store out of an abandoned church. Nixon went to Whittier College, working to pay his way, resenting that he didn't have the money to go somewhere else. He had wavy black hair; small, dark eyes; and heavy, brooding eyebrows. An ace debater, he'd gone after college to Duke Law School, resented all the Wall Street law firms that refused to hire him when he finished, and returned to Whittier. He went away again, to serve in the navy in the South Pacific. And when he got back, serious and strenuously intelligent Lieutenant Commander Nixon, thirty-two, was recruited by a group of California bankers and oilmen to try to defeat five-term Democratic incumbent Jerry Voorhis for a seat in the House. The man from Whittier wanted to go to Washington.

Voorhis, a product of Hotchkiss and Yale and a veteran of Upton Sinclair's EPIC campaign, was a New Dealer who'd first been elected to Congress in 1936, but, ten years later, the New Deal was old news. The midterm elections during Truman's first term—and the fate of his legislative agenda—were tied to heightening tensions between the United States and the Soviet Union. Nixon in California was only one in a small battalion of younger men, mainly ex-servicemen, who ran for office in 1946, the nation's first Cold Warriors. In Massachusetts, another veteran of the war in the Pacific, twenty-nine-year-old John F. Kennedy, ran for a House seat from the Eleventh District. But, unlike Nixon, he'd been readied for that seat from the cradle.

Kennedy, born to wealth and groomed at Choate and Harvard, represented everything Nixon detested: all that Nixon had fought for, by tooth and claw, had been handed to Kennedy, on a platter decorated with a doily. But both Nixon and Kennedy were powerfully shaped by the rising conflict with the Soviet Union, and both understood domestic affairs through the lens of foreign policy. After Stalin broke the promise he'd made at Yalta to allow Poland "free and unfettered elections," it had become clear that he was ruthless, even if the West had, as yet, little knowledge of the purges with which he was overseeing the murder of millions of people. Inside the Truman administration, a conviction grew that the Soviet regime was ideologically and militarily relentless. In February 1946, George Kennan, an American diplomat in Moscow, sent the State Department an 8,000-word telegram in which he reported that the Soviets were resolute in their determination to battle the West in an epic confrontation between capitalism and communism. "We have here a political force committed fanatically to the belief that with US there can be no permanent *modus vivendi* that it is desirable and necessary that the internal harmony of our society be disrupted, our traditional way of life be destroyed, the international authority of our state be broken, if Soviet power is to be secure," Kennan wrote. "This political force has complete power of disposition over energies of one of world's greatest peoples and resources of world's richest national territory, and is borne along by deep and powerful currents of Russian nationalism." Two weeks later, Winston Churchill, speaking in Truman's home state of Missouri, warned of an "iron curtain" falling across Europe.[30]

The postwar peace had been fleeting. As keenly as Roosevelt and Churchill had wanted to avoid repeating the mistakes of the peace made at the end of the First World War, political instability had inevitably trailed behind the devastation of the Second World War. The Soviet Union's losses had been staggering: twenty-seven million Russians died, ninety times as many casualties as were suffered by Americans. Much of Europe and Asia had been ravaged. From ashes and ruins and graveyards, new regimes gathered. In Latin America, Africa, and South Asia, nations and peoples that had been colonized by European powers, began to fight to secure their independence. They meant to choose their own political and economic arrangements. But, in a newly bipolar world, that generally meant choosing between democracy and authoritarianism, between capitalism and communism, between the influence of the United States or the influence of the USSR.[31]

"At the present moment in world history nearly every nation must choose between alternative ways of life," Truman said. He conceived of a choice between freedom and oppression. Much about this conception derived from the history of the United States, a refiguring of the struggle between "freedom" and "slavery" that had divided nineteenth-century America into "free states" and "slave states" and during which opponents of slavery had sought to "contain" it by refusing to admit "slave states" into the Union. In the late 1940s, Americans began applying this rhetoric internationally, pursuing a policy of containing communism while defending the "free world."[32]

The same rhetoric, of course, infused domestic politics. Republicans characterized the 1946 midterm elections as involving a stark choice: "Americanism vs. Communism." In California, scrappy Richard Nixon defeated the diffident Voorhis by debating him on stage a half-dozen times, but especially by painting him as weak on communism and slaughtering him with innuendo and smear. Nixon adopted, in his first campaign, his signature tactic: making false claims and then taking umbrage when his opponent impugned his integrity. Voorhis was blindsided. "Every time that I would say that something wasn't true," he recalled, "the response was always 'Voorhis is using unfair tactics by accusing Dick

Nixon of lying.'" But Nixon, the lunch-bucket candidate, also exploited voters' unease with a distant government run by Ivy League–educated bureaucrats; he found it took only the merest of gestures to convince voters that there was something un-American about people like Voorhis, people like *them*. His campaign motto: "Richard Nixon is one of us."[33]

In November 1946, the GOP won both the House and Senate for the first time since 1932. The few Democrats who were elected, like Kennedy in Massachusetts, had sounded the same themes as Nixon: the United States was soft on communism. As freshmen congressmen, Kennedy and Nixon struck up an unlikely friendship while serving together on the House Education and Labor Committee. Nixon and his fellow Republicans supported a proposed Taft-Hartley Act, regulating the unions and prohibiting certain kinds of strikes and boycotts—an attempt to rein in the power of unions, whose membership had surged before the war, from three million in 1933 to more than ten million in 1941. After Pearl Harbor, the AFL and the CIO had promised to abstain from striking for the duration of the conflict and agreed to wage limits. As soon as the war ended, though, the strikes began. Some five million workers walked out in 1946 alone. Truman opposed Taft-Hartley, and, when Congress passed it, Truman vetoed it. Republicans in Congress began lining up votes for an override. Nixon and Kennedy went to a steel town in western Pennsylvania to debate the question before an audience of union leaders and businessmen. Each man admired the other's style. On the train back to Washington, they shared a sleeping car. Kennedy's half-hearted objections would, in any case, hold no sway against Republicans who succeeded in depicting unionism as creeping communism. Congress overrode the president's veto.[34]

On foreign policy, Truman began to move to the right. Disavowing the legacy of American isolationism, he pledged that the nation would aid any besieged democracy. The immediate cause of this commitment was Britain's decision to stop providing aid to Greece and Turkey, which were struggling against communism. In March of 1947, the president announced what came to be called the Truman Doctrine: the United States would "support free peoples who are resisting subjugation by armed minorities or by outside pressures." (Truman aides later said that the president himself was unpersuaded by the growing fear of communism but was instead concerned about his chances for reelection. "The President didn't attach fundamental importance to the so-called Communist scare," one said. "He thought it was a lot of baloney.") He also urged passage of the Marshall Plan, which provided billions of dollars in aid for rebuilding Western Europe. The Truman Doctrine and the Marshall Plan, the president liked to say, were "two halves of the same walnut." Abroad, the United States would provide aid; at home, it would root out suspected communists. Coining a phrase, the financier and presidential adviser Bernard Baruch in April 1947 said in a speech in South Carolina, "We are today in the midst of a cold war."[35]

Instead of a welfare state, the United States built a national security state. A peace dividend expected after the Allied victory in 1945 never came; instead came the fight to contain communism, unprecedented military spending, and a new military bureaucracy. During Senate hearings on the future of the national defense, military contractors including Lockheed, which had been an object of congressional investigation in the merchants-of-death era of the 1930s and had built tens of thousands of aircraft during the Second World War, argued that the nation required "adequate, continuous, and permanent" funding for military production, pressing not only for military expansion but also for federal government subsidies.[36]

In 1940, when Roosevelt pledged to make the United States an "arsenal of democracy," he meant wartime production. A central political question of postwar American politics would become whether the arsenal was, in fact, compatible with democracy.

After the war, the United States committed itself to military supremacy in peacetime, not only through weapons manufacture and an expanded military but through new institutions. In 1946, the standing committees on military and naval affairs combined to become the Armed Services Committee. The 1947 National Security Act established the Central Intelligence Agency and the National Security Agency; created the position of the chairman of the Joint Chiefs of Staff; and made the War Department, now housed for the first time in a building of its own, into the Department of Defense.

In this political climate, the "one world" vision of atomic scientists, along with the idea of civilian, international control of atomic power, faded fast. Henry Stimson urged the sharing of atomic secrets. "The chief lesson I have learned in a long life," he said, "is the only way you can make a man trustworthy is to trust him; and the surest way you can make a man untrustworthy is to distrust him and to show your distrust." Truman disagreed. Atomic secrets were to be kept secret, and the apparatus of espionage was to be deployed to ferret out scientists who might dissent from that view.[37]

The *Bulletin of the Atomic Scientists* began publishing a Doomsday Clock, an assessment of the time left before the world would be annihilated in an atomic war. In 1947, they set the clock at seven minutes before midnight. Kennan, in a top secret memo to Truman, warned that to use an atomic or hydrogen bomb would be to turn back time. These weapons, Kennan argued, "reach backward beyond the frontiers of western civilization"; "they cannot really be reconciled with a political purpose directed to shaping, rather than destroying, the lives of the adversary"; "they fail to take into account the ultimate responsibility of men for one another."[38]

No caution slowed the development of the weapons program, and Soviet aggression and espionage, along with events in China, aided the case for national security and undercut the argument of anyone who attempted to oppose the military buildup. With every step of communist advance, the United States sought out new alliances, strengthened its defenses, and increased military spending. In 1948, the Soviet-supported Communist Party in Czechoslovakia staged a coup, the Soviets blockaded Berlin, Truman sent in support by air, and Congress passed a peacetime draft. The next year, the United States signed the North Atlantic Treaty, joining with Western Europe in a military alliance to establish, in NATO, a unified front against the USSR and any further Soviet aggression. Months later, the USSR tested its first atomic bomb and Chinese communists won a civil war. In December 1949, Mao Zedong, the chairman of China's Communist Party, visited Moscow to form an alliance with Stalin; in January, Klaus Fuchs, a German émigré scientist who had worked on the Manhattan Project confessed that he was, in fact, a Soviet spy. Between 1949 and 1951, U.S. military spending tripled.[39]

The new spending restructured the American economy, nowhere more than in the South. By the middle of the 1950s, military spending made up close to three-quarters of the federal budget. A disproportionate amount of this spending went to southern states. The social welfare state hadn't saved the South from its long economic decline, but the national security state did. Southern politicians courted federal government contracts for defense plants, research facilities, highways, and airports. The New South led the nation in aerospace and electronics. "Our economy is no longer agricultural," the southern writer William Faulkner observed. "Our economy is the Federal Government."[40]

Nixon staked his political future on becoming an instrument of the national security state. Keen to make a name for himself by ferreting out communist subversives, he gained a coveted spot on the House Un-American Activities Committee, where his early contributions included inviting the testimony of the actor Ronald Reagan, head of the Screen Actors Guild, a Californian two years Nixon's junior. But Nixon's real chance came when the committee sought the testimony of *Time* magazine senior editor and noted anticommunist Whittaker Chambers.

On August 3, 1948, Chambers, forty-seven, told the committee that, in the 1930s, he'd been a communist. *Time*, pressured to fire Chambers, refused, and published this statement: "TIME was fully aware of Chambers' political background, believed in his conversion, and has never since had reason to doubt it." But if Chambers's past was no real surprise, his testimony nevertheless contained a bombshell: Chambers named as a fellow communist the distinguished veteran of the U.S. State Department, former general secretary of a United Nations organizing conference, and now president of the widely respected Carnegie Endowment for International Peace, forty-three-year-old Alger Hiss—news that, by the next morning, was splashed across the front of every newspaper in the country.

Hiss appeared before the committee on August 25 in a televised congressional hearing. He deftly denied the charges and seemed likely to be exonerated, especially after Chambers, who came across as unstable, vengeful, and possibly unhinged, admitted that he had been a Soviet spy (at that point, *Time* publisher Henry Luce accepted his resignation). Chambers having presented no evidence to support his charges against Hiss, the committee was inclined to let it pass—all but Nixon, who seemed to hold a particular animus for Hiss.[41] Rumor had it that in a closed session, not seen on television, Nixon had asked Hiss to name his alma mater.

"Johns Hopkins and Harvard," Hiss answered, and then added dryly, "And I believe your college is Whittier?"[42]

Nixon, who never forgave an Ivy League snub, began an exhaustive investigation, determined to catch his prey, the Sherlock Holmes to

Hiss's Professor Moriarty. Meanwhile, the press and the public forgot about Hiss and turned to the upcoming election, however unexciting it appeared. Hardly anyone expected Truman to win his first full term in 1948 against the Republican presidential nominee, Thomas Dewey, governor of New York. Few Americans were excited about either candidate, but Truman's loss seemed all but inevitable. "We wish Mr. Dewey well without too much enthusiasm," Reinhold Niebuhr said days before the election, "and look to Mr. Truman's defeat without too much regret."[43]

Truman had accomplished little of his domestic agenda, with one exception, which had the effect of alienating him from his own party: he had ordered the desegregation of the military. Aside from that, a Republican-controlled Congress had stymied nearly all of his legislative initiatives, including proposed labor reforms. Truman was so weak a candidate that two other Democrats ran against him on third-party tickets. Henry Wallace ran to Truman's left, as the nominee of the Progressive Party. The *New Republic* ran an editorial with the headline TRUMAN SHOULD QUIT.[44] At the Democratic convention in Philadelphia that summer, segregationists bolted: the entire Mississippi delegation and thirteen members of the Alabama delegation walked out, protesting Truman's stand on civil rights. These southerners, known as Dixiecrats, formed the States' Rights Democratic Party and ran a candidate to Truman's right. They held a nominating convention in Birmingham during which Frank M. Dixon, a former governor of Alabama, said that Truman's civil rights programs would "reduce us to the status of a mongrel, inferior race, mixed in blood, our Anglo-Saxon heritage a mockery." The Dixiecrat platform rested on this statement: "We stand for the segregation of the races and the racial integrity of each race." As its candidate, the States' Rights Party nominated South Carolina governor Strom Thurmond.[45]

Waving aside the challenges from Wallace and Thurmond, Truman campaigned vigorously against Dewey, running on his chief campaign pledge: a national health insurance plan. Dewey, on the other hand, proved about as good a campaigner as a pail of paint. From Kentucky, the *Louisville Courier-Journal* complained, "No presidential candidate in the future will be so inept that four of his major speeches can be boiled down to these historic four sentences. Agriculture is important. Our rivers are full of fish. You cannot have freedom without liberty. Our future lies ahead."[46]

Truman might have felt that the crowds were rallying to him, but every major polling organization predicted that Dewey would defeat him. Truman liked to mock leaders who paid attention to polls. "I wonder how far Moses would have gone if he'd taken a poll in Egypt," he said. "What would Jesus Christ have preached if he'd taken a poll in Israel?"[47] The week before Election Day, George Gallup issued a statement: "We have never claimed infallibility, but next Tuesday the whole world will be able to see down to the last percentage point how good we are."[48] Gallup predicted that Truman would lose. The *Chicago Tribune*, crippled by a strike of typesetters, went to press with the headline DEWEY DEFEATS TRUMAN. A victorious Truman was caught on camera two days later, holding up the paper and wearing a grin as wide as the Mississippi River.

The 1948 election became a referendum on polling, a referendum with considerable consequences because Congress was still debating whether or not to establish a National Science Foundation, and whether such a foundation would provide funding to social science. The pollsters' error likely had to do with undercounting black votes. Gallup routinely failed to poll black people, on the theory that Jim Crow, voter violence, intimidation, and poll taxes prevented most from voting. But blacks who could vote overwhelmingly cast their ballots for Truman, and probably won him the election.

That was hardly the only problem with the polling industry. In 1944, Gallup had underestimated Democratic support in two out of every three states; Democrats charged that he had engineered the poll to favor Republicans. Questioned by Congress, he'd weakly offered that, anticipating a low turnout, he had taken two points off the projected vote for FDR, more or less arbitrarily.[49] Concerned that the federal government might institute regulatory measures, the polling industry had decided to regulate itself by establishing, in 1947, the American Association for Public Opinion Research. But the criticism had continued, especially from within universities, where scholars pointed out that polling was essentially a commercial activity, cloaked in the garb of social science.

The most stinging critiques came from University of Chicago sociologist Herbert Blumer and Columbia political scientist Lindsay Rogers. Public opinion polling is not a form of empirical inquiry, Blumer argued, since it skips over the crucial first step of any inquiry: identifying what it is that is to be studied. As Blumer pointed out, this is by no means surprising, since polling is a business, and an industry run by business-men will create not a science but a product. Blumer argued that pub-lic opinion does not exist, absent its measurement; pollsters created it: "public opinion consists of what public opinion polls poll." The very idea that a quantifiable public opinion exists, Blumer argued, rests on a series of false propositions. The opinions held by any given population are not formed as an aggregation of individual opinions, each given equal weight, as pollsters suppose; they are formed, instead, "as a function of a society in operation"; we come to hold and express the opinions that we hold and express in conversation and especially in debate with other people and groups, over time, and different people and groups influence us, and we them, in different degrees.[50]

Where Herbert Blumer argued that polling rested on a misunder-standing of empirical science, Lindsay Rogers argued that polling rested on a misunderstanding of American democracy. Rogers, a scholar of American political institutions, had started out as a journalist. In 1912, he reported on the Democratic National Convention; three years later, he earned a doctorate in political science from Johns Hopkins. In the 1930s, he'd served as an adviser to FDR. In 1949, in *The Pollsters: Pub-lic Opinion, Politics, and Democratic Leadership*, Rogers argued that he wasn't sold on polling as an empirical science, but that neither was that his particular concern. "My criticisms of the polls go to questions more fundamental than imperfections in sampling methods or inaccuracy in predicting the results of elections," he explained. Even if public opinion could be measured by adding up what people say in interviews over the telephone to people they've never met, legislators using this information to inform their votes in representative bodies would be inconsistent with the Constitution.

"Dr. Gallup wishes his polls to enable the United States to become a mammoth town meeting in which yeses and noes will suffice," Rog-ers wrote. "He assumes that this can happen and that it will be desir-able. Fortunately, both assumptions are wrong." A town meeting has to be small; also, it requires a moderator. Decisions made in town meetings require deliberation and delay. People had said the radio would create a town meeting, too. It had not. "The radio permits the whole population of a country, indeed of the world, to listen to a speaker at the same time. But there is no gathering together. Those who listen are strangers to each other." Nor—and here was Rogers's key argument—would a national town meeting be desirable. The United States has a representative government for many reasons, but among them is that it is designed to protect the rights of minorities against the tyranny of majority opinion. But, as Rogers argued, "The pollsters have dismissed as irrelevant the kind of political society in which we live and which we, as citizens should endeavor to strengthen." That political society requires participation, deliberation, representation, and leadership. And it requires that the government protect the rights of minorities.[51]

Blumer and Rogers offered these critiques before the DEWEY-BEATS-TRUMAN travesty. But after the election, the Social Science Research Council announced that it would begin an investigation. The council, an umbrella organization, brought together economists, anthropologists, historians, political scientists, psychologists, statisticians, and sociologists. Each of these social sciences had grown dependent on the social science survey, the same method used by commercial pollsters: they used weighted samples of larger wholes to measure attitudes and opinions. Many social scientists subscribed to rational choice theory. Newly aided by the power of computers, they used quantitative methods to search for a general theory that could account for the behavior of individuals. In 1948, political scientists at the University of Michigan founded what became the American National Election Survey, the largest, most ambitious, and most significant survey of American voters. Rogers didn't object to this work, but he wasn't persuaded that counting heads is the best way to study politics, and he believed that polling was bad for American democracy. Blumer thought pollsters misunderstood science. But what many other social scientists came to believe, after the disaster of the 1948 election, was that if the pollsters took a fall, social science would fall with them.

The Social Science Research Council warned, "Extended controversy regarding the pre-election polls among lay and professional groups might have extensive and unjustified repercussions upon all types of opinion and attitude studies and perhaps upon social science research generally." Its report, issued in December 1948, concluded that pollsters, "led by false assumptions into believing their methods were much more accurate than in fact they are," were not up to the task of predicting a presidential election, but that "the public should draw no inferences from pre-election forecasts that would disparage the accuracy or usefulness of properly conducted sampling surveys in fields in which the response does not involve expression of opinion or intention to act." That is to say, the polling industry was unsound, but social science was perfectly sound.[52]

Despite social scientists' spirited defense of their work, when the National Science Foundation was finally established in 1950, it did not include a social science division. Even before the founding of the NSF, the federal government had committed itself to fortifying the national security state by funding the physical sciences. By 1949, the Department of Defense and the Atomic Energy Commission represented 96 percent of all federal funds for university research in the physical sciences. Many scientists were concerned about the consequences for academic freedom. "It is essential that the trend toward military domination of our universities be reversed as speedily as possible," two had warned. Cornell physicist Philip Morrison predicted that science under a national security state would become "narrow, national, and secret."[53] The founding of the NSF did not allay these concerns. Although the NSF's budget, capped at $15 million, was a fraction of the funds provided to scientists engaged in military research (the Office of Naval Research alone had an annual research budget of $85 million), the price for receiving an NSF grant was being subjected to a loyalty test, surveillance, and ideological oversight, and agreeing to conduct closeted research. As the Federation of American Scientists put it, "The Foundation which will thus come into existence after 4 years of bitter struggle is a far cry from the hopes of many scientists."[54]

Even without support from the National Science Foundation, of course, social science research proceeded. Political scientists applied survey methods to the study of American politics and relied on the results to make policy recommendations. In 1950, when the distance between the parties was smaller than it has been either before or since—and voters had a hard time figuring out which party was conservative and which liberal—the American Political Science Association's Committee on Political Parties issued a report called "Toward a More Responsible Two-Party System." The problem with American democracy, the committee argued, is that the parties are too alike, and too weak. The report recommended strengthening every element of the party system, from national leadership committees to congressional caucuses, as well as establishing a starker difference between party platforms. "If the two parties do not develop alternative programs that can be executed," the committee warned, "the voter's frustration and the mounting ambiguities of national policy might set in motion more extreme tendencies to the political left and the political right."[55]

The recommendation of political scientists that American voters ought to become more partisan and more polarized did not sit well with everyone. In 1950, in a series of lectures at Princeton, Thomas Dewey, still reeling from his unexpected loss to Truman, damned scholars who "want to drive all moderates and liberals out of the Republican party and then have the remainder join forces with the conservative groups of the South. Then they would have everything neatly arranged, indeed. The Democratic party would be the liberal-to-radical party. The Republican party would be the conservative-to-reactionary party. The results would be neatly arranged, too. The Republicans would lose every election and the Democrats would win every election."[56]

Exactly this kind of sorting did eventually come to pass, not to the favor of one party or the other but, instead, to the detriment of everyone. It may have been the brainchild of quantitative political scientists, but it was implemented by pollsters and political consultants, using computers to segment the electorate. The questions raised by Blumer and Rogers went unanswered. Any pollster might have predicted it: POLLSTERS DEFEAT SCHOLARS.


WHEN TRUMAN BEAT DEWEY, and not the reverse, and Democrats regained control of both houses, and long-eared Lyndon B. Johnson took a seat in the Senate, the American Medical Association panicked and telephoned the San Francisco offices of Campaigns, Inc. In a message to Congress shortly before his inauguration, Truman called for the passage of his national health insurance plan.

The AMA, knowing how stunningly Campaigns, Inc., had defeated Warren's health care plan in California, decided to do exactly what the California Medical Association had done: retain Clem Whitaker and Leone Baxter. The Washington Post suggested that maybe the AMA, at the hands of Whitaker and Baxter, ought to stop "whipping itself into a neurosis and attempting to terrorize the whole American public every time the Administration proposes a Welfare Department or a health program." But the doctors' association, undaunted, hired Whitaker and Baxter for a fee of $100,000 a year, with an annual budget of more than a million dollars. Campaigns, Inc., relocated to a new, national head-quarters in Chicago, with a staff of thirty-seven. To defeat Truman's proposal, they launched a "National Education Campaign." The AMA raised $3.5 million, by assessing twenty-five dollars a year from its mem-bers. Whitaker and Baxter liked to talk about their work as "grass roots campaigning." Not everyone was convinced. "Dear Sirs," one doctor wrote them in 1949. "Is it 2½ or 3½ million dollars you have allotted for your 'grass roots lobby'?"[57]

They started, as always, by drafting a Plan of Campaign. "This must be a campaign to arouse and alert the American people in every walk of life, until it generates a great public crusade and a fundamental fight for freedom," it began. "Any other plan of action, in view of the drift towards socialization and despotism all over the world, would invite disaster." Then, in an especially cunning maneuver, aimed, in part, at silencing the firm's critics, Whitaker had hundreds of thousands of copies of their plan, "A Simplified Blueprint of the Campaign against Compulsory Health Insurance," printed on blue paper—to remind Americans that what they ought to do was to buy Blue Cross and Blue Shield—and distributed it to reporters and editors and to every member of Congress.[58]

The "Simplified Blueprint" wasn't their actual plan; a different Plan of Campaign circulated inside the office, in typescript, marked "CON-FIDENTIAL:— NOT FOR PUBLICATION." While the immediate objective of the campaign was to defeat Truman's proposal, its long-term objective was "to put a permanent stop to the agitation for socialized med-icine in this country by":

(a) awakening the people to the danger of a politically-controlled, government-regulated health system;
(b) convincing the people . . . of the superior advantages of private medicine, as practiced in America, over the State-dominated medical systems of other countries;

(c) stimulating the growth of voluntary health insurance systems to take the economic shock out of illness and increase the availability of medical care to the American people.

As Whitaker and Baxter put it, "Basically, the issue is whether we are to remain a free Nation, in which the individual can work out his own destiny, or whether we are to take one of the final steps toward becoming a Socialist or Communist State. We have to paint the picture, in vivid verbiage that no one can misunderstand, of Germany, Russia—and finally, England."[59]

They mailed leaflets, postcards, and letters across the country, though they were not always well met. "RECEIVED YOUR SCARE LETTER. AND HOW PITYFUL," an angry pharmacist wrote from New York. "I DO HOPE PRESIDENT TRUMAN HAS HIS WAY. GOOD LUCK TO HIM." Truman could have used some luck. Whitaker and Baxter's campaign to defeat his national health insurance plan ended up costing the AMA nearly $5 million and took more than three years. But it worked.[60]

Truman was furious. As to what in his plan could possibly be construed as "socialized medicine," he said, he didn't know what in the Sam Hill that could be. He had one more thing to say: there was "nothing in this bill that came any closer to socialism than the payments the American Medical Association makes to the advertising firm of Whitaker and Baxter to misrepresent my health program."[61]

National health insurance would have to wait for another president, another Congress, and another day. The fight would only get uglier.

## III.

**MOST POLITICAL CAREERS** follow an arithmetic curve. Richard Nixon's rise was exponential: elected to Congress at thirty-three, he won a Senate seat at thirty-six. Two years later, he would be elected vice president.

He had persisted in investigating Whittaker Chambers's claim that Alger Hiss had been a communist. In a series of twists and turns worthy of a Hitchcock film—including microfilm hidden in a hollowed-out pumpkin on Chambers's Maryland farm, the so-called Pumpkin Papers—

Nixon charged that Hiss had been not only communist but, like Chambers, a Soviet spy.[62]

In January 1950, Hiss was convicted of perjury for denying that he had been a communist (the statute of limitations for espionage had expired) and sentenced to five years in prison. Five days after the verdict, on the twenty-sixth, Nixon delivered a four-hour speech on the floor of Congress, a lecture he called "The Hiss Case—A Lesson for the American People." It read like an Arthur Conan Doyle story, recounting the entire history of the investigation, with Nixon as ace detective. Making a bid for a Senate seat, Nixon had the speech printed and mailed copies to California voters.[63]

Nixon sought the Senate seat of longtime California Democrat Sheridan Downey, the "Downey" of the "Uppie-and-Downey" EPIC gubernatorial ticket of 1933, who had decided not to run for reelection. Nixon defeated his opponent, Democrat Helen Gahagan Douglas, by Red-baiting and innuendo-dropping. Douglas, he said, was "Pink right down to her underwear." *The Nation's* Carey McWilliams said Nixon had "an astonishing capacity for petty malice."[64] But what won him the seat was the national reputation he'd earned in his prosecution of Alger Hiss, even if that crusade was soon taken over by a former heavyweight boxer who stood six foot tall and weighed two hundred pounds.

On February 9, a junior senator from Wisconsin named Joseph McCarthy stole whole paragraphs from Nixon's "The Hiss Case—A Lesson for the American People" and used them in an address of his own, in which he claimed to have a list of subversives working for the State Department. In a nod to Nixon, McCarthy liked to say, when he was sniffing out a subversive: "I have found a pumpkin."[65]

McCarthy had big hands and bushy eyebrows, and an unnerving stare. During the war, he'd served as a marine in the Pacific. Although he'd seen little combat and sustained an injury only during a hazing episode, he'd defeated the popular incumbent Robert La Follette Jr., in a 1946 Republican primary by running as a war hero, and had won a Senate seat against the Democrat, Howard McMurray, by claiming, falsely, that McMurray's campaign was funded by communists, as if McMurray wore pink underwear, too.

The first years of McCarthy's term in the Senate had been marked by failure and duplicity. Like Nixon, he tested the prevailing political winds and decided to make his mark by crusading against communism. In his Hiss speech, Nixon had hinted that not only Hiss but many other people in the State Department, and in other parts of the Truman administration, were part of a vast communist conspiracy. When McCarthy delivered his February 9 speech, before the Ohio County Republican Women's Club, in Wheeling, West Virginia, he went further than Nixon. "While I cannot take the time to name all of the men in the State Department who have been named as members of the Communist Party," he said, "I have here in my hand a list of two hundred and five . . . names that were made known to the Secretary of State as members of the Communist Party and who nevertheless are still working and shaping the policy of the State Department."[66] He had no list. He had nothing but imaginary pink underwear.

Three weeks after McCarthy's Wheeling address, John Peurifoy, deputy undersecretary of state, said that while there weren't any communists in the State Department, there *were* ninety-one men, homosexuals, who'd recently been fired because they were deemed to be "security risks" (another euphemism was men whose "habits make them especially vulnerable to blackmail"). It was, in part, Peurifoy's statement that gave credibility to McCarthy's charges: people really had been fired. One Republican representative from Illinois, getting the chronology all wrong, praised McCarthy for the purge: "He has forced the State Department to fire 91 sex perverts."[67]

The purge had begun years earlier, in 1947, under the terms of a set of "security principles" provided to the secretary of state. People known for "habitual drunkenness, sexual perversion, moral turpitude, financial irresponsibility or criminal record" were to be fired or screened out of the hiring process. Thirty-one homosexuals had been fired from the State Department in 1947, twenty-eight in 1948, and thirty-one in 1949. A week after Peurifoy's statement, Roy Blick, the ambitious head of the Washington, DC, vice squad, testified during classified hearings (on "the infiltration of subversives and moral perverts into the executive branch of the United States Government") that there were five thousand homosexuals in Washington. Of these, Blick said, nearly four thousand worked for the federal government. The story was leaked to the press. Blick called for a national task force: "There is a need in this country for a central bureau for records of homosexuals and perverts of all types."[68]

The Nixon-McCarthy campaign against communists can't be separated from the campaign against homosexuals. There had been much intimation that Chambers, a gay man, had informed on Hiss because of a spurned romantic overture. By March of 1950, McCarthy's charges had been reported in newspapers all over the country. The Senate Foreign Relations Committee convened hearings into "whether persons who are disloyal to the United States are or have been employed by the Department of State." The hearings, chaired by Millard Tydings, a Democrat from Maryland, proved unilluminating. In the committee's final report, Tydings called the charges "a fraud and a hoax." This neither dimmed the furor nor daunted McCarthy, who masterfully manipulated the press and escalated fears of a worldwide communist conspiracy and a worldwide network of homosexuals, both trying to undermine "Americanism." (So great was McCarthy's hold on the electorate that, for challenging him, Tydings was defeated when he ran for reelection.) [69]

Who could rein him in? Few critics of McCarthyism were as forceful as Maine senator Margaret Chase Smith, the first woman to serve in both houses of Congress. In June 1950, she rose to speak on the floor of the Senate to deliver a speech later known as the Declaration of Conscience. "I don't want to see the Republican Party ride to political victory on the Four Horsemen of Calumny—Fear, Ignorance, Bigotry, and Smear," said Smith, a moderate Republican in the mold of Wendell Willkie. Bernard Baruch said that if a man had made that speech he would be the next president of the United States. Later, after Smith was jettisoned from the Permanent Subcommittee on Investigations, it was Nixon who took her place. [70]

In September 1950, Congress passed the Internal Security Act, over Truman's veto, requiring communists to register with the attorney general and establishing a loyalty board to review federal employees. That fall, Margaret Chase Smith, who, despite her centrist leanings, had no qualms about the purging of homosexuals, joined North Carolina senator Clyde Hoey's investigation into the "Employment of Homosexuals and Other Sex Perverts in Government." The Hoey committee's conclusion was that such men and women were a threat to national security. [71]

The crusade, at once against communists and homosexuals, was also a campaign against intellectuals in the federal government, derided as "eggheads." The term, inspired by the balding Illinois Democrat Adlai Stevenson, was coined in 1952 by Louis Bromfield to describe "a person of spurious intellectual pretensions, often a professor or the protégé of a professor; fundamentally superficial, over-emotional and feminine in reactions to any problems." The term connoted, as well, a vague homosexuality. One congressman described leftover New Dealers as "short-haired women and long-haired men messing into everybody's personal affairs and lives."[72]

One thing McCarthyism was not was a measured response to communism in the United States. Membership in the Communist Party in the United States was the lowest it had been since the 1920s. In 1950, when the population of the United States stood at 150 million, there were 43,000 party members; in 1951, there were only 32,000. The Communist Party was considerably stronger in, for instance, Italy, France, and Great Britain, but none of those nations experienced a Red Scare in the 1950s. In 1954, Winston Churchill, asked to establish a royal commission to investigate communism in Great Britain, refused.[73]

In 1951, McCarthy's crusade scored a crucial legal victory when the Supreme Court upheld the Smith Act of 1940, ruling 6–2 in *Dennis v. United States* that First Amendment protections of free speech, press, and assembly did not extend to communists. This decision gave the Justice Department a free hand in rounding up communists, who could be convicted and sentenced to prison. In a pained dissent in *Dennis,* Justice Hugo Black wrote, "There is hope, however, that in calmer times, when present pressures, passions and fears subside, this or some later Court will restore the First Amendment liberties to the high preferred place where they belong in a free society." That calm did not come for a very long time. Instead, McCarthy's imagined web of conspiracy grew bigger and stretched further. The Democratic Party itself, he said, was in the hands of men and women "who have bent to the whispered pleas from the lips of traitors." William Jenner, Republican senator from Indiana, said, "Our only choice is to impeach President Truman and find out who is the secret invisible government."[74]

Eggheads or not, Democrats failed to defeat McCarthyism. Lyndon Johnson had become the Democratic Party whip in 1950 and two years later its minority leader; the morning after the 1952 election, he'd called newly elected Democrats before sunrise to get their support. "The guy must never sleep," said a bewildered John F. Kennedy. Johnson became famous for wrangling senators the way a cowboy wrangles cattle. He'd corner them in hallways and lean over them, giving them what a pair of newspaper columnists called "The Treatment." "Its velocity was breathtaking, and it was all in one direction," they wrote. "He moved in close, his face a scant millimeter from his target, his eyes widening and narrowing, his eyebrows rising and falling." Johnson despised McCarthy. "Can't tie his goddam shoes," he said. But, lacking enough support to stop him, Johnson bided his time.[75]

Liberal intellectuals, refusing to recognize the right wing's grip on the American imagination, tended to dismiss McCarthyism as an aberration, a strange eddy in a sea of liberalism. The historian Arthur Schlesinger Jr., writing in 1949, argued that liberals, having been chastened by their earlier delusions about socialism and even Sovietism and their romantic attachment to the ordinary and the everyday, had found their way again to "the vital center" of American politics. Conservatives might be cranks and demagogues, they might have power and even radio programs, but, in the world of ideas, liberal thinkers believed, liberalism had virtually no opposition. "In the United States at this time, liberalism is not only the dominant but even the sole intellectual tradition," insisted literary critic Lionel Trilling. "For it is the plain fact that nowadays there are no conservative or reactionary ideas in general circulation."[76]

This assessment was an error. McCarthyism wasn't an eddy; it was part of a rising tide of American conservatism.[77] Its leading thinkers were refugees from fascist or communist regimes. They opposed collectivism and centralized planning and celebrated personal liberty, individual rights, and the free market. Ayn Rand, born Alisa Rosenbaum, grew up in Bolshevik Russia, moved to the United States in 1926, and went to Hollywood to write screenplays, eventually turning to novels; *The Fountainhead* appeared in 1943 and *Atlas Shrugged* in 1957. Austrian-born Friedrich von Hayek, after nearly twenty years at the London School of Economics, began teaching at the University of Chicago in 1949 (in 1961, he moved to Germany). While engaged in vastly different projects, Hayek and Rand engaged in many of the same rhetorical moves as Whitaker and Baxter, who, like all the most effective Cold Warriors, reduced policy issues like health care coverage to a battle between freedom and slavery. Whitaker and Baxter's rhetoric against Truman's health care plan sounded the same notes as Hayek's "road to serfdom." The facts, Whitaker said in 1949, were these:

> Hitler and Stalin and the socialist government of Great Britain all
> have used the opiate of socialized medicine to deaden the pain of
> lost liberty and lull the people into non-resistance. Old World con-
> tagion of compulsory health insurance, if allowed to spread to our
> New World, will mark the beginning of the end of free institutions
> in America. It will only be a question of time until the railroads, the
> steel mills, the power industry, the banks and the farming industry
> are nationalized.

To pass health care legislation would be to reduce America to a "slave
state."[78]

But perhaps the most influential of the new conservative intellectuals was Richard M. Weaver, a southerner who taught at the University
of Chicago and whose complaint about modernity was that "facts" had
replaced "truth." Weaver's *Ideas Have Consequences* (1948) rejected the
idea of machine-driven progress—a point of view he labeled "hysterical
optimism"—and argued that Western civilization had been in decline
for centuries. Weaver dated the beginning of the decline to the fourteenth century and the denial that there exists a universal truth, a truth
higher than man. "The denial of universals carries with it the denial
of everything transcending experience," Weaver wrote. "The denial of
everything transcending experience means inevitably—though ways are
found to hedge on this—the denial of truth." The only way to answer
the question "Are things getting better or are they getting worse?" is to
discover whether modern man knows more or is wiser than his ancestors, Weaver argued. And his answer to this question was no. With the
scientific revolution, "facts"—particular explanations for how the world
works—had replaced "truth"—a general understanding of the meaning
of its existence. More people could read, Weaver stipulated, but "in a
society where expression is free and popularity is rewarded they read
mostly that which debauches them and they are continuously exposed to
manipulation by controllers of the printing machine." Machines were for
Weaver no measure of progress but instead "a splendid efflorescence of
decay." In place of distinction and hierarchy, Americans vaunted equality, a poor substitute.[79]

If Weaver was conservatism's most serious thinker, nothing better
marked the rising popular tide of the movement than the publication, in

1951, of William F. Buckley Jr.'s *God and Man at Yale: The Superstitions of "Academic Freedom,"* in which Buckley expressed regret over the liberalism of the American university. Faculty, he said, preached anticapitalism, secularism, and collectivism. Buckley, the sixth of ten children, raised in a devout Catholic family, became a national celebrity, not least because of his extraordinary intellectual poise.

Russell Kirk's *The Conservative Mind* appeared in 1953. Kirk, an intellectual historian from Michigan, provided a manifesto for an emerging movement: a story of its origins. *The Conservative Mind* described itself as "a prolonged essay in definition," an attempt at explaining the ideas that have "sustained men of conservative impulse in their resistance against radical theories and social transformation ever since the beginning of the French Revolution." The liberal, Kirk argued, sees "a world that damns tradition, exalts equality, and welcomes changes"; liberalism produces a "world smudged by industrialism; standardized by the masses; consolidated by government." Taking his inspiration from Edmund Burke, Kirk urged those who disagreed with liberalism's fundamental tenets to call themselves "conservatives" (rather than "classical liberals," in the nineteenth-century laissez-faire sense). The conservative, he argued, knows that "civilized society requires orders and classes, believes that man has an evil nature and therefore must control his will and appetite" and that "tradition provides a check on man's anarchic impulse." Conservatism requires, among other things, celebrating the "mystery of human existence."[80]

The battle, then, was a battle not so much for the soul of America as for the mind of America, for mystery over facts, for hierarchy over equality, for the past over the present. In 1955, Buckley founded the *National Review*. Whittaker Chambers joined the staff two years later. Kirk, who decried the "ritualistic liberalism" of American newspapers and magazines, contributed a regular column. In the first issue, Buckley said the magazine "stands athwart history, yelling Stop."[81]

But if it was chiefly men who advanced the ideas and wrote the books of the new conservatism, it was women who carried the placards and worked in the precincts, not yelling, but politely whispering, "Stop, please." Betty Farrington, head of the National Federation of Republican Women's Clubs, filled those clubs with housewives who were ardent in their opposition to communism and support of McCarthy. After Dewey

*Suburban housewives served as the foot soldiers of the conservative movement; here, women rally in support of Joseph McCarthy.*

lost in 1948, Farrington had argued that the GOP needed a strong man: "How thankful we would have been if a leader had appeared to show us the path to the promised land of our hope. The world needs such a man today. He is certain to come sooner or later. But we cannot sit idly by in the hope of his coming. Besides his advent depends partly on us. The mere fact that a leader is needed does not guarantee his appearance. People must be ready for him, and we, as Republican women, in our clubs, prepare for him." Farrington believed McCarthy was that man. It is no accident that McCarthy's Wheeling, West Virginia, speech was an address, made by invitation, to a Republican women's club, nor that his language was the language of the nineteenth-century female crusade. "The great difference between our western Christian world and the atheistic Communist world is not political—it is moral," McCarthy said.[82] Temperance, abolition, suffrage, populism, and prohibition weren't part of Russell Kirk's intellectual genealogy of conservatism, but they were the foundational experiences of its core constituency.

Housewives were to the Republican Party infrastructure what labor union members were to the Democrats'. "If it were not for the National Federation of Republican Women, there would not be a Republican Party," Barry Goldwater admitted. (Nixon couldn't stand them: "I will not go and talk to those shitty ass old ladies!" he'd fume. All the same, gritting his teeth, he went.)[83] By the 1950s, a majority of GOP activists were women, compared to 41 percent of Democratic Party activists. In 1950, Farrington launched the School of Politics, three-day sessions in Washington to train precinct workers; the sessions were open to men and women, but most who attended were women, while, at the same sort of sessions run by the DNC, most attendees were men. In the GOP, party work was women's work, work that the party explained, structured, and justified by calling it housework. Republican Party aspirants were told to "be proud of the women who work on the home front, ringing the doorbells, filling out registration cards, and generally doing the housework of government so that the principles of the Republican Party can be brought to every home." Republican women established Kitchen Kabinets, appointing a female equivalent to every member of the president's cabinet, who shared "political recipes on GOP accomplishments with the housewives in the nation" by way of monthly bulletins on "What's Cooking in Washington."[84] As a senator speaking to the federation of women's clubs suggested, the elephant was the right symbol for the GOP because an elephant has "a vacuum cleaner in front and a rug beater behind."[85]

By the mid-1950s, the conservative critique of the academy as godless and of the press as mindless were in place, along with a defense of the family, and of women's role as housewives, however politicized the role of housewife had become. A moral crusade against homosexuality and in favor of a newly imagined traditional family had begun.

Meanwhile McCarthyism abided: mean-spirited, vulgar, and unhinged. McCarthy's rise, the lunacy of his conspiracy theory, and the size of his following struck many observers as a symptom of a disease at the very heart of American politics. It left George Kennan with a lasting doubt: "A political system and a public opinion, it seemed to me, that could be so easily disoriented by this sort of challenge in one epoch would be no less vulnerable to similar ones in another."[86] What had made so many Americans so vulnerable to such an implausible view of the world?

INSIDE CBS, the plan was known as "Project X." It was top secret until, a month before Election Day in 1952, the television network announced that it would predict the winner using a "giant brain." One local station took out a newspaper ad promising that "A ROBOT COMPUTER WILL GIVE CBS THE FASTEST REPORTING IN HISTORY."[87]

That giant brain was called UNIVAC, the Universal Automatic Computer, and it was the first commercial computer in the history of the world. In May 1951, John Mauchly and Presper Eckert, who'd unveiled ENIAC in 1946, invited members of the press to a demonstration of their new machine; they'd built it for the U.S. Census Bureau. Half the size of ENIAC, UNIVAC was even faster. This lickety-split sorting of the population would prove invaluable to the Census Bureau. Soon, all calculations relating to the federal census were completed by UNIVAC, work that was called "data processing." Commercially applied, UNIVAC and its heirs would transform American business, straightaway cutting costs and accelerating production by streamlining managerial and administrative tasks, such as payroll and inventory, and eventually turning people into consumers whose habits could be tracked and whose spending could be calculated, and even predicted. Politically, it would wreak havoc, splitting the electorate into so many atoms.

The technology that made it possible to sort citizens by "sex, marital status, education, residence, age group, birthplace, employment, income and a dozen other classifications" would make it possible to sort consumers, too. Businesses found that they could both reduce prices and increase profits by sorting markets into segments and pitching the right ad and product to exactly the right consumer. In much the same way that advertisers segmented markets, political consultants would sort voters into different piles, too, and send them different messages.[88]

When Mauchly and Eckert staged their unveiling in 1951, all of this was in the future, and the press was not excited. In a one-paragraph story on the bottom of page twenty-five, the New York Times only dutifully took notice of the "eight-foot-tall mathematical genius," as if it were nothing more than a stunt, like Elektro the Moto-Man.[89]

UNIVAC made its debut at a moment when Americans were increasingly exasperated by automation, the very year that readers waded through White Collar, the sociologist C. Wright Mills's indictment of the fate of the people who worked, surrounded by telephones and Dictaphones, intercoms and Mimeographs, in fluorescent-lit, air-conditioned offices in steel-and-glass skyscrapers or in suburban office parks. Mills argued that machine-driven office work had created a class of desperately alienated workers and that the new office, for all its gadgets, was no less horrible than the old factories of brick and steam. "Seeing the big stretch of office space, with rows of identical desks," Mills wrote, "one is reminded of Herman Melville's description of a nineteenth-century factory: 'At rows of blank-looking counters sat rows of blank-looking girls, with blank, white folders in their blank hands, all blankly folding blank paper.'" Melville had been describing a New England paper mill in 1855; Mills described a modern office a century later: "The new office is rationalized: machines are used, employees become machine attendants; the work, as in the factory, is collective, not individualized," he wrote. "It is specialized to the point of automatization."[90] The minutes of white-collar workers' lives were tapped out by typewriters and adding machines. They had the cheerfulness of robots, having lost the capacity to feel anything except boredom.[91]

"Robotic" having become a term of opprobrium, the people interested in explaining the truly revolutionary capabilities of the UNIVAC had to do something more than write numbers on Ping-Pong balls. Mauchly, disappointed at the bland coverage of UNIVAC's unveiling, wrote a paper called "Are Computers Newsworthy?" Given that the novelty of computers as front-page news had worn off, the best approach would be to find ways to showcase their application to real-world problems, he suggested. He hired a public relations firm. "We must aim our publicity at the public in general because our object is to expand the market until computers become as ordinary as telephone switchboards and bookkeeping machines," he explained. Mauchly's PR team then came up with the very clever plan of bringing to CBS a proposal to predict the outcome of the upcoming election on live television, on Election Night.[92]

In 1948, less than 3 percent of American homes had a television; by 1952, the number was up to 45 percent. By the end of the decade, 90 percent of American homes had a television. The year 1952 marked the first coverage of a presidential election by television, and, if Mauchly had his way, it would be the first whose result would be predicted on television.

It looked to be an especially fascinating election. General Dwight D. Eisenhower, a lifelong military man, a five-star general who during the Second World War had served as Supreme Allied Commander Europe, had refused to run in 1948, on the grounds that professional soldiers ought to abstain from political officeholding. In 1952, at the age of fifty-seven, he was finally persuaded to run against Truman in an election expected to amount to a referendum on U.S. involvement in Korea. In June 1950, North Korean communist forces crossed the thirty-eighth parallel to attack South Korea. Truman sent in troops, led by General Douglas MacArthur, who drove the North Koreans nearly back to the border with China. China responded by providing resources to North Korea, and the American forces lost all of the ground they'd gained. The war was protracted, costly, and unpopular. Eisenhower, a hero from a better war, appeared a perfect candidate for the times.

Clem Whitaker and Leone Baxter managed his campaign. Having worked behind the scenes since its founding in 1933, Campaigns, Inc., had attracted not altogether wanted attention as a consequence of its phenomenal defeat of Truman's national health insurance plan. A three-part exposé, written by Carey McWilliams, had appeared in *The Nation* in 1951. McWilliams admired Whitaker and Baxter, and he also liked them. But he believed that they had too much power, and that they were dangerous, and that what they had created was nothing less than "government by Whitaker and Baxter." After McWilliams's story ran, a number of notable doctors resigned from the AMA, including the head of Massachusetts General Hospital, who explained, in his letter of resignation, that he was no longer willing to pay dues used to support "an activity, which I consider contrary to public welfare and unworthy of a learned profession." That fall, the AMA fired Whitaker and Baxter. That's when Whitaker and Baxter went to work for Eisenhower. [93]

They decided to put Ike on TV. Republicans spent $1.5 million on television advertising in 1952; Democrats spent $77,000. Polls drove the ads; ads drove the polls. George Gallup chose the themes of Eisenhower's TV spots, which took the form of fake documentaries. In "Eisenhower Answers America," a young black man (plucked off the street from Times Square and reading a cue card) says, "General, the Democrats are telling me I never had it so good." Eisenhower replies, "Can that be true, when America is billions in debt, when prices have doubled, when taxes break our backs, and we are still fighting in Korea?" Then, he looks, sternly, straight into the camera. "It's tragic, and it's time for a change." [94]

Eisenhower's politics were moderate, as was his style. He described himself as a "dynamic conservative": "conservative when it comes to money and liberal when it comes to human beings." His Democratic opponent, Illinois governor Adlai Stevenson, found that account of Eisenhower's political commitments wanting: "I assume what it means is that you will strongly recommend the building of a great many schools to accommodate the needs of our children, but not provide the money." Critics called the bald and effete Stevenson an egghead and "fruity"; rumors spread that he was gay. "Eggheads of the world unite!" Stevenson would joke, "You have nothing to lose but your yolks!," not quite appreciating the malice of the campaign against him.[95]

Television became to the 1950s what radio had been to the 1930s. The style of news reporting that had been developed on the radio adapted poorly to the screen, but the audience was so huge that news organizations had every incentive to adapt. In 1949, the Federal Communications Commission established the Fairness Doctrine, a standard for television news that required a "reasonable balance" of views on any issue put before the public. CBS sent Walter Cronkite, a thirty-five-year-old newsman from its Washington affiliate, WTOP-TV, to cover both nominating conventions.

Richard Nixon went to the Republican National Convention in Chicago on board a chartered train from California called the Earl Warren Special, allegedly supporting Warren's bid for the presidential nomination. Whitaker and Baxter had never forgiven Warren for firing them in 1942, and even scuttling his statewide health insurance plan in 1945 had not slaked their thirst for vengeance. During the train ride to Chicago, Nixon secretly swayed California delegates to throw their support behind Eisenhower—a scheme forever after known as the "great train robbery"—and the general had rewarded him with a spot on the ticket. Warren would later call Nixon a "crook and a thief." Eisenhower would find a place for Warren in his administration, as solicitor general.[96]

Nixon had managed to secure the GOP vice presidential nomination, but, weeks later, he'd go on television to try to hold onto it. After the convention, the press revealed that Nixon had an $18,000 slush fund. Eisenhower's advisers urged him to dump Nixon, and asked Nixon to step down. Nixon, facing the end of his political career, decided to make his case to the public. He labored over it, writing the speech of his life. On September 23, 1952, sitting at a pine desk, with his wife looking on from a chintz chair, in what appeared to be his own den but was a stage built at an NBC studio in Los Angeles, he gave a remarkable performance, pained and self-pitying. It reached the largest television audience television ever recorded. Nixon said he intended to do something unprecedented in American politics. He would provide a full financial disclosure, an accounting of "everything I've earned, everything I've spent, and everything I owe." Nearly down to the penny, he then listed his modest income, his loans, and his wealth ("this will surprise you, because it is so little"). He had no stocks, no bonds, a two-year-old Oldsmobile, mortgages, debts to banks, and even a debt to his parents that he was paying back, every month, with interest. Yes, he'd accepted gifts to a campaign fund. But no contributors had gotten special favors for their donations, and "not one cent of the eighteen thousand dollars" had gone to him for his private use. He'd spent it on campaign expenses. He covered his face for a moment, as if offering up a final, humiliating confession. There was one gift he must acknowledge: a man in Texas has sent his daughters a black-and-white spotted cocker spaniel puppy, and his six-year-old daughter, Tricia, had named the dog Checkers. "Regardless of what they say about it," he said, feigning injury, "we're gonna keep it."[97]

Liberals were disgusted, partly because it was something of a sham, but mostly because it was maudlin. Eisenhower was, at the time, president of Columbia University; twenty-three full professors at Columbia, including Allan Nevins, Lionel Trilling, and Richard Hofstadter, issued a statement in which they denounced the Checkers speech, which Nevins described as "so essentially dishonest and emotional an appeal that he confused a great many people as to the issues involved."[98] Walter Lippmann said that watching it was "one of the most demeaning experiences my country has ever had to bear." But the overwhelming majority of people who watched it loved it. Nixon spoke to their experiences and their quiet lives, and to their grievances, too. Plainly, Nixon had saved his career, and more. "In 30 minutes," *Time* reported, "he had changed from a liability to his party to a shining asset."[99]

Nixon had accomplished something else, of greater and more lasting importance. Since the days of Harding and Hoover, the Republican Party had been the party of businessmen, of country club members and stock-holders. The Democratic Party had been the party of the little guy, from Andrew Jackson's self-made man to William Jennings Bryan's farmer to FDR's "forgotten man." Nixon, with that speech, reversed this calculus. That was what so galled liberals: they were no longer the party of the people. Populism had shifted to the right.[100]

The Checkers speech was a landmark in the history of television, and it became a watchword in the history of American politics. Lost in the fog of memory was another epic turn during that election. Nixon decided, after the Checkers speech, that he loved television. As his friend the Hollywood producer Ted Rogers said, "He was the electronic man."[101] But the real electronic man of that year's political season was the UNIVAC.

After the conventions, all three network television broadcasters were looking for a way to do a better job covering election night than they'd done in 1948, which had been widely seen as a dismal failure. There hadn't been much to look at. As one critic put it, "Counting ballots is hardly a function which lends itself to much visual excitement." Added to the clumsiness of the television coverage was the lingering embarrassment of the error of everyone's prediction of the outcome. Broadcasters had made the same error as the DEWEY-BEATS-TRUMAN *Chicago Tribune*; by the time Truman pulled ahead, CBS had already closed down for the night.[102]

CBS agreed to commission UNIVAC as its special guest on Election Night. On November 4, the actual UNIVAC—there was only one—was in Philadelphia, while CBS's Charles Collingwood sat at a blinking console at the network's flagship studio in New York, giving viewers the illusion that he was controlling a computer. "A UNIVAC is a fabulous electronic machine, which we have borrowed to help us predict this election from the basis of early returns as they come in," Collingwood told his audience as the evening's coverage began. "This is not a joke or a trick," he went on, "It's an experiment. We think it's going to work. We don't know. We hope it will work."

Thirty-six-year-old Walter Cronkite read the early, East Coast returns; Edward R. Murrow provided the commentary. Cronkite, born in Missouri, spoke with a gentlemanly midwestern twang. Not long after the East Coast polls closed, CBS announced that Eisenhower was ahead

*CBS News, whose team included Walter Cronkite*
*(right), commissioned the first commercial computer,*
*UNIVAC, to predict the outcome of the election of 1952.*

in the popular vote, Stevenson in the electoral vote. Cronkite then said, "And now to find out perhaps what this all means, at least in the electronic age, let's turn to that electronic miracle, the electronic brain, UNIVAC, with a report from Charles Collingwood."

UNIVAC had been attempting to calculate the likely outcome of the election by comparing early returns to results from the elections of 1944 and 1948. When the camera turned to Collingwood, though, he could get no answer from UNIVAC. Murrow ventured that perhaps UNIVAC was cautious. After all, it was still early in the night. "It may be possible for men or machines to draw some sweeping conclusions from the returns so far," Murrow said, "but I am not able to do it." But then, eyeing the returns from Connecticut, where a great many Democrats had surprisingly voted for the Republican, Murrow, while not offering a sweeping conclusion, suggested that the momentum appeared to be very much in Ike's favor.

At 10:30, Cronkite turned again to Collingwood. UNIVAC was having "a little bit of trouble," Collingwood said with evident embarrassment. At one point UNIVAC predicted that Eisenhower would win by a sizable margin, at another that Stevenson might eke out a win. After Murrow called the election for Eisenhower, UNIVAC changed its mind again and said that the race was close. Cronkite turned to Murrow, who said, "I think it is now reasonably certain that this election is over." Fifteen minutes later, Cronkite offered this update:

> And now, UNIVAC—UNIVAC, our electronic brain—which a moment ago, still thought there was a 7 to 8 for Governor Stevenson, says that the chances are 100 to 1 in favor of General Eisenhower. I might note that UNIVAC is running a few moments behind Ed Murrow, however.

Ike won in a landslide. UNIVAC called it right, in the end, and so did George Gallup, who had gotten the vote wrong by 5 percent in 1948, and got it wrong by 4 percent again in 1952, but this time, Eisenhower's margin of victory was so big that Gallup's margin of error hadn't led him to predict the wrong winner.[103]

The next day, Murrow, speaking on CBS Radio, delivered a sermon about the civic importance of voting, as against the political mischief of polling, political consultants, and electronic brains. "Yesterday the people surprised the pollsters, the prophets, and many politicians," Murrow said. "They demonstrated, as they did in 1948, that they are mysterious and their motives are not to be measured by mechanical means." The election, he thought, had returned to the American voter his sovereignty, stolen by "those who believe that we are predictable." Murrow said, "we are in a measure released from the petty tyranny of those who assert that they can tell us what we think, what we believe, what we will do, what we hope and what we fear, without consulting us—all of us."[104]

Murrow's faith in the American creed, in the triumph of reason over fear, in progress over prophecy, was a hallmark of mid-twentieth-century liberalism. But it was also a shaken faith. Between the unreasoning McCarthy and the coldly calculating computer, where was the independent-minded American voter, weighing facts and searching for truth? The questions about the malleability of public opinion raised by radio were revisited during the rise of television. "Brainwashing" became a household word in the 1950s, when it was used to refer not only to the psychological torture during the Korean War but also to the persuasive powers of television.

When Americans talk about "public opinion," C. Wright Mills argued, they meant the eighteenth-century idea of informed people engaging in free, rational discussion to arrive at truth—the right understanding of an issue—before urging their representatives to take action. But in the middle of the twentieth century, Mills said, this idea had become nothing more than a "fairy tale," as fanciful as Disneyland, because "the public of public opinion is recognized by all those who have considered it carefully as something less than it once was." Like many social scientists of his generation, Mills argued that the United States was far along the road to becoming a fully mass society rather than a community of publics. The way to tell the difference between a mass society and a community of publics is the technology of communication: a community of publics is a population of people who talk to one another; a mass society receives information from the mass media. In a mass society, elites, not the people, make most decisions, long before the people even know there is a decision to be made. The formation of what Mills called "power elites" was directly related to technological shifts, especially the rise of computing. "As the means of information and of power are centralized," Mills wrote, "some men come to occupy positions in American society from which they can look down upon . . . and by their decisions mightily affect the everyday lives of ordinary men and women."[105]

Yet for all the concern about "mass media"—a term coined in derision—there remained sources of optimism, especially in the undeniable observation that investigative television reporting and broadcast television news were usefully informing the electorate, introducing them to candidates and issues, and helping Americans keep abreast of national and world affairs. And McCarthy's own end, after all, came on television.

On February 18, 1954, McCarthy questioned General Ralph Zwicker, a holder of a Purple Heart and a Silver Star. The senator told him the general didn't have "the brains of a five-year-old child" and that his testimony was "a disgrace to the army."[106] Eisenhower had long since lost patience with McCarthy and the damage he had done. But going after the army was the last straw. The next month, on CBS Television's *See It Now*, Murrow narrated an edited selection of McCarthy's speeches before the public and during congressional hearings, revealing the cruelty of the man, his moral shabbiness and pettiness, his brutality. Murrow's thirty-minute presentation of evidence took the form of a carefully

*U.S. Army Chief Counsel Joseph Welch holds his head*
*in his hand as Joseph McCarthy speaks during*
*the Army-McCarthy hearings in 1954.*

planned prosecution. "And upon what meat doth Senator McCarthy feed?" Murrow asked. "Two of the staples of his diet are the investigation, protected by immunity, and the half-truth." (McCarthy was given an opportunity to reply, which he took up, feebly, two weeks later.) Murrow closed with a sermon. "We will not walk in fear, one of another," he said. "We will not be driven by fear into an age of unreason, if we dig deep in our history and our doctrine and remember that we are not descended from fearful men." [107]

One week after Murrow's broadcast, the Senate convened the Army-McCarthy hearings, to investigate charges that McCarthy's chief counsel, Roy Cohn—later Donald Trump's mentor—had attempted to obtain military preferment for another McCarthy aide, David Shine. Lyndon Johnson slyly arranged for the hearings to be televised. The hearings lasted fifty-seven days, of which thirty-six were broadcast. On June 9, when Army Chief Counsel Joseph Welch asked McCarthy if, finally, he had any decency, viewers had seen for themselves that he hadn't. Cohn resigned. Johnson, reelected by a landslide in the fall of 1954, when Democrats regained control of the Senate, decided the moment to strike had finally come. He named a special committee to investigate McCarthy and made sure the committee was dominated by conservatives, so that no one could question that the investigation had been partisan. The committee recommended disciplining McCarthy. That December, the Senate voted 65–22 to censure him. John F. Kennedy, whose brother Robert worked as a McCarthy aide, and whose father had long supported McCarthy, was the only Democrat to not publicly support censure. McCarthy's fall had come.[108]

"It's no longer McCarthyism," said Eisenhower. "It's McCarthy-wasm."[109] McCarthy, struggling with drinking, died three years later, only forty-eight.

**"THIS COUNTRY NEEDS** a revival," House Speaker Sam Rayburn said, "and I believe Billy Graham is bringing it to us." Against the godlessness of communism, before and after McCarthy's fall, Americans turned anew to religion. In the decade following the end of the war, church membership grew from 75 million to 100 million.[110] Much of the growth was driven by Southern Baptists, like Billy Graham, who asserted a growing influence on American life and politics. Between 1941 and 1961, membership in the Southern Baptist Convention doubled. In eight days in the fall of 1949, Graham preached to more than 350,000 people in Los Angeles.

Broad-shouldered and Brylcreemed, Graham left audiences swooning. But he didn't only draw new members to the Southern Baptist Convention; he brought together all manner of white conservative Protestants, North and South, into a new evangelism. For Graham, the Cold War represented a Manichaean battle between Christ and communism. "Do you know that the Fifth Columnists, called Communists, are more rampant in Los Angeles than in any other city in America?" he demanded. "The world is divided into two camps!" Communism "has declared war against God, against Christ, against the Bible, and against all religion! . . . Unless the Western world has an old-fashioned revival, we cannot last!" Communists became the new infidels. [111]

Graham, who'd grown up in North Carolina, romanticized rural America, calling the shepherds of the Bible "hillbillies." His anti-intellectualism aligned well with a broader critique of liberalism. "When God gets ready to shake America, he might not take the Ph.D. and the D.D. and the Th.D.," Graham preached. "God may choose a country boy! God may

*Reverend Billy Graham, here preaching in Washington, DC,*
*in 1952, reached a nationwide audience but boasted an*
*especially strong following in Congress.*

choose a man no one knows . . . a hillbilly, a country boy! Who will sound
forth in a mighty voice to America, 'Thus saith the Lord!'"

Graham himself, though, traveled in powerful, cosmopolitan circles.
In 1950, he began praying before Congress. He held prayer meetings with
senators. He met with presidents. He preached evangelism as Americanism. "If you would be a loyal American," he said, "then become a loyal
Christian." To Graham, the tool of the enemy (and of the devil) was "the
sin of tolerance." "The word 'tolerant' means 'liberal,' 'broad-minded,'" he
said, and "the easy-going compromise and tolerance that we have been
taught by pseudo-liberals in almost every area of our life for years" means
nothing so much as appeasement to communism. "My own theory about
Communism," he said, "is that it is master-minded by Satan."[112]

As Graham's influence grew, Eisenhower came to see his lack of membership in any church as a political liability. Raised a Mennonite, he decided
to convert to Presbyterianism, becoming the first president to be baptized
while in the White House. His administration inaugurated the practice of
national prayer breakfasts. "Our form of government has no sense unless
it is founded in a deeply religious faith, and I don't care what it is," Eisenhower said. During his administration, Congress mandated the inclusion of
"In God We Trust" on all money and added "under God" to the Pledge of
Allegiance.[113]

For more reasons, too, conservatives had high hopes for Eisenhower, whose 1952 campaign had included a promise to repeal New Deal taxes that, he said, were "approaching the point of confiscation."[114] Eisenhower's cabinet included the former president of General Motors. (With Eisenhower's pro-business administration, Adlai Stevenson said, New Dealers made way for car dealers.) Eisenhower was also opposed to national health care, as was his secretary of Health, Education, and Welfare, a longtime conservative Texas Democrat named Oveta Culp Hobby, who'd recently switched parties. She liked to say she'd come to Washington to "bury" socialized medicine. Both Eisenhower and Hobby considered free polio vaccinations socialized medicine, and Hobby argued against the free distribution of the vaccine, a position that would have exposed millions of children to the disease. In the end, after a related scandal, Hobby was forced to resign.[115]

But Eisenhower proved a disappointment to conservatives. From the start, he had his doubts about the nature of the Cold War. A decorated general, Eisenhower was nevertheless the child of pacifists who considered war a sin. And, even as he oversaw a buildup of nuclear weapons, he questioned the possibility of the world surviving an atomic war. "There just aren't enough bulldozers to scrape the bodies off the street," he said. Nor was he so sure that any part of the manufacture of so many weapons could possibly make any kind of sense. In his first major address as president, delivered on April 16, 1953, weeks after Stalin's death—when he may have hoped for warmer relations with the Soviet Union—he reckoned the cost of arms. "Every gun that is made, every warship launched, every rocket fired signifies in the final sense a theft from those who hunger and are not fed, those who are cold and not clothed," he said. "This world in arms is not spending money alone; it is spending the sweat of its laborers, the genius of its scientists, the hopes of its children." He invoked, of all people, William Jennings Bryan, and his cross-of-gold speech. "This is not a way of life at all in any true sense," Eisenhower went on. "Under the clouds of threatening war, it is humanity hanging from a cross of iron."[116] It was Eisenhower's best speech about the arms race, if by no means his last.

"WE'RE ALL IN AGREEMENT on the format," moderator Quincy Howe said in 1956, introducing the first-ever televised debate between two presidential candidates. "There's going to be a three-minute opening statement from each of the two gentlemen here and a five-minute closing." Radio hosts had tried fighting fascism in the 1930s by holding debates over the radio. In the 1950s, television hosts tried to fight communism—and McCarthyism—by doing the same on TV. Howe, a former CBS Radio broadcaster, had been director of the American Civil Liberties Union. In the 1930s, he'd served as a panelist on NBC Radio's *America's Town Meeting of the Air.*[117] He cared about the quality of an argument; he cherished public debate. In 1956, he served as moderator of a debate between Adlai Stevenson and another Democratic presidential prospect, former Tennessee senator Estes Kefauver, broadcast on ABC.

The idea had come from Stevenson and his adviser Newton Minow— later the head of the FCC. In the spirit of radio debates hosted by the League of Women Voters since the 1920s, Stevenson and Minow were convinced that television could educate American voters and model the free and open exchange of political ideas. Stevenson challenged Kefauver; Kefauver agreed, and the two met in a one-hour debate at a studio in Miami. In between opening and closing statements, Howe explained, he'd allow "free-wheeling talk in which I act as a kind of a traffic cop, with the power to hand out parking tickets if anyone stays too long in one place or to enforce speed limits if anyone gets going too fast." The debate took place the day after the United States dropped on the Bikini Atoll a bomb far more powerful than the bomb dropped on Hiroshima. Stevenson said, about the new bomb, "The future is either going to be a future of creativity and of great abundance, or it's going to be a future of total incineration, death and destruction."[118]

The Stevenson-Kefauver debate, like the H-bomb, had been a test. The Republican National Committee chairman called the debate "tired, sorry, and uninspiring." But debating his opponent didn't hurt Stevenson, who won the nomination, and began making a case to the nation that presidential candidates ought to debate one another on television regularly. "I would like to propose that we transform our circus-atmosphere presidential campaign into a great debate conducted in full view of all the people," he later wrote, calling for regular half-hour debates between the major-party candidates.[119]

Meanwhile, Stevenson squared off against Eisenhower and his running mate, Richard Nixon, who'd drawn inward, convinced that the print press was conspiring against him, even though, for a long time, he'd been something of a media darling. "The tall, dark, and—yes—handsome freshman congressman who has been pressuring the House Un-American Activities committee to search out the truth in the Chambers-Hiss affair," is how the *Washington Post* had described him at the beginning of his career. "He was unquestionably one of the outstanding first-termers in the Eightieth Congress." All the same, newspaper columnists had badly drummed Nixon after his Checkers speech, and especially after McCarthy's very bad end, and not always fairly. Syndicated newspaper columnist Drew Pearson had reported that Nixon had taken a bribe from an oil company; the report was based on a letter that turned out to be a forgery. Then there were stories that were simply unwarranted, dumb, and mean. *Time* had gleefully reported that Checkers was not housebroken and had not been spayed and had gotten pregnant by a neighborhood dog. Nixon, fed up, said he wanted to write a memoir called *I've Had It*. But then, in September 1955, Eisenhower had a heart attack, and Nixon decided to hold on, though he had to fight for a spot on the ticket.[120]

He won that spot in San Francisco in 1956 at a Republican convention managed by Whitaker and Baxter. "The key political fact about the gathering now breaking up is that it has made Richard M. Nixon the symbol, if not the center, of authority in the Republican Party," reported Richard Rovere in *The New Yorker*. Campaigns, Inc., had teamed up with the California firm of Baus and Ross. Whitaker and Baxter wrote the copy; Baus and Ross produced the radio and television spots. That same season, they campaigned on behalf of Proposition 4, a ballot measure favoring the oil industry and giving them more license to drill. The measure was written by attorneys for Standard Oil. Whitaker and Baxter succeeded in getting the referendum's name changed to the Oil and Gas Conservation Act. "Political campaigns are too important to leave to politicians," Baus and Ross said. [121]

In a 1956 campaign speech written by economist John Kenneth Galbraith, Stevenson described "Nixonland" as the "land of slander and scare; the land of sly innuendo, the poison pen, the anonymous phone call and hustling, pushing, shoving, the land of smash and grab and anything to win." ("I want you to write the speeches against Nixon," Stevenson had written Galbraith. "You have no tendency to be fair.")[122] But Nixonland was Whitaker and Baxter–land.

In television ads, both the Republican and Democratic presidential campaigns of 1956 acknowledged the confusion that television advertising had itself sown. In one Republican ad, a cartoon voter despairs, "I've listened to everybody. On TV and radio. I've read the papers and magazines. I've tried! But I'm still confused. Who's right? What's right? What should I believe? What are the facts? How can I tell?" A comforting narrator calms down the worried voter and convinces him to like Ike.[123]

Stevenson, in his own television ad, haplessly tried to indict what he considered the callowness and fakery of the medium by exposing the camera, cables, and lights that had been installed in a room in his house in Illinois. He wanted to save Americans from themselves by showing them how what they saw on their screens was produced. "I wish you could see what else is in this room," he said, speaking directly into the camera. "Besides the camera, and the lights over here, there are cables all over the floor." The ad is positively postmodern: self-conscious, uncertain, and troubling. "Thanks to television, I can talk to millions of people that I couldn't reach any other way," Stevenson said, and then he quavered. "I can talk to you, yes, but I can't listen to you. I can't hear about your problems. . . . To do that, I've got to go out and see you in person."[124]

But when Stevenson did go out on the campaign trail, he proved unpersuasive. In Los Angeles, speaking before a primarily black audience, he was booed when he said, "We must proceed gradually, not upsetting habits or traditions that are older than the Republic."[125] In 1952, Eisenhower had beaten Stevenson in the Electoral College 442 to 89; in 1956, he won 457 to 73.

The parties began to drift apart, like continents, loosed. The Republican Party, influenced by conservative suburban housewives, began to move to the right. The Democratic Party, stirred by the moral and political urgency of the struggle for civil rights, began moving to the left. The pace of that drift would be determined by civil rights, the Cold War, television, and the speed of computation.

How and where would Americans work out their political differences? In *Yates v. United States*, the Supreme Court gutted the Smith Act, establishing that the First Amendment protected all political speech, even radical, reactionary, and revolutionary speech, unless it constituted a "clear and present danger." But television broadcasters began to report that their audiences seemed to have an aversion to unpleasant information. "Television in the main is being used to distract, delude, amuse and insulate us," Murrow complained. Magazine and newspaper writers made much the same complaint, finding that their editors were unwilling to run stories critical of American foreign policy. In Guatemala, when the CIA arranged to overthrow the democratically elected government of Jacobo Árbenz Guzmán, who had seized hundreds of thousands of acres of land owned by the United Fruit Company, an American business, American reporters provided only the explanation given by Secretary of State Dulles, who insisted that Árbenz had been overthrown by a popular uprising. Correspondents from China, including John Hersey, protested at the editing of their own reports. From Luce's *Time,* Theodore White threatened to resign.[126]

In a national security state where dissent was declared un-American and political contests were run by advertising firms, it was hard to know what was true. That bewildered cartoon voter had asked, *"Who's right? What's right? What should I believe? What are the facts? How can I tell?"* Maybe computers could tell. Screenwriters Phoebe Ephron and Henry Ephron toyed with that claim in the 1957 film *Desk Set,* starring Spencer Tracy and Katharine Hepburn, and made with the cooperation of IBM. Tracy plays an MIT engineer, a modern Frederick Winslow Taylor, who's invented an "electronic brain." He turns up with a tape measure in the fact-checking department on the twenty-eighth-floor of the Federal Broadcasting Company building. Hepburn, who plays the head of the department, invites him into her office.

"I'm a methods engineer," he says.

"Is that a sort of efficiency expert?"

"Well, that term is a bit obsolete now."

"Oh, forgive me," says Hepburn. "I'm so sorry. I'm the old-fashioned type."

He's come to Hepburn's department to install a giant machine called **E**lectromagnetic **ME**mory and **R**esearch **A**rithmetical **C**alculator, EMERAC, or Emmy for short, which requires pushing aside the desks of her assistants. Hepburn expects that her entire staff, replaced with this newest Office Robot, will be fired. Demonstrating how EMERAC works, Tracy makes a speech to a group of corporate executives.

"Gentlemen, the purpose of this machine of course is to free the worker—"

("You can say that again," Hepburn mutters.)

"—to free the worker from the routine and repetitive tasks and liberate his time for more important work." He points to the walls of books. "You see all those books there? And those up there? Well, every fact in them has been fed into Emmy."

No one will ever need to consult a book again, Tracy promises. In the future, the discovery of facts will require nothing more than asking Emmy. Hepburn, asked what she thinks of Emmy, answers archly: "I think you can safely say that it will provide more leisure for more people."[127]

*Desk Set* played on its audience's fear of automation, of machines that would make workers redundant. But, more bracingly, it offered a proposal about mass democracy and the chaos of facts. Citizens find it impossible to gather all the information they need to make an informed decision about a political issue; they are easily deluded by television and other forms of mass media and mass advertising; they struggle to sort through fact and fiction. But computers have no problem handling a vast store of knowledge; they are animated only by logic; they are immune to persuasion. It seemed possible—it had certainly been Mauchly's dream—that computers would help people become better citizens, that the United States would become a techno-utopia. *Desk Set* wondered, instead, whether computers had about them the whirring mechanical menace of totalitarianism, another cross of iron.

# IV.

THOROUGHGOOD MARSHALL WAS born in Baltimore in 1908, the son of a steward who served at an all-white resort and a kindergarten teacher who taught at all-black schools. He knew all about the color line; he knew about it as intimately as a prisoner knows the walls of his cell. Marshall, who started spelling his name "Thurgood" in the second grade because it was simpler, first read the Constitution when he was made to study it as punishment for raising hell at school. "Instead of making us copy out stuff on the blackboard after school when we misbehaved," Marshall later explained, "our teacher sent us down into the basement to learn parts of the Constitution." He pored over every word. He figured he'd found the key to the lock on that cell door. His parents wanted him to become a dentist, but after working his way through college as a dining-car waiter on the B&O Railroad, he decided he wanted to be a lawyer. He'd learned his pride, and how to argue, from his father during arguments at the dinner table. Whenever he'd say something smart, his father would say, "Why, that's right black of you." [128]

Unable to attend the segregated University of Maryland Law School—a ten-minute trolley ride from his family's house—he instead went to Howard, which required riding in segregated railroad cars, forty miles each way. Graduating first in his class in 1933, he two years later successfully sued, as counsel, the state of Maryland, arguing that, because the state provided no law school for African Americans, it had defied the "separate but equal" doctrine of the Supreme Court's 1896 ruling in *Plessy v. Ferguson.* By 1950, Marshall had convinced the NAACP to abandon this line of argument—demanding equal facilities—in favor of arguing against separation itself.

Marshall started the NAACP's legal and educational defense fund right after he won his case against the state of Maryland. As its chief counsel, he argued hundreds of cases across the South as part of a years-long strategy to end Jim Crow, at one point carrying as many as 450 cases at once. He started with higher education—law schools and professional schools—and worked his way down to colleges with the idea of eventually challenging segregation all the way down to the kind of kindergarten classrooms where his mother had taught. It had taken him a long time to convince colleagues at the NAACP to abandon "equalizing" arguments in favor of integration. (Equalizing had always been a means to end segregation, if gradually, the idea being that states would eventually be broken by the cost of maintaining separate schools if they had to be genuinely equal.) But by 1950, African Americans had challenged Jim Crow in the military and in housing and had also gained more political power. The Great Migration of blacks to the north and west meant that, nationally, anyway, large numbers of black men and women could vote, even if 80 percent of blacks in the South were still disenfranchised. By the middle of the decade, television, too, would argue in favor of making a leap in civil rights litigation: southern racial violence and intimidation, long hidden from view outside the South, could now be seen in living rooms across the country.

Aiming to bring a challenge to segregation in the nation's public schools to the Supreme Court, an objective endorsed by Truman's Justice

Department, Marshall began building a docket of cases in 1951. Several were eventually consolidated under a title case concerning a third grader named Linda Brown, who lived in Topeka, Kansas. Her father, Oliver L. Brown, a welder and part-time pastor, wanted her to go to a school blocks away from their house. But Topeka's segregated school system assigned Linda to a school a long walk and a bus ride away, an hour of travel each way. Oliver Brown agreed to join a civil suit against the Topeka Board of Education, filed by the NAACP's Legal Defense Fund. The case was called *Brown v. Board of Education.*

On the eve of oral arguments in December 1952, Marshall was near to physical collapse from overwork. At the Supreme Court building, a line began to form before dawn, men and women bundled against the morning frost in winter coats and hats. Oral arguments lasted three days. Justice Stanley Reed asked Marshall whether segregation wasn't in the interest of law and order. Marshall was willing to stipulate, for the purpose of argument, that maybe it had been when the court decided *Plessy.* But "even if the concession is made that it was necessary in 1895," he said, "it is not necessary now because people have grown up and understand each other." Marshall offered the court a singularly hopeful picture of American race relations. "I know in the South, where I spent most of my time," he said, "you will see white and colored kids going down the road together to school. They separate and go to different schools, and they come out and they play together. I do not see why there would necessarily be any trouble if they went to school together."

Justice Felix Frankfurter asked Marshall what he meant by "equal." Marshall, six foot four, his wavy black hair slicked back, his thin mustache as pointed as a punctuation mark—*Newsweek* once described him as "a rumpled bear of a man"—answered, with his slight southern drawl, "Equal means getting the same thing, at the same time, and in the same place."

John W. Davis, the seventy-eight-year-old former solicitor general, U.S. ambassador to Britain, and Democratic presidential candidate in 1924, argued the other side, stressing states' rights and precedent. A formidable opponent, Davis had made 139 appearances before the court; this would be his last. He asked, "Is it not a fact that the very strength and fiber of our federal system is local self-government in those matters for which local action is competent?" And, on tradition: "There is no reason assigned here why this Court or any other should reverse the findings of ninety years."[129]

But Marshall's argument, strenuous and intricate, aimed to lift from the shoulders of African Americans the weight of history. Instead of arguing from precedent, Marshall borrowed from Louis Brandeis: he presented the findings of social science. In establishing the constitutionality of Jim Crow laws, *Plessy v. Ferguson* had cited the "customs and traditions of the people." Marshall presented the court with reams of empirical research on the consequences for black children of separate schooling. Jim Crow laws, Marshall told the court, are Black Codes, and the only way the court could possibly uphold them, he said, would be "to find that for some reason Negroes are inferior to all other human beings."[130]

As the court was keenly aware, the case to end segregation was aided by the conditions of the Cold War itself. The United States billed itself as the leader of the "free world," and fought against the Soviets for influence in emerging polities in the third world, but frequently found itself indicted for its racial order at home. When the finance minister of Ghana, on a visit to the United States, stopped at a Howard Johnson's in Delaware and tried to order orange juice, he was told that blacks were not allowed in the restaurant. When the Haitian secretary of agriculture was invited to Biloxi, Mississippi, for a conference, he was told he was unable to stay at the conference hotel. "Can serious people still speak of American democracy?" asked one Haitian newspaper. Newspapers from Bombay to Manila reported on Jim Crow. "The Negro question" was one of the principal themes of Soviet propaganda, the U.S. embassy in Moscow reported. And so, when the Topeka case first reached the Supreme Court, Truman's Justice Department urged the court to overturn *Plessy*, partly on the grounds that legally sanctioned racial discrimination in the United States undermined American foreign policy aims. "Racial discrimination furnishes grist for the Communist propaganda mills," said Attorney General James P. McGranery, "and it raises doubts even among friendly nations as to the intensity of our devotion to the democratic faith." In his brief, the attorney general included two pages written by Dean Acheson, the secretary of state, emphasizing the cost of Jim Crow at home to the United States' reputation around the world. "Racial discrimination in the United States remains a source of constant embarrassment to this Government in the day-to-day conduct of its foreign relations," Acheson reported, "and it jeopardizes the effective maintenance of our moral leadership of the free and democratic nations of the world." Desegregation had become a matter of national security.[131]

As the oral arguments ended, Davis was overheard saying, "I think we've got it won, 5–4, or maybe 6–3." He'd read the bench well. When the justices began their deliberations in closed session, Chief Justice Fred Vinson, a Kentucky Democrat, opened by noting that precedent did indeed support segregation. Vinson thought it would be better if the desegregation of schools came from Congress, and that if the court acted ahead of popular opinion, public schooling in the South might be effectively abolished because segregationists would rather close their schools than admit blacks. Reed, also from Kentucky, said that he thought the time to end segregation would come when the "body of people" thought it was unconstitutional, which hadn't happened yet. Like Reed, Justice Robert Jackson said he thought that if the court had to decide this question, "then representative government has failed." Frankfurter, a longtime liberal who, once on the court, had become its most dogged opponent of judicial activism, wanted—like Texan Tom C. Clark—to delay. Frankfurter had served on the NAACP's Legal Defense Committee and had hired a black law clerk, the court's first, in 1948, but, as much as Frankfurter wanted segregation to end, Marshall hadn't convinced him that it was unconstitutional. Roosevelt appointee and former Columbia University law professor William O. Douglas thought the whole thing was "very simple": the "14th amendment prohibits racial classifications." Hugo Black, from Alabama, was one of the strongest voices in opposition to segregation, even though he himself had been a member of the Klan in the 1920s—a blot that he strained to scrub clean. Had the justices then taken a straw vote (which they did not), it appears likely that four would have found segregation unconstitutional, two would have reaffirmed *Plessy*, and three would have been uncertain. Worried about the political consequences of a divided decision—a worry that extended to mass violence—Vinson decided to reschedule the case, to be reargued in December 1953.[133]

All bets on the outcome of the case were called off, though, when, on September 8, 1953, Vinson died, altogether unexpectedly, of a heart attack. Eisenhower, who had, in an effort to unite the divided Republican

Party, named his rival and Nixon's great political enemy Earl Warren as his solicitor general, had also, at the time, promised Warren a seat on the court. When Vinson died, Eisenhower appointed Warren as chief justice, a position Warren would hold for sixteen years, presiding over the most liberal bench in the court's history. *Brown v. Board* was the first case the Warren Court tackled.

Warren, opening the discussion, saw the case entirely differently than had Vinson. "Separate but equal doctrine rests on [the] basic premise that the Negro race is inferior," he began, agreeing with Marshall that the "only way to sustain *Plessy*" was to agree with the premise of racial inferiority, which was impossible, he said, because "the argument of Negro counsel proves they are not inferior." Warren's vote, added to the four justices who in the earlier session made clear that they believed segregation to be unconstitutional, meant that Warren's argument would prevail, 5–4, even if no other justices joined his side. The justices' clerks nearly unanimously supported Warren's position, all but a young William Rehnquist, as he made plain in a memo to his boss, Justice Jackson. "I realize it is an unpopular and unhumanitarian position, for which I have been excoriated by 'liberal' colleagues," Rehnquist wrote, "but I think Plessy v. Ferguson was right and should be reaffirmed."[133] (Nixon would appoint Rehnquist to the court in 1971.)

The court was scheduled to hand down its decision on May 17, 1954. The NAACP was so uncertain how the court would decide that it prepared two press releases, one for either possible decision. Reporters flooded the galleries. The decision had been made unanimous. Justice Jackson, in the hospital recovering from a heart attack, came to court that day, so committed was the court to a display of unity.[134] Warren delivered the opinion he'd written about the nature of change over time. "In approaching this problem, we cannot turn the clock back to 1868, when the Amendment was adopted, or even to 1896 when *Plessy v. Ferguson* was written," he insisted. "We must consider public education in the light of its full development and its present place in American life throughout the Nation. Only in this way can it be determined if segregation in public schools deprives these plaintiffs of the equal protection of the laws." In assessing the evidence not of the past but of the present—the conditions in American schools—he concluded that "separate educational facilities are inherently unequal."[135] At least on paper, Jim Crow was over.

Much of the public greeted the decision with elation and joy, nowhere better captured than in a photograph of a young mother sitting on the steps of the Supreme Court, cradling her young daughter in the crook of her arm, holding in her lap the next day's newspaper, with its out-sized front-page headline HIGH COURT BANS SEGREGATION IN NATION'S SCHOOLS. Warren's opinion was greeted with near equal pleasure by Cold Warriors, who called it a "blow to communism." Even the Republican National Committee—granting Eisenhower credit for a decision that Truman's Justice Department had pursued—celebrated the court's ruling, stating that "it helps guarantee the Free World's cause."[136]

But not all civil rights activists had supported Marshall and the NAACP's legal strategy, not all African Americans wanted their schools to be desegregated (which often resulted in black teachers losing their jobs), and many who did nevertheless placed greater priority on other political goals. In a 1935 essay called "Does the Negro Need Separate Schools?" W. E. B. Du Bois had written about something almost ineffable in a teacher's understanding of the world of her students. Dissenters within the NAACP found that its willingness to bring the fight for civil rights to the courts came at the expense of securing better jobs, equal pay, and fair housing. In Atlanta, home to five historically black colleges and universities, nearly half the city's public school teachers were black and, of those, three-quarters were black women. Black teachers had been lobbying the legislature for equal pay and for equal funding for black schools. Atlanta lawyer A. T. Walden had begun filing pay equity suits on behalf of the city's teachers in 1942 and the next year had filed a class action suit with Thurgood Marshall. In 1950, when Marshall turned the NAACP strategy to integration and Walden began pursuing desegregation cases, the editor of the *Atlanta Daily World* was among the most outspoken of those black leaders who objected, arguing that much would be lost for black children sent into white schools, especially at a time when the legislature, under growing grassroots pressure, was beginning to move on equalizing funds and opening new black schools. The strongest reservations were those of black schoolteachers; even in Topeka, they "wanted no part of the effort to desegregate the schools." After *Brown*, they continued to be skeptical. Marshall did not hide a frustration laced with contempt. "We will try to convert them to our way of thinking," he said, days after the ruling. "But we will walk over them if they get in our way."[137]

Among whites, especially in the Jim Crow South, *Brown* was met with swift and sustained resistance. Eisenhower had been dismayed by the ruling: "I am convinced that the Supreme Court decision set back progress in the South at least fifteen years," he said privately. "The fellow who tries to tell me you can do these things by FORCE is just plain NUTS." Segregationists prepared for battle. "There is nothing in the United States Constitution that gives the Congress, the President, or the Supreme Court the right to declare that white and colored children must attend the same public schools," said Mississippi senator James Eastland. And a new movement began, called "Impeach Earl Warren."[138]

The court urged schools to desegregate "with all deliberate speed." Some schools in cities and towns like Washington and Baltimore complied. The overwhelming majority did not. In some cities, like Atlanta, where many black families were deeply ambivalent about the NAACP's legal strategy, the school board dragged its feet, and black activists and black teachers' unions didn't press them. In other cities, all-white school boards simply refused to budge. In 1955, in eight states in the South, not a single black child attended school with a white child. The *Richmond News Leader* wrote that year: "In May of 1954, that inept fraternity of politicians and professors known as the United States Supreme Court chose to throw away established law. These nine men repudiated the Constitution, spit upon the Tenth Amendment and rewrote the fundamental law of this land to suit their own gauzy concepts of sociology. If it be said now that the South is flouting the law, let it be said to the high court, *You taught us how.*"[139]

The court could disavow Jim Crow, but it would take a fight to dismantle it. Sometimes that fight took place at the very doors of public schools, where black children were placed on the front lines. It also took place on buses and in restaurants, in the acts of defiance that had become commonplace in the 1940s, even if they had been rarely reported. After *Brown*, reporters took notice. On December 1, 1955, in Montgomery, Alabama, Rosa Parks, a forty-two-year-old seamstress, refused to give up her seat on a bus to a white man. Parks, born in Tuskegee, had joined the NAACP in 1943, when she was thirty; secretary of her chapter, she'd worked on voter registration and the desegregation of transportation. Parks had made a purposeful decision to challenge segregated seating on the city's buses. The driver stopped the bus and asked her to move, and when she again refused, he called for police, who arrested her.

The next night, a twenty-six-year-old minister named Martin Luther King Jr. was drafted to lead a citywide protest that would begin the following Monday, December 5. Born in Atlanta in 1929, the son of a minister and NAACP leader, King had been inspired by American evangelical Christianity, by the liberal theologian Reinhold Niebuhr, and by anticolonialism abroad, particularly by the rhetoric and tactics of nonviolence practiced by Mahatma Gandhi. King had wide-set eyes, short hair, and a pencil mustache. Ordained in 1948, he'd attended a theological seminary in Pennsylvania and then completed a doctoral degree at Boston University in 1955 before becoming pastor at the Dexter Avenue Baptist Church in Montgomery. Lean and quiet as a young man, he'd grown sturdier, and more stirring as he mastered the ancient art of preaching.

On the fifth, with less than half an hour to pull together a speech for a mass meeting to be held at Montgomery's Holt Street Baptist Church, he found himself with a few moments to spare when, on his ride to the church, traffic all but stopped. Cars snaked through the city. More than five thousand people had turned up, thousands more than the church could fit. King climbed to the pulpit. The crowd, while attentive, remained hushed until he found his rhythm. "As you know, my friends," King said, his deep voice beginning to thrum, "there comes a time when people get tired of being trampled over by the iron feet of oppression." Pressed into benches, people began stomping their feet and calling out, "Yes!"

"I want it to be known throughout Montgomery and throughout this nation that we are Christian people," King said as the crowd punctuated his pauses with cries. "The only weapon we have in our hands this evening is the weapon of protest." Joining a tradition of American oratory that dated back to the day Frederick Douglass concluded that he could make a better argument against slavery if he decided the Constitution was on his side instead of against him, King called this protest an American protest. "If we were incarcerated behind the iron curtains of a communistic nation—we couldn't do this," he said, pausing for the thunder of assent. "If we were trapped in the dungeon of a totalitarian regime—we couldn't do this." It was as if the roof might fall. "But the great glory of American democracy," his voice swelled, "is the right to protest for right."

Parks had been arrested on a Thursday; by Monday, 90 percent of the city's blacks were boycotting the buses.[140] Over 381 days, blacks in Montgomery, led by Parks and King, boycotted the city's buses. King, indicted for violating the state's antiboycott law, said, "If we are arrested every day, if we are exploited every day, if we are trampled over every day, don't ever let anyone pull you so low as to hate them." On November 13, 1956, the Supreme Court ruled that the Montgomery bus law was unconstitutional.[141]

Early the next year, King founded the Southern Christian Leadership Conference (SCLC). If the civil rights struggle of the 1950s was aided by the Cold War, it was fueled by a spirit of prophetic Christianity. A political movement and a legal argument, civil rights was also a religious revival. "If you will protest courageously, and yet with dignity and Christian love," King promised his followers, "when the history books are written in future generations, the historians will have to pause and say, 'There lived a great people—a black people—who injected new meaning and dignity into the veins of civilization.'" The historians have obliged: under King's leadership, and by the courage of those who followed him, and those who'd paved the way for him, a commitment to civil rights became not only postwar liberalism's core commitment but the nation's creed.[142]

But blood would be shed. Justice William O. Douglas always blamed Eisenhower for the years of violence that followed the court's ruling in *Brown*, a decision the president, who did not ask Congress for a stronger civil rights bill, never publicly endorsed. Eisenhower, Douglas said, was a national hero, worshipped and adored. "If he had gone to the nation on television and radio telling people to obey the law and fall into line, the cause of desegregation would have been accelerated," Douglas said. Instead, "Ike's ominous silence on our 1954 decision gave courage to the racists who decided to resist the decision, ward by ward, precinct by precinct, town by town, and county by county."[143]

Orval Faubus, Democratic governor of Arkansas, wasn't personally opposed to integration; he sent his own son to an integrated college outside of town. But the sentiment of his constituents—who were nearly all white, in a state where blacks were regularly blocked from voting—led him to consider opposition to school desegregation a political opportunity too good to miss. He sought an injunction against desegregation of

*Elizabeth Eckford was turned away from*
*Central High School in Little Rock, Arkansas, in 1957,*
*by order of the state's governor, Orval Faubus.*

the schools, and the state court agreed to grant it. Thurgood Marshall got a federal district court to nullify the state injunction, but on September 2, 1957, Faubus went on television to announce that he was sending 250 National Guardsmen to Central High School in Little Rock. If any black children tried to get into the school, Faubus warned, "blood will run in the streets."

The next day, before any black children had even arrived, a white mob attacked a group of black newspaper reporters and photographers. Alex Wilson said, as he was knocked to the ground, "I fought for my country, and I'm not running from you." On September 4, when fifteen-year-old Elizabeth Eckford tried to walk to the school, the white students cried, "Lynch her! Lynch her!" Television coverage of black students confronted by armed soldiers and a white mob wielding sticks and stones and worse stunned Americans across the country. The state of Arkansas had authorized armed resistance to federal law.[144]

While Eisenhower dithered over how to handle the crisis in Little Rock, Congress debated the 1957 Civil Rights Act, the first civil rights legislation since Reconstruction. It established a Civil Rights Commission to hear complaints but granted it no authority to do anything about them. It was like "handing a policeman a gun without bullets," said one Justice Department official. Eleanor Roosevelt, as distinctive and influential as an ex–First Lady as she'd been when in the White House, called the law "mere fakery." One senator said it was about as substantial as "soup made from the shadow of a crow which had starved to death." Longtime advocates of civil rights, including Richard Nixon, argued for stronger legislation, to no avail. But the 1957 Civil Rights Act set a precedent, and it was galling enough to segregationists that Strom Thurmond, who filibustered against it for more than twenty-four hours, set a new record. The bill was made possible by the wrangling of Lyndon Johnson. True to his Texas constituency, if not to his principles, Johnson had voted against every civil rights bill that had faced him in his career in the House and Senate, from 1937 to 1957. But he'd never been a segregationist, he'd publicly supported the court's decision in *Brown v. Board*, and he believed the time had come for the Democratic Party to change direction. Johnson was also eyeing a bid for the presidency, and he needed to be seen as a national politician, not a southern Democrat. He courted and counted votes better than any other Senate majority leader ever had, and the bill passed.[145]

"Mob rule cannot be allowed to overrule the decisions of our courts," Eisenhower said on television, and ordered a thousand paratroopers from the 101st Airborne Division to Arkansas, the same division that had dropped from the sky over Normandy on D-Day. On September 25, 1957, U.S. federal troops escorted nine black teenagers to high school. Americans watching on television reeled. They reeled again when, on October 4, 1957, the USSR launched a satellite into orbit. Anyone with a shortwave radio, anywhere in the world, could listen to it, as it made its orbit: it emitted a steady beep, beep, beep, like the ticking of a heart. In the United States, a nation already on edge at the specter of armed paratroopers escorting children into a school, Sputnik also created a political panic: the next obvious step was putting a nuclear weapon in a missile head and firing it by rocket. In both the race to space and the arms race, the Soviets had pulled ahead.

The Cold War would keep overshadowing the civil rights movement, and also propelling it forward. The battle to end segregation in education

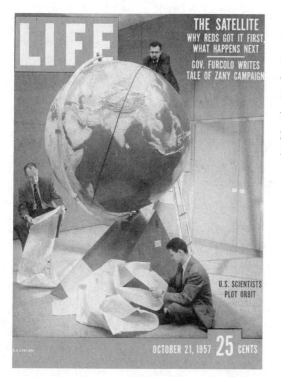

*On the cover of* Life, *MIT scientists attempt to calculate the orbit of the Soviet satellite Sputnik while the magazine promises to explain "Why Reds Got It First."*

was far from over. Faubus—who'd earned the nickname "that sputtering sputnik from the Ozarks"—decided to shut down Little Rock's high schools rather than integrate them. He declared, "The federal government has no authority to require any state to operate public schools."[146]

Two weeks after Sputnik was launched, Eisenhower met with the nation's top scientific advisers, asking them "to tell him where scientific research belonged in the structure of the federal government." That meeting led, in 1958, to the creation of the National Aeronautics and Space Agency. NASA would establish operations in Florida and Texas, and fund research in universities across the former Cotton Belt, the science-and-technology, business-friendly New South, the Sun Belt.[147] That meeting also led to the creation of the Advanced Research Projects Agency as a branch of the Department of Defense. It would be based in the Pentagon. One day, it would build what became the Internet. In February 1958, after Sputnik, and one month after Eisenhower announced ARPA, the *Bulletin of the Atomic Scientists'* Science and Security Board moved the atomic Doomsday Clock to two minutes before midnight.

The hands of time seemed, at once, to be moving both forward and backward. Thurgood Marshall looked back at the late 1950s in dismay. "I had thought, we'd all thought, that once we got the *Brown* case, the thing was going to be over," he said bitterly. "You see, we were always looking for that one case to end it all. And that case hasn't come up yet."[148]

That case did not come. Equality was never going to be a matter of a single case, or even of a long march, but, instead, of an abiding political hope.

*Fourteen*

# RIGHTS AND
# WRONGS

*Vice President Richard Nixon and Soviet premier
Nikita Khrushchev debated the merits of capitalism
and communism in a model American kitchen
on display in Moscow in 1959.*

**N**IKITA **K**HRUSHCHEV, STOUT AND SWAGGERING BENEATH
a wide-brimmed white hat, looked like a circus barker; Richard
Nixon was dressed like an undertaker. "KNOCK THEM DEAD IN
RUSSIA," Nixon's television adviser had cabled him. "THIS IS MOST
IMPORTANT TRIP OF YOUR LIFE."[1]

Nixon, forty-six, went to Moscow in the summer of 1959 eyeing a presidential bid as the unsteady leader of a faltering party. The Republicans
had been badly drubbed in the 1958 midterm elections, losing forty-
eight seats in the House and thirteen in the Senate, and Democrats had
won both Senate seats in the new state of Alaska. Nixon, keen to take
advantage of the spotlight of a televised meeting with the Soviet premier,

wanted to deliver to Americans shaken by Sputnik a technological triumph, or, at the very least, a little machine-made political magic.

Nixon had traveled to Moscow to open an exhibition. The United States and the USSR, unable to launch rockets without risking mutually assured destruction, had agreed to stage a proxy battle of the merits of capitalism and communism. At the Soviet Exhibition of Science, Technology, and Culture, held at the New York Coliseum, the Russians put a space satellite on display alongside a gallery that housed a model Soviet apartment, its kitchen outfitted with a samovar. Its counterpart, the American National Exhibition, mounted inside a ten-acre pavilion in Moscow's Sokolniki Park, answered with electric coffeepots, offering visitors a tour of American consumer goods, especially home appliances of the sort that manufacturers pledged would spare women the drudgery of housework. One American family man, exactly capturing the spirit of the thing, wrote Eisenhower that he had a better idea: "Why don't you let a typical American family make up an exhibit?" He said he'd be happy to bring to Moscow everything anyone in the Soviet Union needed to understand "typical, living, honest to goodness, truthful and democratic loving Americans": striped toothpaste, a Dairy Queen cone, frozen pink lemonade, a GI insurance policy, his set of golf clubs, the family's 1959 Ford station wagon, and "Two plump daughters, ages 10 and 11 complete with hula hoops, Brownie and Girl Scout outfits, and a Monopoly set and polio shots."[2] The president did not take him up on the offer.

In Moscow, a grinning, dark-suited Nixon cut the ribbon to open the American exhibit alongside beaming, stripe-tied Khrushchev. Inside, they sparred over the rewards of capitalism and communism while touring galleries stocked with vacuum cleaners and dishwashers, robots and cake mixes, garbage disposals and frozen dinners, a showcase meant to display the American way of life—abundance, convenience, and choice. The bottles of Pepsi were free.

Stopping at a makeshift television stage, the two men fell into an argument, Khrushchev toying with Nixon like a bear playing with a fish.

"You must not be afraid of ideas," the vice president scolded the premier.

Khrushchev laughed. "The time has passed when ideas scared us."

Nixon pointed out that color television and the video recording of their meeting—American inventions—would lead to great advantages in communication, and that even Khrushchev might learn something from American ingenuity. "Because after all," Nixon said with a stiff smile, "you don't know everything."

"You know absolutely nothing about communism," Khrushchev shot back. "Nothing except fear of it."

Awkwardly, they wandered the exhibit hall.

"I want to show you this kitchen," Nixon said, excitedly ushering the premier to a canary-yellow, appliance-filled room and calling his attention to a washing machine and a television.

"Do your people also have a machine that opens their mouth and chews for them?" Khrushchev prodded.

Nixon dodged and parried. Still, he stood his ground.

The press dubbed it the Kitchen Debate and declared it a draw, but American photographers captured Nixon standing tall and fighting back, poking a finger in Khrushchev's chest, and the visit was a triumph.[3] For the United States, it was, in any event, a triumphant time: at the height of the Cold War, more Americans were earning more, and buying more, than ever before.

*The Affluent Society*, the economist John Kenneth Galbraith called it in 1958. "The fundamental political problems of the industrial revolution have been solved," the sociologist Seymour Martin Lipset wrote confidently in *Political Man* in 1960. For most of human history, the overwhelming majority of people have suffered from want. Industrialism had promised to end that suffering but turned out to produce vast fortunes only for the few, crushing the many under its wheels. Progressives and New Dealers had tried to lift those wheels. They'd legislated all manner of remedies and forms of mitigation, from a graduated federal income tax to maximum-hour and minimum-wage laws, from Social Security to the G.I. Bill. Since 1940, inequalities of wealth and income had been dwindling.[4] Even while checked by the Constitution, the growing power of the state, exercised most dramatically in huge fiscal expenditures, especially military, and funded by a progressive income tax, made possible unprecedented economic growth and a wide distribution of goods and opportunities. By 1960, two out of three Americans owned their own homes. They filled those homes with machines: dishwashers, vacuum cleaners, electric mixers and blenders, refrigerators and freezers, record players, radios, and televisions, the engines of their own abundance. So high a standard of living, so widely distributed, had never been seen before. "Nearly all, throughout history, have been very poor," Galbraith wrote. "The exception, almost insignificant in the whole span of human existence, has been the last few generations in the comparatively small corner of the world populated by Europeans. Here, and especially in the United States, there has been great and quite unprecedented affluence."[5]

The economy a juggernaut, the triumph of liberalism and of Keynesian economics seemed, to many American intellectuals, all but complete. "The remarkable capacity of the United States economy in 1960," one economic historian concluded, "represents the crossing of a great divide in the history of humanity."[6] Not only had the problems of industrialism been solved, many social scientists believed, but so had the problems of mass democracy, with the emergence of a broad and moderate political consensus, as seen on television. Notwithstanding the ongoing struggle over civil rights, Americans fundamentally agreed with one another about their system of government, and most also agreed on an underlying theory of politics. In *The End of Ideology: On the Exhaustion of Political Ideas in the Fifties*, sociologist Daniel Bell argued that socialism and communism had bloomed and withered; ideology, itself, was over. "For ideology, which once was a road to action, has come to be a dead end." Political debates lay ahead, tinkering around the edges, repairs to the appliance of government, and certainly, in Asia and Africa, new ideologies had emerged. But in the West, Bell insisted, the big ideas of the Left had been exhausted, replaced by a consensus: "the acceptance of a Welfare State; the desirability of decentralized power; a system of mixed economy and of political pluralism."[7]

Some younger Americans, Left and Right, found Bell's argument ridiculous. "It's like an old man proclaiming the end of sex," said one. "Because he doesn't feel it anymore, he thinks it has disappeared."[8] Others suggested that Bell had failed to notice a rising tide of conservatism.[9] But Bell hadn't ignored conservatism; he'd discounted it. In 1955, he'd edited a collection of essays called *The New American Right*. Joseph McCarthy, to Bell's contributors, was a man without ideas. "The puzzling thing about McCarthy," Dwight Macdonald wrote, "was that he had no ideology." As for the writings of economists like Friedrich Hayek, Bell dismissed them as nonsense. "Few serious conservatives," wrote Bell, "believe that the Welfare State is the 'road to serfdom.'"[10]

Considerable empirical evidence in fact supported Bell's theory of consensus. At the University of Michigan, political scientists had been conducting interviews with voters every four years since 1948. They'd asked voters questions: "Would you say that either one of the parties is more *conservative* or more *liberal* than the other?" Between 1948 and 1960, many voters could not answer that one. Others answered badly. The researchers had asked a follow-up: "What do people have in mind when they say that the Republicans (Democrats) are more conservative (liberal) than the Democrats (Republicans)?" Voters found this kind of question difficult to answer, too. The bottom 37 percent of respondents "could supply no meaning for the liberal-conservative distinction" and only the top 17 percent gave what the interviewers deemed "best answers." Everyone else fell somewhere in between, but the researchers were pretty sure that a whole bunch of them were just guessing.[11] Ideologically minded politicians and intellectuals talked about liberalism and conservatism, for sure, but to ordinary voters these terms had virtually no meaning.

Elaborating on these findings, which were published in 1960 in a landmark study called *The American Voter,* the political scientist Philip Converse produced an influential essay, "The Nature of Mass Belief Systems in Mass Publics," in which he divided the American electorate into political elites and the mass public. Political elites are exceptionally well informed, follow politics closely, and adhere to a set of political beliefs so coherent—or, as Converse termed, so "constrained"—as to constitute an ideology. But the mass public has only a scant knowledge of politics, resulting in a very loose and unconstrained attachment to any single set of political beliefs. Converse argued that the Michigan voter interviews revealed that political elites know "what-goes-with-what" (laissez-faire with free enterprise, for example) and "what parties stand for" (Democrats favor labor; Republicans, business), but much of the mass public does not. Political elites vote in a more partisan fashion than the mass public: the more a voter knows about politics, the more likely he is to vote in an ideologically consistent way, not just following a party but following a set of constraints dictated by a political ideology. What makes a voter a moderate, Converse concluded, is not knowing very much about politics. In the 1950s, there were a lot of moderates.[12]

What no one could quite see, in 1960, was the gathering strength of two developments that would shape American politics for the next half century. Between 1968 and 1972, both economic inequality and political polarization, which had been declining for decades, began to rise. The fundamental problems of the Industrial Revolution had not, alas, been solved. Nor had the problems of mass democracy. Even as social scientists were announcing the end of ideology, a new age of ideology was beginning.

By 1974, when Richard Nixon announced his resignation from the presidency, sitting before blue drapes in the Oval Office, fifteen years after his debate with Nikita Khrushchev in the canary-yellow kitchen in Moscow, liberalism had begun its long decline, and conservatism its long ascent. And the country was on the way to becoming nearly as divided, and as unequal, as it had been before the Civil War.

# I.

GALBRAITH WASN'T HAPPY about the affluent society. He found it complacent and smug, and too willing to accept poverty as inevitable. The prosperous society, he thought, was a purposeless one. He called for higher taxes to build better hospitals and schools and roads to repair the public sector. Americans shrugged, and turned on their televisions. But beneath the cheerful gurgle of the percolating electric coffeepot could be heard a muffled thrum of despair. It began with a fear of the perils of prosperity: laziness, tastelessness, and purposelessness. "We've grown unbelievably prosperous and we maunder along in a stupor of fat," the historian Eric Goldman complained. One journalist called the 1950s "the age of the slob." It was also the age of the snob. Dwight Macdonald memorably lamented the rise of packed, boxed, and price-tagged, middle-brow mass culture—"masscult," he dubbed it, as if it were a soft drink—especially in the form of trashy paperback novels and ticky-tacky TV shows produced for the sprawling and suburban middle class by corporations, arbitrated not by taste but by sales and ratings. Art is the creation of individuals in communities, Macdonald argued; middlebrow culture is a product manufactured and packaged for the masses. "Masscult is bad in a new way," Macdonald wrote. "It doesn't even have the theoretical possibility of being good."[13]

After Nixon came back from Moscow, the Eisenhower administration announced a new resolve: to discover a national purpose. "The year 1960

*Students from North Carolina A&T College staged a sit-in
at a lunch counter in a Woolworth's in Greensboro.*

was a time when Americans stopped taking their national purpose for
granted and started doing something about it," *Life* reported. Eisenhower
appointed ten eminent men—politicians and editors, business and labor
leaders, and the presidents of universities and charities—to a Commission on National Goals, and asked the commission to identify a set of ten-
year objectives for the United States. A striking measure of the artificial
nature of the era's liberal consensus: every member of the commission
was a white man over the age of forty-five.[14] Yet the goals the commission
would set would be steered, above all, by black college students, who,
beginning in 1960, and without a blue-ribbon committee of eminent men,
made civil rights the nation's purpose.

On Monday, February 1, 1960, two days before Eisenhower named
the members of his Commission on National Goals, four freshmen from
North Carolina A&T in Greensboro, North Carolina, refused to give
up their seats at a lunch counter in a segregated diner inside a Woolworth's store. Theirs wasn't the first sit-in—over the past three years
alone, there'd been sit-ins in sixteen cities—but it was the first to capture
national attention. That night, those four students called NAACP lawyer
Floyd McKissick, who helped spread the word. They went back to Woolworth's the next day, with friends; more came the day after that. They sat

in shifts, at vinyl-and-chrome stools. They set up a command center and kept track of plans being laid in Durham and Raleigh to stage sit-ins of solidarity. By the end of the week, more than four hundred students were involved in the Greensboro sit-in alone. The movement spread to Tennessee, and then across the South, to Georgia, West Virginia, Texas, and Arkansas. It reached forty more cities in March. Within months, fifty thousand students had joined. Hundreds were arrested in Nashville. In South Carolina, police attacked the demonstrators with teargas and fire hoses, arresting nearly four hundred. Even students who'd doubted the philosophy of nonviolent protest began to see its power, as photographers captured images of thuggish whites pouring milk and squeezing ketchup onto the heads of college students sitting quietly at a lunch counter, or of angry, armored policemen beating them with clubs or dragging them down sidewalks. The students' protest even earned the admiration of some hardened pro-segregation southern newspaper editors, including the editor of the *Richmond News Leader*:

> Here were the colored students, in coats, white shirts, ties, and one of them was reading Goethe and one was taking notes from a biology text. And here, on the sidewalk outside, was a gang of white boys come to heckle, a ragtail rabble, slack-jawed, black-jacketed, grinning fit to kill, and some of them, God save the mark, were waving the proud and honored flag of the Southern States in the last war fought by gentlemen. *Eheu!* it gives one pause.

Ella Baker, acting director of the SCLC, arranged to invite the student leaders to an organizing meeting on Easter weekend, in April. Baker, born in Virginia in 1903, had been a longtime organizer for the NAACP, as a field secretary beginning in 1938 and as a director of branches across the South in the 1940s, working on, among many other projects, the campaign to win equal pay for black teachers. She'd agreed to join the SCLC in 1958, to head an Atlanta-based voter registration drive known as the Crusade for Citizenship, but she'd been frustrated by southern preachers' relative inattention to voting rights, and she found Martin Luther King Jr. "too self-centered and cautious." In 1960, when SCLC tried to convince Baker to persuade the students to join as a junior chapter, Baker, in a stirring speech, refused, and instead urged the students to start their own organization. "She didn't say, 'Don't let Martin Luther King tell you what to do,'" Julian Bond later recalled, "but you got the real feeling that that's what she meant." Distancing themselves from both the NAACP and the SCLC, which many students found altogether too conservative, they founded the Student Nonviolent Coordinating Committee (SNCC). They raised an army; their weapon was nonviolent direct action. Baker left the SCLC to join them.[15]

Later in 1960, when Eisenhower's ten distinguished commissioners delivered their report, they wrote that "Discrimination on the basis of race must be recognized as morally wrong, economically wasteful, and in many respects dangerous"; called for federal action to support voting rights; urged the denial of federal funds to employers who discriminate on the basis of race; and insisted upon the urgency of ending segregation in education.[16] Although the final report wasn't published until after the November election, its key findings were released earlier, and more than one observer remarked that the report, while prepared for the Republican White House, aligned very well with the campaign promises made by Democratic presidential candidate John F. Kennedy. "If there were not abundant evidence Senator Kennedy has been fully occupied with other things lately," said CBS's Howard K. Smith, "one would swear he wrote the document."[17]

Before that fall, the presidential prospects for Kennedy, the dashing Irish Catholic from Boston, had not seemed especially good. Liberals distrusted him because of his silence on McCarthyism, and few had much confidence in him. Kennedy, forty-three, was both young and inexperienced. Lyndon Johnson called him "the boy."

Kennedy prevailed, in part, because he was the first packaged, market-tested president, liberalism for mass consumption. Weighing the possible party nominees and its platform, the Democratic National Committee, uncertain how to handle the question of civil rights, turned to a new field, called "data science," a term coined in 1960, to predict the consequences of different approaches to the issue by undertaking the computational simulation of elections. To that end, the DNC in 1959 hired Simulmatics Corporation, a company founded by Ithiel de Sola Pool, a political scientist from MIT. Pool and his team collected old punch cards from the archives of George Gallup and pollster Elmo Roper, the raw data from more than sixty polls conducted during the campaigns of 1952, 1954, 1956, 1958, and 1960, and fed them into a UNIVAC. Using high-speed computation and "a simulation model developed out of historical data," Pool aimed to both advance and accelerate the measurement of public opinion and the forecasting of elections. "This kind of research could not have been conducted ten years ago," Pool and his colleagues reported.

Pool sorted voters into 480 possible types, explaining, "A single voter type might be 'Eastern, metropolitan, lower-income, white, Catholic, female Democrats.' Another might be, 'Border state, rural, upper-income, white, Protestant, male Independents.'" He sorted issues into fifty-two clusters: "Most of these were political issues, such as foreign aid, attitudes toward the United Nations, and McCarthyism," he explained. "Other so-called 'issue clusters' included such familiar indicators of public opinion as 'Which party is better suited for people like you?'"[18]

Simulmatics's work, which continued through the 1960s, marked the advent of a new industry whose implications for American democracy alarmed at least one of his colleagues, the political scientist and novelist Eugene Burdick. Famous for the 1958 best seller he coauthored with William Lederer, *The Ugly American*, and the 1962 novel *Fail-Safe* (written with Harvey Wheeler and made into a film directed by Sidney Lumet), Burdick published a novel called *The 480*, about the work done by Simulmatics, a fictional exposé of what he described as "a benign underworld in American politics":

> It is not the underworld of cigar-chewing pot-bellied officials who mysteriously run "the machine." Such men are still around, but their power is waning. They are becoming obsolete though they have not yet learned that fact. The new underworld is made up of innocent and well-intentioned people who work with slide rules and calculating machines and computers which can retain an almost infinite number of bits of information as well as sort, categorize, and reproduce this information at the press of a button. Most of these people are highly educated, many of them are Ph.D.s, and none that I have met have malignant political designs on the American public. They may, however, radically reconstruct the American political system, build a new politics, and even modify revered and venerable American institutions—facts of which they are blissfully innocent. They are technicians and artists; all of them want, desperately, to be scientists.[19]

The premise of Simulmatics's work, as Burdick saw all too clearly, was that, if voters didn't profess ideologies, if they had no idea of the meaning of the words "liberal" and "conservative," they could nevertheless be sorted into ideological piles, based on their identities—race, ethnicity, hometown, religion, age, and income. Simulmatics's first commission, completed just before the Democratic National Convention, in the summer of 1960, was to conduct a study on "the Negro vote in the North" (so few black people were able to vote in the South that there was no point in simulating their votes, Pool concluded). Pool reported discovering that, between 1954 and 1956, "A small but significant shift to the Republicans occurred among Northern Negroes, which cost the Democrats about 1 per cent of the total votes in 8 key states." The DNC, undoubtedly influenced by the viscerally powerful student sit-ins, absorbed Simulmatics's report, and decided to add civil rights paragraphs to the party's platform at its convention in Los Angeles in July.[20]

Civil rights had not been among Kennedy's priorities as a member of the Senate. But the protests and the predictions altered his course. Needing to win both black votes in the North and white votes in the South, Kennedy decided to run as a civil rights candidate, to woo those northerners, and chose Lyndon Johnson for his running mate, hoping that the Texan could handle the southerners.

The DNC found Simulmatics's initial report sufficiently illuminating that, after the convention, it commissioned Pool to prepare three more reports: on Kennedy's image, on Nixon's image, and on foreign policy as a campaign issue. Simulmatics also ran simulations on different ways Kennedy might talk about his Catholicism. He ought to employ "frankness and directness rather than avoidance," Simulmatics advised.[21] Kennedy therefore gave a frank and direct speech in Houston on September 12, 1960: "I believe in an America where the separation of church and state is absolute—where no Catholic prelate would tell the President (should he be Catholic) how to act, and no Protestant minister would tell his parishioners for whom to vote."[22]

Meanwhile, Nixon, without much help from Eisenhower, who snubbed him, won the Republican nomination. Campaigns, Inc., ran his campaign in California. "The great need is to go on the offensive—and to attack," according to the firm's Plan of Campaign, which advised Nixon to forget "the liberal Democrats who wouldn't vote for Nixon if he received the joint personal endorsement of Jesus Christ and Karl Marx via a séance with Eleanor Roosevelt." In the spirit of going on the offensive, Nixon agreed to debate Kennedy on television, in a series of exchanges. "I would like to propose that we transform our circus-atmosphere presidential campaign into a great debate conducted in full view of all the people," Adlai Stevenson had urged in 1959. But it was Kennedy—a man one notable columnist called "Stevenson with balls"—who made it happen.[23]

On September 26, 1960, Nixon and Kennedy met in a bare CBS television studio in Chicago, without an audience; the event was broadcast live by CBS, NBC, and ABC. By now, nearly nine in ten American households had a television set. Nixon was sick; he'd been in the hospital for twelve days. He was in pain. And he was unprepared. A skilled debater who'd enjoyed nothing but political gain from his appearances on television, and, most lately, from the Kitchen Debate, he'd barely been briefed for his appearance with Kennedy.[24]

The rules were the result of strenuous negotiating. The very scheduling required Congress to temporarily suspend an FCC regulation that required giving equal time to all presidential candidates (there were hundreds). Much negotiation involved seemingly little things. Nixon wanted no reaction shots; he wanted viewers to see only the fellow who was talking, not the other guy. But Kennedy wanted them, and Kennedy prevailed, with this concession: he agreed to Nixon's stipulation that neither man be shown wiping the sweat from his face. Then there were bigger things. Each candidate made an eight-minute opening statement and a three-minute closing statement. The networks wanted Nixon and Kennedy to question each other; both men refused and instead insisted on taking questions from a panel of reporters, one from each network, a format that is more generally known as a parallel press conference. ABC refused to call what happened that night a "debate," billing it instead as a "joint appearance." Everyone else called it a debate, sixty-six million Americans watched Nixon scowl, and the misnomer stuck.[25]

On October 19, two days before the last of the candidates' four scheduled debates, Martin Luther King Jr. was arrested in Atlanta during a lunch counter sit-in. He'd waited a long time before joining the sit-ins. But now he was in, and he was sentenced to four months of hard labor. Kennedy called King's wife, Coretta Scott King. His brother Robert intervened, and got King out of jail. Nixon, who had a much stronger record on

*The joint appearance between Kennedy and Nixon in 1960 was the first televised general election presidential "debate"; another matchup would not take place until 1976.*

civil rights than Kennedy, did nothing. He later came to believe that this lost him the election, one of the closest elections in American history, Kennedy winning by a hairsbreadth, 34,221,000 to 34,108,000.

Nixon came to believe that the result had been rigged, and he may have been right; there appears to have been Democratic voter fraud in Illinois and Texas. Thirteen-year-old Young Republican Hillary Rodham volunteered to look for evidence of fraud in Chicago. "We won, but they stole it from us," Nixon said.[26]

Nixon blamed Democrats. He blamed black voters. And, above all, he blamed the press.

## II.

**THE YOUNGEST MAN** ever elected president, John F. Kennedy replaced the oldest man ever to hold the office. With his hand resting on a Bible carried across the ocean by his Irish immigrant ancestors, Kennedy looked more like a Hollywood movie star than like any man who had ever occupied the Oval Office. Wearing no overcoat, his every exhale visible in the freezing cold, he proclaimed his inauguration, on January 21, 1961, to mark the beginning of a new era: "the torch has been passed to a new generation of Americans—born in this century, tempered by war, disciplined by a hard and bitter peace, proud of our ancient heritage."[27]

Kennedy had taken that torch from Eisenhower. Three days before the inauguration, Eisenhower had delivered a farewell address in which he issued a dire warning about the U.S.-Soviet arms race. "In the councils of government, we must guard against the acquisition of unwarranted influence, whether sought or unsought, by the military-industrial complex," he said. "Only an alert and knowledgeable citizenry can compel the proper meshing of the huge industrial and military machinery of defense with our peaceful methods and goals, so that security and liberty may prosper together." Kennedy, in his inaugural address, echoed his predecessor: "Neither can two great and powerful groups of nations take comfort from our present course—both sides overburdened by the cost of modern weapons, both rightly alarmed by the steady spread of the deadly atom, yet both racing to alter that uncertain balance of terror that stays the hand of mankind's final war."[28]

One of the first acts of his administration was the announcement of the Peace Corps, in March 1961. But during a presidency that began with hope and ended with tragedy, Kennedy set the nation on a path not to peace but to war. In the world-stage struggle between communism and capitalism, Kennedy was determined to win over third world countries that remained, even if only nominally, uncommitted.[29]

In 1951, eyeing a run for the Senate, Kennedy and his brother Bobby had made a seven-week tour of Asia and the Middle East, stopping in Vietnam. Long colonized by the French and occupied by the Japanese beginning in 1940, Vietnam, led by the Communist revolutionary Ho Chi Minh—the man who'd tried to meet with Wilson at the Paris Peace conference in 1919—had declared its independence at the end of the Second World War, but France had launched a campaign to restore colonial rule. The United States viewed the spread of communism in Southeast Asia with alarm, chiefly for ideological reasons, but geopolitical and economic factors played a role, too. China and the USSR were plainly in the best position to exert influence in Southeast Asia, with its population of 170 million, but every Southeast Asian country that became part of the communist bloc threatened a loss of trade for Japan, which had already lost its trading relationship with China, its largest trading partner. The United States, attempting to exert its own influence in the region, redirected its foreign aid from Europe to Asia and Africa. Between 1949 and 1952, three-quarters of American aid went to Europe; between 1953 and 1957, three-quarters went to the third world; by 1962, nine-tenths did. When Indochina began attempting to overthrow French colonial rule, the United States supported France. The United States had been much admired after the war because of FDR's staunch opposition to colonialism; its aid to France led to growing anti-Americanism. France lost the war in 1954. A treaty divided independent Vietnam at the seventeenth parallel; Ho Chi Minh and the Communist Party came to power in the North and U.S.-backed Catholic nationalist Ngo Dinh Diem in the South. Beginning in 1955, South Vietnam became the site of the largest state-building experiment in the world, training a police force and civil servants, building bridges, roads, and hospitals, under the advice of the Michigan State University Vietnam Advisory Group.[30]

In 1958, Kennedy was among a group of senators who handed out to every colleague a copy of Burdick and Lederer's *The Ugly American*, which told the story of American diplomats and military men stationed in the fictional Asian country of Sarkhan, lost in a mire of misunderstanding and failure. In a factual epilogue, Lederer and Burdick reported "a rising tide of anti-Americanism" around the world arguing that the United States could hardly hope to wield political influence when, for one thing, American ambassadors to Asia did not speak the language. "In the whole of the Arabic world—nine nations—only two ambassadors have language qualifications. In Japan, Korea, Burma, Thailand, Vietnam, Indonesia, and elsewhere, our ambassadors must speak and be spoken to through interpreters."[31]

Notwithstanding Burdick and Lederer's caution, the U.S. government escalated its involvement when, by the late 1950s, a communist insurgency had begun in the South. Many people in Vietnam viewed the 1,500 American researchers and advisers in South Vietnam as an early signal that the United States hoped to place Vietnam under its own colonial rule, even though, by 1960, the American military presence consisted of only 685 American troops.[32]

Kennedy understood Vietnam through the lens of modernization schemes endorsed by intellectuals and above all by MIT's Walt Rostow, whose *Stages of Economic Growth* (1960) helped convince Kennedy to commit more resources to Vietnam. Rostow's MIT friend and colleague Ithiel de Sola Pool, having helped get Kennedy elected, turned to the project of using the tools of Simulmatics to help modernize South Vietnam. Convinced that, with enough data, a computer could simulate an entire social and political system, Pool would eventually earn a $24 million contract from ARPA for a multiyear research project in Vietnam.[33] "Modernizing" South Vietnam meant building roads and airstrips. But guaranteeing the security of those roads and airstrips required sending and training soldiers, because the South Vietnamese were engaged in a war with North Vietnam. By the end of 1963, after Ngo Dinh Diem was murdered in a U.S.-sanctioned coup only three weeks before Kennedy was assassinated, 16,000 American troops were stationed in Vietnam. Eventually, winning the war became the mission.[34]

Meanwhile, Kennedy's administration came close to deploying a nuclear weapon in a nearly catastrophic confrontation with Cuba. Eisenhower's administration had developed a plan by which the United States would support an invasion of Cuba by forces opposed to Fidel Castro. Kennedy approved the plan, but in April 1961, Castro's army destroyed the forces that came ashore at the Bay of Pigs. The following summer, American U2s flying over Cuba detected ballistic missiles capable of reaching the United States. They'd been sent by Khrushchev, the latest move in the worldwide Cold War game of chess. On October 22, 1962, in a televised address, Kennedy revealed the existence of the missiles and argued for action. "The 1930s taught us a clear lesson," he said, "aggressive conduct, if allowed to go unchecked and unchallenged, ultimately leads to war." The navy would quarantine Cuba. "It shall be the policy of this nation to regard any nuclear missile launched from Cuba against any nation in the Western Hemisphere as an attack by the Soviet Union on the United States, requiring a full retaliatory response upon the Soviet Union." Two days later, sixteen of nineteen Soviet ships headed for the American naval blockade turned back. The Soviet premier then sent the White House two entirely different messages: one promising that it would withdraw its missiles from Cuba if the United States would end the blockade; the other saying something sterner. Urged by his advisers to ignore the second message, Kennedy responded to the first message. Khrushchev agreed to withdraw the missiles.[35]

As ever, Cold War confrontations abroad formed the backdrop for civil rights battles at home. To test the U.S. government's guarantee of desegregation in interstate transit, the Congress of Racial Equality

(CORE) sent thirteen trained volunteers, seven blacks and six whites—the Freedom Riders—to ride two buses into and across the Deep South. The riders were mostly students, like John Lewis, a theology student, who, although determined to finish his education, explained that "at this time, human dignity is the most important thing in my life." They left Washington, DC, on May 4. Two days later, thirty-five-year-old Robert Kennedy, the president's brother, gave his first public address as attorney general, at the University of Georgia, throwing down a gauntlet to segregationists. "We will move. . . . You may ask, will we enforce the Civil Rights statutes. The answer is: 'Yes, we will.'"[36]

That promise was soon challenged. Eight days later, in Anniston, Alabama, a white mob attacked the Greyhound bus on which one group of the Freedom Riders had been riding, shattering the windows, slashing the tires, and, finally, burning it. "Let's burn them alive," the mob cried. The riders barely escaped with their lives. A Klan posse was waiting for the second bus when it arrived at a Trailways station in Birmingham. Robert Kennedy ordered that the riders, badly beaten, be evacuated. But CORE decided to send in more riders—students from Nashville. Birmingham police commissioner Eugene "Bull" Connor had his troops meet them at the bus station and put them in jail before they could board the bus—there they were held, without having been charged—while the State of Alabama dared the federal government to act.

"As you know, the situation is getting worse in Alabama," the attorney general reported to the president. He convinced the president to call the governor of Alabama, Democrat John Patterson, who'd supported JFK's campaign in 1960. But Patterson, in a shocking act of defiance, refused to take the call. Before he'd become governor, Patterson, as the state's attorney general, had sought to block the NAACP from doing business; in 1958, he'd won the governor's office with the support of the KKK. Robert Kennedy sent an envoy to Montgomery to meet with the governor. "There's nobody in the whole country that's got the spine to stick up to the goddamned niggers except me," Patterson said to the man from the U.S. Justice Department. Told that if the state would not protect the riders, the president would send in federal troops, the governor reluctantly agreed to provide a police escort for the bus on its trip from Birmingham to Montgomery. But when the bus reached the station in Montgomery, another mob was waiting. John Lewis, the first off the bus, began speaking to a crowd of reporters and photographers, only to pause. "It doesn't look right," he whispered to another rider. Vigilantes hidden in the station emerged and began pummeling the press and setting upon the riders, attacking them with pipes, slugging them with fists, braining them with their own suitcases. When the badly beaten and bandaged Freedom Riders and 1,500 blacks met at the First Baptist Church, next to the Alabama State Capitol, to decide what to do next, 3,000 whites surrounded the church, eventually to be dispersed by the Alabama National Guard. The Freedom Riders decided to keep on, and rode all summer long.[37]

Even as 400 Freedom Riders were arrested in Mississippi, and schoolchildren across the South were beaten at the doors of elementary schools, CORE and SNCC and King's Southern Christian Leadership Council continued to press for integration, pursuing a strategy of nonviolence, but they had to answer, more and more, to activists who favored separation and were willing to use force. Elijah Muhammad, the founder and prophet of the Nation of Islam, a Muslim movement begun in Detroit in the 1930s, had called for a black state. His most eloquent disciple, Malcolm X, had been criticizing King since the mid-1950s. He soon gained a new audience.

Malcolm Little, who'd left a juvenile home in Michigan in 1941 to move in with his half-sister in Boston, had been arrested for armed robbery in 1945, when he was twenty. During his six years in prison, he converted to Islam, studied Greek and Latin, and learned how to debate. "Once my feet got wet," he said, "I was gone on debating."[38] Paroled in 1952, he'd gotten a department store job in Detroit and become one of Elijah Muhammad's most talented and devoted followers. Lecturing in Detroit in 1957, he'd drawn crowds 4,000 strong, and, disobeying a Nation of Islam directive not to talk about electoral politics (or even to register to vote), he'd asked, "What would the role and the position of the Negro be if he had a full voting voice?" He'd also drawn the attention of the press, having been featured in *The Hate That Hate Produced*, a five-part 1959 documentary narrated by CBS News's Mike Wallace and reported by the African American television journalist Louis Lomax. (Appalled by the documentary, which he considered delusional to the point of inciting hysteria, Malcolm X compared it to Orson Welles's 1938 adaptation of *The War of the Worlds*.) In the early 1960s, in a series of college-sponsored debates, Malcolm X had taken on integrationists. In 1961, as the Nation of Islam's national spokesman, he debated Bayard Rustin at Howard University and James Farmer, the head of CORE, at Cornell. Farmer, who had spent forty days in jail during the Freedom Ride campaign, insisted on the importance of nonviolent struggle. But Malcolm X had little use for SNCC, CORE, and least of all, SCLC. "Anybody can sit," he liked to say. "It takes a man to stand."[39]

He first reached a national audience in 1962, after police in Los Angeles gunned down seven black Muslims, members of Mosque No. 27—a mosque Malcolm X had organized in the 1950s—who were loading dry cleaning into a car. Ronald X Stokes, a Korean war veteran, was shot with both hands raised. Malcolm X, speaking at a rally, framed the killings in racial, not religious, terms. "It's not a Muslim fight," he said. "It's a black man's fight."[40]

Many in the black community called for armed self-defense, the argument of *Negroes with Guns*, published in 1962. King, preaching Christianity and a sanctified democracy, lamented that black Muslims had "lost faith in America." Meanwhile, white moderates urged SNCC, CORE, and SCLC to slow down. In one poll, 74 percent of whites, but only 3 percent of blacks, agreed with the statement "Negroes are moving too fast."[41]

In April 1963, King led a protest in Birmingham, part of a long-planned campaign in the most violent city in the South. Of the more than two hundred black churches and homes that had been bombed in the South since 1948, more bombs had gone off in Birmingham than in any other city. King had gone to Birmingham to get arrested, but found that support for his planned protest had ebbed. After white liberal clergymen denounced him in the *Birmingham News*, calling the protests "untimely," King wrote a letter from jail, in solitary confinement. He began writing in the margins of the newspaper, adding passages on slips of paper smuggled in by visitors. In the end, the letter reached twenty pages, a soaring piece of American political rhetoric, testament to the urgency of a cause.

"Perhaps it is easy for those who have never felt the stinging darts of segregation to say, 'Wait,'" he conceded, "but when you have seen vicious mobs lynch your mothers and fathers at will and drown your sisters and brothers at whim; when you have seen hate-filled policemen curse, kick and even kill your black brothers and sisters; when you see the vast majority of your twenty million Negro brothers smothering in an airtight cage of poverty in the midst of an affluent society . . . then you will understand why we find it difficult to wait."[42]

George Wallace, Alabama's new governor, more or less answered that King would have to wait until hell froze. In June, Wallace said that if black students tried to enter the campus of the state university in Tuscaloosa, he'd block the door himself.

Wallace, forty-three, ate politics for breakfast, lunch, and dinner; he slept politics and he breathed politics and he smoked politics. He'd been a page in the state senate in 1935, when he was sixteen. At the University of Alabama, he'd been both a star boxer and class president. After studying law, he'd served as an airman in the Pacific during the war. He ran for state congress in 1946, the same year Nixon and Kennedy won seats in the U.S. House of Representatives. A loyal southerner, he'd never been a particularly ardent segregationist. As an alternate at the 1948 Democratic convention, he'd refused to bolt with the rest of the Dixiecrats. He'd endorsed Stevenson. But in 1958, running for governor with "Win with Wallace" as his motto, flanked by Confederate flags, he'd lost the Democratic primary to Patterson, who was more ardently opposed to desegregation; and, as the story goes, Wallace had pledged to his supporters, "No other son of a bitch will out-nigger me again." In 1962, with a speechwriter who doubled as an organizer for the KKK, Wallace had won the governorship, with 96 percent of the vote. In his inaugural in Montgomery, delivered a week before Kennedy was inaugurated in Washington, Wallace stood in the shadow of a statue of the president of the Confederacy, who'd been sworn in on that very spot. "Today I have stood, where once Jefferson Davis stood, and took an oath to my people," Wallace shouted. "And I say, segregation now, segregation tomorrow, segregation forever." He'd followed by meeting with educational leaders in the state and telling them: "If you agree to integrate your schools, there won't be enough state troopers to protect you." In May, when Kennedy celebrated his birthday, his staff gave him a pair of boxing gloves, for his upcoming bout with the heavyweight from Alabama.[43] But when the day came, on June 11, Wallace gave in only three hours after the arrival of the National Guard.

That afternoon, King telegrammed Kennedy that "the Negro's endurance may be at the breaking point." Kennedy, who had been deliberating for months, went to Congress to meet with House members. He decided the time had come to speak to the public. On television that night, he addressed the nation: "If an American, because his skin is dark, cannot eat lunch in a restaurant open to the public; if he cannot send his children to the best public school available; if he cannot vote for the public officials who represent him; if, in short, he cannot enjoy the full and free life which all of us want, then who among us would be content to have the color of his skin changed and stand in his place?" He talked about military service. "When Americans are sent to Viet-Nam or West Berlin, we do not ask for whites only." He invoked history. "One hundred years of delay have passed since President Lincoln freed the slaves, yet their heirs, their grandsons, are not fully free." And he asked Congress for new civil rights legislation.[44] One hundred years had been too long. No longer would Kennedy counsel patience.

To mark the one hundredth anniversary of the Emancipation Proclamation, Bayard Rustin had been charged with planning a March on Washington, scheduled for August 1963. The Kennedy administration, worried about violence, had arranged for military troops to be kept on alert. The District of Columbia had canceled two Washington Senators baseball games. Some 300,000—the largest crowd ever gathered between the Lincoln Memorial and the Washington Monument—assembled on a cloudless summer's day, "this sweltering summer of the Negro's legitimate discontent," King called it. They came by bus and train and subway. One young man roller-skated all the way from Chicago, wearing a sash that read "Freedom." But Rustin had organized the march flawlessly and, by the time it was over, there would be only four march-related arrests; all the arrested were white. [45]

SNCC chairman John Lewis, earnest and only twenty-three, approached the microphone on the makeshift stage on the steps of the Lincoln Memorial. He said he supported the proposed civil rights bill but with great reservations, because there was so much that the federal government had failed to do at every turn. The crowd stirred each time he spoke his speech's refrain: "What did the federal government *do*?"

Television stations that had cut away from earlier speeches resumed coverage when Martin Luther King rose to the stage. It was the first time most Americans had seen King deliver an entire speech. It was the first time that President Kennedy had ever seen King deliver an entire speech.[46]

He began by welcoming "the greatest demonstration for freedom in the history of the nation," honoring Lincoln and the Emancipation Proclamation, and condemning "the manacles of segregation and the chain of discrimination" that still shackled blacks one hundred years later. He spoke slowly and solemnly and formally. The Declaration of Independence and the Constitution were promissory notes, he said, a promise that all men would be guaranteed their rights. "It is obvious today that America has defaulted on this promissory note." It was stock stuff, delivered sternly, and loaded with sorrow. He cautioned the movement about the dangers of the "marvelous new militancy," the loss of the support of whites. He listed grievances. Ten minutes into the speech, his voice rising, he said, "We are not satisfied and will not be satisfied until justice rolls down like waters and righteousness like a mighty stream." He looked down at the cumbersome next lines of his speech—"And so today, let us go back to our communities as members of the international association for the advancement of creative dissatisfaction"—and left them unsaid. Instead, he began to preach. Mahalia Jackson, behind him on the platform, called out "Tell 'em about the dream, Martin." He paused, for an instant. "I still have a dream," he said. "It is a dream deeply rooted in the American dream. I have a dream that one day this nation will rise up and live out the true meaning of its creed: 'We hold these truths to be self-evident, that all men are created equal.'" He found his rhythm, and the depth of his voice, and the spirit of Scripture. "I have a dream today," he said, shaking his head. "I have a dream that one day every valley shall be exalted." The crowd rose, and bowed their heads, and wept. "Let freedom ring!" he cried.[47] It was as if every bell in every tower in every city and town and village had rung: a toll of justice.

# III.

THREE MONTHS LATER, Kennedy was assassinated in Dallas. Less than five years after that, King himself would be shot and killed in Memphis. By then, the dreams of American liberals had been felled in a hail of bullets and a trail of napalm bombs that rained down on the world from the streets of Newark and Detroit to the rice paddies of South Vietnam.

The long arc of American liberalism that began with the inauguration of FDR in 1933 reached its peak, and began its decline, during the
administration of LBJ. Roosevelt pursued a New Deal; Truman promised a Fair Deal; Johnson talked about a Better Deal until he decided
that made him sound like a footnote. He aimed for nothing less than
a Great Society. A great society was more than an affluent society; it
was also a good society, "a place where men are more concerned with
the quality of their goals than the quantity of their goods." Said the
president, "The Great Society rests on abundance and liberty for all. It
demands an end to poverty and racial injustice, to which we are totally
committed in our time."[48]

The day after Kennedy's assassination, Johnson met with Walter
Heller, chairman of the Council of Economic Advisers, and told him that,
contrary to his reputation as a conservative, he was not one. "If you look
at my record, you would know I'm a Roosevelt New Dealer. As a matter
of fact, to tell the truth, John F. Kennedy was a little too conservative to
suit my taste." In his first address to Congress, on November 27, 1963, he
urged action on civil rights. "We have talked long enough in this country about equal rights," he said. "We have talked for one hundred years
or more. It is time now to write the next chapter, and to write it in the
books of law." Johnson always said his slogan was "He gets things done."
He wanted to further Kennedy's agenda, and he had his own agenda, an
"unconditional war on poverty," which he announced in his first State of
the Union address, in January 1964. [49]

Johnson once told reporters, "When I was young, poverty was so common that we didn't know it had a name." But, as Galbraith had pointed
out in *The Affluent Society*, poverty hadn't been eradicated; it had only
been forgotten. "Few things are more evident in modern social history
than the decline of interest in inequality as an economic issue," Galbraith
wrote. "Inequality has ceased to preoccupy men's minds." Some of the
poor were far away from the cities and the suburbs: one-fourth of those
who lived below the "poverty line" worked on farms. In the Kennedy
administration, the War on Poverty had its origins in January 1963, after
Kennedy read a long essay by Dwight Macdonald in *The New Yorker*, "Our
Invisible Poor." No piece of prose did more to make plain the atrocity of
poverty in an age of affluence. Prosperity, Macdonald argued, had left

*Johnson, here touching down in the presidential helicopter
in rural Appalachia, made a Poverty Tour in 1964 to see
what Dwight Macdonald called "our invisible poor."*

the nation both blinded to the plight of the poor and indifferent to their suffering. "There is a monotony about the injustices suffered by the poor that perhaps accounts for the lack of interest the rest of society shows in them," Macdonald wrote, in a scathing indictment of the attitude of the American middle class toward those less well off. "Everything seems to go wrong with them. They never win. It's just boring."[50]

Heller had given Kennedy a copy of Macdonald's article. In February 1963, the entire text of the article had been entered into the *Congressional Record*. Johnson, leveraging the nation's sympathy for the martyred president, pressed Congress for legislation. The next year, he signed the Economic Opportunity Act and the Food Stamp Act. He believed poverty would be eradicated within a decade.

He had more ambitions, too. Wrangling congressmen like cattle, as ever, he secured passage of the Civil Rights Act, which outlawed discrimination based on race, color, religion, sex, or national origin; gave the attorney general power to enforce desegregation; allowed for civil rights cases to move from state to federal courts; and expanded the Civil Rights Commission. "No memorial oration or eulogy could more eloquently honor President Kennedy's memory than the earliest possible passage of the civil rights bill for which he fought so long," Johnson said, in a canny piece of political rhetoric. [51]

Both Martin Luther King and Malcolm X went to Washington to watch the congressional debates over the civil rights bill, a rare bringing together of the two men. Malcolm X had fallen out with the leadership of the Nation of Islam. He'd mocked the August 1963 March on Washington but, disobeying the explicit orders of Elijah Muhammad, had attended anyway. In December, he'd answered reporters who asked him to comment on Kennedy's assassination—despite specific instructions from Muhammad not to speak on the subject. He said Kennedy's assassination sounded to him like "chickens coming home to roost." In the ensuing controversy, Muhammad had ordered Malcolm X to withdraw from all public activity, but in April 1964, having advocated that black men arm themselves, he delivered in Cleveland a speech called "The Ballot or the Bullet," in which he argued that revolution required elections.[52] That vantage had brought him to the halls of Congress.

The congressional debates that Malcolm X and Martin Luther King watched revealed fractures within both parties, with Democrats challenged by their southern flank and Republicans by their Right flank. "I'm not anti-Democrat," Malcolm X said. "I'm not anti-Republican. I'm not anti-anything. I'm just questioning their sincerity." The point is, he said, the time had come to vote.[53] The debates also revealed the worst of American political chicanery. Southern Democrats filibustered for fifty-four days. Strom Thurmond said that the "so-called Civil Rights Proposals, which the President has sent to Capitol Hill for enactment into law, are unconstitutional, unnecessary, unwise and extend beyond the realm of reason."[54] A segregationist from Virginia, Howard Smith, introduced an amendment adding the word "sex" into the bill, a proposal so ridiculous that he was certain it would spell the legislation's defeat. But after Maine Republican Margaret Chase Smith's spirited defense of the amendment, it passed—a momentous if ironic achievement in the battle for equality for women.[55]

Meanwhile, George Wallace, running for the 1964 Democratic nomination, did surprisingly well in early primaries. On the campaign trail, he heard from white voters whose expressions of deep-rooted racial animosity were part of a backlash that would only gain force. At a Wallace rally in Milwaukee, a man named Bronko Gruber said, about the city's blacks, "They beat up old ladies 83-years-old, rape our womenfolk. They mug people. They won't work. They are on relief. How long can we tolerate this? Did I go to Guadalcanal and come back to something like this?"[56]

Wallace's bid for the nomination was ended, not by Johnson's popularity, but by the entry into the race of a conservative Republican. Barry Goldwater, a far right conservative Republican from Arizona, voted against the civil rights bill, making clear that he did so on constitutional grounds alone. "If my vote is misconstrued," he said, "let it be, and let me suffer its consequences."[57] Supporters of the bill eventually broke the filibuster, and on July 2, 1964, Johnson signed the Civil Rights Act into law. Eleven days later, the Republican National Convention met in the Cow Palace, in Daly City, California, and nominated Goldwater as its candidate for president.

In 1960, Goldwater had published a ghostwritten manifesto, *The Conscience of a Conservative*, that had become a best seller. His positions, at the time, occupied the very margin of American political discourse. He called for the abolition of the graduated income tax and recommended that the federal government abandon most of its functions, closing departments and diminishing staffs at a rate of 10 percent a year. Goldwater also opposed the Supreme Court's decision in *Brown v. Board*, insisting on states' rights, a position that aligned him with southern Democrats and also with John Birchers, whose goals included impeaching Earl Warren and withdrawing the United States from the United Nations. Their leader, Robert Welch, had gone so far as to suggest that Eisenhower might be a communist agent; some Birchers believed Sputnik was a hoax. Birchers especially hated Kennedy. Right-wing radio commentator Tom Anderson said in Jackson, Mississippi, "Our menace is not the Big Red Army from without, but the Big Pink Enemy within. Our menace is the KKK—Kennedy, Kennedy, and Kennedy."[58]

Conspiracy theorists who believed Eisenhower was a communist looked like an easy target, and some Kennedy advisers, including Arthur Schlesinger Jr., had urged him to tie the Republican Party to the John Birch Society. In 1961, Kennedy began talking about the "right wing" of the GOP. Daniel Bell, in *The New American Right*, had argued that the "right wing" was fighting nothing so much as modernity itself. Moderate

Republicans, too, had energetically attacked Goldwater. New York governor Nelson Rockefeller warned that a "lunatic fringe" might "subvert the Republican party itself."[59] A matchup between Kennedy and Goldwater would have been interesting. Kennedy, who'd had much success debating Nixon in 1960, had apparently agreed to debate Goldwater if he won the Republican nomination in 1964. Goldwater later said that he and Kennedy had planned to cross the country together, debating at every whistle-stop, "without Madison Avenue, without any makeup or phoniness, just the two of us traveling around on the same airplane."[60]

But Johnson had no reason to agree to debate Goldwater, whose chances of winning the nomination seemed remote. Rockefeller, vying with Goldwater for the nomination, painted him as a Nazi. (In fact, Goldwater had Jewish ancestry.) Liberals said much the same. "We see dangerous signs of Hitlerism in the Goldwater campaign," said Martin Luther King. At the Republican National Convention, Margaret Chase Smith, who sought the nomination herself—the first woman to run for a major-party nomination—refused to release her delegates to Goldwater, in order to prevent him from gaining a unanimous vote.[61]

Richard Nixon did not share Smith's principles. He'd run unsuccessfully for governor of California in 1962 and, having lost two elections in two years, he was in no position to seek the presidential nomination himself. Nevertheless, he set up a clandestine campaign, headquartered in a boiler room in Portland, Oregon. He considered his options. He toyed with running. He toyed with joining the moderate GOP's stop Goldwater campaign. And he toyed with supporting Michigan governor George Romney. When he finally concluded that he had no chance of beating Goldwater, he threw his support behind him. Accepting the party's nomination, Goldwater defended himself against the charge of extremism in language that lost him what little support he might have hoped to enjoy from party moderates. "Extremism in the defense of liberty is no vice," Goldwater said. And "moderation in the pursuit of justice is no virtue." Rockefeller and Romney refused to campaign for Goldwater. Nixon, with his eye on 1968, exerted himself tirelessly: he gave 156 speeches on behalf of the party's nominee.[62]

Johnson was tickled. "In Your Heart, You Know He's Right" was Goldwater's slogan, to which Johnson's campaign answered, "In Your Guts, You Know He's Nuts" or, alluding to Goldwater's enthusiasm for deploying nuclear weapons, "In Your Heart, You Know He Might." Goldwater had campaigned for a constitutional amendment to guarantee Bible reading and prayer in public schools, but Johnson, who had broad support among evangelical Christians, made sure Goldwater had little success with that constituency. Days before the election, Billy Graham's followers urged him to throw his support behind Goldwater, sending him more than a million telegrams and tens of thousands of letters. Johnson pounced. "Billy, you stay out of politics," he told Graham in a phone call, and then invited him to stay the weekend at the White House—far from his mail.[63]

In November, Goldwater lost to Johnson by more than sixteen million votes, winning only his home state of Arizona and five states in the Deep South. So catastrophic was the loss that GOP leaders attempted to purge conservatives from leadership positions with the party. That meant purging conservative women.

Goldwater's nomination had been crucially supported by Phyllis Schlafly, a former Kitchen Kabineter who was president of the National Federation of Republican Women. Born in Missouri in 1924, Schlafly would become one of the most influential women in the history of American politics. During the Second World War, she'd worked as a gunner, test-firing rifles in a munitions plant, to put herself through college, after which she'd earned a graduate degree in political science from Radcliffe. A devout Catholic, she had been an ardent supporter of McCarthy; her husband was president of the World Anti-Communist League. In 1952, she'd run for Congress under the slogan "A Woman's Place Is in the House."[64]

In 1963, Schlafly had nominated Goldwater as the speaker at a celebration of the twenty-fifth anniversary of the federation of Republican women's clubs. During that celebration, she'd also taken a straw poll: out of 293 federation delegates, 262 chose Goldwater as the party's nominee. Conservative women had flocked to the Goldwater campaign's "Crusade for Law and Morality" and to Mothers for Moral America, a fake grassroots organization that recruited Nancy Reagan to its board. But while conservative women had supported Goldwater, the mainstream of the Republican Party had not. The 1964 presidential election was the first in which as many women voted as men. They also voted differently than men. Overall, across parties, women were even more likely to vote against Goldwater than were men. Goldwater Republican women, it seemed, were out of touch not only with the party but with the country.

After Goldwater's ignominious defeat, Elly Peterson, a Michigan party chairman and Romney supporter, set herself the task of keeping Schlafly from the presidency of the National Federation of Republican Women at its next election. This proved difficult, Peterson said, because "the nut fringe is beautifully organized." Schlafly was narrowly defeated, but she contested the results, and police had to remove women from the convention floor when they began attacking one another. The "dame game," *Time* said, had become altogether unladylike.[65]

Schlafly was not so easily defeated. She would never have called herself a feminist, but she believed women should be helping to lead the GOP. "Many men in the Party frankly want to keep the women doing the menial work, while the selection of candidates and the policy decisions are taken care of by the men in the smoke-filled rooms," she complained. The book she wrote about her ouster includes an illustration of a woman standing at a door labeled Republican Party Headquarters, by a sign that reads "Conservatives and Women Please Use Servants' Entrance." Three months after she was kept from the presidency of the women's arm of the GOP, she began writing a monthly newsletter, waging her own crusade for law and morality.[66] It would take her years, but, in the end, she would retake the Republican Party.

Lumbering Lyndon Johnson, flushed with victory, decided to use his sixteen-million-vote margin to shoot for the moon. He had a big Democratic majority in the House, what's known as a fat Congress. He knew his mandate wouldn't last. "Just by the way people naturally think and because Barry Goldwater has simply scared the hell out of them, I've already lost about three of those sixteen," he told his staff in January 1965. "After a fight with Congress or something else, I'll lose another couple of million. I could be down to eight million in a couple of months."[67]

Johnson headed what political scientists call a unified government, in which the executive and legislative branches are controlled by the same party, as opposed to a divided government, in which one party controls the White House and the other Congress. Unified governments and divided governments have legislative agendas of roughly the same size, but unified governments, unsurprisingly, are more productive than divided governments: they get more of their bills passed. Still, no unified government in American history was as productive as LBJ's.[68]

Johnson, who'd begun his career in Washington in 1937, understood

*Johnson applied "The Treatment" to Abe Fortas in July 1965, the month before Fortas took a seat on the Supreme Court.*

the nature of political power better than nearly every other American president. He met with leaders of Congress every week for breakfast. He called senators in the middle of the night. He cajoled and he threatened and he made trades and he made deals. He got Congress to pass an education act, providing millions of dollars to support low-income elementary and high school students. He convinced Congress to amend the Social Security Act to establish Medicare, health insurance for the elderly, and Medicaid, health coverage for the poor—"care for the sick and serenity for the fearful"—and he then flew to Independence, Missouri, so that Truman could witness the signing. "You have made me a very, very happy man," said a deeply moved Truman.[69]

The flurry of bills was hardly limited to social reform. Johnson also persuaded Congress to pass a tax bill, a tax cut that had been introduced into Congress before Kennedy's assassination, the largest tax cut in American history. He hoped it would relieve unemployment. Instead, it undermined his reform programs. It was as if he'd cut off one of his own feet.

"I want to turn the poor from tax eaters to taxpayers," Johnson said, selling his tax cut to Congress. In this formulation, recipients of social programs like Aid to Families with Dependent Children (AFDC), created in 1935, and Medicaid, created in 1965, were the tax eaters. Recipients of other kinds of federal assistance (Medicare, veterans' benefits, farm subsidies) were the taxpayers. By making this distinction, 1960s liberals crippled liberalism. The architects of the War on Poverty, like the New Dealers before them, never defended a broad-based progressive income tax as a public good, in everyone's interest; nor could they separate it from issues of race. They also never referred to Social Security, health care, and unemployment insurance as "welfare." Johnson's Council of Economic Advisers told him that when explaining how the government might fight poverty, he ought to "avoid completely the use of the term 'inequality' or the term 'redistribution.'" The poor were to be referred to as "targets of opportunity."[70]

At first, the tax cut worked: people used the money they once used to pay taxes to buy goods. In 1965, *Time* put Keynes on the cover and announced, "We Are All Keynesians Now."[71] But, as with everything Johnson did, his economic reforms were demolished by his escalation of the war in Vietnam.

When Kennedy died, Robert Kennedy had pressed Johnson not to abandon Vietnam, which had been Johnson's inclination. By the spring of 1965, Johnson had come to understand that he couldn't withdraw without losing, and he didn't want to lose. "I am not going to be the President who saw Southeast Asia go the way China went," he said. In March 1965, the United States began to bomb North Vietnam; that spring Johnson committed to ground forces. But because he didn't want to abandon his domestic agenda, he decided to conceal the escalation. He lied about American involvement, and his administration lied about the war itself. By the end of the year, there were 184,000 troops in Vietnam. College students managed to avoid the draft. Disproportionately, American troops in Vietnam were poor whites and blacks. Johnson deliberately hid the cost of the war. Eventually, paying for the war would require raising taxes. To postpone that inevitability for as long as possible, he cut funding for his social programs. "That bitch of a war," he later said, "killed the lady I really loved—the Great Society." Even as the president insisted that "this is not Johnson's war, this is America's war," protesters chanted, "Hey, hey, LBJ, how many kids did you kill today?"[72]

Johnson, elected in a landslide in 1964, would be so unpopular by 1968 that he'd decide not to run for a second term. And liberalism would

*Americans watched the war in Vietnam*
*from their living rooms.*

be so shattered by Johnson's compromises, by the rise of the New Left, by race riots, by the antiwar movement, by white backlash, and by the Right's calls for law and order, that Nixon would gain the prize he'd been eyeing since his days on the high school debate team in Whittier, California: the White House.

# IV.

"**THERE ARE MORE NEGROES** IN JAIL WITH ME THAN THERE ARE ON THE VOTING ROLLS," read an ad placed in the *New York Times* by the Southern Christian Leadership Conference while Martin Luther King was in prison in Selma, Alabama. Civil rights workers had been trying to register voters in the Deep South for years, without much success. Still, the spirit of protest had spread.

In 1964, Mario Savio, a twenty-one-year-old University of California philosophy major, spent the summer—the Freedom Summer—registering black voters in Mississippi. When he got back to Berkeley that fall, he led a fight against a policy that prohibited political speech on campus by arguing that a public university should be as open for political debate and assembly as a public square. The same right was at stake in both

Mississippi and Berkeley, Savio said: "the right to participate as citizens in a democratic society."[73] After police arrested nearly eight hundred protestors during a sit-in, the university acceded to the students' demands. The principle of allowing political speech on campus was afterward extended from public universities to private ones. Without this principle, students wouldn't have been able to rally on campus for civil rights or against the war in Vietnam, or for or against anything else, then or since.

But the fight for a democratic society divided the Left. When the civil rights movement turned its attention from desegregation to voting rights, it splintered. The fight for voting rights also hit a wall with the Democratic Party. Contesting the Democratic Party's all-white delegation to the party's nominating convention, SNCC set up an alternative party, the Mississippi Freedom Democratic Party. Ella Baker ran its Washington office and delivered the keynote speech at its state nominating convention in Jackson. At the Democratic Party's August 1964 convention in Atlantic City, party leaders refused to seat the Mississippi Freedom Democratic Party delegation. Stokely Carmichael decided to give up on party politics. Carmichael, who'd been a Freedom Rider in 1961, graduated from Howard University in 1964 with a degree in philosophy and was nominated for a Senior Class Humanity Award for his work registering voters in Mississippi; he'd been arrested half a dozen times. "The liberal Democrats are just as racist as Goldwater," he concluded. Borrowing the word "black" from Malcolm X, Carmichael urged a new militancy. "If we can't sit at the table," said one leader of SNCC, "let's knock the fucking legs off." King, and the SCLC, still favored working with white liberals; SNCC, increasingly, favored black consciousness and black power. Selma would be their last stand together.[74]

In January 1965, one hundred years after Congress passed the Thirteenth Amendment, Johnson delivered his inaugural address in Washington, and King went to Selma, where demonstrators had pledged to march all the way to Montgomery, a fifty-five-mile journey that would take them through a county whose population was more than 70 percent black but where hardly any African Americans had so much as attempted to vote since the rise of Jim Crow. On March 7, 1965, they met five hundred Alabama state troopers stationed on the far side of the Pettus Bridge, ordered by George Wallace to arrest anyone who tried to cross.

Malcolm X, who had by now been denounced by the Nation of Islam, flew to Selma. Though SCLC leaders worried that he'd incite violence, he spoke in support of the protesters. Only weeks later, his house was firebombed in New York, and, on February 21, he was assassinated in Manhattan by three men from the Nation of Islam armed with pistols and shotguns. He was shot ten times, once in the ankle, twice in the leg, and seven times in the chest.[75] "I disagreed with him," James Baldwin said, deeply shaken. "But when he talked to the people in the streets," he went on, "if one ignored his conclusions, he was the only person who was describing, making vivid, making a catalog, of the actual situation of the American Negro."[76]

Johnson, pressured by the televised spectacle of Alabama state troopers cracking the skulls of civil rights marchers in Selma as they repeatedly tried to cross the bridge, addressed Congress on March 15. "At times, history and fate meet at a single time in a single place to shape a turning point in man's unending search for freedom," he said. "So it was at Lexington and Concord. So it was a century ago at Appomattox. So it was last week in Selma, Alabama." Calling on Congress to pass a Voting Rights Act, he closed, with his trademark Texas twang: "And we shall overcome." King, watching in Alabama, fell to weeping.[77]

The week before Johnson sent Congress the Voting Rights Act, he'd sent Congress the Law Enforcement Assistance Act, saying he wanted 1965 to be remembered as "the year when this country began a thorough, intelligent, and effective war against crime." The creation of the Law Enforcement Assistance Administration, which funded eighty thousand crime control projects, vastly expanded the police powers of the federal government. "For some time, it has been my feeling that the task of law enforcement agencies is really not much different from military forces; namely, to deter crime before it occurs, just as our military objective is deterrence of aggression," the chair of the Senate Judiciary Committee had said during hearings over the bill. After Johnson signed the act into law, his administration opened a "war on crime," a war in which the police were empowered to act like a military force, using helicopters to patrol city neighborhoods and computer simulations to anticipate crime. Money that had gone to cities for antipoverty measures was used to fight crime. After-school programs and teen centers, instituted as elements of the war on poverty under Johnson, would come, under Nixon, beginning in 1969, to be run by police, elements of the war on crime. More Americans would be sent to prison in the twenty years after LBJ launched his war on crime than went to prison in the entire century before. Blacks and Latinos, 25 percent of the U.S. population, would make up 59 percent of the prison population, in a nation whose incarceration rate would rise to five times that of any other industrial nation. Dismantling the parts of Johnson's program that were aimed to provide services to children and teenagers, Nixon would leave intact only the parts of the program that were aimed to punish them. Running the Great Society became the work of police. Block grants for urban renewal were used, instead, to build prisons. James Baldwin said urban renewal ought to be called "Negro removal."[78]

On August 6, 1965, Johnson signed the Voting Rights Act into law. But the quiet that Johnson had anticipated did not come. The next day, the House Committee on Education and Labor held hearings in Los Angeles's Will Rogers Park Auditorium to find out why the city had failed to implement federal antipoverty programs. A thousand people came; the hearings turned into a rally. Four days later, riots broke out in South Central Los Angeles, in Watts, the first in a series of riots that would shock the nation over four long, hot summers.

King flew to Los Angeles and preached nonviolence; no one really listened. The population density in the city of Los Angeles, outside of Watts, was 5,900 per square mile; in Watts, it was 16,400. The uprising lasted for six days and nights and involved more than 35,000 people. Thirty-four people were killed and nearly a thousand injured as the streets burned. Army tanks and helicopters turned an American city into a war zone. L.A. police chief William Parker said that fighting the people of Watts was "very much like fighting the Viet Cong."[79] Johnson asked, "Is the world topsy-turvy?"[80]

Watts, a neighborhood twice the size of Manhattan, had not a single hospital. An affluent society? Watts was an indigent society. From the outside, it looked as if rights had been answered with riots, as if the entire project of liberalism were collapsing in on itself.

Each riot over those four summers stood alone, but each began with police violence, in a segregated neighborhood in a northern city, where there were hardly any jobs, where the houses were falling down, where the right to vote hadn't ended anyone's misery. In Newark, the biggest city in New Jersey, where the population was 65 percent black, eighteen babies died at the City Hospital in a single year—of diarrhea—in a hospital infested by bats. And yet arguments that the federal government had failed cities like Newark were met with objections: the federal government had spent more on antipoverty programs per capita in Newark than in any other northern city.[81]

Violence begat violence. In the riots that began in Newark in the summer of 1967, police brutality led to protest, which led to looting, which led to shooting. A 4,000-strong force of National Guard sealed off fourteen square miles of the city with roadblocks. In the scenes broadcast on television screens across the country, Newark looked to some American viewers like Vietnam, a mayhem of snipers, of civilians slaughtered. A week and a half later, in riots in Detroit, more than 7,000 people were arrested and more than 2,000 buildings destroyed before order was enforced by 9,600 paratroopers from the 101st and Eighty-Second Airborne Divisions.[82] That summer, a headline on page one of *U.S. News & World Report* read: IS THE U.S. ABLE TO GOVERN ITSELF?[83]

Conservatives had an answer: they could govern with a will of iron. Ronald Reagan, fifty-five and running for governor of California, declared the riots the result of the "philosophy that in any situation the public should turn to government for the answer." Liberalism caused the riots, Reagan suggested, and only conservatism could end them.

Reagan, a man of charm and grace, as dapper as a groom, grew up in Illinois, the son of a shoe salesman who supported his family during the Depression through the largesse of the New Deal. Young Reagan, an ardent Democrat, memorized FDR's speeches, those intimate, confident fireside chats. After graduating from a Christian college, Reagan began working as a radio broadcaster and sports announcer. He turned to film in 1937. During the war, he made films for the Office of War Information. A reliable B-movie actor, widely trusted, in 1947 he was elected president of the Screen Actors Guild, where he was an anticommunist crusader. In 1952, he began supporting Republican candidates. He registered as a Republican in 1962, and by 1964, supporting Goldwater, he'd become a Sun Belt conservative, convert to a new cause.

Other politicians railed; Reagan wooed. In a half-hour televised endorsement for Goldwater, a speech called "A Time for Choosing," Reagan's promise as a politician all but oozes out of the screen. For Reagan, the issue in the 1964 election, as in every election afterward, was a recasting of Alexander Hamilton's question in Federalist 1 in 1787. Reagan asked not whether a people can rule themselves by reason and choice instead of accident and force but "whether we believe in our capacity for self-government or whether we abandon the American Revolution and confess that a little intellectual elite in a far distant capital can plan our lives for us better than we can plan them ourselves."[84] Not reason versus force, but the people versus the government.

Conservative and moderate Republicans didn't agree on much, but they did agree that liberalism was to blame for the violence. King had cried, at the end of the march from Selma to Alabama, "How long? Not long. Because no lie can live forever." In 1966, former college football star Gerald Ford, then the House Republican leader, turned that "how long" around, asking, "How long are we going to abdicate law and order—the backbone of our civilization—in favor of a soft social theory that the man who heaves a brick through your window or tosses a fire bomb into your car is simply the misunderstood and underprivileged product of a broken home?" Reagan went further. "Working men and women should not be asked to carry the additional burden of a segment of society capable of caring for itself but which prefers making welfare a way of life, freeloading at the expense of more conscientious citizens," he said, inciting a racial animosity that came to be known as not backlash but "whitelash."[85]

To run his 1966 gubernatorial campaign, Reagan had hired the California political consulting firm of Spencer-Roberts. The heyday of Whitaker and Baxter had ended; Whitaker died in 1961. But Spencer-Roberts used the Whitaker and Baxter rulebook. "You know something, Stu?" Reagan said to Stuart Spencer. "Politics is just like show business. . . . You begin with a hell of an opening, you coast for a while, and you end with a hell of a closing."[86]

On the stump, Reagan found a new target: college students. He complained about undergraduate "malcontents," and, as Election Day neared, he made a point of publicly denouncing invitations issued by students at the University of California, Berkeley, to two speakers: Robert Kennedy, who was slated to talk about civil rights, and Stokely Carmichael, who had been asked by the Students for a Democratic Society (SDS) to deliver the keynote address at a conference on Black Power. "We cannot have the university campus used as a base from which to foment riots," Reagan warned. He sent a telegram to Carmichael, urging him to decline the invitation, suggesting that the appearance in Berkeley of the head of

SNCC would "stir strong emotions," a clever way to guarantee that Carmichael would come.[87]

The FBI, which had been conducting illegal surveillance on and waging campaigns of harassment against hundreds of civil rights activists, including Martin Luther King, had opened a file on Carmichael in 1964, accelerating its collection in 1966, when he started talking about Black Power and police brutality and urging forms of protest later adopted by the Black Lives Matter movement. The month before Carmichael was scheduled to speak at Berkeley, a white police officer in Atlanta shot and killed a black man. Carmichael organized a protest and spoke at a rally that led to two days of unrest. An FBI informant in Atlanta sent an encrypted telegram to J. Edgar Hoover: "CARMICHAEL BELIEVED NEGROES SHOULD FORM VIGILANTE GROUPS TO OBSERVE POLICE AND SHOULD ANY ACTS OF POLICE BRUTALITY BE OBSERVED, A COMMITTEE SHOULD BE FORMED AMONG THE NEGRO ELEMENT TO PRESS SUCH MATTERS." Carmichael was charged with inciting a riot. Hoover stepped up surveillance of what he described as "black nationalist hate-type groups."[88] Released on bail and challenged by Reagan—baited by Reagan—Carmichael headed to California.

Reagan had by now made his opposition to the free speech movement the centerpiece of his gubernatorial campaign, promising to crack down on Berkeley's "noisy, dissident minority." Urged on by UC regent H. R. Haldeman, Reagan talked about student unrest day after day, much to the dismay of his campaign manager, who told him that the issue hadn't left a trace in the polls. "It's going to," Reagan promised.[89] Three weeks before the election, Reagan's campaign advised him that his prospects would improve "if the disorders boil into public prominence again." Carmichael's proposed visit offered Reagan the opportunity to tie his campaign against student protesters to his denunciation of black militancy. After Reagan issued a public call to Carmichael not to come to California and asked his opponent, the incumbent governor Pat Brown, to join him, knowing that Brown would refuse. Carmichael played right into Reagan's hands.[90]

"This is a student conference, as it should be, held on a campus," Carmichael, twenty-five, lean and grave, told a crowd of ten thousand Berkeley students. Echoing Frederick Douglass's 1860 "Plea for Free Speech," Carmichael said that the regulation of speech amounted to a struggle over "whether or not black people will have the right to use the words they want to use without white people giving their sanction." With Carmichael and the New Left, the civil rights movement changed course. "We been saying freedom for six years, and we ain't got nothing,'" Carmichael said in Berkeley. "What we gonna start saying now is Black Power." SNCC's H. Rap Brown, who called LBJ a "white honky cracker," said, "John Brown was the only white man I could respect and he is dead. The Black Movement has no use for white liberals. We need revolutionaries. Revolutions need revolutionaries." Huey Newton, a founder of the Black Panthers, cited Chairman Mao: "Political Power comes through the Barrel of a Gun."[91]

Reagan won in a landslide and, in the congressional midterm elections, twenty-seven of the forty-eight Democrats who'd been swept into office with LBJ in 1964 failed to win reelection. Republicans won nine out of ten new governorships and gained control of statehouses across the country. But the 1966 election wasn't so much a victory of Republicans over Democrats, it was a victory of conservatives over liberals.

Goldwater's star fell; Reagan's rose. The conservative standard-bearer, Reagan was the first national figure to bring the intensity of the Cold War to domestic politics. He served two terms as governor, held on to his conservative convictions, and bided his time while his party moved rightward. He set as his agenda nothing short of dismantling the New Deal.

From the California governor's office, Reagan didn't let up on either the rhetoric of law and order or his denunciation of free speech on college campuses. In May 1967, when the California legislature was debating a gun control measure, thirty Black Panthers, led by Bobby Seale, walked into the California State House, armed with a Magnum, shotguns, and pistols. "Black people have begged, prayed, petitioned, demonstrated, and everything else to get the racist power structure of America to right the wrongs which have historically been perpetuated against black people," Seale said. "The time has come for black people to arm themselves against this terror before it is too late." Reagan, who went on to sign the law, told the press he saw "no reason why on the street today a citizen should be carrying loaded weapons."[92]

Johnson called for a National Advisory Commission on Civil Disorders to investigate the riots. Chaired by Governor Otto Kerner of Illinois, the Kerner Commission issued a 426-page report calling for $30 billion in urban spending and, as conservatives read it, essentially blaming whites for the violence in black neighborhoods. The commission recommended spending more money on public housing, instituting a massive jobs programs, and committing to desegregation of public education. Kerner and his colleagues warned that failing to change course "could quite conceivably lead to a kind of urban *apartheid* with semimartial law in many major cities, enforced residence of Negroes in segregated areas, and a drastic reduction in personal freedom for all Americans, particularly Negroes." Except for a recommendation about expanding urban policing, Johnson ignored it.[93]

With every instance of racial unrest, with each new form of public protest, Reagan's political capital grew. "Free speech does not require furnishing a podium for the speaker," he said in 1967. "I don't think you should lend these people the prestige of our university campuses for the presentation of their views."[94] Later that year, black students at San Jose College, led by a dashiki-wearing sociology professor and former discus thrower named Harry Edwards, filed a protest against racism on campus and threatened to disrupt the opening day football game. Fearing a riot, the college president called off the game—"the first time a football contest in America had been cancelled because of racial unrest," the *Times* reported. Reagan called the cancellation of the game an "appeasement of lawbreakers," declared Edwards unfit to teach, and called for him to be fired. Edwards called Reagan "unfit to govern," and two months later began organizing a nationwide campaign for black athletes to boycott the 1968 Olympics—beginning with an article in the *Saturday Evening Post* called "Why Negroes Should Boycott Whitey's Olympics"—which led to the clenched-fisted Black Power protest of two medal winners (the inspiration, decades later, for NFL protesters who kneeled during the playing of the national anthem).[95]

Meanwhile, outcry against the escalating war in Vietnam galvanized the New Left, and gave a sprawling and mostly disorganized movement both focus and intensity by bringing together the free speech and civil rights movements. In 1966, John Lewis announced SNCC's opposition to the war in Vietnam, and its support for draft dodgers, described by Lewis as "the men in this country who are unwilling to respond to a military draft which would compel them to contribute their lives to United States aggression in Vietnam in the name of the 'freedom' we find so false in this country." At Berkeley, Stokely Carmichael had called on students to burn their draft cards. World champion heavyweight boxer Muhammad Ali refused to fight in Vietnam, asking, "Why should they ask me to put on a uniform and go ten thousand miles from home and drop bombs and bullets on brown people in Vietnam while so-called Negro people in Louisville are treated like dogs?" And the argument against the war grew both broader and deeper when Martin Luther King joined it in 1967, severing his alliance with Johnson by declaring, "We are fighting an immoral war."[96]

Johnson lost himself in the war. Foreign policy had never been his strength. And he found out far too late that The Treatment didn't work on Ho Chi Minh. By 1967, nearly half a million American combat troops were in Vietnam. That year alone, nine thousand Americans died in Vietnam, and the war consumed $25 billion of the federal budget. To pay for it, Johnson, refusing to raise taxes, having only just convinced Congress to push through a tax cut, starved the Great Society. By the time he was finally willing to ask for a tax increase, he was only able to get it by agreeing to still more spending cuts to his antipoverty programs. And by then, inflation had begun to surge, giving credence to economic theories endorsed by conservatives. By 1968, Robert McNamara, Johnson's secretary of defense, and an architect of Johnson's war, no longer willing to continue, resigned.[97]

In January 1968, during Tet, the Vietnamese new year, the North Vietnamese conducted raids all over South Vietnam, including on the U.S. embassy in Saigon. Johnson had claimed that the North Vietnamese were weak and that the war was nearly won. The Tet Offensive exposed the depth of that lie. In March, *New York Times* columnist James Reston declared, "The main crisis is not Vietnam itself, or in the cities, but in the feeling that the political system for dealing with these things has broken down."[98]

While Americans reeled from news reports from Vietnam, the presidential primary season began. LBJ won the Democratic primary in New Hampshire with only 49 percent of the vote. An antiwar candidate, Minnesota congressman Eugene McCarthy had pulled 42 percent. Emboldened by Johnson's narrow win, Robert Kennedy entered the race. Having urged Johnson in 1963 not to withdraw from Vietnam, Kennedy now ran against it as "Johnson's war." George Wallace entered the race, too. Johnson was being squeezed from the left and from the right, both for what was going on in American cities and for what was going on in Vietnam. Nor were the two often considered separately. In 1966, Wallace had been unable to run for reelection as governor of Alabama because of a law of succession, and had his wife, Lurleen, run in his stead (she won by a margin of two to one). In 1968, when George Wallace decided to campaign for the Democratic nomination, Stokely Carmichael, speaking in Birmingham, said that if the army gives a black soldier a gun and "tells him to shoot his enemy . . . if he don't shoot Lurleen and George and little junior, he's a fool."[99] Johnson was even left to campaign against the ghost of Barry Goldwater. A billboard in Chicago that in 1964 had read, "In Your Heart, You Know He's Right" read four years later, "Now You Know He Was Right."[100]

Disgusted and discouraged, Johnson announced on March 31 that he would not run for reelection. He had decided to dedicate himself to ending the war. "With our hopes and the world's hope for peace in the balance every day," he said in a televised address, "I do not believe that I should devote an hour or a day of my time to any personal partisan causes." The stunned *New York Times* ran a can-you-believe-it, three-tier headline:

JOHNSON SAYS HE WON'T RUN;
HALTS NORTH VIETNAM RAIDS;
BIDS HANOI JOIN PEACE MOVES.[101]

But peace would not come; nor would moderation abide. Four days later, on the balcony of a hotel in Memphis, Martin Luther King was shot by a white ex-convict. As word spread, riots broke out in 130 cities. From California, Reagan, granting barely a moment for mourning, declared that King's assassination was part of the "great tragedy that began when we began compromising with law and order, and people started choosing which laws they'd break." Stokely Carmichael announced that "white America killed Dr. King" and in the doing had "declared war on black America." He told a crowd in Washington to "go home and get your guns."[102]

A stricken Robert Kennedy spoke from the back of a flatbed truck in Indianapolis. "What we need in the United States is not division," he said,

*Young men in Central Park, New York, mourned*
*Martin Luther King Jr. following his assassination*
*in Memphis on April 4, 1968.*

nervously grasping at the slip of paper on which he'd hastily scrawled some notes. "What we need in the United States is not hatred; what we need in the United States is not violence and lawlessness, but love and wisdom and compassion toward one another, and a feeling of justice toward those who still suffer within our country, whether they be white or they be black." Two months later, after winning the California primary, Kennedy was shot while leaving the ballroom of a hotel in Los Angeles.[103]

The nation mourned as Job in the desert, fallen to his knees. What more?

## V.

**RICHARD NIXON'S MOMENT** had come. He would repurpose his anticommunism in the form of a new political rhetoric: antiliberalism. As Reagan had done in the California governor's race two years before, he would stake his campaign for the Republican nomination, and for the presidency, on a pledge to restore law and order. "We have been amply warned that we face the prospect of a war in the making in our own society," he said in a radio address on March 7, 1968, days before the New

Hampshire primary. "We have seen the gathering hate, we have heard the threats to burn and destroy. In Watts and Harlem and Detroit and Newark, we have had a foretaste of what the organizations of insurrection are planning for the summer ahead." He promised that, if elected, he would not cower before those threats. In New Hampshire, he received 79 percent of the Republican vote.[104]

Nixon knew that the more violent the riots, and the worse the news from Vietnam, the better his chances. Deciding that peace would bar his road to the White House, he arranged for Anna Chennault, born in China and the widow of a U.S. general, to act as a conduit to promise South Vietnam that it would get better peace terms if it waited until after the election, and a Nixon victory. Johnson heard rumors about the arrangement, called Nixon, and confronted him. Nixon, lying, denied it. Johnson failed to negotiate a peace; the fighting would last for five more years, at a cost of countless lives. By the time the bombing ended, in 1973, the United States dropped on Vietnam and its neighbors, Laos and Cambodia, more than seven and a half-million tons of bombs, equal to one hundred atom bombs, and three times all the explosives deployed in the Second World War.[105]

Where King and Kennedy had called for love, Nixon, like Carmichael, knew the power of hate. His young political strategist, a number cruncher named Kevin Phillips, explained that understanding politics was all about understanding who hates whom: "That is the secret." Phillips's advice to Nixon was known as the "southern strategy," and it meant winning southern Democrats and giving up on African Americans, by abandoning civil rights for law and order. As Nixon prepared for the Republican National Convention, meeting in Miami in August, he listened to Phillips, who explained that the election would be won or lost on the "law and order/Negro socio-economic revolution syndrome," but that there was no need to talk like George Wallace. This could all be done so much more subtly. In his acceptance speech in Miami, Nixon invoked an apocalypse. "As we look at America, we see cities enveloped in smoke and flame," he said. "We hear sirens in the night." But there was another sound, a quieter sound, a quieter voice—a silenced voice— to which Americans ought to listen. "It is the quiet voice in the tumult and the shouting. It is the voice of the great majority of Americans, the forgotten Americans—the non-shouters; the non-demonstrators. They are not racists or sick; they are not guilty of the crime that plagues the land. . . . They are good people, they are decent people; they work, and they save, and they pay their taxes, and they care."[106]

The GOP adopted a platform plank that billed itself as anticrime (and anti–Kerner Commission): "We must re-establish the principle that men are accountable for what they do, that criminals are responsible for their crimes, that while the youth's environment may help to explain the man's crime, it does not excuse that crime." But as Nixon adviser John Dean later said, "I was cranking out that bullshit on Nixon's crime policy before he was elected. And it was bullshit, too. We knew it. The Nixon campaign didn't call for anything about crime problems that Ramsey Clark [Johnson's attorney general] wasn't already doing under LBJ. We just made more noise."[107]

Two weeks after the Republicans met in Miami, the Democratic National Convention met in Chicago. Antiwar protesters arrived in Chicago, too, along with Students for a Democratic Society, Yippies, anarchists, and hangers-on. They were met with a military police force of an occupying army: some 12,000 Chicago police, 6,000 National Guardsmen, 6,000 army troops, and 1,000 undercover intelligence agents. Richard Daley, the city's mayor, insisted that law and order would prevail.[108] There were armed police, even, in the convention hall. The party had no leader: Johnson had stepped down, Robert Kennedy had been shot. Johnson's vice president, Hubert Humphrey, who had not entered a single primary, won the nomination, defeating Eugene McCarthy and arousing the ire of the party's left flank.

In November, Nixon beat Humphrey by winning those Americans who believed that he was speaking for them, the "Silent Majority." The parties were being sorted by ideology. And they were being sorted by race. In 1960, about three out of every five blue-collar workers had voted Democrat; in 1968, only one in three did. In 1960, one in three African Americans had voted for Nixon over John F. Kennedy; by 1972, only one in ten would vote for Nixon over the Democratic nominee, South Dakota senator George McGovern.[109]

A midcentury era of political consensus had come to an almost unfathomably violent end. After 1968, American politics would be driven once again by division, resentment, and malice. Even Leone Baxter began to have her regrets. Interviewed in the 1960s, she warned that political con-

*Poet and boxer Rodolfo Gonzales, a leader of the Chicano movement, spoke at a rally in Denver in 1970.*

sulting must be kept "in the hands of the most ethical, principled people. People with real concern for the world around them, for people around them or else it will erode into the hands of people who have no regard for the world around them. It could be a very, very destructive thing."[110]

And what of the American past? Was the schoolbook version of American history a lie? The civil rights movement and the war in Vietnam called attention to aspects of American history that had been left out of American history textbooks from the very start. The American Indian Movement, founded in 1968, challenged the story of the nation's origins— the goal of AIM's occupation of an abandoned prison on the island of Alcatraz, an occupation that lasted from the end of 1969 through the middle of 1971, was for the island to become a Native American Studies center. The Black Power movement, the Chicano movement, and a growing Asian American movement made similar demands. In Denver in 1969, Chicano activist Rodolfo Gonzales, who'd founded the Crusade for Justice, led a walkout of Mexican American students in protest over the American history curriculum, insisting that it be revised to "enforce the inclusion in all schools of this city the history of our people, our culture, language, and our contributions to this country."[111] Black studies departments were founded at colleges—the first in 1969, at San Francisco State—followed by Chicano studies and women's studies departments—the first founded at San Diego State in 1970—and sexuality and gender studies. A revolution on the streets produced a revolution in scholarship: a new American past.

A new American history—along with the broadening of research in the social sciences and the humanities more generally—was long overdue. But in the context of the war in Vietnam, questioning academic authority and pointing out the biases of experts began to slip into a cynicism about truth itself. A great deal of university research, not only in engineering and in weapons technology, had been deployed to wage and support the war in Vietnam, a war most Americans deemed ill-judged and many considered immoral. The Cold War had asked many of the nation's scientists and scholars to turn their research to the pursuit of military and foreign policy aims; the Vietnam War had contorted the academy itself. After the Tet Offensive, Senate hearings into military spending revealed, among many other academic scandals, the extent of Simulmatics's years of work in South Vietnam, conducting public opinion surveys and analyzing the dreams of Vietnamese villagers as a way of understanding the insurgency, a project not unrelated to the company's other research, on countering "urban insurgency." Arkansas senator J. William Fulbright, who convened the hearings, denounced social scientists like Ithiel de Sola Pool for failing to provide "an effective counterweight to the military-industrial complex by strengthening their emphasis on the traditional values of our democracy" and instead having "joined the monolith." Noam Chomsky, writing in the *New York Review of Books* in 1969, argued that much of academic life in the United States—the production of knowledge itself—had been suborned for the purpose of waging a grotesque war in which all the courage had been shown by the young, by young soldiers who fought the war, and by young students who protested it. "While young dissenters plead for resurrection of the American promise, their elders continue to subvert it," Fulbright said damningly, charging the nation's intellectuals with "the surrender of independence, the neglect of teaching, and the distortion of scholarship," and accusing the university of abdicating its elemental function, in "not only failing to meet its responsibilities to its students" but in "betraying a public trust."[112]

The academy would have its reckoning. Vietnam convinced a great many American intellectuals to withdraw from public life, on the grounds that the only defensible ethical position was to refuse to engage in discussions of policy and politics. But in colleges and universities, revelations about the betrayals of the Kennedy, Johnson, and Nixon administrations, and about the complicity of scholars and scientists, easily descended into disenchantment and a profound alienation from the idea of America itself. "I learned to despise my countrymen, my government and the entire English speaking world, with its history of genocide and international conquest" said one sixties radical. "I was a normal kid."[113]

In some corners of the left, the idea that everything was a lie became a fashionable truth. Poststructuralism and postmodernism suffused not only American intellectual life but American politics, too. If everything is politics, and politics is a series of lies, then there is no truth. "Suddenly I realized that they did not really believe that there was a nature of things," the social critic Paul Goodman wrote about his students at the end of the 1960s. "There was no knowledge but only the sociology of knowledge. They had so well learned that physical and sociological research is subsidized and conducted for the benefit of the ruling class that they were doubtful that there was such a thing as simple truth."[114] And that was *before* Watergate.

Meanwhile, on the right, a new political wisdom involved a new political math that produced a new and even deeper cynicism. Nixon's 1968 campaign, with its southern strategy, had been singularly divisive. Almost as soon as he entered office, Nixon began thinking about his reelection, planning a still more divisive campaign that would determine the direction of his presidency. Kevin Phillips's *The Emerging Republican Majority* appeared late in 1969. Nixon read it over Christmas and told his chief of staff, H. R. Haldeman, "Go for Poles, Italians, Irish, must learn to understand Silent Majority . . . don't go for Jews & Blacks."[115] (Haldeman, a Californian, had volunteered for Eisenhower-Nixon in 1952 and had left his job to manage Nixon's first presidential campaign: he'd learned how to campaign from Campaigns, Inc. "Whitaker and Baxter was the great old campaign," Haldeman once said, "the granddaddy.")[116]

Democrats plotted their own path to a majority, no less interested in market segmentation. Two Democratic strategists, Richard M. Scammon and Ben J. Wattenberg, published their own manifesto just months after Phillips's book appeared. Like Phillips, Scammon and Wattenberg were using computers to study election returns and public opinion polls. In *The Real Majority* (1970), the two men argued that, in addition to the bread-and-butter issues that had for so long determined how citizens voted, "Americans are apparently beginning to array themselves politically along the axes of certain social situations as well." The GOP was moving to the right, to capitalize on backlash against civil rights, and some in the Democratic Party were planning to move to the left. Scammon and Wattenberg explained, "Under the banner of New Politics there is talk of forming a new coalition of the left, composed of the young, the black, the poor, the well-educated, the socially alienated, minority groups, and intellectuals—while relegating Middle America and especially white union labor to the ranks of 'racists.'" This coalition would be a disaster for the Democratic Party, Scammon and Wattenberg predicted, and they argued strenuously against it. "The great majority of the voters in America are unyoung, unpoor, and unblack; they are the middle-aged, middle-class, middle-minded," they pointed out, and the average voter, statistically speaking, was a forty-seven-year-old Catholic housewife from Dayton, Ohio, married to a machinist:

> To know that the lady in Dayton is afraid to walk the streets alone at night, to know that she has a mixed view about blacks and civil rights because before moving to the suburbs she lived in a neighborhood that became all black, to know that her brother-in-law is a policeman, to know that she does not have the money to move if her new neighborhood deteriorates, to know that she is deeply distressed that her son is going to a community junior college where LSD was found on campus—to know all this is the beginning of contemporary political wisdom.

Scammon and Wattenberg recommended that Democrats move to the center though they feared Democrats wouldn't take their advice, and they were right.[117]

But Nixon did not ignore their advice. He read an advance copy of *The Real Majority* three weeks before it was published. The president "talked about Real Majority and need to get that thinking over to all our people," Haldeman recorded in his notes. "Wants to hit pornography, dope, bad kids." Nixon said, "We should aim our strategy primarily at disaffected

Democrats, at blue-collar workers, and at working-class white ethnics" and "set out to capture the vote of the forty-seven-year-old Dayton house-wife." He decided to change the course of the White House's strategy in the midterm 1970 elections, halting a campaign against Democrats as "big spenders" and replacing it with a campaign for the votes of blue-collar workers, on the basis of social issues, from marijuana to pornography. He charged his vice president, Spiro Agnew, with pushing Democrats out of the political center by calling people like Edward Kennedy "radical liber-als." Nixon's staff crafted this argument into campaign rhetoric, urging him to use this message when talking to voters: "Today, racial minorities are saying that you can't make it in America. What they really mean is that they refuse to start at the bottom of the ladder the way you did. They want to surpass you. . . . They want it handed to them." Eyeing this state of affairs, political scientist Andrew Hacker announced 1970 "the end of the American era," arguing that the nation was no longer a nation but a collection of "two hundred million egos."[118]

Nixon, whose strength had always been foreign policy, wasn't much interested in domestic policy, which he largely relegated to his aide John Ehrlichman. He was interested, though, in using domestic policy to bet-ter divide his opponents. He called the welfare state "building outhouses in Peoria." He chose to address unemployment and the growing ranks of welfare recipients with a proposal first made by the University of Chicago economist Milton Friedman in the 1950s. His chief domestic initiative, announced in August of 1969, was a guaranteed income program that he called the Family Assistance Plan. It would have eradicated the wel-fare system and eliminated social workers and many social programs and replaced them with a cash payment to everyone earning below a certain wage level. Unlike the existing welfare program, the Family Assistance Plan provided an incentive for the poor to work; the cash payment rose with income level. When a Gallup poll asked, "Would you favor or oppose such a plan?" 62 percent said they would oppose it.[119]

During Nixon's first term, opposition within policy circles grew. Con-servatives objected to the Family Assistance Plan because it was a gov-ernment handout; the Left, especially the National Welfare Rights Organization, objected to it because it wasn't generous enough ("Zap FAP," read their placards). Nixon enjoyed watching them battle it out.

And, when the time was right for him politically, he abandoned it. Make a "big play for the plan," he told Haldeman, but "be sure it's killed by Democrats."[120]

Nixon's machinations with Congress weren't all that much more cynical than those of some other American presidents. But his commitment to making sure the American people didn't trust one another really was something distinctive. He often charged Agnew with the nastier part of this work, especially when it came to attacking the press and liberal intellectuals. "Dividing the American people has been my main contribution to the national political scene," Agnew later said. "I not only plead guilty to this charge, but I am somewhat flattered by it."[121]

Many of the means Nixon used to discredit and attack his opponents, both at home and abroad, involved abuses of power that had become commonplace during the Cold War, when anticommunist hysteria and the urgency of national security had triumphed over judgment and the rule of law. Other Cold War presidents had used the CIA to conduct covert operations abroad, the FBI to spy on American citizens, and the IRS to audit political opponents. But Nixon got found out, partly due to his own paranoia, insecurity, and recklessness. And the proof of his duplicity, in the form of tape recordings made in the White House, brought a new kind of historical evidence not only into the archives but into the public mind, a species of evidence much more intimate, and unchecked, than the collection of self-conscious memos and self-serving memoirs that chronicle most presidencies. The tapes would ultimately lead to impeachment proceedings, and Nixon's resignation. But they also altered how Americans understood the presidency, since they altered the historical record, granting a view of even the most casual conversations, which very frequently revealed Nixon's bigotry, suspicion, and mean-spiritedness. Consider a conversation between Nixon and Haldeman about the television talk show host Dick Cavett in June 1971:

HALDEMAN: We've got a running war going with Cavett.
NIXON: Is he just a left-winger? Is that the problem?
HALDEMAN: Yeah.
NIXON: Is he Jewish?
HALDEMAN: I don't know. He doesn't look it.[122]

FDR had holes drilled in the Oval Office floor to allow wires for recording press conferences. Truman had used a microphone hidden in a lampshade on his desk. Eisenhower had recorded conversations in the Oval Office, and bugged his own telephone. Kennedy and Johnson used a recording system installed by the U.S. Army Signal Corps. Nixon, after his inauguration, had ordered Johnson's system dismantled; he didn't like having to remember to turn the switch on and off. Still, his secretary of state, Henry Kissinger, had secretaries listen in to meetings and take notes. In the end, a recording system seemed simpler than a fleet of secretaries, but because Nixon wanted the tapes to serve as a full and accurate chronicle of his presidency, he wanted a system that turned on automatically, at the slightest noise. Early in 1971, Haldeman installed a new, secret tape recording system that was voice-activated, and highly sensitive, to record meetings and telephone conversations in the Oval Office, the Lincoln Sitting Room, and the Cabinet Room. (Only Nixon and Haldeman knew about the system; Kissinger and John Ehrlichman were among those who did not.)[123]

During the very months that Haldeman was arranging for the new recording system at the White House, Daniel Ellsberg, a defense analyst, had been trying to find a way to release to the public a 7,000-page, 47-volume study of the war in Vietnam that had been commissioned by Robert McNamara in 1967, not long before he announced his resignation. The Pentagon Papers, as the report came to be called, was a chronicle of the lies and blunders of one administration after another in pursuing an ill-considered, cruel, and wanton campaign in Vietnam. Ellsberg, who had worked on the report, had made a set of photocopies in hopes that their exposure would bring an end to the war. Beginning in 1969, he had tried to gain the interest of members of Nixon's administration, including Kissinger, to no avail. He had tried to get a member of Congress to leak the report, without success. He finally approached the *New York Times* early in 1971; the paper began publishing excerpts of the report on June 13. "Four succeeding administrations built up the American political, military and psychological stakes in Indochina," the *Times* reported, introducing the chronicle of a decades-long conflict that the U.S. government had conducted to maintain "the power, influence and prestige of the United States . . . irrespective of conditions in Vietnam."[124]

The Pentagon Papers did not indict the Nixon administration; the study ended in 1968. If anything, the release of the papers strengthened Nixon's hand, allowing him to blame Vietnam on Kennedy and Johnson. But Nixon's aides understood the implications of the leaked study. "To the ordinary guy, all this is a bunch of gobbledygook," Haldeman told him. "But out of the gobbledygook comes a very clear thing: you can't trust the government; you can't believe what they say; and you can't rely on their judgment." Nixon, who harbored deep fears of being found out—about anything—became convinced that Ellsberg's leak to the *Times* was part of a conspiracy against him, "a Jewish cabal," as he described it, "the same media that supported Hiss." His aides did not disabuse him of this theory. Kissinger, a German Jew, warned him, "If this thing flies, they're going to do the same to you." Kissinger convinced Nixon to ask the Justice Department to forbid the *Times* to publish any further portions of the report. While that case made its way to the Supreme Court, the *Washington Post* began publishing the papers. On June 30, the Supreme Court ruled that the publication of the papers could continue; the Justice Department nevertheless proceeded with charges against Ellsberg.[125]

Faced with the possibility that their political opponents were gaining power, other presidents had simply called up J. Edgar Hoover and put the FBI on the case. But after the release of the Pentagon Papers, Hoover had grown cautious about engaging in unlawful surveillance and other, still less licit, tactics. The Nixon administration was left to do its own dirty work, much of which it also managed to capture on tape, as when, in July 1971, Nixon ordered his staff to blow up a safe at the Brookings Institution to find files about Vietnam that would embarrass Johnson, a measure motivated by nothing but malice, since he had been out of office for over two years.[126] The administration also established a Special Investigations Unit, headed by a zealot and former aide of Ehrlichman's named G. Gordon Liddy, who was subsequently sent to work for the Committee to Re-elect the President (CRP, popularly known as CREEP). On Saturday, June 17, 1972, Liddy directed five men to break into the offices of Lawrence O'Brien, the DNC chairman, at the Watergate Hotel, to steal documents and repair wiretaps that had earlier been placed on office phones. After finishing that job, the burglars were supposed to proceed to the headquarters of the George McGovern campaign, on Capitol Hill, to do much the same, but they never got there, because they were arrested at the Watergate Hotel. Nixon hadn't known about the break-in before it happened, but six days later, on June 23, he was captured on tape discussing a cover-up with Haldeman.[127]

While the Nixon administration conducted its cover-up in secrecy, secure in its expectation that the president could use executive privilege to prevent anyone from ever hearing anything on its tape recordings, the Nixon reelection campaign proceeded. In November 1972, Nixon won 61 percent of the popular vote and became the first presidential candidate to win forty-nine states, losing only Massachusetts and Washington, DC, to McGovern. Both Nixon's neediness and the way his hunger for approval was fed by his aides are richly illustrated in a conversation he had with Kissinger following McGovern's concession speech, which Nixon considered too scanty in its acknowledgment of his own victory. Nixon called McGovern a "prick."

NIXON: Don't you agree?

KISSINGER: Absolutely. He was ungenerous.

NIXON: Yeah.

KISSINGER: He was petulant.

NIXON: Yeah.

KISSINGER: Unworthy.

NIXON: Right. As you probably know, I responded in a very decent way to him.

KISSINGER: Well, I thought that was a great statement. Year after year the media were harassing you. All the intellectuals were against you and you've come around—

NIXON: That's right.

KISSINGER: —and had the greatest victory.[128]

Five days before his inauguration, in January 1973, Nixon announced the end of the war in Vietnam; the peace treaty would be signed in Paris later that month. In his inaugural address, on the twentieth, he heralded the beginning of a new era of peace and progress, driven by a conservative revolution. "Abroad and at home, the time has come to turn away from the condescending policies of paternalism—of 'Washington knows best,'" he said. "Let us encourage individuals at home and nations abroad to do more for themselves, to decide more for themselves." If Americans had trusted too much in government, this wasn't because government couldn't be trusted, because presidents had lied to the American people; this was because people should do more for themselves. The atrocities waged in the name of the American people in Vietnam, Cambodia, and Laos, the chaos on American streets—these were not the fault of elected officials who made grave mistakes, lied to the press, and obstructed justice. These things were the faults of liberalism, which had taught Americans to expect too much of government. "In trusting too much in government, we have asked of it more than it can deliver," Nixon declared. "This leads only to inflated expectations, to reduced individual effort, and to a disappointment and frustration that erode confidence both in what government can do and in what people can do." Kennedy had urged Americans, "Ask not what your country can do for you—ask what you can do for your country." Nixon urged Americans to ask what they could do for themselves.

Two days after the inauguration, Lyndon Johnson, sixty-four, had a heart attack at his ranch in Texas. Johnson, who had given up his sixty-cigarettes-a-day habit after his first heart attack in 1955, had smoked his first cigarette in fourteen years on the plane ride home from Nixon's first inauguration. Alone at home on January 22, seized with pains in his chest, he telephoned for help, but help arrived too late.

Ten days before his death, in his last interview, with Walter Cronkite, a weary Johnson, in a button-down flannel shirt and thick, wire-framed eyeglasses, had talked with a swelling pride about the role he'd played in advancing civil rights: the Civil Rights Act of 1964, the Voting Rights Act of 1965, the Fair Housing Act of 1968, the "We Shall Overcome" speech he'd made during the crisis at Selma, and his 1967 appointment of Thurgood Marshall to the Supreme Court. "We're living in a fast age, and all of us are rather impatient, and, more important, we're rather intolerant of the opinions of our fellow man and his judgments and his conduct and his traditions and his way of life," Johnson told Cronkite, his languid voice heavy with pain. When Johnson died, Thurgood Marshall said, "He died of a broken heart."[129]

Nixon's own collapse came more slowly, a festering, self-inflicted wound. In February, the Senate voted to convene a special committee to investigate the Watergate burglary. In May, Nixon's incoming attorney general, Elliot Richardson, named Archibald Cox as a special prosecutor. In July, the Senate committee learned about the tapes, but when Cox subpoenaed them, Nixon refused to turn them over, citing executive privilege. The cover-up had gone badly. Charges against Ellsberg were dropped when the Watergate investigation revealed that Liddy's operatives had broken into the office of Ellsberg's psychiatrist in California. Still, Nixon had little fear of impeachment with the notoriously corrupt and much-despised Agnew as his vice president. (He called Agnew the "assassins' dilemma.")[130] But in October, Agnew pled no contest to a charge of tax evasion and resigned. Ten days later, in what became known as the Saturday Night Massacre, Nixon told Richardson to fire Cox; when Richardson refused and resigned instead, Nixon told Deputy Attorney General William Ruckelshaus to do it; Ruckelshaus also resigned. Finally, Nixon got Solicitor General Robert Bork to fire Cox—an abuse of power that would haunt Bork, the FBI, and the Justice Department itself.

"Act like a winner," Nixon wrote in a note to himself, listing his New Year's resolutions. But his efforts to block the release of the tapes failed. Finally, in April 1974, he released 1,200 pages of transcripts to 46 tapes. The public discovered the nature of Nixon's wrath, his pettiness, and his vengefulness. But the June 23, 1972, transcripts were not included, and when the committee demanded them, the White House refused, and the case went to the Supreme Court, in *United States v. Nixon*. While the justices were deliberating, eighty-three-year-old Earl Warren, who had retired from the court five years before, had a heart attack. On July 9, Justices William O. Douglas and William J. Brennan went to see him at Georgetown University Hospital. Warren grabbed Douglas's hand. "If Nixon is not forced to turn over tapes of his conversations with the ring of men who were conversing on their violations of the law," Warren warned, "then liberty will soon be dead in this nation." Brennan and Douglas assured him that the court would order the president to hand over the tapes. Warren died hours later. The Supreme Court delivered its unanimous opinion on July 24 (Nixon nominee William Rehnquist recused himself): the White House had to release the tapes.[131]

The content of the tapes was reported on August 6, 1974. Impeachment seemed certain. To avoid it, Nixon announced his resignation the next day, speaking into television cameras from his desk at the White House. In a brief, curt speech, he touted his foreign policy achievements, which were many, and of deep and abiding significance. He'd opened diplomatic relations with China, after a quarter century. For all that he'd done to prolong it, he had in fact ended the war in Vietnam. He'd improved U.S.

*Nixon left the White House by helicopter*
*on August 9, 1974.*

relations in the Middle East. He'd negotiated arms limitation agreements with the Soviet Union, building on relationships he'd established on his trip to Moscow in 1959. He said nearly nothing about conditions in the United States, except to allude to "the turbulent history of this era"—a turbulence he had done little to alleviate and much to aggravate.[132]

The next morning, bidding farewell to his White House staff, he said, "Always remember, others may hate you—but those who hate you don't win unless you hate them, and then you destroy yourself."[133] Then, carrying on his stooped shoulders the weight of a troubled nation, he walked down a red carpet on the South Lawn to a waiting helicopter, climbed the stairs to its open door, and turned back to deliver his trademark wave, spreading both arms wide. Disappearing inside, he flew away, last seen peering out through a bulletproof window as the whirling helicopter wended its way toward the Washington Monument and over the National Mall, where another man had not so very long ago told a story about a dream.

## *Fifteen*

# BATTLE LINES

*Phyllis Schlafly led a resurgent conservative movement
in the 1970s by making opposition to equal rights
one of its signature issues.*

**B**ETTY FORD AND MORLEY SAFER WERE SITTING ON
either end of a floral sofa in the solarium on the third floor of the
White House on a summer's day in 1975 when the CBS *60 Minutes*
reporter asked the First Lady what she thought about equal rights and
abortion. Safer wore a black suit; Ford, a former fashion model and dancer
with the Martha Graham Dance Company, wore a beige dress: a belted,
gathered smock with a yoked neck. Safer kept apologizing for asking questions about subjects that he described as "taboo," but Ford answered each
question with candor, even though her answers were often at odds with

the views of her husband and, increasingly, of the Republican Party. After the president watched the hour-long interview, he told his wife, "Well, honey, there goes about 20 million votes."[1] He was not entirely wrong.

Betty Ford's *60 Minutes* interview came two years after the Supreme Court's decision in *Roe v. Wade* and at a moment when the Equal Rights Amendment seemed mere months away from becoming law. These two issues would together produce the greatest cleavage in American politics since the debate over slavery.

The origins of the dispute lie in the Constitution itself, but a turning point came in 1963, a year that saw the publication of both Betty Friedan's *The Feminine Mystique* and *American Women,* the official report of the Commission on the Status of Women. The commission, chaired by Eleanor Roosevelt and including Pauli Murray, had been established by JFK in 1961, a step he took to quiet the complaint that he was the first president since Hoover whose cabinet did not include a woman.

In *The Feminine Mystique*, Friedan lamented "the problem that has no name," the suffering of gingham-aproned housewives, frustrated, lonely, and bored. "Each suburban wife struggled with it alone," she wrote.[2] Betty Ford had that problem.

A congressional wife raising four children, Ford began mixing alcohol and painkillers in 1964 and had a nervous breakdown in 1965, the year her husband assumed a new national prominence. "Congress got a new Minority Leader, and I lost a husband," she later said.[3] While Ford struggled with loneliness, Friedan and Murray led a small group of women and men who established the National Organization for Women in 1966.[4] The next year, NOW made the ERA its top priority and added to its agenda the legalization of abortion.

Nothing about equal rights for women, contraception, or abortion is inherently partisan. The public was divided on many issues relating to women, but in the 1960s and 1970s, and well into the 1980s, those divisions did not fall along party lines.[5] Only in 1980 did the leadership of the two parties place legalized abortion on their platforms, Republicans against and Democrats in favor (in their 1976 platforms, both parties equivocated on the issue).[6] But by the 1990s, abortion had become an overwhelmingly partisan issue—a defining issue of a widening divide.[7]

Nor were gun ownership and gun safety legislation partisan issues before the 1970s. But during that decade, political strategists undertook the work of making guns partisan, too. In truth, the very character of partisanship changed. Paul Weyrich, a conservative strategist and a founder of the Heritage Foundation, announced a new war. "It is a war of ideology, it's a war of ideas, and it's a war about our way of life," Weyrich said. "And it has to be fought with the same intensity, I think, and dedication as you would fight a shooting war."[8]

In the waning decades of the twentieth century, liberals and conservatives alike cast the lingering divisions of the 1960s less as matters of law and order than as matters of life and death. Either abortion was murder and guns meant freedom or guns meant murder and abortion was freedom. How this sorted out came to depend upon party affiliation. "The economy, stupid" became the mantra of Bill Clinton's 1992 presidential campaign, when he tried to set aside the guns-and-abortion divide.[9] That proved impossible. Especially after the Cold War came to an end, a domestic cold war began, uncompromising, all or-nothing, murder or freedom, life or death.

# I.

MAKING SOCIAL ISSUES into partisan issues took a great deal of work, much of it done by political strategists and well-paid political consultants and made easier by mainframe and desktop computers. By the 1970s, the Lie Factory that had begun manufacturing public opinion in the 1930s when Campaigns, Inc., opened its doors and George Gallup started conducting polls had grown into a billion-dollar industry that divided the electorate by inciting outrage, having demonstrated that, the more emotional the issue, the likelier voters were to turn up at the polls. And the most emotional issues—those most likely to get out the vote—turned out to be abortion and guns.

In the first decades of the twenty-first century, the Internet would come to function as a polarization machine, fast, efficient, and cheap, and all but automated. But in the last decades of the twentieth century, the work was still done manually. Quite how much labor and money went into the project can only be appreciated by how differently issues like abortion and guns looked before the work began.

Before the 1980s, neither the ERA nor women's health were partisan issues, except insofar as Republicans had historically offered more support to equal rights and family planning than had Democrats. Planned Parenthood, the birth control organization founded by Margaret Sanger in 1916, had forced her out decades before her death in 1966, objecting to her feminism. Beginning in the 1920s, its leaders had been more Republican than Democrat. By the 1950s, many were conservatives—Barry Goldwater and his wife served on the board of Planned Parenthood of Phoenix—family planning having become, politically speaking, a family value. In campaigning for the legalization of contraception, Planned Parenthood also enjoyed the broad support of both doctors and clergymen. In 1958, Alan F. Guttmacher, chief of obstetrics at Mount Sinai Hospital, clinical professor of obstetrics and gynecology at Columbia, and a member of Planned Parenthood's medical advisory board, challenged New York City municipal hospitals to reverse an institutional policy that forbade doctors from giving out contraceptives or contraceptive information. Hospital chaplains lined up behind him. In 1960, Planned Parenthood's Clergymen's National Advisory Council issued a statement, "The Ethics of Family Planning," describing family planning as fulfilling "the will of God" by allowing married couples to enjoy intercourse for the sake of love.[10]

Efforts to legalize abortion were begun in the 1960s, not by women's rights activists, but by the doctors, lawyers, and clergymen who ran Planned Parenthood. In 1962, when Guttmacher became president of Planned Parenthood, he launched a campaign to secure federal government support for family planning programs for the poor, to overturn bans on contraception, and to liberalize abortion law. In 1965, former presidents Eisenhower and Truman, Republican and Democrat, together served as co-chairmen of a Planned Parenthood committee, signaling an across-the-aisle commitment to contraception. That year, in *Griswold v. Connecticut*, the Supreme Court struck down state bans on contraception, overturning the conviction of Estelle Griswold, the head of a Planned Parenthood clinic in Connecticut, who'd been arrested for dispensing contraception. It had been nearly fifty years since Sanger had been arrested on the same charges. But the right to contraception secured in *Griswold* would turn out to be fragile.[11]

The men who wrote and ratified the Constitution had left women, sex, marriage out of it. "Remember the ladies," Abigail Adams had warned her husband in 1776, advice he had ignored. The consequences of writing women out of the republic's founding documents were both lasting and devastating. That the framers of the Constitution had not resolved the question of slavery had led to a civil war. That they regarded women as unequal to men nearly did the same. Over the course of American history, women had often written themselves into the Constitution by way of analogy. Discrimination by sex was like discrimination by race, and language that barred one could be understood to bar another. This, however, was not the argument by which the Supreme Court granted to women the right to contraception and abortion. In *Griswold*, the court based its ruling not on equality but instead on privacy.

"We deal with a right of privacy older than the Bill of Rights," Justice Douglas said in the majority opinion. Although no right to privacy is mentioned in either the Constitution or the Bill of Rights, Douglas maintained that it is nevertheless there, not in words, but in the shadow cast by words, in "penumbras, formed by emanations from those guarantees that help give them life and substance."[12] This would prove a dangerously imperfect support for the many cases that would try to build upon *Griswold* over the next half century.

In 1969, Nixon had asked Congress to increase federal funding for family planning, and in the House, George H. W. Bush, a decorated navy pilot and young Republican congressman from Texas, pressed the case. "We need to make family planning a household word," Bush said. (So known was Bush for his support for family planning that he got the nickname "Rubbers.") In 1972, in *Eisenstadt v. Baird*, the court extended *Griswold*'s notion of privacy from married couples to individuals. "If the right of privacy means anything," Justice Brennan wrote, "it is the right of the individual, married or single, to be free from unwarranted governmental intrusion into matters so fundamentally affecting a person as the decision whether to bear or beget a child."[13]

Between 1967 and 1970, under pressure from doctors and lawyers, often supported by clergy, legislators began lifting restrictions on abortion in sixteen states, including California, where the law was signed by Governor Reagan. When the Catholic Church objected to New York's new abortion law, in apocalyptic terms, Protestant and Jewish clergy asked whether "the cause of ecumenism is best served by attributing to us the advocacy of murder and genocide." In 1970, Nixon signed Title X, which included a provision under which doctors on military bases could perform abortions. "No American woman should be denied access to family planning assistance because of her economic condition," Nixon declared that year.[14]

But if a broad, bipartisan political consensus supported family planning, women themselves had grown divided over many other matters. The "women's movement" of the 1960s and 1970s was really three movements: radical feminism, liberal feminism, and conservative antifeminism. The radical women's movement came out of the New Left, where women had found precious little support for arguments about the oppression of women. "Let them eat cock!" said one Berkeley student leader.[15] Stokely Carmichael, asked about the position of women in the Black Power movement, answered, "The only position for women in the movement is prone." Radical feminists fought for liberation from the bondage of womanhood, the shackles of femininity. Their arguments, at first Marxist and economic, turned swiftly to culture. Emblematically, Shulamith Firestone of the New York Radical Women held a funeral for "Traditional Womanhood," burying a mannequin with blond hair and curlers. Firestone's form of guerrilla theater gained a national audience in 1968 during a protest of the Miss America contest, when radical feminists crowned a sheep Miss America; burned girdles, high-heeled shoes, and *Playboy* magazine in a trash can; and unfurled a "Women's Liberation" banner, shouting, "Freedom for Women!"[16]

Carmichael notwithstanding, radical feminism had been deeply influenced by the Black Power movement, with its disdain for liberalism and its emphasis on separatism and pride, and had close ties, too, to the nascent gay rights movement, which had begun in the 1950s but grew in strength and intensity over the course of the next decade. In 1965, lesbian and gay rights activists picketed the United Nations, Philadelphia's Independence Hall, and the White House (three times). In 1968, at a homosexual rights conference in Chicago, participants, inspired by "Black Is Beautiful," declared, "Gay Is Good." A year after a 1969 police raid of New York's Stonewall Inn, homosexual rights groups held a march from Greenwich Village to Central Park. "We have to come out into the open and stop being ashamed or else people will go on treating us as freaks," said one activist. "This march is an affirmation and declaration of our new pride."[17]

Liberal feminists, by contrast, drew inspiration and borrowed tactics from the suffrage, abolition, and pre–Black Power civil rights movements. In pursuit of equal rights, they wanted to pass laws, amend the Constitution, win court cases, and get women elected to office. In 1971, writer Gloria Steinem, Republican organizer Tanya Melich, and New York congresswomen Bella Abzug and Shirley Chisholm founded the bipartisan National Women's Political Caucus. The next year, a record-breaking number of women ran for office, including Chisholm, who sought the Democratic presidential nomination, and they kept on running. Between 1970 and 1975, the number of women in elected office doubled. The 92nd Congress, which met from 1971 to 1972, passed more women's rights bills than any other Congress, including Title IX and a federal child care bill (which Nixon vetoed). The ERA, first introduced into Congress in 1923, passed in the House in 1971, 354 to 24, and in the Senate in 1972, 84 to 8. Sent to the states for ratification, it won by enormous margins, 205 to 7 in liberal Massachusetts; 31 to 0 in conservative West Virginia; 61 to 0 in independent Colorado.[18]

Liberal feminists made striking gains, too, in the courts, many of them won by Ruth Bader Ginsburg, a brilliant young law school professor born in Brooklyn to Jewish immigrants in 1933. Ginsburg began arguing equal rights cases before the Supreme Court in 1971, relying on and citing Pauli Murray's strategy for using the Fourteenth Amendment to defeat discrimination by sex. Weren't women, after all, "persons"? The next year, Ginsburg launched the ACLU's Women's Rights Project. "I ask no favor for my sex," she told the nine male justices in 1973, quoting the eloquent abolitionist Sarah Grimké. "All I ask of our brethren is that they take their feet off our necks."[19]

A conservative women's movement, best understood as a form of antifeminism, came last, a reaction to both radical and liberal feminism and to the lifting of bans on contraception and the liberalization of abortion laws. In 1970, a woman from Fort Wayne, Indiana, as if conjuring up the ghost of the nineteenth-century anti-vice crusader Anthony Comstock, wrote to Guttmacher, "Everyone is asking, 'What is wrong with our young people in this generation?' Well, I can tell you what is wrong! They are being fed garbage and filth from dirty books, magazines, and movies! But the most tragic thing of all is the fact that many churchmen have joined these non-Christian intellectuals in a new attitude toward sex. It is one of the grave tragedies of our day, and God will surely hold them responsible."[20]

The Constitution, whose framers did not believe women to be political subjects, offered very little guidance. "There is nothing in the United States Constitution concerning birth, contraception, or abortion," Jay Floyd, Texas assistant attorney general, told the court in *Roe v. Wade*, when the case was first argued, in 1971. Floyd spoke on behalf of Wade County, Texas, defending its anti-abortion statute. Floyd was right. But there is also nothing in the Constitution about a great many things on which the court had ruled, from segregated schools to wiretapping. The question became what legal doctrine would be used to talk about the bodies of people that the framers of the Constitution had understood as subject to the rule of men. Men enter the courts as citizens of the Republic; women enter the courts as citizens by sufferance.

Sarah Weddington, the attorney for "Jane Roe," a Texas woman who had sought an abortion, was willing to use any kind of argument the court would accept—liberty, equality, privacy, the First Amendment, the Ninth, the Fourteenth, or the Nineteenth—whatever would work. Asked by Justice Stewart where in the Constitution she placed her argument, she pointed out that the privacy right established in *Griswold* seemed a terribly weak foundation on which to build her case: "Certainly, under the *Griswold* decision, it appears that the members of the Court in that case were obviously divided as to the specific constitutional framework of the right which they held to exist in the *Griswold* decision," Weddington said. She had a few other ideas. "I do feel that the Ninth Amendment is an appropriate place for the freedom to rest," she told the court. "I think the Fourteenth Amendment is equally an appropriate place." Justice Potter Stewart tried to nail her down: did she mean to rely on the due process clause of the Fourteenth Amendment?

"We had originally brought this suit alleging both the due process clause, equal protection clause, the Ninth Amendment, and a variety of others," Weddington answered.

"And anything else that might be applicable?" Stewart asked.

"Yes, right," said Weddington.[21]

As the court neared a ruling on *Roe*, Nixon's advisers saw a political opportunity. In 1971, Nixon speechwriter Patrick Buchanan told the president that abortion was "a rising issue and a gut issue with Catholics," and suggested that the president's prospects for reelection would be improved "if the President should publicly take his stand against abortion, as offensive to his own moral principles." A week later, Nixon, jettisoning his previous support of abortion, issued a statement in which he referred to his "personal belief in the sanctity of human life—including the life of the yet unborn." Exploiting Catholics' opposition to abortion was a deliberate attempt to inject doctrinal absolutism into party politics. Nixon supporters complained, and asked whether Nixon might perhaps return to his original position. Buchanan waved that objection aside: "He will cost himself Catholic support and gain what, Betty Friedan?"[22]

The Supreme Court handed down its decision in *Roe v. Wade* on January 22, 1973, the day LBJ died, finding that the "right of privacy . . . is broad enough to encompass a woman's decision whether or not to terminate her pregnancy."[23] It would turn out to be a monumental decision, salvation to some, sin to others. In the White House, the casual viciousness of the president was caught on tape the next day, when Nixon shared his thoughts on the ruling with an aide. "There are times when abortions are necessary," he said, casting aside, in private, his public invocation of the "sanctity of life." Abortion was necessary in case of rape, for instance, he said, or, here offering his frank, private views on race, in case of a pregnancy resulting from sex between "a black and a white."[24]

Betty Ford, unlike Nixon, didn't express her true views about abortion only behind closed doors. From the moment her husband took office, hours after Nixon resigned, she had been candid about women's rights, abortion, and women's health. She held regular press conferences, something no First Lady had done since Eleanor Roosevelt. Only weeks after she moved into the White House, she found out she had breast cancer and needed an emergency mastectomy. Determined not to be part of a cover-up and to help save the lives of women by encouraging them to get tested—breast cancer was, at the time, the number one killer of women between the ages of twenty-five and forty-five—she disclosed her condition, and allowed herself to be photographed during her recovery. "I thought there are women all over the country like me," she said. "And if I don't make this public, then their lives will be gone or in jeopardy."[25] She earned an intensely loyal following among voters, but especially among women.

*Betty Ford, who attended the National Women's
Conference in Houston in 1977, was among several powerful
Republicans who objected to using women to draw
a line between the political parties.*

Ford's vocal support of the ERA was equally well known. She spent
a great deal of her time making calls to states debating ratification; protesters outside the White House carried signs that read "BETTY FORD,
GET OFF THE PHONE." This caused some strain between the East
and West Wings of the White House, but the president refused to submit
to pressure to quiet his wife and instead joked, "I say one wrong thing
about women's rights and the next state dinner is at McDonald's."[26]

In the summer of 1975, when Betty Ford sat on that floral sofa with
Morley Safer, she did not hold back. "I feel that the Equal Rights Amendment ought to probably pass in our Bicentennial year," she said, hoping
for ratification in 1976. He asked her about abortion; she cited *Roe v.
Wade*: "I feel very strongly that it was the best thing in the world when the
Supreme Court voted to legalize abortion, and in my words, bring it out
of the backwoods and put it in the hospitals where it belongs. I thought it
was a great, great decision."[27]

Neither Betty Ford nor Morley Safer appreciated how tightly these two
issues were being wound together by Phyllis Schlafly, the anticommunist
crusader, McCarthy supporter, and Goldwater promoter. Having been
ousted from Republican Party leadership, Schlafly turned her attention

and prodigious organizing skills to defeating equal rights for women by attaching the ERA to *Roe v. Wade*. Read a headline in a typical issue of the *Phyllis Schlafly Report* in 1974: "ERA Means Abortion and Population Shrinkage."[28]

Betty Ford, ill-judging her adversary, dismissed the Radcliffe-educated Phyllis Schlafly as a crank. Asked whether she'd agree to debate her, the First Lady said, "I wouldn't waste my time."[29]

Schlafly, blond and petite, wore flawlessly pressed pink skirt suits and pumps. She liked to talk about herself as a housewife and mother of six. But she was also ruthless, and she was learned, and people who underestimated her nearly always regretted it. Tying the ERA to abortion was a stroke of political genius. To better debate her opponents, and realizing that much of this political battle would be waged in the courts, Schlafly earned a law degree in the 1970s. She was not a flake; she was as keen as the most cunning battlefield general.

Conservatives had been trying since the 1930s to dismantle the New Deal coalition and to take over the Republican Party. In the 1970s and 1980s, by bringing Catholics, evangelical Christians, and white southern Democrats into their own coalition, they finally succeeded. No small number of conservative political strategists would take credit for this achievement. But it was Schlafly who built the road to the Reagan Revolution, paving it with stones labeled "END ABORTION NOW" and "STOP ERA."

TWO CENTURIES HAD PASSED since Thomas Jefferson declared all men to be equal. "Well, Jerry, I guessed we've healed America," Gerald Ford told himself as he fell asleep on the Fourth of July 1976, after watching a stirring display of fireworks over the Washington Monument on the nation's bicentennial.[30] But the scars of Vietnam and Watergate had not healed, the electorate was growing increasingly polarized, Americans' trust in government had not recovered, and the economy had stalled.

Had American growth peaked? All nations have a rise. In the 1970s, many Americans began to wonder whether their nation's fall had begun. Were its best days in the past? Had its ideals failed?

The economic and moral downturn that would be called a "malaise" during the administration of Democratic president Jimmy Carter, elected in 1976, first became visible to most Americans in 1973, during the OPEC oil embargo. In a matter of months, the cost of gasoline increased by a factor of five, driving up the price of other goods, too. In nine months in 1974, the Dow lost 37 percent of its value. Japanese automobile manufacturers, producing more fuel-efficient cars, out-competed Detroit. Heavy industries, especially steel, closed their doors, or moved to other countries, creating what came to be called the Rust Belt in the Midwest. Economists had to come up with a new name—stagflation— for the strange and puzzling new mix of slow economic growth, high unemployment, and rising inflation that afflicted the American economy in the 1970s.[31]

Liberals blamed the malaise on Nixon and on the abandonment of Johnson's Great Society programs, arguing that if the economy was worsening, it must be because the liberal economic agenda remained unfinished. Conservatives understood the state of the economy as evidence not of the unfinished work of liberalism but of liberalism's failure, and of the wrongheadedness of Keynesian economics: economic planning, taxation, and government regulation, they argued, had shackled the free market.

One explanation that fits some of the evidence, if not all of it, is that the century of economic growth that had begun in 1870 had been driven by inventions, from electricity to the automobile, and was not sustainable. After 1970, the pace of invention slowed and its consequences narrowed. Delivering electricity, gas, telephone, water, and sewer—power, warmth, communication, cleanliness—to every home in the United States, a project completed by about 1940, had ended isolation and produced astonishing improvements in living conditions and economic output. Medical advances made before 1970, which include anesthesia, a public water supply, antiseptic surgery, antibiotics, and X-rays, had saved and lengthened lives. But few inventions after 1970 produced such vast changes; instead, they offered slow, steady improvement. Cellphones were useful, but the telephone had existed since 1876. A Boeing 707 approached the speed of sound in 1958; it's not practical to go faster. Moreover, the growing economic inequality that became a feature of American life after 1970 meant that the economic benefits of newer inventions were disproportionately enjoyed by a very small segment of the population.[32] The rise of the Internet, in the 1990s, would recast some of these arrangements, but it would not yield a return to earlier levels of economic growth; instead, it would contribute to widening income inequality and political instability.

Meanwhile, the economy faltered, in ways that intensified battles over the role and rights of women and, soon enough, over guns. Beginning in 1973, and well into the 1990s, real earnings for all but the very wealthiest Americans remained flat, or declined. The real wages of the average male worker dropped by 10 percent. To make up for shrinking family income, more married women began working outside of the home. They began arguing for government-supported child care. Soon, three out of four women between twenty-five and fifty-four were working for pay.[33]

More women worked, but, for most Americans, family incomes did not rise as a result. Liberals blamed conservatives, conservatives blamed liberals, and Schlafly convinced a lot of people to blame feminists. "Women's lib is a total assault on the role of the American woman as wife and mother, and on the family as the basic unit of society," she wrote in 1972. Schlafly had not at first objected to the ERA. But, she later explained, she'd come to believe that it amounted to a conspiracy against women and the privileges and protections they enjoyed under the law. She tied her opposition to the ERA to anticommunism. Soviet women had "equal rights," she said, which meant a mother being forced "to put her baby in a state-operated nursery or kindergarten so she can join the labor force." George Wallace, who had earlier supported ERA, switched positions when he ran as a third-party candidate that year, with this platform: "Women of the American Party say 'NO' to this insidious socialistic plan to destroy the home, make women slaves of the government, and their children wards of the state."[34]

If the wrenching polarization that would later bring the Republic to the brink of a second civil war has a leading engineer, that engineer was Schlafly. Schlafly's first battle was within the Republican Party—and her first triumph was taking it over. The GOP, founded in 1854 as the party of reform, had been the party of abolition and the party of women's rights. By 1896, it had become the party of big business. It had remained the party most supportive of women's rights. The Equal Rights Amendment had been on the GOP platform since 1940. In 1968, in the first wave of the backlash against the women's movement, the ERA had been left off the party's platform. In 1972, Nixon began turning the GOP into the party opposed to abortion but, long before that effort saw its first successes, Schlafly turned the GOP into the party opposed to equal rights for women.

At the 1972 GOP convention, Republican women fought to restore the party's pro-ERA plank.[35] To outflank them, Schlafly, who had been carefully mustering her troops and stockpiling ideological weapons, formed a women's organization called STOP ERA (STOP stands for Stop Taking Our Privileges) and marched her troops all the way to the front lines. By the 1976 Republican National Convention, a group of thirty GOP feminists had formed the Republican Women's Task Force to fight for platform planks in support of the ERA, reproductive rights, affirmative action, federally funded child care, and the extension of the Equal Pay Act. They also supported the pro-ERA Gerald Ford as the party's nominee over Ronald Reagan. They won only a pyrrhic victory. Ford earned the nomination, but, by a single vote, the platform subcommittee defeated the ERA. Only due to strenuous lobbying from Ford did the ERA plank narrowly pass the general platform committee, 51 to 47.[36]

In the general election, feminists claimed that Ford lost to Carter because, cowed by conservative Republican women, he refused to let his wife campaign for him. (She made only nine campaign stops.) Whatever the cause, Ford's defeat only strengthened Schlafly's hand. Early in 1977, four days after North Carolina's House of Representatives voted in favor of the ERA, Schlafly, speaking in Raleigh, whipped up a crowd of fifteen thousand people to raise their hands and pledge to defeat any member of the legislature who voted for the ERA. North Carolina failed to ratify by two votes.[37]

Schlafly's next battle was with the liberal feminists in both parties who were organizing a National Women's Conference, to be held in November 1977 in Houston. "We simply want for the first time in the history of this country an opportunity for women to meet," said Hawaii congresswoman Patsy Mink, who asked Congress for funds to support the meeting, which was to be preceded by state conventions to nominate delegates. Schlafly protested that neither she nor any women known to be opposed to the ERA had been named to the commission organizing the conference. Darkly, she had hinted at a feminist takeover of the state. After Ford signed Congress's pledge of $5 million to support the conference, the *Phyllis Schlafly Report* ran the headline HOW THE LIBS AND THE FEDS PLAN TO SPEND YOUR MONEY.[38]

The National Women's Conference marked the high point of liberal feminism, a second constitutional convention. It had been a long and arduous century and a quarter since the first women's rights convention in 1848 when three hundred people had met at Seneca Falls for two days. In Houston in 1977, two thousand delegates from fifty states, along with twenty thousand attendees, met for four days, producing a twenty-six-point National Plan of Action. Fifteen hundred reporters gave the conference detailed coverage, not least because it was a who's who of American women, from anthropologist Margaret Mead and tennis champion Billie Jean King to *Roe* lawyer Sarah Weddington and Jean Stapleton from *All in the Family*, an actress whose portrait of Edith Bunker had captured the quiet misery of a blue-collar housewife.

To inaugurate the conference, a relay of more than two thousand female athletes, from long-legged marathon runners to burly field hockey players, carried a torch lit in Seneca Falls the twenty-six hundred miles to Houston, an epic distaff Olympics.[39] They carried, too, a new Declaration of Sentiments, written by the poet Maya Angelou, known to television audiences for her role in the recent blockbuster, Alex Haley's *Roots*. "We promise to accept nothing less than justice for every woman," Angelou had written.[40] In Houston, the last runner delivered the torch to Lady Bird Johnson, Rosalynn Carter, and Betty Ford, three First Ladies, together on a stage.

"I told Jerry I was determined to go to Houston and have my voice here," Betty Ford said. "Jerry answered me, 'Well, naturally.'"[41]

The president of the Girl Scouts of America called the conference to order when she raised a gavel once owned by Susan B. Anthony, on loan from the Smithsonian. Ann Richards, a firebrand Texas county commissioner who would later be elected governor, gave a speech about the ERA in which she talked about her younger daughter, "who cannot find women in the history text of this country in the elementary schools." (Her older daughter, Cecile Richards, would grow up to become president of Planned Parenthood.)[42]

Race had divided and in the end doomed the radical women's movement, and critics expected the Houston conference to fall apart over race, too, which seemed even more likely after the Chicana caucus walked out of a state convention in California. But, in the end, nonwhite women constituted more than a quarter of the delegates in Houston, where the Minority Caucus arguably saved the convention.[43]

"Let this message go forth from Houston, and spread all over the land," said Coretta Scott King, introducing the caucus's Minority Report. "There is a new force, a new understanding, a new sisterhood against all injustice that has been born here. We will not be divided and defeated again."[44]

Schlafly, though, saw plenty of division. Women of color had a place at the convention—as leaders—but conservative women had hardly any place there at all. Schlafly had sent supporters to every state nominating convention, but only one in five women elected as delegates were conservatives.

The conference's two most controversial proposals were a call for government funding for abortion and an endorsement of equal rights for lesbians and gay men. Friedan, in particular, had been deeply hostile to the homosexual rights movement—she thought it would doom the fight for equal rights—and had publicly regretted any perceived ties between feminism and lesbianism. Earlier in the year, Anita Bryant, a pop singer and mother of four, had launched a campaign that she called "Save Our Children." She hoped to save children from the prospect of gay and lesbian schoolteachers (who, she implied, would indoctrinate and sexually abuse children). A former Miss Oklahoma, Bryant, a Southern Baptist living in Florida, objected to a proposed Miami ordinance barring sexual preference–based discrimination in employment, warning of Sodom and Gomorrah. Bryant's campaign backfired. By the time the women's convention opened in Houston, Bryant's crusade against what she described as "a well-organized, highly financed, and politically militant group of homosexual activists" had convinced many liberal feminists, previously reluctant, to throw their support behind homosexual rights.[45]

A hushed silence fell over the floor when Friedan rose during the debate over the gay rights plank. To almost universal surprise, she seconded the resolution to pass it. When the resolution carried in a voice vote, lavender and yellow balloons stamped "We Are Everywhere" rained on the hall.[46]

Not everyone celebrated. "This is a sham," declared a delegate from Illinois. "This conference is run by lesbians and militant feminists." The all-conservative Mississippi delegation knelt in prayer, raising signs that read KEEP THEM IN THE CLOSET. When the abortion plank passed, women carrying a giant blown-up photograph of a fetus rushed the stage while others, in tears, sang, "All we are saying, is give life a chance."[47]

Schlafly was delighted with both votes, which had been taken on the same night. "It is completely apparent now that the women's lib movement means government-financed abortions, government-supported day care and lesbians teaching in our schools," she told reporters. The state conferences, she said, had been so hostile to conservative women that they had driven them into STOP ERA. While the National Women's Conference met in the Sam Houston Coliseum, Schlafly staged a counterconference, across town, in the Astrodome. At the "pro-family, pro-life" rally, fifteen thousand women and men held signs like one that read "God Made Adam and Eve, not Adam and Steve."[48]

Before 1977, abortion and equal rights had remained distinct issues, with distinct constituencies. Pro-life organizations had offered very little support to the campaign to stop the ERA. In 1975, for instance, the National Right to Life Committee defeated an anti-ERA proposal. But by 1977, liberal feminists had driven from their ranks virtually all women who were opposed to abortion, and in Houston, they also drove from their ranks women who were opposed to homosexual rights. Schlafly welcomed these political exiles into her tent. Under a Pro-Woman, Pro-Life banner, she brought together people involved in what had previously been three distinct single-issue campaigns: anti-ERA, anti-abortion, and anti–homosexual rights.[49]

Schlafly provided the organizational strategy for this merger of causes. Her foot soldiers were parishioners in the nation's evangelical churches.

With some exceptions, evangelicals had steered clear of party politics for more than a century. Not since the crusade against slavery had Protestant churches engaged in overt politicking, but in the 1970s, determined to protect the family and the church from the state, evangelicals joined the conservative revolution. A series of decisions issued by the Supreme Court contributed to this turn. In 1961, the court overturned a Maryland law that required an employee to declare his belief in God. In 1962, it declared mandatory school prayer unconstitutional, and in two decisions in 1963 it struck down other forms of mandatory religious expression in schools: Bible reading and the recitation of the Lord's Prayer. Then, in 1971, in *Coit v. Green,* the court ruled that racially segregated private schools were not eligible for tax-exempt status. Under the post–*Coit v. Green* regime, private religious schools no longer provided a refuge for whites opposed to integration. Religious schools in the South investigated by the IRS included Bob Jones University and a school in Lynchburg, Virginia, run by the Southern Baptist Jerry Falwell, who had long since earned a national following as host of the weekly *Old-Time Gospel Hour*, a folksy television program in the tradition of the popular gospel radio shows of the 1920s and 1930s. Falwell, his black hair slicked back, sat before a curtain, his hands resting on his Bible, preaching plainly. *Coit v. Green*, an affirmation with no accompanying opinion, at first received little attention outside the schools affected by it. Later, it became useful to those Cold War conservatives who were segregationists: they attacked it as the latest in a series of rulings that, instead of realizing the constitutional promise of the Fourteenth Amendment and abiding by the court's decision in *Brown v. Board*, promoted communism. "This drive to root God out of our national life is the realization that America cannot be effectively socialized until it is secularized," said Strom Thurmond.[50]

*Green*'s significance, however, was limited. In the end, evangelicals were drawn into the conservative coalition by their religious beliefs, not by opposition to desegregation. In any case, opposition to desegregation did not chiefly come from evangelicals, nor was it limited to the South. Instead, it took different forms in different communities and in different parts of the country. In 1974, whites in Boston rioted over "forced busing," mandatory desegregation of the city's schools, earning for the home of the "cradle of liberty" a new moniker, the "Little Rock of the North," a call back to the terror of 1957. Unable to defeat mandatory desegregation, whites in many cities either sent their children to private schools or left for the suburbs; between 1974 and 1987, the number of white students in Boston's public schools dropped from 45,000 to 16,000.[51]

Paul Weyrich, Heritage Foundation political strategist, and Richard Viguerie, former Goldwater Republican and direct-mail executive, had long been laboring to bring evangelicals into a new conservative coalition by appealing to them on all sorts of issues. They soon recruited Falwell, who in 1979 founded the Moral Majority—the phrase, an echo of Nixon's Silent Majority, was coined by Weyrich—to fight against "secular humanism." Falwell, leaving his plain preaching behind and growing more and more strident, announced, "We are fighting a holy war, and this time we are going to win." To wage that holy war, Falwell rallied his follow-ers around the issues with which Schlafly had already recruited an army: opposition to gay rights, sexual freedom, women's liberation, the ERA, child care, and sex education, and, above all, abortion.[52]

Falwell would later maintain that this political crusade had begun, for him, in 1973, the moment he read of the court's decision in *Roe*. But that was far from the case. Southern Baptists had, in fact, earlier fought for the liberalization of abortion laws. In 1971, the church's national conven-tion, meeting in Missouri, passed this resolution: "We call upon Southern Baptists to work for legislation that will allow the possibility of abortion under such conditions as rape, incest, clear evidence of severe fetal defor-mity, and carefully ascertained evidence of the likelihood of damage to the emotional, mental, and physical health of the mother." The South-ern Baptist Convention reaffirmed this resolution in 1974 and used sim-ilar language in 1976. Pat Robertson, another Southern Baptist minister, founder of the Christian Broadcasting Network, called abortion "a strictly theological matter." Falwell's change of heart and the evangelical turn against abortion struck some Catholics as belated and insincere. In 1982, the founder of the American Life League sneered, "Falwell couldn't spell abortion five years ago."[53]

For the Republican Party, a day of judgment had come. Reagan, sixty-nine, had been the party's most powerful conservative since his election as governor of California in 1966, though he had stood largely in the wings, stage right. Defeated by the moderate Gerald Ford for the pres-idential nomination in 1976, it nevertheless seemed to Reagan and his devoted supporters that his time to lead the nation had finally arrived. He had Schlafly's support. And evangelicals had joined the conservative coalition. During the campaign, Falwell was said to have traveled some three hundred thousand miles; the Moral Majority claimed to have chap-ters in forty-seven states and to have registered four million voters. Pat Robertson, together with Bill Bright, from Campus Crusade for Christ, staged a Washington for Jesus rally, a gathering of a quarter of a million conservative Christians. They took over the leadership of the Southern Baptist Convention and in 1980 passed new resolutions against the ERA, abortion, and homosexuality.[54]

Moderates in the party—especially women—fought back, hoping to retain power. On the first day of the party's 1980 convention in Detroit,

Jill Ruckelshaus, the wife of William Ruckelshaus and sometimes known as the "Gloria Steinem of the Republican Party," spoke at an equal rights rally of 12,000. She wore suffragist white. "My party has endorsed the Equal Rights Amendment for 40 years," Ruckelshaus noted. "Dwight Eisenhower endorsed ERA. Richard Nixon endorsed ERA. Gerald Ford endorsed ERA." And then she pleaded, "Give me back my party!"[55]

Tanya Melich, who had helped found the National Women's Political Caucus, decried a "Republican War against Women," a charge Democrats made their own. Mary Crisp, RNC co-chair, was driven out. She left the party and campaigned for the independent candidate, John Anderson. Said Crisp, of the party of Abraham Lincoln and Susan B. Anthony, "We are reversing our position and are about to bury the rights of over 100 million American women under a heap of platitudes."[56]

They cried in vain. Even as liberal Republicans warned that the GOP was in danger of becoming "God's own party," conservatives seized control—and would hold it for decades. "We've already taken control of the conservative movement, and conservatives have taken control of the Republican Party," Richard Viguerie wrote. "The remaining thing is to see if we can take control of the country."[57]

Reagan won the nomination, and accepted it with his characteristic cheer and resolve, with a voice perfected on the radio and a face made for television. "Three hundred and sixty years ago, in 1620, a group of families dared to cross a mighty ocean to build a future for themselves in a new world," he said. "When they arrived at Plymouth, Massachusetts, they formed what they called a 'compact'; an agreement among themselves to build a community and abide by its laws." Citing divine providence, Reagan proposed a new American covenant. He closed, "I'm going to suggest—I'm more afraid not to—that we begin our crusade joined together in a moment of silent prayer." And then he bowed his head and prayed.[58]

Reagan's genuine warmth suffused that final night of the convention but its days had featured fiery speeches of bitter denunciation and cold calculation. Republican moderate and longtime supporter of equal rights George Romney was reduced to calling supporters of the ERA "moral perverts." The party's platform committee called for a constitutional ban on abortion. Reagan's running mate, George H. W. Bush, in a dramatic turnabout, had changed his position about both ERA and abortion. When asked about his reversals, he waved the question aside: "I'm not going to get nickel-and-dimed to death with detail."[59]

The constitutional rights of women and of fetuses are not mere details. Nor were the Equal Rights Amendment and abortion "wedge" issues. The conservative takeover of the Republican Party—and, later, of Congress, the courts, and the White House—resulted from the use made by political strategists of issues that had come to be understood by advocates on both sides as matters of fundamental rights. As would be the case with the right to bear arms as well, politicians and political strategists needed these issues to *remain* unresolved: describing rights as vulnerable is what got out the vote.

Yet as Viguerie often pointed out, the conservative takeover of the Republican Party also marked a triumph of technology. The first mass-consumer desktop computers, like the Apple II, the Commodore PET, and the TRS-80, appeared in 1977. But long before that, Viguerie was using a mainframe. The Republican technological advantage would last for a long time; the RNC acquired its first mainframe in 1977; the DNC didn't get its own until the 1980s.[60] "Because conservatives have mastered the new technology," Viguerie wrote, "we've been able to bypass the Left's near-monopoly of the national news media." The New Right didn't really have new ideas, Viguerie maintained; it had new tools: "using computers, direct mail, telephone marketing, TV (including cable TV) and radio, cassette tapes and toll-free numbers among other things to ask for contributions and votes." Viguerie was a particular master of the direct-mail campaign, which used the census, campaign finance records, polling, and election data to target individual households. "Conservatives have identified about 4,000,000 contributors," Viguerie reported in 1980, sixteen years after he made his first list, by recording the names and addresses of 12,000 Americans who donated $50 or more to Barry Goldwater. "I estimate that the liberals have identified less than 1,500,000." Direct mail and cable television segmented the electorate and balkanized the public. Conservatives didn't waste their energy talking to voters outside the demographic they hoped to reach, which saved them money and made their campaigns more efficient; new technologies also provided candidates with an incentive for invective. Above all, they allowed conservatives to bypass the mass media, newspapers, and the gatekeepers of broadcast television, which, increasingly, conservatives represented as the enemy.[61]

Nearly as influential in the rise of the New Right was the growth of the polling industry. Beginning in the early 1970s, George Gallup's son, George Jr., a devout Episcopalian, used polls to measure the strength of the evangelical movement, even though, as critics pointed out, polling overrepresented churchgoing Americans, who, civic- and community-minded, were more likely than their fellow citizens to participate. Broader concerns about polling that had been raised in the 1930s reemerged in the 1970s. In 1972, political scientist Leo Bogart demonstrated that most of what polls do is manufacture opinion, given that a sizable portion of Americans know nothing or nearly nothing or else hold no opinion about the subjects and issues raised. "The first question a pollster should ask," Bogart wrote, is "'Have you thought about this at all? Do you *have* an opinion?'" A subsequent congressional investigation into the industry raised, once again, a series of troubling questions about the accuracy of polls, and about their place in a democracy, but a proposed Truth-in-Polling Act failed. Instead, polling grew and spread, as media corporations, equipped with computers, began conducting their own polls. In *Precision Journalism: A Reporter's Introduction to Social Science Methods*, published in 1973, Philip Meyer, Washington correspondent for an Akron, Ohio, newspaper, urged reporters to conduct their own polls: "If your newspaper has a data-processing department, then it has key-punch machines and people to operate them." Two years later, the *New York Times* and CBS released a joint poll—the first media-made poll. Critics pointed out that, ethically, the press, which is supposed to report news, can't also produce it, but media-run polls exploded all the same.[62]

As had been the case in the decades before the Civil War, when evangelicals re-entered politics, partisan politics took on the zeal of religion. Alarmed, political scientists devised new methods for quantifying Americans' growing political fervor, including measuring polarization among members of Congress by analyzing roll-call votes. By that measure, congressional polarization had begun to decline not long after the Civil War, and it continued to decline throughout much of the twentieth century, when Republicans became more moderate. In the 1970s, when Republicans became more conservative, polarization surged. The migration of Southern Democrats to the GOP explains only about a third of this shift. Much of it is better understood as a consequence of the politicization of abortion. Between 1978 and 1984, pro-life Democrats and pro-choice

Republicans were purged from their parties. After Reagan, a so-called gender gap appeared to open. Between 1920, the beginning of women's suffrage, and 1980, women had tended to vote disproportionately for Republican presidential candidates, if by small margins. That changed in 1980, when more women voted for Carter than for Reagan by a gap of 8 percentage points, presumably because the Democratic Party had begun billing itself as the party of women. Republican strategists concluded that, in trading (white) women for (white) men, they'd gotten the better end of the deal. Said one Republican consultant about the Democrats, "They do so badly among men that the fact that we don't do quite as well among women becomes irrelevant."[63]

The change came slowly. Until the late 1980s, Republicans were more pro-choice than Democrats.[64] But before long, the parties were sorted ideologically, and, while conservatives thought of themselves as perfecting targeted political messaging through emerging technologies and liberals believed that they were advancing identity politics, together they amounted to the same thing: a more atomized and enraged electorate, conveniently reached through computer-generated mailing and telephone lists.

The ERA's last chance at ratification expired in 1982. "Ding, Dong, the Witch Is Dead" the amendment's opponents sang at a celebration of its defeat.[65] By then, both parties had abandoned a political settlement necessary to the stability of the Republic—equal rights for women—and descended into a politics of seemingly interminable division that would outlive nearly all of the people who had been its architects, including Phyllis Schlafly, whose last public act, in 2016, at the age of ninety-one, only months before her death, would be to endorse Donald J. Trump as the nation's next president.

## II.

"GOVERNMENT IS NOT the solution to our problem," Ronald Reagan said in his inaugural address, in 1981. "Government is the problem." Two months after he was sworn in as president, he told the Conservative Political Action Conference that his social, economic, and foreign policy agendas were three parts of a whole: "Just as we seek to put our

*Ronald Reagan, a man of immense personal charm,*
*greeted supporters in Indiana during his 1980 campaign.*

financial house in order and rebuild our nation's defenses, so too we seek to protect the unborn, to end the manipulation of schoolchildren by utopian planners, and permit the acknowledgement of a Supreme Being in our classrooms."[66]

Reagan had ridden into office on the back of a revolt against an elaborate and tortured tax code, an accretion of exemptions, preferences, credits, and loopholes. To the extent that the tax code represented a liberal agenda, liberals failed to defend it and, instead, agreed with its critics. Campaigning in 1976, Jimmy Carter called the tax code "a disgrace to the human race." A new American tax revolt began in earnest in 1978, when Californians passed Proposition 13, a ballot measure that cut the state's property tax by 57 percent and eviscerated the state's public education system; California voters endorsed it 2 to 1; the *New York Times* called the referendum a "primal scream by the People against Big Government." Tom Wolfe pronounced the seventies the "Me Decade."[67]

Reagan's economic thinking had been influenced by the writing of Milton Friedman, who, over the course of Reagan's own political career, moved from the academy to celebrity. Friedman earned a PhD at Columbia in 1946 and during the 1940s and 1950s became well known among economists as a contrarian on monetary policy and a vigorous opponent of Keynesianism. In 1962, Friedman published a book aimed at a general audience, *Capitalism and Freedom*, in which he argued that personal freedom can only be assured by the free market system. In his 1967 presidential address to the American Economic Association, Friedman upended conventional thinking about a trade-off between unemployment and inflation; when stagflation arrived in the 1970s, he appeared prescient. From 1966 to 1984, Friedman wrote a regular column for *Newsweek*, a period during which he also was interviewed in *Playboy* (1973), won the Nobel Prize (1976), appeared on *The Phil Donahue Show* (1979), and hosted a PBS series, *Free to Choose* (1980).[68]

Friedman's prominence as a public intellectual lent support to the call for tax cuts made by conservatives who, beginning with Republican congressman and ex–football star Jack Kemp in 1977, endorsed "supply-side economics," arguing that reducing the tax rate would promote economic growth. But the "bible of the Reagan revolution" was *Wealth and Poverty*, a book published in 1981 by George Gilder, the living writer Reagan cited more than any other.[69]

Gilder, born in 1939, had been a speechwriter for Nelson Rockefeller, George Romney, and Richard Nixon in the 1960s, after a stint in the marines and an undergraduate education at Harvard. He wanted to write like Joan Didion, with whom he was infatuated. By the early 1970s, he'd met William F. Buckley and abandoned liberal Republicanism. He achieved the writerly fame he'd wished for as a bad boy of American journalism when he in 1973 published *Sexual Suicide*, a frantic indictment of feminism that earned him the title of Male Chauvinist Pig of the Year, awarded to him by both NOW and *Time*. In *Sexual Suicide*, Gilder argued that the liberation of women would violate what he called the "sexual constitution," the unwritten arrangement that, through sex, binds men to women, who take care of their children for them. "The whole sexual constitution is based on the maternal tie," Gilder wrote. "Women's liberation tries to reject this role." Feminists were ruining this arrangement, he charged, and were to be blamed for "the frustration of the affluent young and their resort to drugs, the breakdown of the family among both the rich and poor, the rising rate of crime and violence." Preserving the sexual constitution, he argued, "may be even more important to the social order than preservation of the legal constitution."[70]

Eight years later, *Wealth and Poverty* served as a bridge between the conservative critique of feminism and the conservative embrace of supply-side economics, in which Gilder attacked fellow conservatives for being too restrained in their approval of capitalism. Steve Forbes compared it, in importance, to Adam Smith's 1776 *The Wealth of Nations*. For Gilder, wealth is always altruistic—"capitalism begins with giving"—and "real poverty is less a state of income than a state of mind," the dependency cultivated by government relief. As Gilder saw it, working women posed a problem not only for the traditional family but for economic growth; by raising family incomes, they contributed to inflation, which had become rampant by the end of the decade. A man's role as primary breadwinner was central to Gilder's social thought in the 1970s; his celebration of the unregulated entrepreneur was central to his economic thought in the 1980s.[71] For his third act, in the 1990s, Gilder would play the role of digital utopian, arguing for a regulation-free Internet.

Influenced by Gilder and supply-side economics, Reagan made tax cuts the centerpiece of his campaign. During his time in office, the top income tax rate, which had been above 90 percent in the 1940s and 1950s, fell from 70 percent to 28 percent. He also slashed certain kinds of federal spending, arguing that Aid to Families with Dependent Children, Medicaid, and other programs promoted dependency and immorality and were destructive of family life, especially by providing counterincentives to marriage. Between 1970 and 1990, the percentage of illegitimate birth rose from 38 percent to 67 percent for blacks and from 6 percent to 17 percent for whites. The number of recipients for AFDC had risen from 7.4 million in 1970 to 10.6 million in 1980. Under Reagan-era reforms, more than a million poor people lost food stamp benefits.[72]

Meanwhile, Reagan's administration doggedly protected other forms of federal assistance, calling programs like Social Security and Medicare, which provided assistance to the elderly rather than to the poor, off-limits. He also vastly expanded military spending by 35 percent from 1981 to 1989, the largest-ever peacetime increase.[73] During Reagan's eight years in office, the national debt tripled, rising from $917 billion to $2.7 trillion; by 1989, it constituted 53 percent of the gross domestic product. The federal government grew, too, as the number of federal employees rose from 2.9 million to 3.1. Deregulating the economy also proved costly. Reagan-era deregulation included allowing savings-and-loan banks to sell junk bonds and high-risk securities. Freed from federal government oversight, many S&Ls acted recklessly and eventually collapsed; the federal government spent $132 billion in taxpayer dollars to bail them out.[74] Conservatives proposed cutting spending and shrinking the federal government. But what came to be called "Reaganomics" did neither. Instead, conservatives consolidated their power by answering the liberal claims for reproductive rights with a different constitutional demand: the right to bear arms.

IN MARCH 1981, outside the Washington Hilton, John Hinckley Jr., the twenty-five-year-old mentally ill son of the president of a Denver oil company, shot Ronald Reagan with a .22-caliber revolver that he'd bought at a pawn shop in Dallas. Hinckley fired six shots in 1.7 seconds, hitting not only the president but also a DC police officer, a Secret Service agent, and James Brady, the White House press secretary. Reagan was rushed into surgery while a worried nation held its breath.

Not only had gun ownership and gun regulation not, historically, been partisan issues, they hadn't been matters of extensive constitutional debate, either. The National Rifle Association, founded in 1871, had fought for state and federal gun safety measures in the 1920s and 1930s. In 1957, when the NRA moved into new headquarters, its motto, at the building's entrance, read, "Firearms Safety Education, Marksmanship Training, Shooting for Recreation." The NRA supported a ban on mail-order gun sales debated by Congress in 1963, after Lee Harvey Oswald assassinated John F. Kennedy with an Italian military surplus rifle that he'd ordered from the NRA magazine, *American Rifleman*. "We do not think that any sane American, who calls himself an American, can object to placing into this bill the instrument which killed the president of the United States," said the NRA's executive vice president, testifying before Congress. The NRA supported the 1968 Gun Control Act, passed after the assassinations of Robert Kennedy and Martin Luther King Jr., banning mail-order sales, restricting certain high-risk people from purchasing guns, and prohibiting the importation of military surplus firearms. Some elements of the legislation "appear unduly restrictive and unjustified in their application to law-abiding citizens," said the NRA's executive vice president, but "the measure as a whole appears to be one that the sports-men of America can live with."[75]

During this debate, the Second Amendment—"A well-regulated militia being necessary to the security of a free State, the right of the people to keep and bear arms shall not be infringed"—had little place, since it had generally been understood to protect the right of citizens to bear arms for the common defense. In the two centuries since the nation's founding, no amendment had received less attention in the courts than the Second, except the Third, which concerns the quartering of troops. This began to change in the 1960s, not because the NRA started talking about the Second Amendment, but because black nationalists did. In 1964, not long before he was shot to death, Malcolm X said, "Article number two of the constitutional amendments provides you and me the right to own a rifle or a shotgun." That same argument animated the founding of the Black Panther Party.[76]

Republicans had been, at that time, as likely as Democrats to support gun safety measures, as part of law and order campaigns. Reagan, as governor of California, had supported gun safety measures, signing the Mulford Act in 1967. And both Nixon's law-and-order campaign and his declared war on drugs involved support for gun regulation. In 1972, Nixon, who believed guns to be "an abomination," urged Congress to pass a ban on "Saturday night specials," privately wished Congress would ban all handguns, and confessed that he found the idea that gun ownership is a constitutional right to be absurd. "I don't know why any individual should have a right to have a revolver in his house," he said, echoing remarks made earlier by Reagan.[77]

The idea that the Second Amendment guarantees an individual's right to carry a gun, rather than the people's right to form armed militias to provide for the common defense, became the official position of the NRA only in the 1970s, and only after a struggle not unlike the contest over abortion among the leaders of the Republican National Committee. Part of the backlash against both feminism and civil rights, gun rights became a conservative political movement, a rights fight for white men.

If, in the 1960s, the gun debate took place in the shadow of the Black Power movement, in the 1970s it took place in the shadow of a growing White Power movement. A whitelash that began as a reaction against the civil rights movement in the 1960s gained strength in the 1970s and 1980s as a reaction to changing patterns of immigration. No federal law had restricted immigration before the 1870s, but the United States had instituted a set of quotas by place of origin, most significantly in the National Origins Act of 1924. By 1970, only 9.6 million Americans, less than 5 percent of the U.S. population, were foreign-born, the lowest percentage in more than a century, and most of these immigrants had come from Europe. By 2000, the number of foreign-born Americans had risen to 28 million, constituting 29 percent of the U.S. population. Most of these newer immigrants were from Latin America and East Asia. Five million immigrants had entered the United States between 1931 and 1965; 4.5 million entered in the 1970s, 7.3 in the 1980s, and 9.1 in the 1990s, not counting those who entered the country illegally.[78] Immigration moved to the center of American political debate.

Immigration patterns had begun to change in the second half of the 1960s as a result of Johnson's 1965 Immigration and Nationality Act, usually classed with the 1964 Civil Rights Act and 1965 Voting Rights Act as his signal accomplishments. Aimed at defeating Jim Crow–era racial discrimination, the 1965 Immigration Act had replaced the old quota system with a new system that did not discriminate on the basis of race or national origins. The new quota system mandated an equivalence: quotas from any country, anywhere in the Eastern Hemisphere, were the same: 20,000 per country. And it also raised the total number of immigrants per year to 290,000. Instead of setting racial and national-origins preferences, the legislation established preferences based on family and occupation. Beginning in 1965, in short, people from the developing world were legally able to immigrate to the United States. They also entered a nation that was redefining citizenship. "Citizenship *is* man's basic right, for it is nothing less than the right to have rights," Earl Warren had written in 1958.

Under the new system, the number of legal immigrants from non-European countries rose, but the number of legal immigrants from Mexico fell. Under the 1924 regime, Mexico and the rest of the Western Hemisphere had been exempt from the quota system; that ended in 1965. And the Bracero Program, which had brought migrant workers from Mexico into the country legally since 1942, was also ended. Under the post-1965 regime, the number of legal immigrants from Mexico fell by 40 percent.

The scale of Mexican immigration, however, remained virtually the same: roughly the same number of Mexicans continued to cross the border after the labor reforms, but two out of every five were now "undocumented" and deemed to be illegal aliens, subject to deportation. Mexican American intellectuals and activists had in the 1960s been at the vanguard of the academic study of ethnicity and the pursuit of immigration reform as an integrationist civil rights struggle, a position that took a turn toward ethnic separatism and nationalism with the emergence of the Chicano movement. By the 1970s, an older generation of Mexican Americans, led by Cesar Chavez and the United Farm Workers, considered illegal Mexican immigrants a threat to unionization efforts, while younger Chicano activists urged the lifting of immigration restriction, classing Immigration and Naturalization Service sweeps as actions of a brutal police state. By the mid-1970s, the Chicano activists had won this debate, both sides agreeing that "to learn how to protect the rights of workers without papers is to learn how to protect ourselves." Nevertheless, by the 1990s, the U.S.-Mexican border had become, effectively, a military zone.[79]

The gun rights movement was tightly bound to anti-immigrant animus. The NRA turned itself from a sporting and hunting association into a powerhouse political interest group during the very years that hostility against immigration was on the rise. In 1975, the NRA created a lobbying arm, the Institute for Legislative Action, and named as its head Harlon Bronson Carter, an award-winning marksman and former chief of the U.S. Border Control. Not long after, the NRA's leadership, objecting to Carter's political aims, decided to force him out and to move the organization's headquarters to Colorado Springs. But at the NRA's annual meeting in 1977, Carter and his allies staged a rebellion and succeeded in ousting the old leadership, rewriting the organization's bylaws and, instead of moving to Colorado, keeping the NRA in Washington. At the door of its headquarters, a new motto appeared, cleaving the second clause of the Second Amendment from the first: "The Right of the People to Keep and Bear Arms Shall Not Be Infringed."[80]

Only after Carter became executive vice president of the NRA did it come out in the press that he had been convicted of murder in Laredo, Texas, in 1931, when he was seventeen years old. He'd come home from school to find his mother distressed about three boys she suspected of

*The lines between the parties hardened over guns and abortion, one meaning freedom and the other murder, though which meant which depended on the party.*

having been involved in stealing the family's car. Carter, armed with a shotgun, found the boys and demanded that they come back to his house with him. Twelve-year-old Salvador Peña testified at Carter's murder trial that after Ramón Casiano, fifteen, pulled out a knife and refused to go, Carter shot Casiano in the chest. Carter was convicted, though the verdict was later overturned on an appeal that rested on the judge's instructions to the jury.[81]

With Carter at its helm, the NRA in 1980 endorsed Reagan, the first time the organization had endorsed a presidential candidate in its century-long history. But, like Oswald's assassination of Kennedy in 1963, Hinckley's attempted assassination of Reagan in 1981 called attention to the ease with which Americans could buy and carry all kinds of guns and ammunition, well past the needs of hunters and sportsmen. Reagan, rushed into surgery, recovered quickly. His press secretary, James Brady, who had been shot in the head with a bullet designed to explode on impact, was permanently paralyzed. He and his wife later founded what would become the Brady Campaign to Prevent Gun Violence. Hinckley was found not guilty by reason of insanity. Despite considerable pressure, Reagan maintained his opposition to legislation that might have banned semiautomatic weapons or prevented their purchase by people with a history of mental illness.[82] Reagan, shot by a handgun-wielding would-be assassin, had become so staunch an opponent of gun laws during his presidency that he advocated for the abolition of the Bureau of Alcohol, Tobacco and Firearms.

Both reproductive rights and gun rights arguments rest on weak constitutional foundations; their very shakiness is what makes them so useful for partisan purposes: gains seem always in danger of being lost. But their foundations are weak for different reasons. And the conservative position on guns rose to the status of party doctrine partly because of the role it played in a conservative strategy to take over the judiciary—and to institutionalize a new way of reading the Constitution.

Conservatives believed that liberals had controlled the federal government, the university, the press, and the courts since the 1930s, and that a conservative revolution would require either taking over these institutions or founding alternatives, or, more practically, accomplishing the first by beginning with the second. Nowhere did conservatives execute this strategy more carefully than with the courts. For a very long time, conservatives had trouble winning elections, a difficulty they often attributed to the role played by a liberal press. Liberals had won their greatest victories in the courts, especially in the rights revolution that began with *Brown v. Board*. Under these circumstances, the best way to win political victories appeared to be by changing the courts, and even constitutional interpretation itself. In the 1970s and 1980s, this campaign took form in the reinterpretation of the Second Amendment, the founding of the Federalist Society, and the development of a new mode of constitutional interpretation, known as originalism.[83]

In 1982, Utah's Orrin Hatch became chairman of the Senate Judiciary Committee's Subcommittee on the Constitution and commissioned a history of the Second Amendment that resulted in a report, *The Right to Keep and Bear Arms*. Hatch's committee concluded that the Second Amendment had been misinterpreted for nearly two centuries. The report concluded, "What the Subcommittee on the Constitution uncovered was clear—and long lost—proof that the second amendment to our Constitution was intended as an individual right of the American citizen to keep and carry arms in a peaceful manner, for protection of himself, his family, and his freedoms."[84]

As late as 1986, the Second Amendment was still known as the "lost amendment." But by 1991, a poll found that Americans were more familiar with the Second Amendment than with the First.[85] Nevertheless, Hatch's committee relied less on anything ever written by James Madison than on very recent scholarship funded by the NRA. Of twenty-seven law review articles published between 1970 and 1989 that were favorable to the NRA's interpretation of the Second Amendment, at least nineteen were written by authors employed or represented by the NRA or other gun rights groups.[86] The argument, that a new interpretation was not new at all but was instead a restoration of an older, long-lost interpretation, was pivotal to the work of self-described constitutional originalists, who sought to scrape away centuries of accreted interpretation to uncover the Constitution's original meaning and the founders' original intentions.

Originalism was, in large part, an answer to the Supreme Court's privacy-based decisions about contraception and abortion; if the left could find rights in penumbras and emanations, the right would find them in ink and parchment. Originalism flowered in law schools, especially through the Federalist Society, founded at the University of Chicago and Yale Law Schools in 1982; a year later, it had chapters at more than seventy law schools. (Nearly every federal judge appointed by Reagan's three Republican successors, George H. W. Bush, George W. Bush, and Donald Trump, had either been a member of, or had been approved by, the Federalist Society.) Originalism also became the official policy of the Reagan Justice Department, headed by his attorney general, Edwin Meese. Meese's Justice Department functioned as a de facto conservative think tank.[87]

In 1985, Meese announced that "the Administration's approach to constitutional interpretation" was to be "rooted in the text of the Constitution as illuminated by those who drafted, proposed, and ratified it." He called this a "jurisprudence of original intention," and contrasted it to the "misuse of history" by jurists, by which he meant liberals, who saw, in the Constitution's "spirit," things like "concepts of human dignity" with which they had turned the Constitution into a "charter for judicial activism."[88] Decisions like *Griswold* and *Roe*, which cited a so-called right to privacy, violated the precepts of originalism. But so, arguably, did *Brown v. Board*, and any number of decisions of the liberal Warren Court.

Liberal jurists and scholars, including historians, answered Meese's call with argument, derision, and disbelief. Justice William Brennan suggested that anyone who had ever studied in the archives or worked with historical records knew better than to believe that the records of the constitutional convention and the ratifying conventions offered so certain, exact, and singular a verdict as that which Meese expected to find there. Brennan called the idea that modern judges could discern the framers' original intention "little more than arrogance cloaked as humility." As to originalists' particular readings, historians tended to find them absurd. In a searing critique of the new interpretation of the Second Amendment, the historian Garry Wills pointed out that the Second Amendment had everything to do with the common defense and nothing to do with hunting: "One does not bear arms against a rabbit."[89]

These arguments did little to narrow the broadening reach of originalism, which the New Right presented to the public as constitutional common sense through a sustained campaign of direct mail, talk radio, and cable television.[90] Many Americans came to believe that originalism was itself original, a mode of constitutional interpretation that dated to the 1790s rather than to the 1980s. The gun debate descended into irrationality. Liberals often reacted hysterically to conservative gun rights arguments, and called for impossible-to-pass gun control measures, measures whose consequences the NRA delightedly exaggerated. Under these circumstances, some gun owners grew genuinely fearful that the federal government intended to seize their guns. Meanwhile, the NRA's interpretation of the Second Amendment, like originalism itself, prevailed. In 1986, Congress repealed parts of the 1968 Gun Control Act in a Firearms Owners' Protection Act that invoked "the rights of citizens . . . to keep and bear arms under the second amendment."[91] In 1991, Warren Burger called the new interpretation of the Second Amendment "one of the greatest pieces of fraud, I repeat the word 'fraud,' on the American public by special interest groups that I have ever seen in my lifetime."[92] It was, indeed, breathtaking. In a few short, violent years, guns became for conservatives what abortion had become for liberals: an emotionally charged matter of a constitutionally guaranteed, individual right with which party operatives could reliably get voters to the polls because, in fact, the constitutional guarantee was no guarantee at all.

———

THE FIRST PRESIDENT to serve two full terms since Dwight Eisenhower, Reagan carried his domestic agenda on the back of his foreign policy successes. The OPEC oil crisis had made plain how desperately American dependence on foreign oil tied the United States to an unstable Middle East. In January 1979, Iranian revolutionaries led by a Muslim cleric named Ayatollah Ruhollah Khomeini had seized control of the government, ousting the shah, a tyrant who had been installed and supported by the United States. In November, rebels took sixty-six Americans hostage at the U.S. embassy and Foreign Ministry offices and demanded that the shah be returned to Iran from his exile in the United States. The crisis, including a tragically failed rescue attempt, was covered nightly on television news; ABC News launched a regular report called *America Held Hostage*. In December 1979, the Soviet Union invaded Afghanistan. By way of sanctions, Carter withdrew from the Senate an arms limitation agreement known as SALT II. In a final rebuke to Carter, the revolutionaries in Tehran released the American hostages as soon as Reagan took office, humiliating Carter, and handing to the incoming president an unearned but powerful political victory.[93]

Every president since Eisenhower had been troubled by the world's growing nuclear arsenal. By the 1980s, fear of a nuclear holocaust had merged with a rising concern about global environmental catastrophe. In the early 1960s, environmental scientists charged with studying the effects of nuclear weapons on the natural world began to notice that nuclear explosions depleted the ozone layer that protects the earth's atmosphere, an effect that could be measured by comparing the ozone layer both before and after the United States and the USSR agreed to stop atmospheric tests of nuclear weapons in 1963. Meanwhile, the publication, in 1962, of Rachel Carson's *Silent Spring* brought to the public a growing scientific concern about the effects of industrial pollution on water, soil, and air. In the wake of *Silent Spring*, the U.S. government formed a number of advisory and oversight organizations, including the Environmental Pollution Panel of the President's Science Advisory Committee. The panel's 1965 report, *Restoring the Quality of Our Environment*, included an appendix on "Atmospheric Carbon Dioxide," laying out, with much alarm, the consequences of "the invisible pollutant" for the planet as a whole.[94] In 1968, S. Fred Singer, an atmospheric physicist and environmental scientist who had worked on satellites and was now a deputy assistant secretary of the interior, organized a symposium on "Global Effects of Environmental Pollution." Four papers were presented at a panel on "Effects of Atmospheric Pollution on Climate."[95] (What would come to be called climate-change science had its origins in the study of nuclear weapons fallout.)

Nuclear weapons research was usually classified; other environmental research was not, and, fueled by that research, the environmental movement exploded. In 1970, Richard Nixon had established the Environmental Protection Agency and expanded the Clean Air Act; two years later, he signed the Clean Water Act. But, especially after the first photographs of the whole earth were taken from space—photographs that became the icon of the environmental movement—environmentalists, pointing out that atmospheric pollution does not honor national boundaries, began to argue for the need for global measures. The same case was made, beginning in the 1970s, by activists who called for nuclear disarmament and a weapons "freeze," an end to all testing, manufacture, and deployment, a proposal that enjoyed the support of hundreds of scientists, congressional Democrats, and mainline Protestant churches, as well as that of sixty-nine Catholic bishops.[96]

The call for a weapons freeze, as much on environmental grounds as on military, moral, or political grounds, soon reached Congress. In 1982, *The New Yorker* published a four-part series by Jonathan Schell called "The Fate of the Earth," which led Tennessee congressman Al Gore to convene House hearings into "The Consequences of Nuclear War on the Global Environment." But Reagan steered the nation in a different direction. In March 1983, he announced a Strategic Defense Initiative, SDI (quickly dubbed "Star Wars"), a plan to defend the United States from nuclear attack with a network of satellite-based missiles. Hoping to break out of the impasse of mutually assured destruction, Reagan proposed, with SDI, that the United States could engage in a "winnable" nuclear war.[97]

But no nuclear war could be winnable if a nuclear explosion would catastrophically affect the atmosphere of the entire planet. Cornell astronomer Carl Sagan, the wildly popular host of a PBS science series, *Cosmos,* became the public face of a body of scientific work that suggested that even a very limited nuclear war could lead to the end of all life on the planet by bringing about a "nuclear winter." Critics charged Sagan with hastening unproven work into publication and, worse, into the popular press. The physicist Edward Teller attacked Sagan in *Nature:* "Highly speculative theories of worldwide destruction—even the end of life on Earth—used as a call for a particular kind of political action serve neither the good reputation of science nor dispassionate political thought." Reagan's assistant secretary of defense, Richard Perle, said he wished Sagan would stop "playing political scientist." A number of environmental scientists challenged the science behind nuclear winter, pointing out that its conclusions were mostly predictions based on models and that the science was, therefore, not certain.[98]

With nuclear winter, conservatives extended their longstanding critique of the "liberal bias" of the media to science. For decades, conservatives, unlikely bedfellows with academic postmodernists, had been arguing against the idea of objectivity. "Fairness and honesty are much to be desired in newspapers of any sort," Russell Kirk wrote in 1969, "but a Utopian 'objectivity' usually is a mask for concealed prejudices and partisanship." Kirk and other conservatives had fought for the overturning of the FCC's 1949 Fairness Doctrine. A 1959 amendment to the Fairness Doctrine had required broadcasters to provide "varying opinions on the paramount issues facing the American people," because regarding "public controversies" the "public has a chance to hear both sides." In the 1950s and 1960s, conservatism itself had been controversial, conservatives pointed out, leaving them at a disadvantage under a regime that misrepresented itself as valuing "fairness." Instead of a public-interest-based rule for broadcasters, conservatives proposed a market-based rule: if people liked it, broadcasters could broadcast it. Ratings, not an "elite" of editors and experts, would become the arbiter of truth (with exactly the sort of malign consequences Walter Lippmann had warned about in the 1920s). Dismantling the Fairness Doctrine became a priority of the Reagan administration, a priority not unrelated to its campaign to discredit scientists like Sagan who opposed the Strategic Defense Initiative.[99]

Scientists who aimed to discredit the theory of nuclear winter deployed against science the argument that conservatives like Kirk had used against journalism: that the claims to objectivity of scientists like Sagan were nothing but thinly disguised partisanship. Significantly, the most prominent critics of the science of nuclear winter would go on to become the most prominent critics of the science of climate change. "Sagan's sce-

nario may well be correct," S. Fred Singer wrote in 1983, "but the range
of uncertainty is so great that the prediction is not particularly useful."
Singer served as a longtime consultant to ARCO, Exxon, Shell Oil, and
Sun Oil, and the Heartland Institute, founded in 1984, and was affiliated
with the Heritage Foundation. (Many scientists, of course, serve on the
boards of corporations and think tanks.)[100] "Most scientists do not believe
human greenhouse gas emissions are a proven threat to the environment
or to human well-being," the Heartland Institute would later announce,
"despite a barrage of propaganda insisting otherwise coming from the
environmental movement and echoed by its sycophants in the mainstream media." In 1984, the George C. Marshall Institute was founded by
NASA physicist Robert Jastrow; Frederick Seitz, a former president of the
National Academy of Sciences; and William Nierenberg, a past director
of the Scripps Institution of Oceanography. They aimed to counter Sagan
by arguing that nuclear winter was not science but politics. "The Nuclear
Winter scenario could not serve the needs of Soviet leaders better if it had
been designed for that purpose," Jastrow wrote. In 1988, funded, in part,
by ExxonMobil, the Marshall Institute turned its attention to challenging
the science behind global warming.[101]

The debate over nuclear winter, in short, established the themes and
battle lines of the debate over climate change, which would rage well
into the twenty-first century, long after the Cold War had ended. That
end came about because, by 1984, the Soviet economy had virtually collapsed. That year, when Reagan ran for reelection, the American economy had finally improved, the stock market at the beginning of a bull
market. Reagan's campaign announced, "It's morning again in America,"
with a television ad that featured farmers and suburban fathers, brides
in white, and American flags. (A sign of the worsening polarization, conservative Georgia congressman Newt Gingrich complained about the ad
campaign: "He should have been running against liberals and radicals.")
Reagan won nearly 60 percent of the popular vote and every state but
Minnesota, his opponent Walter Mondale's home state. (Mondale won
the District of Columbia.)[102]

In 1985, the United States and the USSR together held a stockpile
of more than sixty thousand warheads. Soviet leader Mikhail Gorbachev
began pursuing a policy of *glasnost*, opening the society, and *perestroika*,
restructuring the Soviet Union's collapsed economy. Keen to limit

defense spending, he agreed to a series of arms limitations talks beginning in Geneva. The talks stalled but, plainly, Gorbachev's position had drastically weakened.

The Cold War had lasted nearly half a century. It had been terrible and terrifying. It had lasted so long that it had been nearly impossible to imagine that it would ever end. And when it did, when communism began collapsing across the Soviet bloc, it began to look to many Americans as if Ronald Reagan, with a strong hand and an iron will, had saved the nation, and even the world.


THE FALL OF COMMUNISM liberated Eastern Europe. It also unleashed an unregulated capitalism that would widen economic inequality, destabilize the world order, and eventually threaten America's place in that order. There were precedents for changes on so epic a scale. Capitalism had been unregulated before, at the end of the nineteenth century, only to be subject to regulation once more during the Progressive Era and the New Deal. Empires and nations and ideologies had risen and fallen before, too, as during the Second World War, when a new order had emerged in its aftermath. But if Americans contemplating the consequences of the fall of communism and the end of the Cold War were wise to look to the past to anticipate the future, they were unable to imagine the revolution in information technology that would resist regulation and undermine efforts to establish a new political order.

Reagan, having stockpiled his political capital, set about restructuring the judiciary. Originalism was one strategy for turning back decisions made by the liberal Warren Court. Another strategy was to replace liberal justices with conservative ones, beginning with lower court appointments. While campaigning, Reagan had pledged to appoint only "family values" judges. Liberals read this as coded language meaning "white and Christian." Edwin Meese handled the selection of 369 district and appeals court judges, more than had been appointed by any other president. Of those 369 judges, only twenty-two were nonwhite. By the time Reagan left office, his appointees constituted nearly half of all judges on federal courts.[103]

In 1982, Reagan appointed University of Chicago law professor Antonin Scalia to the DC Circuit Court; four years later, he named him to the Supreme Court. A member of the Federalist Society, Scalia, a father of nine, was also a devout Catholic. Scalia became the Supreme Court's most learned and eloquent proponent of originalism. Between judges interpreting the Constitution and judges trying to figure out what the framers meant, he argued, originalism was plainly the lesser evil. "The purpose of constitutional guarantees . . . is precisely to prevent the law from reflecting certain *changes* in original values that the society adopting the Constitution thinks fundamentally undesirable," Scalia wrote.[104]

Scalia joined the court in 1986, just after it issued a landmark 5–4 decision in *Bowers v. Hardwick,* refusing to overturn a ban on sodomy in Georgia. The gay rights movement had grown during the 1980s in the face of a public health crisis. AIDS as a disease was first identified in 1981; HIV was isolated in 1984. By 1989, the CDC confirmed that AIDS had infected 82,764 Americans and killed 46,344 and estimated that ten times as many cases of infection had not yet been reported. Three out of four cases in the 1980s were gay men. As some leaders of the Christian Coalition called the disease God's vengeance—Pat Buchanan said "nature is exacting an awful retribution"—Reagan kept silent: he didn't speak publicly about AIDS until 1985, when he responded to a question about the disease at a press conference. And still the federal government offered scant support for research and public health services.[105]

*Bowers* had been part of a legal campaign to decriminalize homosexuality by building on the right to privacy established in the chain of cases that began with *Griswold v. Connecticut.* The court rejected this argument: "No connection between family, marriage, or procreation, on the one hand, and homosexual activity, on the other, has been demonstrated"; therefore, the case turned not on a right to privacy but on the claim of a "fundamental right to engage in homosexual sodomy," which, the court determined, did not exist. (Justice Lewis Powell, who joined the majority, said to one of his clerks at the time, "I don't believe I've ever met a homosexual." Unknown to Powell, that clerk, as well as several of Powell's earlier clerks, was a closeted gay man.) Justice Harry Blackmun, dissenting, argued that the case did indeed turn on a right to privacy: "If that right means anything, it means that, before Georgia can prosecute its citizens for making choices about the most intimate aspects of their lives, it must do more than assert that the choice they have made is an 'abominable crime not fit to be named among Christians.'"[106]

Liberal legal scholars and jurists had long been frustrated with the right to privacy as a constitutional argument with which to understand rights having to do with women, sexuality, and the family. In *Griswold*, *Roe*, and *Bowers*, amicus briefs submitted on behalf of the plaintiffs by organizations that included the ACLU, Planned Parenthood, and the Lambda Legal Defense and Education Fund made arguments based on equality that the court simply ignored, instead choosing to base its opinion in these cases on privacy.[107] After the deadline for ratifying the ERA expired in 1982, it appeared that women and gay men would be granted not equality but, at best, privacy. "A right to privacy looks like an injury got up as a gift," the controversial feminist legal theorist Catharine MacKinnon argued in 1983. In 1985, Ruth Bader Ginsburg, then on the U.S. Court of Appeals in DC, regretted that the Supreme Court had "treated reproductive autonomy under a substantive due process/personal autonomy headline not expressly linked to discrimination against women." Ginsburg found the court's opinion in *Roe* wanting for a number of reasons, but among them was its failure to pay any attention at all to discrimination against women, or to a woman's "ability to stand in relation to man, society, and the state as an independent, self-sustaining, equal citizen."[108]

Privacy arguments, long troubling to feminists, were especially troubling to gay rights activists, who, especially given the Reagan administration's seeming indifference to the staggering suffering endured during the AIDS crisis, insisted on the importance and the urgency of visibility, of pride, and of coming out. "Silence=Death" was the slogan of ACT UP, the AIDS Coalition to Unleash Power, which protested in Washington in 1987. The gay rights movement, facing the pro-family rhetoric of the right and observing the limits of the right to privacy in reproductive rights cases, changed course. During the 1990s, privacy remained the watchword of the reproductive rights movement—and abortion became more hidden, and more difficult to procure—while equality became the watchword of the gay rights movement, especially after the antidiscrimination fight to overturn antisodomy laws turned into an equal-rights fight for same-sex marriage.[109]

Each of these battles over sex and reproduction cast light on a disagreement on the Supreme Court over the place of historical analysis in constitutional interpretation. In *Bowers*, Justice Byron White, writing for the majority, argued that the right to engage in homosexual sex was not rooted

*ACT UP demonstrators protested outside*
*New York's city hall in 1988.*

in tradition; instead, *prohibitions* on homosexual sex were rooted in tradition; these prohibitions, he said, have "ancient roots." "I cannot say that conduct condemned for hundreds of years has now become a fundamental right," Justice Powell wrote in a concurring opinion. Justice Blackmun argued against this use of history: "I cannot agree that either the length of time a majority has held its convictions or the passions with which it defends them can withdraw legislation from this court's scrutiny."[110]

The place of originalism in American jurisprudence reached the attention of the public in 1987, during the bicentennial of the constitutional convention and the explosive debate over the nomination of Robert Bork. That May, Justice Thurgood Marshall, the distinguished elder statesman of the civil rights movement, gave a speech in which he suggested that the celebration of the bicentennial "invites a complacent belief that the vision of those who debated and compromised in Philadelphia yielded the 'more perfect Union' it is said we now enjoy." Marshall, who had spent the first half of his career fighting against *Plessy v. Ferguson*, raised a sharp eyebrow at the then-popular dewy nostalgia for the 1787 Constitution and the pieties of originalists.

"I cannot accept this invitation, for I do not believe that the meaning of the Constitution was forever 'fixed' at the Philadelphia Convention,"

Marshall said, with as firm a conviction as he had argued before the court in *Brown v. Board*. "Nor do I find the wisdom, foresight, and sense of justice exhibited by the Framers particularly profound. To the contrary, the government they devised was defective from the start."[111]

Weeks after Marshall's cry of dissent, Reagan nominated Bork to the bench. The best-known conservative legal theorist in the nation, he had been promised a seat by Nixon after the Saturday Night Massacre. His nomination had been strongly supported by the Federalist Society. Bork had a singularly narrow view of constitutional interpretation. No fundamental rights exist outside of those listed in the Constitution, he argued. "Original intent is the only legitimate basis for constitutional decision," he'd written. And, although as late as 1989, Bork would argue that the Second Amendment works "to guarantee the right of states to form militia, not for individuals to bear arms," he did not believe that the right to privacy established in *Griswold* existed and instead believed that privacy had become "an unstructured source of judicial power."[112]

Before Bork, Supreme Court nominations had been all but automatically and often unanimously approved by the Senate Judiciary Committee. The bipartisanship and deference to the separation of powers that such approval represented ended with Bork. Less than an hour after Reagan announced his nominee, Massachusetts senator Edward Kennedy delivered a speech in the Senate in which he declared, "Robert Bork's America is a land in which women would be forced into back-alley abortions, blacks would sit at segregated lunch counters, rogue police could break down citizens' doors in midnight raids, schoolchildren could not be taught about evolution, writers and artists could be censored at the whim of the Government, and the doors of the Federal courts would be shut on the fingers of millions of citizens."[113]

Apocalyptic rhetoric had pervaded American politics from the start. After all, supporters of John Adams had warned that to elect Thomas Jefferson would be to live in a world without God. But with Bork's nomination, the language of the end-of-days came to the courts, as if justice itself had become a kind of dystopia.

Not all of the campaign against Bork was as full-throated as Kennedy's speech. Gregory Peck, best known for his portrayal of an anti-lynching lawyer in *To Kill a Mockingbird*, provided the narration for a temperate television ad that alerted Americans to Bork's support for poll taxes and literacy tests and his opposition to the 1964 Civil Rights Act, and urged them to call their senators to ask them to oppose Bork's nomination.[114] Still, the extraordinary fact was that a judicial nomination had elicited paid political advertising at all. And the Senate Judiciary Committee hearings themselves, also aired on television, proved far from temperate.

The televised Bork hearings offered Americans a sweeping survey of the nation's history—and an argument over it. Bork, with a frizz of combed-over red-and-gray hair and a grizzled beard, parried with the senators on subjects ranging from free speech to women's rights. He quoted Benjamin Franklin's remarks from the closing day of the constitutional convention. He talked about and answered questions on black codes, the committee that drafted the Fourteenth Amendment, *Plessy v. Ferguson*, *Brown v. Board*, and *Griswold v. Connecticut*. (The Connecticut law banning contraception was "nutty," Bork told the committee, but the court's decision in *Griswold* was worse: "It comes out of nowhere and doesn't have any rooting in the Constitution.") He talked about the ERA and about *Bowers*, about originalism and liberalism. In the end, the Senate Judiciary Committee voted down his nomination, 58 to 42.[115]

Five months after Bork's nomination was rejected, he spoke at the annual meeting of the Federalist Society, where members of the audience wore buttons that read "Reappoint Bork." To "bork" became a verb, meaning to destroy a judicial nomination through political campaigning. Ralph Reed of the Christian Coalition promised that conservatives would, one day, "Bork back."[116]

Battle lines between the Left and the Right had been inked on the very pages of the Constitution itself. The lines were new but the questions were old. They had been debated by every generation of Americans. Are women persons? Is separate equal? What is the role of the state in protecting its citizens against discrimination? Is discrimination based on race different from discrimination based on gender or sexuality? Are there limits to free speech?

The Bork hearings and, more broadly, the realignment of the Supreme Court and the politicization of the nomination process marked a turn toward what, in the 1850s, William Seward had called an "irrepressible

*No single act so well captured the end of the Cold War*
*as the dismantling of the Berlin Wall in 1989.*

conflict." Its importance was second only to the other lasting legacy of
the Reagan era: Reagan's role in bringing about the end of the Cold War.
Tragically, the fall of communism, the defeat of an enemy abroad, would
only gird Americans for the battle to come, with one another, at home.

In the last quarter of the twentieth century, rising global temperatures
replaced the possibility of nuclear Armageddon as the chief threat to
the planet. Climate change shaped U.S. foreign policy and its domestic
agenda, too. But it also manifested itself as yet another kind of partisan
division: conservatives rejected the science of climate change and added
environmental science to the list of institutions—like the press and the
courts—that could not be trusted because of their liberal bias.

In June 1987, Reagan, visiting Berlin, demanded, "Mr. Gorbachev,
open this gate! Mr. Gorbachev, tear down this wall!" Months later, the
two leaders signed an agreement to destroy intermediate- and short-range
missiles.[117] The Berlin Wall, a once towering symbol of Soviet power and
communist repression, fell in 1989, reduced to rubble. Gorbachev was
forced out of office in 1991, but by then the Soviet empire had collapsed.

By 1992, more than four decades after it began, the Cold War, unimaginably, was over. Missile by missile, the silos began to close, their caves
abandoned. The skies cleared. And the oceans rose.

# III.

BETWEEN THE END of the Cold War and the beginning of the global war on terror, Americans dragged themselves, bloody and bruised, from one political skirmish to the next. They fought over guns, abortion, religion, gay rights, and the environment. They fought in the schools, the courts, the press, and the university. They fought with words, and they fought over words. They fought by tooth and nail and by hook and by crook and they believed they were fighting for the meaning of America, but, really, they were fighting for raw political power.

"One set of hatreds gives way to the next," Arthur Schlesinger Jr. wrote, wearily. By no means were all Americans animated by ideology; in fact, not very many were. But those who thought ideologically exerted disproportionate influence over American political culture. In their terms, political opponents were no longer mere partisans, equally loyal to the United States; they were enemies of the state. Conservatives, having lost anticommunism as a unifying ideology, leaned more on another, closer to home: opposition to liberalism. "There is no 'after the Cold War' for me," Irving Kristol announced in 1993. "So far from having ended, my cold war has increased in intensity, as sector after sector of American life has been ruthlessly corrupted by the liberal ethos." Liberals engaged in a politics of grievance and contempt: anyone who disagreed with them was racist, sexist, classist, or homophobic—and stupid. On college campuses, they passed "hate speech" codes, banning speech that they deemed offensive. They would brook no dissent.[118]

Everyone seemed to be fighting, somehow, over women, who could not be made to fit into the Constitution but could not be left out of it. Patrick Buchanan, Nixon's former speechwriter, declared war. Buchanan had been fired by Ford but hired by Reagan as his director of communications. At the 1992 Republican National Convention, having lost the party's nomination to George H. W. Bush, he used his endorsement of Bush to rally the party's conservative wing by attacking the Democratic nominee, Arkansas governor Bill Clinton, and his two-for-the-price-of-one wife, Hillary Rodham Clinton, who, campaigning for change, would become the focus of a deep and ugly public animus.[119]

"This, my friends, this is radical feminism, the agenda that Clinton and

Clinton would impose on America," Buchanan said, waving antifeminism as a party flag: "abortion on demand, a litmus test for the Supreme Court, homosexual rights, discrimination against religious schools, women in combat units. That's change, all right, but that's not the kind of change America needs, it's not the kind of change America wants, and it's not the kind of change we can abide in a nation we still call 'God's country.'" The crowd chanted, "Go, Pat, go!" [120]

To many on the right, Bill Clinton and Hillary Rodham Clinton represented the 1960s coming-of-age. Bork called them "the very personifications of the Sixties generation arrived at early middle age with its ideological baggage intact." [121] A backlash against feminism animated much of the Christian Right's pro-family crusade, and Hillary Rodham Clinton proved an easy target. She would remain a target for decades, not only during the campaign and not only during her husband's presidency but through her later career in the Senate, and as secretary of state, and during her own two bids for the presidency, and especially during her ill-fated campaign, in 2016, against Donald Trump.

Hillary Rodham, an astute, uncompromising, and no-nonsense mid-westerner, was born in Chicago in 1947. She started out as a Republican. A precocious politician, Rodham canvassed for Nixon when she was thirteen. At seventeen, she was a "Goldwater Girl." In 1965, she brought her copy of Goldwater's *Conscience of a Conservative* to Welles-ley, where she was elected president of the Young Republicans. As a Capitol Hill intern in 1968, Clinton attended the Republican National Convention in Miami, but her opposition to the war, along with her feminism, slowly drove her away from the GOP. Like many feminists, she began to drift away from the Republican Party when the party began to abandon its support of equal rights for women. In 1969, as president of her class at Wellesley, she became the first student invited to deliver a commencement address; her speech was featured in *Life*. In 1970, she spoke to the League of Women Voters on the occasion of its fiftieth anniversary, wearing a black armband, mourning the students shot by the National Guard at Kent State. The next year, she met Bill Clinton when they were both students at Yale Law School. After graduating, she moved to Washington, DC. She worked as a staffer for the special counsel that was preparing for the possibility of a Nixon impeachment. The next year, she married Clinton, and kept her name. (In 1982, in the

*Bill and Hillary Clinton frequently appeared
together on the campaign trail in 1992.*

interest of her husband's political career, she began referring to herself
as Hillary Rodham Clinton.)[122]

The Republican Party was losing women, fast. But the Democratic
Party that Hillary Rodham joined in 1972 was undergoing a transformation, too, one unprecedented in the twentieth century: it was willfully
kicking its base out from under it. Since the rise of William Jennings
Bryan in 1896, the Democratic Party had been the party of labor. But
early in the 1970s, while the Republican Party was courting blue-collar
white men, especially men who'd lost their manufacturing jobs, the Democratic Party began abandoning blue-collar union workers, especially
white men, in favor of a coalition of women, minorities, and what had
come to be called "knowledge workers," engineers, scientists, and analysts
who wore white collars and tapped away at desktop computers at technology firms, universities, consulting firms, and banks.[123]

Fatefully, the Democratic Party made a bid to become not the party of
labor but the party of knowledge. Party leaders, enthralled by the emerging
high-tech industry, placed their faith in machines to drive demographic
and political change. After the end of the Second World War, with the
decline of industrial production, knowledge workers had become the fastest growing occupational sector. Cold War–era government-funded sci-

ence and technology projects created a civilian offshoot: technology firms grew like weeds in the suburban peripheries of university-rich cities like Boston, New York, New Haven, Philadelphia, Atlanta, Chicago, Seattle, Los Angeles, Ann Arbor, Madison, Austin, Boulder, Chapel Hill, and San Francisco. If small in number, liberals who lived in the suburbs and worked in technology had an outsized influence on the Democratic Party. They favored—and lavishly funded—the campaigns of other highly educated liberals, from George McGovern in 1972 to Michael Dukakis in 1988 to John Kerry in 2004, campaigns that failed miserably.

The new Democratic understanding of the world was technocratic, meritocratic, and therapeutic. They believed that technology could fix political, social, and economic problems, and yet they also believed that they owed their own success to their talents and drive, and that people who had achieved less were less talented and driven. They tended not to see how much of their lives had been shaped by government policies, like government-funded research, or the zoning laws and restrictive covenants that had created high-quality schools in the all-white suburbs or the occasional swank urban pockets in which they typically lived. Notwithstanding all the ways in which government assistance had made possible the conditions of their lives and work, they tended to be opposed to government assistance. Believing in individual achievement and the power of the self, they saw the different political vantages of other people, especially of people who had achieved less, as personal, psychological failings: racism, for instance, they saw not as a structural problem but as a prejudice born of ignorance.[124]

Some of the attitudes of this political class lay in the mystique surrounding the personal computer. Big IBM machines and punch-card computing had looked, to the New Left, bureaucratic, organizational, and inhuman. Students were cogs in the machine of the university, draftees were cogs in the war machine, itself figured as a computer. In 1964, free speech activists demonstrating at Berkeley had strung around their necks punch cards that read "I am a UC student. Please do not fold, bend, spindle or mutilate me."[125] Personal computing, a rejection of those punch cards, came out of the 1960s Bay Area counterculture, a rage against the (IBM) machine. Its loudest promoter was Stewart Brand, who had joined Ken Kesey's Merry Pranksters after graduating from Stanford and founded the *Whole Earth Catalog* in 1967, in Menlo Park, for the tens of thousands of people who were dropping out and moving back to the land, living in communes, and for the much bigger number of people who dreamed of dropping out. (The 1971 *Whole Earth Catalog* won the National Book Award and sold two and a half million copies. It peddled everything from copies of Milton Friedman's *Capitalism and Freedom* for $1.50 to parts for an old Volkswagen, to a "Do-it-Yourself Burial" for $50, to instructions on "How to Build a Working Digital Computer," for $4.45.)[126] "A realm of intimate, personal power is developing," Brand wrote, "power of the individual to conduct his own education, find his own inspiration, shape his own environment, and share his adventure with whoever is interested." For Brand and these New Communalists, dropping out meant plugging in. Mind and consciousness, sun and soil, monitor and keyboard. In 1967, one Haight-Ashbury poet handed out a poem that began: "I like to think (and / the sooner the better!) / of a cybernetic meadow / where mammals and computers / live together in mutually / programming harmony / like pure water/ touching clear sky." Not irrelevantly, this same group of people, whole-earth hippies, usually had quite traditional ideas about the role of women. In the 1960s and 1970s on back-to-the-land communes where people read Brand's *Whole Earth Catalog*, and imagined they were living on an American frontier, women baked bread and spun wool and breast-fed and saved seeds.[127]

Brand was interested in planetary thinking—the "whole earth"—and imagined a worldwide network of computers bringing the world's peoples together, in perfect harmony. That required, first, personal computers, one per person. In 1968, Brand helped produce the Mother of All Demos at a computer industry conference in San Francisco to demonstrate a prototype of a personal computer that Kesey later pronounced "the next thing after acid." Brand wrote about computing for *Rolling Stone* in 1972: "Ready or not, computers are coming to the people."[128] Bill Gates and Paul Allen, who met as boys in Seattle, founded Microsoft in 1975, later adopting the motto "A personal computer on every desk." In Cupertino, Steve Jobs and Stephen Wozniak founded Apple Computer in 1976 and released the Apple II the next year. By 1980, Apple's IPO broke a record held by the Ford Motor Company since 1956.[129] By the 1990s, wealthy Silicon Valley entrepreneurs would lead a Democratic Party that had restructured itself around their priorities. Beginning in 1972, the DNC instituted quotas for its delegations, requiring numbers of women, minorities, and youth but establishing no quotas for union members or the working class. The new rules made it possible for affluent professionals to take over the party, a change of course much influenced by longtime Democratic strategist Frederick Dutton's *Changing Sources of Power* (1971). Dutton argued that the future of the party was young professionals, not old union members.[130] Colorado senator Gary Hart, in 1974, took to mocking "Eleanor Roosevelt Democrats" as fusty and old-fashioned, not hip to the young computer people. The press called Hart's constituency "Atari Democrats."[131]

Personal computing enthusiasts liked to invoke "the power of the people," but they meant the power of the individual person, fortified with a machine. Republicans, the party of big business, remained closely associated with IBM; Democrats, the party of the people, attached themselves to Apple, and jettisoned people without the means or interest in owning their own computer. The knowledge-worker-not-auto-worker wing of the party tried to move to the center, under the auspices of the Democratic Leadership Council, founded in 1985, and soon joined by Bill Clinton and Al Gore. Calling themselves the "New Democrats," they blamed Carter's defeat in 1980 and Mondale's defeat in 1984 on their support for unions and their old-fashioned, New Deal liberalism.[132] "Thanks to the near-miraculous capabilities of micro-electronics, we are vanquishing scarcity," an article in the DLC's *New Democrat* announced in 1995. The class politics of scarcity were dying, and in this new, bright age of the microchip, there would be a "politics of plenty" in which the people left behind—"the losers . . . who cannot or will not participate in the knowledge economy"—would be "like illiterate peasants in the Age of Steam."[133] The party stumbled like a drunken man, delirious with technological utopianism.

BILL CLINTON, FORTY-SIX when he entered the White House and gone already gray, stood six foot two. He had a grin like a 1930s comic-strip scamp, the cadence of a southern Baptist preacher, and the husky voice of a blues singer. He'd grown up poor in Hope, Arkansas—the boy from Hope—and he climbed his way to the White House by dint of charm and hard work and good luck. During the Vietnam War, he'd dodged the draft. After a Rhodes Scholarship and an education at Yale Law School, he'd begun a career in politics, with his young wife at his side. Like many a president before and since, he liked to be liked and he yearned to be admired, although, unlike most presidents, Clinton wore his neediness on his face; he had, all his life, the face of a boy. He was only thirty-two in 1978 when he was elected governor of Arkansas. He appeared to serve as a bridge between the Old Democrats and the New Democrats. A white southerner from a humble background, he appealed to the party's old base. An Ivy League–educated progressive with a strong record on civil rights, he appealed to the party's new base. And yet he was, all along, a rascal.

In 1992, Clinton's campaign for the Democratic nomination had nearly been felled by his reputation as a philanderer. After allegations of one extramarital affair hit the tabloids, he and his wife appeared on *60 Minutes*, sitting together stiffly, and he admitted to "causing pain in my marriage." Citing his right to privacy, he refused to directly answer any questions about infidelity.[134] He also suggested that his candidacy offered an opportunity for the press to turn away from salaciousness.

The year before, the battle for the courts had met the battle of the sexes during the Senate confirmation hearings of Bush's Supreme Court nominee Clarence Thomas. In 1987, Thurgood Marshall, asked at a conference about the increasingly conservative nature of the court, said, "Don't worry, I'm going to outlive those bastards." But, suffering from glaucoma, hearing loss, and other ailments, Marshall retired from the court in 1991.[135] To replace him, Bush nominated Thomas, whom he'd earlier appointed to the DC Circuit Court of Appeals. During the confirmation hearings, law professor Anita Hill accused Thomas, her former boss, of sexual harassment. The televised hearings had included graphic details. Despite Hill's powerful, damning testimony, the Senate confirmed Thomas.

A year later, Clinton attempted to deflect inquiries about his alleged years-long affair with a woman named Gennifer Flowers by piously suggesting that public discourse had been demeaned by televised hearings, proposing to elevate it by refusing to provide details. "This will test the character of the press," Clinton said on *60 Minutes*. "It's not only my character that has been tested." The claim lacked the merest plausibility, not least because on other occasions Clinton had been perfectly willing to discuss matters that other presidential candidates and officeholders would have scorned as demeaning to the dignity of the office. Asked by a high school student at an MTV-sponsored event in 1994 whether he wore boxers or briefs, for instance, he'd not hesitated to supply an answer: "Usually briefs."[136]

Clinton's two terms in office frustrated the Left, enraged the Right, and ended in scandal. He won the 1992 election with the lowest popular vote—43 percent—since Woodrow Wilson. He set as his first task health care reform, which had been on the progressive docket for nearly a century. "If I don't get health care done, I'll wish I didn't run for President," he said. He handed this initiative over to his wife, assigning her to head the Task Force on National Health Care Reform, and calling her his Bobby Kennedy.[137]

Before her husband took office, Hillary Rodham Clinton, a chronic overpreparer, read forty-three biographies of presidential wives to equip herself for her role. After the administration's first one hundred days, *Vanity Fair*, in a profile of the First Lady, described her as holding "unprecedented political ambitions." The magazine reported: "As the first working mother in the White House, the first unapologetic feminist, and arguably the most important woman in the world, she wants not just to have it all, but to do it all." She also changed her name again, going by "Hillary Clinton." Six weeks after Hillary Clinton moved into the White House, Betty Ford came to visit. But Hillary Clinton was no Betty Ford. She had more senior staff assigned to her than did Vice President Al Gore.[138]

Hillary Clinton's task force eventually produced a 1,342-page proposal for what was mainly employer-paid health care. Insurance companies and conservative policy groups, in a rerun of the Whitaker and Baxter campaign of 1949, spent hundreds of millions of dollars in advertising and lobbying campaigns to defeat the proposal. One series of ads featured a couple, Harry and Louise, regretting their lack of choice under "health care plans designed by government bureaucrats," and closed: "KNOW THE FACTS."

Bill Kristol, like his father before him a prominent conservative writer and strategist, urged Republicans to refuse any deal on health care in order to make the case to the public that "Democratic welfare-state liberalism remains firmly in retreat." (Conservatives likely also feared that if the Democrats succeeded in passing health care, its popularity would make the Democratic Party unstoppable.) The First Lady, still a neophyte in the capital, urged her husband to make no compromises; in his 1994 State of the Union address, he promised to veto any bill that did not provide for universal coverage. By the midterm elections, when Republicans took over Congress, winning majorities in both houses for the first time in decades, the proposal, much derided for its intricacies and hobbled by conservatives' distaste for the president's wife, had failed. Felled by the unyielding partisanship of a new political culture, it never even reached a vote.[139]

The failure of Clinton's health care proposal crippled his presidency. His lasting legacy, as a liberal, came in 1993, when he appointed Ruth Bader Ginsburg to the Supreme Court. But Clinton, who had more millionaires in his cabinet even than Bush had, moved to the right—even before the midterms—and much of his agenda amounted to a continuation of work begun by Reagan and Bush.[140] He secured the ratification of the North American Free Trade Agreement (NAFTA), against the opposition of labor unions. He took up the War on Drugs waged by Nixon in 1971 and continued by Reagan with the 1986 Anti-Drug Abuse Act. In 1994, the year Newt Gingrich issued a conservative "Contract with America," Clinton signed a new crime bill that lengthened mandatory sentencing and instituted a 100:1 ratio between sentences for possession of crack and of cocaine. (The bill also included an assault weapons ban, set to expire after ten years.) Some members of the Congressional Black Caucus (CBC) supported the bill; others did not. The NAACP called it a "crime against the American people." The CBC attempted to introduce a Racial Justice Act, to include provisions relating to racial discrimination in sentencing; Republicans threatened a filibuster. When the crime bill passed, liberals boasted about becoming tough on crime. "The liberal wing of the Democratic Party is for 100,000 cops," announced Joe Biden, a hard-bitten senator who grew up in Scranton, Pennsylvania. "The liberal wing of the Democratic Party is for 125,000 new State prison cells."[141]

These bipartisan measures contributed to a social catastrophe, an era of mass incarceration, in which nearly one in every hundred American adults were in prison, the highest rate virtually anywhere in the world, and four times the world average. The 1994 crime bill didn't cause that rise, which had begun much earlier, and, in any case, most people in prison are not convicted of federal crimes (their convictions follow state laws). But the federal crime bill, changes in state and local prosecution rates, and especially the new sentencing regime made the problem worse. Two-thirds of the rise in the prison population between 1985 and 2000 involved drug convictions. The overwhelming majority of Americans convicted of drug offenses are black men. "The Drug War Is the New Jim Crow," read a poster stapled to a telephone booth in California, an observation with which social scientists came, painfully, to agree.[142]

Clinton struck deals on drugs, crime, and guns because he believed in compromise and bipartisanship, but also because he liked and needed to be liked. Especially after the embarrassment of his health care proposal, he moved still further from the center. His political compromises on welfare and the regulation of the economy proved as consequential as his crime bill. In 1996, Clinton and his band of meritocratic New Democrats found common cause with conservatives, led by House Speaker Gingrich, in realizing his campaign pledge to "end welfare as we know it." Siding with those who described welfare as trapping people in poverty through dependence on the government, his administration abolished Aid for Families with Dependent Children. Under the new regime, welfare was left up to the states. (Clinton vetoed a Republican version of the bill that would have ended guaranteed health care to the poor through Medicaid.)[143]

In 1999, in another abdication of the New Deal with far-reaching effects, Clinton signed a measure repealing elements of the Glass-Steagall Act, passed in 1933. The repeal lifted a ban on combinations between commercial and investment banks. Larry Summers, Clinton's Treasury secretary, boasted, "At the end of the 20th century, we will at last be replacing an archaic set of restrictions with a legislative foundation for a 21st-century financial system." The freewheeling securities industry saw record profits in the wake of the repeal. By the end of the decade, the average CEO of a big company earned nearly four hundred times as much as the average worker. And, not long after that, in 2008, during a global financial collapse, Summers's twenty-first-century financial system would be revealed as having been cracked from the start.[144]

Long before the Atari Democrats' financial system failed, and notwithstanding Bill Clinton's forced-grin centrism, the center would not hold. The heated rhetoric of the gun rights and anti-abortion movements fanned rage among extremists. And a new kind of politics came to characterize those on both the Left and the Right.

Identity politics, by other names, goes all the way back to the founding of the Republic. The Constitution, which, for purposes of representation, counted some Americans as worth three-fifths of other Americans, rested on a politics of identity: white supremacy. "This Government was made by our fathers on the white basis," Stephen Douglas had said, debating Abraham Lincoln. "It was made by white men for the benefit of white men and their posterity forever." Lincoln, of course, had disagreed. "There is no reason in the world why the negro is not entitled to all the natural rights enumerated in the Declaration of Independence, the right to life, liberty, and the pursuit of happiness," he'd answered. "I hold that he is as much entitled to these as the white man." Overthrowing Stephen Douglas's brand of identity politics—the identity politics of slaveholders and, later, of the Klan, and of immigration restrictionists, had been the work of more than a century of struggle—for abolition, emancipation, suffrage, and civil rights.

Another self-described identity politics emerged in the middle of the twentieth century, out of the Black Power movement and the gay pride movement, and especially out of feminism. The term was coined in 1977, in a manifesto written by a collective of black lesbian feminists in Cambridge, Massachusetts. "The most profound and potentially most radical politics come directly out of our own identity, as opposed to working to end somebody else's oppression," they wrote.[145] Earlier in the twentieth century, political change from the left had come from coalitions of farmers and laborers. In the 1970s, as animus toward immigrants rose, ethnic groups that had been subjected to longstanding discrimination, including Chicanos, Native Americans, and Asian Americans, found political solidarity, both within and across groups, by emphasizing their difference, not, as with the older identity politics, as racially superior, but as particularly and distinctively oppressed.

By the 1980s, influenced by the psychology and popular culture of trauma, the Left had abandoned solidarity across difference in favor of the meditation on and expression of suffering, a politics of feeling and resentment, of self and sensitivity. The Right, if it didn't describe itself as engaging in identity politics, adopted the same model: the NRA, notably, cultivated the resentments and grievances of white men, feeding, in particular, both longstanding resentment of African Americans and newly repurposed resentment of immigrants. Together, both Left and Right adopted both a politics and a cultural style animated by indictment and indignation.[146]

A nation divided over guns and abortion bred a new generation of domestic terrorists. Between 1977 and 2001, anti-abortion activists, some affiliated with an organization called Operation Rescue, invaded 372 medical clinics that provided abortions, bombed 41 clinics, set 166 clinics on fire, and murdered 7 clinic staff, guards, and volunteers.[147] Groups of white men purporting to defend the right to bear arms formed private militias. In Waco, Texas, in 1993, the Bureau of Alcohol, Tobacco and Firearms laid siege to a religious compound to seize illegal weapons, leading to the brutal deaths of 76 members of a sect headed by a man named David Koresh, including 25 children. Two years later, Timothy McVeigh, who'd fought in the U.S. Army as an infantryman in Kuwait, blew up a federal building in Oklahoma City, killing 168 people, including 15 babies and small children in a day care center. McVeigh said he'd bombed the building in retaliation for the federal government's actions at Waco. Three years before the bombing, he'd written a letter to the editor of a small New York newspaper: "The American Dream of the middle class has all but disappeared, substituted with people struggling just to buy next week's groceries," he wrote. "What is it going to take to open up the eyes of our elected officials? AMERICA IS IN SERIOUS DECLINE."[148]

Meanwhile, the go-go nineties were boom times for dot-commers and hedge fund managers, for Hollywood moguls and global traders. Under Clinton, incomes rose across the board. But the middle class, especially the rural white middle class, really was in decline. What were the causes of that decline? Conservatives blamed liberals, liberals blamed conservatives. Conspiracy theorists blamed a nefarious government of elites. Oklahoma City and Waco launched conservative talk radio host Alex Jones, who started a program called *The Final Edition* in 1996, on which he alleged that the government was behind the Oklahoma City bombing and that the Justice Department had set about to murder Koresh and his followers. Jones professed nonpartisanship. He said, "I don't care if it's Bill Clinton or Governor Bush, they're all elitist filth if you ask me."[149]

Jones's lunatic conspiracy theories lay well outside ordinary political conversation. But the boundaries that separated ordinary political conversation from mayhem and incitement were crumbling. Both new ideas and new forms of political communication cultivated a growing intolerance for differing political opinions and for difference more broadly.

Left identity politics grew especially strong in the academy, where to disagree with the distinctive status of someone belonging to a particular identity group was to violate what conservatives, in an allusion to Stalinism, liked to deride as "political correctness." In his 1987 jeremiad *The Closing of the American Mind,* University of Chicago literary critic Allan Bloom lamented the evisceration of truth: "There is one thing a professor can be absolutely certain of: almost every student entering his university believes, or says he believes, that truth is relative." Veterans of the New Left lamented these developments, too. "The squandering of energy on identity politics, the hardening of boundaries between groups, the insistence that individuals are no more than their labels, is an American tragedy," Todd Gitlin wrote in 1995. Gitlin, who had been president of SDS in the 1960s, pointed out the irony of this tragedy: "the Left, which once stood for universal values, seems to speak today for select identities, while the Right, long associated with privileged interests, claims to defend the common good."[150]

The Left's commitment to open debate unraveled. A "no-platform movement"—the turn during which the Left started sounding like the Right—was founded in 1974 by a British student group that prohibited providing a platform to anyone "holding racist or fascist views." One influence was the German-born American intellectual Herbert Marcuse, who argued in a widely read essay that liberals' commitment to open debate was absurd because free speech had become a form of oppression. Another influence, beginning in the 1980s, was the field of trauma studies, which understood words as harm. By the early 1990s, mostly due to the influence of critical race theory, a theory of unequal speech advanced by black legal scholars including Derrick Bell, more than 350 American colleges and universities adopted hate speech codes. Other black scholars objected. "To be sure, blacks are still on the front lines of First Amendment jurisprudence—but this time we soldier on the other side," Henry Louis Gates Jr. wrote ruefully in 1996. "The byword among many black activists and black intellectuals is no longer the political imperative to protect free speech; it is the moral imperative to suppress 'hate speech.'" Campus hate speech codes were often used against the very people they were designed to protect. The suppression of hate speech, which, a generation before, had been the project of FBI agents who investigated civil rights activists, became the work of the university. In less than two years under the University of Michigan's speech code, more than twenty white students accused black students of racist speech.[151]

At nearly the same time, both the Left and the Right, unwilling to brook dissent, began dismantling structures that nurture fair-minded debate: the Left undermining the university, the Right undermining the press. In 1987, the Reagan administration finally succeeded in its long-sought repeal of the Fairness Doctrine, after the president vetoed a congressional effort to block the repeal. The repeal meant that broadcasters, operating with federal licenses, had no obligation either to dedicate programming to the public interest or to represent opposing points of view. Along with the creation of national toll-free telephone numbers and the opening of the FM band—which meant that music stations largely abandoned AM, opening those stations for other programming—the repeal of the Fairness Doctrine made possible a new kind of conservative talk radio. In 1987, there were some 240 talk radio stations in the country; by 1992, there were 900.[152]

The best-known among the talk radio hosts was the energetic Rush Limbaugh, who began broadcasting nationally, on fifty-six stations, in the summer of 1988. Limbaugh did not generally have guests; he ranted, and he raved, and he fielded phone calls from the public. Caustic and provocative, he gave vent to hatreds and resentments that had been considered unspeakable on the air. "He's saying what I think," listeners said. His popularity could be seen in bumper stickers that read "Rush is Right." Republican political strategist and television producer Roger Ailes met Limbaugh in 1990 and soon began producing a Limbaugh television show, and, although it failed, it convinced Ailes to find a home for conservative television news. In 1992, when Ailes and Limbaugh together visited the White House, President Bush saw fit to carry Limbaugh's bag.[153]

Leone Baxter, who died in 2001 at the age of ninety-five, had worried about men like Ailes, whose early rise she'd witnessed.[154] The Ohio-born Ailes had been working in television when he became an adviser to

Richard Nixon in 1968. He soon moved from entertainment to politics, though what he pioneered was bringing the two together. Between 1980 and 1986, he'd aided the campaigns of thirteen Republican senators and eight members of Congress, including Phil Gramm and Mitch McConnell.[155] At the beginning of the age of talk radio and cable television but a decade before the rise of the Internet and twenty years before social media, Ailes developed a new and prescient theory of communication, which he elaborated on in 1988, in the cowritten book You *Are the Message*. Ailes argued that polling, market research, and the television ratings industry demonstrated that the most saleable pitches are simple, instant, and emotional. This insight applied not only to detergents and sitcoms but also to people. Remote controls for television had become commonplace in the late 1970s, just when cable programming was beginning, and viewers took to flipping through the channels. (The term "sound bite" was coined in the 1970s when, armed with a remote, viewers couldn't be counted on to catch much more than a sentence or a phrase before changing channels.) People are like television programs, Ailes explained: a person has only seven seconds to be likable before someone changes the channel. "It's what I call the like factor," he wrote.[156]

The Like Factor, like the Lie Factory before it, came to drive American political communication, decades before the rise of Facebook, with its "likes." In effect, the Like Factor replaced the Fairness Doctrine. In a transformation long sought by conservatives, ratings trumped the public interest, a change that was perhaps first made evident in televised debates between presidential candidates. After the Kennedy-Nixon debates in 1960, no general election presidential debate had taken place for the sixteen years until Ford agreed to debate Carter in 1976. (Ford believed he had no choice but to agree because after pardoning Nixon, he'd fallen 30 points behind in the all-important polls.) In 1980, when John Anderson ran as an Independent against Carter and Reagan, the League of Women Voters, which sponsored the debates, ruled that to participate in a general election debate, a candidate had to have earned at least 15 percent in a national poll. As even pollsters admitted, this was indefensible, since polls are simply not reliable enough to support that decision. Meanwhile, as part of its campaign to deregulate the FCC, the Reagan administration was determined to allow television broadcasters, rather than nonprofits, to sponsor the debates, notwithstanding a prophetic warning issued by the head of the League of Women Voters, Dorothy Ridings. She told a Senate committee that broadcasters, keen for the highest ratings, would pander both to the candidates and especially to the audience in an attempt to make the debates as zippy and as watchable as possible, without regard to whether or not they would help voters learn about either the candidates or the issues.[157]

As a result of that push, television broadcasters gained control of the primary debates, which grew more raucous, while sponsorship of the general election debates was taken over by a nonpartisan Commission on Presidential Debates. The tone of the debates, though, was set by Ailes. He coached Reagan to disarm Mondale by promising not to make age an issue: "I am not going to exploit for political purposes my opponent's youth and inexperience," Reagan said. He calmed George H. W. Bush's nerves before his first 1988 debate against Michael Dukakis who, as governor of Massachusetts, had supported the repeal of a state law that banned sodomy and bestiality. "If you get in trouble out there, just call him an animal fucker," Ailes whispered to Bush backstage. Even as Bush prepared to take the stage, that night's moderator, Texas-born television newsman Dan Rather, who styled himself in the mold of Edward R. Murrow, looked straight into the camera and apologized to his audience: "This will not be a debate in the sense the word is often used in the English language because all of this is so tightly controlled by the candidates themselves and their managers."[158]

The League of Women Voters issued a press release, denouncing the debates as "a fraud on the American voter." But the debates only got worse. Ratings rose and zingers got zippier. In 1992, the Bill Clinton campaign made sure the candidates were given very big stools, so that Ross Perot would look like a child. Clinton, gregarious and charismatic and quick on his feet, loved a new "town hall" format, in which the candidates take questions from the audience. Reserved, New England–bred Bush did not. Caught on camera looking at his watch, Bush later admitted that he'd been thinking, "only ten more minutes of this crap."[159]

The fiercest indictment came from seventy-four-year-old Walter Cronkite. "The debates are part of the unconscionable fraud that our political campaigns have become," Cronkite said in 1990. "Here is a means to present to the American people a rational exposition of the major issues that face the nation, and the alternate approaches to their

solution. Yet the candidates participate only with the guarantee of a format that defies meaningful discourse. They should be charged with sabo-
taging the electoral process."[160]

Cronkite and other veterans of the golden age of television news
lamented the new age: the rise of cable news. CNN, which provided news
twenty-four hours a day, was launched in 1980 and posted its first profits by 1985. By 1990, it reached fifty-three million households, a number
that only rose after 1991, with its on-the-ground, real-time coverage of
the Persian Gulf War, a U.S.-led operation to push the Saddam Hussein–
led Iraqi army out of neighboring Kuwait. MSNBC started in July 1996,
followed later that year by Fox News, run by Ailes and owned by an Australian tabloid newspaper tycoon and notable conservative named Rupert
Murdoch. The year before, Murdoch had funded a new conservative
magazine, the *Weekly Standard*, published in Washington and coedited
by Bill Kristol. With funding from Murdoch, Ailes started Fox News from
scratch. "We had no news gathering operation," he later recalled. "We had
no studios, no equipment, no employees, no stars, no talent, and no confidence from anybody."[161]

Many found Ailes's venture surprising, since he had no background in
journalism and frequently said that he did not respect journalists. A news
organization run by a political operative—a Republican kingmaker—
would seem to violate basic standards of journalism, and yet Ailes insisted
that Fox News aimed to rescue journalism. "We'd like to restore objectivity where we find it lacking," he said at a press conference. "We expect to
do fine, balanced, journalism."[162]

Liberals shuddered. Senior adviser to the president George Stephanopoulos, asked why Bill Clinton, who had appeared on MSNBC on
its opening day, would not do the same for Fox News, said, "Well, for
one thing, MSNBC's not owned by Rupert Murdoch and run by Roger
Ailes."[163] But MSNBC was not less partisan than Fox News; it was merely
differently partisan.

Entrenched partisanship in cable news eroded the institutions of democratic deliberation. The rise of cable news accelerated the polarization
first of Congress and then of the electorate. During the reign of broadcast television, between 1950 and 1980, when there were only three
major networks, ABC, CBS, and NBC, polarization was the lowest it had
ever been, both before and since. Cable news made voters more parti-

san, by reinforcing their views and limiting their exposure to other views, but cable television had another effect, too: when the only channels on television were ABC, CBS, and NBC, and each network broadcast the news at 6:30 p.m., people who weren't particularly interested in politics, who tended to be moderates, had usually watched, and, as a result, they'd tended to vote. Conservatives denounced broadcast news as liberal, but in fact it was pitched to the widest possible mass audience, made even-handedness its priority, and provided a political education to voters who had not previously been interested in politics. When cable stations offered choices aside from the news, people who weren't interested in the news watched something else, and tended not to vote. The people least interested in politics, and least partisan, dropped out of the electorate.[164]

Meanwhile, the rise of round-the-clock cable news produced a veritable army of political commentators and pundits, and gave officeholders and office seekers nearly endless airtime, creating a political class of television celebrities. "It created a high-profile blur of People on TV whose brands overtook their professional identities," wrote the *New York Times*'s Mark Leibovich. "They were not journalists or strategists or pols per se, but citizens of the green room." They were pretty and handsome and they looked alike, and they sounded alike, too. They never said, "I don't know," or "Let me think about that." They scowled and flared their nostrils and attacked one another, cocks in a cockfight. The White House became a cockfight pit, too. In 1995, Michael McCurry, Clinton's press secretary, began opening daily press briefings to televised coverage. The Clinton campaign was chronicled in *The War Room* and his White House, in a way, on *West Wing*. When people from Clinton's campaign and from his administration left politics, they made piles of money, hawking their access to policymakers. In the two and a half years between when senior adviser Rahm Emanuel left the Clinton White House and when he ran for Congress, he pocketed more than $18 million, chiefly working for an investment banking firm. The opportunities for corruption and ethics violations were endless. The opportunities for ratings, driven by scandal, were limitless. In 1996, CNN had 60 million subscribers; MSNBC, 25 million; and Fox, 17 million. Two years later, a news story broke that led to a 400 percent increase in Fox's prime-time ratings.[165]

Watergate had inaugurated an era of politics by other means, where political opponents attempted, instead of defeating one another's arguments, or winning elections, to oust each other from office by way of ethics investigations. Between 1970 and 1994, the number of federal indictments of public officials rose from virtually zero to more than thirteen hundred. These often meaningless battles, waged in televised hearings, on television talk shows, and in the courts, brought down a great many politicians. They also eroded the public's faith in the institutions to which those politicians belonged, mainly Congress, the presidency, and the Supreme Court.[166]

In July 1995, Monica Lewinsky, a twenty-one-year-old graduate of Oregon's Lewis & Clark College, started an internship at the White House. In November, the president began an affair with her that lasted sixteen months and appears mainly to have involved her performing oral sex on him in or near the Oval Office. Allegedly, she later said her title ought to have been "Special Assistant to the President for Blow Jobs."[167]

Other presidents had affairs. Most of those men, including FDR and JFK, had affairs in an era when the press tacitly agreed not to expose them. Clinton engaged in an affair with Lewinsky at a time when exposing politicians' affairs was the favored weapon of political battle. Not only that, but the nation was in the midst of a campaign against sexual harassment in the workplace. Clinton's foolishness, irresponsibility, and recklessness in this affair was difficult to fathom. He was the first Democratic president to assume office after the rise of right-wing radio. Millions of Americans heard him criticized, daily, for hours. Right-wing attacks on Clinton and his wife were relentless, whether the charges had merit or, more often, no merit at all. Limbaugh accused Hillary Clinton of covering up a murder, a rumor he read in a fax sent to his office. "That's what it said in the fax," Limbaugh said, defending slander.[168] Whatever else other presidents had done, or not done, it was absurd, in such circumstances, for Clinton to believe he would get away with, first, the affair, and, second, the cover-up.

Clinton had been subjected to investigation from the moment he took office. Unrelated investigations into a land deal the Clintons had made in Arkansas, involving Whitewater, a development on the White River, and into a civil suit filed by Paula Jones, a former Arkansas state employee, had been orchestrated by the Conservative Political Action Committee. Jones alleged that Bill Clinton had sexually harassed her in a hotel room in 1991. Beginning in 1994, these charges were investigated

by Bush's former solicitor general Kenneth Starr, appointed as an independent counsel. Jones, who alleged that Clinton had asked her to kiss
his penis, purported to describe its "distinguishing characteristics" in a
sworn affidavit. Jones represented conservatives borking back, after the
Clarence Thomas hearings. The month her story broke, in March 1994,
the nation's three major television news networks aired 126 stories about
Whitewater; from January through March, they had aired 42 stories
about the proposed health care plan.[169]

Critics despaired about a politics of RIP, "Revelation, Investigation,
Prosecution," that led from Watergate to Whitewater. Starr proved an
indefatigable investigator. He spent years and tens of millions of taxpayer
dollars following every lead, right down to a blue dress stained with presidential semen. In 1996, a former White House aide named Linda Tripp
met Lewinsky at the Pentagon, where they both worked. Tripp began
recording her conversations with Lewinsky about Clinton in 1997; she
then gave these recordings to Jones's lawyers. (Tripp also told Lewinsky to
never wash that blue dress.) By this time, Clinton had helped Lewinsky
get a job in New York. On learning about the tapes, Starr began an investigation into a possible obstruction of justice.[170]

The Lewinsky story broke not in a newspaper of record, like the *New
York Times* or the *Wall Street Journal*, but on the Internet, when Matt
Drudge at the Drudge Report revealed the allegations at 11:27 p.m. on
Saturday night, January 17, 1998. Clinton asked his in-house pollster,
Dick Morris, to conduct an instant poll to decide what to do. Morris
told the president that Americans would not forgive him an affair. The
*Washington Post* printed the story on January 21. That afternoon, Clinton agreed to an interview with PBS's Jim Lehrer. Later that night, in a
meeting in the White House solarium, deputy chief of staff Harold Ickes
told the president that the interview had been a disaster. "You look like
a fuckin' dog that's been running all night and someone just kicked the
shit out of you. I've never seen such a performance in my life. Nobody
believed you." Five days later, in the presence of his wife, Clinton delivered an address from the Roosevelt Room and said, "I did not have sexual
relations with that woman." The next morning, on the *Today* show, Hillary Clinton attributed the allegations to a "vast right-wing conspiracy."[171]

To cover the Lewinsky story, Ailes launched a new 6:00 p.m. news-
cast, *Special Report*, hosted by Brit Hume, and moved commentator Bill

O'Reilly's *The O'Reilly Factor* from 6:00 to 8:00 p.m. By the time the story had played out, Fox News had beaten MSNBC in the ratings war and was on its way to beating CNN. Partisan coverage produced partisan opinion: by the time the House voted on impeachment, 58 percent of Independents and 84 percent of Democrats would oppose it, while some two out of three Republicans would support it. But Fox News had no monopoly on in-depth coverage of the Lewinsky affair. Broadcast and televisions news, magazines and newspapers, all covered each new detail of the president's encounters with his intern, which included inserting a cigar into her vagina and then, as most Americans believed, lying about it on national television and before a grand jury. "The country is awash in the muck of the White House nastiness," columnist A. M. Rosenthal wrote in the *Times*, and "dirty with the cynicism that flows from it." In September 1998, Starr submitted to the House his 445-page report, along with 2,600 pages of documentary evidence. The details, both of the affair and of Clinton's efforts to cover it up, were at once ridiculous, embarrassing, and terrible. Columnist Andrew Sullivan wrote: "Clinton is a cancer on the culture, a cancer of cynicism, narcissism, and deceit."[172] But the cause of the cancer lay elsewhere.

The United States had endured eras of heightened partisanship before, in the 1790s, say, or the 1850s. But beginning in the 1990s, the nation started a long fall into an epistemological abyss. The conservative media establishment, founded on the idea that the existing media establishment was biased, had built into its foundation a rejection of the idea that truth could come from weighing different points of view, which, after all, is the whole point of partisan disputation. Instead, the conservative media establishment engineered a fail-safe against dissent. As one historian explained, "When an outlet like the *New York Times* criticized a liberal policy, conservative media activists presented it not as evidence of the paper's even-handedness but as evidence of the policy's failure. *Even the liberal* New York Times *had to admit.* . . . Thus evidence that seemed to undermine the charge of liberal bias could be reinterpreted to support it."[173]

The nation had lost its way in the politics of mutually assured epistemological destruction. There was no truth, only innuendo, rumor, and bias. There was no reasonable explanation; there was only conspiracy. The White House hired private detectives to find dirt about Starr and other investigators. Voters found the investigation as reprehensible as Clinton, or more so. By a margin of two to one, women thought the press coverage had gone too far. Still, they blamed Republicans for making a spectacle of the presidency. Republicans, who'd hoped to gain seats in the 1998 midterms, lost them. After the election, House Speaker Gingrich, who was already on his second wife, learned that his own affair with a congressional aide twenty-three years his junior was about to be exposed, and resigned, blaming "cannibals who had 'blackmailed' him into quitting."[174]

The Lewinsky scandal indelibly left something else in its aftermath. It diminished liberalism. Liberals defended Clinton almost at all cost, depicting him as a victim. Steinem and other prominent feminists who had crusaded against Clarence Thomas as a perpetrator of sexual harassment waved aside Clinton's dalliances, often with young women, including women in his employ, at some sizable cost to the cause of feminism. Thomas had at one point suggested he was being subjected to "a high-tech lynching." Writing about the Lewinsky investigation in *The New Yorker*, Toni Morrison said that, "white skin notwithstanding, this is our first black President"—he was so cool, so hip, so long-suffering—and compared the investigation to a lynching. "Serious as adultery is, it is not a national catastrophe," Morrison said.[175] Adultery is not a national catastrophe, but Bill Clinton was no more subjected to a lynching than was Clarence Thomas.

On February 12, 1999, the Senate narrowly defeated two charges of impeachment: on perjury and obstruction of justice. Four days later, Paul Weyrich circulated a letter in which he announced the failure of the Christian Right. The Christian Coalition fell into debt, and, investigated by both the FEC and the IRS, its membership numbers had plummeted by 1997. But that wasn't the kind of failure Weyrich was talking about. Even if the Christian Coalition had fallen apart, conservatives had won elections and appointed judges. But they hadn't been able to stop what Weyrich called the "collapse of the culture" into an "ever-widening sewer." "I no longer believe that there is a moral majority," Weyrich wrote. "I do not believe that a majority of Americans actually shares our values." If they did, he said, "Bill Clinton would have been driven out of office months ago."[176]

A curtain closed on the culture wars. "People on the political right set out to unseat a president, and they almost succeeded," Anthony Lewis wrote in the *New York Review of Books*. "In his folly, Clinton played into their hands. But that does not alter the fact that this country came close to a *coup d'état*."[177] The most that many Americans began to expect Congress to accomplish in any given session was, possibly, to avoid a shutdown and, at best, to agree on a budget. The government had been reduced to a shambles. Attempting to stage a *coup d'état* became an ordinary part of every American presidency. Opponents of each of the next three presidents, George W. Bush, Barack Obama, and Donald J. Trump, would call them "unconstitutional." Members of the House of Representatives would call for impeachment proceedings. Collectors of political paraphernalia interested in documenting this turn could have compiled, by attending political rallies during any year after 1994, calls for an end to each American presidential administration. IMPEACH CLINTON! The signs came in every color. IMPEACH BUSH! They came in block letters and cursive. IMPEACH OBAMA! They were staked in front yards. IMPEACH TRUMP! They were duct-taped to mailboxes.

In the summer of 1999, in a nation consumed by the politics of scandal, celebrity, pettiness, and vengeance, rumors began to spread that Donald Trump, fifty-three, intended to run for president. Born in 1947, Trump was the son of a real-estate man from Queens. In 1964, he graduated from military school, where he'd been known as a "ladies' man." He considered going to the University of Southern California, to study film, but ended up studying first at Fordham University, then business at Wharton, graduating in 1968. [178] He spent most of his time reading the listings of foreclosures on federally financed housing projects, he later said. He joined his father's business and set out to conquer Manhattan. In 1973, the Department of Justice charged Trump and his father with violating the 1968 Fair Housing Act. "We never have discriminated," Trump told the *New York Times*, "and we never would."[179] During the years when the parties swapped women for men, and Hillary Rodham left the Republican Party to become a Democrat, Donald Trump did the reverse. In the 1970s, Trump began making donations to the Democratic Party. "The simple fact is that contributing money to politicians is very standard and accepted for a New York City developer," he explained in *The Art of the Deal*, his best-selling business book, published in 1987, the year he first toyed with running for president. At the time, Trump was a larger-than-life media presence, a huckster chronically in and out of bankruptcy court but a reliable ratings booster on the talk show circuit, where he was usually referred to as a "hustler." An avid participant in the world of professional wrestling, Trump's forays into politics were generally greeted as stunts. In 1984, he'd offered to serve as an arms negotiator with the Soviet Union. "It would take an hour-and-a-half to learn everything there is to learn about missiles," he told the *Washington Post*. "I think I know most of it anyway."[180] In 1987, Trump had flown to New Hampshire, where he was greeted by "Trump for President" signs. "I'm not here because I'm running for President," he said. "I'm here because I'm tired of our country being kicked around." He promised to eliminate the budget deficit by making countries like Japan, Saudi Arabia, and Kuwait pay their debts: "There is a way you can ask them and they will give it, if you have the right person asking."[181]

In the 1990s, the American economy thrived, at least by some measures. Dot-com stock was booming. By the end of Clinton's second term, unemployment had fallen to 4.1 percent and the United States was producing nearly a quarter of the world's output, a share never seen before, not even by the British Empire at its peak, in 1913, when it produced 8 percent of the world's output. And still, for Americans without a college education and especially for those without a high school diploma, real wages were stagnant or falling. And yet a worship of the very rich was everywhere, from *Lifestyles of the Rich and Famous*, which aired from 1984 to 1995, to the rising fame of gold-plated New York real estate tycoon Donald Trump.[182]

During the Lewinsky scandal, Trump, known as "a twice-divorced, doll-chasing socialite," gleefully offered his opinions, as a famous cad, about the affair. The Lewinsky scandal had elevated Trump from pop culture celebrity businessman to political commentator. "Paula Jones is a loser," he said on NBC's *Hardball with Chris Matthews*. "But the fact is that she may be responsible for bringing down a president indirectly." Clinton's statement was "a disaster," Trump said, and he should have taken the Fifth Amendment. He'd have had more respect for Bill Clinton, Trump said, if he'd had sex with a supermodel instead of with Lewinsky.[183]

Keen to remain in the spotlight, Trump published a new book, *The America We Deserve*, that had all the trappings of a campaign manifesto. In a chapter called "Should I Run," Trump pointed to a survey that documented his name recognition: "It was no surprise to me that 97 percent of the American people knew who I was." His supporters launched a website, www.thedonald2000.org. The *National Enquirer* conducted a poll of one hundred people, who very much liked Trump. Readers of the *Enquirer*, Trump said, were "the real people." He said, "I think the kind of people who support me are the workers, the construction workers, the taxicab driver. Rich people don't like me." The *National Enquirer* survey allowed Trump to report, "The polls have been unbelievable."[184]

Trump knew exactly what he was up to. He said that he'd choose Oprah Winfrey as his running mate and if the establishment laughed, that was their error. The establishment did laugh. "Mr. Trump is trying to determine whether there is a place in American political life for a rogue," the *New York Times* reported. But Trump knew that Americans were disillusioned. "I am considering a run only because I am convinced that the major parties have lost their way," he explained. "The Republicans, especially those in Congress, are captives of their right wing. The Democrats are captive of their left wing. I don't hear anyone speaking for the working men and women in the center. There is very little contact between the concerns and interests of ordinary people and the agendas of politicians."[185]

Trump boasted of his legendary deal making, but his real attraction to voters, he told the columnist Maureen Dowd, was his personality, and his sex appeal. "I think the only difference between me and the other candidates," he said, "is that I'm more honest and my women are more beautiful." His candidacy didn't go much beyond talking points, but he did offer policy proposals: to close the budget deficit, he suggested raising $5.7 trillion with a onetime 14.25 percent tax on the net worth of people and trusts worth $10 million or more. As for the rest of his economic plan, he said, "That would be determined and worked out." In remarks outlining his possible foreign policy, he insulted France ("a terrible partner"), Germany ("they failed militarily"), Japan ("ripping us big league"), and Saudi Arabia ("I mean, the money they make") and suggested that, if elected president, he would double as U.S. trade representative, "and I guarantee you," he said on Fox News, "the rip-off of the United States would end."[186]

Serious political commentators did not even elevate his candidacy to that of a crank; they considered him a buffoon. "The only thing standing between Donald Trump and the presidency," wrote syndicated columnist Mark Shields, "is the good judgment of the American people." By January 2000, www.thedonald2000.org was for sale. "Are these people stiffs, or what?" Trump said later that month, watching a GOP primary debate. "They're losers," he said. "Who the hell wants to have a person like this for president?"[187]

The Republican who did win the nomination that year was George W. Bush, the governor of Texas and former president's son. With the younger Bush, a Yale graduate and a devout born-again Christian, conservatism got a new face, a new voice, and a new slogan: "compassionate conservatism." "Big government is not the answer," Bush said at the Republican convention. "But the alternative to bureaucracy is not indifference. It is to put conservative values and conservative ideas into the thick of the fight for justice and opportunity." Republican speechwriter David Frum proved skeptical, joking: "Love conservatism but hate arguing about abortion? Try our new *compassionate conservatism*—great ideological taste, now with less controversy."[188]

Less controversy there would not be. The nation, long divided, turned out to be divided quite evenly. The 2000 election was a nail-biter to end all nail-biters. After it was all over, it was by no means clear that the voters had decided the outcome. Instead, the two most dauntingly powerful forces on the battleground of American politics—cable television and the Supreme Court—made the first and eventually the final call.

Just before 8:00 p.m. on Election Night, the networks announced that Gore had won Florida in a very close vote. Later that night, Fox News countermanded the networks' prediction of a Gore victory. Ailes had hired John Ellis, Bush's first cousin, to head Fox News's "decision desk." Shortly after 2:00 a.m., after getting off the phone with Bush's brother, Jeb Bush, the governor of Florida, Ellis cried out, "Jebbie says we got it!" (Later, before a House committee, Ailes said that there had not been anything inappropriate in his employing Ellis. "Quite the contrary," he said. "I see this as a good journalist talking to his very high-level sources on election night.")[189] Fox News then called the election for Bush.

Four minutes later, ABC, CBS, NBC, and CNN followed Fox's lead, naming Bush the next president. A crestfallen Gore conceded, but then, in yet another twist of a tale as tangled as seaweed, Gore un-conceded, telling Bush, in a second phone call, "Your little brother is not the ultimate authority on this." A report commissioned by CNN damned the television coverage that night as a "news disaster that damaged democracy and journalism" and "played an important part in creating the ensuing cli-

*A battle over a recount in the election of 2000*
*left the outcome in doubt for weeks.*

mate of rancor and bitterness."[190] The report missed the point. Television coverage of American politics had helped create that climate, for sure, but years before Bush faced Gore.

Gore contested the election. No one disputed that he had won the popular vote by more than half a million ballots. That meant that the election turned on a handful of votes needed to capture the electoral vote in Florida. The Florida Supreme Court supported Gore's demand for a manual recount in four counties. There followed thirty-six days of doubt about the outcome of the election—and of the American presidency itself—while a recount was held. Then, astonishingly, on December 12, the Supreme Court called off the recount, overruling the lower court in a bitterly argued 5–4 decision.

In September of 1787, when Americans were first asked to debate the Constitution, many had wondered at the power granted to the Supreme Court. Many wondered, again, in December of 2000, when the court exercised a power never before known. The five justices that formed the majority had all been named by Reagan or Bush. They rested their decision on the equal protection clause of the Fourteenth Amendment, an amendment that had been written and ratified to guarantee the rights of African Americans.[191] "Although we may never know with complete certainty the identity of the winner of this year's Presidential election, the identity of the loser is perfectly clear," Justice John Paul Stevens, eighty, and a Ford appointee, wrote, in a blistering dissent. "It is the Nation's confidence in the judge as an impartial guardian of the rule of law." [192]

On the final day of his presidency, Clinton made one last deal in which, in exchange for immunity from prosecution, he admitted to having lied under oath. He and his wife left the White House with more than $190,000 in gifts. An editorial in the *Washington Post* urged George W. and Laura Bush to count the White House spoons and described the Clintons as having "no capacity for embarrassment." Hillary got an $8 million book deal; she and Bill bought two multimillion-dollar homes. [193]

"Our nation must rise above a house divided," the new president said, after Gore conceded. [194] But the nation, its houses newly wired for the Internet, was about to come apart, two towers collapsing.

## *Sixteen*

# AMERICA,
# DISRUPTED

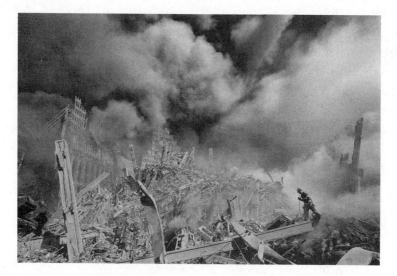

*Firefighters searched Ground Zero
long after the collapse of both towers.*

THE FIRST PLANE CRASHED INTO THE TOP FLOORS OF
the north tower of the World Trade Center in New York at 8:46 a.m.
on September 11, 2001. CNN broke into a commercial to show live footage of the tower, gray smoke billowing out of a black gash in the steel and
glass against a nearly cloudless blue sky. On an ordinary day, some fifty
thousand people worked in the Twin Towers, more than one hundred stories high; by a quarter to nine on that particular Tuesday, nearly twenty
thousand people had already shown up, wearing hats and pumps, carrying
laptops and briefcases. Orders to evacuate or not to evacuate, and whether
to go up or go down, conflicted; most people decided to leave, and headed
down. As more than a thousand firefighters, EMTs, and police officers

raced to the scene and began rescue efforts, some people trapped on the upper floors, facing insufferable heat and unable to breathe, leapt to their deaths rather than be burned alive. One couple held hands as they fell. From far away, they looked like paper dolls.

At 8:52 a.m., Peter Hanson, a passenger on another plane, United Airlines Flight 175, was able to call his father. He asked him to report to authorities that his flight had been hijacked. Hanson, thirty-two, was flying with his wife and their two-and-a-half-year-old daughter: they were going to Disneyland. "I think they've taken over the cockpit," Hanson whispered to his father. The passengers were thinking about trying to gain control of the plane from the terrorists, who'd used knives and Mace and said they had a bomb and appeared to have killed the pilots. At 9:00, Hanson called his father again. "I think we are going down," he said. "My God, my God," he gasped. Three minutes later, United 175 crashed into the south tower of the World Trade Center.

Television stations had been covering the fire in the north tower live; announcers and reporters watched in horror as the plane hit the south tower and burst into a fireball. It looked impossible, something out of a 1950s Hollywood disaster film, props, models, wires, and tin, something that could not happen, King Kong swinging from the Empire State Building, Godzilla climbing the Statue of Liberty. "My God, my God," said a host on ABC News. "Oh Lord." Sirens shrieked, and from the streets there came a wailing.

At 9:37 a.m., in Washington, DC, a third hijacked plane, traveling at 530 miles per hour, crashed into the Pentagon. The hijackers had intended to crash a fourth plane, United Flight 93, into the Capitol or the White House. This flight, unlike the first three, all of which had departed on time, was running more than half an hour late; it took off at 8:42 a.m. At 9:23, a United flight dispatcher sent out a message: "Beware any cockpit intrusion." At 9:26, the pilot on Flight 93 responded with seeming disbelief: "Confirm latest mssg plz." Two minutes later, the hijackers stormed the cockpit. In the moments that followed, ten of the flight's thirty-three passengers and the two surviving members of the crew managed to make phone calls. They learned about the attacks on the World Trade Center; they decided to fight back. At 9:47, CeeCee Lyles, a flight attendant and mother of four, called her husband and left him a message. "I hope to be able to see your face again, baby," she said, her voice breaking. "I love you." Ten minutes later, the passengers and crew, having taken a vote about what to do, charged the cockpit. The plane began to roll. At 10:03, United Flight 93 plowed into a field in Shanksville, Pennsylvania, twenty minutes outside of Washington. Everyone on all four planes died.

In New York, emergency workers had entered the towers, evacuating thousands of people, but the burning jet fuel, at over a thousand degrees, was weakening the skyscrapers' steel girders. At 9:58 a.m., the south tower collapsed into itself, falling straight to the ground like an elevator shaft, crushing everyone inside. CNN, which had been covering the crash at the Pentagon, cut back to New York, the TV screen showing nothing but cloud upon cloud; for a moment, watching the screen felt like looking out the window of a plane, flying through the white. The north tower fell at 10:28. CNN: "There are no words."

It seemed altogether possible that there were more attacks to come. "We have some planes," one of the hijackers had said. Poor communication between the civilian aviation authority and the military's aerospace command—and the lack of any experience with or protocol for a suicide hijacking—meant that the U.S. military had been unable to mount a defense. About 10:15, the vice president authorized the air force to shoot down United Flight 93, unaware that it had already met its horrible end. By noon, all flights from all U.S. airports were grounded, federal buildings were evacuated, embassies were shuttered, and millions of prayers were whispered. The vice president was moved from the White House to an underground bunker, and the president, who had been visiting an elementary school in Florida, was flown to a secure location in Omaha, Nebraska. Nearly three thousand people had been killed.[1]

"America Under Attack," ran the headline on CNN.com, whose coverage that day included videos, a photo gallery, a timeline, statements from leaders around the world, and emergency resources.[2] NYTimes.com posted a slideshow, maps, a flight tracker, and a list of places to donate blood.[3] The Drudge Report's homepage displayed a pair of police sirens and the question "Who Did This?!"[4] And Foxnews.com began an ongoing special report, "Terrorism Hits America."[5]

That night, a resolved president delivered a televised address. "A great people has been moved to defend a great nation," George W. Bush said. Even before night had fallen, he committed the United States to waging a "war against terrorism."[6]

Nineteen men, trained by al Qaeda, an Islamic terrorist organization led by Saudi millionaire Osama bin Laden, had conducted the attacks. Bush's rhetoric and that of the neoconservatives in his administration characterized the "war on terror" as an inevitable conflict that was part of a "clash of civilizations," predicted by political scientist Samuel P. Huntington in a 1993 article in *Foreign Affairs*. Once, there had been wars between kings, then wars between peoples, then wars between ideologies, Huntington argued, but those ages had passed, and the future would be characterized by clashes between the world's great civilizations, first along the fault line between Western civilization and the Islamic world. Western dependence on Arab oil and the rise of Islamic fundamentalism had already led to the 1979 U.S. hostage crisis in Iran and the Soviet invasion of Afghanistan, and, in 1990, to the First Persian Gulf War.[7]

"America was targeted for attack because we're the brightest beacon for freedom and opportunity in the world," Bush said.[8] Barack Obama, an Illinois state senator and constitutional law professor, offered a different interpretation in a Chicago newspaper. "The essence of this tragedy," he said, "derives from a fundamental absence of empathy on the part of the attackers," a deformation that "grows out of a climate of poverty and ignorance, helplessness and despair."[9]

It became something of a national myth, later, to describe the American people, long divided, as newly united after 9/11. More accurate would be to say that, in those first days, politicians and writers who expressed views that strayed far from the mournful stoicism that characterized the response of both Bush, on an international stage, and Obama, in a neighborhood newspaper, were loudly denounced. These included Susan Sontag, who traced the origins of the attack to U.S. foreign policy in the Middle East—the propping up of tyrants, the CIA toppling of Middle Eastern leaders, and the ongoing bombing of Iraq. "Where is the acknowledgment that this was not a 'cowardly' attack on 'civilization' or 'liberty' or 'humanity' or 'the free world' but an attack on the world's self-proclaimed superpower, undertaken as a consequence of specific American alliances and actions?" Sontag asked in *The New Yorker*. "In the matter of courage (a morally neutral virtue): whatever may be said of the perpetrators of Tuesday's slaughter, they were not cowards."[10] In the *Washington Post*, Charles Krauthammer accused Sontag of "moral obtuseness."[11] From the right, Ann Coulter, a columnist who'd earlier worked for Paula Jones's legal team, wrote in the *National Review*, in an article posted online on September 13, that drawing any distinctions between anyone in the Arab world was unnecessary, as was any investigation into the attacks. "This is no time to be precious about locating the exact individuals directly involved in this particular terrorist attack," Coulter wrote. "We don't need long investigations of the forensic evidence to determine with scientific accuracy the person or persons who ordered this specific attack. . . . We should invade their countries, kill their leaders and convert them to Christianity."[12] Two weeks later, the editor of the *National Review* announced that it regretted publishing Coulter's piece, and stopped publishing her column.[13] "I really believe the pagans and abortionists, and the feminists and the gays and the lesbians who are actively trying to make that an alternative lifestyle, the ACLU, People for the American Way, all of them who have tried to secularize America, I point the finger in their face and say, 'You helped this happen,'" Jerry Falwell said immediately after the attacks.[14] But he, too, was condemned, including by the president.[15]

Alex Jones, cluster-bomb radio host, flew in under the radar of this opprobrium. On the afternoon of the attacks, he broadcast across the country, live from Austin, to nearly a hundred affiliated stations, for five hours. He began, not with sympathy, not with grief, not with horror, but with gleeful self-congratulation: "Well, I've been warning you about it for at least five years, all terrorism that we've looked at from the World Trade Center and Oklahoma City to Waco, has been government actions," Jones crowed. "They need this as a pretext to bring you and your family martial law. They're either using provocateur Arabs and allowing them to do it or this is full complicity with the federal government: the evidence is overwhelming." (Earlier that summer, Jones had issued a warning. "Please!" he'd screamed. "Call Congress. Tell 'em we *know* the government is planning terrorism.") On September 11, he reported the morning's events as if reading from an incidents log, adding details of his own—"dead bodies up to six blocks away, arms, legs, you name it"—interrupting with updates, and cutting to eyewitnesses, in coverage that sounded straight out of Orson Welles's *The War of the Worlds*. Like Welles, Jones asserted his own credibility by frequently sounding notes of caution—"we don't know how many of these reports are accurate"—while making singularly outrageous and vicious claims, even as surgeons in New York were amputating limbs and nurses were cleaning burned skin and firefighters, falling down from exhaustion, were digging through rubble, looking for survivors. "I'll tell you the bottom-line," Jones growled. "Ninety-eight percent chance this was a government-orchestrated, controlled bombing."[16]

Between 2001 and 2016, the demise of the daily newspaper, following the spiraling decline of broadcast television, contributed to a dizzying political disequilibrium, as if the world of news were suddenly revealed to be contained within a bouncy castle at an amusement park. New sources of news and opinion appeared like so many whirling, vertiginous rides, neon-bright, with screams of fright and delight, from blogs and digital newspapers to news aggregators and social media, roller coasters and water slides and tea-cup-and-saucer spinners. Facebook launched in 2004, YouTube in 2005, Twitter in 2006, the iPhone in 2007. By 2008, Twitter had a million users, and one in six Americans had a smartphone. Six years later, those numbers had climbed teeteringly high: Twitter had 284 million users, and two out of three Americans owned smartphones. They clutched them in their hands as they rode and rolled, thrilled by the G-force drop and the eardrum-popping rise and the sound of their own shrieking.

New sources of news tended to be unedited, their facts unverified, their politics unhinged. "Alternative" political communities took the 1990s culture wars online; Tumblr on the left and 4chan on the right, trafficking in hysteria and irony, hatred and contempt, Tumblr performing the denunciation of white privilege with pious call-outs and demanding trigger warnings and safe spaces, 4chan pronouncing white supremacy and antifeminism by way of ironic memes and murderous trolls.[17] In a throwback to the political intrigues of the Cold War, Russia-sponsored hackers and trolls, posing as Americans, created fake Twitter and Facebook accounts whose purpose was to undermine the authority of the mainstream news, widen the American partisan divide, stoke racial and religious animosity, and incite civil strife. Under these circumstances, the fevered rants of deranged conspiracy theorists reached a new and newly receptive audience but, in a much broader and deeper sense, in an age of ceaseless online spectacle and massive corporate and government surveillance, nearly all political thinking became conspiratorial.

Jones, in retrospect, was the least but also the worst of this, the amusement park's deadly but absurd Stephen King clown. After 9/11, he briefly lost some of his affiliates, but he didn't especially need a radio network. In 1999, he'd launched a website called Infowars, where he presented himself to the world as a citizen journalist, a fighter for the truth by way of the new, no-holds-barred medium of the Internet. On September 11, Infowars warned, of the federal government, "They Are Preparing to Radically Re-engineer Our Society Forever." That day, Jones inaugurated what came to be called the truther movement, a faction of conspiracy theorists who believed that the United States government was behind the 9/11 attacks. The vice president, Jones would later elaborate, had been disappointed by the passenger revolt on United Flight 93. "If it would have hit its target," Jones said, "the government would have been completely decapitated and the president could have declared total martial law."[18]

Jones, wild with malice, cut through the American political imagination with a chainsaw rigged to a broom handle, flailing and gnashing. In 2008, when Barack Obama sought the Democratic nomination for president in a close competition with Hillary Clinton, Jones and other truthers became birthers: they argued that Obama, who was born in Hawaii—an event reported in two Hawaiian newspapers and recorded on his birth certificate—had been born in Kenya. The truthers were on the far fringes, but even the broader American public raised an eyebrow at Obama's name, Barack Hussein Obama, at a time when the United States's declared enemies were Osama bin Laden and Saddam Hussein. Urged to change his name, Obama refused. Instead, he joked about it. "People call me 'Alabama,'" he'd say on the campaign trail. "They call me 'Yo Mama.' And that's my supporters!"[19]

So far from changing his name, Obama made his story his signature. His 2008 campaign for "Hope" and "Change" was lifted by soaring storytelling about the nation's long march to freedom and equality in which he used his own life as an allegory for American history, in the tradition of Benjamin Franklin, Andrew Jackson, and Frederick Douglass. But Obama's story was new. "I am the son of a black man from Kenya and a white woman from Kansas," he said. "These people are a part of me. And they are a part of America." Obama's American family was every color, and part of a very big world. "I have brothers, sisters, nieces, nephews, uncles and cousins, of every race and every hue, scattered across three continents, and for as long as I live, I will never forget that in no other country on Earth is my story even possible."[20]

Obama's election as the United States' first black president was made possible by centuries of black struggle, by runaways and rebellions, by war and exile, by marches and court cases, by staggering sacrifices. "Barack Obama is what comes at the end of that bridge in Selma," said the much-admired man who had marched at Selma, John Lewis.[21] His victory seemed to usher in a new era in American history, a casting off of the nation's agonizing legacy of racial violence, the realizing, at long last, of the promises made in the nation's founding documents. Yet as he took office in 2009, Obama inherited a democracy in disarray. The United States was engaged in two distant wars with little popular support and few achievable objectives, fought by a military drawn disproportionately from the poor—as if they were drones operated by richer men. The economy had collapsed in one of the worst stock market crashes in American history. The working class had seen no increase in wages for more than a generation. One in three black men between the ages of twenty and twenty-nine was in prison or on probation.[22] Both parties had grown hollow—hard and partisan on the outside, empty on the inside—while political debate, newly waged almost entirely online, had become frantic, desperate, and paranoid. Between 1958 and 2015, the proportion of Americans who told pollsters that they "basically trust the government" fell from 73 percent to 19 percent.[23] Forty years of a relentless conservative attack on the government and the press had produced a public that trusted neither. Forty years of identity politics had shattered Rooseveltian liberalism; Obama walked on shards of glass.

Even as Obama embraced a family of cousins scattered across continents, nationalism and even white supremacy were growing in both the United States and Europe in the form of populist movements that called for immigration restriction, trade barriers, and, in some cases, the abdication of international climate accords. New movements emerged from the right—the Tea Party in 2009 and the alt-right in 2010—and from the left: Occupy in 2011, Black Lives Matter in 2013. Activists on the left, including those aligned with an antifascist resistance known as antifa, self-consciously cast their campaigns as international movements, but the new American populism and a resurgent white nationalism had their counterparts in other countries, too. Whatever their political differences, they shared a political style. In a time of accelerating change, both the Far Left and the Far Right came to understand history itself as a plot, an understanding advanced by the very formlessness of the Internet, anonymous and impatient. Online, the universe appeared to be nothing so much as an array of patterns in search of an explanation, provided to people unwilling to trust to any authority but that of their own fevered, reckless, and thrill-seeking political imaginations.

In 2011, during Obama's second term, the aging New York business-man, television star, and on-again, off-again presidential candidate Donald Trump aligned himself with the truthers and the birthers by questioning the president's citizenship. In a country where the Supreme Court had ruled, in *Dred Scott*, that no person born of African descent could ever be an American citizen, to say that Obama was not a citizen was to call upon centuries of racial hatred. Like 9/11 conspiracy theorists, Obama con-spiracy theorists (who were in many cases the same people) were forever adding details to their story: the president was born in Nairobi; he was educated at a madrasa in Jakarta; he was secretly a Muslim; he was, still more secretly, an anti-imperialist African nationalist, like his father; he was on a mission to make America African.[24] "The most powerful country in the world," right-wing pundit Dinesh D'Souza warned, "is being gov-erned according to the dreams of a Luo tribesman of the 1950s."[25]

Trump, bypassing newspapers and television and broadcasting directly to his supporters, waged this campaign online, through his Twitter account. "An 'extremely credible source' has called my office and told me that @BarackObama's birth certificate is a fraud," he tweeted in 2012.[26] Trump did not back off this claim as he pursued the Republican nomi-nation in 2015.[27] The backbone of his campaign was a promise to build a wall along the U.S.-Mexican border. After 9/11, a white nationalist move-ment that had foundered for decades had begun to revive, in pursuit of two goals: preserving the icons of the Confederacy, and ending the immi-gration of dark-skinned peoples.[28] Trump, announcing his candidacy from New York's Trump Tower, gave a speech in which he called Mexi-cans trying to enter the United States "rapists," borrowing from a book by Ann Coulter called *¡Adios, America!*[29] (On immigration and much else, Coulter promoted herself as a courageous teller of truths in a world of lies. "Every single elite group in America is aligned against the public— the media, ethnic activists, big campaign donors, Wall Street, multimil-lionaire farmers, and liberal 'churches,'" Coulter wrote. "The media lie about everything, but immigration constitutes their finest hour of collec-tive lying.")[30] Obama had promised hope and change. Trump promised to Make America Great Again.

Hillary Clinton, having lost the Democratic nomination to Obama in 2008, won it in 2016 and hoped to become the first female president. Her campaign misjudged Trump and not only failed to address the suffering of blue-collar voters but also insulted Trump's supporters, dismissing half of them as a "basket of deplorables." Mitt Romney had done much the same thing as the Republican nominee in 2012, when, with seething contempt, he dismissed the "47 percent" of the U.S. population—Obama's supporters—as people "who believe they are victims."[31] Party politics had so far abandoned any sense of a national purpose that, within the space of four years, each of the party's presidential nominees declared large portions of the population of the United States unworthy of their attention and beneath their contempt.

Trump, having secured the nomination, campaigned against Clinton, aided by the UK data firm Cambridge Analytica, by arguing that she belonged in jail. "She is an abject, psychopathic, demon from Hell that as soon as she gets into power is going to try to destroy the planet," said Jones, who sold "Hillary for Prison" T-shirts. "Lock Her Up," Trump's supporters said at his rallies.[32]

American history became, in those years, a wound that bled, and bled again. Gains made toward realizing the promise of the Constitution were lost. Time seemed to be moving both backward and forward. Americans fought over matters of justice, rights, freedom, and America's place in the world with a bitter viciousness, and not only online. Each of the truths on which the nation was founded and for which so many people had fought was questioned. The idea of truth itself was challenged. The only agreed-upon truth appeared to be a belief in the ubiquity of deception. The 2008 Obama campaign assembled a Truth Team.[33] "You lie!" a South Carolina congressman called out to President Obama, during a joint session of Congress in 2011. "You are fake news!" Trump said to a CNN reporter at an event at the White House.[34]

"Let facts be submitted to a candid world," Jefferson had written in the Declaration of Independence, founding a nation by appealing to truth. But whatever had been left of a politics of reasoned debate, of inquiry and curiosity, of evidence and fair-mindedness, seemed to have been eradicated when, on December 2, 2015, Trump appeared on Infowars by Skype from Trump Tower. In an earlier campaign rally, Trump had said that on 9/11 he'd been watching television from his penthouse, and had seen footage of "thousands and thousands of people," Muslims, cheering from rooftops in New Jersey.[35] Jones began by congratulating Trump on being vindicated on this point. (Trump had not, in fact, been vindicated, and no such footage has ever been found.) Jones, sputtering, gushed about the historic nature of Trump's campaign.

"What you're doing is epic," Jones told Trump. "It's George Washington level."

"Your reputation's amazing," Trump told Jones, promising, "I will not let you down."[36]

Five days later, Trump called for a "total and complete shutdown of the entry of Muslims to the United States."[37] In place of towers, there would be walls.

Between the attacks on September 11, 2001, and the election of Donald Trump fifteen years later, on November 9, 2016, the United States lost its way in a cloud of smoke. The party system crashed, the press crumbled, and all three branches of government imploded. There was real fear that the American political process was being run by Russians, as if, somehow, the Soviets had won the Cold War after all. To observers who included the authors of books like *How Democracy Ends, Why Liberalism Failed, How the Right Lost Its Mind,* and *How Democracies Die,* it seemed, as Trump took office, as if the nation might break out in a civil war, as if the American experiment had failed, as if democracy itself were in danger of dying.[38]

# I.

IT BEGAN, in the year 1999, with a panic. Computer programmers predicted that at one second after midnight on January 1, 2000, all the world's computers, unable to accommodate a year that did not begin with "19," would crash. Even before the twenty-first century began, even before no small number of political dystopians forecast a thousand-year clash of civilizations or the imminent death of democracy, Americans were subjected to breathless warnings of millennial doom, a ticking clock catastrophe, not the global annihilation timed by the atomic age's Doomsday Clock but a disaster, a "Y2K bug," embedded into the programs written to run on the microprocessor tucked into the motherboard of the hulking computer

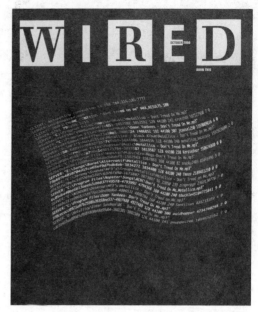

*Wired magazine began appearing in 1993 and by 2000 announced that the Internet had ushered in "One Nation, Interconnected."*

perched on every desktop. After much rending of garments and gnashing of teeth, this bug was quietly and entirely fixed. The end of the world averted, digital prophets next undertook to predict the exact date of the arrival of an Aquarian age of peace, unity, and harmony, ushered in by, of all things, the Internet.

In the spring of 2000, *Wired*, the slick, punk, Day-Glo magazine of the dot-com era, announced that the Internet had, in fact, already healed a divided America: "We are, as a nation, better educated, more tolerant, and more connected because of—not in spite of—the convergence of the Internet and public life. Partisanship, religion, geography, race, gender, and other traditional political divisions are giving way to a new standard—wiredness—as an organizing principle for political and social attitudes."[39] Of all the wide-eyed technological boosterism in American history, from the telegraph to the radio, few pronouncements rose to such dizzying rhetorical heights.

Over the course of the twentieth century, the United States had assumed an unrivaled position in the world as the defender of liberal states, democratic values, and the rule of law. From NATO to NAFTA, relations between states had been regulated by pacts, free trade agreements, and restraint. But, beginning in 2001, with the war on terror, the United States undermined and even abdicated the very rules it had helped to establish, including prohibitions on torture and wars of aggression.[40] By 2016, a "by any means necessary" disregard for restraints on conduct had come to characterize American domestic politics as well. "If you see somebody getting ready to throw a tomato," Trump told supporters at a campaign rally in Iowa, "knock the crap out of them, would you?"[41] Countless factors contributed to these changes. But the crisis of American moral authority that began with the war on terror at the start of the twenty-first century cannot be understood outside of the rise of the Internet, which is everything a rule-based order is not: lawless, unregulated, and unaccountable.

What became the Internet had begun in the late 1960s, with ARPANET. By the mid-1970s, the Department of Defense's Advanced Research Projects Agency's network had grown to an international network of networks: an "internet," for short. In 1989, in Geneva, Tim Berners-Lee, an English computer scientist, proposed a protocol to link pages on what he called the World Wide Web. The first web page in the United States was created in 1991, at Stanford. Berners-Lee's elegant protocol spread fast, first across universities and then to the public. The first widely available web browser, Mosaic, was launched in 1993, making it possible for anyone with a personal computer wired to the Internet to navigate web pages around the world, click by astonishing click.[42]

*Wired*, launched in March 1993, flaunted cyberculture's countercultural origins. Its early contributors included Stewart Brand and John Perry Barlow, a gold-necklace- and scarf-wearing bearded mystic who for many years wrote lyrics for the Grateful Dead. In *Wired*, the counterculture's dream of a nonhierarchical, nonorganizational world of harmony found expression in a new digital utopianism, as if every Internet cable were a string of love beads. Brand, writing in an article in *Time*, "We Owe It All to the Hippies," announced that "the real legacy of the sixties generation is the computer revolution."[43]

But between the 1960s and the 1990s, the revolution had moved from the far left to the far right. *Wired* was edited by Louis Rossetto, a libertarian and former anarchist known to lament the influence of the "mainstream media." In the magazine's inaugural issue, Rossetto predicted that the Internet would bring about "social changes so profound their only parallel is probably the discovery of fire." The Internet would create a new, new world order, except it wouldn't be an order; it would be an open market, free of all government interference, a frontier, a Wild West. In 1990, Barlow had helped found the Electronic Frontier Foundation, to promote this vision. (The EFF later became chiefly concerned with matters of intellectual property, free speech, and privacy.) In 1993, *Wired* announced that "life in cyberspace seems to be shaping up exactly like Thomas Jefferson would have wanted: founded on the primacy of individual liberty and a commitment to pluralism, diversity and community."[44]

The digital utopians' think tank was Newt Gingrich's Progress and Freedom Foundation, established in 1993 (and later the subject of an ethics inquiry); its key thinker was an irrepressible George Gilder, resurrected. Gingrich appeared on the cover of *Wired* in 1995, Gilder in 1996. Gingrich was battling in Congress for a new Telecommunications Act, the first major revision of the FCC-founding 1934 Federal Communications Act (itself a revision of the 1927 Federal Radio Act); his objective was to insure that, unlike radio or television, the new medium would lie beyond the realm of government regulation. At a 1994 meeting of Gingrich's Progress and Freedom Foundation in Aspen, Gilder, along with futurists Alvin Toffler and Esther Dyson and the physicist George Keyworth, Reagan's former science adviser, drafted a "Magna Carta for the Knowledge Age."[45] It established the framework of the act Gingrich hoped to pass. Announcing that "cyberspace is the latest American frontier," the writers of the new Magna Carta contended that while the industrial age might have required government regulation, the knowledge age did not. "If there is to be an 'industrial policy for the knowledge age,'" their Magna Carta proclaimed, "it should focus on removing barriers to competition and massively deregulating the fast-growing telecommunications and computing industries."[46]

Gingrich got his wish. On February 8, 1996, Bill Clinton signed the Telecommunications Act in the reading room of the Library of Congress; he signed on paper and then, electronically, with a digital pen, an event reported in real time on the Internet.[47] If little noticed at the time, Clinton's approval of this startling piece of legislation would prove a lasting and terrible legacy of his presidency: it deregulated the communications industry, lifting virtually all of its New Deal antimonopoly provisions, allowing for the subsequent consolidation of media companies and prohibiting regulation of the Internet with catastrophic consequences.

Nevertheless, that the U.S. government would even presume to legislate the Internet—even if only to promise not to regulate it—alarmed the Internet libertarians. On the day Clinton signed the bill, Barlow, ex-hippie become the darling of world bankers and billionaires, watching from the World Economic Forum in Davos, Switzerland, wrote a Declaration of Independence of Cyberspace:

> Governments of the Industrial World, you weary giants of flesh and steel, I come from Cyberspace, the new home of Mind. On behalf of the future, I ask you of the past to leave us alone. You are not welcome among us. You have no sovereignty where we gather. . . . Governments derive their just powers from the consent of the governed. You have neither solicited nor received ours. We did not invite you. You do not know us, nor do you know our world. Cyberspace does not lie within your borders.[48]

He posted this statement on the web, where it became one of the very first posts to spread, as was said, like a virus, an infection.

Cyberutopians who had no use for government ignored the altogether inconvenient fact that of course not only the Internet itself but also nearly all the tools used to navigate it, along with the elemental inventions of the digital age, had been built or subsidized by taxpayer-funded, government-sponsored research. The iPhone, taking only one example, depended on the unquestionable and extraordinary ingenuity of Apple, but it also depended on U.S. government–funded research that had earlier resulted in several key technological developments, including GPS, multi-touch screens, LCD displays, lithium-ion batteries, and cellular networks. Nevertheless, Barlow and his followers believed that the Internet existed entirely outside of government, as if it had sprung up, *mirabile dictu*, out of nowhere, before and outside of civil society and the rule of law, in the borderless psychedelic fantasy world of cyberspace. "I ask you of the past to leave us alone," Barlow pleaded. But if the futurists were uninterested in the past, they seemed also strangely incautious about the future. With rare exception, early Internet boosters, who fought for deregulation and antitrust measures even as they benefited from the munificence of the

federal government, evidenced little concern about the possible consequences of those measures on income inequality and political division in
the United States and around the world.[49]

The Internet, a bottomless sea of information and ideas, had profound
effects on the diffusion of knowledge, and especially on its speed and
reach, both of which were accelerated by smartphones. If not so significant to human history as the taming of fire, it was at least as significant
as the invention of the printing press. It accelerated scholarship, science,
medicine, and education; it aided commerce and business. But in its
first two decades, its unintended economic and political consequences
were often dire. Stability, in American politics, had depended not on the
wealth of the few but on the comfort of the many, not on affluence but
on security, and a commitment to the notion of a commonwealth. The
Internet did not destroy the American middle class, but it did play a role
in its decline. It fueled economic growth and generated vast fortunes for
a tiny clutch of people at a time when the poor were becoming poorer
and the middle class disappearing. It turned out that the antimonopoly regulations of the industrial era, far from being obsolete, were sorely
needed in the information age. And the vaunted promise of Internet connection, the gauzy fantasy of libertarians and anarchists who imagined a
world without government, produced nothing so much as a world discon-
nected and distraught.

Silicon Valley, as it grew, earned a reputation as a liberal enclave, but it
also drew a younger generation of libertarians, who had come not from the
counterculture but from the New Right. Peter Thiel, born in Germany in
1967, had gone to Stanford, and then to Stanford Law School, where in
1987 he had founded the *Stanford Review* with funding from Irving Kristol. It aimed to counter campus multiculturalism, feminism, and political
correctness, whose rise at Stanford Thiel had lamented in *The Diversity
Myth*, a 1990s update and dilution of *God and Man at Yale*. George Gilder
and Robert Bork were among Thiel's heroes. (Bork's writings on the error
of antitrust laws informed much Silicon Valley libertarianism.) After a
brief career as a lawyer and a stock trader, Thiel had returned to California in 1996, just in time for the dot-com boom, which followed the lifting
of restrictions on commercial traffic on the Internet. Ten thousand websites were launched every day, poppies in a field. In 1996, Bob Dole, an
unlikely but bold pioneer, became the first presidential candidate to have

a website. Amazon was founded in 1994, Yahoo! in 1995, Google in 1998. In 1998, Thiel cofounded PayPal, hoping that it would free the citizens of the world from government-managed currency. "PayPal will give citizens worldwide more direct control over their currencies than they ever had before," he promised.[50]

The Silicon Valley entrepreneur—almost always a man—became the unrivaled hero of the Second Gilded Age. He was a rescued man, the male breadwinner defended by George Gilder in the 1970s against the forces of feminism, saved, and newly seen as saving the nation itself. Multibillion-dollar Internet deals were made every day. In four years, the value of dot-coms, many of which had not earned a profit, rose by as much as 3,000 percent. By 1999, Bill Gates, at forty-three, had become the richest man in the world, and Microsoft the first corporation in history valued at more than half a trillion dollars.[51]

Inventors from Benjamin Franklin to Thomas Edison had been called "men of progress." Silicon Valley had "disruptive innovators." The language was laden, freighted with the weight of centuries. Historically, the idea of innovation has been opposed to the idea of progress. From the Reformation through the Enlightenment, progress, even in its secular usage, connoted moral improvement, a journey from sin to salvation, from error to truth. Innovation, on the other hand, meant imprudent and rash change. Eighteenth-century conservatives had called Jacobinism "an innovation in politics," Edmund Burke had derided the French Revolution as a "revolt of innovation," and Federalists, opposing Jefferson, had declared themselves to be "enemies to innovation."[52] Over the nineteenth century, the meaning of progress narrowed, coming, more often, to mean merely technological improvement. In the twentieth century, innovation began to replace progress, when used in this sense, but it also meant something different, and more strictly commercial. In 1939 the economist Joseph Schumpeter, in a landmark study of business cycles, used "innovation" to mean bringing new products to market, a usage that spread only slowly, and only in the specialized scholarly literatures of economics and business. In 1942, Schumpeter theorized about "creative destruction," language that, after Hiroshima, had virtually no appeal.[53] Progress, too, accreted critics; in the age of the atom bomb, the idea of progress seemed, to many people, obscene: salvation had not, in fact, been found in machines; to the contrary. Innovation gradually emerged as an all-purpose replacement, progress without goodness. Innovation might make the world a better place, or it might not; the point was, innovation was not concerned with goodness; it was concerned with novelty, speed, and profit.

"Disruption" entered the argot in the 1990s. To disrupt something is to take it apart. The chief proselytizer of "disruptive innovation" (a rebranding of "creative destruction") was Clayton M. Christensen, a professor at Harvard Business School. In 1997, Christensen published *The Innovator's Dilemma,* a business bible for entrepreneurs, in which he argued that companies that make only "sustaining innovations" (careful, small, gradual refinements) are often overrun by companies that make "disruptive innovations": big changes that allow them to produce a cheaper, poorerquality product for a much larger market. IBM made sustaining innovations in its mainframe computers, a big, expensive product marketed to big businesses; Apple, selling a personal computer that ordinary people could afford, made a disruptive innovation.[54]

After 9/11, disruptive innovation, a theory that rested on weak empirical evidence, became gospel, a system of belief, a way of reckoning with uncertainty in an age of rapid change, an age of terror. Terrorism was itself a kind of disruptive innovation, cheaper and faster than conventional war. The gospel of disruptive innovation applauded recklessness and heedlessness. Mark Zuckerberg founded Facebook in 2004, when he was not yet twenty, partly with funding from Thiel. "Unless you are breaking stuff, you aren't moving fast enough," he said, embracing the heedlessness of disruptive innovation. "Don't be evil" was Google's motto, though how to steer clear of iniquity appears to have been left to market forces. Companies and whole industries that failed were meant to fail; disruptive innovation aligned itself with social Darwinism. Above all, the government was to play no role in restraining corporate behavior: that had been a solution for the industrial age, and this was an age of knowledge.[55]

One of the first casualties of disruptive innovation, from the vantage of American democracy, was the paper newspaper, which had supplied the electorate with information about politics and the world and a sense of political community since before the American Revolution. "Printers are educated in the Belief, that when Men differ in Opinion," Benjamin Franklin had once written, "both Sides ought equally to have the Advantage of being heard by the Publick; and that when Truth and Error have fair Play, the former is always an overmatch for the latter."[56] There had been great newspapers and there had been lousy newspapers. But the Republic had never known a time without newspapers, and it was by no means clear that the Republic could survive without them, or at least without the freedom of the press on which they were established, the floor on which civil society stands. Nevertheless, neither that history nor that freedom—nor any manner of editorial judgment whatsoever—informed decisions made by the disruptive innovators who declared the newspaper dead.

The deregulation of the communications industry had allowed for massive mergers: General Electric bought RCA and NBC; Time merged with Warner, and then with AOL. Newspapers housed within this giant corporation became less accountable to their readers than to stockholders. (The *New York Times*, the *Washington Post*, and National Public Radio were among a handful of exceptions.) Fast-growing dot-coms had been a chief source of newspaper advertising revenue; during the dot-com bust, those companies either slashed their advertising budgets or eliminated them; they also turned to advertising online instead. Readers found that they could get their news without paying for it, from news aggregators that took reported stories from the newspapers and reprinted them. Papers began laying off a generation of experienced editors and reporters, then whole bureaus, and then the papers began closing their doors.[57]

"The Internet is the most democratizing innovation we've ever seen," Democratic presidential candidate Howard Dean's campaign manager said in 2004, "more so even than the printing press." At the time, many journalists agreed. Tom Brokaw talked about the "democratization of news," and conservative journalists, in particular, celebrated the shattering of the "power of elites" to determine what is news and what is not.[58] Compared to newspapers and broadcast television news, the information available on the Internet was breathtakingly vast and thrilling; it was also uneven, unreliable, and, except in certain cases, unrestrained by standards of reporting, editing, and fact-checking. The Internet didn't leave seekers of news "free." It left them brutally constrained. It accelerated the transmission of information, but the selection of that information—the engine that searched for it—was controlled by the biggest unregulated monopoly in the history of American business. Google went public in 2004. By 2016, it controlled nearly 90 percent of the market.[59]

The Internet transformed the public sphere, blurring the line between what political scientists had for decades called the "political elite" and the "mass public," but it did not democratize politics. Instead, the Internet hastened political changes that were already under way. A model of citizenship that involved debate and deliberation had long since yielded to a model of citizenship that involved consumption and persuasion. With the Internet, that model yielded to a model of citizenship driven by the hyperindividualism of blogging, posting, and tweeting, artifacts of a new culture of narcissism, and by the hyperaggregation of the analysis of data, tools of a new authoritarianism. Data collected online allowed websites and search engines and eventually social media companies to profile "users" and—acting as companies selling products rather than as news organizations concerned with the public interest—to feed them only the news and views with which they agreed, and then to radicalize them. Public opinion polling by telephone was replaced by the collection and analysis of data. Social media, beginning with Facebook, moving fast and breaking things, exacerbated the political isolation of ordinary Americans while strengthening polarization on both the left and the right, automating identity politics, and contributing, at the same time, to a distant, vague, and impotent model of political engagement.[60] In a wireless world, the mystic chords of memory, the ties to timeless truths that held the nation together, faded to ethereal invisibility.

**"OUR WAR ON TERROR** begins with al Qaeda, but it does not end there," Bush said when he addressed Congress and a shaken nation on September 20, 2001. "It will not end until every terrorist group of global reach has been found, stopped, and defeated." Bush pledged to destroy not only the perpetrators of the attacks on 9/11 but terrorism itself. This was not merely the saber rattling of a moment. By 2006, the stated objective of the National Security Strategy of the United States was to "end tyranny." Like a war on poverty, a war on crime, and a war on drugs, a war on terror could imagine no end.[61]

Terrorism respected no borders and recognized no laws. Fighting it risked doing the same. In 1980, twenty-three-year-old Osama bin Laden had joined a resistance movement against the Soviet occupation of Afghanistan, supplying funds and building a network of supporters. In 1988, when the mujahideen triumphed and the Soviet Union agreed to withdraw from Afghanistan, bin Laden formed al Qaeda as a base for future jihads, or holy wars. Bin Laden was not a cleric and did not in any way speak for the religion of Islam. But he did describe his movement in religious terms, as a form of political incitement. At a time of economic decline, political unrest, and violent sectarianism throughout the Arab world, he called for a jihad against Americans, whom he described as a godless, materialist people. Bin Laden argued that Americans had defiled the Islamic world and undermined the Muslim faith by causing wars between Muslims in Europe, Asia, Africa, and the Middle East. "It is saddening to tell you that you are the worst civilization witnessed by the history of mankind," he wrote in a letter to America. In 1990, he urged the Saudi monarchy to support a jihad to retake Kuwait after the Americans ousted Saddam Hussein; instead, the Saudis welcomed U.S. forces into Saudi Arabia. Bin Laden denounced the American "occupation" and recruited and trained forces for terrorist acts that included suicide bombings. The CIA formed a special unit to work against al Qaeda and bin Laden in 1996, by which time bin Laden had declared war on the United States and found refuge with the Taliban, radical Islamic fundamentalists who had taken over Afghanistan and remade it as a religious state. In 1998, bin Laden called for a fatwa against all Americans, describing the murder of Americans as the "individual duty for every Muslim who can do it in any country," in the name of a "World Islamic Front."[62]

After 9/11, the Bush administration demanded that the Taliban hand over bin Laden. The Taliban refused. On October 7, 2001, the United States began a war in Afghanistan. The immediate end of the war, aided by coalition partners, was to defeat al Qaeda; its more distant aim was to replace the Taliban with a democratically elected, pro-Western government.[63] It became the longest war in American history.

The Bush administration conceived of the war on terror as an opportunity to strike against hostile regimes all over the world, on the grounds that they harbored and funded terrorists. Between 1998 and 2011, military spending nearly doubled, reaching more than $700 billion a year— more, in adjusted dollars, than at any time since the Allies were fighting the Axis. In his 2002 State of the Union address, Bush described Iraq, Iran, and North Korea as another axis. "States like these, and their terrorist allies, constitute an axis of evil, arming to threaten the peace of the world," he said. "By seeking weapons of mass destruction, these regimes

pose a grave and growing danger. They could provide these arms to terrorists, giving them the means to match their hatred." For all his fierce rhetoric, Bush took great pains and care not to denounce Islam itself, steering
clear of inciting still more hatred. "All Americans must recognize that the
face of terror is not the true face of Islam," he said later that year. "Islam is
a faith that brings comfort to a billion people around the world. It's a faith
that has made brothers and sisters of every race. It's a faith based upon
love, not hate."[64]

The Bush administration soon opened a second front in the war on
terror. In 2003, another U.S.-led coalition invaded Iraq, with the aim of
eradicating both Saddam Hussein and his weapons of mass destruction.
The architects of this war were neoconservatives who regretted what
they saw as George H. W. Bush's premature withdrawal from the Middle
East, his failing to occupy Iraq and topple Hussein after pushing him out
of Kuwait. With few exceptions, Democrats and Republicans alike supported the wars in Afghanistan and Iraq, but support for the Iraq war was,
from the start, more limited, and dwindled further after it became clear
that Hussein in fact had no weapons of mass destruction. "In 2003, the
United States invaded a country that did not threaten us, did not attack
us, and did not want war with us, to disarm it of weapons we have since
discovered it did not have," wrote Pat Buchanan, placing the blame for the
war on the neocons' hijacking of the conservative movement, whose influence he greatly regretted. He complained, "Neoconservatives captured
the foundations, think tanks, and opinion journals of the Right and were
allowed to redefine conservatism."[65]

The war on terror differed from every earlier American war. It was
led, from Washington, by men and women who had never served in
the military, and it was fought, in the Middle East, by an all-volunteer
force whose sacrifices American civilians did not share or know or even,
finally, consider. In both Afghanistan and Iraq, the United States' regime-
building efforts failed. Vietnam had been a bad war, and a distant war,
and its sacrifices had been unevenly borne, but they had been shared—
and protested. Far distant from the United States, in parts of the world
that few Americans had ever visited, the wars in Afghanistan and Iraq
were fought by a tiny slice of the American population; between 2001 and
2011, less than one-half of 1 percent of Americans saw active duty. Hardly
any members of Congress had ever seen combat, or had family members

*The Iraq War mired U.S. soldiers in
counterinsurgency campaigns.*

who had. "God help this country when someone sits in this chair who
doesn't know the military as well as I do," Eisenhower once said. George
H. W. Bush was the last president of the United States to have served in
the U.S. military, to fear and loathe war because of knowing war.[66] His
successors lacked that knowledge. During the Vietnam War, George W.
Bush had avoided combat by serving in the Texas Air National Guard. Bill
Clinton and Donald Trump had dodged the draft. Obama came of age
after that war was over. None of these men had sons or daughters who
served in the military.[67]

The war on terror had its dissenters: among them were those who
fought it. A 2011 Pew study reported that half of veterans of Afghanistan
and Iraq thought the war in Afghanistan wasn't worth fighting, nearly 60
percent thought the war in Iraq wasn't worth it, and a third thought neither war was worth what it cost.[68] One of the war on terror's severest critics was Andrew J. Bacevich, a West Point graduate and career army officer
who, after fighting in Vietnam in 1970 and 1971, had risen to the rank of
colonel and become a history professor. Bacevich's only son was killed
in Iraq. A Catholic and a conservative, Bacevich argued that while few
Americans served in the military, Americans and the American government had "fallen prey to militarism, manifesting itself in a romanticized

view of soldiers, a tendency to see military power as the truest measure of national greatness, and outsized expectations regarding the efficacy of force." Somehow, Bacevich wrote, Americans accepted that it was the fate of the United States to engage in permanent war, without dissent: "The citizens of the United States have essentially forfeited any capacity to ask first-order questions about the fundamentals of national security policy."[69]

By no means had the wars in Afghanistan and Iraq gone unquestioned, but one reason there had been relatively little debate had to do not only with a widening gap between the civilian and the military populations but also with the consequences of disruptive innovation. In many parts of the country, the daily paper, with its side-by-side op-ed essays, had vanished. Voters had been sorted into parties, the parties had been sorted, ideologically, and a new political establishment, the conservative media, having labeled and derided the "mainstream media" as biased, abdicated dispassionate debate. Rigorous studies of newspapers had not, up to that point, been able to discern a partisan bias. Nevertheless, the conservative establishment insisted that such bias existed, warned their audiences away from nonconservative media outlets, and insulated their audience from the possibility of persuasion by nonconservative outlets by insisting that anything except the conservative media was the "liberal media."[70] This critique applied not only to the news but to all manner of knowledge. "Science has been corrupted," Rush Limbaugh said on the radio in 2009. "We know the media has been corrupted for a long time. Academia has been corrupted. None of what they do is real. It's all lies!"[71]

Limbaugh, who came of age during the Vietnam War but did not serve in the military (apparently due to a cyst), strenuously supported the war on terror.[72] Roger Ailes, who, like Limbaugh, had neither seen combat in Vietnam nor served in the military (Ailes suffered from hemophilia), strongly supported U.S. military action in both Afghanistan and Iraq. And his network, Fox News, did more than report the wars; it promoted them. After 9/11, when Fox News anchors and reporters began wearing flag pins, some journalists, including CBS's Morley Safer, condemned the practice. Ailes brushed him off: "I'm a little bit squishy on killing babies, but when it comes to flag pins I'm pro-choice." When the United States invaded Iraq, Fox News adopted an on-air chyron: "The War on Terror." John Moody, Fox's vice president for news, circulated morning memos with directives for the day's coverage. On June 3, 2003, he wrote, "The

president is doing something that few of his predecessors dared undertake: putting the US case for Mideast peace to an Arab summit. It's a dis-
tinctly skeptical crowd that Bush faces. His political courage and tactical
cunning are worth noting in our reporting through the day." On March 23,
2004, following early reports that the 9/11 commission was investigating
the degree of negligence involved in the Bush administration leading up
to the attacks, Moody wrote: "Do not turn this into Watergate. Remember
the fleeting sense of national unity that emerged from this tragedy. Let's
not desecrate that." Moody's editorial directives included prohibitions on
certain words. On April 28, 2004, he wrote: "Let's refer to the US marines
we see in the foreground as 'sharpshooters,' not snipers, which carries a
negative connotation." Walter Cronkite said of the memos, after they were
leaked: "I've never heard of any other network nor any other legitimate
news organization doing that, newspaper or broadcast."[73]

The conservative media establishment broadcast from a bunker, garri-
soned against dissenters. Those who listened to Rush Limbaugh, and who
only years before had also gotten news from their local newspapers and
from network television, were now far more likely to watch only Fox News
and, if they read a newspaper, to read only the *Wall Street Journal*, which,
like Fox, was owned, as of 2007, by Rupert Murdoch. The conservative
websites to which search engines directed listeners of Limbaugh, watch-
ers of Fox News, and readers of the *Wall Street Journal* only reinforced
this view. "It's a great way to have your cake and eat it too," wrote Matt
Labash in the *Weekly Standard* in 2003. "Criticize other people for not
being objective. Be as subjective as you want. It's a great little racket. I'm
glad we found it actually."[74]

Other administrations, of course, had lied, as the Pentagon Papers had
abundantly demonstrated. But in pursuing regime change in the Middle East, the Bush administration dismissed the advice of experts and
took the radically postmodern view that all knowledge is relative, a matter of dueling political claims rather than of objective truth. That view
had characterized not only its decision to go to war in Iraq but also the
campaign's argument against the recount in 2000, and Bush's withdrawal
from the Kyoto Protocol, a climate change agreement, in 2001.[75] In 2002,
a senior Bush adviser told a reporter for the *New York Times* that journalists "believe that solutions emerge from your judicious study of discernible reality" but that "that's not the way the world works anymore.

We're an empire now, and when we act, we create our own reality."[76] The culture and structure of the Internet made it possible for citizens to live in their own realities, too.

Jaundiced journalists began to found online political fact-checking sites like PolitFact, which rated the statements of politicians on a Truth-O-Meter. "I'm no fan of dictionaries or reference books: they're elitist," the satirist Stephen Colbert said in 2005, when he coined "truthiness" while lampooning George W. Bush. "I don't trust books. They're all fact, no heart. And that's exactly what's pulling our country apart today."[77] But eventually liberals would respond to the conservative media by imitating them—two squirrels, chasing each other down a tree.

WHAT DID HE *know and when did he know it?* had been the pressing question of the Watergate investigation. *What does anyone know anymore, and what is knowledge, anyway?* became the question of the Bush era.

The United States' position as the leader of a liberal world order based on the rule of law entered a period of crisis when, pursuing its war on terror, the country defied its founding principles and flouted the Geneva Conventions, international law, and human rights through the torture of suspected terrorists and their imprisonment without trial.

On October 26, 2001, Bush signed the Patriot Act, granting the federal government new powers to conduct surveillance and collect intelligence to prevent and investigate terrorist acts. It passed both houses less than two months after the 9/11 attacks, in a frenzied climate in which legislators who dared to break ranks were labeled unpatriotic. Outside the Capitol, the ACLU and the Electronic Frontier Foundation were among the many vocal opponents of the act, citing violations of civil liberties, especially as established under the Fourth Amendment, and of civil rights, especially the due process provision of the Fourteenth Amendment. John Ashcroft, Bush's attorney general, defended the Patriot Act, citing the war on drugs as a precedent for the war on terror. "Most Americans expect that law enforcement tools used for decades to fight organized crime and drugs be available to protect lives and liberties from terrorists," Ashcroft said.[78]

In November 2001, Bush signed a military order concerning the "Detention, Treatment, and Trial of Certain Non-Citizens in the War Against Terrorism." Suspected terrorists who were not citizens of the

United States were to be "detained at an appropriate location designated by the Secretary of Defense." If brought to trial, they were to be tried and sentenced by military commissions. The ordinary rules of military law would not apply. Nor would the laws of war, nor the laws of the United States.[79]

The conduct of war will always challenge a nation founded on a commitment to justice. It will call back the nation's history, its earlier struggles, its triumphs and failures. There were shades, during the war on terror, of the Alien and Sedition Acts passed in 1798 during the Quasi-War with France, of the Espionage Act of the First World War, and of FDR's Japanese internment order during the Second World War. But with Bush's November 2001 military order, the war on terror became, itself, like another airplane, attacking the edifice of American law, down to its very footings, the ancient, medieval foundations of trial by jury and the battle for truth.

"You've got to be kidding me," Ashcroft said when he read a draft of the order. He'd expected the prosecution of people involved in planning the attacks on 9/11 to be handled criminally, by his department—as had been done successfully with earlier terrorism cases, with due process. National security adviser Condoleezza Rice and Secretary of State Colin Powell only learned that Bush had signed the order when they saw it on television. In the final draft, the Department of Justice was left out of the prosecutions altogether: suspected terrorists were to be imprisoned without charge, denied knowledge of the evidence against them, and, if tried, sentenced by courts following no established rules. The order deemed "the principles of law and the rules of evidence generally recognized in the trial of criminal cases in the United States district courts" to be impractical. The means by which truth was to be established and justice secured, traditions established and refined over centuries, were deemed inconvenient. "Now, some people say, 'Well, gee, that's a dramatic departure from traditional jurisprudence in the United States,'" Vice President Cheney said, but "we think it guarantees that we'll have the kind of treatment of these individuals that we believe they deserve."[80]

The Bush administration's course of action with the wars in Afghanistan and Iraq and with the military tribunals and with the Patriot Act rested on an expansive theory of presidential power. The party in control of the White House tends to like presidential power, only to change its mind when it loses the White House. From Woodrow Wilson through FDR and Lyndon Johnson, Democrats had liked presidential power, and had tried to extend it, while Republicans had tried to limit it. Beginning with the presidency of Richard Nixon, Democrats and Republicans switched places, Republicans extending presidential power with Nixon and Reagan. But the conservative effort to expand the powers of the presidency reached a height in the George W. Bush administration, in powers seized while the nation reeled from an unprecedented attack.[81]

Beginning in the fall of 2001, the U.S. military dropped flyers over Afghanistan offering bounties of between $5,000 and $25,000 for the names of men with ties to al Qaeda and the Taliban. "This is enough money to take care of your family, your village, your tribe, for the rest of your life," one flyer read. (The average annual income in Afghanistan at the time was less than $300.) The flyers fell, Secretary of Defense Donald Rumsfeld said, "like snowflakes in December in Chicago." (Unlike many in Bush's inner circle, Rumsfeld was a veteran; he served as a navy pilot in the 1950s.)[82] As hundreds of men were rounded up abroad, the Bush administration considered where to put them. Taking over the federal penitentiary at Leavenworth, Kansas, and reopening Alcatraz, closed since 1963, were both considered but rejected because, from Kansas or California, suspected terrorists would be able to appeal to American courts and under U.S. state and federal law. Diego Garcia, an island in the Indian Ocean, was rejected because it happened to be a British territory, and therefore subject to British law. In the end, the administration chose Guantánamo, a U.S. naval base on the southeastern end of Cuba. No part of either the United States or of Cuba, Guantánamo was one of the known world's last no-man's-lands. Bush administration lawyer John Yoo called it the "legal equivalent of outer space."[83]

On January 9, 2002, Yoo and a colleague submitted to the Department of Defense the first of what came to be called the torture memos, in which they concluded that international treaties, including the Geneva Conventions, "do not apply to the Taliban militia" because, although Afghanistan had been part of the Geneva Conventions since 1956, it was a "failed state." International treaties, the memo maintained, "do not protect members of the al Qaeda organization, which as a non-State actor cannot be a party to the international agreements governing war." Two days later, the first twenty prisoners, shackled, hooded, and blindfolded, arrived at Guantánamo. More camps were soon built to house more prisoners, eventually 779, from 48 countries. They weren't called criminals, because criminals have to be charged with a crime; they weren't called prisoners, because prisoners of war have rights. They were "unlawful combatants" who were being "detained" in what White House counsel Alberto Gonzales called "a new kind of war," although it was as ancient as torture itself.[84]

The White House answered terrorism, an abandonment of the law of war, with torture, an abandonment of the rule of law. Aside from the weight of history, centuries of political philosophy and of international law, and, not least, its futility as a means for obtaining evidence, another obstacle to torture remained: the Convention against Torture and other Cruel, Inhuman or Degrading Treatment or Punishment, a treaty the United States had signed in 1988. This objection was addressed in a fifty-page August 2002 memo to Gonzales that attempted to codify a distinction between acts that are "cruel, inhuman, or degrading" and acts that constitute torture. "Severe pain," for instance, was defined as pain that caused "death, organ failure, or permanent damage resulting in the loss of significant bodily functions." ("If the detainee dies, you're doing it wrong," the chief counsel for the CIA's counterterrorism center advised, according to meeting minutes later released by the Senate Armed Services Committee.) Methods described in the torture memos included stripping, shackling, exposure to extremes of temperature and light, sexual humiliation, threats to family members, near-drowning, and the use of dogs. Many of these forms of torment, including sleep deprivation and semi-starvation, came from a 1957 U.S. Air Force study called "Communist Attempts to Elicit False Confessions From Air Force Prisoners of War," an investigation of methods used by the Chinese Communists who tortured American prisoners during the Korean War. Top security advisers, including Colin Powell, objected to what the White House called "enhanced interrogation techniques." Others, including Ashcroft, urged discretion. "Why are we talking about this in the White House?" he is said to have asked at one meeting, warning, "History will not judge this kindly." But the position of the secretary of defense prevailed. On a list of interrogation techniques approved for the use of U.S. military, Rumsfeld wrote: "I stand for 8–10 hours a day. Why is standing limited to 4 hours? D.R."[85]

Torture wasn't confined to Guantánamo. In Iraq, American forces inflicted torture at Abu Ghraib, and in Afghanistan, in a CIA prison in Kabul and at Bagram Air Base, where, in 2002, two men died while chained to the ceiling of their cells. Within the legal academy and among civil liberties organizations, opposition both to provisions of the Patriot Act and to the treatment of suspected terrorists had been ongoing. During Barack Obama's 2003 Senate bid, he called the Patriot Act "a good example of fundamental principles being violated," and objected to the lack of due process in the arrest and trials of suspected terrorists. Glimpses of what was happening only reached the American public in 2004, after *The New Yorker* and *60 Minutes* reported on abuses at Abu Ghraib and the ACLU published the torture memos. In June 2006, in *Hamdan v. Rumsfeld*, the Supreme Court ruled that, without congressional authorization, the president lacked the power to establish the military commissions. Six months later, Congress authorized the commissions, but in 2008, the court found this act unconstitutional as well.[86] Still, something crucial about the fundamental institutions on which the nation had been founded had been very badly shaken.

The Supreme Court's ruling had neither righted the Republic nor healed its divisions. During Bush's two terms in office, income inequality widened and polarization worsened, as they had during the Clinton years and the Reagan years, and as they would under Obama and Trump. A Bush-era tax cut granted 45 percent of its savings to the top 1 percent of income earners, and 13 percent to the poorest 60 percent. In 2004 and again in 2008, the percentage of voters who did things like post campaign yard signs in front of their houses or paste bumper stickers onto their cars was higher than it had been at any time since people had been counting those things, in 1952. Members of Congress no longer regretted hyperpartisanship but instead celebrated it, outgoing Republican House majority leader Tom DeLay insisting in his 2006 farewell address that "the common lament over the recent rise in political partisanship is often nothing more than a veiled complaint instead about the recent rise of political conservatism."[87]

DeLay had been indicted for money laundering and had also been tied to all manner of other political grubbiness in connection with the Russian government and with lobbyists. Political insiders like DeLay had a financial stake in heightened partisanship: the more partisan the country, the more money they could raise for reelection, and the more money they could make after they left office. Before the 1990s, "change elections," when a new party took over Congress or the White House or both, meant that politicians who were thrown out of office left town, along with their staff. That stopped happening. Instead, politicians stayed in Washington and became pundits, or political consultants, or management consultants, or, most likely, lobbyists, or—for those with the least scruples—all of the above. They made gargantuan sums of money, through speaking fees, or selling their memoirs, or hawking their connections, or appearing on television: the cable stations, compelled to fill twenty-four hours of airtime, needed talking heads at all hours of every day, the angrier and more adversarial the talk, the higher the ratings. "Insiders have always been here," the New York Times's Mark Leibovich observed in 2013. "But they are more of swarm now: bigger, shinier, online, and working it all that much harder."[88]

Bush's presidency ended with a global economic collapse, the explosion of a time bomb that had begun ticking during the Reagan administration. Clinton's administration had not managed to defuse that bomb; instead, it had contributed to the deregulation of the financial services industry by repealing parts of the New Deal's Glass-Steagall Act. Like all financial collapses in the long course of American history, starting with the Panic of 1792, it seemed to come suddenly, but, looking back, it appeared inevitable.

Wall Street totters from the top. Most of the suffering happens at the bottom. The first to fall were financial services giants Bear Stearns, Lehman Brothers, and Merrill Lynch, which had been wildly leveraged in high-risk subprime mortgages. The Dow Jones Industrial Average, 14,164 in October 2007, had fallen to 8,776 by the end of 2008. Unemployment rose by nearly 5 percentage points. Home values fell by 20 percent. In the last years of Bush's administration, nearly 900,000 properties were repossessed. Millions of Americans lost their homes.[89]

In yards once festooned with campaign placards, Bush/Cheney '04 or "Kerry/Edwards: A Stronger America," Foreclosure and For Sale signs waved in front of doors boarded with plywood. Here and there the tails of yellow ribbons fluttered from trees, in remembrance of soldiers. Here and there were staked flags, and signs painted red, white, and blue: Bring Our Troops Home. And still, in the faraway and troubled lands of Afghanistan and Iraq, the wars dragged on, seen occasionally on Americans' flickering, hand-held screens in fleeting footage of ruin and rubble.

# II.

BARACK OBAMA HAD a narrow face and big ears and copper-colored skin, and sometimes he spoke like a preacher and sometimes he spoke like a professor, but he always spoke with a studied equanimity and a determined forbearance. "We, the people, have remained faithful to the ideals of our forebears, and true to our founding documents," he said in his inaugural address in 2009, speaking to the largest crowd ever recorded in the nation's capital, more than one-and-a-half-million people, on a terribly cold Tuesday in January. The day of hope and change was a day of hats and mittens.

His voice rose and fell with the cadences of Martin Luther King Jr. and held fast with the resolve of Franklin Delano Roosevelt. People had driven for hours, for tens of hours, to see him sworn in. "I just feel like if you had the opportunity to be there for the Gettysburg Address or when Hank Aaron hit his historic home run, would you take it?" Dennis Madsen, a thirty-nine-year-old urban planner from Atlanta, told CNN. Eight-year-old Bethany Dockery, from Memphis, wore a pink hat and coat, and jumped up and down when Obama took the oath of office. "It makes us feel good," her mother said, crying, "because we have a chance."[90]

The time had come, Obama said, "to choose our better history."[91] For Obama, that better history meant the long struggle against adversity and inequality, the work that generations of Americans had done for prosperity and justice. His inauguration marked a turn in American history, but just around that bend lay a hairpin.

He'd wanted to be a writer. He'd written his first book, *Dreams from My Father: A Story of Race and Inheritance*, when he was thirty-three, long before running for office. "His life is an open book," his wife, Michelle, later said. "He wrote it and you can read it." He'd been reckoning with race and inheritance since he was a little boy. "To some extent," he once told a reporter, "I'm a symbolic stand-in for a lot of the changes that have been made."[92] But he'd also made himself that stand-in, by writing about it.

Obama's mother's father, Stanley Dunham, born in Wichita, Kansas, in 1918, was named after the explorer Henry Morton Stanley, whose books included *In Darkest Africa*, which was published right around the time

*Barack Obama's inauguration in 2009 drew the largest
crowd ever assembled on the Mall.*

that Obama's father's father, Hussein Obama, was born in Kanyadhiang, Kenya. During the Second World War, Hussein Obama worked as a cook for the British Army in Burma, and Stanley Dunham enlisted in the U.S. Army and went to Europe while, in Wichita, his wife, Madelyn, helped build B-29s for Boeing. Obama's father, Barack Hussein Obama, was born in 1936; his mother, Stanley Ann Dunham, in 1942. On September 26, 1960, the day Richard M. Nixon first debated John F. Kennedy, seventeen-year-old Stanley Ann Dunham met twenty-three-year-old Barack Hussein Obama in an elementary Russian class at the University of Hawaii. By Election Day, she was pregnant. They married on February 2, 1961, two weeks after Kennedy's inauguration, in the Wailuku County courthouse. In twenty-one states, that marriage would have been illegal, as a violation of miscegenation laws that were not overturned by the Supreme Court until 1967, in *Loving v. Virginia*. Neither family approved of the marriage. As recorded on his birth certificate, Barack Hussein Obama II was born at the Kapi'olani Maternity and Gynecological Hospital, in Honolulu, on August 4, 1961, at 7:24 p.m.[93]

As a boy, living with his grandparents in Hawaii—his parents had divorced—young Barack Obama became a reader. He soaked up James Baldwin and W. E. B. Du Bois. "At night I would close the door to my room," he later wrote, and "there I would sit and wrestle with words, locked in suddenly desperate argument, trying to reconcile the world as I'd found it with the terms of my birth." After graduating from Columbia, he worked as a community organizer on the South Side of Chicago, planting roots in a city that had just elected its first black mayor. He joined a black Baptist church and began dating an ambitious young lawyer named Michelle Robinson, descended from men and women who had been held in slavery. At Harvard Law School, he worked as a research assistant for Laurence Tribe, who'd been looking for common ground between what appeared to be incommensurable arguments; this would become Obama's signature move, too: reconciling seemingly irreconcilable differences.[94]

Not since Woodrow Wilson had Americans elected a scholar as president. At the University of Chicago Law School, Obama taught a seminar on race and law that amounted to a history of the United States itself, from Andrew Jackson and Indian removal through Reconstruction and Jim Crow, from civil rights to Ronald Reagan and affirmative action. Later, during the campaign, when the course syllabus was posted online, constitutional scholars from both the right and the left applauded its evenhandedness. Obama, as a professor, cultivated the values of engaged, open-minded debate: students were to be graded for their ability "to draw out the full spectrum of views," for their display of "a thorough examination of the diversity of opinion" and for evidence of having broken "some sweat trying to figure out the problem in all its wonderful complexity."[95] By no means was it clear that what worked in a law school seminar room would work in Washington.

In 1996, the professor sought a seat in the state senate and offered this bridge across the American divide: the Right had "hijacked the higher moral ground with this language of family values and moral responsibility," and the Left had ceded that ground and needed to gain it back, because a language of moral responsibility was what the whole nation needed, together. "We have to take this same language—these same values that are encouraged within our families—of looking out for one another, of sharing, of sacrificing for each other—and apply them to a larger society," he said.[96]

Obama brought together the language of the nation's founding with the language of its religious traditions. Elected to the U.S. Senate, where he became its only black member, he was tapped to deliver the keynote address at the 2004 Democratic National Convention. He wrote a speech that drew as much on the Bible—"I am my brother's keeper"—as on the Declaration of Independence: "We hold these truths to be self-evident"; and he recited both as prayers. (Like William Jennings Bryan before him, Obama had worked with a Shakespearean speech coach.) Part preacher, part courtroom lawyer, he electrified the crowd. "There are those who are preparing to divide us, the spin masters and negative ad peddlers who embrace the politics of anything goes," he said. "Well, I say to them tonight, there is not a liberal America and a conservative America; there is a United States of America." [97]

Obama-mania began that night. He was young and handsome and glamorous; his rhetoric soared. Reporters, especially, swooned. Before he'd even taken his seat in the Senate, Obama was asked if he intended to run for president, a question he waved away. He did not enjoy his time in the Senate. If, after the end of his term, he stayed in Washington, he told a friend, "Shoot me." [98] He found bloody-minded partisanship maddening. Liberals were fools if they thought they could defeat conservatives by treating them like enemies. The American people, he insisted, "don't think George Bush is mean-spirited or prejudiced." Instead, he went on, "they are angry that the case to invade Iraq was exaggerated, are worried that we have unnecessarily alienated existing and potential allies around the world, and are ashamed by events like those at Abu Ghraib, which violate our ideals as a country." [99]

Obama ran for the Democratic nomination in 2008 with a slogan adapted from the 1972 United Farm Workers campaign of Cesar Chavez and Dolores Huerta, "Sí, se puede": Yes we can. His resume for the job was thin. He ran on his talent, his character, and his story. Some people said he was too black, some people said he wasn't black enough. In a heated and very close primary race against sixty-year-old Hillary Clinton, he benefited from having opposed the Iraq War, which Clinton, then in the Senate, had voted to authorize. And while Clinton began with deep support from African American voters and leaders, that support was squandered by her husband. Threatened by Obama's poise and charm—a cooler, blacker, and more upright version of himself—Bill Clinton alienated black voters by accusing Obama and his supporters of deviousness: "I think they played the race card on me," the former president complained. [100]

In an age of extremes, Obama projected reasonableness and equanimity in politics and candor about religion. His faith, he said, "admits doubt, and uncertainty, and mystery." His belief in the United States—"a faith in simple dreams, an insistence on small miracles"—admitted no doubt.[101] In a time of war and of economic decline, he projected the optimism of Reagan and held the political commitments, it appeared, of FDR.

Obama's candidacy stirred an apathetic electorate. It also changed the nature of campaigning. Turnout in 2008 was the highest since 1968. Against the much-admired long-term Republican senator from Arizona, John McCain, who had been a prisoner of war in Vietnam, Obama won by more than nine million votes. He also defeated McCain on social media. McCain, seventy-two, a man of his generation, hadn't yet grasped the power of new forms of political communication. Obama's campaign had four times as many followers as McCain on Facebook, the social media juggernaut, and an astounding twenty-three times as many on Twitter. His digital team registered voters at a website called Vote for Change. His supporters, who texted "HOPE" to join his list, received three texts on Election Day alone. When he won, more than a million Americans received a text that read "All of this happened because of you. Thanks, Barack."[102]

Obama had promised hope and change. He seemed, at first, poised to deliver both. He swept into office with majorities in both the House and the Senate and the wind of history at his back. It proved a fickle wind.

To address the global financial collapse that had torqued the markets during Bush's last months in office, he asked Congress to approve a stimulus program of $800 billion that reporters dubbed the New New Deal. The *Economist* announced "Roosevelt-mania." But Obama was no FDR. His administration did not prosecute the people whose wrongdoing had led to the financial disaster. His economic program rescued the banks, but it didn't rescue people who'd lost their savings. During Obama's first year in office, while ordinary Americans lost their jobs, their houses, and their retirement money, executives at Wall Street's thirty-eight largest companies earned $140 billion and the nation's top twenty-five hedge fund managers earned an average of $464 million.[103]

Obama's biggest initiative was the Affordable Health Care Act, which passed the Senate at the end of 2009 and the House at the beginning of 2010 in a razor-thin, party-line vote, 219 to 212. It had been a century since American Progressives first proposed national health care. Hillary

Clinton's own proposal had failed, badly, in 1994. (Obama, inspired by a biography of Lincoln, who put his political rivals in his cabinet, had named Clinton his secretary of state.) But the win was diminished by the fury of the campaign to repeal it, a campaign begun even before the legislation passed.

The day before Obama's inauguration, Fox News launched a new program hosted by a radio talk show celebrity named Glenn Beck. Beck compared Obama to Mussolini. He turned his television studio into an old-fashioned one-room schoolhouse, with chalk and a blackboard, and oak desks, and lectured his viewers about American history, and how everything Obama stood for was a betrayal of the founding fathers. If Beck's campaign was different from Alex Jones and the truthers, it drew on the same animus and exploited the same history of racial hatred. In March, Beck launched a movement called 9/12, whose purpose was to restore the unity Americans had supposedly felt the day after the attacks on the Twin Towers. Opponents of Obama's economic plan and of health care reform called for a new Tea Party, to resist the tyranny of the federal government. In the spring of 2009, Tea Partiers across the country held rallies on town commons and city streets, waving copies of the Constitution. They dressed up as George Washington, Thomas Jefferson, and Benjamin Franklin, in tricornered hats and powdered wigs, knee breeches and buttoned waistcoats. They believed American history was on their side. They wanted, in words that would later become Donald Trump's slogan, to make America great again.

With the Tea Party, the conservative media and the conservative movement merged: the Tea Party was, in some ways, a political product manufactured by Fox News. Former Alaska governor Sarah Palin, who'd gained a place in the national spotlight when McCain named her as his running mate in 2008, signed a one-million-dollar-per-year contract with Fox, and then began speaking at Tea Party rallies. Glenn Beck began holding Founders' Fridays. Fox News host Sean Hannity began invoking the Liberty Tree.[104]

But the Tea Party was much more than a product of Fox News; it was also an earnest, grassroots movement. Some Tea Partiers cherished the NRA's interpretation of the Second Amendment, or cared deeply about prayer in schools, or were opposed to same-sex marriage. Some held grievances against globalization, about immigration and trade deals, echoes of

*Tax Day protests held on April 15, 2009, marked the
birth of the Tea Party movement, which countered
Obama's call for change with a call for a return
to the principles of the founding fathers.*

fears from the isolationist and nativist 1920s. Most had plenty of long-standing populist grievances, about taxes, in particular, and their objections to a federally run health care program, like the plans for such a program, dated back more than a century.

In the twenty-first century, the Tea Party married nineteenth-century populism to twentieth-century originalism. As populists, they blamed a conspiracy of federal government policymakers and Wall Street fat cats for their suffering. As originalists, they sought a remedy for what ailed them in a return to the original meaning of the Constitution.

Not irrelevantly, the movement was overwhelmingly white and it imagined a history that was overwhelmingly white, too. This is not to say that Tea Partiers were racists—though many liberals did say this, often without the least foundation—but, instead, that the story of American history had been impoverished by not being told either fully or well. Whole parts, too, had been rejected. "The American soil is full of corpses of my ancestors, through 400 years and at least three wars," James Baldwin had written in 1965. Wrote Baldwin, "What one begs American people to do, for all sakes, is simply to accept our history."[105] That acceptance had not come.

If most Tea Partiers were mainly worried about their taxes, a few really did object to the changing nature of the Republic, on the ground that it was becoming less white. They objected to the very idea of a black president. It was as if they had resurrected Roger Taney's argument from *Dred Scott* in 1857, when he ruled that no person of African descent could ever become an American citizen. "Impeach Obama," their signs read. "He's unconstitutional."[106]

IN DECEMBER 2010, sixty-nine-year-old Vermont senator Bernie Sanders delivered an eight-and-a-half-hour speech on the floor of the Senate—without eating or drinking, or sitting down, or taking a bathroom break. He had no audience but the cameras. Sanders wasn't speaking to his fellow senators; he was trying to reach the public directly, through social media. "My speech was the most Twittered event in the world on that day," Sanders said later.

Sanders, born in Brooklyn in 1941, had been a civil rights and anti-war activist at the University of Chicago, leading sit-ins against segregated housing on campus and working for SNCC. After Chicago, he moved to Vermont, where he ran for mayor of Burlington. He took office the same year Reagan was inaugurated. Ten years later, he went to Washington as Vermont's only member of Congress. There were perks to being the only socialist in Congress, he told the *New York Times*. "I can't get punished," he said. "What are they going to do? Kick me out of the party?"[107] Sanders's career in the Senate began in 2007—Obama had campaigned for him in 2006—and had been undistinguished. But during the recession, he emerged as one of the few prominent people in Washington, a city flooded with money, willing to speak about poverty.

The numbers were staggering. In 1928, the top 1 percent of American families earned 24 percent of all income; in 1944, they earned 11 percent, a rate that remained flat for several decades but began to rise in the 1970s. By 2011, the top 1 percent of American families was once again earning 24 percent of the nation's income. In 2013, the U.S. Census Bureau reported a Gini index of .476, the highest ever recorded in any affluent democracy. Nations with income inequality similar to that in the United States at the time included Uganda, at .447, and China, at .474.[108]

Sanders was a socialist; his hero was Eugene Debs. He'd once made a recording of Debs delivering his most famous speech, during the First World War: "I am opposed to every war but one," Debs had said then. "I am for that war, with heart and soul, and that is the worldwide war of the social revolution. In that war, I am prepared to fight any way the revolution the ruling class may make necessary, even to the barricades." Sanders, nearly a century later, offered his echo, as if history were a reel of tape, winding and rewinding and winding again: "There is a war going on in this country," Sanders said. "I am not referring to the war in Iraq or the war in Afghanistan. I am talking about a war being waged by some of the wealthiest and most powerful people against working families, against the disappearing and shrinking middle class of our country."[109]

In 2010, in a series of deals that made possible the passage of health care reform, Democrats agreed to extend the Bush-era tax cuts, and Sanders was one of the few members of Congress to object. "President Obama has said he fought as hard as he could against the Republican tax breaks for the wealthy and for an extension in unemployment," he said during his eight-hour speech. "Well, maybe. But the reality is that fight cannot simply be waged inside the Beltway. Our job is to appeal to the vast majority of the American people and to stand up and to say: Wait a minute."[110]

By 2011, Sanders was no longer a lone voice in the wilderness. Protests against the bailout and against tuition hikes and budget cuts had started at the University of California in 2009, where students occupying a campus building carried signs that read "Occupy Everything, Demand Nothing." The Occupy movement spread on social media, adopting the slogan, "We are the 99%." Occupy Wall Street, an encampment in Zuccotti Park in downtown New York, begun in September 2011, drew thousands. Within months, Occupy protests had been staged in more than six hundred American communities and in hundreds more cities around the world. "We desperately need a coming together of working people to stand up to Wall Street, corporate America, and say enough is enough," Sanders said during Occupy Wall Street. "We need to rebuild the middle class in this country."[111]

Occupy, for all its rhetoric, was not a coming together of a representative array of working people. It was overwhelmingly and notably urban and white, and most protesters were students or people with jobs. It also had no real leadership, favoring a model of direct democracy, and lacked particular, achievable policy goals, preferring loftier objectives, like reinventing politics. *Demand nothing.* But it did propel Sanders to national prominence, and established the foundations for a movement that would lead him to one of the most remarkable progressive presidential campaigns since Theodore Roosevelt in 1912.

If the Tea Party married populism to originalism, Occupy married populism to socialism. The Tea Party on the right and Occupy on the left together offered an assault on Washington, sharing the conviction that the federal government had grown indifferent to the lives of ordinary Americans. Neither Republicans nor Democrats were able to unseat that conviction.

Obama's team had gone to Washington disdainful of "insider Washington," with its moneymakers and its dealmakers and its partisanship-for-hire. This piety did not last. David Plouffe, Obama's 2008 campaign manager, called the GOP "a party led by people who foment anger and controversy to make a name for themselves and to make a buck." In 2010, Plouffe earned $1.5 million; his income included management consulting work for Boeing and GE and speaking gigs booked through the Washington Speakers Bureau. Nor did the press, on the whole, hold politicians to account. Reporters had become "embedded" journalists in Iraq; more were embedded in Washington. So breezily did the press socialize with White House and congressional staff that a politician's wife issuing an invitation to a child's birthday party might take pains to announce that it would be "off the record." But, in truth, hardly anything was off the record, and the record was blaring. The race-car pace of online news—the daily email newsletters, the blogs, and then Twitter—made for frantic, absurd fixations and postures, both grand and petty. "Never before has the so-called permanent establishment of Washington included so many people in the media," reported Mark Leibovich. "They are, by and large, a cohort that is predominantly white and male." They held iPhones in their hands and wore wireless receivers in their ears. They reported in breathless bursts. "They are aggressive, technology-savvy, and preoccupied by the quick bottom lines," wrote Leibovich. "Who's winning? Who's losing? Who gaffed?"[112]

The mantras of Obama's University of Chicago Law School syllabus were not the watchwords of a jacked-up, Bluetoothed, wallet-stuffed Washington. "Draw out the full spectrum of views on the issue you're dealing with," he'd instructed his students. "Display a thorough examination of the diversity of opinion that exists on the issue or theme." House members raising money for reelection and booking their next television appearance didn't think that way. Obama's administration, unsurprisingly, found it difficult to gain traction with Congress, and the new president's commitment to calm, reasoned deliberation proved untenable in a madcap capital.

The president's aloofness kept him from the fray. Then, too, his signature health care act was a complicated piece of legislation, a feast for people who could make money by mocking it or explaining it, or both. Sarah Palin said that Obama's health care plan would lead to "death panels," which, while both absurd and untrue, was simply put. This, and the Democratic response, was the sort of outrageous assertion that generated a lot of web traffic, which had become a kind of virtual currency. Madness meant money. "We get paid to get Republicans pissed off at Democrats, which they rightfully are," one Republican lobbyist told the *Huffington Post*. "It's the easiest thing in the world. It's like getting paid to get you to love your mother." The intricacies of reforming health care insurance, which constituted a fifth of the American economy, chiefly served the interests of lobbyists. "Complication and uncertainty is good for us," said Democratic lobbyist Tony Podesta, the brother of Bill Clinton's former chief of staff, John Podesta.[113] It meant more clients.

More money was made by more people interested in profiting from political decay after the Supreme Court ruled, in a 2010 case called *Citizens United v. Federal Election Commission*, that restrictions on spending by political action committees and other groups were unconstitutional. Roscoe Conkling's fateful maneuver of 1882—telling the Supreme Court that when he'd helped draft the Fourteenth Amendment, the committee had changed the word "citizens" to "persons" in order to protect the rights of corporations—would make judicial history, time and time again. Where earlier rulings had granted corporations, as "persons," certain liberties (especially the *Lochner*-era liberty of contract), *Citizens United* granted corporations a First Amendment right to free speech. By 2014, the court would grant corporations First Amendment rights to freedom of religious expression. In a landmark case, corporations owned by people who objected to contraception on religious grounds were allowed to refuse to provide insurance coverage for birth control to their employees, citing their corporation's First Amendment rights.[114]

And yet on college and university campuses, students continued to protest not for but against free speech. Every hate speech code that had been instituted since the 1990s that had been challenged in court had been found unconstitutional.[115] Some had been lifted, others disavowed. In 2014, the University of Chicago issued a report on freedom of expression: "The University's fundamental commitment is to the principle that debate or deliberation may not be suppressed because the ideas put forth are thought by some or even by most members of the University community to be offensive, unwise, immoral, or wrongheaded."[116] Nevertheless, a generation of younger Americans who had been raised with hate speech codes rejected debate itself. They attempted to silence visiting speakers, including not only half-mad provocateurs but scholars and serious if controversial public figures, from Condoleezza Rice to longtime political columnist George Will to former FBI director James Comey.

While campus protesters squashed the free speech rights of people, the Supreme Court protected the free speech rights of corporations. When *Citizens United* demolished the constitutional dam, money flooded the vast plains of American politics, from east to west. The Tea Party movement was soon overwhelmed by political grifters. Within five years of the movement's founding, its leading organizations, including the Tea Party Express and the Tea Party Patriots, were spending less than 5 percent of their funds on campaigns and elections.[117]

All that money bought nothing so much as yet more rage. Liberal columnist E. J. Dionne detected a pattern: candidates and parties made big promises, and when they gained power and failed to make good on those promises, they blamed some kind of conspiracy—any sort of conspiracy: a conspiracy of the press, a conspiracy of the rich, a conspiracy of the "deep state" (including, during Trump's first term, a conspiracy of the FBI). Then they found media organizations willing to present readers with evidence of such a conspiracy, however concocted. Conservative commentator David Frum offered a not dissimilar diagnosis: "The media culture of the U.S. has been reshaped to become a bespoke purveyor of desired facts."[118] Under these circumstances, it was difficult for either party to hold a majority for long. Democrats lost the House in 2010, the Senate in 2014, and the White House in 2016.

———

WHEN DONALD TRUMP was out of the White House, he railed at the government. When he was in the White House, he railed at the press. He railed at Congress. He railed at immigrants. He railed at North Korea. He railed at his staff. He grew red in the face with railing.

Well known in the world of professional wrestling, Trump brought to politics the tactics of the arena, which borrowed its conventions of melodrama from reality television, another genre with which Trump was well acquainted, having starred, beginning in 2004, in a reality program called *The Apprentice*. On *The Apprentice*, Trump's signature line was "You're fired." In professional wrestling, a hero known as a face battles his exact opposite, a villain known as a heel; every time they meet, they act out another chapter of their story together. They say their lines, they take their bows.

Not long into Obama's presidency, Trump began staging bouts, as if he were the face and the president his heel. He taunted. He smirked. He swaggered. He wanted Obama to be fired. Early in 2011, he called for Obama to release to the public his "long-form" birth certificate, intimating that the president had something to hide. "He doesn't have a birth certificate, or if he does, there's something on that certificate that is very bad for him," Trump said. "Now, somebody told me—and I have no idea if this is bad for him or not, but perhaps it would be—that where it says 'religion' it might have 'Muslim.'"[119]

These performances reached a ready-made audience. If the polls could be trusted, a dubious proposition, even before Trump began his imaginary bout with Obama, more than two in five Republicans believed that the president was either definitely or probably born in another country. Another difficult-to-credit poll reported that more than one in three Americans believed, about that time, that it was either "somewhat likely" or "very likely" that "federal officials either participated in the attacks on the World Trade Center and the Pentagon, or took no action to stop them."[120]

Both the truther conspiracy theory and the birther conspiracy theory had long been peddled by Alex Jones. By 2011, by which time the Drudge Report had begun linking to Infowars, Jones's audience was bigger than the audiences of Rush Limbaugh and Glenn Beck put together. (Jones had no use for either man. "What a whore Limbaugh is," he said). "Our investigation of the purported Obama birth certificate released by Hawaiian authorities today reveals the document is a shoddily contrived hoax," Jones wrote after the White House released the long-form certificate at the end of April 2011. The Drudge Report linked to the story. After the release, another Gallup poll reported—again, dubiously—that nearly one in four Republicans still believed that Obama was definitely or probably born outside of the United States.[121]

On February 26, 2012, in a national atmosphere of racial incitement, a twenty-eight-year-old man named George Zimmerman, prowling around the neighborhood outside Orlando, Florida, called 911 to report seeing "a real suspicious guy." He'd seen seventeen-year-old Trayvon Martin, who was walking to a nearby store. Zimmerman got out of his car and shot Martin, who was unarmed, with a 9mm handgun. Zimmerman told the police that Martin attacked him. Zimmerman weighed 250 pounds; Martin weighed 140. Martin's family said that the boy, heard over a cellphone, had begged for his life. Martin did not survive. Zimmerman was not charged for six weeks. On March 8, Trayvon Martin's father, Tracy Martin, held a press conference in Orlando and demanded the release of recordings of calls to 911. "We feel justice has not been served," he said.[122]

Martin's death might not have gained national attention if it had not been for yet another shooting. The day after George Zimmerman killed Trayvon Martin, a seventeen-year-old boy named T. J. Lane walked into the cafeteria at Chardon High School, about thirty miles outside of Cleveland, pulled out a .22-caliber pistol, and fired, killing three students and badly injuring two more.[123]

By then, the United States had the highest rate of private gun ownership in the world, twice that of the country with the second highest rate, which was Yemen. The United States also had the highest homicide rate of any affluent democracy, nearly four times higher than France or Germany, six times higher than the United Kingdom. In the United States at the start of the twenty-first century, guns were involved in two-thirds of all murders.[124] None of these facts had dissuaded the Supreme Court from ruling, in 2008, in *District of Columbia v. Heller*, that DC's 1975 Firearms Control Regulations Act was unconstitutional, Justice Scalia writing, "The Second Amendment protects an individual right to possess a firearm unconnected with service in a militia." Anticipating openings on the court, the new head of the NRA told *American Rifleman* that the 2012 presidential election was "perhaps the most crucial election, from a Second Amendment standpoint, in our lifetimes."[125]

There were shootings on street corners, in shopping malls, in hospitals, in movie theaters, and in churches. The nation had been mourning shootings in schools since 1999, when two seniors at a high school in Columbine, Colorado, shot and killed twelve students, a teacher, and themselves. In 2007, twenty-three-year-old Seung Hui-Cho, a senior at Virginia Tech, shot fifty people in Blacksburg, killing thirty-two people before he killed himself.[126] The shooting in an Ohio high school, the day after Martin was killed in Florida, was, by comparison with Virginia Tech, a lesser tragedy, but it cast in a very dark light the claims coming out of Florida that George Zimmerman had a right to shoot Trayvon Martin.

Between 1980 and 2012, forty-nine states had passed laws allowing gun owners to carry concealed weapons outside their homes for personal protection. (Illinois was the sole holdout.) In 2004, Bush had allowed the 1994 Brady Bill's ban on the possession, transfer, or manufacture of semiautomatic assault weapons to expire. In 2005, Florida passed a "stand your ground" law, exonerating from prosecution citizens who use deadly force when confronted by an assailant, even if they could have safely retreated. More states followed.[127] Carrying a concealed weapon for self-defense came to be understood not as a failure of civil society, to be mourned, but as an act of citizenship, to be vaunted, law and order, man by man.

Obama refused to cede this argument. "If I had a son," the president said at a press conference on March 23, visibly shaken, "he'd look like Trayvon."[128] Later that day, Rick Santorum, a Republican presidential aspirant, spoke outside at a firing range in West Monroe, Louisiana, where he shot fourteen rounds from a Colt .45. He told the crowd, "What I was able to exercise was one of those fundamental freedoms that's guaranteed in our Constitution, the right to bear arms." A woman called out, "Pretend it's Obama."[129]

On April 2, thousands of students rallied in Atlanta, carrying signs that read "I am Trayvon Martin" and "Don't Shoot!"[130] Even as they were rallying, a forty-three-year-old man named One Goh walked into a classroom in a small Christian college in Oakland, took out a .45-caliber semiautomatic pistol, lined the students against the wall, said, "I'm going to kill you all," and fired. That same morning, in Tulsa, five people were shot on the street. An investigation called "Operation Random Shooter" led the Tulsa police to Jake England, nineteen, whose father had been shot to death two years before. By Easter Sunday, two college students had been shot to death in Mississippi.[131]

On March 20, the U.S. Justice Department announced that it would conduct an investigation into the death of Trayvon Martin. On April 7, Martin's parents appeared on *Good Morning America*. Five days later, Newt Gingrich, seeking the 2012 Republication nomination, called the Second Amendment a "universal human right." Trump found this a suitable moment to cast doubt, once more, on the president's birth certificate. "A lot of people do not think it was an authentic certificate," Trump said that May, just before endorsing Mitt Romney as the GOP nominee.[132]

Obama won reelection in 2012, even as Democrats lost control of the Senate. Weeks later, on a woeful day in December in the snow-dusted New England town of Newtown, Connecticut, a mentally ill twenty-year-old shot his mother and then went to his former elementary school, fully armed. He shot and killed six teachers and staff and twenty very young children, as young as five, a massacre of first graders.

"I know there's not a parent in America who doesn't feel the same overwhelming grief that I do," Obama said at the White House. He could not stop himself from weeping. "Our hearts are broken."[133] And yet the Obama administration had no success getting gun safety measures through a Republican Congress, which staunchly defended the right to bear arms at all costs, calling the massacre of little children the price of freedom.

**OBAMA'S SECOND TERM** was marked by battles over budgets and the mire of the Middle East. In 2011, U.S. forces had found and killed Osama bin Laden, and Obama withdrew the last American troops from Iraq. Yet Obama's foreign policy looked aimless and haphazard and tentative, which diminished both his stature and that of his secretary of state, Hillary Clinton. While war in Afghanistan wore on, Islamic militants attacked U.S. government facilities in Libya in 2012, and by 2014 a new terrorist group, calling itself the Islamic State, had gained control of territory in Iraq. America's nation-building project in the Middle East had failed. Obama, who had been an early critic of the Patriot Act, of the prison at Guantánamo, and of the Iraq War, led an administration that stepped up surveillance through a secret program run by the National Security Agency, prosecuted whistle-blowers who leaked documents that revealed U.S. abuses in the Middle East, and used drones to commit assassinations. Critics argued that the war on terror had been an unmitigated disaster, that occupying Arab countries had only produced more terrorists, and that the very idea of a war on terror was an error. Terrorism is a criminal act, historian Andrew Bacevich argued, and required police action and diplomacy, not military action.[134]

With a massive defense budget, the federal government proved unmovable on tax policy and all but unable even to discuss its spending priorities. House leader Paul Ryan, a Wisconsin Republican, proposed capping the top income tax rate at 25 percent, a rate not seen in the United States since the days of Andrew Mellon. Of 248 Republican members of Congress and 47 Republican senators, all but 13 signed a pledge swearing to oppose any income tax increase. The Obama administration wanted to raise the top rate to 39 percent, a recommendation supported by the nonpartisan Congressional Research Service. But Senate Republicans objected to the CRS's report (finding, for instance, the phrase "tax cuts for the rich" to be biased) and, in a move without precedent in the century-long history of the Congressional Research Service, forced the report's withdrawal.[135]

While Congress fought over the implications of the phrase "tax cuts for the rich," political scientists raised a distressing question: how much inequality of wealth and income can a democracy bear? In 2004, a task force of the American Political Science Association had concluded that growing economic inequality was threatening fundamental American political institutions. Four years later, a 700-page collection of scholarly essays presented its argument as its title, *The Unsustainable American State*. A 2013 report by the United Nations reached the conclusion that growing income equality was responsible not only for political instability around the world but also for the slowing of economic growth worldwide. The next year, when the Pew Research Center conducted its annual survey about which of five dangers people in forty-four countries considered to be the "greatest threat to the world," most countries polled put religious and ethnic hatred at the top of their lists, but Americans chose inequality.[136]

As the 2016 election neared, inequality seemed poised to gain the candidates' full attention. Bernie Sanders, seeking the Democratic nomination, would make inequality the centerpiece of his campaign, leading a movement that called for Progressive-style economic reform. But Hillary Clinton, the eventual Democratic nominee, would fail to gain any real traction on the problem. And the unlikely Republican nominee, Donald Trump, would blame immigrants.

A movement to fight gun violence began during Obama's second term, but it wasn't a gun control movement; it was a movement for racial justice. In 2013, after a jury in Florida acquitted George Zimmerman of all charges related to the death of Trayvon Martin, organizers began tweeting under the hashtag #BlackLivesMatter. African Americans had been fighting against domestic terrorism, state violence, and police brutality since before the days of Ida B. Wells's anti-lynching crusade. Black Lives Matter was Black Power, with disruptively innovative technologies: smartphones and apps that could capture and stream candid footage live over the Internet. If stand your ground laws encouraged vigilantism, data service providers encouraged do-it-yourself reporting. Newt Gingrich insisted that the Second Amendment was a human right, but data plans promoted the idea that all users of the Internet were reporters, every man his own muckraker, and that uploading data was itself a human right. "A billion roaming photojournalists uploading the human experience, and it is spectacular," said the voice-over in an ad for a data plan, over images of a vast mosaic of photographs. "My iPhone 5 can see every point of view, every panorama, the entire gallery of humanity. I need, no, I have the right, to be unlimited."[137]

Black Lives Matter made visible, through photography, the experience of African Americans, maybe even in the very way that Frederick Douglass had predicted a century and a half earlier. With photography, witnesses and even the victims themselves captured the experiences of young black men who for generations had been singled out by police, pulled over in cars, stopped on street corners, pushed, frisked, punched, kicked, and even killed. In 2014, police in Ferguson, Missouri, not far from St. Louis, shot and killed eighteen-year-old Michael Brown in the middle of the street. Witnesses captured the shooting on their smartphones. All over the country, witnesses captured one police shooting after another. Police shot and killed Tamir Rice, age twelve, in a city park in Cleveland; he was carrying a toy gun. Minnesota police shot and killed Philando Castile in his car; he had a licensed handgun in his glove compartment and was trying to tell them about it. Castile's girlfriend livestreamed the shooting. "Social media helps Black Lives Matter fight the power," announced *Wired*. Yet legal victories eluded the movement. One killing after another was captured on film and posted on the Internet, but in nearly all cases where officers were charged with wrongdoing, they were acquitted.[138]

Black Lives Matter called urgent attention to state-sanctioned violence against African Americans, in forms that included police brutality, racially discriminatory sentencing laws, and mass incarceration. Unsurprisingly, perhaps, the movement did not make gun control legislation a priority, not least because its forebears included the Black Panthers, who had argued that black men had to arm themselves, and advanced that argument by interpreting the Second Amendment in a way that would later be adopted by the NRA. Meanwhile, hair-trigger fights along the battle lines first drawn in the 1970s, over guns and abortion, continued to be waged on the streets and at the ballot box, but especially in the courts. A pattern emerged. Second Amendment rights—a de facto rights fight led for and by white men—gathered strength. Civil rights for black people, women, and immigrants stalled and even fell back. And gay rights advanced.

In the early years of the twenty-first century, while other civil rights claims failed, the gay rights movement, newly styled the LGBT movement, won signal victories, chiefly by appropriating the pro-family rhetoric that had carried conservatives to victories since Phyllis Schlafly's STOP ERA campaign. In 2003, in *Lawrence v. Texas*, the Supreme Court overruled its 1986 decision in *Bowers* by declaring a Texas sodomy law unconstitutional. In a concurring opinion, Justice Sandra Day O'Connor said she based her decision on a Fourteenth Amendment equal protection argument, asserting that the Texas law constituted sex discrimination: a man could not be prosecuted for engaging in a particular activity with a woman but could be prosecuted for engaging in that same activity with a man. O'Connor's reasoning marked the way forward for LGBT litigation, which turned, increasingly, to marriage equality. Less than a year after the ruling in *Lawrence*, the Massachusetts Supreme Judicial Court made the commonwealth the first state to guarantee same-sex marriage as a constitutional right.[139]

The *Brown v. Board* for same-sex marriage came in the spring of 2015, fifty years after the court's landmark decision on contraception in *Griswold v. Connecticut*. The case, *Obergefell v. Hodges*, consolidated the petitions of four couples who had sought relief from state same-sex marriage bans in Kentucky, Michigan, Ohio and Tennessee. In 2004, Ohio had passed a law stating that "Only a union between one man and one woman may be a marriage valid in or recognized by this state." Ohioans James Obergefell and John Arthur had been together for nearly twenty years when Arthur was diagnosed with ALS, a wrenching and terminal illness, in 2011. In 2013, they flew to Maryland, a state without a same-sex marriage ban, and were married on the tarmac at the airport. Arthur died four months later, at the age of forty-eight. To his widower he was, under Ohio law, a stranger.[140]

In its ruling in *Obergefell v. Hodges*, the Supreme Court declared state bans on same-sex marriage unconstitutional. At New York's Stonewall Inn, the movement's holy site, people gathered by candlelight, hugged one another, and wept. It had been a long and dire struggle and yet the victory, when it came, felt as unexpected and as sudden as the fall of the Berlin Wall. One minute there was a wall; the next, sky.

A triumph for a half century of litigation over reproductive and gay rights, *Obergefell* marked, for conservative Christians, a landmark defeat in a culture war that had begun with the sexual revolution in the 1960s. Between *Griswold* and *Obergefell*, Christians had joined and transformed the Republican Party and yet had not succeeded in stopping a tectonic cultural shift. Many felt betrayed, and even abandoned, by a secular world hostile to the basic tenets of their faith. Conservative Christians had long identified Hollywood, for its celebrating sex and violence on film and television, as an agent of that change. But as entertainment, including pornography, moved online, conservative Christians, like everyone else, began to wonder about the effects of the Internet on belief, tradition, and community. In a book outlining "a strategy for Christians in a post-Christian nation," Rod Dreher, an editor at the *American Conservative*, wrote, "To use technology is to participate in a cultural liturgy that, if we aren't mindful, trains us to accept the core truth claim of modernity: that the only meaning there is in the world is what we choose to assign it in our endless quest to master nature."[141]

Exactly what role the Internet had played in the political upheaval of the first decades of the twenty-first century remained uncertain, but in the aftermath of the 9/11 attacks, Americans believed in conspiracies and feared invasions. Different people feared different conspiracies, but their fears took the same form: intruders had snuck into American life and undermined American democracy. Wasn't that invader the Internet itself? Cyberutopians said no, and pointed to Obama's 2008 campaign, the Tea Party, the Occupy movement, Black Lives Matter, the Arab Spring, and political hackers from Anonymous to WikiLeaks as evidence that the long-predicted democratization of politics had at last arrived. "A new Information Enlightenment is dawning," Heather Brooke wrote, in *The Revolution Will Be Digitised*. "Technology is breaking down traditional social barriers of status, class, power, wealth and geography, replacing them with an ethos of collaboration and transparency."[142]

Instead, social media had provided a breeding ground for fanaticism, authoritarianism, and nihilism. It had also proved to be easily manipulated, not least by foreign agents. On the Internet, everything looked new, even though most of it was very old. The alt-right, a term coined in 2008 by Richard Spencer, was nothing so much as the old right, with roots in the anti–civil rights Ku Klux Klan of the 1860s and the anti-immigration Klan of the 1920s. It stole its style—edgy and pornographic— from the counterculture of the 1960s. The alt-right, less influenced by conservatism than by the sexual revolution, considered itself to be transgressive, a counterculture that had abandoned the moralism of the Moral Majority— or any kind of moralism—and deemed the security state erected by neoconservatives to be insufficient to the clash of civilizations; instead, it favored authoritarianism.[143]

Spencer had been a History PhD student at Duke before leaving in 2007 to become an editor and a leader of what he described as "a movement of consciousness and identity for European people in the 21st century." The alt-right, fueled by the ideology of white supremacy and by disgust with "establishment conservatism," turned misogyny into a rhetorical style and made opposition to immigration its chief policy issue. In 2011, Spencer became the president of the National Policy Institute, whose website announced in 2014, "Immigration is a kind of proxy war— and maybe a last stand—for White Americans who are undergoing a painful recognition that, unless dramatic action is taken, their grandchildren will live in a country that is alien and hostile."[144]

About the only thing that was new about the alt-right was the home it found online, on forums like Reddit and especially 4chan, where users, mostly younger white men, mocked PC culture, bemoaned the decline of

*Supporters of Bernie Sanders, many of them also affiliated with the Occupy movement, insisted on their right to protest outside the 2016 Democratic National Convention in Philadelphia.*

Western civilization, attacked feminism, trolled women, used neo-Nazi memes, and posted pornography, and also on new, disruptive media sites, especially Breitbart, which was started in 2007 and was for a time one of the most popular websites in the United States.[145]

The alt-right's online counterpart, sometimes called the alt-left, had one foot in the online subculture of Tumblr and other platforms, and the other foot in the campus politics of endless pieties over smaller and smaller stakes. If the favored modes of the alt-right were the women-hating troll and the neo-Nazi meme, the favored modes of the alt-left were clickbait and the call-out, sentimental, meaningless outrage—"8 Signs Your Yoga Practice Is Culturally Appropriated"—and sanctimonious accusations of racism, sexism, homophobia, and transphobia. In 2014, Facebook offered users more than fifty different genders to choose from in registering their identities; people who were baffled by this were accused online of prejudice: public shaming as a mode of political discourse was every bit as much a part of the online Far Left as it was of the online Far Right, if not more. After fourteen people were killed in a terrorist attack on a gay nightclub in San Bernardino, California, the alt-left spent its energies in the aftermath of this tragedy attacking one another for breaches of the rules of "intersectionality," which involve intricate, identity-based hierarchies of suffering and virtue. "One Twitter-famous intersectionalist admonished those who had called it the worst mass shooting in US history by reminding them that 'the worst was wounded knee,'" the writer Angela Nagle reported. "Other similar tweeters raged against the use of the term Latina/o instead of Latinx in the reporting, while still others made sure to clarify that it was the shooter's mental illness, not his allegiance to ISIS and the caliphate, that caused the shooting. Not to be outdone, others then tweeted back angrily about the ableism of those who said the shooter had a mental illness."[146]

Millennials, a generation of Americans who grew up online, found their political style on the Internet. At the time of the 2016 election, a majority of younger eligible voters got their news from Facebook's News Feed, which had been launched in 2006. Not many of them—fewer than in any generation before them—believed in political parties, or churches, or public service. The mantra of the counterculture, "question authority," had lost its meaning; few institutions any longer wielded authority. Sellers of data plans suggested that people could upload all of themselves onto the Internet, a self of selfies and posts, an abdication of community and of inquiry. Sellers of search engines suggested that all anything anyone needed to know could be found out with a click. "Eventually you'll have an implant," Google cofounder Larry Page promised, "where if you think about a fact, it will just tell you the answer."[147] But online, where everyone was, in the end, utterly alone, it had become terribly difficult to know much of anything with any certainty, except how to like and be liked, and, especially, how to hate and be hated.

# III.

**"I'VE SAT AROUND** these tables with some of these other guys before," Jeb Bush's campaign manager said. In a room about the size of a tennis court, its walls painted martini-olive green, the campaign managers of the candidates for president of the United States in 2016 sat around a broad conference table to debrief after the election. They were warriors, after the war, standing atop a mountain of dead, remorseless. They had gathered at Harvard's Kennedy School, as campaign managers had done after every presidential election since 1972, for a two-day tell-all. Most of what

*Not long after his
2017 inauguration,
President Trump
greeted visitors to
the White House in
front of a portrait
of Hillary Clinton.*

they said was shop talk, some of it was loose talk. No one said a word about the United States or its government or the common good. Sitting in that room, watching, was like being a pig at a butchers' convention: there was much talk of the latest technology in knives and the best and tastiest cuts of meat, but no one pretended to bear any love for the pig.

The election of 2016 was a product of technological disruption: the most significant form of political communication during the campaign was Donald Trump's Twitter account. It involved a crisis in the press, whose standards of evidence and accountability were challenged by unnamed sources and leaks, some of which turned out to have been part of a campaign of political interference waged by the Russian government, in what came to be called troll factories. The election dredged from the depths of American politics the rank muck of ancient hatreds. It revealed the dire consequences of a dwindling middle class. It suggested the cost, to the Republic's political stability, of the unequal constitutional status of women. It marked the end of the conservative Christian Coalition. And it exposed the bleak emptiness of both major political parties.

Seventeen candidates had vied for the Republican nomination. At the debrief, the campaign managers talked about their candidates and the campaign the way jockeys talk about their horses, and the conditions on the race track. "Our strategy was to keep our head down," said Florida senator Marco Rubio's manager. Wisconsin governor Scott Walker's manager said, "The path was going to be the long game." Ted Cruz's manager talked about what lane his horse was racing in. Trump's former campaign manager, CNN analyst Corey Lewandowski, spoke the longest. His horse was the best, the prettiest, the fastest, and ran "the most unconventional race in the history of the presidency." He told a story, likely apocryphal, about how in 2012 Mitt Romney had been driven in a limo to campaign events but then, at the last minute, he'd jump into a Chevy. Not Trump. Trump went everywhere in his jet. "Our goal was to make sure we were going to run as the populist, to run on our wealth and not run from it, and to monopolize the media attention by using social media unlike anybody else," Lewandowski gloated. "What we know is that when Donald Trump put out a tweet, Fox News would cover it live." Field organizing was over, he said. Newspapers, newspaper advertisements? Irrelevant, he said. "Donald Trump buys ink by the television station," he said. Trump hadn't run in any lane. Trump had run from a plane.[148]

South Carolina senator Lindsey Graham's manager pointed out that much had turned on Fox News's decision to use polls to determine who participated in the primary debates, and where each candidate would stand on the stage, and how much camera time each candidate would get. In the 2016 election, the polls had been a scandal of near Dewey-Beats-Truman proportion, a scandal that people in the industry had seen coming. During the 2012 presidential election, twelve hundred polling organizations had conducted thirty-seven thousand polls by making more than three billion phone calls. Most Americans—more than 90 percent— had refused to speak to them. Mitt Romney's pollsters had believed, even on the morning of the election, that Romney would win. A 2013 study—a poll—found that three out of four Americans distrusted polls. But nine of ten people, presumably, distrusted the polls so much that they had refused to answer the question, which meant that the results of that poll meant nothing at all.[149]

"Election polling is in near crisis," a past president of the American Association for Public Opinion Research had written just months before the 2016 election. When George Gallup founded the polling industry in the 1930s, the response rate—the number of people who answer a pollster as a percentage of those who are asked—was well above 90. By the 1980s, it had fallen to about 60 percent. By the election of 2016, the response rate had dwindled to the single digits. Time and again, predictions failed.

In 2015, polls failed to predict Benjamin Netanyahu's victory in Israel, the Labour Party's loss in the United Kingdom, and a referendum in Greece. In 2016, polls failed to predict Brexit, the vote to withdraw Great Britain and Northern Ireland from the European Union.[150]

The more unreliable the polls became, the more the press and the parties relied on them, which only made them less reliable. In 2015, during the primary season, Fox News announced that, in order to participate in its first prime-time debate, Republican candidates had to "place in the top 10 of an average of the five most recent national polls," and that where the candidates would be placed on the debate stage would be determined by their polling numbers. (Standing in the polls had earlier been used to exclude third-party candidates from debates—a practice that had led to a raft of complaints filed with the Federal Election Commission—but not major-party candidates.) The Republican National Committee didn't object, but the decision had alarmed reputable polling organizations. The Marist Institute for Public Opinion called the Fox News plan "a bad use of public polls." Scott Keeter, Pew's director of Survey Research, said, "I just don't think polling is really up to the task of deciding the field for the headliner debate." Pew, Gallup, and the *Wall Street Journal*/NBC pollsters refused to participate.[151]

Polls admitted Trump into the GOP debates, polls placed him at center stage, and polls declared him the winner. "Donald J. Trump Dominates *Time* Poll," the Trump campaign posted on its website following the first debate, referring to a story in which *Time* reported that 47 percent of respondents to a survey it had conducted said that Trump had won. *Time*'s "poll" was conducted by PlayBuzz, a viral content provider that embedded "quizzes, polls, lists and other playful formats" onto websites to attract traffic. PlayBuzz collected about seventy thousand "votes" from visitors to *Time*'s website in its instant opt-in Internet poll. *Time* posted this warning: "The results of this poll are not scientific."[152] Less reputable websites did not bother with disclaimers.

Efforts to call attention to the weakness of the polls, or to make distinctions between one kind of poll and another, were both unsuccessful and halfhearted. The *New York Times* ran a story called "Presidential Polls: How to Avoid Getting Fooled." Polls drove polls. Good polls drove polls, and bad polls drove polls and when bad polls drove good polls, they weren't so good anymore. Then, too, warning their readers, listeners, or

viewers about the problems with polls hadn't prevented news organizations from compounding them. In August 2015, the day after the first
GOP debate, *Slate* published a column called "Did Trump Actually Win
the Debate? How to Understand All Those Instant Polls That Say Yes,"
even as *Slate* conducted its own instant poll: "Now that the first Republican presidential debate is over, pundits and politicos will be gabbing
about what it all means for each candidate's campaign. Who triumphed?
Who floundered? Who will ride the debate to electoral glory, and who
is fated to fizzle?" They made the same populist promises Gallup had
made in the 1930s. "TV talking heads won't decide this election," promised *Slate*'s pollster (whose title was "Interactives Editor"). "The American people will."[153]

Every major polling organization miscalled the 2016 election, predicting a win for Hillary Clinton. It had been a narrow contest. Clinton won
the popular vote; Trump won in the Electoral College. The Kennedy
School post-election debrief served as one of the earliest formal reckon-
ings with what, exactly, had happened.

After the Republican campaign managers finished taking stock, the
Democrats spoke. "Hillary, a lot of people don't recall, came to electoral
politics late in her career," her campaign manager, Robby Mook, said.
"She got her start with the Children's Defense Fund . . ." Clinton's campaign had failed to say much of anything new about Hillary Clinton, a
candidate Americans knew only too well. Mook apparently had little
to add. Bernie Sanders's manager looked wan. He shook his head. "We
almost did it."[154]

The more obvious explanations for Clinton's loss went, on the whole,
unstated. Obama had failed to raise up a new generation of political talent. The Democratic National Committee, believing Clinton's nomination and even her victory to be inevitable, had suppressed competition.
Clinton, dedicating her time to fund-raising with wealthy coastal liberals
from Hollywood to the Hamptons, failed to campaign in swing states and
hardly bothered to speak to blue-collar white voters. After Trump won the
nomination, she failed to do much of anything except to call out his flaws
of character, even though Trump's most vocal supporters had pointed out,
from the very beginning, that a call-out approach would fail.

The Clinton campaign believed Trump's political career had come to
an end when an audio recording was leaked in which he said that the

best way to approach women was to "grab 'em by the pussy." But even this hadn't stopped conservative Christians from supporting him. "Although the media tried to portray Trump's personality as a cult of personality, ironically, the one thing voters weren't wild about was his personality," wrote Ann Coulter, in *In Trump We Trust*, a hastily written campaign polemic that, like her earlier work, waved aside even the vaguest interest in evidence: "I'm too busy to footnote." As for charges of Trump's depravity and deceit, Coulter rightly predicted that his supporters would be untroubled: "There's nothing Trump can do that won't be forgiven," she wrote. "Except change his immigration policies." [155]

Phyllis Schlafly, the grande dame of American conservatism, had provided Trump with one of his earliest and most important endorsements, at a rally in St. Louis in March of 2016. At ninety-one, her voice quavered but her powers were undiminished. In a pink blazer, her blond bouffant as flawless as ever, she told the crowd that Trump was a "true conservative." Trump, to Schlafly, represented the culmination of a movement she had led for so long, from the anticommunist crusade of the 1950s and the Goldwater campaign of the 1960s to STOP ERA in the 1970s and the Reagan Revolution in the 1980s. Since 9/11, Schlafly had been calling for an end to immigration, and for a fence along the border, and Trump's call for a wall had won her loyalty. "Donald Trump is the one who has made immigration the big issue that it really is," Schlafly said. "Because Obama wants to change the character of our country." [156]

That summer, Schlafly had attended the Republican National Convention to celebrate Trump's historic nomination. In a wheelchair, she looked weak and pale and yet she spoke with her trademark determination. She said she wanted to be remembered for "showing that the grassroots can rise up and defeat the establishment, because that's what we did with the Equal Rights Amendment, and I think that's what we're going to do with electing Donald Trump." Schlafly died only weeks later, on September 5, 2016. Her endorsement, *The Conservative Case for Trump*, published the day after her death, called on conservative Christians to support Trump because of his positions on immigration and abortion: "Christianity is under attack around the world—most dramatically from Islamists, but also insidiously here at home with attacks on religious freedom." [157]

Only weeks before the election, Trump delivered the opening remarks at Schlafly's funeral, at a gothic cathedral in St. Louis. "With Phyllis, it was America first," said Trump from the altar. He raised a finger, as if making a vow: "We will never, ever let you down." On Election Day, at least according to exit polls, 52 percent of Catholics and 81 percent of evangelicals voted for Trump.[158]

Trump's election marked a last and abiding victory for the woman who stopped the ERA. Yet dissenting conservative Christians argued that it also marked the end of Christian conservatism. "Though Donald Trump won the presidency in part with the strong support of Catholics and evangelicals, the idea that someone as robustly vulgar, fiercely combative, and morally compromised as Trump will be an avatar for the restoration of Christian morality and social unity is beyond delusional," wrote Rod Dreher after the election. "He is not a solution to the problem of America's cultural decline, but a symptom of it."[159]

Dreher called on Christians to engage in "digital fasting as an ascetic practice." Other conservatives who had not supported Trump wrestled with the consequences of the right-wing attack on traditional sources of authority and knowledge but especially the press. "We had succeeded in convincing our audiences to ignore and discount any information whatsoever from the mainstream media," former conservative talk radio host Charlie Sykes reported after the election, in an act of apostasy called *How the Right Lost Its Mind*.[160]

The Left placed blame elsewhere. Hillary Clinton mainly attributed her defeat to a scandal over her email, for which she blamed the FBI, though she and her supporters also blamed Bernie Sanders, for dividing the Democratic Party.[161] At the Kennedy School post-election conference, neither the Clinton campaign nor the mainstream media was ready to reckon with its role in the election. At an after-dinner discussion about the role of the media in the election. Jeff Zucker, the president of CNN, rebuffed every suggestion that CNN might have made mistakes in its coverage—for instance, in the amount of airtime it gave to Trump, including long stretches when, waiting for the candidate to appear somewhere, the network broadcast footage of an empty stage. "Frankly, respectfully, I think that's bullshit," Zucker said of the complaints. "Donald Trump was on CNN a lot. That's because we asked him to do interviews and he agreed to do them. We continuously asked the other candidates to come on and do interviews and they declined."[162]

"You showed empty podiums!" someone hollered from the audience.

Zucker refused to back down. "Donald Trump was asked to come on, and he agreed to come on, and he took the questions. These other candidates were asked—"

"That's not true!" screamed another campaign manager.

Zucker: "I understand that emotions continue to run high. . . ."[163]

The moderator, Bloomberg Politics writer Sasha Issenberg, called for calm. "Let's move to a less contentious subject—fake news."[164]

During the campaign, voters who got their news online had been reading a great many stories that were patently untrue, pure fictions, some of them written by Russian propagandists. Russian president Vladimir Putin disliked Clinton; Trump admired Putin. During Trump's first year in office, Congress would investigate whether the Trump campaign had colluded with the Russian government, and even whether the meddling affected the outcome of the election, but the meddling, which appeared to consist of stoking partisan fires and igniting racial and religious animosity, had a larger aim: to destroy Americans' faith in one another and in their system of government.[165]

In any event, not all writers of fake news were Russians. Paul Horner, a thirty-seven-year-old aspiring comedian from Phoenix, wrote fake pro-Trump news for profit, and was amazed to find that Trump staff like Lewandowski reposted his stories on social media. "His campaign manager posted my story about a protester getting paid $3,500 as fact," Horner told the *Washington Post*. "Like, I made that up. I posted a fake ad on Craigslist." Horner, who did not support Trump, later said, "All the stories I wrote were to make Trump's supporters look like idiots for sharing my stories." (Horner died not long after the election, possibly of a drug overdose.)[166]

Horner may have been surprised that people reposted his hoaxes as news, but a great deal of reposting was done not by people but by robots. In the months before the election, Twitter had as many as 48 million fake accounts, bots that tweeted and retweeted fake news. On Facebook, a fake news story was as likely as a real news story to be posted in Facebook's News Feed.[167]

At the Kennedy School forum, moderator Issenberg turned to Elliot Schrage, Facebook's vice president of global communications, marketing, and public policy.

"At what point did you recognize there was a problem with fake news?" Issenberg asked.

"The issue of our role as a news dissemination organization is something that really surfaced over the course of the past year," Schrage said.[168]

Congress would subsequently conduct an investigation into what Facebook knew, and when it knew it, and why it didn't do more about it.[169] Mark Zuckerberg, who appeared to be exploring the possibility of some day running for president of the United States, had at first dismissed the notion that Facebook played any role in the election as "crazy." During a subsequent congressional investigation, Facebook would reluctantly admit that a Kremlin-linked misinformation organization, the Internet Research Agency, whose objective was to divide Americans and interfere with the election, had bought inflammatory political ads from Facebook that had been seen by more than 126 million Americans.[170] It later came out that Facebook had provided the private data of more than 87 million of its users to Cambridge Analytica, a data firm retained by the Trump campaign.

Schrage, however, didn't speak to any of that. Facebook had only very recently begun to wonder whether it ought to think of itself as a "news organization"—"I'd say probably in the last three or six months," he explained—and it showed. Schrage, a corporate lawyer who specialized in acquisitions and mergers, displayed little evidence of any particular understanding of news, reporting, editing, editorial judgment, or the public interest. When he dithered about photographs with nipples that Facebook's algorithms had classified as pornography, but which might really be legitimate news stories, the Associated Press's Kathleen Carroll interjected witheringly.[171]

"Can I just say that news judgment is a lot more complicated than nipples?"[172]

Schrage shrank in his chair.

At the start of Trump's second year in office, the Justice Department would indict thirteen Russian nationals involved with the Internet Research Agency, charging them with "posing as U.S. persons and creating false U.S. persons," as well as using "the stolen identities of real U.S. persons" to operate and post on social media accounts "for purposes of interfering with the U.S. political system," a strategy that included "supporting the presidential campaign of then-candidate Donald J. Trump . . .

and disparaging Hillary Clinton." They were also charged with undermining the campaigns of Republican candidates Ted Cruz and Marco Rubio, supporting the campaigns of Bernie Sanders and Green Party candidate Jill Stein, using Facebook and Twitter to sow political dissent in forms that included fake Black Lives Matter and American Muslim social media accounts, and organizing pro-Trump, anti-Clinton rallies, posting under hashtags that included #Trump2016, #TrumpTrain, #IWontProtectHillary and #Hillary4Prison.[173] More revelations would follow.

At the post-election panel, Issenberg asked Marty Baron, esteemed editor of the *Washington Post*, whether he had considered not publishing the content of Democratic National Committee emails released by WikiLeaks, an anonymous source site established in 2006. WikiLeaks founder Julian Assange, an Australian computer programmer, styled himself after Daniel Ellsberg, the former RAND analyst who had leaked the Pentagon Papers, but Assange, living in the Ecuadorian embassy in London, bore not the remotest resemblance to Ellsberg. Russian hackers had broken into the DNC's servers, Assange had released the hacked emails on WikiLeaks, and the *Post* was among the media outlets that decided to quote from emails that would turn out to have been hacked by a sovereign nation-state.[174]

Baron, otherwise serene and oracular, grew testy, evading Issenberg's question and pointing out, irrelevantly, that the *Post* had not hesitated to release the contents of the emails because "the Clinton campaign never said that they had been falsified."[175]

Issenberg asked Schrage why Facebook hadn't fact-checked purported news stories before moving them in the News Feed rankings. Schrage talked about Facebook's "learning curve." Mainly, he dodged. "It is not clear to me that with 1.8 billion people in the world in lots of different countries with lots of different languages, that the smart strategy is to start hiring editors," he said.[176] As congressional hearings would subsequently confirm, Facebook had hardly any strategy at all, smart or otherwise, except to maximize its number of users and the time they spent on Facebook.

"Where's news judgment?" called out someone from the audience, directing the question at the entire panel.

Zucker shrugged. "At the end of the day, it is up to the viewer."[177] He was answered by groans.

Carroll, a longtime eminence in the profession of journalism and a member of the Pulitzer board, summed up the discussion. "I know that there are some organizations or some journalists or some observers who feel like the media ought to put on a hair shirt," she said. "I think that's crap."[178] And the evening ended, with no one from any of the campaigns, or from cable news or social media or the wire services, having expressed even an ounce of regret, for anything.

The election had nearly rent the nation in two. It had stoked fears, incited hatreds, and sown doubts about American leadership in the world, and about the future of democracy itself. But remorse would wait for another day. And so would a remedy.

*If we should perish, the ruthlessness of the foe would be only the secondary cause of the disaster. The primary cause would be that the strength of a giant nation was directed by eyes too blind to see all the hazards of the struggle; and the blindness would be induced not by some accident of nature or history but by hatred and vainglory.*

—Reinhold Niebuhr,
*The Irony of American History,*
1952

*Glenn Ligon's 2012* Double America, *in neon and paint,
was partly inspired by the opening words of Charles Dickens's* A Tale
of Two Cities: *"It was the best of times, it was the worst of times."*

# THE QUESTION ADDRESSED

I T HAD BEEN UNUSUALLY WARM IN PHILADELPHIA THE summer of the constitutional convention, but by the middle of September, when the last delegates mounted their horses and headed for home, the weather had begun to turn. By October, when *The Federalist Papers* began appearing in newspapers, asking Americans to debate the question of "whether societies of men are really capable or not of establishing good government from reflection and choice, or whether they are forever destined to depend for their political constitutions on accident and force," the air was as crisp as an autumn apple. In November, as the last apples were pressed into cider, the temperature began to plummet. The day after Christmas, ice closed the Delaware River and kept it shut for months, over a winter so cold that the ground froze as far south as Savannah.[1]

It's been hotter in the years since. The climate of the Constitution is gone. The average annual temperature in Philadelphia at the time of the constitutional convention was 52 degrees Fahrenheit.[2] By the end of Barack Obama's presidency, it had risen to 59 degrees.[3] When the world began to warm, the temperature over land rose faster than the temperature over water, but the oceans heated up, too. Ice caps melted, seas rose, storms grew.[4] Not long after Donald Trump announced that he would withdraw the United States from the nearly two-hundred-member-nation Paris climate accord, a declaration he described as "a reassertion of America's sovereignty," a trillion-ton iceberg the size of the state of Delaware broke off of Antarctica.[5]

For millions of years the continents had drifted away from one another. In 1492 they'd met again, in America, a new world. Sixteenth-century conquerors debated the nature of justice. Seventeenth-century dissenters hoped to find nearness to God. Eighteenth-century rationalists, cleaving themselves from the past, hoped to found a new beginning, a place out of time.

The United States began with an act of severing: "When in the Course of human events it becomes necessary for one people to dissolve the political bands which have connected them with another . . . a decent respect to the opinions of mankind requires that they should declare the causes which impel them to the separation." Its Constitution aspired to create a more perfect union, but it was slaves and the descendants of slaves who, by dissolving the bonds of tyranny, helped to realize the promise of that union, in bonds of equality. Those new bonds tied Americans to one another, and to the world. Telegraph wires stretched across the Atlantic, sunk to the ocean's floor. Then came steamships, airplanes, supersonic jets, satellites, pollution, atomic bombs, the Internet. "In the beginning, all the world was America," John Locke had written. By the close of the Cold War, some commentators concluded that America had become all the world, as if the American experiment had ended, in unrivaled triumph.

The American experiment had not ended. A nation born in revolution will forever struggle against chaos. A nation founded on universal rights will wrestle against the forces of particularism. A nation that toppled a hierarchy of birth only to erect a hierarchy of wealth will never know tranquillity. A nation of immigrants cannot close its borders. And a nation born in contradiction, liberty in a land of slavery, sovereignty in a land of conquest, will fight, forever, over the meaning of its history.

And still the waters rose. Trump's election started a tidal wave. Not a few political commentators announced the end of the Republic. Trump's rhetoric was apocalyptic and absolute; the theme of his inaugural address was "American carnage." The rhetoric of his critics was no less dystopian—angry, wounded, and without hope.[6]

As Trump began his term in office, Americans fought over immigration and guns, sex and religion. They fought, too, over statues and monuments, plaques and names. The ghosts of American history rattled their chains. In Frederick, Maryland, a Chevy pickup truck carted a bronze bust of Roger Taney, the judge who'd made the decision in *Dred Scott*, from the city hall to a cemetery outside of town. In St. Louis, cranes pulled up two Confederate memorials—their plinths spray-painted "BLACK LIVES MATTER" and "END RACISM"—and put them into storage. New Orleans planned to take down statues of four Confederate leaders, which led to mayhem, seepage from what secessionists once described as a "sea of blood," the bursting of a dam. In Charlottesville, Virginia, where a statue of Robert E. Lee had been slated to come down, armed white supremacists marched through the city; one ran down a counter-protester and killed her, as if the Civil War had never ended, she the last of the Union dead.[7]

The truths on which the nation was founded—equality, sovereignty, and consent—had been retold after the Civil War. Modern liberalism came out of that political settlement, and the United States, abandoning isolationism, had carried that vision to the world: the rule of law, individual rights, democratic government, open borders, and free markets. The fight to make good on the promise of the nation's founding truths held the country together for a century, during the long struggle for civil rights. And yet the nation came apart all the same, all over again.

Conservatives based their claim to power on liberalism's failure, which began in the 1960s, when the idea of identity replaced the idea of equality. Liberals won gains in the courts while losing state houses, governors' offices, and congressional seats. By the 1990s, conservative Robert Bork insisted, "Modern liberalism is fundamentally at odds with democratic government because it demands results that ordinary people would not freely choose. Liberals must govern, therefore, through institutions that are largely insulated from the popular will."[8] But the problem wasn't that liberals did not succeed in winning popular support; the problem was that liberals did not try, spurning electoral politics in favor of judicial remedies, political theater, and purity crusades.

Conservatives rested their claim to political power on winning elections and winning history. The *National Review*, William F. Buckley had written in 1955, "stands athwart history, yelling Stop." From wanting it to stop, conservatives began wanting history to turn back, not least by making a fetish of the nation's founding, in the form of originalism. "From the arrival of English-speaking colonists in 1607 until 1965," Newt Gingrich wrote in 1996, "from the Jamestown colony and the Pilgrims, through de Tocqueville's *Democracy in America*, up to Norman Rockwell's paintings of the 1940s and 1950s, there was one continuous civilization built around commonly accepted legal and cultural principles."[9] Since 1965, the year Lyndon Johnson signed the Immigration Act, Gingrich argued, that civilization had come undone. Gingrich's account of America's past was a fantasy, useful to his politics, but useless as history—heedless of difference and violence and the struggle for justice. It also undermined and belittled the American experiment, making it less bold, less daring, less interesting, less violent, a daffy, reassuring bedtime story instead of a stirring, terrifying, inspiring, troubling, earth-shaking epic. And yet that fairy tale spoke to the earnest yearnings and political despair of Americans who joined the Tea Party, and who rallied behind Donald Trump's promise to "make American great again." Nor was the nostalgia limited to America alone. All over the world, populists seeking solace from a troubled present sought refuge in imagined histories. The fate of the nation-state itself appearing uncertain; nationalists, who had few proposals for the future, gained power by telling fables about the greatness of the past.

Barack Obama had urged Americans "to choose our better history," a longer, more demanding, messier, and, finally, more uplifting story. But a nation cannot choose its past; it can only choose its future. And in the twenty-first century, it was no longer clear that choice, in the sense that Alexander Hamilton meant, had much to do with the decisions made by an electorate that had been cast adrift on the ocean of the Internet. Can a people govern themselves by reflection and choice? Hamilton had wanted to know, or are they fated to be ruled, forever, by accident and force, lashed by the violence of each wave of a surging sea?

The ship of state lurched and reeled. Liberals, blown down by the slightest breeze, had neglected to trim the ship's sails, leaving the canvas to flap and tear in a rising wind, the rigging flailing. Huddled belowdecks, they had failed to plot a course, having lost sight of the horizon and their grasp on any compass. On deck, conservatives had pulled up the ship's planking to make bonfires of rage: they had courted the popular will by demolishing the idea of truth itself, smashing the ship's very mast.

It would fall to a new generation of Americans, reckoning what their forebears had wrought, to fathom the depths of the doom-black sea. If they meant to repair the tattered ship, they would need to fell the most majestic pine in a deer-haunted forest and raise a new mast that could pierce the clouded sky. With sharpened adzes, they would have to hew timbers of cedar and oak into planks, straight and true. They would need to drive home nails with the untiring swing of mighty arms and, with needles held tenderly in nimble fingers, stitch new sails out of the rugged canvas of their goodwill. Knowing that heat and sparks and hammers and anvils are not enough, they would have to forge an anchor in the glowing fire of their ideals. And to steer that ship through wind and wave, they would need to learn an ancient and nearly forgotten art: how to navigate by the stars.

# ACKNOWLEDGMENTS

IT IS A TRUISM THAT EVERY BOOK TAKES AN AUTHOR A LIFE to write. In this case, the truism is apt. I've been teaching much of the material in this book for decades and my first thanks is to my students, whose searching questions have deepened my curiosity, challenged my assumptions, and sharpened my understanding.

My next thanks is to my colleagues. To write this book, I undertook the incredibly delightful and joyful work of learning and writing about many people, events, ideas, and institutions I'd never studied before and reading the work of generations of distinguished American historians and political scientists. I leaned on their expertise in other ways, too. Extraordinarily generous colleagues read drafts, pointed me to readings, and talked me through trouble spots. Special thanks to David Armitage, David Blight, Tomiko Brown-Nagin, Davíd Carrasco, Linda Colley, Nancy Cott, Noah Feldman, Gary Gerstle, Annette Gordon-Reed, John Harpham, Elizabeth Hinton, Adam Hochschild, Tony Horwitz, Maya Jasanoff, Walter Johnson, Jane Kamensky, James Kloppenberg, Ann Marie Lipinski, Louis Menand, Charles Maier, Lisa McGirr, Julie Miller, Martha Minow, Benjamin Naddaff-Hafrey, Latif Nasser, Sarah Phillips, Leah Price, Emma Rothschild, Bruce Schulman, Erik Seeman, Rogers Smith, and Sean Wilentz.

I benefited, as well, from immensely helpful comments from audiences who listened to me present versions of this work as the George Bancroft Memorial Lecture at the U.S. Naval Academy; the Spencer Trask Lecture at Princeton University; the Patten Lectures at Indiana University; the Richard Leopold Lecture on Public Affairs at Northwestern University; the Theodore H. White Lecture on Press and Politics at Harvard's Kennedy School of Government; the F.E.L. Priestley Memorial Lectures in the History of Ideas at the University of Toronto; the Distinguished Visiting Fellow Lecture at the University of Connecticut, Storrs; and the

Callahan Distinguished Lecture at Case Western Reserve University. I received particularly crucial suggestions during seminars at Harvard, including in the History Department, at the Nieman Foundation, and at the Program on Constitutional Government, as well as during presentations at the American History Seminar at the University of Cambridge and at the American Wing of the Metropolitan Museum of Art, New York.

All books of this scope represent the culmination of long-waged labors. To write this book, I in many cases revisited stories that I have told before—in lectures, in essays, and in books—about everything from the histories of taxation, debt, and political consulting to the lives of Jane Franklin, Andrew Jackson, Woodrow Wilson, and Barack Obama. I have drawn freely from my earlier teaching, research, and writing, especially from articles originally written for *The New Yorker*. My boundless thanks, as ever, to my editor there, Henry Finder. Readers of the magazine may recognize the ghosts of old magazine essays haunting these pages, brought to life in new form and for an altogether different purpose—and with endnotes clattering after them like chains.

Jon Durbin at Norton asked me if I would write this book and I thought he was crazy but I'm glad he asked. Thanks as well to Tina Bennett, for cheering me on. Peter Pellizzari, Thera Webb, and Sean Lavery checked facts, saving me from many an error. Janet Byrne copyedited with peerless care and judiciousness. The amazing Pembroke Herbert compiled illustrations; Rebecca Karamehmedovic tracked down permissions. Marie Pantojan and Don Rifkin at Norton miraculously kept everything on track. The passion and wisdom of my editor at Norton, Robert Weil, are without rival.

Abiding thanks to dear friends: Adrianna Alty, Elise Broach, Jane Kamensky, Elisabeth Kanner, Lisa Lovett, Liz McNerney, Bruce Schulman, Rachel Seidman, and Denise Webb. Paul and Doris Leek have become my own parents. And to Gideon, Simon, Oliver, and Tim Leek: love, everlasting.

# NOTES

## A Note about the Notes

This book draws on innumerable primary sources and a sprawling scholarly literature. I have tried both to identify my chief sources and to keep citations brief. I have favored citing primary sources over secondary literature. Full titles appear only at the initial citation. For well-known speeches and public documents that are easily available online—for example, inaugural addresses, nomination acceptance speeches, party platforms, and online editions of manuscript collections—I have generally provided a citation but not a URL. In instances where I have drawn on research I conducted for essays written for *The New Yorker*, I have provided citations to my original sources rather than to the essays.

### Introduction: THE QUESTION STATED

1. *New-York Packet*, October 30, 1787.
2. September 12, 1787, *The Records of the Federal Convention of 1787*, ed. Max Farrand, 3 vols. (New Haven, CT: Yale University Press, 1911), 2:588.
3. "An Old Whig IV," [Philadelphia] *Independent Gazetteer*, October 27, 1787.
4. James Madison to William Eustis, July 6, 1819, in *The Papers of James Madison*, Retirement Series, ed. David B. Mattern, J. C. A. Stagg, Mary Parke Johnson, and Anne Mandeville Colony, 12 vols. (Charlottesville: University of Virginia Press, 2009), 1:478–80.
5. *New-York Packet*, October 30, 1787.
6. Ibid.
7. Michael Holler, *The Constitution Made Easy* (n.p.: The Friends of Freedom, 2008).
8. Benjamin Franklin, "Observations on Reading History," May 9, 1731, in *The Papers of Benjamin Franklin* (hereafter *PBF*), online edition at Franklinpapers.org.
9. David Hume, "An Enquiry Concerning Human Understanding [1748]," *Essays and Treatises on Various Subjects* (Boston: J. P. Mendum, 1868), 54.
10. For example, Ross Douthat, "Who Are We?," *New York Times* [hereafter *NYT*], February 4, 2017.
11. Thucydides, *History of the Peloponnesian War*, Book I, ch. 1; Herodotus, *The Essential Herodotus*, translation, introduction, and annotations by William A. Johnson (New

York: Oxford University Press, 2017), 2; Ibn Khaldûn, *The Muqaddimah: An Intro-duction to History*, trans. Franz Rosenthal (1967; Princeton, NJ: Princeton University Press, 2005), 5.

12. Sir Walter Ralegh, *The Historie of the World* (London: Walter Burre, 1614), 4.

13. Thomas Paine, *Common Sense* (Philadelphia: R. Bell, 1776), 17, 12. James Madison, Federalist No. 14 (1787).

14. Paine, *Common Sense*, 18.

15. Carl Degler, *Out of Our Past: The Forces That Shaped Modern America* (New York: Harper & Brothers, 1959), xi.

16. The letter was originally published as James Baldwin, "A Letter to My Nephew," *The Progressive*, January 1, 1962; a revision appears in James Baldwin, *The Fire Next Time* (1963; New York: Vintage International, 1993), 3–5.

17. Ibid.

## *One:* THE NATURE OF THE PAST

1. Christopher Columbus, *The* Diario *of Christopher Columbus's First Voyage to America, 1492–1493, Abstracted by Fray Bartolomé de Las Casas*, transcribed and translated by Oliver Dunn and James E. Kelly Jr. (Norman: University of Oklahoma Press, 1989); Las Casas, summarizing a passage by Columbus, wrote "vireon gente desnuda" ("they saw naked people"); I have changed this to "we saw naked people," which, as is supposed, is what Columbus wrote. On the history of the diary, see Samuel E. Morison, "Texts and Translations of Columbus's of the Journal of Columbus's First Voyage," *Hispanic American Historical Review* 19 (1939): 235–61.

2. Columbus, *Diario,* 63–69.

3. Columbus, "The Admiral's Words [c. 1496]," in Ramón Pané, *An Account of the Antiquities of the Indians* [1498], ed. José Juan Arrom, trans. Susan C. Griswold (Durham, NC: Duke University Press, 1999), appendix.

4. Pané, *Antiquities of the Indians*, 3.

5. Ibid., introduction.

6. Ibid., 3, 11–12, 17.

7. Ibid., 20.

8. Gonzalo Fernández de Oviedo, *Historia General y Natural de las Indias*, as excerpted in *1492: Discovery, Invasion, Encounter: Sources and Interpretations*, ed. Marvin Lunefeld (1529; Lexington, MA: D.C. Heath and Company, 1991), 152–53.

9. Pané, *Antiquities of the Indians*, 31.

10. David A. Zinniker, Mark Pagani, and Camille Holmgren, "The Stable Isotopic Composition of Taxon-Specific Higher Plant Biomarkers in Ancient Packrat Middens: Novel Proxies for Seasonal Climate in the Southwest US," *Geological Society of America* 39 (2007): 271.

11. Charles Darwin, *On the Origin of Species by Means of Natural Selection*, 4th ed. (London, 1866), 375.

12. On the debate over population figures, see Charles C. Mann, *1491: New Revelations of the Americas before Columbus* (New York: Knopf, 2005), 92–96, 132–33.

13. Useful sources include *Handbook of North American Indians* (Washington, DC: Smithsonian Institution, 1978, 2008); Alvin M. Josephy Jr., *America in 1492: The World of the Indian Peoples before the Arrival of Columbus* (New York: Vintage Books, 1991); and Daniel K. Richter, *Facing East from Indian Country: A Native History of Early America* (Cambridge, MA: Harvard University Press, 2001).

14. Irving Rouse, *The Tainos: Rise and Decline of the People Who Greeted Columbus* (New Haven, CT: Yale University Press, 1992).

15. Broadly, see Charles Maier, *Once within Borders: Territories of Power, Wealth, and Belonging since 1550* (Cambridge, MA: Harvard University Press, 2016).

16. George Bancroft, *The Necessity, the Reality, and the Promise of the Progress of the Human Race* (New York: New York Historical Society, 1854), 29.

17. On the native peoples of North America, see Daniel K. Richter, *Before the Revolution: America's Ancient Pasts* (Cambridge, MA: Harvard University Press, 2011). On Zheng He, see, for example, Louise Levathes, *When China Ruled the Seas: The Treasure Fleet of the Dragon Throne, 1405–1433* (New York: Simon & Schuster, 1994). On the Maya, see Inga Clendinnen, *Ambivalent Conquests: Maya and Spaniard in Yucatan, 1517–1570* (New York: Cambridge University Press, 1987). On West Africans, see John Thornton, *Africa and Africans in the Making of the Atlantic World, 1400–1680* (New York: Cambridge University Press, 1992).

18. Samuel Purchas, *Purchas His Pilgrimage; Or, Relations of Man . . . from the Creation unto This Present* (London, 1614).

19. Samuel Purchas, "A Discourse of the diversity of Letters used by the divers Nations in the World," in *Hakluytus Posthumus, or Purchas His Pilgrimes*, 20 vols. (Glasgow: James MacLehose & Sons, 1905), 1:486.

20. *Diario*, 63–69.

21. Stephen Greenblatt, *Marvelous Possessions: The Wonder of the New World* (Chicago: University of Chicago Press, 1991), ch. 3.

22. See Tzvetan Todorov, *The Conquest of America: The Question of the Other*, trans. Richard Howard (New York: Harper and Row, 1984).

23. Quoted in J. H. Elliott, *The Old World and the New, 1492–1650* (1970; New York: Cambridge University Press, 1992), 10.

24. Amerigo Vespucci, *Mundus Novus: Letter to Lorenzo Pietro di Medici*, trans. George Tyler Northrup (Princeton, NJ: Princeton University Press, 1916), 1.

25. Sir Thomas More, *Utopia*, ed. Edward Surtz (New Haven, CT: Yale University Press, 1964). On the traveler's voyage with Vespucci, see 12–13.

26. Isidore of Seville, *The Etymologies of Isidore of Seville*, translated and introduced by Stephen A. Barney et al. (New York: Cambridge University Press, 2006), introduction.

27. John R. Hébert, "The Map That Named America," *Library of Congress Information Bulletin* 62 (September 2003).

28. Quoted in Eric Williams, *Capitalism and Slavery* (Chapel Hill: University of North Carolina Press, [1944] 1994), 4.

29. Pané, *Antiquities of the Indians*, 35.

30. All of these numbers are estimates and all are contested. On European migration, a useful introduction is Bernard Bailyn, *The Peopling of British America: An Introduction* (New York: Knopf, 1986). For African numbers, see David Eltis, *The Rise of African Slavery in the Americas* (New York: Cambridge University Press, 2000), a study of the Voyages Database: Estimates, *Voyages: The Trans-Atlantic Slave Trade Database*, http://www.slavevoyages.org, accessed June 2, 2017. For the continuing controversy over indigenous population, see, for example, Jeffrey Ostler, "Genocide and American Indian History," *Oxford Research Encyclopedia of American History* (New York: Oxford University Press, 2016).

31. Quoted in Elliott, *The Old World and the New*, 76.

32. Elliott, *The Old World and the New*, 59–61; Adam Smith, *An Inquiry into the Nature and Causes of the Wealth of Nations*, 3 vols. (1776; New York: Collier, 1902), 2:394. On the rise of capitalism, see Joyce Appleby, *The Relentless Revolution: A History of Capitalism* (New York: Norton, 2010). On the long history of slavery, see David Brion Davis, *The Problem of Slavery in Western Culture* (Ithaca, NY: Cornell University Press, 1966), and David Brion Davis, *Inhuman Bondage: The Rise and Fall of Slavery in the New World* (New York: Oxford University Press, 2006).

33. Thornton, *Africa and Africans in the Making of the Atlantic World*, chs. 3 and 4.

34. Columbus, *Diario*, 75.

35. On the environmental consequences of 1492, see Alfred W. Crosby, *The Columbian Exchange: Biological Consequences of 1492* (Westport, CT: Greenwood, 1972), and

Alfred W. Crosby, *Ecological Imperialism: Biological Expansion of Europe, 900–1900* (Cambridge: Cambridge University Press, 1986). The quotation is from Crosby, *Ecological Imperialism,* 166.

36. Quoted in Crosby, *Ecological Imperialism,* 175.

37. Crosby, *Ecological Imperialism,* ch. 9.

38. David J. Weber, *The Spanish Frontier in North America* (New Haven, CT: Yale University Press, 1992), 1–4.

39. Quoted in Crosby, *Ecological Imperialism,* 215, 208.

40. Aristotle, *Politics,* Book One, parts 1, 3–7. And, broadly, see Anthony Pagden, *Spanish Imperialism and the Political Imagination* (New Haven, CT: Yale University Press, 1990), ch. 1; Lewis Hanke, *The Spanish Struggle for Justice in the Conquest of America* (Philadelphia: University of Pennsylvania Press, 1949); James Muldoon, *Popes, Lawyers, and Infidels: The Church and the Non-Christian World, 1250–1550* (Philadelphia: University of Pennsylvania Press, 1979); and James Muldoon, *The Americas in the Spanish World Order: The Justification for Conquest in the Seventeenth Century* (Philadelphia: University of Pennsylvania Press, 1994).

41. Antonio de Montesinos, December 21, 1511, Hispaniola, as quoted in Justo L. González and Ondina E. González, *Christianity in Latin America: A History* (New York: Cambridge University Press, 2007), 30. On the relationship between Christianity and human rights, see Samuel Moyn, *Christian Human Rights* (Philadelphia: University of Pennsylvania Press, 2015). Moyn writes: "Without Christianity, our commitment to the moral equality of human beings is unlikely to have come about, but by itself this had no bearing on most forms of political equality—whether between Christians and Jews, whites and blacks, civilized and savage, or men and women" (6).

42. The Requerimiento, 1513, in *Major Problems in American Indian History: Documents and Essays,* ed. Albert L. Hurtado and Peter Iverson (Boston: Houghton Mifflin, 2001), 58.

43. Miguel León-Portilla, *The Broken Spears: The Aztec Accounts of the Conquest of Mexico* (1962; Boston: Beacon Press, 2006), 137.

44. Weber, *The Spanish Frontier in North America,* 14–17.

45. Bartolomé de Las Casas, *A Short Account of the Destruction of the Indies,* ed. and trans. Nigel Griffin (1552; New York: Penguin Books, 1992).

46. Lewis Hanke reconstructs the debate in *All Mankind Is One: A Study of the Disputation between Bartolomé de Las Casas and Juan Ginés de Sepúlveda in 1550 on the Intellectual and Religious Capacity of the American Indians* (DeKalb: Northern Illinois University Press, 1974). For the arguments made by Las Casas and Sepúlveda, see Bartolomé de Las Casas, *In Defense of the Indians,* ed. and trans. Stafford Poole (1542; DeKalb: Northern Illinois University Press, 1974), and Juan Ginés de Sepúlveda, *Democrates Alter: Or, On the Just Causes for War Against the Indians* (1544).

47. Richard Hakluyt (the Younger), "Discourse of Western Planting," 1584, in *Envisioning America: English Plans for the Colonization of North America, 1580–1640,* ed. Peter C. Mancall (Boston: Bedford Books, 1995), 45–61.

48. Constance Jordan, "Woman's Rule in Sixteenth-Century British Political Thought," *Renaissance Quarterly* 40 (1987): 421–51; Natalie Zemon Davis, "Women on Top," in *Society and Culture in Early Modern France* (Stanford, CA: Stanford University Press, 1975), 124–51.

49. Ken MacMillan, *Sovereignty and Possession in the English New World: The Legal Foundations of Empire, 1576–1640* (New York: Cambridge University Press, 2006), 82.

50. On this triangulation, see Jill Lepore, *The Name of War: King Philip's War and the Origins of American Identity* (New York: Knopf, 1998), 9.

51. See Stephen Greenblatt and Peter G. Platt, eds., *Shakespeare's Montaigne: The Florio Translation of the Essays: A Selection* (New York: New York Review of Books, 2014); on Ralegh reading Montaigne, see Alfred Horatio Upham, *The French Influence on English Literature from the Accession of Elizabeth to the Restoration* (New York: Columbia University Press, 1908), 289–93.

52. Michel Montaigne, *The Complete Essays of Montaigne*, trans. Donald M. Frame (Palo Alto, CA: Stanford University Press, 1965), 80, 152.

53. Quoted in Karen Kupperman, *Roanoke: The Abandoned Colony* (Totowa, NJ: Rowman and Allanheld, 1984), 17. See also Kathleen Donegan, *Seasons of Misery: Catastrophe and Colonial Settlement in Early America* (Philadelphia: University of Pennsylvania Press, 2014), ch. 1.

## *Two:* THE RULERS AND THE RULED

1. Gregory A. Waselkov, "Indian Maps of the Colonial Southeast," in *Powhatan's Mantle: Indians of the Colonial Southeast*, ed. Waselkov et al. (Lincoln: University of Nebraska Press, 2006), 453–57.

2. James Stuart, *The True Law of Free Monarchies* in *The Political Works of James I*, ed. Charles Howard McIlwain (Cambridge, MA: Harvard University Press, [1598] 1918), 310. And see Glenn Burgess, "The Divine Right of Kings Reconsidered," *English Historical Review* 107 (1992): 837–61.

3. "The First Charter of Virginia, April 10, 1606," in *The Federal and State Constitutions, Colonial Charters, and Other Organic Laws*, ed. Francis Newton Thorpe, 7 vols. (Washington, DC: U.S. Government Printing Office, 1909), 3:3783. On Jamestown, see James P. Horn, *Adapting to a New World: English Society in the Seventeenth-Century Chesapeake* (Chapel Hill: University of North Carolina Press, 1994), and Karen Kupperman, *The Jamestown Project* (Cambridge, MA: Harvard University Press, 2007).

4. "The First Charter of Virginia, April 10, 1606."

5. Ibid.

6. David Armitage, *The Ideological Origins of the British Empire* (New York: Cambridge University Press, 2000); Linda Colley, *Captives: Britain, Empire and the World, 1600–1850* (London: Jonathan Cape, 2002); David Armitage and Michael J. Braddick, eds., *The British Atlantic World, 1500–1800* (New York: Palgrave Macmillan, 2002).

7. Daniel J. Hulsebosch, "English Liberties Outside England: Floors, Doors, Windows, and Ceilings in the Legal Architecture of Empire," in *The Oxford Handbook of Law and Literature, 1500–1700*, ed. Lorna Hutson (Oxford: Oxford University Press, 2017), ch. 38.

8. John Locke in *Second Treatise of Government and a Letter Concerning Toleration*, ed. Mark Goldie (1690; New York: Oxford University Press, 2016), 4, 63.

9. Paine, *Common Sense*, 12.

10. Edward Coke, *The First Part of the Institutes* (1628; London, 1684), 97b. On the process of preparing charters, see Ken MacMillan, *Sovereignty and Possession in the English New World: The Legal Foundations of Empire, 1576–1640* (New York: Cambridge University Press, 2006), 79–86. On Coke, see Daniel J. Hulsebosch, "The Ancient Constitution and the Expanding Empire: Sir Edward Coke's British Jurisprudence," *Law and History Review* 21 (2003): 439–82. For a dissenting view on Coke's contribution to the 1606 charter, see Mary S. Bilder, "Charter Constitutionalism: The Myth of Edward Coke and the Virginia Charter," *North Carolina Law Review* 94 (2016): 1545–98, especially 1558–60.

11. John Smith, *Complete Works of Captain John Smith*, ed. Philip L. Barbour, 2 vols. (Chapel Hill: University of North Carolina Press, 1986), 1:lviii. I discuss Smith and the Jamestown colony in *The Story of America: Essays on Origins* (Princeton, NJ: Princeton University Press, 2012), ch. 1.

12. Kupperman, *The Jamestown Project*, 58, 64–68.

13. John Smith, *Captain John Smith*, ed. James Horn (New York: Penguin Group, 2007), 44.

14. Ibid., 42; Smith, *Complete Works*, 1:207.

15. Edmund S. Morgan, *American Slavery, American Freedom: The Ordeal of Colonial Virginia* (New York: Norton, 1975), chs. 3 and 4.

16. Morgan, *American Slavery, American Freedom*, 78.

17. *A True Declaration of the Estate of the Colonie in Virginia* (London, 1610), 11.

18. Smith, *Complete Works*, 2:128–29.

19. Smith, *Captain John Smith*, 1100–1101; Smith, *Complete Works*, 1:xlv.

20. Thomas Hobbes, *Leviathan* (1651; Oxford: Clarendon Press, 1909), 96–97. On Hobbes and the Virginia Company, see Noel Malcolm, "Hobbes, Sandys, and the Virginia Company," in *Aspects of Hobbes* (New York: Oxford University Press, 2002), 53–79.

21. Morgan, *American Slavery, American Freedom*, 108–9, 158–59.

22. Martha McCartney, "Virginia's First Africans," *Encyclopedia Virginia*, Virginia Foundation for the Humanities, July 5, 2017.

23. Sowande' M. Mustakeem, *Slavery at Sea: Terror, Sex and Sickness in the Middle Passage* (Urbana: University of Illinois Press, 2016), introduction and ch. 5 (quotation, 117). Also see Marcus Rediker, *The Slave Ship: A Human History* (New York: Viking, 2007).

24. Samuel Morison, introduction to William Bradford, *Of Plymouth Plantation, 1620–1647* (New York: Knopf, 1952), xxvi–xxvii.

25. Bradford, *Of Plymouth Plantation*, 3, chs. 9 and 10.

26. Stephen Church, *King John: And the Road to Magna Carta* (New York: Basic Books, 2015), 21.

27. Quoted in Nicholas Vincent, ed., *Magna Carta: A Very Short Introduction* (Oxford: Oxford University Press, 2012), 15–16. And on the general question, see R. C. van Caenegem, *The Birth of the English Common Law* (Cambridge: Cambridge University Press, 1973), 2–3.

28. Vincent, *Magna Carta*, 12.

29. David Carpenter, *Magna Carta* (New York: Penguin, 2015), 252.

30. Quoted in Carpenter, *Magna Carta*, ch. 7.

31. Church, *King John*, 148; Carpenter, *Magna Carta*, 81; Nicholas Vincent, ed., *Magna Carta: The Foundation of Freedom, 1215–2015* (London: Third Millennium Publishing, 2015), 61–63.

32. Church, *King John*, 210.

33. Magna Carta, 1215, in G. R. C. Davis, *Magna Carta* (London: British Museum, 1963), 23–33.

34. Quoted in *The [Cobbett's] Parliamentary History of England*, ed. William Cobbett and J. Wright, 36 vols. (London, 1806–20), 2:357.

35. On this transformation, see Leonard W. Levy, *The Palladium of Justice: Origins of Trial by Jury* (Chicago: I. R. Dee, 1999); John H. Langbein, *Torture and the Law of Proof* (1977; Chicago: University of Chicago Press, 2006); Paul R. Hyams, "Trial by Ordeal: The Key to Proof in the Early Common Law," in *On the Laws and Customs of England: Essays in Honor of Samuel E. Thorne*, ed. Morris S. Arnold et al. (Chapel Hill: University of North Carolina Press, 1981); Robert Bartlett, *Trial by Fire and Water: The Medieval Judicial Ordeal* (Oxford: Clarendon Press, 1986).

36. Barbara J. Shapiro, "The Concept 'Fact': Legal Origins and Cultural Diffusion," *Albion* 26 (1994): 227–52; Barbara J. Shapiro, *A Culture of Fact: England, 1550–1720* (Ithaca, NY: Cornell University Press, 2000). See also Lorraine Daston, "Marvelous Facts and Miraculous Evidence in Early Modern Europe," *Critical Inquiry* 18 (1991): 93–124; Mary Poovey, *A History of the Modern Fact: Problems of Knowledge in the Sciences of Wealth and Society* (Chicago: University of Chicago Press, 1998); Lorraine Daston, "Strange Facts, Plain Facts, and the Texture of Scientific Experience in the Enlightenment," in *Proof and Persuasion: Essays on Authority, Objectivity, and Evidence* ([Tournai]: Brepols, 1996), 42–59.

37. James I, Speech in the Star Chamber, June 20, 1616, in J. R. Tanner, *Constitutional Documents of the Reign of James I: 1603–1625* (Cambridge: Cambridge University Press, 1960), 19.

38. Vincent, *Magna Carta*, 4, 90. Vincent, *Magna Carta: The Foundation of Freedom*, 108.

39. John Winthrop, *A Modell of Christian Charity* (Boston: Massachusetts Historical Soci-

ety, [1630] 1838), 31–48. See also Edmund S. Morgan, *The Puritan Dilemma: The Story of John Winthrop* (Boston: Little, Brown, 1958).

40. Quoted in Karen Kupperman, *Providence Island, 1630–1641: The Other Puritan Colony* (New York: Cambridge University Press, 1993), 18.

41. Winthrop, *A Modell of Christian Charity*; Edward Winslow, *Good News from New England*, ed. Kelly Wisecup (1624; Amherst: University of Massachusetts Press, 2014), 114; John Winthrop, February 26, 1638, *Winthrop's Journal "History of New England," 1630–1649*, ed. James Kendall Hosmer (New York: Scribner, 1908), 260. On the conversion mission, see Lepore, *The Name of War*. On New England and slavery, see Wendy Warren, *New England Bound: Slavery and Colonization in Early America* (New York: Liveright, 2016).

42. John Harpham, "The Intellectual Origins of American Slavery," PhD thesis, Harvard University, 2018, ch. 2.

43. Quoted in Harpham, "Intellectual Origins of American Slavery," 28, 32.

44. Harpham, "Intellectual Origins of American Slavery," 34.

45. Quoted in Vincent Brown, *The Reaper's Garden: Death and Power in the World of Atlantic Slavery* (Cambridge, MA: Harvard University Press, 2008), 5. For slavery, broadly, see also Davis, *The Problem of Slavery in Western Culture*; Winthrop Jordan, *White over Black: American Attitudes toward the Negro, 1550–1812* (Chapel Hill: University of North Carolina Press, 1968); Peter Kolchin, *American Slavery 1619–1877* (New York: Hill and Wang, 1993); Ira Berlin, *Many Thousands Gone: The First Two Centuries of Slavery in North America* (Cambridge, MA: Harvard University Press, 1998).

46. Quoted in Stanley Engerman, Seymour Drescher, and Robert Paquette, eds., *Slavery* (New York: Oxford University Press, 2001), 105–13.

47. Quoted in A. Leon Higginbotham Jr., *Shades of Freedom: Racial Politics and Presumptions of the American Legal Process* (New York: Oxford University Press, 1996), 18–27.

48. Annette Gordon-Reed, *The Hemingses of Monticello: An American Family* (New York: Norton, 2008), 45.

49. "Massachusetts Body of Liberties of 1641," in *The Colonial Laws of Massachusetts*, ed. W. H. Whitmore (Boston, 1890), clause 91 on 53.

50. Edmund S. Morgan, *Inventing the People: The Rise of Popular Sovereignty in England and America* (New York: Norton, 1988), chs. 3 and 4.

51. Ibid., 72–87.

52. John Milton, *Areopagitica: A Speech of Mr. John Milton for the Liberty of Unlicens'd Printing, to the Parliament of England* (London, 1644), 30.

53. Roger Williams to the Town of Providence, January 15, 1655, in *The Complete Writings of Roger Williams*, 7 vols. (New York: Russell and Russell, 1963), 6:278–79.

54. William Penn, *The Frame of the Government of the Province of Pennsilvania* [sic] *in America* (London, 1682), 11.

55. Although the *Second Treatise* was not published until 1689–90, Locke wrote parts of it in or around 1682, including the chapter "Of Property," at a time when he was revising *The Fundamental Constitutions of Carolina*. David Armitage, "John Locke, Carolina, and the 'Two Treatises of Government,'" *Political Theory* 32 (2004): 602–27.

56. "Charter of Carolina and Fundamental Constitutions of Carolina," in *The Federal and State Constitutions, Colonial Charters, and Other Organic Laws*, 5:2743, 2783–84.

57. Armitage, "John Locke, Carolina, and the 'Two Treatises of Government.'"

58. Sir Thomas More, *Utopia*, ed. Edward Surtz (New Haven, CT: Yale University Press, 1964), 76.

59. Armitage, "John Locke, Carolina, and the 'Two Treatises of Government.'" And, broadly, see also John Dunn, *The Political Thought of John Locke: An Historical Account of the Argument of* Two Treatises of Government (Cambridge: Cambridge University Press, 1969), and Jeremy Waldron, *God, Locke, and Equality: Christian Foundations of John Locke's Political Thought* (Cambridge: Cambridge University Press, 2002).

60. *Great Newes from the Barbadoes, or, A True and Faithful Account of the Grand Conspiracy of the Negroes Against the English* (London: Printed for L. Curtis, 1676), 9–10; Nathaniel Saltonstall, *A New and Further Narrative of the State of New-England* (London, 1676), 71–74; Lepore, *The Name of War*, 167–68. And see also Stephen Saunders Webb, *1676: The End of American Independence* (New York: Knopf, 1984).

61. Christine Daniels, "'Without Any Limitacon of Time': Debt Servitude in Colonial America," *Labor History* 36 (1995): 232–50.

62. Quoted in Berlin, *Many Thousands Gone*, 97.

63. Mary Beth Norton, *In the Devil's Snare: The Salem Witchcraft Crisis of 1692* (New York: Knopf, 1998), quotations on 58–59.

64. "A Full and Particular Account of the Negro Plot in Antigua," *New-York Weekly Journal*, March 28, April 4, April 11, April 18, April 25, 1737. And see David Barry Gaspar, *Bondmen and Rebels: A Study of Master-Slave Relations in Antigua* (Durham, NC: Duke University Press, 1993), 3–62. I discuss some of these episodes and write, broadly, on fears of Indian wars and slave rebellions and their influence on the origins of American politics in Jill Lepore, *New York Burning: Liberty, Slavery, and Conspiracy in Eighteenth-Century Manhattan* (New York: Knopf, 2005).

65. *New-York Weekly Journal*, March 28, 1737; *Pennsylvania Gazette*, October 19 and 20, 1738.

66. Quoted in Alan Taylor, *American Colonies* (New York: Viking, 2001), 238.

67. On Stono, see Peter Wood, *Negroes in Colonial South Carolina from 1670 through the Stono Rebellion* (New York: Norton, 1974); Peter Charles Hoffer, *Cry Liberty: The Great Stono River Slave Rebellion of 1739* (New York: Oxford University Press, 2010); Jack Shuler, *Calling Out Liberty: The Stono Slave Rebellion and the Universal Struggle for Human Rights* (Jackson: University Press of Mississippi, 2009).

68. "An Act for the Better Ordering and Governing Negroes," 1740, in David J. McCord, ed., *The Statutes at Large of South Carolina*, 22 vols. (Columbia, SC: A. S. Johnston, 1840), 7:397.

69. Most usefully, see Charles E. Clark, *The Public Prints: The Newspaper in Anglo-American Culture, 1665–1740* (New York: Oxford University Press, 1994).

70. On Jane Franklin, and on her relationship with her brother, see Carl Van Doren, *Jane Mecom, the Favorite Sister of Benjamin Franklin* (New York: Viking, 1950), and Jill Lepore, *Book of Ages: The Life and Opinions of Jane Franklin* (New York: Knopf, 2013). Much of their correspondence is reproduced in *The Letters of Benjamin Franklin and Jane Mecom*, ed. Carl Van Doren (Princeton, NJ: Princeton University Press, 1950), but here I instead cite the online *PBF*. Van Doren refers to Jane Franklin throughout, by her married name, Jane Mecom; but for clarity I here refer to her throughout as Jane Franklin.

71. Cotton Mather quoted in J. A. Leo Lemay, *The Life of Benjamin Franklin*, 3 vols. (Philadelphia: University of Pennsylvania Press, 2006), 1:114. And see Perry Miller, introduction to *The New-England Courant: A Selection of Certain Issues* (Boston: Academy of Arts and Sciences, 1956), 5–9; and Thomas C. Leonard, *The Power of the Press: The Birth of American Political Reporting* (New York: Oxford University Press, 1986), ch. 1.

72. John Trenchard and Thomas Gordon, *Cato's Letters: Or, Essays on Liberty*, 4 vols. (4th ed.; London: W. Wilkins et al., 1737), Letter No. 15, 1:96.

73. Benjamin Franklin, "Apology for Printers," *Pennsylvania Gazette*, June 10, 1731.

74. Hobbes, *Leviathan*, 64.

75. Lepore, *New York Burning*, preface. My brief discussion here of Zenger's trial and the 1741 slave conspiracy follows this earlier, book-length account of these same two signal events.

76. Ibid., xii–xvii.

77. Ibid., ch. 4.

78. Ibid., xii–xvi.

79. Ibid., xi–xii, 89–90.

80. Benjamin Franklin to Richard Partridge, May 9, 1754, and The Albany Plan of Union, 1754, *PBF*. See also Taylor, *American Colonies*, 424–28.

81. Benjamin Franklin, "A Proposal for Promoting Useful Knowledge," May 14, 1743, *PBF*.

82. Alexander Hamilton, *Gentleman's Progress: The Itinerarium of Dr. Alexander Hamilton, 1744*, ed. Carl Bridenbaugh (Pittsburgh: University of Pittsburgh Press, 1948), 199.

83. Quoted in Albert David Belden, *George Whitefield, the Awakener* (New York: Macmillan, 1953), 4–5.

84. Gilbert Tennent, *A Solemn Warning to the Secure World, from the God of Terrible Majesty* (Boston, 1735), 102.

85. Benjamin Franklin, "Observations concerning the Increase of Mankind, Peopling of Countries, &c.," 1751, *PBF*.

86. Benjamin Franklin, *The Autobiography of Benjamin Franklin*, *PBF*.

## *Three:* OF WARS AND REVOLUTIONS

1. Benjamin Lay, *All Slave-Keepers* (Philadelphia: B. Franklin, 1738), 16, 61, 271.

2. "To be SOLD, by Benjamin Lay," advertisement, *American Weekly Mercury*, October 19, 1732. And on Lay's reading practices, see Marcus Rediker, *The Fearless Benjamin Lay: The Quaker Dwarf Who Became the First Revolutionary Abolitionist* (Boston: Beacon Press, 2017), ch. 5.

3. Lay, *All Slave-Keepers*, 21.

4. Roberts Vaux, *Memoirs of the Lives of Benjamin Lay and Ralph Sandiford: Two of the Earliest Public Advocates for the Emancipation of the Enslaved Africans* (Philadelphia, 1815), 1–55. Rediker, *Fearless Benjamin Lay*, 2.

5. Advertisement for *All Slave-Keepers* ["Sold by B. Franklin"], *American Weekly Mercury*, September 7, 1738.

6. *New York Gazette*, January 29, 1750. *Boston Gazette*, November 13, 1753. *Pennsylvania Gazette*, July 8, 1754. *Maryland Gazette*, February 6, 1755. *Virginia Gazette*, August 27, 1756.

7. Franklin, *Autobiography*.

8. Benjamin Franklin, Last Will and Testament, April 28, 1757, *PBF*. On Franklin and slavery, see David Waldstreicher, *Runaway America: Benjamin Franklin, Slavery, and the American Revolution* (New York: Hill and Wang, 2004), and Gary B. Nash, "Franklin and Slavery," *Proceedings of the American Philosophical Society* 150 (2006): 618–35. Benjamin Franklin to Deborah Franklin, June 10, 1758, *PBF*. Rediker, *Fearless Benjamin Lay*, 121–23.

9. [Benjamin Rush], "An Account of Benjamin Lay," *Columbian Magazine*, March 1790, reprinted in *Pennsylvania Mercury*, April 29, 1790, and later published in *Dr. Rush's Literary, Moral, and Philosophical Essays* (1798).

10. Vaux, *Memoirs*, 51.

11. Anthony Benezet, *Observations on the Inslaving, Importing and Purchasing of Negroes* (Germantown, PA: Christopher Sower, 1759), 7.

12. Quoted in John Mack Faragher et al., *Out of Many: A History of the American People*, 2nd ed., 2 vols. (Upper Saddle River, NJ: Prentice Hall, 2000), 1:90.

13. Quoted in Jane Kamensky, *A Revolution in Color: The World of John Singleton Copley* (New York: Norton, 2016), 52.

14. Quoted in Kamensky, *Revolution in Color*, 65; emphasis in original.

15. Franklin, *Autobiography*.

16. Ibid.

17. Fred Anderson, *A People's Army: Massachusetts Soldiers and Society in the Seven Years' War* (Chapel Hill: University of North Carolina Press, 1984), 111–20.

18. Quoted in James T. Kloppenberg, *Toward Democracy: The Struggle for Self-Rule in European and American Thought* (New York: Oxford University Press, 2016), 295.

19. *The Debates in the Several State Conventions on the Adoption of the Federal Constitution*, ed. Jonathan Elliot, 5 vols. (Philadelphia: J. B. Lippincott Company, 1901), 1:443. Pinckney's human property is listed on an inventory from 1787: https://www.nps.gov/chpi/planyourvisit/upload/African_Americans_at_Snee_Farm.pdf.

20. King George quoted in Gordon Wood, *The Radicalism of the American Revolution* (New York: Vintage Books, 1991), 14. See also Fred Anderson, *Crucible of War: The Seven Years' War and the Fate of Empire in British North America, 1754–1766* (New York: Knopf, 2000). For more on the empire-wide context, see David Armitage and Sanjay Subrahmanyam, eds., *The Age of Revolutions in Global Context, c. 1760–1840* (New York: Palgrave Macmillan, 2010); Eliga H. Gould, *Among the Powers of the Earth: The American Revolution and the Making of a New World Empire* (Cambridge, MA: Harvard University Press, 2012); P. J. Marshall, *The Making and Unmaking of Empires: Britain, India, and America c. 1750–1783* (New York: Oxford University Press, 2005).

21. Benjamin Franklin, *Poor Richard's Almanack* (Philadelphia: B. Franklin, 1737).

22. James Otis to the Boston Town Meeting, 1763, quoted in James Grahame, *The History of the Rise and Progress of the United States*, 4 vols. (London: Smith, Elder and Co., 1836), 4:447.

23. Delaware prophet Neolin, in James Kenny journal entry, December 12, 1762, in "Journal of James Kenny, 1761–1763," ed. John W. Jordan, *Pennsylvania Magazine of History and Biography* 37 (1913): 175.

24. Broadly, see Carolyn Webber and Aaron Wildavsky, *A History of Taxation and Expenditure in the Western World* (New York: Simon & Schuster, 1986).

25. Samuel Adams, "Instructions of the Town of Boston to its Representatives in the General Court, May 1764," in *The Writings of Samuel Adams*, ed. Harry Alonzo Cushing, 4 vols. (New York: Putnam, 1904), 1:5.

26. Benjamin Franklin, *Poor Richard's Almanack for 1757, PBF.*

27. Richard Ford, "Imprisonment for Debt," *Michigan Law Review* 25 (1926): 24–25. Bruce Mann, *Republic of Debtors: Bankruptcy in the Age of American Independence* (Cambridge, MA: Harvard University Press, 2002), 286n8. See also Margot Finn, *The Character of Credit: Personal Debt in English Culture, 1740–1914* (New York: Cambridge University Press, 2003), 110.

28. Edwin T. Randall, "Imprisonment for Debt in America: Fact and Fiction," *Mississippi Valley Historical Review* 39 (June 1952): 89–102; George Philip Bauer, "The Movement Against Imprisonment for Debt in the United States," PhD dissertation, Harvard University, 1935.

29. Quoted in Kamensky, *Revolution in Color*, 99.

30. T. H. Breen, *Tobacco Culture: The Mentality of the Great Tidewater Planters on the Eve of Revolution* (Princeton, NJ: Princeton University Press, 1985), esp. chs. 4 and 5.

31. Smith, *The Wealth of Nations*, 3:322–23. See also Trevor Burnard, *Planters, Merchants, and Slaves: Plantation Societies in British America, 1650–1820* (Chicago: University of Chicago Press, 2015).

32. Smith, *The Wealth of Nations*, 3:245.

33. *Boston Gazette*, October 14, 1765.

34. Benjamin Franklin to David Hall, February 14, 1765, *PBF.*

35. *Journal of the First Congress of the American Colonies, in Opposition to the Tyrannical Acts of the British Parliament. Held at New York, October 7, 1765* (New York, 1845), 28.

36. Bauer, "The Movement Against Imprisonment for Debt," 77.

37. *The Examination of Doctor Benjamin Franklin, before an August Assembly, relating to the Repeal of the Stamp Act, &c.* (Philadelphia, 1766).

38. Donna Spindel, "The Stamp Act Crisis in the British West Indies," *Journal of American Studies* 11 (1977): 214–15. And, broadly, see Andrew Jackson O'Shaughnessy, *An Empire Divided: The American Revolution and the British Caribbean* (Philadelphia: University of Pennsylvania Press, 2000), and Selwyn H. H. Carrington, *The British West Indies during the American Revolution* (Providence, RI: Foris, 1988).

39. Quoted in O'Shaughnessy, *Empire Divided*, 153.

40. John Adams diary, January 2, 1766, Adams Family Papers, Massachusetts Historical Society (hereafter AFP); O'Shaughnessy, *Empire Divided*, 99.

41. Kender Mason to the Treasury, December 22, 1765, T 1/452/291–294, National Archives (Kew), London, England. With thanks to Peter Pellizzari.

42. Quoted in T. R. Clayton, "Sophistry, Security, and Socio-Political Structures in the American Revolution; or Why Jamaica Did Not Rebel," *Historical Journal* 29 (1986): 328.

43. James Otis, *The Rights of the British Colonies Asserted and Proved* (Boston: Edes and Gill, 1764), 43–44.

44. Benjamin Franklin to John Waring, December 17, 1763, *PBF*; George Mason to George Washington, December 23, 1765, in *The Papers of George Washington*, ed. Philander D. Chase, 24 vols. (Charlottesville: University Press of Virginia, 1987), 7:424–25. And see Philip D. Morgan, "'To Get Quit of Negroes': George Washington and Slavery," *Journal of American Studies* 39 (2005): 414.

45. Lay, *All Slave-Keepers*, 146. Otis, *The Rights of the British Colonies Asserted and Proved*, 4.

46. Jane Franklin to Benjamin Franklin, April 2, 1789, *PBF*.

47. Jane Franklin to Benjamin Franklin, December 1, 1767, *PBF*.

48. John Adams diary, November 11, 1766, AFP.

49. Benjamin Franklin to Jane Franklin, March 1, 1766, *PBF*.

50. *Journals of the House of Representatives of Massachusetts*, 50 vols. (Boston: Massachusetts Historical Society, 1974), 43:xii.

51. Jane Franklin to Benjamin Franklin, November 7, 1768, *PBF*; "Boston Town Meeting Instructions to its Representatives in the General Court," May 15, 1770, in Record Commissioners of the City of Boston, *Boston Town Records*, 1770–1777 (Boston: Rockwell and Churchill, 1887), 26; O'Shaughnessy, *Empire Divided*, 51.

52. Samuel Cooke, *A Sermon Preached at Cambridge* (Boston, 1770), 42; James Warren to John Adams, June 22, 1777, in *The Papers of John Adams*, ed. Robert J. Taylor, 18 vols. (Cambridge, MA: Harvard University Press, 2006), 5:231.

53. "Peter Bestes and Other Slaves Petition for Freedom, April 20, 1773," in Howard Zinn, *Voices of a People's History of the United States* (New York: Seven Stories Press, 2004), 55; *Virginia Gazette*, September 30, 1773.

54. Noah Feldman, *The Three Lives of James Madison: Genius, Partisan, President* (New York: Random House, 2017), 9–12, 18.

55. Morgan, "'To Get Quit of Negroes,'" 410.

56. George Washington to Robert Mackenzie, October 10, 1774, in *The Writings of George Washington*, ed. John C. Fitzpatrick, 39 vols. (Washington, DC: U.S. Government Printing Office, 1931–44), 3:246.

57. Feldman, *Three Lives of James Madison*, 19.

58. Patrick Henry quoted in John Adams Diary 22A, "Notes of Debates in the Continental Congress," September 6, 1774, AFP.

59. The Petition of Jamaica to the King, *London Gazette*, December 1775.

60. Address to the Assembly of Jamaica, July 25, 1775, Journals of the Continental Congress; Samuel Johnson, *Taxation No Tyranny: An Answer to the Resolutions and Address of the American Colonies* (London, 1775), 89; Johnson's toast is quoted in Kamensky, *Revolution in Color*, 323; Rush is quoted in Peter A. Dorsey, *Common Bondage: Slavery as Metaphor in Revolutionary America* (Knoxville: University of Tennessee Press, 2009), 105.

61. Peter Edes, *A Diary of Peter Edes* (Bangor, ME: Samuel Smith, 1837).

62. Jane Franklin to Benjamin Franklin, May 14, 1775, *PBF*.

63. Benjamin Franklin to Jane Franklin, June 17, 1775, *PBF*.

64. James Madison to William Bradford, June 19, 1775, quoted in Feldman, *Three Lives of James Madison*, 24.

65. Douglas B. Chambers, *Murder at Montpelier: Igbo Africans in Virginia* (Jackson: University of Mississippi Press, 2005), 9–10.
66. Morgan, "'To Get Quit of Negroes,'" 411.
67. Cassandra Pybus, *Epic Journeys of Freedom: Runaway Slaves of the American Revolution and Their Global Quest for Liberty* (Boston: Beacon Press, 2006), 218.
68. Lund Washington to George Washington, December 3, 1775, in *The Papers of George Washington*, 2:477–82; Pybus, *Epic Journeys*, 11.
69. Pybus, *Epic Journeys*, 212.
70. Edward Rutledge to Ralph Izard, December 8, 1775, in *Correspondence of Mr. Ralph Izard* (New York, 1884), 165.
71. Maya Jasanoff, *Liberty's Exiles: American Loyalists in the Revolutionary World* (New York: Knopf, 2011), 8.
72. Paine, *Common Sense*, ii, 17, 12.
73. Thomas Paine, "The Forester's Letters, III: 'To Cato'" in *The Writings of Thomas Paine*, ed. Moncure Daniel Conway, 4 vols. (New York: G. P. Putnam's Sons, 1894), 1:151; Paine, *Common Sense*, 31–32.
74. Paine, *Common Sense*, 2–3.
75. Feldman, *Three Lives of James Madison*, 26–7.
76. The first draft: *The Papers of George Mason*, 3 vols. (Chapel Hill: University of North Carolina Press, 1970), 1:277. The final draft: *Papers of George Mason*, 1:287; "Have the effect of abolishing": quoted in Gary B. Nash, *The Unknown American Revolution: The Unruly Birth of Democracy and the Struggle to Create America* (New York: Penguin Books, 2006), 11.
77. Abigail Adams to John Adams, March 31, 1776, and John Adams to Abigail Adams, April 14, 1776, AFP.
78. John Dickinson, Draft of the Articles of Confederation, June 1776, Historical Society of Pennsylvania.
79. Jeremy Bentham, "Short Review of the Declaration," in David Armitage, *The Declaration of Independence: A Global History* (Cambridge, MA: Harvard University Press, 2007), 173. And see David Armitage, *Foundations of Modern International Thought* (New York: Cambridge University Press, 2013), ch. 10.
80. On the Declaration, see Carl Becker, *The Declaration of Independence: A Study in the History of Political Ideas* (New York, 1922); Pauline Maier, *American Scripture: Making the Declaration of Independence* (New York: Knopf, 1997); Armitage, *The Declaration of Independence*.
81. Gary B. Nash, *The Forgotten Fifth: African Americans in the Age of Revolution* (Cambridge, MA: Harvard University Press, 2006), 28.
82. Quoted in David Hackett Fischer, *Liberty and Freedom: A Visual History of America's Founding Ideas* (New York: Oxford University Press, 2004), 87.
83. Pybus, *Epic Journeys*, 8.
84. O'Shaughnessy, *Empire Divided*, 197–98.
85. Holger Hoock, *Scars of Independence: America's Violent Birth* (New York: Crown, 2017), 111.
86. Quoted in Kamensky, *Revolution in Color*, 323.
87. Christopher Gadsden to Samuel Adams, July 6, 1779, in *The Writings of Christopher Gadsden, 1746–1805*, ed. Richard Walsh (Columbia: University of South Carolina Press, 1966), 166.
88. Jasanoff, *Liberty's Exiles*, 5–6, 8, 91–93.
89. "Inspection Roll of Negroes Book No. 2," The Miscellaneous Papers of the Continental Congress, 1774–1789, National Archives, Washington, DC.
90. Joseph Plumb Martin, *A Narrative of a Revolutionary Soldier: The Narrative of Joseph Plumb Martin* (New York: Dover Publications, [1830] 2006), 136; Comte Jean-François-Louis de Clermont-Crèvecoeur, "Journal of the War in America," in *American Campaigns of Rochambeau's Army 1780, 1781, 1782, 1783*, trans. and ed. Howard C. Rice Jr.

and Anne S. K. Brown, 2 vols. (Princeton, NJ: Princeton University Press, 1972), 1:64; Simon Schama, *Rough Crossings: Britain, the Slaves, and the American Revolution* (New York: Ecco, 2006), 155; Nash, *Forgotten Fifth*, 39–43.

91. Henry Wiencek, *An Imperfect God: George Washington, His Slaves, and the Creation of America* (New York: Farrar, Straus and Giroux, 2003), 259; Jasanoff, *Liberty's Exiles*, 88; Nash, *Forgotten Fifth*, 45–47.

92. Marquis de Lafayette to George Washington, February 5, 1783; and Washington to Lafayette, April 5, 1783, in *Writings of George Washington*, 26:300.

93. Quoted in Shane White, *Somewhat More Independent: The End of Slavery in New York City, 1770–1810* (Athens: University of Georgia Press, 2012), 56.

94. Quoted in Eva Sheppard Wolf, *Race and Liberty in the New Nation: Emancipation in Virginia from the Revolution to Nat Turner's Rebellion* (Baton Rouge: Louisiana State University Press, 2006), 54.

95. James Madison to James Madison Sr., March 30, 1782, in *The Papers of James Madison*, 4:127. And see Edwin Wolf, "The Dispersal of the Library of William Byrd of Westover," *Proceedings of the American Antiquarian Society* 68 (1958): 19–106, and Eric Slauter, *The State as a Work of Art: The Cultural Origins of the Constitution* (Chicago: University of Chicago Press, 2009), 48, fig. 6.

96. Feldman, *Three Lives of James Madison*, 50–52. On Henrietta Gardener, see James A. Bear and Lucia C. Stanton, eds., *Jefferson's Memorandum Books, Volume 2: Accounts, with Legal Records and Miscellany, 1767–1826* (Princeton, NJ: Princeton University Press, 2017), 808.

97. "Memoirs of the Life of Boston King," *Methodist Magazine*, May 1798, 209; Jasanoff, *Liberty's Exiles*, 172–75.

98. Jane Franklin to Benjamin Franklin, April 29, 1783, *PBF*.

99. See Christopher Brown, *Moral Capital: Foundations of British Abolitionism* (Chapel Hill: University of North Carolina Press, 2006).

100. *Independent New-York Gazette*, November 29, 1783.

## *Four:* THE CONSTITUTION OF A NATION

1. David O. Stewart, *The Summer of 1787: The Men Who Invented the Constitution* (New York: Simon & Schuster, 2007), ch. 4.

2. James Madison to Thomas Jefferson, May 15, 1787, *Republic of Letters: The Correspondence between Thomas Jefferson and James Madison*, ed. James Morton Smith, 3 vols. (New York: Norton, 1995), 1:477.

3. James Madison, "Origin of the Constitutional Convention," in *The Writings of James Madison*, ed Gaillard Hunt, 9 vols. (New York: G. P. Putnam's Sons, 1900), 2:410–11.

4. Jean Jacques Rousseau, *A Treatise on the Social Compact; or The Principles of Politic Law* (London, 1764), 151.

5. *The Craftsmen* 395 (January 26, 1733): 100.

6. "Letter CCXXI," March 29, 1750, in *The Letters of the Earl of Chesterfield to His Son*, ed. Charles Strachey (London, 1901), 42.

7. Thomas Paine, *Rights of Man: Part the First, Being an Answer to Mr. Burke's Attack on the French Revolution* (London, 1791), 27.

8. Thomas Paine, *Rights of Man: Part the Second, Combining Principle and Practice* (London, 1792), 28.

9. "Constitution of New Hampshire," January 5, 1776, in *The Federal and State Constitutions, Colonial Charters, and Other Organic Laws of the United States*, 4:2452.

10. Thomas Jefferson to Thomas Nelson, May 16, 1776, in *The Papers of Thomas Jefferson*, ed. Julian P. Boyd et al., 60 vols. projected (Princeton, NJ: Princeton University Press, 1950), 1:292–93. And see Francis Cogliano, "'The Whole Object of the Present Controversy': The Early Constitutionalism of Paine and Jefferson," in Simon P. Newman

and Peter S. Onuf, eds., *Paine and Jefferson in the Age of Revolutions* (Charlottesville: University of Virginia Press, 2013), 26–48.

11. John Adams diary entry, June 2, 1775, in *The Diary of John Adams*, ed. L. H. Butterfield, 4 vols. (Cambridge, MA: Harvard University Press, 1962), 3:352; John Adams, "Thoughts on Government," April 1776, in *The Papers of John Adams*, 4:92. See also Pauline Maier, *Ratification: The People Debate the Constitution, 1787–88* (New York: Simon & Schuster, 2010); Linda Colley, "Empires of Writing: Britain, America and Constitutions, 1776–1848," *Law and History Review* 32 (2014): 237–66.

12. The Constitution of Pennsylvania—1776, in *The Federal and State Constitutions, Colonial Charters, and Other Organic Laws*, 5:3082; "Constitution or Form of Government for the Commonwealth of Massachusetts—1780," in *The Federal and State Constitutions, Colonial Charters, and Other Organic Laws*, 3:1888–89.

13. Fisher Ames quoted in Ralph Waldo Emerson, *Essays and Poems* (New York: Harcourt, Brace and Co., 1921), 254.

14. John Adams to James Sullivan, May 26, 1776, in *The Papers of John Adams*, 4:210.

15. "Constitution or Form of Government for the Commonwealth of Massachusetts—1780," in *The Federal and State Constitutions, Colonial Charters, and Other Organic Laws*, 3:1893–1906; The Constitution of Pennsylvania—1776, in *The Federal and State Constitutions, Colonial Charters, and Other Organic Laws*, 5:3084–90.

16. Emilie Piper and David Levinson, *One Minute a Free Woman: Elizabeth Freeman and the Struggle for Freedom* (Salisbury, CT: Upper Housatonic Valley National Heritage Area, 2010).

17. Nash, *The Unknown American Revolution*, 282.

18. Samuel Chase in "Notes of Proceedings in the Continental Congress," July 12, 1776, in *The Papers of Thomas Jefferson*, 1:320–21; Thomas Lynch in "Notes of Debates on the Articles of Confederation, Continued," July 30, 1776, in *The Diary of John Adams*, 2:246; Benjamin Franklin in *The Journals of the Continental Congress, 1774-1789*, ed. Worthington Chauncey Ford et al., 34 vols. (Washington, DC: U.S. Government Printing Office, 1906), July 30, 1776, 6:1080.

19. Smith, *The Wealth of Nations*, 1:86; *The Journals of the Continental Congress*, June 28, 1787, 25:948–49; *The Records of the Federal Convention of 1787*, 1:444.

20. For the prehistory of the convention and origins of the Constitution, see Sean Condon, *Shays's Rebellion: Authority and Distress in Post-Revolutionary America* (Baltimore: Johns Hopkins University Press, 2015).

21. Jane Franklin to Benjamin Franklin, October 12, 1786, *PBF*.

22. Quoted in Feldman, *Three Lives of James Madison*, 82–83, 94.

23. James Madison to Thomas Jefferson, March 18, 1786, in *Republic of Letters*, 1:413. Madison, "Ancient & Modern Confederacies [April–May 1786]," in *The Writings of James Madison*, 2:369–90.

24. James Madison to Thomas Jefferson, August 12, 1786, in *Republic of Letters*, 1:432.

25. "Proceedings of Commissioners to Remedy Defects of the Federal Government," September 11, 1786, in *Documents Illustrative of the Formation of the Union of the American States*, ed. Charles C. Tansill (Washington, DC: U.S. Government Printing Office, 1927), 43.

26. See Jack Rakove, *The Beginnings of National Politics: An Interpretive History of the Continental Congress* (New York: Knopf, 1979).

27. James Madison, "Vices of the Political System of the United States," April 1787, in *The Papers of James Madison*, 9:355.

28. Jane Franklin to Benjamin Franklin, May 22, 1787, *PBF*.

29. Benjamin Franklin to Jane Franklin, May 30, 1787, *PBF*.

30. Ibid.

31. Jane Franklin to Benjamin Franklin, May 22 1787, *PBF*; Lepore, *Book of Ages*, 221, 246.

32. Wiencak, *Imperfect God*, 112–13.

33. On Washington's apotheosis, see Paul K. Longman, *The Invention of George Wash-ington* (Berkeley and Los Angeles: University of California Press, 1988), and François Furstenberg, *In the Name of the Father: Washington's Legacy, Slavery, and the Making of a Nation* (New York: Penguin Press, 2006).

34. *The Records of the Federal Convention of 1787*, 1:18, 19, 30.

35. *The Records of the Federal Convention of 1787*, 1:26; *The Debates in the Several State Conventions on the Adoption of the Federal Constitution*, 5:138; *The Records of the Federal Convention of 1787*, 1:48.

36. *The Records of the Federal Convention of 1787*, 1:133.

37. *The Records of the Federal Convention of 1787*, 2:201; James Madison, Federalist No. 57 (1788).

38. *The Records of the Federal Convention of 1787*, 1:177, 182, 199.

39. Ibid., 1:486.

40. Ibid., 1:134–35.

41. Ibid., 1:183.

42. Benjamin Franklin to Granville Sharp, and to Richard Price, June 9, 1787, *PBF*.

43. *The Records of the Federal Convention of 1787*, 1:596, 587. And see Margo J. Anderson, *The American Census: A Social History* (New Haven, CT: Yale University Press, 2015).

44. Akhil Reed Amar, *America's Constitution: A Biography* (New York: Random House, 2005), 89–98.

45. Feldman, *Three Lives of James Madison*, 156–57.

46. Henry Adams, *The History of the United States of America during the Administration of Thomas Jefferson* (New York, 1891), 2:231–32, and Carl Van Doren, *The Great Rehearsal* (New York: Viking, 1948), 88.

47. Nash, *Forgotten Fifth*, 76–77.

48. *The Records of the Federal Convention of 1787*, 2:364, 371, 415, 222–23.

49. John Dickinson, "Notes for a Speech by John Dickinson (II)," in *Supplement to Max Farrand's The Records of the Federal Convention of 1787*, ed. James H. Hutson (New Haven, CT: Yale University Press, 1987), 158–59. And see David Waldstre-icher, *Slavery's Constitution: From Revolution to Ratification* (New York: Hill and Wang, 2009); John P. Kaminski, ed., *A Necessary Evil?: Slavery and the Debate over the Constitution* (Madison, WI: Madison House, 1995); and François Furstenberg, "Beyond Freedom and Slavery: Autonomy, Virtue, and Resistance in Early Amer-ican Political Discourse," *Journal of American History* [hereafter *JAH*] 89 (2003): 295–1330.

50. *The Records of the Federal Convention of 1787*, 2:641–43.

51. Ibid., 2:648.

52. James Madison, Federalist No. 40 (1788).

53. *The Debates in the Several State Conventions on the Adoption of the Federal Constitu-tion*, 2:200.

54. *The Records of the Federal Convention of 1787*, 2:588; Thomas Jefferson to James Mad-ison, December 20, 1787, in *The Papers of James Madison*, 10:337.

55. *The Papers of John Adams*, 4:87; "Address by Denatus," in Herbert J. Storing, ed., *The Complete Anti-Federalist*, 7 vols. (Chicago: University of Chicago Press, 1981), 5:262. Patrick Henry is in Herbert J. Storing, *What the Anti-Federalists Were For* (Chi-cago: University of Chicago Press, 1981), 54. See also Christopher M. Duncan, *The Anti-Federalists and Early American Political Thought* (DeKalb: Northern Illinois Uni-versity Press, 1995); Albert Furtwangler, *The Authority of Publius: A Reading of the Federalist Papers* (Ithaca, NY: Cornell University Press, 1984); Saul Cornell, *The Other Founders: Anti-Federalism and the Dissenting Tradition in America, 1788–1828* (Chapel Hill: University of North Carolina Press, 1999).

56. Luther Martin, *Genuine Information*, delivered to the Maryland legislature on Novem-ber 29, 1787, printed in *The Records of the Federal Convention of 1787*, 3:197. And see Nash, *Forgotten Fifth*, 77.

57. James Madison, Federalist No. 54 (1788).

58. Jane Franklin to Benjamin Franklin, November 9, 1787, *PBF*.

59. "A Plebeian: An Address to the People of the State of New York," April 17, 1788, in *The Documentary History of the Ratification of the Constitution*, Commentaries on the Constitution, ed. John P. Kaminski, Gaspare J. Saladino, et al., 29 vols. (Madison: The State Historical Society of Wisconsin, 1995), 17:149; *The Debates in the Several State Conventions on the Adoption of the Federal Constitution*, 3:44.

60. James Wilson in *Pennsylvania Gazette*, July 9, 1788. North Carolina rejected the Constitution in 1788 but ratified it at a second convention in November 1789, and Rhode Island eventually gave its consent to the nation's new frame of government in May of 1790, by which time the government was already in place.

61. *Independent Gazetteer* [Philadelphia], August 7, 1788; *New-Jersey Journal*, August 13, 1788; *Essex Journal* [Newburyport, Massachusetts], August 6, 1788.

62. Louis Torres, "Federal Hall Revisited," *Journal of the Society of Architectural Historians* 29 (1970): 327–38.

63. *The Records of the Federal Convention of 1787*, 2:653; The Constitution of Pennsylvania, September 28, 1776, in *The Federal and State Constitutions, Colonial Charters, and Other Organic Laws*, 5:3085. And see Michael Schudson, *The Rise of the Right to Know: Politics and the Culture of Transparency, 1945–1975* (Cambridge, MA: Harvard University Press, 2015), 5. By the mid-1790s, the doors of the Senate were open, too.

64. U.S. Senate Journal, 1st Cong., 1st Session, April 30, 1789, 18–19.

65. Robert Darnton, *George Washington's False Teeth* (New York: Norton, 2003), ch. 1; and Morgan, "'To Get Quit of Negroes,'" 421–22.

66. *The Records of the Federal Convention of 1787*, 2:659; Amendments to the Constitution, in *The Papers of James Madison*, 12:209. And, broadly, see Akhil Reed Amar, *The Bill of Rights: Creation and Reconstruction* (New Haven, CT: Yale University Press, 1998).

67. Alexander Hamilton, Federalist No. 78 (1788).

68. I. N. Phelps Stokes, *The Iconography of Manhattan Island, 1498–1909*, 6 vols. (New York, 1915), 1:368, 377, 380.

69. U.S. Senate Journal, 1st Cong., 1st Session, February 12, 1790, 157; U.S. House Journal, 1st Cong., 1st Session, March 23, 1790, 180.

70. Vincent Carretta, *Equiano, the African: Biography of a Self-Made Man* (Athens: University of Georgia Press, 2005), 231; Schama, *Rough Crossings*, 322.

71. Pybus, *Epic Journeys of Freedom*, 150, 182; Schama, *Rough Crossings*, 310–11, 328, 390, 394–95; Jasanoff, *Liberty's Exiles*, 300–3.

72. U.S. House Journal, 1st Cong., 1st Session, March 23, 1790, 180.

73. Benjamin Franklin to Jane Franklin, July 1, 1789, *PBF*.

74. Benjamin Franklin, "To the Editor of the Federal Gazette," March 23, 1790, in *Memoirs of the Life and Writings of Benjamin Franklin* (London, 1818), 406.

75. Thomas Jefferson, "A Bill for Establishing Religious Freedom" in *The Papers of Thomas Jefferson*, 2:545–46; James Madison, "A Memorial and Remonstrance Against Religions Assessments," ca. June 20, 1785, in *The Papers of James Madison*, 8:299.

76. "The Fundamental Orders of Connecticut, 1638–39," in *The Federal and State Constitutions, Colonial Charters, and Other Organic Laws*, 1:519. And, broadly, see Frank Lambert, *The Founding Fathers and the Place of Religion in America* (Princeton, NJ: Princeton University Press, 2003).

77. Bauer, "The Movement Against Imprisonment for Debt," 90–91.

78. Alexander Hamilton to John Jay, November 13, 1790, in *The Papers of Alexander Hamilton*, ed. Harold C. Syrett, 27 vols. (New York: Columbia University Press, 1963), 7:149.

79. Thomas Jefferson to Pierre Samuel Du Pont de Nemours, April 15, 1811, *The Papers of Thomas Jefferson*, Retirement Series, ed. J. Jefferson Looney, 14 vols. (Princeton, NJ: Princeton University Press, 2006), 3:560.

80. James Grant Wilson, *John Pintard, Founder of the New York Historical Society* (New York: Printed for the Society, 1902), 17; David L. Sterling, "William Duer, John Pintard, and the Panic of 1792," in Joseph R. Frese and Jacob Judd, eds., *Business Enterprise in Early New York* (Tarrytown, NY: Sleepy Hollow Press, 1979), 99–132; Robert Sobel, *Panic on Wall Street: A Classic History of America's Financial Disasters with a New Exploration of the Crash of 1987* (New York: Truman Talley Books/Dutton, 1988), 17–19, 28; James Ciment, "In the Light of Failure: Bankruptcy, Insolvency and Financial Failure in New York City, 1790–1860," PhD dissertation, City University of New York, 1992, 42, 160.

81. Page Smith, *James Wilson, Founding Father, 1742–1798* (Chapel Hill: University of North Carolina Press, 1956), ch. 15.

82. George W. Johnston, "John Pintard," typescript biographical essay dated January 16, 1900, Pintard Papers, New-York Historical Society, Box 3, in a folder titled "Notes on John Pintard and Governor Clinton."

83. *The Complete Writings of Thomas Paine*, ed. Philip S. Foner, 2 vols. (New York: Citadel Press, 1969), 1:286, 344, 404–5; Paine, *Rights of Man: Part the First*, 76; John Keane, *Tom Paine: A Political Life* (Boston: Little Brown, 1995), xiii.

84. Donald R. Hickey, "America's Response to the Slave Revolt in Haiti, 1791–1806," *Journal of the Early Republic* 2 (1982): 361–79.

85. Declaration of the Rights of Man, 1789, Article 1.

86. *The Complete Writings of Thomas Paine*, 1:464, 599.

87. Hickey, "America's Response to the Slave Revolt in Haiti, 1791–1806," 361–79; Tim Matthewson, "Abraham Bishop, 'the Rights of Black Men,' and the American Reaction to the Haitian Revolution," *Journal of Negro History* 67 (1982): 148–54. And see C. L. R. James, *The Black Jacobins: Toussaint L'Ouverture and the San Domingo Revolution* (New York: Dial Press, 1938); Robin Blackburn, "Haiti, Slavery, and the Age of the Democratic Revolution," *William and Mary Quarterly* 63 (2006): 643–74; Laurent Dubois, *Avengers of the New World: The Story of the Haitian Revolution* (Cambridge, MA: Harvard University Press, 2004).

88. Thomas Jefferson to James Madison, February 12, 1799, in *Republic of Letters*, 2:1095.

89. James Madison, Federalist No. 10 (1787).

90. James Madison, "Public Opinion," *National Gazette*, December 19, 1791.

91. Jeffrey L. Pasley, *"The Tyranny of Printers": Newspaper Politics in the Early American Republic* (Charlottesville: University Press of Virginia, 2001), 33 and Appendix 2.

92. Marcus Daniel, *Scandal and Civility: Journalism and the Birth of American Democracy* (New York: Oxford University Press, 2009), 8.

93. *Connecticut Bee*, October 1, 1800. And see Eric Burns, *Infamous Scribblers: The Founding Fathers and the Rowdy Beginnings of American Journalism* (New York: Public Affairs, 2006), 14.

94. Thomas Jefferson to James Madison, February 5, 1799, in *The Papers of Thomas Jefferson*, 31:10.

95. Washington's Farewell Address, 1796. And see Matthew Spalding, "George Washington's Farewell Address," *Wilson Quarterly* 20 (1996): 65–71.

96. Nash, *Forgotten Fifth*, 62–65.

97. Morgan, "'To Get Quit of Negroes,'" 403–5; Nash, *Forgotten Fifth*, 66.

98. Schama, *Rough Crossings*, 390–95; Pybus, *Epic Journeys*, 202; Cassandra Pybus, "Mary Perth, Harry Washington, and Moses Wilkinson: Black Methodists Who Escaped from Slavery and Founded a Nation," in Alfred F. Young, Gary B. Nash, and Ray Raphael, eds., *Revolutionary Founders: Rebels, Radicals, and Reformers in the Making of the Nation* (New York: Knopf, 2011), 168; Janet Polasky, *Revolutions without Borders: The Call to Liberty in the Atlantic World* (New Haven, CT: Yale University Press, 2015), 109; Jasanoff, *Liberty's Exiles*, 305.

99. Slauter, *The State as a Work of Art*, 297–99.

### Five: A DEMOCRACY OF NUMBERS

1. John Adams to Thomas Jefferson, December 6, 1787, *The Adams-Jefferson Letters*, ed. Lester J. Cappon, 2 vols. (Chapel Hill: University of North Carolina Press, 1959), 1:213–14.
2. Ibid., 213.
3. Quotations from James E. Lewis Jr., "'What Is to Become of Our Government?': The Revolutionary Potential of the Election of 1800," in James J. Horn, Jan Ellen Lewis, and Peter S. Onuf, eds., *The Revolution of 1800: Democracy, Race, and the New Republic* (Charlottesville: University of Virginia Press, 2002), 10–11, 19, 13–14.
4. John Adams, *A Defense of the Constitutions of Government of the United States of America*, 3 vols. (London, 1787), 3:299.
5. Thomas Jefferson, "II. The Response," February 12, 1790, *The Papers of Thomas Jefferson*, 16:179.
6. Adams, *A Defense of the Constitutions*, 1:iii.
7. Benjamin Franklin, "Advice to a Young Tradesman," 1748, *PBF*.
8. Adams, *A Defense of the Constitutions*, 1:preface.
9. *The Records of the Federal Convention of 1787*, 3:166.
10. *The Records of the Federal Convention of 1787*, 2:57, 29.
11. On numbers and the census, see Margo J. Anderson, *The American Census: A Social History*, 2nd ed. (1988; New Haven, CT: Yale University Press, 2016); Hyman Alterman, *Counting People: The Census in History* (New York: Harcourt, Brace and World, 1969); Patricia Cline Cohen, *A Calculating People: The Spread of Numeracy in Early America* (Chicago: University of Chicago Press, 1982). On the rise of quantification more broadly, see Theodore M. Porter, *Trust in Numbers: The Pursuit of Objectivity in Science and Public Life* (Princeton, NJ: Princeton University Press, 1995); I. Bernard Cohen, *The Triumph of Numbers: How Counting Shaped Modern Life* (New York: Norton, 2005); and Alfred W. Crosby, *The Measure of Reality: Quantification and Western Society, 1250–1600* (New York: Cambridge University Press, 1997).
12. *Gazette of the United States*, December 15, 1796.
13. John Adams to Elbridge Gerry, December 6, 1777, in *The Papers of John Adams*, 5:346.
14. "Resolutions Adopted by the Kentucky General Assembly," November 10, 1798, in *The Papers of Thomas Jefferson*, 30:554.
15. Thomas Pickering to Rufus King, March 12, 1799, in *The Life and Correspondence of Rufus King*, ed. Charles R. King, 6 vols. (New York: G. P. Putnam's Sons, 1895), 2:557; Timothy Dwight, "Triumph of Democracy," January 1, 1801, in James G. Basker, ed., *Amazing Grace: An Anthology of Poems About Slavery, 1660–1810* (New Haven, CT: Yale University Press, 2002), 488.
16. "Letter from Alexander Hamilton, Concerning the Public Conduct and Character of John Adams, Esq., President of the United States," October 24, 1800, in *The Papers of Alexander Hamilton*, 25:186, 190.
17. *Carolina Gazette*, August 14, 1800.
18. Edward J. Larson, *A Magnificent Catastrophe: The Tumultuous Election of 1800* (New York: Free Press, 2007), 185, 171–72; *Federal Observer* [Portsmouth, New Hampshire], May 1, 1800; Thomas Jefferson, *Notes on the State of Virginia* (London, 1787), 265. And see also Susan Dunn, *Jefferson's Second Revolution: The Election Crisis of 1800 and the Triumph of Republicanism* (Boston: Houghton Mifflin, 2004), and John Ferling, *Adams vs. Jefferson: The Tumultuous Election of 1800* (New York: Oxford University Press, 2004).
19. *Aurora*, October 14, 1800.
20. Larson, *A Magnificent Catastrophe*, 134–35.
21. Spencer Albright, *The American Ballot* (Washington, DC: American Council on Public Affairs, 1942), 16; Charles Gross, "The Early History of the Ballot in England," *American Historical Review* 3 (April 1898): 456–63. And see Robert J. Dinkin, *Voting in Pro-*

*vincial America: A Study of Elections in the Thirteen Colonies, 1689–1776* (Westport, CT: Greenwood, 1977), ch. 6.

22. Andrew Robertson and Phil Lampi, "The Election of 1800 Revisited," paper presented at the Annual Meeting of the American Historical Association, Chicago, Illinois, January 9, 2000.

23. Alexander Keyssar, *The Right to Vote: The Contested History of Democracy in the United States* (New York: Basic Books, 2000), 24 and Tables A.1 and A.2.

24. Alexander Hamilton to James A. Bayard, January 16, 1801, in *The Papers of Alexander Hamilton*, 25:319.

25. Quoted in Arthur M. Schlesinger Jr., ed., *History of American Presidential Elections, 1789–1968*, 4 vols. (New York: Chelsea House, 1971), 1:111.

26. Schlesinger, *History of American Presidential Elections, 1789–1968*, 129–30.

27. Garry Wills, "'*Negro President': Jefferson and the Slave Power* (Boston: Houghton Mifflin, 2003), 1 (John Quincy Adams is quoted).

28. John Adams to Thomas Jefferson, February 20, 1801, in *The Papers of Thomas Jefferson*, 33:23.

29. *The Mercury and New-England Palladium* [Boston, Massachusetts], January 20, 1801.

30. Quoted in Larson, *A Magnificent Catastrophe*, 274.

31. "Causes of the American Discontents before 1768," *London Chronicle*, January 5–7, 1768, *PBF*.

32. John Adams, *Thoughts on Government: Applicable to the Present State of the American Colonies. In a Letter from a Gentleman to His Friend* (Philadelphia, 1776), in *The Papers of John Adams*, 4:91.

33. Jed Handelsman Shugerman, *The People's Courts: Pursuing Judicial Independence in America* (Cambridge, MA: Harvard University Press, 2012), chs. 1 and 2.

34. "Brutus, Essay 11," *New York Journal*, January 31, 1788. And see Shugerman, *The People's Court*, 25–26.

35. Alexander Hamilton, Federalist No. 78 (1788).

36. Quoted in Suzy Maroon and Fred J. Maroon, *The Supreme Court of the United States* (New York: Thomasson-Grant and Lickle, 1996), 110.

37. Quoted in Clare Cushman, *Courtwatchers: Eyewitness Accounts in Supreme Court History* (Lanham, MD: Rowman and Littlefield, 2011), 2, 5–6.

38. Quoted in Cushman, *Courtwatchers*, 10.

39. Maroon, *Supreme Court*, 173, 20; Cushman, *Courtwatchers*, 16.

40. Quoted in Alexandra K. Wigdor, *The Personal Papers of Supreme Court Justices* (New York: Garland Publishing, 1986), 9.

41. *Marbury v. Madison*, 5 U.S. 137 (1803).

42. Jefferson, *Notes on the State of Virginia*, 274. Thomas Malthus, *An Essay on the Principle of Population* (London, 1798), 346. On Jefferson and Jeffersonianism, see Drew R. McCoy, *The Elusive Republic: Political Economy in Jacksonian America* (New York: Norton, 1980); Gordon Wood, *Empire of Liberty: A History of the Early Republic, 1789–1815* (New York: Oxford University Press, 2009); and Annette Gordon-Reed and Peter S. Onuf, "'Most Blessed of the Patriarchs': Thomas Jefferson and the Empire of the Imagination* (New York: Liveright, 2016).

43. Joyce Appleby, *The Relentless Revolution: A History of Capitalism* (New York: W. W. Norton, 2010), ch. 5.

44. Thomas Jefferson to Wilson Cary Nicholas, September 7, 1803, in *The Papers of Thomas Jefferson*, 41:347. And, broadly, see Steven Hahn, *A Nation Without Borders: The United States and Its World in an Age of Civil Wars, 1830–1910* (New York: Viking, 2016).

45. Thomas Jefferson to Thomas Cooper, February 24, 1804, and to Benjamin Chambers, December 28, 1805, quoted in Drew McCoy, *The Elusive Republic: Political Economy in Jeffersonian America* (Chapel Hill, NC: University of North Carolina Press, 1980), 194, 203.

46. Thomas Jefferson to John Adams, January 21, 1812, *The Papers of Thomas Jefferson*,

4:428; Thomas Jefferson to James Jay, April 7, 1809, *The Papers of Thomas Jefferson*, Retirement Series, 1:110–11.

47. Thomas Jefferson to James Maury, June 16, 1815, in *The Papers of Thomas Jefferson*, Retirement Series, 8:544. On cotton, see Sven Beckert, *Empire of Cotton: A Global History* (New York: Knopf, 2014).

48. *The Constitution of the United States together with An Account of Its Travels Since September 17, 1787*, compiled by David C. Mearns and Verner W. Clapp (Washington, DC: Library of Congress, 1958), 1–17.

49. [Sereno Edwards Dwight], *Slave Representation by Boreas, Awake! O Spirit of the North* (New Haven, CT: 1812), 1.

50. *Slave Representation*, 1. Alan Taylor, *The Civil War of 1812: American Citizens, British Subjects, Irish Rebels, & Indian Allies* (New York: Knopf, 2010); Matthew Mason, "'Nothing Is Better Calculated to Excite Divisions': Federalist Agitation against Slave Representation during the War of 1812," *New England Quarterly* 75 (2002): 531–61.

51. Jefferson, *Notes on the State of Virginia*, 270–71. And see Gordon-Reed, *The Hemingses of Monticello*.

52. Thomas Jefferson to John Norvell, June 11, 1807, in *The Papers of Thomas Jefferson*, 11:222.

53. Thomas Jefferson to Elbridge Gerry, March 29, 1801, in *The Papers of Thomas Jefferson*, 33:491.

54. James Thomas Callender, "The President, Again," *Richmond Recorder*, September 1, 1802.

55. Thomas Jefferson to Francis C. Gray, March 4, 1815, in *The Papers of Thomas Jefferson*, Retirement Series, 8:311. Gordon-Reed, *The Hemingses of Monticello*, 599–600.

56. American Colonization Society, *The Tenth Annual Report of the American Society for Colonizing the Free People of Colour of the United States* (Washington, DC, 1827), 79.

57. Josiah Quincy, *Memoir of the Life of John Quincy Adams* (Boston, 1859), 115.

58. 15 Annals of Cong. 1204 (February 16, 1819).

59. James Madison to Robert Walsh, November 27, 1819, in *The Papers of James Madison*, Retirement Series, 557.

60. 16 Annals of Cong. 228 (January 20, 1820).

61. Gordon-Reed, *Thomas Jefferson and Sally Hemings*, 246. See also Gordon-Reed, *The Hemingses of Monticello*, 557–60.

62. Daniel Raymond, *Thoughts on Political Economy* (Baltimore, 1820), 456. Daniel Raymond, *The Missouri Question* (Baltimore, 1819), 6–7.

63. 16 Annals of Cong. 428 (February 1, 1820); Raymond, *The Missouri Question*, 10.

64. John Quincy Adams diary entry, January 10, 1810, in *The Diaries of John Quincy Adams: A Digital Collection*, 51 vols., Massachusetts Historical Society, 31:245.

65. John Adams to John Quincy Adams, April 23, 1794, in *The Adams Family Correspondence*, ed. Margaret A. Hogan et. al., 13 vols. (Cambridge, MA: Harvard University Press, 2011), 10:151.

66. *The National Journal* [Washington, DC], April 28, 1824.

67. As the constitutional scholar Alexander Bickel once explained, "The populist idea, identified in the American political tradition with Andrew Jackson and in some measure with everyone else ever since, is that the ills of society and its government will be cured by giving a stronger and more certain direction of affairs to a popular majority" (Bickel, "Is Electoral Reform the Answer?," *Commentary*, December 1968, 41). On populism, broadly, see Michael Kazin, *The Populist Persuasion: An American History* (New York: Basic Books, 1995), and Charles Postel, *The Populist Vision* (New York: Oxford University Press, 2007).

68. John Quincy Adams diary entry, June 18, 1833, in *The Diaries of John Quincy Adams*, 39:98.

69. Thomas Jefferson as quoted by Daniel Webster, December 1824, in *The Private*

*Correspondence of Daniel Webster*, ed. Fletcher Webster (Boston: Little, Brown, 1857), 371.

70. Robert L. Brunhouse, ed., "David Ramsay, 1749–1815: Selections from His Writings," *Transactions of the American Philosophical Society* 55 (1965), 27; Frank L. Owsley Jr., "Editor's Introduction" to John Reid and John Henry Eaton, *The Life of Andrew Jackson* (Tuscaloosa: University of Alabama Press, [1974] 2007), v–vii; John Eaton, *The Life of Andrew Jackson: Major General in the Service of the United States* (Philadelphia: M. Carey and Son, 1817); Margaret Bayard Smith, 1828, as quoted in Catherine Allgor, *Parlor Politics: In Which the Ladies of Washington Help Build a City and a Government* (Charlottesville: University Press of Virginia, 2000), 200.

71. John Eaton, *The Life of Andrew Jackson* (Philadelphia: S. F. Bradford, 1824); Owsley, "Editor's Introduction," *The Life of Andrew Jackson*, x (Owsley's annotated edition marks out the changes between the 1817 and 1824 editions). On campaign buttons: M. J. Heale, *The Presidential Quest: Candidates and Images in American Political Culture, 1787–1852* (London: Longman, 1982), 50. On campaigning, broadly: Robert J. Dinkin, *Campaigning in America: A History of Election Practices* (New York: Greenwood, 1989), 42. I also discuss Jackson's campaign biography and its influence in *The Story of America*, ch. 10.

72. Benjamin Austin, *Constitutional Republicanism, in Opposition to Fallacious Federalism* (Boston, 1803), 87.

73. On the rise of the nominating convention: James S. Chase, *Emergence of the Presidential Nominating Convention, 1789–1832* (Urbana, IL: University of Illinois Press, 1973); *National Party Conventions, 1831–1984*, 4th ed. (Washington, DC: Congressional Quarterly Inc., 1987); Stan M. Haynes, *The First American Political Conventions: Transforming Presidential Nominations, 1832–1872* (Jefferson, NC: McFarland, 2012).

74. James Kent quoted in *Reports of the Proceedings and Debates of the Convention of 1821, Assembled for the Purpose of Amending the Constitution of the State of New-York* (Albany, 1821), 221.

75. Quoted in David McCullough, *John Adams* (New York: Simon & Schuster, 2001), 639–40.

76. Quoted in *The Proceedings and Debates of the Virginia State Convention of 1829–30* (Richmond, 1830), 316. And see Daniel Rodgers, *Contested Truths: Keywords in American Politics Since Independence* (New York: Basic Books, 1987), 80–111.

77. George Bancroft, "The Office of the People in Art, Government, and Religion," An Oration Delivered before the Adelphi Society of Williamstown College in August 1835, in Thomas Breed et al., eds., *Modern Eloquence*, 15 vols. (Philadelphia: John D. Morris and Company, 1900), 7:79; George Bancroft, *Oration Delivered on the Fourth of July, 1826, at Northampton, Massachusetts* (Northampton, 1826), 20.

78. *Connecticut Herald*, July 11, 1826.

79. Gordon-Reed, *Hemingses of Monticello*, 655–56, 661–62.

80. Joseph Ellis, *American Sphinx: The Character of Thomas Jefferson* (New York: Knopf, 1997), 287–90; McCullough, *John Adams*, 644–47.

81. John Randolph to John Brockenbrough, January 12, 1829, in *The Collected Letters of John Randolph of Roanoke to Dr. John Brockenbrough*, ed. Kenneth Shorey (1988; New Brunswick, NJ: Transaction Books, 2015), 317.

82. *Alexandria Gazette*, March 4, 1829.

83. Margaret Bayard Smith to Jane Bayard Kirkpatrick, March 11, 1829, in *The First Forty Years of Washington Society Portrayed by the Family Letters of Mrs. Samuel Harrison Smith (Margaret Bayard)*, ed. Gaillard Hunt (New York: Charles Scribner's Sons, 1906), 290–94; Andrew Jackson, "First Annual Message," December 8, 1829, *The American Presidency Project* (online), comp. John T. Woolley and Gerhard Peters; Joseph Story to Mrs. Joseph Story (Sarah Waldo Wetmore), March 7, 1829, in *The Life and Letters of Joseph Story*, ed. William M. Story, 2 vols. (Boston: Charles C. Little and James Brown, 1851), 1:563.

84. Bayard Smith to Bayard Kirkpatrick, March 11, 1829.

### *Six:* THE SOUL AND THE MACHINE

1. Maria W. Stewart, "Religion and the Pure Principles of Morality, The Sure Foundation on Which We Must Build," October 1831, in *Maria W. Stewart: America's First Black Woman Political Writer*, ed. Marilyn Richardson (Bloomington: Indiana University Press, 1987), 40.
2. Richardson, *Maria W. Stewart*, 29, 38. Garrison's impressions of Stewart are recorded in a letter he later wrote in support of her widow's pension application: William Lloyd Garrison to Maria W. Stewart, April 4, 1879, ibid., 89–90.
3. On the Second Great Awakening, see especially Mary P. Ryan, *The Cradle of the Middle Class: The Family in Oneida County, New York, 1790–1865* (New York: Cambridge University Press, 1981), and Daniel Howe, *What Hath God Wrought: The Transformation of America, 1815–1848* (New York: Oxford University Press, 2007).
4. Quoted in Paul Johnson, *A Shopkeeper's Millennium: Society and Revivals in Rochester, New York, 1815–1837*, 1st rev. ed. (New York: Hill and Wang, 2004), 5.
5. Ibid., 3.
6. Maria W. Stewart, "Mrs. Stewart's Farewell Address to Her Friends in the City of Boston," in Richardson, *Maria W. Stewart*, 70.
7. Thomas Jefferson to William Ludlow, September 6, 1824, in *The Writings of Thomas Jefferson*, ed. Andrew A. Lipscomb and Albert Ellery Bergh, 20. vols. (Washington, DC: Thomas Jefferson Memorial Association of the United States, 1903–7), 16:74–76.
8. Jacob Bigelow, *The Useful Arts*, 3 vols. (New York: Harper and Brothers, 1855), 1:18–19.
9. Jeanne Boydston, *Home and Work: Housework, Wages, and the Ideology of Labor in the Early Republic* (New York: Oxford University Press, 1990). See also Alan Dawley, *Class and Community: The Industrial Revolution in Lynn* (Cambridge, MA: Harvard University Press, 1976).
10. George B. Ellenberg, *Mule South to Tractor South: Mules, Machines, and the Transformation of the Cotton South* (Tuscaloosa: University of Alabama Press, 2007), 146.
11. Walter Isaacson, *The Innovators: How a Group of Inventors, Hackers, Geniuses, and Geeks Created the Digital Revolution* (New York: Simon & Schuster, 2014), ch. 1.
12. On the business history, see Robert Dalzell, *Enterprising Elite: The Boston Associates and the World They Made* (Cambridge, MA: Harvard University Press, 1987).
13. Howe, *What Hath God Wrought*, 216–17.
14. Johnson, *A Shopkeeper's Millennium*, 18, 42.
15. Ryan, *Cradle of the Middle Class*, 146–47, 155–58.
16. See Kathryn Kish Sklar, *Catharine Beecher: A Study in American Domesticity* (New Haven, CT: Yale University Press, 1973).
17. Charles Grandison Finney, *Memoirs of Rev. Charles G. Finney* (New York: A. S. Barnes & Company, 1876), 20; Johnson, *A Shopkeeper's Millennium*, 108, 122.
18. Ruth Cowan, *A Social History of American Technology* (New York: Oxford University Press, 1997), 138, 210. And on technological determinism in American politics and culture, broadly, see David Nye, *American Technological Sublime* (Cambridge, MA: MIT Press, 1994); Robert Friedel, *A Culture of Improvement: Technology and the Western Millennium* (Cambridge, MA: MIT Press, 2008); Robert L. Heilbroner, "Do Machines Make History?," *Technology and Culture* 8 (1967): 335–45; Leo Marx, *The Machine in the Garden: Technology and the Pastoral Ideal in America* (New York: Oxford University Press, 1964).
19. Jacob Bigelow, *Elements of Technology* (Boston, 1829); Jacob Bigelow, *An Address on the Limits of Education Read before the Massachusetts Institute of Technology* (Boston: E. P. Dutton & Company, 1865), 4. See also Thomas Misa, *Leonardo to the Internet: Technology and Culture from the Renaissance to the Present* (Baltimore: Johns Hopkins University Press, 2004), 204; Marx, "The Idea of Technology"; Howard P. Segal, *Technological Utopianism in American Culture* (Chicago: University of Chicago Press, 1985), 180–81.

20. Thomas Carlyle, "Signs of the Times," *Edinburgh Review* 49 (June 1829): 457.
21. Timothy Walker, "A Defense of Mechanical Philosophy," *North American Review* 33 (July 1831): 122–27.
22. Quoted in Sean Wilentz, *The Rise of American Democracy: Jefferson to Lincoln* (New York: Norton, 2005), 425.
23. Bancroft quoted in Russel Nye, *George Bancroft: Brahmin Rebel* (New York: Knopf, 1944), 100; Sullivan quoted in *New York Morning News*, February 27, 1845.
24. Stewart, "Religion and the Pure Principles of Morality," October 1831, in Richardson, *Maria W. Stewart*, 39.
25. Quoted in Valerie C. Cooper, *Word, Like Fire: Maria Stewart, the Bible, and the Rights of African Americans* (Charlottesville: University of Virginia Press, 2012), 4.
26. Quoted in Richardson, introduction to *Maria W. Stewart*, 14.
27. Benjamin Rush to John Adams, June 15, 1789, in *The Letters of Benjamin Rush*, ed. L. H. Butterfield, 2 vols. (Princeton, NJ: Princeton University Press, 1951), 1:516.
28. James Madison to the General Assembly of the Commonwealth of Virginia, "A Memorial and Remonstrance," ca. June 20, 1785, in *The Papers of James Madison*, Congressional Series, ed. J. C. A. Stagg et al., 17 vols. (Charlottesville: University of Virginia Press, 2010), 8:301.
29. Article 11, Treaty of Peace and Friendship, signed at Tripoli, November 4, 1796, in *Treaties and Other International Acts of the United States of America*, ed. Hunter Miller, 8 vols. (Washington, DC: U.S. Government Printing Office, 1931–48), 2:365.
30. Stewart, "Cause for Encouragement" in Richardson, *Maria W. Stewart*, 43.
31. Lyman Beecher, "Lecture VII: The Republican Elements of the Old Testament," in *Lectures on Political Atheism and Kindred Subjects* (Boston, 1852), 189.
32. Nathan O. Hatch, *The Democratization of American Christianity* (New Haven, CT: Yale University Press, 1989), 4.
33. Thomas Jefferson to Samuel Kercheval, July 12, 1816, in *The Papers of Thomas Jefferson*, Retirement Series, 10:226.
34. William Lloyd Garrison, "Address to the Colonization Society," July 4, 1829, in *Selections from the Writings and Speeches of William Lloyd Garrison* (Boston: R. F. Wallcut, 1852), 53.
35. Richardson, *Maria W. Stewart*, introduction.
36. Wilentz, *The Rise of American Democracy*, 221; Walter Johnson, *River of Dark Dreams: Slavery and Empire in the Cotton Kingdom* (Cambridge, MA: Harvard University Press, 2013), 41–42, 152–54; Sven Beckert, *Empire of Cotton: A Global History* (New York: Knopf, 2014), ch. 5.
37. Douglas R. Egerton and Robert L. Paquette, eds., *The Denmark Vesey Affair: A Documentary History* (Gainesville: University Press of Florida, 2017). See also Michael P. Johnson, "Denmark Vesey and His Co-Conspirators," *William and Mary Quarterly* 58 (2001): 915–76.
38. Henry Highland Garnet, *Walker's Appeal* (New York: J. H. Tobitt, 1848), vi.
39. *Freedom's Journal*, March 16, 1827.
40. David Walker, *Walker's Appeal in Four Articles; Together with a Preamble, to the Coloured Citizens of the World, but in Particular, and Very Expressly, to Those of the United States of America*, September 28, 1829 (Boston, 1829), 73–74, 18, 66, 55, 47, 28, 21, and 27. See also *David Walker's Appeal to the Coloured Citizens of the World*, ed. Peter P. Hinks (University Park: Pennsylvania State University Press, 2000), introduction. And, on the idea of the "colored citizen," see Stephen Kantrowitz, *More Than Freedom: Fighting for Black Citizenship in a White Republic, 1829–1889* (New York: Penguin Press, 2012), 28–40.
41. *David Walker's Appeal*, ed. Hinks, xiv–xxv.
42. Ibid., xxxix–xl; *The Liberator* [Boston, Massachusetts], January 1, 1831.
43. *The Confessions of Nat Turner with Related Documents*, 2nd ed., ed. Kenneth S. Greenberg (1831; Boston: Bedford/St. Martin's, 2017), 44; James M'Dowell Jr., *Speech of*

*James M'Dowell Jr. (of Rockbridge) in the House of Delegates of Virginia, on the Slave Question* (Richmond: Thomas W. White, 1832), 29.

44. Alexis de Tocqueville, *Democracy in America*, 2 vols. (New York: Knopf, 1956), 2:256.

45. Quoted in Stefan M. Wheelock, *Barbaric Culture and Black Critique: Black Antislavery Writers, Religion, and the Slaveholding Atlantic* (Charlottesville: University of Virginia Press, 2015), ch. 4.

46. William Lloyd Garrison, "Declaration of Sentiments of the American Anti-Slavery Convention, December 6, 1833," in *Selections from the Writings of William Lloyd Garrison*, 70.

47. Catherine Beecher, *An Essay on Slavery and Abolitionism, with Reference to the Duty of American Females* (Philadelphia: Henry Perkins, 1837), 121.

48. Wilentz, *The Rise of American Democracy*, 356–57, 419–20; Howe, *What Hath God Wrought*, 539–40.

49. Wilentz, *The Rise of American Democracy*, 283; Charles Sellers, *The Market Revolution: Jacksonian America, 1815–1846* (New York: Oxford University Press, 1991), 238.

50. Quoted in Carl N. Degler, *Out of Our Past: The Forces That Shaped Modern America*, rev. ed. (New York: Harper and Row, [1959] 1970), 275–76.

51. Quoted in Carl Kaestle, *Pillars of the Republic: Common Schools and American Society, 1780–1860* (New York: Farrar, Straus and Giroux, 2011), 80.

52. Quoted in Daniel Boorstin, *The Americans: The Democratic Experience* (New York: Random House, 1973), 257.

53. Samuel F. B. Morse, *Imminent Dangers to the Free Institutions of the United States through Foreign Immigration* (New York, 1835), 28. And on Morse, see Jill Lepore, *A is for American: Letters and Other Characters in the Newly United States* (New York: Knopf, 2002), ch. 6.

54. Quoted in Daniel J. Czitrom, *Media and the American Mind: From Morse to McLuhan* (Chapel Hill: University of North Carolina Press, 1982), 11–12.

55. Barnet Schecter, *The Devil's Own Work: The Civil War Draft Riots and the Fight to Reconstruct America* (New York: Walker & Company, 2005), 78.

56. On the common school movement, see Kaestle, *Pillars of the Republic*; Ira Katznelson and Margaret Weir, *Schooling for All: Class, Race, and the Decline of the Democratic Ideal* (New York: Basic Books, 1983).

57. Quoted in Kaestle, *Pillars of the Republic*, 163, 139.

58. Ibid., 176, 179.

59. Christopher B. Daly, *Covering America: A Narrative History of a Nation's Journalism* (Amherst, MA: University of Massachusetts Press, 2012), 59–63; Michael Schudson, *Origins of the Ideal of Objectivity in the Professions: Studies in the History of American Journalism and American Law, 1830–1940* (PhD dissertation, 1976; New York: Garland, 1990), 36–40.

60. Tocqueville, *Democracy in America*, 2:42.

61. Joseph Story to Judge Fay, February, 18, 1834, in *The Life and Letters of Joseph Story*, 2:154. Asher Robbins quoted in Michael G. Kammen, *A Machine That Would Go of Itself: The Constitution in American Culture* (1986; New Brunswick, NJ: Transaction Publishers, 2006), 50.

62. Joseph Story, *A Discourse Pronounced at the Request of the Essex Historical Society on the 18th of September, 1828, in Commemoration of the First Settlement of Salem* (Boston: Hilliard, Gray, Little, and Wilkins, 1828), 74–75. On Indian removal see Ronald N. Satz, *American Indian Policy in the Jacksonian Era* (Lincoln: University of Nebraska Press, 1975); Anthony F. C. Wallace, *The Long, Bitter Trail: Andrew Jackson and the Indians* (New York: Hill and Wang, 1993); Theda Perdue, *The Cherokee Nation and the Trail of Tears* (New York: Viking, 2007).

63. "Instructions to a Deputation of Our Warriors . . . to Proceed On and Visit Our Father the President of the United States," Fortville, Cherokee Nation, September 19, 1817, in Walter Lowrie and Walter S. Franklin, eds., *American State Papers, Documents, Leg-*

*islative and Executive, of the Congress of the United States* (Washington, DC: Gale and Seaton, 1834), 145.

64. Quoted in Althea Bass, *Cherokee Messenger* (Norman: University of Oklahoma Press, 1996), 31.

65. On the Cherokees in this era, see William G. McLoughlin, *Cherokee Renascence in the New Republic* (Princeton, NJ: Princeton University Press, 1986). On Sequoyah, see Lepore, *A is for American,* ch. 3.

66. Response of the Cherokee Council to U.S. Commissioners Duncan G. Campbell and James Meriwether, October 20, 1823, in *American State Papers, Documents, Legislative and Executive, of the Congress of the United States,* Indian Affairs, 2 vols. (Washington, DC: Gales and Seaton, 1834), 2:469; U.S. Commissioners to the Cherokee Chiefs, December 9, 1824, in *American State Papers*, Indian Affairs, 2:570; and Cherokee Council to U.S. Commissioners, February 11, 1824, in *American State Papers*, Indian Affairs, 2:474.

67. John Howard Payne, "The Cherokee Cause [1835]," reprinted in the *Journal of Cherokee Studies* 1 (1976): 19.

68. Speech of Senator Theodore Frelinghuysen, April 7–9, 1830, in *Speeches of the Passage of the Bill for the Removal of the Indians, Delivered in the Congress of the United States, April and May, 1830* (Boston: Perkins and Marvin, 1830), 8.

69. *Cherokee Nation v. Georgia*, 30 U.S. 1 (1831), and *Worcester v. Georgia*, 31 U.S. 515 (1832).

70. *An Indian's Appeal to the White Men of Massachusetts* is reprinted in William Apess, *On Our Own Ground: The Writings of William Apess, a Pequot,* ed. by Barry O'Connell (Amherst, MA: University of Massachusetts Press, 1992), 205. And see my discussion of the broader cultural and political context for the Mashpee and Penobscot claims in *The Name of War*, ch. 7.

71. Edward Everett, *An address delivered at Bloody Brook, in South Deerfield, September 30, 1835* (Boston: Russell, Shattuck, & Williams, 1835), 8, 10–11. And see Edward Everett, "The Cherokee Case," *North American Review* 33 (1831): 136–53.

72. Andrew Jackson, First Annual Message, December 8, 1829.

73. Jon Meacham, *American Lion: Andrew Jackson in the White House* (New York: Random House, 2008), 204.

74. Perdue, *The Cherokee Nation and the Trail of Tears*, 139–40. General Winfield Scott, "Extracts from General Orders, or the Address to the Troops," May 17, 1838, in *Memoirs of Lieut.-General Winfield Scott*, ed. Timothy D. Johnson (Knoxville: University of Tennessee Press, 2015), 166.

75. Harriet Martineau, *Retrospect of Western Travel*, 3 vols. (London: Saunders and Otley, 1838), 1:147.

76. Quoted in Kerry S. Walters, *Explosion on the Potomac: The 1844 Calamity Aboard the USS Princeton* (Charleston, SC: The History Press, 2013), 85.

77. Johnson, *River of Dark Dreams*, ch. 10.

78. Wilentz, *The Rise of American Democracy*, 319–22.

79. *Memoirs of General Andrew Jackson Seventh President of the United States* (Auburn, NY: James C. Derby & Co., 1845), 202, 208.

80. Wilentz, *The Rise of American Democracy*, 387, 430.

81. James S. Chase, *Emergence of the Presidential Nominating Convention, 1789–1832* (Urbana: University of Illinois Press, 1973), 27–34.

82. Stan M. Haynes, *The First American Political Conventions: Transforming Presidential Nominations, 1832–1872* (Jefferson, NC: McFarland, 2012), 29.

83. On the Panic of 1837 and the Bank War, see Reginald Charles McGrane, *The Panic of 1837: Some Financial Problems of the Jacksonian Era* (New York: Russell and Russel, Inc., 1924, 1965); Marc Shell, *Money, Language and Thought: Literary and Philosophic Economies from the Medieval to the Modern Era* (Baltimore and London: Johns Hopkins University Press, 1982); and Alasdair Roberts, *America's First Great Depression: Eco-*

*nomic Crisis and Political Disorder after the Panic of 1837* (Ithaca, NY: Cornell University Press, 2012).

84. Wilentz, *The Rise of American Democracy*, 365.

85. *The Correspondence of Nicholas Biddle*, ed. Reginald C. McGrane (Boston: Houghton Mifflin Company, 1919), 93; Wilentz, *The Rise of American Democracy*, 361.

86. Wilentz, *The Rise of American Democracy*, 368, 372.

87. U.S. Senate Journal, 22d Cong., 1st Sess., July 10, 1832.

88. Wilentz, *The Rise of American Democracy*, 398.

89. Robert Sobel, *Panic on Wall Street: A Classic History of America's Financial Disasters* (Washington, DC: Beard Books, [1968, Macmillan], 1999), 38–40, 47.

90. Andrew Jackson, "Fourth Annual Message," December 4, 1832.

91. *Speech of Mr. Kennedy, of Indiana, on the Oregon Question Delivered in the House of Representatives, January 10, 1846* (Washington, 1846), 7. Also quoted in Donald William Meinig, *The Shaping of America: A Geographical Perspective on 500 Years of History, vol. 2: Continental America, 1800–1867*, 4 vols. (New Haven, CT: Yale University Press, 1993), 2:222.

92. Meinig, *The Shaping of America*, 2:135; Hahn, *A Nation Without Borders*, 12. On the War with Mexico, see, Rachel St. John, *Line in the Sand: A History of the Western U.S.-Mexico Border* (Princeton, NJ: Princeton University Press, 2011). And see Patricia Nelson Limerick, *The Legacy of Conquest: The Unbroken Past of the American West* (New York: Norton, 2006), ch. 7.

93. Quoted in Walter R. Borneman, *Polk: The Man Who Transformed the Presidency and America* (New York: Random House, 2008), 73.

94. Donald J. Ratcliffe, "Thomas Morris," *American National Biography Online*; Thomas Morris, *Speech in Reply to the Speech of Henry Clay, February 9, 1839* (New York, 1839).

95. Haynes, *The First American Political Conventions*, 1; Chase, *Emergence of the Presidential Nominating Convention*, 40.

96. Frank E. Hagen and Elmo Scott Watson, "The Origin of Ruckerize," *Cambridge* [MA] *Sentinel*, September 12, 1936.

97. Sobel, *Panic on Wall Street*, 51, 67.

98. Bauer, "The Movement Against Imprisonment for Debt." See also Charles Warren, *Bankruptcy in United States History* (Cambridge, MA: Harvard University Press, 1935); James Ciment, "In the Light of Failure: Bankruptcy, Insolvency and Financial Failure in New York City, 1790–1860"; Edward J. Balleisen, *Navigating Failure: Bankruptcy and Commercial Society in Antebellum America* (Chapel Hill: University of North Carolina Press, 2001).

99. Wilentz, *The Rise of American Democracy*, 492–93.

100. [Richard Hildreth], *The People's Presidential Candidate; or The Life of William Henry Harrison, of Ohio* (Boston, 1839), 14–16, 194. Robert Gray Gunderson, *The Log Cabin Campaign* (Lexington: University of Kentucky Press, 1957), 73–79; 129–33.

101. Quoted in Wilentz, *The Rise of American Democracy*, 547. And see Milton C. Sernett, *North Star Country: Upstate New York and the Crusade for African American Freedom* (Syracuse, NY: Syracuse University Press, 2002), 115.

102. Mary P. Ryan, *Women in Public: Between Banners and Ballots, 1825–1880* (Baltimore: Johns Hopkins University Press, 1990), 134; and see Jo Freeman, *A Room at a Time: How Women Entered Party Politics* (Lanham, MD: Rowman & Littlefield, 2000).

103. Dinkin, *Campaigning in America*, 33.

104. Ralph Waldo Emerson, *The Journals and Miscellaneous Notebooks of Ralph Waldo Emerson*, ed. A. W. Plumstead, Harrison Hayford, et al., 16 vols. (Cambridge, MA: Harvard University Press, 1969), 7:482.

105. "The Telegraph," *New York Sun*, November 6, 1847, in Morse's scrapbook, Samuel Morse Papers, Library of Congress, Washington, DC.

106. Daly, *Covering America*, 77; Daniel Webster, "Opening of the Northern Railroad to Lebanon, N.H. [1847]," in *Works of Daniel Webster*, 11th ed., 6 vols. (Boston: Little Brown, 1858), 2:419.
107. Karl Marx, "Estranged Labour," in *Economic and Philosophic Manuscripts of 1844*, ed. Martin Milligan (1961; New York: Dover Publications, 2007), 69.
108. *Ralph Waldo Emerson: Updated Edition*, ed. Harold Bloom (New York: Chelsea House, 2007), 127.
109. Quoted in James D. Hart, "They All Were Born in Log Cabins," *American Heritage* 7 (1956): 32.
110. Henry David Thoreau, *Walden; or, Life in the Woods* (Boston: Ticknor and Fields, 1854), 118, 54, 118, 57, 102, 107, 58–59.
111. Thoreau, *Walden*, 175, 352; Review of *Walden*, *The New York Churchman*, September 2, 1854.
112. Thoreau, *Walden*, 57.

## Seven: OF SHIPS AND SHIPWRECKS

1. Walters, *Explosion on the Potomac*, 9–10.
2. Quoted in Dan Monroe, *The Republican Vision of John Tyler* (College Station: Texas A&M University Press, 2003), 63.
3. Charles Dickens, *American Notes for General Circulation*, edited and with an introduction by Patricia Ingham (1842; New York: Penguin, 2000), 138.
4. Daniel Webster, "Letter to the Citizens of Worcester County, Massachusetts," January 23, 1844, in *The Writings and Speeches of Daniel Webster*, ed. Edward Everett, National Edition, 18 vols. (Boston: Little, Brown, 1903), 16:423.
5. Quoted in Walters, *Explosion on the Potomac*, 31, 32.
6. Quoted in Jay Sexton, *The Monroe Doctrine: Empire and Nation in Nineteenth-Century America* (New York: Hill and Wang, 2011), 62.
7. "Speech of Mr. McDuffie, July 6, 1844," in *Niles' National Register*, ed. William Ogden Niles, 75 vols. (Baltimore, 1839–48), 66:303. On Greeley, see Daly, *Covering America*, 66–72. And on American expansion in this era, see Hahn, *A Nation Without Borders*, and John Robert Van Atta, *Securing the West: Politics, Public Lands, and the Fate of the Old Republic: 1785–1850* (Baltimore: Johns Hopkins University Press, 2014).
8. John Quincy Adams diary entry, April 22, 1844, in *The Diaries of John Quincy Adams*, 44:303.
9. Henry Clay to Stephen F. Miller, July 1, 1844, in *The Private Correspondence of Henry Clay*, ed. Calvin Colton (Boston: Frederick Parker, 1856), 491.
10. John Quincy Adams diary entry, February 19, 1845, in *The Diaries of John Quincy Adams*, 45:50.
11. "Nuptials of the President of the United States," *New York Herald*, June 27, 1844; Walters, *Explosion on the Potomac*, 105–6.
12. Quoted in Haynes, *The First American Political Conventions*, 70.
13. Haynes, *First American Political Conventions*, 89. And see Charles Sellers, "Election of 1844," in Schlesinger, *History of American Presidential Elections, 1789–1968*, 1:761–66.
14. Speech by Daniel Webster, "On Mr. Foot's Resolution," January 26–27, 1830, Register of Debates, Senate, 21st Cong., 1st Sess. (1830).
15. Joseph Story, *Commentaries on the Constitution of the United States . . . Abridged by the Author for the Use of Colleges and High Schools* (Boston: Hilliard, Gray, and Company, 1833), 595. And see Arnold Bennett, *The Constitution in School and College* (New York: G. P. Putnam's Sons, 1935).
16. Tocqueville, *Democracy in America*, 1:251–52. And, broadly, see Kammen, *A Machine That Would Go of Itself*; Larry D. Kramer, *The People Themselves: Popular Constitu-*

*tionalism and Judicial Review* (Oxford: Oxford University Press, 2004); Daniel Levin, *Representing Popular Sovereignty: The Constitution in American Political Culture* (Albany: State University of New York Press, 1999).

17. William Grimes, *Life of William Grimes, the Runaway Slave* [1825], ed. William L. Andrews and Regina E. Mason (New York: Oxford University Press, 2008), 103.

18. Colley, "Empires of Writing," 237–38.

19. "The Sage of Montpelier Is No More!," *Charleston Courier,* July 7, 1836.

20. David W. Houpt, "Securing a Legacy: The Publication of James Madison's Notes from the Constitutional Convention," *Virginia Magazine of History and Biography* 118 (2010): 4–39.

21. Quoted in Kammen, *A Machine That Would Go of Itself,* 97–100.

22. Quoted in ibid., 103, 83.

23. Hahn, *A Nation Without Borders,* introduction.

24. Webster, "Letter to Citizens of Worcester County, Massachusetts," in *The Writings and Speeches of Daniel Webster,* 16:423.

25. Quoted in Johnson, *River of Dark Dreams,* 322.

26. Eugene McCormac, *James K. Polk: A Political Biography* (Berkeley: University of California Press, 1922), 705. In 1845, a Florida senator had asked Congress to negotiate with Spain for Cuba; while the War with Mexico continued, Congress set this request aside. But by 1848 Polk was writing in his diary, "I am decidedly in favour of purchasing Cuba & making it one of the States of the Union": James K. Polk diary entry, May 10, 1848, in *The Diary of James K. Polk During His Presidency, 1845–1849,* ed. Milo Milton Quaife, Chicago Historical Society Collection, 4 vols. (Chicago: A. C. McClurg & Co, 1910), 3:446. And on southern imperial ambitions, see especially Matthew Karp, *This Vast Southern Empire: Slaveholders at the Helm of American Foreign Policy* (Cambridge, MA: Harvard University Press, 2016).

27. Quoted in Hahn, *A Nation Without Borders,* 122. And see Bernard DeVoto, *The Year of Decision, 1846* (Boston: Little Brown, 1943), and William Ghent, *The Road to Oregon: A Chronicle of the Great Emigrant Trail* (New York: Longmans and Green and Co., 1929).

28. John O'Sullivan, "Annexation," *United States Magazine and Democratic Review* 17 (July–August 1845): 5–10.

29. James K. Polk, "Special Message to Congress on Mexican Relations," May 11, 1846.

30. Daly, *Covering America,* 78–79.

31. Dickens, *American Notes,* 134.

32. Joanne Freeman, "The Field of Blood: Violence in Congress," paper delivered at the Gilder Lehrman Center for the Study of Slavery, Resistance, and Abolition, Yale University, November 4, 2017.

33. Speech by John C. Calhoun, "Conquest of Mexico," 30 Cong. Globe 51 (January 4, 1848).

34. Charles Sumner to Salmon P. Chase, February 7, 1848, Chase Papers, Library of Congress—quoted in James M. McPherson, *Battle Cry of Freedom: The Civil War Era* (New York: Oxford University Press, 1988), 60; Speech of B. R. Wood, "The Wilmot Proviso," 29 Cong. Globe 345 (February 10, 1847), appendix.

35. Quoted in Meinig, *Shaping of America,* 2:300–301.

36. Theodore Parker, *A Sermon of Mexican War, Preached at the Melodeon, on Sunday, June 7, 1846* (Boston: I. R. Butts, 1846), 32, 30.

37. Henry David Thoreau, "Civil Disobedience," in *The Writings of Henry David Thoreau,* ed. Horace Elisha Scudder et al., 11 vols. (Boston: Houghton Mifflin Company, [1863] 1893), 10:141, 149.

38. Ralph Waldo Emerson, "Ode, Inscribed to William H. Channing," in *The Oxford Book of American Poetry,* ed. David Lehman (New York: Oxford University Press, 2006), 35.

39. Maurice S. Lee, ed., *The Cambridge Companion to Frederick Douglass* (New York: Cambridge University Press, 2009), 15.

40. John Stauffer, Zoe Trodd, and Celeste-Marie Bernier, *Picturing Frederick Douglass: An Illustrated Biography of the Nineteenth Century's Most Photographed American* (New York: Liveright, 2015).

41. Frederick Douglass, *Narrative of the Life of Frederick Douglass*, ed. David W. Blight (New York: St. Martin's/Bedford Books in American History, 1993), 16.

42. Daly, *Covering America*, 93.

43. Frederick Douglass, "The War with Mexico," *The North Star*, January 21, 1848.

44. Frederick Douglass, Editorial, *The North Star*, April 28, 1848.

45. Quoted in Czitrom, *Media and the American Mind*, 12.

46. Daly, *Covering America*, 81.

47. Speech by Lewis Cass, 29 Cong. Globe 369 (February 10, 1847).

48. David G. Gutiérrez, *Walls and Mirrors: Mexican Americans, Mexican Immigrants, and the Politics of Ethnicity* (Berkeley: University of California Press, 1995), ch. 1.

49. Rachel St. John, *Line in the Sand: A History of the Western U.S.-Mexico Border* (Princeton, NJ: Princeton University Press, 2011), 21–22.

50. James DeBow, *The Seventh Census of the United States: 1850* (Washington, DC: Robert Armstrong, 1853), xxix.

51. Ralph Waldo Emerson, *Selected Writings of Ralph Waldo Emerson*, ed. William H. Gilman (New York: Signet Classics, 1965), 116.

52. Lynn Hudson Parsons, "The 'Splendid Pageant': Observations on the Death of John Quincy Adams," *New England Quarterly* 53 (December 1980), 464–82.

53. Ralph Waldo Emerson, *Emerson in His Journals*, selected and edited by Joel Porte (Cambridge, MA: Harvard University Press, 1984), 303.

54. "Letter XII: Human Rights Not Founded on Sex," in Angelina Grimké, *Letters to Catherine Beecher, in Reply to an Essay on Slavery and Abolitionism Addressed to A. E. Grimké* (Boston: Isaac Knapp, 1838), 114.

55. Sarah Grimké, *Letters on the Equality of the Sexes, and the Condition of Woman* (Boston: Isaac Knapp, 1838), 11, 45. And see Ellen Carol DuBois, *Feminism and Suffrage: The Emergence of an Independent Women's Movement in America, 1848–1869* (1979; Ithaca, NY: Cornell University Press, 1999).

56. Margaret Fuller, *Woman in the Nineteenth Century* (New York: Greeley & McElrath, 1845), 26.

57. On Fuller, see especially Charles Capper, *Margaret Fuller: An American Romantic Life* (New York: Oxford University Press, 2007), and Megan Marshall, *Margaret Fuller: A New American Life* (New York: Houghton Mifflin Harcourt, 2013).

58. Zachary Taylor to Capt. J. S. Allison, April 22, 1848, in *The Papers of Henry Clay*, ed. Melba Porter Hay, 11 vols. (Lexington: University Press of Kentucky, 1991), 10:343. See also Eric Foner, *Free Soil, Free Labor, Free Men: The Ideology of the Republican Party before the Civil War* (1970; New York: Oxford University Press, 1995).

59. Quoted in Haynes, *First American Political Conventions*, 101.

60. Quoted in ibid., 105.

61. Quoted in Kloppenberg, *Toward Democracy*, 655.

62. Lincoln, Address before the Wisconsin State Agricultural Society, Milwaukee, Wisconsin, September 30, 1859.

63. Quoted in Foner, *Free Soil, Free Labor, Free Men*, 14–16.

64. Quoted in ibid., 72, 45, 41, 46.

65. Frederick Douglass, *The Claims of the Negro, Ethnologically Considered* (Rochester, NY: 1854), 13. And see Randall Fuller, *The Book That Changed America: How Darwin's Theory of Evolution Ignited a Nation* (New York: Viking, 2017), ch. 9.

66. George Fitzhugh, *Sociology for the South, or the Failure of Free Society* (Richmond, VA: A. Morris, 1854), 177, 179, 183, 158.

67. George Fitzhugh, *Cannibals All! or, Slaves Without Masters* (Richmond, VA: A. Morris, 1857), 31, 29. See also Larry E. Tise, *Proslavery: A History of the Defense of Slavery in America, 1701–1840* (Athens: University of Georgia Press, 1987).

68. Salmon P. Chase to Charles Sumner, March 24, 1850, in "The Diary and Correspondence of Salmon P. Chase," Annual Report, American Historical Association (Washington, DC: U.S. Government Printing Office, 1903), 205.

69. *Report of the Woman's Rights Convention, Held at Seneca Falls, N.Y., July 19th and 20th, 1848* (Rochester, NY: John Dick, 1848), 7–9.

70. "Bolting Among the Ladies," *Oneida Whig*, August 1, 1848. And see DuBois, *Feminism and Suffrage*, and Melanie Susan Gustafson, *Women and the Republican Party, 1854–1924* (Urbana: University of Illinois Press, 2001).

71. Capper, *Margaret Fuller*, 505–14.

72. Longfellow to John Greenleaf Whittier, September 6, 1844, in *The Letters of Henry Wadsworth Longfellow*, ed. Andrew Hilen, 6 vols. (Cambridge, MA: Harvard University Press, 19), 3:44.

73. Henry Wadsworth Longfellow Dana, "'Sail On, O Ship of State!': How Longfellow Came to Write These Lines 100 Years Ago," *Colby Library Quarterly* 2 (1950): 209–214. On the relationship between Sumner and Longfellow, see Frederick J. Blue, "The Poet and the Reformer: Longfellow, Sumner, and the Bonds of Male Friendship, 1837–1874," *Journal of the Early Republic* 15 (1995): 273–297, and Jill Lepore, "Longfellow's Ride," in *The Story of America: Essays on Origins*, ch. 15.

74. John Marshall to Joseph Story, September 22, 1832, *Proceedings of the Massachusetts Historical Society*, Second Series, 14 (1950): 352; *Debates and Proceedings of the Constitutional Convention of the State of California*, vol. 3 (Sacramento: J. D. Young, 1881), 1191.

75. Stephen Douglas, Chicago, July 9, 1858, in *Political Debates Between Hon. Abraham Lincoln and Hon. Stephen A. Douglas* (Columbus, OH: Follett, Foster, 1860), 6.

76. Harriet Jacobs, *Incidents in the Life of a Slave Girl* (Boston, 1861), 286.

77. *The Letters of Henry Wadsworth Longfellow*, 4:3.

78. Manisha Sinha, *The Slave's Cause: A History of Abolition* (New Haven, CT: Yale University Press, 2016); Tubman quoted in Eric Foner, *Gateway to Freedom: The Hidden Story of the Underground Railroad* (New York: Norton, 2015), 191.

79. Lee, *Cambridge Companion to Frederick Douglass*, 23.

80. Frederick Douglass, "What to the Slave is the Fourth of July?," July 5, 1852.

81. *The Letters of Stephen A. Douglas*, ed. Robert W. Johannsen (Urbana: University of Illinois Press, 1961), 399.

82. King quoted in Michael S. Green, *Politics and America in Crisis: The Coming of the Civil War* (Santa Barbara, CA: Praeger, 2010), 77. Hamlin quoted in Mark Scroggins, *Hannibal: The Life of Abraham Lincoln's First Vice President* (Lanham, MD: University Press of America, 1994), 107.

83. Samuel F. B. Morse, *The Present Attempt to Dissolve the American Union, a British Aristocratic Plot* (New York, 1862), 38.

84. Samuel F. B. Morse to Sidney Morse, December 29, 1857, in *Samuel F. B. Morse: His Letters and Journals*, ed. Edward Lind Morse, 2 vols. (Boston: Houghton Mifflin, 1914), 2:331.

85. Abraham Lincoln, "Fragment on Slavery," [April 1, 1854], in *The Collected Works of Abraham Lincoln*, 2:222–23; Eric Foner, *The Fiery Trial: Abraham Lincoln and American Slavery* (New York: Norton, 2010); John Stauffer, *Giants: The Parallel Lives of Frederick Douglass and Abraham Lincoln* (New York: Twelve, 2009); Robert Levine, *The Lives of Frederick Douglass* (Cambridge, MA: Harvard University Press, 2016).

86. Gustafson, *Women and the Republican Party*, 1, 24–30.

87. Abraham Lincoln, Peoria Speech, October 16, 1854, in *The Collected Works of Abraham Lincoln*, 2:266, 255, 275, 276.

88. Lincoln, "Fragment on Slavery," [July 1, 1854], in *The Collected Works of Abraham Lincoln*, 2:222–23.

89. Abraham Lincoln to Joshua Speed, August 24, 1855, in *The Collected Works of Abraham Lincoln*, 2:323.

90. Charles Sumner, *The Crime Against Kansas* (Boston, 1856); Longfellow to Sumner, May 28, 1856, *The Letters of Henry Wadsworth Longfellow*, 3:540; Excerpts from Longfellow's Account Books, transcribed from the original account books at the Houghton Library, Harvard University by James M. Shea, Director/Museum Curator, Longfellow National Historic Site, Cambridge, Massachusetts.
91. Quoted in McPherson, *Battle Cry of Freedom*, 150.
92. Quoted in Haynes, *The First American Political Conventions*, 138, 173.
93. Quoted in Gustafson, *Women and the Republican Party*, 20.
94. "President Polk's Diary," *Atlantic Monthly*, August 1895, 237.
95. James Buchanan, Inaugural Address, March 4, 1857.
96. *New York Herald*, March 5, 1857.
97. *Scott v. Sandford*, 60 U.S. 393 (1857).
98. *New York Evening Journal* [Albany, New York], March 7, 1857; *The Liberator*, March 13, 1857; *The National Era* [Washington, DC], March 19, 1857; *The Independent* [New York], March 19, 1857.
99. *Philadelphia Inquirer*, March 5, 1857.
100. Longfellow to Sumner, February 24, 1858, *The Letters of Henry Wadsworth Longfellow*, 4:65.
101. Abraham Lincoln, Speech at Springfield, Illinois, June 26, 1857.
102. Frederick Douglass, "The Dred Scott Decision," Speech delivered before the American Anti-Slavery Society, New York, May 14, 1857, in *Frederick Douglass: Selected Speeches and Writings*, ed. Philip S. Foner; abridged and adapted by Yuval Taylor (Chicago: Lawrence Hill Books, 1999), 347–48, 351, 350.

### *Eight:* THE FACE OF BATTLE

1. Samuel F. B. Morse to Sidney Morse, March 9, 1839, in *Samuel F. B. Morse: His Letters and Journals*, 2:129; and see Stauffer et al., *Picturing Frederick Douglass*.
2. "New Discovery—Engraving, and Burnet's Cartoons," *Blackwood's Edinburgh Magazine* (London, 1839), 384.
3. Quoted in Alan Trachtenberg, *Lincoln's Smile and Other Enigmas* (New York: Hill and Wang, 2007), 27.
4. Horace Traubel, *With Walt Whitman in Camden*, 2 vols. (New York: Mitchell Kennerley, 1915), Wednesday, August 8, 1888, 2:107.
5. Douglass's essays on photography are reprinted in Stauffer et al., *Picturing Frederick Douglass* (quotations, xv, 127, 140–41).
6. Quoted in Trachtenberg, *Lincoln's Smile and Other Enigmas*, 26.
7. *The Liberator*, September 10, 1858; Reverend Dr. Bellows, Speech, in Charles T. McClenachan, *Detailed Report of the Proceedings Had in Commemoration of the Successful Laying of the Atlantic Telegraph Cable, by Order of the Common Council of the City of New York* (New York: Edmund Jones & Co., Corporation Printers, 1863), 244.
8. Samuel F. B. Morse to Norvin Green, July 1855, in *Samuel F. B. Morse: His Letters and Journals*, 2:345.
9. The statistics are from J. Cutler Andrews, "The Southern Telegraph Company, 1861–65: A Chapter in the History of Wartime Communication," *Journal of Southern History* 30 (1964): 319.
10. Rens Bod, *A New History of the Humanities: The Search for Principles and Patterns from Antiquity to the Present* (New York: Oxford University Press, 2013), 34.
11. Kathleen Hall Jamieson, *Presidential Debates: The Challenge of Creating an Informed Electorate* (New York: Oxford University Press, 1988), 40, 21, 78.
12. Caleb Bingham, *The Columbian Orator* (1797; Troy, NY: 1803), 240–42.
13. Frederick Douglass, *My Bondage and My Freedom* (New York, 1855), 89.

14. Dan Monroe and Bruce Tap, *Shapers of the Great Debate on the Civil War: A Biographical Dictionary* (Westport, CT: Greenwood, 2005), 106–7.

15. The correspondence is reprinted in David Henry Leroy, ed., *Mr. Lincoln's Book: Publishing the Lincoln-Douglas Debates* (New Castle, DE: Oak Knoll Press, 2009).

16. Lincoln during the seventh debate, Alton, Illinois, October 15, 1858.

17. Leroy, *Mr. Lincoln's Book*, ch. 1.

18. Quoted in Tony Horwitz, *Midnight Rising: John Brown and the Raid That Sparked the Civil War* (New York: Henry Holt, 2011), 81.

19. *Baltimore Sun*, October 31, 1857, and July 31, 1858.

20. Oregon State Constitution, Article II, Section 6, in *The Constitution of the State of Oregon and Official Register of State, District, and County Officers*, compiled and issued by Frank W. Benson (Salem, OR: Willis S. Duniway, State Printer, 1908), 14.

21. Leonidas W. Spratt, "Report on the Slave Trade, Made to the Southern Convention at Montgomery by L. W. Spratt," *DeBow's Review* 24 (June 1858): 477, 585; Johnson, *River of Dark Dreams*, ch. 14 (quotations, 398, 399).

22. George Fitzhugh, "The Conservative Principle; or, Social Evils and Their Remedies, Part II: The Slave Trade," *DeBow's Review* 22 (1857): 449, 455. See also Johnson, *River of Dark Dreams*, 413.

23. Quoted in Johnson, *River of Dark Dreams*, 291.

24. Freeman, "The Field of Blood."

25. William H. Seward, Speech delivered at Rochester, October 25, 1858. And see Horwitz, *Midnight Rising*, 273.

26. Frederick Douglass, *Life and Times of Frederick Douglass, Written by Himself* (Hartford, CT: Park Publishing Co., 1881), 389.

27. Horwitz, *Midnight Rising*, 142–43, 192, 153.

28. Robert L. Tsai, "John Brown's Constitution," *Boston College Law Review* 51 (2010): Appendix C, 205.

29. Douglass, *Life and Times of Frederick Douglass*, 315. Henry David Thoreau, "A Plea for Captain John Brown," Read to the Citizens of Concord, Massachusetts, October 30, 1859, in Henry David Thoreau, *A Yankee in Canada, with Anti-Slavery and Reform Papers* (Boston: Ticknor and Fields, 1866), 178, 167.

30. Fuller, *The Book That Changed America*, especially ch. 14.

31. Quoted in Horwitz, *Midnight Rising*, 213–15.

32. Samuel Longfellow, *Life of Henry Wadsworth Longfellow, with Extracts from his Journals and Correspondence*, 2 vols. (Boston, 1886), 2:341–42.

33. On "Paul Revere's Ride" as a fugitive slave narrative, see Lepore, "Longfellow's Ride," in *The Story of America*, ch. 15.

34. Quoted in Horwitz, *Midnight Rising*, 256.

35. Reuben Davis, *Speech of the Honorable Reuben Davis on the State of the Union ...* [December 8, 1859] (Washington, DC: 1859), 5–6.

36. Abraham Lincoln, Speech delivered at Cooper Institute, New York City, February 27, 1860, in *The Collected Works of Abraham Lincoln*, 3:544.

37. Leroy, *Mr. Lincoln's Book*, 76.

38. Foner, *Free Soil, Free Labor, Free Men*, 257.

39. Haynes, *The First American Political Conventions*, 173.

40. William Dean Howells, *Life of Abraham Lincoln* (summer 1860; reprint edition, Springfield: Illinois, 1938), v.

41. Howells, *Life of Abraham Lincoln*, 17–18.

42. Ibid., 47.

43. Quoted in Haynes, *President-Making in the Gilded Age: The Nominating Conventions of 1876–1900* (Jefferson, NC: McFarland, 2016), 151–57.

44. *Official Proceedings of the Democratic National Convention, Held in 1860, at Charleston and Baltimore*, prepared and published under the direction of John G. Parkhurst (Cleveland, 1860), 155.

45. Longfellow, *Life of Henry Wadsworth Longfellow*, 2:358.
46. Frederick Douglass, "A Plea for Freedom of Speech in Boston," December 9, 1860, in *Frederick Douglass Papers*, Series One, *Speeches, Debates, and Interviews*, ed. John W. Blassingame et al., 5 vols. (New Haven, CT: Yale University Press, 1979–92), 3:420–24.
47. William W. Freehling, *The Road to Disunion, Volume II: Secessionists Triumphant* (New York: Oxford University Press, 2007), 340, 345.
48. *Journal of the Provisional Congress of the Confederate States of America, 1861–1865*, first of 7 vols. of *Journal of the Congress of the Confederate States of America, 1861–1865* (Washington, DC: U.S. Government Printing Office, 1904–5), 1:7.
49. "The Last Years of Sam Houston," *Harper's New Monthly Magazine*, December 1865–May 1866 (New York: Harper & Brothers, 1866), 634.
50. Longfellow, *Life of Henry Wadsworth Longfellow*, 2:361.
51. Jefferson Davis, Speech in Montgomery, Alabama, February 18, 1861, in *Jefferson Davis: The Essential Writings*, ed. William J. Cooper Jr. (New York: Random House, [2003] 2004), 202.
52. Alexander H. Stephens, "Cornerstone Address," Savannah, Georgia, March 21, 1861, *Macon Telegraph* [Macon, Georgia], March 25, 1861.
53. Abraham Lincoln, First Inaugural Address, March 4, 1861, in *The Collected Works of Abraham Lincoln*, 4:268–69, 272.
54. Douglass, "A Plea for Freedom of Speech in Boston."
55. Stephanie McCurry, *Confederate Reckoning: Power and Politics in the Civil War South* (Cambridge, MA: Harvard University Press, 2010), 1.
56. Quoted in McCurry, *Confederate Reckoning*, 40.
57. James DeBow, *The Interest in Slavery of the Southern Non-Slaveholder* (Charleston: Evans & Cogswell, 1860), 9. See also McCurry, *Confederate Reckoning*, 45.
58. Freehling, *The Road to Disunion, Volume II*, 533.
59. Abraham Lincoln, First Inaugural Address; "May the Union be Perpetuated," quoted in Lepore, *A Is for American*, 154.
60. Jefferson Davis, 36 Cong. Globe 917 (1860).
61. Quoted in Drew Gilpin Faust, *This Republic of Suffering: Death and the American Civil War* (New York: Knopf, 2008), 62.
62. Faust, *This Republic of Suffering*, 125, 323; *NYT*, October 20, 1862. And see Jeff L. Rosenheim, *Photography and the American Civil War* (New York: Metropolitan Museum of Art, 2013); J. Matthew Gallman and Gary W. Gallagher, eds., *Lens of War: Exploring Iconic Photographs of the Civil War* (Athens: University of Georgia Press, 2015); George Sullivan, *In the Wake of Battle: The Civil War Images of Mathew Brady* (New York: Prestel, 2004).
63. Daly, *Covering America*, 106.
64. Alexander Gardner, *Gardner's Photographic Sketch Book of the War* (Washington, DC: Philp & Solomons, 1866), 4.
65. Garry Wills, *Lincoln at Gettysburg: The Words That Remade America* (New York: Simon & Schuster, 1992, 2012), prologue.
66. Abraham Lincoln, "Address Delivered at the Dedication of the Cemetery at Gettysburg," November 19, 1863, in *The Collected Works of Abraham Lincoln*, 7:24.
67. Quoted in Chandra Manning, *What This Cruel War Was Over: Soldiers, Slavery, and the Civil War* (New York: Knopf, 2007), 3.
68. W. E. B. Du Bois, "The Freedman's Bureau," *Atlantic Monthly*, March 1901, 354.
69. "The Slaves of Jefferson Davis Coming on to the Camp at Vicksburg," *Frank Leslie's Illustrated Newspaper*, August 8, 1863; and see Harold Holzer, *The Civil War in 50 Objects* (New York: Penguin), ch. 29. And, more broadly, see Ira Berlin, Barbara Fields, et al., eds., *Slaves No More: Three Essays on Emancipation and the Civil War* (New York: Cambridge University Press, 1992).
70. Quoted in John Hope Franklin, *The Emancipation Proclamation* (1963; Wheeling, IL: Harlan Davidson, 1995), xiv.

71. *New York Tribune,* September 24, 1862; Abraham Lincoln to Hannibal Hamlin, September 28, 1862, in *The Collected Works of Abraham Lincoln,* 5:443. Franklin, *The Emancipation Proclamation,* 48.

72. Franklin, *The Emancipation Proclamation,* 101, 67–68; Harold Holzer, Edna Greene Medford, and Frank J. Williams, eds., *The Emancipation Proclamation: Three Views* (Baton Rouge: Louisiana State University Press, 2006), 17.

73. Frederick Douglass, "January First 1863," *Douglass' Monthly* (January 1863); Abraham Lincoln, Annual Message to Congress, December 1, 1862, in *The Collected Works of Abraham Lincoln,* 5:538; Franklin, *The Emancipation Proclamation,* 92, 97.

74. Lincoln quoted in Franklin, *The Emancipation Proclamation,* 80.

75. Franklin, *The Emancipation Proclamation,* 94–95. And see Mitch Kachun, *Festivals of Freedom: Meaning and Memory in African American Emancipation Celebrations, 1808–1915* (Boston: University of Massachusetts Press, 2003), 103; Edna Greene Medford, "Imagined Promises, Bitter Realities: African Americans and the Meaning of the Emancipation Proclamation," in *The Emancipation Proclamation: Three Views,* 21, 22.

76. Medford, "Imagined Promises," 23; *Douglass' Monthly,* March 21, 1863.

77. McCurry, *Confederate Reckoning,* 152, 154.

78. Quoted in Manning, *What This Cruel War Was Over,* 208–9.

79. Schuyler Colfax, 37 Cong. Globe 306 (1861). And see McCurry, *Confederate Reckoning,* 155–56 and 206–7.

80. Quoted in McCurry, *Confederate Reckoning,* 143, 150, 171, 175, 183.

81. McCurry, *Confederate Reckoning,* 207–9; Theda Skocpol, *Protecting Soldiers and Mothers: The Political Origins of Social Policy in the United States* (Cambridge, MA: Harvard University Press, 1992), ch. 2, especially 139–43.

82. Lincoln to Horace Greeley, August 1862, *The Collected Works of Abraham Lincoln,* 5:388.

83. DuBois, *Feminism and Suffrage,* 53.

84. A collection of Lincoln's 1864 campaign buttons is held in the Prints and Photographs Division of the Library of Congress.

85. Haynes, *The First American Political Conventions,* 194.

86. Quoted in Manning, *What This Cruel War Was Over,* 183–86.

87. James S. Rollins, 38 Cong. Globe 260 (1865); Manning, *What This Cruel War Was Over,* 190.

88. Benn Pitman, ed., *The Assassination of President Lincoln and the Trial of the Conspirators* (1865; Clark, NJ: Lawbook Exchange, 2005), 45.

89. Quoted in Richard Wightman Fox, *Lincoln's Body: A Cultural History* (New York: Norton, 2015), 67.

90. Ibid., 64, 65.

91. Quotes are in ibid., 88, and Martha Hodes, *Mourning Lincoln* (New Haven, CT: Yale University Press, 2015), 78, 186.

92. Hodes, *Mourning Lincoln,* 186.

93. Quoted in Foner, *The Fiery Trial,* 317.

## *Nine:* OF CITIZENS, PERSONS, AND PEOPLE

1. Edward Bates, *Opinion of Attorney General Bates on Citizenship* (Washington, DC: U.S. Government Printing Office, 1862), 3. And, broadly, see Rogers M. Smith, *Civil Ideals: Conflicting Visions of Citizenship in U.S. History* (New Haven, CT: Yale University Press, 1997).

2. Quoted in William J. Novak, "The Legal Transformation of Citizenship in Nineteenth-Century America," in Meg Jacobs et al., eds., *The Democratic Experiment: New Directions in American Political History* (Princeton, NJ: Princeton University Press, 2003), 85–119.

3. William Jay, *The Life of John Jay: With Selections from His Correspondence and Miscellaneous Papers* (New York: J. & J. Harper, 1833), 194.

4. James Madison, Federalist No. 52 (1788).

5. Levi Morton, Speech in the House, 46 Cong. Rec. 2664 (April 22, 1880).

6. Alexander Hamilton, Federalist No. 80 (1788).

7. Charles Sumner, "Equality before the Law," in *Charles Sumner: His Complete Works*, 20 vols. (Boston: Lee and Shepard, 1900) 3:65–66.

8. Gustafson, *Women and the Republican Party*, 22.

9. Gaillard Hunt, *The American Passport: Its History* (Washington, DC: U.S. Government Printing Office, 1898), 131–32.

10. Hunt, *The American Passport*, 15. The term "free persons of color" entered the American lexicon by way of French Louisiana, where it generally referred to people of mixed ancestry. In 1810, the first U.S. Census conducted after the Louisiana Purchase counted free persons of color in the new territory. The term really only entered U.S. legal discourse in the 1810s, when, in slave states, free persons of color were required to register with the local government. "In the early nineteenth century, the term 'persons of color' included free blacks, persons suspected of having African ancestry, or, in a state that was still very rural and sometimes suspicious of strangers, any non-white person whose antecedents were locally unknown. The legal terms 'free black' and 'free person of color' referred to the civil status of a black who was either born free or legally manumitted after birth" (Mary R. Bullard, "Deconstructing a Manumission Document: Mary Stafford's Free Paper," *Georgia Historical Quarterly* 89 [2005]: 287). By the 1830s, the designation "free person of color" had become commonplace in state laws— see, for example, McCord, *The Statutes at Large of South Carolina*, 7:468 (citing a law from 1834); *Laws of the Republic of Texas Passed at the Session of the Fourth Congress* (Houston: Telegraph Power Press), 151 (citing a law from 1840).

11. Hunt, *American Passport*, 50; Craig Robertson, *The Passport in America: The History of a Document* (New York: Oxford University Press, 2010), 131; *The United States Passport: Past, Present, Future* (Washington, DC: Passport Office, Department of State, 1976).

12. *Rules Governing Applications for Passports* (Washington, DC: U.S. Department of State, 1896).

13. Steven Hahn, *A Nation under Our Feet: Black Political Struggles in the Rural South from Slavery to the Great Migration* (Cambridge, MA: Harvard University Press, 2003), 79, 106, 129.

14. *The Selected Papers of Thaddeus Stevens*, ed. Beverly Wilson Palmer and Holly Byers Ochoa, 2 vols. (Pittsburgh: University of Pittsburgh Press, 1998), 2:16.

15. "The Colored People of Virginia," *The Anti-Slavery Reporter*, October 2, 1865, 250.

16. Eric Foner, *Nothing but Freedom: Emancipation and Its Legacy*, with a foreword by Steven Hahn (Baton Rouge: Louisiana State University Press/Walter Lynwood Fleming Lectures in Southern History, 2007), 50; Wyn Craig Wade, *The Fiery Cross: The Ku Klux Klan in America* (New York: Oxford University Press, 1998), 22. And see W. E. B. Du Bois, *Black Reconstruction: An Essay toward a History of the Part Which Black Folk Played in the Attempt to Reconstruct Democracy in America, 1860–1880* (New York: Russell & Russell, 1935).

17. Quoted in Wade, *Fiery Cross*, 35. And see Michael Newton, *White Robes and Burning Crosses: A History of the Ku Klux Klan from 1866* (Jefferson, NC: Macfarland, 2014); Jacqueline Goldsby, *A Spectacular Secret: Lynching in American Life and Literature* (Chicago: University of Chicago Press, 2006).

18. *The Papers of Andrew Johnson*, ed. Paul H. Bergeron, 16 vols. (Knoxville: University of Tennessee Press, 1967–2000), 10:42–48.

19. On the rise of state power, see Richard Franklin Bensel, *Yankee Leviathan: The Origins of Central State Authority in America, 1859–1877* (New York: Cambridge University Press, 1990); Gary Gerstle, *Liberty and Coercion: The Paradox of American Govern-*

*ment* (Princeton, NJ: Princeton University Press, 2016); Nell Irvin Painter, *Standing at Armageddon: The United States, 1877–1919* (New York: Norton, 1987); Martin J. Sklar, *The Corporate Reconstruction of American Capitalism, 1890–1916* (1988).

20. U.S. Const. amend. 14.

21. Quoted in DuBois, *Feminism and Suffrage*, 60–63. And, broadly, see also Melanie Gustafson, Kristie Miller, and Elisabeth I. Perry, eds., *We Have Come to Stay: American Women and Political Parties 1880–1960* (Albuquerque: University of New Mexico Press, 1999); Jo Freeman, *We Will be Heard: Women's Struggles for Political Power in the United States* (Lanham, MD: Rowan and Littlefield, 2008); and Gustafson, *Women and the Republican Party.*

22. Quoted in Martin Gruberg, *Women in American Politics: An Assessment and Sourcebook* (Oshkosh, WI: Academia Press, 1968), 3–4. DuBois, *Feminism and Suffrage*, 60–63.

23. U.S. Const. amend 14.

24. 39 Cong. Globe 2767 (1866).

25. Quoted in Hahn, *A Nation under Our Feet*, 205.

26. Ibid., 215; Richard Goldstein, *Mine Eyes Have Seen: A First-Person History of the Events That Shaped America.* (New York: Simon & Schuster, 1997), 126.

27. On the history and force of impeachment, see Lawrence Tribe and Joshua Matz, *To End a Presidency: The Power of Impeachment* (New York: Basic Books, 2018).

28. On Chinese immigration and exclusion, see Earl M. Maltz, "The Federal Government and the Problem of Chinese Rights in the Era of the Fourteenth Amendment," *Harvard Journal of Law and Public Policy* 17 (1994): 223–52; John Hayakawa Torok, "Reconstruction and Racial Nativism: Chinese Immigrants and the Debates on the Thirteenth, Fourteenth, and Fifteenth Amendments and Civil Rights Laws," *Asian Law Journal* 3 (1996): 55–103; Najia Aarim-Heriot, *Chinese Immigrants, African Americans, and Racial Anxiety in the United States, 1848–1882* (Urbana: University of Illinois Press, 2003); Bill Ong Hing, *Making and Remaking Asian America through Immigration Policy, 1850–1990* (Stanford, CA: Stanford University Press, 1993).

29. *People v. Hall*, 4 Cal. 399 (1854).

30. United States Supreme Court, *United States Reports: Cases Adjudged in the Supreme Court* (Banks & Bros., Law Publishers, 1898), 697.

31. 39 Cong. Globe 1026 (1866). And see Garrett Epps, *Democracy Reborn: The Fourteenth Amendment and the Fight for Equal Rights in Post-Civil War America* (New York: Henry Holt, 2006), 172.

32. Stephen K. Williams, ed., *United States Supreme Court Reports: Cases Argued and Decided in the Supreme Court of the United States* (Newark, NJ: Lawyers Co-operative Publishing Company, 1854), 1071.

33. 40 Cong. Globe 287 (1869), appendix.

34. Edward McPherson, *A Political Manual for 1869* (Washington, DC: Philp & Solomons, 1869), 401.

35. 40 Cong. Globe 1009 (1869).

36. *Frederick Douglass Papers*, 4:13. And, broadly, see Edlie L. Wong, *Racial Reconstruction: Black Inclusion, Chinese Exclusion, and the Fictions of Citizenship* (New York: New York University Press, 2015).

37. U.S. Const. amend. 15.

38. Ellen Fitzpatrick, *The Highest Glass Ceiling: Women's Quest for the American Presidency* (Cambridge, MA: Harvard University Press, 2016), 9, 42. Gustafson, *Women and the Republican Party,* 52.

39. The quotations are from *National Party Conventions, 1831–1984*, 4th ed. (Washington, DC: Congressional Quarterly, Inc., 1987), 48–49; Gustafson, *Women and the Republican Party*, 49; Haynes, *President-Making in the Gilded Age*, 17–18.

40. Haynes, *President-Making in the Gilded Age*, 10, 65, 29.

41. Isabel Wilkerson, *The Warmth of Other Suns: The Epic Story of America's Great Migration* (New York: Random House, 2010), 45.

42. William A. White, *The Autobiography of William Allen White* (New York: Macmillan, 1946), 218–19; Brooke Speer Orr, "Mary Elizabeth Lease: Nineteenth-Century Populist and Twentieth-Century Progressive," PhD dissertation, George Washington University, 2002, 145, 155–56; Mary E. Lease, speech to the National Council of Women of the United States, Washington, DC, February 24, 1891, in Rachel Avery Foster, ed., *Transactions of the National Council of Women of the United States: Assembled in Washington, D.C., February 22 to 25, 1891* (Philadelphia: J. B. Lippincott, 1891), 157.

43. Quoted in Orr, "Mary Elizabeth Lease," 18.

44. Mary E. Lease, speech to the National Council of Women of the United States, Washington, DC, February 24, 1891.

45. See Paula Baker, "The Domestication of Politics: Women and American Political Society, 1780–1920," *American Historical Review* 89 (1984): 620–47; and Michael McGerr, "Political Style and Women's Power, 1830–1930," *JAH* 77 (1990): 864–85.

46. Hahn, *A Nation Without Borders*, 334–36.

47. Gerstle, *Liberty and Coercion*, 111. And, on the sweep of this era, see Patricia Nelson Limerick, *The Legacy of Conquest: The Unbroken Past of the American West* (New York: Norton, 1987), especially chs. 2, 3, and 4; Hahn, *A Nation Without Borders*, especially chs. 7, 8, and 9; and William Cronon, *Nature's Metropolis: Chicago and the Great West* (New York: Norton, 1992), especially chs. 2, 3, and 5.

48. Quoted in Judith Freeman Clark, *The Gilded Age* (New York: Facts On File, 2006), 101.

49. Orr, "Mary Elizabeth Lease," 22–23.

50. Hahn, *A Nation Without Borders*, 318–24.

51. Orr, "Mary Elizabeth Lease," 30.

52. "Farmers' Declaration of Independence," *Pacific Rural Press* [San Francisco], August 30, 1873.

53. Quoted in Orr, "Mary Elizabeth Lease," 25.

54. Quoted in Jefferson Cowie, *The Great Exception: The New Deal & the Limits of American Politics* (Princeton, NJ: Princeton University Press/ Politics and Society in Twentieth-Century America, 2016), 42.

55. Quoted in Limerick, *The Legacy of Conquest*, 264.

56. Painter, *Standing at Armageddon*, 60.

57. Hahn, *A Nation Without Borders*, 377–87.

58. United States, Department of the Interior, *Annual Reports of the Department of the Interior* (Washington, DC, 1883), 732.

59. Hahn, *A Nation Without Borders*, 357–58; Painter, *Standing at Armageddon*, 72.

60. Conkling's chicanery is fully recounted in Adam Winkler, *We the Corporations: How American Businesses Won Their Civil Rights* (New York: Liveright, 2017).

61. Ibid.

62. Ibid.

63. Quoted in Cowie, *The Great Exception*, 37.

64. Orr, "Mary Elizabeth Lease," 165. Orr's language was both commonplace and consequential: as I argue in *The Secret History of Wonder Woman* (New York: Knopf, 2014), the nineteenth-century notion of female superiority served as an inspiration for the comic book superhero Wonder Woman, created in 1941.

65. Orr, "Mary Elizabeth Lease," 31–32.

66. Freeman, *A Room at a Time*, 34–35; Frances Willard, *My Happy Half-Century: The Autobiography of an American Woman* (London: Ward, Lock, and Bowden, 1894), 312.

67. Sarah E. V. Emery, *Seven Financial Conspiracies Which Have Enslaved the American People* (Lansing, MI: Robert Smith and Co., 1888), 8. And see Russell B. Nye, "Sarah Elizabeth Van de Vort Emery," in *Notable American Women, 1607–1950*, ed. Edward T. James et al., 3 vols. (Cambridge, MA: Harvard University Press, 1971), 3:582–83.

68. Quoted in Haynes, *President-Making in the Gilded Age*, 78.

69. Gustafson, *Women and the Republican Party*, 59; Freeman, *We Will be Heard*, 86–87; Gustafson et al., *We Have Come to Stay*, 6–7.

70. On George's life, see Edward J. Rose, *Henry George* (New York: Twayne, 1968), and David Montgomery, "Henry George," *American National Biography Online*.

71. Henry George, "What the Railroad Will Bring Us," in *Henry George: Collected Journalistic Writings*, ed. Kenneth C. Wenzer, 4 vols. (Armonk, NY: M. E. Sharp, 2003), 1:15–26; Rose, *Henry George*, 54.

72. Rose, *Henry George*, 40.

73. Henry George, "Money in Elections," *North American Review* 136 (March 1883): 211.

74. Roy G. Saltman, *The History and Politics of Voting Technology: In Quest of Integrity and Public Confidence* (New York: Palgrave Macmillan, 2006), 84, 91–92.

75. Henry George, "Bribery in Elections," *Overland Monthly* 7 (December 1871): 497–504.

76. Rose, *Henry George*, 121; Orr, "Mary Elizabeth Lease," 53.

77. Orr, "Mary Elizabeth Lease," 62, 60, 201.

78. Mary E. Lease, *The Problem of Civilization Solved* (Chicago: Laird and Lee, 1895). And see Orr, "Mary Elizabeth Lease," 131–33.

79. Quoted in John Henry Wigmore, *The Australian Ballot System* (Boston: C. C. Soule, 1889), 23–24; Lionel E. Fredman, *The Australian Ballot: The Story of an American Reform* (East Lansing, MI: Michigan State University, 1968), ix.

80. Fredman, *The Australian Ballot*, 42–43.

81. Herbert J. Bass, '*I Am a Democrat*': *The Political Career of David Bennett Hill* (Syracuse, NY: Syracuse University Press, 1961), 149; *New York Herald*, January 17, February 9, 1890 and *NYT*, March 4, 29, 1890.

82. Fredman, *The Australian Ballot*, 53–55; Mia Bay, *To Tell the Truth Freely: The Life of Ida B. Wells* (New York: Hill and Wang, 2009), 79; John Crowley, "Uses and Abuses of the Secret Ballot in the American Age of Reform," in Romain Bertrand, Jean-Louis Briquet, and Peter Pels, eds., *Cultures of Voting: The Hidden History of the Secret Ballot* (London: C. Hurst & Co., 2007), 59.

83. Quoted in Jack Beatty, *Age of Betrayal: The Triumph of Money in America, 1865–1900* (New York: Knopf, 2007), 200.

84. Michael Kazin, *A Godly Hero: The Life of William Jennings Bryan* (New York: Knopf, 2006), 7–20.

85. Quoted in Kazin, *A Godly Hero*, 48–49.

86. Orr, "Mary Elizabeth Lease," 76–77.

87. Russell B. Nye, "Sarah Elizabeth Van de Vort Emery," in *Notable American Women, 1607–1950*, edited by Edward T. James et al., 3 vols. (Cambridge, MA: Harvard University Press, 1971), 3:582–83.

88. Quoted in Orr, "Mary Elizabeth Lease," 81.

89. Donnelly's speech appears in Scott J. Hammond et al., *Classics of American Political and Constitutional Thought* (Indianapolis, IN: Hackett Pub., 2007), 229.

90. National People's Party Platform, Omaha, Nebraska, July 4, 1892.

91. Quoted in Orr, "Mary Elizabeth Lease," 93, 115.

92. Quoted in Robert C. McMath Jr., *American Populism: A Social History, 1877–1898* (New York: Hill and Wang, 1993), 181.

93. Quoted in Orr, "Mary Elizabeth Lease," 121.

94. William Jennings Bryan, "An Income Tax," 1894, in *Speeches of William Jennings Bryan*, 2 vols. (New York: Funk and Wagnalls, 1909), 2:178.

95. Kazin, *A Godly Hero*, 51; *Pollock v. Farmers' Loan and Trust Company*, 57 U.S. 429 (1895).

96. Broadly, see Julie A. Reuben, *The Making of the Modern University: Intellectual Transformation and the Marginalization of Morality* (Chicago: University of Chicago Press, 1996); Dorothy Ross, *The Origins of American Social Science* (New York: Cambridge University Press/Ideas in Context, 1991); Peter Novick, *That Noble Dream: The "Objectivity Question" and the American Historical Profession* (New York: Cambridge University Press, 1988).

97. A. Scott Berg, *Wilson* (New York: G. P. Putnam's Sons, 2013), 107. Cooper writes:

"He really had only one subject, which he studied with quiet obsessiveness: How does power really work?" See John Milton Cooper Jr., ed., *Reconsidering Woodrow Wilson: Progressivism, Internationalism, War and Peace* (Baltimore: Johns Hopkins University Press, 2008), 17.

98. Quoted in Daly, *Covering America*, 155.

99. Ibid., 112–16, 125–27.

100. Michael Schudson, *Discovering the News: A Social History of American Newspapers* (New York: Basic Books, 1978), 110.

101. Julius Chambers, *News Hunting on Three Continents* (New York: Mitchell Kennerley, 1921), 7. Schudson, *Origins of the Ideal of Objectivity*, 170–80.

102. "Expressions of Regret," *NYT,* October 30, 1897.

103. 1896 Democratic Party Platform.

104. William Jennings Bryan and Robert W. Cherny, *The Cross of Gold: Speech Delivered before the National Democratic Convention at Chicago, July 9, 1896* (Lincoln: University of Nebraska Press, 1997).

105. "Repudiation Has Won," *NYT,* July 10, 1896.

106. Quoted in Kazin, *A Godly Hero,* 63–65.

107. Quoted in Richard Franklin Bensel, *Passion and Preferences: William Jennings Byran and the 1896 Democratic National Convention* (New York: Columbia University Press, 2008), 304; Orr, "Mary Elizabeth Lease," 178–79.

108. Kazin, *A Godly Hero,* 66–77.

109. Orr, "Mary Elizabeth Lease," 198, 190, 200–2.

110. "Brief History of the AHA," https://www.historians.org/about-aha-and-membership/aha-history-and-archives/brief-history-of-the-aha, accessed June 24, 2017.

111. Max Weber and C. Wright Mills, *From Max Weber: Essays in Sociology* (New York: Routledge, 2009), 51.

112. Quoted in Edward J. Larson, *Summer for the Gods: The Scopes Trial and America's Continuing Debate over Science and Religion* (New York: Basic Books, 1997), 34.

113. Frances FitzGerald, *The Evangelicals: The Struggle to Shape America* (New York: Simon & Schuster, 2017), 115.

114. Frederick Jackson Turner, *The Significance of the Frontier in American History* (Wisconsin, 1893).

115. Isaacson, *The Innovators,* 35–36. And see Geoffrey D. Austrian, *Herman Hollerith: Forgotten Giant of Information Processing* (New York: Columbia University Press, 1982).

116. Turner, *The Significance of the Frontier.*

117. Anna R. Paddon and Sally Turner, "African Americans and the World's Columbian Exposition," *Illinois Historical Journal* 88 (1995): 19–36.

118. Frederick Douglass, *The Reason Why the Colored Man Is Not in the Columbian Exposition* (Chicago: Privately printed, 1893), introduction.

119. Darlene Clark Hine, *Black Women in American History: From Colonial Times through the Nineteenth Century,* 4 vols. (Brooklyn, NY: Carlson Pub., 1990), 3:336.

120. On Wells's life, see Bay, *To Tell the Truth Freely.* For her writings, see Ida B. Wells-Barnett, *The Light of Truth: Writings of an Anti-lynching Crusader,* ed. Mia Bay and Henry Louis Gates Jr. (New York: Penguin Books, 2014). Frederick Douglass, Letter, in Ida B. Wells, *Southern Horrors: Lynch Law in All Its Phases* (New York: The New Age, 1891), 51.

121. Douglass, *The Reason Why the Colored Man Is Not in the Columbian Exposition,* introduction.

122. Paddon and Turner, "African Americans and the World's Columbian Exposition."

123. Quoted in William S. McFeely, *Frederick Douglass* (New York: Norton, 1991), 371.

124. Frederick Douglass, "The Blessings of Liberty and Education," Manassas, Virginia, September 3, 1894, in *Frederick Douglass Papers,* 5:629.

125. "Death of Fred Douglass," *NYT,* February 21, 1895.

126. "Tributes of Two Races," *NYT,* February 26, 1895.

127. "The Duty of the Bar to Uphold the Constitutional Guarantees of Contracts and Private Property," *American Law Review* 26 (1892): 674.

128. *Plessy v. Ferguson*, 163 U.S. 57 (1896).

129. W. E. B. Du Bois, *The Souls of Black Folk* (Chicago: A. McClurg, 1903), 3.


## *Ten:* EFFICIENCY AND THE MASSES

1. Ronald Steel, *Walter Lippmann and the American Century* (New Brunswick, NJ: Transaction, 1999), 282, xv, 280, 175; on the House of Truth, see 120–23 and Brad Snyder, *The House of Truth: A Washington Political Salon and the Foundations of American Liberalism* (New York: Oxford University Press, 2017), especially ch. 5.

2. Snyder, *House of Truth*, 3. On the Progressive urge, see Robert Wiebe, *The Search for Order, 1877–1920* (New York: Hill and Wang, 1967).

3. See the *OED*. The quotation is from "Merchants Hold a Radio Luncheon," *NYT*, March 18, 1927.

4. Quoted in Michael Kazin, *The Populist Persuasion: An American History* (Ithaca, NY: Cornell University Press, 1998), 27; "Candidate Watson's Book," *Indianapolis News*, July 27, 1896.

5. Quoted in George McKenna, *The Puritan Origins of American Patriotism* (New Haven, CT: Yale University Press, 2007), 242.

6. For discussions of distinctions among these groups, see Richard Hofstadter, *The Age of Reform: From Bryan to F.D.R.* (New York: Vintage, 1955); Richard L. McCormick, *The Party Period and Public Policy: American Politics from the Age of Jackson to the Progressive Era* (New York: Oxford University Press, 1986); James T. Kloppenberg, *Uncertain Victory: Social Democracy and Progressivism in European and American Thought, 1870–1920* (New York: Oxford University Press, 1986); and Glenda Gilmore, ed., *Who Were the Progressives?* (New York: Palgrave, 2002).

7. Elizabeth Sanders, *Roots of Reform: Farmers, Workers, and the American State, 1877–1917* (Chicago: University of Chicago Press, 1999), 154; Robert Post, *Citizens Divided: Campaign Finance Reform and the Constitution* (Cambridge, MA: Harvard University Press, 2014), 30; Painter, *Standing at Armageddon*, 270.

8. Martin E. Marty, *Modern American Religion: The Irony of It All, 1893–1919*, 3 vols. (Chicago: University of Chicago Press, 1997), 1:286, 362n10; Henry George, *Progress and Poverty: An Inquiry into the Cause of Industrial Depressions, and of Increase of Want with Increase of Wealth, the Remedy* (London: W. Reeves, 1884), 426; Clarence Darrow, *The Story of My Life* (New York: Charles Scribner's Sons, 1932), 52.

9. Gladden is quoted in Gary J. Dorrien, *Social Ethics in the Making: Interpreting an American Tradition* (Malden, MA: Wiley-Blackwell, 2009), 65.

10. Degler, *Out of Our Past*, 346; FitzGerald, *The Evangelicals*, 65–69.

11. Kazin, *A Godly Hero*, 124.

12. Daly, *Covering America*, 132–38.

13. Emilio Aguinaldo to the Philippine People, February 5, 1899, in Daniel B. Schirmer and Stephen Rosskamm Shalom, eds., *The Philippines Reader: A History of Colonialism, Neocolonialism, Dictatorship, and Resistance* (Boston: South End Press, 1987), 20–21; Bryan, "Will It Pay?," *New York Journal*, January 15, 1899; Kazin, *A Godly Hero*, 91.

14. Albert J. Beveridge, "In Support of an American Empire," 56 Cong. Rec. 704–12 (January 9, 1900); Ben Tillman, 56 Cong. Rec. 836–37 (January 20, 1899).

15. [Unsigned] black soldier to the *Wisconsin Weekly Advocate*, May 17, 1900; and Rienzi B. Lemus to the *Richmond Planet*, November 4, 1899, in Willard B. Gatewood Jr., ed., *"Smoked Yankees" and the Struggle for Empire: Letters from Negro Soldiers, 1898–1902* (Fayetteville: University of Arkansas Press, 1987), 279–81, 246–47.

16. C. Vann Woodward, *The Strange Career of Jim Crow* (New York: Oxford University Press, 1955), 82; Wilkerson, *The Warmth of Other Suns*, 26, 29, 31, 26–27, 37, 45–46,

40; Twain quoted in Kathleen Dalton, *Theodore Roosevelt: A Strenuous Life* (New York: Knopf, 2002), 203; Richard Rothstein, *The Color of Law: A Forgotten History of How Our Government Segregated America* (New York: Liveright, 2017), 41–45.

17. W. E. B. Du Bois, "The Study of the Negro Problems," *Annals of the American Academy of Political and Social Science* 11 (1898): 1. On the early history of surveys, see Robert Wuthnow, *Inventing American Religion: Polls, Surveys, and the Tenuous Quest for a Nation's Faith* (New York: Oxford University Press, 2015), 8–9, and especially 15–43. David Levering Lewis, *W. E. B. Du Bois: Biography of a Race, 1868–1919* (New York: Henry Holt, 1993), 226.

18. Bay, *To Tell the Truth Freely*, 95; Wilkerson, *The Warmth of Other Suns*, 10; Lewis, *W. E. B. Du Bois*, 411.

19. Theodore Roosevelt, "Address of President Roosevelt at the Laying of the Corner Stone of the Office Building of the House of Representatives" ("The Man with the Muck-Rake"), April 14, 1906; Roosevelt, "The Man with the Muck-Rake," *The Outlook*, April 21, 1906.

20. Ida M. Tarbell, *All in the Day's Work: An Autobiography* (Urbana: University of Illinois Press, 2003), 241; Weinberg, *Taking on the Trust*, 227; Daly, *Covering America*, 148.

21. Tarbell, *All in the Day's Work*, 6; Ida M. Tarbell, *The History of the Standard Oil Company*, 2 vols. (1902; New York: Macmillan, 1925), 1:vii, 37.

22. Quoted in Kazin, *A Godly Hero*, 125.

23. Berg, *Wilson*, 44, 49, 73, 78, 81, 103–5; Mark Benbow, "Wilson the Man," in Ross A. Kennedy, ed., *A Companion to Woodrow Wilson* (Malden, MA: John Wiley & Sons, 2013), 9–37.

24. Woodrow Wilson, *Congressional Government: A Study in American Politics* (Boston: Houghton Mifflin, 1885), 110–11; Woodrow Wilson, *Constitutional Government in the United States* (New York: Columbia University Press, 1911), 56, 60, 69.

25. Quoted in Dalton, *Theodore Roosevelt*, 203; Kazin, *A Godly Hero*, 105–6.

26. Nikil Saval, *Cubed: A Secret History of the Workplace* (New York: Doubleday, 2014), 41, 13, 36, 42, 266; Ann Douglas, *Terrible Honesty: Mongrel Manhattan in the 1920s* (London: Picador, 1995), 4; Lynn Dumenil, *The Modern Temper: American Culture and Society in the 1920s* (New York: Hill and Wang, 1995), 11; Kazin, *A Godly Hero*, 114.

27. Dalton, *Theodore Roosevelt*, 125, 207, 213–14; Kazin, *A Godly Hero*, 114.

28. Quoted in Dalton, *Theodore Roosevelt*, 225.

29. Robert Stanley, *Dimensions of Law in the Service of Order: Origins of the Federal Income Tax, 1861–1913* (New York: Oxford University Press, 1993), 180, table 5-1. Bryan's speech is reproduced in Paolo E. Coletta, "The Election of 1908," in Schlesinger, *History of American Presidential Elections, 1789–1968*, 3:2115. On his reception, see Kazin, *A Godly Hero*, 145–46.

30. Quoted in Steven R. Weisman, *The Great Tax Wars: Lincoln, Teddy Roosevelt, Wilson: How the Income Tax Transformed America* (New York: Simon & Schuster, 2004), 227.

31. Stanley, *Dimensions of Law*, 211–12, table 5-5; "History of the 1040," *Chicago Tribune*, March 27, 1994.

32. Theda Skocpol, *Protecting Soldiers and Mothers: The Political Origins of Social Policy in the United States* (Cambridge, MA: Harvard University Press, 1992), 65, 156, 375.

33. *Lochner v. New York*, 198 U.S. 45 (1905).

34. Shugerman, *The People's Courts*, 173; 62 Cong. Rec. 472 (1912), appendix.

35. On this point, especially, see Skocpol, *Protecting Soldiers and Mothers*, ch. 5.

36. Irving Fisher, "The Need for Health Insurance," *American Labor Legislation Review* 7 (1917): 9–23.

37. Arthur J. Viseltear, "Compulsory Health Insurance in California, 1915–1918," *Journal of the History of Medicine and Allied Sciences* (1969): 170–71; Odin W. Anderson, "Health Insurance in the United States, 1910–1920," *Journal of the History of Medicine and Allied Sciences* 5 (1950): 370–71; Ronald Numbers, "The Specter of Socialized Medicine: American Physicians and Compulsory Health Insurance," in Numbers,

ed. *Compulsory Health Insurance: The Continuing American Debate* (Westport, CT: Greenwood, 1982), 3–24.

38. Nancy Woloch, *Muller v. Oregon: A Brief History with Documents* (Boston: Bedford Books, 1996), 5.

39. Skocpol, *Protecting Soldiers and Mothers*, 333–40 (quotation, 337).

40. Quoted in Woloch, *Muller v. Oregon*, 17.

41. Woloch, *Muller v. Oregon*, 8.

42. Skocpol, *Protecting Soldiers and Mothers*, 394–95.

43. "The Brandeis Brief," Louis D. Brandeis School of Law Library, https://louisville.edu/law/library/special-collections/the-louis-d.-brandeis-collection/the-brandeis-brief-in-its-entirety, accessed July 9, 2017.

44. This element of Brandeis's argument is quoted and discussed in Sally J. Kenney, *For Whose Protection? Reproductive Hazards and Exclusionary Politics in the United States and Britain* (Ann Arbor: University of Michigan Press, 1992), 45–46.

45. Skocpol, *Protecting Soldiers and Mothers*, 10, and see also ch. 8.

46. Louis Brandeis, "Efficiency and Social Ideas," 1914, in Philippa Strum, ed., *Brandeis on Democracy* (Lawrence: University Press of Kansas, 1995), 33.

47. Frederick W. Taylor, "The Gospel of Efficiency," *American Magazine* 71 (1911): 479–80, 570–81. And see Frederick Winslow Taylor, *The Principles of Scientific Management* (New York: Harper & Bros., 1911).

48. Matthew Stewart, *The Management Myth: Debunking Modern Business Philosophy* (New York: Norton, 2009), 48–50.

49. On immigration in this era, see John Higham, *Strangers in the Land: Patterns of American Nativism, 1860–1925* (Rutgers, NJ: Rutgers University Press, 1955), and John Bodnar, *The Transplanted: A History of Immigrants in Urban America* (Bloomington: Indiana University Press, 1985).

50. Painter, *Standing at Armageddon*, xix.

51. Stephen P. Meyer, *The Five Dollar Day: Labor Management and Social Control in the Ford Motor Company, 1908–1921* (Albany, NY: State University of New York Press, 1981), 2, 5, 12. Chrysler is quoted in Maury Klein, *Rainbow's End: The Crash of 1929* (New York: Oxford University Press, 2001), 29.

52. Quoted in Janet F. Davidson et al., *On the Move: Transportation and the American Story* (New York: National Geographic, 2003), 165.

53. Jill Lepore, *The Mansion of Happiness: A History of Life and Death* (New York: Knopf, 2012), ch. 6.

54. Meyer, *The Five Dollar Day*, 6, 99, 156.

55. Philippa Strum, *Louis D. Brandeis: Justice for the People* (Cambridge, MA: Harvard University Press, 1984), 160.

56. Edna Yost, *Frank and Lillian Gilbreth: Partners for Life* (New Brunswick, NJ: Rutgers University Press, 1949), 185–88; "Roads Could Save $1,000,000 a Day," *NYT*, November 22, 1910; Strum, *Louis D. Brandeis: Justice for the People*, 166–67.

57. Robert Kanigel, *The One Best Way: Frederick Winslow Taylor and the Enigma of Efficiency* (New York: Viking, 2007), 3–4, 474–77.

58. Painter, *Standing at Armageddon*, 265, 257.

59. Woodrow Wilson, Inaugural Address, March 4, 1913; Theodore Roosevelt, "New Nationalism," Speech, Osawatomie, Kansas, 1910; Berg, *Wilson*, 294.

60. "Women Leap Suddenly Into Political Favor, Now Courted by All Parties" *New York Herald*, August 11, 1912.

61. McGerr, "Political Style and Women's Power."

62. Quoted in Geoffrey Cowan, *Let the People Rule: Theodore Roosevelt and the Birth of the Presidential Primary* (New York: Norton, 2016), 99.

63. Quotations from Cowan, *Let the People Rule*, 208, 259.

64. Roosevelt's senior thesis at Harvard in 1880 was titled "Practicability of Equalizing Men and Women before the Law"; Freeman, *We Will be Heard*, 23, 30, 37, 52, 55.

65. Quotations from Gustafson, *Women and the Republican Party*, 123, 173.

66. Sidney Milkis, *Theodore Roosevelt, the Progressive Party, and the Transformation of American Democracy* (Lawrence: University Press of Kansas, 2009).

67. Wilson, Inaugural Address.

68. Louis Brandeis, *Other People's Money: and How the Bankers Use It* (New York: F. A. Stokes, 1913), 33, 99; Strum, *Brandeis on Democracy*, 15.

69. David W. Blight, *Race and Reunion: The Civil War in American Memory* (Cambridge, MA: Harvard University Press, 2001), 9–11, 384–390.

70. James Weldon Johnson, "President Wilson's 'New Freedom' and the Negro," in *The Selected Writings of James Weldon Johnson*, ed. Sondra Kathryn Wilson, 2 vols. (New York: Oxford University Press, 1995), 1 (*The New York Age Editorials, 1914–1923*):182.

71. Eric Rauchway, *Blessed Among Nations: How the World Made America* (New York: Hill and Wang, 2006), 7.

72. Henry James to Rhoda Broughton, August 10, 1914, in *The Letters of Henry James*, selected and edited by Percy Lubbock, 2 vols. (New York: Charles Scribner's Sons, 1920), 2:389.

73. See, for example, the reckoning in Eric Hobsbawn, *The Age of Extremes: A History of the World, 1914–1991* (New York: Pantheon, 1994), 6–7.

74. Quoted in Darren Dochuk, *From Bible Belt to Sun Belt: Plain-Folk Religion, Grassroots Politics, and the Rise of Evangelical Conservatism* (New York: Norton, 2011), 30.

75. Quotations from FitzGerald, *The Evangelicals*, 71–79, 97, 113.

76. Quotations from ibid., 113; Kazin, *A Godly Hero*, 263–64; Larson, *Summer for the Gods*, 39.

77. Quoted in Jon Butler et al., *Religion in American Life: A Short History* (New York: Oxford University Press, 2011), 329.

78. Charles Benedict Davenport, *Eugenics, the Science of Human Improvement by Better Breeding* (New York: Henry Holt, 1910); Carl N. Degler, *In Search of Human Nature: The Decline and Revival of Darwinism in American Social Thought* (New York: Oxford University Press, 1991), 42–43.

79. Madison Grant, *The Passing of the Great Race; Or, the Racial Basis of European History* (New York: Scribner, 1916), 10. And see Mark A. Largent, *Breeding Contempt: The History of Coerced Sterilization in the United States* (New Brunswick, NJ: Rutgers University Press, 2008).

80. Quotations from FitzGerald, *The Evangelicals*, 102–14.

81. Quoted in Kazin, *A Godly Hero*, 215.

82. Quoted in Berg, *Wilson*, 417.

83. Ibid., 384, 412, 404–5.

84. Charlotte Perkins Gilman, "A Woman's Party," *The Suffragist* 8 (1920): 8–9; Campaign in Colorado Donkey with National Woman's Party sign advocating opposition to Democratic Party, Colorado, United States, 1916, Library of Congress; "Last Minute Activities of the Woman's Party," *The Suffragist* 4 (1916): 4–5; Berg, *Wilson*, 417; Cooper, *Reconsidering Woodrow Wilson*, 126.

85. Lepore, *The Secret History of Wonder* Woman, 93–95; Mary Chapman and Angela Mills, *Treacherous Texts: U.S. Suffrage Literature, 1846–1946* (New Brunswick, NJ: Rutgers University Press, 2011), 294.

86. Mary Alexander and Marilyn Childress, "The Zimmerman Telegram," *Social Education* 45, 4 (April 1981): 266.

87. Wilson, War Message to Congress, April 2, 1917; Kenneth Whyte, *Hoover: An Extraordinary Life in Extraordinary Times* (New York: Knopf, 2017), 181.

88. Robert Lansing, *Address before the Reserve Officers' Training Corps . . . July 29, 1917* (Washington, DC: U.S. Government Printing Office, 1917), 5.

89. John Dewey, "Conscription of Thought," *The New Republic* [hereafter *TNR*], September 1, 1917, 128–29; Ronald Schaffer, *America in the Great War: The Rise of the War Welfare State* (New York: Oxford University Press, 1991), 4. And see Jonathan Auer-

bach, *Weapons of Democracy: Propaganda, Progressivism, and American Public Opinion* (Baltimore: Johns Hopkins University Press, 2015).

90. Quoted in Schaffer, *America in the Great War*, 15.

91. W. E. B. Du Bois, "The African Roots of War," *Atlantic Monthly*, May 1915; Lewis, *W. E. B. Du Bois*, 554–56; Schaffer, *America in the Great War*, 75.

92. Billie Holiday, "Strange Fruit," 1939. The poem was published as "Bitter Fruit" (1937).

93. On Lippmann's role in the Inquiry, see Steel, *Walter Lippmann*, ch. 11.

94. W. Elliot Brownlee, *Federal Taxation in America: A Short History* (New York: Cambridge University Press, 1996), 62–63; Weisman, *Great Tax Wars*, 333, 337; Webber and Wildavsky, *History of Taxation and Expenditure in the Western World*, 421; "War Savings Societies—A Home Defense," *Medical Times* 46 (1918): 24. The war advanced what the historian Julia C. Ott has called the ideology of an "investors' democracy": Ott, *When Wall Street Met Main Street: The Quest for an Investors' Democracy* (Cambridge, MA: Harvard University Press, 2011). And see also Meg Jacobs, "Pocketbook Politics: Democracy and the Market in Twentieth-Century America," in Meg Jacobs et al., eds., *The Democratic Experiment: New Directions in American Political History* (Princeton, NJ: Princeton University Press, 2003).

95. Rauchway, *Blessed Among Nations*, 148; Schaffer, *America in the Great War*, 58, 66.

96. Schaffer, *America in the Great War*, 101, 97; Allan M. Brandt, *No Magic Bullet: A Social History of Venereal Disease in America Since 1880* (New York: Oxford University Press, 1995), especially ch. 2; Lisa McGirr, *The War on Alcohol: Prohibition and the Rise of the American State* (New York: Norton, 2016), xviii–xxi. And Darrow as quoted in John A. Farrell, *Clarence Darrow: Attorney for the Damned* (New York: Doubleday, 2011), 327.

97. Quoted in Steel, *Walter Lippmann*, 143, 147, 148.

98. Hobsbawn, *The Age of Extremes*, 13, 97.

99. Theodore Roosevelt, *Roosevelt in the Kansas City Star; War-time Editorials* (Boston: Houghton Mifflin Company, 1921), 274.

100. Steel, *Walter Lippmann*, 152; Fredrik Logevall, *Embers of War: The Fall of an Empire and the Making of America's Vietnam* (New York: Random House, 2012), 3–4; Erez Manela, *The Wilsonian Moment: Self-Determination and the International Origins of Anticolonial Nationalism* (New York: Oxford University Press, 2007), 141–58.

101. Lewis, *W. E. B. Du Bois*, 367, 561–78; Painter, *Standing at Armageddon*, 365.

102. Berg, *Wilson*, 568–70.

103. H. G. Wells, *Outline of History* (London, 1920), 1066–67.

104. Steel, *Walter Lippmann*, 158; John Maynard Keynes, *The Economic Consequences of the Peace* (New York: Harcourt, Brace and Howe, 1920), 41, 228.

105. Berg, *Wilson*, 605–7.

106. Ibid., 613–14.

107. Ibid., 619, 633–38, 664; Cooper, *Reconsidering Woodrow Wilson*, 16.

108. Walter Lippmann, "The Basic Problem of Democracy," *Atlantic Monthly*, November 1919, 616.

109. Walter Lippmann, *Public Opinion* (New York: Harcourt, Brace and Company, 1922), 364.

110. Walter Lippmann, *Public Opinion*, with a new foreword by Ronald Steel (1922; New York: Free Press, 1997), 356; intelligence bureaus: 242–51.

111. Quoted in McGerr, "Political Style and Women's Power," 833.

112. Woloch, *Muller v. Oregon*, 58–59; Kenney, *For Whose Protection?*, 46–47.

113. Warren G. Harding, Inaugural Address, March 4, 1921; David C. Mearns and Verner W. Clapp, comp., *The Constitution of the United States together with An Account of Its Travels Since September 17, 1787* (Washington, DC: Library of Congress, 1958), 1–17; Kammen, *A Machine That Would Go of Itself*, 252.

114. James M. Beck, *The Constitution of the United States: A Brief Study of the Genesis, Formulation and Political Philosophy of the Constitution of the United States* (New York:

George H. Doran Company, 1922), 110; Thomas Reed Powell, "Constitutional Metaphors, a Review of James M. Beck's *The Constitution of the United States*, Originally Published in *TNR* on February 11, 1925. And see the typescript, "Constitutional Metaphors," and the poem, "The Constitution Is a Dock," in Thomas Reed Powell Papers, Special Collections, Harvard Law School, Box F, Folder 11.

115. Elmer Rice, *The Adding Machine: A Play in Seven Scenes* (Garden City, N. Y.: Doubleday, Page and Company, 1923), 9.

116. "Thomas Watson," IBM Archives: Transcript of Thomas Watson comments on "THINK," https://www-03.ibm.com/ibm/history/multimedia/think_trans.html, accessed July 5, 2017.

117. Harding, Inaugural Address.

118. Klein, *Rainbow's End*, 28.

119. Brownlee, *Federal Taxation in America*, 73n13; Andrew W. Mellon, *Taxation: The People's Business* (New York: Macmillan, 1924), 18, 137; "Taxpayers' League Target of Attack before Committee," *Atlanta Constitution*, November 10, 1927; "Clashes Electrify Estate Tax Hearing," *NYT*, November 9, 1927. On the Mellon family as funders of the League, see "W. L. Mellon Listed as Tax Lobby Donor," *NYT*, November 6, 1929. Holmes on taxation: *Compañía General de Tabacos de Filipinas v. Collector of Internal Revenue*, 275 U.S. 87 (1927). Webber and Wildavsky, *History of Taxation and Expenditure in the Western World*, 423.

120. Whyte, *Hoover*, 226, 206, 233–37.

121. Ibid., 206, 257–58; Ellis W. Hawley, "Herbert Hoover, the Commerce Secretariat, and the Vision of an 'Associative State,' 1921–1928," *JAH* 61 (1974): 116–40 (quotation, 121); Dumenil, *The Modern Temper*, 36–38.

122. Samuel Strauss, "Things Are in the Saddle," *Atlantic Monthly*, July 1924, 579.

123. League of Nations, *Industrialization and Foreign Trade* (Geneva: League of Nations, 1945), 13.

124. Eric Rauchway, *The Great Depression and the New Deal: A Very Short Introduction* (New York: Oxford University Press, 2008), 8–9, 28–32.

125. Rauchway, *The Great Depression and the New Deal*, 11.

126. Quoted in Steel, *Walter Lippmann*, 285.

127. Daniel Levin, "Federalists in the Attic: Original Intent, the Heritage Movement, and Democratic Theory," *Law and Social Inquiry* 29 (2004): 308.

128. Ott, *When Wall Street Met Main Street*, 36–54, and see also Morrison H. Heckscher, "The American Wing Rooms in the Metropolitan Museum of Art," *Winterthur Portfolio* 46 (2012): 161–78; and Wendy Kaplan, "R. T. H. Halsey: An Ideology of Collecting American Decorative Arts," *Winterthur Portfolio* 17 (1982): 43–53.

129. Gary Gerstle, *American Crucible: Race and Nation in the Twentieth Century* (Princeton, NJ: Princeton University Press, 2001, 2017), 105, 118.

130. David G. Gutiérrez, *Walls and Mirrors: Mexican Americans, Mexican Immigrants, and the Politics of Ethnicity* (Berkeley: University of California Press, 1995), 39–55.

131. Mae Ngai, *Impossible Subjects: Illegal Aliens and the Making of Modern America* (Princeton, NJ: Princeton University Press, 2004), introduction and chs. 1 and 2; Gutiérrez, *Walls and Mirrors*, 52–53, 55.

132. Linda Gordon, *The Second Coming of the KKK: The Ku Klux Klan of the 1920s and the American Political Tradition* (New York: Liveright, 2017); Robert K. Murray, *The 103rd Ballot: Democrats and the Disaster in Madison Square Garden* (New York: Harper & Row, 1976).

133. Du Bois, *The Souls of Black Folk*, 13.

134. Alain LeRoy Locke and Winold Reiss, *The New Negro: An Interpretation* (New York: Albert and Charles Boni, 1925), 5; the author of "The Negro Digs Up His Past" was the historian and writer Arturo Alfonso Schomburg, whose collection became an important part of the New York Public Library's Schomburg Center (originally the Division of Negro Literature, History and Prints); Douglas, *Terrible Honesty*, 93.

135. W. E. B. Du Bois and Lothrop Stoddard, *Report of Debate Conducted by the Chicago Forum: "Shall the Negro be encouraged to seek cultural equality?"* (Chicago: Chicago Forum Council, 1929).

136. George Lloyd Bird and Frederic Eaton Merwin, *The Newspaper and Society: A Book of Readings* (New York: Prentice-Hall, 1942), 30; Daly, *Covering America*, 148–49; Schudson, *Origins of the Ideal of Objectivity*, 249, citing Ivy Ledbetter Lee, *Publicity: Some of the Things It Is and Is Not* (New York: Industries Publishing Co., 1925), 21.

137. Frank Luther Mott, *A History of American Magazines*, 5 vols. (Cambridge, MA: Harvard University Press, 1968), 5 (1905–1930):294–95; Isaiah Wilner, *The Man Time Forgot: A Tale of Genius, Betrayal, and the Creation of* Time *Magazine* (New York: HarperCollins, 2006), 83–86; Alan Brinkley, *The Publisher: Henry Luce and His American Century* (New York: Knopf, 2010), 99; Daly, *Covering America*, 195.

138. Mott, *A History of American Magazines*, 5:230, 319–21; Sarah Smith, "Lessons Learned: Fact-Checking Disasters of the Past," https://netzwerkrecherche.org/files/nr-werkstatt -16-fact-checking.pdf#page=24.

139. Douglas, *Terrible Honesty*, 35; Ben Yagoda, *About Town: The* New Yorker *and the World It Made* (New York: Scribner, 2000), 202–3. And see especially Sarah Cain, "'We Stand Corrected': *New Yorker* Fact-Checking and the Business of American Accuracy," in *Writing for the* New Yorker: *Critical Essays on an American Periodical*, ed. Fiona Green (Edinburgh: Edinburgh University Press, 2015), 36–57.

140. Larry Tye, *The Father of Spin: Edward L. Bernays and the Birth of Public Relations* (New York: Crown, 1998), 78 79; Ernest Gruening, "The Higher Hokum," *The Nation*, April 16, 1924, 450; Edward L. Bernays, "Putting Politics on the Market," *The Independent*, May 19, 1928, 470–72; Edward L. Bernays, "This Business of Propaganda," *The Independent*, September 1, 1928, 198–99.

141. Edward Bernays, "Propaganda and Impropaganda," June 1928, Edward L. Bernays Papers, Library of Congress, Container 422: 1919–1934, Folder: Speech and Article File, 1919–1962.

142. Edward L. Bernays, *Propaganda* (New York: Horace Liveright, 1928), 9.

143. Quoted in Larson, *Summer for the Gods*, 32.

144. Quoted in ibid., 7, 32; Elizabeth Sanders, *Roots of Reform*, 55; FitzGerald, *The Evangelicals*, 125–27.

145. Richard J. Jensen, *Clarence Darrow: The Creation of an American Myth* (New York: Greenwood, 1992), 3; Farrell, *Clarence Darrow: Attorney for the Damned*, 13; Darrow, *The Story of My Life*, 244.

146. Quoted in Farrell, *Clarence Darrow: Attorney for the Damned*, 341.

147. Farrell, *Clarence Darrow: Attorney for the Damned*, 362; Lawrence W. Levine, *Defender of the Faith* (New York: Oxford University Press, 1965), vii–viii.

148. Darrow, *The Story of My Life*, 249.

149. Marquis James, "Dayton, Tennessee," *The New Yorker* [hereafter *TNY*], July 4, 1926. Mencken is quoted in FitzGerald, *The Evangelicals*, 135.

150. For the trial, see Jeffrey P. Moran, *The Scopes Trial: A Brief History with Documents* (New York: Palgrave, 2002).

151. Kazin, *A Godly Hero*, 287–95; John Nimick, "Great Commoner Bryan Dies in Sleep," UPI, July 27, 1925.

152. Nimick, "Great Commoner Bryan Dies in Sleep"; H. L. Mencken, Editorial, *American Mercury*, October 1925, 158–60. Mencken is quoted in Kazin, *A Godly Hero*, 298.

153. Irving Stone, *Clarence Darrow for the Defense* (Garden City, NY: Doubleday, Doran & Company, Inc., 1941), 493.

154. Walter Lippmann, *American Inquisitors: A Commentary on Dayton and Chicago* (New York: Macmillan, 1928), 11–12, 14.

155. Ibid., 39.

156. Ibid., 105.

157. Clarence Darrow, *The Woodworkers' Conspiracy Case* (Chicago, 1898), 79.

## *Eleven:* A CONSTITUTION OF THE AIR

1. Dumenil, *The Modern Temper*, 38.
2. David Halberstam, *The Powers That Be* (Urbana: University of Illinois Press, 2000), 14–15; Joan Hoff Wilson, *Herbert Hoover: Forgotten Progressive* (Boston: Little, Brown, 1975), 140.
3. Herbert Hoover, *The Memoirs of Herbert Hoover*, 3 vols. (New York: Macmillan, 1951–52), 2:144. And see also Hoff Wilson, *Herbert Hoover*, 112–13; Mark Goodman and Mark Gring, "The Radio Act of 1927: Progressive Ideology, Epistemology, and Praxis," *Rhetoric and Public Affairs* 3 (2000): 397–418.
4. Hoover, *Memoirs*, 2:146; J. G. Harbord, "Radio and Democracy," *Forum* 81 (April 1929): 214.
5. Hoover, *Memoirs*, 2:184; Klein, *Rainbow's End*, 4, 5, 11.
6. Quoted in Whyte, *Hoover*, 371.
7. Whyte, *Hoover*, 377–82, 405–6.
8. Tye, *The Father of Spin*, 63–69.
9. Phillip G. Payne, *Crash!: How the Economic Boom and Bust of the 1920s Worked* (Baltimore: Johns Hopkins University Press, 2015); David Kennedy, *Freedom from Fear: The American People in Depression and War, 1929–1945* (New York: Oxford University Press, 1999), 41; Michael A. Bernstein, "Why the Great Depression Was Great: Toward a New Understanding of the Interwar Economic Crisis in the United States," in Steve Fraser and Gary Gerstle, eds., *The Rise and Fall of the New Deal Order, 1930–1980* (Princeton, NJ: Princeton University Press, 1989), 32–54.
10. Quoted in Rauchway, *The Great Depression and the New Deal*, 32.
11. Quoted in ibid., 28–33; John E. Moser, *The Global Great Depression and the Coming of World War II* (Boulder, CO: Paradigm Publishers, 2015), 50; Cass R. Sunstein, *The Second Bill of Rights: FDR's Unfinished Revolution and Why We Need It More Than Ever* (New York: Perseus, 2004), 36–37.
12. "The Press vs. The Public," *TNR* 90 (March 17, 1937), 178–91; Ira Katznelson, *Fear Itself: The New Deal and the Origins of Our Time* (New York: Liveright, 2013), 105.
13. Frankfurter: Schudson, *Discovering the News*, 125; Toynbee: Kiran Klaus Patel, *The New Deal: A Global History* (Princeton, NJ: Princeton University Press, 2016), 43; Laski: Schudson, *Discovering the News*, 125.
14. Moser, *The Global Great Depression*, 77; Mussolini quoted in Katznelson, *Fear Itself*, 5.
15. Walter Lippmann, "Today and Tomorrow," *San Bernardino Sun*, March 24, 1933.
16. Charles A. Beard, "The Historical Approach to the New Deal," *American Political Science Review* [hereafter *APSR*] 28 (1934): 11–15; Katznelson, *Fear Itself*, 114, quoting Reinhold Niebuhr, *Reflections on the End of an Era* (New York: Charles Scribner's Sons, 1934).
17. Hoff Wilson, *Herbert Hoover*, 139–41; Herbert Hoover, Radio Address to the Nation on Unemployment Relief, October 18, 1931.
18. Alonzo L. Hamby, *Man of Destiny: FDR and the Making of the American Century* (New York: Basic Books, 2015), 160; Robert J. Brown, *Manipulating the Ether: The Power of Broadcast Radio in Thirties America* (Jefferson, NC: McFarland, 1988), 28–29.
19. Alan Brinkley, "Roosevelt, Franklin Delano," *American National Biography Online*.
20. Franklin Delano Roosevelt quoted in Kennedy, *Freedom from Fear*, 373.
21. Franklin Delano Roosevelt, Address Accepting the Presidential Nomination at the Democratic National Convention in Chicago, July 2, 1932.
22. Republican: Brown, *Manipulating the Ether*, 27; Hoover: Kazin, *A Godly Hero*, xix; Roosevelt: Degler, *Out of Our Past*, 349.
23. Audio from Stephen Drury Smith, "The First Family of Radio: Franklin and Eleanor Roosevelt's Historic Broadcasts," American Radio Works, November 2014, http://www.americanradioworks.org/documentaries/roosevelts/.

24. Charlotte Perkins Gilman, "A Woman's Party," *The Suffragist* 8 (1920): 8–9.

25. Freeman, *A Room at a Time*, 125; Susan Ware, *Partner and I: Molly Dewson, Feminism, and New Deal Politics* (New Haven, CT: Yale University Press, 1987), 148.

26. Stephen Drury Smith, ed., *First Lady of Radio: Eleanor Roosevelt's Historic Broadcasts* (New York: The New Press, 2014), 33.

27. Gustafson et al., *We Have Come to Stay*, 179.

28. "Mrs. Roosevelt Going to Write Book Now," *Boston Globe*, January 4, 1933.

29. Eleanor Roosevelt, *It's Up to the Women* (1933; New York: The Nation Press, 2017), 173. More about the publication of the book, and its reception, can be found in my introduction to this edition.

30. Franklin D. Roosevelt, Inaugural Address, March 4, 1933.

31. Quoted in Steel, *Walter Lippmann*, 300.

32. *Gabriel over the White House* (MGM, 1933).

33. Quoted in Katznelson, *Fear Itself*, 118–19.

34. Dorothy Thompson, *I Saw Hitler!* (New York: Farrar & Rinehart, 1932), 14; Peter Kurth, *American Cassandra: The Life of Dorothy Thompson* (Boston: Little, Brown, 1990), 163. And see Daly, *Covering America*, 227–31. By 1939, Thompson's columns appeared in 196 newspapers. She also spoke every week on NBC Radio.

35. Horst J. P. Bergmeier and Rainer E. Lotz, *Hitler's Airwaves: The Inside Story of Nazi Radio Broadcasting and Propaganda Swing* (New Haven, CT: Yale University Press, 1997), 3–6; Kennedy, *Freedom from Fear*, 383–84, 412–13.

36. Quoted in Alan Brinkley, *The End of Reform: New Deal Liberalism in Recession and War* (New York: Vintage, 1995), 65.

37. Leila A. Sussmann, *Dear FDR: A Study of Political Letter-Writing* (Totowa, NJ: The Bedminster Press, 1963), 10; Brandon Rottinghaus, "'Dear Mr. President': The Institutionalization and Politicization of Public Opinion Mail in the White House," *Political Science Quarterly* 121 (2006): 456–58.

38. Hoover's mail had been "tremendously big," people said at the time; FDR's mail was, even on a quiet day, an order of magnitude bigger. Leila A. Sussmann, "FDR and the White House Mail," *Public Opinion Quarterly* 20 (1956): 5.

39. Lowell Thomas, *Fan Mail* (New York: Dodge, 1935), x; Jeanette Sayre, "Progress in Radio Fan-Mail Analysis," *Public Opinion Quarterly* 3 (1939): 272–78; Leila A. Sussmann, "Mass Political Letter Writing in America: The Growth of an Institution," *Public Opinion Quarterly* 23 (1959): 203–12.

40. Frances Perkins, *The Roosevelt I Knew* (New York: Viking, 1946), 113.

41. Franklin Delano Roosevelt, First Fireside Chat ("The Banking Crisis"), March 12, 1933.

42. Brown, *Manipulating the Ether*, 5, 11, 16, 18–19.

43. Perkins quoted in Steve Fraser, "The 'Labor Question,'" in Fraser and Gerstle, *The Rise and Fall of the New Deal Order*, 68–69.

44. Sarah T. Phillips, *This Land, This Nation: Conservation, Rural America, and the New Deal* (New York: Cambridge University Press, 2007), 61; FDR quoted in Bruce J. Schulman, *From Cotton Belt to Sunbelt: Federal Policy, Economic Development, and the Transformation of the American South* (New York: Oxford University Press, 1991), 3.

45. Beard, "The Historical Approach to the New Deal," 11–12; George McJimsey, *Harry Hopkins: Ally of the Poor and Defender of Democracy* (Cambridge, MA: Harvard University Press, 1987), 77; Ronald L. Numbers, "The Third Party: Health Insurance in America," in Judith Walzer Leavitt and Ronald L. Numbers, eds., *Sickness and Health in America: Readings in the History of Medicine and Public Health* (Madison: University of Wisconsin Press, 1997), 273; Morris Fishbein, Editorial, *Journal of the American Medical Association* 99 (1932).

46. Franklin D. Roosevelt, *Franklin D. Roosevelt's Own Story: Told in His Own Words from His Private and Public Papers*, selected by Donald Day (Boston: Little, Brown, 1951), 202; Molly C. Michelmore, *Tax and Spend: The Welfare State, Tax Politics, and the*

*Limits of American Liberalism* (Philadelphia: University of Pennsylvania Press, 2012), 5, 6, 10.

47. William Downs Jr., comp., *Stories of Survival: Arkansas Farmers during the Great Depression* (Fayetteville, AK: University of Arkansas Press, 2015), 183, 218–19, 226–27.

48. Manning Marable, *Malcolm X: A Life of Reinvention* (New York: Viking, 2011), 23–36; Gordon, *The Second Coming of the KKK*, 93–94; *The Portable Malcolm X Reader*, ed. Manning Marable and Garrett Felber (New York: Penguin, 2013), 3–33; Erik S. McDuffie, "The Diasporic Journeys of Louise Little: Grassroots Garveyism, the Midwest, and Community Feminism," *Women, Gender, and Families of Color* 4 (2016): 146–70.

49. Brown, *Manipulating the Ether*, 2–3.

50. David A. Taylor, *Soul of a People: the WPA Writers' Project Uncovers Depression America* (New York: Wiley, 2009), 12. And see Monty Noam Penkower, *The Federal Writers' Project: A Study in Government Patronage of the Arts* (Urbana: University of Illinois Press, 1977); Jerre Mangione, *The Dream and the Deal: The Federal Writers' Project, 1935–1943* (Philadelphia: University of Pennsylvania Press, 1983); Jerrold Hirsch, *Portrait of America: A Cultural History of the Federal Writers' Project* (Chapel Hill: University of North Carolina Press, 2003).

51. James Truslow Adams, *The Epic of America,* with an introduction by Howard Schneiderman (1931; New Brunswick, NJ: Transaction Publishers, 2012), xx; Jim Cullen, *The American Dream: A Short History of an Idea That Shaped a Nation* (New York: Oxford University Press, 2003), 3–4, 191–92; Allan Nevins, *James Truslow Adams: Historian of the American Dream* (Urbana: University of Illinois Press, 1968), 66–72. For the radio play, see WPA Radio Scripts, 1936–1940, New York Public Library, Billy Rose Theatre Division, Series XXV: The Epic of America; and Federal Theatre Project Collection, Library of Congress, Music Division, Containers 873–74.

52. "Introduction: American Life Histories: Manuscripts from the Federal Writers' Project, 1936–1940," Library of Congress. And see Federal Writers' Project, *These Are Our Lives, as Told by the People and Written by Members of the Federal Writers' Project of the Works Progress Administration in North Carolina, Tennessee and Georgia* (Chapel Hill: University of North Carolina Press, 1939). Linda Gordon, *Dorothea Lange: A Life Beyond Limits* (New York: Norton, 2010), 201.

53. Bruce J. Schulman, *Lyndon B. Johnson and American Liberalism: A Brief Biography with Documents* (Boston: Bedford Books, 1995), 5–18; Brown, *Manipulating the Ether*, 37.

54. Phillips, *This Land, This Nation*, 151–69.

55. Lidia Ceriani and Paolo Verme, "The Origins of the Gini Index: Extracts from *Variabilità e Mutabilità* (1912) by Corrado Gini," *Journal of Economic Inequality* 10 (2012): 421–43. And see Anthony B. Atkinson and Andrea Brandolini, "Unveiling the Ethics behind Inequality Measurement," *The Economic Journal* 125 (2015): 1–12.

56. Thomas Piketty and Emmanuel Saez, "Income Inequality in the United States, 1913–1998," *Quarterly Journal of Economics* 118 (2003): 1–39; see table 2.

57. Jean-Guy Prévost, *A Total Science: Statistics in Liberal and Fascist Italy* (Montreal: McGill-Queens University Press, 2009), 204–7, 224–25, 250–51.

58. Katznelson, *Fear Itself*, 14; Kurth, *American Cassandra*, 285; Richard Wright, "The FB eye blues" (1949), *Harris Broadsides,* Brown Digital Repository, Brown University Library, https://repository.library.brown.edu/studio/item/bdr:294360/. And see William J. Maxwell, *F. B. Eyes: How J. Edgar Hoover's Ghostreaders Framed African American Literature* (Princeton, NJ: Princeton University Press, 2015).

59. Joshua Polster, *Stages of Engagement: U.S. Theatre and Performance, 1898–1949* (New York: Routledge, 2015) 220–21.

60. Historians have long debated whether the New Deal order marked a continuation of the American experiment or a temporary departure from it. Arguments that it was an exception include Cowie, *The Great Exception.* For an excellent introduction to the

debate, see Fraser and Gerstle, *The Rise and Fall of the New Deal Order.* The terms of this debate derive from the idea that American politics cycles between eras of liberalism and eras of conservatism, a view that many scholars have lately disregarded, insisting, instead, that "the liberal and the conservative are always and essentially intertwined" (Bruce J. Schulman, ed., *Making the American Century: Essays on the Political Culture of Twentieth-Century America* [New York: Oxford University Press, 2014], 5).

61. Alan Brinkley, *Liberalism and Its Discontents* (Cambridge, MA: Harvard University Press, 1998), especially the introduction and "The Problem of American Conservatism."

62. Adam Winkler, *Gunfight: The Battle over the Right to Bear Arms in America* (New York: Norton, 2011), 165–73.

63. Winkler, *Gunfight,* 63–65, 215–16; *U.S. v. Miller,* 307 U.S. 174 (1939).

64. James Ledbetter, *Unwarranted Influence: Dwight D. Eisenhower and the Military-Industrial Complex* (New Haven, CT: Yale University Press, 2011), 22–24; Kim Phillips-Fein, *Invisible Hands: The Making of the Conservative Movement from the New Deal to Reagan* (New York: Norton, 2009), 5.

65. Phillips-Fein, *Invisible Hands,* 14; Wendy Wall, *Inventing the "American Way": The Politics of Consensus from the New Deal to the Civil Rights Movement* (New York: Oxford University Press, 2008), 55.

66. Sharon Beder, *Free Market Missionaries: The Corporate Manipulation of Community Values* (London: Routledge, 2006), 20; Richard S. Tedlow, "The National Association of Manufacturers and Public Relations during the New Deal," *Business History Review* 50 (1976): 25–45.

67. Beder, *Free Market Missionaries,* 20.

68. Phillips-Fein, *Invisible Hands,* 13–22.

69. Donald T. Critchlow, *The Conservative Ascendancy: How the GOP Right Made Political History* (Cambridge, MA: Harvard University Press, 2007), 9–10.

70. Stanley Kelley Jr., *Professional Public Relations and Political Power* (Baltimore: Johns Hopkins University Press, 1956), 44, 12–13.

71. Ben Proctor, *William Randolph Hearst, Final Edition, 1911–1951* (New York: Oxford University Press, 2007), vii., 5, 195; Howard K. Beale, ed., *Charles A. Beard: An Appraisal* (Lexington: University of Kentucky Press, 1954), 245–46.

72. Orson Welles, Deposition taken in Casablanca, May 4, 1949, *Ferdinand Lundberg v. Orson Welles, Herman J Mankiewicz, and R.K.O. Radio Pictures, Inc.,* U.S. District Court for the Southern District of New York, Civil Case Files-Docket No. Civ. 44-62, Boxes: 700780A and 700781A, National Archives, New York. In an essay published in *TNY* in 1971, Pauline Kael argued that Welles's contributions to the screenplay were minimal: Pauline Kael, "Raising Kane," *TNY,* February 20 and 27, 1971. But the film scholar Robert L. Carringer, working with the RKO archives, demonstrated, in *The Making of Citizen Kane* (Berkeley: University of California Press, 1985), 21–22, 153n12, that Welles really did deserve the writing credit. See also Robert L. Carringer, "The Scripts of 'Citizen Kane,'" *Critical Inquiry* 5 (1978): 369–400.

73. The two best sources on the early history of the firm are the Whitaker & Baxter Campaigns, Inc., Records, California State Archives, Sacramento, California; and Carey McWilliams, "Government by Whitaker and Baxter," *The Nation,* April 14 and 21 and May 5, 1951, 346–48, 366–69, 419–21.

74. Upton Sinclair, "I, Governor of California: And How I Ended Poverty—A True Story of the Future," 4, https://depts.washington.edu/epic34/docs/I_governor_1934.pdf.

75. Possibly out of loyalty to Robert Whitaker (Clem Whitaker's uncle and a friend of Upton Sinclair's), Sinclair never named Whitaker and Baxter as the authors of his political doom; he leaves the name of the firm out of all of his accounts of the race. See, for example, Upton Sinclair, *The Autobiography of Upton Sinclair* (New York: Harcourt, Brace & World, Inc., 1962), 272.

76. The fullest accounts of this campaign can be found in Sinclair's writing, but for Whita-

ker and Baxter's end of it, see Irwin Ross, "The Supersalesmen of California Politics: Whitaker and Baxter," *Harper's*, 1959, 56–57; Kelley, *Professional Public Relations and Political Power*, ch. 4; and especially Greg Mitchell, *The Campaign of the Century: Upton Sinclair's Race for Governor of California and the Birth of Media Politics* (New York: Random House, 1992).

77. Mitchell, *The Campaign of the Century*, 128; Sinclair, "I, Candidate," 145–46.

78. Upton Sinclair, *Love's Pilgrimage: A Novel* (New York: Mitchell Kennerley, 1911), 650.

79. Sinclair, *I, Candidate for Governor: And How I Got Licked* (New York: Farrar & Rinehart, 1934), 144; on the serialization: James N. Gregory, introduction to a 1994 reprint edition of the book (Berkeley: University of California Press), x–xi. Sinclair actually also explained how he was losing while he was losing, in Upton Sinclair, *The Lie Factory Starts* (Los Angeles: End Poverty League, 1934).

80. Sinclair, *I, Candidate for Governor*, 144; Sinclair, *Autobiography*, 272.

81. Ross, "Supersalesmen," 56–57; Carey McWilliams, "The Politics of Utopia [1946]," in *Fool's Paradise: A Carey McWilliams Reader*, ed. Dean Stewart and Jeannine Gendar (Santa Clara and Berkeley: Santa Clara University and Heyday Books, 2001), 65.

82. James Harding, *Alpha Dogs: The Americans Who Turned Political Spin into a Global Business* (New York: Farrar, Straus and Giroux, 2008), 64.

83. "The Partners," *Time*, December 26, 1955: "In nearly 25 years, the firm of Whitaker & Baxter has managed 75 political campaigns (all but two confined to California) and has lost only five." And see Dan Nimmo, *The Political Persuaders: The Techniques of the Modern Election Campaign* (Englewood Cliffs, NJ: Prentice-Hall, 1970), 36.

84. McWilliams, "Government by Whitaker and Baxter," May 5, 1951, 419; Ross, "Supersalesmen," 57; Clem Whitaker and Leone Baxter, "What Will We Do with the Doctor's $25.00?," *Dallas Medical Journal*, April 1949, 57.

85. Kelley, *Professional Public Relations and Political Power*, 51; Ross, "Supersalesmen," 58; McWilliams, "Government by Whitaker and Baxter," May 5, 1951, 419; Whitaker, speech before the Los Angeles Area Chapter of the Public Relations Society of America, July 13, 1948, quoted in Kelley, *Professional Public Relations and Political Power*, 50.

86. Transcripts of separate oral histories of Clem Whitaker Jr. and Leone Baxter (hers is entitled "Mother of Political Public Relations"), conducted in 1988 and 1972, respectively, by Gabrielle Morris, Regional Oral History Office, The Bancroft Library, University of California, Berkeley, 57, 15; Kelley, *Professional Public Relations and Political Power*, 48–49; Whitaker, speech before the Los Angeles Area Chapter of the Public Relations Society of America, July 13, 1948; Leone Baxter, "Public Relations Precocious Baby," *Public Relations Journal* 6 (1950): 22.

87. Clem Whitaker, "Professional Political Campaign Management," *Public Relations Journal* 6 (1950): 19; Whitaker, speech before the Los Angeles Area Chapter of the Public Relations Society of America, July 13, 1948.

88. Bergmeier and Lotz, *Hitler's Airwaves*, 3, 8–9.

89. Claude E. Robinson, *Straw Votes: A Study of Political Prediction* (New York: Columbia University Press, 1932), 46–51. See also John M. Fenton, *In Your Opinion: The Managing Editor of the Gallup Poll Looks at Polls, Politics and the People from 1945 to 1960*, with a foreword by Dr. George Gallup (Boston: Little, Brown and Company, 1960), ch. 1; George Gallup and Saul Forbes Rae, *The Pulse of Democracy: The Public-Opinion Poll and How It Works* (New York: Simon & Schuster, 1940), ch. 3.

90. Melvin G. Holli, *The Wizard of Washington: Emil Hurja, Franklin Roosevelt, and the Birth of Public Opinion Polling* (New York: Palgrave, 2002), 41–47.

91. Holli, *Wizard of Washington*, 47–48.

92. Reminiscences of George Gallup (1962–63), Columbia University Oral History Research Office Collection, 17–22; George Horace Gallup, "An Objective Method for Determining Reader Interest in the Content of a Newspaper," PhD dissertation, University of Iowa, 1928, 1–17, 55, 56; Wuthnow, *Inventing American Religion*, 54, 5–6.

93. Reminiscences of George Gallup, 101–15.

94. Gallup and Rae, *The Pulse of Democracy*; E. B. White, Talk of the Town, *TNY*, November 13, 1948; David W. Moore, *The Opinion Makers: An Insider Exposes the Truth Behind the Polls* (Boston: Beacon Press, 2008), 39.

95. Brown, *Manipulating the Ether*, 13; Michael Zalampas, *Adolf Hitler and the Third Reich in American Magazines, 1923–1939* (Bowling Green, OH: Bowling Green State University Popular Press, 1989), 43–44; Bergmeier and Lotz, *Hitler's Airwaves*, ch. 3.

96. Some representative usages: "Britain Demands Russian Apology for Fake News," *Chicago Daily Tribune*, December 8, 1932; "Press Parley Acts to Bar Fake News," *NYT*, November 12, 1933; "Fake News," *Chicago Daily Tribune*, August 3, 1942 (this last is an indictment of the OWI).

97. Quoted in Brown, *Manipulating the Ether*, 11, 14.

98. Frankfurter to FDR, in *Roosevelt and Frankfurter: Their Correspondence, 1928–1945*, annotated by Max Freedman (Boston: Little Brown, 1968), 214.

99. Franklin D. Roosevelt, Acceptance Speech for the Renomination for the Presidency, Philadelphia, Pennsylvania, June 27, 1936.

100. Kennedy, *Freedom from Fear*, 19; Katznelson, *Fear Itself*, 142.

101. Sarah E. Igo, *The Averaged American: Surveys, Citizens, and the Making of a Mass Public* (Cambridge, MA: Harvard University Press, 2007), 138–39.

102. Katznelson, *Fear Itself*, 166–68.

103. Quoted in Brinkley, *The End of Reform*, 166–67.

104. Reminiscences of George Gallup, 117–18; "Polls on Trial," *Time*, November 18, 1940.

105. Reminiscences of George Gallup, 120, 70–80; George Gallup, *Public Opinion in a Democracy* (Princeton, NJ: Princeton University Press, 1939), 5, 15. Roper as cited in Igo, *The Averaged American*, 121.

106. "Hurja Poll," *Time*, May 25, 1939; Gallup, *Public Opinion*, 1, 10.

107. Igo, *The Averaged American*, 169; Amy Fried, *Pathways to Polling: Crisis, Cooperation and the Making of Public Opinion Professions* (New York: Routledge, 2012), 68, 71, 73, 76–77, 146n7.

108. For example, "*America's Town Meeting of the Air*: Personal Liberty and the Modern State," YouTube video, 59:27, from a radio broadcast on December 12, 1935, posted by "A Room with a View" on November 9, 2014, https://www.youtube.com/watch?v=jE6zSfGbzLE; "*America's Town Meeting of the Air*—Does America Need Compulsory Health Insurance?," YouTube video, 59:50, from a radio broadcast on January 15, 1940, posted by "YSPH1" on February 27, 2015, https://www.youtube.com/watch?v=gKa2dYgqd68; Brown, *Manipulating the Ether*, 149; Jamieson, *Presidential Debates*, 88.

109. Joel L. Swerdlow, *Beyond Debate: A Paper on Televised Presidential Debates* (New York: The Twentieth Century Fund, 1984), 27; Jamieson, *Presidential Debates*, 99.

110. Hadley Cantril and Gordon W. Allport, *The Psychology of Radio* (New York, London: Harper & Brothers, 1935), 20.

111. Joel A. Carpenter, *Revive Us Again: The Reawakening of American Fundamentalism* (New York: Oxford University Press, 1997), 21–24, 126–27.

112. Alan Brinkley, *Voices of Protest: Huey Long, Father Coughlin, and the Great Depression* (New York: Vintage Books, 1983), 135.

113. Brown, *Manipulating the Ether*, 84–86.

114. "Prof. J. H. Holmes of Swarthmore Declares That Laws Should Be 'Altered More Easily,'" *NYT*, December 28, 1931, 12; Kammen, *A Machine That Would Go of Itself*, 276.

115. "Hoover Lays Supreme Court Cornerstone," *NYT*, October 14, 1932.

116. James F. Simon, *FDR and Chief Justice Hughes: The President, the Supreme Court, and the Epic Battle over the New Deal* (New York: Simon & Schuster, 2012), 40.

117. Ibid., 225, 235, 243, 246.

118. Ibid., 254–56.

119. Ibid., 258–64.

120. Cushman, *Courtwatchers*, 108–9, 130; James MacGregor Burns, *Packing the Court:*

*The Rise of Judicial Power and the Coming Crisis of the Supreme Court* (New York: Penguin Press, 2009), 143, 143; James Mussatti, *New Deal Decisions of the United States Supreme Court* (Los Angeles: California Publications, 1936), v.

121. Burns, *Packing the Court*, 144; Simon, *FDR and Chief Justice Hughes*, 307.

122. Simon, *FDR and Chief Justice Hughes*, 301.

123. Quoted in Brinkley, *The End of Reform*, 19–20.

124. Franklin Delano Roosevelt, Fireside Chat, March 9, 1937; Simon, *FDR and Chief Justice Hughes*, 317, 324.

125. Alan Brinkley, "Introduction," *American Historical Review* 110 (2005): 1047; Simon, *FDR and Chief Justice Hughes*, 327.

126. H. L. Mencken, "A Constitution for the New Deal," *American Mercury*, June 1937, 129–36. And see Robert G. McCloskey, *The American Supreme Court* (Chicago: University of Chicago Press, 1960), 149–50; Laura Kalman, "The Constitution, the Supreme Court, and the New Deal," *American Historical Review* 110 (2005): 1052–80.

127. Quoted in Brinkley, *End of Reform*, 65, 66, 22.

128. Bergmeier and Lotz, *Hitler's Airwaves*, 23.

129. Dan D. Nimmo and Cheville Newsome, *Political Commentators in the United States: A Bio-Critical Sourcebook* (Westport, CT: Greenwood, 1997), 135–39.

130. Audio excerpts can be found at "The Munich Crisis," *Old Time Radio*, http://www.otr.com/munich.html.

131. Quoted in David Clay Large, *Between Two Fires: Europe's Path in the 1930s* (New York: Norton, 1990), 355.

132. Benjamin Naddaff-Hafrey, "Telling 'the Electrified Fable': Experimental Radio Drama, Interwar Social Psychology, and Imagining Invasion in *The War of the Worlds*," senior thesis, Harvard College, 2013.

133. Quoted in Brown, *Manipulating the Ether*, 247.

134. "23-Year-Old Author Aghast at Hysteria His Skit Created," *Atlanta Constitution*, November 1, 1938.

135. Quoted in Brown, *Manipulating the Ether*, 226–27.

136. Dorothy Thompson, "On the Record," November 14, 1938, as quoted in Kurth, *American Cassandra*, 283. And see Martin Gilbert, *Kristallnacht: Prelude to Destruction* (New York: HarperCollins, 2006).

137. Franklin D. Roosevelt, Excerpts from the Press Conference, November 5, 1938.

## Twelve: THE BRUTALITY OF MODERNITY

1. "World of Tomorrow, 1939 World's Fair," YouTube video, 9:27, from a newsreel from 1939, posted by "PeriscopeFilm," May 12, 2015, https://www.youtube.com/watch?v=HcfgvzwaDHc.

2. James Mauro, *Twilight at the World of Tomorrow: Genius, Madness, Murder, and the 1939 World's Fair on the Brink of War* (New York: Ballantine, 2010), xx; "Metro, The Westinghouse Moto-Man," YouTube video, 3:47, posted by "RobynDexterNSteve," April 2, 2008, https://www.youtube.com/watch?v=soO9CR1NiZk.

3. Mauro, *Twilight at the World of Tomorrow*, xxi, 142–54; E. B. White, "The World of Tomorrow," in *One Man's Meat* (Gardiner, ME: Tilbury House, 1997), 58–64 (quotation, 58).

4. Mauro, *Twilight at the World of Tomorrow*, xxiii–xxiv.

5. Ibid., xx; *The Book of Record of the Time Capsule of Cupaloy* (New York: Westinghouse Electric & Manufacturing Company, 1938).

6. Albert Einstein, *Ideas and Opinions* (New York: Three Rivers Press, 1995), 18.

7. Robert A. Divine, *Second Chance: The Triumph of Internationalism in America During World War II* (New York: Atheneum, 1967), 29, 41, 32.

8. Kennedy, *Freedom from Fear*, 398–99.

9. Quotations from Meacham, *Franklin and Winston*, 134, and Kennedy, *Freedom from Fear*, 392–93.

10. Kennedy, *Freedom from Fear*, 429; Franklin D. Roosevelt, "Message to Congress on Appropriations for National Defense," January 12, 1939; Albert Einstein to FDR, August 2, 1939, reprinted in William Lanouette with Bela Silard, *Genius in the Shadows: A Biography of Leo Szilard, the Man Behind the Bomb* (New York: Skyhorse Publishing, 2013), 211–13; Richard G. Hewlett and Oscar E. Anderson Jr., *The New World, 1939–1946* (*A History of the United States Atomic Energy Commission*, in 2 vols.) (University Park, PA: Pennsylvania State University Press, 1962), 1:20.

11. Quoted in Daly, *Covering America*, 243.

12. Katznelson, *Fear Itself*, 282, 286.

13. Alan Brinkley, *Voices of Protest: Huey Long, Father Coughlin, and the Great Depression* (New York: Vintage, 1983), especially Appendix I: "The Question of Anti-Semitism and the Problem of Fascism."

14. Katznelson, *Fear Itself*, 56–57; Kurth, *American Cassandra*, 285–88.

15. Brown, *Manipulating the Ether*, 87.

16. Katznelson, *Fear Itself*, 276–77; "The War of 1939," *Fortune*, October 1939.

17. "The War of 1939," and "The *Fortune* Survey: Supplement on War," *Fortune*, October 1939. And see also Sister Mary Gertina Feffer, "American Attitude toward World War II during the Period from September 1939 to December 1941," master's thesis, Loyola University, 1951, 35–64.

18. Lindbergh quoted in Kennedy, *Freedom from Fear*, 433.

19. Kennedy, *Freedom from Fear*, 448; Vandenberg quoted in Patel, *The New Deal*, 50.

20. Meacham, *Franklin and Winston*, x–xv, 44–46, 246 (quotation).

21. Churchill quoted in Kennedy, *Freedom from Fear*, 441.

22. Franklin D. Roosevelt, Address at University of Virginia, June 10, 1940.

23. Willkie-McNary Speakers Manual, Campaigns Inc. Records, Box 1, Folder 53; Kennedy, *Freedom from Fear*, 459.

24. Dorothy Thompson, "On the Record," *New York Herald Tribune*, October 9, 1940.

25. U.S. Department of State, *Peace and War: United States Foreign Policy, 1931–1941* (Washington, DC: U.S. Government Printing Office, 1943), 571–72; Statement by the Secretary of State on the Tripartite Pact, September 27, 1940.

26. Pendleton Herring, *Presidential Leadership* (New York: Rinehart and Company, 1940), as quoted in Katznelson, *Fear Itself*, 8.

27. Franklin Delano Roosevelt, Fireside Chat, December 29, 1940.

28. *The FBI's RACON: Racial Conditions in the United States During World War II*, ed. Robert A. Hill (Boston: Northeastern University Press, 1995), 2.

29. FDR to Winston Churchill, January 20, 1941, Churchill Additional Papers, Churchill Archives Centre, Cambridge, UK; Churchill as quoted in Doris Kearns Goodwin, *No Ordinary Time: Franklin & Eleanor Roosevelt: The Home Front in World War II* (New York: Simon & Schuster, 1994), 213.

30. Goodwin, *No Ordinary Time*, 214.

31. Henry Luce, "The American Century," *Life*, February 1941.

32. Quoted in Max Wallace, *The American Axis: Henry Ford, Charles Lindbergh, and the Rise of the Third Reich* (New York: St. Martin's, 2003), 259.

33. Brown, *Manipulating the Ether*, 108–9; Wallace, *The American Axis*, 279.

34. Goodwin, *No Ordinary Time*, 214; Kennedy, *Freedom from Fear*, 474–75, citing *NYT*, March 12, 1941.

35. Katznelson, *Fear Itself*, 313–14; Wallace, *The American Axis*, 274–75, 277, 289, 291; Critchlow, *The Conservative Ascendancy*, 12.

36. Quoted in Bacevich, *The New American Militarism*, 14–15.

37. Jon Meacham, *Franklin and Winston: An Intimate Portrait of an Epic Friendship* (New York: Random House, 2003), 105.

38. Ibid., 107–20; FDR and Churchill, Atlantic Charter, August 14, 1941; Elizabeth Borgwardt, *A New Deal for the World: America's Vision for Human Rights* (Cambridge, MA: Harvard University Press, 2005), 4–6.

39. Meacham, *Franklin and Winston*, 130.

40. Ibid., 131.

41. Franklin Delano Roosevelt, Pearl Harbor Address to the Nation, December 8, 1941; Franklin Delano Roosevelt, Fireside Chat, December 9, 1941.

42. Elaine Tyler May, "Rosie the Riveter Gets Married," in *The War in American Culture: Society and Consciousness during World War II*, ed. Lewis A. Erenberg and Susan E. Hirsch (Chicago: University of Chicago Press, 1996), 130; Patel, *The New Deal*, 261.

43. Patel, *The New Deal*, 262.

44. John Morton Blum, *V Was for Victory: Politics and American Culture During World War II* (New York: Harcourt Brace & Co., 1976), 91–94; Alan Brinkley, "World War II and American Liberalism," in Erenberg and Hirsch, *The War in American Culture*, 315; Patel, *The New Deal*, 262; John P. Broderick, "Business Dropping Off as Wage Scales Rise," *Wall Street Journal*, October 1, 1942.

45. Katznelson, *Fear Itself*, 337–39; Stone quoted in Alan Brinkley, "The New Deal and the Idea of the State," in Fraser and Gerstle, *The Rise and Fall of the New Deal*, 103.

46. Brownlee, *Federal Taxation in America*, 124–48; Michelmore, *Tax and Spend*, 11–12; Thomas L. Hungerford, "Taxes and the Economy: An Economic Analysis of the Top Tax Rates Since 1945," Congressional Research Service, September 14, 2012.

47. Patel, *The New Deal*, 262–66; Katznelson, *Fear Itself*, 346–47.

48. Jytte Klausen, "Did World War II End the New Deal? A Comparative Perspective on Postwar Planning Initiatives," in *The New Deal and the Triumph of Liberalism* (Amherst, MA: University of Massachusetts Press, 2002), 197.

49. Allan M. Winkler, *The Politics of Propaganda: The Office of War Information, 1942–1945* (New Haven, CT: Yale University Press, 1978), 2–3.

50. Blum, *V Was for Victory*, 21–24.

51. Edmond Taylor, *The Strategy of Terror: Europe's Inner Front* (Boston: Houghton Mifflin, 1940), 9, 211.

52. Blum, *V Was for Victory*, 30; Archibald MacLeish, *Collected Poems, 1917–1952* (Boston: Houghton Mifflin, 1952), 13.

53. Quoted in Winkler, *The Politics of Propaganda*, 11–12.

54. Office of Facts and Figures, *Divide and Conquer* (Washington, DC: Office of Facts and Figures, 1942), 3.

55. Kurth, *American Cassandra*, 159; Dorothy Thompson, "Problems of Journalism," 1935, quoted in Michael J. Kirkhorn, "Dorothy Thompson: Withstanding the Storm," [Syracuse University Library] *Courier* 22 (1988):16.

56. Quoted in Winkler, *The Politics of Propaganda*, 23.

57. Archibald MacLeish, *A Time to Act: Selected Addresses* (Boston: Houghton Mifflin, 1943), 23–31.

58. Winkler, *The Politics of Propaganda*, 42; Blum, *V Was for Victory*, 27, 22–23.

59. Gerd Horten, *Radio Goes to War: The Cultural Politics of Propaganda During World War II* (Berkeley: University of California Press, 2002), 2, 43–48.

60. Quotations from Blum, *V Was for Victory*, 31–45.

61. Divine, *Second Chance*, 48; Meacham, *Franklin and Winston*, xviii.

62. Divine, *Second Chance*, 49–51, 63, 72, 104, 119.

63. Quotations from Daly, *Covering America*, 272–74.

64. Quoted in Blum, *V Was for Victory*, 67.

65. Katznelson, *Fear Itself*, 327–28.

66. Ibid., 339.

67. Richard Cahan and Michael Williams, *Un-American: The Incarceration of Japanese Americans During World War II: Images by Dorothea Lange, Ansel Adams, and Other*

*Government Photographers* (Chicago: Cityfiles Press, 2016)—quotations, 24–25; Jasmine Alinder, *Moving Images: Photography and the Japanese American Incarceration* (Urbana: University of Illinois Press, 2009), ch. 1; Linda Gordon, "Dorothea Lange Photographs the Japanese American Internment," in *Impounded: Dorothea Lange and the Censored Images of the Japanese American Internment*, ed. Linda Gordon and Gary Y. Okihiro (New York: Norton, 2008), 5–45.

68. *Hirabayashi v. United States*, 320 U.S. 81 (1943); Mitchell T. Maki, Harry H. L. Kitano, and S. Megan Berthold, *Achieving the Impossible Dream: How Japanese Americans Obtained Redress* (Urbana: University of Illinois Press, 1999), 35.

69. *Korematsu v. United States*, 323 U.S. 214 (1944); Maki et al., *Achieving the Impossible Dream*, 35–38.

70. Lewis, *W. E. B. Du Bois*, 554–56. The letter to Roosevelt is reprinted in Hill, *The FBI's RACON*, 1–2.

71. Blum, *V Was for Victory*, 184–185. Baldwin quoted in Hill, *The FBI's RACON*, 30.

72. Pauli Murray, *The Negro Woman in the Quest for Equality* (New York, 1964); Rosalind Rosenberg, *Jane Crow: The Life of Pauli Murray* (New York: Oxford University Press, 2017), 157–61; Mark V. Tushnet, *Making Civil Rights Law: Thurgood Marshall and the Supreme Court, 1936–1961* (New York: Oxford University Press, 1994), 123.

73. Bayard Rustin, interviewed by Ed Edwin, January 24, 1985, New York, New York, published as *The Reminiscences of Bayard Rustin* (Alexandria, VA: Alexander Street Press, 2003), 2: 43–6.

74. William H. Hastie and Thurgood Marshall, "Negro Discrimination and the Need for Federal Action [1942]," in *Thurgood Marshall: His Speeches, Writings, Arguments, Opinions, and Reminiscences*, ed. Mark V. Tushnet (Chicago: Lawrence Hill Books, 2001), 80.

75. 77 Cong. Rec. 7457 (1942).

76. Declassified in 1980, the report was published in full in 1997 as *The FBI's RACON*. Hoover's June 22, 1942, memo to field agents is reprinted in an addendum, 622–24.

77. Thomas J. Sugrue, *Sweet Land of Liberty: The Forgotten Struggle for Civil Rights in the North* (New York: Random House, 2008), 63, 66–69.

78. Pauli Murray, "Mr. Roosevelt Regrets (Detroit Riot, 1943)," in *Dark Testament and Other Poems* (Norwalk, CT: Silvermine, 1970), 34.

79. Rosenberg, *Jane Crow*, 157–61.

80. Franklin D. Roosevelt, "State of the Union Message to Congress," January 11, 1944; Katznelson, *Fear Itself*, 196, 221–22.

81. Brinkley, *The End of Reform*, 169; Gunnar Myrdal, *An American Dilemma* (New York: McGraw-Hill, 1964), 997.

82. Reed Ueda, "The Changing Path to Citizenship: Ethnicity and Naturalization during World War II," in Erenberg and Hirsch, *The War in American Culture*, 202–3; Lary May, "Making the American Consensus: The Narrative of Conversion and Subversion in World War II Films," in Erenberg and Hirsch, *The War in American Culture*, 71–72, 76.

83. Quoted in Brinkley, *The End of Reform*, 167.

84. Divine, *Second Chance*, 157–59; Meacham, *Franklin and Winston*, 248–66.

85. Franklin Delano Roosevelt, "State of the Union Message to Congress, January 11, 1944"; Rauchway, *The Great Depression and the New Deal*, 127.

86. Borgwardt, *A New Deal for the World*, 50; Patel, *The New Deal*, 268; Brinkley, *The End of Reform*, 129–35.

87. Brinkley, *The End of Reform*, 141; Gerstle, *American Crucible*, 158.

88. "States Moving to Limit U.S. Taxing Power," *Chicago Tribune*, March 12, 1939.

89. Godfrey N. Nelson, "Ceiling Is Sought for Federal Taxes," *NYT*, October 3, 1943.

90. Michelmore, *Tax and Spend*, 34.

91. *Expenditures by Corporations to Influence Legislation. A Report of the House Select Committee on Lobbying Activities, House of Representatives, Eighty-First Congress, Sec-*

*ond Session. Created Pursuant to H. Res. 298. October 13, 1950,* 50; Martin, "Redistributing Toward the Rich," 15–16; Michelmore, *Tax and Spend,* 33–34.

92. "D-Day: 'The Great Crusade,'" multimedia program, https://www.army.mil/d-day/history.html#.

93. Quoted in Borgwardt, *A New Deal for the World,* 95.

94. Moser, *The Global Great Depression,* 2.

95. Hoover quoted in Katznelson, *Fear Itself,* 235–36.

96. Quoted in Brinkley, *The End of Reform,* 158–59.

97. Quoted in Crichtlow, *The Conservative Ascendancy,* 15–16.

98. Alan Brinkley, "World War II and American Liberalism," in Erenberg and Hirsch, *The War in American Culture,* 321; Brinkley, *The End of Reform,* 164–65.

99. Allen J. Matusow, *The Unraveling of America: A History of Liberalism in the 1960s* (Athens: University of Georgia Press, 1984, 2009), 5–6.

100. S. M. Plokhy, *Yalta: The Price of Peace* (New York: Viking, 2010), 4–6, 18–19.

101. Whittaker Chambers, *Ghosts on the Roof: Selected Journalism,* edited and with an introduction by Terry Teachout (Washington, DC: National Book Network, 1989), xxxiv–xxxv, 111–15.

102. Plokhy, *Yalta,* xxiv, 36, 91.

103. Franklin D. Roosevelt, Address to Congress on the Yalta Conference, March 1, 1945.

104. Quoted in Kennedy, *Freedom from Fear,* 806–8.

105. Brown, *Manipulating the Ether,* 125; Meacham, *Franklin and Winston,* 345.

106. "Buchenwald: Report from Edward R. Murrow," April 16, 1945, http://www.jewishvirtuallibrary.org/report-from-edward-r-murrow-on-buchenwald, accessed July 22, 2017.

107. Daly, *Covering America,* 234, 250, 252.

108. Kennedy, *Freedom from Fear,* 797.

109. "Buchenwald: Report from Edward R. Murrow."

110. Quoted in Peter S. Novick, *The Holocaust in American Life* (Boston: Houghton Mifflin, 1999), 65.

111. General Eisenhower to General Marshall concerning his visit to a Germany internment camp near Gotha (Ohrdruf), April 15, 1945, emphasis in original, Dwight D. Eisenhower's Pre-Presidential Papers, Principal File (Box 80, Marshall George C.), Dwight D. Eisenhower Presidential Library, Museum, and Boyhood Home.

112. Novick, *The Holocaust in American Life,* 63–65.

113. Daly, *Covering America,* 286.

114. Henry Stimson to Harry S. Truman, April 24, 1945, Truman Papers, Confidential File, War Department, Box 1, Giangreco, Dennis—Correspondence Between Harry S. Truman, George C. Marshall, Henry Stimson, and Others Regarding Strategy for Ending the War Against Japan, 1945, Harry S. Truman Library and Museum.

115. Plokhy, *Yalta,* 71–72, 228, 381, 392–93.

116. Mauro, *Twilight at the World of Tomorrow,* xx.

117. Divine, *Second Chance,* prologue, 299.

118. Borgwardt, *A New Deal for the World,* 7, 11, 79; Winkler, *The Politics of Propaganda* 155–56.

119. H. G. Wells, *The World Set Free: A Story of Mankind* (New York: Dutton, 1914), 63–64.

120. A Petition to the President of the United States, July 17, 1945, Truman Library and Museum, and quoted in Dan Zak, *Almighty: Courage, Resistance, and Existential Peril in the Nuclear Age* (New York: Blue Rider Press, 2016), 68–69. On Szilard and Wells, see Philip L. Cantelon et al., eds., *The American Atom: A Documentary History of Nuclear Policies from the Discovery of Fission to the Present, 1939–1984* (Philadelphia: University of Pennsylvania Press, 1984), 3–7.

121. Divine, *Second Chance,* 283.

122. *Watchtower Over Tomorrow,* dir. Alfred Hitchcock, Office of War Information, 1945.

123. William M. Rigdon, "President's Trip to the Berlin Conference (July 6, 1945 to August 7, 1945)," Harry S. Truman Library and Museum.

### Thirteen: A WORLD OF KNOWLEDGE

1. John Hersey, "Hiroshima," *TNY*, August 31, 1946.
2. Paul Boyer, *By the Bomb's Early Light: American Thought and Culture at the Dawn of the Atomic Age* (Chapel Hill: University of North Carolina Press, 1985, 1991), 3; James T. Patterson, *Grand Expectations: The United States, 1945–1974* (New York: Oxford University Press, 1996), 3–4.
3. Editorial, *Newsweek*, August 20, 1945; Boyer, *By the Bomb's Early Light*, 3, 7, 22.
4. T. R. Kennedy Jr., "Electronic Computer Flashes Answers, May Speed Engineering," *NYT*, February 15, 1946.
5. Alan Turing, "On Computable Numbers, with an Application to the Entscheidungs-problem," *Proceedings of the London Mathematical Society* 41 (1936): 241.
6. Martin Campbell-Kelly et al., *Computer: A History of the Information Machine* (Boulder, CO: Westview Press, 2014), 41; Grace Murray Hopper, "The Education of a Computer," *Proceedings of the Association for Computing Machinery Conference* (May 1952), 271–81.
7. Isaacson, *The Innovators*, 45–46, 50–52, 76–79, 96, 72–75, 112.
8. Ibid., 219.
9. Vannevar Bush, *Science, the Endless Frontier* (Washington, DC: U.S. Government Printing Office, 1945), 19, 10.
10. *Hearings on Science Legislation (S. 1297 and Related Bills): Hearings before a Subcommittee of the Committee on Military Affairs, U.S. Senate, 79th Congress, 1st Session, Pursuant to S. Res. 107 (78th Congress) and S. Res. 146 (79th Congress) Authorizing a Study of the Possibilities of Better Mobilizing the National Resources of the United States* (Washington, DC: The Committee, 1945), 144. And see Jessica Wang, "Liberals, the Progressive Left, and the Political Economy of Postwar American Science: The National Science Foundation Debate Revisited," *Historical Studies in the Physical and Biological Sciences* 26 (1995): 139–66.
11. Albert Einstein, "The Real Problem Is in the Hearts of Men," interview by Michael Amrine, *NYT*, June 23, 1946; Jessica Wang, "Scientists and the Problem of the Public in Cold War America, 1945–1960," *Osiris* 17 (2002): 323–47; Wang, "Liberals, the Progressive Left, and the Political Economy of Postwar American Science"; Jessica Wang, *American Science in an Age of Anxiety: Scientists, Anticommunism, and the Cold War* (Chapel Hill: University of North Carolina Press, 1999); Federation of Atomic Scientists, *One World or None: A Report to the Public on the Full Meaning of the Atomic Bomb* (New York: McGraw-Hill, 1946), 77.
12. Isaacson, *The Innovators*, 112–15; Kennedy, "Electronic Computer Flashes Answers, May Speed Engineering."
13. Kennedy, *Freedom from Fear*, 786–87; Hilary Herbold, "Never a Level Playing Field: Blacks and the GI Bill," *Journal of Blacks in Higher Education* 6 (Winter 1994–1995): 104.
14. Lizabeth Cohen, *A Consumers' Republic: The Politics of Mass Consumption in Postwar America* (New York: Vintage, 2004), 119, 214.
15. John Updike, *Collected Poems 1953–1993* (New York: Knopf, 1993), 270.
16. Randy Bright, *Disneyland: Inside Story* (New York: Harry N. Abrams, 1987), chs. 1 and 2 (quotation, 73).
17. Elaine Tyler May, "Cold War—Warm Hearth: Politics and the Family in Postwar America," in Fraser and Gerstle, *The Rise and Fall of the New Deal Order*, 153–81 (quotation, 161). And see Elaine Tyler May, "Rosie the Riveter Gets Married," in Erenberg and Hirsch, *The War in American Culture*, 128–43.
18. Cohen, *Consumers' Republic*, 137–42; Margot Canaday, "Building a Straight State: Sexuality and Social Citizenship under the 1944 G.I. Bill," *JAH* 90 (2003): 936–57.
19. Herbold, "Never a Level Playing Field," 104–8.
20. Patterson, *Grand Expectations*, 26–27, 333; Matusow, *The Unraveling of America*,

xii; William E. Leuchtenburg, "Consumer Culture and Cold War: American Society, 1945–1960," in *The Unfinished Century: America Since 1900* (Boston: Little, Brown, 1973), 750.

21. Patterson, *Grand Expectations*, 23; Langston Hughes, "Adventures in Dining," *Chicago Defender*, June 2, 1945, reprinted in *Langston Hughes and the* Chicago Defender: *Essays on Race, Politics, and Culture, 1942–62*, ed. Chris C. De Santis (Urbana: University of Illinois Press, 1995), 55–56.

22. Sugrue, *Sweet Land of Liberty*, 99–100.

23. Harry S. Truman, "Special Message to the Congress Recommending a Comprehensive Health Program," Washington, DC, November 19, 1945.

24. Carey McWilliams, "The Education of Earl Warren," *The Nation*, October 12, 1974; on the apology, see G. Edward White, *Earl Warren: A Public Life* (New York: Oxford University Press, 1982), 76, 81; weeping during a 1972 interview is mentioned by Paul Finkelman in his entry for Warren in *American National Biography Online*; Clem Whitaker, Plan of Campaign for Earl Warren, 1942, in Campaigns, Inc., Records, Box 1, Folder 3, 2–3; Earl Warren, *The Memoirs of Chief Justice Earl Warren* (1977; Lanham, MD: Madison Books, 2001), 163–65; Whitaker, oral history, 48–49.

25. Warren, *The Memoirs of Chief Justice Earl Warren*, 187–88.

26. Baxter, oral history, 1972, 89; White, *Earl Warren*, 112. But see also McWilliams's attempts to understand Warren's political transformation, including McWilliams, "Strange Doings in California," February 1945, in *Fool's Paradise*, 210; McWilliams, "The Education of Earl Warren," *The Nation*, October 12, 1974, 325–26; and McWilliams to Freda Kirchwey, October 12, 1947, *The Nation* Records, Houghton Library, Harvard, Box 25, Folder 4953.

27. McWilliams, "Government by Whitaker and Baxter," April 21, 1951, 366–67; Whitaker from *Medical Economics* (1948) as quoted in Kelley, *Professional Public Relations and Political Power*, 57; Whitaker, oral history, 1988–89, 14–16.

28. Campaigns, Inc., Records, California Medical Association, 1945–1949, Box 5, Folder 20.

29. Warren, *The Memoirs of Chief Justice Earl Warren*, 188.

30. "The Yalta Conference," The Avalon Project. David F. Trask, "The Imperial Republic: America in World Politics, 1945 to the Present," in Leuchtenberg, *The Unfinished Century*, 583; George Kennan to the U.S. Department of State, telegram, February 22, 1946; Winston Churchill, "Sinews of Peace," Fulton, Missouri, March 5, 1946.

31. John Lewis Gaddis, *The Cold War: A New History* (New York: Penguin, 2005), 9–10.

32. Harry S. Truman, "Special Message to the Congress on Greece and Turkey: The Truman Doctrine," Washington, DC, March 12, 1947; Trask, "The Imperial Republic," 577–87, 597.

33. Zelizer, *Arsenal of Democracy*, 66; John A. Farrell, *Richard Nixon: The Life* (New York: Doubleday, 2017), 23, 34–38.

34. Brinkley, *The End of Reform*, 201; Nelson Lichtenstein, "From Corporatism to Collective Bargaining: Organized Labor and the Eclipse of Social Democracy During the Postwar Era," in Fraser and Gerstle, *The Rise and Fall of the New Deal Order*, 122–52; Farrell, *Richard Nixon*, 83–84.

35. Zelizer, *Arsenal of Democracy*, 63–66, 68–71; James T. Patterson, *America in the Twentieth Century: A History*, 5th ed. (Fort Worth, TX: Harcourt College Publishers, 2000), 314.

36. Patel, *The New Deal*, 279; William D. Hartung, *Prophets of War: Lockheed Martin and the Making of the Military-Industrial Complex* (New York: Nation Books, 2011, 2012), 29, 252, 259, 263, 43–47, 52–59.

37. Zelizer, *Arsenal of Democracy*; Patterson, *America in the Twentieth Century*, 312. And see Michael S. Sherry, *In the Shadow of War: The United States Since the 1930s* (New Haven, CT: Yale University Press, 1995).

38. Kennan quoted in Gaddis, *The Cold War*, 47.

39. Gaddis, *The Cold War*, 39.

40. John L. Boies, *Buying for Armageddon: Business, Society, and Military Spending Since the Cuban Missile Crisis* (New Brunswick, NJ: Rutgers University Press, 1994), 1. Faulkner quoted in Schulman, *From Cotton Belt to Sunbelt*, 135, and, more broadly, see ch. 6.

41. Chambers, *Ghosts on the Roof*, xxxvi–xxxvii.

42. Farrell, *Richard Nixon*, 98, 115–24.

43. Patterson, *America in the Twentieth Century*, 161.

44. Ibid., 317; Michael Straight, "Truman Should Quit," *TNR*, April 5, 1948.

45. *National Party Conventions*, 96–97.

46. Patterson, *America in the Twentieth Century*, 319.

47. Quoted in Michael A. Genovese and Matthew J. Streb, eds., *Polls and Politics: The Dilemmas of Democracy* (Albany: State University of New York Press, 2004), 18.

48. Gallup quoted in Lindsay Rogers, *The Pollsters: Public Opinion, Politics, and Democratic Leadership* (New York: Knopf, 1949), vi.

49. Fried, *Pathways to Polling*, 79–80.

50. Herbert Blumer, "Public Opinion and Public Opinion Polling," *American Sociological Review* 13 (1948): 524–49.

51. Rogers, *The Pollsters*, vi, 37, 65, 71, 46, 61. On Rogers, see Amy Fried, "The Forgotten Lindsay Rogers and the Development of American Political Science," *APSR* 100 (2006): 555–56. Although *The Pollsters* appeared in 1949, Rogers wrote it in 1948, before the election.

52. Fredrick Mosteller et al., *The Pre-Election Polls of 1948: Report to the Committee on Analysis of Pre-election Polls and Forecasts* (New York: Social Science Research Council, 1949), vii, Appendix A.

53. Wang, *American Science in an Age of Anxiety*, 39–40.

54. Wang, "Liberals, the Progressive Left, and the Political Economy of Postwar American Science," 156–64.

55. "Summary of Conclusions and Proposals," *APSR* 44 (September 1950): 1–14 (quotation, 14). And see Evron M. Kirkpatrick, "'Toward a More Responsible Two-Party System': Political Science, Policy Science, or Pseudo-Science?," *APSR* 65 (December 1971): 965–90.

56. Dewey quoted in V. O. Key, *Politics, Parties and Pressure Groups* (New York: Thomas Y. Crowell Company, 1942), 220–21.

57. "Medicine Show," *Washington Post*, August 30, 1949; McWilliams, "Government by Whitaker and Baxter," April 14, 1951, 346. A typescript titled "AMA's Plan of Battle: An Outline of Strategy and Policies in the Campaign against Compulsory Health Insurance," and identified as written by W&B, Directors of the National Education Campaign of the AMA, February 12, 1949, Campaigns, Inc., Records, Box 9, Folder 27, 2. On the numbers of pamphlets, see Whitaker and Baxter, "What Will We Do with the Doctor's $25.00?," *Dallas Medical Journal*, April 1949. Daniel Cameron to the National Education Campaign, September 3, 1949, in Campaigns, Inc., Records, Box 9, Folder 40.

58. Campaign Procedures, Campaigns, Inc., Records, Box 9, Folder 27. "AMA's Plan of Battle," 1; Whitaker, "Professional Political Campaign Management," 19—a copy of the printed version is in Campaigns, Inc., Records, Box 9, Folder 26; McWilliams, "Government by Whitaker and Baxter," April 21, 1951, 368.

59. "Plan of Campaign Against Compulsory Health Insurance," written by W&B and dated January 8, 1949 (CONFIDENTIAL: NOT FOR PUBLICATION), Campaigns, Inc., Records, Box 9, Folder 27.

60. I. Isquith, Pharmacist, Stamford, NY, to the NEC, May 22, 1949, Campaigns, Inc., Records, Box 9, Folder 40. Whitaker and Baxter spent $4,678,000, according to Ross, "Supersalesmen," 60.

61. "Truman Blames A.M.A. for Defeat of Security Bill," *Boston Globe*, May 22, 1952.

62. Farrell, *Richard Nixon*, 98, 115–24.

63. Richard Nixon, "The Hiss Case: A Lesson for the American People [January 26, 1950]," in *Speeches, Writings, Documents*, edited and introduced by Rick Perlstein (Princeton, NJ: Princeton University Press, 2010), 19–59.

64. Rick Perlstein, *Nixonland: The Rise of a President and the Fracturing of America* (New York: Scribner, 2008), 34; Farrell, *Richard Nixon*, 159.

65. Farrell, *Richard Nixon*, 143.

66. Geoffrey R. Stone, *Perilous Times: Free Speech in Wartime, from the Sedition Act of 1798 to the War on Terrorism* (New York: Norton, 2004), 331.

67. David K. Johnson, *The Lavender Scare: The Cold War Persecution of Gays and Lesbians in the Federal Government* (Chicago: University of Chicago Press, 2004), 19.

68. Ibid., 21, 79–80, 86–87.

69. Robert Griffith, *The Politics of Fear: Joseph R. McCarthy and the Senate* (Lexington: University Press of Kentucky, 1970), 60; Arthur Herman, *Joseph McCarthy: Reexamining the Life and Legacy of America's Most Hated Senator* (New York: Free Press, 2000), 135.

70. Fitzgerald, *Highest Glass Ceiling*, 109, 115; Farrell, *Richard Nixon*, 163.

71. U.S. Congress, Senate, Committee on Expenditures in the Executive Departments, Subcommittee on Investigations, *Employment of Homosexuals and Other Sex Perverts in Government*, 81 Cong., 2d Sess. (1950).

72. Johnson, *The Lavender Scare*, 25–34, 114–116, 93. And see Aaron Lecklider, *Inventing the Egghead: The Battle over Brainpower in American Culture* (Philadelphia: University of Pennsylvania Press, 2013), ch. 7.

73. Stephen J. Whitfield, *The Culture of the Cold War* (Baltimore: John Hopkins University Press, 1996), 2–4.

74. *Dennis v. United States*, 341 U.S. 494 (1951); Patterson, *America in the Twentieth Century*, 323–34.

75. Schulman, *Lyndon B. Johnson and American Liberalism*, 43–48.

76. Arthur M. Schlesinger and Alfred D. Chandler, *The Vital Center: The Politics of Freedom* (Boston: Houghton Mifflin, 1949); Lionel Trilling, *The Liberal Imagination* (New York: Viking, 1950), ix. And see Matusow, *The Unraveling of America*, 3–5.

77. Critchlow, *The Conservative Ascendancy*, 2–7.

78. "Socialized Medicine 'Opiate,' 200 Physicians Warned Here," *Boston Globe*, March 28, 1949. And see "Welfare State Hit as a Slave State," *NYT*, November 12, 1949.

79. Richard M. Weaver, *Ideas Have Consequences* (1948; Chicago: University of Chicago Press, 2013), 4–12 and see especially ch. 2.

80. Russell Kirk, *The Conservative Mind, from Burke to Santayana* (Chicago: H. Regnery, 1953), 3, 4, 8; Critchlow, *The Conservative Ascendancy*, 19–22.

81. George H. Nash, *The Conservative Intellectual Movement in America Since 1945* (New York: Basic Books, 1976), 72, 142, 150–51; William Buckley, "Publisher's Statement," *National Review*, November 19, 1955.

82. Catherine E. Rymph, *Republican Women: Feminism and Conservatism from Suffrage through the Rise of the New Right* (Chapel Hill: University of North Carolina Press, 2006), 117, 113.

83. Perlstein, *Nixonland*, 85.

84. Rymph, *Republican Women*, 138, 162.

85. Ibid., 94, 107, 117, 131–38.

86. Kennan quoted in Patterson, *America in the Twentieth Century*, 324.

87. Ira Chinoy, "Battle of the Brains: Election-Night Forecasting at the Dawn of the Computer Age," PhD diss., University of Maryland, 2010, 244–45, 256, 260.

88. "Briefs . . . ," *Journal of Accountancy* 92 (1951): 142; Cohen, *Consumers' Republic*, 292–344.

89. "8-Foot 'Genius' Dedicated," *NYT*, June 15, 1951.

90. Saval, *Cubed*, 128–131, 144–47; C. Wright Mills, *White Collar: The American Middle Classes* (New York: Oxford University Press, 1951), 209. The quotation is from a Melville story called "The Paradise of Bachelors and the Tartarus of Maids," which appeared in *Harper's* in 1855 (volume 10; quotation, 675).

91. Mills discusses "The Cheerful Robot" in *The Sociological Imagination* (New York: Oxford University Press, 1959, 2000), 171–76, but introduces it in *White Collar*, in a section called "The Morale of the Cheerful Robot" (233–34).

92. Chinoy, "Battle of the Brains," 206–7.

93. Whitaker and Baxter to Carey McWilliams, May 1, 1951, in Campaigns Inc. Records, Box 10, Folder 3; McWilliams, "Government by Whitaker and Baxter," May 5, 1951, 420; McWilliams, "Government by Whitaker and Baxter," April 21, 1951, 368; Frances Burns, "Mass. General Chief, Dr. Means, Quits AMA Over Health Insurance," *Boston Globe*, June 21, 1951. Whitaker and Baxter reported to McWilliams that his exposé had been sent, anonymously, to the president of the AMA, "probably from someone who thinks W&B should be fired forthwith!" (Whitaker and Baxter to Carey McWilliams, May 1, 1951). Editorial, "Whitaker and Baxter Bow Out," *New England Journal of Medicine*, 247 (1951): 577.

94. Larry J. Sabato, *The Rise of Political Consultants: New Ways of Winning Elections* (New York: Basic Books, 1981), 112, 113, 117, 114; Citizens for Eisenhower, "Eisenhower Answers America," *The Living Room Candidate: Presidential Campaign Commercials 1952–2016*, Museum of the Moving Image.

95. Johnson, *Lavender Scare*, 121–22; Lecklider, *Inventing the Egghead*, 206–7; Daly, *Covering America*, 290.

96. Perlstein, *Nixonland*, 35–36; Farrell, *Richard Nixon*, 199–200; Bernard Schwartz and Stephan Lesher, *Inside the Warren Court* (Garden City, NY: Doubleday, 1983), 17.

97. Richard Nixon, Checkers speech, September 23, 1952.

98. "23 Professors Score Nixon Campaign Fund," *Columbia Spectator*, October 6, 1952. And see Philip Ranlet, *Richard B. Morris and American History in the Twentieth Century* (Dallas: University Press of America, 2004), 63–5. But see Farrell, *Richard Nixon*, 200.

99. Perlstein, *Nixonland*, 41; Farrell, *Richard Nixon*, 194–5.

100. Perlstein, *Nixonland*, 38–43; Farrell, *Richard Nixon*, 198–9.

101. Farrell, *Richard Nixon*, 208.

102. Chinoy, "Battle of the Brains," 210, 194–196.

103. Ibid., 369–88. And see "CBS News Election Coverage: November 4, 1952." YouTube video, 31:02, posted by "NewsActive3," December 17, 2015, https://www.youtube.com/watch?v=5vjD0d8D9Ec; Wuthnow, *Inventing American Religion*, 64.

104. Murrow, quoted in Ibo, *Averaged American*, 180–81.

105. C. Wright Mills, "The Mass Society" in *The Power Elite* (New York: Oxford University Press, 1956), 298–324.

106. Farrell, *Richard Nixon*, 222.

107. "A Report on Senator Joseph R. McCarthy," *See It Now*, CBS, March 9, 1954.

108. Schulman, *Lyndon B. Johnson and American Liberalism*, 47–49.

109. Farrell, *Richard Nixon*, 225.

110. Sydney E. Ahlstrom and Daniel Aaron, *A Religious History of the American People* (New Haven, CT: Yale University Press, 1972), 952.

111. FitzGerald, *The Evangelicals*, 145, 236, 169; Whitfield, *Culture of the Cold War*, 87, 77.

112. FitzGerald, *The Evangelicals*, 170, 177, 186; Whitfield, *Culture of the Cold War*, 80–81.

113. FitzGerald, *The Evangelicals*, 204, 184–85; Whitfield, *Culture of the Cold War*, 88.

114. Marc Linder, "Eisenhower-Era Marxist-Confiscatory Taxation: Requiem for the Rhetoric of Rate Reduction for the Rich," *Tulane Law Review* 70 (1995–96): 905.

115. Whitfield, *The Culture of the Cold War*, 23–4. Leuchtenberg, "Consumer Culture and

Cold War," 763; David M. Oshinsky, *Polio: An American Story* (New York: Oxford University Press, 2005), 217–18.

116. Ledbetter, *Unwarranted Influence*, 45–46; Zak, *Almighty*, 47–49; *The Future of the U.S. Military Ten Years After 9/11 and the Consequences of Defense Sequestration: Prepared for the Use of the Committee on Armed Services of the House of Representatives* (Washington, DC: U.S. Government Printing Office, 2011), 35.

117. The year was 1938, and the subject was how democracies should respond to dictatorships, http://xroads.virginia.edu/~1930s/Radio/TownMeeting/TownMeeting.html.

118. Newton N. Minow and Craig L. LaMay, *Inside the Presidential Debates: Their Improbable Past and Promising Future* (Chicago: University of Chicago Press, 2008), 18–19; "Adlai Stevenson and Estes Kefauver—First Televised Debate, 1956," broadcast by WTVJ on May 21, 1956.

119. "GOP Calls Debate 'Flop,'" *NYT*, May 23, 1956; Minow and LaMay, *Inside the Presidential Debates*, 20.

120. William E. Porter, *Assault on the Media: The Nixon Years* (Ann Arbor: University of Michigan Press, 1976), 9–17; Farrell, *Richard Nixon*, 206–7, 217, 233–34.

121. Richard Rovere, "Letter from San Francisco," *TNY*, September 1, 1956; Herbert M. Baus and William R. Ross, *Politics Battle Plan* (New York: Macmillan, 1968), 258. On Proposition 4, see the files in Campaigns, Inc., Records, Box 29, Folders 23–25.

122. Farrell, *Richard Nixon*, 243. Perlstein, *Nixonland*, 46.

123. Citizens for Eisenhower, "Cartoon Guy," *The Living Room Candidate: Presidential Campaign Commercials 1952–2016*, Museum of the Moving Image.

124. Democratic National Committee television advertisement, "The Man from Libertyville," available for viewing at the online exhibit *The Living Room Candidate: Presidential Campaign Commercials 1952–2016*, Museum of the Moving Image.

125. Whitfield, *Culture of the Cold War*, 21.

126. Ibid., 155–60.

127. *Desk Set*, dir. Walter Lang (20th Century Fox, 1957); *The Desk Set: Screenplay*, filmscript, March 14 1957.

128. Linda Greenhouse, "Thurgood Marshall, Civil Rights Hero, Dies at 84," *NYT*, January 25, 1993; Michael D. Davis and Hunter R. Clark, *Thurgood Marshall: Warrior at the Bar, Rebel on the Bench* (New York: Carol Publishing Group, 1992), 9.

129. Greenhouse, "Thurgood Marshall, Civil Rights Hero, Dies at 84"; Davis and Clark, *Thurgood Marshall*, 9, 160–65.

130. *Brown v. Board of Education*, 347 U.S. 483 (1954).

131. Leuchtenberg, "Consumer Culture and Cold War," 765; Mary L. Dudziak, "Desegregation as a Cold War Imperative," *Stanford Law Review* 41 (1988–89): 81–93, 111.

132. Michael J. Klarman, *Brown v. Board of Education and the Civil Rights Movement* (New York: Oxford University Press, 2007), ch. 3.

133. "Supreme Court: Memo from Rehnquist," *Newsweek*, December 13, 1971. On how word of the memo leaked, see Jill Lepore, "The Great Paper Caper," *TNY*, December 2, 2014, and my note on sources at https://scholar.harvard.edu/files/jlepore/files/lepore_great_paper_caper_bibliography.pdf.

134. Klarman, *Brown v. Board of Education and the Civil Rights Movement*, ch. 3.

135. In one footnote, Warren wrote, "And see generally Myrdal, *An American Dilemma*": *Brown v. Board of Education*, 347 U.S. 483 (1954).

136. Dudziak, "Desegregation as a Cold War Imperative," 65, 115.

137. Tomiko Brown-Nagin, *Courage to Dissent: Atlanta and the Long History of the Civil Rights Movement* (New York: Oxford University Press, 2011), ch. 4.

138. Emmet John Hughes, *The Ordeal of Power: A Political Memoir of the Eisenhower Years* (New York: Atheneum, 1963), 201; "Divergent Views of Public Men," *Life*, September 17, 1956, 119–20; Jim Newton, *Justice for All: Earl Warren and the Nation He Made* (New York: Riverhead Books, 2006), 386.

139. Leuchtenberg, "Consumer Culture and Cold War," 766–67.
140. Taylor Branch, *The King Years: Historic Moments in the Civil Rights Movement* (New York: Simon & Schuster, 2013), ch. 1.
141. Harvard Sitkoff, *The Struggle for Black Equality* (New York: Hill and Wang, 2008), 50.
142. Leuchtenberg, "Consumer Culture and Cold War," 771–72; Harvard Sitkoff and Eric Foner, *The Struggle for Black Equality, 1945–1992* (New York: Macmillan, 1993), 45–46. And, broadly, see David L. Chappell, *Stone of Hope: Prophetic Religion and the Death of Jim Crow* (Chapel Hill: University of North Carolina Press, 2004).
143. Davis and Clark, *Thurgood Marshall*, 191.
144. Klarman, *Brown v. Board of Education*, 187–91; Davis and Clark, *Thurgood Marshall*, 458.
145. Schulman, *Lyndon B. Johnson and American Liberalism*, 53–54; Dan T. Carter, *The Politics of Rage: George Wallace, the Origins of the New Conservatism, and the Transformation of American Politics* (Baton Rouge: Louisiana State University Press, 1995, 2000), 96–97.
146. Klarman, *Brown v. Board of Education*, 191; Leuchtenberg, "Consumer Culture and the Cold War," 770; Orval E. Faubus, "Speech on School Integration" (1958).
147. Schulman, *From Cotton Belt to Sunbelt*, 147–48.
148. Thurgood Marshall, oral history interview, 1977, in *Thurgood Marshall*, ed. Tushnet, 463.

### *Fourteen:* RIGHTS AND WRONGS

1. Farrell, *Richard Nixon*, 269–71.
2. Jerry Marlatt to Dwight Eisenhower, July 10, 1969, in Shane Hamilton and Sarah Phillips, *The Kitchen Debate and Cold War Consumer Politics: A Brief History with Documents* (Boston: Bedford Books, 2014), 41–43.
3. Hamilton and Phillips, *The Kitchen Debate*; "The Kitchen Debate," July 24, 1959, posted by "Richard Nixon Foundation," August 26, 2012, https://www.youtube.com/watch?v=XRgOz2x9c08.
4. Michael B. Katz and Mark J. Stern, *One Nation Divisible: What America Was and What It Is Becoming* (New York: Russell Sage, 2006), 66.
5. John Kenneth Galbraith, *The Affluent Society and Other Writings* (New York: Library of America, 2010), 355.
6. Leuchtenberg, "Consumer Culture and Cold War," 678–80.
7. Daniel Bell, *The End of Ideology: On the Exhaustion of Political Ideas in the Fifties* (Glencoe, IL: Free Press, 1960), 393, 402.
8. Patterson, *America in the Twentieth Century*, 351.
9. Robert Haber, *The End of Ideology as Ideology* (New York: Students for a Democratic Society, c. 1960).
10. Daniel Bell, "The End of Ideology in the West: An Epilogue," in *The End of Ideology: On the Exhaustion of Political Ideas in the Fifties* (1960; Cambridge, MA: Harvard University Press, 2000), 393–407; Macdonald quoted in Richard H. Pells, *The Liberal Mind in a Conservative Age* (Middletown, CT: Wesleyan University Press, 1989), 330.
11. Philip E. Converse, "The Nature of Belief Systems in Mass Publics," in *Ideology and Discontent*, ed. David E. Apter (1964): 207–60; Angus Campbell and Philip E. Converse, *The American Voter* (New York: Wiley, 1960), 193–94.
12. Converse, "The Nature of Belief Systems in Mass Publics." And see Alan Abramowitz and Kyle Saunders, "Is Polarization a Myth?," *Journal of Politics* 70 (2008): 542.
13. Galbraith, *The Affluent Society and Other Writings*, 356; Patterson, *America in the Twentieth Century*, 339; Dwight Macdonald, "Masscult and Midcult," in *Against the American Grain* (New York, NY: Random House, 1962), 4.
14. William Miller, "Provocative Goals," *Life*, December 12, 1960.

15. Taylor Branch, *Parting the Waters: America in the King Years, 1954–63* (New York: Simon & Schuster, 1988), 271–74; Clayborne Carson, *In Struggle: SNCC and the Black Awakening of the 1960s* (Cambridge, MA: Harvard University Press, 1981); Leuchtenberg, "Consumer Culture and Cold War," 772; Susan Gushee O'Malley, "Baker, Ella Josephine," *American Biography Online.*

16. *Goals for Americans: Programs for Action in the Sixties* (Englewood Cliffs, NJ: Prentice-Hall, 1960), 3, 42–48.

17. William Miller, "Provocative Goals," *Life,* December 12, 1960.

18. Ithiel de Sola Pool and Robert Abelson, "The Simulmatics Project," *Public Opinion Quarterly* 25 (1961): 167–83; Ithiel de Sola Pool, Robert Abelson, and Samuel L. Popkin, *Candidates, Issues, and Strategies: A Computer Simulation of the 1960 and 1964 Presidential Election* (Cambridge, MA: MIT Press, 1965).

19. Eugene Burdick, *The 480* (New York: McGraw-Hill, 1964), vii.

20. 1960 Democratic Party Platform, July 11, 1960.

21. Pool and Abelson, "The Simulmatics Project"; Pool, Abelson, and Popkin, *Candidates, Issues, and Strategies.*

22. John F. Kennedy, Address of Senator John F. Kennedy to the Greater Houston Ministerial Association, Houston, Texas, September 12, 1960.

23. Memo, James Dorais to Clem Whitaker Jr. and Newton Stearns, 1960 Nixon Plan of Campaign, Campaigns, Inc., Records, Box 60, Folder 25; Minow and LaMay, *Inside the Presidential Debates,* 20; Farrell, *Richard Nixon,* 299.

24. Perlstein, *Nixonland,* 52.

25. Newton N. Minow and Clifford M. Sloan, *For Great Debates: A New Plan for Future Presidential TV Debates* (New York: Priority Press Publications, 1987), 9–10, 13–14.

26. Farrell, *Richard Nixon,* 287–89, 294–98.

27. John F. Kennedy, Inaugural Address, January 20, 1961.

28. Dwight D. Eisenhower, Farewell Address, January 17, 1961; Kennedy, Inaugural Address.

29. Fredrik Logevall, *Embers of War: The Fall of an Empire and the Making of America's Vietnam* (New York: Random House, 2012), xi–xii.

30. James M. Carter, *Inventing Vietnam: The United States and State Building, 1954–1968* (New York: Cambridge University Press, 2008), 79.

31. Carter, *Inventing Vietnam,* 113–14, 31–32, 97–98; William J. Lederer and Eugene Burdick, *The Ugly American* (New York: Norton, 1958), 272–73, 282.

32. Logevall, *Embers of War,* xiii.

33. Joy Rohde, "The Last Stand of the Psychocultural Cold Warriors: Military Contract Research in Vietnam," *Journal of the History of the Behavioral Sciences* 47 (2011): 232–50.

34. Carter, *Inventing Vietnam,* 33–34, 139–42.

35. Trask, "The Imperial Republic," 638–45; John F. Kennedy, "Radio and Television Report to the American People on the Soviet Arms Buildup in Cuba," October 22, 1962.

36. Robert F. Kennedy, Speech, University of Georgia, May 6, 1961.

37. *Freedom Riders,* dir. Stanley Nelson, American Experience, PBS, May 16, 2011; Branch, *Parting the Waters,* 428–91.

38. Alex Haley, *The Autobiography of Malcolm X* (New York: Ballantine, 1965), 200.

39. Marable, *Malcolm X,* chs. 3–6 (quotation, 133); *Portable Malcolm X Reader,* 34–71, 97–117, 145–65, 184–98.

40. *Portable Malcolm X Reader,* 199–206.

41. Robert F. Williams, *Negroes with Guns* (New York: Marzani and Munsell, 1962); Taylor Branch, *Pillar of Fire: America in the King Years, 1963–1965* (New York: Simon & Schuster, 1998), 13, 136.

42. Carter, *The Politics of Rage,* 115; Branch, *Parting the Waters,* 737–45; Martin Luther King Jr., "Letter from a Birmingham Jail," April 16, 1963.

43. Carter, *The Politics of Rage,* 90–6, 11, 112, 133.

44. Branch, *King Years,* 49–57; John F. Kennedy, "Radio and Television Report to the American People on Civil Rights," June 11, 1963.

45. Bayard Rustin, *I Must Resist: Bayard Rustin's Life in Letters,* introduced and edited by Michael G. Long (San Francisco: City Lights Books, 2012), 257, 261–64.

46. Branch, *Pillar of Fire,* 133.

47. Martin Luther King Jr., "I Have a Dream," speech delivered at the March on Washington for Jobs and Freedom, Washington, DC, August 28, 1963; Branch, *King Years,* 61–67.

48. Schulman, *Lyndon B. Johnson and American Liberalism,* 83–84; Lyndon B. Johnson, "Remarks at the University of Michigan," Ann Arbor, May 22, 1964.

49. Matusow, *The Unraveling of America,* 56; Leuchtenburg, "The Travail of Liberalism," 824; Lyndon B. Johnson, Annual Message to the Congress on the State of the Union, Washington, DC, January 8, 1964.

50. Leuchtenburg, "The Travail of Liberalism," 810; Galbraith, *The Affluent Society,* 419; Leuchtenberg, "Consumer Culture and Cold War," 726; Dwight Macdonald, "Our Invisible Poor," *TNY,* January 19, 1963. And see Jill Lepore, "How a *New Yorker* Article Launched the First Shot in the War against Poverty," *Smithsonian Magazine,* September 2012.

51. Lyndon B. Johnson, Address before a Joint Session of the Congress, Washington, DC, November 27, 1963.

52. *Portable Malcolm X Reader,* 311–26.

53. Ibid., 318.

54. Thurgood Marshall, Glenn L. Starks, and F. Erik Brooks, *Thurgood Marshall: A Biography* (Santa Barbara, CA: Greenwood, 2012), 42.

55. Robert O. Self, *All in the Family: The Realignment of American Democracy Since the 1960s* (New York: Hill and Wang, 2012), 25.

56. Carter, *The Politics of Rage,* 206–7.

57. Critchlow, *The Conservative Ascendancy,* 72.

58. Ibid., 53.

59. Ibid., 67.

60. Ibid., 67.

61. Ibid. 70–71; Fitzgerald, *Highest Glass Ceiling,* 142.

62. Perlstein, *Nixonland,* 63–64; Barry Goldwater, Acceptance Speech, 28th Republican National Convention, Daly City, California, July 17, 1964.

63. Patterson, *America in the Twentieth Century,* 395; Leuchtenburg, "The Travail of Liberalism," 812–13; FitzGerald, *The Evangelicals,* 243–44.

64. Marjorie J. Spruill, *Divided We Stand: The Battle Over Women's Rights and Family Values That Polarized American Politics* (New York: Bloomsbury, 2017), 77.

65. Critchlow, *The Conservative Ascendancy,* 41; Donald T. Critchlow, *Phyllis Schlafly and Grassroots Conservatism: A Woman's Crusade* (Princeton, NJ: Princeton University Press, 2005), 145; Rymph, *Republican Women,* 182.

66. Rymph, *Republican Women,* 166–87.

67. Schulman, *Lyndon Johnson and American Liberalism,* 82.

68. Sarah A. Binder, *Stalemate: Causes and Consequences of Legislative Gridlock* (Washington, DC: Brookings Institution Press, 2003), ch. 4, and see also Binder, "The Dynamics of Legislative Gridlock, 1947–96," *APSR* 93 (1999): 519–33, and David R. Jones, "Party Polarization and Legislative Gridlock," *Political Research Quarterly* 54 (2001): 125–41.

69. Schulman, *Lyndon B. Johnson and American Liberalism,* 90.

70. Michelmore, *Tax and Spend,* 48–50, 62–63; Brownlee, *Federal Taxation in America,* 123.

71. Matusow, *The Unraveling of America,* 57.

72. Trask, "The Imperial Republic," 647; Carter, *Inventing Vietnam,* 161; Schulman, *Lyndon B. Johnson and American Liberalism,* 101.

73. Steve Warshaw, *The Trouble in Berkeley* (Berkeley, CA: Diablo Press, 1965), 27.

74. Perlstein, *Nixonland,* 96.
75. Branch, *Pillar of Fire,* 578–79; *Portable Malcolm X Reader,* 394.
76. James Baldwin's remarks on the death of Malcolm X can be seen at https://www.you tube.com/watch?v=cHm31kOWFec.
77. Lyndon B. Johnson, "The American Promise": Address before a Joint Session of the Congress, Washington, DC, March 15, 1965.
78. Elizabeth Hinton, *From the War on Poverty to the War on Crime: The Making of Mass Incarceration in America* (Cambridge, MA: Harvard University Press, 2016), 1–5, 13–16, 65, 79, 90–98, 106–7, 119–21; Patterson, *America in the Twentieth Century,* 414.
79. Hinton, *From the War on Poverty to the War on Crime,* 66–69.
80. Schulman, *Lyndon B. Johnson and American Liberalism,* 111–12.
81. Leuchtenburg, "The Travail of Liberalism," 829.
82. Perlstein, *Nixonland,* 189–96.
83. Leuchtenberg, "The Travail of Liberalism," 874.
84. Ronald Reagan, "Time for Choosing," Speech, televised campaign address for Goldwater presidential campaign, October 27, 1964.
85. Martin Luther King Jr., "Our God Is Marching On," speech delivered at the Selma to Montgomery March, Montgomery, Alabama, March 25, 1965; John Herbers, "Right Backers Fear a Backlash," *NYT,* September 21, 1966; Gerald R. Ford, Illinois State Fair Address, August 17, 1966, Ford Congressional Papers, Press Secretary and Speech File, Gerald R. Ford Presidential Library, Box D20, Folder "Illinois State Fair"; Perlstein, *Nixonland,* 71, 83, 114.
86. Quoted in David Chagall, *The New King-Makers* (New York: Harcourt Brace Jovanovich, 1981), 3.
87. "Reagan Urges Carmichael Not to Speak at UC," *Los Angeles Times,* October 19, 1966; Richard Bergholz, "Reagan Criticizes UC for Permitting Bob Kennedy Talk," *Los Angeles Times,* October 21, 1966.
88. Redacted to Hoover, September 4, 1966, decoded telegram, Stokely Carmichael FBI file, FBI Vault (vault.fbi.gov), Part 3, page 5. Special Agent in Charge, Atlanta, to Hoover, September 20, 1966, Carmichael's FBI file, FBI Vault, Part 4, page 9. The FBI was trying to find a way to deport Carmichael, who had been born in Trinidad.
89. Stuart Spencer, oral history, November 15–16, 2001, Miller Center, University of Virginia. Reagan told a slightly different story: Gerard J. De Groot, "Ronald Reagan and Student Unrest in California, 1966–1970," *Pacific Historical Review* 65 (1996): 107–29.
90. Michelle Reeves, "'Obey the Rules or Get Out': Ronald Reagan's 1966 Gubernatorial Campaign and the 'Trouble in Berkeley,'" *Southern California Quarterly* 92 (2010): 295. And see Stanley G. Robertson, "LA Confidential," *Los Angeles Sentinel,* November 3, 1966.
91. Stokeley Carmichael, speech at Berkeley, October 1966, https://www.youtube.com/watch?v=uWsgT67-RM4; James Reston, "Berkeley, California: The University and Politics," *NYT,* October 23, 1966; Patterson, *America in the Twentieth Century,* 416–19.
92. Adam Winkler, "The Secret History of Guns," *Atlantic,* September 2011.
93. Hinton, *From the War on Poverty to the War on Crime,* 123–27.
94. Quoted in De Groot, "Ronald Reagan and Student Unrest," 116.
95. Arnold Hano, "The Black Rebel Who 'Whitelists" the Olympics," *NYT,* May 12, 1968.
96. Perlstein, *Nixonland,* 97; David Remnick, *King of the World: Muhammad Ali and the Rise of an American Hero* (New York: Knopf, 2014), 289; Sandra Millner, *The Dream Lives On: Martin Luther King, Jr.* (New York: MetroBooks, 1999), 44.
97. Schulman, *Lyndon B. Johnson and American Liberalism,* 126, 139, 241.
98. Leuchtenburg, "The Travail of Liberalism," 874.
99. Carter, *Politics of Rage,* 306.
100. Perlstein, *Nixonland,* 163–65.
101. "Lyndon Johnson Says He Won't Run," *NYT,* April 1, 1968.
102. Schulman, *Lyndon B. Johnson and American Liberalism,* 119; Perlstein, *Nixonland,* 257;

Bruce J. Schulman, *The Seventies: The Great Shift in American Culture* (New York: Free Press, 2001), 2–3; Ben. A. Franklin, "Army Troops in Capital as Negroes Riot," *NYT*, April 5, 1968.

103. Robert F. Kennedy, "Statement on Assassination of Martin Luther King, Jr.," Indianapolis, Indiana, April 4, 1968.

104. Perlstein, *Nixonland*, 239–41; Ronald Reagan, radio address, March 7, 1968.

105. Farrell, *Richard Nixon*, 343–44, 367.

106. Carter, *Politics of Rage*, 379; Farrell, *Richard Nixon*, 330, 336; Richard Nixon, Address Accepting the Presidential Nomination at the Republican National Convention in Miami Beach, Florida, August 8, 1968.

107. Hinton, *From the War on Poverty to the War on Crime*, 139–40.

108. Schulman, *The Seventies*, 12. The best account is Norman Mailer, *Miami and the Siege of Chicago: An Informal History of the Republican and Democratic Conventions of 1968* (New York: New American Library, 1968).

109. Schulman, *Lyndon B. Johnson and American Liberalism*, 161; Keith T. Poole and Howard Rosenthal, "On Party Polarization in Congress," *Daedalus* 136 (2007): 104–7.

110. Baxter, oral history, 1972, 17, 22–4.

111. Quoted in Hartman, *War for the Soul of America*, 25.

112. Noam Chomsky, "The Menace of Liberal Scholarship," *The New York Review of Books*, January 2, 1969; Rohde, "The Last Stand of the Psychocultural Cold Warriors," 246. Chomsky refers to Simulmatics's "urban insurgency" work as confidential; Rohe cites Simulmatics's "Urban Insurgency file" in *Armed with Expertise: The Militarization of American Social Research During the Cold War* (Ithaca, NY: Cornell University Press, 2013), 169n5.

113. Schulman, *The Seventies*, 16.

114. Leuchtenburg, "The Travail of Liberalism," 873.

115. This was on January 8, 1970; Carter, *Politics of Rage*, 380.

116. H. R. Haldeman, transcript of an oral history, conducted 1991 by Dale E. Trevelen, State Government Oral History Program, California State Archives, 317.

117. Richard M. Scammon and Ben J. Wattenberg, *The Real Majority* (New York: Coward-McCann, Inc., 1970), 20–21, 280–81.

118. Schulman, *The Seventies*, 38; James M. Naughton, "Nixon, Confident of Gains in '70, Planning Same Tactics for '72," *NYT*, October 23, 1970; Farrell, *Richard Nixon*, 388; Andrew Hacker, *The End of the American Era* (New York: Atheneum, 1970), ch. 2.

119. Perlstein, *Nixonland*, 393–96.

120. Schulman, *The Seventies*, 34–35; Carter, *Politics of Rage*, 398–99.

121. Farrell, *Richard Nixon*, 413.

122. Ibid., 418.

123. *The Nixon Tapes, 1971–1972*, edited and annotated by Douglas Brinkley and Luke A. Nichter (Boston: Houghton Mifflin, 2014), ix–x.

124. Neil Sheehan, "Pentagon Study Traces 3 Decades of Growing U.S. Involvement," *NYT*, June 13, 1971.

125. Farrell, *Richard Nixon*, 420–26.

126. Audio, https://www.nixonlibrary.gov/virtuallibrary/tapeexcerpts/534-2(3)-brookings.mp 3; transcript, https://www.nixonlibrary.gov/forresearchers/find/tapes/watergate/trial/exhibit_12.pdf; Schulman, *The Seventies*, 44.

127. Farrell, *Richard Nixon*, 465–84. For the June 23 conversation: "The Smoking Gun Tape," Watergateinfo, http://watergate.info/1972/06/23/the-smoking-gun-tape.html, accessed August 17, 2017.

128. Farrell, *Richard Nixon*, 497–98.

129. LBJ, interview with Walter Cronkite, January 12, 1973, https://www.youtube.com/watch?v=vW5PemdbcT8; Schulman, *Lyndon B. Johnson and American Liberalism*, 164.

130. Farrell, *Richard Nixon*, 519.

131. Ibid., 523–57; *U.S. v. Nixon*, 418 U.S. 683 (1974).

132. Richard Nixon, Resignation Speech, Washington, DC, August 8, 1974.

133. Farrell, *Richard Nixon*, 532.


## Fifteen: BATTLE LINES

1. Betty Ford to Lesley Stahl, in a 1997 interview, CBS News, "The Remarkable Mrs. Ford," August 17, 2015, https://www.cbsnews.com/news/the-remarkable-mrs-ford/, accessed August 21, 2017.

2. Betty Friedan, *The Feminine Mystique* (New York: Dell, 1963), 11.

3. Betty Ford with Chris Chase, *The Times of My Life* (New York: Harper & Row, 1978), 120. And on these years, see also John Robert Greene, *Betty Ford: Candor and Courage in the White House* (Lawrence: University Press of Kansas, 2004), ch. 2.

4. On Murray's role in NOW's founding and mission, see Rosenberg, *Jane Crow*, 298–300.

5. An August 1972 Gallup poll reported that 68 percent of Republicans and 58 percent of Democrats agreed that "the decision to have an abortion should be made solely by a woman and her physician" (Jack Rosenthal, "Survey Finds Majority, in Shift, Now Favors Liberalized Laws," *NYT*, August 25, 1972), a poll that Supreme Court Justice Harry Blackmun included in his *Roe v. Wade* case file; Linda Greenhouse and Reva B. Siegel, "Before (and After) *Roe v. Wade*: New Questions About Backlash," *Yale Law Journal* 120 (2011): 2031.

6. "The Republican Party favors a continuance of the public dialogue on abortion and supports the efforts of those who seek enactment of a constitutional amendment to restore protection of the right to life for unborn children" (Republican Party Platform of 1976, August 18, 1976). "We fully recognize the religious and ethical nature of the concerns which many Americans have on the subject of abortion. We feel, however, that it is undesirable to attempt to amend the U.S. Constitution to overturn the Supreme Court decision in this area" (1976 Democratic Party Platform, July 12, 1976).

7. Byron W. Daynes and Raymond Tatlovich, "Presidential Politics and Abortion, 1972–1988," *Presidential Studies Quarterly* 22 (1992): 545–61.

8. Richard A. Viguerie, *The New Right: We're Ready to Lead* (Falls Church, VA: Viguerie, 1981), 55; on the culture wars, broadly, see Andrew Hartman, *A War for the Soul of America: A History of the Culture Wars* (Chicago: University of Chicago Press, 2015).

9. Michael Kelly, "The 1992 Campaign," *NYT*, October 31, 1992.

10. Editor's note in Margaret Sanger, *The Selected Papers of Margaret Sanger*, ed. Esther Katz et al., 4 vols. (Urbana: University of Illinois Press, 2010), 3:469. And see James W. Reed, Interview with Mary Steichen Calderone, MD, August 7, 1974, transcript, Schlesinger-Rockefeller Oral History Project, Schlesinger Library, Radcliffe, Reel A-1, 2; Tom Davis, *Sacred Work: Planned Parenthood and Its Clergy Alliances* (New Brunswick, NJ: Rutgers University Press, 2005), 89.

11. James W. Reed, interviews with Loraine Lesson Campbell, December 1973–March 1974, Schlesinger-Rockefeller Oral History Project, Reel A-1, 71, 83; Alan F. Guttmacher, "Memoirs," typescript, November 1972, Planned Parenthood Federation of America (PPFA) Records, Smith College, PPFA 2, Administration, Guttmacher, A. F., Autobiography, Rough Draft, Box 117, Folder 39; David M. Kennedy, *Birth Control in America; the Career of Margaret Sanger* (New Haven, CT: Yale University Press, 1970), vii; *Griswold v. Connecticut*, 381 U.S. 479 (1965).

12. *Griswold v. Connecticut*, 381 U.S. 479 (1965).

13. Bush quoted in Gloria Feldt with Carol Trickett Jennings, *Behind Every Choice Is a Story* (Denton: University of North Texas Press, 2002), 94. Spruill, *Divided We Stand*, 286; *Eisenstadt v. Baird*, 405 U.S. 438 (1972).

14. Greenhouse and Siegel, "Before (and After) *Roe*," 2047–49; Linda Gordon, *The Moral Property of Women: A History of Birth Control Politics in America* (Urbana and Chicago:

University of Illinois Press, 2002), 289; Richard Nixon: "Special Message to the Congress on Problems of Population Growth," July 18, 1969.

15. "F. J. Bardacke on The Woman Question," *San Francisco Express Times*, September 25, 1968.

16. Alice Echols, *Daring To Be Bad: Radical Feminism in America, 1967–1975* (Minneapolis: University of Minnesota Press, 1989), 56–57, 92–96, 120.

17. Vern L. Bullough, *Before Stonewall: Activists for Gay and Lesbian Rights in Historical Context* (New York: Harrington Park Press, 2002); Frank Kameny and Michael G. Long, *Gay Is Good: The Life and Letters of Gay Rights Pioneer Franklin Kameny* (Syracuse, NY: Syracuse University Press, 2014), 93, 165, 173–74; Lacey Fosburgh, "Thousands of Homosexuals Hold a Protest Rally in Central Park," *NYT*, June 29, 1970. And, on the transition from the 1950s homophile movement to the 1960s gay rights movement, see Gregory Andrew Briker, "The Right to Be Heard: *One* Magazine, Obscenity Law, and the Battle over Homosexual Speech," AB thesis, Harvard University, 2017.

18. Spruill, *Divided We Stand*, 14, 29–33.

19. Irin Carmon and Shana Knizhnik, *Notorious RBG: The Life and Times of Ruth Bader Ginsburg* (New York: William Morrow, 2015), 46.

20. Pauline M. Trowbridge to Alan Guttmacher, August 2, 1970, Alan Guttmacher Papers, Countway Library, Harvard Medical School, Box 2, Folder 10.

21. *Roe v. Wade*, 410 U.S. 113 (1973).

22. Greenhouse and Siegel, "Before (and After) *Roe*," 2053–54.

23. *Roe v. Wade*, 410 U.S. 113 (1973).

24. Richard Nixon to Charles Colson, January 23, 1976, in *The Nixon Tapes: 1973*, edited and annotated by Douglas Brinkley and Luke A. Nichter (New York: Houghton Mifflin Harcourt, 2015), 17–18.

25. "The First Lady," *60 Minutes*, August 10, 1975, transcript of an interview with Betty Ford by Morley Safer, Box 11, Folder "Ford, Betty—General," Ron Nessen Papers, Ford Presidential Library, https://www.fordlibrarymuseum.gov/library/docu ment/0204/1511773.pdf. And on her cancer, see Ford, *The Times of My Life*, ch. 26.

26. Spruill, *Divided We Stand*, 43–45.

27. "The First Lady," *60 Minutes*, August 10, 1975.

28. Greene, *Betty Ford*, 59. And on this point, generally, see Spruill, *Divided We Stand*.

29. Greene, *Betty Ford*, 67.

30. Sean Wilentz, *The Age of Reagan: A History, 1974–2008* (New York: HarperCollins, 2008), 14.

31. Ibid., 35; Patterson, *Restless Giant*, 7.

32. For this thesis and its evidence, see Robert J. Gordon, *The Rise and Fall of American Growth: The U.S. Standard of Living since the Civil War* (Princeton, NJ: Princeton University Press, 2016).

33. Piketty and Saez, "Income Inequality in the United States, 1913–1998," 1–41; Self, *All in the Family*, 314.

34. Spruill, *Divided We Stand*, 71, 80, 85.

35. Rymph, *Republican Women*, 198–99.

36. Republican Party Platform of 1976, August 18, 1976; Freeman, *We Will be Heard*, 122–25; Rymph, *Republican Women*, 189, 205, 207, 209–10, 223.

37. Spruill, *Divided We Stand*, 127.

38. Rymph, *Republican Women*, 215–16; Self, *All in the Family*, 312, 313. For chronicles of the conference, see Alice S. Rossi, *Feminists in Politics: A Panel Analysis of the First National Women's Conference* (New York: Academic Press, 1982), and Shelah Gilbert Leader and Patricia Rusch Hyatt, *American Women on the Move: The Inside Story of the National Women's Conference, 1977* (Lanham, NJ: Levington Books, 2016).

39. "The Torch Relay," in National Commission on the Observance of International Women's Year, *The Spirit of Houston: The First National Women's Conference* (Washington, DC: U.S. Government Printing Office, March 1978), 193–203.

40. Maya Angelou, "To Form a More Perfect Union," in *The Spirit of Houston*, 195.

41. "Speech by Betty Ford, National Commissioner and Former First Lady, First Plenary Session," in *The Spirit of Houston*, 220–21.

42. Self, *All in the Family*, 217; Spruill, *Divided We Stand*, 225.

43. Self, *All in the Family*, 318; Spruill, *Divided We Stand*, 7.

44. "The Minority Caucus: 'It's Our Movement Now,'" in *The Spirit of Houston*, 156–57.

45. Anita Bryant, *The Anita Bryant Story: The Survival of Our Nation's Families and the Threat of Militant Homosexuality* (Old Tappan, NJ: Felming H. Revell Company, 1977), 17, 21.

46. Spruill, *Divided We Stand*, 228–29.

47. Anna Quindlen, "Women's Conference Approves Planks on Abortion and Rights for Homosexuals," *NYT*, November 21, 1977; Self, *All in the Family*, 320–21.

48. Carolyn Kortge, "Schlafly Says Women's Movement Is Dying in an Anti-Feminist Surge," *Eagle & Beacon*, August 3, 1977, reprinted in *National Women's Conference Official Briefing Book: Houston, Texas, November 18 to 21, 1977* (Washington, DC: National Commission on the Observance of International Women's Year, 1977), 228. Self, *All in the Family*, 319.

49. Spruill, *Divided We Stand*, 152.

50. Critchlow, *The Conservative Ascendancy*, 132–33.

51. Patterson, *Restless Giant*, 21.

52. Critchlow, *The Conservative Ascendancy*, 128; John D'Emilio and Estelle B. Freedman, *Intimate Matters: A History of Sexuality* (Chicago: University of Chicago Press, 1988), 349–50; FitzGerald, *The Evangelicals*, 291, 302.

53. "Resolution On Abortion: St. Louis, Missouri, 1971," Southern Baptist Convention, http://www.sbc.net/resolutions/13/resolution-on-abortion); FitzGerald, *The Evangelicals*, 299; Robert C. Post and Reva C. Siegel, "*Roe* Rage: Democratic Constitutionalism and Backlash," 2007, Faculty Scholarship Series, Yale University, Paper 169, 420–21.

54. FitzGerald, *The Evangelicals*, 291–94.

55. Spruill, *Divided We Stand*, 288–89.

56. Rymph, *Republican Women*, 221, 228, 237–38.

57. Self, *All in the Family*, 358–60.

58. Ronald Reagan, Address Accepting the Presidential Nomination at the Republican National Convention in Detroit, July 17, 1980.

59. Spruill, *Divided We Stand*, 287.

60. Kenneth Janda, "Innovations in Information Technology in American Party Politics Since 1960," in Guy Lachapelle and Philippe J. Maarek, eds. *The Political Parties in the Digital Age: The Impact of New Technologies in Politics* (Boston: De Gruyter Oldenbourg, 2015).

61. Viguerie, *The New Right*, 12, 21, 32, 35, 91–93.

62. Wuthnow, *Inventing American Religion*, 99–100; Leo Bogart, *Silent Politics: Polls and the Awareness of Public Opinion* (New York: Wiley and Sons, 1972), 101; Philip Meyer, *Precision Journalism: A Reporter's Introduction to Social Science Methods* (Bloomington: Indiana University Press, 1973)—quotation, 191; David W. Moore, *The Opinion Makers: An Insider Exposes the Truth Behind the Polls* (Boston: Beacon, 2008), xvii.

63. Nolan M. McCarty, Keith T. Poole, and Howard Rosenthal, "Polarized Politicians," in *Polarized America: The Dance of Ideology and Unequal Riches* (Cambridge, MA: MIT Press, 2006), 15–70; Sinclair, *Party Wars*, 16; Self, *All in the Family*, 371; Rymph, *Republican Women*, 231.

64. Greg D. Adams, "Abortion: Evidence of an Issue Evolution," *American Journal of Political Science* 41 (1997): 718, 723; Greenhouse and Siegel, "Before (and After) *Roe*," 2069–70.

65. Hartman, *War for the Soul of America*, 134.

66. Ronald Reagan, Inaugural Address, January 20, 1981; Crichtlow, *Conservative Ascendancy*, 199.

67. Michelmore, *Tax and Spend*, 122, 138–39; Brownlee, *Federal Taxation in America*, 134; Patterson, *Restless Giant*, 66–69.

68. H. W. Brands, *Reagan: The Life* (New York: Doubleday, 2015), 179; Alan O. Ebenstein, *Milton Friedman: A Biography* (New York: Palgrave Macmillan, 2007), 208; Reagan's introduction to Friedman's television series, "President Reagan on Dr. Friedman and Free to Choose," YouTube video, 1:09, posted by "Free to Choose Network," July 18, 2013, https://www.youtube.com/watch?v=um-p3ZhiO60; Eamonn Butler, *Milton Friedman: A Guide to His Economic Thought* (New York: Universe Books, 1985).

69. Larissa MacFarquhar, "The Gilder Effect," *TNY*, May 29, 2000. For a skeptical view of the rise of supply-side economics, see Jonathan Chait, *The Big Con: The True Story of How Washington Got Hoodwinked and Hijacked by Crackpot Economics* (Boston: Houghton Mifflin, 2007).

70. MacFarquhar, "The Gilder Effect"; George F. Gilder, *Sexual Suicide* (New York: Quadrangle, 1973), 5–6, 92–93, 131, 241–42.

71. George Gilder, *Wealth and Poverty: A New Edition for the Twenty-First Century* (New York: Regnery, 2012), foreword by Steve Forbes, x, 27, 15, 17.

72. Patterson, *Restless Giant*, 48–49.

73. Daniel Wirls, *Irrational Security: The Politics of Defense from Reagan to Obama* (Baltimore: Johns Hopkins University Press, 2010), 19; Michelmore, *Tax and Spend*, 141, 147.

74. Patterson, *Restless Giant*, 158–59, 165, 175.

75. Winkler, *Gunfight*, 65, 248, 253, but see Siegel, "Dead or Alive," n58.

76. Winkler, *Gunfight*, 233–235.

77. William Safire, "An Appeal for Repeal," *NYT*, June 10, 1999. Nixon Library, White House Tapes, Nixon to H. R. Haldeman, June 1, 1971, tape 256; Nixon Oval Office Conversation with Aides, May 19, 1972, tape 726; Nixon phone calls, June 15, 1972, tape 256.

78. Patterson, *Restless Giant*, 25–6, 293–95.

79. Gutiérrez, *Walls and Mirrors*, ch. 6 (quotation, 203); Ngai, *Impossible Subjects*, ch. 7.

80. Winkler, *Gunfight*, 67–68.

81. John M. Crewdson, "Hard-Line Opponent of Gun Laws Wins New Term at Helm of Rifle Association," *NYT*, May 4, 1981.

82. Ronald Reagan, Kiron K Skinner, Annelise Graebner Anderson, and Martin Anderson, *Reagan: A Life in Letters* (New York: Free Press, 2003), 368. *Public Papers of the Presidents of the United States, Ronald Reagan: 1981–1988/89* (Washington, DC: U.S. Government Printing Office, 1992), 388.

83. Steven M. Teles, *The Rise of the Conservative Legal Movement: The Battle for Control of the Law* (Princeton, NJ: Princeton University Press, 2008) and Amanda Hollis-Brusky, *Ideas with Consequences: The Federalist Society and the Conservative Counterrevolution* (New York: Oxford University Press, 2015).

84. *The Right to Keep and Bear Arms: Report of the Subcommittee on the Constitution of the Committee on the Judiciary, United States Senate, Ninety-seventh Congress, Second Session* (Washington, DC: U.S. Government Printing Office, 1982).

85. Robert A. Sprecher, "The Lost Amendment," *American Bar Association Journal* 51 (1965): 665–69. Both party platforms supported gun control in 1968. The Republican platform only began to oppose gun control in 1980. On polling, see Carl T. Bogus, "The Hidden History of the Second Amendment," *U.C. Davis Law Review* 31 (1998): 312.

86. Carl T. Bogus, "The History and Politics of Second Amendment Scholarship: A Primer," in *The Second Amendment in Law and History*, edited by Carl T. Bogus (New York: New Press, 2000), 1, 4.

87. Michael Avery and Danielle McLaughlin, *The Federalist Society: How Conservatives Took the Law Back from Liberals* (Nashville, TN: Vanderbilt University Press, 2013), 2. And see Teles, *The Rise of the Conservative Legal Movement*.

88. Edwin Meese, Address to the Federalist Society's Lawyers Division, Washington, DC, November 15, 1985.

89. Steven F. Hayward, *The Age of Reagan. The Conservative Counterrevolution, 1980–1989* (New York: Crown Forum, 2009), 414; William J. Brennan, "The Constitution of the United States: Contemporary Ratification," reprinted in *Interpreting the Constitution: The Debate over Original Intent*, ed. Jack N. Rakove (Boston: Northeastern University Press, 1990); Garry Wills, "To Keep and Bear Arms," *New York Review of Books*, September 21, 1995.

90. Jamal Greene, "Selling Originalism," *Georgetown Law Journal* 97 (2009): 708.

91. Reva B. Siegel, "Dead or Alive: Originalism as Popular Constitutionalism in Heller," Faculty Scholarship Series, 2008, Paper 1133, 216.

92. Warren Burger, "2nd Amendment Fraud," YouTube video, 0:57, from an interview on *The MacNeil/Lehrer NewsHour*, televised by PBS on December 16, 1991, posted by "Frank Staheli," August 28, 2016, https://www.youtube.com/watch?v=Eya_k4P-iEo.

93. Patterson, *Restless Giant*, 123–26.

94. Rachel Carson, *Silent Spring* (New York: Fawcett Crest, 1962); President's Science Advisory Committee, Environmental Pollution Panel, *Restoring the Quality of Our Environment* (Washington, DC: White House, 1965), appendix, "Atmospheric Carbon Dioxide."

95. S. Fred Singer, and the American Association for the Advancement of Science, *Global Effects of Environmental Pollution; a Symposium Organized by the American Association for the Advancement of Science, Held in Dallas, Texas, December 1968* (Dordrecht, Holland: D. Reidel, 1970).

96. FitzGerald, *The Evangelicals*, 321–32.

97. Naomi Oreskes and Erik M. Conway, *Merchants of Doubt: How a Handful of Scientists Obscured the Truth on Issues from Tobacco Smoke to Global Warming* (New York: Bloomsbury, 2010), 45.

98. Badash, *A Nuclear Winter's Tale*, 66, 122; Edward Teller, "Widespread After-Effects of Nuclear War," *Nature* 310 (August 23, 1984): 621–24.

99. Nicole Hemmer, *Messengers of the Right: Conservative Media and the Transformation of American Politics* (Philadelphia: University of Pennsylvania Press, 2016), 115–17.

100. Singer is quoted in Badash, *Nuclear Winter's Tale*, 142. His career is discussed at some length in Oreskes, *Merchants of Doubt*. For Singer's more recent views, see Ashley Thorne, "The Father of Global Warming Skepticism: An Interview with S. Fred Singer," *National Association of Scholars*, January 3, 2011, https://www.nas.org/articles/The_Father_of_Global_Warming_Skepticism_An_Interviewwith_S_Fred_Singer.

101. "Climate Change," Heartland Institute, July 27, 2016, https://www.heartland.org/topics/climate-change/, accessed August 28, 2017; Jastrow is quoted in Oreskes, *Merchants of Doubt*, 59.

102. Reagan-Bush '84, "Prouder, Stronger, Better," 1984, Museum of the Moving Image; Gingrich quoted in Ronald Brownstein, *The Second Civil War: How Extreme Partisanship Has Paralyzed Washington and Polarized America* (New York: Penguin, 2007), 143.

103. Patterson, *Restless Giant*, 174.

104. Antonin Scalia, "Originalism: The Lesser Evil," *University of Cincinnati Law Review* 57 (1989): 849–65.

105. Patterson, *Restless Giant*, 179; Buchanan is quoted in Crichtlow, *Conservative Ascendancy*, 217; Randy Shilts, *And the Band Played on: Politics, People, and the AIDS Epidemic* (New York: St. Martin's, 2000), 173, 294–99; on spending: Craig A. Rimmerman, *From Identity to Politics: The Lesbian and Gay Movements in the United States* (Philadelphia: Temple University Press, 2002), 93.

106. Jeffrey Toobin, *The Nine: Inside the Secret World of the Supreme Court* (New York: Doubleday, 2007), 218–19; *Bowers v. Hardwick*, 478 U.S. 186 (1986), Blackmun, dissenting.

107. See, for example, Elizabeth M. Schneider, "The Synergy of Equality and Privacy in Women's Rights," *University of Chicago Legal Forum* 137 (2002): 137–154, especially 140n12.

108. Catharine A. MacKinnon, "Privacy v. Equality: Beyond *Roe v. Wade* (1983)," in *Feminism Unmodified: Discourses on Life and Law* (Cambridge, MA: Harvard University Press, 1987), 93–102 (quotations, 100, 93); Ruth Bader Ginsburg, "Some Thoughts on Autonomy and Equality in Relation to *Roe v. Wade*," *North Carolina Law Review* 63 (1984–85): 375–86 (quotation, 383).

109. Self, *All in the Family*, 385, 391–93. And see Nancy F. Cott, *Public Vows: A History of Marriage and the Nation* (Cambridge, MA: Harvard University Press, 2000).

110. *Bowers v. Hardwick*, 478 U.S. 186 (1986). And on the place of historical analysis in the court during this era, see Erwin Chemerinsky, "History, Tradition, the Supreme Court, and the First Amendment," *Hastings Law Journal* 44 (1993): 919.

111. Thurgood Marshall, Bicentennial Speech, Annual Seminar of the San Francisco Patent and Trademark Law Association, Maui, Hawaii, May 6, 1987.

112. Robert Bork, *Saving Justice: Watergate, the Saturday Night Massacre, and Other Adventures of a Solicitor General* (New York: Encounter Books, 2013), 86; Robert Bork, "The Great Debate," University of San Diego Law School, San Diego, California, November 18, 1985; guns: Reva B. Siegel, "Dead or Alive: Originalism as Popular Constitutionalism in *Heller*," Bork quoted on 224.

113. United States Congress, Senate, Committee on the Judiciary, *Nomination of Robert H. Bork to Be Associate Justice of the United States Supreme Court: Hearings before the Committee on the Judiciary, United States Senate, One Hundredth Congress, First Session, on the Nomination of Robert H. Bork to Be Associate Justice of the Supreme Court of the United States* (Washington, DC: U.S. Government Printing Office, 1987), 2818.

114. The People for the American Way, Anti-Bork Commercial, 1987, www.pfaw.org.

115. John Corry, "Evaluating Bork on TV," *NYT*, September 17, 1987; Linda Greenhouse, "The Bork Battle: Visions of the Constitution," *NYT*, October 4, 1987. Footage from the PBS *NewsHour* at https://www.youtube.com/watch?v=5ffTtOMIJAk.

116. Michael Avery and Danielle McLaughlin, *The Federalist Society: How Conservatives Took the Law Back from Liberals* (Nashville, TN: Vanderbilt University Press, 2013), 26–27.

117. Patterson, *Restless Giant*, 214–16.

118. Arthur M. Schlesinger Jr., *The Disuniting of America: Reflections on a Multicultural Society* (New York: Norton, 1991, 1992, 1998), 11; Irving Kristol, "My Cold War," *National Interest* 31 (1993): 141–44. On the history of hate speech codes, see Erwin Chemerinsky and Howard Gillman, *Free Speech on Campus* (New Haven, CT: Yale University Press, 2017).

119. Maureen Dowd, "The 1992 Campaign," *NYT*, May 18, 1992.

120. Patrick Buchanan, "Culture War," Republican National Convention, Houston, Texas, August 17, 1992.

121. Robert H. Bork, *Slouching Towards Gomorrah: Modern Liberalism and American Decline* (New York: ReganBooks, 1996), 2.

122. Carl Bernstein, *A Woman in Charge: The Life of Hillary Rodham Clinton* (New York: Alfred A. Knopf, 2007), 30–38, 54–56, 69; Mark Leibovich, "In Turmoil of '68, Clinton Found a New Voice," *NYT*, September 5, 2007; on the history of her name, see Janell Ross, "The Complicated History Behind Hillary Clinton's Evolving Name," *Washington Post*, July 25, 2015.

123. The term was coined by Peter Drucker in 1962 (Saval, *Cubed*, 197, 201).

124. Lily Geismer, *Don't Blame Us: Suburban Liberals and the Transformation of the Democratic Party* (Princeton, NJ: Princeton University Press, 2015), 1–9.

125. Fred Turner, *From Counterculture to Cyberculture: Stewart Brand, the Whole Earth Network, and the Rise of Digital Utopianism* (Chicago: University of Chicago Press, 2006), 2.

126. Ibid., 81; *The Last Whole Earth Catalog: Access to Tools* (Menlo Park, CA: Portola Institute, distributed Random House, 1971), 344, 248–49, 225, 389.

127. Turner, *From Counterculture to Cyberculture*, 38, 76–77, 98. And see, for example, "Kibbutz: Venture in Utopia," *Whole Earth Catalog* (San Rafael, CA: Point Foundation, 1998), 42.

128. Isaacson, *The Innovators*, 268–81.

129. Patterson, *Restless Giant*, 59–60.

130. Frederick G. Dutton, *Changing Sources of Power: American Politics in the 1970s* (New York: McGraw-Hill, 1971), ch. 7.

131. Thomas Frank, *Listen, Liberal: Or, What Ever Happened to the Party of the People?* (New York: Metropolitan Books, 2016), 46–53.

132. Crichtlow, *Conservative Ascendancy*, 203; Al From and Alice McKeon, *The New Democrats and the Return to Power* (New York City: Palgrave Macmillan, 2013), especially ch. 5; Patterson, *Restless Giant*, 190.

133. Michael Rothschild, "Beyond Repair: The Politics of the Machine Age Are Hopelessly Obsolete," *New Democrat*, July/August 1995, 8–11.

134. Patterson, *Restless Giant*, 249; "Stories of Bill," *Frontline*, http://www.pbs.org/wgbh/pages/frontline/shows/choice/bill/greenberg.html, accessed August 28, 2017.

135. Davis and Clark, *Thurgood Marshall*, 5.

136. Bill Clinton and Hillary Clinton, interview by Steve Kroft, *60 Minutes*, CBS, January 26, 1992; Patterson, *Restless Giant*, 256.

137. Patterson, *Restless Giant*, 253; Bob Woodward, *The Agenda: Inside the Clinton White House* (New York: Simon & Schuster, 1994), 117.

138. Margaret Carlson, "A Hundred Days of Hillary," *Vanity Fair*, June 1, 1993. On the name, see Ross, "The Complicated History Behind Hillary Clinton's Evolving Name."

139. "Harry and Louise on Clinton's Health Plan," YouTube video, 1:00, aired 1994, posted by "danieljbmitchell," July 15, 2007, https://www.youtube.com/watch?v=Dt31nhleeCg; William Kristol to Republican Leaders, December 2, 1993, Memo, https://www.scribd.com/document/12926608/William-Kristol-s-1993-Memo-Defeating-President-Clinton-s-Health-Care-Proposal; Brownstein, *Second Civil War*, 155; Patterson, *Restless Giant*, 328–30.

140. Frank, *Listen, Liberal*, 78–79.

141. Biden quoted in Frank, *Listen, Liberal*, 93; Elizabeth Hinton, Julilly Kohler-Hausmann, and Vesla M. Weaver, "Did Blacks Really Endorse the 1994 Crime Bill?," *NYT*, April 13, 2016.

142. Kleiman, *When Brute Force Fails*, 1; Michelle Alexander, *The New Jim Crow: Mass Incarceration in the Age of Colorblindness* (New York: The New Press, 2010, 2012), 3–60.

143. William J. Clinton, "Statement on Signing the Personal Responsibility and Work Opportunity Reconciliation Act of 1996," Washington, DC, August 22, 1996.

144. Stephen Labaton, "A New Financial Era," *NYT*, October 23, 1999; Frank, *Listen, Liberal*, 119.

145. "What We Believe," Combahee River Collective, April 1977, http://circuitous.org/scraps/combahee.html. Combahee is a river associated with Harriet Tubman's rescue missions.

146. On the rise of trauma, see Anne Rothe, *Popular Trauma Culture: Selling the Pain of Others in the Mass Media* (New Brunswick, NJ: Rutgers University Press, 2011), and especially Ruth Leys, *Trauma: A Genealogy* (Chicago: University of Chicago Press, 2000). And for a jaundiced view, see Mark Lilla, *The Once and Future Liberal: After Identity Politics* (New York: Harper, 2017).

147. Gordon, *Moral Property*, 309.

148. Mark Hamm, *Apocalypse in Oklahoma: Waco and Ruby Ridge Revenged* (Boston: Northeastern University Press, 1997), 158.

149. Jonathan Kay, *Among the Truthers: A Journey into the Growing Conspiracist Underground of 9/11 Truthers, Birthers, Armagheddonites, Vaccine Hysterics, Hollywood Know-Nothings and Internet Addicts* (New York: HarperCollins, 2011), 27–29; Lee Nichols, "Libertarians on TV," *Austin Chronicle*, August 7, 1998.

150. Allan Bloom, *The Closing of the American Mind* (1987; New York: Simon & Schuster, 2008), 25; Todd Gitlin, *The Twilight of Common Dreams: Why America Is Wracked by Culture Wars* (New York: Metropolitan Books, 1995), 35–36; and on the history of political correctness, 169–71.

151. Chemerinsky and Gillman, *Free Speech on Campus*, 71; Herbert Marcuse, "Repressive Tolerance," in Robert Paul Wolff, Barrington Moore Jr., and Herbert Marcuse, *A Critique of Pure Tolerance* (Boston: Beacon, 1965); Henry Louis Gates Jr., "Critical Race Theory and the Freedom of Speech," *The Future of Academic Freedom*, ed. Louis Menard (Chicago: University of Chicago Press, 1996), ch. 5.

152. Hemmer, *Messengers of the Right*, 258–59; Daly, *Covering America*, 412.

153. Philip Seib, *Rush Hour: Talk Radio, Politics, and the Rise of Rush Limbaugh* (Fort Worth, TX: The Summit Group, 1993), 4, 27, 59; Ze'ev Chafets, *Roger Ailes: Off Camera* (New York, New York: Sentinel, 2013), 62–63; Charles J. Sykes, *How the Right Lost Its Mind* (New York: St. Martin's, 2017), 135.

154. Baxter, oral history, 1972, 17, 22–4.

155. Sherman, *Loudest Voice*, 115–16.

156. Roger Ailes with Jon Kraushar, You *Are the Message: Getting What You Want by Being Who You Are* (New York: Crown Business, 1988, 1995), 17, 82.

157. Minow and Sloan, *For Great Debates*, 28; Dorothy S. Ridings to Editorial Page Editors and Writers, September 23, 1983, Dorothy Ridings Papers, Schlesinger Library, Radcliffe, Box 1.

158. Ailes, You *Are the Message*, 23–24; Chafets, *Roger Ailes*, 48; George Farah, *No Debate: How the Republican and Democratic Parties Secretly Control the Presidential Debates* (New York: Seven Stories Press, 2004), 89.

159. Bush in an interview with James Lehrer, *Debating Our Destiny: 40 Years of Presidential Debate* (Washington, DC: MacNeil/Lehrer Productions, 2000).

160. Cronkite made his original remarks in the 1990 Theodore H. White lecture at Harvard's Kennedy School; Farah, *No Debate*, 32–33, 90, 93.

161. Daly, *Covering America*, 401–15; Gabriel Sherman, *The Loudest Voice in the Room: How the Brilliant, Bombastic Roger Ailes Built Fox News—and Divided a Country* (New York: Random House, 2014), 183.

162. Ken Auletta, "Vox Fox," *TNY*, May 26, 2003. Sherman, *Loudest Voice*, 175. Jane Hall, "Murdoch Will Launch 24-Hour News Channel; Roger Ailes Will Head the New Service," *Los Angeles Times*, January 30, 1996.

163. Sherman, *Loudest Voice*, 230.

164. Markus Prior, *Post-Broadcast Democracy: How Media Choice Increase Inequality in Political Involvement and Polarizes Elections* (New York: Cambridge University Press, 2007).

165. Leibovich, *This Town*, 101–7; Sherman, *Loudest Voice*, 200, 229.

166. Benjamin Ginsberg and Martin Shefter, *Politics by Other Means: Politicians, Prosecutors, and the Press from Watergate to Whitewater*, revised and updated edition (New York: Norton, 1990, 1999), figure 1.1., 27.

167. Kenneth Starr, and United States Office of the Independent Counsel. *The Starr Report: The Findings of Independent Counsel Kenneth W. Starr on President Clinton and the Lewinsky Affair* (New York: Public Affairs, 1998), 49–50. The quotation is attributed to Lewinsky by David Halberstam, *War in a Time of Peace: Bush, Clinton, and the Generals* (New York: Scribner, 2001), 372.

168. Johnson, *Best of Times*, 254.

169. Ibid., 259.

170. Ibid., 272–73.

171. Ibid., 232–33, 292; William J. Clinton, interview by Jim Lehrer, *The NewsHour with Jim Lehrer*, PBS, January 21, 1998; Patterson, *Restless Giant*, 390; *Today* show, interview with Matt Lauer, January 27, 1998.

172. Sherman, *Loudest Voice*, 236–38, 245; Brownstein, *Second Civil War*, 171; A. M. Rosenthal, "Risking the Presidency," *NYT*, March 17, 1998; Andrew Sullivan, "Lies That Matter," *TNR*, September 14, 21, 1998.

173. Hemmer, *Messengers of the Right*, xiii–xiv.

174. Johnson, *The Best of Times*, 328–30, 373–74, 397; Steven M. Gillon, *The Pact: Bill Clinton, Newt Gingrich, and the Rivalry That Defined a Generation* (New York: Oxford University Press, 2008), 249; Katharine Q. Seelye, "The Speaker Steps Down," *NYT*, November 7, 1998.

175. Gloria Steinem, "Why Feminists Support Clinton," *NYT*, March 22, 1998; Toni Morrison, "On the First Black President," *TNY*, October 5, 1998.

176. Patterson, *Restless Giant*, 267; "Letter to Conservatives" from Paul M. Weyrich, February 16, 1999, in Direct Line, http://www.rfcnet.org/archives/weyrich.htm.

177. Anthony Lewis, "Nearly a Coup," *New York Review of Books*, April 13, 2000.

178. "I decided real estate was a much better business," he later explained: Donald J. Trump with Tony Schwartz, *The Art of the Deal* (New York: Random House, 1987), 77.

179. Ibid., 77–81; David Dunlap, "Meet Donald Trump," *NYT [Insider]*, July 30, 2015.

180. Luis Romano, "Donald Trump, Holding All the Cards," *Washington Post*, November 15, 1984.

181. Trump, *The Art of the Deal*, 105, 107; Fox Butterfield, "New Hampshire Speech Earns Praise for Trump," *NYT*, October 23, 1987.

182. Patterson, *Restless Giant*, 357; Lawrence R. Samuel, *Rich: The Rise and Fall of American Wealth Culture* (New York: American Management Association, 2009), 224–31.

183. Carl Rowan, "The Uglification of Presidential Politics," *Titusville (PA) Herald*, November 3, 1999; Donald Trump, interview by Chris Matthews, *Hardball with Chris Matthews*, NBC News, August 27, 1998; Adam Nagourney, "President? Why Not?," *NYT*, September 25, 1999.

184. Donald J. Trump with Dave Shiflett, *The America We Deserve* (Los Angeles: Renaissance Books, 2000), 261; The Donald 2000, https://web.archive.org/web/19991104133242/http://thedonald2000.org/; "In to Win? Trump Eyes Candidacy," *Harrisburg (PA) Daily News Record*, October 8, 1999; Nagourney, "President? Why Not?"; Chris Matthews, "Gotham Hero," *Corbin Times Tribune*, December 1, 1999; Tony Kornheiser, "Look Who's Running for President," *The Titusville Herald*, October 13, 1999.

185. Trump, *The America We Deserve*, 271–72; Adam Nagourney, "President? Why Not?"

186. Maureen Dowd, "Behold the Flirtation of the Trumpster," *Lowell Sun*, November 18, 1999; Adam Nagourney, "Trump Proposes Clearing Nation's Debt at Expense of the Rich," *NYT*, November 10, 1999; William Mann, "If Donald Trump Were President," *Syracuse (New York) Post-Standard*, November 1, 1999.

187. Mark Shields, "A Wonderful Holiday," *Daily Herald Chicago*, November 24, 1999; The Donald 2000, https://web.archive.org/web/20000116042120/http://www.thedonald2000.org/.https://web.archive.org/web/20000116042120/http://www.thedonald2000.org/; Michael Janofsky, "Trump Speaks Out About Just About Everything," *NYT*, January 8, 2000.

188. George W. Bush, Address Accepting the Presidential Nomination, Republican National Convention, Philadelphia, Pennsylvania, August 3, 2000; Frum quoted in Kevin M. Kruse, "Compassionate Conservatism: Religion in the Age of George W. Bush," in Julian E. Zelizer, ed., *The Presidency of George W. Bush: A First Historical Assessment* (Princeton, NJ: Princeton University Press, 2010), 230.

189. Sherman, *Loudest Voice*, 253, 259–60; Jane Mayer, "Dept. of Close Calls: George W.'s Cousin," *TNY*, November 20, 2000.

190. Jeffrey Toobin, *Too Close to Call: The Thirty-Six Day Battle to Decide the 2000 Election* (New York: Random House, 2001), 25; Johnson, *Best of Times*, 523–24.

191. Toobin, *Too Close to Call*, 266–67.

192. Patterson, *Restless Giant*, 410–16; *Bush v. Gore*, 531 U.S. 98 (2000) (Stevens dissenting).

193. "Count the Spoons," *Washington Post*, January 24, 2001; Johnson, *The Best of Times*, 546–47.

194. George W. Bush, Address in Austin Accepting Election as the 43rd President of the United States, Austin, Texas, December 13, 2000. Linda Greenhouse, "Bush Prevails," *NYT*, December 13, 2000.

### *Sixteen:* AMERICA, DISRUPTED

1. This account derives chiefly from *The 9/11 Commission Report: Final Report of the National Commission on Terrorist Attacks upon the United States* (New York: Norton, 2004), chs. 1 and 9; and Understanding 9/11: A Television Archive, https://archive.org/details/911. "F93 Attendent CeeCee Lyles Leaves a Message for Her Husband," YouTube video, 0:45, posted by "911NeverForget," May 21, 2008, https://www.youtube.com/watch?v=fUrxsrTKHN4.

2. "America Under Attack," CNN.com, September 11, 2001.

3. "World Trade Center Toppled in Attack," *NYT*, September 11, 2001, and "Terrorists Attack New York and Washington," *NYT*, September 11, 2001.

4. "America Under Attack," Drudge Report, http://www.drudgereportarchives.com/data/specialreports/EFG/20010911_0855.htm.

5. "Terrorism Hits America," FOX News, September 11, 2001.

6. George W. Bush, 9/11 Address to the Nation, Washington, DC, September 11, 2001.

7. Samuel P. Huntington, "Clash of Civilizations?," *Foreign Affairs*, Summer 1993. And see Huntington, *The Clash of Civilizations and the Remaking of World Order* (New York: Simon & Schuster, 1996, 2011).

8. Bush, 9/11 Address to the Nation.

9. Quoted in David Remnick, *The Bridge: The Life and Rise of Barack Obama* (New York: Knopf, 2010), 337.

10. Susan Sontag, "Tuesday, And After," *TNY*, September 24, 2001.

11. Charles Krauthammer, "Voices of Moral Obtuseness," *Washington Post*, September 21, 2001. And for a roundup, see Celeste Bohlen, "Think Tank: In New War on Terrorism, Words Are Weapons, Too," *NYT*, September 29, 2001.

12. Ann Coulter, "This Is War," *National Review* (online), September 13, 2001, and in print September 17, 2001.

13. Jonah Goldberg, "L'Affaire Coulter," *National Review*, October 2, 2017.

14. Quoted in Leonard Zeskind, *Blood and Politics: The History of the White Nationalist Movement from the Margins to the Mainstream* (New York: Farrar, Straus and Giroux, 2009), 516.

15. Laurie Goodstein, "After the Attacks," *NYT*, September 15, 2001; John F. Harris, "Falwell Apologizes for Remarks," *Washington Post*, September 18, 2001.

16. https://archive.org/details/TheAlexJonesRadioShowOn9-11-2001. And see Alexander Zaitchik, "Meet Alex Jones," *Rolling Stone*, March 2, 2011.

17. Angela Nagle, *Kill All Normies: The Online Culture Wars from Tumblr and 4chan to the Alt-Right and Trump* (Washington, DC: Zero Books, 2017).

18. Infowars, September 11, 2001, https://web.archive.org/web/20011201080653/http://infowars.com:80/archive_wtc.htm; Jones in his 2005 film, *Martial Law 9-11*, is quoted in Sykes, *How the Right Lost Its Mind*, 108.

19. Remnick, *The Bridge,* 362, 370.

20. Barack Obama, "A More Perfect Union," Speech, Philadelphia, Pennsylvania, March 18, 2005.

21. David Remnick, "The President's Hero," *TNY*, June 19, 2017.

22. Marc Mauer, *Young Black Americans and the Criminal Justice System: Five Years Later* (Washington DC: The Sentencing Project, 1995).

23. Kay, *Among the Truthers*, xvii.

24. David Maraniss, *Barack Obama: The Story* (New York: Simon & Schuster, 2012), xxiii.

25. Dinesh D'Souza, *The Roots of Obama's Rage* (Washington, DC: Regnery, 2010), 26–27, 34, 215, 198.

26. Gregory Krieg, "14 of Trump's Most Outrageous 'Birther' Claims—Half from after 2011," CNN Politics, September 16, 2016.

27. David Graham, "The Unrepentent Birtherism of Donald Trump," *Atlantic*, September 16, 2016.

28. Leonard Zeskind, *Blood and Politics: The History of the White Nationalist Movement from the Margins to the Mainstream* (New York: Farrar Straus Giroux, 2009), 519–27.

29. Trump got the Coulter material via Corey Lewandowski, according to Sykes, *How the Right Lost Its Mind*, 155–56.

30. Ann Coulter, ¡*Adios, America! The Left's Plan to Turn Our Country into a Third World Hellhole* (New York: Regnery, 2015), 1–2.

31. Seema Mehta, "Transcript: Clinton's Full Remarks as She Called Half of Trump Supporters 'Deplorables.'" *Los Angeles Times*, September 10, 2016; Romney: http://www.politifact.com/truth-o-meter/statements/2012/sep/18/mitt-romney/romney-says-47-percent-americans-pay-no-income-tax/.

32. Jones is quoted in Sykes, *How the Right Lost Its Mind*, 109; Tessa Stuart, "How 'Lock Her Up!' Became a Mainstream GOP Rallying Cry," *Rolling Stone,* July 21, 2016.

33. Stephanie Condon, "Obama Campaign Launches 'Truth Team,'" CBS News, February 13, 2012.

34. Katharine Q. Seelye, "Wilson Calls His Outburst 'Spontaneous,'" *NYT*, September 10, 2009; Barney Henderson, David Lawler, and Louise Burke, "Donald Trump Attacks Alleged Russian Dossier as 'Fake News' and Slams Buzzfeed and CNN at Press Conference," *Telegraph*, January 11, 2017.

35. "Fact-Checking Trump's Claim That Thousands in New Jersey Cheered When World Trade Center Tumbled," PolitiFact, November 21, 2015.

36. Eric Hananoki and Timothy Johnson, "Donald Trump Praises Leading Conspiracy Theorist Alex Jones And His 'Amazing' Reputation," Media Matters for America, December 2, 2015.

37. Trump called for this ban on December 7, 2016 but after court challenges to his administration's travel ban, the call was erased from his website. Laurel Raymond, "Trump, Who Campaigned on a Muslim Ban, Says to Stop Calling It a Muslim Ban," ThinkProgress, January 30, 2017, https://thinkprogress.org/trump-who-campaigned-on-a-muslim-ban-says-to-stop-calling-it-a-muslim-ban-630961d0fbcf/.

38. David Runciman, *How Democracy Ends* (New York: Basic Books, 2018); Patrick Deneen, *Why Liberalism Failed* (New Haven, CT: Yale University Press, 2018); Sykes, *How the Right Lost Its Mind*; Steven Levitsky and Daniel Ziblatt, *How Democracies Die* (New York: Crown, 2018).

39. Karen Breslau, "One Nation, Interconnected," *Wired*, May 2000, 154.

40. Broadly, see G. John Ikenberry, *Liberal Leviathan: The Origins, Crisis, and Transformation of the American World Order* (Princeton, NJ: Princeton University Press, 2011).

41. Sam Reisman, "Trump Tells Crowd to 'Knock the Crap Out' of Protesters, Offers to Pay Legal Fees," *Mediaite*, February 1, 2016. And see Louis Jacobson and Manuela Tobias, "Has Donald Trump Never 'Promoted or Encouraged Violence'?," PolitiFact, July 5, 2017.

42. Isaacson, *The Innovators*, ch. 7.

43. Stewart Brand, "We Owe It All to the Hippies," *Time*, March 1, 1995, 54.

44. Fred Turner, *From Counterculture to Cyberculture: Stewart Brand, the Whole Earth Network, and the Rise of Digital Utopianism* (Chicago: University of Chicago Press, 2006), 216–18; Louis Rossetto, "Why Wired?," *Wired*, March 1993. On Rossetto's biog-

raphy and politics, see Turner, *From Counterculture to Cyberculture*, 209–11; Owen Thomas, "'The Ultimate Luxury Is Meaning and' . . . Chocolate?," *Gawker*, December 12, 2007. And see Mitchell Kapor, "Where Is the Digital Highway Really Heading?," *Wired*, July & August 1993.

45. Roger Parloff, "Newt Gingrich and His Sleazy Ways: A History Lesson," *Fortune*, December 5, 2011; Esther Dyson, "Friend and Foe," *Wired*, August 1995; Po Bronson, "George Gilder," *Wired*, March 1996; Turner, *From Counterculture to Cyberculture*, 208, 215, 222–24.

46. Esther Dyson et al., "Cyberspace and the American Dream: A Magna Carta for the Knowledge Age," The Progress & Freedom Foundation, August 22, 1994, http://www .pff.org/issues-pubs/futureinsights/fi1.2magnacarta.html.

47. Guy Lamolinara, "Wired for the Future: President Clinton Signs Telecom Act at LC," *Library of Congress Information Bulletin*, February 19, 1996. And see Andy Greenberg, "It's Been 20 Years Since John Perry Barlow Declared Cyberspace Independence," *Wired*, June 3, 2017, https://www.wired.com/2016/02/its-been-20-years-since-this -man-declared-cyberspace-independence/.

48. John Perry Barlow, "A Declaration of the Independence of Cyberspace," Electronic Frontier Foundation, February 8, 1996, https://www.eff.org/cyberspace-independence.

49. Mariana Mazzucato, *The Entrepreneurial State: Debunking Private v. Public Sector Myths* (London: Anthem Press, 2013); A. B. Atkinson, *Inequality: What Can Be Done?* (Cambridge, MA: Harvard University Press, 2015), 82, 118.

50. David O. Sacks and Peter A. Thiel, *The Diversity Myth: Multiculturalism and Political Intolerance on Campus* (Oakland, CA: The Independent Institute, 1995, 1998); Haynes Johnson, *The Best of Times: America in the Clinton Years* (New York: Harcourt, Inc., 2001), 25; WorldWideWeb SLAC Home Page, December 24, 1993, https://swap .stanford.edu/19940102000000/http://slacvm.slac.stanford.edu/FIND/slac.html; George Packer, *The Unwinding: An Inner History of the New America* (New York: Farrar, Straus and Giroux, 2013), 129–34.

51. Johnson, *Best of Times,* 25, 57; Turner, *From Counterculture to Cyberspace,* 214.

52. Edmund Burke to Chevalier de Rivarol, June 1, 1791, in *Correspondence of the Right Honourable Edmund Burke,* ed. Earl Fitzwilliam and Sir Richard Bourke, KCB, 4 vols. (London, 1844), 3:211; *Gazette of the United States,* June 10, 1800.

53. See Joseph A. Schumpeter, *Essays on Entrepreneurs, Innovations, Business Cycles, and the Evolution of Capitalism,* ed. Richard V. Clemence (1951; New Brunswick, NJ: Transaction Publishers, 1989). Regarding the origins of innovation studies, see Benoît Godin, "'Innovation Studies': The Invention of a Specialty," *Minerva* 50 (2012): 397–421, and especially Jan Fagerberg et al., eds., *The Oxford Handbook of Innovation* (New York: Oxford University Press, 2006), introduction—note, in particular, figure 1.1 (a graph of scholarly articles with the word "innovation" in the title, 1955–2005); and Box 1.2 (on Schumpeter as the theorist of innovation).

54. Clayton M. Christensen, *The Innovator's Dilemma: The Revolutionary Book That Will Change the Way You Do Business* (1997; New York: HarperBusiness, 2011). For an earlier usage, see Jean-Marie Dru, *Disruption: Overturning Conventions and Shaking Up the Marketplace* (New York: Wiley, 1996).

55. I discuss the shaky evidence for "disruptive innovation" in "The Disruption Machine," *TNY*, June 23, 2014; a bibliography for that article can be found at https://scho lar.harvard.edu/files/jlepore/files/lepore_disruption_bibliography_6_16_14_0.pdf. On heedlessness, see, for example, Jonathan Taplin, *Move Fast and Break Things: How Facebook, Google, and Amazon Cornered Culture and Undermined Democracy* (New York: Little, Brown, 2017).

56. Franklin, "Apology for Printers."

57. Daly, *Covering America*, ch. 13.

58. Quoted in Matthew Hindman, *The Myth of Digital Democracy* (Princeton NJ: Princeton University Press, 2009), 2.

59. Taplin, *Move Fast and Break Things*, 6, 21. And see Ken Auletta, *Googled: The End of the World as We Know It* (New York: Penguin Press, 2009).

60. See, broadly, Hindman, *Myth of Digital Democracy*; Cass Sunstein, *Republic.com* (Princeton, NJ: Princeton University Press, 2001); Nathan Heller, "The Failure of Facebook Democracy," *TNY*, November 18, 2016.

61. George W. Bush, Address before a Joint Session of the Congress on the United States Response to the Terrorist Attacks of September 11, Washington, DC, September 20, 2001; "The National Security Strategy of the United States of America," March 2006, http://web.archive.org/web/20060517140100/www.whitehouse.gov/nsc/nss/2006/nss2006.pdf.

62. Stephen E. Atkins, *The 9/11 Encyclopedia: Second Edition* (Santa Barbara: ABC-CLIO, LLC, 2011), 741; *The 9/11 Commission Report: Final Report of the National Commission on Terrorist Attacks Upon the United States* (Washington, DC: National Commission on Terrorist Attacks upon the United States, 2004), ch. 2.

63. Daniel Wirls, *Irrational Security: The Politics of Defense from Reagan to Obama* (Baltimore: Johns Hopkins University Press, 2010), 17.

64. Wirls, *Irrational Security*, 134–35; Melvin A. Goodman, *National Insecurity: The Cost of American Militarism* (San Francisco: City Lights, 2013), 279, 327; Timothy Naftali, "George W. Bush and the 'War on Terror,'" in Zelizer, *The Presidency of George W. Bush*, 59–87; George W. Bush, "Remarks at the Embassy of Afghanistan," Washington, DC, September 10, 2002.

65. Fredrik Logevall, "Anatomy of an Unnecessary War: The Iraq Invasion," in Zelizer, *The Presidency of George W. Bush*, 88–113; Patrick J. Buchanan, *Where the Right Went Wrong: How Neoconservatives Subverted the Reagan Revolution and Hijacked the Presidency* (New York: St. Martin's, 2004), 6, 233.

66. Pew Research, "The Military-Civilian Gap," November 23, 2011, http://www.pewsocialtrends.org/2011/11/23/the-military-civilian-gap-fewer-family-connections/; Goodman, *National Insecurity*, 8–9, 30, 211.

67. Katharine Q. Seeyle and Ralph Blumenthal, "Documents Suggest Special Treatment for Bush in Guard," *NYT*, September 9, 2004; "Bill Clinton's Vietnam Test," *NYT*, February 14, 1992; Steven Eder and Dave Philipps, "Donald Trump's Draft Deferments," *NYT*, August 1, 2016; Marvin Kalb, "The Other War Haunting Obama," *NYT*, October 8, 2011.

68. "War and Sacrifice in the Post-9/11 Era," Pew Research Center's Social & Demographic Trends Project, October 04, 2011, http://www.pewsocialtrends.org/2011/10/05/war-and-sacrifice-in-the-post-911-era/.

69. Andrew J. Bacevich, *The New American Militarism: How Americans Are Seduced by War* (New York: Oxford University Press, 2005), 2; Andrew J. Bacevich, *Washington Rules: America's Path to Permanent War* (New York: Metropolitan Books, 2010), 27.

70. Kathleen Hall Jamieson and Joseph N. Cappella, *Echo Chamber: Ross Limbaugh and the Conservative Media Establishment* (New York: Oxford University Press, 2008), x–xiii.

71. Quoted in David Roberts, "Donald Trump and the Rise of Tribal Epistemology," *Vox*, May 19, 2017, https://www.vox.com/policy-and-politics/2017/3/22/14762030/donald-trump-tribal-epistemology.

72. For a sample wartime transcript, see "Excuse Us for Taking the War on Terror Seriously," *Rush Limbaugh Show*, July 31, 2006, https://www.rushlimbaugh.com/daily/2006/07/31/excuse_us_for_taking_the_war_on_terror_seriously/. For a discussion of his Vietnam draft status, see (citing Limbaugh's biographer), "Rush Limbaugh Avoided the Draft Due to Pilonidal Cyst?," *Snopes*, June 17, 2014, https://www.snopes.com/politics/military/limbaugh.asp.

73. Chafets, *Roger Ailes*, 96; Alexandra Kitty, *Outfoxed* (New York: Disinformation, 2005), ch. 7; Daly, *Covering America*, 418, 419, https://www.mediamatters.org/research/2004/07/14/33-internal-fox-editorial-memos-reviewed-by-mmf/131430.

74. "Interview with Matt Labash, *The Weekly Standard*—May 2003," JournalismJobs.com, October 3, 2003, http://web.archive.org/web/20031003110233/http://www.journalism jobs.com/matt_labash.cfm. And see David Greenberg, "Creating Their Own Reality: The Bush Administration and Expertise in a Polarized Age," in Zelizer, *The Presidency of George W. Bush*, 202.

75. Greenberg, "Creating Their Own Reality," 210–18.

76. Ron Suskind, "Faith, Certainty and the Presidency of George W. Bush," *NYT*, October 17, 2004. And see Greenberg: "The Right thus found itself in the Bush years promoting a radical epistemological relativism: the idea that established experts' claims lacked empirical foundation and represented simply a political choice. In this position, conservatives were espousing a notion resembling that of postmodernism—or at least that strand of postmodernism that denies the possibility of objective truth claims" ("Creating Their Own Reality," 203–4).

77. Stephen Colbert, "The Word," *The Colbert Report*, 2:40, October 17, 2005. http://www .cc.com/video-clips/63ite2/the-colbert-report-the-word---truthiness.

78. John Ashcroft, "Remarks on the Patriot Act," Speech, Boise, Idaho, August 25, 2003. https://www.justice.gov/archive/ag/speeches/2003/082503patriotactremarks.htm.

79. Military Order of November 13, 2001, Detention, Treatment, and Trial of Certain Non-Citizens in the War Against Terrorism, *Federal Register*, November 16, 2001, 66, 222; Jess Bravin, *The Terror Courts: Rough Justice at Guantanamo Bay* (New Haven, CT: Yale University Press, 2013), 39.

80. Ashcroft is quoted in Bravin, *Terror Courts*, 41; on when Rice and Powell learned Bush had signed the order, see pp. 41–44; Military Order of November 13, 2001; Cheney is quoted in Bravin, 47.

81. Julian Zelizer, "Establishment Conservative: The Presidency of George W. Bush," in Zelizer, *The Presidency of George W. Bush*, 1–14.

82. On Rumsfeld's early career, see James Mann, "Close-Up: Young Rumsfeld," *Atlantic*, November 2003.

83. Mahvish Khan, *My Guantánamo Diary: The Detainees and the Stories They Told Me* (New York: PublicAffairs, 2008), 55–57; Bravin, *Terror Courts*, 76. And see Jonathan Hafetz, *Habeas Corpus after 9/11: Confronting America's New Global Detention System* (New York: New York University Press, 2011), 28–29.

84. John Yoo and Robert J. Delahunty to William J. Haynes II, Memorandum re: Applications of Treaties and Laws to al Qaeda and Taliban Detainees, January 9, 2002, http:// www.gwu.edu/~nsarchiv/NSAEBB/NSAEBB127/02.01.09.pdf; Bravin, *Terror Courts*, 62–63, 71, 74–75, 76–77; Gonzales, January 24, 2002, quoted in Hafetz, *Habeas Corpus*, 20. And see Mary L. Dudziak, "A Sword and a Shield: The Uses of Law in the Bush Administration," in Zelizer, *The Presidency of George W. Bush*, 39–58.

85. Hafetz, *Habeas Corpus*, 21, 23–4, 37–8, 267n56; Donald Rumsfeld, Memorandum to James T. Hill, U.S. Southern Command, April 2003, http://www.gwu.edu/~nsarchiv/ NSAEBB/NSAEBB127/03.04.16.pdf; Scott Shane, "China Inspired Interrogations at Guantánamo," *NYT*, July 2, 2008; Bravin, *Terror Courts*, 161.

86. Eliza Griswold, "Black Hole; The Other Guantanamo," *TNR*, May 7, 2007; "Barack Obama 2003: National Security vs Civil Rights," YouTube video, 3:08, from an interview televised on the Illinois Channel on November 6, 2003, posted by "IllinoisChannelTV," June 12, 2013, https://www.youtube.com/watch?v=xWeLUPd9vVg; Hafetz, *Habeas Corpus*, 63.

87. James T. Patterson, "Transformative Economic Policies: Tax Cutting, Stimuli, and Bailouts," in Zelizer, ed., *The Presidency of George W. Bush*, 122; Alan I. Abramowitz, *The Polarized Public: Why Our Government Is So Dysfunctional* (Upper Saddle River, NJ: Pearson, 2013), 8; Ronald Brownstein, *The Second Civil War: How Extreme Partisanship Has Paralyzed Washington and Polarized America* (New York: Penguin, 2007), 4.

88. Mark Leibovich, *This Town: Two Parties and a Funeral—Plus Plenty of Valet Parking!— in America's Gilded Capital* (New York: Blue Rider Press, 2013), 8.

89. Patterson, "Transformative Economic Policies," 134–35.

90. "Inauguration Prompts Travel Rush to Washington," CNN, November 19, 2008; Mary Anne Ostrom, "Obama's Inauguration: Record Crowd Gathers on Mall to Celebrate 'Achievement for the Nation,'" *San Jose Mercury News*, January 20, 2009.

91. Barack Obama, Inaugural Address, January 20, 2009.

92. Remnick, *The Bridge*, 207–8, 227, 230.

93. Maraniss, *The Story of Obama*, 68, 162, 175–76, 193; State of Hawaii Department of Health, certificate of birth number 151 (4 August 1961), Barack Hussein Obama, II. http://static.politifact.com/files/birth-certificate-long-form.pdf.

94. Barack Obama, *Dreams from My Father: A Story of Race and Inheritance* (New York: Broadway Books, 2004), 85; Remnick, *The Bridge*, 193–96.

95. Remnick, *The Bridge*, 263–65; James T. Kloppenberg, *Reading Obama: Dreams, Hope, and the American Political Tradition* (Princeton, NJ: Princeton University Press, 2012), ch. 1; Barack Obama, "Current Issues in Racism and the Law" (syllabus, University of Chicago Law School, Chicago, IL, 1994), http://www.nytimes.com/packages/pdf/poli tics/2008OBAMA_LAW/Obama_CoursePk.pdf.

96. Quoted in Remnick, *The Bridge*, 294.

97. Remnick, *The Bridge*, 394; Barack Obama, Keynote Address, Democratic National Convention, Boston, Massachusetts, July 27, 2004.

98. Leibovich, *This Town*, 45.

99. Barack Obama, "Tone, Truth, and the Democratic Party," *Daily Kos*, September 30, 2005.

100. Remnick, *The Bridge*, 371, 510–13.

101. Ibid., 458; Barack Obama, Keynote Address, Democratic National Convention, July 27, 2004.

102. Jennifer Aaker and Victoria Chang, "Obama and the Power of Social Media and Technology," *European Business Review*, May & June 2010.

103. Frank, *Listen, Liberal*, 140–41; Jacob S. Hacker and Paul Pierson, *Winner-Take-All Politics: How Washington Made the Rich Richer—And Turned Its Back on the Middle Class* (New York: Simon & Schuster, 2010), 1.

104. Hemmer, *Messengers of the New Right*, 273.

105. James Baldwin, "The American Dream and the American Negro," *NYT*, March 7, 1965.

106. Jill Lepore, *The Whites of Their Eyes: The Tea Party's Revolution and the Battle over American History* (Princeton, NJ: Princeton University Press, 2010), 126.

107. Elizabeth Kolbert, "Political Outsider Coping with Life as an Insider," *NYT*, August 18, 1991.

108. Piketty and Saez, "Income Inequality in the United States, 1913–1998"; Alfred Stepan and Juan J. Linz, "Comparative Perspectives on Inequality and the Quality of Democracy in the United States," *Perspectives on Politics* 9 (2011): 844; Distribution of family income—Gini index 2014 country comparisons, November 11, 2014, http://www.pho tius.com/rankings/economy/distribution_of_family_income_gini_index_2014_0.html.

109. Bernard Sanders, *The Speech: A Historic Filibuster on Corporate Greed and the Decline of Our Middle Class* (New York: Nation Books, 2011), 20.

110. Ibid., 1, 19.

111. Aaron Bady and Mike Konczal, "From Master Plan to No Plan: The Slow Death of Higher Public Education," *Dissent*, Fall 2012, 10–16; Bernie Sanders on *Countdown with Keith Olbermann*, MSNBC, September 29, 2011.

112. Leibovich, *This Town*, 43, 52, 107.

113. Ibid., 98.

114. *Citizens United v. FEC*, 558 U.S. 310 (2010); *Burwell v. Hobby Lobby Stores*, 572 U.S. _ (2014).

115. Chemerinsky and Gillman, *Free Speech on Campus*, 97–100.

116. Report of the Committee on Freedom of Expression, University of Chicago, 2014,

http://provost.uchicago.edu/sites/default/files/documents/reports/FOECommitteeRe port.pdf.

117. Sykes, *How the Right Lost Its Mind,* 67.

118. E. J. Dionne, *Why the Right Went Wrong: Conservatism—from Goldwater to the Tea Party and Beyond* (New York: Simon & Schuster, 2016), 2; Frum (in 2012), quoted in Hemmer, *Messengers of the Right,* 274.

119. Alana Abramson, "How Donald Trump Perpetuated the 'Birther' Movement for Years," ABC News, September 16, 2016; "Donald Trump 'Proud' to Be a Birther," YouTube video, 5:59, from an interview on *The Laura Ingraham Show* on September 1, 2016, posted by "Laura Ingraham," March 30, 2011, https://www.youtube.com/watch?v=Wqa S9OCoTZs.

120. Kay, *Among the Truthers,* xxi.

121. Sykes, *How the Right Lost its Mind,* 111–13; Alexander Zaitchik, "Meet Alex Jones," *Rolling Stone,* March 2, 2011; Kurt Nimmo, "New Obama Birth Certificate Is a Forgery," Infowars, April 28, 2011, https://www.infowars.com/new-obama-birth-certificate -is-a-forgery/; Lymari Morales, "Obama's Birth Certificate Convinces Some, but Not All, Skeptics," Gallup, May 13, 2011, http://www.gallup.com/poll/147530/ obama-birth-certificate-convinces-not-skeptics.aspx.

122. Judd Legum, "What Everyone Should Know About Trayvon Martin (1995–2012)," ThinkProgress, March 18, 2012; "Timeline of Events in Trayvon Martin Case," CNN, April 11, 2012; "Timeline: The Trayvon Martin Shooting," *Orlando Sentinel,* March 26, 2012.

123. Karen Farkas, "Chardon High School Video Shows Students Being Shot in Cafeteria," Cleveland.com, February 27, 2012, http://www.cleveland.com/chardon-shooting/index .ssf/2012/02/chardon_high_school_video_show.html.

124. On ownership, see the 2007 Small Arms Survey (smallarmssurvey.org), which is conducted by an organization in Geneva, and is comparative; the most useful appendix of that report is http://www.smallarmssurvey.org/fileadmin/docs/A-Yearbook/2007/en/Small-Arms -Survey-2007-Chapter-02-annexe-4-EN.pdf. Some of that year's survey is reported in Laura MacInnis, "U.S. Most Armed Country," Reuters, August 28, 2007. The Small Arms Survey reports the sources of its estimates at http://www.smallarmssurvey.org/ fileadmin/docs/A-Yearbook/2007/en/Small-Arms-Survey-2007-Chapter-02-annexe -3-EN.pdf. For some slightly older but useful data, see Philip J. Cook and Jens Ludwig, *Guns in America: National Survey on Private Ownership and Use of Firearms* (Washington, DC: National Institute of Justice, 1997). On the involvement of guns in murders, see, for example, http://www.fbi.gov/ucr/cius2008/offenses/expanded_information/ data/shrtable_07.html. And see my discussion of the U.S. homicide rate in *The Story of America,* ch. 20.

125. *District of Columbia v. Heller,* 554 U.S. 570 (2008); Henry Martin, "Changing of the Guard," *American Rifleman,* September 2011, 94–97; Ronald Kessler, "David Keene Takes Over the NRA," *Newsmax,* March 28, 2011; David Keene, interview with the author, March 30, 2012.

126. Laura Johnston, "Chardon High School Emergency Plan Prepared Community for Shooting Tragedy," Cleveland.com, February 27, 2012, http://www.cleveland.com/ chardon-shooting/index.ssf/2012/02/chardon_community_prepared_for.html.

127. Cora Currier, "23 Other States Have 'Stand Your Ground' Laws, Too," *Atlantic,* March 22, 2012.

128. Krissah Thompson and Scott Wilson, "Obama on Trayvon Martin: 'If I Had a Son, He'd Look Like Trayvon," *Washington Post,* March 23, 2012.

129. John Hoeffel, "Woman at Gun Range Event Tells Santorum to 'Pretend It's Obama,'" *Los Angeles Times,* March 23, 2012.

130. "New Claims Cast Trayvon Martin as the Aggressor," Fox News, March 27, 2012, http://www.foxnews.com/us/2012/03/27/new-claims-cast-trayvon-martin-as-aggres sor/?intcmp=obinsite.

131. Jay Barmann, "Police Recover Gun Believed Used in Oakland Shooting Spree; Goh's Alleged Target Revealed," SFist, April 6, 2012, http://sfist.com/2012/04/06/police_recover_gun_believed_used_in.php; Olivia Katrandjian, "Two Men Arrested, Facebook Clues in Tulsa Shooting Spree," ABC News, April 8, 2012, http://abcnews.go.com/US/tulsa-oklahoma-men-arrested-shooting-spree/story?id=16096391#.T4HAY5j1Lgo; "2 Mississippi College Students Killed in Separate Shootings over Weekend," Fox News, March 26, 2012, http://www.foxnews.com/us/2012/03/26/2-mississippi-college-students-killed-in-separate-shootings-over-weekend/?intcmp=obinsite.

132. James Rainey, "Sorting out Truth from Fiction in the Trayvon Martin Case," *Detroit Free Press*, April 7, 2012; Lucy Madison, "Gingrich: Everyone in the World Should Have Right to a Gun," CBS News, April 13, 2012; "Blitzer and Trump Go at It Over Trump's Birther Claims," CNN, May 29, 2012.

133. Barack Obama, Speech, Sandy Hook Prayer Vigil, Newtown, CT, December 16, 2012.

134. Andrew Bacevich, *America's War for the Greater Middle East: A Military History* (New York: Random House, 2016).

135. House Budget Committee, "The Path to Prosperity," March 20, 2012, http://budget.house.gov/uploadedfiles/pathtoprosperity2013.pdf; Thomas L. Hungerford, *Taxes and the Economy: An Economic Analysis of the Top Tax Rates Since 1945* (Washington, DC: Congressional Research Service, 2012), 1; Jonathan Weisman, "Nonpartisan Tax Report Withdrawn After G.O.P. Protest," *NYT*, November 1, 2012.

136. American Political Science Association and Russell Sage Foundation, *American Democracy in an Age of Rising Inequality* (Washington, DC: American Political Science Association, 2004); Lawrence Jacobs and Desmond King, eds., *The Unsustainable American State* (Oxford: Oxford University Press, 2009); United Nations, Department of Economic Social Affairs, *Inequality Matters: Report of the World Social Situation 2013* (New York: United Nations, 2013); Joseph Stiglitz, *The Price of Inequality* (New York: Norton, 2012); "Greatest Dangers in the World," Pew Research Center's Global Attitudes Project, October 16, 2014, http://www.pewglobal.org/2014/10/16/greatest-dangers-in-the-world/.

137. "I Am Unlimited," online and television advertisement, Sprint, 2013, https://www.youtube.com/watch?v=C9qxjBlL3ko.

138. Bijan Stephen, "Social Media Helps Black Lives Matter Fight the Power," *Wired*, November 2015; Jordan T. Camp and Christina Heatherton, eds., *Policing the Planet: Why the Policing Crisis Led to Black Lives Matter* (London: Verso, 2016).

139. *Lawrence v. Texas*, 539 U.S. 558 (2003); *Goodridge v. Dept. of Public Health*, 798 NE 2d 941 (Mass. 2003).

140. Brief for Petitioners, *Obergefell v. Hodges & Henry v. Hodges*, http://www.americanbar.org/content/dam/aba/publications/supreme_court_preview/BriefsV5/14-556_pet.auth checkdam.pdf.

141. Rod Dreher, *The Benedict Option: A Strategy for Christians in a Post-Christian Nation* (New York: Sentinel, 2017), 3–9 and quotation, 219.

142. Nagle, *Kill All Normies*, 10. And see Ralph D. Berenger, ed., *Social Media Go to War: Rage, Rebellion and Revolution in the Age of Twitter* (Spokane, WA: Marquette Books, 2013); Heather Brooke, *The Revolution Will Be Digitised: Dispatches from the Information War* (London: William Heinemann, 2011), ix.

143. Nagle, *Kill All Normies*, 64.

144. Adrian Florido, "The White Nationalist Origins of the Term 'Alt-Right'—and the Debate Around It," NPR, November 27, 2016; Richard Spencer, "Become Who We Are," conference remarks, Washington, DC, November 2016; Southern Poverty Law Center, *Alt-Right: The White Nationalist's Alternative to American Conservatism* (Montgomery, AL: Southern Poverty Law Center, 2016), 4–7; Josh Harkinson, "Meet the White Nationalist Trying to Ride the Trump Train to Lasting Power," *Mother Jones*, June 23, 2017.

145. By 2015, Breitbart was "one of the top 1,000 most popular websites on the Internet,

and just outside the top 200 most popular websites in the United States" (Southern Poverty Law Center, *Alt-Right*, 15). And see Stephen Piggott, "Is Breitbart.com Becoming the Media Arm of the 'Alt-Right?'," April 28, 2016, https://www.splcenter.org/hate watch/2016/04/28/breitbartcom-becoming-media-arm-alt-right.

146. Maisha E. Johnson and Nisha Ahuja, "8 Signs Your Yoga Is Culturally Appropriated—and Why It Matters," everydayfeminism, May 25, 2016, http://everydayfeminism .com/2016/05/yoga-cultural-appropriation/. On the rise of clickbait and listicles, see Tim Wu, *The Attention Merchants: The Epic Scramble to Get Inside Our Heads* (New York: Knopf, 2016), chs. 22 and 26; Nagle, *Kill All Normies*, 77.

147. Steven Levy, *In the Plex: How Google Thinks, Works, and Shapes Our Lives* (New York: Simon & Schuster, 2011), 67.

148. Institute of Politics, Harvard Kennedy School, *Campaign for President: The Managers Look at 2016* (Lanham, MD: Rowman and Littlefield, 2017), 13, 16, 28–29, 59. Hereafter IOP, *Campaign for President*.

149. Robert Wurthnow, "In Polls We Trust," *First Things*, August 2015; Dan Wagner, Civis Analytics, interview with the author, August 17, 2015; Elizabeth Wilner, "Kantar's Path to Public Opinion," Kantar, September 4, 2013, http://us.kantar.com/public-affairs/pol itics/2013/kantars-path-to-public-opinion/.

150. Cliff Zukin, "What's the Matter with Polling?," *NYT*, June 20, 2015; "Details of Opinion Poll Inquiry Announced," British Polling Council, May 22, 2015, http://www .britishpollingcouncil.org/details-of-opinion-poll-inquiry-announced/; Doug Rivers, YouGov, interview with the author, August 3, 2015; Scott Horsley, "Changing Polling Metrics to Decide GOP's Presidential Debate Lineup," NPR, August 3, 2015; "Election 2015: Inquiry into Opinion Poll Failures," BBC News, May 8, 2015; "Poll Measures Americans' Trust in Public Opinion Polls," C-SPAN.org, September 4, 2013, https:// www.c-span.org/video/?314837-1/poll-measures-americans-trust-public-opinion-polls; Mark Blumenthal, "Why the Polls in Greece Got It Wrong," *Huffington Post*, July 8, 2015; Oren Liebermann, "Why Were the Israeli Election Polls So Wrong?," CNN, March 18, 2015.

151. "Fox News and Facebook Partner to Host First Republican Presidential Primary Debate of 2016 Election," Fox News, May 20, 2015; Ann Ravel, Chair, FEC, interview with the author, August 21, 2015; Doyle McManus, "Fox Appoints Itself a GOP Primary Gatekeeper," *Los Angeles Times*, May 30, 2015; Rebecca Kaplan, "Marist Doesn't Want Its Poll Used for Fox Debate Criteria," CBS News, August 3, 2015; Scott Keeter, interview with the author, August 20, 2015; Bill McInturff, interview with the author, August 21, 2015.

152. Donald J. Trump for President, August 8, 2015, https://web.archive.org/web/2015 0808202314/https://www.donaldjtrump.com/; Playbuzz—Authoring Platform for Interactive Storytelling, https://publishers.playbuzz.com/, accessed September 12, 2017; "Republican Debate Poll: Who Won First Fox GOP Debate?," *Time*, August 7, 2015, http:// time.com/3988073/republican-debate-fox-first-gop/, accessed September 12, 2017.

153. Brendan Nyhan, "Presidential Polls: How to Avoid Getting Fooled," *NYT*, July 30, 2015; Michael W. Traugott, "Do Polls Give the Public a Voice in a Democracy?," in Genovese and Streb, *Polls and Politics*, 85–86. Gallup's own defense against the critics (including charges of bandwagoning and underdogging) is best read in Gallup and Rae, *The Pulse of Democracy*, ch. 18. "The conventional wisdom that politicians habitually respond to public opinion when making major policy decisions is wrong," is the argument of the political scientists Lawrence R. Jacobs and Robert Y. Shapiro, *Politicians Don't Pander: Political Manipulation and the Loss of Democratic Responsiveness* (Chicago: University of Chicago Press, 2000), xii–xv. Chris Kirk, "Who Won the Republican Debate? You Tell Us," *Slate*, August 6, 2015; Josh Voorhees, "Did Trump Actually Win the Debate? How to Understand All Those Instant Polls That Say Yes," *Slate*, August 7, 2015.

154. This report is based on the author's presence at the Kennedy conference. For a transcript of the proceedings, see IOP, *Campaign for President*. Transcript of the campaign

managers' roundtable, 11–60. Outbursts from the audience at this roundtable and at other events held during the conference that are not found in the transcript come from notes taken by the author while attending.

155. Ann Coulter, *In Trump We Trust: E Pluribus Awesome!* (New York: Sentinel, 2016), 2–5, 21.

156. Phyllis Schlafly, Speech in St. Louis, March 13, 2016.

157. https://www.youtube.com/watch?v=DCGLXku15x0; Phyllis Schlafly, Ed Martin, and Brett M. Decker, *The Conservative Case for Trump* (Washington, DC: Regnery, 2016).

158. The remarks of Donald Trump at the funeral of Phyllis Schlafly, September 10, 2016, https://www.youtube.com/watch?v=1Bng_6HZlPM; Spruill, *Divided We Stand*, 336–41; Rod Dreher, *The Benedict Option: A Strategy for Christians in a Post-Christian Nation* (New York: Sentinel, 2017), 80.

159. Dreher, *The Benedict Option*, 79.

160. Ibid., 226; Sykes, *How the Right Lost Its Mind*, 17.

161. Hillary Clinton, *What Happened* (New York: Simon & Schuster, 2017).

162. IOP, *Campaign for President*, 67.

163. Ibid., 68.

164. Ibid., 69.

165. Nicholas Confessore and Daisuke Wakabayashi, "How Russia Harvested American Rage to Reshape U.S. Politics," *NYT*, October 9, 2017.

166. Caitlyn Dewey, "Facebook Fake-News Writer," *Washington Post*, November 17, 2016. And on his death: http://www.phoenixnewtimes.com/arts/paul-horner-dead-at-38-9716641.

167. Tim Wu, "Please Prove You're Not a Robot," *NYT*, July 15, 2017.

168. IOP, *Campaign for President*, 70.

169. Mike Isaac and Scott Shane, "Facebook's Russia-Linked Ads Came in Many Disguises," *NYT*, October 2, 2017. And see, for example, Zeynep Tufekci, "Zuckerberg's Preposterous Defense of Facebook," *NYT*, September 29, 2017.

170. Cecilia Kang, Nicholas Fandos, and Mike Isaac, "Tech Executives Are Contrite About Election Meddling, but Make Few Promises on Capitol Hill," *NYT*, October 31, 2017.

171. IOP, *Campaign for President*, 70.

172. Ibid., 71.

173. Indictment, *U.S. v. Internet Research Agency et al.*, 18 USC §§ 2, 371, 1349, 1028A, February 16, 2018.

174. On Assange, see Raffi Khatchadourian, "Julian Assange, a Man Without a Country," *TNY*, August 21, 2017.

175. IOP, *Campaign for President*, 76.

176. Ibid., 83.

177. Ibid., 87.

178. Ibid., 89.

## Epilogue: THE QUESTION ADDRESSED

1. Alexander Hamilton, Federalist No. 1 (1788); Edward R. Garriott, *Cold Waves and Frost in the United States* (Washington, DC: Weather Bureau, 1906), 10.

2. Charles Pierce, *A Meteorological Account of the Weather in Philadelphia from January 1, 1790, to January 1, 1847* (Philadelphia: Lindsay and Blakiston, 1847), 264. My thanks to Charles Cullen and the Historical Society of Pennsylvania and to Peter Huybers of Harvard's Department of Earth and Planetary Sciences.

3. Average annual temperatures from 1948 to 2017 can be found at NOAA National Centers for Environmental Information, Climate at a Glance: U.S. Time Series, Average Temperature, published July 2017, http://www.ncdc.noaa.gov/cag/, accessed July 23, 2017.

4. Michael Carlowicz, "World of Change: Global Temperatures: Feature Articles," NASA, https://earthobservatory.nasa.gov/Features/WorldOfChange/decadaltemp.php, accessed September 12, 2017.

5. "President Trump Announces U.S. Withdrawal from the Paris Climate Accord," The White House, June 1, 2017, https://www.whitehouse.gov/blog/2017/06/01/president -donald-j-trump-announces-us-withdrawal-paris-climate-accord; "President Trump Decides to Pull U.S. Out of Paris Climate Agreement," *All Things Considered*, NPR, June 1, 2017; Justin Worland, "The Enormous Ice Sheet that Broke Off of Antarctica Won't Be the Last to Go," *Time*, July 13, 2017.

6. Andrew Sullivan, "The Republic Repeals Itself," *New York*, November 9, 2016; Donald J. Trump, Inaugural Address, January 20, 2017; Samuel Moyn and David Priestland, "Trump Isn't a Threat to Our Democracy; Hysteria Is," *NYT*, August 11, 2017.

7. Jessica Anderson, "Taney Statue Is Moved from Outside Frederick City Hall," *Baltimore Sun*, March 18, 2017; Celeste Bott, "Remaining Pieces of Confederate Monument Removed from Forest Park," *St. Louis Post-Dispatch*, June 28, 2017; Richard Fausset, "Tempers Flare over Removal of Confederate Statues in New Orleans," *NYT*, May 2, 2017; Sheryl Gay Stolberg and Brian M. Rosenthal, "Man Charged After White Nationalist Rally in Charlottesville Ends in Deadly Violence," *NYT*, August 12, 2017.

8. Bork, *Slouching Towards Gomorrah*, 317–18.

9. Newt Gingrich, *To Renew America* (New York: HarperCollins, 1996), 7.

# ILLUSTRATION CREDITS

Frontispiece  Americans assembled on the National Mall for the 1963 March on Washington. Warren K. Leffler / Library of Congress.

xxii  John Durand painted the precocious six-year-old New Yorker Jane Beekman in 1767, holding a book and seized with inspiration. Jane Beekman by John Duran, 1767, oil on canvas. Photo © New York Historical Society.

3  "America" first appeared as the name of an undefined land mass on a map of the world made in 1507. Martin Waldseemüller / Library of Congress.

4  On an ink-splotched sketch of northwest Haiti, Columbus labeled "la española," Hispaniola, "the little Spanish island." The Granger Collection.

15  A drawing originally made in the seventh century by Isidore of Seville became, in 1472, the first printed map of the world; twenty years later, it was obsolete. British Library, London, UK, © British Library Board. All Rights Reserved / Bridgeman Images.

16  Artists working for the sixteenth-century mestizo Diego Muñoz Camargo illustrated the Spanish punishment for native converts who abandoned Christianity. Glasgow University Library, Scotland / Bridgeman Images.

21  An Aztec artist rendered the Spanish conquistadors, led by Cortés, invading Mexico. The Granger Collection.

24  Mexican casta, or caste, paintings purported to chart sixteen different possible intermarriages of Spanish, Indian, and African men and women and their offspring. Museo Nacional del Virreinato, Tepotzotlan, Mexico / Courtesy of Schalkwijk / Art Resource, NY.

31  This deerskin cloak, likely worn by Powhatan, was by the middle of the seventeenth century housed in a museum in Oxford, England. Ashmolean Museum, University of Oxford, UK / Bridgeman Images.

35  The Virginia Company recruited colonists with advertisements that lavishly promised an Eden-like bounty. Library of Congress.

44  In 1629, Massachusetts Bay adopted a colony seal that, by way of justifying settlement, pictured a nearly naked Indian, begging the English to "Come Over and Help Us." Massachusetts Archives.

46  European slave traders inspecting people for purchase sometimes licked their skin, believing it possible to determine whether they were healthy or sick by the taste of their sweat. Traite General du Commerce de l'Amerique by Chambon. Bibliothèque Municipale, Nantes France (PRC BW).

51  In 1681, Charles II granted lands to the English Quaker William Penn, who founded a "holy experiment" in the eponymous colony of Pennsylvania. Library of Congress.

65  Benjamin Franklin's 1754 woodcut served as both a political cartoon and a map of the colonies. Library of Congress.

68  George Whitefield's preaching stirred ordinary Americans and set them swooning, but it also inspired study, and intellectual independence, repre-

sented here in the form of a woman, in the lower left, wearing spectacles to study Scripture. Private Collection / Bridgeman Images.

72    Boston-born artist John Singleton Copley left the colonies in 1774, never to return; in 1783, while living in London, he depicted the 1781 Battle of Jersey in a 12 × 8 foot painting—only a detail is shown here—and offered his own argument about American liberty by picturing, near its center, a black man firing a gun. © Tate, London 2018.

73    In protest of slavery, Benjamin Lay rejected anything produced by slave labor, became a hermit, and lived in a cave. William Williams / National Portrait Gallery.

80    London-printed maps commemorating the treaty that ended the Seven Years' War in 1763 marked out the importance of both the Caribbean and the continent. Library of Congress.

85    People held in slavery in Jamaica rebelled throughout the middle decades of the eighteenth century, leaving Jamaican slave owners reliant on British military protection and unwilling to join colonists on the continent in rebelling against British rule. Bibliothéque Nationale, Paris, France / Bridgeman Images.

89    A British minister with the 1774 bill closing the port of Boston in his pocket pours tea down the throat of "America"—here, and often, depicted as a naked Indian woman—while another looks under her skirt. American Antiquarian Society.

101   This political cartoon, published in London, shows "Britain," on one side of the scale, warning, "No one injures me with impunity," while, on the other side, "America," trampled by her allies (Spain, France, and the Netherlands), cries, "My Ingratitude is Justly punished." American Antiquarian Society.

103   Benjamin West, American-born History Painter to the King, began a painting of the British and American peace commissioners—including Benjamin Franklin, John Adams, and John Jay—but never finished the canvas. Courtesy, Winterthur; painting: *American Commissioners of the Preliminary Peace Negotiations with Great Britain* by Benjamin West (1783–1819), oil paint on canvas, London, England, gift of Henry Francis du Pont, 1957.856.

109   Printers published the proposed Constitution as a broadside but also included it in newspapers, almanacs, and pamphlets. Gilder Lehrman.

115   The value of paper currency fluctuated wildly, and by the end of the Revolutionary War, money printed on behalf of the Continental Congress had become nearly worthless. American Antiquarian Society.

118   James Madison took copious notes on the proceedings of the constitutional convention. James Madison / Library of Congress.

129   A 1787 engraving pictures Federalists and Anti-Federalists pulling in two different directions a wagon labeled "Connecticut," stuck in a ditch and loaded with debts and (worthless) paper money. Amos Doolittle / Library of Congress.

132   George Washington was inaugurated on the balcony of Federal Hall, formerly New York's city hall. Courtesy, Winterthur; etching: *FEDERAL HALL / The Seat of CONGRESS* by Amos Doolittle, Peter Lacour, 1790, New Haven, CT, ink, watercolor on laid paper, bequest of Henry Francis du Pont, 1957.816.

143   Federalists and Anti-Federalists had different reactions to the Haitian revolution. Bibliothéque Nationale, Paris, France, Roger-Viollet, Paris / Bridgeman Images.

148   An 1800 print commemorating the life of Washington pictures him hold-

ing the "The American Constitution," a tablet etched in stone. Library of Congress.

150     Arthur Fitzwilliam Tate's 1854 canvas *Arguing the Point* depicts a hunter and a farmer debating an election while reading a paper brought by a townsman, while the farmer's daughter tries to break in on the conversation. *Arguing the Point; Settling the Presidency* by Arthur Fitzwilliam Tait (1819–1905); photo: R. W. Norton Art Gallery.

153     Philadelphians of all ranks celebrate the Fourth of July in 1812 in this watercolor by John Lewis Krimmel, a German immigrant. *Fourth of July Celebration in Center Square* by John Lewis Krimmel, HSP large graphics collection [V65] / Historical Society of Pennsylvania.

160     An election of 1800 campaign banner for Thomas Jefferson, promised "John Adams No More." Smithsonian Institution, Washington, D.C.#45-553 (PRC CT).

169     Jefferson imagined an "empire of liberty," a republic of yeoman farmers, equal and independent. Library of Congress.

174     This political caricature, engraved and inked in Massachusetts about 1804 and sold in New Hampshire by 1807, depicts Jefferson as a rooster and Sally Hemings as his hen, testament to how widespread were rumors about the president's relationship with one of his slaves. American Antiquarian Society.

183     Andrew Jackson's 1824 bid for the presidency introduced all manner of paraphernalia, including this campaign sewing box. David Frent Collection / Photo courtesy of Heritage Auctions, HA.com.

184     Paper ballots were in general use by the 1820s, usually in the form of "party tickets" for an entire slate of candidates, like this Democratic Party ticket from Ohio in 1828. Library of Congress.

187     Jackson's inauguration in 1829 brought an unprecedented crowd to the Capitol—a crowd that followed him to the White House. Robert Cruikshank / Library of Congress.

189     In the 1830s, railroads emerged as a symbol of progress, pictured, as in this engraving, as if cutting through the wilderness and carrying civilization across the continent. LC-USZ62-51439 (b&w film copy neg.).

194     The textile mills of Lowell, Massachusetts, on the banks of the Merrimack River, were the first in the United States to use power looms. Library of Congress.

196     The tent meetings of the Second Great Awakening had much in common with Jacksonian-era political rallies, but, where men dominated party politics, women dominated the revival movement. The Granger Collection.

200     An unidentified woman, about the age of Maria W. Stewart when she first wrote for the *Liberator*, posed for a daguerreotype, holding a book, an emblem of her learnedness. Courtesy of the George Eastman Museum.

213     The Cherokees devised their own writing system, adopted their own constitution, and began printing their own newspaper, the *Phoenix*, in 1828. Library of Congress.

222     Pioneers heading west gathered at settlements like Major John Dougherty's trading post on the Missouri River. Denver Public Library, Western History Division #F3226 (PRC B/W).

225     During the Panic of 1837, a destitute family cowers when debt collectors come to the door, demanding hard money; fading portraits of Jackson and Van Buren hang on the wall behind them. Library of Congress.

227     An 1848 cartoon pictured William Henry Harrison as the engine of a train fueled by hard cider and pulling a log cabin while President Martin Van Buren, driving "Uncle Sam's Cab," pulled by a blindered horse, stumbles on a pile of (Henry) Clay. Robert N. Elton/ Library of Congress.

232      In Richard Caton Woodville's 1848 painting, a crowd gathers on the porch of the "American Hotel"—a symbol of the Union—eagerly awaiting the "War News from Mexico." Crystal Bridges Museum of American Art, Bentonville, Arkansas #2010.74.

237      President Tyler officiates at a wedding between the Texas star and America in a political cartoon from a New Orleans newspaper in 1844—the year Tyler himself married. Andrew Jackson Houston Papers #3445, Courtesy of Texas State Library and Archives Commission.

245      Zachary Taylor tries to balance the congressional scales between the "Wilmot Proviso" and "Southern Rights." Library of Congress.

246      Americans who objected to the extension of slavery often pictured Texans (and Mexicans) as mixed-race and brutal. In this political cartoon, "young Texas," whose tattoos read "Murder," "Slavery," and "Rape," sits on a whipped and manacled slave. E. Jones / The Beinecke Rare Book & Manuscript Library, Yale University.

248      Frederick Douglass, the most photographed man in antebellum America, believed photography to be a democratic art. The Art Institute of Chicago, IL, USAMajor Acquisitions Centennial Endowment / Bridgeman Images.

253      The leading 1848 presidential candidates race to the White House by telegraph (Lewis Cass) and railroad (Zachary Taylor); Henry Clay tries to gain on them in a rowboat; laggard Martin Van Buren follows on a skinny horse; and a black man, representing abolition, lies facedown in the dirt, defeated. Edwin Forrest Durang / Library of Congress.

272      Photographs like the Alexander Gardner's portraits of the dead at Antietam chronicled the war and its many devastations. Alexander Gardner / Library of Congress.

280      African American photographer Augustus Washington captured this likeness of John Brown in his daguerreotype studio in Connecticut in 1846 or 1847. Brown, his right hand raised as if taking an oath, stands in front of the flag of the Subterranean Pass-Way, his more militant version of the Underground Railroad. Augustus Washington.

286      Mathew Brady's 1860 daguerreotype of Abraham Lincoln, cropped, was reproduced as a campaign button. Mathew B. Brady / Library of Congress.

289      Broadsides printed early in 1861 notified citizens of the seceding states that their legislatures had dissolved the Union by repealing their ratification of the 1787 Constitution. Library of Congress.

294      Alexander Gardner, another kind of sharpshooter, took this photograph of a dead Confederate sharpshooter at Gettysburg. Alexander Gardner / Library of Congress.

298      On Emancipation Day, January 1, 1863, black men, women, and children celebrated outside Beaufort, South Carolina. Timothy H. O'Sullivan.

302      *Frank Leslie's Illustrated Newspaper*, a Northern paper, in 1863 ran this before-and-after illustration of Southern women first urging their men to rebellion and later staging bread riots. Library of Congress.

306      Mourners lined New York's Union Square in 1865 as Lincoln's funeral procession passed by while, perched on a rooftop, a photographer captured a bird's-eye shot of the scene. Library of Congress.

308      The growing power of the federal government was extravagantly displayed at increasingly lavish presidential inaugurations. Universal History Archive / UIG / Bridgeman Images.

311      Residents of Richmond, Virginia, celebrated the anniversary of Emancipation Day in 1888, beneath a banner of Abraham Lincoln. Cook Collection, Valentine Museum #1388.

316      Lew Wa Ho worked at a dry goods shop in St. Louis; the photograph was

included in his Immigration Service case file as evidence of employment. National Archives, Pacific Region (Seattle) Records of the Immigration and Naturalization Service.

319    A pamphlet published in 1916 celebrated "the noble ride of the Ku Klux Klan of the Reconstruction Period" and insisted on its "rightful place in history as the saviour of the South, and, thereby, the saviour of the nation." Collection of the Smithsonian National Museum of African American History and Culture # 2011.155.15.

325    In an 1886 cartoon, Uncle Sam kicks Chinese immigrants out of the United States, demonstrating the intensity of anti-Chinese feeling in the first decade of the Chinese Exclusion Act. Shober & Carqueville / Library of Congress.

331    A family unable to pay the mortgage on a farm in western Kansas headed back east to Illinois, having chronicled the journey on the canvas of their wagon: "left Nov. 20, 1894; arrived Dec. 26, 1894." Kansas Historical Society.

351    *Judge* magazine in 1896 pictured William Jennings Bryan bearing his cross of gold, wielding a crown of thorns, and standing on an open Bible while a follower, behind him, waves a flag that reads "Anarchy." Grant E. Hamilton / Library of Congress.

357    Ida B. Wells's indictment of lynching was first published in 1892. Udo J. Keppler / Library of Congress.

361    The 120-acre Ford Motor plant in Highland Park, Michigan, opened in 1910, the largest manufacturing site in the world. From the Collections of The Henry Ford.

367    In 1898, newspaper publishers Joseph Pulitzer and William Randolph Hearst both used the war to increase circulation. Leon Barritt / Library of Congress.

370    Charles Mitchell was lynched in Urbana, Ohio, in 1897, one of thousands of black men lynched during the Jim Crow era. Harvard Art Museums / Fogg Museum, Transfer from the Carpenter Center for the Visual Arts, 2.2002.3604; photo: Imaging Department © President and Fellows of Harvard College.

372    In a 1910 magazine cover, top-hatted banker J. Pierpont Morgan grabs at all of New York City's banks—even a toddler's piggy bank. Frank A. Nankivell / Library of Congress.

374    A 1900 cartoon depicts Theodore Roosevelt as a centaur, branded "GOP," bucking wildly while firing two guns, one labeled "Speeches," the other, "Wild Talk." Udo J. Keppler / Library of Congress.

385    Photographer Jesse Tarbox Beals took this shot of a suffrage parade in New York in 1910. Jessie Tarbox Beals / Schlesinger Library, Radcliffe Institute, Harvard University.

408    A 1921 cartoon depicts Uncle Sam deploying a funnel to stanch the flow of immigrants from Europe. Library of Congress.

415    *Shall Christianity Remain Christian?*, a pamphlet published in 1922, pictured a journey from doubt to atheism as an inevitable descent. Ernest James Pace / Courtesy of Presbyterian Historical Society.

421    A family in Hood River, Oregon, gathers around the radio in 1925. National Archives.

425    Dorothea Lange photographed farmers on relief in California's Imperial Valley in 1936. Dorothea Lange, Courtesy Harvard Art Museums / Fogg Museum, Transfer from the Carpenter Center for the Visual Arts, Sedgewick Memorial Collection.

429    Franklin Delano Roosevelt bypassed the press and spoke to the people

| | directly by radio. Library of Congress, Prints & Photographs Division, photograph by Harris & Ewing. |
| 432 | Eleanor Roosevelt created an entirely new role for the First Lady, not least by spending time touring the country. In May 1935, she toured a coal mine in Bellaire, Ohio. AP Photo. |
| 439 | Sharecroppers were evicted from their homes in 1936 in Arkansas after joining a tenant farmers' union. John Vachon / Library of Congress. |
| 453 | Joseph Goebbels, Germany's minister of propaganda, made especially effective use of radio, here used to address Hitler Youth. Hulton-Deutsch / Hulton-Deutsch Collection / Corbis / Getty Images. |
| 468 | Newspapers around the country reported a panic during the 1938 broadcast of Orson Welles's *The War of the Worlds*. NY Daily News Archive / Getty Images. |
| 472 | The day after the United States bombed Hiroshima, the *St. Louis Post-Dispatch* ran, as an editorial, a crayon drawing titled *A New Era in Man's Understanding of Nature's Forces*. Daniel Robert Fitzpatrick / Courtesy State Historical Society of Missouri. |
| 485 | A 1943 Office of War Information poster celebrated the combined strength of the Allied forces. US Army, Signal Corps / Courtesy Schlesinger Library, Radcliffe Institute, Harvard University. |
| 486 | Wartime mobilization called on women to join the military, as in this U.S. Navy recruiting poster from 1942. Henry Koerner / Library of Congress. |
| 493 | Soldiers communicated from the trenches by way of radio, here in the Philippine island of Leyte in 1944. John Philip Falter / Library of Congress. |
| 495 | Dorothea Lange photographed the forced relocation of Japanese Americans in California in 1942. Dorothea Lange / National Archives. |
| 500 | A billboard in Detroit in 1942 called for the continuation of segregated housing. Office of War Information, Arthur Siegel, Courtesy of Harry S. Truman Library. |
| 509 | FDR and Winston Churchill conferred on a warship at the outset of the Yalta Conference in 1945. Courtesy the Franklin D. Roosevelt Presidential Library & Museum. |
| 513 | In 1945, General Dwight D. Eisenhower and other U.S. generals stopped at a newly liberated concentration camp at Ohrdruf, where the remains of burned bodies were found on railroad tracks. United States Holocaust Memorial Museum, courtesy of National Archives and Records Administration, College Park. |
| 518 | John Mauchly's ENIAC, sometimes called the Giant Brain, marked the beginning of the age of information. Bettmann Archive / Getty Images. |
| 521 | In an era of American abundance, TV sets in a store window broadcast Eisenhower's announcement of his decision to run for reelection in 1956. Grey Villet / The LIFE Picture Collection / Getty Images. |
| 524 | Vassar mathematician Grace Murray Hopper programmed Mark I. Grace Murray Hopper Collection, Archives Center, National Museum of American History, Smithsonian Institution. |
| 528 | The G.I. Bill made it possible for a generation of Americans to attend college. In September 1947, three jubilant former servicemen leave a student union at Indiana University, waving their notices of admission. Indiana University Photographic Services Neg # 47-1082 (PRC has B/W). |
| 533 | Leone Baxter and Clem Whitaker, who founded Campaigns, Inc., in California in 1933, attained national prominence at the end of the 1940s through their successful defeat of Truman's health insurance plan. George Skadding / The LIFE Picture Collection / Getty Images. |
| 556 | Suburban housewives served as the foot soldiers of the conservative |

movement; here, women rally in support of Joseph McCarthy. Bettmann Archive / Getty Images.

564    CBS News, whose team included Walter Cronkite, commissioned the first commercial computer, UNIVAC, to predict the outcome of the election of 1952. Keystone-France / Gamma-Keystone / Getty Images.

567    U.S. Army Chief Counsel Joseph Welch holds his head in his hand as Joseph McCarthy speaks during the Army-McCarthy hearings in 1954. Robert Phillips / The LIFE Images Collection / Getty Images.

569    Reverend Billy Graham, here preaching in Washington, DC, in 1952, reached a nationwide audience but boasted an especially strong following in Congress. Mark Kauffman / The LIFE Premium Collection / Getty Images.

585    Elizabeth Eckford was turned away from Central High School in Little Rock, Arkansas, in 1957, by order of the state's governor, Orval Faubus. Francis Miller / The LIFE Picture Collection / Getty Images.

587    On the cover of *Life*, MIT scientists attempt to calculate the orbit of the Soviet satellite Sputnik while the magazine promises to explain "Why Reds Got It First." Dmitri Kessel / *Life* magazine, Copyright Time Inc. / The LIFE Premium Collection / Getty Images.

589    Vice President Richard Nixon and Soviet premier Nikita Khrushchev debated the merits of capitalism and communism in a model American kitchen on display in Moscow, 1959. Photo by Howard Sochurek / The LIFE Picture Collection / Getty Images #50475727.

595    Students from North Carolina A&T College staged a sit-in at a lunch counter in a Woolworth's in Greensboro. Bettman Archive / Getty Images.

601    The joint appearance between Kennedy and Nixon in 1960 was the first televised presidential "debate"; another matchup would not take place until 1976. CBS Photo Archive / Getty Images.

612    Johnson, here touching down in the presidential helicopter in rural Appalachia, made a Poverty Tour in 1964 to see what Dwight Macdonald called "our invisible poor." Lyndon B. Johnson Presidential Library.

618    Johnson applied "The Treatment" to Abe Fortas in July 1965, the month before Fortas took a seat on the Supreme Court. Lyndon B. Johnson Presidential Library photo by Yoichi Okamoto.

620    Americans watched the war in Vietnam from their living rooms. Library of Congress.

631    Young men in Central Park, New York, mourned Martin Luther King Jr. following his assassination in Memphis on April 4, 1968. Benedict Fernandez, Courtesy Harvard Art Museums / Fogg Museum, Transfer from the Carpenter Center for the Visual Arts, Beinecke Fund.

634    Poet and boxer Rodolfo Gonzales, a leader of the Chicano movement, spoke at a rally in Denver in 1970. Dave Buresh / The Denver Post / Getty Images.

645    Nixon left the White House by helicopter on August 9, 1974. Bettmann Archive / Getty Images.

646    Phyllis Schlafly led a resurgent conservative movement in the 1970s by making opposition to equal rights one of its signature issues. Bettman Archive / Getty Images.

655    Betty Ford, who attended the National Women's Conference in Houston in 1977, was among several powerful Republicans who objected to using women to draw a line between the political parties. Bettye Lane / Schlesinger Library, Radcliffe Institute, Harvard University.

669    Ronald Reagan, a man of immense personal charm, greeted supporters in Indiana during his 1980 campaign. Kristoffer Tripplaar / Alamy Stock Photo.

676    The lines between the parties hardened over guns and abortion, one meaning freedom and the other murder, though which meant which depended on the party. Courtesy Ronald Reagan Library.

687    ACT UP demonstrators protested outside New York's city hall in 1988. Bettye Lane / Schlesinger Library, Radcliffe Institute, Harvard University.

690    No single act so well captured the end of the Cold War as the dismantling of the Berlin Wall in 1989. Luis Veiga / Getty Images.

693    Bill and Hillary Clinton frequently appeared together on the campaign trail in 1992. Cynthia Johnson / Liason / Getty Images.

717    A battle over a recount in the election of 2000 left the outcome in doubt for weeks. LeFranc / Gamma-Rapho / Getty Image.

719    Firefighters searched Ground Zero long after the collapse of both towers. Photo by James Nachtwey '70 The Hood Museum of Art at Dartmouth.

730    *Wired* magazine began appearing in 1993 and by 2000 announced that the Internet had ushered in "One Nation, Interconnected." *Wired* © Condé Nast.

741    The Iraq War mired U.S. soldiers in counterinsurgency campaigns. Matt Cardy / Getty Images.

751    Barack Obama's inauguration in 2009 drew the largest crowd ever assembled on the Mall. Robyn Beck / AFP / Getty Images.

756    Tax Day protests held on April 15, 2009, marked the birth of the Tea Party movement, which countered Obama's call for change with a call for a return to the principles of the founding fathers. Emmanuel Dunand / AFP / Getty Images.

773    Not long after his 2017 inauguration, President Trump greeted visitors to the White House in front of a portrait of Hillary Clinton. Aude Guerrucci-Pool / Getty Images.

784    Glenn Ligon's 2012 *Double America*, in neon and paint, was partly inspired by the opening words of Charles Dickens's *A Tale of Two Cities*: "It was the best of times, it was the worst of times." © Glenn Ligon; Courtesy of the artist, Luhring Augustine, New York, Regen Projects, Los Angeles, and Thomas Dane Gallery, London.

# INDEX

Page numbers in *italics* refer to illustrations.

ABC list, 494
Abenakis, 57
abolitionists, 205, 252
  constitutional convention damned by, 241
  evolution and, 284
  founders judged by, 201
  Texas annexation opposed by, 238, 241–42
  women as, 207, 228
abortion:
  anti-abortion terrorism, 702
  and anti-feminist women's movement, 652–53
  Betty Ford on, 654, 655
  and evangelical churches, 664
  history of, 649–50
  and National Women's Conference, 661, 662
  and 1960s political consensus, 647, 649
  and Nixon, 653–54, 658
  and political polarization, 647, 658, 667–68, 676
  and right to privacy, 650, 678, 685–86, 688
  and Schlafly, 656
  Supreme Court on, 647, 653–54, 655, 656, 678
abstinence, 197
Abu Ghraib, 748
Abzug, Bella, 652
academia:
  hate speech codes, 703–4, 763
  and identity politics, 703
  and 1960s activism, 634–35
  postmodernism, 636
  and Vietnam War, 635–36
  *see also* universities
academic freedom, 545, 553, 554–55, 557
*Account of the Antiquities of the Indians, An* (Pané),
    5–7, 24
Acheson, Dean, 578–79
ACLU (American Civil Liberties Union), 415–16,
    744
  and right to privacy, 686
  and women's rights, 652
Act for the Better Ordering and Governing Negroes,
    An (South Carolina colony), 59
Act Prohibiting the Teaching of the Evolution The-
    ory, 418

ACT UP, 686, 687
Adams, Abigail, 650
  on women's equality, 96–97
Adams, James Truslow, 441
Adams, John, 82, 84–85, 87, 88, 92, 93, 94, 96–97,
    98, 101, 102, *103*, 111–12, 113, 114, 129,
    180, 185
  Alien and Sedition Acts and, 158
  death of, 185–86, 190, 199
  in debate with Jefferson on Constitution, 153–
    54
  on Declaration of Independence, 98
  in election of 1796, 158
  in election of 1800, 154, 160–62, 164
  Haiti revolution and, 159
  on lack of established religion, 200–201
  majority rule feared by, 155
  Marshall appointed chief justice by, 165, 167
  vanity of, 98, 155, 158, 160
Adams, John Quincy, 164, 176, 185, 217, 288
  acquisition of Texas opposed by, 223, 236
  death of, 251
  desire to negotiate Mexican border, 222
  election of, 184
  in election of 1824, 180–81
  in election of 1828, 186
  in election of 1836, 224
  Monroe Doctrine crafted by, 234–35
Adams, Samuel, 81, 92, 165
Addams, Jane, 368, 377, 380, 387
*Adding Machine, The* (Rice), 404
Advanced Research Projects Agency (ARPA), 587
advertising, 448, 534, 560, 572–73
Advisory Committee on Post-War Foreign Policy,
    492
AFDC (Aid to Families with Dependent Children),
    618–19, 671, 700
*Affluent Society, The* (Galbraith), 591, 611
Afghanistan, 738–40, 742, 746
Affordable Health Care Act (2010), 754–55
Africa, 456, 462
  Portuguese exploration of, 11
  slave trade in, 11–12, 17–18, 38, 46

African Americans, 530–32, 541, 542, 575–88, 767
  Black Power movement, 625–26, 627, 628, 651, 673, 701
  black studies, 634–35
  and criminal justice policy, 623, 700
  and presidential election (1968), 633
  and presidential elections, 599
  race riots, 623–24, 627–28
  and southern strategy, 632
  voting rights of, 163
  see also civil rights movement; specific people
African Free School, 210
African Labor Supply Association, 281
African Methodist Episcopal Church, 202, 203
Agassiz, Louis, 256, 284
Age of Machinery, 198
Age of Reason, The (Paine), 142
Agnew, Spiro, 638, 639, 644
Agreement of the People, An (1647), 49
Agriculture Adjustment Act, 437, 438
agriculture companies, 336
Agriculture Department, U.S., 473–74
Aguinaldo, Emilio, 367–68
AIDS, 685, 687
Aid to Dependent Children, 439
Aid to Families with Dependent Children (AFDC), 618–19, 671, 700
Aiken, Howard, 523
Ailes, Roger, 704–5, 706, 707, 710–11, 716, 742
Alabama, 531
  gun laws in, 445
  income tax in, 301
  Indians in, 213
  movement to, 221
  secession of, 290
  slaves sold to, 202
  as slave state, 179
Albany Congress (1754), 66, 70–71, 77, 91
Albany Journal, 269
Alcatraz occupation (1969–71), 634
Alexander, James, 61–62
Algonquians, 55–56
Ali, Muhammad, 629
Alien and Sedition Acts (1798), 158–59, 164, 165, 395, 745
Allen, Paul, 695
Allport, Gordon W., 460
All Slave-Keepers That keep the Innocent in Bondage, Apostates (Lay), 74
Almonté, Juan, 233, 238
Alpine race, 392
al Qaeda, 722, 738–39, 746–47
Alta California, 243
Amazon, 735
America, first use of term, 3, 14
America Firsters, 481, 482
American Academies of Arts and Sciences, 155
American Anti-Slavery Society:
  founding of, 206
  Texas annexation opposed by, 223
American Association for Labor Legislation, 37

American Association for Public Opinion Research, 542
American Bankers' League, 405, 504
American Bar Association, 359
American Board of Commissioners of Foreign Missions, 213
American Civil Liberties Union, see ACLU
American colonies, British:
  British troops in, 84, 87
  credit crisis in, 81–82
  Elizabeth I's desire for, 25, 26, 28
  English king's claim to dominion over, 34
  ethos of, 44–45
  European migration to, 44, 45
  expansion of, 43–44
  extent of, 33–34
  growth of literacy in, 59
  Indian attacks in, 55–57
  individual liberties in, 33, 34
  James I's charter for, 32–33, 34–35
  mortality rates in, 67
  newspapers in, 59
  popular sovereignty in, 50
  racial dimension of slavery in, 69–70
  religious and political freedom in, 49–53
  religious revival in, 67–69, 68
  in Seven Years' war, see French and Indian War
  slavery in, 45–46, 48
  Spanish conquest vs., 33
  taxation of, 78, 81, 88–89, 91–92
  see also specific colonies
American Colonization Society, 176, 177, 178–79, 204, 240
American Dilemma, An (Myrdal), 501
American Dream, 441
American Equal Rights Association, 328
American Eugenics Society, 410
American Federation of Labor (AFL), 537
American Freedmen's Inquiry Commission, 317
American Geographical Society, 396, 400
American Historical Association, 353
American history, 1960s challenges, 634–35
American Indian Movement (AIM), 634
American Institute of Public Opinion, 455
American Liberty League, 447
American Magazine, 77
American Medical Association (AMA), 438, 546–48, 560
American National Election Survey, 544
American National Exhibition (1959), 590–91
American Party, 263
American Philosophical Society, 67, 155
American Political Science Association, 545–46
American Revolution:
  Caribbean and, 101–2, 103
  Continental currency printed in, 334
  expectation of British victory in, 100, 101
  first fighting in, 92–93
  France and, 101–2
  global dimensions of, 100–101
  institution of slavery challenged by, 105–6

Loyalists in, *see* Loyalists
Native Americans and, 102
peace negotiations in, 103, *103*, 107
seeds of, 75, 92
slavery and, 93–95, 100, 108
southern theater in, 102–3
American Taxpayers' Association, 504–5
American Taxpayers' League, 405
*American Voter, The,* 593
*American Women* (Commission on the Status of Women), 647
Americas:
European extraction of wealth from, 17
European migration to, 16–17
European voyages to, 11
introduction of European animal and plants into, 18–19
native population of, 8–9
slavery in, 17
Spanish conquest of, *see* Spanish conquest
*America's Town Meeting of the Air,* 459–60, 571
*America We Deserve, The* (Trump), 714
Ames, Fisher, 112
Analytical Engine (Babbage), 193–94
"Ancient & Modern Confederacies" (Madison), 117
Anderson, John, 221, 665, 705
Angelou, Maya, 660
Angola, 38
Annapolis Convention (1786), in call for constitutional convention, 117–18
Anschluss, 466
Anthony, Susan B., 358
citizenship of women desired by, 321
National Woman Suffrage Association founded by, 328
Thirteenth Amendment pushed by, 303
women's suffrage desired by, 340
anthropology, 348
anticolonialism, 583
Anti-Drug Abuse Act (1986), 699
Anti-Federalists, 129–30, *129*, 131, 137, *143*, 145
anti-feminist women's movement, *646,* 652–53, 661–62
Antigua, 34
slave rebellion in, 57–58, 63
Anti-Imperialist League, 368
Anti-Mason Party, 218–19
antislavery movement:
in Britain, 107–8
in New England, 87, 88
antitrust act, 388
antiwar movement, *see* peace movement
Apaches, 222
"Apology for Printers" (Franklin), 61
*Appeal to the Colored Citizens of the World, but in Particular, and Very Expressly, to those of the United States of America* (Walker), 203, 204–5, 218, 256
Apple Computer, 695, 733
*Apprentice, The,* 762
Arabs, 399

Arbenz Guzmán, Jacobo, 574
"Are Computers Newsworthy?" (Mauchly), 559
*Arguing the Point* (Tate), *152*
Aristotle, 21, 47, 112, 155
Arizona, 260–61, 394, 494
creation of, 332
irrigated land in, 409
women's voting rights in, 386
Arkansas, 281, 584–87
black voting in, 344
free blacks banned from, 280
movement to, 221
sharecroppers in, *439*
Arkansas National Guard, 585
Armed Services Committee, 538
Armenians, 390, 399
arms control, 680, 681
arms race, 570, 586
Army-McCarthy hearings (1954), 567, *567*
Arnold, Thurman, 462
ARPANET, 731
Arthur, John, 769
Articles of Confederation, 97–98, 114, 121, 128, 290
attempted revisions of, 115, 117
artifacts, 8
*Art of the Deal, The* (Trump), 713
Ashcroft, John, 744, 745, 747
Ashley, John, 113
Asia, 407
Associated Press, 490
Atlanta, Ga., 302, 581, 582
*Atlanta Daily World,* 581
Atlantic Charter, 482–83
*Atlantic Monthly,* 448
*Atlas Shrugged* (Rand), 553
Atomic Age Conferences, 526
atomic bomb, 514, 515–16, 517, 521–23, 531, 532, 538–39, 571, 587
Atomic Energy Commission (AEC), U.S., 545
atomic power, 526
atomization, 527
*Augusta,* 483
*Aurora,* 161–62
Auschwitz, 513
Australia, 342, 344, 456
Austria, 466–67, 471, 473
Austrian Empire, 426
*Autobiography* (Franklin), 211
automatic weapons, 445
automation, 558–59, 574–75
Axis, 466, 479
Aztecs, 8, *21*
Cortés's defeat of, 22–23

Babbage, Charles, 193–94, 523
Bacevich, Andrew J., 741–42
Bacon, Nathaniel, rebellion of, 56
Bagram Air Base, 748
Baker, Ella, 596–97
Baker, Ray Stannard, 349, 371

Baldwin, James, xix–xx, 497, 622, 623, 756
Ball, Charles, 202–3
"Ballot or the Bullet, The" (Malcolm X), 613
Baltimore, Md., 287, 303, 582
*Baltimore Sun*, 417
Bancroft, George, 10, 185, 198–99, 353–54
Bank Act, 239
bankers, 343
Bankhead-Jones Act, 442
banking, 334
Bank of the United States (first), 138–39, 141
bankruptcy laws, 141
bankruptcy protection, 226
banks, 231, 363, 364
    closing in the Depression of, 436
    failure in the Depression of, 425–26
    regulation of, 388
Baptists, 50, 201, 568
Barbados, 34, 46, 47
    slavery in, 73
    slave rebellion in, 56, 63
Barber, Francis, 92
Barbour, James, 179
Barlow, John Perry, 731, 732, 733
Barlowe, Arthur, 30
Barnum's Museum, 274
Baruch, Bernard, 538, 551
"Basic Problem of Democracy, The" (Lippmann),
    309
Bates, Fred, 467
Baus and Ross, 572
Baxter, Leone, 448, 449, 450, 451–52, 456, 478,
    532–34, 533, 546–48, 553–54, 560, 561,
    572, 704
    *see also* Campaigns, Inc.
Bay of Pigs, 604
BBC, 467
Beacon Hill, 202
Beals, Jesse Tarbox, 385
Beard, Charles, 427, 438, 441, 449
Beaton, Ark., 439–40
Beaufort, S.C., 298
Beck, Glenn, 755, 762
Beck, James Montgomery, 403, 404
Beecher, Catherine, 197, 207, 215, 252
Beecher, Lyman, 195, 197, 201, 204
    anti-Catholic views of, 208
Beekman, Jane, 2
Belgium, 473
Bell, Daniel, 592, 593, 614
Bell, Derrick, 703
Benezet, Anthony, 76
Bennett, James Gordon, 211, 229
Benthan, Jeremy, 98
Berkeley, William, 56
Berlin Airlift (1948–49), 539
Bermuda, 34
Bernays, Edward, 413–14, 424, 456, 457
Berners-Lee, Tim, 731
Bethlehem, Pa., 366
Bethlehem Steel, 382, 412

Bett (Elizabeth Freeman), 113–14
Beveridge, Albert J., 368
Biddle, Nicholas, 220
Biden, Joe, 699
Bigelow, Jacob, 198, 203
Big Oil, 363
Bikini Atoll hydrogen bomb test (1946), 571
bill of rights, xii, 127, 129, 130
Bill of Rights, U.S., 48, 134
    established religion forbidden by, 200
    150th anniversary of, 490–91
    ratification of, 135, 137–38
Biloxi, Miss., 578
bin Laden, Osama, 722, 725, 738–39, 765
birth control, 386, 394
    *see also* contraception
birther movement, 727, 762–63
Bishop, Abraham, 143
Black, Hugo, 339, 552, 579
black churches, 202
black codes, 318, 320, 578
black colleges and schools, 576, 581
Black Lives Matter, 726, 767–68
Blackmun, Harry, 685, 687
Black Panthers, 627, 768
Black Power movement, 625–26, 627, 628, 651, 673,
    701, 767
blacks, 409, 411
    citizenship of, 314, 317, 321–22
    and colonization issue, 204, 205
    in Colored Farmers' Alliance, 336
    as cowboys, 334
    in the Depression, 440
    excluded from common schools, 210
    excluded from New Deal, 440, 457–58
    Grant supported by, 324
    and populist movement, 343–44
    Republicans supported by, 323, 386–87
    voting rights of, 320, 326, 330, 353, 501
    women, 190
    in World War II, 496–503, *500*, 508
    *see also* Jim Crow
Bleecker, Leonard, 140
Bleeding Kansas, 266
Bletchley Park, 523–24
Blick, Roy, 550
Bloom, Allan, 703
Blue Cross and Blue Shield, 547
"blue discharge," 530
Blumer, Herbert, 542–43, 544, 546
Board of Trade, Chicago, 275
Bob Jones College, 461
Bob Jones University, 663
Body of Liberties, 48
Bogart, Leo, 667
Bolshevists, 363
Bond, Julian, 597
Booth, John Wilkes, 285, 305
Border Patrol, U.S., 410
border states, 303, 304, 318
Bork, Robert, 644, 687–90, 692, 734

bosses, 195
Boston, Mass.:
  British troops in, 87
  free black community in, 202
  Irish in, 209
  newspapers in, 59–60
  segregation in, 259
  siege of, 92
  top 1 percent in, 207
*Boston Gazette*, 82–83, 92
*Boston Globe*, 433
Boston Harbor, closing of, 89, *89*
*Boston News-Letter*, 59
Boston Tea Party, 89
Botkin, Benjamin, 441
Boukman (Haitian slave), 143
*Bowers v. Hardwick*, 685, 686–87, 768
Bracero Program, 674
Braddock, Edward, 77–78
Bradford, William, 38–39, 90, 93
Brady, James, 672, 676
Brady, Mathew, 285, *286*, 294
Brady Campaign to Prevent Gun Violence, 676
brainwashing, 565
Brand, Stewart, 694–95, 731
Brandeis, Louis, 381, 382, 384, 388–89, 578
Brazil, 281
Breckinridge, John, 288
Brennan, William J., 644, 650, 679
Bretton Woods, 483, 506
*Brevísima Relación de la Destrucción de las Indias*
      (Las Casas), 24
*Brides*, 528
Bright, Bill, 664
British Empire:
  American Revolution and, 100–101, 107
  credit crisis in, 82, 88
  slavery abolished in, 235
broadcasting, 422
Brokaw, Tom, 737
Bromfield, Louis, 551–52
Brooke, Heather, 770
Brooks, Preston, 266–67
Brown, H. Rap, 627
Brown, John, 279–80, *280*, 281, 282–85, 288
Brown, Linda, 577
Brown, Michael, 767
Brown, Oliver L., 577
Brown, Pat, 626
*Brown v. Board of Education*, 382, 577–82, 586,
      588, 614, 663, 677, 678
Bryan, William Jennings, 345–46, 430, 563, 570, 693
  desire to stay out of World War I, 393
  in election of 1896, 350–52, *351*, 366, 374–75
  fundamentalism and, 354, 391, 418
  imperialism protested by, 366, 368
  income tax supported by, 347–48, 376
  made secretary of state, 387–88
  Rockefeller boycotted by, 373
  in Scopes trial, 414–19
  in Spanish-American War, 367

Bryant, Anita, 661
Buchanan, James, 290
  and election of 1848, 253
  in election of 1856, 267–68
Buchanan, Pat, 654, 685, 691, 740
*Buchanan v. Warley*, 369
Buchenwald, 511, 512, 513
Buckley, William F., 554–55, 670
buffalo, 333–34
"Building of the Ship, The" (Longfellow), 259–60,
      271, 480
Bulgaria, 426
*Bulletin of the Atomic Scientists*, 539, 587
Bunyan, John, 192
Burdick, Eugene, 598–99, 603
Bureau of Efficiency, 363
Bureau of Refugees, Freedmen, and Abandoned
      Lands, 317, 319–20
Bureaus of Intelligence, 402
Burger, Warren, 679
Burgoyne, John, 101
Burke, Edmund, 110, 555, 735
Burnham, James, 504
Burr, Aaron, 163
  in election of 1800, 164
Bush, George H. W., 740
  and abortion, 665–66
  and contraception, 650
  and judiciary, 678
  and presidential election (1988), 706
  and presidential election (1992), 691, 706
  and talk radio, 704
Bush, George W., 739, 741, 743
  and judiciary, 678
  9/11 attacks and, 721, 722
  and presidential election (2000), 716–17
  war on terror and, 738–40, 744–45
Bush, Jeb, 716, 772
Bush, Vannevar, 524, 525
business machines, 558–59
busing, 663
Butler, Andrew, 266
Butler, William, 254
Byrne, Ethel, 394
Byron, George Gordon, Lord, 194

cable television, 666, 679, 705, 707–8, 710–11
  and presidential election (2000), 716
Cabot, John, 25
Caesar (slave), 3, 64, 83, 131
Cahokia, 8
Calhoun, John C., 224, 238
  annexation of Cuba desired by, 242
  annexation of Texas desired by, 236
  in election of 1824, 182
  and Indian removal policies, 214, 217
  as John Quincy Adams's pallbearer, 251
  on necessity of slavery, 218, 255
  nullification pushed by, 217–18, 239
  opposed to granting citizenship to Mexico, 244,
      245

Calhoun, Patrick, 233
California, 243, 250, 260, 450–51, 494, 532–34, 533, 535, 546, 549, 561
  Chinese immigrants in, 324, 325
  irrigated land in, 409
  universal health care in, 379–80
  women's voting rights in, 386
California Medical Association, 533–37, 546
California State of the State Address (1945), 533
California Street (San Francisco), 406
Callender, James, 162, 174–75
Cambridge Analytica, 728, 780
campaign biographies, Jackson's introduction of, 181–82
campaign financing, 562
Campaigns, Inc., 448, 449–50, 532–34, 533, 546–48, 560, 572, 625, 633–34, 636, 648
Campus Crusade for Christ, 664
Canada, 69
  Loyalists in, 104, 107
canals, 195, 221
Cantril, Hadley, 460
Cape Cod, Mass., 39
capital gains tax, 405
capitalism, 230, 315, 331, 332, 335–36, 343, 427, 535, 555
  idea of progress and, 156
*Capitalism and Freedom* (Friedman), 670
Capitol News Bureau, 449
Caribbean, 108
  American Revolution and, 101–2, 103
  black mortality rate in, 102
  British colonies in, 34
  British troops in, 84, 87–88
  colonists' boycott of goods from, 85
  Continental Congress's ban on trade with, 91
  mortality rates in, 67
  slave rebellions in, 56, 57–58, 63, 84, 99
  slavery in, 46, 64, 142
  Stamp Act in, 84
  sugar plantations in, 45, 46, 47, 82, 102, 142
Carlyle, Thomas, 198, 203
Carmichael, Stokely, 621, 625–27, 629, 630, 651
Carnegie, Andrew, 336, 368
Carnegie Endowment for International Peace, 540
Carolina colony, Locke as secretary of, 52
*Carolina Gazette*, 160–61
Carson, Rachel, 680
Carter, Harlon Bronson, 675–76
Carter, Jimmy:
  and arms control, 680
  and Iranian hostage crisis, 680
  and 1970s economic malaise, 656–57
  and presidential election (1976), 659, 705
  and presidential election (1980), 668, 696
  and tax policy, 669
Carter, Rosalynn, 660
Cass, Lewis, 250, 253, 253
Castille, Philando, 767–68
Castro, Fidel, 604
Catholic Church, and abortion, 650, 653–54, 664

Catholicism, 26
Catholics, 50, 263, 410
  immigrants, 208–9
  Muslim wars with, 36
  in riots, 209
  rumors of plots by, 208–9
*Cato's Letters* (Trenchard and Gordon), 60, 61, 63
Catt, Carrie Chapman, 431
caucuses, opposition to, 182
"Causes and Proposed Remedies of Poverty, The," 366
Cayton, Horace, 502
CBS, 422, 467, 469–71, 491, 511, 557–59, 563–65, 564, 566
censure, 568
census, 125, 168
  of 1790, 157
Census Bureau, U.S., 355, 558
Central Intelligence Agency (CIA), 538, 574
  and Cold War, 639
*Challenge to Liberty, The* (Hoover), 506
Chamberlain, Neville, 467, 468
Chambers, Julius, 349
Chambers, Whittaker, 509, 540–41, 548–49, 555, 572
*Changing Sources of Power* (Dutton), 696
Chardon High School, 763
charitable aid societies, 207
Charles I, king of England, 44, 48
  divine right of kings claimed by, 43
  execution of, 49
Charles II, king of England, 50–51, 51
Charleston, S.C., 86, 102, 104, 105, 203, 204, 287
  AME church in, 202, 203
*Charleston Courier*, 240
Charter of Liberties, English, 40–41
Chase, Salmon, 256–57
  Emancipation Proclamation amended by, 298
Chase, Samuel, 115
Chavez, Cesar, 675
Cheever, John, 441
Cheney, Dick, 745
Chennault, Anna, 632
Cherokee Nation, 213–16, 218
*Cherokee Nation v. Georgia*, 215
Cherokees, 212–13, 213, 214–16, 337
Chicago, Ill., 287, 333, 334, 371
  transcontinental railroad through, 262
Chicago, University of, 354, 763
Chicago Gospel Tabernacle, 460
*Chicago Record-Herald*, 453
*Chicago Tribune*, 349, 488, 542, 563
Chicago World's Fair, 353–57
Chicano movement, 634, 634, 635, 660, 675
Chickasaw Bayou, 297
Chickasaws, 181, 212–13
child labor, 388
*Children in Bondage* (Creel), 395
Chile, 260
China, 260, 482, 539, 560
  and creation of United Nations, 492

in United Nations, 503
U.S. food sent to, 486
China, ancient, 11, 12
Chinese, 399
Chinese Americans, 326–27
Chinese Exclusion Act, 325, 336, 359, 407, 409
Chinese immigrants, 281, 324–25, 325, 326–27, 342, 409
Knights of Labor's opposition to, 336
Chisholm, Shirley, 652
Chocktaws, 181, 212–13
Chomsky, Noam, 635
Christensen, Clayton M., 736
Christian Coalition, 685, 712
Christianity, 190–91, 568–69, 584
Christy, David, 281–82
Chrysler, Walter, 383
Churchill, Winston, 468, 477, 478, 479, 480–81, 508, 536
Atlantic Charter negotiated by, 483
and creation of United Nations, 491–92
Hitler's underestimation of, 485
Lend-Lease praised by, 481
and Pearl Harbor attack, 484
at Tehran Conference, 502–3
at Yalta Conference, 508–10, 509
church membership, 200
Church of England, 43
dissenters from, 38
Cincinnati Enquirer, 453
Cincinnati Gazette, 267
Citizen Kane (film), 449
citizenship, 311–16, 528, 575
of black people, 314, 317, 321–22
defined by Civil Rights Act, 319
defined by Fourteenth Amendment, 321–22
Douglass on, 327
of women, 314, 315, 321–22
Citizens United v. Federal Election Commission, 760, 763
Civilian Conservation Corps, 504
Civil Rights Act (1866), 319–20
Civil Rights Act (1957), 585–86
Civil Rights Act (1964), 322, 612–13
Civil Rights Commission, U.S., 586
civil rights movement, 530–32, 541, 573, 575–88, 595–97
and Black Power movement, 627
Civil Rights Act (1964), 612–13
FBI surveillance, 626
Freedom Riders, 604–6
and George Wallace, 608, 613–14
Greensboro sit-in (1960), 595–96, 595
and Johnson administration, 611, 612–13, 614, 622
and Kennedy administration, 608–9
King arrest (1960), 600–601
and Malcolm X, 606–7, 613, 621–22
March on Washington (1963), 609–10, 613
and political polarization, 637
and presidential election (1960), 599, 600–601

and presidential election (1964), 613–14
Selma march (1965), 621–22
voter registration, 620–21
and White Power movement, 673–74
Civil War, U.S.:
black men in, 300
casualties of, 272, 293–94, 294, 390
draft riots in, 300
emancipation in, 296–97
federal government expanded by, 301, 316–17, 337–38
Lincoln's claims to war powers in, 487
photography from, 272, 274, 294, 294, 295
slavery as cause of, 296, 389
start of, 292, 293
Clark, Ramsey, 633
Clark, Tom C., 579
Clark, Victor S., 409
Clarke, George, 63
"classical liberalism," 555
Clay, Henry, 176, 178, 179, 184, 253
American Colonization Society founded by, 204
annexation of Texas opposed by, 236, 238
Compromise of 1850 of, 260–61
in election of 1824, 182
in election of 1832, 219, 220
in election of 1844, 237–38
in election of 1848, 254
Clean Air Act, 681
Clean Water Act, 681
Cleveland, Ohio, 371
climate change:
and conservatism, 690
and science, 680–81, 682–83
Clinton, Bill, 732, 741
background of, 696–97
and criminal justice policy, 699–700
and Democratic Party, 696
economic policy, 699, 700
ethics investigations, 697–98, 709–13, 714, 718
and health care, 698–99
marriage of, 692–93
and media, 707, 708
and presidential election (1992), 648, 693, 697, 698, 706
and social issues, 648
and welfare, 700
and women's rights, 691–92
Clinton, Henry, 102
Clinton, Hillary Rodham, 601, 725, 728, 753, 754–55, 765, 767
background of, 692–93
and ethics investigations, 710
and health care, 698, 699
and presidential election (1992), 693
and presidential election (2016), 692
right-wing attacks on, 709
and women's rights, 691–92
Closing of the American Mind, The (Bloom), 703
CNN, 707, 716–17, 719, 721
Coast Guard, 363

Cobb, Thomas R. R., 292
code breaking, 523
Coercive Acts (1774), 89, 89, 90, 91
Cohn, Roy, 567
*Coit v. Green*, 662–63
Coke, Edward, 34–35
    divine right of kings challenged by, 40, 41, 43
Colbert, Stephen, 744
Cold War, 525, 535–38, 553, 568, 570, 573, 578,
        581, 584, 586–87
    and academia, 635
    Bay of Pigs, 604
    Cuban Missile Crisis, 604
    end of, 683–84, 690, 690
    and Kennedy administration, 602
    and knowledge workers, 693–94
    and Nixon-Khrushchev meeting (1959), 589–91
    and political polarization, 639
    and Reagan, 627
    and school desegregation, 663
    and women's rights, 658
Colfax, Schuyler, 301
collectivism, 555
Collingwood, Charles, 563–64
colonialism, and Vietnam War, 602, 603
Colonial Revival, 407, 411
colonization movement, 176, 177, 178
Colonization Society, 201
Colorado, 325
    women's voting rights in, 386
Colored Farmers' Alliance, 336
Colored Orphan Asylum, 300
Colored People's Day, 356
*Columbian Almanack*, xviii
Columbian Exposition, 353–57
*Columbian Orator*, 276
Columbia University, 348, 562
Columbus, Christopher, xviii, 17, 18, 337
    diary of, 3–4, 12, 23–24
    in 1492 arrival at Haiti, 3–4
    second voyage of, 5, 18
    sketch map of Haiti by, 4
    Spanish sponsorship of, 12
    western voyage proposed by, 12
Columbus, Ferdinand, 5, 16
Comey, James, 761
Commission on National Goals, 594–95, 597
Commission on the Status of Women, 647
Committee for Constitutional Government, 504–5
Committee on Political Parties, 545–46
Committee on Social Insurance, 379
Committee to Re-elect the President (CRP), 641
common schools, 209–10
*Common Sense* (Paine), xvii, 95–96, 130
communism, 482, 527, 534–41, 548–57, 565–68,
        571, 581
*Communist Manifesto* (Marx and Engels), 254
Communist Party USA (CPUSA), 552
Company of Royal Adventures of England Trading
        with Africa, 46
compassionate conservatism, 716

Compromise of 1850, 260–61
computers, 193–94, 521, 523–27, 524, 544, 557–59,
        563–65, 573, 574–75, 587, 667, 694–95
Computing-Tabulating-Recording Company, 404
Comrie, L. J., 523
Comstock, Anthony, 652–53
concealed weapons, 446
Confederate States of America:
    draft in, 300–301
    formation of, 289–90
    Hitler's admiration for, 476
    pardoning of leaders of, 318
    taxes in, 300, 301
    welfare in, 302–3
    women in, 301–3, 302
Congregationalists, 201
Congress, U.S., 525, 529, 531, 535, 538, 541, 542,
        546, 547, 548, 549, 566, 568, 569, 569, 572,
        579, 582, 584, 585–86
    Dickens's criticism of, 243–44
    inventory of manufacturing instituted by, 172
    national bank charter renewed by, 234
    slave trade abolished by, 172
    war declared on Spain by, 366–67
Congress, U.S., First, 131–34
    antislavery petitions and, 135, 136–37
    Bill of Rights and, 134
    debt assumption plan passed by, 140
    and founding of Washington, DC, 139–40
    Hamilton's bank plan passed by, 138–39
Congressional Black Caucus (CBC), 699
*Congressional Government* (Wilson), 373, 388
*Congressional Record*, 132, 408
Congress of Industrial Organizations (CIO), 537
Congress of Racial Equality (CORE), 604–5, 606,
        607
Conkling, Roscoe, 329, 338
Connecticut, 654
    suffrage sold in, 342
*Connecticut Bee*, 145
Connecticut colony, 44
Connecticut compromise, 125
Connor, Eugene "Bull," 605
*Conscience of a Conservative, The* (Goldwater), 614
conscription of thought, 395–96
conservatism, 332, 364, 529, 552–57, 556, 560–63,
        568, 570, 573, 579–80, 581
    and Constitution, 677–79
    and George W. Bush administration, 716
    and gun control debate, 672–74, 675–78, 679
    and health care, 698–99
    and inflation, 629
    New Deal vs., 444–45, 446–47
    and 1960s political consensus, 592
    and Nixon administration, 638
    and political polarization, 711
    and polling industry, 667
    and presidential election (1964), 613–15
    and race, 662–63
    and race riots (1960s), 623
    and Reagan, 624–25, 627

Republican Party takeover of, 658–59, 664–68
and science, 682–83
and technology, 666
Weyrich on failure of, 712
*see also* culture wars; political polarization
*Conservative Mind, The* (Kirk), 555
Constitution, Confederate, 290
Constitution, U.S., xi, 52, 287, 543, 552, 573, 575,
     579, 582, 583, 728
Article I of, 139, 157
Article VI of, 138
bill of rights as originally lacking in, 127, 129,
     130
commerce clause of, 462
and conservatism, 677–79, 684, 685, 686–87
and establishment of Cherokee Nation, 215
evolution and, 373
fundamentalist view of, 403, 404
God absent from, 200
New Deal and debate over, 462–66
originalism, 677, 678–79, 684, 685, 687–88
and payment of congressmen, 122
preamble to, xi–xii
property requirements for federal office holders
     rejected by, 122
publication of, *109*, 128
ratification debate over, 128–31, 166
ratification of, xii–xiv
repeal of ratification by seceding states, 289–90,
     *289*
rival interpretations of, 411–12
signing of, 128
slavery and, 127
slavery in, 191, 241, 256–57, 261–62, 268
slave trade and, 136
and state sovereignty, 217–18
three-fifths clause in, 130, 157, 173, 175
treated as scripture, 201
voting rights and, 122
and white supremacy, 701
and women's rights, 650, 653, 691
*see also* Bill of Rights, U.S.; *specific amendments*
constitutional convention (1787), xi, 109–10, 119–28
adjournment of, 128
apportionment issue at, 123, 125
conflicts between states as issue at, 121
Connecticut compromise at, 125
debate at, 275
debt and taxation as issue at, 121
free speech discussed at, 291
Madison's notes on, 110, 111, *118*, 149, 240–41,
     256–57
Northwest Ordinance enacted by, 124–25
representation as issue at, 121–22, 123, 124–25
secrecy pledge at, 121
slavery as issue at, 123–27
slave trade as issue at, 125–26
three-fifths rule adopted by, 125
Virginia Plan and, 120
*Constitutional Courant*, 83
constitutional crisis of 1840s and 1850s, 238–41

"Constitution for the New Deal," 466
Constitution of the Air, 422–23
constitutions, 112, 240
English, 110
constitutions, state, 111–13
branches of government in, 113
Declarations of Rights in, 112, 113, 114
slavery and, 113–14
voting rights in, 112–13
constitutions, use of term, 110
consumers, 380–81
consumer spending, 528, 558
Continental army, 93
Continental Congress, 92, 93, 97–98, 128
Articles of Confederation enacted by, 114
boycott of British goods by, 91
and calculation of states' share of taxes, 115–16
Caribbean trade banned by, 91
and foreign demands for repayment of debts, 114,
     116
paper money issued by, *115*, 116
and question of representation, 90–91
taxing authority lacked by, 114–15
Continental currency, 334
contraception, 386, 394
history of, 649
1970s activism, 647
and right to privacy, 650, 678, 685–86, 688
Supreme Court on, 649, 650, 653, 678
*see also* birth control
contract, liberty of, 378
Converse, Philip, 593
Cooke, Henry, 335
Cooke, Jay, 335
Coolidge, Calvin:
efficiency of taxation by, 405
propaganda used by, 414
Cooper, James Fenimore, 212
Cooper Union, 285
Copley, John Singleton, 72
CORE (Congress of Racial Equality), 604–5, 606,
     607
Cornwallis, Lord, surrender of, 103, 104
Coronado, Francisco Vásquez de, 23
corporations, 330, 333, 336–37
as people, 339, 348
people vs., 348
taxing of, 336
"corrupt bargain" (1828), 236
corruption, 708
Cortés, Hernán, *21*, 22–23
Corwin, Norman, 491
Cosby, William, 61, 62–63
*Cosmos* (TV show), 681
cotton, 203
doubling of production of, 202
export of, 217
Cotton Belt, 438
cotton gin, 172
*Cotton Is King* (Christy), 281
Coughlin, Charles, 461, 476, 479

Coulter, Ann, 722–23, 727
Council on Foreign Relations, 474
counting and measuring, *see* quantification
Country Party (New York), 62, 63
Court Party (New York), 62
courts, *see* judiciary; Supreme Court
cowboys, 334
Cox, Archibald, 643–44
Cox, James, 403
Coxe, Tench, 172
Creeks, 212
Creek War, 213, 214
Creel, George, 395, 396, 414, 488, 496
"Crime Against Kansas, The" (Sumner), 266
Crimean War, 301
criminal justice policy:
    and Clinton administration, 699–700
    and gun control debate, 673
    and Johnson administration, 622–23
    mass incarceration, 699–700
    NFL kneeling protests, 628
    and presidential election (1968), 632–33
*Crisis*, 371, 396, 497
Crisp, Mary, 665
critical race theory, 703
Cronkite, Walter, 561, 563–64, 563, 565, 643,
    706–7, 743
"cross-of-gold" speech, 570
CRP (Committee to Re-elect the President), 641
Crusade for Justice, 634
Cruz, Ted, 774
Cuba, 370, 374
    filibusters in, 281
    missionaries in, 366
    Polk's desire to annex, 242
Cuban Missile Crisis, 604
Cudjoe, 58
Cugoano, Quobna Ottobah, 136
Culpeper, Va., 297
culture wars, 647–48, 676
    and anti-feminist women's movement, *646*,
        652–53, 661–62
    and conservative Republican Party takeover,
        658–59, 664–68
    and Constitution, 653–54, 677–79
    end of, 712–13
    and evangelical churches, 662–64
    and immigration, 674, 675
    and National Women's Conference, 661–62
    and 1960s political consensus, 649–51, 672–73
    and 1970s economic malaise, 658
    and Schlafly, 655–56, 658–59, 661, 662, 664
    and White Power movement, 673–74
    and women's rights activism, 646–47, 651–52,
        654–55
Cushing, Caleb, 288
Czechoslovakia, 400, 467–68, 473, 475

Dachau, 513
Daguerre, Louis, 272–73
daguerreotype, 272–74

Dakota Sioux, 333
Daley, Richard, 633
dams, 442
*Darkest Africa* (Stanley), 750–51
Darrow, Clarence, 365, 420
    Prohibition opposed by, 398
    at Scopes trial, 416–19
Darwin, Charles, 8, 284, 417, 419
data processing, 557–59
data science, 597–99, 603–4, 635
Davenport, Charles, 392
Davis, Elmer, 491
Davis, Garrett, 326
Davis, Jeff, 365
Davis, Jefferson:
    inauguration of, 290
    made president of Confederacy, 289–90
    slavery defended by, 293
    slaves of, 296–97
Davis, John W., 411, 577–78, 579
Davis, Reuben, 285
Davis's Hotel (Washington), 176
Dawes, Henry Laurens, 337
Dawes Severalty Act, 337
D-Day, 505–6, 586
*Dead of Antietam, The* (exhibit), 294
Dean, Howard, 737
Dean, John, 633
debate, 275–76, 459–60
DeBow, James D. B., 292
Debs, Eugene, 352, 384, 385, 395–96, 416–17,
    757–58
debt, national, Hamilton's plan for repayment of,
    138–40
debt, as slavery, 81, 82, 83
debtors' prison, 141, 226
Declaration of Independence, xiv–xv, xvii, 75, 98–99,
    112, 128, 154, 165, 227, 257–58, 280, 287, 728
    and black Americans, 203–4
    centennial of, 329
    considered scripture, 202
    criticism of, 256
    fiftieth anniversary celebration of, 185
    fiftieth anniversary of, 189–90, 199
    Garrison's praise of, 206
    Jefferson's draft of, 99
    slavery ignored by, 99
Declaration of Independence of Cyberspace, 733
Declaration of Liberty by the Representatives of
    the Slave Population of the United States of
    America, 283
Declarations of Rights, 112, 113, 114
Defense Department, U.S., 538, 545
*Defense of the Constitutions of Government of the
    United States* (Adams), 155
defense spending, *see* military spending
Degler, Carl, xviii
Delaware, 578
DeLay, Tom, 748
"Demands of the Vietnamese People, The," 399
de Mier y Terán, Manuel, 222

democracy, xviii
   doubts in the Depression about, 426
   measurement of public opinion and, 452–57
   Nazism vs., 434
   negative connotation of term, 112, 121
   peace and, 395
   public relations and, 402
   republicanism vs., 181
   spread of, 191, 192
   and television, 592
   World War II fought for, 492
Democratic Leadership Council, 696
Democratic National Committee (DNC), 431, 432,
      454, 456–57, 557
Democratic Party, U.S., 264, 282, 331
   and Civil Rights Act, 613–14
   congressional majority of, 537, 549, 552–53,
      567–68
   conservative opposition to, 556, 557, 563
   1832 convention of, 219
   1860 conventions of, 287
   1864 convention of, 303
   1876 convention of, 345
   1880 convention of, 340
   1896 convention of, 350–52, *351*
   1912 convention of, 543
   in election of 1836, 224
   in election of 1840, 227, 228
   and gender gap, 668
   Irish in, 209
   and labor unions, 693, 696
   and Mississippi Freedom Democratic Party, 621
   1924 convention of, 410–11
   1928 convention of, 428
   1932 convention of, 429–30
   People's Party fused into, 346–47, 350
   popular support for, 541–46, 560, 563, 564, 571,
      572–73, 586
   Populists folded into, 364–65
   presidential election (1960), 597
   presidential election (1964), 621
   presidential election (1968), 633
   rearrangement of, 431
   rise of, 211
   and southern strategy, 632, 636, 656, 667
   southern white support for, 323
   and technology, 693–96
   Truman as leader of, 531, 541–46, 552
   2004 convention of, 253
   women's rights supported by, 529
Democratic Party (Jacksonian), 186
Democratic-Republican Party, see Republicans
      (Jeffersonian)
*Democratic Review*, 243
demography, 157
denationalization, 526
Denmark, 473
*Dennis v. United States*, 552
deregulation, 671–72, 705–6
desegregation, racial, 530–31, 541, 575–88, 585,
      663

*Desk Set* (film),574–75
Detroit, Mich., 383, 499, *500*
   Great Migration to, 371
Dewey, John, 395
Dewey, Thomas E., 541–46, 555–56, 563
Dias, Bartolomeu, 12, 17
Dickens, Charles, 234, 243–44
Dickinson, Anna, 264
Dickinson, John, 97, 127
Dies, Martin, Jr., 443–44, 498–99, 504
Difference Engine (Babbage), 193, 523
differential analyzer, 524
Diggers, 50
digital electronic computers, 524
direct mail, 666, 679
diseases, European, catastrophic effect on Native
      Americans of, 19–20
Disney, Walt, 528–29
Disneyland, 528–29, 566
disruption, economic, 735–36
*District of Columbia v. Heller*, 763–64
*Divide and Conquer* (MacLeish), 489
divine right of kings, 48, 54
Dixiecrats, 541
Dixon, Frank M., 541
Dodge City, Kans., 445
"Does the Negro Need Separate Schools?" (Du Bois),
      581
Dole, Bob, 734–35
domestic economy, 197
Donnelly, Ignatius, 346
Doomsday Clock, 539, 587
Dougherty, John, *222*
Douglas, Helen Gahagan, 549
Douglas, Stephen:
   Compromise of 1850 of, 260–61
   in election of 1858, 265, 275, 276–79
   in election of 1860, 288
   and identity politics, 701
   Kansas-Nebraska Act proposed by, 262
   Lincoln's criticism of, 285
   Lincoln's debates with, 275, 276–79, 286
Douglas, William O., 579, 584, 644, 650
Douglass, Frederick, 247–49, *248*, 374, 417, 583,
      767
   black men urged to join Union army by, 300
   Brown's meeting with, 282, 283, 284
   on citizenship rights, 327
   Civil Rights Act pushed by, 319–20
   on Columbian Exposition, 356–57
   on constitutionality of slavery, 261–62
   debate studied by, 276
   *Dred Scott* decision denounced by, 270, 271
   on Emancipation Proclamation, 297–98
   escape from slavery, 314
   Jim Crow's rise explained by, 353, 355–56, 358
   Lincoln's study of, 264–65
   on photography, *248*, 273–74, 460
   on separate creation of races, 256
   worries about Reconstruction, 329
Dow Jones Industrial Average, 424

Downey, Sheridan, 449, 450, 549
draft riots, 300
Drake, Francis, 29
*Dreams from My Father* (Obama), 750
*Dred Scott v. Sandford*, 268–70, 291, 314, 360, 464, 727, 757
Dreher, Rod, 769, 778
Dresser, Robert B., 504–5
drought, in the Depression, 426, 439–40
Drudge, Matt, 710
Drudge Report, 763
drug laws, 376
drug policy, 699, 700
D'Souza, Dinesh, 727
Duane, William, 161–62
Du Bois, W. E. B., 296, 360, 369–70, 371, 396, 411, 496, 581
    at Paris Peace Conference, 399
Duer, William, 140–41, 335
Dukakis, Michael, 694, 706
Duke Law School, 534
Dulles, John Foster, 574
Dunham, Stanley, 750–51
Dunham, Stanley Ann, 751
Dunmore, Lord, 93, 94–95
Du Pont, 448
du Pont, Irénée, 445, 446
du Pont, Lammont, 445, 446, 447
du Pont, Pierre, 445, 446
Durand, John, 2
Dutton, Frederick, 696
Dwight, Timothy, 159
Dyson, Esther, 732

"Earl Warren Special," 561
Earp, Wyatt, 445
earth, geological history of, 7
East Asia Tin Works, 521–22
East India Company, 82, 88–89
Eastland, James, 582
Eaton, John, 181–82
Eckert, Presper, 524, 526–27, 558
Eckford, Elizabeth, 585, 585
*Economic Consequences of the Peace, The* (Keynes), 400
economic inequality:
    and end of Cold War, 684
    and Internet, 657–58
    and Kennedy administration, 611–12
    late 1960s increase in, 594
    and 1970s economic malaise, 657, 658
    1990s increase in, 702
    *see also* poverty
Economic Opportunity Act (1964), 612
economic policy:
    Clinton administration, 699, 700
    deregulation, 671–72, 705–6
    Keynesian, 592, 619, 657, 670
    NAFTA, 699
    Reagan administration, 669–72, 705–6

supply-side economics, 670, 671
economics, 348
economic situation:
    early 1960s affluence, 591–92
    late 1960s inflation, 629
    1970s malaise, 656–57
    1990s improvement, 714
    and Reagan administration, 683
Edes, Benjamin, 92–93
Edison, Thomas, 424
Edison Institute, 424
Editors' Research Bureau, 455
Edmunds, George F., 327
education, 527–30, 545, 553, 554–55, 557, 576, 579
    of women, 386
Edward, Harry, 628
efficiency, 382
"eggheads," 551–52, 561
Egyptians, 399
Ehrlichman, John, 638, 640
eight-hour workday, 346, 377, 388
Einstein, Albert, 474, 475, 526
Eisenhower, Dwight D., 741
    and abortion, 649
    and Cold War, 602
    Commission on National Goals, 594–95, 597
    conservative support for, 570, 579–80, 581
    D-Day overseen by, 505
    McCarthy as viewed by, 566, 568
    and nuclear weapons, 680
    Ohrduf visited by, 512, 513, 513
    presidential campaign of (1952), 559–60, 562, 565
    presidential campaign of (1956), 571–72
    and presidential election (1960), 599, 602
    racial policies of, 582, 584, 585–86
    recording system, 640
    religious affiliation of, 569
    scientific research supported by, 587
"Eisenhower Answers America," 560
*Eisenstadt v. Baird*, 650
Election Day, 342
election forecasts, 557–59, 563–65, 564
elections, California, 1934, 450–51
elections, direct, 156
elections, Illinois, 1858, 265
elections, indirect, 156–57
elections, U.S., 156–58
    of 1789, 133
    of 1796, 154, 158
    of 1800, 154–55, 159–64, 160
    of 1824, 180–85
    of 1828, 185, 186
    of 1832, 218–19
    of 1836, 224–25
    of 1840, 226–29, 257
    of 1844, 236–38, 243, 257
    of 1848, 253–54, 256–57
    of 1856, 267
    of 1860, 285, 286, 287–88

of 1864, 303
of 1866, 323
of 1868, 324
of 1876, 329–30
of 1896, 350–53, *351*, 362, 366
of 1908, 376, 384
of 1912, 385–87, 543
of 1916, 393
of 1920, 403, 428
of 1928, 421–22, 423
of 1930, 427
of 1932, 429–31, 454, 536
of 1933, 549
of 1936, 447, 462, 503, 535
of 1938, 503
of 1940, 478
of 1942, 503
of 1944, 531, 542, 564
of 1946, 534–37, 549
of 1948, 541–46, 555–56, 559–60, 563, 564
of 1952, 552, 557–59, 561–65, *564*, 570
of 1954, 567
of 1956, 570–73
"party tickets" in, *184*, 186
Electoral College, 218, 573
    in 1824 election, 184
    in election of 1800, 154, 164
    election of delegates to, 158, 163–64, 183, 186
    three-fifths rule and, 157–58, 164
electrification, 404–5
Electronic Frontier Foundation (EFF), 732, 744
Elektro the Moto-Man, 526, 558
"Elements of Technology, The" (Bigelow) 198
Elizabeth I, queen of England, 25–26, *26*, 27
Ellis, John, 716
Ellison, Ralph, 441
Ellsberg, Daniel, 640–41, 644
Ellsworth, Oliver, 122, 126
El Salvador, 281
emancipation:
    implications for citizenship of, 311–12
    *see also* slaver
Emancipation Day, *311*
Emancipation Proclamation, 297–300, 303, 329
Emanuel, Rahm, 708
Embargo Act (1807), 171–72
Emergency Banking Act (1933), 437
*Emerging Republican Majority, The* (Phillips), 636
Emerson, Ralph Waldo, 229, 230, 247, 252
Emery, Sarah E. V., 340, 346
*Emigrants' Guide to Oregon and California* (Hastings), 242
empiricism, 349
*End of Ideology, The* (Bell), 592
End Poverty in California (EPIC), 450
Engels, Friedrich, 380
England, *see* Great Britain
England, Jake, 765
English Civil War, 48
English common law, 35, 47

Glanville on, 40
    slavery and, 88
English North America, racism in, 23
ENIAC (Electronic Numerical Integrator and Computer), *520*, 523–27, 558
Enigma machine, 524
Enlightenment, 256
environmental movement, 681
Environmental Protection Agency, 681
Ephron, Henry, 574
Ephron, Phoebe, 574
EPIC campaign, 535, 549
*Epic of America, The* (Adams), 441
Episcopalians, 201
equality, 205–6, 360
    criticism of, 256
    and *Dred Scott* decision, 270
    as moral idea, xv
    political, *see* political equality
    U.S. democracy's reliance on, 341–42
equal pay, 581
Equal Pay Act, 659
equal protection of the law, 580
Equal Rights Amendment, *see* ERA
Equal Rights Leagues, 318
Equal Rights Party, 328, 340
Equal Rights Association, 402
ERA (Equal Rights Amendment), 402, 403, 529
    Betty Ford on, 655
    and conservative Republican Party takeover, 659, 664, 665, 668
    and liberal feminism, 652
    and NOW, 647
    and right to privacy, 686
    and Schlafly, 656, 658
Erie Canal, 195
espionage, 539, 540–41, 548–49
*Essay on Slavery and Abolitionism, with Reference to the Duty of American Females, An* (Beecher), 207
*Essay on the Principle of Population* (Malthus), 157, 171
estate tax, 405
ethics investigations, 708–13, 714
"Ethics of Family Planning, The," 649
Ethiopia, 427
*Etymologiae* (Isidore of Seville), 14
eugenics, 391–92, 394, 410
*Eugenics* (Davenport), 392
Europe:
    American voyages of, 11
    before 1492, 9
    extraction of wealth from Americas by, 17
Europe, Western, 537–38, 539
evangelical Christianity, 568–69, 584
    and AIDS crisis, 685
    Christian origin of U.S. claimed by, 201
    and culture wars, 662–64
    spread of, 199
    *see also* Second Great Awakening

Evans, Walker, 441
Everett, Edward, 216, 220, 295
evidence:
    in determinate of truth, 41–42
    historical, xvii–xviii, 4
    scientific, xvii
    truth and, 61
evolution, 284, 348, 354, 390, 391
    applied to Constitution, 373
    in Scopes trial, 414–19
excess profits tax, 405
executive branch, FDR's reorganization of, 466
Executive Order 8802, 498

Facebook, 736
fact-checking, 412–13
factions, 129
    Madison on, 144
factories, 191, 193, 194–95, 202, 426
*Fail-Safe* (Burdick and Wheeler), 598
"Failure of Free Society, The," debate, 276
Fair Deal, 532
Fairness Doctrine, 561, 682, 704
faith, history vs., xvi–xvii, xix
Falwell, Jerry, 663–64, 723
family, 196–97, 529, 557
Family Assistance Plan, 638–39
Far East, 456
farm cooperatives, 336
Farmer, James, 607
farmers, 343
    declining number of, 375
    in the Depression, 425, 426, 437–38
    federal aid to, 388
    in World War II, 486
Farmers' Alliance, 340
Farmers' Declaration of Independence, 335
Farmers' Independence Council, 447
Farm Security Administration (FSA), 438, 441, 494
Farrington, Betty, 555–56, 557
fascism, 571
"Fate of the Earth, The" (Schell), 681
Faubus, Orval, 584–87, 585
Faulkner, William, 540
Fay, John Dewey, 226
"FB Eye Blues, The" (Wright), 443
Federal Bureau of Investigation (FBI), 443, 494, 495
    and Black Power movement, 626
    and Cold War, 639
Federal Communications Commission (FCC), 422,
        470, 561, 571
Federal Council of Churches, 366
Federal Deposit Insurance Corporation, 437
Federal Firearms Act, 445
federal funding, 526
Federal Hall (New York City), 131–32, *132*
Federalist No. 52, 312
*Federalist Papers*, xiii–xiv, 128–29, 134, 166,
        624–25

Federalists, 129, *129*, 130–31, 137, *143*, 144, 145,
        211
    as anti-slavery, 176
    in election of 1796, 158
    in election of 1800, 154–55, 160–62, 164
    Louisiana Purchase and, 170
Federalist Society, 677, 678, 684, 688, 689
Federal Radio Act, 422
Federal Radio Commission, 422–23
Federal Reserve Bank, 364
Federal Theatre of the Air, 441
Federal Theatre Project, 437, 441, 444
Federal Writers' Project, 437, 441, 444
Federation of American Scientists, 545
Federation of Atomic Scientists, 526
Female Anti-Slavery Societies, 207
*Feminine Mystique, The* (Friedan), 647
feminism, 635, 652–53
    and Clinton ethics investigations, 712
    and identity politics, 701
    *see also* women's rights
Ferdinand and Isabella, monarchs of Spain, 12, 18
Ferguson, John, 358
Ferguson, Mo., 767
fertility rates, 196–97
Fifteenth Amendment, 326, 327, 328, 337, 476
Fifth Avenue (New York City), 406
Fifty-Fourth Massachusetts Infantry, 300
filibusters, 281
Fillmore, Millard, 267
Filmer, Robert, 54
film industry, government influence on, 501–2
*Final Edition, The* (radio show), 702
finance, 335–36
Finland, 400
Finney, Charles Grandison, 197, 202, 204
Firearms Owners' Protection Act (1986), 679
Firestone, Shulamith, 651
First Amendment, 137–38, 395, 552, 573
*First Battle, The* (Bryan), 353
First Maroon War, 58
First National Bank, 388
First Persian Gulf War, 722
First South Carolina Volunteer Infantry, 299
First U.S. Volunteer Cavalry Regiment, 367
Fisher, Irving, 379
Fitzhugh, George, 256, 276
Flanagan, Hallie, 443–44
Florida, 58
    gun laws in, 445
    income tax in, 301
    Indians in, 213
    Polk's desire to admit as a slave state, 242
    secession of, 289
    Spanish in, 25
Flowers, Gennifer, 697
Floyd, Jay, 653
Flynn, James T., 516
food laws, 376
Food Stamp Act (1964), 612

Forbes, Steve, 671
Force Act, 327
Ford, Betty, 646–47, 654–55, 655, 656, 660
Ford, Edsel, 405
Ford, Gerald:
    and ERA, 659
    and political polarization, 656
    and presidential election (1972), 659
    and presidential election (1976), 664, 705
    and race riots, 625
    and women's rights, 660
Ford, Henry, 383–84, 405, 407, 424, 481
Ford Motor plant, *361*
*Foreign Affairs*, 722
Forest Service, 363
*Forlorn Hope*, 138
Fortas, Abe, *618*
Fort Duquesne, British attack on, 77–78
Fort Sumter, 292, 293
*Fortune*, 477, 489, 522
fossil record, 8
Foster, Judith Ellen, 340–41
founding principles, U.S., xiv–xv, xix
    disagreement about, xvi
*Fountainhead, The* (Rand), 553
4chan, 724
*480, The* (Burdick), 598–99
Four Freedoms, 480, 483
Four Powers Pact, 467–68
Fourteen Points, 396–97, 491
Fourteenth Amendment, 321–23, 324, 326, 336,
    337, 359, 369, 579
    as applied to corporations, 338–39
    Hitler's desire for repeal of, 476
    liberty of contract and, 378
Fourth of July celebrations, *see* July Fourth cele-
    brations
Fox News, 742–43, 755, 774
    and Clinton ethics investigations, 710–11
    founding of, 707
    and presidential election (2000), 716
"Fragments on Government" (Lincoln), 151
Frame of Government, Pennsylvania colony, 51
France, 223, 473, 745
    American Revolution and, 101–2
    British wars with, 65–66, 76–77, 170, 171, 172
    constitution of, 240
    economy of, 406
    in Four Powers Pact, 467–68
    India alliances with, 66
    invasion of, 505–6
    in Munich crisis, 467, 474
    at Paris Peace Conference, 400
    repayment of American debt demanded by, 116
    U.S. arms used by, 475
    U.S. food sent to, 486
    war on Germany declared by, 476–77
    in World War I, 398
Frankfurter, Felix, 426, 457, 465, 577, 579
*Frank Leslie's Illustrated Newspaper*, 302

Franklin, Benjamin, xv, 59, 83, 86, 93, 98, 101, *103*,
    115, 156, 165, 211, 736
    abolition urged by, 135, 137
    autobiography of, 75
    childhood and youth of, 59–60
    at constitutional convention, 119–20, 122,
        124–25, 127–28
    diffusion of knowledge promoted by, 66
    "JOIN, or DIE" woodcut of, 65, 65, 66, 71, 76
    in move to Philadelphia, 60–61
    as newspaper publisher printer and, 60–61
    in Paris peace negotiations, 107
    Philadelphia house of, 119–20
    as Philadelphia postmaster, 66, 67
    Plan of Union of, 70–71, 77
    on race, 70
    slaves owned by, 74
    Stamp Act opposed by, 82
Franklin, Deborah, 75
Franklin, James, 60, 75
Franklin, Jane, 59, 60, 93, 107, 116, 120, 130
    and women's equality, 87
free blacks, as political problem, 176–78
Freedmen's Bureau, *see* Bureau of Refugees, Freed-
    men, and Abandoned Lands
freedom, 536, 552, 553, 573
    truth and, 49–50
freedom from fear, in Four Freedoms, 480
freedom from want, in Four Freedoms, 480
freedom of religion, in Four Freedoms, 480
freedom of speech, in Four Freedoms, 480
Freedom Riders, 604–6
*Freedom's Journal*, 203
Freedom Summer (1964), 620
free labor, 255
*Freeman*, 447
Freeman, Elizabeth (Bett), 113–14
free markets, xviii, 364–65
Free Silver, 347
Free-Soil Party, 254, 255, 256–57, 259, 261, 264,
    282
*Free Speech*, 356
free speech, and gag rule on antislavery tracts, 223,
    276, 291
Free Speech Movement (1964–65), 620–21,
    625–27, 694
free trade, 223
    slavery and, 281–82
Frémont, John C., 242
    in election of 1856, 267, 268
French and Indian War, 77
    American troops in, 78–79
    British troops in, 77–78
    and taxation of American colonies, 78, 81
    Washington's skirmish with French in, 76–77
French Resistance, 506
French Revolution, 142
Freud, Sigmund, 413
Friedan, Betty, 647, 661
Friedman, Milton, 638, 669–70

frontier, 354–55
Frontierland, 528–29
Frum, David, 716
Fuchs, Klaus, 539
Fugitive Slave Law, 261
Fulbright, J. William, 635
Fuller, Margaret, 252, 254, 257, 258
*Fundamental Constitutions of Carolina* (Locke), 52–53, 55
fundamentalism, 390–91, 392–93, 418
    on radio, 460–61
*Fundamentals, The: A Testimony to the Truth*, 391, 414
*Futurama*, 473

Gabriel (slave), 159
*Gabriel Over the White House* (film), 434
Galbraith, John Kenneth, 572, 591, 592, 594, 611
Gallup, George, 454–56, 457, 458–59, 542, 543, 560, 565, 597, 774
Gallup, George, Jr., 667
Gandhi, Mohandas K., 583
Gardener, William (Billey), 106–7, 125
Gardiner, David, 236
Gardner, Alexander, 272, 294, 295, 304
*Gardner's Photographic Sketch Book of the War* (Gardner), 295
Garnet, Henry Highland, 256, 299
Garrison, William Lloyd, 190, 201, 247, 248, 269
    American Anti-Slavery Society founded by, 206
    Constitution damned by, 241, 262
Gates, Bill, 695, 735
Gates, Henry Louis, Jr., 703–4
gay rights movement, 768–69
    and AIDS crisis, 685, 686, 687
    and evangelical churches, 664
    growth of, 651–52
    and identity politics, 701
    and liberal feminism, 661–62
    and Supreme Court, 685, 686–87
*Gazette of the United States*, 161
gender gap, 616, 668
General Land Office, 221
General Motors, 447, 570
Genesis, 7, 9
Geneva Conventions, 746–47
Genoa, 12
George, David, 107, 136
George, Henry, 341–43, 350, 365
George C. Marshall Institute, 683
George III, king of England, 79
    accession of, 79
    factory visited by, 193
Georgia, 34, 531
    Indians in, 213, 214, 215–16, 218
    secession of, 289, 292
German educational model, 348
German immigrants, 208, 209–10, 313
Germany, 379, 548
    American Revolution and, 101
    in Axis, 466, 479

economy of, 406
Kristallnacht in, 471
Poland invaded by, 473, 474, 487
punished at Peace Conference, 400
rise of Nazis in, 427, 434
Soviet Union invaded by, 481–82
Sudetenland seized by, 467–68
unemployment in, 426–27
in World War I, 390, 391–92, 393, 394, 398
Geronimo, 337
Gerry, Elbridge, 121
Gettysburg, Battle of, 294–95, *294*, 389
Gettysburg Address, 295–96, 307
Ghana, 578
ghettos, 530
"Giant Brain," 520
G. I. Bill, 527–30, *528*
Gilded Age, 336, 363
Gilder, George, 670–71, 734, 735
Gingrich, Newt, 683, 699, 700, 712, 732, 765
Gini, Corrado, 442
Gini index, 442–43
Ginsburg, Ruth Bader, 652, 686, 699
Gitlin, Todd, 703
Gladden, Washington, 305, 354, 365
Glanville, Ranulf de, 40–41
Glass-Steagall Act (1933), 437, 700, 749
Gobright, Lawrence, 249
*God and Man at Yale: The Superstitions of "Academic Freedom"* (Buckley), 554–55
Goddard, William, 83
Godfrey, Arthur, 511
Goebbels, Joseph, 434, 452, *453*, 456, 466
gold, 214–15
gold-bugs, 220
*Golden Hour of the Little Flower, The* (radio show), 461
Goldman, Eric, 594
Goldmark, Alice, 381
Goldmark, Josephine, 381
gold rush, 260, 324
gold standard, 334, 351
Goldwater, Barry, 556, 614–16, 624, 630, 649, 666
Gonzales, Alberto, 747
Gonzales, Rodolfo, 634, *634*
Goodman, Paul, 636
Google, 736
Gorbachev, Mikhail, 683–84
Gordon, Thomas, 60
Gore, Al, 681, 696, 716–17
Gospel of Efficiency, 382–84, 404
government, Locke on role of, 53–54
Graham, Billy, 461, 568–69, *569*, 616
Graham, Lindsey, 774
grain, 335
Grange, 335, 336
Grant, Madison, 392, 408
Grant, Ulysses S., 329
    black support for, 324
    on Civil War casualties, 293

corrupt administration of, 334
in election of 1868, 324
Lee's surrender to, 305
grass-roots campaigns, 547
Great Basin, 333
Great Britain, 223, 537, 548, 554
American colonies of, *see* American colonies,
British
antislavery movement in, 107–8
and creation of United Nations, 492
economy of, 406
in Four Powers Pact, 467–68
French wars with, 65–66, 76–77, 170, 171, 172
individual liberties in, 27, 33
in Munich crisis, 467, 474
Oregon Territory claimed by, 235, 242
at Paris Peace Conference, 400
political principles of, 27
as Protestant country, 26–27
repayment of American debt demanded by, 114
Restoration in, 50–51
in slave trade, 45–48
in United Nations, 503
U.S. arms used by, 475, 477, 480, 481
U.S. food sent to, 486
war on Germany declared by, 476–77
welfare state in, 378, 379
in World War I, 398
Great Depression, 424–25, *425*, 436–44, 515, 529
end of, 486–87
"Great Lawsuit, The: Man *versus* Women" (Fuller),
252
Great Migration, 371, 576
Great Nebraska Silver Train, 350
Great Society, 611, 619, 623, 629, 657
"great train robbery," 561
Greece, 537
Greeks, ancient, 11
Greeley, Horace, 235, 252, 303
Bleeding Kansas named by, 266
Emancipation Proclamation praised by, 297
slavery criticized by, 255
greenbacks, 334
Greenleaf, Thomas, 131
Grimes, William, 239–40
Grimké, Angelina, 252, 275
Grimké, Sarah, 652
*Griswold v. Connecticut*, 649, 653, 678, 685, 686,
688, 689, 768
Gruber, Bronko, 614
Guadalcanal, Battle of, 494
Guadalupe Hidalgo, Treaty of, 250, 251
Guantánamo Bay, 746–47, 766
Guatemala, 281, 574
Guatícabanú, 5, 16
*Gulliver*, 492
Gun Control Act (1968), 672, 679
gun control debate:
and Black Power movement, 627, 673
and conservatism, 672–74, 675–78

and originalism, 688
and political consensus, 672–73
and political polarization, 647–48, 676, 679
gun laws, 445–46
Gutenberg, Johannes, 13
Guttmacher, Alan F., 649

Hacker, Andrew, 638
Hadden, Briton, 412, 413
Haiti, 18, 337, 578
Columbus's 1492 arrival at, 3–4
Columbus's return to, 5
Columbus's sketch map of, *4*
constitution of, 240
French withdrawal from, 170
independence of, 203
revolution in, 254
revolution of 1791 in, 142–43, *143*, 159
sugar plantations in, 142
Hakluyt, Richard, 25–26, 27–28
Haldeman, H. R., 626, 636, 637, 639, 640, 642
Haley, Alex, 660
Halifax, 136
Halsey, R. T. H., 407
*Hamdan v. Rumsfeld*, 748
Hamilton, Alexander, xiii–xiv, xvii, 117, 122, 134,
145, 154, 160, 163–64, 167, 624–25
on citizenship, 313
economic plan of, 334
as *Federalist Papers* coauthor, 128–29, 134, 166
and founding of Washington, DC, 139–40
on judiciary's powers, 134–35
on self-rule by people, 420
U.S. Bank plan of, 138–39
Washington's Farewell Address and, 146
Washington's inaugural address written by, 133
Hamilton, Alexander (doctor), 67
Hamilton, Andrew, Zenger trial and, 62–63
Hancock, John, 92
Hanna, Mark, 374
Hannity, Sean, 755
Hanson, Peter, 720
Harbord, James G., 423
Harding, Warren G., 394, 504, 562
in election of 1920, 403
government efficiency desired by, 404–5
Harlan, John Marshall, 359–60
Harlem Renaissance, 411
Harpers Ferry, Va., 282–83, 284
Harrison, William Henry, 227, 234
in election of 1840, 227–28, 229
Hart, Gary, 696
Hartford Convention (1814), 173, 217
Harvard College, 45
Hastings, Lansford W., 242
Hatch, Orrin, 677, 678
hate speech codes, 703–4, 763
*Hate That Hate Produced, The* (TV documentary),
606
Hatfield, George, 450

Hayek, Friedrich A., 506, 507, 553, 592
Hayes, Rutherford B.:
    in election of 1876, 329
    strike broken by, 338
Haywood, Bill, 395
health care, and Clinton administration, 698–99
health insurance, 377, 378, 379–80, 438, 532–34,
        533, 541, 546–48, 553–54, 560, 561, 570
Hearst, Phoebe Apperson, 380
Hearst, William Randolph, 349, 366, 367, 434, 437,
        448–49, 453, 463, 475–76, 479
Heartland Institute, 683
Heller, Walter, 611, 612
Hemings, Beverly, 178
Hemings, Elizabeth, 174
Hemings, Eston, 186
Hemings, Harriet, 178, 186, 187
Hemings, John, 186
Hemings, Madison, 178, 186
Hemings, Sally, 174
    Jefferson's children with, 173–76, 178, 186
Henry, Patrick, 91, 94, 130–31, 167
Henry, prince of Portugal, 11
Henry I, king of England, 40
Henry VIII, king of England, 26
Hepburn, Katharine, 574–75
Hercules (slave), 147
Heritage Foundation, 648, 663, 683
Herodotus, xvi
Herring, Pendleton, 479
Hersey, John, 494, 521–22, 574
Hewitt, Abram, 343
Higby, William, 326
Hill, Anita, 697
Hill, David, 344
Hinckley, John, Jr., 672, 676
*Hindoo*, 341
hippies, 695
Hirabayashi, Gordon, 495
*Hirabayashi v. United States*, 495
Hiroshima bombing (1945), 517, 521–22, 571
Hispaniola, *see* Haiti
Hiss, Alger, 509–10, 515, 540–41, 548–49, 550, 641
"Hiss Case—A Lesson for the American People,
    The" lecture (Nixon), 549
historical studies, 353–54
history:
    ancient concept of, xvi
    artifacts and, 8
    faith vs., xvi–xvii, xix
    as form of heritage, xix
    as form of inquiry, xvi–xviii
    fossil record and, 8
    founders' study of, xv
    geological, 7
    importance of counting and measuring in, 16–18
    as inheritance, xx
    as study of what remains, 4
    writing and, 12–13, 15
*History of the American People* (Wilson), 374
*History of the United States* (Beard), 441

*History of the United States from the Discovery of the
    American Continent to the Present* (Bancroft),
    10, 198–99, 353–54
*History of the World* (Ralegh), xvi
Hitchcock, Alfred, 502, 516–17
Hitler, Adolf, 427, 434, 449, 467, 468, 474, 516, 554
    Anschluss announced by, 466
    Coughlin's admiration for, 476
    Soviet Union invaded by, 481–82
    U.S. disdained by, 475
    war on U.S. declared by, 485
Ho, Lew Wa, 316
Hobbes, Thomas, 37, 61, 106
Hobby, Oveta Culp, 570
Ho Chi Minh, 399, 602, 603, 629
Hodge, A. A., 391
Hodge, Charles, 390–91
Hoey, Clyde, 551
Hofstadter, Richard, 562
Holiday, Billie, 396
Holland:
    American Revolution and, 101
    repayment of American debt demanded by, 116
Hollerith, Herman, 355, 404
Holmes, John Haynes, 522
Holmes, Oliver Wendell, 362, 378, 405, 462
Holocaust, 529
Holt Street Baptist Church, 583
home, work vs., 193, 195, 196–97
home loans, 530
Home Owners' Loan Corporation, 504
Home Protection Party, 340
Homestead Act, 317, 332, 333
*Homo sapiens* (modern humans), evolution and
        migration of, 8
homosexuality, 530, 550–52
Honduras, 462
Hood River, Oreg., 421
Hoover, Herbert, 362, 433, 506, 562
    and building of new Supreme Court building,
        462
    efficiency of government by, 405, 406, 423–24
    in election of 1928, 421–22, 423
    in election of 1932, 430–31
    Federal Radio Act pushed by, 422, 423
    inauguration of, 423
    made secretary of commerce, 405–6
    New Deal criticism of, 506–7
    radio addresses of, 427–28
    relief work by, 421
    response to the Depression of, 424–25
Hoover, J. Edgar, 443, 499, 626, 641
Hopkins, Elizabeth, 39
Hopkins, Harry, 438
Hopper, Grace Murray, 523, 524
Horsmanden, Daniel, 62, 63–64
Hose, Sam, 370
House of Burgesses, 37–38, 48
House of Representatives, U.S., 125, 535, 537, 540,
        572, 586
    Committee on Foreign Relations of, 481

Education and Labor Committee of, 537
and 1924 election, 184
Indian removal voted on in, 215
as open to speculators, 132
in presidential election of 1800, 164
Special Committee to Investigate the Taylor and
    Other Systems of Shop Management, 384
Texas annexation voted on by, 238
Ways and Means Committee of, 301, 317
House of Truth, 405
House Un-American Activities Committee
    (HUAC), 443, 498–99, 540, 572
housing, 530, 576
Houston, Sam, 223, 290
Howard, Jacob, 322, 326–27
Howard Johnson's restaurants, 578
Howard University Law School, 576
Howe, Julia Ward, 328
Howe, Quincy, 570–71
Howe, William, 100, 101
Howells, William Dean, 287–88
Hughes, Charles Evans, 393, 462–63, 465
Hughes, Langston, 531
Hull House, 380
human rights, xviii, 313, 503
    Locke on, 53–55
    slavery and, 86
    as U.S. founding principle, xiv–xv
"Human Rights Not Founded on Sex" (Grimké), 252
Hume, Brit, 710
Hume, David, xv
Humphrey, Hubert, 633
Hungarians, 409
Hungary, 383, 426
Huntington, Samuel P., 722
Hurja, Emil, 454
Hurston, Zora Neale, 441
Hussein, Saddam, 740
Hutchinson, Thomas, 79
hydrogen bomb, 524–25, 539, 571

*I, Candidate for Governor: And How I Got Licked*
    (Sinclair), 450
IBM, 523
Ickes, Harold, 710
Idaho, 242, 324
    creation of, 332
    women's voting rights in, 386
*Ideas Have Consequences* (Weaver), 554
identity politics, 668
    and political polarization, 701–2, 703
"I Have a Dream" speech (King), 609–10
Illinois, 221
    eight-hour workday in, 377
    movement to, 221
*Immigrant Dangers to the Free Institutions of the
    United States through Foreign Immigrants*
    (Morse), 208, 263
immigrant labor, 383
immigrants:
    encouraging of, 208

nineteenth-century rise in, 208
    and populist movement, 344
immigration, 314, 727
    and identity politics, 701
    restrictions on, 325, 336, 359, 407–11, *408*
    and White Power movement, 674
Immigration Act, 409
Immigration and Nationality Act (1965), 674
"Impeach Earl Warren" campaign, 582
*Imperial Hearst* (Lundberg), 449
imperialism, 366, 482
Incas, 8
income inequality, 757–58, 766–67
income tax, 347
    in Civil War, 301
    graduated, 345, 346
    opposition to, 504–5
    passage of Sixteenth Amendment on, 376–77
    in Progressive Era, 364
    TR's endorsement of, 376
Independence, Mo., 531
*Independent*, 269
Indiana:
    as free state, 176
    gun laws in, 445
    movement to, 221
    suffrage sold in, 342
Indiana University, 528
Indian immigrants, 409
*Indian's Appeal to the White Men of Massachusetts,
    An*, 215
Indonesia, 456
industrial accident compensation, 377
industrialization, 366, 529
    economic security vs., 377
    rise in 1920s of, 404
    slavery and, 191
Industrial Workers of the World (IWW), 395
industry, 334
inflation, 629
influenza epidemic, 398
information age, 520
    *see also* computers
Infowars, 724–25, 728–29, 762
infrastructure, 337–38
"In God We Trust" motto, 569
*In His Steps: What Would Jesus Do?* (Sheldon), 366
*Innovator's Dilemma, The* (Christensen), 736
Inquiry, 396
Inquisition, 12
Institute for Legislative Action, 675
intellectuals, 551–55, 561, 568–69
Inter-Allied Board, 398
*Interest in Slavery of the Southern Non-Slaveholder,
    The* (DeBow), 292
Internal Revenue Bureau, 301, 377
Internal Revenue Service (IRS), 405
Internal Security Act (1950), 551
International Business Machines (IBM), 355, 404
Internet, 587, 731–38, 744, 769–70
    and Clinton ethics investigations, 710

Internet (*continued*)
  and economic inequality, 657–58
  Gilder on, 671
  and political polarization, 648
Interstate Commerce Committee, 384
inventors, 198
Iowa:
  farm cooperatives in, 336
  immigrants recruited to, 208
Iowa method, 455
Iranian hostage crisis, 680, 722
Iraq, 740, 765
Iraq War, 740–42, *741*, 753, 766
Ireland, famine in, 209
Irish immigrants, 208, 209, 313
Iron Curtain, 536
Iroquois confederation (Six Nations), 66
  in French and Indian War, 80
Isidore, Archbishop of Seville, 14, *15*
Islamic fundamentalism, 722, 739–40
Islamic State, 765
isolationism, 406–7, 477, 481–82, 492, 537
Italians, 383, 409
Italy, 383, 427, 462, 517
  in Axis, 466, 479
  Ethiopia invaded by, 427
  in Four Powers Pact, 467–68
  invasion of, 502
  at Paris Peace Conference, 400
*It's Up to the Women* (Eleanor Roosevelt), 433

Jackson, Andrew, 173, 176, *225*, 268, 332, 563
  criticism of, 198, 208, 212
  in election of 1824, 180–85, *183*
  in election of 1828, 186
  in election of 1832, 218–19
  and election of 1836, 224–25
  inauguration of, 186–88, *187*
  Indian removal policies of, 212–13, 214–15,
    216–17, 337
  Lincoln's opposition to, 288
  majority rule as principle of, 187
  national bank opposed by, 219–20, 239
  nullification opposed by, 217, 218
  Panic of 1837 caused by, 226, 227
  people's support for, 212
  populism and, 181
  and progress, 198, 199
  Tyler's criticism of, 233
Jackson, James, 135
Jackson, Mahalia, 610
Jackson, Robert, 579, 580
Jackson, Robert H., 446
Jacksonianism, and Second Great Awakening, 191
Jacobs, Harriet, 261
Jacquard, Joseph-Marie, 193
Jamaica, 34, 91
  Maroon Wars in, 58
  slave rebellions in, 63, 84, 85, 99
James, Henry, 390
James, William, 361, 368

James I, king of England, 32, 41
  divine right of kings claimed by, 32, 39–40, 42
  Virginia charter of, 32–33, 34
James River, 36
Jamestown, Bacon's burning of, 56
Jane Crow, 500
Japan:
  atomic bomb dropped on, 517
  in Axis, 466, 479
  Manchuria invaded by, 427, 481–82
  Nanking invaded by, 481–82
  in Pacific War, 493–94
  Pearl Harbor attacked by, 484, 487, 494
Japanese Americans, internment of, 494–96, *495*, 532
Japanese immigrants, 409
Jastrow, Robert, 683
Jay, John, 101, *103*, 106, 163–64
  as chief justice, 166–67
  citizenship desired limited by, 312
  as *Federalist Papers* coauthor, 129
Jay Cooke & Company, 335
Jefferson, Martha Wayles, 173
Jefferson, Thomas, xiv, xvii, 110, 111, 116, 117, 129,
    134, 137–38, 139, 145, 159, *169*, *174*, 184–85,
    212, 332, 360, 363, 728
  Alien and Sedition Acts and, 158–59
  death of, 185–86, 190, 199
  in debate with Adams on Constitution, 153–54
  and Declaration of Independence, 98–99
  1807 embargo and, 171–72
  in election of 1796, 158
  in election of 1800, 154–55, 160–62, *160*, 164
  expansionism of, 168
  farming promoted over manufacturing by, 168–
    70, 171–72
  on Haitian revolution, 143, 144
  Hemings children of, 173–76, 178, 186
  inaugural address of, 165
  inauguration of, 164–65
  Kentucky and Virginia Resolves written by, 217
  language of liberty used by, 235
  Louisiana Territory purchased by, 170–71
  on majority rule, 418–20
  majority rule advocated by, 155
  population theory of, 343
  on progress, 192, 216
  racial formula of, 175
  religious freedom and, 161
  slaves owned by, 104, 161, 186
  tariffs and, 140
  Turner influenced by, 354
  on worship of Founders, 201
Jemmy (slave), 58, 63
Jenner, William, 552
Jersey, Battle of (1781), 72
Jesus Christ, 568
Jews, 12, 383, 399, 409, 410, 529
  in American colonies, 50, 51
  anti-Semitism vs., 448
  Lindberg's criticism of, 482
  in Nazi Germany, 435, 466

Jim Crow, 330, *370*, 499, 501
  Douglass on, 353, 355–56, 358
  and European immigrants, 410
  and *Plessy v. Ferguson*, 359, 360
  Progressives' lack of discussion of, 364, 371–72,
      386–87
  and war in Philippines, 369
  Wells's resistance to, 356
  in World War I, 496
Jim Crow laws, 531, 542, 575–88
Jobs, Steve, 695
Jobson, Richard, 46
John, king of England, 40–41
John Birch Society, 614
Johns Hopkins University, 348
Johnson, Andrew:
  Douglass's visit to, 320
  impeachment of, 324
  Radical Republicans vs., 320, 323
  South protected by, 318
  Stanton vs., 323–24
Johnson, James Weldon, 389
Johnson, Lady Bird, 660
Johnson, Lyndon B., 546, 552–53, 567–68, 586,
      *618*
  and civil rights movement, 611, 612–13, 614,
      622
  and criminal justice policy, 622–23
  death of, 643
  Great Society, 611, 619, 623
  and immigration, 674
  liberalism of, 444, 611
  New Deal projects of, 442, 443
  political power of, 617–18
  and poverty, 611, *611*, 618–19, 622–23, 657
  and presidential election (1960), 597, 599
  and presidential election (1964), 615–17
  and presidential election (1968), 629–30
  and race riots, 627–28
  recording system, 640
  and Vietnam War, 619, 629–30, 632
Johnson, Reverdy, 322
Johnson, Samuel, 92
Johnston, Eric, 501–2
Joint Chiefs of Staff, U.S., 538
Joint Committee on Reconstruction, 321, 338–39
Joint United States and Mexican Boundary Com-
      mission, 251
Jones, Alex, 702–3, 723–25, 729, 762–63
Jones, Mary, 301–2
Jones, Paula, 709–10
journalism, Taylorism in, 412–13
*Journalist*, 349
journalistic exposé, 363–64
*Journal of the American Medical Association*, 379,
      438
Judge, Ona, 147
judicial recall, 378
judicial review, 239, 358–59
judiciary:
  and conservatism, 677

and Reagan administration, 684–90
  separation of powers and, 165–66
Judiciary Act (1789), 134, 166
Judiciary Act (1801), 167
Judiciary Committee, 388
July Fourth celebrations, *153*
  of 1826, 185–86
*Jungle, The* (Sinclair), 450
Justice Department, U.S., 376, 395, 552, 576–77,
      578, 581, 745

Kansas, 331, *331*
  creation of, 262
  farm cooperatives in, 336
  violence in, 266–67
  women's voting rights in, 386
Kansas City, Mo., 333
Kansas-Nebraska Act, 262–64, 265, 267, 276
Karski, Jan, 512
Kefauver, Estes, 570–71
Kelley, Florence, 377, 380, 381, 382
Kemp, Jack, 670
Kennan, George F., 535, 539, 557
Kennedy, Edward, 638, 688
Kennedy, John F., 535, 537, 552, 568
  assassination of, 610, 613, 672
  and civil rights movement, 600–601, 608–9
  and Cold War, 602
  and Commission on National Goals, 597
  and conservatism, 614, 615
  and Cuban Missile Crisis, 604
  inauguration of, 601–2
  and presidential election (1960), 597, 600–601,
      *601*
  recording system, 640
  and Vietnam War, 602–4
  War on Poverty, 611–12
  and women's rights, 647
Kennedy, Patrick, 209
Kennedy, Robert F., 568
  assassination of, 631, 672
  and civil rights movement, 600, 605, 625,
      630–31
  and presidential election (1968), 629, 631
  and Vietnam War, 602, 619
Kent, James, 183
Kentucky, 579
  gun laws in, 445
  secret ballots in, 344
Kentucky Resolves, 217
Kerner Commission, 627–28, 633
Kerry, John, 694
Kesey, Ken, 694, 695
Keynes, John Maynard, 400, 435, 466
  *see also* Keynesian economics
Keynesian economics, 592, 619, 657, 670
Keyworth, George, 732
Khaldun, Ibn, xvi
Khomeini, Ayatollah Ruhollah, 680
Khrushchev, Nikita, 604
  Nixon meeting (1959), 589–91, *589*

Kiernan, W. C., 476
Kilgore, Harley M., 526
King, Billie Jean, 660
King, Boston, 105, 107
King, Coretta Scott, 661
King, Martin Luther, Jr., 441, 583–84, 750
    arrest of (1960), 600–601
    assassination of, 610, 630, *631*, 672
    and Civil Rights Act, 613
    FBI surveillance, 626
    "Letter from Birmingham Jail," 607–8
    March on Washington, 609–10
    and Nation of Islam, 606, 607
    and peace movement, 629
    and presidential election (1964), 615
    and Selma march, 621–22, 625
    and SNCC, 597
    and Watts riots, 623
King, Rufus, 125
King George's War (1744–48), 66
King Philip's War (1675), 55–56
King William's War (1689–97), 66
Kirk, Russell, 555, 556, 682
Kissinger, Henry, 640, 642
Kitchen Debate (1959), 589–91, *589*
"Kitchen Kabinets," 557
Klan Act, 327
Knights of Labor, 336, 340
knowledge workers, 693–94
Know-Nothing Party, 263
Knox, Henry, 134
*Knoxville Chancellor*, 349
Koreans, 399
Korean War, 560, 565, 747
Korematsu, Fred Toyosaburo, 496
*Korematsu v. United States*, 496
Koresh, David, 702
Krauthammer, Charles, 722
Krimmel, John Lewis, *153*
Kristallnacht, 471
Kristol, Bill, 698–99, 707
Kristol, Irving, 691, 734
KTSA, 442
Ku Klux Klan (KKK), 318–19, *319*, 323, 324, 327,
    330, 410, 440, 579, 605, 608, 701, 770
Kurds, 399
Kursk, Battle of, 502
Kuwait, 739
Kwangtung Province, China, 324
Kyoto Protocol, 743

Labash, Matt, 743
labor force, 529
labor laws, 380–82
labor unions, 537, 541, 556
    and Clinton administration, 699
    and Democratic Party, 693, 696
    and immigration, 675
Ladies' Department, 190
Lafayette, Marquis de, 103, 105, 128
La Follette, Robert, 386, 447

La Follette, Robert, Jr., 549
La Follette Committee, 447
laissez-faire, 378, 427, 446
La Malinche, 23
Lambda Legal Defense and Education Fund, 686
Landon, Alf M., 447
land tax, 301
Lane, Isaac, 297
Lane, Ralph, 29
Lane, T. J., 763
Lange, Dorothea, *425*, 441, 494–95, *495*
Lansing, Robert, 395
Las Casas, Bartolomé de, 3, 4, 5, 13, 23–25, 28,
    47, 337
Laski, Harold, 426
*Last of the Mohicans, The* (Cooper), 212
Latin America, 456
Law Enforcement Assistance Act (1965), 622–23
*Lawrence v. Texas*, 768
Law to Remedy the Distress of People and Reich,
    434–35
Lay, Benjamin, 73, 92
    background of, 72–73
    as bookseller, 73
    slavery denounced by, 73–74, 75–76
    on women's equality, 86–87
League of Gileadites, 279
League of Nations, 397, 400, 427, 435, 474, 515
League of Women Voters, 431, 571, 705, 706
Lease, Charles, 334–35
Lease, Evelyn Louise, 346
Lease, Mary E., 330–32, 334–35, 336, 339, 340,
    341, 342, 388
    Bryan mistrusted by, 346
    Bryan supported by, 352
    in campaign for George, 350
    Democratic Party hated by, 331, 346
    McKinley criticized by, 352–53
    monopolism opposed by, 343
    People's Party formed by, 343
    socialist views of, 347
    Union Labor Party joined by, 342
Lederer, William, 598, 603
Lee, Ivy, 412
Lee, Richard Henry, 98
Lee, Robert E.:
    Gettysburg defeat of, 294–95
    Harpers Ferry retaken by, 283
    surrender of, 305
Legal Defense Fund, 577, 579
legal precedents, 479
Leibovich, Mark, 708, 749, 759
Lemus, Rienzi B., 369
Lend-Lease Act, 480, 481
L'Enfant, Pierre Charles, 132
"Letter from Birmingham Jail" (King), 607–8
*Letters concerning Toleration* (Locke), 52
Levellers, 49, 50
*Leviathan, The* (Hobbes), 37, 61, 106
Lewandowski, Corey, 774
Lewinsky, Monica, 709, 710, 712, 714

Lewis, Anthony, 712–13
Lewis, John, 605–6, 609, 628, 726
Lewis, William, 490–91
Lexington and Concord, Battles of, 92
Leyte, *493*
liberal arts, 275
liberal feminism, 652, 659
    and abortion, 662
    and gay rights, 661, 662
    National Women's Conference (1977), 659–62
liberalism, 427, 429, 554–55, 561, 565, 568–69,
        580, 584
    and Clinton ethics investigations, 712
    and judiciary, 677, 685–86
    Nazism vs., 434
    in New Deal, 444
    and New Democrats, 696
    1960s decline of, 591, 592, 594, 610, 619–20
    and 1970s economic malaise, 657
    and originalism, 678–79
    and presidential election (1968), 631
    and race riots, 623, 625
    and tax policy, 669
    and technology, 694
    and Vietnam War, 610
    and War on Poverty, 619
    after World War II, 504–5, 507–8
    *see also* political polarization
liberal world order, xviii
*Liberator*, 189–90, *200*, 206, 247, 269
Liberia, 179
liberty:
    idea of, slavery and, 10, 64, 86, 88, 92, 96,
        105–6
    language of, 235
Liberty and Victory Bonds, 397
Library Company of Philadelphia, 66, 90
Liberty Party, 228, 238, 259
Libya, 765
Liddy, G. Gordon, 641, 644
Lie Factory, 448, 450–51, 456
*Life*, 481, 587
*Lifeboat* (film), 502
*Life of Abraham Lincoln* (Howells), 287–88
*Life of Andrew Jackson* (Eaton), 182
lightbulb, 424
Light's Golden Jubilee, 424
Like Factor, 705
Limbaugh, Rush, 704, 742, 743, 762
Lincoln, Abraham, xix, 151, *311*
    assassination and funeral of, 305–7, *306*
    Cooper Union speech of, 285
    Douglas's debates with, 275, 276–79, 286
    Douglass studied by, 264–65
    *Dred Scott* decision denounced by, 270
    in election of 1858, 265, 275, 276–79
    in election of 1860, 285, 286, 287–88
    in election of 1864, 303–4
    Emancipation Proclamation supported by,
        297–300, 303, 329
    Gettysburg Address of, 295–96, 307
    inaugurations of, 290, 304–5
    Internal Revenue Bureau created by, 302
    John Quincy Adams's funeral organized by, 251
    on labor, 255
    Longfellow praised by, 260
    Mexican War opposed by, 243, 263
    photographs of, 273
    slavery criticized by, 255, 263–66
    Tarbell's biography of, 371
    Thirteenth Amendment pushed by, 304
    vindictive peace disdained by, 317–18
    war powers claimed by, 487
Lindbergh, Charles, 477, 479, 481, 482
Lippmann, Walter, 361–63, 371, 427, 457, 562, 682
    Bernays influenced by, 414
    Hoover praised by, 405
    on majority rule, 309, 362–63, 364, 418–20,
        423
    on need for dictatorial powers, 434
    peace proposal drawn up by, 396–97, 398, 400
    on tariffs, 407
Lipset, Seymour Martin, 591
literacy, 210–11
*Literary Digest*, 453, 454, 458
Lithuania, 426
Little, Earl, 440
Little Rock Central High School desegregation
        (1957), 584–87, *585*
Liverpool, U.K., 202
living standards, 527–28
Livingston, Robert R., 98
*Lochner v. New York*, 378, 380
Locke, Alain, 411
Locke, John, 1, 30–31, 34, 95
    as Carolina colony secretary, 52
    egalitarianism of, 53, 54
    on human (natural) rights, 53–55
    political philosophy of, 52–53
    on slavery, 54–55
Lockheed Corp., 538
Lockwood, Belva, 340
Lodge, Henry Cabot, 401
Lomax, Louis, 606
London, German bombing of, 479, 512
Long, Huey, 461–62
Longfellow, Henry Wadsworth, 259–60, 261, 267,
        270, 271, 480
    on Brown's death, 284–85
    on dissolution of Union, 290
    on Lincoln's election, 288
Los Alamos National Laboratory, 524–25
Los Angeles, Calif., 371, 568, 573
*Los Angeles Times*, 450
Louisiana, 281, 531
    black governor of, 323
    black voter registration in, 344
    Indians in, 213
    movement to, 221
    secession of, 289
    slaves sold to, 202
    as slave state, 176

Louisiana Purchase, 251
Louisiana Territory, 69, 80, 170, 173
    Jefferson's purchase of, 170–71
    *see also* New France
*Louisville Courier-Journal*, 541
Louis XVI, king of France, beheading of, 142
Louverture, Toussaint, 143, 170
Lovejoy, Elijah, 221
Lovelace, Ada, 194
*Love's Pilgrimage* (Sinclair), 450
*Loving v. Virginia*, 751
Lowell, Francis Cabot, 194, 195
Lowell, Mass., 194–95, *194*
Loyalists, 92, 94, 102, 103–4
    in flight to Canada and Britain, 104, 107
loyalty tests, 545
Luce, Henry, 412, 413, 481, 540, 574
Luxembourg, 473
Lyles, CeeCee, 720–21
Lynch, Thomas, 115
lynching, 356, 368, 370, 396, 399
    FDR's failure on, 458
    Twain's denunciation of, 369
lynchings, 531

MacArthur, Douglas, 560
Macdonald, Dwight, 592, 594, 611–12
*Machine Age*, 444
machine guns, 445
MacKinnon, Catharine, 686
MacLeish, Archibald, 488–91, 504, 511, 512, 516
Madison, Ambrose, 94
Madison, Dolley, 233, 240
Madison, James, xii, xvii, 93, 116, 130, 156, 177,
        363
    Alien and Sedition Acts and, 158–59
    antislavery petitions and, 135, 136–37
    Bill of Rights authored by, 134, 137
    on citizenship, 322
    on citizenship requirements for Congress, 312
    on colonization, 343
    at constitutional convention, 109, 111, *118*,
        119–23, 125–26, 128, 149
    on dangers of majority rule, 118–19, 123–24
    on established religion, 200
    on factions, 144
    as *Federalist Papers* coauthor, 129
    on importance of newspapers, 144–45
    Kentucky and Virginia Resolves written by, 217
    notes on constitutional convention kept by, *118*,
        240–41, 256–57
    political history studied by, 117, 118
    in proposal to count slaves as three-fifths of a
        person, 116
    on religious freedom, 96
    on religious liberty, 89–90
    on republicanism, 144–45
    slaves owned by, 105–6
    Virginia Plan drafted by, 120
    and War of 1812, 172

Madsen, Dennis, 750
Magby, Willis, 439–40
Magna Carta, 83–84, 95
    Coke's resurrection of, 40, 41, 43
    and right to trial by jury, 41–42
*Maine*, 366
Maine, as free state, 179
majority rule, 155, 187
    Madison on dangers of, 118–19, 123–24
Malcolm X, 440, 613, 621–22
    assassination of, 622
    background of, 606–7
    and gun control debate, 673
Malthus, Thomas, 157, 168, 171, 343
*Managerial Revolution, The* (Burnham), 504
Manchuria, 427, 481–82
Mandeville, John, 13
Manhattan Project, 516, 523
manifest destiny, 10, 199
"Manifesto of Fascist Intellectuals," 443
Mansfield, Lord, 88
"Manual for the Motion Picture Industry, A,"
        501–2
manufacturing, 192
    Hamilton's emphasis on, 140
    inventory of, 172
    Jefferson's distaste for, 169, 171–72
    slavery as form of, 169
    in World War II, 486
Mao Zedong, 539
maps, mapmakers, 14
*Marbury v. Madison*, 168, 239, 268–69, 378
March on Washington (1963), 609–10, 613
Mark I computer, 523, *524*
Marlowe, Christopher, 444
marriage, 529
Married Women's Property Act, 257
Marshall, John:
    Cherokee National recognized by, 215–16
    as chief justice, 165, 167–68, 187
    federal law overturned by, 239
    on preservation of Union, 260
Marshall, Thurgood, 497, 575–88
    on Johnson, 643
    on originalism, 687–88
    retirement of, 697
Marshall Plan, 538
Martin, Jim, 505–6
Martin, Luther, 125–26, 130
Martin, Tracy, 763
Martin, Trayvon, 763, 765, 767
Marx, Karl, 230, 231, 254, 255
Mary I, queen of England, 26–27
Maryland, 576
    income tax in, 301
Maryland, University of, Law School, 576
Maryland colony, 44
Mashpees, 212, 215
Mason, George, xii, 86, 96, 99, 122, 128
    bill of rights proposal of, 127

Massachusetts:
    constitution of, 111, 112, 114, 128
    Know-Nothings in, 263
    ratification debate in, 130
    Revolutionary War debt of, 116
    secret ballot in, 344
    Shays's Rebellion in, 116, 118
    slavery outlawed in, 114
Massachusetts Assembly, 88
Massachusetts Bay colony, 43–44, *44*
Massachusetts General Colored Association, 203
Massachusetts General Hospital, 560
Massachusetts Institute of Technology (MIT), 524, 587
mass advertising, 401
    and campaign of 1912, 387
mass communication, 363, 420, 566
mass consciousness, 363
mass consumption, 363
mass delusion, 364
*Masses*, 362
mass hysteria, 363
mass incarceration, 699–700
mass migration, 363
mass production, 363, 444
Mather, Cotton, 57, 60
mattresses, 195
Mauchly, John, 520, 524, 526–27, 558, 559, 575
maximum-hour laws, 346, 377, 381, 382
Maya, 8, 11
*Mayflower*, 43
    voyage of, 38–39
Mayflower Compact, 39, 43
McAllum, Sam, 317
McCain, John, 752
McCarthy, Eugene, 629, 633
McCarthy, Joseph, 504, 549–52, 553, 555, 556, 557, 565–68, 567, 571, 572, 592
McCarthyism, 592, 597
McClellan, George, 303, 304
McClure, Samuel Sidney, 371
*McClure's*, 371
McCormick, Anne O'Hare, 423, 457
McCurry, Michael, 708
McGovern, George, 633, 642, 694
McGranery, James P., 578
McKellar, Kenneth, 39
McKinley, William:
    assassination of, 375
    in election of 1896, 352, 374, 375
    warship sent to Cuba by, 366
McKissick, Floyd, 595
McMurray, Howard, 549
McNamara, Robert, 629, 640
McVeigh, Timothy, 702
McWilliams, Carey, 549, 560
Mead, Margaret, 660
measurement, *see* quantification
"Measurement of Inequality, The" (Gini), 443
*Mechanics Magazine*, 210

Mecom, Edward, 87
media:
    and Ailes, 704–5, 742–43
    consolidation of, 732–33
    deregulation of, 737
    Fairness Doctrine, 682, 704
    and political polarization, 704, 707–8, 724
    republicanism's faith in, 144–45
    Wilson's relationship with, 388
Medicaid, 619, 671, 700
Medicare, and Reagan administration, 671
Meese, Edwin, 678–79, 684
*Mein Kampf* (Hitler), 489
Melich, Tanya, 652, 665
Mellon, Andrew W., 405, 443
Melville, Herman, 559
"Memorial Remonstrance against Religious Assessments" (Madison), 137
*Menace of Modernism, The* (Riley), 392–93
Mencken, H. L., 417, 418, 466
Mennonites, 569
*Merchants of Death* (Engelbrecht and Hanighen), 445
*Mercury Theatre on the Air* (radio show), 468–69
Merriam, Frank, 450, 451
Mesoamerica, 12
Mesopotamia, 12
Metacom ("King Philip"), 55–56
Methodists, 201, 366
Metropolitan Museum of Art, 407
Mexicans, 409–10
    as cowboys, 334
Mexican War, 232, 241, 244, 368, 482
    casualties of, 293
    declaration of, 243
    Douglass's opposition to, 249
    protests against, 246, 259, 263
    and Wilmot Proviso, 244–46, *245*
Mexico, 281, 394
    Cortés's invasion of, 22–23
    immigration from, 674–75
    movement of Americans into, 221–22
    negotiation of border with, 222
    Oregon Territory claimed by, 242
    shrinking of, 250–51
    Texas's rebellion against, 222–23, 233
Mexico City, 250
Meyer, Philip, 667
Michigan, 208, 255
    movement to, 221
Michigan, University of, 348, 544
Michigan Avenue (Chicago), 406
Microsoft, 695, 735
middle class, 529
Middle East, 11
Midway, Battle of, 494
military desegregation, 541
military spending, and Reagan administration, 671
militias, 702
Miller, Ola Babcock, 455

Millionaire's Amendment, 505
Mills, C. Wright, 558–59, 566
Milton, John, 49, 291
Milwaukee, Wis., 371
minimum wage, 364
Ministry of Propaganda, German, 434, 452, 456, 481
Mink, Patsy, 659
Minnesota:
    farm cooperatives in, 336
    immigrants recruited to, 208
minorities, 544
    *see also specific minorities*
*Minor v. Happersett*, 328
Minow, Newton, 571
missionaries, 366
Mississippi, 281, 541, 578
    flood in, 421
    Indians in, 213
    movement to, 221
    secession of, 289
    slaves sold to, 202
    as slave state, 176
    Understanding Clause in constitution of, 344
Mississippi Freedom Democratic Party, 621
Mississippi River, navigation rights on, 170
Missouri:
    battle over statehood for, 176–80
    movement to, 221
Missouri Compromise, 179–80, 253, 262–63
*Missouri Question* (Raymond), 178–79
Mitchell, Charles, 370
Mobile, Ala., 302
"Model of Christian Charity, A" (Winthrop), 43
Modern Efficiency Desk, 404
modernism, 354, 390
modernization, and Vietnam War, 603–4
Mondale, Walter, 683, 696, 706
monogenists, 256
monopolies, 335, 343, 363, 449, 526
Monroe, James, 172, 176
Monroe Doctrine, 180, 234–35
Montaigne, Michel de, 28
Montana, 325
    blacks in, 369
    creation of, 332
Montesinos, Antonio de, 21–22, 23
Montesquieu, 129, 135
Montgomery, Ala., bus boycott (1955–56), 582–84
Montreal, 79
Moody, John, 742–43
Moore, Mary, 302
moral crusades, 557
Moral Majority, 663–64
More, Thomas, 14, 54
Morgan, J. Pierpont, 372, 388
Mormons, 201
Morris, Dick, 710
Morris, Gouverneur, 119, 126–27
Morris, Robert, 109
Morris, Thomas, 223–24

Morrison, Philip, 545
Morrison, Toni, 712
Morse, Samuel F. B., 208–9, 229, 249, 263, 272–73
    telegraph lauded by, 274–75
mortgages, 343
Morton, Levi, 313
Mosaic, 731
Mothers for Moral America, 616
Motion Picture Association of America, 501
Mount Vernon, 233, 236
MSNBC, 707
muckrakers, 371–73, 448
Muhammad, Elijah, 606, 613
mulattoes, 409
Muller, Curt, 381
*Muller v. Oregon*, 381–82
*Mundus Novus* (Vespucci), 14
Munich crisis, 467, 474
Munitions Committee, 445
Muñoz Camargo, Diego, *16*
Murdoch, Rupert, 707, 743
Murphy, Frank, 495–96
Murray, Pauli, 497–98, 499–500, 647, 652
Murrow, Edward R., 511–12, 522, 563, 564–67, 574
Muslims, 11, 12
    in American colonies, 50
    Catholic wars with, 36
Mussolini, Benito, 427, 449, 467, 474, 514
Mutual network, 461
Myrdal, Gunnar, 501, 502

NAFTA (North American Free Trade Agreement), 699
Nagasaki bombing (1945), 517, 522
Nanking, 481–82
Napoleon Bonaparte, 371
Napoleon I, emperor of France, 170
Napoleonic Wars, 170, 171, 172
*Narrative of the Life of Frederick Douglass* (Douglass), 248
*Nation*, 344, 414, 434, 502
National Advisory Commission on Civil Disorders (Kerner Commission), 627–28
National Aeronautics and Space Agency (NASA), 587
National Association for the Advancement of Colored People (NAACP), 371, 389, 396, 399, 497, 577, 579, 580, 581, 582, 583, 595, 596, 605
    on criminal justice policy, 699
National Association of Manufacturers, 446
national bank, 233
    renewal of charter of, 234
National Bank Act, 333
National Broadcasting Corporation (NBC), 422, 435, 467, 473, 476, 562, 571
National Bureau of Standards, 363
National City Bank, 388
National Congress of Mothers, 380
National Convention of Colored Men, 238, 317
national debt, World War II growth of, 487

National Defense Research Committee (NDRC), 488, 525
"National Education Campaign," 547
*National Era*, 269
National Farmers' Alliance, 336
National Federation of Republican Women's Clubs, 555–57
National Firearms Act, 445
National Insurance Act, 379
National Organization for Women (NOW), 647
National Origins Act, 407–8
National Photographic Portrait Gallery, 294
national prayer breakfasts, 569
National Press Association, 356
*National Radio Chapel* (radio show), 460
National Recovery Administration, 463
National Republican Party, 219
*National Review*, 555, 723
National Rifle Association (NRA), 445–46, 672–73, 675–76, 678
National Science Foundation (NSF), 525, 542, 545
National Security Act (1947), 538
National Security Agency (NSA), 538
National Urban League, 497
National War Labor Board, 397, 487
National Welfare Rights Organization, 638
National Woman's Alliance, 346
National Woman's Party, 394, 431
National Woman Suffrage Association, 328, 329
National Women's Conference (1977), 659–62
National Women's Political Caucus, 652
National Youth Administration, 504
Nation of Islam, 606–7, 613, 621, 622
nation-states, 525
    and fiction of common ancestry, 9–10
    rise of, 9
Native Americans, 399
    American Revolution and, 102
    catastrophic effect of European diseases on, 19–20
    as cowboys, 334
    declining territory of, 337
    enslavement of, 48
    European disease in, 17
    excluded by populism, 336
    French alliances with, 66
    in human zoos, 354
    legal and moral right as issue for, 55
    Locke on rights of, 53
    1960s activism, 634
    path to citizenship of, 337
    removal of, 192, 212–16
    on reservations, 337
    sovereignty and, 53–54
    in wars with colonists, 55–56
nativism, 263
Naturalization Act (1798), 314
natural rights, *see* human rights
"Nature of Mass Belief Systems in Mass Publics, The" (Converse), 593
Navy, U.S., *486*

Nazi Party, 427, 434–35
    genocide by, 511–13, *513*
Ndongo, 38
Neal, Claude, 458
Nebraska:
    creation of, 262
    farm cooperatives in, 336
    women protected in, 380–81
Negro March on Washington, 498
*Negroes with Guns*, 607
Negro Seaman Acts, 203
Netherlands, 240, 473
Neutrality Acts, 474, 475
Nevada, 260–61, 324
    creation of, 332
    irrigated land in, 409
Nevins, Allan, 562
Nevis, 84
*New American Right, The* (Bell), 592, 614
Newby, Dangerfield, 283
New Communalism, 695
New Conservation, 437
New Deal, 429–30, 437–38, 444, 479, 504, 515, 526, 527, 531–32, 535, 552, 570
    blacks excluded from, 440, 457–58
    and Clinton administration, 700
    conservatism vs., 444–45, 446–47, 656
    and debate over Constitution, 462–66
    first hundred days of, 462
    Herbert Hoover's criticism of, 506–7
    liberalism of, 444
    and New Democrats, 696
    and Reagan agenda, 627
    redistribution under, 443
    Supreme Court vs., 463–66
New Democrats, 696
New Departure, 324
New Echota, Ga., 214–15
New England:
    abolition of slavery in, 123
    antislavery movement in, 87, 88
    Caribbean sugar plantations and, 45
    dissenters' settlement of, 39, 40, 43
    Indian removal and, 215
    Indian wars in, 55–56
    Pequot War in, 45
    slavery in, 45, 48
*New-England Courant*, 60
*New Forum*, 346
Newfoundland, 34
New France, Métis in, 69
New Hampshire, constitution of, 111, 128
New Hampshire colony, 44
New Haven colony, 44
New Jersey colony, 51
New Left, 627, 628–29, 637, 651, 694
    and identity politics, 703
New Mexico, 243, 260–61, 394
*New Negro, The* (Locke), 411
New Netherland, 44
New Orleans, Battle of, 173, 181

New Orleans, La., 170, 204
*New Orleans Bee*, 289
*New Republic*, 362, 396–97, 400, 403, 426, 541
New South, 587
New Spain, 17, 20, 26
    free blacks in, 69
    racial caste system in, 23, *24*
newspapers, 211, 533–34, 540–41, 551, 552, 555,
    557, 558, 563, 571–72, 580
    growth of, 145
    Madison on importance of, 144–45
    partisanship of, 145
    political campaigning and, 160–61
    two-party system and, 145
    *see also* media; press, freedom of
New Sweden, 44
*Newsweek*, 522, 577
New Theology, 354
Newton, Huey, 627
Newtown, Ct., 765
New Women, 386
New York, debtors' prison abolished by, 226
New York, N.Y., 104, 105
    corruption in, 342
    draft riots in, 300
    Federal Hall in, 131–32, *132*
    slaves in, 61, 62, 63–64
    supposed slave conspiracy in, 63–64
    top 1 percent in, 207
New York, secret ballot in, 344
*New York American*, 182
New York colony, 51
*New Yorker, The*, 413, 521, 572, 722
*New York Herald*, 210, 211, 229, 236, 349, 385,
    453, 458
*New York Herald Tribune*, 479, 490
*New York Journal*, 349, 367
*New York Observer*, 273
*New-York Packet*, xi, xii–xiii, xviii
New York Power Authority, 438
New York state, slavery in, 123
New York Stock Exchange, 141–42, 407, 424, 436
*New York Sun*, 211, 229
*New York Times*, 255, 295, 297, 340, 342, 349, 350,
    352, 363, 387, 445, 505, 523, 527, 558
*New York Tribune*, 235, 252
*New-York Weekly Journal*, 61–62
*New York World*, 349–50, 375
Ngo Dinh Diem, 603, 604
Nicaragua, 281
Niebuhr, Reinhold, 427, 541, 583
Nierenberg, William, 683
*Nine Old Men, The*, 464
Nineteenth Amendment, 402, 431
Nixon, Richard M.:
    and abortion, 653–54, 658
    as anticommunist, 540–41, 548–51
    background of, 534–35, 540–41
    "Checkers speech" of, 561–63, 572
    congressional campaign of (1946), 534–37

    and contraception, 650
    and criminal justice policy, 622, 673
    and economic malaise, 657
    and environmental movement, 681
    and gun control debate, 673
    inauguration (1973), 642–43
    Khrushchev meeting (1959), 589–91, *589*
    and Pentagon Papers, 640–41
    and political polarization, 636, 637–39, 643
    and presidential election (1960), 589, 599–601,
        *601*
    and presidential election (1964), 615
    and presidential election (1968), 631–33, 636
    and presidential election (1972), 641–42
    as Republican leader, 536–37, 556–57, 572–73
    resignation of, 594, 644–45, *645*
    as vice president, 571–72, 579–80, 586
    vice-presidential campaign of (1952), 561–63
    vice-presidential campaign of (1956), 571–72
    and Vietnam War, 632, 642
    War on Drugs, 699
    Watergate scandal, 641–42, 643–45, 688
    White House surveillance, 639–40
"Nixonland," 572
Nock, Albert Jay, 447–48
Non-Importation Act (1806), 171
no-platform movement, 703
Nordic race, 392
Norfolk, Va., 299
Norris, J. Frank, 390, 392
North:
    antislavery societies in, 205
    Indians in, 212
North, Lord, 91–92, 101
North Africa, 11
North America, English colonization of, *see* Ameri-
    can colonies, British
North American Free Trade Agreement (NAFTA),
    699
North Atlantic Treaty (1949), 539
North Atlantic Treaty Organization (NATO), 539
North Carolina, income tax in, 301
North Carolina, University of, 497
North Dakota:
    creation of, 332
    farm cooperatives in, 336
Northern Democratic Party, 288
Northern Pacific Railway, 335
North Korea, 560
*North Star*, 249
North Vietnam, 399
Northwestern University, 340
Northwest Ordinance, 124–25
Northwest Territory, 114, 124–25
Norton, Louise, 440
Norton, Malcolm, 440
Norwegian Americans, 208
*Notes* (Madison), 240–41, 256–57
*Notes on the State of Virginia* (Jefferson), 161
Nova Scotia, free blacks in, 107

nuclear war, 522, 524–25, 531, 532, 538–39, 570, 571, 586, 587
nuclear weapons, 680, 681–82, 683
nuclear winter, 681–83
Nueces Strip, 243
nullification, 217–18, 239
Nuremberg Laws, 466
Nye, Gerald P., 445, 446

Obama, Barack, 441, 519, 722, 725–26, 728, 748, 750–55, *751*, 759–60, 763, 764, 765–66
Obama, Hussein, 751
Obama, Michelle Robinson, 752
Obergefell, James, 769
*Obergefell v. Hodges*, 768–69
Oberlin College, 366
"Objective Method for Determining Reader Interest in the Content of a Newspaper, An" (Gallup), 454–55
*Observation on the Inslaving, Importing and Purchasing of Negroes* (Benezet), 76
"Observations concerning the Increase of Mankind, Peopling of Countries, &c" (Franklin), 69
"Observations on Reading History" (Franklin), xv
Occupy movement, 726, 758–59
Ochs, Adolph, 349
Office of Facts and Figures, 488, 489–91
Office of Naval Research, U.S., 545
Office of Price Administration, 487
Office of Scientific Research and Development, 488
Office of War Information, *485*, 491, 492, 515
Ohio:
   as free state, 176
   gun laws in, 445
   movement to, 221
Ohio Country Republican Women's Club, 550, 556
Ohrduf, 512, 513, *513*
Oil and Gas Conservation Act, 572
oil crisis (1970s), 657, 680
oil industry, 572
O.K. Corral, 445
Oklahoma, gun laws in, 445
Old-age Home Guard of the United States Army, 377
old-age pensions, 377, 378
*Old Fashioned Revival Hour* (radio show), 461
*Old-Time Gospel Hour* (TV show), 663
Olympics (1968), 628
Omaha, Neb., 333
"On Computable Numbers" (Turing), 523
One Goh, 764–65
101st Airborne Division, U.S., 586
*One World or None: A Report on the Full Meaning of the Atomic Bomb*, 526
*One World* (Willkie), 492
"one world" vision, 538
*On the Origin of Species* (Darwin), 284, 348
OPEC oil embargo, 657, 680
Operation Rescue, 702

Oppenheimer, J. Robert, 516, 526
Oregon, 242, 260, 324, 494
   blacks barred from, 280–81
   female ten-hour law in, 381
   women's voting rights in, 386
Oregon Territory, 235, 242
Oregon Trail, 242
originalism, 677, 678–79, 684, 685, 687–88
origin stories, 6–7, 9
*Orion*, 508
O'Sullivan, John, 199, 243
*Other People's Money and How the Bankers Use It* (Brandeis), 388
Otis, James, Jr., 80, 86, 88
   on women's equality, 87
Ottoman Empire, 390, 426
*Our Enemy, the State* (Nock), 447
"Our Invisible Poor" (Macdonald), 611–12
Outer Banks, N.C., 28–29
*Out of Our Past* (Degler), xviii
Owen, Robert, 194

Pacific Gas and Electric, 449
Pacific Railway Act, 332–33
Pacific Telephone and Telegraph, 450
"Packaged Society," 528
Paine, Thomas, xvii, 34, 95–96, 110–11, 142
   French Revolution and, 142
   on right of revolution, 95–96
Palin, Sarah, 755, 760
Pan-American Congress, 399
Pané, Ramón, 5–7, 13, 16, 24
Panic of 1792, 140, 141–42, 335, 749
Panic of 1809, 226
Panic of 1819, 207
Panic of 1837, 225–26, *225*
Panic of 1873, 335
Panic of 1893, 347
paper currency, 220–21, 333
paper mills, 559
Parent Teacher Association (PTA), 380
Paris, Treaty of (1783), 107, 114, 123
Paris Peace Conference, 398–400, 414
Parker, Alton B., 376
Parker, Theodore, 246–47
Parker, William, 623
Parks, Rosa, 582–84
Parliament:
   Coercive Acts passed by, 89, 90, 91
   divine right of kings challenged by, 39–40, 42
   English Civil War and, 48
   Franklin's appearance before, 83–84
   popular sovereignty and, 49
   slave trade abolished by, 172
   and taxation of American colonies, 81, 82, 88–89, 91–92
partisanship, *see* political polarization
party caucuses, 159–60
party system, 211
*Passing of the Great Race, The* (Grant), 392, 408

passports, 314–16
Patent Office, U.S., 198
Patman, Wright, 505
*Patriarcha* (Filmer), 54
Patriot Act (2001), 744, 748, 765
Patterson, John, 605, 608
Patton, George, 512
Paul, Alice, 393, 394, 431
"Paul Revere's Ride" (Longfellow), 285
PayPal, 735
payroll taxes, 439, 532
peace, democracy and, 395
Peace Corps, 602
peace dividend, 538
peace movement, and Vietnam War, 628–29, 633
peace societies, 207
Pearl Harbor attack (1941), 484, 487, 494, 537
Peck, Gregory, 688–89
Penn, William, 51, *51*
Pennsylvania:
    abolition law in, 106
    constitution of, 112–13
    income tax in, 301
    slavery in, 123
Pennsylvania, University of, 530
Pennsylvania Abolition Society, 135
Pennsylvania colony, Charter of, *51*
*Pennsylvania Gazette*, 61, 137
Pennsylvania Society for the Promoting the Abolition of Slavery, 92, 114, 124
Penobscots, 215, 216
pensions, 377, 378
Pentagon, 487, 720, 722
Pentagon Papers, 640–41, 743
People's Party, 343–44, 346–47, 350, 364
*People's Presidential Candidate, The*, 227–28
*People v. Hall*, 325
Pequots, enslavement of, 45, 48
Pequot War (1637), 45, 48
Perkins, Frances, 436, 437
Perle, Richard, 682
Perlman, Nathan D., 408
Permanent Indian Territory, 262–63
Perot, Ross, 706
Persian Gulf War, 707
Peters, Frank, 136
Peterson, Elly, 617
Peurifoy, John, 550
Philadelphia, Pa.:
    AME church opened in, 202
    British capture of, 101
    free blacks in, 106
    Great Migration to, 371
    religious riots in, 209
    Working Men's Party formed in, 207
Philadelphia & Reading Rail Road, 347
*Philadelphia Inquirer*, 268
*Philadelphia Negro, The* (Hose), 370
Philippine-American War, 368–69
Philippines:
    missionaries in, 366

    in Spanish-American War, 367–68
Philippine Sea, Battle of, 506
Phillips, Carl, 469
Phillips, Kevin, 632, 636
Phillips, Wendell, 276, 321
*philosophes*, 256
*Phoenix*, 213
photography, *248*, 272–74, 460
Pickering, Timothy, 159, 164
Pierce, Walter, 459
*Pilgrim's Progress* (Bunyan), 192, 371
Pinckney, Charles Cotesworth, 160, 164
    slaves of, 79
Pinckney, Thomas, 158
Pintard, John, 140–41
Pitt, William, the Elder, 78
*Pittsburgh Courier*, 501
Plains, 337
Planned Parenthood, 649, 686
Plan of Campaign, 532, 547
plantations, 202
Plato, 50
"Plea for Captain John Brown, A" (Thoreau), 284
"Plea for Free Speech" (Douglass), 288–89, 291
"Plea for the Temperance Ballot for Women, A," speech (Lease), 339
Pledge of Allegiance, 569
Plessy, Homer, 358
*Plessy v. Ferguson*, 358–60, 369, 381, 498, 576, 578, 579, 687
Plouffe, David, 759
Plymouth colony, 40
Plymouth Company, 33
Podesta, Tony, 760
Poe, Edgar Allan, 252
*Poems on Slavery* (Longfellow), 284–85
Poland, 240, 400, 426, 427, 535
    German invasion of, 473, 474, 487
polio vaccinations, 570
political campaigning:
    election of 1800 and, 159, 160, *160*
    Jackson and, 182
    newspapers and, 160–61
    paraphernalia of, *183*
political consensus (1960s), 591–93, 633–34, 672–73
political consulting, 448–52
    Democratic Party, 636–37
    and Nixon, 632, 636
    and Reagan, 625
    and social issues, 648
political correctness, 703
*Political Debates Between Hon. Abraham Lincoln and Hon. Stephen A. Douglas*, 286–87
political equality:
    Locke and, 34
    Paine on, 34
    as U.S. founding principle, xiv–xv
*Political Man* (Lipset), 591
political parties:
    ratification debate and, 129

rise of, 62, 63
  Washington's warning against, 146
  *see also* two-party system
political polarization, 545–46
  and abortion, 647, 658, 667–68, 676
  and Clinton ethics investigations, 710–11
  and gun control debate, 647–48, 676, 679
  and identity politics, 701–2, 703
  and Internet, 648
  late 1960s increase in, 594, 636–39
  and media, 704, 707–8
  and 1970s economic malaise, 658
  1990s, 691–92
  and Nixon administration, 636, 637–39, 643
  and polling industry, 667
  and Reagan administration, 683
  and Schlafly, 658–59
  and southern strategy, 636, 656, 667
  and Supreme Court, 688–90
  and technology, 666, 668
  and Vietnam War, 643
  and women's rights, 691–92
  *see also* culture wars
political science, 348
politics:
  change in, 525–26
  debates in, 570–71
  domestic, 536
  issues in, 565–66, 570–71
  parties in, 545–46
  power in, 522, 576
  quantification of, 156
  "vital center" of, 553
  warfare and, 539
*Politics* (Aristotle), 21
Polk, James K.:
  desire for empire of, 242–43, 250
  in election of 1844, 237, 238, 243
polling industry, 667, 705
*Pollock v. Farmers' Loan and Trust Company*, 348,
    376
polls, opinion, 542–46, 557, 560, 565–66
*Pollsters: Public Opinion, Politics, and Democratic
    Leadership, The* (Rogers), 543–44
poll taxes, 542
pollution, 680
Polo, Marco, 13
polygenists, 256
Pontiac, 81
Pool, Ithiel de Sola, 597–99, 603–4, 635
*Poor Richard's Almanack*, 66, 79, 81
Pope, Alexander, 62
popular sovereignty, 261
  in American colonies, 50
  as legal fiction, 48
  representation and, 49, 83, 122
  as U.S. founding principle, xiv–xv
populism, 563
  Jackson and, 181
populist movement, 330–32, 336–38, 364
  Coughlin's radio show on, 461

folded into Democratic Party, 364–65
  gradual income tax pushed by, 345, 346
  monopolies opposed by, 343
  Progressives vs., 364–65, 371
  racism of, 343–44
  secret ballot pushed by, 344
  state as bulwark against, 348–49
  TR's pursuit of policies of, 375–76
  women in, 332, 339–40
Porfirio Díaz, José de la, 409
*Portland Oregonian*, 449
Portugal:
  in exploration of Africa, 11
  in slave trade, 11–12, 18, 38, 46
  territorial claims of, 15–16
postmodernism, 636
poststructuralism, 636
poverty:
  and Johnson administration, 611, *611*, 612,
    618–19, 622–23, 629
  and Kennedy administration, 611–12
  and Reagan administration, 671
Powell, Colin, 745
Powell, Lewis, 685, 687
Powell, Thomas, 403
"power elites," 566
power looms, 193, *194*
Powhatan, 31–32, *31*, 36–37, 54
"Practicability of Equalizing Men and Women
    Before the Law, The" (Roosevelt), 343
prayer meetings, 569
*Precision Journalism* (Meyer), 667
Preliminary Emancipation Proclamation, 297
Presbyterianism, 51, 201, 569
president, U.S.:
  duties of, 134
  elections of, 156–58
presidential elections:
  and data science, 597–99
  debates, 705–7
  1960, 597–601, *601*
  1964, 613–17, 621
  1968, 629–30, 631–33
  1972, 641–42
  1976, 659, 664–66, 705
  1980, 669, 676, 696, 705
  1984, 683, 696, 706
  1988, 706
  1992, 648, 693, 697, 698, 706
  2000, 715–18, *717*
  *see also* elections, U.S.; *specific presidents, politi-
    cians, and political parties*
press, freedom of the, 49–50, 59, 60, 137
  Alexander's advocacy of, 61–62
  Franklin's advocacy of, 61
  Stamp Act and, 82–83
  Zenger trial and, 62–63, 64
  *see also* media
*Prince of Wales*, 483
*Princeton*, USS, 232–33, 236, 238
*Principles of Scientific Management, The* (Taylor), 382

Pringle, Henry, 491
printing press, invention of, 13
privacy, right to, 650, 678, 685, 688
*Problem of Civilization Solved, The* (Lease), 343–44
*Profits of Religion, The* (Sinclair), 451
progress, 192, 197–99, 229–30
    idea of, capitalism and, 156
Progress and Freedom Foundation, 732
*Progress and Poverty* (George), 341, 365
Progressive Era, 363–64
Progressive Party, 541
Progressives, 362
    fundamentalists mocked by, 392–93
    Jim Crow ignored by, 364, 371–72, 38607
progressivism, 348–49, 526
    in election of 1912, 385–87
    muckraking in, 373
    Populists vs., 364–65, 371
    reaction against, 403–4
    roots of, 364
Prohibition, 397–98
Prohibition Party, 339–40
"Project X," 557–59
propaganda, 414, 434, 452, 456–57, 578
    in World War II, 488
*Propaganda* (Bernays), 414
property:
    Locke on, 53–54
    sovereignty and, 53–54
    voting rights and, 56, 112–13, 122, 182–83
*Proposal for Promoting Useful Knowledge among the British Plantations in America, A* (Franklin), 66–67
Proposition 4, 572
Proposition 13 (California), 669
*Prospect before Us, The* (Callender), 162
Protestantism, 26, 365, 568–69
Protestants, 50
    in riots, 209
Ptolemy, Claudius, 11
Public Credit Act, 334
*Publick Occurrences*, 59
public opinion, 457–59
    democracy vs., 452–57
*Public Opinion* (Lippmann), 401–2, 414, 454
"Public Opinion" (Madison), 144
Public Proclamation 1, 494
public relations, 402, 414
public relations campaigns, 532–34, 546–48, 553–54, 557, 559, 560–61, 572
public schools, 576, 579, 580–87
public transportation, 582–84
Public Works Administration, 437
Pulitzer, Joseph, 349, 350, 352, 366, 367, 375
Pumpkin Papers, 548–49
Purchas, Samuel, 12–13, 59
Puritans, 43, 45
Purnell, Fred S., 408
Pyle, Ernie, 493, 513

Quakers, 50, 51, 113, 135, 205
    slavery banned by, 92
    slavery denounced by, 75–76
quantification:
    historical importance to, 16–18
    of politics, 156
Quebec, 25, 84
    British and American victory at, 79
Queen Anne's War (1702–13), 66
*Quest for Security, The* (Rubinow), 438
*Quincy*, USS, 508
quota sampling, 458

race, 409
    and Constitution, 701
    Franklin on, 70
    Jefferson's formula for, 175
    politics of, 176–78
    slavery and, 55, 56–57, 69–70, 86, 143
    and women's rights, 660–61
    *see also* civil rights movement
"Race Problem in America, The" (Douglass), 356
race riots (1960s), 623–24, 627–28, 630
    and political polarization, 643
    and presidential election (1968), 632, 633
racism, 530–31, 541, 575–88, 756
    in English North America, 23, *24*
    in New Spain, 23
radical feminism, 651, 660
Radical Republicans, 317, 318, 320
    in election of 1866, 323
radio, *421*, 422–23, 427–29, 429, 430, 435, 436–37, 465, 479–80, 543–44, 561, 571, 572, 584, 704
    debates on, 459–60
    in the Depression, 440
    fundamentalism on, 460–61
    populism nourished by, 461
Radio Corporation of America (RCA), 422, 473
railroads, *189*, 191, 231, 249, 255, 333–34, 336, 341, 347, 363, 364
    desire for public ownership of, 346, 347
    government support for, 338
    income from, 406
    regulation of, 376
    taxing of, 336, 338
    transcontinental, 262
Ralegh, Walter, xvi, 35
    Roanoke colony of, 28–30
Ramsay, David, 181
Rand, Ayn, 553
Randolph, A. Philip, 498
Randolph, Edmund, 119, 121, 134
Randolph, John, 186
Randolph, Peyton, 94
Randolph, Thomas Jefferson, 205
Rather, Dan, 706
Rayburn, Sam, 568
Raymond, Daniel, 178–79
*Reader's Digest*, 507

readjustment benefit, 527–28, 528
Reagan, Nancy, 616
Reagan, Ronald, 540
　and abortion, 650
　and AIDS crisis, 685
　assassination attempt, 672, 676
　background of, 624
　economic policy, 669–72, 705–6
　and end of Cold War, 683–84, 690
　and Free Speech Movement, 625–26
　gubernatorial race (1966), 625–27
　and gun control debate, 673, 676–77
　inauguration (1981), 668–69
　and Iranian hostage crisis, 680
　and judiciary, 684–90
　and King's assassination, 630
　and media, 682, 704, 705–6
　military spending, 681
　and political polarization, 683
　and presidential election (1976), 664, 665
　and presidential election (1980), 669
　and presidential election (1984), 683, 706
　and race riots, 624
　War on Drugs, 699
*Real Majority, The* (Scammon and Wattenberg),
　636–37
*Reason Why the Colored American Is Not in the
　Columbian Exposition, The*, 356–57
Reconstruction, 337, 368, 585–86
　failure of, 329–30, 389
Reconstruction Acts, 323
Redeemers, 330
Red Scare, 415–16, 443–44
Reed, Ralph, 689
Reed, Stanley, 577, 579
*Reflections on the End of an Era* (Niebuhr), 427
Reformation, 42
Rehnquist, William, 580, 644
Reid, John, 181
Reign of Terror, 142
religion:
　and abortion, 649–50, 664
　evangelical churches, 662–64
　lack of established, 200–201
　and presidential election (1964), 616
　slavery and, 17
religion, freedom of, 49–53, 137–38
　as fundamental right, 96
　Jefferson and, 161
　Madison and, 89–90
*Report of an Exploration . . . between the Missouri
　River and the Rocky Mountains* (Frémont), 242
*Report of the Exploring Expedition to Oregon and
　California* (Frémont), 242
representation:
　constitutional convention and, 121–22, 123,
　124–25
　popular sovereignty and, 49, 83, 122
　sovereignty and, 90–91
　taxation and, 81, 83

three-fifths rule and, 125, 130, 157
reproductive rights, *see* abortion; contraception;
　culture wars
*Republic* (Plato), 50
Republican clubs, 318
republicanism:
　democracy vs., 181
　Madison on, 144–45
Republican National Committee (RNC), 571, 581
Republican National Conventions:
　of 1952, 561
　of 1956, 572
Republican Party, U.S.:
　and abortion, 668
　black support for, 323, 386–87
　business interests supported by, 562–63, 570,
　572
　conservative support for, 560–63, 570, 579–80,
　581
　conservative takeover, 658–59, 664–68
　and contraception, 649
　creation of, 264
　1860 convention of, 287
　1864 convention of, 303
　and expansion west, 32–33
　1912 convention of, 386–87
　and Nixon-Khrushchev meeting (1959), 589
　popular support for, 541–46, 564
　and presidential election (1960), 599–600
　and presidential election (1968), 631–33
　and presidential election (1976), 664–65
　and Reagan, 624
　rearrangement of, 431
　and Schlafly, 616–17, 658–59
　southern strategy, 632, 636, 656, 667
　women as supporters of, 529, 551, 555–57
　and women's rights, 658–59, 665, 692
　*see also* Radical Republicans
Republican Party (first), 211
Republicans (Jeffersonian), 144, 145–46, 159
　in election of 1800, 154–55, 160–62, 164
　Louisiana Purchase and, 170
　political dominance of, 172
　as pro-slavery, 176
Republican Women's Task Force, 659
Requerimiento, 22, 23
reservations, 337
Reston, James, 629
*Restoring the Quality of Our Environment* (Environ-
　mental Pollution Panel), 680
restrictive covenants, 530
return to normalcy, 407, 504
Revenue Act, 487–88
revolution, right of, 99
　Paine on, 95–96
revolutions of 1848, 254
Rhineland, 427, 466
Rhode Island colony, 44
　religious and political freedom in, 49–50
Rice, Condoleezza, 745, 763

Rice, Tamir, 767
Richards, Ann, 660
Richardson, Elliot, 643, 644
Richmond, Va., 302, *311*
*Richmond Examiner*, 297
*Richmond News Leader*, 582
*Richmond Recorder*, 175
Ridings, Dorothy, 706
"Rights of Black Man, The" (Bishop), 143
*Rights of Man* (Paine), 142
*Rights of the British Colonists Asserted* (Otis), 86
"Right to Equal Opportunity in Employment, The" (Murray), 500
*Right to Keep and Bear Arms* (Subcommittee on the Constitution), 677
Riley, William B., 392–93
*Rising Tide of Color Against the White World-Supremacy, The* (Stoddard), 411
RKO, 473–74
*Road to Serfdom, The* (Hayek), 57, 506
Roanoke colony, 28–30
Roberts, Owen, 463, 465, 496
Robertson, Pat, 664
robots, 559
Rochester, N.Y., 195–96, 197, 202
Rochester Society for the Promotion of Temperance, 195–96
Rockefeller, John D., 352, 372–73, 412
Rockefeller, John D., Jr., 405
Rockefeller, Nelson, 615
*Roe v. Wade*, 647, 653, 654, 655, 656, 664, 678, 686
Rogers, Lindsay, 542, 543–44, 546
Rogers, Ted, 563
Rollins, James S., 304
Roman law, slavery in, 21–22, 47, 48
Romney, George, 615, 665
Romney, Mitt, 728, 765, 774
Roosevelt, Eleanor, 428, 431–33, *432*, 483, 504, 586
    and Commission on the Status of Women, 647
Roosevelt, Franklin Delano, 750
    "arsenal of democracy" concept of, 538
    Atlantic Charter negotiated by, 482–83
    Churchill's courting of, 478
    and colonialism, 603
    convention attended by, 219
    court-packing plan of, 464–65, 479
    death of, 508, 510–11, 523, 531
    in election of 1920, 403, 428
    in election of 1932, 429–31, 454
    in election of 1936, 462
    executive branch reorganized by, 466
    fight for civil rights by, 500–501
    "forgotten man" concept of, 563
    Hitler's underestimation of, 485
    inauguration of (1933), 433
    influenced by populist movement, 332
    Keynes's letters to, 435, 466
    letters to, 435–36
    letter to Churchill from, 480–81
    and liberalism, 611
    on limits of welfare state, 438–39
    New Deal policies of, 526, 527, 531–32, 535, 552, 570
    and Pearl Harbor attack, 484
    plan to arm Europe, 475
    political consultants vs., 457
    presidential campaign of (1944), 542
    public opinion surveys relied on by, 457–58
    racial polices of, 531
    radio addresses of, 428–29, *429*, 430, 432, 436–37, 465, 479–80
    radio debates refused by, 460
    recording system, 640
    scientific research supported by, 525
    at Tehran Conference, 502–3
    United Nations plans of, 491–92, 502–3
    urged to be dictator, 434
    war powers claimed by, 487
    on World's Fair, 473
    at Yalta Conference, 508–10, *509*
Roosevelt, Franklin Delano, Jr., 478
Roosevelt, Theodore, 374, 428
    in election of 1896, 374–75
    in election of 1912, 386, 387
    judicial recall supported by, 378
    mothers praised by, 380
    muckrakers named by, 371
    on need to control commercial forces, 365
    on Paris Peace Conference, 398–99
    reforms pursued by, 375–76
    in Spanish-American War, 367, 374
    on women's equality, 343
*Roots* (TV show), 660
Roper, Elmo, 597
Rosenthal, A. M., 711
Ross, Harold, 413
Rossetto, Louis, 731–32
Rostow, Walt, 603
Rousseau, Jean-Jacques, 110
Rovere, Richard, 572
Rubinow, Isaac M., 379, 438
Ruckelshaus, Jill, 665
Ruckelshaus, William, 644
Rucker, Edward, 225
rule, nature of, 15
rule of law, xviii
    *see also* English common law
Rumsfeld, Donald, 746
Rush, Benjamin, 75, 200
    on liberty and slavery, 92
Russia, 242, 426
Russian Revolution, 362
Rustin, Bayard, 498, 607, 609
Rutledge, Edward, 94
Rutledge, John, 126, 167

*Sacramento Union*, 448
Safer, Morley, 646–47, 655, 742
Sagan, Carl, 681–82, 683
Saint-Dominque, *see* Haiti

Saintes, Battle of, 103
St. John's, slave rebellion in, 57
St. Kitts, 84, 88
St. Louis, Mo., 333, 522
*St. Louis Post-Dispatch*, 472
*St. Louis Republic*, 453
Salem, Mass., witchcraft trials in, 57
Salisbury, N.C., 302
SALT II, 680
same-sex marriage, 686
Sandburg, Carl, 412
Sanders, Bernie, 757–58, 766–67
Sandys, George, 36
San Francisco, Calif., 342, 522
    earthquake in, 376
*San Francisco Chronicle*, 379–80
*San Francisco Examiner*, 349, 448, 449
*San Francisco Times*, 341
Sanger, Margaret, 386, 394, 649
San Juan Hill, 367
Santa Anna, Antonio López de, 223, 250
*Santa Clara County v. Southern Pacific Railroad*, 339
Santayana, George, 361
Santorum, Rick, 764
*Sao João Bautista*, 38
Saratoga, Battle of (1777), 101
Sasaki, Toshiko, 521–22
Satan, 569
*Saturday Evening Post*, 507
Saturday Night Massacre, 644, 688
Saudi Arabia, 739
Savannah, Ga., 102, 104, 105, 204
Save Our Children, 661
savings and loan crisis, 672
Savio, Mario, 620–21
Scalia, Antonin, 684–85, 763
Scammon, Richard M., 636–37
Schell, Jonathan, 681
Schlafly, Phyllis, *646*, 655–56
    and evangelical churches, 664
    and National Women's Conference, 659, 661,
        662
    and presidential election (1976), 664
    and Republican Party, 616–17, 658–59
    and Trump, 668
Schlesinger, Arthur, Jr., 553, 614, 691
school desegregation, 608, 628, 662–63
School of Politics, 557
school prayer, 662
schools, common, 209–10
school shootings, 764
Schumpeter, Joseph, 735
science:
    and climate change, 680–81, 682–83
    and conservatism, 682–83
    and environmental movement, 680
    and nuclear weapons, 682
"Science, the Endless Frontier" (Bush), 525
SCLC (Southern Christian Leadership Confer-
    ence), 596–97, 606, 607, 620, 622

Scopes, John, 414–19
Scott, Dred, 268–69, 270–71
Scott, Walter, 373
Scott, Winfield, 216, 250
SDI (Strategic Defense Initiative), 681
SDS (Students for a Democratic Society), 625, 633
Seale, Bobby, 627
secession:
    difficulty of decision, 292
    push for, 289
Second Amendment, 673, 675, 677–78, 679, 688,
        764–65, 768
Second Bank of the United States, 219–21
Second Bill of Rights, 532
Second Great Awakening, 190–91, 195–98, *196*, 345
    and alleged Christian origin of U.S., 201
*Second Treatise on Government* (Locke), 1
secret ballot, 344, 353, 386
Secret Service, 234
secularism, 555
Securities Exchange Commission, 437, 446
Sedgwick, Theodore, 113
sedition, 395
*See It Now* (TV show), 566–67
segregation, racial, 530–31, 541, 575–88, 585
    start of, 330
Seitz, Frederick, 683
Selma march (1965), 621–22, 625
Seminoles, 181, 212-13
Senate, U.S., 125, 157, 529, 531, 537, 538, 546, 547,
        548, 549, 551, 567–68, 586
    Civil Rights Act (1866) passed by, 319–20
    direct election to, 346, 364
    Indian removal voted on in, 215
    rule over Philippines discussed in, 368
    Texas annexation vote of, 233
    Versailles Treaty rejected by, 400–401
Senate Foreign Relations Committee, 401, 551
Senate Judiciary Committee, 465–66
Senate Permanent Subcommittee on Investigations,
        551
Seneca Falls convention, 257–58
"separate but equal" doctrine, 359–60, 576–77,
        579, 580
separation of powers, 157
    judiciary and, 165–66
    in World War II, 479
September 11, 2001, terrorist attacks, xviii, 719–29,
        *719*
Sepúlveda, Juan Ginés de, 25, 47, 337
Sequoyah, 214
Serviceman's Readjustment Act (1944), 527
*Seven Financial Conspiracies Which Have Enslaved
        the American People* (Emery), 340
Seventeenth Amendment, 157
Seven Years' War:
    cost of, 78, 80
    global arena of, 77
    in North America, *see* French and Indian War
    1763 treaty in, 79–80, *80*

Seward, William, 689–90
   "irrepressible conflict" speech of, 282
   on passports, 315
   slavery criticized by, 255
sexual harassment, 697, 709, 712
*Sexual Suicide* (Gilder), 670
Shaftesbury, Earl of, 52
Shakers, 201
*Shall Christianity Remain Christian?*, 415
Shanghai, 427
sharecroppers, *439*
Share Our Wealth Society, 461–62
Shays, Daniel, 116
Shays's Rebellion, 116, 118
Sheldon, Charles, 366
Sherman, John, 345
Sherman, Roger, 98
Sherman Antitrust Act, 345
Shields, Mark, 715
Shiloh, Battle of, 293
Shiloh Presbyterian Church, 299
Shine, David, 567
Short, Mercy, 57
Shotwell, James T., 506
Sierra Leone, 135–36, 147–48
"Significance of the Frontier in American History,
   The" (Turner), 354–55
*Silent Spring* (Carson), 680
Silicon Valley, 695–96
silver, 347, 352
"Simplified Blueprint of the Campaign against
   Compulsory Health Insurance, A" (Whitaker
   and Baxter), 547–48
Simulmatics, 598–99, 603–4, 635
Sinclair, Upton, 412, 450–51, 535
Singer, S. Fred, 680–81, 683
Sioux, 335
Six Nations (Iroquois confederation), 66
Sixteenth Amendment, 376–77, 504
skyscrapers, 406
slave owners, 223
*Slave Pen, Alexandria, Virginia*, 295
slave rebellions:
   of Turner, 205, 206
   of Vesey, 203
*Slave Representation*, 173
slavery, 536, 553, 554, 583
slaves, slavery, xiii, 10
   American Revolution and, 93–95, 100, 108
   and annexation of Texas, 235, 236, *246*
   Aristotle on, 21, 47
   in Caribbean, 46
   as cause of Civil War, 296, 389
   Compromise of 1850 on, 260–61
   and Constitution, 191, 241, 256–57, 261–62, 268
   constitutional convention and, 123–27
   Constitution and, 127
   Davis's defense of, 293
   death toll of, 47
   debt as, 81, 82, 83
   Declaration of Independence's ignoring of, 99

   defenses of, 255–56
   democracy vs., 191
   efforts to silence dissent on, 223–24
   and election of 1840, 228
   in election of 1860, 287
   and English common law, 88
   and European extraction of wealth from Ameri-
      cas, 17
   Federalist/Republican divide on, 176
   forbidden to read, 205
   as form of manufacturing, 169
   as form of politics, 64
   free labor vs., 255
   free trade and, 281–82
   global history of, 17–18
   idea of liberty and, 10, 86, 88, 92, 96, 105–6
   in industrializing U.S., 202–3
   legal and moral right as issue in, 10, 15–16,
      20–22, 45–48, 55, 74, 86, 108, 133, 177
   liberty and, 64
   Lincoln's criticism of, 255, 263–66
   Locke on, 54–55
   in Loyalist exodus from U.S., 104–5, 107
   Missouri statehood and, 176–80
   Morse's defense of, 263
   New Deal recordings of, 441
   in New England, 45, 48
   opposition to, 199–200
   post-Revolution increase in, 123
   price of, 280, 281
   Quakers' ban on, 92
   race and, 55, 56–57, 69–70, 86, 143
   Raymond's predicted growth of, 179
   rebellions by, 3, 55, 56–59, 63, 84, 85, 99, 159
   religion and, 17
   under Roman law, 21–22, 47, 48
   runaway, 74–75, 94, 100, 104, 203
   in Spanish America, 18, 21–22
   state constitutions and, 113–14
   as three-fifths of a person, 116, 125, 130, 157,
      173, 175
   torture of, 58, 63, 73
   in Virginia, 38
   Walker's denunciation of, 203–4
   in West, 221, 267
slave trade, 29, *46*
   in Africa, 11–12, 17–18, 38, 46
   American colonies and, 48
   Atlantic crossing in, 38, 47
   British in, 45–48, 73
   closing of, 202
   Constitution and, 136
   death toll in, 47
   desire to reopen, 281
   as issue at constitutional convention, 125–26
   Portuguese in, 11–12, 18, 38, 46
   within U.S., 123
Slavs, 383
smallpox, 19–20
Smith, Adam, 17, 82, 115–16
Smith, Howard, 613

Smith, John, 36
Smith, Margaret Bayard, 182, 187–88
Smith, Margaret Chase, 551, 613, 615
Smith, William Loughton, 135
Smith Act (1940), 552, 573
SNCC (Student Nonviolent Coordinating Committee), 597, 606, 607, 621, 625–26, 627, 628–29
Social Creed, 366
social Darwinism, 343, 378, 379, 391
Social Gospel movement, 365–66, 391
social insurance, 377
Social Insurance (Rubinow), 379
socialism, 384–85, 504, 553
"socialized medicine," 547–48, 553–54, 570
social media, 770
social purity movement, 397
Social Science Research Council, 544–45
social sciences, 348, 349, 354, 542–46, 566, 578
Social Security, 447, 533
    and Reagan administration, 671
Social Security Act, 438, 439, 465
Social Statics (Spencer), 378
Society for the Relief of Distressed Debtors, 140
Society for the Relief of Free Negroes Unlawfully Held in Bondage, see Pennsylvania Society for Promoting the Abolition of Slavery
sociology, 348
Sojourner Truth Homes, 499
Solomon Islands, 494
Somerset, James, 88
Somerset v. Stewart, 88
Somme, Battle of, 390
Sons of Liberty, 82, 84–85, 86, 87, 299
Sontag, Susan, 722
South, 203
    antislavery societies in, 205
    black codes in, 318, 320
    black voting rights in, 320
    cotton production in, 202, 217
    defense of slavery in, 255–56
    divided into military districts, 323
    exports from, 217
    freedmen denied rights in, 317
    Great Migration from, 371
    Indian removal in, 212–16
    movement into Mexico from, 221–22
    secret ballot in, 344
South Carolina, 203
    black "apprenticeship" in, 318
    black politicians in, 323
    desire to reopen slave trade of, 281
    income tax in, 301
    nullification and, 218
    percentage of slaves in, 218
    secession of, 289
    slaves sold downriver from, 202
    women arrested for voting in, 328
South Carolina colony:
    slave rebellion in, 63
    Stono Rebellion in, 58–59
South Dakota:
    creation of, 332
    farm cooperatives in, 336
Southeast Asia, 456
Southern Baptist Convention, 568, 664
Southern Christian Leadership Conference (SCLC), 584, 596–97, 606, 607, 620, 622
Southern Commercial Convention, 281
Southern Democratic Party, 288
Southern Horrors: Lynch Law in All Its Phases (Wells), 356, 357
Southern Pacific Railroad Company, 338
South Korea, 560
sovereignty:
    legal and moral right as issue in, 32, 39–43, 48, 53–54, 55
    of the people, see popular sovereignty
    representation and, 90–91
Soviet Exhibition of Science, Technology, and Culture (1959), 590
Soviet Union, 535–39, 548, 570, 578, 586
    and creation of United Nations, 492
    German invasion of, 481
    invasion of Afghanistan by, 680, 722, 738
    in United Nations, 503
    U.S. food sent to, 486
Spain, 221, 242, 462
    American Revolution and, 101
    as Catholic country, 26
    civil war in, 474
    expulsion of Muslims and Jews from, 12
    and Polk's desire for Cuba, 242
    territorial claims of, 15–16
Spanish-American War, 366–67, 367, 374, 482
Spanish conquest, 18–25, 21, 26
    British colonies vs., 33
    debate over morality and legality of, 23–25
    Florida and, 25
    impact of European diseases in, 19–20
    legal and moral right as issue in, 15–16, 20–22, 47
    Requerimiento in, 22, 23
    slavery in, 18, 21–22
    see also New Spain
Special Report (TV show), 710–11
speculation, 140, 141
speech, freedom of, 49–50, 60, 62, 131, 137, 552, 573, 763
Spencer, Herbert, 343, 365, 378
Spencer, Richard, 770
Spencer, Sarah, 329
Spencer-Roberts, 625
Spirit of the Laws, The (Montesquieu), 129
Spooner, Lysander, 241
Spratt, Leonidas, 281
Sputnik launch (1957), 586, 587
Stages of Economic Growth (Rostow), 603
stagflation, 657
Stalin, Josef:
    at Tehran Conference, 502–3
    at Yalta Conference, 508–10, 514

Stalin, Joseph, 535, 539, 554, 570
Stalinism, 482
Stamp Act (1765), 82–87, 90
    repeal of, 87
Stamp Act Congress (1765), 83, 91, 131
standard of living, 1960s, 591–92
Standard Oil, 371, 372–73, 412, 448, 449, 572
"stand your ground" laws, 764
Stanley, Henry Morton, 750–51
Stanton, Edwin, 317, 324
Stanton, Elizabeth Cady, 257–58, 329
    citizenship of women desired by, 320–21
    National Woman Suffrage Association founded
        by, 328
    Thirteenth Amendment pushed by, 303
Stapleton, Jean, 660
Starnes, Joseph, 443–44
Starr, Kenneth, 710, 711
State, The (Wilson), 348
State Department, U.S., 134, 474, 492, 535–36,
    540, 549, 550–51
state power, 1960s, 591
state primaries, 386
states' rights, 223, 389, 577
States' Rights Democratic Party, 541
Statistical Methods, with Special Reference to Biolog-
    ical Variation (Davenport), 392
Statute of Religious Freedom (Virginia), 137–38
steam, 192–93, 198, 347
steamboat, 18, 221
Steel, U.S., 363
steel companies, 336
steel production, 406
Steffens, Lincoln, 371
Steinbeck, John, 502
Steinem, Gloria, 652, 712
Stephanopoulos, George, 707
Stephens, Alexander, 290
Stevens, John Paul, 718
Stevens, Thaddeus, 317
Stevenson, Adlai, 551–52, 561, 565, 570–73, 600
Stewart, Charles, 88
Stewart, James W., 190, 202, 204, 205
Stewart, Jimmy, 491
Stewart, Maria W., 189–90, 192, 199, 200, 201,
    202, 204, 205, 206
    address to mixed audience given by, 206
    speeches given up by, 207
Stewart, Potter, 653
Stimson, Henry, 514
Stimson, Henry L., 538–39
stock market, 407, 423, 424, 436
stock market crashes, of 1792, 141
Stoddard, Lothrop, 411
Stokes, Ronald X, 607
Stone, Harlan, 495
Stone, I. F., 487, 504
Stone, Lucy, 328
Stonewall riots (1969), 651, 769
Stono Rebellion, 58–59, 63
STOP ERA, 659, 662

Story, Joseph, 187, 212, 239
Stow, Marietta, 340
Strachey, William, 36
Strategic Defense Initiative (SDI), 681
Strategy of Terror, The (Taylor), 488
strikes, labor, 537
strikes, railroad, 338
Strong, George Templeton, 209
Student Nonviolent Coordinating Committee
    (SNCC), 597, 606, 607, 621, 625–26, 627,
    628–29
Students for a Democratic Society (SDS), 625,
    633
"Study of the Negro Problems, The" (Hose), 370
Subterranean Pass-Way, 280
Sudetenland, 467–68, 471
Sugar Act (1764), 81, 82
Sullivan, Andrew, 711
Summers, Larry, 700
Sumner, Charles, 210, 259, 270, 480
    beating of, 266–67
    on citizenship, 313
    Compromise of 1850 despised by, 261
    Wilmot Proviso criticized by, 245
    worried about Emancipation Proclamation, 298
Sun Belt, 587
supply-side economics, 670, 671
"Supreme Court, The: They Will Mould the Gov-
    ernment into Almost Any Shape They Please,"
    166
Supreme Court, U.S., 530, 552, 573, 576, 577–82,
    584
    on abortion, 647, 653–54, 655, 656, 678
    bankruptcy law ruled unconstitutional by, 226
    Bork nomination, 687–90
    and Clinton administration, 699
    and constitutionality of laws, 159, 168
    constitutionality of Second Bank upheld by, 220
    on contraception, 649, 650, 653, 678
    court-packing plan for, 464–65, 479
    first meeting of, 135
    on gay rights, 685, 686–87
    income tax ruled unconstitutional by, 348
    and Indian removal policies, 215–17
    limited constitutional powers of, 134–35
    Marbury decision of, 168
    market beliefs of, 364–65
    new building for, 462–63
    New Deal vs., 463–66
    and originalism, 687–88
    and political polarization, 688–90
    and presidential election (2000), 716, 717–18
    Progressive labor legislation struck down by,
        377–78
    and Reagan administration, 684–90
    and religion, 662
    and right to privacy, 685–86
    and school desegregation, 614, 662–63, 677
    and Watergate scandal, 644
    see also specific cases
Survey of Racial Conditions in the United States, 499

survival of the fittest, 365
Switzerland, 240
Szilard, Leo, 475, 515, 516, 526

Tabulating Machine Company, 355, 404
Tacky (slave), 84
Taft, Robert, 482, 487
Taft, William Howard:
    in election of 1908, 376
    in election of 1912, 386, 387
    Hughes appointed to Supreme Court by, 463
    income tax supported by, 376
Taft-Hartley Act (1947), 537
Taíno, 8–9, 16
    near extinction of, 7
    origin stories of, 6–7
    Pané's report on, 5–7
Taliban, 739, 746
talk radio, 679, 704, 709
Tallmadge, James, 177
Taney, Roger, 268–69, 270, 291, 757
Tarbell, Ida, 371, 372, 412
tariff:
    nullification and, 217–18
    slavery and, 281–82
    Wilson's lowering of, 388
Tariff Act (1930), 425
tariffs, 140, 347, 407
task management, 382–84
Tate, Arthur Fitzwilliam, 152
Taxation: The People's Business (Mellon), 405
Taxation No Tyranny (Johnson), 92
taxes:
    capital gains, 405
    of corporations, 336
    efficiency brought to, 405
    excess profits, 405
    estate, 405
    on imports, 407
    income, see income tax
    payroll, 439
    of railroads, 336, 338
taxes, taxation:
    of American colonies, 78, 81, 88–89, 91–92
    calculation of states' share of, 115–16
    Continental Congress's lack of authority for, 114–15
    representation and, 81, 83
taxes, World War II growth of, 487–88
tax policy:
    and Johnson administration, 618–19, 629
    and Reagan administration, 669, 670, 671
Taylor, Edward, 410, 488
Taylor, Frederick Winslow, 382, 384, 404, 412
Taylor, Zachary:
    in election of 1848, 253, 254
    in Mexican War, 243, 245, 250
Tea Act (1773), 88–89
Tea Party, 726, 755–57, 756, 759, 761
technology, 198, 199
    and Democratic Party, 693–96
    and political polarization, 666, 668

Tehran Conference, 502–3
Telecommunications Act (1996), 732–33
telegraph, 191, 229, 231, 249, 272, 347
    as allegedly bringing peace, 274–75
    in Civil War, 293
    transatlantic, 274–75, 347
television, 557–59, 560, 561–67, 570–74, 575, 576, 584
    and conservatism, 666
    and democracy, 592
    and elections, 708
    and presidential debates, 706
    and presidential election (1960), 600, 601
    and Supreme Court, 688–89
Teller, Edward, 682
temperance, 195–96, 206, 228, 342
    women in, 339–40
Tennessee:
    Fourteenth Amendment ratified by, 322–23
    gun laws in, 445
    Indians in, 213
    Jim Crow laws in, 330
Tenochtitlán, 8
10 percent plan, 318
Tenth Amendment, 139
Tenure of Office Act, 324
terrorism, 721–23, 738–39, 746–47
Tet Offensive (1968), 629, 635
Texas, 250, 394
    annexation of, 237, 238, 241–42, 243, 246, 259
    annexation proposed for, 232–33, 234
    gun laws in, 445
    rebellion against Mexico in, 222–23, 233
    secession of, 289
    territory yielded to New Mexico by, 260
Texas longhorns, 334
textiles, 194, 194
Theory of Employment, Interest, and Money (Keynes), 437
These Are Our Lives (Federal Writers' Project), 441
Thiel, Peter, 734–35, 736
Things to Come (film), 516
Thirteenth Amendment, 303, 306, 320
This Is War! (Corwin), 491
Thomas, Clarence, 697, 710, 712
Thompson, Dorothy, 434, 468, 470, 471, 476, 479, 489
Thoreau, Henry David, 230–31, 247, 255, 258, 284, 497
Thucydides, xvi
Thurmond, Strom, 541, 586, 613, 663
Tilden, Samuel, 329
Tillman, Ben, 368–69
Time, 412, 413, 459, 503, 509, 540, 562, 574, 731
time, quantification of, 156
Title IX, 652
tobacco, Virginia and, 37
Tocqueville, Alexis de, 206, 211–12, 226, 239
    on economic equality, 341–42
    language of liberty used by, 235
Toffler, Alvin, 732

Tombstone, Ariz., 445
Toombs, Robert, 297
Topeka, Kans., Board of Education, 577, 581
Torrey, R. A., 414
torture, 746–48
   of rebellious slaves, 58, 63, 73
*To Secure These Rights*, 531–32
"Toward a More Responsible Two-Party System,"
   545–46
*Town Meeting of the Air*, 459–60
town meetings, 543–44
Townshend Acts (1767–68), 87
Toynbee, Arnold J., 426
Tracy, Spencer, 574–75
trade, collapse in the Depression of, 425
Trail of Tears, 216
transatlantic cable, 274–75
trauma studies, 703
Treasury Department, U.S., 134, 389
*Treasury of American Folklore, A* (Botkin), 441
Tremont Temple, 288
Trenchard, John, 60
trial by jury, 58
   right to, 41–42
Tribe, Laurence, 752
Trilling, Lionel, 553, 562
Tripoli, Treaty of, 200–201
Tripp, Linda, 710
*True Law of Free Monarchies, The* (James I), 32
Truman, Harry S., 618
   and abortion, 649
   atomic bomb decision of, 522
   atomic bomb dropped by, 515–16, 517
   communism as viewed by, 552
   and creation of United Nations, 514–15
   as Democratic leader, 531, 541–46, 552
   domestic policies of, 535, 537, 541
   foreign policy of, 535, 537–39
   health insurance program of, 532–34, 533, 541,
      546–48, 553–54, 560, 561
   learning about atomic bomb, 514
   made president, 511
   presidential campaign of (1948), 541–46, 560,
      563
   racial policies of, 531–32, 576–77, 578, 581
   recording system, 640
   scientific research supported by, 525
   vetoes by, 551
   as vice president, 523, 531
   *see also* Truman administration
Truman Doctrine, 537–39
Trumbull, Lyman, 326
Trump, Donald J., 567, 727–29, 731, 762, 765, 773
   background of, 713–14
   and Clinton ethics investigations, 714
   and judiciary, 678
   1990s campaign plans, 714–16
   and presidential election (2016), 692, 773–74
   and Schlafly, 668
truth:
   as determined by evidence, 41–42, 61

freedom and, 49–50
   nature of, 15
truther movement, 725, 727, 762
Tubman, Harriet, 261
Tumblr, 724
Turing, Alan, 523–24
Turkey, 537
Turner, Frederick Jackson, 353–55, 374
Turner, Nat, 205, 206
Twain, Mark, 273, 368, 369
Tweed, William Magear, 342
Twelfth Amendment, 164
Twenty-Fifth Infantry, 369
two-party system, 165
   election of 1800 and, 154
   Federalist/Anti-Federalists factions and, 129,
      *129*, 145
   newspapers and, 145
*Two Treatises on Civil Government* (Locke), 52,
   53–54
Tydings, Millard, 551
Tyler, John, 178, 229, 232–34
   and annexation of Texas, 234–35, 237
   in election of 1844, 236–38
Tyler, Julia, 236, 238

*Ugly American, The* (Burdick and Lederer), 598, 603
unconscious, Freud's theory of, 413
*Unconstitutionality of Slavery, The* (Spooner), 241
"under God" phrase, 569
Underground Railroad, 261, 279
Union Labor Party, 342–43
Union Leagues, 318
Union Party, 461–62
unions, 371, 379
   of tenant farmers, *439*
   in World War II, 488
United Airlines Flight 93, 720–21, 725
United Airlines Flight 175, 720
United Farm Workers, 675
United Fruit Co., 574
United Mine Workers, 416
United Nations, 517
   charter of, 483
   creation of, 491–92, 514–15
   plan for, 502–3
United Negro Improvement Association, 440
United States:
   anticommunism in, 534–41, 548–57, 565–68,
      571, 581
   British recognition of, 107
   budget of, 527, 539
   Columbus's voyage as origin of, 10
   as democracy, 525, 536, 537, 543–46, 565–66,
      575, 578, 583
   division between industrial North and agricul-
      tural South in, 169–70
   economic prosperity of, 527–28
   federal government of, 526, 527, 531, 545
   and fiction of common ancestry, 9–10
   foreign policy of, 535, 537–39, 574, 578–79

founding principles of, *see* founding principles, U.S.
free blacks in, 108
growing population of, 250
isolationism in, 537
mass society in, 566
military spending by, 538–40
mixed heritage of, xv–xvi
national security of, 538–39, 574
population of, 168
public opinion in, 542–46, 557, 560, 565–66, 579, 584
religious morality in, 568–69
slavery in, *see* slaves, slavery, in U.S.
southern states of, 531, 539–40, 546, 575–88
in space race, 586–87, 587
taxation in, 527, 532, 542, 570
technological progress in, 522, 525–26, 554, 557–59, 566, 586, 587
violent beginnings of, 10
as welfare state, 538
westward expansion of, 10
*United States v. Wong Kim Ark,* 326
UNIVAC (Universal Automatic Computer), 557–59, 563–65, *564*
Universalists, 201
universal truths, 554
universities, 348, 354
   *see also see* academia
university research, 526
Updike, John, 528
"Uppie and Downie," 549
Upshur, Abel, 232, 233, 234, 235, 236
uranium, 475
*U.S. v. Miller,* 446
Utah, 260–61
   irrigated land in, 409
   women's voting rights in, 386
Utes, 222
*Utopia* (More), 54

Vallee, Rudy, 491
Van Buren, Martin, 225, 227, 253
   in election of 1832, 219
   in election of 1836, 225
   in election of 1840, 226–27
   in election of 1848, 254
   and nullification issue, 217
   Tyler's criticism of, 233
Vandenberg, Arthur, 460
vegetarian societies, 207
Verdun, Battle of, 390
Vermont:
   constitution of, 113
   slavery outlawed in, 113, 114
Versailles, Treaty of, 400–401, 466, 491
Vesey, Denmark, 203
Vespucci, Amerigo, 14
Vetal, Albert H., 409–10
Veterans Administration (VA), U.S., 6
"Vices of the Political System of the United States" (Madison), 118

Vicksburg, Battle of, 297
Vietnam War, 740, 741, 742
   and academia, 635–36
   end of, 642
   and Johnson administration, 619
   and Kennedy administration, 602–4
   and liberalism, 610
   peace movement, 628–29, 633
   Pentagon Papers, 640–41
   and political polarization, 643
   and presidential election (1968), 629, 632
Viguerie, Richard, 663, 665, 666
Vinson, Fred, 579–80
Virginia:
   black voting in, 323
   constitution of, 112
   1800 slave rebellion in, 159
   gun laws in, 445
   income tax in, 301
   Nat Turner's rebellion in, 205, 206
   ratification debate in, 130–31
   secession of, 292–93
   slaves sold downriver from, 202
Virginia charter, 32–33, 34
Virginia colony:
   founding of, 36–37
   House of Burgesses of, *see* House of Burgesses
   slavery in, 38
   starvation in, 37
   tobacco and, 37
Virginia Company, 33, 35, 35, 36, 37
Virginia Declaration of Rights, 99
Virginia Declaration of Rights and Form of Government, 96
Virginia Plan, 120
Virginia Resolves, 217
*Voice to the Married, A,* 196–97
"Voluntary Health Insurance Week," 534
von Ranke, Leopold, 254
Voorhis, Jerry, 535, 536–37
voter eligibility, in election of 1800, 163
voters, 545–46, 565, 573, 574
voter turnout, in 1828 election, 185, 186
voting rights, 333
   on black people, 320, 326, 330, 353, 501
   of blacks, 163
   Constitution and, 122
   after Panic of 1819, 207
   property and, 56, 112–13, 122, 182–83
   and property qualifications, 206
   of white men, 191, 209
   of women, 163, 206, 315, 324, 328, 339–40, 342, 346, 353, 364, 385–86, 387, 393, 402
Voting Rights Act (1965), 622, 623

Waco siege (1993), 702
Wade-Davis Bill (1864), 318
wage limits, 537
wage workers, 343
Walden, A. T., 581
Walden Pond, 230–31, 247

Waldseemüller, Martin, 14
Walker, David, 202, 203–5, 215, 218, 256
Walker, Timothy, 198
Wallace, George, 608, 613–14, 621, 632
    and ERA, 658
    and presidential election (1968), 629, 630
Wallace, Henry, 474, 526, 541
Wallace, Mike, 606
*Wall Street Journal*, 406, 423, 487, 743
war, causes of, 274–75
"War Aims and Peace Terms It Suggests, The"
    (Lippman), 396–97
war bonds, 335
War Department, U.S., 134, 523, 524
*War of the Worlds, The* (radio play; Welles), 468–71,
    468, 474, 475
War on Drugs, 699
War of 1812, 172–73, 190, 217
War on Poverty, 611–12, 619, 623
war on terror, 730–31, 738–47
War Production Board, 487
War Relocation Authority (WRA), 494–95
Warren, Earl, 532–34, 546, 561, 579–81, 582, 644,
    674, 678, 684
*War Room, The* (film), 708
war veterans, 530–31
*War without Violence* (Murray), 497
Washington, 242, 324, 494
    women's voting rights in, 386
Washington, August, 279, 280
Washington, Bushrod, 176
Washington, DC, 569, 582
    British burning of, 172–73
    Davis's Hotel in, 176
    founding of, 139–40
    Jefferson's inauguration in, 164–65
    slavery abolished in, 260
Washington, George, 86, 90, 105, 108, 116, 134,
    148, 233
    as commander of Continental army, 93
    at constitutional convention, 109, 119, 120
    death of, 147–48
    in decision not to seek third term, 145–46
    in failure to emancipate his slaves, 133–34
    Farewell Address of, 146, 148
    in first skirmish with French, 76–77
    inaugural address of, 133
    inauguration of, 132, 133
    slaves owned by, 94, 104
    will of, and freeing of slaves, 147
Washington, Harry (former slave), 94, 100, 104,
    107
    as leader of Sierra Leone rebels, 147–48
    in move to Sierra Leone, 135–36
Washington, Martha, 146–47
*Washington Bee*, 389
Washington for Jesus rally (1976), 664
*Washington Giving the Laws to America*, 148, 149
*Washington Post*, 455, 546–47, 572, 722
*Waste in Industry* (Hoover), 406
*Watchtower Over Tomorrow* (film), 516–17

water cure, 368
Watergate scandal, 641–42, 643–45, 688, 708–9, 744
water wheels, 192
Watson, Thomas, 404
Watt, James, 192–93
Wattenberg, Ben J., 636–37
Watts riots (1965), 623
WAVES, 486
*Wealth and Poverty* (Gilder), 670–71
*Wealth of Nations* (Smith), 17, 82, 115–16
weapons trajectories, 523, 525
Weaver, James, 346
Weaver, Richard, 136
Weaver, Richard M., 554
Webster, Daniel, 230, 234, 239, 242
    and Compromise of 1850, 261
    in election of 1848, 254
    on labor, 255
Weddington, Sarah, 653–54, 660
*Weekly Standard*, 707, 743
*We Hold These Truths* (Corwin), 491
Weisenberger, Walter W., 446–47
Welch, Joseph, 567, 567
welfare, 618–19
    and Clinton administration, 700
    and Nixon administration, 638–39
    and Reagan administration, 671
welfare program, 377
    in Civil War, 301
    in Confederacy, 302–3
welfare state, 378
    in the Depression, 438–39
Welles, Orson, 444, 449, 468–71, 468, 474, 475,
    491
Wells, H. G., 400, 515–16
Wells, Ida B., 356, 357, 371
Weltrundfunksender, 456
West:
    movement of people to, 221, 255
    populist movement in, 332
    Republican expansion of, 332–33
    slavery in, 221, 267
    U.S. economy transformed by, 333–34
West, Benjamin, 103
*West Coast Hotel Co. v. Parrish*, 465
West Indies, *see* Caribbean
Westinghouse, 473–74
West Virginia, creation of, 293
*West Wing* (TV show), 708
Weyrich, Paul, 648, 663, 712
"What's Cooking in Washington," 557
"What the Railroad Will Bring Us" (George), 341
Wheaton College, 461
Wheeler, Harvey, 598
Wheeling, W. Virg., 550, 556
Whig Party, 226, 264, 282
    collapse of, 267
    in election of 1836, 224, 225
    in election of 1840, 227, 228, 257
    in election of 1844, 257
    rise of, 211

Whitaker, Clem, 448, 449, 450, 451–52, 456, 478, 532–34, 533, 546–48, 553–54, 560, 561, 572
Whitaker and Baxter, *see* Campaigns, Inc.
White, Byron, 686–87
White, E. B., 473
White, John, 29–30
White, Theodore, 574
White, Walter, 458
*White Collar* (Mills), 558–59
white-collar employees, 558–59
Whitefield, George, 67–69, *68*
White House, 173, *187*
   public admitted to, 188
*White Lion*, 38
White Power movement, 673–74, 702
Whitewater, 709, 710
Whitman, Walt, 228
Whitney, Eli, 198
Whittier College, 534
*Whole Earth Catalog* (Brand), 695
Wichita, Kans., 445
Wilkeson, Samuel, 295
Wilkinson, Moses, 107, 136
Will, George, 762
Willard, Frances, 339–40
William Jennings Bryan University, 461
Williams, Roger, 44
   religious and political freedom espoused by, 49–50
Willkie, Wendell, 478–79, 480, 481, 482, 492, 551
Wills, Garry, 679
Wilmington, N.C., 202, 204
Wilmot, David, 244, 246
Wilmot Proviso, 244–46, *245*, 263
Wilson, Alex, 585
Wilson, Edith, 400, 401
Wilson, James, 119, 122, 124, 131, 141, 156, 167
Wilson, William B., 377, 384
Wilson, Woodrow, 348, 491
   books on American democracy by, 373–74
   desire to stay out of World War I, 393
   in election of 1912, 385, 387
   in election of 1916, 393
   on evolution of Constitution, 373
   Fourteen Points proposed by, 396–97
   Geneva sculpture of, 474
   good relationship with press, 388
   inauguration of, 387–88
   on industrialization, 378
   at Paris Peace Conference, 398–400, 414
   on Progressives, 365
   racial inequality endorsed by, 389
   strokes of, 401
   tax bill of, 397
windmills, 192
*Winning of the West, The* (Roosevelt), 374
Winslow, Edward, 45
Winthrop, John, 20, 43, 44, 45
*Wired*, 730, *730*, 731–32

Wisconsin, immigrants recruited to, 208
Wise, Henry, 292
WOKO, 428
Wolfe, Tom, 669
*Woman in the Nineteenth Century* (Fuller), 252
*Woman of Destiny*, 444
*Woman Rebel, The*, 386
Woman's Crusade, 339–40
Woman's Independent Political Party, 340
women, 190, 252–53
   citizenship of, 314, 315, 321–22
   as computer programmers, 524–25
   in Confederacy, 301–3, *302*
   as consumers, 380–81
   education of, 529–30
   and election of 1912, 387
   in electoral politics, 615, 616–17
   equal rights and, 402–3
   equal rights for, 529
   as housewives, 529, 555–57, *556*, 573
   lack of property rights of, 196
   in manufacturing jobs, 380
   in munitions manufacturing, 485–86, *486*
   political influence of, 529, 551, 555–57, 573
   political party desired by, 340–41
   in populist movement, 332, 339–40
   Radical Republicans supported by, 320–21
   in reform societies, 195–96, 206–7, 228
   as Republicans, 529, 551, 555–57
   in revival movement, 196, *196*, 197
   in temperance movement, 339–40
   tilted toward Democratic Party, 433
   voting rights of, 163, 206, 315, 324, 328, 339–40, 342, 346, 353, 364, 385–86, 387, 393, 402
   at Whig conventions, 228
   *see also specific people*
women, equality of, 86–87
   Abigail Adams on, 96–97
Women's Army Corps, 486
Women's Christian Temperance Union (WCTU), 339–40
Women's League for Equal Opportunity, 402
Women's National Republican Association, 341
Women's Peace Parade, 393
women's rights:
   Betty Ford on, 646–47, 654
   Gilder on, 670
   and hippies, 695
   National Women's Conference (1977), 659–62
   and political polarization, 691–92
   Schlafly activism, *646*
   *see also* culture wars; ERA; feminism
women's studies, 635
Woodhull, Victoria, 328
Woodville, Richard Caton, *232*
Worcester Town Meeting, 88
*Worcester v. Georgia*, 215
workingmen, 207–8
Working Men's Party, 207
Workingmen's Party of California, 336

Works Progress Administration (WPA), 441, 443–44, 465, 497, 504
World of Tomorrow, 472–73, 514
World's Christian Fundamentals Association, 392–93
World's Fair (1939), 472–74, 514, 526
World Trade Center, 719–20, 721
World War I, 362, 389–90, 393, 394, 531, 536, 745
    Armistice, 398–99
    Jim Crow in, 496
    power of government expanded by, 397
    U.S. entry into, 394–95
World War II, 523–24, 525, 527, 536, 537, 538, 586, 745
    Allied need for U.S. in, 477–78
    blacks in, 496–503, *500*, 508
    meaning of, 492–93
    mobilization for, 485–87
    Pacific War in, 493–94
    power of government expanded by, 487–88
    start of, 473
    turning of tide of, 502–3
World Wide Web, 731
Wozniak, Stephen, 695
Wright, Fanny, 228

Wright, Richard, 441, 443
Wright, Silas, 225, 241
writing:
    history and, 12–13, 15
    invention of, 12

Y2K bug, 729–30
Yalta Conference (1945), 508–10, *509*, 514, 535
Yancey, William, 281
Yaqui Indians, 222
*Yates v. United States*, 573
Yoo, John, 746–47
Yorktown, Va., Cornwallis's surrender in, 103, 104
<u>You</u> *Are the Message* (Ailes), 705
Yugoslavia, 400

Zenger, John Peter, 61–63, 83, 131, 291
    arrest and trial of, 62–63, 64
Zheng He, 11
Zimmerman, Alice, 394
Zimmerman, George, 763, 767
Zuckerberg, Mark, 736
Zuni, 23
Zwicker, Ralph, 566

# ABOUT THE AUTHOR

**JILL LEPORE** is the David Woods Kemper '41 Professor of American History at Harvard University. She is also a staff writer at *The New Yorker*.

The daughter of public school teachers, Lepore always wanted to be a writer, but spent years working odd jobs: newspaper girl, chambermaid, prep cook, secretary, public opinion survey caller, and shoe store clerk. She went to Tufts University on an ROTC scholarship as a math major but ended up graduating with a BA in English in 1987. After an MA in American culture from the University of Michigan, she finished a PhD in American Studies at Yale University in 1995.

She began teaching at Harvard in 2003 and started writing for *The New Yorker* in 2005. Her books and essays have been widely translated, including in German, Spanish, Italian, Portuguese, Latvian, Swedish, French, Chinese, and Japanese. In 2012, she was named Harvard College Professor, in recognition of distinction in undergraduate teaching; she also teaches at Harvard Law School. A member of the American Academy of Arts and Sciences and the American Philosophical Society, she is also past president of the Society of American Historians.

Much of Lepore's scholarship explores absences and asymmetries of evidence in the historical record. She likes to think about how people know what they know. Her earlier work includes a political history trilogy: *The Name of War: King Philip's War and the Origins of American Identity* (1998), winner of the Bancroft Prize; *New York Burning: Liberty, Slavery, and Conspiracy in Eighteenth-Century Manhattan* (2005), a finalist for the Pulitzer Prize; and *Book of Ages: The Life and Opinions of Jane Franklin* (2013), a finalist for the 2013 National Book Award for Nonfiction. Her 2014 book, *The Secret History of Wonder Woman*, was a national bestseller and winner of the American History Book Prize.

She lives in Cambridge, Massachusetts, with her husband and three sons.